Published by Neal-Schuman Publishers, Inc.
23 Leonard Street
New York, NY 10013

Copyright © 1991 by Mary Hovas Munroe, Judith Rogers Banja

All rights reserved. Reproduction of this book, in whole or in part, without written permission of the publisher is prohibited.

Printed and bound in the United States of America

Library of Congress Cataloging-in-Publication Data

Munroe, Mary Hovas
    The birthday book : [birthdates, birthplaces, and biographical sources for American authors and illustrators of children's books] / Mary Hovas Munroe and Judith Rogers Banja
        p. cm.
     Includes index.
     ISBN 1-55570-051-9
     1. Children's literature, American--Bio-bibliography--Indexes.
  2. Authors, American--Biography--Indexes. 3. Birthplaces--Indexes.
    4. Birthdays--Indexes. I. Banja, Judith Rogers. II. Title
PS490.M8 1991
810.9'9287--dc20
[B]   90-20019
                                       CIP

To
Mary McReynolds
With Admiration and Appreciation

Contents

Acknowledgments	vi
Preface	vii
How To Use This Book	ix
Abbreviations for Sources	x
Index to Authors	1
Birth Month Index	371
Birth Year Index	411
Geographical Index	451

Acknowledgments

We would like to acknowledge the help of many people in this effort. To Georgia State University's Pullen Library (especially Virginia Moreland and William Meneely) for providing its facilities and much support, to Jane Hobson and the ILL staff for patient gathering of material, to our children, Mike, Christopher, Sara, and Rebecca, for tolerating thrown-together meals and distracted mothers, and to Neal-Schuman for patience while Topsy grew. We would particularly like to thank our husbands, John Banja and Charles Munroe—John for editing and sage advice about publishing and Charles for many hours of careful help in programming, problem-solving, and printing—all cheerfully and lovingly given.

Preface

The idea for *The Birthday Book: Birthdates, Birthplaces, and Biographical Sources for American Authors and Illustrators of Children's Books* came from Mary McReynolds, a lifelong children's librarian. She had struggled for years to answer questions about the birthdates and birthplaces of American authors of books for children. "My teacher asked me to write a letter to an author, Mrs. McReynolds. Which authors were born in my birth month?" Like most children's librarians, Mrs. McReynolds pointed out the bio-bibliography collection, and the child read entries until he or she found an author born in the appropriate month. More challenging were the questions from other librarians: "I've been asked for a list of Georgia authors. The only lists I can find are at least 20 years old! Can you help me?" Frustrated, Mrs. McReynolds suggested that we make a list of the birthdates and birthplaces of children's authors. The list grew and grew until it outgrew stacks and boxes of cards and found its way into a database where it could grow some more.

The Birthday Book includes biographical information on 7,219 American authors and illustrators. The criteria for inclusion were adopted for reasons of convenience to our readers (U.S. Postal Service domestic rates) and necessity to us (an 80 megabyte hard disk): Authors must have been born in the United States or its territories or have lived a significant portion of their adult lives in the United States. Authors must also have been included in one or more of the standard biographical sources we consulted. A list of these sources and the abbreviations we used for them can be found on page xiii.

A quick glance through this book to count question marks—questionable birthdates and birthplaces—will convince anyone that biography is not an exact science. Most authors of biographical reference sources attempt to clear copy with biographees prior to publication. But many biographees do not wish to publish their birthdates or birthplaces; some falsify dates on purpose; others simply do not correct and return a biographical summary. Where we have been able to verify information in—or supply data from—published sources, we have done so. *The Birthday Book,* however, is an index to published collective biographies, and we have not attempted to plough new ground. The information in this book is limited by the sources available in academic and public libraries in the Atlanta area, but we left no available stone unturned in our quest for answers to all the questions.

SAMPLE ENTRY

(1) ALDEN, ISABELLA (2) (MACDONALD)

(3) (Pansy)

(4) Birthdate: 11/3/1841

(5) Birthplace: Rochester, NY

(6) Deathdate: 8/5/1930

(7) Information Available in These Sources: DLB 42, YABC

(8) PANSY
See Alden, Isabella (Macdonald)

How to Use This Book

The Birthday Book is designed to help the user find biographical information about children's authors. The indexes have been designed so users can approach this information in several ways.

The largest part of *The Birthday Book* is the Index to Authors, arranged alphabetically by last name. The first item in the entry is the full name of the author, insofar as it is known (see Sample Entry #1). Because many authors have married (see #2), used several pseudonyms, or used variations of their birth name, the second item in the entry is a list of pseudonyms or variations that the author is known to use (see #3). Each of the pseudonyms or variants is listed separately with a *see* reference to the main entry (see #8). This main entry is intended to be the legal name of the author insofar as the authors of this book have been able to determine it. The fourth and fifth items in the entry are the birthdate (see #4) and birthplace (see #5) of the author. If this information is not included, it was unavailable. If the author is deceased, the deathdate has also been added (see #6). Next are the abbreviations of sources in which further information about the author may be obtained (see #7). The user should consult the following Abbreviations for Sources for a full citation to the source. Finally, if more than one birthdate or deathdate has been reported in several different sources, the entry will cite the variations; for example, 4/2/1959 or 4/3/1959 means that the birthdate has been listed in both ways in several sources.

The authors of *The Birthday Book* have discovered that many users are interested in locating authors born in a particular month or on a particular day. To assist them, there is a Month Index, arranged by month of birth and then by day of the month. The only listing in this index is the name of the author. The user may refer to the author index to locate full information.

Users who wish to locate authors born in a particular year will find that information in the Year Index. The entries are arranged by birthdate within a particular year. Again, the user will need to refer to the author index for complete information.

Finally, users who wish to locate authors born in a particular state or city may refer to the Geographical Index where authors are listed by state or country and then by city. The user will retrieve a list of authors, for whom full information is available in the author index.

Abbreviations for Sources

ABYP 1	*Authors of Books for Young People.* Martha E. Ward and Dorothy A. Marquardt. New York and London: The Scarecrow Press, Inc., 1964.
ABYP 2, 3, and 4	*Authors of Books for Young People.* Martha E. Ward and Dorothy A. Marquardt. Metuchen, N.J.: The Scarecrow Press, Inc., 1967, 1971, and 1979.
AICB	*Authors and Illustrators of Children's Books: Writings on Their Lives and Works.* Miriam Hoffman and Eva Samuels. New York: Bowker, 1972.
BABP	*Books Are By People:* Interviews with One Hundred and Four Authors and Illustrators of Books for Young Children. Lee Bennett Hopkins. New York: Citation Press, 1969.
BAI	*Black Authors and Illustrators of Children's Books.* Barbara Rollock. New York and London: Garland Publishing Company, 1988.
BC	*Behind the Covers. Interviews with Authors and Illustrators of Books for Children and Young Adults.* Jim Roginski. Littleton, Colo.: Libraries Unlimited, Inc., 1985.
CFB	*The Child's First Books: A Critical Study of Pictures and Text.* Donna Rae McCann and Olga Richards. New York: H. W. Wilson, 1973.
CICB	*Contemporary Illustrators of Children's Books.* Bertha E. Mahony and Elinor Whitney, compilers. Detroit: Gale Research, 1978, © 1930.
DACF	*Dictionary of American Children's Fiction, 1960-1984:* Recent Books of Recognized Merit. Alethea K. Helbig and Agnes Regan Perkins. New York: Greenwood Press, 1986.
DLB 22, 42, 52, 61	*Dictionary of Literary Biography.* Detroit: Gale Research, 1978-.
FLTYP	*Famous Literary Teams for Young People.* Norah Smaridge. New York: Dodd, Mead & Company, 1968.
FSYP	*Famous Storytellers for Young People.* Laura Benet. New York: Dodd, Mead & Company, 1977.
IBYP 1 and 2	*Illustrators of Books for Young People.* Martha E. Ward and Dorothy A. Marquardt. Metuchen, N.J.: The Scarecrow Press, 1970, and 1975.
ICB 1	*Illustrators of Children's Books, 1744-1945.* Bertha E. Mahony, Louise Payson Latimer and Beulah Folmsbee, compilers. Boston: Horn Book, 1970, © 1947.
ICB 2	*Illustrators of Children's Books, 1946-1956.* Ruth Hill Viguers, Marcia Dalphin, and Bertha E. Mahony Miller, compilers. Boston: Horn Book, 1958.
ICB 3	*Illustrators of Children's Books, 1957-1966.* Lee Kingman, Joanna

	Foster, and Ruth Giles Lontoft, compilers. Boston: Horn Book, 1968.
ICB 4	*Illustrators of Children's Books, 1767-1976.* Lee Kingman, Grace Allen Hogarth, and Harriet Quimby, compilers. Boston: Horn Book, 1978.
JBA 1	*Junior Book of Authors.* Stanley Kunitz, editor. New York: H.W. Wilson Co., 1934
JBA 2	*Junior Book of Authors.* Second edition, revised. Stanley Kunitz and Howard Haycraft, editors. New York: H.W. Wilson Co., 1951.
JBA 3	*Third Book of Junior Authors.* Doris De Montreville and Donna Hill, editors. New York: H.W. Wilson Co., 1972.
JBA 4	*Fourth Book of Junior Authors and Illustrators.* Doris de Montreville and Elizabeth D. Crawford, editors. New York: H.W. Wilson Co., 1978.
JBA 5	*Fifth Book of Junior Authors and Illustrators.* Sally Holmes Holtze, editor. New York: H.W. Wilson Co., 1983.
JBA 6	*Sixth Book of Junior Authors and Illustrators.* Sally Holmes Holtze, editor. New York: H.W. Wilson Co., 1989.
MBMP	*More Books by More People: Interviews with Sixty-Five Authors of Books for Children.* Lee Bennett Hopkins. New York: Citation Press, 1974.
MJA	*More Junior Authors.* Muriel Fuller, editor. New York: H.W. Wilson Co., 1963.
SATA 1-60	*Something About the Author.* Detroit: Gale Research, 1971- .
SVC 2	*Story and Verse for Children.* Revised edition. Mirian Blanton Huber, editor. New York: The Macmillan Company, 1955.
SVC 3	*Story and Verse for Children.* Third edition. Mirian Blanton Huber. New York: The Macmillan Company, 1965.
TCCW 1	*Twentieth Century Cildren's Writers.* New York: St. Martin's Press, 1979.
TCCW 2	*Twentieth Century Cildren's Writers.* Second edition. New York: St. Martin's Press, 1983.
TCCW 3	*Twentieth Century Cildren's Writers.* Third edition. New York: St. Martin's Press, 1989.
WC	*Writers for Children. Critical Studies of Major Authors Since the Seventeenth Century.* Jane M. Bingham, editor. New York: Charles Scribner's Sons, 1988.
WCL	*Who's Who of Children's Literature.* Brian Doyle, compiler and editor. New York: Schocken Books, 1968.
YABC	*Yesterday's Authors of Books for Children: Facts and Pictures About Authors and Illustrators of Books for Young People, From Early Times to 1960.* 2 volumes. Anne Commire, editor. Detroit: Gale Research, © 1977-78.

Index to Authors

A, DR.
See Silverstein, Alvin

AARDEMA, VERNA (NORBERG)
(Verna Aardema Vugteveen)
Birthdate: 6/6/1911
Birthplace: New Era, MI
Information Available in These Sources: ABYP 4, JBA 5, SATA 4

AARON, CHESTER
Birthdate: 5/9/1923
Birthplace: Butler, PA
Information Available in These Sources: SATA 9, ABYP 4, JBA 3, TCCW 2, TCCW 3

AASENG, NATE
See Aaseng, Nathan

AASENG, NATHAN
(Nate Aaseng)
Birthdate: 7/7/1953
Birthplace: Park Rapids, MN
Information Available in These Sources: JBA 6, SATA 38, SATA 51

ABBOTT, ALICE
See Speicher, Helen Ross (Smith) and Borland, Kathryn Kilby

ABBOTT, JACOB
Birthdate: 11/13/1803 or 11/14/1803
Birthplace: Hallowell, ME
Deathdate: 10/31/1879
Information Available in These Sources: DLB 42, JBA 1, SATA 22, TCCW 3

ABBOTT, R. TUCKER
See Abbott, Robert Tucker

ABBOTT, ROBERT TUCKER
(R. Tucker Abbott)
Birthdate: 9/28/1919
Birthplace: Watertown, MA
Information Available in These Sources: ABYP 4

ABBOTT, SARAH
See Zolotow, Charlotte S(hapiro)

ABDUL, RAOUL
Birthdate: 11/7/1929
Birthplace: Cleveland, OH
Information Available in These Sources: BAI, SATA 12

ABEL, RAYMOND
Birthdate: 9/19/1911
Birthplace: Chicago, IL
Information Available in These Sources: ICB 4, SATA 12

ABELS, HARRIETTE SHEFFER
(H. R. Sheffer)
Birthdate: 12/1/1926
Birthplace: Port Chester, NY
Information Available in These Sources: SATA 50

ABERCROMBIE, BARBARA (MATTES)
Birthdate: 4/6/1939
Birthplace: Evanston, IL
Information Available in These Sources: SATA 16

ABERNETHY, ROBERT G(ORDON)
Birthdate: 11/5/1927
Birthplace: Geneva, Switzerland
Information Available in These Sources: SATA 5

ABISCH, ROSLYN KROOP
(Roz Abisch, Mr. McGillicuddy, A. K. Roche, Mr. Sniff)
Birthdate: 4/2/1927
Birthplace: Brooklyn, NY
Information Available in These Sources: ABYP 4, SATA 9

ABISCH, ROZ
See Abisch, Roslyn Kroop

ABODAHER, DAVID J. (NAIPH)
Birthdate: 2/1/1919
Birthplace: Streator, IL
Information Available in These Sources: ABYP 4, SATA 17

ABRAHAMS, ROBERT D(AVID)
Birthdate: 9/24/1905
Birthplace: Philadelphia, PA
Information Available in These Sources: ABYP 2, ABYP 3, SATA 4

ABRAMOVITZ, ANITA (ZELTNER BROOKS)
See Brooks, Anita

ABRAMS, JOY
Birthdate: 3/17/1941
Birthplace: New York, NY
Information Available in These Sources: SATA 16

ABRAMS, LAWRENCE F.
Birthdate: 3/1/1944
Birthplace: Detroit, MI
Information Available in These Sources: SATA 47, SATA 58

ABRAMS, LESTER
Information Available in These Sources: IBYP 2

ABRASHKIN, RAYMOND
(Ray Ashley)
Birthdate: 1911
Birthplace: Brooklyn, NY
Deathdate: 8/25/1960
Information Available in These Sources: ABYP 4, SATA 50

ACHESON, PATRICIA CASTLES
Birthdate: 5/24/1924
Birthplace: New York, NY
Information Available in These Sources: ABYP 2, ABYP 3

ACKER, HELEN
Birthplace: Niagara Falls, NY
Information Available in These Sources: ABYP 2, ABYP 3

ACKERMAN, EUGENE (FRANCIS)
Birthdate: 1/1/1888
Birthplace: Huntingdon, IN
Deathdate: 5/2/1974
Information Available in These Sources: SATA 10

ACKLEY, PEGGY JO
Birthdate: 10/18/1955
Birthplace: Sacramento, CA
Information Available in These Sources: SATA 58

ACUFF, SELMA BOYD
(Selma Boyd)
Birthdate: 4/10/1924
Birthplace: Chicago, IL
Information Available in These Sources: SATA 45

ADA, ALMA FLOR
Birthdate: 1/3/1938
Birthplace: Camaguey, Cuba
Information Available in These Sources: SATA 43

ADAIR, MARGARET WEEKS
Birthplace: Portland, OR
Deathdate: 12/19/1971
Information Available in These Sources: SATA 10

ADAM, CORNEL
See Lengyel, Cornel Adam

ADAMS, ADRIENNE
(Adrienne Adams Anderson)
Birthdate: 2/8/1906
Birthplace: Fort Smith, AR
Information Available in These Sources: BABP, FLTYP, IBYP 1, IBYP 2, ICB 2, ICB 3, ICB 4, JBA 3, SATA 8

ADAMS, ANDY
Birthdate: 5/3/1859
Birthplace: Whitley County, IN
Deathdate: 9/26/1935
Information Available in These Sources: JBA 1, JBA 2, YABC

ADAMS, BARBARA JOHNSTON
Birthdate: 8/24/1943
Birthplace: Bronxville, NY
Information Available in These Sources: SATA 60

ADAMS, CHARLOTTE
Birthdate: 12/8/1899
Birthplace: Ridgewood, NJ
Information Available in These Sources: ABYP 4

ADAMS, DALE
See Quinn, Elisabeth

ADAMS, HARRIET S(TRATEMEYER)
(Victor Appleton II, May Hollis Barton, Franklin W. Dixon, Laura Lee Hope, Carolyn Keene, Helen Louise Thorndyke)
Birthdate: 12/6/1894
Birthplace: Newark, NJ
Deathdate: 3/27/1982
Information Available in These Sources: SATA 1, SATA 29

ADAMS, HARRISON
See Stratemeyer, Edward L.

ADAMS, HAZARD
Birthdate: 2/15/1926
Birthplace: Cleveland, OH
Information Available in These Sources: SATA 6

ADAMS, JULIA DAVIS
(Julia Davis, F. Draco)
Birthdate: 7/23/1904
Birthplace: Clarksburg, WV
Information Available in These Sources: JBA 1, JBA 2, SATA 6

ADAMS, KATHARINE
Birthplace: Elmira, NY
Information Available in These Sources: JBA 1, JBA 2

ADAMS, LAURIE
(Laurie Schneider)
Birthdate: 9/29/1941
Birthplace: New York, NY
Information Available in These Sources: SATA 33

ADAMS, LOWELL
See Joseph, James (Herz)

ADAMS, NOEL
See Barrows, R(uth) M(arjorie)

ADAMS, PAULINE BATCHELDER
Birthdate: 1897
Information Available in These Sources: IBYP 2

ADAMS, RUTH JOYCE
Information Available in These Sources: ABYP 2, ABYP 3, SATA 14

ADAMS, SAMUEL HOPKINS
Birthdate: 1/26/1871
Birthplace: Dunkirk, NY
Deathdate: 11/15/1958
Information Available in These Sources: ABYP 2, ABYP 3

ADAMS, WILLIAM TAYLOR
(Warren T. Ashton, Irving Brown, Clingham Hunter, M.D., Brooks McCormick, Oliver Optic, Gayle Winterton)
Birthdate: 7/30/1822
Birthplace: Bellingham (Medway), MA
Deathdate: 3/27/1897
Information Available in These Sources: DLB 42, SATA 28

ADAMSON, GEORGE WORSLEY
Birthdate: 2/7/1913
Birthplace: New York, NY
Information Available in These Sources: ICB 4, SATA 30

ADAMSON, WENDY WRISTON
Birthdate: 6/25/1942
Birthplace: Glens Falls, NY
Information Available in These Sources: SATA 22

ADDAMS, CHARLES (SAMUEL)
Birthdate: 1/7/1912
Birthplace: Westfield, NJ
Deathdate: 9/29/1988
Information Available in These Sources: SATA 55

ADDONA, ANGELO F.
Birthdate: 11/18/1925
Birthplace: CT
Information Available in These Sources: SATA 14

ADDY, TED
See Winterbotham, R(ussell) R(obert)

ADELBERG, DORIS
See Orgel, Doris (Adelberg)

ADELSON, LEONE
Birthdate: 6/13/1908
Birthplace: New York, NY
Information Available in These Sources: ABYP 2, ABYP 3, SATA 11

ADKINS, JAN
Birthdate: 11/7/1944
Birthplace: Gallipolis, OH
Information Available in These Sources: ABYP 4, ICB 4, JBA 5, SATA 8

ADLER, C(AROLE) S(CHWERDTFEGER)
Birthdate: 2/23/1932
Birthplace: Long Island, NY
Information Available in These Sources: JBA 6, SATA 26

ADLER, DAVID A.
Birthdate: 4/10/1947
Birthplace: New York, NY
Information Available in These Sources: JBA 6, SATA 14

ADLER, IRENE
See Penzler, Otto

ADLER, IRVING
See Adler, Robert Irving

ADLER, LARRY
Birthdate: 7/10/1939
Birthplace: White Plains, NY
Information Available in These Sources: SATA 36

ADLER, PEGGY
(Peggy Adler Walsh)
Information Available in These Sources: ABYP 2, ABYP 3, SATA 22

ADLER, ROBERT IRVING
(Irving Adler, Robert Irving)
Birthdate: 4/27/1913
Birthplace: New York, NY
Information Available in These Sources: ABYP 1, ABYP 3, JBA 3, SATA 1 SATA 29

ADLER, RUTH
Birthdate: 4/20/1915
Birthplace: Sullivan County, NY
Deathdate: 3/30/1968
Information Available in These Sources: ABYP 1, ABYP 3, JBA 3, SATA 1

ADOFF, ARNOLD
Birthdate: 7/16/1935
Birthplace: Bronx, NY
Information Available in These Sources: JBA 4, MBMP, SATA 5, SATA 57, TCCW 2, TCCW 3

ADOFF, VIRGINIA HAMILTON
See Hamilton, Virginia (Esther)

ADORJAN, CAROL (MADDEN)
Birthdate: 8/17/1934
Birthplace: Chicago, IL
Information Available in These Sources: SATA 10

ADRIAN, MARY
See Jorgensen, Mary Venn

AGAPIDA, FRAY ANTONIO
See Irving, Washington

AGARD, NADEMA
Birthdate: 9/10/1948
Birthplace: New York, NY
Information Available in These Sources: SATA 18

AGLE, NAN HAYDEN
(Anna Bradford Hayden)
Birthdate: 4/13/1905
Birthplace: Baltimore, MD
Information Available in These Sources: ABYP 1, ABYP 3, JBA 4, SATA 3

AGNEW, EDITH J(OSEPHINE)
(Marcelino)
Birthdate: 10/13/1897
Birthplace: Denver, CO
Information Available in These Sources: SATA 11

AGNEW, SETH MARSHALL
Birthdate: 1921?
Information Available in These Sources: ABYP 4

AHERN, MARGARET MCCROHAN
(Peg O'Connell)
Birthdate: 2/16/1921
Birthplace: New York, NY
Information Available in These Sources: SATA 10

AHL, ANNA MARIA
Birthdate: 3/26/1926
Birthplace: Chicago, IL
Information Available in These Sources: SATA 32

AHNSTROM, D(ORIS) N.
Birthdate: 8/4/1915
Birthplace: Muskegon, MI
Information Available in These Sources: ABYP 2, ABYP 3

AHRENHOLD, NOVIE MOFFAT
Information Available in These Sources: IBYP 2

AIKEN, CLARISSA (LORENZ)
Birthdate: 1/28/1899
Birthplace: Milwaukee, WI
Information Available in These Sources: SATA 12

AIKEN, CONRAD (POTTER)
(Samuel Jeake, Jr.)
Birthdate: 8/5/1899
Birthplace: Savannah, GA
Deathdate: 8/17/1973
Information Available in These Sources: ABYP 2, ABYP 3, SATA 3, SATA 30

AINSWORTH, CATHERINE HARRIS
(Catherine Harris)
Birthdate: 10/5/1910
Birthplace: Elkin, NC
Information Available in These Sources: SATA 56

AINSWORTH, NORMA
(Norma Paul Ruedi)
Birthplace: Clinton, MO
Information Available in These Sources: SATA 9

AITKEN, AMY
Birthdate: 10/19/1952
Information Available in These Sources: SATA 40, SATA 54

AITKEN, DOROTHY (LOCKWOOD)
Birthdate: 7/19/1916
Birthplace: CO
Information Available in These Sources: SATA 10

AKERS, FLOYD
See Baum, L(yman) Frank

ALAIN
See Brustlein, Daniel

ALAJALOV, CONSTANTIN
Birthdate: 11/18/1900
Birthplace: Rostovna-Donu, Russia
Deathdate: 10/24/1987
Information Available in These Sources: IBYP 2, ICB 1, ICB 2, SATA 53

ALBERT, BURTON, JR.
(Brooks Healey)
Birthdate: 9/25/1936
Birthplace: Pittsfield, MA
Information Available in These Sources: SATA 22

ALBERT, MARVIN H.
(Anthony Rome)
Birthdate: 1924
Birthplace: Philadelphia, PA
Information Available in These Sources: ABYP 2, ABYP 3

ALBERTS, FRANCES JACOBS
Birthdate: 1/14/1907
Birthplace: Lennox, SD
Information Available in These Sources: SATA 14

ALBION, LEE SMITH
(Lee Smith)
Birthplace: Rochester, NY
Information Available in These Sources: IBYP 2, ICB 3, SATA 29

ALBRECHT, LILLIE (VANDERVEER)
Birthdate: 1/2/1894
Birthplace: Monroe, NY
Information Available in These Sources: SATA 12

ALCOCK, GUDRUN
Birthdate: 4/18/1908
Birthplace: Stockholm, Sweden
Information Available in These Sources: SATA 33, SATA 56

ALCORN, JOHN
Birthdate: 2/10/1935
Birthplace: Corona, NY
Information Available in These Sources: IBYP 1, IBYP 2, ICB 3, JBA 3, SATA 30, SATA 31

ALCOTT, LOUISA MAY
Birthdate: 11/29/1832
Birthplace: Germantown, PA
Deathdate: 3/6/1888
Information Available in These Sources: ABYP 2, ABYP 3, DLB 42, JBA 1 SVC 2, SVC 3, TCCW 2, TCCW 3, WC, YABC

ALDA, ARLENE
Birthdate: 3/12/1933
Birthplace: Bronx, NY
Information Available in These Sources: SATA 36, SATA 44

ALDEN, ISABELLA (MACDONALD)
(Pansy)
Birthdate: 11/3/1841
Birthplace: Rochester, NY
Deathdate: 8/5/1930
Information Available in These Sources: DLB 42, YABC

ALDEN, JACK
See Barrows, R(uth) M(arjorie)

ALDERMAN, CLIFFORD LINDSEY
Birthdate: 8/5/1902
Birthplace: Springfield, MA
Information Available in These Sources: ABYP 2, ABYP 3, SATA 3

ALDERSON, SUE ANN
Birthdate: 9/11/1940
Birthplace: New York, NY
Information Available in These Sources: SATA 48, SATA 59, TCCW 3

ALDIS, DOROTHY (KEELEY)
Birthdate: 3/13/1896 or 3/13/1897
Birthplace: Chicago, IL
Deathdate: 7/4/1966
Information Available in These Sources: ABYP 1, ABYP 3, DLB 22, JBA 1 JBA 2, SATA 2, SVC 2, SVC 3

ALDON, ADAIR
See Meigs, Cornelia Lynde

ALDRICH, ANN
See Meaker, Marijane

ALDRICH, BESS STREETER
Birthdate: 2/17/1881
Birthplace: Cedar Falls, IA
Deathdate: 8/3/1954
Information Available in These Sources: JBA 1

ALDRICH, THOMAS BAILEY
Birthdate: 11/11/1836
Birthplace: Portsmouth, NH
Deathdate: 3/19/1907
Information Available in These Sources: ABYP 4, DLB 42, JBA 1, SATA 17TCCW 2, TCCW 3

ALDRIDGE, JOSEPHINE HASKELL
Information Available in These Sources: ABYP 2, ABYP 3, SATA 14

ALEGRIA, RICARDO E.
Birthdate: 4/14/1921
Birthplace: San Juan, PR
Information Available in These Sources: SATA 6

ALEX, MARLEE
(Marlee)
Birthdate: 12/29/1948
Birthplace: Pratt, KS
Information Available in These Sources: SATA 45

ALEXANDER, ANNA B(ARBARA COOKE)
(Anne Alexander, Barbara Cooke)
Birthdate: 10/6/1913
Birthplace: Shanghai, China
Information Available in These Sources: ABYP 1, ABYP 3, SATA 1

ALEXANDER, ANNE
See Alexander, Anna B(arbara Cooke)

ALEXANDER, DAVID
Birthdate: 4/21/1907
Birthplace: Shelbyville, KY
Deathdate: 3/21/1973
Information Available in These Sources: ABYP 4

ALEXANDER, FRANCES (LAURA)
Birthdate: 2/12/1888
Birthplace: Blanco, TX
Information Available in These Sources: SATA 4

ALEXANDER, JOCELYN (ANNE ARUNDEL)
(Jocelyn Arundel)
Birthdate: 6/16/1930
Birthplace: Washington, DC
Information Available in These Sources: ABYP 2, ABYP 3, SATA 22

ALEXANDER, LINDA
Birthdate: 2/4/1935
Birthplace: Carthage, MO
Information Available in These Sources: SATA 2

ALEXANDER, LLOYD (CHUDLEY)
Birthdate: 1/30/1924
Birthplace: Philadelphia, PA
Information Available in These Sources: ABYP 2, ABYP 3, DACF, DLB 52, JBA 3, MBMP, SATA 3, SATA 49, TCCW 1, TCCW 2, TCCW 3

ALEXANDER, MARTHA
Birthdate: 5/25/1920
Birthplace: Augusta, GA
Information Available in These Sources: BC, IBYP 1, IBYP 2, JBA 4, SATA 11

ALEXANDER, RAE PACE
See Alexander, Raymond Pace

ALEXANDER, RAYMOND PACE
(Rae Pace Alexander)
Birthdate: 10/13/1898
Birthplace: Philadelphia, PA
Deathdate: 11/23/1974
Information Available in These Sources: SATA 22

ALEXANDER, SUE
Birthdate: 8/20/1933
Birthplace: Tucson, AZ
Information Available in These Sources: JBA 6, SATA 12

ALEXANDER, VINCENT ARTHUR
Birthdate: 11/4/1925
Birthplace: Wyckoff, NJ
Deathdate: 5/22/1980
Information Available in These Sources: SATA 23

ALGER, HORATIO, JR.
(Arthur Lee Putnam)
Birthdate: 1/13/1832
Birthplace: Revere, MA
Deathdate: 7/18/1899
Information Available in These Sources: DLB 42, SATA 16, TCCW 2, TCCW 3

ALGER, LECLAIRE (GOWANS)
(Sorche NicLeodhas)
Birthdate: 5/20/1898
Birthplace: Youngstown, OH
Deathdate: 11/14/1969
Information Available in These Sources: ABYP 2, ABYP 3, JBA 3, SATA 15

ALIKI
See Brandenberg, Aliki (Liacouras)

ALKEMA, CHESTER JAY
Birthdate: 7/17/1932
Birthplace: Martin, MI
Information Available in These Sources: SATA 12

ALLARD, HARRY
See Allard, Harry G(rover), Jr.

ALLARD, HARRY G(ROVER), JR.
(Harry Allard)
Birthdate: 1/27/1928
Birthplace: Evanston, IL
Information Available in These Sources: ABYP 4, JBA 5, SATA 42

ALLEE, MARJORIE HILL
Birthdate: 6/2/1890
Birthplace: Carthage, IN
Deathdate: 4/30/1945
Information Available in These Sources: JBA 1, JBA 2, SATA 17

ALLEN, ADAM
See Epstein, Beryl (M. Williams) and Epstein, Samuel

ALLEN, ALEX B.
See Heide, Florence Parry

ALLEN, ALLYN
See Eberle, Irmengarde

ALLEN, BETSY
See Cavanna, Betty

ALLEN, GERTRUDE E(LIZABETH)
Birthdate: 7/18/1888
Birthplace: Detroit, MI
Information Available in These Sources: SATA 9

ALLEN, GRACE
See Hogarth, Grace (Weston Allen)

ALLEN, HENRY WILSON
(Clay Fisher, Will Henry)
Birthdate: 1912
Birthplace: Kansas City, MO
Information Available in These Sources: ABYP 4

ALLEN, JEFFREY (YALE)
Birthdate: 9/3/1948
Birthplace: Detroit, MI
Information Available in These Sources: SATA 42

ALLEN, LAURA JEAN
Birthplace: Collingswood, NJ
Information Available in These Sources: SATA 53

ALLEN, LEE
Birthdate: 1/12/1915
Birthplace: Cincinnati, OH
Deathdate: 5/20/1969
Information Available in These Sources: ABYP 2, ABYP 3

ALLEN, LEROY
Birthdate: 7/13/1912
Birthplace: McLeansboro, IL
Information Available in These Sources: SATA 11

ALLEN, MARIE LOUISE
Birthplace: Cleveland, OH
Information Available in These Sources: ABYP 2, ABYP 3

ALLEN, MARJORIE
Birthdate: 12/8/1931
Birthplace: Manchester, NH
Information Available in These Sources: SATA 22

ALLEN, MAURY
Birthdate: 5/2/1932
Birthplace: Brooklyn, NY
Information Available in These Sources: SATA 26

ALLEN, MEL
Birthdate: 2/14/1913
Birthplace: Birmingham, AL
Information Available in These Sources: ABYP 2, ABYP 3

ALLEN, MERRITT PARMALEE
Birthdate: 7/2/1892
Birthplace: Bristol, VT
Deathdate: 12/26/1954
Information Available in These Sources: ABYP 1, ABYP 3, JBA 2, SATA 22

ALLEN, NINA (STROMGREN)
Birthdate: 9/17/1935
Birthplace: Copenhagen, Denmark
Information Available in These Sources: SATA 22

ALLEN, RICHARD J.
Birthplace: New York, NY
Information Available in These Sources: ABYP 2, ABYP 3

ALLEN, RODNEY F.
Birthdate: 11/2/1938
Birthplace: Wilmington, DE
Information Available in These Sources: SATA 27

ALLEN, RUTH
See Peterson, Esther (Allen)

ALLEN, SAMUEL (WASHINGTON)
(Paul Vesey)
Birthdate: 12/9/1917
Birthplace: Columbus, OH
Information Available in These Sources: SATA 9

ALLEN, STEPHEN VALENTINE PATRICK WILLIAM
(Steve Allen)
Birthdate: 12/26/1921
Birthplace: New York, NY
Information Available in These Sources: ABYP 4

ALLEN, STEVE
See Allen, Stephen Valentine Patrick William

ALLEN, T(ERRIL) D(IENER)
(Terry D. Allen)
Birthdate: 8/13/1908
Birthplace: Douglas, OK
Information Available in These Sources: SATA 35

ALLEN, TERRY D.
See Allen, T(erril) D(iener)

ALLEN, THOMAS B(ENTON)
(Tom Allen)
Birthdate: 3/20/1929
Birthplace: Bridgeport, CT
Information Available in These Sources: SATA 45

ALLEN, TOM
See Allen, Thomas B(enton)

ALLERTON, MARY
See Govan, Christine Noble

ALLINGTON, RICHARD L(LOYD)
Birthdate: 5/13/1947
Birthplace: Grand Rapids, MI
Information Available in These Sources: SATA 35, SATA 39

ALLISON, BOB
Birthplace: NY
Information Available in These Sources: ABYP 2, ABYP 3, SATA 14

ALLISON, LINDA
Birthdate: 7/7/1948
Birthplace: San Bernardino, CA
Information Available in These Sources: SATA 43

ALLISON, RAND
See McCormick, Wilfred

ALLMENDINGER, DAVID F(REDERICK), JR.
Birthdate: 5/13/1938
Birthplace: Wooster, OH
Information Available in These Sources: SATA 35

ALLRED, GORDON T.
Birthdate: 12/27/1930
Birthplace: Iowa City, IA
Information Available in These Sources: SATA 10

ALLYN, ALLEN
See Eberle, Irmengarde

ALMOND, LINDA STEVENS
Birthdate: 1881?
Birthplace: Seaford, DE
Deathdate: 1/10/1987
Information Available in These Sources: SATA 50

ALMQUIST, DON
Birthdate: 7/21/1929
Birthplace: Hartford, CT
Information Available in These Sources: IBYP 1, IBYP 2, SATA 11

ALOISE, FRANK E.
Information Available in These Sources: IBYP 1, IBYP 2

ALSOP, MARY O'HARA
(Mary O'Hara, Mary Sture-Vasa)
Birthdate: 7/12/1885
Birthplace: Cape May Point, NJ
Deathdate: 10/14/1980 or 10/15/1980
Information Available in These Sources: SATA 2, SATA 24, SATA 34, TCCW 1, TCCW 2, TCCW 3

ALSOP, REESE FELL
Birthdate: 1913
Birthplace: New York, NY
Information Available in These Sources: ABYP 2, ABYP 3

ALTER, JUDITH (MACBAIN)
(Judy Alter)
Birthdate: 7/22/1938
Birthplace: Chicago, IL
Information Available in These Sources: SATA 52

ALTER, JUDY
See Alter, Judith (MacBain)

ALTER, ROBERT EDMOND
(Robert Raymond, Robert Retla)
Birthdate: 12/10/1925
Birthplace: San Francisco, CA
Deathdate: 5/26/1965
Information Available in These Sources: ABYP 2, ABYP 3, SATA 9

ALTSCHULER, FRANZ
Birthdate: 10/2/1923
Birthplace: Mannheim, Germany
Information Available in These Sources: SATA 45

ALTSHELER, JOSEPH A(LEXANDER)
Birthdate: 4/29/1862
Birthplace: Three Springs, KY
Deathdate: 6/5/1919
Information Available in These Sources: ABYP 1, ABYP 2, JBA 1, TCCW 2 TCCW 3, YABC

ALVAREZ, JOSEPH A.
Birthdate: 10/2/1930
Birthplace: New York, NY
Information Available in These Sources: SATA 18

ALVAREZ-DEL REY, RAMON FELIPE SAN JUAN MARIO SILVO ENRICO
See del Rey, Lester

ALZADA, JUAN SANCHEZ
See Joseph, James (Herz)

AMBROSE, STEPHEN E(DWARD)
Birthdate: 1/10/1936
Birthplace: Decatur, IL
Information Available in These Sources: SATA 40

AMERMAN, LOCKHART
Birthdate: 9/11/1911
Birthplace: New York, NY
Deathdate: 11/20/1969
Information Available in These Sources: ABYP 2, ABYP 3, SATA 3

AMES, EVELYN
Birthdate: 6/26/1908
Birthplace: Hamden, CT
Information Available in These Sources: SATA 13

AMES, GERALD
Birthdate: 10/17/1906
Birthplace: Rochester, NY
Information Available in These Sources: ABYP 4, BABP, JBA 3, SATA 11

AMES, LEE J(UDAH)
(Jonathan David)
Birthdate: 1/8/1921
Birthplace: New York, NY
Information Available in These Sources: ABYP 2, ABYP 3, ICB 2, ICB 3, ICB 4, JBA 6, SATA 3

AMES, MILDRED
Birthdate: 11/2/1919
Birthplace: Bridgeport, CT
Information Available in These Sources: JBA 5, SATA 22

AMES, ROSE WYLER
See Wyler, Rose

AMON, ALINE
Birthdate: 10/15/1928
Birthplace: Paris, France
Information Available in These Sources: ABYP 4, SATA 9

AMOSS, BERTHE (MARKS)
Birthdate: 9/26/1925
Birthplace: New Orleans, LA
Information Available in These Sources: DACF, SATA 5

AMUNDSEN, RICHARD E.
Information Available in These Sources: IBYP 2

ANASTASIO, DINA
Birthdate: 10/9/1941
Birthplace: Des Moines, IA
Information Available in These Sources: SATA 30, SATA 37

ANCONA, GEORGE
Birthdate: 12/4/1929
Birthplace: New York, NY
Information Available in These Sources: ABYP 4, JBA 6, SATA 12

ANDERSDATTER, KARLA M(ARGARET)
(Karla Margaret)
Birthdate: 4/9/1938
Birthplace: San Francisco, CA
Information Available in These Sources: SATA 34

ANDERSEN, TED
See Boyd, Waldo T.

ANDERSEN, YVONNE
Birthdate: 9/7/1932
Birthplace: Long Beach, CA
Information Available in These Sources: ABYP 4, SATA 27

ANDERSON, ADRIENNE ADAMS
See Adams, Adrienne

ANDERSON, BERNICE G(OUDY)
Birthdate: 11/17/1894
Birthplace: Lawrence, KS
Information Available in These Sources: SATA 33

ANDERSON, BRAD
See Anderson, Bradley Jay

ANDERSON, BRADLEY JAY
(Brad Anderson)
Birthdate: 5/14/1924
Birthplace: Jamestown, NY
Information Available in These Sources: SATA 31, SATA 33

ANDERSON, C(LARENCE) W(ILLIAM)
Birthdate: 4/12/1891
Birthplace: Wahoo, NE
Deathdate: 3/26/1971
Information Available in These Sources: ABYP 1, ABYP 3, BABP, ICB 1, ICB 2, ICB 3, JBA 2, JBA 3, SATA 11, SVC 2, SVC 3, TCCW 2 TCCW 3

ANDERSON, CLIFFORD
See Gardner, Richard (M.)

ANDERSON, DAVE
See Anderson, David Poole

ANDERSON, DAVID POOLE
(Dave Anderson)
Birthdate: 5/6/1929
Birthplace: Troy, NY
Information Available in These Sources: SATA 60

ANDERSON, ELOISE ADELL
Birthdate: 5/13/1927
Birthplace: Warren, MN
Information Available in These Sources: SATA 9

ANDERSON, ETHEL TODD
Birthplace: OH
Information Available in These Sources: ABYP 2, ABYP 3

ANDERSON, GRACE FOX
(Grace Fox)
Birthdate: 5/14/1932
Birthplace: Melrose Park, IL
Information Available in These Sources: SATA 43

ANDERSON, GUNNAR (DONALD)
Birthdate: 3/3/1927
Birthplace: Berkeley, CA
Information Available in These Sources: IBYP 2

ANDERSON, HELEN JEAN
(Jean Anderson)
Birthdate: 10/12/1931
Birthplace: Raleigh, NC
Information Available in These Sources: ABYP 4

ANDERSON, JEAN
See Anderson, Helen Jean

ANDERSON, JOHN LONZO
(Lonzo Anderson)
Birthdate: 3/1/1905
Birthplace: Ellijay, GA
Information Available in These Sources: ABYP 4, BABP, FLTYP, JBA 3, SATA 2

ANDERSON, JOY
Birthdate: 7/22/1928
Birthplace: Los Angeles, CA
Information Available in These Sources: SATA 1

ANDERSON, LAVERE (FRANCIS SHOENFELT)
Birthdate: 4/15/1907
Birthplace: Muskogee, OK
Information Available in These Sources: SATA 27

ANDERSON, LEONE CASTELL
Birthdate: 8/12/1923
Birthplace: Los Angeles, CA
Information Available in These Sources: SATA 49, SATA 53

ANDERSON, LONZO
See Anderson, John Lonzo

ANDERSON, LUCIA (LEWIS)
(Lucia Z. Lewis)
Birthdate: 8/9/1922
Birthplace: Pittsburgh, PA
Information Available in These Sources: SATA 10

ANDERSON, MADELYN KLEIN
Birthplace: New York, NY
Information Available in These Sources: SATA 28

ANDERSON, MARGARET J(EAN)
Birthdate: 12/24/1931
Birthplace: Gorebridge, Scotland
Information Available in These Sources: JBA 5, SATA 27

ANDERSON, MARY (QUIRK)
Birthdate: 1/20/1939
Birthplace: New York, NY
Information Available in These Sources: ABYP 4, JBA 6, SATA 7

ANDERSON, NEIL
See Beim, Jerrold

ANDERSON, NORMAN (DEAN)
Birthdate: 1/29/1928
Birthplace: Dickens, IA
Information Available in These Sources: SATA 22

ANDERSON, POUL (WILLIAM)
(A. A. Craig, Michael Karageorge, Winston P. Sanders)
Birthdate: 11/25/1926
Birthplace: Bristol, PA
Information Available in These Sources: ABYP 4, SATA 39

ANDERSON, RUTH I(RENE)
Birthdate: 4/17/1919
Birthplace: Millertown, PA
Information Available in These Sources: ABYP 2, ABYP 3

ANDRE, EVELYN M(ARIE)
Birthdate: 7/13/1924
Birthplace: PA
Information Available in These Sources: SATA 27

ANDREWS, BENNY
Birthdate: 11/13/1930
Birthplace: Madison, GA
Information Available in These Sources: IBYP 1, IBYP 2, SATA 31

ANDREWS, F(RANK) EMERSON
Birthdate: 1/26/1902
Birthplace: Lancaster, PA
Deathdate: 8/7/1978
Information Available in These Sources: SATA 22

ANDREWS, JULIE
See Edwards, Julie (Andrews)

ANDREWS, MARY RAYMOND SHIPMAN
Birthdate: 1860 or 1865
Birthplace: Mobile, AL
Deathdate: 8/2/1936
Information Available in These Sources: JBA 1

ANDREWS, ROY CHAPMAN
Birthdate: 1/26/1884
Birthplace: Beloit, WI
Deathdate: 3/11/1960
Information Available in These Sources: ABYP 1, ABYP 3, SATA 19

ANDREWS, V. C.
See Andrews, Virginia Cleo

ANDREWS, VIRGINIA CLEO
(V. C. Andrews)
Birthdate: 6/6/1924
Birthplace: Portsmouth, VA
Deathdate: 12/19/1986
Information Available in These Sources: SATA 50

ANDRIOLA, ALFRED J.
Birthdate: 5/24/1912
Birthplace: New York, NY
Deathdate: 3/29/1983
Information Available in These Sources: SATA 34

ANDRIST, RALPH K.
Birthdate: 1/11/1914
Birthplace: Crookston, MN
Information Available in These Sources: ABYP 4, SATA 45

ANGELES, PETER A.
Birthdate: 2/21/1931
Birthplace: Ambridge, PA
Information Available in These Sources: SATA 40

ANGELL, JUDIE
Birthdate: 7/10/1937
Birthplace: New York, NY
Information Available in These Sources: JBA 6, SATA 22

ANGELL, MADELINE
Birthdate: 1/6/1919
Birthplace: Devils Lake, ND
Information Available in These Sources: SATA 18

ANGELO, VALENTI
Birthdate: 6/23/1897
Birthplace: Massarosa, Tuscany, Italy
Information Available in These Sources: ABYP 1, ABYP 3, ICB 1, ICB 2, ICB 3, JBA 2, SATA 14, TCCW 1, TCCW 2

ANGELOU, MAYA
Birthdate: 4/4/1928
Birthplace: St. Louis, MO
Information Available in These Sources: SATA 49

ANGIER, BRADFORD
Birthdate: 5/13/1910
Birthplace: Boston, MA
Information Available in These Sources: ABYP 4, SATA 12

ANGLE, PAUL M(CCLELLAND)
Birthdate: 12/25/1900
Birthplace: Mansfield, OH
Deathdate: 5/11/1975
Information Available in These Sources: SATA 20

ANGLUND, JOAN WALSH
Birthdate: 1/3/1926
Birthplace: Hinsdale, IL
Information Available in These Sources: ABYP 1, ABYP 3, ICB 3, JBA 3, SATA 2, TCCW 1

ANGRIST, STANLEY W(OLFF)
Birthdate: 6/3/1933
Birthplace: Dallas, TX
Information Available in These Sources: SATA 4

ANITA
See Daniel, Anita

ANNETT, CORA
See Scott, Cora Annett (Pipitone)

ANNIXTER, JANE
See Sturtzel, Jane Levington

ANNIXTER, PAUL
See Sturtzel, Howard A(llison)

ANTELL, WILL D.
Birthdate: 10/2/1935
Birthplace: White Earth, MN
Information Available in These Sources: SATA 30

ANTHONY, EDWARD
Birthdate: 8/4/1895
Birthplace: New York, NY
Deathdate: 8/16/1971
Information Available in These Sources: ABYP 2, ABYP 3, SATA 21

ANTICAGLIA, ELIZABETH
Birthdate: 9/14/1939
Birthplace: New York, NY
Information Available in These Sources: SATA 12

ANTOLINI, MARGARET FISHBACK
(Margaret Fishback)
Birthdate: 3/10/1904
Birthplace: Washington, DC
Deathdate: 9/25/1985
Information Available in These Sources: SATA 45

ANTON, MICHAEL J(AMES)
Birthdate: 12/6/1940
Birthplace: Memphis, TN
Information Available in These Sources: SATA 12

ANTONACCI, ROBERT JOSEPH
Birthdate: 1/21/1916
Birthplace: Toluca, IL
Information Available in These Sources: SATA 37, SATA 45

ANTONCICH, BETTY (KENNEDY)
Birthdate: 12/1/1913
Birthplace: Seattle, WA
Information Available in These Sources: ABYP 2, ABYP 3

AODHAGAIN, EAMON MAC
See Egan, Edward Welstead

APFEL, NECIA H(ALPERN)
Birthdate: 7/31/1930
Birthplace: Mount Vernon, NY
Information Available in These Sources: SATA 41

APHRODITE, J.
See Livingston, Carole

APIKUNI
See Schultz, James Willard

APILADO, TONY
Birthplace: HI
Information Available in These Sources: IBYP 2

APPEL, BENJAMIN
Birthdate: 9/13/1907
Birthplace: New York, NY
Deathdate: 4/3/1977
Information Available in These Sources: SATA 21, SATA 39

APPEL, DAVID H.
Information Available in These Sources: ABYP 2, ABYP 3

APPEL, MARTIN E(LIOT)
(Marty Appel)
Birthdate: 8/7/1948
Birthplace: Brooklyn, NY
Information Available in These Sources: SATA 45

APPEL, MARTY
See Appel, Martin E(liot)

APPLE, MARGOT
Birthplace: Detroit, MI
Information Available in These Sources: SATA 42

APPLEBAUM, STAN
(Robert Keith)
Birthdate: 3/1/1929
Birthplace: Newark, NJ
Information Available in These Sources: SATA 45

APPLETON, VICTOR
See Garis, Howard R(oger) and Stratemeyer, Edward L.

APPLETON, VICTOR II
See Adams, Harriet S(tratemeyer) and Stratemeyer, Edward L.

APPLEYARD, DEV
Birthplace: NE
Information Available in These Sources: IBYP 2

APSLER, ALFRED
Birthdate: 11/13/1907
Birthplace: Vienna, Austria
Information Available in These Sources: ABYP 4, SATA 10

ARAGONES, SERGIO
Birthdate: 9/6/1937
Birthplace: Castellon, Spain
Information Available in These Sources: SATA 39, SATA 48

ARBEITER, JEAN S(ONKIN)
Birthdate: 1/13/1937
Birthplace: New York, NY
Information Available in These Sources: ABYP 4

ARBUCKLE, DOROTHY FRY
Birthdate: 1/23/1910
Birthplace: Eldred, IL
Deathdate: 11/14/1982
Information Available in These Sources: SATA 33

ARBUTHNOT, MAY HILL
Birthdate: 8/27/1884
Birthplace: Mason City, IA
Deathdate: 10/2/1969
Information Available in These Sources: ABYP 1, ABYP 3, SATA 2

ARCHAMBAULT, JOHN
Birthplace: Pasadena, CA
Information Available in These Sources: JBA 6

ARCHER, FRANK
See O'Connor, Richard

ARCHER, JULES
Birthdate: 1/27/1915
Birthplace: New York, NY
Information Available in These Sources: ABYP 2, ABYP 3, JBA 5, SATA 4

ARCHER, MARION FULLER
Birthdate: 2/9/1917
Birthplace: Eugene, OR
Information Available in These Sources: SATA 11

ARCHIBALD, JOE
See Archibald, Joseph S(topford)

ARCHIBALD, JOSEPH S(TOPFORD)
(Joe Archibald)
Birthdate: 9/2/1898
Birthplace: Newington, NH
Deathdate: 3/1/1986
Information Available in These Sources: ABYP 1, ABYP 3, SATA 3, SATA 47

ARDEN, BARBI(E)
See Stoutenberg, Adrien (Pearl)

ARDEN, WILLIAM
See Lynds, Dennis

AREHART-TREICHEL, JOAN
Birthdate: 5/19/1942
Birthplace: Louisville, KY
Information Available in These Sources: SATA 22

ARENELLA, ROY
Birthdate: 7/3/1939
Birthplace: Brooklyn, NY
Information Available in These Sources: SATA 14

ARKHURST, JOYCE (COOPER)
Birthdate: 10/20/1921
Birthplace: Seattle, WA
Information Available in These Sources: BAI, ABYP 4

ARKIN, ALAN (WOLF)
(Roger Short)
Birthdate: 3/26/1934
Birthplace: New York, NY
Information Available in These Sources: SATA 32, SATA 59

ARKIN, DAVID
Birthdate: 12/19/1906
Birthplace: New York, NY
Information Available in These Sources: ABYP 4

ARMER, ALBERTA (ROLLER)
Birthdate: 2/11/1904
Birthplace: Huntingburg, IN
Information Available in These Sources: SATA 9

ARMER, LAURA (ADAMS)
Birthdate: 1/12/1874
Birthplace: Sacramento, CA
Deathdate: 3/3/1963
Information Available in These Sources: ABYP 1, ABYP 3, ICB 1, JBA 2, SATA 13, TCCW 2, TCCW 3

ARMER, SIDNEY
Birthdate: 4/28/1871
Birthplace: San Francisco, CA
Information Available in These Sources: ICB 1

ARMOUR, RICHARD (WILLARD)
Birthdate: 7/25/1906
Birthplace: San Pedro, CA
Information Available in These Sources: ABYP 2, ABYP 3, JBA 5, SATA 14TCCW 1

ARMSTRONG, GEORGE D.
Birthdate: 5/26/1927
Birthplace: Chicago, IL
Information Available in These Sources: SATA 10

ARMSTRONG, GERRY (BREEN)
Birthdate: 10/28/1929
Birthplace: Detroit, MI
Information Available in These Sources: SATA 10

ARMSTRONG, LOUISE
Information Available in These Sources: ABYP 4, SATA 33, SATA 43

ARMSTRONG, THOMAS E.
(Tom Armstrong)
Birthdate: 1935
Information Available in These Sources: IBYP 2

ARMSTRONG, TOM
See Armstrong, Thomas E.

ARMSTRONG, WILLIAM H(OWARD)
Birthdate: 9/14/1914
Birthplace: Lexington, VA
Information Available in These Sources: ABYP 3, DACF, MBMP, JBA 3, SATA 4, TCCW 1, TCCW 2, TCCW 3

ARNDT, URSULA (MARTHA H.)
Birthplace: Dusseldorf, Germany
Information Available in These Sources: IBYP 1, IBYP 2, SATA 39, SATA 56

ARNESON, D. J.
See Arneson, Don Jon

ARNESON, DON JON
(D. J. Arneson)
Birthdate: 8/15/1935
Birthplace: Montevideo, MN
Information Available in These Sources: SATA 37

ARNETT, CAROLINE
See Cole, Lois Dwight

ARNO, ENRICO
Birthdate: 7/16/1913
Birthplace: Mannheim, Germany
Deathdate: 4/30/1981
Information Available in These Sources: IBYP1, IBYP 2, ICB 2, ICB 3, JBA 4, SATA 28, SATA 43

ARNOLD, CAROLINE
Birthdate: 5/16/1944
Birthplace: Pittsburgh, PA
Information Available in These Sources: SATA 34, SATA 36

ARNOLD, ELLIOTT
Birthdate: 9/13/1912
Birthplace: New York, NY
Deathdate: 5/13/1980
Information Available in These Sources: ABYP 2, ABYP 3, SATA 5, SATA 22

ARNOLD, EMILY
See McCully, Emily Arnold

ARNOLD, OREN
Birthdate: 7/20/1900
Birthplace: Minden, TX
Information Available in These Sources: SATA 4

ARNOLD, SUSAN (RISER)
Birthdate: 10/11/1951
Birthplace: Salt Lake City, UT
Information Available in These Sources: SATA 58

ARNOLDY, JULIE
See Bischoff, Julia Bristol

ARNOSKY, JIM
Birthdate: 9/1/1946
Birthplace: New York, NY
Information Available in These Sources: JBA 5, SATA 22

ARNOV, BORIS, JR.
Birthdate: 10/17/1926
Birthplace: Los Angeles, CA
Information Available in These Sources: ABYP 1, ABYP 3, SATA 12

ARNOW, HARRIETTE (LOUISA) SIMPSON
(Harriette Simpson)
Birthdate: 7/7/1908
Birthplace: Wayne County, KY
Deathdate: 3/22/1986
Information Available in These Sources: SATA 42, SATA 47

ARNSTEIN, HELEN S(OLOMON)
Birthdate: 4/23/1915
Birthplace: New York, NY
Information Available in These Sources: SATA 12

ARNTSON, HERBERT E(DWARD)
Birthdate: 4/8/1911
Birthplace: Tacoma, WA
Information Available in These Sources: SATA 12

ARONIN, BEN
Birthdate: 1904
Deathdate: 8/26/1980
Information Available in These Sources: SATA 25

ARORA, SHIRLEY LEASE
Birthdate: 6/3/1930
Birthplace: Youngstown, OH
Information Available in These Sources: DACF, SATA 2

ARQUETTE, LOIS
See Duncan, Lois S(teinmetz)

ARQUETTE, LOIS S(TEINMETZ)
See Duncan, Lois S(teinmetz)

ARRE, HELEN
See Ross, Z(ola) H(elen Girdey)

ARROWOOD, CLINTON
See Arrowood, McKendrick Lee Clinton

ARROWOOD, MCKENDRICK LEE CLINTON
(Clinton Arrowood)
Birthdate: 10/16/1939
Birthplace: Price, UT
Information Available in These Sources: SATA 19

ARTHUR, ROBERT
See Feder, Robert Arthur

ARTHUR, T. S.
See Arthur, Timothy Shay

ARTHUR, TIMOTHY SHAY
(T. S. Arthur)
Birthdate: 6/6/1809
Birthplace: Orange County, NY
Deathdate: 3/6/1885
Information Available in These Sources: DLB 42

ARTIS, VICKI KIMMEL
Birthdate: 12/14/1945
Birthplace: Milwaukee, WI
Information Available in These Sources: SATA 12

ARTZYBASHEFF, BORIS (MIKLAILOVICH)
Birthdate: 5/25/1899
Birthplace: Kharkov, Ukraine, Russia
Deathdate: 7/16/1965
Information Available in These Sources: ABYP 2, ABYP 3, ICB 1, JBA 1, JBA 2, SATA 14, SVC 2, SVC 3

ARUEGO, ARIANE
See Dewey, Ariane

ARUEGO, JOSE
Birthdate: 8/9/1932
Birthplace: Manila, Philippines
Information Available in These Sources: IBYP 2, ICB 4, JBA 4, SATA 6

ARUNDEL, JOCELYN
See Alexander, Jocelyn (Anne Arundel)

ASCH, FRANK
Birthdate: 8/6/1946
Birthplace: Somerville, NJ
Information Available in These Sources: ABYP 4, ICB 4, JBA 4, SATA 5, TCCW 3

ASHABRANNER, BRENT (KENNETH)
Birthdate: 11/3/1921
Birthplace: Shawnee, OK
Information Available in These Sources: JBA 6, SATA 1

ASHER, SANDY (FENICHEL)
Birthdate: 10/16/1942
Birthplace: Philadelphia, PA
Information Available in These Sources: SATA 34, SATA 36

ASHLEY, RAY
See Abrashkin, Raymond

ASHLEY, ROBERT P(AUL) JR.
Birthdate: 4/15/1915
Birthplace: Baltimore, MD
Information Available in These Sources: ABYP 2, ABYP 3

ASHMEAD, GORDON (B.)
Information Available in These Sources: ABYP 2, ABYP 3

ASHMUN, MARGARET ELIZA
Birthdate: 1875
Birthplace: Waupaca County, WI
Deathdate: 3/13/1940
Information Available in These Sources: JBA 1, JBA 2

ASHTON, WARREN T.
See Adams, William Taylor

ASIMOV, ISAAC
(Paul French)
Birthdate: 1/2/1920
Birthplace: Petrovichi, USSR
Information Available in These Sources: ABYP 1, ABYP 3, BC, JBA 3, SATA 1, SATA 26

ASIMOV, JANET
See Jeppson, J(anet) O(pal)

ASINOF, ELIOT
Birthdate: 7/13/1919
Birthplace: New York, NY
Information Available in These Sources: SATA 6

ATENE, ANNA
See Atene, Rita Anna

ATENE, RITA ANNA
(Anna Atene)
Birthdate: 4/24/1922
Birthplace: Philadelphia, PA
Information Available in These Sources: SATA 12

ATKIN, FLORA B(LUMENTHAL)
Birthdate: 5/15/1919
Birthplace: Baltimore, MD
Information Available in These Sources: TCCW 1

ATKINSON, ALLEN
Birthdate: 1953?
Birthplace: Norwalk, CT
Deathdate: 6/22/1987
Information Available in These Sources: SATA 46, SATA 60

ATKINSON, ELEANOR (STACKHOUSE)
Birthdate: 1863
Birthplace: Rensselaer, IN
Deathdate: 11/4/1942
Information Available in These Sources: JBA 1

ATKINSON, MARGARET FLEMING
Birthplace: Washington, DC
Information Available in These Sources: ABYP 2, ABYP 3, SATA 14

ATWATER, FLORENCE (HESSELTINE CARROLL)
Information Available in These Sources: SATA 16

ATWATER, FREDERICK MUND
See Atwater, Richard (Tupper)

ATWATER, MONTGOMERY MEIGS
Birthdate: 10/21/1904
Birthplace: Baker, OR
Information Available in These Sources: ABYP 1, ABYP 3, MJA, SATA 15

ATWATER, RICHARD (TUPPER)
(Frederick Mund Atwater, Riq)
Birthdate: 12/29/1892
Birthplace: Chicago, IL
Deathdate: 8/21/1948 or 8/21/1938
Information Available in These Sources: SATA 27, SATA 54, TCCW 1, TCCW 2, TCCW 3

ATWOOD, ANN (MARGARET)
Birthdate: 2/12/1913
Birthplace: Heber, CA
Information Available in These Sources: ABYP 4, JBA 4, SATA 7

AUERBACH, MARJORIE (HOFFBERG)
Birthdate: 12/10/1932
Birthplace: Astoria, NY
Information Available in These Sources: ABYP 4, ICB 2

AUGELLI, JOHN P(AT)
Birthdate: 1/30/1921
Birthplace: Italy
Information Available in These Sources: SATA 46

AULT, PHIL
See Ault, Phillip H(alliday)

AULT, PHILLIP H(ALLIDAY)
(Phil Ault)
Birthdate: 4/26/1914
Birthplace: Maywood, IL
Information Available in These Sources: ABYP 4, SATA 23

AULT, ROSALIE SAIN
(Roz Ault)
Birthdate: 4/22/1942
Birthplace: Abington, PA
Information Available in These Sources: SATA 38

AULT, ROZ
See Ault, Rosalie Sain

AUSLANDER, JOSEPH
Birthdate: 10/11/1897
Birthplace: Philadelphia, PA
Deathdate: 6/22/1965
Information Available in These Sources: JBA 1

AUSTIN, ELIZABETH S(CHLING)
Birthdate: 1/23/1907
Birthplace: New York, NY
Information Available in These Sources: ABYP 4, SATA 5

AUSTIN, JANE GOODWIN
See Austin, Mary Jane Goodwin

AUSTIN, MARGOT
Birthplace: Portland, OR
Information Available in These Sources: ABYP 1, ABYP 2, MJA, SATA 11

AUSTIN, MARY (HUNTER)
Birthdate: 9/9/1868
Birthplace: Carlinville, IL
Deathdate: 8/14/1934
Information Available in These Sources: SVC 2, SVC 3

AUSTIN, MARY C(ARRINGTON)
Birthdate: 1/10/1915
Birthplace: Sherrill, NY
Information Available in These Sources: JBA 1

AUSTIN, MARY JANE GOODWIN
(Jane Goodwin Austin)
Birthdate: 2/25/1831
Birthplace: Worcester, MA
Deathdate: 3/30/1894
Information Available in These Sources: JBA 1

AUSTIN, OLIVER L(UTHER) JR.
Birthdate: 5/24/1903
Birthplace: Tuckahoe, NY
Deathdate: 12/31/1988
Information Available in These Sources: ABYP 4, SATA 7, SATA 59

AUSTIN, PHIL
Birthdate: 1/27/1910
Birthplace: Waukegan, IL
Information Available in These Sources: IBYP 1, IBYP 2

AUSTIN, R. G.
See Gelman, Rita Golden

AUSTIN, TOM
See Jacobs, Linda C.

AUTH, TONY
See Auth, William Anthony, Jr.

AUTH, WILLIAM ANTHONY, JR.
(Tony Auth)
Birthdate: 5/7/1942
Birthplace: Akron, OH
Information Available in These Sources: SATA 49

AVERILL, ESTHER (HOLDEN)
(John Domino)
Birthdate: 7/24/1902
Birthplace: Bridgeport, CT
Information Available in These Sources: ABYP 1, ABYP 2, ICB 2, ICB 3, ICB 4, JBA 2, SATA 1, SATA 28 TCCW 1, TCCW 2, TCCW 3

AVERY, A. A.
See Montgomery, Rutherford (George)

AVERY, AL
See Montgomery, Rutherford (George)

AVERY, KAY
Birthdate: 9/29/1908
Birthplace: Middletown, VT
Information Available in These Sources: SATA 5

AVERY, LYNN
See Cole, Lois Dwight

AVI
See Wortis, Avi

AVINOFF, ANDREY
Birthdate: 2/14/1884
Birthplace: Tulchin, Russia
Deathdate: 7/16/1949
Information Available in These Sources: ICB 1

AVISON, GEORGE (ALFRED)
Birthdate: 5/6/1885
Birthplace: Norwalk, CT
Information Available in These Sources: CICB, IBYP 1, IBYP 2, ICB 1, ICB 2

AXEMAN, LOIS
Birthplace: Chicago, IL
Information Available in These Sources: IBYP 2

AYARS, JAMES S(TERLING)
Birthdate: 11/17/1898
Birthplace: Wilmette, IL
Information Available in These Sources: ABYP 2, ABYP 3, SATA 4

AYER, JACQUELINE (BRANDFORD)
Birthdate: 5/2/1930
Birthplace: New York, NY
Information Available in These Sources: IBYP 2, ICB 3, JBA 3, SATA 13 TCCW 1

AYER, MARGARET
Birthdate: 1903
Birthplace: New York, NY
Deathdate: 4/24/1981
Information Available in These Sources: IBYP 2, ICB 2, MJA, SATA 15

AYLESWORTH, JIM
Birthdate: 2/21/1943
Information Available in These Sources: SATA 38

AYLESWORTH, THOMAS G(IBBONS)
Birthdate: 11/5/1927
Birthplace: Valparaiso, IN
Information Available in These Sources: ABYP 4, SATA 4

AYLWARD, WILLIAM JAMES
Birthdate: 9/5/1875
Birthplace: Milwaukee, WI
Deathdate: 2/26/1956
Information Available in These Sources: ICB 1

AYMAR, BRANDT
Birthdate: 5/8/1911
Birthplace: New York, NY
Information Available in These Sources: SATA 22

AYRES, CAROLE BRIGGS
See Briggs, Carole S(uzanne)

AYRES, PATRICIA MILLER
Birthdate: 1923
Birthplace: Tampico, Mexico
Deathdate: 9/17/1985
Information Available in These Sources: SATA 46

AZAID
See Zaidenberg, Arthur

B

BABBITT, NATALIE (MOORE)
Birthdate: 7/28/1932
Birthplace: Dayton, OH
Information Available in These Sources: ABYP 4, DACF, DLB 52, ICB 4, JBA 4, MBMP, SATA 6, TCCW 1, TCCW 2, TCCW 3

BABCOCK, DENNIS ARTHUR
Birthdate: 6/16/1948
Birthplace: Berkeley, CA
Information Available in These Sources: SATA 22

BACH, ALICE (HENDRICKS)
Birthdate: 4/6/1942
Birthplace: New York, NY
Information Available in These Sources: ABYP 4, JBA 5, SATA 27, SATA 30

BACH, RICHARD DAVID
Birthdate: 6/23/1936
Birthplace: Oak Park, IL
Information Available in These Sources: SATA 13

BACHARACH, HERMAN ILFELD
Birthdate: 8/5/1899
Birthplace: Las Vegas, NV
Information Available in These Sources: CICB

BACHELLER, IRVING (ADDISON)
Birthdate: 9/26/1859
Birthplace: Pierpont, NY
Deathdate: 2/24/1950
Information Available in These Sources: JBA 1

BACHMAN, FRED
Birthdate: 1/24/1949
Birthplace: Niles, MI
Information Available in These Sources: SATA 12

BACHMAN, RICHARD
See King, Stephen (Edwin)

BACMEISTER, RHODA W(ARNER)
Birthdate: 2/28/1893
Birthplace: Northampton, MA
Information Available in These Sources: SATA 11

BACON, ELIZABETH
(Betty Morrow)
Birthdate: 9/15/1914
Birthplace: Los Angeles, CA
Information Available in These Sources: SATA 3

BACON, JOAN CHASE
See Bowden, Joan Chase

BACON, JOSEPHINE DODGE (DASKAM)
(Josephine Dodge Daskam, Ingraham Lovell)
Birthdate: 2/17/1876
Birthplace: Stamford, CT
Deathdate: 7/29/1961
Information Available in These Sources: SATA 48, SVC 2, SVC 3

BACON, MARGARET FRANCES
(Peggy Bacon)
Birthdate: 5/2/1895
Birthplace: Ridgefield, CT
Deathdate: 1/4/1987
Information Available in These Sources: CICB, IBYP 2, ICB 1, ICB 2, ICB 3, SATA 2, SATA 50, SVC 2 SVC 3

BACON, MARGARET HOPE
Birthdate: 4/7/1921
Birthplace: New York, NY
Information Available in These Sources: SATA 6

BACON, MARTHA SHERMAN
Birthdate: 4/2/1917
Birthplace: Berkeley, CA
Information Available in These Sources: ABYP 4, DACF, SATA 18, SATA 27TCCW 1, TCCW 2, TCCW 3

BACON, PAUL
Birthdate: 1913
Birthplace: MD
Information Available in These Sources: ABYP 1, ABYP 3

BACON, PEGGY
See Bacon, Margaret Frances

BADER, BARBARA (BRENNER)
Birthplace: New York, NY
Information Available in These Sources: ABYP 4

BAERG, HARRY J(OHN)
Birthdate: 5/17/1909
Birthplace: Waldheim, Saskatchewan, Canada
Information Available in These Sources: SATA 12

BAHLKE, VALERIE WORTH
See Worth, Valerie

BAHR, ROBERT
Birthdate: 10/29/1940
Birthplace: Newark, NJ
Information Available in These Sources: SATA 38

BAHTI, TOM
Birthdate: 6/23/1926
Birthplace: South Range, MI
Information Available in These Sources: IBYP 2, SATA 31, SATA 57

BAILEY, ALICE COOPER
Birthdate: 12/9/1890
Birthplace: San Diego, CA
Information Available in These Sources: SATA 12

BAILEY, BERNADINE FREEMAN
Birthdate: 1901
Birthplace: Mattoon, IL
Information Available in These Sources: ABYP1, ABYP 3, SATA 14

BAILEY, CAROLYN SHERWIN
Birthdate: 10/25/1875
Birthplace: Hoosick Falls, NY
Deathdate: 12/23/1961
Information Available in These Sources: ABYP 1, ABYP 3, JBA 2, SATA 14SVC 2, SVC 3, TCCW 1, TCCW 2, TCCW 3

BAILEY, FLORA
Information Available in These Sources: ABYP 1, ABYP 3

BAILEY, FREDERICK AUGUSTUS WASHINGTON
See Douglass, Frederick

BAILEY, JANE H(ORTON)
Birthdate: 5/14/1916
Birthplace: Chicago, IL
Information Available in These Sources: SATA 12

BAILEY, JOHN (SWARTWOUT)
Birthdate: 1907
Birthplace: OH
Information Available in These Sources: ABYP 2, ABYP 3

BAILEY, MATILDA
See Radford, Ruby L(orraine)

BAILEY, RALPH EDGAR
Birthdate: 9/24/1893
Birthplace: East Greenwich, RI
Information Available in These Sources: SATA 11

BAILEY-JONES, BERYL
Birthdate: 11/9/1912
Birthplace: New York, NY
Information Available in These Sources: IBYP 2, ICB 2

BAIN, EDWARD USSICK
(Edward Ustick Bain)
Information Available in These Sources: ABYP 1, ABYP 3

BAIN, EDWARD USTICK
See Bain, Edward Ussick

BAIRD, BIL
(William Britton Baird)
Birthdate: 8/14/1904
Birthplace: Grand Island, NE
Deathdate: 3/18/1987
Information Available in These Sources: SATA 30, SATA 52

BAIRD, EVA-LEE
Information Available in These Sources: ABYP 4

BAIRD, THOMAS (P.)
Birthdate: 4/22/1923
Birthplace: Omaha, NE
Information Available in These Sources: ABYP 4, SATA 39, SATA 45

BAIRD, WILLIAM BRITTON
See Baird, Bil

BAITY, ELIZABETH CHESLEY
Birthdate: 3/5/1907
Birthplace: Hamilton, TX
Information Available in These Sources: MJA, SATA 1

BAKACS, GEORGE
Birthplace: Budapest, Hungary
Information Available in These Sources: IBYP 2

BAKELESS, JOHN (EDWIN)
Birthdate: 12/30/1894
Birthplace: Carlisle Barracks, PA
Deathdate: 8/8/1978
Information Available in These Sources: ABYP 1, ABYP 3, SATA 9

BAKELESS, KATHERINE LITTLE
Birthdate: 12/5/1895
Birthplace: Bloomsburg, PA
Information Available in These Sources: SATA 9

BAKER, ALAN
Birthdate: 11/14/1951
Birthplace: London, England
Information Available in These Sources: SATA 22

BAKER, AUGUSTA (BRAXSTON)
Birthdate: 4/1/1911
Birthplace: Baltimore, MD
Information Available in These Sources: BAI, SATA 3

BAKER, BETTY (LOU)
(Betty Lou Baker Venturo)
Birthdate: 6/20/1928
Birthplace: Bloomsburg, PA
Deathdate: 11/6/1987
Information Available in These Sources: ABYP 2, ABYP 3, DACF, JBA 3, SATA 5, SATA 54, TCCW 1, TCCW 2, TCCW 3

BAKER, CHARLOTTE
Birthdate: 8/31/1910
Birthplace: Nacogdoches, TX
Information Available in These Sources: ABYP 1, ABYP 3, DACF, ICB 2, SATA 2

BAKER, ELIZABETH
See Baker, Mary Elizabeth (Gillette)

BAKER, EMILIE (ADDOMS) KIP
Birthplace: Brooklyn, NY
Information Available in These Sources: SVC 2, SVC 3

BAKER, EUGENE H.
Information Available in These Sources: SATA 50

BAKER, GAYLE C(UNNINGHAM)
Birthdate: 4/23/1950
Birthplace: Elmhurst, IL
Information Available in These Sources: SATA 39

BAKER, JAMES W.
(Jim Baker)
Birthdate: 6/24/1924
Birthplace: Owensboro, KY
Information Available in These Sources: SATA 22

BAKER, JANICE E(DLA)
Birthdate: 6/18/1941
Birthplace: Shreveport, LA
Information Available in These Sources: SATA 22

BAKER, JEFFREY J(OHN) W(HEELER)
Birthdate: 2/2/1931
Birthplace: Montclair, NJ
Information Available in These Sources: SATA 5

BAKER, JIM
See Baker, James W.

BAKER, LAURA NELSON
Birthdate: 1/7/1911
Birthplace: Humboldt, IA
Information Available in These Sources: ABYP 2, ABYP 3, SATA 3

BAKER, LIVA
Birthdate: 6/25/1930
Birthplace: Plymouth, PA
Information Available in These Sources: ABYP 4

BAKER, MARY ELIZABETH (GILLETTE)
(Elizabeth Baker)
Birthdate: 11/14/1923
Birthplace: Rochester, NY
Information Available in These Sources: ABYP 4, SATA 7

BAKER, NINA (BROWN)
Birthdate: 12/31/1888
Birthplace: Galena, KS
Deathdate: 9/1/1957
Information Available in These Sources: ABYP 1, ABYP 3, JBA 2, SATA 15

BAKER, RACHEL (MININBERG)
Birthdate: 3/1/1904
Birthplace: Chernigov, Ukraine, Russia
Deathdate: 7/7/1978
Information Available in These Sources: ABYP 1, ABYP 3, MJA, SATA 2, SATA 26

BAKER, RAY STANNARD
(David Grayson)
Birthdate: 4/17/1870
Birthplace: Lansing, MI
Deathdate: 7/12/1946
Information Available in These Sources: JBA 1

BAKER, SAMM S(INCLAIR)
Birthdate: 7/29/1909
Birthplace: Paterson, NJ
Information Available in These Sources: SATA 12

BAKER, WILLIAM C.
Birthdate: 1891
Information Available in These Sources: ABYP 2, ABYP 3

BALCH, GLENN
Birthdate: 12/11/1902
Birthplace: Venus, TX
Information Available in These Sources: ABYP 1, ABYP 3, MJA, SATA 3

BALDRIDGE, CYRUS LEROY
Birthdate: 5/27/1889
Birthplace: Alton, NY
Information Available in These Sources: IBYP 1, IBYP 2, ICB 1, ICB 2, SATA 29

BALDUCCI, CAROLYN FELEPPA
Birthdate: 2/13/1946
Birthplace: Pelham, NY
Information Available in These Sources: ABYP 4, SATA 5

BALDWIN, ANNE NORRIS
Birthdate: 3/25/1938
Birthplace: Philadelphia, PA
Information Available in These Sources: ABYP 4, SATA 5

BALDWIN, ARTHUR H.
Information Available in These Sources: ABYP 1, ABYP 3

BALDWIN, CLARA
Birthplace: Ironton, MO
Information Available in These Sources: SATA 11

BALDWIN, GORDO
See Baldwin, Gordon C.

BALDWIN, GORDON C.
(Gordo Baldwin, Lew Gordon)
Birthdate: 6/5/1908
Birthplace: Portland, OR
Information Available in These Sources: ABYP 4, SATA 12

BALDWIN, JAMES
(Robert Dudley)
Birthdate: 12/15/1841
Birthplace: Hamilton County, IN
Deathdate: 8/30/1925
Information Available in These Sources: ABYP 1, ABYP 3, JBA 1, JBA 2, SATA 24

BALDWIN, JAMES (ARTHUR)
Birthdate: 8/2/1924
Birthplace: New York, NY
Deathdate: 8/2/1987
Information Available in These Sources: SATA 9, SATA 54

BALDWIN, MARGARET
See Weis, Margaret (Edith)

BALDWIN, STAN(LEY C.)
Birthdate: 12/17/1929
Birthplace: Bend, OR
Information Available in These Sources: SATA 28

BALDWIN-FORD, PAMELA
(Pamela Baldwin Ford)
Information Available in These Sources: IBYP 1, IBYP 2

BALES, CAROL ANN
Birthdate: 11/9/1940
Birthplace: St. Louis, MO
Information Available in These Sources: SATA 29, SATA 57

BALET, JAN (BERNARD)
Birthdate: 7/20/1913
Birthplace: Bremen, Germany
Information Available in These Sources: ABYP 1, ABYP 3, ICB 2, JBA 3, SATA 11

BALIAN, LORNA (KOHL)
Birthdate: 12/14/1929
Birthplace: Milwaukee, WI
Information Available in These Sources: ABYP 4, JBA 5, SATA 9

BALL, JOHN (DUDLEY), JR.
Birthdate: 7/8/1911
Birthplace: Schenectady, NY
Information Available in These Sources: ABYP 2, ABYP 3

BALL, ROBERT
Birthdate: 1918
Birthplace: New York, NY
Information Available in These Sources: IBYP 2, ICB 2

BALL, ZACHARY
See Masters, Kelly Ray

BALLANTINE, LESLEY FROST
See Frost, Lesley

BALLARD, LOWELL CLYNE
Birthdate: 12/29/1904
Birthplace: Bisbee, AZ
Deathdate: 9/20/1986
Information Available in These Sources: SATA 12, SATA 49

BALLARD, MIGNON FRANKLIN
Birthdate: 10/29/1934
Birthplace: Calhoun, GA
Information Available in These Sources: SATA 49

BALOW, TOM
Birthdate: 7/2/1931
Birthplace: Michigan City, IN
Information Available in These Sources: SATA 12

BAMMAN, HENRY A.
Birthdate: 6/13/1918
Birthplace: Macon, MO
Information Available in These Sources: SATA 12

BANCROFT, GRIFFING
Birthdate: 2/18/1907
Birthplace: San Diego, CA
Information Available in These Sources: ABYP 3, SATA 6

BANCROFT, LAURA
See Baum, L(yman) Frank

BANDEL, BETTY
Birthdate: 7/28/1912
Birthplace: Washington, DC
Information Available in These Sources: SATA 47

BANER, SKULDA V(ANADIS)
Birthdate: 11/23/1897
Birthplace: Ironwood, MI
Deathdate: 1/31/1964
Information Available in These Sources: SATA 10

BANG, BETSY (GARRETT)
Birthdate: 7/9/1912
Birthplace: SC
Information Available in These Sources: JBA 5, SATA 37, SATA 48

BANG, GARRETT
See Bang, Molly Garrett

BANG, MOLLY GARRETT
(Garrett Bang)
Birthdate: 12/29/1943
Birthplace: Princeton, NJ
Information Available in These Sources: JBA 5, SATA 24

BANKS, LAURA STOCKTON VOORHEES
Birthdate: 1908?
Birthplace: Washington, DC
Deathdate: 6/18/1980
Information Available in These Sources: SATA 23

BANKS, SARA (JEANNE GORDON HARRELL)
(Sara Gordon Harrell)
Birthdate: 11/7/1937
Birthplace: Tuscaloosa, AL
Information Available in These Sources: SATA 26

BANNER, RACHEL
See Roddy, Lee

BANNING, EVELYN I.
Birthdate: 12/10/1903
Birthplace: Oakdale, MA
Information Available in These Sources: SATA 36

BANNISTER, PAT
See Davis, Lou Ellen

BANNON, LAURA (MAY)
Birthplace: Acme, MI
Deathdate: 12/14/1963
Information Available in These Sources: ABYP 1, ABYP 3, ICB 1, ICB 2, ICB 3, MJA, SATA 6

BARBE, WALTER BURKE
Birthdate: 10/30/1926
Birthplace: Miami, FL
Information Available in These Sources: SATA 45

BARBER, LINDA
See Graham-Barber, Lynda

BARBERA, JOE
See Barbera, Joseph Roland

BARBERA, JOSEPH ROLAND
(Joe Barbera)
Birthdate: 3/24/1911
Birthplace: New York, NY
Information Available in These Sources: SATA 49

BARBOUR, RALPH HENRY
(Richard Stillman Powell)
Birthdate: 11/13/1870
Birthplace: Cambridge, MA
Deathdate: 2/19/1944
Information Available in These Sources: ABYP 1, ABYP 3, DLB 22, JBA 1 JBA 2, SATA 16

BARD, ANNE ELIZABETH CAMPBELL
See MacDonald, Betty (Heskett Bard)

BARE, ARNOLD EDWIN
Birthdate: 6/20/1920
Birthplace: New York, NY
Information Available in These Sources: IBYP 2, ICB 1, ICB 2, SATA 16

BARE, COLLEEN STANLEY
Birthplace: Oakland, CA
Information Available in These Sources: SATA 32

BARISH, MATTHEW
Birthdate: 10/19/1907
Birthplace: Jersey City, NJ
Information Available in These Sources: ABYP 4, SATA 12

BARKER, ALBERT W.
(Reefe King, Hawk Macrae)
Birthdate: 1900
Information Available in These Sources: SATA 8

BARKER, MELVERN (J.)
Birthdate: 11/24/1907
Birthplace: Providence, RI
Information Available in These Sources: ICB 2, SATA 11

BARKER, S(QUIRE) OMAR
(Jose Canusi, Dan Scott, Phil Squires)
Birthdate: 6/16/1894
Birthplace: Beulah, NM
Information Available in These Sources: SATA 10

BARKER, WILL
(Doug Demarest)
Birthdate: 3/25/1908
Birthplace: Troy, NY
Deathdate: 9/14/1983
Information Available in These Sources: ABYP 2, ABYP 3, SATA 8

BARKIN, CAROL
(Elizabeth Carroll, Beverly Hastings)
Birthdate: 12/22/1944
Birthplace: Fort Worth, TX
Information Available in These Sources: SATA 42, SATA 52

BARKLEY, JAMES EDWARD
Birthdate: 4/19/1941
Birthplace: New York, NY
Information Available in These Sources: IBYP 2, ICB 4, SATA 6

BARKS, CARL
Birthdate: 3/27/1901
Birthplace: Merrill, OR
Information Available in These Sources: SATA 37

BARKSDALE, LENA
Birthdate: 1887
Birthplace: Philadelphia, PA
Information Available in These Sources: ABYP 2, ABYP 3

BARLOW, GENEVIEVE
Birthdate: 6/10/1910
Birthplace: Gardena, CA
Information Available in These Sources: ABYP 4

BARLOW, ROGER
See Leckie, Robert (Hugh)

BARNABY, RALPH S(TANTON)
Birthdate: 1/21/1893
Birthplace: Meadville, PA
Information Available in These Sources: ABYP 4, SATA 9

BARNER, BOB
Birthdate: 11/11/1947
Birthplace: Tuckerman, AR
Information Available in These Sources: SATA 29

BARNES, CATHERINE J.
Birthdate: 6/6/1918
Birthplace: Philadelphia, PA
Information Available in These Sources: IBYP 2, ICB 2

BARNES, ERIC WOLLENCOTT
See Barnes, Frank Eric Wollencott

BARNES, FRANK ERIC WOLLENCOTT
(Eric Wollencott Barnes)
Birthdate: 5/7/1907
Birthplace: Little Rock, AR
Deathdate: 12/31/1962
Information Available in These Sources: ABYP 2, ABYP 3, SATA 22

BARNETT, L. DAVID
See Laschever, Barnett D.

BARNETT, LEO
Birthdate: 1/3/1925
Birthplace: New York, NY
Information Available in These Sources: ABYP 4

BARNETT, LINCOLN (KINNEAR)
Birthdate: 2/12/1909
Birthplace: New York, NY
Deathdate: 9/8/1979
Information Available in These Sources: SATA 36

BARNETT, MONETA
Birthdate: 1922?
Birthplace: Brooklyn, NY
Deathdate: 11/16/1976
Information Available in These Sources: BAI, IBYP 2, ICB 4, SATA 33

BARNETT, NAOMI
(Naomi Barnett Buchheimer)
Birthdate: 12/14/1927
Birthplace: Cincinnati, OH
Information Available in These Sources: SATA 40

BARNEY, MAGINEL WRIGHT
(Maginel Wright Enright)
Birthdate: 6/19/1881
Birthplace: Weymouth, MA
Deathdate: 4/18/1966
Information Available in These Sources: ICB 1, SATA 32, SATA 39

BARNHART, CLARENCE L(EWIS)
Birthdate: 12/30/1900
Birthplace: Plattsburg, MO
Information Available in These Sources: SATA 48

BARNHART, NANCY
Birthdate: 2/17/1889
Birthplace: St. Louis, MO
Information Available in These Sources: ICB 1, ICB 2

BARNOUW, ADRIAAN JACOB
Birthdate: 10/9/1877
Birthplace: Amsterdam, Holland
Deathdate: 9/27/1968
Information Available in These Sources: ABYP 1, ABYP 3, SATA 27

BARNOUW, VICTOR
Birthdate: 5/25/1915
Birthplace: The Hague, Netherlands
Information Available in These Sources: SATA 28, SATA 43

BARNSTONE, WILLIS
Birthdate: 11/13/1927
Birthplace: Lewiston, ME
Information Available in These Sources: SATA 20

BARNUM, JAY HYDE
Birthdate: 1888?
Birthplace: Geneva, OH
Information Available in These Sources: ABYP 1, ABYP 3, ICB 2, SATA 20

BARNUM, RICHARD
See Stratemeyer, Edward L.

BARNWELL, D. ROBINSON
Birthdate: 4/16/1915
Birthplace: Pageland, SC
Information Available in These Sources: ABYP 4, DACF

BARON, VIRGINIA OLSEN
Birthdate: 7/5/1931
Birthplace: Wilkes-Barre, PA
Information Available in These Sources: ABYP 4, SATA 28, SATA 46

BARR, DONALD
Birthdate: 8/2/1921
Birthplace: New York, NY
Information Available in These Sources: ABYP 4, SATA 20

BARR, GEORGE
Birthdate: 11/11/1907
Birthplace: Brooklyn, NY
Information Available in These Sources: ABYP 2, ABYP 3, SATA 2

BARR, JENE
See Cohen, Jene Barr

BARRER, GERTRUDE
See Barrer-Russell, Gertrude

BARRER-RUSSELL, GERTRUDE
(Gertrude Barrer)
Birthdate: 3/11/1921
Birthplace: New York, NY
Information Available in These Sources: SATA 27

BARRETT, ETHEL
Birthdate: 1914?
Information Available in These Sources: SATA 44

BARRETT, JUDI(TH)
Birthdate: 1941
Birthplace: Brooklyn, NY
Information Available in These Sources: ABYP 4, JBA 6, SATA 26

BARRETT, RON
Birthdate: 7/25/1937
Birthplace: Bronx, NY
Information Available in These Sources: IBYP 2, ICB 4, JBA 6, SATA 14

BARRETT, WILLIAM E(DMUND)
Birthdate: 11/16/1900
Birthplace: New York, NY
Deathdate: 9/14/1986
Information Available in These Sources: SATA 49

BARRINGER, DANIEL MOREAU, JR.
Birthdate: 1900
Birthplace: Philadelphia, PA
Information Available in These Sources: ABYP 4

BARRIOS, DAVID
Information Available in These Sources: IBYP 2

BARRIS, GEORGE
Birthdate: 11/20/1925
Birthplace: Chicago, IL
Information Available in These Sources: ABYP 4, SATA 47

BARROL, GRADY
See Bograd, Larry

BARROWS, MARJORIE
See Barrows, R(uth) M(arjorie)

BARROWS, R(UTH) M(AJORIE)
(Noel Adams, Jack Alden, Marjorie Barrows, Ruth Dixon, Hugh Graham)
Birthdate: 1892?
Birthplace: Chicago, IL
Deathdate: 3/29/1983
Information Available in These Sources: ABYP 1, ABYP 3

BARROWS, R. M.
See Barrows, Ruth Marjorie

BARRY, JAMES E.
Birthplace: NY
Information Available in These Sources: IBYP 1, IBYP 2

BARRY, JAMES P(OTVIN)
Birthdate: 10/23/1918
Birthplace: Alton, IL
Information Available in These Sources: SATA 14

BARRY, KATHARINA (MARIA WATJEN)
Birthdate: 3/31/1936
Birthplace: Berlin, Germany
Information Available in These Sources: ABYP 1, ABYP 3, ICB 3, SATA 4

BARRY, ROBERT (EVERETT)
Birthdate: 10/7/1931
Birthplace: Newport, RI
Information Available in These Sources: ABYP 1, ABYP 3, ICB 3, SATA 6

BARRY, SCOTT
Birthdate: 12/1/1952
Birthplace: Flushing, NY
Information Available in These Sources: SATA 32

BARSS, WILLIAM
Birthdate: 7/1/1916
Birthplace: Syracuse, NY
Information Available in These Sources: IBYP 2, ICB 3

BARTENBACH, JEAN
Birthdate: 8/12/1918
Birthplace: Brooklyn, NY
Information Available in These Sources: SATA 40

BARTH, EDNA (SMITH)
(Edna Weiss)
Birthdate: 3/13/1914
Birthplace: Marblehead, MA
Deathdate: 10/1/1980
Information Available in These Sources: ABYP 4, SATA 7, SATA 24

BARTHELME, DONALD
Birthdate: 4/7/1931
Birthplace: Philadelphia, PA
Information Available in These Sources: ABYP 4, SATA 7

BARTHOLOMEW, BARBARA (G.)
Birthdate: 1941
Birthplace: OK
Information Available in These Sources: SATA 42

BARTHOLOMEW, JEAN
See Beatty, Patricia (Robbins)

BARTLETT, PHILIP A.
See Stratemeyer, Edward L.

BARTLETT, ROBERT MERRILL
Birthdate: 12/23/1899 or 12/23/1898
Birthplace: Kingston, IN
Information Available in These Sources: SATA 12

BARTON, BYRON (THEODORE VARTANIAN)
Birthdate: 9/8/1930
Birthplace: Pawtucket, RI
Information Available in These Sources: ABYP 4, ICB 4, JBA 5, SATA 9

BARTON, HARRIETT
Birthplace: Picher, OK
Information Available in These Sources: SATA 43

BARTON, MAY HOLLIS
See Adams, Harriet S(tratemeyer) and Stratemeyer, Edward L.

BARUCH, DOROTHY W(ALTER)
Birthdate: 8/5/1899
Birthplace: San Francisco, CA
Deathdate: 9/4/1962
Information Available in These Sources: SATA 21, SVC 2, SVC 3

BASHEVIS, ISAAC
See Singer, Isaac (Bashevis)

BASILEVSKY, HELEN
Birthdate: 1939
Birthplace: Brussels, Belgium
Information Available in These Sources: IBYP 1, IBYP 2

BASKIN, LEONARD
Birthdate: 8/15/1922
Birthplace: New Brunswick, NJ
Information Available in These Sources: ICB 4, JBA 5, SATA 27, SATA 30

BASON, LILLIAN
Birthdate: 10/17/1913
Birthplace: Albany, NY
Information Available in These Sources: ABYP 4, SATA 20

BASSETT, JENI (CRISLER)
(Jeni (Crysler) Bassett)
Birthdate: 1960
Information Available in These Sources: SATA 43

BASSETT, JENI (CRYSLER)
See Bassett, Jeni (Crisler)

BASSETT, JOHN KEITH
See Keating, Lawrence A(lfred)

BATE, LUCY
Birthdate: 3/19/1939
Birthplace: Washington, DC
Information Available in These Sources: SATA 18

BATE, NORMAN (ARTHUR)
Birthdate: 1/3/1916
Birthplace: Buffalo, NY
Information Available in These Sources: ABYP 2, ABYP 3, ICB 2, SATA 5

BATES, BARBARA S(NEDEKER)
(Stephen Cuyler, Jim Roberts)
Birthdate: 4/28/1919
Birthplace: Philadelphia, PA
Information Available in These Sources: SATA 12

BATES, BETTY
Birthdate: 10/5/1921
Birthplace: Evanston, IL
Information Available in These Sources: SATA 19

BATES, KATHARINE LEE
Birthdate: 8/12/1859
Birthplace: Falmouth, MA
Deathdate: 3/28/1929
Information Available in These Sources: JBA 1

BATEY, TOM
(Jasper Tomkins)
Birthdate: 12/19/1946
Birthplace: Des Moines, IA
Information Available in These Sources: SATA 41, SATA 52

BATHERMAN, MURIEL
See Sheldon, Muriel

BATIUK, THOMAS M(ARTIN)
Birthdate: 3/14/1947
Birthplace: Akron, OH
Information Available in These Sources: SATA 40

BATSON, LARRY
Birthdate: 2/17/1930
Birthplace: Aguilar, CO
Information Available in These Sources: SATA 35

BATTAGLIA, AURELIUS
Information Available in These Sources: IBYP 2, SATA 33, SATA 50

BATTEN, MARY
Birthdate: 1/19/1937
Birthplace: Smithfield, VA
Information Available in These Sources: ABYP 4, SATA 5

BATTERBERRY, ARIANE RUSKIN
(Ariane Ruskin)
Birthdate: 9/18/1935
Birthplace: New York, NY
Information Available in These Sources: ABYP 2, ABYP 3, SATA 7, SATA 13

BATTERBERRY, MICHAEL (CARVER)
Birthdate: 4/8/1932
Birthplace: Newcastle, England
Information Available in These Sources: ABYP 4, SATA 32

BATTLES, EDITH
See Battles, Roxy Edith (Baker)

BATTLES, ROXY EDITH (BAKER)
(Edith Battles)
Birthdate: 3/29/1921
Birthplace: Spokane, WA
Information Available in These Sources: ABYP 4, SATA 7

BAUER, CAROLINE FELLER
Birthdate: 5/12/1935
Birthplace: Washington, DC
Information Available in These Sources: SATA 46, SATA 52

BAUER, FRED
Birthdate: 3/30/1934
Birthplace: Montpelier, OH
Information Available in These Sources: SATA 36

BAUER, HELEN
Birthdate: 8/14/1900
Birthplace: DeQueen, AR
Information Available in These Sources: SATA 2

BAUER, MARION DANE
Birthdate: 11/20/1938
Birthplace: Oglesby, IL
Information Available in These Sources: DCAF, JBA 5, SATA 20

BAUERNSCHMIDT, MARJORIE
Birthdate: 11/19/1926
Birthplace: Baltimore, MD
Information Available in These Sources: IBYP 2, ICB 2, SATA 15

BAUM, ALLYN Z(ELTON)
Birthdate: 10/22/1924
Birthplace: Chicago, IL
Information Available in These Sources: SATA 20

BAUM, BETTY
Information Available in These Sources: ABYP 2, ABYP 3

BAUM, L(YMAN) FRANK
(Floyd Akers, Laura Bancroft, Louis F. Baum, John Estes Cooke, Captain Hugh Fitzgerald, Suzanne Metcalf, Schuyler Staunton, Edith VanDyne)
Birthdate: 5/15/1856
Birthplace: Chittenango, NY
Deathdate: 5/6/1919
Information Available in These Sources: ABYP 3, DLB 22, FSYP, JBA 3, SATA 18, TCCW 1, TCCW 2, TCCW 3, WC, WCL

BAUM, LOUIS F.
See Baum, L(yman) Frank

BAUM, PATRICIA
Information Available in These Sources: ABYP 4

BAUM, WILLI
Birthdate: 3/10/1931
Birthplace: Bern (Biel), Switzerland
Information Available in These Sources: SATA 4

BAYER, JANE E.
Deathdate: 2/3/1985
Information Available in These Sources: SATA 44

BAYLOR, BYRD
(Baylor Byrd Schweitzer)
Birthdate: 3/28/1924
Birthplace: San Antonio, TX
Information Available in These Sources: ABYP 2, ABYP 3, ABYP 4, JBA 4 SATA 16

BAYNES, ERNEST HAROLD
(Harold Baynes)
Birthdate: 5/1/1868
Birthplace: Calcutta, India
Deathdate: 1/21/1925
Information Available in These Sources: JBA 1, JBA 2, SVC 2, SVC 3

BAYNES, HAROLD
See Baynes, Ernest Harold

BEACH, CHARLES
See Reid, Thomas Mayne

BEACH, CHARLES AMORY
See Stratemeyer, Edward L.

BEACH, EDWARD L(ATIMER)
Birthdate: 4/20/1918
Birthplace: New York, NY
Information Available in These Sources: SATA 12

BEACH, STEWART TAFT
Birthdate: 12/17/1899
Birthplace: Pontiac, MI
Deathdate: 2/21/1979
Information Available in These Sources: ABYP 1, ABYP 3, SATA 23

BEAGLE, PETER S.
Birthdate: 4/20/1939
Birthplace: New York, NY
Information Available in These Sources: SATA 60

BEALER, ALEX W(INKLER III)
Birthdate: 3/6/1921
Birthplace: Valdosta, GA
Deathdate: 3/17/1980
Information Available in These Sources: ABYP 4, SATA 8, SATA 22

BEALS, CARLETON
Birthdate: 11/13/1893
Birthplace: Medicine Lodge, KS
Deathdate: 6/26/1979
Information Available in These Sources: ABYP 1, ABYP 3, SATA 12

BEALS, FRANK LEE
Birthdate: 9/2/1881
Birthplace: Morganton, TN
Deathdate: 8/31/1972
Information Available in These Sources: SATA 26

BEAME, RONA
Birthdate: 12/8/1934
Birthplace: New York, NY
Information Available in These Sources: SATA 12

BEAMER, CHARLES
See Beamer, George Charles, Jr.

BEAMER, GEORGE CHARLES, JR.
(Charles Beamer)
Birthdate: 8/16/1942
Birthplace: Kansas City, MO
Information Available in These Sources: SATA 43

BEARD, CHARLES AUSTIN
Birthdate: 11/27/1874
Birthplace: Knightstown, IN
Deathdate: 9/1/1948
Information Available in These Sources: SATA 18

BEARD, DAN(IEL CARTER)
Birthdate: 6/21/1850
Birthplace: Cincinnati, OH
Deathdate: 6/11/1941
Information Available in These Sources: ABYP 4, JBA 1, SATA 22

BEARDEN, ROMARE (HOWARD)
Birthdate: 9/2/1912 or 9/2/1914
Birthplace: Charlotte, NC
Deathdate: 3/11/1988
Information Available in These Sources: BAI, SATA 22, SATA 56

BEARMAN, JANE (RUTH)
Birthdate: 9/12/1917
Birthplace: Minneapolis, MN
Information Available in These Sources: SATA 29

BEATTY, ELIZABETH
See Holloway, Teresa (Bragunier)

BEATTY, HETTY BURLINGAME
Birthdate: 10/8/1907
Birthplace: New Canaan, CT
Deathdate: 8/20/1971
Information Available in These Sources: ABYP 1, ABYP 3, ICB 2, ICB 3, ICB 4, MJA, SATA 5

BEATTY, JEROME, JR.
Birthdate: 12/9/1918
Birthplace: New Rochelle, NY
Information Available in These Sources: ABYP 2, ABYP 3, SATA 5

BEATTY, JOHN (LOUIS)
Birthdate: 1/24/1922
Birthplace: Portland, OR
Deathdate: 3/23/1975
Information Available in These Sources: DACF, JBA 3, SATA 6, SATA 25, TCCW 1, TCCW 2, TCCW 3

BEATTY, PATRICIA (ROBBINS)
(Jean Bartholomew)
Birthdate: 8/26/1922
Birthplace: Portland, OR
Information Available in These Sources: ABYP 2, ABYP 3, DACF, JBA 3, SATA 1, SATA 30, TCCW 1, TCCW 2, TCCW 3

BEATY, JOHN YOCUM
Birthdate: 12/12/1884
Birthplace: Finchford, IA
Information Available in These Sources: ABYP 1, ABYP 3

BECHTEL, LOUISE SEAMAN
Birthdate: 6/29/1894
Birthplace: Brooklyn, NY
Deathdate: 4/12/1985 or 4/13/1985
Information Available in These Sources: SATA 4, SATA 43

BECK, BARBARA L.
Birthdate: 3/25/1927
Birthplace: Boston, MA
Information Available in These Sources: SATA 12

BECKER, BERIL
Birthdate: 8/24/1901
Birthplace: Slonim, Russia
Information Available in These Sources: ABYP 4, SATA 11

BECKER, JOHN (LEONARD)
Birthdate: 12/12/1901
Birthplace: Chicago, IL
Information Available in These Sources: ABYP 2, ABYP 3, SATA 12

BECKER, JOYCE
Birthdate: 8/27/1936
Birthplace: Brooklyn, NY
Information Available in These Sources: SATA 39

BECKER, MAY LAMBERTON
Birthdate: 8/26/1873
Birthplace: New York, NY
Deathdate: 4/27/1958
Information Available in These Sources: JBA 1, SATA 33

BECKETT, SHEILA
Birthdate: 9/3/1913
Birthplace: Vancouver, B.C., Canada
Information Available in These Sources: SATA 33

BECKHARD, ARTHUR J.
Birthplace: New York, NY
Information Available in These Sources: ABYP 2, ABYP 3

BECKMAN, DELORES
Birthdate: 8/12/1914
Birthplace: Grover Hill, OH
Information Available in These Sources: DACF, SATA 49

BEDFORD, A(NNIE) N(ORTH)
See Watson, Jane Werner

BEE, CLAIR (FRANCIS)
Birthdate: 3/2/1900
Birthplace: Grafton, WV
Deathdate: 5/20/1983
Information Available in These Sources: ABYP 2, ABYP 3

BEEBE, B(URDETTA) F(AYE)
See Johnson, B(urdetta) F(aye)

BEEBE, CHARLES WILLIAM
(William Beebe)
Birthdate: 7/29/1877
Birthplace: Brooklyn, NY
Deathdate: 6/4/1962
Information Available in These Sources: JBA 1, SATA 19, SVC 2, SVC 3

BEEBE, RACHEL IRENE
See Sutton, Margaret (Beebe)

BEEBE, WILLIAM
See Beebe, Charles William

BEEBY, BETTY
Birthdate: 3/26/1923
Birthplace: Detroit, MI
Information Available in These Sources: SATA 25

BEECH, LINDA
Birthplace: New York, NY
Information Available in These Sources: ABYP 4

BEECH, WEBB
See Butterworth, W(illiam) E(dmund III)

BEECROFT, JOHN WILLIAM RICHARD
Birthdate: 6/22/1902
Birthplace: Superior, WI
Deathdate: 9/21/1966
Information Available in These Sources: ABYP 1, ABYP 3

BEELER, NELSON F(REDERICK)
Birthdate: 4/5/1910
Birthplace: Adams, MA
Information Available in These Sources: ABYP 1, ABYP 3, MJA, SATA 13

BEERS, DOROTHY SANDS
Birthdate: 6/17/1917
Birthplace: Rye, NY
Information Available in These Sources: SATA 9

BEERS, LORNA
Birthdate: 5/10/1897
Birthplace: Maple Plain, MN
Information Available in These Sources: SATA 14

BEERS, V(ICTOR) GILBERT
Birthdate: 5/6/1928
Birthplace: Sidell, IL
Information Available in These Sources: SATA 9

BEGAY, HARRISON
Birthdate: 1917
Birthplace: White Cone, AZ
Information Available in These Sources: IBYP 1, IBYP 2

BEGLEY, KATHLEEN A(NNE)
Birthdate: 3/28/1948
Birthplace: Philadelphia, PA
Information Available in These Sources: SATA 21

BEHN, GILES
See Behn, Harry

BEHN, HARRY
(Giles Behn)
Birthdate: 9/24/1898
Birthplace: Prescott(McCabe), AZ
Deathdate: 9/6/1973
Information Available in These Sources: ABYP 2, ABYP 3, DACF, DLB 61, ICB 2, ICB 3, MBMP, MJA, SATA 2, SATA 34, SVC 2, SVC 3 TCCW 1, TCCW 2, TCCW 3

BEHNKE, FRANCES L. (BERRY)
Birthdate: 9/6/1919
Birthplace: Fayette, AL
Information Available in These Sources: SATA 8

BEHR, JOYCE
Birthdate: 12/18/1929
Birthplace: New York, NY
Information Available in These Sources: SATA 15

BEHRENS, JUNE YORK
Birthdate: 4/25/1925
Birthplace: Maricopa, CA
Information Available in These Sources: ABYP 2, ABYP 3, SATA 19

BEHRMAN, CAROL (HELEN)
Birthdate: 8/24/1925
Birthplace: Brooklyn, NY
Information Available in These Sources: SATA 14

BEIM, JERROLD
(Neil Anderson)
Birthdate: 1910
Birthplace: Newark, NJ
Deathdate: 3/2/1957
Information Available in These Sources: ABYP 1, ABYP 3, JBA 2

BEIM, LORRAINE LEVY
Birthdate: 1909
Birthplace: Syracuse, NY
Information Available in These Sources: ABYP 3, JBA 2

BEISER, ARTHUR
Birthdate: 2/16/1931
Birthplace: New York, NY
Information Available in These Sources: ABYP 1, ABYP 3, SATA 22

BEISER, GERMAINE (BOUSQUET)
Birthdate: 3/2/1931
Birthplace: Cambridge, MA
Information Available in These Sources: ABYP 1, ABYP 3, SATA 11

BEITLER, STANLEY (SAMUEL)
Birthdate: 3/7/1924
Birthplace: New York, NY
Information Available in These Sources: ABYP 1, ABYP 3

BELAIR, RICHARD L.
Birthdate: 6/11/1934
Birthplace: Central Falls, RI
Information Available in These Sources: SATA 45

BELDEN, SHIRLEY
Information Available in These Sources: ABYP 1, ABYP 3

BELDEN, WILANNE SCHNEIDER
Birthdate: 10/14/1925
Birthplace: Pittsburgh, PA
Information Available in These Sources: SATA 56

BELKNAP, B. H.
See Ellis, Edward S(ylvester)

BELL, CLARE
Birthdate: 1952
Birthplace: England
Information Available in These Sources: DACF

BELL, CORYDON WHITTEN
Birthdate: 7/16/1894
Birthplace: Tiffin, OH
Information Available in These Sources: ABYP 2, ABYP 3, IBYP 2, ICB 2 ICB 3, JBA 3, SATA 3

BELL, EMILY MARY
See Cason, Emille Mabel Earp

BELL, FREDERIC
Birthdate: 1928
Birthplace: Bronxville, NY
Information Available in These Sources: ABYP 4

BELL, GERTRUDE (WOOD)
Birthdate: 1/28/1911
Birthplace: Liberty, MO
Information Available in These Sources: ABYP 4, SATA 12

BELL, GINA
See Iannone, Jeanne (Koppel)

BELL, JANET
See Clymer, Eleanor (Lowenton)

BELL, JOSEPH N.
Birthdate: 7/4/1921
Birthplace: Bluffton, IN
Information Available in These Sources: ABYP 1, ABYP 3

BELL, KENSIL
Birthdate: 1907
Birthplace: Camden, NJ
Information Available in These Sources: ABYP 1, ABYP 3

BELL, MARGARET E(LIZABETH)
Birthdate: 12/29/1898
Birthplace: Thorn Bay, AK
Information Available in These Sources: ABYP1, ABYP 3, MJA, SATA 2

BELL, NEILL
Birthdate: 1/19/1946
Birthplace: Washington, DC
Information Available in These Sources: SATA 50

BELL, NORMAN (EDWARD)
Birthdate: 7/26/1899
Birthplace: Winnemucca, NV
Information Available in These Sources: SATA 11

BELL, RAYMOND MARTIN
Birthdate: 3/21/1907
Birthplace: Weatherly, PA
Information Available in These Sources: SATA 13

BELL, THELMA HARRINGTON
Birthdate: 7/3/1896
Birthplace: Detroit, MI
Information Available in These Sources: ABYP 2, ABYP 3, JBA 3, SATA 3

BELL-ZANO, GINA
See Iannone, Jeanne (Koppel)

BELLAIRS, JOHN
Birthdate: 1/17/1938
Birthplace: Marshall, MI
Information Available in These Sources: JBA 5, SATA 2

BELLVILLE, CHERYL WALSH
Birthdate: 8/27/1944
Birthplace: Deming, NM
Information Available in These Sources: SATA 49, SATA 54

BELPRE, PURA
(Pura Belpre White)
Birthdate: 2/2/1899
Birthplace: Cidra, PR
Deathdate: 7/1/1982
Information Available in These Sources: ABYP 1, ABYP 3, BABP, JBA 4, SATA 16, SATA 30

BELTING, NATALIA MAREE
Birthdate: 7/11/1915
Birthplace: Oskaloosa, IA
Information Available in These Sources: ABYP 1, ABYP 3, JBA 3, SATA 6

BELTON, JOHN RAYNOR
Birthdate: 11/30/1931
Birthplace: Milwaukee, WI
Information Available in These Sources: SATA 22

BEMELMANS, LUDWIG
Birthdate: 4/27/1898
Birthplace: Meran, Tirol, Austria
Deathdate: 10/1/1962
Information Available in These Sources: ABYP 1, ABYP 3, AICB, CFB, DLB 22, IBYP 1, IBYP 2, ICB 1 ICB 2, ICB 3, MJA, SATA 15, TCCW 1, TCCW 2, TCCW 3, WC

BENAGH, JIM
Birthdate: 10/10/1937
Birthplace: Flint, MI
Information Available in These Sources: ABYP 4

BENARY, MARGOT
See Benary-Isbert, Margot

BENARY-ISBERT, MARGOT
(Margot Benary)
Birthdate: 12/2/1889
Birthplace: Saarbruecken, Germany
Deathdate: 5/27/1979
Information Available in These Sources: ABYP 1, ABYP 3, MJA, SATA 2, SATA 21

BENASUTTI, MARION
Birthdate: 8/2/1908
Birthplace: Philadelphia, PA
Information Available in These Sources: SATA 6

BENCHLEY, NATHANIEL (GODDARD)
Birthdate: 11/13/1915
Birthplace: Newton, MA
Deathdate: 12/14/1981
Information Available in These Sources: ABYP 4, DACF, JBA 4, SATA 3, SATA 25, SATA 28, TCCW 1, TCCW 2, TCCW 3

BENCHLEY, PETER B(RADFORD)
Birthdate: 5/8/1940
Birthplace: New York, NY
Information Available in These Sources: SATA 3

BENDA, WLADYSLAW THEODORE
Birthdate: 1/15/1873
Birthplace: Poznaw, Poland
Deathdate: 12/2/1948
Information Available in These Sources: ICB 1

BENDER, LUCY ELLEN
Birthdate: 6/11/1942
Birthplace: Grantsville, MD
Information Available in These Sources: SATA 22

BENDICK, JEANNE
Birthdate: 2/25/1919
Birthplace: New York, NY
Information Available in These Sources: ABYP 2, ABYP 3, BABP, ICB 2, ICB 3, MJA, SATA 2

BENDICK, ROBERT L(OUIS)
Birthdate: 2/8/1917
Birthplace: New York, NY
Information Available in These Sources: ABYP 2, ABYP 3, MJA, SATA 11

BENEDICT, DOROTHY POTTER
Birthdate: 4/15/1889
Birthplace: Chicago, IL
Deathdate: 12/4/1979
Information Available in These Sources: SATA 11, SATA 23

BENEDICT, LOIS TRIMBLE
Birthdate: 6/29/1902
Birthplace: North Tonawanda, NY
Deathdate: 4/8/1967
Information Available in These Sources: SATA 12

BENEDICT, REX (ARTHUR)
Birthdate: 6/27/1920
Birthplace: Jet, OK
Information Available in These Sources: ABYP 4, SATA 8, TCCW 1, TCCW 2TCCW 3

BENEDICT, STEWART H(URD)
Birthdate: 12/27/1924
Birthplace: Mineola, NY
Information Available in These Sources: SATA 26

BENENSON, LAWRENCE A.
Information Available in These Sources: ABYP 2, ABYP 3

BENET, LAURA
Birthdate: 6/13/1884
Birthplace: Brooklyn (Fort Hamilton), NY
Deathdate: 2/17/1979
Information Available in These Sources: ABYP 2, ABYP 3, JBA 2, SATA 3 SATA 23

BENET, STEPHEN VINCENT
Birthdate: 7/22/1898
Birthplace: Bethelehem, PA
Deathdate: 3/13/1943
Information Available in These Sources: ABYP 4, JBA 1, SVC 2, SVC 3, YABC

BENET, SULA
Birthdate: 9/24/1903
Birthplace: Warsaw, Poland
Deathdate: 11/12/1982
Information Available in These Sources: ABYP 2, ABYP 3, SATA 21, SATA 33

BENEZRA, BARBARA (BEARDSLEY)
Birthdate: 4/2/1921
Birthplace: Woodman, CO
Information Available in These Sources: SATA 10

BENJAMIN, NORA
See Kubie, Nora (Gottheil) Benjamin

BENNETT, EVE
Birthplace: Neligh, NE
Information Available in These Sources: ABYP 1, ABYP 3

BENNETT, JAY
Birthdate: 12/24/1912
Birthplace: Brooklyn, NY
Information Available in These Sources: ABYP 4, DACF, JBA 6, SATA 27, SATA 41

BENNETT, JOHN
Birthdate: 5/17/1865
Birthplace: Chillicothe, OH
Deathdate: 12/28/1956
Information Available in These Sources: CICB, DLB 42, ICB 1, JBA 1, JBA 2, JBA 4, YABC

BENNETT, LERONE, JR.
Birthdate: 1928
Birthplace: Clarksdale, MS
Information Available in These Sources: BAI

BENNETT, RACHEL
See Hill, Margaret (Ohler)

BENNETT, RAINEY
Birthdate: 7/26/1907 or 7/20/1907
Birthplace: Marion, IN
Information Available in These Sources: IBYP 2, ICB 3, ICB 4, JBA 4, SATA 15

BENNETT, RICHARD
Birthdate: 7/22/1899
Birthplace: Ireland
Information Available in These Sources: IBYP 2, ICB 1, ICB 2, JBA 2, SATA 21

BENNETT, RUSSELL H(ORADLEY)
Birthdate: 11/30/1896
Birthplace: Minneapolis, MN
Information Available in These Sources: SATA 25

BENNETT, SUSAN
Birthplace: MN
Information Available in These Sources: IBYP 1, IBYP 2

BENSON, MILDRED W.
Birthplace: Ladora, IA
Information Available in These Sources: ABYP 2, ABYP 3

BENSON, SALLY
(Esther Evarts)
Birthdate: 9/3/1900
Birthplace: St. Louis, MO
Deathdate: 7/19/1972
Information Available in These Sources: SATA 1, SATA 27, SATA 35

BENTEL, PEARL B(UCKLEN)
Birthdate: 10/23/1901
Birthplace: Rochester, PA
Information Available in These Sources: ABYP 1, ABYP 3

BENTLEY, JUDITH (MCBRIDE)
Birthdate: 4/8/1945
Birthplace: Indianapolis, IN
Information Available in These Sources: SATA 40

BENTON, THOMAS HART
Birthdate: 4/15/1889
Birthplace: Neosho, MO
Deathdate: 1/19/1975
Information Available in These Sources: ICB 1, ICB 2

BERELSON, HOWARD
Birthdate: 2/7/1940
Birthplace: Brooklyn, NY
Information Available in These Sources: IBYP 2, SATA 5

BERENDS, POLLY BERRIEN
Birthdate: 12/1/1939
Birthplace: Chicago, IL
Information Available in These Sources: SATA 38, SATA 50

BERENSTAIN, JAN(ICE GRANT)
Birthdate: 7/26/1923
Birthplace: Philadelphia, PA
Information Available in These Sources: ABYP 2, ABYP 3, JBA 5, SATA 12

BERENSTAIN, MICHAEL
Birthdate: 12/21/1951
Birthplace: Philadelphia, PA
Information Available in These Sources: SATA 45

BERENSTAIN, STAN(LEY)
Birthdate: 9/29/1923
Birthplace: Philadelphia, PA
Information Available in These Sources: ABYP 2, ABYP 3, JBA 5, SATA 12

BERG, BJORN
Birthdate: 9/17/1923
Birthplace: Munich, Germany
Information Available in These Sources: JBA 4, SATA 47

BERG, DAVE
See Berg, David

BERG, DAVID
(Dave Berg)
Birthdate: 6/12/1920
Birthplace: Brooklyn, NY
Information Available in These Sources: SATA 27

BERG, JEAN HORTON
Birthdate: 5/30/1913
Birthplace: Clairton, PA
Information Available in These Sources: ABYP 4, SATA 6

BERG, JOAN
See Victor, Joan Berg

BERGAUST, ERIK
Birthdate: 3/23/1925
Birthplace: Baerum, Oslo, Norway
Deathdate: 3/1/1978
Information Available in These Sources: ABYP 1, ABYP 3, SATA 20

BERGER, BARBARA HELEN
Birthdate: 3/1/1945
Birthplace: Lancaster, CA
Information Available in These Sources: JBA 6

BERGER, GILDA
Information Available in These Sources: SATA 42

BERGER, JOSEF
(Jeremiah Digges)
Birthdate: 5/12/1903
Birthplace: Denver, CO
Deathdate: 11/11/1971
Information Available in These Sources: SATA 36

BERGER, MELVIN H.
Birthdate: 8/23/1927
Birthplace: Brooklyn, NY
Information Available in These Sources: ABYP 2, ABYP 3, JBA 5, SATA 5

BERGER, PHIL
Birthdate: 4/1/1942
Birthplace: Brooklyn, NY
Information Available in These Sources: ABYP 4

BERGER, TERRY
Birthdate: 8/11/1933
Birthplace: New York, NY
Information Available in These Sources: SATA 8

BERGER, WILLIAM MERRITT
Birthdate: 2/14/1872
Birthplace: Union Springs, NY
Information Available in These Sources: CICB

BERGERE, THEA LINDGREN
Birthdate: 5/28/1933
Birthplace: New York, NY
Information Available in These Sources: ABYP 2, ABYP 3

BERGERON, VICTOR (JULES, JR.)
(Trader Vic)
Birthdate: 12/10/1902
Birthplace: San Francisco, CA
Deathdate: 10/11/1984
Information Available in These Sources: ABYP 4

BERGEY, ALYCE (MAE)
Birthdate: 3/25/1934
Birthplace: Lanesboro, MN
Information Available in These Sources: SATA 45

BERKEBILE, FRED D(ONOVAN)
(William Donovan, William Ernest, Don Stauffer)
Birthdate: 10/7/1900
Birthplace: Kanter, PA
Information Available in These Sources: SATA 26

BERKEY, BARRY ROBERT
Birthdate: 9/28/1935
Birthplace: New Kensington, PA
Information Available in These Sources: SATA 24

BERKOWITZ, FREDA PASTOR
Birthdate: 10/11/1910
Birthplace: Newark, NJ
Information Available in These Sources: ABYP 2, ABYP 3, SATA 12

BERLINER, DON
Birthdate: 7/3/1930
Birthplace: Columbus, OH
Information Available in These Sources: SATA 33

BERLITZ, CHARLES L. (FRAMBACH)
Birthdate: 11/22/1913
Birthplace: New York, NY
Information Available in These Sources: SATA 32

BERMAN, LINDA
Birthdate: 5/25/1948
Birthplace: Hempstead, Long Island, NY
Information Available in These Sources: SATA 38

BERNARD, JACQUELINE (DE SIEYES)
Birthdate: 5/5/1921
Birthplace: Le Bourget du Lac, Savole, France
Deathdate: 8/1/1983
Information Available in These Sources: ABYP 4, SATA 8, SATA 45

BERNAYS, ANNE
See Kaplan, Anne Bernays

BERNSTEIN, JOANNE E(CKSTEIN)
Birthdate: 4/21/1943
Birthplace: New York, NY
Information Available in These Sources: SATA 15

BERNSTEIN, RALPH
Birthdate: 1921
Birthplace: Philadelphia, PA
Information Available in These Sources: ABYP 1, ABYP 3

BERNSTEIN, THEODORE M(ENLINE)
Birthdate: 11/17/1904
Birthplace: New York, NY
Deathdate: 6/27/1979
Information Available in These Sources: SATA 12, SATA 27

BERRIEN, EDITH HEAL
See Heal, Edith

BERRILL, JACQUELYN (BATSEL)
Birthdate: 11/5/1905
Birthplace: South Carrollton, KY
Information Available in These Sources: ABYP 1, ABYP 3, ICB 3, SATA 12

BERRY, B(ARBARA) J.
Birthdate: 2/17/1937
Birthplace: Westfield, NY
Information Available in These Sources: SATA 7

BERRY, ERICK
See Best, Evangel Allena Champlin

BERRY, JAMES
(Jim Berry)
Birthdate: 1/16/1932
Birthplace: Oak Park, IL
Information Available in These Sources: ABYP 4

BERRY, JANE COBB
(Jane Cobb)
Birthdate: 1915?
Deathdate: 3/31/1979
Information Available in These Sources: SATA 22

BERRY, JIM
See Berry, James

BERRY, JOY WILT
(Joy Wilt)
Birthdate: 4/15/1944
Birthplace: Southgate, CA
Information Available in These Sources: SATA 46, SATA 58

BERRY, WILLIAM D(AVID)
Birthdate: 5/20/1926
Birthplace: San Mateo, CA
Information Available in These Sources: ABYP 2, ABYP 3, ICB 3, SATA 14

BERSON, HAROLD
Birthdate: 11/21/1926 , 11/23/1926 or 11/28/1926
Birthplace: Los Angeles, CA
Information Available in These Sources: IBYP 2, ICB 3, ICB 4, JBA 4, SATA 4

BERWICK, JEAN
See Meyer, Jean Shepherd

BESS, CLAYTON
See Locke, Robert

BEST, ALLENA CHAMPLIN
See Best, Evangel Allena Champlin

BEST, EVANGEL ALLENA CHAMPLIN
(Erick Berry, Allena Champlin Best, Anne Maxon)
Birthdate: 1/4/1892
Birthplace: New Bedford, MA
Deathdate: 2/, /1974
Information Available in These Sources: ABYP 1, ABYP 3, CICB, ICB 1, ICB 2, JBA 1, JBA 2, SATA 2, SATA 25

BEST, HERBERT
See Best, Oswald Herbert

BEST, OSWALD HERBERT
(Herbert Best)
Birthdate: 3/25/1894
Birthplace: Chester, England
Deathdate: 1981
Information Available in These Sources: ABYP 2, ABYP 3, JBA 1, JBA 2, SATA 2

BESTON, HENRY B.
(Henry Beston Sheahan)
Birthdate: 6/1/1888
Birthplace: Quincy, MA
Deathdate: 4/15/1968
Information Available in These Sources: JBA 1, JBA 2

BETANCOURT, JEANNE
Birthdate: 10/2/1941
Birthplace: Burlington, VT
Information Available in These Sources: SATA 43, SATA 54

BETH, MARY
See Miller, Mary Beth

BETHANCOURT, T(OMAS) ERNESTO
(Tom Paisley, Thomas E. Passailaigue)
Birthdate: 10/2/1932
Birthplace: Brooklyn, NY
Information Available in These Sources: JBA 5, SATA 11

BETHEL, DELL
Birthdate: 11/22/1929
Birthplace: Chicago, IL
Information Available in These Sources: SATA 52

BETHELL, JEAN (FRANKENBERRY)
Birthdate: 2/12/1922
Birthplace: Sharon, PA
Information Available in These Sources: SATA 8

BETHERS, RAY
Birthdate: 4/25/1902
Birthplace: Corvallis, OR
Information Available in These Sources: ABYP 1, ABYP 3, SATA 6

BETHUNE, J. G.
See Ellis, Edward S(ylvester)

BETTMANN, OTTO LUDWIG
Birthdate: 10/15/1903
Birthplace: Leipzig, Germany
Information Available in These Sources: SATA 46

BETTS, JAMES
See Haynes, Betsy

BETZ, BETTY
Birthdate: 3/28/1920
Birthplace: Chicago, IL
Information Available in These Sources: ABYP 1, ABYP 3, MJA

BETZ, EVA KELLY
(Caroline Peters)
Birthdate: 3/11/1897
Birthplace: Fall River, MA
Deathdate: 4/7/1968
Information Available in These Sources: SATA 10

BEVANS, MARGARET (VAN DOREN)
Birthdate: 1917
Information Available in These Sources: ABYP 2, ABYP 3

BEVANS, MICHAEL H.
Birthplace: New York, NY
Information Available in These Sources: ABYP 1, ABYP 3

BEYER, AUDREY WHITE
Birthdate: 11/12/1916
Birthplace: Portland, ME
Information Available in These Sources: DACF, SATA 9

BIALK, ELISA
See Krautter, Elisa (Bialk)

BIANCO, MARGERY (WILLIAMS)
Birthdate: 7/22/1881
Birthplace: London, England
Deathdate: 9/4/1944
Information Available in These Sources: JBA 2, SATA 15, SVC 2, SVC 3, WC

BIANCO, PAMELA
Birthdate: 12/31/1906
Birthplace: London, England
Information Available in These Sources: ABYP 2, ABYP 3, ICB 1, JBA 1, JBA 2, SATA 28

BIBLE, CHARLES
Birthdate: 4/22/1937
Birthplace: Waco, TX
Information Available in These Sources: BAI, IBYP 2, SATA 13

BIEMILLER, CARL LUDWIG
Birthdate: 12/16/1912
Birthplace: Haddonfield, NJ
Deathdate: 10/2/1979
Information Available in These Sources: ABYP 4, SATA 21, SATA 40

BIENENFELD, FLORENCE L(UCILLE)
Birthdate: 12/29/1929
Birthplace: Los Angeles, CA
Information Available in These Sources: SATA 39

BIERHORST, JOHN (WILLIAM)
Birthdate: 9/2/1936
Birthplace: Boston, MA
Information Available in These Sources: ABYP 4, JBA 5, SATA 6

BILECK, MARVIN
Birthdate: 3/3/1920
Birthplace: Passaic, NJ
Information Available in These Sources: IBYP 1, IBYP 2, ICB 2, ICB 3, JBA 4, SATA 40

BILL, ALFRED HOYT
Birthdate: 5/5/1879
Birthplace: Rochester, NY
Deathdate: 8/10/1964
Information Available in These Sources: JBA 1, JBA 2, SATA 44

BILLINGS, CHARLENE W(INTERER)
Birthdate: 1/11/1941
Birthplace: Manchester, NH
Information Available in These Sources: SATA 41

BILLINGS, HENRY
Birthdate: 7/13/1901
Birthplace: Bronxville, NY
Information Available in These Sources: ICB 2, MJA

BILLINGTON, ELIZABETH T(HAIN)
Birthplace: New York, NY
Information Available in These Sources: SATA 43, SATA 50

BILLOUT, GUY RENE
Birthdate: 7/7/1941
Birthplace: Decize, France
Information Available in These Sources: SATA 10

BINDER, EANDO
See Binder, Otto O(scar)

BINDER, OTTO O(SCAR)
(Eando Binder, John Coleridge, Gordon A. Giles, Dean D. O'Brien)
Birthdate: 8/26/1911
Birthplace: Bessemer, MI
Deathdate: 10/14/1974
Information Available in These Sources: ABYP 2, ABYP 3

BINGHAM, CALEB
Birthdate: 4/15/1757
Birthplace: Salisbury, CT
Deathdate: 4/6/1817
Information Available in These Sources: DLB 42

BINKLEY, ANNE
See Rand, Ann(e Binkley)

BINN, MARK
Information Available in These Sources: IBYP 2

BINZEN, BILL
See Binzen, William

BINZEN, WILLIAM
(Bill Binzen)
Birthplace: NJ
Information Available in These Sources: ABYP 4, SATA 24

BIRCH, REGINALD B(ATHURST)
Birthdate: 5/2/1856
Birthplace: London, England
Deathdate: 6/17/1943
Information Available in: CICB, JBA 2, SATA 19

BIRD, ALICE
Information Available in These Sources: IBYP 1, IBYP 2

BIRD, E(LZY) J(AY)
Birthdate: 4/3/1911
Birthplace: Salt Lake City, UT
Information Available in These Sources: SATA 58

BIRD, TRAVELLER
See Tsisghwanai, Traveller Bird

BIRMINGHAM, LLOYD
Birthdate: 8/23/1924
Birthplace: Buffalo, NY
Information Available in These Sources: SATA 12

BISCHOFF, ILSE MARTHE
Birthdate: 11/21/1901 or 11/21/1903
Birthplace: New York, NY
Information Available in These Sources: ABYP 1, ABYP 3, CICB, ICB 1, ICB 2, MJA

BISCHOFF, JULIA BRISTOL
(Julie Arnoldy)
Birthdate: 3/2/1909
Birthplace: Almont, MI
Deathdate: 3/10/1970
Information Available in These Sources: ABYP 2, ABYP 3, SATA 12

BISHOP, BONNIE
Birthdate: 8/24/1943
Birthplace: Meriden, CT
Information Available in These Sources: SATA 37

BISHOP, CLAIRE HUCHET
Birthplace: Brittany, France
Information Available in These Sources: ABYP 1, ABYP 3, BABP, JBA 2, SATA 14, TCCW 1, TCCW 2, TCCW 3

BISHOP, CURTIS (KENT)
(Curt Brandon, Curt Carroll)
Birthdate: 11/10/1912
Birthplace: Bolivar, TN
Deathdate: 3/17/1967
Information Available in These Sources: ABYP 1, ABYP 3, DACF, SATA 6

BISHOP, ELIZABETH
Birthdate: 2/8/1911
Birthplace: Worcester, MA
Deathdate: 10/6/1979
Information Available in These Sources: ABYP 4, JBA 4, SATA 24

BISHOP, GRACE (EYRES)
Information Available in These Sources: ABYP 2, ABYP 3

BISHOP, JACK
See Dorman, Michael

BITTER, GARY G(LEN)
Birthdate: 2/2/1940
Birthplace: Hoisington, KS
Information Available in These Sources: SATA 22

BIXBY, WILLIAM (COURTNEY)
Birthdate: 6/15/1920
Birthplace: San Diego, CA
Deathdate: 2/11/1986
Information Available in These Sources: ABYP 2, ABYP 3, SATA 6, SATA 47

BJERREGAARD-JENSEN, VILHELM HANS
See Hillcourt, William

BJORKLUND, KARNA L.
Information Available in These Sources: ABYP 4

BJORKLUND, LORENCE F.
Birthdate: 7/16/1913
Birthplace: St. Paul, MN
Deathdate: 5/7/1978
Information Available in These Sources: IBYP 1, IBYP 2, ICB 2, ICB 3, SATA 32, SATA 35

BLACK, ALGERNON DAVID
Birthdate: 11/19/1900
Birthplace: New York, NY
Information Available in These Sources: SATA 12

BLACK, IRMA S(IMONTON)
Birthdate: 6/6/1906
Birthplace: Paterson, NJ
Deathdate: 6/18/1972
Information Available in These Sources: ABYP 1, ABYP 3, SATA 2, SATA 25

BLACK, MANSELL
See Trevor, Elleston

BLACK, SUSAN ADAMS
Birthdate: 2/17/1953
Birthplace: Cincinnati, OH
Information Available in These Sources: SATA 40

BLACKBURN, CLAIRE
See Jacobs, Linda C.

BLACKBURN, EDITH H.
Birthplace: Denver, CO
Information Available in These Sources: ABYP 2, ABYP 3

BLACKBURN, JOHN(NY) BREWTON
Birthdate: 8/19/1952
Birthplace: Nashville, TN
Information Available in These Sources: SATA 15

BLACKBURN, JOYCE KNIGHT
Birthdate: 11/1/1920
Birthplace: Mount Vernon, IN
Information Available in These Sources: SATA 29

BLACKTON, PETER
See Wilson, Lionel

BLADOW, SUZANNE WILSON
Birthdate: 10/2/1937
Birthplace: Des Moines, IA
Information Available in These Sources: SATA 14

BLAINE, JOHN
See Goodwin, Harold Leland and Harkins, Philip

BLAINE, MARGE(RY KAY)
Birthdate: 12/20/1937
Birthplace: New York, NY
Information Available in These Sources: ABYP 4, SATA 11

BLAIR, ANNE DENTON
Birthdate: 2/4/1914
Birthplace: Oakmont, PA
Information Available in These Sources: SATA 46

BLAIR, HELEN
Birthdate: 12/29/1910
Birthplace: Hibbing, MN
Information Available in These Sources: IBYP 2, ICB 2, SATA 29

BLAIR, JAY
Birthdate: 1/21/1953
Birthplace: Omaha, NE
Information Available in These Sources: SATA 45

BLAIR, MARY ROBINSON
Birthdate: 10/21/1911
Birthplace: McAlester, OK
Information Available in These Sources: ICB 2

BLAIR, RUTH VAN NESS
Birthdate: 6/9/1912
Birthplace: St. Michael, AK
Information Available in These Sources: ABYP 4, SATA 12

BLAIR, SHANNON
See Kaye, Marilyn

BLAIR, WALTER
Birthdate: 4/21/1900
Birthplace: Spokane, WA
Information Available in These Sources: ABYP 2, ABYP 3, SATA 12

BLAISDELL, ELINORE
Birthdate: 1904
Birthplace: Brooklyn, NY
Information Available in These Sources: IBYP 2, ICB 1, ICB 2

BLAKE, OLIVE
See Supraner, Robyn

BLAKE, ROBERT
Birthdate: 5/10/1949
Birthplace: Paterson, NJ
Information Available in These Sources: SATA 42

BLAKE, WALTER E.
See Butterworth, W(illiam) E(dmund III)

BLAKELEY, GWENDOLYN ELIZABETH BROOKS
See Brooks, Gwendolyn

BLANE, GERTRUDE
See Blumenthal, Gertrude

BLANTON, CATHERINE
See Blanton, Martha Catherine

BLANTON, MARTHA CATHERINE
(Catherine Blanton)
Birthdate: 3/3/1907
Birthplace: San Angelo, TX
Information Available in These Sources: ABYP 2, ABYP 3

BLASSINGAME, WYATT (RAINEY)
(W. B. Rainey)
Birthdate: 2/6/1909
Birthplace: Demopolis, AL
Deathdate: 1/8/1985
Information Available in These Sources: ABYP 2, ABYP 3, SATA 1, SATA 34, SATA 41

BLAUER, ETTAGALE LAURE
Birthdate: 6/8/1940
Birthplace: New York, NY
Information Available in These Sources: SATA 49

BLEEKER, SONIA
(Sonia Bleeker Zim)
Birthdate: 11/28/1909
Birthplace: Starchevicvhi, White Russia
Deathdate: 11/13/1971
Information Available in These Sources: BABP, MJA, SATA 2, SATA 26

BLEGVAD, ERIK
Birthdate: 3/3/1923
Birthplace: Copenhagen, Denmark
Information Available in These Sources: FLTYP, IBYP 1, IBYP 2, ICB 2, ICB 3, ICB 4, JBA 3, SATA 14

BLEGVAD, LENORE (HOCHMAN)
Birthdate: 5/8/1926
Birthplace: New York, NY
Information Available in These Sources: FLTYP, JBA 3, SATA 14

BLISS, CORINNE D(EMAS)
Birthdate: 5/14/1947
Birthplace: New York, NY
Information Available in These Sources: SATA 37

BLISS, RONALD G(ENE)
Birthdate: 8/12/1942
Birthplace: Atwood, KS
Information Available in These Sources: SATA 12

BLIVEN, BRUCE
Birthdate: 7/27/1889
Birthplace: Emmetsburg, IA
Deathdate: 5/27/1977
Information Available in These Sources: ABYP 2, ABYP 3

BLIVEN, BRUCE, JR.
Birthdate: 1/31/1916
Birthplace: Los Angeles, CA
Information Available in These Sources: SATA 2

BLOCH, LUCIENNE
Birthdate: 1/5/1909
Birthplace: Geneva, Switzerland
Information Available in These Sources: IBYP 1, IBYP 2, ICB 1, ICB 2, SATA 10

BLOCH, MARIE HALUN
Birthdate: 12/1/1910
Birthplace: Komarno, Ukraine, Russia
Information Available in These Sources: ABYP 1, ABYP 3, DACF, JBA 4, SATA 6, TCCW 1

BLOCH, ROBERT
Birthdate: 4/5/1917
Birthplace: Chicago, IL
Information Available in These Sources: SATA 12

BLOCHMAN, LAWRENCE G(OLDTREE)
Birthdate: 2/17/1900
Birthplace: San Diego, CA
Deathdate: 1/22/1975
Information Available in These Sources: SATA 22

BLOCK, IRVIN
Birthdate: 4/1/1917
Birthplace: Pittsburgh, PA
Information Available in These Sources: SATA 12

BLOCKSMA, MARY
Birthdate: 1/19/1942
Information Available in These Sources: SATA 44

BLOOD, CHARLES LEWIS
Birthdate: 12/24/1929
Birthplace: NJ
Information Available in These Sources: SATA 28

BLOOM, FREDDY
Birthdate: 2/6/1914
Birthplace: New York, NY
Information Available in These Sources: SATA 37

BLOOM, LLOYD
Birthdate: 1/10/1947
Birthplace: New York, NY
Information Available in These Sources: JBA 6, SATA 43

BLOOME, ENID P.
Birthdate: 7/29/1925
Birthplace: New York, NY
Information Available in These Sources: ABYP 4

BLOS, JOAN W(INSOR)
Birthdate: 12/9/1928
Birthplace: New York, NY
Information Available in These Sources: ABYP 4, DACF, JBA 5, SATA 27, SATA 33, TCCW 3

BLOUGH, GLENN O(RLANDO)
Birthdate: 9/5/1907
Birthplace: Edmore, MI
Information Available in These Sources: ABYP 2, ABYP 3, MJA, SATA 1

BLOW, MICHAEL
Information Available in These Sources: ABYP 4

BLUE, ROSE
(Rose Bluestone)
Birthdate: 12/3/1931
Birthplace: New York, NY
Information Available in These Sources: ABYP 4, DACF, SATA 5

BLUESTONE, ROSE
See Blue, Rose

BLUMBERG, LEDA
Birthdate: 7/19/1956
Birthplace: Mount Kisco, NY
Information Available in These Sources: SATA 59

BLUMBERG, RHODA
Birthdate: 12/14/1917
Birthplace: New York, NY
Information Available in These Sources: JBA 6, SATA 35

BLUME, JUDY (SUSSMAN)
Birthdate: 2/12/1938
Birthplace: Elizabeth, NJ
Information Available in These Sources: ABYP 4, DACF, DLB 52, JBA 4, SATA 2, SATA 31, TCCW 1, TCCW 2, TCCW 3

BLUMENTHAL, GERTRUDE
(Gertrude Blane)
Birthdate: 1907
Deathdate: 12/27/1971
Information Available in These Sources: SATA 27

BLUMENTHAL, SHIRLEY
Birthdate: 10/9/1943
Birthplace: New York, NY
Information Available in These Sources: SATA 46

BLUST, EARL R.
Birthplace: Harrisburg, PA
Information Available in These Sources: IBYP 1, IBYP 2

BLUTIG, EDUARD
See Gorey, Edward St. John

BLY, JANET (CHESTER)
Birthdate: 2/23/1945
Birthplace: Visalia, CA
Information Available in These Sources: SATA 43

BLY, ROBERT W(AYNE)
Birthdate: 7/21/1957
Birthplace: Paterson, NJ
Information Available in These Sources: SATA 48

BLY, STEPHEN A(RTHUR)
Birthdate: 8/17/1944
Birthplace: Visalia, CA
Information Available in These Sources: SATA 43

BOARDMAN, FON WYMAN, JR.
Birthdate: 7/28/1911
Birthplace: Bolivar, NY
Information Available in These Sources: SATA 6

BOARDMAN, GWENN R.
Birthdate: 11/16/1924
Birthplace: London, England
Information Available in These Sources: SATA 12

BOATNER, MARK MAYO, III
Birthdate: 6/28/1921
Birthplace: Alexandria, VA
Information Available in These Sources: SATA 29

BOBBE, DOROTHIE (DE BEAR)
Birthdate: 3/1/1905
Birthplace: London, England
Deathdate: 3/19/1975
Information Available in These Sources: SATA 1, SATA 25

BOBRI
See Bobritsky, Vladimir

BOBRI, V(LADIMIR)
See Bobritsky, Vladimir

BOBRITSKY, VLADIMIR
(Bobri, V(ladimir) Bobri)
Birthdate: 5/13/1898
Birthplace: Charkov, Ukraine, Russia
Information Available in These Sources: IBYP 1, IBYP 2, ICB 1, ICB 2, ICB 3, SATA 32, SATA 47

BOCK, HAL
See Bock, Harold I.

BOCK, HAROLD I.
(Hal Bock)
Birthdate: 5/11/1939
Birthplace: New York, NY
Information Available in These Sources: SATA 10

BOCK, VERA
Birthdate: 4/1/1905
Birthplace: St. Petersburg, Russia
Information Available in These Sources: CICB, IBYP 2, ICB 1, ICB 2, ICB 3, MJA

BOCK, WILLIAM SAUTS NETAMUX'WE
(Netamuxwe)
Birthdate: 9/18/1939
Birthplace: Hatfield, PA
Information Available in These Sources: IBYP 2, ICB 4, SATA 14

BODE, JANET
Birthdate: 7/14/1943
Birthplace: Penn Yan, NY
Information Available in These Sources: SATA 60

BODECKER, N(IELS) M(OGENS)
Birthdate: 1/13/1922
Birthplace: Copenhagen, Denmark
Deathdate: 2/1/1988
Information Available in These Sources: IBYP 1, IBYP 2, ICB 2, ICB 3, ICB 4, JBA 6, SATA 8, SATA 54 TCCW 1, TCCW 2, TCCW 3

BODIE, IDELLA F(ALLAW)
Birthdate: 12/2/1925
Birthplace: Ridge Spring, SC
Information Available in These Sources: SATA 12

BOECKMAN, CHARLES
Birthdate: 11/9/1920
Birthplace: San Antonio, TX
Information Available in These Sources: ABYP 4, SATA 12

BOEGEHOLD, BETTY (DOYLE)
(Donovan Doyle)
Birthdate: 9/15/1913
Birthplace: New York, NY
Deathdate: 4/7/1985
Information Available in These Sources: ABYP 2, ABYP 3, SATA 42

BOESCH, MARK J(OSEPH)
Birthdate: 10/31/1917
Information Available in These Sources: SATA 12

BOESEN, VICTOR
(Jesse Hall, Eric Harald)
Birthdate: 9/7/1908
Birthplace: Plainfield, IN
Information Available in These Sources: ABYP 4, SATA 16

BOGAN, LOUISE
Birthdate: 8/11/1897
Birthplace: Livermore Falls, ME
Deathdate: 2/4/1970
Information Available in These Sources: ABYP 2, ABYP 3

BOGEN, CONSTANCE
Birthplace: New York, NY
Information Available in These Sources: ABYP 4

BOGGS, RALPH STEELE
Birthdate: 11/17/1901
Birthplace: Terre Haute, IN
Information Available in These Sources: ABYP 2, ABYP 3, SATA 7

BOGRAD, LARRY
(Grady Barrol)
Birthdate: 5/5/1953
Birthplace: Denver, CO
Information Available in These Sources: SATA 33

BOHLEN, NINA
Birthdate: 3/5/1931
Birthplace: Boston, MA
Information Available in These Sources: SATA 58

BOKER, IRVING
Information Available in These Sources: IBYP 2

BOLDEN, JOSEPH
Information Available in These Sources: IBYP 1, IBYP 2

BOLES, PAUL DARCY
Birthdate: 3/5/1919 or 3/5/1916
Birthplace: Auburn, IN
Deathdate: 5/4/1984
Information Available in These Sources: SATA 9, SATA 38

BOLIAN, POLLY
Birthdate: 9/20/1925
Birthplace: MS
Information Available in These Sources: IBYP 2, SATA 4

BOLLEN, ROGER
Birthdate: 6/27/1941
Birthplace: Cleveland, OH
Information Available in These Sources: SATA 29

BOLOGNESE, DON(ALD ALAN)
Birthdate: 1/6/1934
Birthplace: New York, NY
Information Available in These Sources: IBYP 1, IBYP 2, ICB 3, JBA 4, SATA 24

BOLOGNESE, ELAINE RAPHAEL (CHIONCHIO)
(Elaine Raphael)
Birthdate: 3/14/1933
Birthplace: Brooklyn, NY
Information Available in These Sources: ICB 3, JBA 4, SATA 23

BOLTON, CAROLE (ROBERTS)
Birthdate: 1/10/1926
Birthplace: Uniontown, PA
Information Available in These Sources: ABYP 4, SATA 6

BOLTON, ELIZABETH
See Johnston, Norma

BOLTON, EVELYN
See Bunting, A(nne) E(velyn Bolton)

BOLTON, HENRY CARRINGTON
Birthdate: 1/28/1843
Birthplace: New York, NY
Deathdate: 11/19/1903
Information Available in These Sources: SVC 2, SVC 3

BOLTON, ISABEL
See Miller, Mary Britton

BOLTON, IVY MAY
Birthdate: 1879
Birthplace: England
Information Available in These Sources: ABYP 1, ABYP 3

BOND, FELICIA
Birthdate: 7/18/1954
Birthplace: Yokohama, Japan
Information Available in These Sources: JBA 6, SATA 49

BOND, GLADYS BAKER
(Jo Mendel, Holly Beth Walker)
Birthdate: 5/7/1912
Birthplace: Berryville, AR
Information Available in These Sources: SATA 14

BOND, J. HARVEY
See Winterbotham, R(ussell) R(obert)

BOND, JEAN CAREY
Birthplace: New York, NY
Information Available in These Sources: ABYP 4, BAI

BOND, NANCY (BARBARA)
Birthdate: 1/8/1945
Birthplace: Bethesda, MD
Information Available in These Sources: ABYP 4, DACF, JBA 5, SATA 22, TCCW 2, TCCW 3

BONESTELL, CHESLEY
Birthdate: 1888
Birthplace: San Francisco, CA
Deathdate: 6/11/1986
Information Available in These Sources: SATA 48

BONHAM, BARBARA (THOMAS)
Birthdate: 9/27/1926
Birthplace: Franklin, NE
Information Available in These Sources: SATA 7

BONHAM, FRANK
Birthdate: 2/25/1914
Birthplace: Los Angeles, CA
Deathdate: 12/16/1988
Information Available in These Sources: ABYP 2, ABYP 3, DACF, JBA 3, MBMP, SATA 1, SATA 49, TCCW 1 TCCW 3

BONI, MARGARET BRADFORD
Birthdate: 1893?
Birthplace: Birmingham, AL
Deathdate: 12/1/1974
Information Available in These Sources: ABYP 4

BONNELL, DOROTHY HAWORTH
Birthdate: 10/12/1914
Birthplace: Buffalo, NY
Information Available in These Sources: ABYP 4

BONNER, MARY GRAHAM
Birthdate: 9/5/1895 or 9/5/1890
Birthplace: Cooperstown, NY
Deathdate: 2/12/1974
Information Available in These Sources: ABYP 1, ABYP 3, SATA 19

BONNERS, SUSAN
Birthdate: 4/8/1947
Birthplace: Chicago, IL
Information Available in These Sources: JBA 6, SATA 48

BONSALL, CROSBY (BARBARA NEWELL)
(Crosby Newell)
Birthdate: 1/2/1921
Birthplace: New York, NY
Information Available in These Sources: IBYP 1, IBYP 2, ICB 3, JBA 3, SATA 23, TCCW 1, TCCW 2, TCCW 3

BONTEMPS, ARNA(UD WENDELL)
Birthdate: 10/13/1902
Birthplace: Alexandria, LA
Deathdate: 6/4/1973
Information Available in These Sources: ABYP 1, ABYP 3, BAI, JBA 2, MBMP, SATA 2, SATA 24, SATA 44SVC 2, SVC 3, TCCW 3, WC

BOOHER, DIANNA DANIELS
Birthdate: 1/13/1948
Birthplace: Hillsboro, TX
Information Available in These Sources: SATA 33

BOOKMAN, CHARLOTTE
See Zolotow, Charlotte S(hapiro)

BOONE, CHARLES EUGENE
See Boone, Pat

BOONE, PAT
(Charles Eugene Boone)
Birthdate: 6/1/1934
Birthplace: Jacksonville, FL
Information Available in These Sources: SATA 7

BOORMAN, LINDA (KAY)
Birthdate: 4/28/1940
Birthplace: Boston, MA
Information Available in These Sources: SATA 46

BOORSTIN, DANIEL J(OSEPH)
Birthdate: 10/1/1914
Birthplace: Atlanta, GA
Information Available in These Sources: SATA 52

BOOTH, ERNEST SHELDON
Birthdate: 10/8/1915
Birthplace: Lehman, PA
Deathdate: 5/??/1984
Information Available in These Sources: SATA 43

BOOTH, GRAHAM (CHARLES)
Birthdate: 7/24/1935
Birthplace: London, England
Information Available in These Sources: IBYP 1, IBYP 2, ICB 3, SATA 37

BORDEN, CHARLES A.
Birthdate: 4/29/1912
Birthplace: Oakland, CA
Deathdate: 6/??/1968
Information Available in These Sources: ABYP 2, ABYP 3

BORHEGYI, SUZANNE CATHERINE SIMS DE
(Suzanne C(atherine) Sims DeBorhegyi)
Birthdate: 11/15/1926
Birthplace: Pittsburgh, PA
Information Available in These Sources: ABYP 2, ABYP 3

BORING, MEL
Birthdate: 9/12/1939
Birthplace: St. Clair Shores, MI
Information Available in These Sources: SATA 35

BORJA, CORINNE
Birthdate: 7/19/1929
Birthplace: Chicago, IL
Information Available in These Sources: IBYP 1, IBYP 2, SATA 22

BORJA, ROBERT
Birthdate: 5/31/1923
Birthplace: Chicago, IL
Information Available in These Sources: IBYP 1, IBYP 2, SATA 22

BORLAND, HAL
See Borland, Harold Glen

BORLAND, HAROLD GLEN
(Hal Borland, Ward West)
Birthdate: 5/14/1900
Birthplace: Sterling, NE
Deathdate: 2/22/1978
Information Available in These Sources: SATA 5, SATA 24

BORLAND, KATHRYN KILBY
(Alice Abbott, Jane Land, Ross Land)
Birthdate: 8/14/1916
Birthplace: Pullman, MI
Information Available in These Sources: SATA 16

BORNSCHLEGEL, RUTH
Information Available in These Sources: IBYP 1, IBYP 2

BORNSTEIN, RUTH
(Ruth Bornstein-Lercher)
Birthdate: 4/28/1927
Birthplace: Milwaukee, WI
Information Available in These Sources: ABYP 4, ICB 4, SATA 14

BORNSTEIN-LERCHER, RUTH
See Bornstein, Ruth

BORSKI, LUCIA MERECKA
Birthdate: 8/2/1903
Birthplace: Warsaw, Poland
Information Available in These Sources: SATA 18

BORTEN, HELEN JACOBSON
Birthdate: 6/20/1930
Birthplace: Philadelphia, PA
Information Available in These Sources: ABYP 1, ABYP 3, ICB 3, ICB 4, SATA 5

BORTON, ELIZABETH
(Elizabeth B(orton) de Trevino)
Birthdate: 9/2/1904
Birthplace: Bakersfield, CA
Information Available in These Sources: ABYP 2, ABYP 3, DACF, JBA 3, MBMP, SATA 1, SATA 29, TCCW 1, TCCW 2, TCCW 3

BORTSTEIN, LARRY
Birthdate: 11/25/1942
Birthplace: Bronx, NY
Information Available in These Sources: SATA 16

BOSHINSKI, BLANCHE
Birthdate: 11/28/1922
Birthplace: Fort Morgan, CO
Information Available in These Sources: SATA 10

BOSSE, MALCOLM J(OSEPH)
Birthdate: 5/6/1933
Birthplace: Detroit, MI
Information Available in These Sources: JBA 5, SATA 35

BOSSOM, NAOMI
Birthdate: 8/26/1933
Birthplace: Brooklyn, NY
Information Available in These Sources: SATA 35

BOSTELMANN, ELSE W. VON ROEDER
(Else W. VonRoeder-Bostelmann)
Birthdate: 1882
Birthplace: Leipzig, Germany
Deathdate: 1961
Information Available in These Sources: ICB 1

BOSWORTH, J. ALLAN
Birthdate: 1925
Birthplace: CA
Information Available in These Sources: ABYP 2, ABYP 3, SATA 19

BOTHWELL, JEAN
Birthdate: 11/??/????
Birthplace: Winside, NE
Deathdate: 3/2/1977
Information Available in These Sources: ABYP 1, ABYP 3, JBA 2, SATA 2

BOTKIN, B(ENJAMIN) A(LBERT)
Birthdate: 2/7/1901
Birthplace: Boston, MA
Deathdate: 7/30/1975
Information Available in These Sources: SATA 40

BOTTNER, BARBARA
Birthdate: 5/25/1943
Birthplace: New York, NY
Information Available in These Sources: ABYP 4, JBA 6, SATA 14

BOUCHARD, LOIS KALB
Birthdate: 8/1/1938
Birthplace: New York, NY
Information Available in These Sources: ABYP 4

BOULET, SUSAN SEDDON
Birthdate: 7/10/1941
Birthplace: Sao Paulo, Brazil
Information Available in These Sources: SATA 50

BOURDON, DAVID
Birthdate: 10/15/1934
Birthplace: Glendale, CA
Information Available in These Sources: SATA 46

BOURGEOIS, FLORENCE
Birthdate: 3/16/1904
Birthplace: Ventnor City, NJ
Information Available in These Sources: ICB 1

BOURNE, MIRIAM ANNE (YOUNG)
Birthdate: 3/4/1931
Birthplace: Buffalo, NY
Information Available in These Sources: ABYP 4, SATA 16

BOVA, BEN(JAMIN WILLIAM)
Birthdate: 11/8/1932
Birthplace: Philadelphia, PA
Information Available in These Sources: ABYP 4, JBA 5, SATA 6

BOWDEN, JOAN CHASE
(Joan Chase Bacon, Jane Godfrey, Charlotte Graham, Kathryn Kenny)
Birthdate: 5/1/1925
Birthplace: London, England
Information Available in These Sources: SATA 38, SATA 51

BOWEN, BETTY MORGAN
See West, Betty

BOWEN, CATHERINE DRINKER
Birthdate: 1/1/1897
Birthplace: Haverford, PA
Deathdate: 11/1/1973
Information Available in These Sources: SATA 7

BOWEN, DAVID
See Bowen, Joshua David

BOWEN, IRENE
See Robinson, Irene Bowen

BOWEN, JOSHUA DAVID
(David Bowen)
Birthdate: 1930
Information Available in These Sources: ABYP 2, ABYP 3, SATA 22

BOWEN, R(OBERT) SYDNEY
(James Robert Richard, Robert Sydney Bowen)
Birthdate: 1900
Birthplace: Boston, MA
Deathdate: 4/11/1977
Information Available in These Sources: ABYP 2, ABYP 3, SATA 21

BOWEN, ROBERT SIDNEY
See Bowen, R(obert) Sydney

BOWLER, JAN BRETT
See Brett, Jan (Churchill)

BOWMAN, JAMES CLOYD
Birthdate: 1/18/1880
Birthplace: Leipsic, OH
Deathdate: 9/27/1961
Information Available in These Sources: ABYP 2, ABYP 3, JBA 2, SATA 23SVC 2, SVC 3

BOWMAN, JOHN S(TEWART)
Birthdate: 5/30/1931
Birthplace: Cambridge, MA
Information Available in These Sources: ABYP 4, SATA 16

BOWMAN, KATHLEEN (GILL)
Birthdate: 12/19/1942
Birthplace: Minneapolis, MN
Information Available in These Sources: SATA 40, SATA 52

BOXER, DEVORAH
Birthplace: Troy, NY
Information Available in These Sources: ABYP 2, ABYP 3

BOYCE, GEORGE A(RTHUR)
Birthdate: 1/20/1898
Birthplace: Scranton, PA
Information Available in These Sources: SATA 19

BOYD, CANDY DAWSON
Birthdate: 1946
Birthplace: Chicago, IL
Information Available in These Sources: BAI

BOYD, EDNA MCGUIRE
See McGuire, Edna

BOYD, EVALINE
See Ness, Evaline (Michelow)

BOYD, FRANK
Birthdate: 2/16/1893
Birthplace: St. John, New Brunswick, Canada
Information Available in These Sources: CICB

BOYD, LORENZ
Information Available in These Sources: ABYP 4

BOYD, MILDRED WORTHY
Birthdate: 4/20/1921
Birthplace: Ranger, TX
Information Available in These Sources: ABYP 4

BOYD, PAULINE
See Schock, Pauline

BOYD, SELMA
See Acuff, Selma Boyd

BOYD, WALDO T.
(Ted Andersen, Robert Parker)
Birthdate: 2/4/1918
Birthplace: Wiergor Township, WI
Information Available in These Sources: ABYP 4, SATA 18

BOYER, ROBERT E(RNST)
Birthdate: 8/3/1929
Birthplace: Palmerton, PA
Information Available in These Sources: SATA 22

BOYESEN, HJALMAR HJORTH
Birthdate: 9/23/1848
Birthplace: Frederiksvarn, Norway
Deathdate: 10/4/1895
Information Available in These Sources: JBA 1

BOYLE, ANN (PETERS)
Birthdate: 1/21/1916
Birthplace: Independence, MO
Information Available in These Sources: SATA 10

BOYLSTON, HELEN (DORE)
Birthdate: 4/4/1895
Birthplace: Portsmouth, NH
Deathdate: 9/30/1984
Information Available in These Sources: ABYP 1, ABYP 3, JBA 2, SATA 23, SATA 39, TCCW 1, TCCW 2, TCCW 3

BOYNTON, SANDRA (KEITH)
Birthdate: 4/3/1953
Birthplace: Orange, NJ
Information Available in These Sources: SATA 38, SATA 57

BOYTON, NEIL
Birthdate: 11/30/1884
Birthplace: New York, NY
Deathdate: 2/1/1956
Information Available in These Sources: ABYP 2, ABYP 3

BOZE, CALVIN
Information Available in These Sources: IBYP 2

BOZZO, FRANK
Birthdate: 9/21/1937
Birthplace: Chicago, IL
Information Available in These Sources: IBYP 1, IBYP 2, ICB 4

BRACKER, CHARLES EUGENE
Birthdate: 10/16/1895
Birthplace: Rochester, NY
Information Available in These Sources: ICB 1

BRADBURY, BIANCA
(Jane Wyatt, Molly Wyatt)
Birthdate: 12/4/1908
Birthplace: Mystic, CT
Deathdate: 5/29/1982
Information Available in These Sources: ABYP 2, ABYP 3, JBA 4, SATA 3 SATA 56

BRADBURY, RAY (DOUGLAS)
Birthdate: 8/22/1920
Birthplace: Waukegan, IL
Information Available in These Sources: SATA 11

BRADDY, NELLA
Birthdate: 1894
Birthplace: GA
Information Available in These Sources: ABYP 1, ABYP 3

BRADFIELD, JOLLY ROGER
See Bradfield, Roger

BRADFIELD, ROGER
(Jolly Roger Bradfield)
Birthdate: 9/22/1924
Birthplace: White Bear, MN
Information Available in These Sources: ABYP 4

BRADFORD, ADAM
See Wassersug, Joseph D(avid)

BRADFORD, ANN (LIDDELL)
Birthdate: 11/9/1917
Birthplace: San Leandro, CA
Information Available in These Sources: SATA 38, 56

BRADFORD, LOIS J(EAN)
Birthdate: 5/29/1936
Birthplace: Griswold, IA
Information Available in These Sources: SATA 36

BRADFORD, RICHARD (ROARK)
Birthdate: 5/1/1932
Birthplace: Chicago, IL
Information Available in These Sources: SATA 59

BRADLEY, DUANE
See Sanborn, Duane

BRADLEY, VIRGINIA
Birthdate: 12/2/1912
Birthplace: Omaha, NE
Information Available in These Sources: SATA 23

BRADLEY, WILL(IAM H.)
Birthdate: 7/10/1868
Birthplace: Boston, MA
Deathdate: 1962
Information Available in These Sources: ICB 1

BRADY, ESTHER WOOD
(Esther Wood)
Birthdate: 8/24/1905
Birthplace: Akron, NY
Deathdate: 6/30/1987
Information Available in These Sources: JBA 2, SATA 31, SATA 53

BRADY, IRENE
Birthdate: 12/29/1943
Birthplace: Ontario, OR
Information Available in These Sources: ICB 4, JBA 6, SATA 4

BRADY, LILLIAN
Birthdate: 1902
Birthplace: Eagle Grove, IA
Information Available in These Sources: SATA 28

BRADY, MAXINE L.
Birthdate: 7/22/1941
Birthplace: Brooklyn, NY
Information Available in These Sources: ABYP 4

BRADY, RITA G.
Information Available in These Sources: ABYP 1, ABYP 3

BRAGDON, ELSPETH (MACDUFFIE)
(Elspeth)
Birthdate: 5/6/1897
Birthplace: Springfield, MA
Information Available in These Sources: SATA 6

BRAGDON, LILLIAN (JACOT)
Birthplace: NJ
Information Available in These Sources: ABYP 1, ABYP 3, SATA 24

BRAGG, CHARLES
Birthdate: 1931
Information Available in These Sources: IBYP 2

BRAGG, MABEL CAROLINE
(Watty Piper)
Birthdate: 9/15/1870
Birthplace: Milford, MA
Deathdate: 4/25/1945
Information Available in These Sources: DLB 22, JBA 4, SATA 24

BRAHM, SUMISHTA
Birthdate: 8/1/1954
Birthplace: Wiesbaden, Germany
Information Available in These Sources: SATA 58

BRAM, ELIZABETH
Birthdate: 12/5/1948
Birthplace: New York, NY
Information Available in These Sources: SATA 30

BRANCATO, ROBIN F(IDLER)
Birthdate: 3/19/1936
Birthplace: Reading, PA
Information Available in These Sources: JBA 5, SATA 23

BRAND, OSCAR
Birthdate: 2/7/1920
Birthplace: Winnipeg, Manitoba, Canada
Information Available in These Sources: ABYP 2, ABYP 3

BRANDENBERG, ALIKI (LIACOURAS)
(Aliki)
Birthdate: 9/3/1929
Birthplace: Wildwood Crest, NJ
Information Available in These Sources: ABYP 2, ABYP 3, ICB 3, JBA 3, SATA 2, SATA 35

BRANDENBERG, FRANZ
Birthdate: 2/10/1932
Birthplace: Lachen, Switzerland
Information Available in These Sources: JBA 5, SATA 8, SATA 35

BRANDHORST, CARL T(HEODORE)
Birthdate: 8/24/1898
Birthplace: Lincoln, NE
Information Available in These Sources: SATA 23

BRANDON, BRUMSIC, JR.
Birthdate: 4/10/1927
Birthplace: Washington, DC
Information Available in These Sources: SATA 9

BRANDON, CURT
See Bishop, Curtis (Kent)

BRANDT, CATHARINE
Birthdate: 1/23/1905
Birthplace: Jacksonville, IL
Information Available in These Sources: SATA 40

BRANDT, KEITH
See Sabin, Louis

BRANDT, SUE R(EADING)
Birthdate: 6/16/1916
Birthplace: Curryville, MO
Information Available in These Sources: SATA 59

BRANLEY, FRANKLYN M(ANSFIELD)
Birthdate: 6/5/1915
Birthplace: New Rochelle, NY
Information Available in These Sources: ABYP 1, ABYP 3, BABP, MJA, SATA 4

BRANN, ESTHER
Birthplace: New York, NY
Information Available in These Sources: ABYP 1, ABYP 3, CICB, JBA 1, JBA 2

BRANSCUM, ROBBIE
Birthdate: 6/17/1937
Birthplace: Big Flats, AR
Information Available in These Sources: DACF, JBA 5, SATA 23

BRANSOM, JOHN PAUL
(Paul Bransom)
Birthdate: 7/26/1885
Birthplace: Washington, DC
Deathdate: 7/12/1979
Information Available in These Sources: CICB, IBYP 1, IBYP 2, ICB 1, ICB 2, MJA, SATA 43

BRANSOM, PAUL
See Bransom, John Paul

BRASIER, VIRGINIA
Birthdate: 7/31/1910
Birthplace: Toronto, Ontario, Canada
Information Available in These Sources: SVC 2, SVC 3

BRATTON, HELEN
Birthdate: 7/17/1899
Birthplace: Albany, NY
Information Available in These Sources: SATA 4

BRATTON, KARL H(ENRY)
Birthdate: 1/29/1906
Birthplace: Lawrence, KS
Information Available in These Sources: ABYP 1, ABYP 3

BRAUDE, MICHAEL
Birthdate: 3/6/1936
Birthplace: Chicago, IL
Information Available in These Sources: SATA 23

BRAUN, KATHY
Birthplace: New York, NY
Information Available in These Sources: ABYP 2, ABYP 3

BRAUN, SAUL M.
Information Available in These Sources: ABYP 2, ABYP 3

BRAUN, WERNHER VON
Birthdate: 3/23/1912
Birthplace: Wirsitz, Germany
Deathdate: 6/16/1977
Information Available in These Sources: ABYP 1, ABYP 3

BRAUTIGAN, RICHARD (GARY)
Birthdate: 1/30/1935
Birthplace: Spokane, WA
Deathdate: 9/??/1984
Information Available in These Sources: SATA 56

BRAWLEY, BENJAMIN GRIFFITH
Birthdate: 4/22/1882
Birthplace: Columbia, SC
Deathdate: 2/1/1939
Information Available in These Sources: BAI

BRAYMER, MARJORIE (ELIZABETH)
Birthdate: 3/21/1911
Birthplace: Chicago, IL
Information Available in These Sources: SATA 6

BRAZOS, WACO
See Jennings, Michael

BRECHT, EDITH
Birthdate: 4/7/1895
Birthplace: Lancaster, PA
Deathdate: 8/16/1975
Information Available in These Sources: SATA 6, SATA 25

BRECK, VIVIAN
See Breckenfeld, Vivian Gurney

BRECKENFELD, VIVIAN GURNEY
(Vivian Breck)
Birthdate: 1/5/1895
Birthplace: San Francisco, CA
Information Available in These Sources: ABYP 2, ABYP 3, MJA, SATA 1

BREDA, TJALMAR
See DeJong, David C(ornel)

BREETVELD, JIM PATRICK
(Avery Mann)
Birthdate: 1/30/1925
Birthplace: New York, NY
Information Available in These Sources: ABYP 2, ABYP 3

BREISKY, WILLIAM J(OHN)
Birthdate: 10/27/1928
Birthplace: Pittsburgh, PA
Information Available in These Sources: SATA 22

BRENNAN, DENNIS
Birthplace: Lockport, IL
Information Available in These Sources: ABYP 4

BRENNAN, GALE PATRICK
Birthdate: 3/12/1927
Birthplace: Manitowoc, WI
Information Available in These Sources: SATA 53

BRENNAN, JOSEPH GERARD
Birthdate: 11/2/1910
Birthplace: Boston, MA
Information Available in These Sources: ABYP 2, ABYP 3

BRENNAN, JOSEPH L(OMAS)
(Steve Lomas)
Birthdate: 5/26/1903
Birthplace: Easton, PA
Information Available in These Sources: SATA 6

BRENNAN, TIM
See Conroy, Jack (Wesley)

BRENNER, BARBARA (JOHNES)
Birthdate: 6/26/1925
Birthplace: Brooklyn, NY
Information Available in These Sources: ABYP 2, ABYP 3, JBA 4, SATA 4 SATA 42

BRENNER, FRED
Birthdate: 4/4/1920
Birthplace: Newark, NJ
Information Available in These Sources: IBYP 2, JBA 4, SATA 34, SATA 36

BRENT, HOPE
Birthdate: 1935?
Deathdate: 8/17/1984
Information Available in These Sources: SATA 39

BRENT, STUART
Birthplace: Chicago, IL
Information Available in These Sources: ABYP 2, ABYP 3, SATA 14

BRETT, GRACE N(EFF)
Birthdate: 2/11/1900
Birthplace: Chicago, IL
Deathdate: 12/27/1975
Information Available in These Sources: SATA 23

BRETT, HAROLD M.
Birthdate: 12/13/1880 or 12/13/1882
Birthplace: Middleboro, MA
Deathdate: 1955
Information Available in These Sources: CICB, ICB 1

BRETT, JAN (CHURCHILL)
(Jan Brett Bowler)
Birthdate: 12/1/1949
Birthplace: Hingham, MA
Information Available in These Sources: JBA 6, SATA 42

BREVANNES, MAURICE
Birthdate: 9/14/1904
Birthplace: Paris, France
Information Available in These Sources: IBYP 2, ICB 2

BREWER, SALLY KING
Birthdate: 11/14/1947
Birthplace: Iowa City, IA
Information Available in These Sources: SATA 33

BREWSTER, BENJAMIN
See Folsom, Franklin (Brewster) and Elting, Mary

BREWSTER, PATIENCE
Birthdate: 10/26/1952
Birthplace: Plymouth, MA
Information Available in These Sources: SATA 51

BREWTON, JOHN E(DMUND)
Birthdate: 12/19/1898
Birthplace: Brewton, AL
Information Available in These Sources: SATA 5

BREY, CHARLES
Birthplace: Kansas City, MO
Information Available in These Sources: IBYP 2

BRICK, JOHN
Birthdate: 1/1/1922
Birthplace: Newburgh, NY
Deathdate: 10/15/1973
Information Available in These Sources: ABYP 1, ABYP 2, SATA 10

BRIDGERS, SUE ELLEN
Birthdate: 9/20/1942
Birthplace: Greenville, NC
Information Available in These Sources: DACF, DLB 52, JBA 5, SATA 22, TCCW 3

BRIDGES, LAURIE
See Bruck, Lorraine

BRIDGES, WILLIAM (ANDREW)
Birthdate: 1/27/1901
Birthplace: Franklin, IN
Deathdate: 3/28/1984
Information Available in These Sources: ABYP 1, ABYP 3, SATA 5

BRIDWELL, NORMAN
Birthdate: 2/15/1928
Birthplace: Kokomo, IN
Information Available in These Sources: SATA 4

BRIER, HOWARD M(AXWELL)
Birthdate: 3/20/1903
Birthplace: River Falls, WI
Deathdate: 10/3/1969
Information Available in These Sources: ABYP 1, ABYP 3, MJA, SATA 8

BRIGGS, BARBARA A.
(Kuumba)
Information Available in These Sources: ABYP 1, ABYP 3

BRIGGS, CAROLE S(UZANNE)
(Carole Briggs Ayres)
Birthdate: 6/26/1950
Birthplace: Janesville, WI
Information Available in These Sources: SATA 47

BRIGGS, PETER
Birthdate: 4/15/1921
Birthplace: St. Paul, MN
Deathdate: 7/18/1975
Information Available in These Sources: SATA 31, SATA 39

BRIGHAM, GRACE A.
Birthdate: 12/3/1909
Information Available in These Sources: IBYP 2

BRIGHT, ROBERT
(Michael Douglas)
Birthdate: 8/5/1902
Birthplace: Sandwich, MA
Deathdate: 11/21/1988
Information Available in These Sources: IBYP 2, ICB 2, ICB 3, MJA, SATA 24, SATA 60, TCCW 1, TCCW 2, TCCW 3

BRIGHTFIELD, RICHARD
(Rick Brightfield)
Birthdate: 9/28/1927
Birthplace: Baltimore, MD
Information Available in These Sources: SATA 53

BRIGHTFIELD, RICK
See Brightfield, Richard

BRIMBERG, STANLEE
Birthdate: 7/7/1947
Birthplace: New York, NY
Information Available in These Sources: SATA 9

BRIN, RUTH F(IRESTONE)
Birthdate: 5/5/1921
Birthplace: St. Paul, MN
Information Available in These Sources: SATA 22

BRINCKLOE, JULIE (LORRAINE)
Birthdate: 4/25/1950
Birthplace: Mare Island, CA
Information Available in These Sources: IBYP 2, SATA 13

BRINDEL, JUNE (RACHUY)
Birthdate: 6/5/1919
Birthplace: Little Rock (near), IA
Information Available in These Sources: ABYP 4, SATA 7

BRINDZE, RUTH
Birthdate: 1903
Birthplace: New York, NY
Information Available in These Sources: ABYP 2, ABYP 3, MJA, SATA 23

BRINK, CAROL RYRIE
Birthdate: 12/28/1895
Birthplace: Moscow, ID
Deathdate: 8/15/1981
Information Available in These Sources: ABYP 1, ABYP 3, JBA 2, MBMP, SATA 1, SATA 27, SATA 31, SVC 2, SVC 3, TCCW 1, TCCW 2, TCCW 3, WC

BRISCO, PAT A.
See Matthews, Patricia

BRISCO, PATTY
See Matthews, Patricia

BRISCOE, JILL (PAULINE)
Birthdate: 6/29/1935
Birthplace: Liverpool, England
Information Available in These Sources: SATA 47, SATA 56

BRISTOW, JOAN
Birthplace: PA
Information Available in These Sources: ABYP 4

BRITT, ALBERT
Birthdate: 11/26/1874
Birthplace: Utah, IL
Deathdate: 2/18/1969
Information Available in These Sources: SATA 28

BRITT, DELL
Birthdate: 4/29/1934
Birthplace: Arkadelphia, AR
Information Available in These Sources: SATA 1

BRITTAIN, BILL
See Brittain, William

BRITTAIN, WILLIAM
(Bill Brittain, James Knox)
Birthdate: 12/16/1930
Birthplace: Rochester, NY
Information Available in These Sources: DACF, JBA 5, SATA 36, TCCW 3

BRITTON, KATE
See Stegeman, Janet Allais

BRITTON, LOUISA
See McGuire, Leslie (Sarah)

BRO, MARGUERITTE (HARMON)
Birthdate: 8/5/1894
Birthplace: David City, NE
Deathdate: 2/21/1977
Information Available in These Sources: MJA, SATA 19, SATA 27

BROADHEAD, HELEN CROSS
(Helen Reeder Cross)
Birthdate: 8/26/1913
Birthplace: Wilmington, NC
Information Available in These Sources: SATA 25

BROCK, BETTY (CARTER)
Birthdate: 8/31/1923
Birthplace: Biltmore, NC
Information Available in These Sources: ABYP 4, SATA 4, SATA 7

BROCK, DELIA
See Ephron, Delia

BROCK, EMMA L(ILLIAN)
Birthdate: 6/11/1886
Birthplace: Fort Shaw, MT
Deathdate: 8/17/1974
Information Available in These Sources: ABYP 1, ABYP 3, CICB, ICB 1, ICB 2, JBA 1, JBA 2, SATA 8, SVC 2, SVC 3

BROCK, VIRGINIA
Birthplace: CA
Information Available in These Sources: ABYP 4

BROCKMAN, C(HRISTIAN) FRANK
Birthdate: 6/4/1902
Information Available in These Sources: SATA 26

BRODERICK, DOROTHY M.
Birthdate: 6/23/1929
Birthplace: Bridgeport, CT
Information Available in These Sources: ABYP 2, ABYP 3, SATA 5

BRODIE, SALLY
See Cavin, Ruth (Brodie)

BRODIN, PIERRE EUGENE
Birthdate: 9/19/1909
Birthplace: Paris, France
Information Available in These Sources: ABYP 4

BRODSKY, BEVERLY
See McDermott, Beverly Brodsky

BROEKEL, RAINER LOTHAR
(Ray Broekel)
Birthdate: 3/24/1923
Birthplace: Dresden, Germany
Information Available in These Sources: SATA 38

BROEKEL, RAY
See Broekel, Rainer Lothar

BROKAMP, MARILYN
(Mary Lynn)
Birthdate: 9/9/1920
Birthplace: Covington, KY
Information Available in These Sources: SATA 10

BROMHALL, WINIFRED
Birthplace: Walsall, Staffordshire, England
Information Available in These Sources: CICB, IBYP 2, ICB 1, ICB 2, MJA, SATA 26

BROMLEY, DUDLEY
Birthdate: 12/9/1948
Birthplace: Odessa, TX
Information Available in These Sources: SATA 51

BROMMER, GERALD F(REDERICK)
Birthdate: 1/8/1927
Birthplace: Berkeley, CA
Information Available in These Sources: SATA 28

BRONDFIELD, JEROME
(Jerry Brondfield)
Birthdate: 12/9/1913
Birthplace: Cleveland, OH
Information Available in These Sources: SATA 22

BRONDFIELD, JERRY
See Brondfield, Jerome

BRONOWSKI, JACOB
Birthdate: 1/18/1908
Birthplace: Poland
Deathdate: 8/22/1974
Information Available in These Sources: SATA 54

BRONSON, LYNN
See Lampman, Evelyn (Sibley)

BRONSON, WILFRID SWANCOURT
Birthdate: 10/24/1894
Birthplace: Chicago (Morgan Park), IL
Deathdate: 4/23/1985
Information Available in These Sources: ABYP 1, ABYP 3, ICB 1, ICB 2, JBA 1, JBA 2, SATA 43, SVC 2, SVC 3

BROOKE-HAVEN, P.
See Wodehouse, P(elham) G(renville)

BROOKINS, DANA (MARTIN)
Birthdate: 2/22/1931
Birthplace: St. Louis, MO
Information Available in These Sources: DACF, SATA 28

BROOKS, ANITA
(Anita (Zeltner Brooks) Abramovitz)
Birthdate: 1/7/1914
Birthplace: Forest Hills, Long Island, NY
Information Available in These Sources: ABYP 2, ABYP 3, SATA 5

BROOKS, ANNE (TEDLOCK)
(Anne Carter, Cynthia Millburn)
Birthdate: 1905
Birthplace: New York, NY
Information Available in These Sources: ABYP 4

BROOKS, BARBARA
See Simons, Barbara B(rooks)

BROOKS, BRUCE
Birthdate: 1950
Birthplace: VA
Information Available in These Sources: JBA 6, SATA 53

BROOKS, CHARLOTTE K.
Birthdate: 6/5/1918
Birthplace: Washington, DC
Information Available in These Sources: ABYP 3, SATA 24

BROOKS, ELBRIDGE STREETER
Birthdate: 4/14/1846
Birthplace: Lowell, MA
Deathdate: 1/7/1902
Information Available in These Sources: JBA 1

BROOKS, GWENDOLYN
(Gwendolyn Elizabeth Brooks Blakeley)
Birthdate: 6/7/1917
Birthplace: Topeka, KS
Information Available in These Sources: BAI, JBA 4, SATA 6

BROOKS, JEROME
Birthdate: 7/17/1931
Birthplace: Chicago, IL
Information Available in These Sources: SATA 23

BROOKS, LESTER
Birthdate: 11/8/1924
Birthplace: Des Moines, IA
Information Available in These Sources: ABYP 4, SATA 7

BROOKS, MAURICE (GRAHAM)
Birthdate: 6/16/1900
Birthplace: French Creek, WV
Information Available in These Sources: SATA 45

BROOKS, NOAH
(Uncle Noah)
Birthdate: 10/24/1830
Birthplace: Castine, ME
Deathdate: 8/16/1903
Information Available in These Sources: DLB 42, JBA 1

BROOKS, POLLY SCHOYER
Birthdate: 8/11/1912
Birthplace: South Orleans, MA
Information Available in These Sources: SATA 12

BROOKS, TERRY
Birthdate: 1/8/1944
Birthplace: Sterling, IL
Information Available in These Sources: SATA 60

BROOKS, THOMAS R(EED)
Birthdate: 4/25/1925
Birthplace: Shrewsbury, MA
Information Available in These Sources: ABYP 4

BROOKS, WALTER R(OLLIN)
Birthdate: 1/9/1886
Birthplace: Rome, NY
Deathdate: 8/17/1958
Information Available in These Sources: JBA 2, SATA 17, TCCW 1, TCCW 2TCCW 3

BROSNAN, JAMES PATRICK
(Jim Brosnan)
Birthdate: 10/24/1929
Birthplace: Cincinnati, OH
Information Available in These Sources: ABYP 4, SATA 14

BROSNAN, JIM
See Brosnan, James Patrick

BROTHER ERNEST
Birthdate: 1897
Birthplace: Elyria, OH
Information Available in These Sources: ABYP 1, ABYP 3

BROTHERS HILDEBRANDT, THE
See Hildebrandt, Greg; Hildebrandt, Tim(othy)

BROUN, EMILY
See Sterne, Emma Gelders

BROUN, HEYWOOD CAMPBELL
Birthdate: 12/7/1888
Birthplace: Brooklyn, NY
Deathdate: 12/18/1939
Information Available in These Sources: ABYP 4

BROW, THEA
Birthdate: 7/23/1934
Birthplace: Rhinelander, WI
Information Available in These Sources: SATA 60

BROWER, MILLICENT
Birthplace: Jersey City, NJ
Information Available in These Sources: SATA 8

BROWER, PAULINE (YORK)
Birthdate: 12/9/1929
Birthplace: Long Beach, CA
Information Available in These Sources: SATA 22

BROWIN, FRANCES WILLIAMS
(Frances B. Williams)
Birthdate: 9/13/1898
Birthplace: Media, PA
Information Available in These Sources: ABYP 2, ABYP 3, SATA 5

BROWN, ABBIE FARWELL
Birthdate: 1872 or 1875
Birthplace: Boston, MA
Deathdate: 3/4/1927
Information Available in These Sources: JBA 1

BROWN, ALICE
Birthdate: 12/5/1857
Birthplace: Hampton Falls, NH
Deathdate: 6/21/1948
Information Available in These Sources: JBA 1

BROWN, BILL
See Brown, William Louis

BROWN, BILLYE WALKER
See Cutchen, Billye Walker

BROWN, BOB
See Brown, Robert Joseph

BROWN, BUCK
Birthdate: 2/3/1936
Birthplace: Morrison, TN
Information Available in These Sources: SATA 45

BROWN, CONRAD
Birthdate: 1922
Birthplace: OR
Information Available in These Sources: ABYP 2, ABYP 3, SATA 31

BROWN, DAVID
See Myller, Rolf

BROWN, DEE (ALEXANDER)
Birthdate: 2/28/1908
Birthplace: LA
Information Available in These Sources: ABYP 4, SATA 5

BROWN, DROLLENE P.
Birthdate: 9/24/1939
Birthplace: South Charleston, WV
Information Available in These Sources: SATA 53

BROWN, EDNA ADELAIDE
Birthdate: 3/7/1875
Birthplace: Providence, RI
Deathdate: 6/23/1944
Information Available in These Sources: JBA 1, JBA 2

BROWN, ELEANOR FRANCES
Birthdate: 5/28/1908
Birthplace: Spokane, WA
Information Available in These Sources: ABYP 1, ABYP 3, SATA 3

BROWN, ELIZABETH M(YERS)
Birthdate: 12/31/1915
Birthplace: Brooklyn, NY
Information Available in These Sources: SATA 43

BROWN, FERN G.
Birthdate: 12/23/1918
Birthplace: Chicago, IL
Information Available in These Sources: SATA 34

BROWN, FLETCH
See Brown, Robert Fletch

BROWN, GEORGE EARL
Birthdate: 2/12/1883
Birthplace: Toronto, KS
Deathdate: 10/28/1964
Information Available in These Sources: SATA 11

BROWN, HELEN (EVANS)
Birthdate: 1904
Information Available in These Sources: ABYP 2, ABYP 3

BROWN, IRENE BENNETT
Birthdate: 1/31/1932
Birthplace: Topeka, KS
Information Available in These Sources: DACF, SATA 3

BROWN, IRVING
See Adams, William Taylor

BROWN, JEFF
See Brown, Sevellon III

BROWN, JOE DAVID
Birthdate: 5/12/1915
Birthplace: East Lake, AL
Deathdate: 4/22/1976
Information Available in These Sources: SATA 44

BROWN, JOSEPH E(DWARD)
Birthdate: 12/14/1929
Birthplace: San Francisco, CA
Information Available in These Sources: SATA 51

BROWN, JUDITH GWYN
Birthdate: 10/15/1933
Birthplace: New York, NY
Information Available in These Sources: ABYP 2, ABYP 3, ICB 3, ICB 4, SATA 20

BROWN, LAURENE KRASNY
(Laurene Krasny Meringoff)
Birthdate: 12/16/1945
Birthplace: New York, NY
Information Available in These Sources: SATA 54

BROWN, LLOYD ARNOLD
Birthdate: 5/5/1907
Birthplace: Providence, RI
Deathdate: 3/30/1966
Information Available in These Sources: ABYP 1, ABYP 3, SATA 36

BROWN, MARC (TOLON)
Birthdate: 11/25/1946
Birthplace: Erie, PA
Information Available in These Sources: JBA 5, SATA 10, SATA 53, TCCW 3

BROWN, MARCIA (JOAN)
Birthdate: 7/13/1918
Birthplace: Rochester, NY
Information Available in These Sources: ABYP 1, ABYP 3, BABP, CFB, DLB 61, IBYP 1, IBYP 2, ICB 2 ICB 3, ICB 4, MJA, SATA 7, SATA 47, TCCW 3

BROWN, MARGARET WISE
(Timothy Hay, Golden MacDonald, Juniper Sage)
Birthdate: 5/23/1910
Birthplace: Brooklyn, NY
Deathdate: 11/13/1952
Information Available in These Sources: ABYP 1, ABYP 3, AICB, DLB 22, JBA 2, TCCW 1, TCCW 2, TCCW 3 YABC

BROWN, MARGERY (W.)
Birthplace: Durham, NC
Information Available in These Sources: SATA 5

BROWN, MARION MARSH
Birthdate: 7/22/1908
Birthplace: Brownville, NE
Information Available in These Sources: ABYP 1, ABYP 3, SATA 6

BROWN, MYRA BERRY
Birthdate: 10/27/1918
Birthplace: Minneapolis, MN
Information Available in These Sources: ABYP 2, ABYP 3, SATA 6

BROWN, PALMER
Birthdate: 5/10/1919
Birthplace: Chicago, IL
Information Available in These Sources: IBYP 2, ICB 2, ICB 3, JBA 5, SATA 36, TCCW 2, TCCW 3

BROWN, PAUL
Birthdate: 11/27/1893
Birthplace: Mapleton, MN
Deathdate: 12/25/1958
Information Available in These Sources: ABYP 1, ABYP 3, ICB 1, ICB 2, JBA 2

BROWN, PHILIP S.
Information Available in These Sources: ABYP 2, ABYP 3

BROWN, REGINA MARGARET
Information Available in These Sources: ABYP 2, ABYP 3

BROWN, RICH(ARD ERIC)
Birthdate: 10/25/1946
Information Available in These Sources: ICB 4

BROWN, ROBERT FLETCH
(Fletch Brown)
Birthdate: 5/28/1923
Birthplace: New York, NY
Information Available in These Sources: SATA 42

BROWN, ROBERT JOSEPH
(Bob Brown)
Birthdate: 8/19/1907
Birthplace: Rockwood, TN
Information Available in These Sources: SATA 14

BROWN, ROSALIE (GERTRUDE) MOORE
(Rosalie Moore)
Birthdate: 10/8/1910
Birthplace: Oakland, CA
Information Available in These Sources: ABYP 2, ABYP 3, SATA 9

BROWN, ROSWELL
See Webb, Jean Francis (III)

BROWN, SEVELLON III
(Jeff Brown)
Birthdate: 4/23/1913
Birthplace: Washington, DC
Deathdate: 7/20/1983
Information Available in These Sources: ABYP 2, ABYP 3

BROWN, VINSON
Birthdate: 12/7/1912
Birthplace: Reno, NV
Information Available in These Sources: ABYP 1, ABYP 3, SATA 19

BROWN, VIRGINIA SUGGS
Birthdate: 1924
Information Available in These Sources: BAI

BROWN, WALTER R(EED)
Birthdate: 8/25/1929
Birthplace: Oklahoma City, OK
Information Available in These Sources: SATA 19

BROWN, WILLIAM LOUIS
(Bill Brown)
Birthdate: 4/5/1910
Birthplace: Myrtle Point, OR
Deathdate: 9/28/1964
Information Available in These Sources: ABYP 2, ABYP 3, SATA 5

BROWNE, DIK
See Browne, Richard

BROWNE, RICHARD
(Dik Browne)
Birthdate: 8/11/1917
Birthplace: New York, NY
Information Available in These Sources: SATA 38

BRUCE, MARY
Birthdate: 9/12/1927
Birthplace: New Boston, TX
Information Available in These Sources: ABYP 4, SATA 1

BRUCHAC, JOSEPH III
Birthdate: 10/16/1942
Birthplace: Sarasota Springs, NY
Information Available in These Sources: SATA 42

BRUCK, LORRAINE
(Laurie Bridges)
Birthdate: 3/16/1921
Birthplace: Omaha, NE
Information Available in These Sources: SATA 46, 55

BRUNER, RICHARD W(ALLACE)
Birthdate: 6/26/1926
Birthplace: Burlington, IA
Information Available in These Sources: ABYP 4

BRUSSEL-SMITH, BERNARD
Birthdate: 3/1/1914
Birthplace: New York, NY
Information Available in These Sources: IBYP 2, ICB 2, SATA 58

BRUSTLEIN, DANIEL
(Alain)
Birthdate: 9/11/1904
Birthplace: Mulhouse, France
Information Available in These Sources: IBYP 2, ICB 2, ICB 3, SATA 40

BRUSTLEIN, JANICE TWORKOV
(Janice)
Information Available in These Sources: ABYP 2, ABYP 3, SATA 40

BRYAN, ASHLEY F.
Birthdate: 7/13/1923
Birthplace: Bronx, NY
Information Available in These Sources: BAI, ICB 4, JBA 5, SATA 31

BRYAN, DOROTHY M(ARIE)
Birthdate: 1896?
Birthplace: Washington, DC
Deathdate: 9/12/1984
Information Available in These Sources: FLTYP, SATA 39

BRYAN, JOSEPH (III)
Birthdate: 4/30/1904
Birthplace: Richmond, VA
Information Available in These Sources: ABYP 1, ABYP 3

BRYAN, MARGUERITE
Deathdate: 1948
Information Available in These Sources: FLTYP

BRYANT, BERNICE (MORGAN)
Birthdate: 4/6/1908
Birthplace: St. Louis, MO
Information Available in These Sources: SATA 11

BRYANT, GERTRUDE THOMSON
Birthplace: East Orange, NJ
Information Available in These Sources: ABYP 2, ABYP 3

BRYANT, WILLIAM CULLEN
Birthdate: 1794
Deathdate: 1878
Information Available in These Sources: SVC 2, SVC 3

BRYSON, BERNARDA
(Bernarda Bryson Shahn)
Birthdate: 3/7/1905 or 3/7/1903
Birthplace: Athens, OH
Information Available in These Sources: IBYP 1, IBYP 2, ICB 2, ICB 3, JBA 3, SATA 9

BUBA, JOY FLINSCH
Birthdate: 7/25/1904
Birthplace: Lloyd's Neck, NY
Information Available in These Sources: IBYP 2, ICB 2, SATA 44

BUCHAN, STUART
Birthdate: 8/30/1942
Birthplace: Sydney, Australia
Deathdate: 10/15/1987
Information Available in These Sources: SATA 54

BUCHANAN, WILLIAM
See Buck, William Ray

BUCHHEIMER, NAOMI BARNETT
See Barnett, Naomi

BUCHWALD, ANN (MCGARRY)
Information Available in These Sources: ABYP 4

BUCHWALD, ART(HUR)
Birthdate: 10/20/1925
Birthplace: Mount Vernon, NY
Information Available in These Sources: ABYP 4, SATA 10

BUCHWALD, EMILIE
Birthdate: 9/6/1935
Birthplace: Vienna, Austria
Information Available in These Sources: SATA 7

BUCK, LEWIS
Birthdate: 2/16/1925
Birthplace: Norfolk, VA
Information Available in These Sources: SATA 18

BUCK, MARGARET WARING
Birthdate: 6/3/1910
Birthplace: Brooklyn, NY
Information Available in These Sources: ABYP 2, ABYP 3, SATA 3

BUCK, PEARL S(YDENSTRICKER)
(John Sedges)
Birthdate: 7/26/1892
Birthplace: Hillsboro, WV
Deathdate: 3/6/1973
Information Available in These Sources: ABYP 1, ABYP 3, SATA 1, SATA 25

BUCK, WILLIAM RAY
(William Buchanan)
Birthdate: 1/10/1930
Birthplace: Bloomington, IL
Information Available in These Sources: ABYP 2, ABYP 3

BUCKHOLTZ, EILEEN (GARBER)
(Alyssa Howard, Amanda Lee, Rebecca York, Samantha Chase)
Birthdate: 2/1/1949
Birthplace: Atlanta, GA
Information Available in These Sources: SATA 47, SATA 54

BUCKLEY, HELEN E(LIZABETH)
Birthdate: 6/6/1918
Birthplace: Syracuse, NY
Information Available in These Sources: SATA 2

BUCKMASTER, HENRIETTA
See Stephens, Henrietta Henkle

BUDD, LILLIAN (PETERSON)
Birthdate: 7/21/1897
Birthplace: Chicago, IL
Information Available in These Sources: ABYP 1, ABYP 3, SATA 7

BUEHR, WALTER FRANKLIN
Birthdate: 5/14/1897
Birthplace: Chicago, IL
Deathdate: 1/2/1971
Information Available in These Sources: ABYP 1, ABYP 3, ICB 2, ICB 3, JBA 3, SATA 3

BUELL, ELLEN LEWIS
Birthdate: 6/9/1905
Birthplace: Marietta, OH
Information Available in These Sources: ABYP 2, ABYP 3

BUELL, HAL
See Buell, Harold G.

BUELL, HAROLD G.
(Hal Buell)
Birthdate: 4/28/1931
Birthplace: Chicago, IL
Information Available in These Sources: ABYP 4

BUFANO, REMO
Birthdate: 11/12/1894
Birthplace: Italy
Deathdate: 6/17/1948
Information Available in These Sources: ABYP 2, ABYP 3

BUFF, CONRAD
Birthdate: 1/15/1886
Birthplace: Speicher, Switzerland
Deathdate: 1975
Information Available in These Sources: ABYP 1, ABYP 3, FLTYP, ICB 1, ICB 2, ICB 3, JBA 2, SATA 19, SVC 2, 3

BUFF, MARY MARSH
Birthdate: 4/10/1890
Birthplace: Cincinnati, OH
Deathdate: 11/??/1970
Information Available in These Sources: ABYP 1, ABYP 3, FLTYP, JBA 2 SATA 19, SVC 2, SVC 3, TCCW 1

BUGBEE, EMMA
Birthdate: 1888?
Birthplace: Shippensburg, PA
Deathdate: 10/6/1981
Information Available in These Sources: ABYP 1, ABYP 3, SATA 29

BULFINCH, THOMAS
Birthdate: 7/15/1796
Birthplace: Newton, MA
Deathdate: 5/27/1867
Information Available in These Sources: SATA 35

BULL, CHARLES LIVINGSTON
Birthdate: 1874
Birthplace: NY
Deathdate: 3/22/1932
Information Available in These Sources: CICB

BULLA, CLYDE ROBERT
Birthdate: 1/9/1914
Birthplace: King City, MO
Information Available in These Sources: ABYP 1, ABYP 3, AICB, BABP, DACF, MJA, SATA 2, SATA 41, TCCW 1, TCCW 2, TCCW 3

BULLARD, MARION (RORTY)
Birthplace: Middletown, NY
Deathdate: 1950
Information Available in These Sources: CICB

BUNCE, WILLIAM HARVEY
Birthdate: 8/27/1903
Birthplace: Stillwater, NY
Information Available in These Sources: ABYP 1, ABYP 3

BUNIN, CATHERINE
Birthdate: 2/24/1967
Birthplace: New York, NY
Information Available in These Sources: SATA 30

BUNIN, SHERRY
Birthdate: 2/24/1925
Birthplace: Tarboro, NC
Information Available in These Sources: SATA 30

BUNTAIN, RUTH JAEGER
Birthplace: Chicago, IL
Information Available in These Sources: ABYP 2, ABYP 3

BUNTING, A(NNE) E(VELYN BOLTON)
(Evelyn Bolton, Eve Bunting)
Birthdate: 12/19/1928
Birthplace: Maghera, Ireland
Information Available in These Sources: ABYP 4, JBA 5, SATA 18, TCCW 2TCCW 3

BUNTING, EVE
See Bunting, A(nne) E(velyn Bolton)

BUNTING, GLENN (DAVISON)
Birthdate: 11/28/1957
Birthplace: Belfast, Ireland
Information Available in These Sources: SATA 22

BURACK, SYLVIA K.
(Sylvia E. Kamerman)
Birthdate: 12/16/1916
Birthplace: Hartford, CT
Information Available in These Sources: SATA 35

BURANELLI, MARGUERITE
Information Available in These Sources: ABYP 4

BURBANK, ADDISON (BUSWELL)
Birthdate: 6/1/1895
Birthplace: Los Angeles, CA
Deathdate: 10/4/1961
Information Available in These Sources: ICB 1, ICB 2, JBA 2, SATA 37

BURCH, GLADYS
Birthdate: 1899
Information Available in These Sources: ABYP 2, ABYP 3

BURCH, ROBERT (JOSEPH)
Birthdate: 6/26/1925
Birthplace: Inman, GA
Information Available in These Sources: ABYP 2, ABYP 3, DACF, DLB 52, JBA 3, MBMP, SATA 1, TCCW 1, TCCW 2, TCCW 3

BURCHARD, MARSHALL (GAINES)
Information Available in These Sources: ABYP 4

BURCHARD, PETER D(UNCAN)
Birthdate: 3/1/1921
Birthplace: Washington, DC
Information Available in These Sources: ABYP 2, ABYP 3, DACF, ICB 2, ICB 3, ICB 4, JBA 3, SATA 5

BURCHARD, SUE (HUSTON)
Birthdate: 11/23/1937
Birthplace: Oak Park, IL
Information Available in These Sources: ABYP 4, SATA 22

BURCHARDT, NELLIE
Birthdate: 5/13/1921
Birthplace: Philadelphia, PA
Information Available in These Sources: SATA 7

BURCHELL, S. C.
Information Available in These Sources: ABYP 4

BURCKMYER, ELIZABETH
Birthplace: CA
Information Available in These Sources: IBYP 1, IBYP 2

BURD, CLARA M(ILLER)
Birthplace: New York, NY
Information Available in These Sources: CICB

BURDICK, EUGENE (LEONARD)
Birthdate: 12/12/1918
Birthplace: Sheldon, IA
Deathdate: 7/26/1965
Information Available in These Sources: SATA 22

BURGER, CARL (VICTOR)
Birthdate: 6/18/1888
Birthplace: Maryville, TN
Deathdate: 12/??/1967
Information Available in These Sources: ICB 3, SATA 9

BURGESS, ANN MARIE
See Gerson, Noel B(ertram)

BURGESS, EM
See Burgess, Mary Wyche

BURGESS, F(RANK) GELETT
(Gelett Burgess)
Birthdate: 1/30/1866
Birthplace: Boston, MA
Deathdate: 9/18/1951
Information Available in These Sources: CICB, ICB 1, ICB 2, SATA 30, SATA 32

BURGESS, GELETT
See Burgess, F(rank) Gelett

BURGESS, MARY WYCHE
(Em Burgess)
Birthdate: 11/6/1916
Birthplace: Greenville, SC
Information Available in These Sources: SATA 18

BURGESS, MICHAEL
See Gerson, Noel B(ertram)

BURGESS, ROBERT F(ORREST)
Birthdate: 11/30/1927
Birthplace: Grand Rapids, MI
Information Available in These Sources: ABYP 4, SATA 4

BURGESS, STARLING
See Tudor, Tasha

BURGESS, THORNTON W(ALDO)
(W. B. Thornton)
Birthdate: 1/14/1874
Birthplace: Sandwich, MA
Deathdate: 6/5/1965
Information Available in These Sources: ABYP 2, ABYP 3, DLB 22, JBA 1, JBA 2, SATA 17, TCCW 2, TCCW 3, WCL

BURGESS, TREVOR
See Trevor, Elleston

BURGLON, NORA
Birthdate: 1896
Birthplace: MN
Information Available in These Sources: JBA 2

BURGOYNE, LEON E.
Birthdate: 1916
Information Available in These Sources: ABYP 1, ABYP 3

BURGWYN, MEBANE H(OLOMAN)
Birthdate: 12/10/1914
Birthplace: Rich Square, NC
Information Available in These Sources: SATA 7

BURKE, JOHN
See O'Connor, Richard

BURKE, LYNN
Birthdate: 1943?
Information Available in These Sources: ABYP 1, ABYP 3

BURKERT, NANCY EKHOLM
Birthdate: 2/16/1933
Birthplace: Sterling, CO
Information Available in These Sources: IBYP 1, IBYP 2, ICB 3, ICB 4, JBA 3, SATA 24

BURLAND, BRIAN (BERKELEY)
Birthdate: 4/23/1931
Birthplace: Paget, Bermuda
Information Available in These Sources: ABYP 2, ABYP 3, SATA 34

BURLEIGH, ROBERT
Birthdate: 1/4/1936
Birthplace: Chicago, IL
Information Available in These Sources: SATA 55

BURLESON, ELIZABETH
Birthdate: 11/2/1912
Birthplace: Kerrville, TX
Deathdate: 10/2/1979
Information Available in These Sources: DACF

BURLINGAME, ROGER
See Burlingame, William Roger

BURLINGAME, WILLIAM ROGER
(Roger Burlingame)
Birthdate: 5/7/1889
Birthplace: New York, NY
Deathdate: 3/19/1967
Information Available in These Sources: ABYP 4, SATA 2

BURMAN, ALICE CADDY
(Alice Caddy)
Birthdate: 1896
Birthplace: Hamilton, Ontario, Canada
Deathdate: 8/3/1977
Information Available in These Sources: ICB 2, SATA 24

BURMAN, BEN LUCIEN
Birthdate: 12/12/1895 or 12/12/1896
Birthplace: Covington, KY
Deathdate: 11/12/1984
Information Available in These Sources: SATA 6, SATA 40, TCCW 2, TCCW 3

BURN, DORIS
Birthdate: 4/24/1923
Birthplace: Portland, OR
Information Available in These Sources: ICB 3, SATA 1

BURNETT, CONSTANCE BUEL
Birthdate: 5/15/1893
Birthplace: New York, NY
Deathdate: 1/2/1975
Information Available in These Sources: ABYP 2, ABYP 3, SATA 36

BURNETT, FRANCES (ELIZA) HODGSON
Birthdate: 11/24/1849
Birthplace: Cheetham Hill, Manchester, England
Deathdate: 10/29/1924
Information Available in These Sources: ABYP 1, ABYP 3, DLB 42, JBA 1, TCCW 1, TCCW 2, TCCW 3, YABC

BURNS, IRENE
Birthplace: Boston, MA
Information Available in These Sources: IBYP 1, IBYP 2

BURNS, MARILYN
Information Available in These Sources: SATA 33

BURNS, PAUL C(LAY)
Birthdate: 1923
Birthplace: Catlettsburg, KY
Information Available in These Sources: SATA 5

BURNS, RAY(MOND HOWARD)
Birthdate: 4/21/1924
Birthplace: New York, NY
Information Available in These Sources: SATA 9

BURNS, WILLIAM A(LOYSIUS)
Birthdate: 10/7/1909
Birthplace: New York, NY
Information Available in These Sources: ABYP 4, SATA 5

BURR, LONNIE
Birthdate: 5/31/1943
Birthplace: Dayton, KY
Information Available in These Sources: SATA 47

BURRIS, BURMAH
Information Available in These Sources: IBYP 1, IBYP 2

BURROUGHS, EDGAR RICE
Birthdate: 9/1/1875
Birthplace: Chicago, IL
Deathdate: 3/19/1950
Information Available in These Sources: SATA 41

BURROUGHS, JEAN MITCHELL
Birthdate: 12/4/1908
Birthplace: Bonham, TX
Information Available in These Sources: SATA 28

BURROUGHS, JOHN
Birthdate: 4/3/1837
Birthplace: Roxbury, NY
Deathdate: 3/29/1921
Information Available in These Sources: JBA 1

BURROUGHS, MARGARET TAYLOR G.
(Margaret Taylor)
Birthdate: 11/1/1917
Birthplace: St. Rose, LA
Information Available in These Sources: ABYP 2, ABYP 3, BAI

BURROUGHS, POLLY
Birthdate: 1/8/1925
Birthplace: Waterbury, CT
Information Available in These Sources: SATA 2

BURROWAY, JANET (GAY)
Birthdate: 9/21/1936
Birthplace: Tucson, AZ
Information Available in These Sources: ABYP 4, SATA 23

BURSTEIN, JOHN
(Slim Goodbody)
Birthdate: 12/25/1949
Birthplace: Mineola, NY
Information Available in These Sources: SATA 40, 54

BURT, JESSE CLIFTON
Birthdate: 8/29/1921
Birthplace: Nashville, TN
Deathdate: 11/20/1976
Information Available in These Sources: SATA 20, SATA 46

BURT, NATHANIEL
Birthdate: 11/21/1913
Birthplace: Moose, WY
Information Available in These Sources: ABYP 2, ABYP 3

BURT, OLIVE WOOLLEY
Birthdate: 5/26/1894
Birthplace: Ann Arbor, MI
Information Available in These Sources: ABYP 1, ABYP 3, SATA 4

BURTON, KATHERINE (KURZ)
Birthdate: 1890 or 1887
Birthplace: Cleveland, OH
Deathdate: 1969
Information Available in These Sources: ABYP 2, ABYP 3

BURTON, LESLIE
See McGuire, Leslie (Sarah)

BURTON, MARILEE ROBIN
Birthdate: 12/27/1950
Birthplace: Los Angeles, CA
Information Available in These Sources: SATA 46

BURTON, VIRGINIA LEE
Birthdate: 8/30/1909
Birthplace: Newton Center, MA
Deathdate: 10/15/1968
Information Available in These Sources: ABYP 1, ABYP 3, AICB, CFB, DLB 22, IBYP 1, IBYP 2, ICB 1, ICB 2, JBA 2, SATA 2, TCCW 1, TCCW 2, TCCW 3, WC

BURTON, WILLIAM H(ENRY)
Birthdate: 10/9/1890
Birthplace: Fort Worth, TX
Deathdate: 4/3/1964
Information Available in These Sources: SATA 11

BUSBY, EDITH (A. LAKE)
Birthplace: Terre Haute, IN
Deathdate: 11/16/1964
Information Available in These Sources: ABYP 1, ABYP 3, SATA 29

BUSCH, PHYLLIS S.
Birthdate: 10/6/1909
Birthplace: New York, NY
Information Available in These Sources: SATA 30

BUSH-BROWN, LOUISE
Birthdate: 1896?
Deathdate: 12/15/1973
Information Available in These Sources: ABYP 2, ABYP 3

BUSHMILLER, ERNIE
Birthdate: 8/23/1905
Birthplace: New York, NY
Deathdate: 8/15/1982
Information Available in These Sources: SATA 31

BUSONI, RAFAELLO
Birthdate: 2/1/1900
Birthplace: Berlin, Germany
Deathdate: 3/17/1962
Information Available in These Sources: ABYP 1, ABYP 3, ICB 1, ICB 2, ICB 3, JBA 2, SATA 16

BUTLER, BEVERLY (KATHLEEN)
Birthdate: 5/4/1932
Birthplace: Fond du Lac, WI
Information Available in These Sources: ABYP 1, ABYP 3, JBA 6, SATA 7

BUTLER, ELLIS PARKER
Birthdate: 12/5/1869
Birthplace: Muscatine, IA
Deathdate: 9/13/1937
Information Available in These Sources: JBA 1

BUTLER, HAL
Birthdate: 1/3/1913
Birthplace: St. Louis, MO
Information Available in These Sources: ABYP 2, ABYP 3

BUTLER, MILDRED ALLEN
Birthdate: 5/23/1897
Birthplace: Newton, MA
Information Available in These Sources: ABYP 4

BUTLER, WILLIAM
Birthdate: 1929
Birthplace: Portland, OR
Information Available in These Sources: ABYP 4

BUTTERS, DOROTHY GILMAN
(Dorothy Gilman)
Birthdate: 6/25/1923
Birthplace: New Brunswick, NJ
Information Available in These Sources: ABYP 2, ABYP 3, SATA 5

BUTTERWORTH, EMMA MACALIK
Birthdate: 9/5/1928
Birthplace: Vienna, Austria
Information Available in These Sources: SATA 43

BUTTERWORTH, HEZEKIAH
Birthdate: 12/22/1839
Birthplace: Warren, RI
Deathdate: 9/5/1905
Information Available in These Sources: DLB 42

BUTTERWORTH, OLIVER
Birthdate: 5/23/1915
Birthplace: Hartford, CT
Information Available in These Sources: ABYP 4, DACF, JBA 4, SATA 1, TCCW 2, TCCW 3

BUTTERWORTH, W(ILLIAM) E(DMUND III)
(Webb Beech, Walker E. Blake, James McM. Douglas, Edmund O. Scholefield, Patrick J. Williams)
Birthdate: 11/10/1929
Birthplace: Newark, NJ
Information Available in These Sources: ABYP 4, JBA 5, SATA 5

BUXTON, RALPH
See Silverstein, Virginia B(arbara Opshelor)

BYARD, CAROLE (MARIE)
Birthdate: 7/22/1941
Birthplace: Atlantic City, NJ
Information Available in These Sources: BAI, SATA 57

BYARS, BETSY (CROMER)
Birthdate: 8/7/1928
Birthplace: Charlotte, NC
Information Available in These Sources: ABYP 2, ABYP 3, DACF, JBA 3, MBMP, SATA 4, SATA 46, TCCW 1, TCCW 2, TCCW 3

BYFIELD, BARBARA NINDE
Birthdate: 3/28/1930
Birthplace: Abilene, TX
Information Available in These Sources: IBYP 2, SATA 8

BYRD, ELIZABETH
Birthdate: 12/8/1912
Birthplace: St. Louis, MO
Information Available in These Sources: SATA 34

BYRD, GRADY
Information Available in These Sources: IBYP 2

BYRD, ROBERT (JOHN)
Birthdate: 1/11/1942
Birthplace: Atlantic City, NJ
Information Available in These Sources: SATA 33

BYRNE, DONN
(Brian Oswald Donn-Byrne)
Birthdate: 11/20/1899
Birthplace: New York, NY
Deathdate: 6/18/1928
Information Available in These Sources: JBA 1

C

CABLE, MARY
Birthdate: 1/24/1920
Birthplace: Cleveland, OH
Information Available in These Sources: SATA 9

CABRAL, O(LGA) M(ARIE)
Birthdate: 9/14/1909
Birthplace: Port of Spain, Trinidad, West Indies
Information Available in These Sources: SATA 46

CADDY, ALICE
See Burman, Alice Caddy

CADWALLADER, SHARON
Birthdate: 1/12/1936
Birthplace: Jamestown, ND
Information Available in These Sources: SATA 7

CADY, HARRISON
See Cady, Walter Harrison

CADY, WALTER HARRISON
(Harrison Cady)
Birthdate: 7/??/1877 or 7/??/1879
Birthplace: Gardner, MA
Deathdate: 12/9/1970
Information Available in These Sources: ICB 1, SATA 19

CAEN, HERB (EUGENE)
Birthdate: 4/3/1916
Birthplace: Sacramento, CA
Information Available in These Sources: ABYP 4

CAFFREY, NANCY
Birthdate: 10/19/1929
Birthplace: Stamford, CT
Information Available in These Sources: ABYP 2, ABYP 3

CAGLE, MALCOLM W(INFIELD)
Birthdate: 9/26/1918
Birthplace: Grand Junction, CO
Information Available in These Sources: SATA 32

CAHN, RHODA
Birthdate: 3/29/1922
Information Available in These Sources: SATA 37

CAHN, WILLIAM
Birthdate: 5/12/1912
Birthplace: New York, NY
Information Available in These Sources: SATA 37

CAIN, ARTHUR H(OMER)
(Arthur King)
Birthdate: 7/30/1913
Birthplace: Atlanta, GA
Information Available in These Sources: ABYP 4, SATA 3

CAIN, CHRISTOPHER
See Fleming, Thomas J(ames)

CAINES, JEANNETTE (FRANKLIN)
Birthdate: 1938
Birthplace: New York, NY
Information Available in These Sources: BAI, SATA 43

CALAPAI, LETTERIO
Birthdate: 3/29/1903 or 3/29/1902
Birthplace: Boston, MA
Information Available in These Sources: ICB 2

CALDER, LYN
See Calmenson, Stephanie

CALDWELL, JOHN C(OPE)
Birthdate: 11/27/1913
Birthplace: Futsing, China
Information Available in These Sources: ABYP 1, ABYP 3, SATA 7

CALHOUN, MARY HUISKAMP
(Mary Huiskamp Calhoun Wilkins)
Birthdate: 8/3/1926
Birthplace: Keokuk, IA
Information Available in These Sources: ABYP 2, ABYP 3, JBA 3, SATA 2

CALL, HUGHIE FLORENCE
Birthdate: 4/20/1890
Birthplace: Trent, TX
Deathdate: 1969
Information Available in These Sources: SATA 1

CALLAHAN, CLAIRE WALLIS
(Ann Kilborn Cole, Nancy Hartwell)
Birthdate: 4/10/1890
Birthplace: Philadelphia, PA
Information Available in These Sources: ABYP 2, ABYP 3

CALLAHAN, DOROTHY M(ONAHAN)
Birthdate: 12/24/1934
Birthplace: Bronx, NY
Information Available in These Sources: ABYP 2, ABYP 3, SATA 35, SATA 39

CALLAHAN, PHILIP S(ERNA)
Birthdate: 8/29/1923
Birthplace: Fort Benning, GA
Information Available in These Sources: ABYP 4, SATA 25

CALLAN, JAMIE
Birthdate: 1/26/1954
Birthplace: Long Island, NY
Information Available in These Sources: SATA 59

CALLAWAY, KATHY
Birthdate: 2/19/1943
Birthplace: Chicopee, MA
Information Available in These Sources: SATA 36

CALLEN, LARRY
See Callen, Lawrence Willard, Jr.

CALLEN, LAWRENCE WILLARD, JR.
(Larry Callen)
Birthdate: 4/3/1927
Birthplace: New Orleans, LA
Information Available in These Sources: JBA 5, SATA 19

CALMENSON, STEPHANIE
(Lyn Calder)
Birthdate: 11/28/1952
Birthplace: Brooklyn, NY
Information Available in These Sources: SATA 37, SATA 51

CALVERT, JAMES
Birthdate: 9/8/1920
Birthplace: Cleveland, OH
Information Available in These Sources: ABYP 2, ABYP 3

CALVERT, JOHN
See Leaf, Wilbur Munro

CALVERT, PATRICIA
(Peter J. Freeman)
Birthdate: 7/22/1931
Birthplace: Great Falls, MT
Information Available in These Sources: JBA 6, SATA 45

CAMERON, ANN
Birthdate: 10/21/1943
Birthplace: Rice Lake, WI
Information Available in These Sources: SATA 27

CAMERON, EDNA M.
Birthdate: 9/1/1905
Birthplace: Fredonia, TX
Information Available in These Sources: SATA 3

CAMERON, ELEANOR FRANCES (BUTLER)
Birthdate: 3/23/1912
Birthplace: Winnipeg, Manitoba, Canada
Information Available in These Sources: ABYP 2, ABYP 3, DACF, JBA 3, SATA 1, SATA 25, TCCW 1, TCCW 2, TCCW 3

CAMERON, ELIZABETH
See Nowell, Elizabeth Cameron

CAMERON, POLLY (MCQUISTON)
Birthdate: 10/14/1928
Birthplace: Walnut Creek, CA
Information Available in These Sources: ABYP 1, ABYP 3, ICB 3, ICB 4, JBA 4, SATA 2

CAMP, CHARLES LEWIS
Birthdate: 3/12/1893
Birthplace: Jamestown, ND
Deathdate: 8/14/1975
Information Available in These Sources: SATA 31

CAMP, MADELEINE L'ENGLE
See L'Engle, Madeleine

CAMP, WALTER (CHAUNCEY)
Birthdate: 4/7/1859
Birthplace: New Britain, CT
Deathdate: 3/14/1925
Information Available in These Sources: JBA 1, JBA 2, YABC

CAMPBELL, ANN R.
Birthdate: 1/30/1925
Birthplace: Boston, MA
Information Available in These Sources: SATA 11

CAMPBELL, BARBARA
Birthdate: 1939
Birthplace: AR
Information Available in These Sources: BAI

CAMPBELL, BRUCE
See Epstein, Samuel

CAMPBELL, CAMILLA
Birthdate: 4/15/1905
Birthplace: Fort Worth, TX
Information Available in These Sources: SATA 26

CAMPBELL, ELIZABETH A(NDERSON)
Information Available in These Sources: ABYP 2, ABYP 3

CAMPBELL, HOPE
(Virginia Hughes, G. McDonald Wallis, Helen Wells)
Birthdate: 6/17/1925
Birthplace: Seattle, WA
Information Available in These Sources: SATA 20

CAMPBELL, JANE
See Edwards, Jane Campbell

CAMPBELL, JUDY PIUSSI
See Piussi-Campbell, Judy

CAMPBELL, M. RUDOLPH
Birthplace: South Bend, IN
Information Available in These Sources: ABYP 4

CAMPBELL, PATRICIA J(EAN)
(Patty Campbell)
Birthdate: 11/20/1930
Birthplace: Hollywood, CA
Information Available in These Sources: SATA 45

CAMPBELL, PATTY
See Campbell, Patricia J(ean)

CAMPBELL, R(OSEMAE) W(ELLS)
Birthdate: 5/4/1909
Birthplace: Brooklyn, NY
Information Available in These Sources: ABYP 2, ABYP 3, SATA 1

CAMPBELL, VIRGINIA
Birthdate: 2/17/1914
Birthplace: New Orleans, LA
Information Available in These Sources: IBYP 1, IBYP 2, ICB 2

CAMPBELL, WANDA JAY
Birthplace: Trent, TX
Information Available in These Sources: ABYP 1, ABYP 3

CAMPION, NARDI REEDER
Birthdate: 6/27/1917
Birthplace: Honolulu, HI
Information Available in These Sources: ABYP 1, ABYP 3, SATA 22

CANDELL, VICTOR
Birthdate: 5/11/1903
Birthplace: Budapest, Hungary
Deathdate: 2/15/1977
Information Available in These Sources: SATA 24

CANDY, ROBERT
See Candy, William Robert

CANDY, WILLIAM ROBERT
(Robert Candy)
Birthdate: 3/18/1920
Birthplace: Milton, MA
Information Available in These Sources: ABYP 1, ABYP 3, ICB 2

CANFIELD, DOROTHY
See Fisher, Dorothy (Frances) Canfield

CANFIELD, JANE WHITE
Birthdate: 4/29/1897
Birthplace: Syracuse, NY
Deathdate: 5/23/1984
Information Available in These Sources: SATA 32, SATA 38

CANIFF, MILTON (ARTHUR)
Birthdate: 2/28/1907
Birthplace: Hillsboro, OH
Deathdate: 4/3/1988
Information Available in These Sources: SATA 58

CANNON, BETTIE (WADDELL)
Birthdate: 11/13/1922
Birthplace: Detroit, MI
Information Available in These Sources: SATA 59

CANNON, CORNELIA (JAMES)
Birthdate: 11/17/1876
Birthplace: St. Paul, MN
Deathdate: 12/7/1969
Information Available in These Sources: JBA 1, SATA 28

CANNON, RAVENNA
See Mayhar, Ardath

CANOE, JOHN
See Kirkpatrick, Oliver Austin

CANTY, MARY
Information Available in These Sources: ABYP 4

CANUSI, JOSE
See Barker, S(quire) Omar

CAPLIN, ALFRED GERALD
(Al Capp)
Birthdate: 9/28/1909
Birthplace: New Haven, CT
Deathdate: 11/5/1979
Information Available in These Sources: SATA 21

CAPP, AL
See Caplin, Alfred Gerald

CAPPEL, CONSTANCE
(Constance Montgomery)
Birthdate: 6/22/1936
Birthplace: Dayton, OH
Information Available in These Sources: SATA 22

CAPPS, BENJAMIN (FRANKLIN)
Birthdate: 6/11/1922
Birthplace: Dundee, TX
Information Available in These Sources: SATA 9

CAPTAIN DUCK
See Pinkwater, Daniel Manus

CAPTAIN KANGAROO
See Keeshan, Robert J.

CARAFOLI, MARCI
See Ridlon, Marci

CARAS, ROGER A(NDREW)
(Roger Sarac)
Birthdate: 5/24/1928
Birthplace: Methuen, MA
Information Available in These Sources: SATA 12

CARAWAY, CAREN
Birthdate: 8/8/1939
Birthplace: Madison, WI
Information Available in These Sources: SATA 57

CARBONNIER, JEANNE
Birthdate: 11/25/1894
Birthplace: Paris, France
Deathdate: 5/19/1974
Information Available in These Sources: SATA 3, SATA 34

CARDEN, PRISCILLA
Birthplace: Boston, MA
Information Available in These Sources: ABYP 1, ABYP 3

CARDOZO, LOIS (STEINMETZ)
See Duncan, Lois S(teinmetz)

CARDWELL, PAUL, JR.
Birthdate: 1933
Birthplace: Dallas, TX
Information Available in These Sources: ABYP 4

CAREW, JAN (RYNVELD)
Birthdate: 9/24/1925
Birthplace: Agricola, Guyana
Information Available in These Sources: SATA 40, SATA 51

CAREY, BONNIE
Birthdate: 6/9/1941
Birthplace: Concord, NH
Information Available in These Sources: SATA 18

CAREY, ERNESTINE (MOLLER) GILBRETH
Birthdate: 4/5/1908
Birthplace: New York, NY
Information Available in These Sources: SATA 2

CAREY, M(ARY) V(IRGINIA)
Birthdate: 5/19/1925
Birthplace: New Brighton, England
Information Available in These Sources: SATA 39, SATA 44

CAREY, VALERIE SCHO
Birthdate: 8/6/1949
Birthplace: Pittsburgh, PA
Information Available in These Sources: SATA 60

CARINI, EDWARD
Birthdate: 5/27/1923
Birthplace: Glastonbury, CT
Information Available in These Sources: SATA 9

CARLE, ERIC
Birthdate: 6/25/1929
Birthplace: Syracuse, NY
Information Available in These Sources: IBYP 2, ICB 4, JBA 4, SATA 4, TCCW 3

CARLETON, BARBEE OLIVER
Birthdate: 8/17/1917
Birthplace: Thomaston, ME
Information Available in These Sources: DACF

CARLETON, CAPTAIN L. C.
See Ellis, Edward S(ylvester)

CARLETON, L. C.
See Ellis, Edward S(ylvester)

CARLETON, R(EGINAL) MILTON
Birthdate: 8/16/1899
Birthplace: Chicago, IL
Deathdate: 9/3/1986
Information Available in These Sources: ABYP 4

CARLEY, V(AN NESS) ROYAL
Birthdate: 8/14/1906
Birthplace: Bridgeport, CT
Deathdate: 8/15/1976
Information Available in These Sources: SATA 20

CARLISLE, CLARK
See Holding, James (Clark Carlisle, Jr.)

CARLISLE, OLGA A(NDREYEV)
Birthdate: 1/22/1930
Birthplace: Paris, France
Information Available in These Sources: ABYP 4, SATA 35

CARLSEN, G(EORGE) ROBERT
Birthdate: 4/15/1917
Birthplace: Bozeman, MT
Information Available in These Sources: SATA 30

CARLSEN, RUTH C(HRISTOFFER)
Birthdate: 2/21/1918
Birthplace: Milwaukee, WI
Information Available in These Sources: ABYP 4, SATA 2

CARLSON, AL(BERT W. D.)
Information Available in These Sources: IBYP 2

CARLSON, BERNICE WELLS
Birthdate: 7/21/1910
Birthplace: Clare, MI
Information Available in These Sources: ABYP 1, ABYP 3, SATA 8

CARLSON, DALE BICK
Birthdate: 5/24/1935
Birthplace: New York, NY
Information Available in These Sources: ABYP 4, SATA 1

CARLSON, DANIEL
Birthdate: 10/20/1960
Birthplace: New York, NY
Information Available in These Sources: SATA 27

CARLSON, ESTHER ELISABETH
Birthdate: 12/3/1920
Birthplace: Belmont, MA
Information Available in These Sources: ABYP 1, ABYP 3

CARLSON, NANCY LEE
Birthdate: 10/10/1953
Birthplace: Minneapolis, MN
Information Available in These Sources: SATA 45, SATA 56

CARLSON, NATALIE SAVAGE
Birthdate: 10/3/1906
Birthplace: Winchester, VA
Information Available in These Sources: ABYP 1, ABYP 3, AICB, DACF, MBMP, MJA, SATA 2, TCCW 1, TCCW 2, TCCW 3

CARLSON, VADA F.
(Florella Rose)
Birthdate: 2/27/1897
Birthplace: Cody, NE
Information Available in These Sources: ABYP 4, SATA 16

CARLSTROM, NANCY WHITE
Birthdate: 8/4/1948
Birthplace: Washington, PA
Information Available in These Sources: JBA 6, SATA 48, SATA 53

CARLYON, RICHARD
Information Available in These Sources: SATA 55

CARMER, CARL (LAMSON)
Birthdate: 10/16/1893
Birthplace: Cortland, NY
Deathdate: 9/11/1976
Information Available in These Sources: ABYP 1, ABYP 3, SATA 30, SATA 37, SVC 2, SVC 3

CARMER, ELIZABETH BLACK
Birthdate: 6/14/1904
Birthplace: New Orleans, LA
Information Available in These Sources: ABYP 2, ABYP 3, ICB 2, SATA 24

CARMICHAEL, CARRIE
See Carmichael, Harriet

CARMICHAEL, HARRIET
(Carrie Carmichael)
Birthdate: 1/31/1944
Birthplace: Plainfield, NJ
Information Available in These Sources: SATA 40

CARMICHAEL, JOEL
Birthdate: 12/31/1915
Birthplace: New York, NY
Information Available in These Sources: ABYP 4

CARNAHAN, MARJORIE R.
Information Available in These Sources: ABYP 2, ABYP 3

CAROL, BILL J.
See Knott, William Cecil, Jr.

CARONA, PHILIP B(EN)
Birthdate: 1/2/1925
Birthplace: Dickinson, TX
Information Available in These Sources: ABYP 2, ABYP 3

CAROSELLI, REMUS F(RANCIS)
Birthdate: 10/4/1916
Birthplace: Providence, RI
Information Available in These Sources: DACF, SATA 36

CARPENTER, ALLAN
See Carpenter, John Allan

CARPENTER, EDMUND SNOW
Birthdate: 1922?
Information Available in These Sources: ABYP 4

CARPENTER, FRANCES
Birthdate: 4/30/1890
Birthplace: Washington, DC
Deathdate: 11/2/1972
Information Available in These Sources: ABYP 2, ABYP 3, MJA, SATA 3, SATA 27

CARPENTER, JOHN
Birthdate: 1/16/1948
Birthplace: Carthage, NY
Information Available in These Sources: SATA 58

CARPENTER, JOHN ALLAN
(Allan Carpenter)
Birthdate: 5/11/1917
Birthplace: Waterloo, IA
Information Available in These Sources: SATA 3

CARPENTER, PATRICIA (HEALY EVANS)
(Patricia Healy Evans)
Birthdate: 5/22/1920
Birthplace: Milwaukee, WI
Information Available in These Sources: ABYP 2, ABYP 3, SATA 11

CARR, HARRIETT H(ELEN)
Birthdate: 1/4/1899
Birthplace: Ann Arbor, MI
Information Available in These Sources: ABYP 2, ABYP 3, DACF, MJA, SATA 3

CARR, MARY JANE
Birthdate: 4/23/1899
Birthplace: Portland, OR
Deathdate: 1/4/1988
Information Available in These Sources: ABYP 1, ABYP 3, JBA 2, SATA 2 SATA 55

CARR, RACHAEL
See Carr, Rachel (Elizabeth)

CARR, RACHEL (ELIZABETH)
(Rachael Carr)
Birthdate: 1921
Birthplace: Hankow, China
Information Available in These Sources: ABYP 4

CARRICK, CAROL (HATFIELD)
Birthdate: 5/20/1935
Birthplace: Queens, NY
Information Available in These Sources: JBA 4, SATA 7

CARRICK, DONALD
Birthdate: 4/7/1929
Birthplace: Dearborn, MI
Information Available in These Sources: IBYP 2, ICB 4, JBA 4, SATA 7

CARRIER, LARK
Birthdate: 3/27/1947
Birthplace: MT
Information Available in These Sources: SATA 50

CARRIGHAR, SALLY
Birthplace: Cleveland, OH
Information Available in These Sources: SATA 24

CARRIS, JOAN DAVENPORT
Birthdate: 8/18/1938
Birthplace: Toledo, OH
Information Available in These Sources: SATA 42, SATA 44

CARROLL, ARCHER LATROBE
(Latrobe Carroll, Archer Latrobe)
Birthdate: 1/5/1894
Birthplace: Washington, DC
Information Available in These Sources: MJA, SATA 7

CARROLL, CURT
See Bishop, Curtis (Kent)

CARROLL, ELIZABETH
See Barkin, Carol and James, Elizabeth

CARROLL, LATROBE
See Carroll, Archer Latrobe

CARROLL, LAURA
See Parr, Lucy

CARROLL, RAYMOND
Information Available in These Sources: SATA 47

CARROLL, RUTH (ROBINSON)
Birthdate: 9/24/1899
Birthplace: Lancaster, NY
Information Available in These Sources: IBYP 2, ICB 2, ICB 3, MJA

CARRUTH, ELIA (KAISER)
Birthplace: Cleveland, OH
Information Available in These Sources: ABYP 4

CARRUTH, HAYDEN
Birthdate: 8/3/1921
Birthplace: Waterbury, CT
Information Available in These Sources: SATA 47

CARRYL, CHARLES E(DWARD)
Birthdate: 12/30/1841
Birthplace: New York, NY
Deathdate: 7/3/1920
Information Available in These Sources: DLB 42, JBA 1, SVC 2, SVC 3

CARSE, ROBERT
Birthdate: 7/9/1902
Birthplace: New York, NY
Deathdate: 1/14/1971
Information Available in These Sources: SATA 5

CARSON, J(OHN) FRANKLIN
Birthdate: 8/2/1920
Birthplace: Indianapolis, IN
Information Available in These Sources: ABYP 2, ABYP 3, SATA 1

CARSON, JULIA MARGARET (HICKS)
Birthdate: 1899
Birthplace: Columbus, OH
Information Available in These Sources: ABYP 2, ABYP 3

CARSON, RACHEL (LOUISE)
Birthdate: 5/27/1907
Birthplace: Springfield, PA
Deathdate: 4/14/1964
Information Available in These Sources: SATA 23

CARSON, ROSALIND
See Chittenden, Elizabeth F. and Chittenden, Margaret

CARSON, S. M.
See Gorsline, S(ally) M(arie)

CARSWELL, EVELYN M(EDICUS)
Birthdate: 2/1/1919
Birthplace: Baltimore, MD
Information Available in These Sources: ABYP 2, ABYP 3

CARTER, ANNE
See Brooks, Anne (Tedlock)

CARTER, DOROTHY SHARP
Birthdate: 3/22/1921
Birthplace: Chicago, IL
Information Available in These Sources: SATA 8

CARTER, FORREST
Birthdate: 1927 or 1925
Birthplace: TN
Deathdate: 6/7/1979
Information Available in These Sources: SATA 32

CARTER, HELENE
Birthdate: 1887
Birthplace: Toronto, Ontario, Canada
Deathdate: 12/31/1960 or 12/31/1961
Information Available in These Sources: ICB 1, ICB 2, MJA, SATA 15

CARTER, HODDING
See Carter, William Hodding

CARTER, JAMES H.
See Carter, Katharine J(ones)

CARTER, KATHARINE J(ONES)
(James H. Carter, Davney Hancock, Katharine Mary Jones, Mary E. Nelson)
Birthdate: 2/25/1905
Birthplace: Greenbackville, VA
Information Available in These Sources: SATA 2

CARTER, MARY KENNEDY
Birthdate: 1934
Birthplace: Franklin, OH
Information Available in These Sources: BAI

CARTER, NICK
See Lynds, Dennis

CARTER, PAGE
Information Available in These Sources: ABYP 4

CARTER, PHYLLIS ANN
See Eberle, Irmengarde

CARTER, SAMUEL III
Birthdate: 10/6/1904
Birthplace: New York, NY
Deathdate: 12/28/1988
Information Available in These Sources: SATA 37, SATA 60

CARTER, WILLIAM E(ARL)
Birthdate: 4/29/1927 or 4/29/1926
Birthplace: Dayton, OH
Deathdate: 8/14/1983
Information Available in These Sources: ABYP 2, ABYP 3, SATA 1, SATA 35

CARTER, WILLIAM HODDING
(Hodding Carter)
Birthdate: 2/3/1907
Birthplace: Hammond, LA
Deathdate: 4/4/1972
Information Available in These Sources: ABYP 2, ABYP 3, SATA 2, SATA 27

CARTEY, WILFRED GEORGE ONSLOW
Birthdate: 7/19/1931
Birthplace: Port-of-Spain, Trinidad
Information Available in These Sources: BAI

CARTWRIGHT, SALLY
Birthdate: 11/25/1923
Birthplace: New York, NY
Information Available in These Sources: ABYP 4, SATA 9

CARTY, LEO
Birthdate: 1931
Birthplace: New York, NY
Information Available in These Sources: BAI, IBYP 2

CARVER, JOHN
See Gardner, Richard (M.)

CARWELL, L'ANN
See McKissack, Patricia (L'Ann) C(arwell)

CARY
See Cary, Louis F(avreau)

CARY, BARBARA KNAPP
Birthdate: 1912
Deathdate: 5/4/1975
Information Available in These Sources: SATA 31

CARY, LOUIS F(AVREAU)
(Cary)
Birthdate: 3/13/1915
Birthplace: Brockton, MA
Information Available in These Sources: SATA 9

CARY, M(ARY) V(IRGINIA)
See Carey, M(ary) V(irginia)

CARYL, JEAN
See Kaplan, Jean Caryl Korn

CASE, ELINOR RUTT
Birthdate: 6/18/1914
Birthplace: Sharpsburg, IA
Information Available in These Sources: ABYP 2, ABYP 3

CASE, MARSHAL T(AYLOR)
Birthdate: 2/21/1941
Birthplace: Buffalo, NY
Information Available in These Sources: SATA 9

CASE, MICHAEL
See Howard, Robert West

CASELEY, JUDITH
Birthdate: 10/17/1951
Birthplace: Rahway, NJ
Information Available in These Sources: SATA 53

CASEWIT, CURTIS
(D. Green, D. Vernor, K. Werner)
Birthdate: 3/21/1922
Birthplace: Mannheim, Germany
Information Available in These Sources: SATA 4

CASEY, BRIGID
Birthdate: 1/11/1950
Birthplace: New York, NY
Information Available in These Sources: SATA 9

CASON, EMILLE MABEL EARP
(Emily Mary Bell, Mabel Earp Cason)
Birthdate: 3/7/1892
Birthplace: Corpus Christi, TX
Deathdate: 4/25/1965
Information Available in These Sources: SATA 10

CASON, MABEL EARP
See Cason, Emille Mabel Earp

CASSEDY, SYLVIA
Birthdate: 1/29/1930
Birthplace: Brooklyn, NY
Deathdate: 4/6/1989
Information Available in These Sources: ABYP 4, JBA 6, SATA 27, TCCW 3

CASSEL, LILI
See Wronker, Lili (Cassel)

CASTELLANOS, JANE MOLLIE (ROBINSON)
Birthdate: 8/6/1913
Birthplace: Lansing, MI
Information Available in These Sources: ABYP 4, SATA 9

CASTELLON, FEDERICO
Birthdate: 9/14/1914
Birthplace: Alhabia, Almeria, Spain
Deathdate: 7/29/1971
Information Available in These Sources: ICB 2, SATA 48

CASTILLO, EDMUND LUIS
Birthdate: 11/13/1924
Birthplace: Toledo, OH
Information Available in These Sources: ABYP 2, ABYP 3, SATA 1

CASTLE, LEE
See Ogan, George F. and Ogan, Margaret E. (Nettles)

CASTLE, PAUL
See Howard, Vernon (Linwood)

CASTLEMON, HARRY
See Fosdick, Charles Austin

CASTOR, HENRY
Birthdate: 7/17/1909
Birthplace: Philadelphia, PA
Information Available in These Sources: ABYP 2, ABYP 3

CASWELL, HELEN (RAYBURN)
Birthdate: 3/16/1923
Birthplace: Long Beach, CA
Information Available in These Sources: ABYP 4, SATA 12

CATHER, CAROLYN
Information Available in These Sources: IBYP 1, IBYP 2

CATHER, WILLA (SIBERT)
Birthdate: 12/7/1873 or 12/7/1876
Birthplace: Black Creek Valley, VA
Deathdate: 4/24/1947
Information Available in These Sources: JBA 1, SATA 30

CATHERWOOD, MARY HARTWELL
Birthdate: 12/16/1847
Birthplace: Luray, OH
Deathdate: 12/26/1902
Information Available in These Sources: JBA 1

CATHON, LAURA E(LIZABETH)
Birthdate: 10/17/1908
Birthplace: Pittsburgh, PA
Information Available in These Sources: SATA 27

CATLIN, WYNELLE
Birthdate: 7/29/1930
Birthplace: TX
Information Available in These Sources: SATA 13

CATTON, BRUCE
See Catton, Charles Bruce

CATTON, CHARLES BRUCE
(Bruce Catton)
Birthdate: 10/9/1899
Birthplace: Petoskey, MI
Deathdate: 8/28/1978
Information Available in These Sources: SATA 2, SATA 24

CATZ, MAX
See Glaser, Milton

CAUDELL, MARIAN
Birthdate: 10/8/1930
Birthplace: Mitchell, IN
Information Available in These Sources: SATA 52

CAUDILL, REBECCA
Birthdate: 2/2/1899
Birthplace: (Poor Fork) Cumberland, KY
Deathdate: 10/2/1985
Information Available in These Sources: ABYP 1, ABYP 3, DACF, MJA, SATA 1, SATA 44, TCCW 1, TCCW 2, TCCW 3

CAULEY, LORINDA BRYAN
Birthdate: 7/2/1951
Birthplace: Washington, DC
Information Available in These Sources: JBA 6, SATA 43, SATA 46

CAULFIELD, PEGGY F.
Birthdate: 4/10/1926
Birthplace: Hartford, CT
Deathdate: 9/18/1987
Information Available in These Sources: SATA 53

CAUMAN, SAMUEL
Birthdate: 6/29/1910
Birthplace: Boston, MA
Deathdate: 3/6/1971
Information Available in These Sources: SATA 48

CAVALLO, DIANA
Birthdate: 11/3/1931
Birthplace: Philadelphia, PA
Information Available in These Sources: SATA 7

CAVANAGH, HELEN (CAROL)
Birthdate: 12/4/1939
Birthplace: Quincy, MA
Information Available in These Sources: SATA 37, SATA 48

CAVANAH, FRANCES
Birthdate: 9/26/1899
Birthplace: Princeton, IN
Deathdate: 5/2/1982
Information Available in These Sources: ABYP 1, ABYP 3, MJA, SATA 1, SATA 31

CAVANNA, BETTY
(Betsy Allen, Elizabeth Allen Cavanna, Elizabeth Headley)
Birthdate: 6/24/1909
Birthplace: Camden, NJ
Information Available in These Sources: ABYP 1, ABYP 3, DACF, MJA, SATA 1, SATA 30, TCCW 1, TCCW 2, TCCW 3

CAVANNA, ELIZABETH ALLEN
See Cavanna, Betty

CAVIN, RUTH (BRODIE)
(Sally Brodie, Jennie Soble)
Birthdate: 10/15/1918
Birthplace: Pittsburgh, PA
Information Available in These Sources: SATA 38

CAZET, DENYS
Birthdate: 3/22/1938
Birthplace: Oakland, CA
Information Available in These Sources: SATA 41, SATA 52

CEBULASH, MEL
(Ben Farrell, Glen Harlan, Jared Jansen, Jeanette Mara)
Birthdate: 8/24/1937
Birthplace: Jersey City, NJ
Information Available in These Sources: SATA 10

CEDER, GEORGIANA DORCAS
(Ana Dor)
Birthplace: Chicago, IL
Information Available in These Sources: SATA 10

CELESTINO, MARTHA LAING
(Martha Laing)
Birthdate: 7/9/1951
Birthplace: Delhi, NY
Information Available in These Sources: SATA 39

CELLINI, EVA
Birthplace: Budapest, Hungary
Information Available in These Sources: IBYP 1, IBYP 2, ICB 3

CELLINI, JOSEPH
Birthdate: 6/13/1924
Birthplace: Budapest, Hungary
Information Available in These Sources: IBYP 1, IBYP 2, ICB 3

CERF, BENNETT (ALFRED)
Birthdate: 5/25/1898
Birthplace: New York, NY
Deathdate: 8/27/1971
Information Available in These Sources: ABYP 1, ABYP 3, SATA 7

CERF, CHRISTOPHER (BENNETT)
Birthdate: 8/19/1941
Birthplace: New York, NY
Information Available in These Sources: SATA 2

CERMAK, MARTIN
See Duchacek, Ivo D(uka)

CETIN, FRANK STANLEY
Birthdate: 12/15/1921
Birthplace: Kemmerer, WY
Information Available in These Sources: SATA 2

CHACONAS, D(ORIS) J.
Birthdate: 3/11/1938
Information Available in These Sources: ABYP 4

CHADWICK, LESTER
See Stratemeyer, Edward L.

CHAFETZ, HENRY
Birthdate: 5/2/1916
Birthplace: New York, NY
Deathdate: 1/5/1978
Information Available in These Sources: ABYP 1, ABYP 3

CHAFFEE, ALLEN
(Antoinette Gurney)
Birthdate: 1919
Birthplace: Farragut, IA
Information Available in These Sources: SATA 3

CHAFFIN, LILLIE D(ORTON)
(Randall Chaffin, Lila Day, Lena Winston)
Birthdate: 2/1/1925
Birthplace: Varney, KY
Information Available in These Sources: ABYP 4, DACF, SATA 4

CHAFFIN, RANDALL
See Chaffin, Lillie D(orton)

CHAIKIN, MIRIAM
Birthdate: 12/8/1928
Birthplace: Jerusalem, Israel (Palestine)
Information Available in These Sources: JBA 6, SATA 24

CHALMERS, AUDREY
Birthdate: 5/27/1899 or 5/27/1893
Birthplace: Montreal, Canada
Deathdate: 11/27/1957
Information Available in These Sources: ABYP 1, ABYP 3, ICB 1, ICB 2

CHALMERS, MARY (EILEEN)
Birthdate: 3/16/1927
Birthplace: Camden, NJ
Information Available in These Sources: ABYP 2, ABYP 3, ICB 2, ICB 3, JBA 3, SATA 6, TCCW 2, TCCW 3

CHAMBERLAIN, ELINOR
Birthdate: 6/21/1901
Birthplace: Muskegon, MI
Information Available in These Sources: ABYP 2, ABYP 3

CHAMBERLIN, JO HUBBARD
Information Available in These Sources: ABYP 2, ABYP 3

CHAMBERS, BRADFORD
Birthdate: 2/4/1922
Birthplace: New York, NY
Deathdate: 9/22/1984
Information Available in These Sources: ABYP 4, SATA 39

CHAMBERS, C. BOSSERON
Birthdate: 5/13/1883
Birthplace: St. Louis, MO
Information Available in These Sources: CICB

CHAMBERS, CATHERINE E.
See Johnston, Norma

CHAMBERS, JOHN W.
Birthdate: 9/29/1933
Birthplace: New York, NY
Information Available in These Sources: SATA 46, SATA 57

CHAMBERS, ROBERT WARNER
Birthdate: 10/27/1924
Birthplace: Oakland, CA
Information Available in These Sources: ABYP 2, ABYP 3

CHAN, PLATO
Birthdate: 1931
Birthplace: New York, NY
Information Available in These Sources: ICB 1

CHANDLER, CAROLINE A(UGUSTA)
Birthdate: 12/7/1906
Birthplace: Ford City, PA
Deathdate: 12/18/1979
Information Available in These Sources: ABYP 2, ABYP 3, SATA 22, SATA 24

CHANDLER, DAVID PORTER
Birthdate: 2/7/1933
Birthplace: New York, NY
Information Available in These Sources: SATA 28

CHANDLER, EDNA WALKER
Birthdate: 11/16/1908
Birthplace: Macksville, KS
Deathdate: 9/14/1982
Information Available in These Sources: ABYP 2, ABYP 3, SATA 11, SATA 31

CHANDLER, LINDA S(MITH)
Birthdate: 2/4/1929
Birthplace: Wadesboro, NC
Information Available in These Sources: SATA 39

CHANDLER, RUTH FORBES
Birthdate: 7/17/1894
Birthplace: New Bedford, MA
Deathdate: 12/29/1978
Information Available in These Sources: ABYP 1, ABYP 3, SATA 2, SATA 26

CHANDLER, THOMAS
Birthdate: 1911
Birthplace: Los Angeles, CA
Information Available in These Sources: ABYP 2, ABYP 3

CHANELES, SOL
Birthdate: 9/23/1926
Birthplace: New York, NY
Information Available in These Sources: ABYP 4

CHAPIAN, MARIE
Birthdate: 10/10/1938
Birthplace: Minneapolis, MN
Information Available in These Sources: SATA 29

CHAPIN, ALENE OLSEN DALTON
(Alene Dalton)
Birthdate: 1915
Birthplace: Brigham City, UT
Deathdate: 6/3/1986
Information Available in These Sources: SATA 47

CHAPIN, HENRY
Birthdate: 1893
Birthplace: Toledo, OH
Deathdate: 9/4/1983
Information Available in These Sources: ABYP 2, ABYP 3

CHAPMAN, ALLEN
See Stratemeyer, Edward L.

CHAPMAN, FRANK MICHLER
Birthdate: 6/12/1864
Birthplace: Englewood, NJ
Deathdate: 11/15/1945
Information Available in These Sources: JBA 1

CHAPMAN, FREDERICK TRENCH
Birthdate: 7/24/1887
Birthplace: Windsor, CA
Deathdate: 1983
Information Available in These Sources: ICB 2

CHAPMAN, JOHN STANTON HIGHAM
(Maristan Chapman, Kirk Connell, Dent Ilsley, Jane Selkirk)
Birthdate: 5/21/1891
Birthplace: London, England
Deathdate: 10/13/1972
Information Available in These Sources: ABYP 1, ABYP 2, ABYP 3, SATA 27

CHAPMAN, MARISTAN
See Chapman, John Stanton Higham

CHAPMAN, MARY HAMILTON ILLSLEY
Birthdate: 9/10/1895
Birthplace: Chattanooga, TN
Information Available in These Sources: ABYP 1, 2, 3

CHAPMAN, WALKER
See Silverberg, Robert

CHAPPELL, WARREN
Birthdate: 7/9/1904
Birthplace: Richmond, VA
Information Available in These Sources: IBYP 1, IBYP 2, ICB 1, ICB 2, ICB 3, ICB 4, JBA 3, SATA 6

CHARDIET, BERNICE (KROLL)
Birthdate: 11/12/1930 or 11/12/1927
Birthplace: New York, NY
Information Available in These Sources: SATA 27

CHARLES, DONALD
See Meighan, Donald Charles

CHARLES, NICHOLAS
See Kuskin, Karla (Seidman)

CHARLIP, REMY
Birthdate: 1/10/1929
Birthplace: Brooklyn (Brownsville), NY
Information Available in These Sources: ABYP 1, ABYP 3, ICB 2, ICB 3, ICB 4, JBA 3, SATA 4

CHARLOT, JEAN
Birthdate: 2/7/1898
Birthplace: Paris, France
Deathdate: 3/20/1979
Information Available in These Sources: IBYP 2, ICB 1, ICB 2, ICB 3, ICB 4, MJA, SATA 8, SATA 31

CHARMATZ, BILL
Birthdate: 11/15/1925
Birthplace: New York, NY
Information Available in These Sources: SATA 7

CHAROSH, MANNIS
Birthdate: 11/9/1906
Birthplace: New York, NY
Information Available in These Sources: SATA 5

CHASE, ADAM
See Marlowe, Stephen

CHASE, ALICE (ELIZABETH)
See McHargue, Georgess

CHASE, ANYA SETON
See Seton, Anya

CHASE, EMILY
See Sachs, Judith

CHASE, MARY (COYLE)
Birthdate: 2/25/1907
Birthplace: Denver, CO
Deathdate: 10/20/1981
Information Available in These Sources: ABYP 2, ABYP 3, SATA 17, SATA 29

CHASE, MARY ELLEN
Birthdate: 2/24/1887
Birthplace: Bluehill, ME
Deathdate: 7/28/1973
Information Available in These Sources: ABYP 2, ABYP 3, JBA 4, SATA 10

CHASE, RHODA (CAMPBELL)
Information Available in These Sources: CICB

CHASE, RICHARD
Birthdate: 2/15/1904
Birthplace: Huntsville, AL
Information Available in These Sources: ABYP 4, MJA

CHASE, SAMANTHA
See Buckholtz, Eileen (Garber)

CHASEK, JUDITH
Birthplace: Newark, NJ
Information Available in These Sources: ABYP 4

CHASINS, ABRAM
Birthdate: 8/17/1903
Birthplace: New York, NY
Information Available in These Sources: ABYP 4

CHASTAIN, MADYE LEE
Birthdate: 12/15/1908
Birthplace: Texarkana, TX
Information Available in These Sources: ICB 2, MJA, SATA 4

CHEN, ANTHONY YOUNG
(Tony Chen)
Birthdate: 1/3/1929
Birthplace: Kingston, Jamaica, West Indies
Information Available in These Sources: ICB 4, JBA 5, SATA 6

CHEN, TONY
See Chen, Anthony Young

CHENAULT, NELL
See Smith, Linell Nash

CHENERY, JANET (DAI)
Birthdate: 4/10/1923
Birthplace: New Rochelle, NY
Information Available in These Sources: SATA 25

CHENEY, CORA
Birthdate: 12/20/1916
Birthplace: Birmingham, AL
Information Available in These Sources: ABYP 2, ABYP 3, SATA 3

CHENEY, TED
See Cheney, Theodore Albert

CHENEY, THEODORE ALBERT
(Ted Cheney)
Birthdate: 1/1/1928
Birthplace: Milton, MA
Information Available in These Sources: SATA 11

CHENG, JUDITH
Birthdate: 9/25/1955
Birthplace: Hong Kong
Information Available in These Sources: SATA 36

CHERMAYEFF, IVAN
Birthdate: 6/6/1932
Birthplace: London, England
Information Available in These Sources: ICB 3, SATA 47

CHERNOFF, DOROTHY A.
See Ernst, Lyman John

CHERNOFF, GOLDIE TAUB
Birthdate: 5/8/1909
Birthplace: Austria
Information Available in These Sources: SATA 10

CHERRY, LYNNE
Birthdate: 1/5/1952
Birthplace: Philadelphia, PA
Information Available in These Sources: SATA 34

CHERRYHOLMES, ANNE
See Price, Olive (M.)

CHESLER, BERNICE
Birthdate: 10/3/1932
Birthplace: New Bedford, MA
Information Available in These Sources: SATA 59

CHESNUTT, CHARLES WADDELL
Birthdate: 1858
Birthplace: Cleveland, OH
Deathdate: 1932
Information Available in These Sources: BAI

CHESS, VICTORIA (DICKERSON)
Birthdate: 11/16/1939
Birthplace: Chicago, IL
Information Available in: ICB 4, JBA 6, SATA 33

CHESSARE, MICHELE
Birthdate: 1921
Information Available in These Sources: SATA 42

CHESTER, MICHAEL (ARTHUR)
Birthdate: 11/23/1928
Birthplace: New York, NY
Information Available in These Sources: ABYP 2, ABYP 3

CHETIN, HELEN
Birthdate: 7/6/1922
Information Available in These Sources: SATA 6

CHETWIN, GRACE
Birthplace: Nottingham, England
Information Available in These Sources: SATA 50

CHEVALIER, CHRISTA
Birthdate: 3/25/1937
Birthplace: Limbach, Germany
Information Available in These Sources: SATA 35

CHEW, RUTH
(Ruth Silver)
Birthdate: 4/8/1920
Birthplace: Minneapolis, MN
Information Available in These Sources: JBA 6, SATA 7

CHIANG, YEE
Birthdate: 5/19/1903
Birthplace: Kiu-Kiang, China
Deathdate: 10/17/1977
Information Available in These Sources: ICB 2

CHICKERING, MARJORIE
Birthplace: Walden, VT
Information Available in These Sources: ABYP 4

CHIDSEY, DONALD BARR
Birthdate: 5/14/1902
Birthplace: Elizabeth, NJ
Information Available in These Sources: SATA 3, SATA 27

CHIEFARI, JANET D.
Birthdate: 10/24/1942
Birthplace: Saratoga Springs, NY
Information Available in These Sources: SATA 58

CHILD, CHARLES JESSE
Birthdate: 1/15/1901
Birthplace: Montclair, NJ
Information Available in These Sources: ICB 1

CHILD, LYDIA MARIA
Birthdate: 2/11/1802
Birthplace: Medford, MA
Deathdate: 10/20/1880
Information Available in These Sources: SVC 2, SVC 3

CHILDREN'S SHEPHERD, THE
See Westphal, Arnold Carl

CHILDRESS, ALICE
Birthdate: 10/12/1920
Birthplace: Charleston, SC
Information Available in These Sources: ABYP 4, BAI, DACF, JBA 5, SATA 7, SATA 48, TCCW 3

CHILDS, FAY
See Childs, Halla Fay (Cochrane)

CHILDS, HALLA FAY (COCHRANE)
(Fay Childs)
Birthdate: 8/31/1890
Birthplace: Chambers, NE
Deathdate: 10/??/1971
Information Available in These Sources: SATA 1, SATA 25

CHILDS, JOHN FARNSWORTH
Birthdate: 11/24/1909
Birthplace: New York, NY
Information Available in These Sources: ABYP 1, ABYP 3

CHIN, RICHARD (M.)
Birthdate: 12/9/1946
Birthplace: Canton, China
Information Available in These Sources: SATA 52

CHITTENDEN, ELIZABETH F.
(Rosalind Carson)
Birthdate: 11/4/1903
Birthplace: Brandon, VT
Information Available in These Sources: SATA 9

CHITTENDEN, MARGARET
(Rosalind Carson)
Birthdate: 1/31/1933
Birthplace: London, England
Information Available in These Sources: SATA 28

CHITTUM, IDA (HOOVER)
Birthdate: 4/6/1918
Birthplace: Canton, OH
Information Available in These Sources: ABYP 4, SATA 7

CHOATE, FLORENCE
Birthplace: Florence, NJ
Information Available in These Sources: CICB

CHOATE, JUDITH (NEWKIRK)
Birthdate: 1/1/1940
Birthplace: La Junta, CO
Information Available in These Sources: SATA 30

CHORAO, ANN MCKAY (SPROAT)
(Kay Chorao)
Birthdate: 1/7/1936 or 1/7/1937
Birthplace: Elkhart, IN
Information Available in These Sources: IBYP 2, ICB 4, JBA 4, SATA 8

CHORAO, KAY
See Chorao, Ann McKay (Sproat)

CHORON, JACQUES
Birthdate: 1/8/1904
Birthplace: Shavli, Russia
Deathdate: 3/30/1972
Information Available in These Sources: ABYP 2, ABYP 3

CHORPENNING, CHARLOTTE (LEE BARROWS)
Birthdate: 1/3/1872
Deathdate: 1/??/1955
Information Available in These Sources: SATA 37, TCCW 1, TCCW 2, TCCW 3

CHRISMAN, ARTHUR BOWIE
Birthdate: 7/16/1899
Birthplace: White Post, VA
Deathdate: 2/24/1953
Information Available in These Sources: ABYP 1, ABYP 3, JBA 1, JBA 2, TCCW 2, TCCW 3, YABC

CHRISTELOW, EILEEN
Birthdate: 4/22/1943
Birthplace: Washington, DC
Information Available in These Sources: SATA 35, SATA 38

CHRISTENSEN, GARDELL DANO
Birthdate: 8/31/1907
Birthplace: Shelley, ID
Information Available in These Sources: ABYP 2, ABYP 3, ICB 2, SATA 1

CHRISTESEN, BARBARA
Birthdate: 3/7/1940
Birthplace: New York, NY
Information Available in These Sources: SATA 40

CHRISTGAU, ALICE ERICKSON
Birthdate: 11/15/1902
Birthplace: Scandia, MN
Information Available in These Sources: SATA 13

CHRISTIAN, MARY BLOUNT
Birthdate: 2/20/1933
Birthplace: Houston, TX
Information Available in These Sources: SATA 9

CHRISTIAN, SAMUEL T(ERRY)
Birthdate: 12/4/1937
Birthplace: Huntington, WV
Information Available in These Sources: ABYP 4

CHRISTOPHER, LOUISE
See Hale, Arlene

CHRISTOPHER, MATT(HEW) F.
(Fredric Martin)
Birthdate: 8/16/1917 or 8/6/1917
Birthplace: Bath, PA
Information Available in These Sources: ABYP 2, ABYP 3, JBA 5, MBMP, SATA 2, SATA 47

CHRISTOPHER, MILBOURNE
Birthdate: 1914?
Birthplace: Baltimore, MD
Deathdate: 6/17/1984
Information Available in These Sources: SATA 46

CHRISTY, HOWARD CHANDLER
Birthdate: 1/10/1873
Birthplace: Morgan County, OH
Deathdate: 3/4/1952
Information Available in These Sources: ICB 1, SATA 21

CHRYSTIE, FRANCES NICHOLSON
Birthdate: 1904
Birthplace: New York, NY
Deathdate: 11/27/1986
Information Available in These Sources: ABYP 1, ABYP 3, SATA 60

CHU, DANIEL
Birthdate: 6/11/1933
Birthplace: Nanking, China
Information Available in These Sources: SATA 11

CHURCH, CAROL BAUER
Information Available in These Sources: ABYP 4

CHURCHILL, E. RICHARD
Birthdate: 5/25/1937
Birthplace: Greeley, CO
Information Available in These Sources: SATA 11

CHUTE, B(EATRICE) J(OY)
Birthdate: 1/3/1913
Birthplace: Minneapolis, MN
Deathdate: 9/6/1987
Information Available in These Sources: MJA, SATA 2, SATA 53

CHUTE, MARCHETTE (GAYLORD)
Birthdate: 8/16/1909
Birthplace: Wayzata, MN
Information Available in These Sources: ABYP 1, ABYP 3, MJA, SATA 1, SVC 2, TCCW 1, TCCW 2, TCCW 3

CHWAST, JACQUELINE (WEINER)
Birthdate: 1/1/1932
Birthplace: Newark, NJ
Information Available in These Sources: IBYP 1, IBYP 2, ICB 3, JBA 4, SATA 6

CHWAST, SEYMOUR
Birthdate: 8/18/1931
Birthplace: Bronx, NY
Information Available in These Sources: IBYP 2, ICB 3, ICB 4, JBA 4, SATA 18

CIARDI, JOHN (ANTHONY)
Birthdate: 6/24/1916
Birthplace: Boston, MA
Deathdate: 3/30/1986
Information Available in These Sources: ABYP 1, ABYP 3, BABP, JBA 3, SATA 1, SATA 46, SVC 3, TCCW 1TCCW 2, TCCW 3

CIMINO, MARIA (PIA)
Information Available in These Sources: ABYP 4

CLAFLIN, EDWARD
Birthdate: 4/14/1949
Birthplace: Stamford, CT
Information Available in These Sources: ABYP 4

CLAGETT, JOHN (HENRY)
Birthdate: 4/6/1916
Birthplace: Bowling Green, KY
Information Available in These Sources: ABYP 2, ABYP 3

CLAMPETT, BOB
See Clampett, Robert

CLAMPETT, ROBERT
(Bob Clampett)
Birthdate: 5/8/1914?
Birthplace: San Diego, CA
Deathdate: 5/2/1984
Information Available in These Sources: SATA 38, SATA 44

CLANCY, HOLLING ALLISON
See Holling, Holling C(lancy)

CLANCY, JOSEPH P(ATRICK)
Birthdate: 3/8/1928
Birthplace: New York, NY
Information Available in These Sources: ABYP 4

CLAPP, PATRICIA
Birthdate: 6/9/1912
Birthplace: Boston, MA
Information Available in These Sources: DACF, JBA 5, SATA 4, TCCW 1, TCCW 2, TCCW 3

CLARK, ANN NOLAN
Birthdate: 12/5/1896 or 12/5/1898
Birthplace: Las Vegas, NM
Information Available in These Sources: ABYP 1, ABYP 3, AICB, JBA 2, MBMP, SATA 4, SVC 2, SVC 3, TCCW 1, TCCW 2, TCCW 3

CLARK, CHAMP
Birthdate: 8/24/1923
Birthplace: St. Louis, MO
Information Available in These Sources: SATA 47

CLARK, DAVID ALLEN
See Ernst, Lyman John

CLARK, ELECTA
Birthdate: 5/17/1910
Birthplace: Chicago, IL
Information Available in These Sources: ABYP 4

CLARK, FRANK J(AMES)
Birthdate: 8/4/1922
Birthplace: Brooklyn, NY
Information Available in These Sources: ABYP 2, ABYP 3, SATA 18

CLARK, GAREL
See Garelick, May

CLARK, MARGARET GOFF
Birthdate: 3/7/1913
Birthplace: Oklahoma City, OK
Information Available in These Sources: ABYP 2, ABYP 3, SATA 8

CLARK, MARY HIGGINS
Birthdate: 12/24/1929
Birthplace: New York, NY
Information Available in These Sources: SATA 46

CLARK, MERLE
See Gessner, Lynne

CLARK, PATRICIA (FINROW)
Birthdate: 1/3/1929
Birthplace: Walla Walla, WA
Information Available in These Sources: SATA 11

CLARK, VAN D(EUSEN)
Birthdate: 12/26/1909
Birthplace: Deming, NM
Information Available in These Sources: SATA 2

CLARK, VIRGINIA
See Gray, Patricia (Clark)

CLARK, WALTER VAN TILBURG
Birthdate: 8/3/1909
Birthplace: East Oreland, ME
Deathdate: 11/11/1971
Information Available in These Sources: SATA 8

CLARKE, CLORINDA
Birthdate: 3/4/1917
Birthplace: Utica, NY
Information Available in These Sources: SATA 7

CLARKE, FRED G.
Birthdate: 1964
Information Available in These Sources: ABYP 4

CLARKE, JOHN
See Laklan, Carli (Laughlin Aiello)

CLARKE, MARY STETSON
Birthdate: 12/27/1911
Birthplace: Melrose, MA
Information Available in These Sources: SATA 5

CLARKE, MICHAEL
See Newlon, Frank Clarke

CLARKE, REBECCA SOPHIA
(Sophie May)
Birthdate: 2/22/1833
Birthplace: Norridgewock, ME
Deathdate: 8/16/1906
Information Available in These Sources: DLB 42

CLAY, PATRICE
Birthdate: 4/8/1947
Birthplace: McKeesport, PA
Information Available in These Sources: SATA 47

CLAYPOOL, JANE
See Miner, Jane Claypool

CLAYTON, BARBARA
See Pluff, Barbara (Littlefield)

CLEARY, BEVERLY (BUNN)
Birthdate: 4/12/1916
Birthplace: McMinnville, OR
Information Available in These Sources: ABYP 1, ABYP 3, AICB, DACF, MBMP, MJA, SATA 2, SATA 43, TCCW 1, TCCW 2, TCCW 3

CLEAVER, BILL
See Cleaver, William Joseph

CLEAVER, CAROLE
Birthdate: 5/21/1934
Birthplace: Ridgewood, NJ
Information Available in These Sources: SATA 6

CLEAVER, VERA (ALLEN)
Birthdate: 1/6/1919
Birthplace: Virgil, SD
Information Available in These Sources: ABYP 3, DACF, JBA 4, SATA 22, TCCW 1, TCCW 2, TCCW 3

CLEAVER, WILLIAM JOSEPH
(Bill Cleaver)
Birthdate: 3/24/1920
Birthplace: Seattle, WA
Deathdate: 8/20/1981
Information Available in These Sources: ABYP 3, DACF, JBA 4, SATA 22, SATA 27, TCCW 1, TCCW 2, TCCW 3

CLELAND, MABEL
See Widdemer, Mabel Cleland

CLEMENS, SAMUEL LANGHORNE
See Twain, Mark

CLEMENS, VIRGINIA PHELPS
Birthdate: 4/7/1941
Birthplace: Bronxville, NY
Information Available in These Sources: SATA 35

CLEMENT, CLARLES
Birthdate: 8/15/1921
Birthplace: New York, NY
Information Available in These Sources: ICB 2

CLEMENTS, BRUCE
Birthdate: 11/25/1931
Birthplace: New York, NY
Information Available in These Sources: ABYP 4, DACF, JBA 5, SATA 27, TCCW 2, TCCW 3

CLEMONS, ELIZABETH
See Nowell, Elizabeth Cameron

CLEVELAND, BOB
See Cleveland, George

CLEVELAND, GEORGE
(Bob Cleveland, Cappy Dick)
Birthdate: 1903?
Birthplace: Peoria, IL
Deathdate: 4/29/1985
Information Available in These Sources: SATA 43

CLEVEN, CATHERINE
See Cleven, Kathryn Seward

CLEVEN, KATHRYN SEWARD
(Catherine Cleven)
Birthdate: 11/26/1906
Birthplace: Dayton, OH
Information Available in These Sources: SATA 2

CLIFFORD, ETH
See Rosenberg, Ethel (Clifford)

CLIFFORD, HAROLD B(URTON)
(Burt Farnham)
Birthdate: 5/21/1893
Birthplace: Winthrop, ME
Information Available in These Sources: SATA 10

CLIFFORD, M(ARGARET) C(ORT)
(Peggy Clifford, M. C. Cort)
Birthdate: 9/20/1929
Birthplace: Cincinnati, OH
Information Available in These Sources: SATA 1

CLIFFORD, MARY LOUISE (BENEWAY)
Birthdate: 8/15/1926
Birthplace: Ontario, NY
Information Available in These Sources: ABYP 4, SATA 23

CLIFFORD, PEGGY
See Clifford, M(argaret) C(ort)

CLIFTON, G.
See Wisler, G(ary) Clifton

CLIFTON, LUCILLE
(Thelma Sayles)
Birthdate: 6/27/1936
Birthplace: Depew, NY
Information Available in These Sources: BAI, JBA 5, SATA 20, TCCW 1, TCCW 2, TCCW 3

CLIMO, SHIRLEY
Birthdate: 11/25/1928
Birthplace: Cleveland, OH
Information Available in These Sources: SATA 35, SATA 39

CLISH, LEE MARIAN
(Marian Clish, Marian Lee)
Birthdate: 9/27/1946
Birthplace: Madison, WI
Information Available in These Sources: SATA 43

CLISH, MARIAN
See Clish, Lee Marian

CLOKEY, ART
Birthdate: 1921
Birthplace: Detroit, MI
Information Available in These Sources: SATA 59

CLYMER, ELEANOR (LOWENTON)
(Janet Bell, Elizabeth Kinsey)
Birthdate: 1/7/1906
Birthplace: New York, NY
Information Available in These Sources: ABYP 1, ABYP 3, DACF, JBA 4, SATA 9, TCCW 1, TCCW 2, TCCW 3

CLYNE, PATRICIA EDWARDS
(P. E. Edwards, Allison Parker)
Birthdate: 5/2/1935
Birthplace: New York, NY
Information Available in These Sources: ABYP 4, SATA 31

COALSON, GLO
Birthdate: 3/19/1946
Birthplace: Abilene, TX
Information Available in These Sources: IBYP 2, ICB 4, SATA 26

COATES, BELLE
Birthdate: 11/11/1896
Birthplace: Victor, IA
Information Available in These Sources: SATA 2

COATES, RUTH ALLISON
Birthdate: 5/18/1915
Birthplace: Mt. Carmel, IL
Information Available in These Sources: SATA 11

COATSWORTH, ELIZABETH (JANE)
Birthdate: 5/31/1893
Birthplace: Buffalo, NY
Deathdate: 8/31/1986, or 9/2/1986
Information Available in These Sources: ABYP 1, ABYP 3, AICB, DACF, DLB 22, JBA 1, JBA 2, MBMP, SATA 2, SATA 49, SATA 56, SVCC 2, SVC 3, TCCW 1, TCCW 2 TCCW 3

COBB, JANE
See Berry, Jane Cobb

COBB, VICKI (WOLF)
Birthdate: 8/19/1938
Birthplace: New York, NY
Information Available in These Sources: ABYP 4, JBA 5, SATA 8

COBER, ALAN E(DWIN)
Birthdate: 5/18/1935
Birthplace: New York, NY
Information Available in These Sources: IBYP 1, ICB 3, ICB 4, JBA 4, SATA 7

COBLENTZ, CATHERINE CATE
Birthdate: 1897
Birthplace: VT
Deathdate: 1951
Information Available in These Sources: JBA 2

COBURN, JOHN BOWEN
Birthdate: 9/27/1914
Birthplace: Danbury, CT
Information Available in These Sources: ABYP 4

COCHRAN, BOBBYE A.
Birthdate: 11/4/1949
Birthplace: New Albany, IN
Information Available in These Sources: SATA 11

COCONIS, TED
Birthdate: 1927
Birthplace: Chicago, IL
Information Available in These Sources: IBYP 2, ICB 4

COE, DOUGLAS
See Epstein, Beryl (M. Williams) and Epstein, Samuel

COE, LLOYD
Birthdate: 8/23/1899
Birthplace: Edgartown, MA
Deathdate: 10/10/1976
Information Available in These Sources: ICB 2, SATA 30

COEN, RENA NEUMANN
Birthdate: 2/22/1925
Birthplace: New York, NY
Information Available in These Sources: SATA 20

COERR, ELEANOR (PAGE)
(Eleanor B. Hicks, Eleanor Page)
Birthdate: 5/29/1922
Birthplace: Kamsack, Saskatchewan, Canada
Information Available in These Sources: ABYP 4, JBA 6, SATA 1

COFFIN, GEOFFREY
See Mason, F(rancis) van Wyck

COFFIN, JOSEPH (JOHN)
Birthdate: 8/9/1899
Birthplace: Whitestone, NY
Information Available in These Sources: ABYP 4

COFFIN, ROBERT P. TRISTRAM
Birthdate: 3/18/1892
Birthplace: Brunswick, ME
Deathdate: 1/20/1955
Information Available in These Sources: SVC 2, SVC 3

COFFMAN, RAMON PEYTON
(Uncle Ray)
Birthdate: 7/24/1896
Birthplace: Indianapolis, IN
Information Available in These Sources: SATA 4

COGGINS, HERBERT LEONARD
Information Available in These Sources: ABYP 2, ABYP 3

COGGINS, JACK BANHAM
Birthdate: 7/10/1911
Birthplace: London, England
Information Available in These Sources: ABYP 1, ABYP 3, MJA, SATA 2

COHEN, BARBARA (KAUDER)
Birthdate: 3/15/1932
Birthplace: Asbury Park, NJ
Information Available in These Sources: ABYP 4, JBA 5, SATA 10, TCCW 3

COHEN, DANIEL
Birthdate: 3/12/1936
Birthplace: Chicago, IL
Information Available in These Sources: ABYP 4, JBA 6, SATA 8

COHEN, JENE BARR
(Jene Barr)
Birthdate: 7/28/1900
Birthplace: Kobrin, Russia
Deathdate: 4/5/1985
Information Available in These Sources: ABYP 1, ABYP 3, SATA 16, SATA 42

COHEN, JOAN LEBOLD
Birthdate: 8/19/1932
Birthplace: Highland Park, IL
Information Available in These Sources: SATA 4

COHEN, JOEL H.
Information Available in These Sources: ABYP 4

COHEN, MIRIAM
Birthdate: 10/14/1926
Birthplace: Brooklyn, NY
Information Available in These Sources: JBA 5, SATA 29

COHEN, MORTON N(ORTON)
(John Moreton)
Birthdate: 2/27/1921
Birthplace: Calgary, Alberta, Canada
Information Available in These Sources: ABYP 4

COHEN, PAUL S.
Birthdate: 11/13/1945
Birthplace: Brooklyn, NY
Information Available in These Sources: SATA 58

COHEN, PETER ZACHARY
Birthdate: 10/27/1931
Information Available in These Sources: SATA 4

COHEN, ROBERT CARL
Birthdate: 9/24/1930
Birthplace: Laguna Beach, CA
Information Available in These Sources: ABYP 4, SATA 8

COHN, ANGELO
Birthdate: 9/21/1914
Birthplace: Bucharest, Romania
Information Available in These Sources: SATA 19

COIT, MARGARET LOUISE
Birthdate: 5/30/1919
Birthplace: Norwich, CT
Information Available in These Sources: ABYP 1, ABYP 3, SATA 2

COLABELLA, VINCENT
Information Available in These Sources: IBYP 2

COLBY, C(ARROLL) B(URLEIGH)
Birthdate: 9/7/1904
Birthplace: Claremont, NH
Deathdate: 10/31/1977
Information Available in These Sources: ABYP 1, ABYP 3, MJA, SATA 3, SATA 35

COLBY, JEAN POINDEXTER
Birthdate: 7/26/1909
Birthplace: Pine Orchard, CT
Information Available in These Sources: ABYP 4, SATA 23

COLE, ANN KILBORN
See Callahan, Claire Wallis

COLE, ANNETTE
See Steiner, Barbara A(nnette)

COLE, BROCK
Birthdate: 5/29/1938
Birthplace: Charlotte, MI
Information Available in These Sources: JBA 6

COLE, DAVIS
See Elting, Mary

COLE, JACK
See Stewart, John (William)

COLE, JACKSON
See Schisgall, Oscar

COLE, JENNIFER
See Zach, Cheryl (Byrd)

COLE, JOANNA
(Ann Cooke)
Birthdate: 8/11/1944
Birthplace: Newark, NJ
Information Available in These Sources: JBA 5, SATA 37, SATA 49

COLE, LOIS DWIGHT
(Caroline Arnett, Lynn Avery, Nancy Dudley, Allan Dwight, Anne Eliot)
Birthdate: 1903
Birthplace: New York, NY
Deathdate: 7/20/1979
Information Available in These Sources: ABYP 2, ABYP 3, SATA 10, SATA 26

COLE, SHEILA R(OTENBERG)
Birthdate: 1/5/1939
Birthplace: Toronto, Ontario, Canada
Information Available in These Sources: SATA 24

COLE, WALTER
Birthdate: 11/26/1891
Birthplace: New York, NY
Information Available in These Sources: ICB 1

COLE, WILLIAM (ROSSA)
Birthdate: 11/20/1919
Birthplace: Staten Island, NY
Information Available in These Sources: ABYP 2, ABYP 3, BABP, JBA 4, SATA 9

COLEMAN, PAULINE (HODGKINSON)
Birthdate: 10/17/1911
Birthplace: Long Beach, CA
Information Available in These Sources: ABYP 1, ABYP 3

COLEMAN, WILLIAM L(EROY)
Birthdate: 9/25/1938
Birthplace: Barkhill, MD
Information Available in These Sources: SATA 34, SATA 49

COLERIDGE, JOHN
See Binder, Otto O(scar)

COLES, ROBERT (MARTIN)
Birthdate: 10/12/1929
Birthplace: Boston, MA
Information Available in These Sources: ABYP 4, SATA 23

COLLIER, CHRISTOPHER
Birthdate: 1/29/1930
Birthplace: New York, NY
Information Available in These Sources: ABYP 4, DACF, JBA 5, SATA 16

COLLIER, EDMUND
Information Available in These Sources: ABYP 1, ABYP 3

COLLIER, ETHEL
Birthdate: 7/24/1903
Birthplace: Toledo, OH
Information Available in These Sources: ABYP 2, ABYP 3, SATA 22

COLLIER, JAMES LINCOLN
(Charles Williams)
Birthdate: 6/27/1928
Birthplace: New York, NY
Information Available in These Sources: ABYP 4, DACF, JBA 5, SATA 8, TCCW 3

COLLIER, JANE
See Collier, Zena

COLLIER, ZENA
(Jane Collier, Zena Shumsky)
Birthdate: 1/21/1926
Birthplace: London, England
Information Available in These Sources: SATA 23

COLLINGS, ELLSWORTH
Birthdate: 10/23/1887
Birthplace: McDonald County, MO
Information Available in These Sources: ABYP 1, ABYP 3

COLLINS, DAVID (RAYMOND)
Birthdate: 2/29/1940
Birthplace: Marshalltown, IA
Information Available in These Sources: ABYP 4, SATA 7

COLLINS, HENRY HILL
Birthdate: 1907
Information Available in These Sources: ABYP 2, ABYP 3

COLLINS, HUNT
See Hunter, Evan

COLLINS, MICHAEL
See Lynds, Dennis

COLLINS, MICHAEL
Birthdate: 10/31/1930
Birthplace: Rome, Italy
Information Available in These Sources: SATA 58

COLLINS, PAT LOWERY
Birthdate: 10/6/1932
Birthplace: Los Angeles, CA
Information Available in These Sources: SATA 31

COLLINS, RUTH PHILPOTT
Birthdate: 3/17/1890
Birthplace: Canada
Deathdate: 1/10/1975
Information Available in These Sources: SATA 30

COLMAN, HILA (CRAYDER)
(Teresa Crayder)
Birthplace: New York, NY
Information Available in These Sources: ABYP 2, ABYP 3, DACF, JBA 3, MBMP, SATA 1, SATA 53, TCCW 3

COLMAN, MORRIS
Birthdate: 1899?
Deathdate: 3/5/1981
Information Available in These Sources: SATA 25

COLONIUS, LILLIAN
Birthdate: 3/19/1911
Birthplace: Irvine, CA
Information Available in These Sources: SATA 3

COLORADO, ANTONIO JULIO
See Colorado (Capella), Antonio Julio

COLORADO (CAPELLA), ANTONIO JULIO
(Antonio Julio Colorado)
Birthdate: 2/13/1903
Birthplace: San Juan, PR
Information Available in These Sources: SATA 23

COLT, MARTIN
See Epstein, Beryl (M. Williams) and Epstein, Samuel

COLUM, PADRAIC
Birthdate: 12/8/1881
Birthplace: Longford, Ireland
Deathdate: 1/12/1972
Information Available in These Sources: ABYP 1, ABYP 3, JBA 1, JBA 2, SATA 15, SVC 2, SVC 3, WC

COLUMELLA
See Moore, Clement Clarke

COLVER, ALICE MARY (ROSS)
(Mary Randall)
Birthdate: 8/28/1892
Birthplace: Plainfield, NJ
Information Available in These Sources: ABYP 1, ABYP 3

COLVER, ANNE
(Polly Anne (Colver) Graff, Colver Harris, Polly Ann (Colver) Harris)
Birthdate: 6/20/1908
Birthplace: Cleveland, OH
Information Available in These Sources: ABYP 1, ABYP 3, SATA 7

COMBS, ROBERT
See Murray, John

COMFORT, BARBARA
Birthdate: 9/4/1916
Birthplace: Nyack, NY
Information Available in These Sources: ICB 2

COMFORT, JANE LEVINGTON
See Sturtzel, Jane Levington

COMFORT, MILDRED HOUGHTON
Birthdate: 12/11/1886
Birthplace: Winona, MN
Information Available in These Sources: SATA 3

COMINS, ETHEL M(AE)
Birthdate: 5/16/1901
Birthplace: Clayton, NY
Information Available in These Sources: SATA 11

COMINS, JEREMY
Birthdate: 5/8/1933
Birthplace: OH
Information Available in These Sources: SATA 28

COMMAGER, HENRY STEELE
Birthdate: 10/25/1902
Birthplace: Pittsburgh, PA
Deathdate: 4/2/1984
Information Available in These Sources: ABYP 1, ABYP 3, SATA 23

COMMINS, DOROTHY BERLINER
Information Available in These Sources: ABYP 2, ABYP 3

COMPERE, JANET
Birthplace: NY
Information Available in These Sources: IBYP 2

CONDIT, MARTHA OLSON
Birthdate: 9/8/1913
Birthplace: East Orange, NJ
Information Available in These Sources: SATA 28

CONE, FERNE GELLER
Birthdate: 10/9/1921
Birthplace: Portland, OR
Information Available in These Sources: SATA 39

CONE, MOLLY (LAMKEN)
(Caroline More)
Birthdate: 10/3/1918
Birthplace: Tacoma, WA
Information Available in These Sources: ABYP 1, ABYP 3, DACF, JBA 3, SATA 1, SATA 28

CONFORD, ELLEN (SCHAFFER)
Birthdate: 3/20/1942
Birthplace: New York, NY
Information Available in These Sources: ABYP 4, JBA 5, SATA 6, TCCW 2 TCCW 3

CONGER, LESLEY
See Suttles, Shirley (Smith)

CONGER, MARION
Birthdate: 1915
Birthplace: IN
Information Available in These Sources: ABYP 2, ABYP 3

CONKLIN, GLADYS (PLEMON)
Birthdate: 5/30/1903
Birthplace: Harpster, ID
Information Available in These Sources: ABYP 2, ABYP 3, JBA 4, SATA 2

CONKLIN, PAUL (S.)
Birthplace: Louisville, KY
Information Available in These Sources: ABYP 4, SATA 33, SATA 43

CONKLING, FLEUR
Information Available in These Sources: ABYP 1, ABYP 3

CONKLING, HILDA
Birthdate: 10/8/1910
Birthplace: Catskill-on-Hudson, NY
Information Available in These Sources: SATA 23, SVC 2, SVC 3

CONLY, ROBERT LESLIE
(Robert C. O'Brien)
Birthdate: 1/11/1918
Birthplace: Brooklyn, NY
Deathdate: 3/5/1973
Information Available in These Sources: ABYP 4, DACF, JBA 4, SATA 23, TCCW 1, TCCW 2, TCCW 3

CONN, FRANCES (GOLDBERG)
Birthdate: 1/28/1925
Birthplace: Oil City, PA
Information Available in These Sources: ABYP 4

CONNELL, KIRK
See Chapman, John Stanton Higham

CONNELLY, MARC(US COOK)
Birthdate: 12/13/1890
Birthplace: McKeesport, PA
Deathdate: 12/21/1980
Information Available in These Sources: SATA 25

CONNOLLY, JEROME P(ATRICK)
Birthdate: 1/14/1931
Birthplace: Minneapolis, MN
Information Available in These Sources: IBYP 1, IBYP 2, ICB 3, SATA 8

CONNOR, JAMES
Birthdate: 1944
Birthplace: Philadelphia, PA
Information Available in These Sources: ABYP 4

CONOVER, CHRIS
Birthdate: 2/12/1950
Birthplace: New York, NY
Information Available in These Sources: ABYP 4, ICB 4, JBA 6, SATA 31

CONRAD, ARTHUR S.
Birthdate: 2/8/1907
Birthplace: Chicago, IL
Information Available in These Sources: ICB 2

CONRAD, PAM(ELA)
Birthdate: 6/18/1947
Birthplace: New York, NY
Information Available in These Sources: JBA 6, SATA 49, SATA 52

CONRAD, SYBIL
Birthdate: 6/16/1921
Birthplace: New York, NY
Information Available in These Sources: ABYP 2, ABYP 3

CONROY, JACK (WESLEY)
(Tim Brennan, John Conroy, John Norcross)
Birthdate: 12/5/1899
Birthplace: Moberly (near), MO
Information Available in These Sources: SATA 19

CONROY, JOHN
See Conroy, Jack (Wesley)

CONROY, ROBERT
See Goldston, Robert (Conroy)

CONSTANT, ALBERTA WILSON
Birthdate: 9/16/1908
Birthplace: Dalhart, TX
Information Available in These Sources: ABYP 4, SATA 22, SATA 28

CONTRERAS, JERRY
Information Available in These Sources: IBYP 2

CONWAY, HELENE
Birthplace: Roxbury, MA
Information Available in These Sources: ABYP 1, ABYP 3

COOK, BERNADINE
Birthdate: 9/6/1924
Birthplace: Saginaw, MI
Information Available in These Sources: SATA 11

COOK, FRED J(AMES)
Birthdate: 3/8/1911
Birthplace: Point Pleasant, NJ
Information Available in These Sources: ABYP 1, ABYP 3, SATA 2

COOK, GLADYS EMERSON
Birthdate: 11/7/1901 or 11/7/1899
Birthplace: Haverhill, MA
Information Available in These Sources: ABYP 2, ABYP 3, ICB 2

COOK, HOWARD NORTON
Birthdate: 7/16/1901
Birthplace: Springfield, MA
Deathdate: 6/24/1980
Information Available in These Sources: ICB 1

COOK, JOSEPH J(AY)
Birthdate: 2/19/1924
Birthplace: Brooklyn, NY
Information Available in These Sources: ABYP 2, ABYP 3, SATA 8

COOK, LOUISE DREW
See Yap, Weda

COOK, MARION BELDEN
Birthplace: Brooklyn, NY
Information Available in These Sources: ABYP 2, ABYP 3

COOK, OLIVE RAMBO
Birthdate: 8/26/1892
Birthplace: Avalon, MO
Information Available in These Sources: ABYP 1, ABYP 3

COOK(E), SHERMAN R(OBLEY)
Information Available in These Sources: ABYP 2, ABYP 3

COOKE, ANN
See Cole, Joanna

COOKE, BARBARA
See Alexander, Anna B(arbara Cooke)

COOKE, CHARLES HARRIS
Birthdate: 1904?
Deathdate: 10/18/1977
Information Available in These Sources: ABYP 4

COOKE, DAVID COXE
Birthdate: 6/7/1917
Birthplace: Wilmington, DE
Information Available in These Sources: ABYP 2, ABYP 3, SATA 2

COOKE, DONALD EWIN
Birthdate: 8/5/1916
Birthplace: Philadelphia, PA
Deathdate: 8/17/1985
Information Available in These Sources: ABYP 1, ABYP 3, SATA 2, SATA 45

COOKE, JOHN ESTES
See Baum, L(yman) Frank

COOKE, SARAH (PALFREY) FABYAN
(Sarah Palfrey)
Birthdate: 1913
Birthplace: Sharon, MA
Information Available in These Sources: ABYP 4

COOLEY, LYDIA
Information Available in These Sources: IBYP 2

COOLIDGE, OLIVIA E(NSOR)
Birthdate: 10/16/1908
Birthplace: London, England
Information Available in These Sources: ABYP 1, ABYP 3, MJA, SATA 1, SATA 26, TCCW 1

COOLIDGE, SUSAN
See Woolsey, Sarah Chauncy

COOMBS, CHARLES I(RA)
(Chick Coombs)
Birthdate: 6/27/1914
Birthplace: Los Angeles, CA
Information Available in These Sources: ABYP 1, ABYP 3, SATA 3, SATA 43

COOMBS, CHICK
See Coombs, Charles I(ra)

COOMBS, PATRICIA
Birthdate: 7/23/1926
Birthplace: Los Angeles, CA
Information Available in These Sources: IBYP 2, ICB 3, ICB 4, JBA 5, SATA 3, SATA 51

COOMER, ANNE
Birthplace: MO
Information Available in These Sources: ABYP 4

COONEY, BARBARA
Birthdate: 8/6/1917
Birthplace: Brooklyn, NY
Information Available in These Sources: ABYP 1, ABYP 3, BABP, IBYP 1, IBYP 2, ICB 1, ICB 2, ICB 3, ICB 4, MJA, SATA 6, SVC 3

COONEY, CAROLINE B.
Birthdate: 5/10/1947
Information Available in These Sources: SATA 41, SATA 48

COONEY, NANCY EVANS
Birthdate: 9/9/1932
Birthplace: Northfork, WV
Information Available in These Sources: SATA 42

COONTZ, OTTO
Birthdate: 11/29/1946
Birthplace: Worcester, MA
Information Available in These Sources: SATA 33

COOPER, ELIZABETH KEYSER
Birthdate: 2/16/1916
Birthplace: Erie, PA
Information Available in These Sources: JBA 4, SATA 47

COOPER, JAMES FENIMORE
(Jane Morgan)
Birthdate: 9/15/1789
Birthplace: Burlington, NJ
Deathdate: 9/14/1851
Information Available in These Sources: ABYP 2, ABYP 3, SATA 19, WC, WCL

COOPER, JOHN R.
See Stratemeyer, Edward L.

COOPER, KAY
Birthdate: 7/26/1941
Birthplace: Cleveland, OH
Information Available in These Sources: SATA 11

COOPER, LEE (PELHAM)
Birthdate: 11/4/1926
Birthplace: Mangum, OK
Information Available in These Sources: ABYP 2, ABYP 3, SATA 5

COOPER, LESTER (IRVING)
Birthdate: 1/20/1919
Birthplace: New York, NY
Deathdate: 6/6/1985
Information Available in These Sources: SATA 32, SATA 43

COOPER, M. E.
See Davis, Maggie S.

COOPERSMITH, JEROME
Birthdate: 8/11/1925
Birthplace: New York, NY
Information Available in These Sources: ABYP 4

COPELAND, FRANCES VIRGINIA
Information Available in These Sources: ABYP 1, ABYP 3

COPELAND, HELEN
Birthdate: 4/23/1920
Birthplace: Rochester, MN
Information Available in These Sources: SATA 4

COPELAND, PAUL W(ORTHINGTON)
Birthplace: New York, NY
Information Available in These Sources: ABYP 2, ABYP 3, SATA 23

COPELON, ALLAN
See Sherman, Allan

COPPOCK, CHARLES
Birthdate: 1906
Birthplace: Kerrville, TX
Information Available in These Sources: ABYP 2, ABYP 3

CORBETT, SCOTT
(Winfield Scott Corbett)
Birthdate: 7/27/1913
Birthplace: Kansas City, MO
Information Available in These Sources: ABYP 2, ABYP 3, DACF, JBA 4, SATA 2, SATA 42, TCCW 1, TCCW 2, TCCW 3

CORBETT, WINFIELD SCOTT
See Corbett, Scott

CORBIN, SABRA LEE
See Malvern, Gladys

CORBIN, WILLIAM
See McGraw, William Corbin

CORCORAN, BARBARA
(Paige Dixon, Gail Hamilton)
Birthdate: 4/12/1911
Birthplace: Hamilton, MA
Information Available in These Sources: ABYP 4, DACF, JBA 5, SATA 3

CORCOS, LUCILLE
Birthdate: 9/21/1908
Birthplace: New York, NY
Deathdate: 8/25/1973
Information Available in These Sources: ABYP 2, ABYP 3, ICB 2, ICB 3, ICB 4, SATA 10

COREY, DOROTHY
Birthplace: Rush Lake, Saskatchewan, Canada
Information Available in These Sources: SATA 23

COREY, ROBERT
Information Available in These Sources: IBYP 1, IBYP 2

CORMACK, MARIBELLE B.
Birthdate: 1/11/1902
Birthplace: Buffalo, NY
Information Available in These Sources: ABYP 1, ABYP 3, JBA 2, SATA 39

CORMIER, ROBERT (EDMUND)
(John Fitch IV)
Birthdate: 1/17/1925
Birthplace: Leominster, MA
Information Available in These Sources: DACF, DLB 52, JBA 5, SATA 10, SATA 45, TCCW 2, TCCW 3

CORNELIUS, CAROL
Birthdate: 11/18/1942
Birthplace: St. Joseph, MO
Information Available in These Sources: SATA 40

CORNELL, J(EFFREY)
Birthdate: 9/22/1945
Birthplace: Bridgeport, CT
Information Available in These Sources: SATA 11

CORNELL, JAMES (CLAYTON, JR.)
Birthdate: 9/25/1938
Birthplace: Niagara Falls, NY
Information Available in These Sources: SATA 27

CORNELL, JEAN GAY
Birthdate: 8/17/1920
Birthplace: Streator, IL
Information Available in These Sources: SATA 23

CORNISH, SAM(UEL JAMES)
Birthdate: 12/22/1935
Birthplace: Baltimore, MD
Information Available in These Sources: BAI, SATA 23

CORREY, LEE
See Stine, G(eorge) Harry

CORRIGAN, ADELINE
See Corrigan, Helen Adeline

CORRIGAN, BARBARA
Birthdate: 4/30/1922
Birthplace: Attleboro, MA
Information Available in These Sources: SATA 8

CORRIGAN, HELEN ADELINE
(Adeline Corrigan)
Birthdate: 5/31/1909
Birthplace: Cleveland, OH
Information Available in These Sources: SATA 23

CORT, M. C.
See Clifford, M(argaret) C(ort)

CORWIN, JUDITH HOFFMAN
Birthdate: 11/14/1946
Birthplace: New York, NY
Information Available in These Sources: SATA 10

CORWIN, JUNE ATKIN
Birthdate: 6/1/1935
Birthplace: New York, NY
Information Available in These Sources: ICB 3

COSGRAVE, JOHN O'HARA II
Birthdate: 10/10/1908
Birthplace: San Francisco, CA
Deathdate: 5/9/1968
Information Available in These Sources: IBYP 2, ICB 1, ICB 2, ICB 3, ICB 4, MJA, SATA 21

COSGROVE, MARGARET (LEOTA)
Birthdate: 6/3/1926
Birthplace: Sylvania, OH
Information Available in These Sources: ABYP 2, ABYP 3, ICB 3, ICB 4, JBA 4, SATA 47

COSGROVE, STEPHEN E(DWARD)
Birthdate: 7/26/1945
Birthplace: Spokane, WA
Information Available in These Sources: SATA 40, SATA 53

COSKEY, EVELYN
Birthdate: 11/16/1932
Birthplace: Jersey City, NJ
Information Available in These Sources: ABYP 4, SATA 7

COSNER, SHAARON
Birthdate: 2/10/1940
Birthplace: Albuquerque, NM
Information Available in These Sources: SATA 43

COSTABEL, EVA DEUTSCH
Birthdate: 11/20/1924
Birthplace: Zagreb, Yugoslavia
Information Available in These Sources: SATA 45

COSTAIN, THOMAS B(ERTRAM)
Birthdate: 5/8/1885
Birthplace: Brantford, Ontario, Canada
Deathdate: 10/8/1965
Information Available in These Sources: ABYP 2, ABYP 3

COSTELLO, DAVID (FRANCIS)
Birthdate: 9/1/1904
Birthplace: NE
Information Available in These Sources: SATA 23

COTT, JONATHAN
Birthdate: 12/24/1942
Birthplace: New York, NY
Information Available in These Sources: ABYP 4, SATA 23

COTTAM, CLARENCE
Birthdate: 1/1/1899
Birthplace: St. George, UT
Deathdate: 3/30/1974
Information Available in These Sources: SATA 25

COTTLER, JOSEPH
Birthdate: 10/26/1899
Birthplace: Russia
Information Available in These Sources: SATA 22

COUGHLAN, MARGARET N(OURSE)
Birthdate: 6/21/1925
Birthplace: Baltimore, MD
Information Available in These Sources: ABYP 4

COURLANDER, HAROLD
Birthdate: 9/18/1908
Birthplace: Indianapolis, IN
Information Available in These Sources: ABYP 2, ABYP 3, MJA, SATA 6

COURTIS, STUART APPLETON
Birthdate: 5/15/1874
Birthplace: Wyandotte, MI
Deathdate: 10/19/1969
Information Available in These Sources: SATA 29

COUSINS, MARGARET
(Avery Johns, William Masters, Mary Parrish)
Birthdate: 1/26/1905
Birthplace: Munday, TX
Information Available in These Sources: ABYP 2, ABYP 3, SATA 2

COVARRUBIAS, MIGUEL
Birthdate: 1904
Birthplace: Mexico City, Mexico
Deathdate: 2/4/1957
Information Available in These Sources: ICB 1, ICB 2

COVILLE, BRUCE
Birthdate: 5/16/1950
Birthplace: Syracuse, NY
Information Available in These Sources: SATA 32

COVINGTON, JOHN (P.)
Birthplace: Darby Township, PA
Information Available in These Sources: ABYP 4

COWEN, EVE
See Werner, Herma

COWLES, KATHLEEN
See Krull, Kathleen

COX, DONALD WILLIAM
Birthdate: 4/16/1921
Birthplace: Rutherford, NJ
Information Available in These Sources: SATA 23

COX, PALMER
Birthdate: 4/28/1840
Birthplace: Granby, Quebec, Canada
Deathdate: 7/24/1924
Information Available in These Sources: ABYP 4, DLB 42, JBA 1, SATA 24

COX, VICTORIA
See Garretson, Victoria Diane

COX, WALLACE MAYNARD
(Wally Cox)
Birthdate: 12/6/1924
Birthplace: Royal Oak, MI
Deathdate: 2/15/1973
Information Available in These Sources: SATA 25

COX, WALLY
See Cox, Wallace Maynard

COX, WILLIAM R(OBERT)
(Willard d'Arcy, Mike Frederic, John Parkhill, Joel Reeve, Wayne Robbins, Roger G. Spellman, Jonas Ward)
Birthdate: 4/14/1901
Birthplace: Peapack, NJ
Deathdate: 8/7/1988
Information Available in These Sources: ABYP 2, ABYP 3, SATA 31, SATA 46, SATA 57

COY, HAROLD
Birthdate: 9/24/1902
Birthplace: La Habra, CA
Information Available in These Sources: ABYP 1, ABYP 3, SATA 3

CRAIG, A. A.
See Anderson, Poul (William)

CRAIG, ALISA
See MacLeod, Charlotte (Matilda Hughes)

CRAIG, M. JEAN
Birthdate: 1915
Birthplace: New York, NY
Information Available in These Sources: ABYP 2, ABYP 3, JBA 4, SATA 17

CRAIG, MARGARET MAZE
Birthdate: 1/16/1911
Birthplace: Ridgway, PA
Deathdate: 12/5/1964
Information Available in These Sources: MJA, SATA 9

CRAIG, MARY FRANCIS
See Shura, Mary Francis

CRAM, BILL
See Cram, L. D.

CRAM, L. D.
(Bill Cram)
Birthdate: 5/18/1898
Birthplace: OR
Information Available in These Sources: ICB 2

CRANCH, CHRISTOPHER PEARSE
Birthdate: 3/8/1813
Birthplace: Washington, DC
Deathdate: 1/20/1892
Information Available in These Sources: DLB 42

CRANE, ALAN (HORTON)
Birthdate: 11/14/1901
Birthplace: Brooklyn, NY
Information Available in These Sources: ABYP 2, ABYP 3

CRANE, BARBARA J.
Birthdate: 6/2/1934
Birthplace: Trenton, NJ
Information Available in These Sources: SATA 31

CRANE, CAROLINE
Birthdate: 10/30/1930
Birthplace: Chicago, IL
Information Available in These Sources: ABYP 4, SATA 11

CRANE, FLORENCE
Information Available in These Sources: ABYP 2, ABYP 3

CRANE, IRVING (DONALD)
Birthdate: 11/13/1913 or 11/13/1914
Birthplace: Livonia, NY
Information Available in These Sources: ABYP 2, ABYP 3

CRANE, M. A.
See Wartski, Maureen (Ann Crane)

CRANE, ROY(STON CAMPBELL)
Birthdate: 11/22/1901
Birthplace: Abilene, TX
Deathdate: 7/7/1977
Information Available in These Sources: SATA 22

CRANE, STEPHEN (TOWNLEY)
(Johnston Smith)
Birthdate: 11/1/1871
Birthplace: Newark, NJ
Deathdate: 6/4/1900
Information Available in These Sources: YABC

CRANE, WILLIAM D(WIGHT)
Birthdate: 12/6/1892
Birthplace: New York, NY
Information Available in These Sources: SATA 1

CRARY, ELIZABETH (ANN)
Birthdate: 5/18/1942
Birthplace: New Orleans, LA
Information Available in These Sources: SATA 43

CRARY, MARGARET (COLEMAN)
Birthdate: 9/27/1906
Birthplace: Carthage, SD
Information Available in These Sources: ABYP 2, ABYP 3, SATA 9

CRAVEN, THOMAS
Birthdate: 1/6/1889
Birthplace: Salina, KS
Deathdate: 2/27/1969
Information Available in These Sources: ABYP 2, ABYP 3, SATA 22

CRAWFORD, CHARLES P.
Birthdate: 1/23/1945
Birthplace: Wayne, PA
Information Available in These Sources: SATA 28

CRAWFORD, DEBORAH
Birthdate: 1/16/1922
Birthplace: Elizabeth, NJ
Information Available in These Sources: SATA 6

CRAWFORD, JOHN E(DMUND)
Birthdate: 1/21/1904
Birthplace: Pittsburgh, PA
Deathdate: 10/12/1971
Information Available in These Sources: SATA 3

CRAWFORD, MEL
Birthdate: 9/10/1925
Birthplace: Toronto, Ontario, Canada
Information Available in These Sources: SATA 33, 44

CRAWFORD, PHYLLIS
(Josie Turner)
Birthdate: 2/8/1899
Birthplace: Little Rock, AR
Information Available in These Sources: JBA 2, SATA 3

CRAWFORD, THELMAR WYCHE
Birthdate: 5/24/1905
Birthplace: Longview, TX
Information Available in These Sources: ABYP 2, ABYP 3

CRAWFORD, WILL
Birthdate: 1869
Birthplace: Washington, DC
Deathdate: 1944
Information Available in These Sources: CICB

CRAWFORD-SEEGER, RUTH PORTER
See Seeger, Ruth Porter (Crawford)

CRAYDER, DOROTHY
Birthdate: 9/12/1906
Birthplace: New York, NY
Information Available in These Sources: ABYP 4, SATA 7

CRAYDER, TERESA
See Colman, Hila (Crayder)

CRAYON, GEOFFREY
See Irving, Washington

CRAZ, ALBERT G.
Birthdate: 6/26/1926
Birthplace: New York, NY
Information Available in These Sources: ABYP 2, ABYP 3, SATA 24

CRECY, JEANNE
See Williams, J(eanne R.)

CREDLE, ELLIS
Birthdate: 8/18/1902
Birthplace: Sladesville, NC
Information Available in These Sources: ABYP 1, ABYP 3, ICB 1, ICB 2, JBA 2, SATA 1, SVC 3

CREEKMORE, RAYMOND (L.)
Birthdate: 5/5/1905
Birthplace: Portsmouth, VA
Information Available in These Sources: ICB 2

CRESPI, PACHITA
Birthdate: 8/25/1900
Birthplace: Costa Rica
Information Available in These Sources: ABYP 1, ABYP 3

CRETAN, GLADYS (YESSAYAN)
Birthdate: 11/11/1921
Birthplace: Reedley, CA
Information Available in These Sources: ABYP 4, SATA 2

CREW, FLEMING H.
Birthdate: 1882
Birthplace: McConnelsville, OH
Information Available in These Sources: JBA 2

CREW, HELEN (CECILIA) COALE
Birthdate: 12/8/1866
Birthplace: Baltimore, MD
Deathdate: 5/1/1941
Information Available in These Sources: JBA 1, JBA 2, YABC

CREWS, DONALD
Birthdate: 8/30/1938
Birthplace: Newark, NJ
Information Available in These Sources: BAI, BC, IBYP 2, ICB 4, JBA 5 SATA 30, SATA 32

CRICHLOW, ERNEST T.
Birthdate: 6/19/1914
Birthplace: Brooklyn, NY
Information Available in These Sources: BAI, IBYP 1, IBYP 2, ICB 3, JBA 4

CRICHTON, J. MICHAEL
(Michael Crichton, Jeffrey Hudson, John Lange)
Birthdate: 10/23/1942
Birthplace: Chicago, IL
Information Available in These Sources: SATA 9

CRICHTON, MICHAEL
See Crichton, J. Michael

CRILE, HELGA SANDBURG
See Sandburg, Helga

CRINER, BEATRICE (HALL)
Birthdate: 11/25/1915
Birthplace: Hamilton, IL
Information Available in These Sources: ABYP 4

CRINER, CALVIN
Information Available in These Sources: ABYP 4

CRISS, MILDRED
Birthdate: 1890
Birthplace: Orange, NJ
Information Available in These Sources: ABYP 1, ABYP 3

CRIST, EDA (SZECSKAY)
Birthdate: 1909
Information Available in These Sources: ABYP 2, ABYP 3

CRIST, RICHARD HARRISON
Birthdate: 1909
Information Available in These Sources: ABYP 2, ABYP 3

CROCKETT, LUCY HERNDON
Birthdate: 4/4/1914
Birthplace: Honolulu, HI
Information Available in These Sources: ICB 1, ICB 2

CROFUT, BILL
See Crofut, William E. III

CROFUT, WILLIAM E. III
(Bill Crofut)
Birthdate: 12/14/1934
Birthplace: Cleveland, OH
Information Available in These Sources: SATA 23

CROLL, CAROLYN
Birthdate: 5/20/1945
Birthplace: Sioux Falls, SD
Information Available in These Sources: SATA 52, SATA 56

CROMAN, DOROTHY YOUNG
See Rosenberg, Dorothy

CROMIE, ALICE HAMILTON
(Alice Hamilton, Vivian Mort)
Birthdate: 5/29/1914
Birthplace: Chariton, IA
Information Available in These Sources: ABYP 4, SATA 24

CROMIE, WILLIAM J(OSEPH)
Birthdate: 3/12/1930
Birthplace: New York, NY
Information Available in These Sources: ABYP 4, SATA 4

CROMPTON, ANNE ELIOT
Birthdate: 4/6/1930
Birthplace: Northhampton, MA
Information Available in These Sources: ABYP 4, SATA 23

CRONBACH, ABRAHAM
Birthdate: 2/16/1882
Birthplace: Indianapolis, IN
Deathdate: 4/2/1965
Information Available in These Sources: SATA 11

CRONE, RUTH
Birthdate: 6/24/1919
Birthplace: Lincoln, NE
Information Available in These Sources: ABYP 3, SATA 4

CROOK, BEVERLY COURTNEY
Birthplace: Baltimore, MD
Information Available in These Sources: SATA 35, SATA 38

CROS, EARL
See Rose, Carl

CROSBY, ALEXANDER L.
Birthdate: 6/10/1906
Birthplace: Catonsville, MD
Deathdate: 1/31/1980
Information Available in These Sources: ABYP 1, ABYP 3, MBMP, SATA 2, SATA 23

CROSBY, PHOEBE
Information Available in These Sources: ABYP 2, ABYP 3

CROSS, HELEN REEDER
See Broadhead, Helen Cross

CROSS, WILBUR LUCIUS III
Birthdate: 8/17/1918
Birthplace: Scranton, PA
Information Available in These Sources: SATA 2

CROSSCUP, RICHARD
Birthdate: 1905
Birthplace: Boston, MA
Information Available in These Sources: ABYP 4

CROUSE, ANNA (ERSKINE)
Information Available in These Sources: ABYP 2, ABYP 3

CROUSE, RUSSELL M.
Birthdate: 2/20/1893
Birthplace: Findlay, OH
Deathdate: 4/3/1966
Information Available in These Sources: ABYP 2, ABYP 3

CROUSE, WILLIAM H(ARRY)
Birthdate: 12/19/1907
Birthplace: Anderson, IN
Information Available in These Sources: ABYP 1, ABYP 3

CROUT, GEORGE C(LEMENT)
Birthdate: 2/10/1917
Birthplace: Middletown, OH
Information Available in These Sources: SATA 11

CROW, DONNA FLETCHER
(Elizabeth Paul)
Birthdate: 11/15/1941
Birthplace: Nampa, ID
Information Available in These Sources: SATA 40

CROW, FRANCIS LUTHER
See Luther, Frank

CROWE, BETTINA LUM
(Peter Lum(m))
Birthdate: 4/27/1911
Birthplace: Minneapolis, MN
Information Available in These Sources: ABYP 1, ABYP 2, ABYP 3, SATA 6

CROWE, JOHN
See Lynds, Dennis

CROWELL, ANN
Information Available in These Sources: ABYP 4

CROWELL, GRACE NOLL
Birthdate: 10/31/1877
Birthplace: Inland, IA
Deathdate: 3/31/1969
Information Available in These Sources: SATA 34

CROWELL, PERS
Birthdate: 3/28/1910
Birthplace: Pasco, WA
Deathdate: 11/26/1965
Information Available in These Sources: IBYP 2, ICB 2, MJA, SATA 2

CROWFIELD, CHRISTOPHER
See Stowe, Harriet (Elizabeth) Beecher

CROWLEY, ARTHUR M(CBLAIR)
Birthdate: 9/19/1945
Birthplace: Dallas, TX
Information Available in These Sources: SATA 38

CROWNFIELD, GERTRUDE
Birthdate: 10/26/1867
Birthplace: Baltimore, MD
Deathdate: 6/2/1945
Information Available in These Sources: ABYP 2, ABYP 3, JBA 1, JBA 2, YABC

CRUICKSHANK, HELEN GERE
Birthdate: 2/20/1907
Birthplace: Brooklyn, PA
Information Available in These Sources: ABYP 2, ABYP 3

CRUMP, FRED H., JR.
Birthdate: 6/7/1931
Birthplace: Houston, TX
Information Available in These Sources: SATA 11

CRUMP, IRVING
See Crump, J(ames) Irving

CRUMP, J(AMES) IRVING
(Irving Crump)
Birthdate: 12/7/1887
Birthplace: Saugerties, NY
Deathdate: 7/3/1979
Information Available in These Sources: ABYP 2, ABYP 3, JBA 1, JBA 2, SATA 21, SATA 57

CRUTCHER, CHRIS(TOPHER C.)
Birthdate: 7/17/1946
Birthplace: Cascade, ID
Information Available in These Sources: SATA 52

CRUZ, RAY(MOND)
Birthdate: 6/30/1933
Birthplace: New York, NY
Information Available in These Sources: IBYP 2, ICB 4, SATA 6

CUFFARI, RICHARD
Birthdate: 3/2/1925
Birthplace: Brooklyn, NY
Deathdate: 10/10/1978
Information Available in These Sources: IBYP 1, IBYP 2, ICB 4, JBA 5, SATA 6, SATA 25

CULLEN, COUNTEE PORTER
Birthdate: 5/30/1903
Birthplace: New York, NY
Deathdate: 1/9/1946
Information Available in These Sources: BAI, JBA 4, SATA 18

CULLUM, ALBERT
Information Available in These Sources: ABYP 4

CULP, LOUANNA MCNARY
Birthdate: 7/11/1901
Birthplace: PA
Information Available in These Sources: SATA 2

CUMMINGS, BETTY SUE
Birthdate: 7/12/1918
Birthplace: Big Stone Gap, VA
Information Available in These Sources: DACF, JBA 5, SATA 15

CUMMINGS, E(DWARD) E(STLIN)
Birthdate: 10/14/1894
Birthplace: Cambridge, MA
Deathdate: 9/3/1962
Information Available in These Sources: ABYP 2, ABYP 3

CUMMINGS, PARKE
Birthdate: 10/8/1902
Birthplace: West Medford, MA
Information Available in These Sources: SATA 2

CUMMINGS, PAT (MARIE)
Birthdate: 11/9/1950
Birthplace: Chicago, IL
Information Available in These Sources: BAI, JBA 6, SATA 42

CUMMINGS, RICHARD
See Gardner, Richard (M.)

CUMMINS, MARIA SUSANNA
Birthdate: 4/9/1827
Birthplace: Salem, MA
Deathdate: 10/1/1866
Information Available in These Sources: DLB 42, WCL, YABC

CUNLIFFE, MARCUS (FALKNER)
Birthdate: 7/5/1922
Information Available in These Sources: SATA 37

CUNNINGHAM, CAPTAIN FRANK
See Glick, Carl (Cannon)

CUNNINGHAM, CATHY
See Cunningham, Chet

CUNNINGHAM, CHET
(Cathy Cunningham)
Birthdate: 12/9/1928
Birthplace: Shelby, NE
Information Available in These Sources: SATA 23

CUNNINGHAM, DALE S(PEERS)
Birthdate: 5/27/1932
Birthplace: Elmira, NY
Information Available in These Sources: SATA 11

CUNNINGHAM, E. V.
See Fast, Howard (Melvin)

CUNNINGHAM, JULIA W(OOLFOLK)
Birthdate: 10/4/1916
Birthplace: Spokane, WA
Information Available in These Sources: ABYP 1, ABYP 3, DACF, JBA 3, MBMP, SATA 1, SATA 26, TCCW 1 TCCW 2, TCCW 3

CUNNINGHAM, MARY
See Pierce, Mary Cunningham (Fitzgerald)

CUNNINGHAM, VIRGINIA
See Holmgren, Virginia C(unningham)

CURIAE, AMICUS
See Fuller, Edmund (Maybank)

CURLEY, DANIEL
Birthdate: 10/4/1918
Birthplace: East Bridgewater, MA
Information Available in These Sources: SATA 23

CURRY, JANE L(OUISE)
Birthdate: 9/24/1932
Birthplace: East Liverpool, OH
Information Available in These Sources: ABYP 2, ABYP 3, DACF, JBA 4, SATA 1, SATA 52, TCCW 1, TCCW 2, TCCW 3

CURRY, JOHN STEUART
Birthdate: 11/14/1897
Birthplace: Dunavant, KS
Deathdate: 8/29/1946
Information Available in These Sources: ICB 1

CURRY, PEGGY SIMSON
Birthdate: 12/30/1911
Birthplace: Dunure, Ayrshire, Scotland
Deathdate: 1/20/1987
Information Available in These Sources: SATA 8, SATA 50

CURTIS, ALICE (TURNER)
Birthdate: 1860
Birthplace: Sullivan, ME
Deathdate: 1958
Information Available in These Sources: ABYP 2, ABYP 3

CURTIS, ALICE BERTHA
Birthplace: IA
Information Available in These Sources: ABYP 2, ABYP 3

CURTIS, BRUCE (RICHARD)
Birthdate: 12/21/1944
Birthplace: Roslyn Heights, NY
Information Available in These Sources: SATA 30

CURTIS, ELIZABETH
Birthplace: New York, NY
Information Available in These Sources: CICB

CURTIS, PATRICIA
Birthdate: 7/31/1921
Birthplace: Orange, NJ
Information Available in These Sources: SATA 23

CURTIS, RICHARD (ALAN)
(Ray Lilly, Curtis Richards, Morton Stultifer, Melanie Ward)
Birthdate: 6/23/1937
Birthplace: Bronx, NY
Information Available in These Sources: ABYP 4, SATA 29

CURTIS, ROBERT H.
Birthdate: 1922
Birthplace: New York, NY
Information Available in These Sources: ABYP 4

CURTIS, WADE
See Pournelle, Jerry (Eugene)

CUSACK, MARGARET
Birthdate: 8/1/1945
Birthplace: Chicago, IL
Information Available in These Sources: SATA 58

CUSHMAN, JEROME
Birthdate: 6/1/1914
Birthplace: Chicago, IL
Information Available in These Sources: ABYP 4, SATA 2

CUTCHEN, BILLYE WALKER
(Billye Walker Brown)
Birthdate: 4/23/1930
Birthplace: Oklahoma City, OK
Information Available in These Sources: SATA 15

CUTCHENS, JUDY
Birthdate: 12/6/1947
Birthplace: New Orleans, LA
Information Available in These Sources: SATA 59

CUTLER, ANN
Information Available in These Sources: ABYP 2, ABYP 3

CUTLER, SAMUEL
See Folsom, Franklin (Brewster)

CUYLER, MARGERY STUYVESANT
(Daisy Wallace)
Birthdate: 12/31/1948
Birthplace: Princeton, NJ
Information Available in These Sources: BC, SATA 39

CUYLER, STEPHEN
See Bates, Barbara S(nedeker)

D

D'AMATO, ALEX
Birthdate: 2/4/1919
Birthplace: Italy
Information Available in These Sources: ABYP 4, SATA 20

D'AMATO, JANET (POTTER)
Birthdate: 6/5/1925
Birthplace: Rochester, NY
Information Available in These Sources: ABYP 4, SATA 9

D'ANDREA, KATE
See Steiner, Barbara A(nnette)

D'ARCY, WILLARD
See Cox, William R(obert)

D'ATTILIO, ANTHONY
Birthdate: 7/2/1909
Birthplace: Rodi, Italy
Information Available in These Sources: IBYP 1, IBYP 2

D'AULAIRE, EDGAR PARIN
Birthdate: 9/30/1898
Birthplace: Munich, Germany
Deathdate: 5/1/1986
Information Available in These Sources: ABYP 1, ABYP 3, BABP, DLB 22, FLTYP, IBYP 1, IBYP 2, ICB 1, ICB 2, ICB 3, ICB 4, JBA 1, JBA 2, SATA 5, SATA 47, SVC 2 SVC 3, TCCW 1, TCCW 2, TCCW 3

D'AULAIRE, INGRI (MAARTENSON)
Birthdate: 12/27/1904
Birthplace: Kongsberg, Norway
Deathdate: 10/24/1980
Information Available in These Sources: ABYP 1, ABYP 3, BABP, DLB 22, FLTYP, IBYP 1, IBYP 2, ICB 1, ICB 2, ICB 3, ICB 4, JBA 1, JBA 2, SATA 5, SATA 24, SVC 2 SVC 3, TCCW 1, TCCW 2, TCCW 3

D'HARNONCOURT, RENE
Birthdate: 5/17/1901
Birthplace: Vienna, Austria
Information Available in These Sources: ICB 1

D'IGNAZIO, FRED(ERICK)
Birthdate: 1/6/1949
Birthplace: Bryn Mawr, PA
Information Available in These Sources: SATA 35, SATA 39

DABCOVICH, LYDIA
Birthplace: Bulgaria
Information Available in These Sources: SATA 47, SATA 58

DAHL, BORGHILD
Birthdate: 2/5/1890
Birthplace: Minneapolis, MN
Deathdate: 2/20/1984
Information Available in These Sources: ABYP 2, ABYP 3, JBA 3, SATA 7, SATA 37

DAHL, MARY B(ARTLETT)
Birthplace: Providence, RI
Information Available in These Sources: ABYP 4

DAHLSTEDT, MARDEN (ARMSTRONG)
Birthdate: 8/14/1921
Birthplace: Pittsburgh, PA
Information Available in These Sources: ABYP 4, SATA 8

DAIN, MARTIN J.
Birthdate: 9/20/1924
Birthplace: Cambridge, MA
Information Available in These Sources: SATA 35

DALE, RUTH BLUESTONE
Information Available in These Sources: ABYP 2, ABYP 3

DALGLIESH, ALICE
Birthdate: 10/7/1893
Birthplace: Trinidad, British West Indies
Deathdate: 6/11/1979
Information Available in These Sources: ABYP 1, ABYP 3, JBA 1, JBA 2, SATA 17, SATA 21, SVC 2, SVC 3TCCW 1, TCCW 2, TCCW 3

DALTON, ALENE
See Chapin, Alene Olsen Dalton

DALY, KATHLEEN N(ORAH)
Birthplace: London, England
Information Available in These Sources: ABYP 4, SATA 37

DALY, MAUREEN (MCGIVERN)
Birthdate: 3/15/1921
Birthplace: Castle Caulfield, County Tyrone, Ireland
Information Available in These Sources: ABYP 1, ABYP 3, MJA, SATA 2, TCCW 1, TCCW 2, TCCW 3

DALY, SHEILA JOHN
Birthdate: 1929 or 1927
Information Available in These Sources: ABYP 2, ABYP 3

DAMROSCH, HELEN THERESE
See Tee-Van, Helen Damrosch

DANA, BARBARA
Birthdate: 12/28/1940
Birthplace: New York, NY
Information Available in These Sources: SATA 22

DANA, RICHARD HENRY, JR.
Birthdate: 8/1/1815
Birthplace: Cambridge, MA
Deathdate: 1/6/1882
Information Available in These Sources: SATA 26

DANGERFIELD, BALFOUR
See McCloskey, John Robert

DANIEL, ANITA
(Anita)
Birthdate: 1893?
Birthplace: Lassy, Romania
Deathdate: 6/17/1978
Information Available in These Sources: ABYP 2, ABYP 3, SATA 23, SATA 24

DANIEL, ANNE
See Steiner, Barbara A(nnette)

DANIEL, BECKY
(Rebecca Daniel)
Birthdate: 9/5/1947
Birthplace: Ottumwa, IA
Information Available in These Sources: SATA 56

DANIEL, HAWTHORNE
Birthdate: 1/20/1890
Birthplace: Norfolk, NE
Information Available in These Sources: JBA 1, JBA 2, SATA 8

DANIEL, MILLY HAWK
Information Available in These Sources: ABYP 4

DANIEL, REBECCA
See Daniel, Becky

DANIELS, GUY
Birthdate: 5/11/1919
Birthplace: Gilmore City, IA
Information Available in These Sources: ABYP 4, SATA 7, SATA 11

DANIELS, JOHN S.
See Overholser, Wayne D.

DANIELS, JONATHAN
Birthdate: 4/26/1902
Birthplace: Raleigh, NC
Deathdate: 11/6/1981
Information Available in These Sources: ABYP 1, ABYP 3

DANK, GLORIA RAND
Birthdate: 10/5/1955
Birthplace: Toledo, OH
Information Available in These Sources: SATA 46, SATA 56

DANK, LEONARD DEWEY
Birthdate: 12/21/1929
Birthplace: Birmingham, AL
Information Available in These Sources: SATA 44

DANK, MILTON
Birthdate: 9/12/1920
Birthplace: Philadelphia, PA
Information Available in These Sources: SATA 31

DANNAY, FREDERIC
(Daniel Nathan, Ellery Queen, Barnaby Ross)
Birthdate: 10/20/1905
Birthplace: Brooklyn, NY
Deathdate: 9/3/1982
Information Available in These Sources: ABYP 3

DANSKA, HERBERT
Birthdate: 10/16/1927 , 10/16/1926, or 10/16/1928
Birthplace: New York, NY
Information Available in These Sources: IBYP 2, ICB 2, ICB 3

DANZIGER, PAULA
Birthdate: 8/18/1944
Birthplace: Washington, DC
Information Available in These Sources: JBA 5, SATA 30, SATA 36, TCCW 3

DARBY, ADA CLAIRE
Birthdate: 12/31/1883
Birthplace: St. Joseph, MO
Deathdate: 12/23/1953
Information Available in These Sources: ABYP 1, ABYP 3

DARBY, J. N.
See Govan, Christine Noble

DARBY, PATRICIA (PAULSEN)
Information Available in These Sources: ABYP 3, SATA 14

DARBY, RAY(MOND) K.
Birthdate: 3/9/1912
Birthplace: Edmonton, Alberta, Canada
Information Available in These Sources: ABYP 2, ABYP 3, SATA 7

DAREFF, HAL
(Scott Foley)
Birthdate: 5/8/1920
Birthplace: Brooklyn, NY
Information Available in These Sources: ABYP 2, ABYP 3

DARINGER, HELEN FERN
Birthdate: 6/24/1892
Birthplace: Mattoon, IL
Information Available in These Sources: MJA, SATA 1

DARLEY, F(ELIX) O(CTAVIUS) C(ARR)
Birthdate: 6/23/1822
Birthplace: Philadelphia, PA
Deathdate: 3/27/1888
Information Available in These Sources: SATA 35

DARLING, KATHY
See Darling, Mary Kathleen

DARLING, LOIS (MACINTYRE)
Birthdate: 8/15/1917
Birthplace: New York, NY
Information Available in These Sources: ABYP 2, ABYP 3, ICB 3, ICB 4, MJA, SATA 3

DARLING, LOUIS, JR.
Birthdate: 4/26/1916
Birthplace: Stamford, CT
Deathdate: 1/21/1970
Information Available in These Sources: ABYP 2, ABYP 3, ICB 2, ICB 3, MJA, SATA 3, SATA 23

DARLING, MARY KATHLEEN
(Kathy Darling)
Birthdate: 9/8/1943
Birthplace: Hudson, NY
Information Available in These Sources: SATA 9

DARLING, RICHARD L(EWIS)
Birthdate: 1/19/1925
Birthplace: Great Falls, MT
Information Available in These Sources: ABYP 4

DARROW, WHITNEY, JR.
Birthdate: 8/22/1909
Birthplace: Princeton, NJ
Information Available in These Sources: ABYP 4, SATA 13

DARWIN, BEATRICE
Birthplace: Boston, MA
Information Available in These Sources: IBYP 1, IBYP 2

DARWIN, LEN
See Darwin, Leonard

DARWIN, LEONARD
(Len Darwin)
Birthdate: 1916
Information Available in These Sources: IBYP 1, IBYP 2, SATA 24

DASKAM, JOSEPHINE DODGE
See Bacon, Josephine Dodge (Daskam)

DAUER, ROSAMOND
Birthdate: 6/29/1934
Birthplace: New York, NY
Information Available in These Sources: SATA 23

DAUGHERTY, CHARLES MICHAEL
Birthdate: 11/17/1914
Birthplace: New York, NY
Information Available in These Sources: ABYP 2, ABYP 3, ICB 2, SATA 16

DAUGHERTY, HARRY R.
Birthdate: 1883
Birthplace: Trymville, PA
Information Available in These Sources: ICB 2

DAUGHERTY, JAMES (HENRY)
Birthdate: 6/1/1889
Birthplace: Asheville, NC
Deathdate: 2/21/1974 or 2/12/1974
Information Available in These Sources: ABYP 1, ABYP 3, BABP, ICB 1, ICB 2, ICB 3, ICB 4, JBA 1, JBA 2, SATA 13, SVC 2, SVC 3, TCCW 1, TCCW 2, TCCW 3, WC

DAUGHERTY, RICHARD D(EO)
Birthdate: 3/31/1922
Birthplace: Aberdeen, WA
Information Available in These Sources: SATA 35

DAUGHERTY, SONIA MEDWEDEFF
Birthplace: Moscow, Russia
Deathdate: 5/4/1971
Information Available in These Sources: SATA 27

DAVENPORT, MARCIA (GLUCK)
Birthdate: 6/9/1903
Birthplace: New York, NY
Information Available in These Sources: ABYP 2, ABYP 3

DAVES, MICHAEL
Birthdate: 3/4/1938
Birthplace: Wichita Falls, TX
Information Available in These Sources: ABYP 4, SATA 40

DAVID, EUGENE
Information Available in These Sources: ABYP 2, ABYP 3

DAVID, JONATHAN
See Ames, Lee J(udah)

DAVIDSON, ALICE JOYCE
Birthdate: 9/22/1932
Birthplace: Cincinnati, OH
Information Available in These Sources: SATA 45, 54

DAVIDSON, BILL
See Davidson, William

DAVIDSON, ELISABETH WENNING
See Wenning, Elisabeth

DAVIDSON, JESSICA
Birthdate: 10/3/1915
Birthplace: New York, NY
Information Available in These Sources: SATA 5

DAVIDSON, JUDITH
Birthdate: 9/21/1953
Birthplace: Portland, OR
Information Available in These Sources: SATA 40

DAVIDSON, MARGARET (COMPERE)
(Mickie Davidson)
Birthdate: 5/14/1936
Birthplace: New York, NY
Information Available in These Sources: ABYP 4, SATA 5

DAVIDSON, MARION
See Garis, Howard R(oger)

DAVIDSON, MARY R.
Birthdate: 12/20/1885
Birthplace: Auburndale, MA
Deathdate: 1973
Information Available in These Sources: SATA 9

DAVIDSON, MICKIE
See Davidson, Margaret (Compere)

DAVIDSON, R(AYMOND)
Birthdate: 8/7/1926
Birthplace: Brooklyn, NY
Information Available in These Sources: SATA 32

DAVIDSON, ROSALIE
Birthdate: 7/25/1921
Birthplace: Paoli, IN
Information Available in These Sources: SATA 23

DAVIDSON, SANDRA CALDER
Birthdate: 4/20/1935
Birthplace: Concord, MA
Information Available in These Sources: ABYP 4

DAVIDSON, WILLIAM
(Bill Davidson)
Birthdate: 1918
Birthplace: Jersey City, NJ
Information Available in These Sources: ABYP 2, ABYP 3

DAVIES, BETTILU D(ONNA)
Birthdate: 3/30/1942
Birthplace: Pontiac, MI
Information Available in These Sources: SATA 33

DAVIS, BARBARA STEINCROHN
See Davis, Maggie S.

DAVIS, BETTE J.
Birthdate: 4/18/1923
Birthplace: Joplin, MO
Information Available in These Sources: IBYP 1, IBYP 2, SATA 15

DAVIS, BURKE
Birthdate: 7/24/1913
Birthplace: Durham, NC
Information Available in These Sources: ABYP 1, ABYP 3, SATA 4

DAVIS, CHRISTOPHER
Birthdate: 10/23/1928
Birthplace: Philadelphia, PA
Information Available in These Sources: ABYP 4, SATA 6

DAVIS, CLIVE E(DWARD)
Birthdate: 10/19/1914
Birthplace: New South Berlin, NY
Information Available in These Sources: ABYP 2, ABYP 3

DAVIS, D(ELBERT) DWIGHT
Birthdate: 12/30/1908
Birthplace: Rockford, IL
Deathdate: 2/6/1965
Information Available in These Sources: SATA 33

DAVIS, DANIEL S(HELDON)
Birthdate: 9/15/1936
Birthplace: New York, NY
Information Available in These Sources: SATA 12

DAVIS, ELIZABETH
See Davis, Lou Ellen

DAVIS, EMMA
See Davis, Maggie S.

DAVIS, GIBBS
Birthdate: 11/16/1953
Birthplace: Milwaukee, WI
Information Available in These Sources: SATA 41, SATA 46

DAVIS, GRANIA
(Mama G.)
Birthdate: 7/17/1943
Birthplace: Milwaukee, WI
Information Available in These Sources: SATA 50

DAVIS, HUBERT J(ACKSON)
Birthdate: 4/30/1904
Birthplace: Richlands, VA
Information Available in These Sources: ABYP 4, SATA 31

DAVIS, JAMES ROBERT
(Jim Davis)
Birthdate: 7/28/1945
Birthplace: Marion, IN
Information Available in These Sources: SATA 32

DAVIS, JIM
See Davis, James Robert

DAVIS, JULIA
See Adams, Julia Davis

DAVIS, LAVINIA (RIKER)
(Wendell Farmer)
Birthdate: 2/7/1909
Birthplace: New York, NY
Deathdate: 8/14/1961
Information Available in These Sources: ABYP 1, ABYP 3, JBA 2

DAVIS, LOU ELLEN
(Pat Bannister, Elizabeth Davis)
Birthdate: 11/9/1936
Birthplace: Pittsburgh, PA
Information Available in These Sources: ABYP 4

DAVIS, LOUISE LITTLETON
Birthdate: 9/7/1921
Birthplace: Paris, TN
Information Available in These Sources: SATA 25

DAVIS, MAGGIE S.
(M. E. Cooper, Barbara Steincrohn Davis, Emma Davis)
Birthdate: 5/30/1943
Birthplace: Hartford, CT
Information Available in These Sources: SATA 57

DAVIS, MARGUERITE
Birthdate: 2/10/1889
Birthplace: Quincy, MA
Information Available in These Sources: CICB, ICB 1, ICB 2, SATA 34

DAVIS, MARY GOULD
Birthdate: 2/13/1882
Birthplace: Bangor, ME
Deathdate: 4/15/1956
Information Available in These Sources: ABYP 2, ABYP 3, JBA 1, JBA 2

DAVIS, MARY L(EE)
Birthdate: 3/21/1935
Birthplace: Worthington, MN
Information Available in These Sources: ABYP 4, SATA 9

DAVIS, MARY OCTAVIA
(Dutz)
Birthdate: 5/11/1901
Birthplace: Castroville, TX
Information Available in These Sources: SATA 6

DAVIS, OSSIE
Birthdate: 1917
Birthplace: Cogdell, GA
Information Available in These Sources: BAI

DAVIS, PAXTON
Birthdate: 5/7/1925
Birthplace: Winston-Salem, NC
Information Available in These Sources: SATA 16

DAVIS, REDA
Birthplace: San Francisco, CA
Information Available in These Sources: ABYP 1, ABYP 3

DAVIS, RICHARD HARDING
Birthdate: 4/18/1864
Birthplace: Philadelphia, PA
Deathdate: 4/11/1916
Information Available in These Sources: JBA 1

DAVIS, ROBERT
Birthdate: 7/28/1881
Birthplace: Beverly, MA
Deathdate: 9/25/1949
Information Available in These Sources: JBA 2, YABC

DAVIS, RUSSELL G(ERARD)
Birthdate: 10/29/1922
Birthplace: Boston, MA
Information Available in These Sources: SATA 3

DAVIS, VERNE T(HEODORE)
Birthdate: 8/14/1889
Birthplace: MI
Deathdate: 7/15/1973
Information Available in These Sources: SATA 6

DAVIS, WILLIAM STEARNS
Birthdate: 4/30/1877
Birthplace: Amherst, MA
Deathdate: 2/15/1930
Information Available in These Sources: JBA 1

DAWSON, ELMER A.
See Stratemeyer, Edward L.

DAWSON, MITCHELL
Birthdate: 5/13/1890
Birthplace: Chicago, IL
Deathdate: 1956
Information Available in These Sources: ABYP 2, ABYP 3

DAY, A(RTHUR) GROVE
Birthdate: 4/29/1904
Birthplace: Philadelphia, PA
Information Available in These Sources: SATA 59

DAY, BETH (FEAGLES)
(Elizabeth Feagles)
Birthdate: 5/25/1924
Birthplace: Fort Wayne, IN
Information Available in These Sources: ABYP 4, SATA 33

DAY, LILA
See Chaffin, Lillie D(orton)

DAY, MAURICE
Birthdate: 7/2/1892
Birthplace: Damariscotta, ME
Deathdate: 1983
Information Available in These Sources: CICB, ICB 1, SATA 30

DAZEY, AGNES J(OHNSTON)
(Agnes Christine Johnston)
Birthplace: Swissville, PA
Information Available in These Sources: ABYP 4, SATA 2

DAZEY, FRANK M.
Birthplace: Quincy, IL
Information Available in These Sources: ABYP 4, SATA 2

DEAN, ANABEL
Birthdate: 5/24/1915
Birthplace: Deming, NM
Information Available in These Sources: SATA 12

DEAN, GRAHAM M.
Birthdate: 8/10/1904
Birthplace: Lake View, IA
Information Available in These Sources: ABYP 2, ABYP 3

DEAN, KAREN STRICKLER
Birthdate: 11/24/1923
Birthplace: Los Angeles, CA
Information Available in These Sources: SATA 49

DEAN, LEIGH
Information Available in These Sources: ABYP 4

DEAN, NELL MARR
(Virginia Roberts)
Birthdate: 9/28/1910
Birthplace: Tulsa, OK
Information Available in These Sources: ABYP 2, ABYP 3

DEANGELI, MARGUERITE (LOFFT)
Birthdate: 3/14/1889
Birthplace: Lapeer, MI
Deathdate: 6/16/1987
Information Available in These Sources: ABYP 1, ABYP 3, AICB, DLB 22, ICB 1, ICB 2, ICB 3, ICB 4, JBA 2, MBMP, SATA 1, SATA 27, SATA 51, TCCW 1, TCCW 2, TCCW 3

DEARMAND, FRANCES ULLMANN
Birthdate: 1904?
Birthplace: Springfield, MO
Deathdate: 4/14/1984
Information Available in These Sources: ABYP 2, ABYP 3, SATA 10, SATA 38

DEBORHEGYI, SUZANNE C(ATHERINE) SIMS
See Borhegyi, Suzanne Catherine Sims de

DEBRUYN, MONICA
Birthdate: 5/12/1952
Birthplace: Chicago, IL
Information Available in These Sources: SATA 13

DECAMP, CATHERINE C(ROOK)
Birthdate: 11/6/1907
Birthplace: New York, NY
Information Available in These Sources: SATA 12

DECAMP, L(YON) SPRAGUE
(Lyman R. Lyon, J. Wellington Wells)
Birthdate: 11/27/1907
Birthplace: New York, NY
Information Available in These Sources: ABYP 2, SATA 9

DECKER, DUANE (WALTER)
(Richard Wayne)
Birthdate: 7/28/1910
Birthplace: Bridgeport, CT
Deathdate: 8/21/1964
Information Available in These Sources: ABYP 1, ABYP 3, SATA 5

DECLEMENTS, BARTHE
Birthdate: 10/8/1920
Birthplace: Seattle, WA
Information Available in These Sources: JBA 6, SATA 35

DEEDY, JOHN
Birthdate: 8/17/1923
Birthplace: Worcester, MA
Information Available in These Sources: SATA 24

DEEGAN, PAUL JOSEPH
(Sean O'Reilly)
Birthdate: 3/19/1937
Birthplace: Mankato, MN
Information Available in These Sources: SATA 38, SATA 48

DEFOREST, CHARLOTTE B(URGIS)
Birthdate: 2/23/1879
Birthplace: Osaka, Japan
Deathdate: 1971
Information Available in These Sources: ABYP 4

DEFRANCE, ANTHONY
See DiFranco, Anthony (Mario)

DEGARZA, PATRICIA
Information Available in These Sources: ABYP 4

DEGEN, BRUCE N.
Birthdate: 6/14/1932 or 6/14/1945
Birthplace: Brooklyn, NY
Information Available in These Sources: JBA 6, SATA 47, SATA 57

DEGENS, T.
Birthplace: East Germany
Information Available in These Sources: JBA 5

DEGERING, ETTA (FOWLER)
Birthdate: 1/7/1898
Birthplace: Arcadia, NE
Information Available in These Sources: ABYP 2, SATA 7

DEGRAZIA
See DeGrazia, Ted

DEGRAZIA, ETTORE
See DeGrazia, Ted

DEGRAZIA, TED
(DeGrazia, Ettore DeGrazia)
Birthdate: 6/14/1909
Birthplace: Morenci, AZ
Deathdate: 9/17/1982
Information Available in These Sources: SATA 39

DEGROAT, DIANE L.
Birthdate: 5/24/1947
Birthplace: Newton, NJ
Information Available in These Sources: ICB 4, JBA 5, SATA 31

DEGROS, J. H.
See Villiard, Paul

DEGRUMMOND, LENA YOUNG
Birthplace: Centerville, LA
Information Available in These Sources: ABYP 2, SATA 6

DEISS, JOSEPH JAY
Birthdate: 1/25/1915
Birthplace: Twin Falls, ID
Information Available in These Sources: SATA 12

DEJONG, DAVID C(ORNEL)
(Tjalmar Breda)
Birthdate: 6/9/1905
Birthplace: Blija, Friesland, Netherlands
Deathdate: 9/5/1967
Information Available in These Sources: ABYP 2, ABYP 3, SATA 10

DEJONG, DOLA
Birthdate: 10/10/1911
Birthplace: Arnhem, Holland, Netherlands
Information Available in These Sources: ABYP 1, ABYP 3, DACF, MJA, SATA 7

DEJONG, MEINDERT
Birthdate: 3/4/1906
Birthplace: Wierum, Netherlands
Information Available in These Sources: ABYP 1, ABYP 3, AICB, DACF, DLB 52, MBMP, MJA, SATA 2, TCCW 1, TCCW 2, TCCW 3

DEJONGE, JOANNE E.
Birthdate: 5/18/1943
Birthplace: Paterson, NJ
Information Available in These Sources: SATA 56

DEKAY, ORMONDE, JR.
Birthdate: 12/17/1923
Birthplace: New York, NY
Information Available in These Sources: SATA 7

DEKKER, CARL
See Lynds, Dennis

DEKRUIF, PAUL (HENRY)
Birthdate: 3/2/1890
Birthplace: Zeeland, MI
Deathdate: 2/28/1971
Information Available in These Sources: JBA 1, SATA 5, SATA 50

DEL REY, LESTER
(Ramon Felipe San Juan Mario Silvo, Enrico Alvarez-del Rey, Philip St. John, Erik VanLhin, Kenneth Wright)
Birthdate: 6/2/1915
Birthplace: Clydesdale, MN
Information Available in These Sources: ABYP 1, ABYP 3, JBA 3, SATA 22

DELACRE, LULU
Birthdate: 12/20/1957
Birthplace: PR
Information Available in These Sources: SATA 36

DELAGE, IDA
Birthdate: 7/16/1918
Birthplace: New York, NY
Information Available in These Sources: SATA 11

DELANEY, NED
Birthdate: 7/6/1951
Birthplace: Glenridge, NJ
Information Available in These Sources: SATA 28

DELANO, HUGH
Birthdate: 12/14/1933
Birthplace: Cranford, NJ
Information Available in These Sources: SATA 20

DELARREA, VICTORIA
Birthdate: 11/21/1933
Birthplace: New York, NY
Information Available in These Sources: IBYP 1, IBYP 2

DELATORRE, LILLIAN
See McCue, Lillian Bueno

DELATORRE-BUENO, LILLIAN
See McCue, Lillian Bueno

DELAUNE, JEWEL LYNN (DE GRUMMOND)
(Lynn Delaune)
Birthdate: 1924
Birthplace: Canterville, LA
Information Available in These Sources: ABYP 2, ABYP 3, SATA 7

DELAUNE, LYNN
See Delaune, Jewel Lynn (de Grummond)

DELAURENTIS, LOUISE BUDDE
Birthdate: 10/5/1920
Birthplace: Stafford, KS
Information Available in These Sources: SATA 12

DELEAR, FRANK J.
Birthdate: 1/21/1914
Birthplace: Boston, MA
Information Available in These Sources: ABYP 4

DELEEUW, ADELE (LOUISE)
Birthdate: 8/12/1899
Birthplace: Hamilton, OH
Deathdate: 6/12/1988
Information Available in These Sources: ABYP 1, ABYP 3, FLTYP, JBA 2, SATA 1, SATA 30, SATA 56

DELEEUW, CATEAU (WILHELMINA)
(Kay Hamilton, Jessica Lyon)
Birthdate: 9/22/1903
Birthplace: Hamilton, OH
Deathdate: 6/2/1975
Information Available in These Sources: ABYP 1, ABYP 3, FLTYP, JBA 2

DELESSERT, ETIENNE
Birthdate: 1/4/1941
Birthplace: Lausanne, Switzerland
Information Available in These Sources: IBYP 2, ICB 4, JBA 6, SATA 27 SATA 46

DELMAR, ROY
See Wexler, Jerome (LeRoy)

DELORIA, VINE (VICTOR), JR.
Birthdate: 3/26/1933
Birthplace: Martin, SD
Information Available in These Sources: SATA 21

DELTON, JUDY
Birthdate: 5/6/1931
Birthplace: St. Paul, MN
Information Available in These Sources: ABYP 4, JBA 5, SAIA 14

DELULIO, JOHN
Birthdate: 3/29/1938
Information Available in These Sources: IBYP 2, SATA 15

DELVING, MICHAEL
See Williams, Jay

DEMAREST, CHRIS(TOPHER) L(YNN)
Birthdate: 4/18/1951
Birthplace: Hartford, CT
Information Available in These Sources: SATA 44, SATA 45

DEMAREST, DOUG
See Barker, Will

DEMARTELLY, JOHN STOCKTON
Birthdate: 9/10/1903
Birthplace: Philadelphia, PA
Information Available in These Sources: ICB 1

DEMAS, VIDA
Birthdate: 3/30/1927
Birthplace: Pittsburgh, PA
Information Available in These Sources: SATA 9

DEMEJO, OSCAR
Birthdate: 8/22/1911
Birthplace: Trieste, Italy
Information Available in These Sources: SATA 40

DEMESSIERES, NICOLE
Birthdate: 1/26/1930
Birthplace: Ales, France
Information Available in These Sources: SATA 39

DEMI
See Hunt, Charlotte Dumaresq

DEMIJOHN, THOM
See Disch, Thomas M(ichael)

DEMING, DOROTHY
Birthdate: 6/8/1893
Birthplace: New Haven, CT
Information Available in These Sources: ABYP 1, ABYP 3

DEMING, RICHARD
(Max Franklin, Emily Moor)
Birthdate: 4/25/1915
Birthplace: Des Moines, IA
Information Available in These Sources: ABYP 4, SATA 24

DEMISKEY, JULIAN
Birthdate: 12/21/1908
Birthplace: Csabdi, Hungary
Deathdate: 5/21/1976
Information Available in These Sources: ICB 3, ICB 4

DEMUTH, FLORA NASH
Birthdate: 9/7/1888
Birthplace: Hartford, PA
Information Available in These Sources: ICB 2

DEMUTH, PATRICIA BRENNAN
Birthdate: 3/16/1948
Birthplace: Sioux City, IA
Information Available in These Sources: SATA 49

DENGLER, SANDY
Birthdate: 6/8/1939
Birthplace: Newark, OH
Information Available in These Sources: SATA 40, 54

DENISON, CAROL (HAMILTON)
Birthplace: Kansas City, MO
Information Available in These Sources: ABYP 1, ABYP 3

DENMAN, FRANK
Birthdate: 1897?
Deathdate: 1968
Information Available in These Sources: ABYP 2, ABYP 3

DENMARK, HARRISON
See Zelazny, Roger (Joseph Christopher)

DENNING, PATRICIA
See Willis, Corinne (Denney)

DENNIS, MORGAN
Birthdate: 2/27/1891, 2/27/1892, or 2/27/1893
Birthplace: Boston, MA
Deathdate: 10/22/1960
Information Available in These Sources: ABYP 2, ABYP 3, ICB 1, ICB 2, MJA, SATA 18

DENNIS, WESLEY
Birthdate: 5/16/1903
Birthplace: Falmouth, MA
Deathdate: 9/5/1966
Information Available in These Sources: ABYP 2, ABYP 3, ICB 1, ICB 2, ICB 3, MJA, SATA 18

DENNISTON, ELINORE
(Rae Foley)
Birthdate: 9/20/1900
Birthplace: Medora, ND
Deathdate: 5/24/1978
Information Available in These Sources: SATA 24

DENSEN-GERBER, JUDIANNE
Birthdate: 11/13/1934
Birthplace: New York, NY
Information Available in These Sources: ABYP 4

DENSLOW, W(ILLIAM) W(ALLACE)
Birthdate: 5/5/1856
Birthplace: Philadelphia, PA
Deathdate: 3/29/1915
Information Available in These Sources: JBA 4, SATA 16

DENZEL, JUSTIN F(RANCIS)
Birthdate: 1/15/1917
Birthplace: Clifton, NJ
Information Available in These Sources: SATA 38, SATA 46

DENZER, ANN WISEMAN
See Wiseman, Ann (Sayre)

DEOSMA, LUPE
Birthplace: Costa Rica
Information Available in These Sources: ABYP 2, ABYP 3

DEPAOLA, THOMAS ANTHONY
(Tomie DePaola)
Birthdate: 9/15/1934
Birthplace: Meriden, CT
Information Available in These Sources: DLB 61, IBYP 1, IBYP 2, ICB 3 ICB 4, JBA 5, SATA 11, SATA 59TCCW 2, TCCW 3

DEPAOLA, TOMIE
See DePaola, Thomas Anthony

DEPAUW, LINDA GRANT
Birthdate: 1/19/1940
Birthplace: New York, NY
Information Available in These Sources: ABYP 4, SATA 24

DEREGNIERS, BEATRICE SCHENK
(Tamara Kitt)
Birthdate: 8/16/1914
Birthplace: Lafayette, IN
Information Available in These Sources: ABYP 1, ABYP 3, BABP, MJA, SATA 2, TCCW 1, TCCW 2, TCCW 3

DERLETH, AUGUST (WILLIAM)
(Stephen Grendon, Tally Mason)
Birthdate: 2/24/1909
Birthplace: Sauk City, WI
Deathdate: 7/4/1971
Information Available in These Sources: ABYP 2, ABYP 3, SATA 5

DERMAN, SARAH AUDREY
Birthdate: 8/28/1915
Birthplace: Rock Island, IL
Information Available in These Sources: SATA 11

DESCHWEINITZ, KARL
Birthdate: 11/26/1887
Birthplace: Northfield, MN
Deathdate: 4/20/1975
Information Available in These Sources: ABYP 4

DESMOND, ALICE CURTIS
Birthdate: 9/19/1897
Birthplace: Southport, CT
Information Available in These Sources: ABYP 1, ABYP 3, SATA 8

DETWILER, SUSAN DILL
Birthdate: 1/7/1956
Birthplace: Fort Knox, KY
Information Available in These Sources: SATA 58

DEUCHER, SYBIL
Birthplace: New York, NY
Information Available in These Sources: MJA

DEUTSCH, BABETTE
Birthdate: 9/22/1895
Birthplace: New York, NY
Deathdate: 11/13/1982
Information Available in These Sources: MJA, SATA 1, SATA 33

DEVANEY, JOHN
Birthdate: 3/15/1926
Birthplace: New York, NY
Information Available in These Sources: ABYP 4, SATA 12

DEVEAUX, ALEXIS
Birthdate: 9/24/1948
Birthplace: New York, NY
Information Available in These Sources: BAI

DEVEREUX, FREDERICK L(EONARD), JR.
Birthdate: 4/20/1914
Birthplace: New York, NY
Information Available in These Sources: SATA 9

DEVEYRAC, ROBERT
Birthdate: 10/1/1901
Birthplace: France
Information Available in These Sources: ICB 1

DEVLIN, DOROTHY WENDE
(Wende Devlin)
Birthdate: 4/27/1918
Birthplace: Buffalo, NY
Information Available in These Sources: FLTYP, IBYP 2, SATA 11

DEVLIN, HARRY
Birthdate: 3/22/1918
Birthplace: Jersey City, NJ
Information Available in These Sources: FLTYP, IBYP 1, IBYP 2, SATA 11

DEVLIN, WENDE
See Devlin, Dorothy Wende

DEWAARD, E(LLIOTT) JOHN
Birthdate: 3/30/1935
Birthplace: Sault Ste. Marie, MI
Information Available in These Sources: SATA 7

DEWEESE, GENE
See DeWeese, Thomas Eugene

DEWEESE, JEAN
See DeWeese, Thomas Eugene

DEWEESE, THOMAS EUGENE
(Gene DeWeese, Jean DeWeese, Thomas Stratton, Victoria Thomas)
Birthdate: 1/31/1934
Birthplace: Rochester, IN
Information Available in These Sources: SATA 45, SATA 46

DEWEY, ARIANE
(Ariane Aruego)
Birthdate: 8/17/1937
Birthplace: Chicago, IL
Information Available in These Sources: IBYP 2, ICB 4, JBA 4, SATA 7

DEWEY, JENNIFER (OWINGS)
Birthdate: 10/2/1941
Birthplace: Chicago, IL
Information Available in These Sources: SATA 48, SATA 58

DEWEY, KEN(NETH FRANCIS)
Birthdate: 10/5/1940
Birthplace: New York, NY
Information Available in These Sources: SATA 39

DEWIT, DOROTHY (MAY KNOWLES)
Birthdate: 5/24/1916
Birthplace: Youngstown, OH
Deathdate: 6/19/1980
Information Available in These Sources: SATA 28, SATA 39

DEWITT, CORNELIUS HUGH
Birthdate: 6/6/1905
Birthplace: Cassel, Germany
Information Available in These Sources: ICB 1, ICB 2

DEWITT, JAMES
See Lewis, Mildred D.

DEYNEKA, ANITA
Birthdate: 7/7/1943
Birthplace: Seattle, WA
Information Available in These Sources: SATA 24

DEYRUP, ASTRITH JOHNSON
Birthdate: 4/22/1923
Birthplace: Nyack, NY
Information Available in These Sources: ABYP 4, SATA 24

DI CERTO, JOSEPH JOHN
Birthdate: 2/27/1933
Birthplace: New York, NY
Information Available in These Sources: SATA 60

DIAMOND, DONNA
Birthdate: 10/19/1950
Birthplace: New York, NY
Information Available in These Sources: ICB 4, JBA 5, SATA 30, SATA 35

DIAMOND, PETRA
See Sachs, Judith

DIAMOND, REBECCA
See Sachs, Judith

DIAS, EARL JOSEPH
Birthdate: 3/23/1916
Birthplace: New Bedford, MA
Information Available in These Sources: SATA 41

DICK, CAPPY
See Cleveland, George

DICK, TRELLA LAMSON
Birthdate: 5/29/1889
Birthplace: Orleans, NE
Deathdate: 5/10/1974
Information Available in These Sources: ABYP 1, ABYP 3, SATA 9

DICKENS, MONICA (ENID)
Birthdate: 5/10/1915
Birthplace: London, England
Information Available in These Sources: ABYP 4, SATA 4

DICKERSON, ROY ERNEST
Birthdate: 4/3/1886
Birthplace: Versailles, IN
Deathdate: 11/8/1965
Information Available in These Sources: SATA 26

DICKINSON, EMILY (ELIZABETH)
Birthdate: 12/10/1830
Birthplace: Amherst, MA
Deathdate: 5/15/1886
Information Available in These Sources: SATA 29, SVC 2, SVC 3

DICKMEYER, LOWELL A.
Birthdate: 5/14/1939
Birthplace: Fort Wayne, IN
Information Available in These Sources: SATA 51

DICKSON, MARGUERITE (STOCKMAN)
Birthdate: 11/14/1873
Birthplace: Portland, ME
Deathdate: 10/11/1953
Information Available in These Sources: ABYP 1, ABYP 3, MJA

DICKSON, NAIDA
(Grace Lee Richardson)
Birthdate: 4/18/1916
Birthplace: Thatcher, AZ
Information Available in These Sources: SATA 8

DIETZ, BETTY WARNER
See Dietz, Elisabeth H.

DIETZ, DAVID H(ENRY)
Birthdate: 10/6/1897
Birthplace: Cleveland, OH
Deathdate: 12/9/1984
Information Available in These Sources: SATA 10, SATA 41

DIETZ, ELISABETH H.
(Betty Warner Dietz)
Birthdate: 5/12/1908
Birthplace: Chicago, IL
Information Available in These Sources: ABYP 2, ABYP 3, ABYP 4

DIETZ, LEW
Birthdate: 5/22/1907
Birthplace: Pittsburgh, PA
Information Available in These Sources: ABYP 2, ABYP 3, SATA 11

DIFIORI, LARRY
See DiFiori, Lawrence

DIFIORI, LAWRENCE
(Larry DiFiori)
Birthplace: Philadelphia, PA
Information Available in These Sources: IBYP 2

DIFRANCO, ANTHONY (MARIO)
(Anthony DeFrance)
Birthdate: 8/29/1945
Birthplace: New York, NY
Information Available in These Sources: SATA 42

DIGGES, JEREMIAH
See Berger, Josef

DIGGINS, JULIA E.
Information Available in These Sources: ABYP 2, ABYP 3

DIGRAZIA, THOMAS
Birthplace: NJ
Deathdate: 3/10/1983
Information Available in These Sources: IBYP 2, ICB 4, SATA 32

DILLARD, ANNIE
Birthdate: 4/30/1945
Birthplace: Pittsburgh, PA
Information Available in These Sources: SATA 10

DILLARD, POLLY (HARGIS)
Birthdate: 4/22/1916
Birthplace: Somerset, KY
Information Available in These Sources: SATA 24

DILLER, ANGELA
Birthdate: 8/1/1877
Birthplace: Brooklyn, NY
Deathdate: 5/1/1968
Information Available in These Sources: ABYP 1, ABYP 3

DILLON, BARBARA
Birthdate: 9/2/1927
Birthplace: Montclair, NJ
Information Available in These Sources: SATA 39, SATA 44

DILLON, CORINNE BOYD
Birthplace: Louisville, KY
Information Available in These Sources: IBYP 1, IBYP 2, ICB 2

DILLON, DIANE (C.)
Birthdate: 3/13/1933
Birthplace: Glendale, CA
Information Available in These Sources: ABYP 4, ICB 4, JBA 5, SATA 15 SATA 51

DILLON, LEO
Birthdate: 3/2/1933
Birthplace: Brooklyn, NY
Information Available in These Sources: ABYP 4, BAI, ICB 4, JBA 5, SATA 15, SATA 51

DILLON, SHARON SASEEN
See Saseen, Sharon (Dillon)

DILSON, JESSE
Birthdate: 12/23/1914
Birthplace: Brooklyn, NY
Information Available in These Sources: SATA 24

DINES, GLEN
See Dines, Harry Glen

DINES, HARRY GLEN
(Glen Dines)
Birthdate: 11/19/1925
Birthplace: Casper, WY
Information Available in These Sources: ABYP 2, ABYP 3, ICB 2, ICB 3, SATA 7

DINNERSTEIN, HARVEY
Birthdate: 4/3/1928
Birthplace: Brooklyn, NY
Information Available in These Sources: SATA 42

DIRKS, RUDOLPH
Birthdate: 2/26/1877
Birthplace: Heide, Germany
Deathdate: 4/20/1968
Information Available in These Sources: SATA 31

DIRKSEN, EVERETT MCKINLEY
Birthdate: 1/4/1896
Birthplace: Pekin, IL
Deathdate: 9/7/1969
Information Available in These Sources: ABYP 4

DISALVO-RYAN, DYANNE
Birthdate: 10/3/1954
Birthplace: Brooklyn, NY
Information Available in These Sources: SATA 59

DISCH, THOMAS M(ICHAEL)
(Thom Demijohn, Leonie Hargrave, Cassandra Kaye)
Birthdate: 2/2/1940
Birthplace: Des Moines, IA
Information Available in These Sources: SATA 54

DISKA, PAT
Birthplace: New York, NY
Information Available in These Sources: ABYP 4

DISNEY, WALT(ER ELIAS)
(Retlaw Yensid)
Birthdate: 12/5/1901
Birthplace: Chicago, IL
Deathdate: 12/15/1966
Information Available in These Sources: DLB 22, SATA 27, SATA 28, WCL

DITMARS, RAYMOND LEE
Birthdate: 6/20/1876
Birthplace: Newark, NJ
Deathdate: 5/12/1942
Information Available in These Sources: ABYP 1, ABYP 3, JBA 1, JBA 2

DITZEL, PAUL C(ALVIN)
Birthdate: 11/11/1926
Birthplace: Buffalo, NY
Information Available in These Sources: ABYP 4

DIVALENTIN, MARIA (MESSURI)
Birthdate: 10/29/1911
Birthplace: New York, NY
Information Available in These Sources: SATA 7

DIX, BEULAH MARIE
Birthdate: 12/25/1876
Birthplace: Kingston, MA
Deathdate: 9/25/1970
Information Available in These Sources: JBA 1, JBA 2

DIXON, FRANKLIN W.
See Adams, Harriet S(tratemeyer), Stratemeyer, Edward L. and Svenson, Andrew E.

DIXON, JEANNE
(Mary Wood Harper, Josephine Rector Stone)
Birthdate: 7/18/1936
Birthplace: Two Medicine, MT
Information Available in These Sources: SATA 31

DIXON, PAIGE
See Corcoran, Barbara

DIXON, PETER L.
Birthdate: 8/19/1931
Birthplace: New York, NY
Information Available in These Sources: SATA 6

DIXON, RUTH
See Barrows, R(uth) M(arjorie)

DOANE, PELAGE
Birthdate: 4/11/1906
Birthplace: Palmyra, NJ
Deathdate: 12/9/1966
Information Available in These Sources: ABYP 1, ABYP 3, ICB 1, ICB 2, MJA, SATA 7

DOBBS, ROSE
Information Available in These Sources: ABYP 2, ABYP 3

DOBIAS, FRANK
Birthdate: 1902
Birthplace: Styria Mountains, Austria
Information Available in These Sources: ICB 1

DOBIE, J(AMES) FRANK
Birthdate: 9/26/1888
Birthplace: Live Oaks County, TX
Deathdate: 9/18/1964
Information Available in These Sources: SATA 43

DOBKIN, ALEXANDER
Birthdate: 5/1/1908
Birthplace: Genoa, Italy
Deathdate: 3/21/1975
Information Available in These Sources: ICB 2, SATA 30

DOBLER, LAVINIA G.
Birthdate: 7/3/1910
Birthplace: Riverton, WY
Information Available in These Sources: MBMP, SATA 6

DOBRIN, ARNOLD (JACK)
Birthdate: 6/6/1928
Birthplace: Omaha, NE
Information Available in These Sources: ABYP 4, ICB 3, SATA 4

DOCKERY, WALLENE T.
Birthdate: 12/15/1941
Birthplace: Lineville, AL
Information Available in These Sources: SATA 27

DOCKTOR, IRV
Birthdate: 7/10/1918
Birthplace: Philadelphia, PA
Information Available in These Sources: ICB 2

DODD, ED(WARD BENTON)
Birthdate: 11/7/1902
Birthplace: LaFayette, GA
Information Available in These Sources: SATA 4

DODDS, JOHN W(ENDELL)
Birthdate: 7/20/1902
Birthplace: Grove City, PA
Information Available in These Sources: ABYP 4

DODGE, BERTHA S(ANFORD)
Birthdate: 3/23/1902
Birthplace: Cambridge, MA
Information Available in These Sources: ABYP 2, ABYP 3, SATA 8

DODGE, MARY (ELIZABETH) MAPES
Birthdate: 1/26/1831 , 1/26/1830, or 1/26/1838
Birthplace: New York, NY
Deathdate: 8/21/1905
Information Available in These Sources: ABYP 1, ABYP 3, DLB 42, FSYP, JBA 1, SATA 21, TCCW 1, TCCW 2TCCW 3, WC, WCL

DODSON, KENNETH M(ACKENZIE)
Birthdate: 10/11/1907
Birthplace: Luanda, Angola, Africa
Information Available in These Sources: SATA 11

DODSON, SUSAN
Birthdate: 1/19/1941
Birthplace: Pittsburgh, PA
Information Available in These Sources: SATA 40, SATA 50

DODWORTH, DOROTHY L.
Information Available in These Sources: ABYP 2, ABYP 3

DOHERTY, JOHN STEPHEN
Information Available in These Sources: ABYP 1, ABYP 3

DOLAN, EDWARD F(RANCIS), JR.
Birthdate: 2/10/1924
Birthplace: Oakland, CA
Information Available in These Sources: ABYP 4, SATA 31, SATA 45

DOLBIER, MAURICE (WYMAN)
Birthdate: 5/5/1912
Birthplace: Skowhegan, ME
Information Available in These Sources: ABYP 1, ABYP 3, MJA

DOLCH, EDWARD WILLIAM
Birthdate: 8/4/1889
Birthplace: St. Louis, MO
Information Available in These Sources: SATA 50

DOLCH, MARGUERITE PIERCE
Birthdate: 12/16/1891
Birthplace: St. Louis, MO
Deathdate: 3/??/1978
Information Available in These Sources: SATA 50

DOLEZAL, CARROLL
Birthplace: New London, CT
Information Available in These Sources: IBYP 1, IBYP 2

DOLIM, MARY N(UZUM)
Birthdate: 8/15/1925
Birthplace: Timberhill, KS
Information Available in These Sources: ABYP 2, ABYP 3

DOLLAR, DIANE (HILLS)
Birthdate: 4/25/1933
Birthplace: Kansas City, MO
Information Available in These Sources: SATA 57

DOLSON, HILDEGARDE
Birthdate: 8/31/1908
Birthplace: Franklin, PA
Information Available in These Sources: SATA 5

DOMANSKA, JANINA
(Janina Domanska Laskowski)
Birthplace: Warsaw, Poland
Information Available in These Sources: ABYP 2, ABYP 3, ICB 3, ICB 4, JBA 3, SATA 6

DOMBROWSKI, BARONESS
See Dombrowski, Kathe Schonberger von

DOMBROWSKI, KATHARINE VON
See Dombrowski, Kathe Schonberger von

DOMBROWSKI, KATHE SCHONBERGER VON
(Baroness Dombrowski, Katharine von Dombrowski, K. O. S., Kathe Olshausen Schonberger)
Birthdate: 6/11/1881
Birthplace: Vienna (near), Austria
Information Available in These Sources: ICB 1

DOMINO, JOHN
See Averill, Esther (Holden)

DOMJAN, JOSEPH
Birthdate: 3/15/1907
Birthplace: Budapest, Hungary
Information Available in These Sources: SATA 25

DONAHEY, MARY (AUGUSTA) DICKERSON
Birthdate: 9/22/1876
Birthplace: New York, NY
Deathdate: 3/31/1962
Information Available in These Sources: ABYP 1

DONAHEY, WILLIAM
Birthdate: 10/19/1884 or 10/19/1883
Birthplace: Westchester, OH
Deathdate: 1970
Information Available in These Sources: ABYP 1, ABYP 3

DONALDS, GORDON
See Shirreffs, Gordon D(onald)

DONN-BYRNE, BRIAN OSWALD
See Byrne, Donn

DONNA, NATALIE
Birthdate: 12/25/1934
Birthplace: New York, NY
Deathdate: 2/9/1979
Information Available in These Sources: ABYP 2, ABYP 3, SATA 9

DONOVAN, FRANK (ROBERT)
Birthdate: 6/6/1906
Birthplace: New York, NY
Deathdate: 9/26/1975
Information Available in These Sources: ABYP 2, ABYP 3, SATA 30

DONOVAN, JOHN
Birthdate: 1928
Information Available in These Sources: DACF, JBA 5, SATA 29, TCCW 1, TCCW 2, TCCW 3

DONOVAN, WILLIAM
See Berkebile, Fred D(onovan)

DONZE, SARA LEE (HATHAWAY)
Birthdate: 11/12/1925
Birthplace: East Liberty, OH
Information Available in These Sources: ABYP 4

DOOB, LEONARD W(ILLIAM)
Birthdate: 3/3/1909
Birthplace: New York, NY
Information Available in These Sources: ABYP 4, SATA 8

DOR, ANA
See Ceder, Georgiana Dorcas

DOREMUS, ROBERT
Birthdate: 6/3/1913
Birthplace: Union Springs, NY
Information Available in These Sources: IBYP 1, IBYP 2, SATA 30

DOREN, MARION (WALKER)
Birthdate: 7/10/1928
Birthplace: Glen Ridge, NJ
Information Available in These Sources: SATA 57

DORIAN, EDITH M(CEWEN)
Birthdate: 5/5/1900
Birthplace: Newark, NJ
Information Available in These Sources: SATA 5

DORIAN, MARGUERITE
Birthplace: Bucharest, Romania
Information Available in These Sources: ABYP 1, SATA 7

DORIN, PATRICK C(ARBERRY)
Birthdate: 2/12/1939
Birthplace: Chicago, IL
Information Available in These Sources: SATA 52, SATA 59

DORMAN, MICHAEL
(Jack Bishop)
Birthdate: 10/9/1932
Birthplace: New York, NY
Information Available in These Sources: ABYP 4, SATA 7

DORMAN, N. B.
Birthdate: 7/12/1927
Birthplace: IA
Information Available in These Sources: SATA 39

DORSON, RICHARD M(ERCER)
Birthdate: 3/12/1916
Birthplace: New York, NY
Information Available in These Sources: SATA 30

DOS SANTOS, JOYCE AUDY
See Zarins, Joyce Audy

DOSS, HELEN (GRIGSBY)
Birthdate: 8/9/1918
Birthplace: Sanderstead, Surrey, England
Information Available in These Sources: ABYP 2, ABYP 3, SATA 20

DOSS, MARGOT PATTERSON
Birthdate: 8/22/1922
Birthplace: St. Paul, MN
Information Available in These Sources: ABYP 4, SATA 6

DOTTIG
See Grider, Dorothy

DOTTS, MARYANN J.
Birthdate: 11/11/1933
Birthplace: Pittsburgh, PA
Information Available in These Sources: SATA 35

DOTY, JEAN SLAUGHTER
(Jean Slaughter)
Birthdate: 3/19/1929 or 1924
Information Available in These Sources: ABYP 4, SATA 28

DOTY, ROY
Birthdate: 9/10/1922
Birthplace: Chicago, IL
Information Available in These Sources: IBYP 2, SATA 28

DOTZENKO, GRISHA F.
(Grisha)
Birthplace: Ukraine, Russia
Information Available in These Sources: IBYP 2

DOUGHERTY, CHARLES
Birthdate: 5/1/1922
Birthplace: Chicago, IL
Information Available in These Sources: SATA 18

DOUGHERTY, JOANNA FOSTER
See Foster, Joanna

DOUGHTIE, CHARLES
Birthplace: VA
Information Available in These Sources: ABYP 2, ABYP 3

DOUGLAS, EMILY (TAFT)
Birthdate: 4/19/1899
Birthplace: Chicago, IL
Information Available in These Sources: ABYP 1

DOUGLAS, JAMES MCM.
See Butterworth, W(illiam) E(dmund III)

DOUGLAS, JOHN SCOTT
Birthdate: 5/16/1905
Birthplace: Seattle, WA
Information Available in These Sources: ABYP 2, ABYP 3

DOUGLAS, KATHRYN
See Ewing, Kathryn

DOUGLAS, MARJORY STONEMAN
Birthdate: 4/7/1890
Birthplace: Minneapolis, MN
Information Available in These Sources: SATA 10

DOUGLAS, MICHAEL
See Bright, Robert

DOUGLAS, WILLIAM O(RVILLE)
Birthdate: 10/16/1898
Birthplace: Maine, MN
Deathdate: 1/19/1980
Information Available in These Sources: ABYP 2, ABYP 3

DOUGLASS, BARBARA
Birthdate: 4/27/1930
Birthplace: Wilmar, CA
Information Available in These Sources: SATA 40

DOUGLASS, FREDERICK
(Frederick Augustus Washington Bailey)
Birthdate: 2/, /1817
Birthplace: Tuckahoe, MD
Deathdate: 2/20/1895
Information Available in These Sources: SATA 29

DOUGLASS, RALPH
Birthdate: 12/29/1895
Birthplace: St. Louis, MO
Information Available in These Sources: ICB 1, ICB 2

DOUTY, ESTHER M(ORRIS)
Birthdate: 3/24/1911
Birthplace: Mount Vernon, NY
Deathdate: 12/13/1978
Information Available in These Sources: ABYP 4, SATA 8, SATA 23

DOW, EMILY R.
Birthdate: 5/26/1904
Birthplace: Exeter, NH
Information Available in These Sources: SATA 10

DOWD, VICTOR
Information Available in These Sources: IBYP 1, IBYP 2

DOWDELL, DOROTHY (FLORENCE) KARNS
Birthdate: 5/5/1910
Birthplace: Reno, NV
Information Available in These Sources: SATA 12

DOWDEN, ANNE OPHELIA (TODD)
(Anne Ophelia Todd)
Birthdate: 9/17/1907
Birthplace: Denver, CO
Information Available in These Sources: ABYP 2, ABYP 3, ICB 4, JBA 5, SATA 7

DOWDEY, LANDON GERALD
Birthdate: 8/2/1923
Birthplace: Washington, DC
Information Available in These Sources: SATA 11

DOWDY, MRS. REGERA
See Gorey, Edward St. John

DOWLING, VICTOR J.
Birthdate: 4/21/1906
Birthplace: New York, NY
Information Available in These Sources: IBYP 2, ICB 2

DOWNER, MARION
Birthdate: 1892
Deathdate: 10/6/1971
Information Available in These Sources: ABYP 2, ABYP 3, SATA 25

DOWNEY, FAIRFAX D(AVIS)
Birthdate: 11/28/1893
Birthplace: Salt Lake City, UT
Information Available in These Sources: ABYP 2, ABYP 3, SATA 3

DOWNIE, MARY ALICE (DAWE)
(Dawe Hunter)
Birthdate: 2/12/1934
Birthplace: Alton, IL
Information Available in These Sources: SATA 13, TCCW 1

DOYLE, DONOVAN
See Boegehold, Betty (Doyle)

DR. A
See Silverstein, Alvin

DRACO, F.
See Adams, Julia Davis

DRAGER, GARY
See Edens, Cooper

DRAGONWAGON, CRESCENT (ZOLOTOW)
Birthdate: 11/25/1952
Birthplace: New York, NY
Information Available in These Sources: JBA 6, SATA 11, SATA 41

DRAPER, NANCY
Birthdate: 1916
Birthplace: NY
Information Available in These Sources: ABYP 2, ABYP 3

DRESANG, ELIZA (CAROLYN TIMBERLAKE)
Birthdate: 10/21/1941
Birthplace: Atlanta, GA
Information Available in These Sources: SATA 19

DRESCHER, HENRIK
Birthdate: 12/15/1955
Birthplace: Denmark
Information Available in These Sources: JBA 6

DRESCHER, JOAN E(LIZABETH)
Birthdate: 3/6/1939
Birthplace: New York, NY
Information Available in These Sources: SATA 30

DRESSER, LAWRENCE
Birthplace: WI
Information Available in These Sources: IBYP 2

DREVES, VERONICA R.
Birthdate: 10/29/1927
Birthplace: Sioux City, IA
Deathdate: 9/30/1986
Information Available in These Sources: SATA 50

DRIAL, J. E.
See Laird, Jean E(louise)

DRIMMER, FREDERICK
Birthplace: Brooklyn, NY
Information Available in These Sources: SATA 60

DRIVING HAWK, VIRGINIA
See Sneve, Virginia Driving Hawk

DRUCKER, MALKA
Birthdate: 3/14/1945
Birthplace: Tucson, AZ
Information Available in These Sources: SATA 29, SATA 39

DRUMMOND, A. H.
(Lee Drummond)
Birthdate: 1927
Information Available in These Sources: ABYP 4

DRUMMOND, LEE
See Drummond, A. H.

DRUMMOND, WALTER
See Silverberg, Robert

DRURY, ROGER W(OLCOTT)
Birthdate: 3/3/1914
Birthplace: Boston, MA
Information Available in These Sources: ABYP 4, DACF, SATA 15

DRYDEN, PAMELA
See Johnston, Norma

DUANE, DIANE (ELIZABETH)
See Duane-Smyth, Diane (Elizabeth)

DUANE-SMYTH, DIANE (ELIZABETH)
(Diane Duane)
Birthdate: 5/18/1952
Birthplace: New York, NY
Information Available in These Sources: SATA 46, SATA 58

DUBANEVICH, ARLENE
Birthdate: 12/6/1950
Birthplace: Springfield, VT
Information Available in These Sources: SATA 56

DUBKIN, LOIS (KNUDSON)
Birthdate: 2/5/1911
Birthplace: Chicago, IL
Information Available in These Sources: ABYP 4

DUBOIS, ROCHELLE HOLT
See Holt, Rochelle Lynn

DUBOIS, SHIRLEY GRAHAM
(Shirley Graham)
Birthdate: 11/11/1907 , 11/11/1906, or 11/11/1908
Birthplace: Indianapolis, IN
Deathdate: 3/27/1977
Information Available in These Sources: ABYP 2, ABYP 3, MJA, SATA 24, SVC 2, SVC 3

DUBOIS, THEODORA (MCCORMICK)
Birthdate: 9/14/1890
Birthplace: Brooklyn, NY
Information Available in These Sources: ABYP 2, ABYP 3

DUBOIS, W(ILLIAM) E(DWARD) B(URGHARDT)
Birthdate: 2/23/1868
Birthplace: Great Barrington, MA
Deathdate: 8/27/1963
Information Available in These Sources: SATA 42

DUBOIS, WILLIAM (SHERMAN) PENE
Birthdate: 5/9/1916
Birthplace: Nutley, NJ
Information Available in These Sources: ABYP 1, ABYP 3, DACF, DLB 61, ICB 1, ICB 2, ICB 3, ICB 4, JBA 2, SATA 4, SVC 2, SVC 3, TCCW 1, TCCW 2, TCCW 3

DUBOSE, LAROCQUE (RUSS)
Birthdate: 4/24/1926
Birthplace: San Antonio, TX
Information Available in These Sources: SATA 2

DUCAS, DOROTHY
Birthdate: 6/9/1905
Birthplace: New York, NY
Information Available in These Sources: ABYP 2, ABYP 3

DUCHACEK, IVO D(UKA)
(Ivo Duka, Martin Cermak)
Birthdate: 2/27/1913
Birthplace: Prostejov, Czechoslovakia
Deathdate: 3/3/1988
Information Available in These Sources: SATA 55

DUCHAILLU, PAUL (BELLONI)
Birthdate: 7/31/1831 or 7/31/1835
Birthplace: Paris, France
Deathdate: 4/30/1903
Information Available in These Sources: JBA 1, SATA 26

DUCK, CAPTAIN
See Pinkwater, Daniel Manus

DUCORNET, ERICA
(Rikki Ducornet)
Birthdate: 4/19/1943
Birthplace: Canton, NY
Information Available in These Sources: ABYP 4, SATA 7

DUCORNET, GUY
Information Available in These Sources: ABYP 4

DUCORNET, RIKKI
See Ducornet, Erica

DUDLEY, MARTHA WARD
Birthdate: 1909?
Birthplace: Rochester, NY
Deathdate: 11/22/1985
Information Available in These Sources: SATA 45

DUDLEY, NANCY
See Cole, Lois Dwight

DUDLEY, ROBERT
See Baldwin, James

DUDLEY, RUTH H(UBBELL)
Birthdate: 5/14/1905
Birthplace: Champlain, NY
Information Available in These Sources: SATA 11

DUELAND, JOY V(IVIAN)
Birthplace: Brooklyn, NY
Information Available in These Sources: SATA 27

DUFF, ANNIS (JAMES)
Birthdate: 1904?
Birthplace: Toronto, Ontario, Canada
Deathdate: 8/10/1986
Information Available in These Sources: SATA 49

DUFF, MAGGIE
See Duff, Margaret K.

DUFF, MARGARET K.
(Maggie Duff)
Birthdate: 1/4/1916
Birthplace: Walton, IN
Information Available in These Sources: JBA 6, SATA 37

DUJARDIN, ROSAMOND NEAL
Birthdate: 7/22/1902
Birthplace: Fairland, IL
Deathdate: 3/27/1963
Information Available in These Sources: ABYP 1, ABYP 4, MJA, SATA 2

DUKA, IVO
See Duchacek, Ivo D(uka)

DUKE, WILL
See Gault, William Campbell

DUKERT, JOSEPH M(ICHAEL)
Birthdate: 9/19/1929
Birthplace: Baltimore, MD
Information Available in These Sources: ABYP 1, ABYP 3

DUNBAR, PAUL LAURENCE
Birthdate: 6/27/1872
Birthplace: Dayton, OH
Deathdate: 2/9/1906
Information Available in These Sources: BAI, SATA 34

DUNBAR, ROBERT E(VERETT)
Birthdate: 11/24/1926
Birthplace: Quincy, MA
Information Available in These Sources: SATA 32

DUNCAN, GREGORY
See McClintock, Marshall

DUNCAN, LOIS S(TEINMETZ)
(Lois Arquette, Lois (Steinmetz) Cardozo, Lois Kerry)
Birthdate: 4/28/1934
Birthplace: Philadelphia, PA
Information Available in These Sources: ABYP2, ABYP 3, DACF, JBA 5, SAIA 1, SATA 36, TCCW 2, TCCW 3

DUNCAN, NORMAN
Birthdate: 7/2/1871
Birthplace: Brantford, Ontario, Canada
Deathdate: 10/18/1916
Information Available in These Sources: JBA 1, JBA 2, YABC

DUNLAP, HOPE
Birthdate: 2/26/1880
Birthplace: Topeka, KS
Information Available in These Sources: ICB 1

DUNLAP, LON
See McCormick, Wilfred

DUNN, HARVEY T(HOMAS)
Birthdate: 3/8/1884
Birthplace: Manchester, SD
Deathdate: 10/29/1952
Information Available in These Sources: ICB 1, SATA 34

DUNN, JUDY
See Spangenberg, Judith Dunn

DUNN, MARY LOIS
Birthdate: 8/18/1930
Birthplace: Uvalde, TX
Information Available in These Sources: ABYP 4, DACF, SATA 6

DUNNAHOO, TERRY
Birthdate: 12/8/1927
Birthplace: Fall River, MA
Information Available in These Sources: SATA 7

DUNNE, MARY COLLINS
(Regina Moore)
Birthdate: 1/15/1914
Birthplace: County Down, Ireland
Information Available in These Sources: ABYP 4, SATA 11

DUNNING, ARTHUR STEPHEN, JR.
(Stephen Dunning)
Birthdate: 10/31/1924
Birthplace: Duluth, MN
Information Available in These Sources: ABYP 4

DUNNING, STEPHEN
See Dunning, Arthur Stephen, Jr.

DUNNINGTON, TOM
Information Available in These Sources: IBYP 1, IBYP 2

DUNREA, OLIVIER
Birthdate: 9/22/1953
Birthplace: Virginia Beach, VA
Information Available in These Sources: SATA 46, 59

DUPUY, T(REVOR) N(EVITT)
Birthdate: 5/3/1916
Birthplace: New York, NY
Information Available in These Sources: ABYP 2, ABYP 3, SATA 4

DURANT, JOHN
Birthdate: 1/10/1902
Birthplace: Waterbury, CT
Information Available in These Sources: ABYP 1, ABYP 3, SATA 27

DURELL, ANN
Birthdate: 9/20/1930
Birthplace: Belleplain, NJ
Information Available in These Sources: ABYP 2, ABYP 3

DURLACHER, ED(WIN)
Information Available in These Sources: ABYP 1, ABYP 3

DUSOE, ROBERT C(OLEMAN)
Birthdate: 11/, /1892
Birthplace: Los Angeles, CA
Deathdate: 1958
Information Available in These Sources: MJA, YABC

DUTZ
See Davis, Mary Octavia

DUVAL, KATHERINE
See James, Elizabeth

DUVALL, EVELYN MILLIS
Birthdate: 7/28/1906
Birthplace: Oswego, NY
Information Available in These Sources: SATA 9

DUVOISIN, ROGER (ANTOINE)
Birthdate: 8/28/1904
Birthplace: Geneva, Switzerland
Deathdate: 6/30/1980
Information Available in These Sources: ABYP 1, ABYP 3, AICB, BABP, DLB 61, IBYP 1, IBYP 2, ICB 1 ICB 2, ICB 3, ICB 4, JBA 2, SATA 2, SATA 23, SATA 30, SVC 2, SVC 3, TCCW 1, TCCW 2

DWIGGINS, DON
Birthdate: 11/15/1913
Birthplace: Plainfield, NJ
Deathdate: 12/10/1988
Information Available in These Sources: ABYP 4, SATA 4, SATA 60

DWIGGINS, WILLIAM ADDISON
Birthdate: 6/19/1880
Birthplace: Martinsville, OH
Deathdate: 12/25/1956
Information Available in These Sources: ICB 1, ICB 2

DWIGHT, ALLAN
See Cole, Lois Dwight

DYER, T(HOMAS) A(LLAN)
Birthdate: 8/19/1947
Birthplace: Newburg, OR
Information Available in These Sources: DACF

DYGARD, THOMAS J.
Birthdate: 8/10/1931
Birthplace: Little Rock, AR
Information Available in These Sources: JBA 6, SATA 24

E

EAGER, EDWARD (MCMAKEN)
Birthdate: 1911
Birthplace: Toledo, OH
Deathdate: 10/23/1964
Information Available in These Sources: ABYP 1, ABYP 3, DACF, DLB 22, MJA, SATA 17, TCCW 1, TCCW 2, TCCW 3, WCL

EAGER, GEORGE B.
Birthdate: 4/4/1921
Birthplace: Valdosta, GA
Information Available in These Sources: SATA 56

EAGLE, MIKE
Birthdate: 4/26/1942
Birthplace: Yonkers, NY
Information Available in These Sources: SATA 11

EAMES, GENEVIEVE TORREY
Birthplace: Pasadena, CA
Information Available in These Sources: ABYP 1, ABYP 3

EARLE, ALICE MORSE
See Earle, Mary Alice Morse

EARLE, EYVIND
Birthdate: 4/26/1916
Birthplace: New York, NY
Information Available in These Sources: ICB 2

EARLE, MARY ALICE MORSE
(Alice Morse Earle)
Birthdate: 4/27/1853
Birthplace: Worcester, MA
Deathdate: 2/16/1911
Information Available in These Sources: ABYP 4

EARLE, OLIVE (LYDIA)
Birthdate: 1888
Birthplace: London, England
Information Available in These Sources: IBYP 2, ICB 2, ICB 3, ICB 4, MJA, SATA 7

EARLE, VANA
Birthdate: 4/6/1917
Information Available in These Sources: ICB 2

EASTMAN, CHARLES A(LEXANDER)
(Ohiyesa)
Birthdate: 1858
Birthplace: Redwood Falls, MN
Deathdate: 1/8/1939
Information Available in These Sources: JBA 1, JBA 2, YABC

EASTMAN, P(HILIP) D(EY)
Birthdate: 11/25/1909
Birthplace: Amherst, MA
Deathdate: 1/7/1986
Information Available in These Sources: ABYP 1, ABYP 3, ICB 3, SATA 33 SATA 46

EATON, ANNE T(HAXTER)
Birthdate: 5/8/1881
Birthplace: Beverly Farms, MA
Deathdate: 5/3/1971
Information Available in These Sources: SATA 32

EATON, GEORGE L.
See Verral, Charles Spain

EATON, JANET
See Givens, Janet E(aton)

EATON, JEANETTE
Birthdate: 11/30/1886
Birthplace: Columbus, OH
Deathdate: 2/19/1968
Information Available in These Sources: ABYP 4, JBA 1, JBA 2, SATA 24 SVC 2, SVC 3

EATON, TOM
Birthdate: 3/2/1940
Birthplace: Wichita, KS
Information Available in These Sources: IBYP 2, SATA 22

EATON, WALTER PRITCHARD
Birthdate: 1878
Deathdate: 1957
Information Available in These Sources: JBA 1, SVC 2

EBEL, ALEX
Birthdate: 11/14/1927
Birthplace: Mexico City, Mexico
Information Available in These Sources: SATA 11

EBERLE, IRMENGARDE
(Allyn Allen, Phyllis Ann Carter)
Birthdate: 11/11/1898
Birthplace: San Antonio, TX
Deathdate: 2/27/1979
Information Available in These Sources: ABYP 1, ABYP 3, JBA 2, SATA 2 SATA 23

EBERSTADT, CHARLES F.
(Frederick Eberstadt)
Birthdate: 1914
Deathdate: 6/29/1974
Information Available in These Sources: ABYP 1, ABYP 3

EBERSTADT, FREDERICK
See Eberstadt, Charles F.

EBERSTADT, ISABEL (NASH)
(Isabel Nash)
Birthdate: 1934?
Information Available in These Sources: ABYP 1, ABYP 3

EBY, LOIS CHRISTINE
(Patrick Lawson)
Birthdate: 1908
Birthplace: Wabash, IN
Information Available in These Sources: ABYP 1, ABYP 3

ECKBLAD, EDITH BERVEN
Birthdate: 4/14/1923
Birthplace: Baltic, SD
Information Available in These Sources: SATA 23

ECKERT, ALLAN W.
Birthdate: 1/30/1931
Birthplace: Buffalo, NY
Information Available in These Sources: ABYP 4, DACF, JBA 4, SATA 27, SATA 29

ECONOMAKIS, OLGA
Birthplace: San Francisco, CA
Information Available in These Sources: ABYP 2, ABYP 3

EDDINGS, CLAIRE NEFF
Information Available in These Sources: ABYP 4

EDELL, CELESTE
Information Available in These Sources: SATA 12

EDELMAN, ELAINE
Birthplace: Minneapolis, MN
Information Available in These Sources: SATA 50

EDELMAN, LILY (JUDITH)
Birthdate: 9/2/1915
Birthplace: San Francisco, CA
Deathdate: 1/22/1981
Information Available in These Sources: ABYP 1, ABYP 3, SATA 22

EDELSON, EDWARD
Birthdate: 9/10/1932
Birthplace: New York, NY
Information Available in These Sources: ABYP 4, SATA 51

EDENS, BISHOP DAVID
Birthdate: 2/11/1926
Birthplace: Sumter, SC
Information Available in These Sources: SATA 39

EDENS, COOPER
(Gary Drager)
Birthdate: 9/25/1945
Birthplace: Washington, DC
Information Available in These Sources: SATA 49

EDEY, MAITLAND A(RMSTRONG)
Birthdate: 2/13/1910
Birthplace: New York, NY
Information Available in These Sources: SATA 25

EDGUN
See Wulff, Edgun Valdemar

EDLER, TIMOTHY
Birthdate: 4/6/1948
Birthplace: New Iberia, LA
Information Available in These Sources: SATA 56

EDMONDS, I(VY) G(ORDON)
(Gary Gordon)
Birthdate: 2/15/1917
Birthplace: Frost, TX
Information Available in These Sources: ABYP 4, SATA 8

EDMONDS, RICHARD W.
Information Available in These Sources: ABYP 1, ABYP 3

EDMONDS, WALTER D(UMAUX)
Birthdate: 7/15/1903
Birthplace: Boonville, NY
Information Available in These Sources: ABYP 1, ABYP 3, DACF, MBMP, MJA, SATA 1, SATA 27, TCCW 1, TCCW 2, TCCW 3

EDMONDSON, MADELEINE
Information Available in These Sources: ABYP 4

EDMUND, SEAN
See Pringle, Laurence P.

EDSALL, MARIAN S(TICKNEY)
Birthdate: 4/24/1920
Birthplace: Chicago, IL
Information Available in These Sources: ABYP 4, SATA 8

EDWARDS, AGNES
See Pratt, Agnes Edwards Rothery

EDWARDS, AL
See Nourse, Alan E(dward)

EDWARDS, ALEXANDER
See Fleischer, Leonore

EDWARDS, ANNE
Birthdate: 8/20/1927
Birthplace: Port Chester, NY
Information Available in These Sources: SATA 35

EDWARDS, AUDREY
Birthdate: 4/21/1947
Birthplace: Tacoma, WA
Information Available in These Sources: BAI, SATA 31, SATA 52

EDWARDS, BRONWEN ELIZABETH
See Rose, Wendy

EDWARDS, CECILE (PEPIN)
Birthdate: 6/24/1916
Birthplace: Medfield, MA
Information Available in These Sources: ABYP 1, ABYP 3, SATA 25

EDWARDS, GEORGE WHARTON
Birthdate: 3/14/1869
Birthplace: Fairhaven, CT
Deathdate: 1/18/1950
Information Available in These Sources: ICB 1

EDWARDS, HARVEY
Birthdate: 5/10/1929
Birthplace: Long Beach, NY
Information Available in These Sources: ABYP 4, SATA 5

EDWARDS, JANE CAMPBELL
(Jane Campbell)
Birthdate: 3/31/1932
Birthplace: Miles City, MT
Information Available in These Sources: SATA 10

EDWARDS, JULIE (ANDREWS)
(Julie Andrews)
Birthdate: 10/1/1935
Birthplace: Walton-on-Thames, Surrey, England
Information Available in These Sources: ABYP 4, MBMP, SATA 7

EDWARDS, LINDA STRAUSS
Birthdate: 6/16/1948
Birthplace: White Plains, NY
Information Available in These Sources: SATA 42, SATA 49

EDWARDS, MARGARET (ALEXANDER)
Birthdate: 10/23/1902
Birthplace: Childress, TX
Deathdate: 4/19/1988
Information Available in These Sources: SATA 56

EDWARDS, P. E.
See Clyne, Patricia Edwards

EDWARDS, PAGE L., JR.
Birthdate: 1/15/1941
Birthplace: Gooding, ID
Information Available in These Sources: SATA 59

EDWARDS, SALLY (CARY)
Birthdate: 7/28/1929
Birthplace: Spartanburg, SC
Information Available in These Sources: SATA 7

EDWARDS, SAMUEL
See Gerson, Noel B(ertram)

EGAN, E(DWARD) W(ELSTEAD)
(Eamon Mac Aodhagain)
Birthdate: 3/26/1922
Birthplace: New York, NY
Information Available in These Sources: SATA 35

EGGENBERGER, DAVID
Birthdate: 7/25/1918
Birthplace: Pontiac, IL
Information Available in These Sources: SATA 6

EGGENHOFER, NICHOLAS
Birthdate: 1897
Birthplace: Bavaria
Information Available in These Sources: IBYP 1, IBYP 2

EGGLESTON, EDWARD
Birthdate: 12/10/1837
Birthplace: Vevay, IN
Deathdate: 9/3/1902
Information Available in These Sources: JBA 1, SATA 27

EGIELSKI, RICHARD
Birthdate: 7/16/1952
Birthplace: New York, NY
Information Available in These Sources: ICB 4, JBA 6, SATA 11, SATA 49

EGYPT, OPHELIA SETTLE
Birthdate: 2/20/1903
Birthplace: Clarksville, TX
Deathdate: 5/25/1984
Information Available in These Sources: BAI, SATA 16, SATA 38

EHLERT, LOIS (JANE)
Birthdate: 11/9/1934
Birthplace: Beaver Dam, WI
Information Available in These Sources: ICB 3, ICB 4, SATA 35

EHRLICH, AMY
Birthdate: 7/24/1942
Birthplace: New York, NY
Information Available in These Sources: SATA 25

EICHENBERG, FRITZ
Birthdate: 10/24/1901
Birthplace: Cologne, Germany
Information Available in These Sources: IBYP 2, ICB 1, ICB 2, ICB 3, ICB 4, MJA, SATA 9, SATA 50, SVC 2, SVC 3

EICHNER, JAMES A.
Birthdate: 11/30/1927
Birthplace: Rochester, NY
Information Available in These Sources: SATA 4

EICKE, EDNA
Birthplace: Montclair, NJ
Information Available in These Sources: IBYP 1, IBYP 2

EIFERT, VIRGINIA (LOUISE) S(NIDER)
Birthdate: 1/23/1911
Birthplace: Springfield, IL
Deathdate: 6/17/1966
Information Available in These Sources: ABYP 1, ABYP 3, SATA 2

EINSEL, NAIAD
Birthplace: Philadelphia, PA
Information Available in These Sources: SATA 10

EINSEL, WALTER
Birthdate: 10/10/1926
Birthplace: New York, NY
Information Available in These Sources: ABYP 2, ABYP 3, SATA 10

EISEMAN, ALBERTA
Birthdate: 11/2/1925
Birthplace: Venice, Italy
Information Available in These Sources: ABYP 4, SATA 15

EISENBERG, AZRIEL
Birthdate: 8/29/1903
Birthplace: Russia
Information Available in These Sources: ABYP 1, ABYP 3, SATA 12

EISENBERG, LISA
Birthdate: 4/19/1949
Birthplace: Flushing, NY
Information Available in These Sources: SATA 50, SATA 57

EISENBERG, PHYLLIS ROSE
Birthdate: 1/26/1924 or 6/26/1924
Birthplace: Chicago, IL
Information Available in These Sources: SATA 41

EISNER, VIVIENNE
See Margolis, Vivienne

EISNER, VIVIENNE
See Margolis, Vivienne

EISNER, WILL(IAM ERWIN)
(Will Erwin, Willis Rensie)
Birthdate: 3/16/1917
Birthplace: New York, NY
Information Available in These Sources: SATA 31

EITZEN, ALLAN
Birthdate: 5/25/1928
Birthplace: Mountain Lake, MN
Information Available in These Sources: IBYP 1, IBYP 2, SATA 9

EITZEN, RUTH (CARPER)
Birthdate: 7/20/1924
Birthplace: Lititz, PA
Information Available in These Sources: SATA 9

ELAM, RICHARD M(ACE, JR.)
Birthdate: 7/16/1920
Birthplace: Richmond, VA
Information Available in These Sources: SATA 9

ELBERT, VIRGINIA FOWLER
Birthdate: 2/8/1912
Birthplace: Brooklyn, NY
Information Available in These Sources: ABYP 4

ELFMAN, BLOSSOM
Birthdate: 11/4/1925
Birthplace: New York, NY
Information Available in These Sources: SATA 8

ELGIN, KATHLEEN
Birthdate: 1/13/1923
Birthplace: Trenton, NJ
Information Available in These Sources: IBYP 2, ICB 2, ICB 3, SATA 39

ELIOT, ANNE
See Cole, Lois Dwight

ELIOT, FRANCES
Birthdate: 9/2/1901
Birthplace: Mt. Desert, ME
Information Available in These Sources: ICB 1

ELISOFON, ELIOT
Birthdate: 4/17/1911
Birthplace: New York, NY
Deathdate: 4/7/1973
Information Available in These Sources: SATA 21

ELIZABETH, ANNE
See Fleur, Anne (Elizabeth)

ELKIN, BENJAMIN
Birthdate: 8/10/1911
Birthplace: Baltimore, MD
Information Available in These Sources: ABYP 1, ABYP 3, JBA 4, SATA 3

ELKINS, DOV PERETZ
Birthdate: 12/7/1937
Birthplace: Philadelphia, PA
Information Available in These Sources: ABYP 2, ABYP 3, SATA 5

ELLEN, BARBARA
Birthdate: 12/19/1938
Birthplace: Brooklyn, NY
Information Available in These Sources: ABYP 2, ABYP 3

ELLENTUCK, SHAN
Birthplace: Brooklyn, NY
Information Available in These Sources: ABYP 4

ELLIOTT, ELIZABETH SHIPPEN GREEN
(Elizabeth Shippen Green)
Birthdate: 1871
Birthplace: Philadelphia, PA
Deathdate: 1954
Information Available in These Sources: CICB, ICB 1

ELLIOTT, SARAH M(CCARN)
Birthdate: 3/6/1930
Birthplace: Chicago, IL
Information Available in These Sources: ABYP 4, SATA 14

ELLIS, EDWARD S(YLVESTER)
(B. H. Belknap, J. G. Bethune, Captain L. C. Carleton, L. C. Carleton, Colonel H. R. Gordon, H. R. Gordon, Captain R. M. Hawthorne, R. M. Hawthorne, Lieutenant R. H. Jayne, R. H. Jayne, C. E. Lassalle, Seward D. Lisle, Billex Muller, J. H. Randolph, Lieutenant J. H. Randolph, Seelin Robins, Emerson Rodman, Captain Wheeler)
Birthdate: 4/11/1840
Birthplace: Geneva, OH
Deathdate: 6/20/1916
Information Available in These Sources: DLB 42, YABC

ELLIS, ELLA THORP
Birthdate: 7/14/1928
Birthplace: Los Angeles, CA
Information Available in These Sources: ABYP 4, JBA 5, SATA 7

ELLIS, HARRY BEARSE
Birthdate: 12/9/1921
Birthplace: Springfield, MA
Information Available in These Sources: ABYP 2, 3, SATA 9

ELLIS, HERBERT
See Wilson, Lionel

ELLIS, MEL(VIN RICHARD)
Birthdate: 2/21/1912
Birthplace: Beaver Dam, WI
Deathdate: 9/1/1984
Information Available in These Sources: SATA 7, SATA 39

ELLISON, LUCILE WATKINS
Birthdate: 1907?
Birthplace: Pennington, AL
Deathdate: 12/20/1979
Information Available in These Sources: SATA 22, 50

ELLISON, VIRGINIA HOWELL
(Virginia Tier Howell, Mary A. Mapes Virginia T. H. Mussey, V. H. Soskin, Leong Gor Yung)
Birthdate: 2/4/1910
Birthplace: New York, NY
Information Available in These Sources: ABYP 4, SATA 4

ELLSBERG, EDWARD
Birthdate: 11/21/1891
Birthplace: New Haven, CT
Deathdate: 1/24/1983
Information Available in These Sources: ABYP 1, ABYP 3, JBA 1, JBA 2, SATA 7

ELMER, IRENE (ELIZABETH)
Birthdate: 3/1/1937
Birthplace: Portland, OR
Information Available in These Sources: ABYP 2, ABYP 3

ELMORE, CAROLYN PATRICIA
(Patricia Elmore)
Birthdate: 11/21/1933
Birthplace: Miami, FL
Information Available in These Sources: SATA 35, SATA 38

ELMORE, PATRICIA
See Elmore, Carolyn Patricia

ELSPETH
See Bragdon, Elspeth (MacDuffie)

ELTING, MARY
(Benjamin Brewster, Davis Cole, Campbell Tatham)
Birthdate: 6/21/1906
Birthplace: Creede, CO
Information Available in These Sources: ABYP 2, ABYP 3, MJA, SATA 2

ELWART, JOAN POTTER
Birthdate: 8/27/1927
Birthplace: Detroit, MI
Information Available in These Sources: SATA 2

ELWOOD, ANN
Birthdate: 1/3/1931
Birthplace: Ridgewood, NJ
Information Available in These Sources: SATA 52, SATA 55

ELWOOD, ROGER
Birthdate: 1/13/1943
Birthplace: Atlantic City, NJ
Information Available in These Sources: ABYP 4, SATA 58

EMBERLEY, BARBARA A(NNE COLLINS)
Birthdate: 12/12/1932
Birthplace: Chicago, IL
Information Available in These Sources: BABP, FLTYP, JBA 3, SATA 8

EMBERLEY, ED(WARD RANDOLPH)
Birthdate: 10/19/1931
Birthplace: Malden, MA
Information Available in These Sources: ABYP 1, ABYP 3, AICB, BABP, FLTYP, IBYP 1, IBYP 2, ICB 3, ICB 4, JBA 3, SATA 8

EMBERLEY, MICHAEL
Birthdate: 6/2/1960
Birthplace: Boston, MA
Information Available in These Sources: SATA 34

EMBRY, MARGARET (JACOB)
Birthdate: 8/28/1919
Birthplace: Salt Lake City, UT
Information Available in These Sources: ABYP 4, SATA 5

EMERSON, ALICE B.
See Stratemeyer, Edward L.

EMERSON, CAROLINE D(WIGHT)
Birthdate: 3/14/1891
Birthplace: Amherst, MA
Deathdate: 12/19/1973
Information Available in These Sources: ABYP 1, ABYP 3

EMERSON, RALPH WALDO
Birthdate: 5/25/1803
Birthplace: Boston, MA
Deathdate: 4/27/1882
Information Available in These Sources: SVC 2, SVC 3

EMERSON, SYBIL (DAVIS)
Birthdate: 1895
Birthplace: Worcester, MA
Information Available in These Sources: ICB 1

EMERSON, WILLIAM K(EITH)
Birthdate: 5/1/1925
Birthplace: San Diego, CA
Information Available in These Sources: SATA 25

EMERY, ANNE (ELEANOR MCGUIGAN)
Birthdate: 9/1/1907
Birthplace: Fargo, ND
Information Available in These Sources: ABYP 1, ABYP 3, MJA, SATA 1, SATA 33

EMERY, RUSSELL GUY
Birthdate: 1908
Birthplace: MN
Information Available in These Sources: ABYP 1, ABYP 3

EMMENS, CAROL ANN
Birthdate: 10/12/1944
Birthplace: Newark, NJ
Information Available in These Sources: SATA 39

EMRICH, DUNCAN (BLACK MACDONALD)
(Blackie Macdonald)
Birthdate: 4/11/1908
Birthplace: Mardin, Turkey
Information Available in These Sources: ABYP 4, SATA 11

EMRY-PERROTT, JENNIFER
See Perrott, Jennifer

ENDERLE, JUDITH (ANN)
Birthdate: 11/26/1941
Birthplace: Detroit, MI
Information Available in These Sources: SATA 38

ENFIELD, CARRIE
See Smith, Susan Vernon

ENGDAHL, SYLVIA LOUISE
Birthdate: 11/24/1933
Birthplace: Los Angeles, CA
Information Available in These Sources: ABYP 4, DACF, JBA 4, SATA 4, TCCW 1, TCCW 2, TCCW 3

ENGELHART, MARGARET S(TEVENS)
Birthdate: 6/19/1924
Birthplace: Flint, MI
Information Available in These Sources: SATA 59

ENGEMAN, JOHN T.
Birthdate: 1901
Information Available in These Sources: ABYP 2, ABYP 3

ENGLE, ELOISE KATHERINE
Birthdate: 4/12/1923
Birthplace: Seattle, WA
Information Available in These Sources: SATA 9

ENGLISH, JAMES W(ILSON)
Birthdate: 1/13/1915
Birthplace: Phoenix, AZ
Information Available in These Sources: SATA 37

ENGVICK, WILLIAM
Birthplace: Oakland, CA
Information Available in These Sources: ABYP 2, ABYP 3

ENRIGHT, ELIZABETH (WRIGHT)
Birthdate: 9/17/1909
Birthplace: Oak Park, IL
Deathdate: 6/8/1968
Information Available in These Sources: ABYP 1, ABYP 3, DACF, DLB 22, ICB 1, ICB 2, JBA 2, SATA 9, TCCW 1, TCCW 2, TCCW 3, WC

ENRIGHT, MAGINEL WRIGHT
See Barney, Maginel Wright

EPHRON, DELIA
(Delia Brock)
Birthdate: 7/12/1944
Birthplace: Los Angeles, CA
Information Available in These Sources: SATA 50

EPPENSTEIN, LOUISE (KOHN)
Birthdate: 1892
Deathdate: 7/14/1987
Information Available in These Sources: SATA 54

EPPLE, ANNE ORTH
Birthdate: 2/9/1927
Birthplace: Tuckahoe, NY
Information Available in These Sources: SATA 20

EPSTEIN, ANNE MERRICK
Birthdate: 10/3/1931
Birthplace: Alplaus, NY
Information Available in These Sources: SATA 20

EPSTEIN, BERYL (M. WILLIAMS)
(Adam Allen, Douglas Coe, Martin Colt, Charles Strong, Beryl Williams)
Birthdate: 11/15/1910
Birthplace: Columbus, OH
Information Available in These Sources: ABYP 1, ABYP 3, MJA, SATA 1, SATA 31

EPSTEIN, PERLE S(HERRY)
Birthdate: 8/21/1938
Birthplace: New York, NY
Information Available in These Sources: ABYP 4, SATA 27

EPSTEIN, SAMUEL
(Adam Allen, Bruce Campbell, Douglas Coe, Martin Colt, Charles Strong)
Birthdate: 11/22/1909
Birthplace: Boston, MA
Information Available in These Sources: ABYP 1, ABYP 3, MJA, SATA 1, SATA 31

ERDMAN, LOULA GRACE
Birthplace: Alma, MO
Information Available in These Sources: ABYP 1, ABYP 3, MJA, SATA 1

ERDOES, RICHARD
Birthdate: 7/7/1912
Birthplace: Vienna, Austria
Information Available in These Sources: IBYP 1, IBYP 2, ICB 3, SATA 28SATA 33

ERHARD, WALTER
Birthdate: 6/14/1920
Birthplace: Mount Vernon, NY
Information Available in These Sources: ICB 3, SATA 30

ERICKSON, PHOEBE
Birthdate: 11/23/1907
Birthplace: North Bay, WI
Information Available in These Sources: ABYP 1, ABYP 3, ICB 2, SATA 59

ERICKSON, RUSSELL E(VERETT)
Birthdate: 7/8/1932
Birthplace: Hartford, CT
Information Available in These Sources: ABYP 4, SATA 27

ERICKSON, SABRA R(OLLINS)
(Sabra Holbrook)
Birthdate: 2/12/1912
Birthplace: Worcester, MA
Information Available in These Sources: SATA 35

ERICSON, WALTER
See Fast, Howard (Melvin)

ERIKSON, MEL
Birthdate: 3/3/1937
Birthplace: Brooklyn, NY
Information Available in These Sources: IBYP 2, SATA 31

ERLANGER, BABA
See Trahey, Jane

ERLANGER, ELLEN (LOUISE)
Birthdate: 11/14/1950
Birthplace: Canton, OH
Information Available in These Sources: SATA 52

ERLICH, LILLIAN (FELDMAN)
Birthdate: 3/7/1910
Birthplace: Johnstown, PA
Information Available in These Sources: ABYP 1, ABYP 3, SATA 10

ERNEST, BROTHER
See Brother Ernest

ERNEST, WILLIAM
See Berkebile, Fred D(onovan)

ERNST, KATHRYN (FITZGERALD)
Birthdate: 11/12/1942
Birthplace: New York, NY
Information Available in These Sources: SATA 25

ERNST, LISA CAMPBELL
Birthdate: 3/13/1957
Birthplace: Bartlesville, OK
Information Available in These Sources: SATA 44, SATA 55

ERNST, LYMAN JOHN
(Dorothy A. Chernoff, David Allen Clark)
Birthdate: 9/1/1940
Birthplace: New York, NY
Information Available in These Sources: SATA 39

ERVIN, JANET HALLIDAY
Birthdate: 5/29/1923
Birthplace: Muncie, IN
Information Available in These Sources: SATA 4

ERWIN, BETTY K.
Information Available in These Sources: ABYP 4, DACF

ERWIN, WILL
See Eisner, Will(iam Erwin)

ESBENSEN, BARBARA JUSTER
Information Available in These Sources: SATA 53

ESHERICK, JOSEPH
Birthdate: 12/28/1914
Birthplace: Philadelphia, PA
Information Available in These Sources: ABYP 4

ESHMEYER, R(EINHART) E(RNST)
Birthdate: 5/2/1898
Birthplace: Knoxville (near), OH
Information Available in These Sources: SATA 29

ESPELAND, PAMELA (LEE)
Birthdate: 8/19/1951
Birthplace: Oak Park, IL
Information Available in These Sources: SATA 38, SATA 52

ESPENSHADE, EDWARD BOWMAN, JR.
Birthdate: 10/23/1910
Birthplace: Chicago, IL
Information Available in These Sources: ABYP 4

ESPY, WILLARD R(ICHARDSON)
Birthdate: 12/11/1910
Birthplace: Olympia, WA
Information Available in These Sources: SATA 38

ESTEP, IRENE (COMPTON)
Birthdate: 1/28
Birthplace: Wood River, NE
Information Available in These Sources: SATA 5

ESTES, ELEANOR (RUTH)
Birthdate: 5/9/1906
Birthplace: West Haven, CT
Deathdate: 7/15/1988
Information Available in These Sources: ABYP 1, ABYP 3, DACF, DLB 22, ICB 2, JBA 2, MBMP, SATA 4, SATA 7, SATA 56, SVC 2, SVC 3 TCCW 1, TCCW 2, TCCW 3

ETCHEMENDY, NANCY
Birthdate: 2/19/1952
Birthplace: Reno, NV
Information Available in These Sources: SATA 38

ETCHISON, BIRDIE L(EE)
(Leigh Hunter, Catherine Wood)
Birthdate: 6/22/1937
Birthplace: San Diego, CA
Information Available in These Sources: SATA 38

ETS, MARIE HALL
Birthdate: 12/16/1893 or 12/16/1895
Birthplace: Milwaukee (N. Greenfield), WI
Information Available in These Sources: ABYP 1, ABYP 3, AICB, BABP, DLB 22, IBYP 1, IBYP 2, ICB 1 ICB 2, ICB 3, ICB 4, JBA 2, SATA 2, SVC 2, SVC 3, TCCW 1, TCCW 2, TCCW 3

EUNSON, DALE
Birthdate: 8/15/1904
Birthplace: Neillsville, WI
Information Available in These Sources: SATA 5

EUNSON, ROBY
Birthplace: Globe, AZ
Information Available in These Sources: ABYP 4

EVANOFF, VLAD
Birthdate: 12/12/1906
Birthplace: New York, NY
Information Available in These Sources: SATA 59

EVANS, EDNA HOFFMAN
Birthdate: 1913
Information Available in These Sources: ABYP 1, ABYP 3

EVANS, EVA KNOX
Birthdate: 8/17/1905
Birthplace: Roanoke, VA
Information Available in These Sources: ABYP 1, ABYP 3, MJA, SATA 27

EVANS, KATHERINE (FLOYD)
Birthdate: 1/2/1899 or 1/2/1901
Birthplace: Sedalia, MO
Deathdate: 8/8/1964
Information Available in These Sources: ABYP 1, ABYP 3, ICB 3, SATA 5

EVANS, MARI
Birthdate: 7/16/1923 or 7/16/1926
Birthplace: Toledo, OH
Information Available in These Sources: ABYP 4, BAI, SATA 10

EVANS, MARK
Birthplace: St. Louis, MO
Information Available in These Sources: SATA 19

EVANS, PATRICIA HEALY
See Carpenter, Patricia (Healy Evans)

EVANS, PAULINE RUSH
Information Available in These Sources: ABYP 4

EVANS, SHIRLEE
Birthdate: 9/4/1931
Birthplace: Centralia, WA
Information Available in These Sources: SATA 58

EVARTS, ESTHER
See Benson, Sally

EVARTS, HAL G. (,JR.)
Birthdate: 2/8/1915
Birthplace: Hutchinson, KS
Information Available in These Sources: ABYP 4, DACF, SATA 6

EVERETT, GAIL
See Hale, Arlene

EVERNDEN, MARGERY
Birthdate: 6/6/1916
Birthplace: Okeechobee, FL
Information Available in These Sources: SATA 5

EVERS, ALF
Birthdate: 1905
Information Available in These Sources: ABYP 1, ABYP 3

EVSLIN, BERNARD
Birthdate: 4/9/1922
Birthplace: Philadelphia, PA
Information Available in These Sources: ABYP 4, SATA 28, SATA 45

EWEN, DAVID
Birthdate: 11/26/1907
Birthplace: Lwow, Austria
Deathdate: 12/28/1985
Information Available in These Sources: ABYP 2, ABYP 3, SATA 4, SATA 47

EWING, KATHRYN
(Kathryn Douglas)
Birthdate: 4/12/1921
Birthplace: Jenkintown, PA
Information Available in These Sources: ABYP 4, SATA 20

EYERLY, JEANETTE HYDE
(Jeannette Griffith)
Birthdate: 6/7/1908
Birthplace: Topeka, KS
Information Available in These Sources: ABYP 4, DACF, JBA 5, SATA 4

EYRE, DOROTHY
See McGuire, Leslie (Sarah)

EYRE, KATHERINE WIGMORE
Birthdate: 9/23/1901
Birthplace: Los Angeles, CA
Deathdate: 2/27/1970
Information Available in These Sources: MJA, SATA 26

EZZELL, MARILYN
Birthdate: 3/11/1937
Birthplace: Teaneck, NJ
Information Available in These Sources: SATA 38, SATA 42

F

FABE, MAXENE
Birthdate: 5/22/1943
Birthplace: Atlanta, GA
Information Available in These Sources: SATA 15

FABELL, WALTER C.
Information Available in These Sources: ABYP 2, ABYP 3

FABER, DORIS (GREENBERG)
Birthdate: 1/29/1924
Birthplace: New York, NY
Information Available in These Sources: ABYP 1, ABYP 3, SATA 3

FABER, HAROLD
Birthdate: 9/12/1919
Birthplace: New York, NY
Information Available in These Sources: ABYP 3, SATA 5

FABRES, OSCAR
Birthdate: 7/5/1900
Birthplace: Santiago, Chile
Information Available in These Sources: IBYP 2, ICB 2

FABRIZIUS, PETER
See Knight, Max

FACKLAM, MARGERY METZ
Birthdate: 9/6/1927
Birthplace: Buffalo, NY
Information Available in These Sources: ABYP 4, SATA 20

FADIMAN, CLIFTON (PAUL)
Birthdate: 5/15/1904
Birthplace: Brooklyn, NY
Information Available in These Sources: SATA 11

FAIRMAN, JOAN A(LEXANDRA)
Birthdate: 4/11/1935
Birthplace: Philadelphia, PA
Information Available in These Sources: SATA 10

FAITHFULL, GAIL
(Gail Faithfull Keller)
Birthdate: 11/20/1936
Birthplace: New York, NY
Information Available in These Sources: SATA 8

FALKNER, LEONARD
Birthdate: 7/7/1900
Birthplace: Cleveland, OH
Deathdate: 2/22/1977
Information Available in These Sources: SATA 12

FALL, THOMAS
See Snow, Donald Clifford

FALLS, C(HARLES) B(UCKLES)
Birthdate: 12/10/1874
Birthplace: Fort Wayne, IN
Deathdate: 4/15/1960
Information Available in These Sources: ABYP 2, ABYP 3, ICB 1, ICB 2, JBA 1, JBA 2, SATA 27, SATA 38

FALSTEIN, LOUIS
Birthdate: 5/1/1909
Birthplace: Nemirov, Ukraine, Russia
Information Available in These Sources: SATA 37

FANNING, LEONARD M(ULLIKEN)
Birthdate: 7/4/1888
Birthplace: New Rockford, ND
Deathdate: 12/29/1967
Information Available in These Sources: SATA 5

FARALLA, DANA
(Dorothy W. Faralla, Dana Wilma)
Birthdate: 8/4/1909
Birthplace: Renville, MN
Information Available in These Sources: SATA 9

FARALLA, DOROTHY W.
See Faralla, Dana

FARB, PETER
Birthdate: 7/25/1929
Birthplace: New York, NY
Deathdate: 4/8/1980
Information Available in These Sources: ABYP 4, SATA 12, SATA 22

FARBER, NORMA
Birthdate: 8/6/1909
Birthplace: Boston, MA
Deathdate: 3/21/1984
Information Available in These Sources: ABYP 4, DLB 61, JBA 5, SATA 25SATA 38, TCCW 2, TCCW 3

FARGO, LUCILE FOSTER
Birthdate: 10/18/1880
Birthplace: Madison, WI
Deathdate: 7/5/1962
Information Available in These Sources: ABYP 1, ABYP 3

FARLEY, CAROL (J. MCDOLE)
(Carol McDole)
Birthdate: 12/20/1936
Birthplace: Ludington, MI
Information Available in These Sources: ABYP 4, DACF, JBA 5, SATA 4

FARLEY, WALTER (LORIMER)
Birthdate: 6/26/1915 , 6/26/1920, or 6/26/1922
Birthplace: Syracuse, NY
Information Available in These Sources: ABYP 1, ABYP 3, DLB 22, JBA 2 MBMP, SATA 2, SATA 43, TCCW 1 TCCW 2, TCCW 3

FARMER, WENDELL
See Davis, Lavinia (Riker)

FARNHAM, BURT
See Clifford, Harold B(urton)

FARQUHAR, MARGARET C(UTTING)
Birthdate: 10/6/1905
Birthplace: Worcester, MA
Information Available in These Sources: SATA 13

FARQUHARSON, ALEXANDER
Birthdate: 6/13/1944
Birthplace: Boston, MA
Information Available in These Sources: SATA 46

FARQUHARSON, MARTHA
See Finley, Martha

FARR, FINIS (KING)
Birthdate: 12/31/1904
Birthplace: Lebanon, TN
Deathdate: 1/3/1982
Information Available in These Sources: SATA 10

FARRAR, JOHN C(HIPMAN)
(John Prosper)
Birthdate: 2/25/1896
Birthplace: Burlington, VT
Deathdate: 11/6/1974
Information Available in These Sources: SVC 2, SVC 3

FARRAR, SUSAN CLEMENT
Birthdate: 11/10/1917
Birthplace: Billerica, MA
Information Available in These Sources: SATA 33

FARRELL, BEN
See Cebulash, Mel

FARRINGTON, S(ELWYN) KIP, JR.
Birthdate: 5/7/1904
Birthplace: Orange, NJ
Deathdate: 2/7/1983
Information Available in These Sources: ABYP 1, ABYP 3, SATA 20

FASSLER, JOAN (GRACE)
Birthdate: 9/23/1931
Birthplace: New York, NY
Information Available in These Sources: SATA 11

FAST, HOWARD (MELVIN)
(E. V. Cunningham, Walter Ericson)
Birthdate: 11/11/1914
Birthplace: New York, NY
Information Available in These Sources: ABYP 1, ABYP 3, SATA 7

FATHER XAVIER
See Hurwood, Bernhardt J.

FATIGATI, EVELYN DE BUHR
See Fatigati, Frances Evelyn de Buhr

FATIGATI, FRANCES EVELYN DE BUHR
(Evelyn de Buhr Fatigati)
Birthdate: 2/4/1948
Birthplace: Washington, MO
Information Available in These Sources: SATA 24

FATIO, LOUISE
Birthdate: 8/18/1904
Birthplace: Lausanne, Switzerland
Information Available in These Sources: BABP, MJA, SATA 6, TCCW 1, TCCW 2, TCCW 3

FAULHABER, MARTHA
Birthdate: 9/6/1926
Birthplace: Dayton, OH
Information Available in These Sources: SATA 7

FAULKNER, ANNE IRVIN
See Faulkner, Nancy (Anne Irvin)

FAULKNER, GEORGENE
(Story lady)
Birthdate: 10/6/1873
Birthplace: Chicago, IL
Information Available in These Sources: ABYP 2, ABYP 3

FAULKNER, JOHN
Birthdate: 1922
Information Available in These Sources: IBYP 1, IBYP 2

FAULKNER, NANCY (ANNE IRVIN)
(Anne Irvin Faulkner)
Birthdate: 1/8/1906
Birthplace: Lynchburg, VA
Information Available in These Sources: ABYP 1, ABYP 3, DACF, JBA 4, SATA 23

FAUSET, JESSIE (REDMON)
Birthdate: 1884?
Birthplace: Snow Hill, NJ
Deathdate: 4/30/1961
Information Available in These Sources: BAI

FAVA, RITA F.
Birthdate: 6/2/1932
Birthplace: Rome, Italy
Information Available in These Sources: ICB 2

FAX, ELTON CLAY
Birthdate: 10/9/1909
Birthplace: Baltimore, MD
Information Available in These Sources: BAI, ICB 4, SATA 25

FAXON, LAVINIA
See Russ, Lavinia

FEAGLES, ANITA MACRAE
(Travis MacRae)
Birthdate: 9/27/1927 or 9/27/1926
Birthplace: Chicago (Galesburg), IL
Information Available in These Sources: ABYP 2, ABYP 3, JBA 4, SATA 9

FEAGLES, ELIZABETH
See Day, Beth (Feagles)

FEAGUE, MILDRED H.
Birthdate: 5/30/1915
Birthplace: Sharon, PA
Information Available in These Sources: SATA 14

FEASER, DANIEL DAVID
Birthdate: 5/28/1920
Birthplace: Dauphin, PA
Information Available in These Sources: IBYP 1, IBYP 2, ICB 3

FEDER, PAULA (KURZBAND)
Birthdate: 11/5/1935
Birthplace: New York, NY
Information Available in These Sources: SATA 26

FEDER, ROBERT ARTHUR
(Robert Arthur)
Birthdate: 11/1/1909
Birthplace: New York, NY
Deathdate: 4/28/1969
Information Available in These Sources: ABYP 4, SATA 35

FEELINGS, MURIEL (GREY)
Birthdate: 7/31/1938
Birthplace: Philadelphia, PA
Information Available in These Sources: BAI, FLTYP, JBA 4, SATA 16

FEELINGS, THOMAS
(Tom Feelings)
Birthdate: 5/19/1933
Birthplace: Brooklyn, NY
Information Available in These Sources: BABP, BAI, FLTYP, IBYP 1, IBYP 2, ICB 4, JBA 3, SATA 8

FEELINGS, TOM
See Feelings, Thomas

FEHRENBACH, T(HEODORE) R(EED, JR.)
Birthdate: 1/12/1925
Birthplace: San Benito, TX
Information Available in These Sources: SATA 33

FEIFFER, JULES
Birthdate: 1/26/1929
Birthplace: Bronx, NY
Information Available in These Sources: SATA 8

FEIG, BARBARA KRANE
Birthdate: 11/8/1937
Birthplace: Mitchell, SD
Information Available in These Sources: SATA 34

FEIKEMA, FEIKE
See Manfred, Frederick F(eikema)

FEIL, HILA
Birthdate: 6/29/1942
Birthplace: New York, NY
Information Available in These Sources: SATA 12

FEILEN, JOHN
See May, Julian

FEINBERG, BARBARA JANE
(Barbara Silberdick Feinberg)
Birthdate: 6/1/1938
Birthplace: New York, NY
Information Available in These Sources: SATA 58

FEINBERG, BARBARA SILBERDICK
See Feinberg, Barbara Jane

FELDER, ELEANOR
Information Available in These Sources: ABYP 4

FELDMAN, ANNE (RODGERS)
Birthdate: 7/19/1939
Birthplace: Pittsburgh, PA
Information Available in These Sources: SATA 19

FELLER, ROBERT WILLIAM ANDREW
Birthdate: 11/3/1918
Birthplace: Van Meter, IA
Information Available in These Sources: ABYP 2, ABYP 3

FELLNER, RUDOLPH
Information Available in These Sources: ABYP 2, ABYP 3

FELLOWS, MURIEL H.
Information Available in These Sources: ABYP 1, ABYP 3, SATA 10

FELSEN, GREGOR
See Felsen, Henry Gregor

FELSEN, HENRY GREGOR
(Gregor Felsen, Angus Vicker)
Birthdate: 8/16/1916
Birthplace: Brooklyn, NY
Information Available in These Sources: ABYP 1, ABYP 3, JBA 2, SATA 1

FELT, SUE
Birthdate: 12/7/1924
Birthplace: Oakland, CA
Information Available in These Sources: ICB 2

FELTON, HAROLD W(ILLIAM)
Birthdate: 4/1/1902
Birthplace: Neola, IA
Information Available in These Sources: ABYP 2, ABYP 3, MJA, SATA 1

FELTS, SHIRLEY
Birthdate: 3/1/1934
Birthplace: WV
Information Available in These Sources: SATA 33

FENDERSON, LEWIS H.
Birthdate: 7/22/1907
Birthplace: Baltimore, MD
Deathdate: 12/12/1983
Information Available in These Sources: SATA 37, SATA 47

FENNER, CAROL (ELIZABETH)
(Carol Williams)
Birthdate: 9/30/1929
Birthplace: New York (Almond), NY
Information Available in These Sources: ICB 3, ICB 4, SATA 7

FENNER, PHYLLIS REID
Birthdate: 10/24/1899
Birthplace: Almond, NY
Deathdate: 2/26/1982
Information Available in These Sources: ABYP 1, ABYP 3, SATA 1, SATA 29

FENTEN, BARBARA D(ORIS)
Birthdate: 8/25/1935
Birthplace: New York, NY
Information Available in These Sources: SATA 26

FENTEN, D(ONALD) X.
Birthdate: 1/3/1932
Birthplace: New York, NY
Information Available in These Sources: ABYP 4, SATA 4

FENTON, CARROLL LANE
Birthdate: 2/12/1900
Birthplace: Parkersburg, IA
Deathdate: 11/16/1969
Information Available in These Sources: ABYP 1, ABYP 3, FLTYP, MJA, SATA 5

FENTON, EDWARD
Birthdate: 7/7/1917
Birthplace: New York, NY
Information Available in These Sources: ABYP 3, DACF, JBA 3, SATA 7, TCCW 1, TCCW 2, TCCW 3

FENTON, MILDRED ADAMS
Birthdate: 1899
Birthplace: West Branch (Near), IA
Information Available in These Sources: ABYP 1, ABYP 3, FLTYP, MJA, SATA 21

FENWICK, PATTI
See Grider, Dorothy

FERAVOLO, ROCCO VINCENT
Birthdate: 5/12/1922
Birthplace: Newark, NJ
Information Available in These Sources: ABYP 1, ABYP 3, SATA 10

FERBER, EDNA
Birthdate: 8/15/1887
Birthplace: Kalamazoo, MI
Deathdate: 4/16/1968
Information Available in These Sources: JBA 1, SATA 7

FERGUSON, BOB
See Ferguson, Robert Bruce

FERGUSON, CECIL
Birthdate: 3/13/1931
Birthplace: Chicago, IL
Information Available in These Sources: SATA 45

FERGUSON, ROBERT BRUCE
(Bob Ferguson)
Birthdate: 12/30/1927
Birthplace: Willow Springs, MO
Information Available in These Sources: SATA 13

FERGUSON, WALTER (W.)
Birthdate: 7/14/1930
Birthplace: New York, NY
Information Available in These Sources: IBYP 1, IBYP 2, ICB 2, SATA 34

FERGUSSON, ERNA
Birthdate: 1/10/1888
Birthplace: Albuquerque, NM
Deathdate: 7/30/1964
Information Available in These Sources: SATA 5

FERMI, LAURA (CAPON)
Birthdate: 6/16/1907
Birthplace: Rome, Italy
Deathdate: 12/26/1977
Information Available in These Sources: ABYP 1, ABYP 3, SATA 6, SATA 28

FERN, EUGENE A.
Birthdate: 9/29/1919
Birthplace: Detroit, MI
Deathdate: 9/6/1987
Information Available in These Sources: SATA 10, SATA 54

FERRIER, LUCY
See Penzler, Otto

FERRIS, HELEN JOSEPHINE
Birthdate: 11/19/1890
Birthplace: Hastings, NE
Deathdate: 9/28/1969
Information Available in These Sources: ABYP 1, ABYP 3, JBA 1, JBA 2, SATA 21, SVC 2

FERRIS, JAMES CODY
See Stratemeyer, Edward L.

FERRIS, JEAN
Birthdate: 1/24/1939
Birthplace: Fort Leavenworth, KS
Information Available in These Sources: SATA 50, SATA 56

FERRY, CHARLES
Birthdate: 10/8/1927
Birthplace: Chicago, IL
Information Available in These Sources: SATA 43

FETZ, INGRID
Birthdate: 3/8/1915
Birthplace: New York, NY
Information Available in These Sources: IBYP 1, IBYP 2, ICB 3, SATA 30

FEYDY, ANNE LINDBERGH
See Sapieyevski, Anne Lindbergh

FIAMMENGHI, GIOIA
Birthdate: 9/29/1929
Birthplace: New York, NY
Information Available in These Sources: IBYP 1, IBYP 2, ICB 2, ICB 3, ICB 4, SATA 9

FIAROTTA, NOEL
(Noel Ficarotta)
Birthdate: 3/13/1944
Birthplace: Meriden, CT
Information Available in These Sources: SATA 15

FIAROTTA, PHYLLIS
(Phyllis Ficarotta)
Birthdate: 8/21/1942
Birthplace: Meriden, CT
Information Available in These Sources: SATA 15

FICAROTTA, NOEL
See Fiarotta, Noel

FICAROTTA, PHYLLIS
See Fiarotta, Phyllis

FICHTER, GEORGE S.
(Matt Warner)
Birthdate: 9/17/1922
Birthplace: Reily, OH
Information Available in These Sources: ABYP 4, SATA 7

FIEDEL, ROSLYN
Information Available in These Sources: ABYP 4

FIEDLER, JEAN(NETTE FELDMAN)
Birthdate: 1923
Birthplace: Pittsburgh, PA
Information Available in These Sources: SATA 4

FIELD, EDWARD
Birthdate: 6/7/1924
Birthplace: Brooklyn, NY
Information Available in These Sources: SATA 8

FIELD, ELINOR WHITNEY
(Whitney Field)
Birthdate: 1889
Deathdate: 11/24/1980
Information Available in These Sources: SATA 28

FIELD, EUGENE
Birthdate: 9/3/1850
Birthplace: St. Louis, MO
Deathdate: 11/4/1895
Information Available in These Sources: ABYP 2, ABYP 3, DLB 42, JBA 1 SATA 16, SVC 2, SVC 3

FIELD, GANS T.
See Wellman, Manly Wade

FIELD, PETER
See Hobson, Laura Z(ametkin)

FIELD, RACHEL (LYMAN)
Birthdate: 9/19/1894
Birthplace: New York, NY
Deathdate: 3/15/1942
Information Available in These Sources: ABYP 1, ABYP 3, DLB 22, JBA 1 JBA 2, SATA 15, SVC 2, SVC 3, TCCW 1, TCCW 2, TCCW 3, WC

FIELD, WHITNEY
See Field, Elinor Whitney

FIFE, DALE (ODILE)
Birthdate: 8/24/1910
Birthplace: Toledo, OH
Information Available in These Sources: ABYP 4, JBA 4, SATA 18

FIGUEROA, PABLO
Birthdate: 1/26/1938
Birthplace: Santurce, PR
Information Available in These Sources: SATA 9

FIJAN, CAROL
Birthdate: 2/18/1918
Birthplace: Milwaukee, WI
Information Available in These Sources: SATA 12

FILLMORE, PARKER H(OYSTED)
Birthdate: 9/21/1878
Birthplace: Cincinnati, OH
Deathdate: 6/5/1944
Information Available in These Sources: JBA 1, JBA 2, YABC

FILSTRUP, CHRIS
See Filstrup, E(dward) Christian

FILSTRUP, E(DWARD) CHRISTIAN
(Chris Filstrup)
Birthdate: 5/9/1942
Birthplace: Hollywood, CA
Information Available in These Sources: SATA 43

FILSTRUP, JANE MERRILL
See Merrill, Jane

FILSTRUP, JANIE
See Merrill, Jane

FINEMAN, MORTON
Information Available in These Sources: ABYP 4

FINGER, CHARLES J(OSEPH)
Birthdate: 12/25/1869 or 12/25/1871
Birthplace: Willesden, Sussex, England
Deathdate: 1/7/1941
Information Available in These Sources: ABYP 1, ABYP 3, JBA 1, SATA 42TCCW 2, TCCW 3

FINK, WILLIAM B(ERTRAND)
Birthdate: 5/11/1916
Birthplace: Yonkers, NY
Information Available in These Sources: SATA 22

FINKE, BLYTHE F(OOTE)
Birthdate: 12/24/1922
Birthplace: Pasadena, CA
Information Available in These Sources: SATA 26

FINLAYSON, ANN
Birthdate: 3/25/1925
Birthplace: New York, NY
Information Available in These Sources: SATA 8

FINLEY, MARTHA
(Martha Farquharson)
Birthdate: 4/26/1828
Birthplace: Chillicothe, OH
Deathdate: 1/30/1909
Information Available in These Sources: DLB 42, SATA 43, TCCW 2, TCCW 3, WCL

FINNEY, GERTRUDE E. (BRIDGEMAN)
Birthdate: 5/13/1892
Birthplace: Morocco, IN
Information Available in These Sources: ABYP 2, ABYP 3

FINTA, ALEXANDER
Birthdate: 6/12/1881
Birthplace: Turkeve, Hungary
Information Available in These Sources: ICB 1

FISCHBACH, JULIUS
Birthdate: 4/25/1894
Birthplace: Huntington, WV
Information Available in These Sources: SATA 10

FISCHER, ANN A.
Birthplace: Peoria, IL
Information Available in These Sources: IBYP 1, IBYP 2

FISCHER, ANTON OTTO
Birthdate: 2/23/1882
Birthplace: Munich, Germany
Deathdate: 3/26/1964
Information Available in These Sources: ICB 1, ICB 2

FISCHLER, STAN(LEY I.)
Birthdate: 1932
Information Available in These Sources: SATA 36

FISCHSTROM, HARVEY
See Zemach, Harve

FISCHSTROM, MARGOT ZEMACH
See Zemach, Margot

FISHBACK, MARGARET
See Antolini, Margaret Fishback

FISHER, AILEEN (LUCIA)
Birthdate: 9/9/1906
Birthplace: Iron River, MI
Information Available in These Sources: ABYP 2, ABYP 3, BABP, MJA, SATA 1, SATA 25, TCCW 1, TCCW 2, TCCW 3

FISHER, BARBARA
(Barbara Fisher Perry)
Birthdate: 12/10/1940
Birthplace: New York, NY
Information Available in These Sources: SATA 34, SATA 44

FISHER, CALVIN C(ARGILL)
Birthdate: 7/12/1912
Birthplace: Arlington, NJ
Information Available in These Sources: SATA 24

FISHER, CLAY
See Allen, Henry Wilson

FISHER, DOROTHY (FRANCES) CANFIELD
(Dorothy Canfield)
Birthdate: 2/17/1879
Birthplace: Lawrence, KS
Deathdate: 11/9/1958
Information Available in These Sources: ABYP 4, JBA 1, TCCW 1, TCCW 2 TCCW 3, YABC

FISHER, LAURA HARRISON
Birthdate: 5/11/1934
Birthplace: Malad, ID
Information Available in These Sources: SATA 5

FISHER, LEONARD EVERETT
Birthdate: 6/24/1924
Birthplace: New York, NY
Information Available in These Sources: ABYP 2, ABYP 3, DLB 61, ICB 2 ICB 3, ICB 4, JBA 3, MBMP, SATA 4, SATA 34

FISHER, LOIS I.
Birthdate: 12/8/1948
Birthplace: Bronx, NY
Information Available in These Sources: SATA 35, SATA 38

FISHLER, MARY (SHIVERICK)
Birthdate: 9/2/1920
Birthplace: Chicago, IL
Information Available in These Sources: ABYP 4

FITCH, CLARKE
See Sinclair, Upton (Beall)

FITCH, FLORENCE MARY
Birthdate: 2/17/1875
Birthplace: Stratford, CT
Deathdate: 6/2/1959
Information Available in These Sources: ABYP 1, ABYP 3, MJA

FITCH, JOHN IV
See Cormier, Robert (Edmund)

FITSCHEN, DALE
Birthdate: 10/13/1937
Birthplace: St. Louis, MO
Information Available in These Sources: SATA 20

FITZ-RANDOLPH, JANE (CURRENS)
Birthdate: 6/23/1915
Birthplace: Boulder, CO
Information Available in These Sources: SATA 51

FITZALAN, ROGER
See Trevor, Elleston

FITZGERALD, CAPTAIN HUGH
See Baum, L(yman) Frank

FITZGERALD, CATHLEEN
Birthdate: 7/1/1932
Birthplace: Dublin, Ireland
Deathdate: 1/11/1987
Information Available in These Sources: SATA 50

FITZGERALD, EDWARD EARL
Birthdate: 9/10/1919
Birthplace: New York, NY
Information Available in These Sources: ABYP 2, ABYP 3, SATA 20

FITZGERALD, F(RANCIS) A(NTHONY)
Birthdate: 1/13/1940
Birthplace: Queens, NY
Information Available in These Sources: SATA 15

FITZGERALD, JOHN D(ENNIS)
Birthdate: 1907 or 1906
Birthplace: UT
Deathdate: 5/21/1988
Information Available in These Sources: ABYP 4, DACF, JBA 5, SATA 20, SATA 56, TCCW 2, TCCW 3

FITZHUGH, LOUISE (PERKINS)
Birthdate: 10/5/1928
Birthplace: Memphis, TN
Deathdate: 11/19/1974
Information Available in These Sources: ABYP 2, ABYP 3, DACF, JBA 3, SATA 1, SATA 24, SATA 45, TCCW 1, TCCW 2, TCCW 3

FITZSIMMONS, ROBERT
Birthplace: Newark, NJ
Information Available in These Sources: ABYP 2, ABYP 3

FLACK, MARJORIE
Birthdate: 10/23/1897
Birthplace: Greenport, Long Island, NY
Deathdate: 8/29/1958
Information Available in These Sources: ABYP 1, ABYP 3, ICB 1, ICB 2, JBA 1, JBA 2, SVC 2, SVC 3, TCCW 1, TCCW 2, TCCW 3, YABC

FLACK, NAOMI (JOHN WHITE)
(Naomi John, Naomi (John) Sellers)
Birthplace: OK
Information Available in These Sources: SATA 35, SATA 40

FLAHERTY, ROBERT JOSEPH
Birthdate: 2/16/1884
Birthplace: Iron Mountain, MI
Deathdate: 7/13/1951
Information Available in These Sources: ABYP 4

FLEISCHER, LENORE
(Alexander Edwards, Mike Roote, Allison Thomas)
Birthdate: 1934
Birthplace: New York, NY
Information Available in These Sources: SATA 47

FLEISCHER, MAX
Birthdate: 7/17/1889
Birthplace: Vienna, Austria
Deathdate: 9/11/1972
Information Available in These Sources: SATA 30

FLEISCHMAN, ALBERT SID(NEY)
(Sid Fleischman)
Birthdate: 3/16/1920
Birthplace: Brooklyn, NY
Information Available in These Sources: ABYP 2, ABYP 3, DACF, JBA 3, SATA 8, SATA 59, TCCW 1, TCCW 2, TCCW 3

FLEISCHMAN, PAUL (TAYLOR)
Birthdate: 9/5/1952
Birthplace: Monterey, CA
Information Available in These Sources: JBA 5, SATA 32, SATA 39, TCCW 3

FLEISCHMAN, SEYMOUR
Birthdate: 1/29/1918
Birthplace: Chicago, IL
Information Available in These Sources: IBYP 1, IBYP 2, ICB 2, ICB 3, SATA 32

FLEISCHMAN, SID
See Fleischman, Albert Sid(ney)

FLEISCHMANN, GLEN HARVEY
Birthdate: 2/23/1909
Birthplace: Manley, NE
Information Available in These Sources: ABYP 4

FLEISHER, ROBBIN
Birthdate: 1/6/1951
Birthplace: Brooklyn, NY
Deathdate: 4/26/1977
Information Available in These Sources: SATA 49, SATA 52

FLEMING, ALICE MULCAHEY
Birthdate: 12/21/1928
Birthplace: New Haven, CT
Information Available in These Sources: ABYP 2, ABYP 3, SATA 9

FLEMING, ELIZABETH P.
Birthdate: 1888
Birthplace: Morioka, Japan
Deathdate: 12/16/1985
Information Available in These Sources: ABYP 2, ABYP 3, SATA 48

FLEMING, RONALD LEE
Birthdate: 5/13/1941
Birthplace: Los Angeles, CA
Information Available in These Sources: SATA 56

FLEMING, SUSAN
Birthdate: 6/12/1932
Birthplace: Eliot, ME
Information Available in These Sources: SATA 32

FLEMING, THOMAS J(AMES)
(Christopher Cain, T. F. James, J. F. Thomas)
Birthdate: 7/5/1927
Birthplace: Jersey City, NJ
Information Available in These Sources: ABYP 4, SATA 8

FLENDER, HAROLD
Birthdate: 10/29/1924
Birthplace: New York, NY
Information Available in These Sources: ABYP 4

FLESCH, YOLANDE (CATARINA)
(Yvonne Greene)
Birthdate: 8/20/1950
Birthplace: Arnheim, Netherlands
Information Available in These Sources: SATA 55

FLETCHER, ALAN MARK
Birthdate: 5/19/1928
Birthplace: Conklin, NY
Information Available in These Sources: ABYP 4

FLETCHER, BEALE
Birthplace: Asheville, NC
Information Available in These Sources: ABYP 1, ABYP 3

FLETCHER, CHARLIE MAY HOGUE
(Charlie May (Hogue) Simon)
Birthdate: 8/17/1897
Birthplace: Monticello, AR
Information Available in These Sources: ABYP 1, ABYP 3, JBA 2, SATA 3

FLETCHER, COLIN
Birthdate: 3/14/1922
Birthplace: Cardiff, Wales
Information Available in These Sources: SATA 28

FLETCHER, HELEN JILL
(Carol Lee, Charles Morey)
Birthdate: 2/25/1911
Birthplace: New York, NY
Information Available in These Sources: ABYP 2, ABYP 3, SATA 13

FLETCHER, RICHARD E.
(Rick Fletcher)
Birthdate: 1917
Deathdate: 3/16/1983
Information Available in These Sources: SATA 34

FLETCHER, RICK
See Fletcher, Richard E.

FLEUR, ANNE (ELIZABETH)
(Anne Elizabeth, Anne Fleur Lancaster, Sari)
Birthdate: 1901
Birthplace: Lancaster, PA
Information Available in These Sources: IBYP 2, ICB 2, SATA 31

FLEURET, SEBASTIAN
See Wegen, Ron(ald)

FLEXNER, JAMES THOMAS
Birthdate: 1/13/1908
Birthplace: New York, NY
Information Available in These Sources: SATA 9

FLITNER, DAVID P(ERKINS)
Birthdate: 1/3/1949
Birthplace: Boston, MA
Information Available in These Sources: SATA 7

FLOETHE, LOUISE LEE
Birthdate: 3/13/1913
Birthplace: New York, NY
Information Available in These Sources: ABYP 1, ABYP 3, SATA 4

FLOETHE, RICHARD
Birthdate: 9/2/1901
Birthplace: Essen, Germany
Information Available in These Sources: ICB 1, ICB 2, ICB 3, ICB 4, MJA, SATA 4

FLOHERTY, JOHN JOSEPH
Birthdate: 4/28/1882
Birthplace: Ireland
Deathdate: 12/3/1964
Information Available in These Sources: ABYP 1, ABYP 3, JBA 2, SATA 25

FLOOD, FLASH
See Robinson, Jan M.

FLORA, JAMES (ROYER)
Birthdate: 1/25/1914
Birthplace: Bellefontaine, OH
Information Available in These Sources: ABYP 4, CFB, IBYP 2, ICB 2, ICB 3, JBA 3, SATA 1, SATA 30 TCCW 1, TCCW 2, TCCW 3

FLORENCE
See Wabbes, Maria

FLORIAN, DOUGLAS
Birthdate: 3/18/1950
Birthplace: New York, NY
Information Available in These Sources: SATA 19, JBA6

FLORY, JANE TRESCOTT
Birthdate: 6/29/1917
Birthplace: Wilkes-Barre, PA
Information Available in These Sources: ABYP 4, SATA 22

FLOURNOY, VALERIE R.
Birthdate: 1952
Birthplace: Palmyra, NJ
Information Available in These Sources: BAI

FLYNN, BARBARA
Birthdate: 10/12/1928
Birthplace: Culver City, CA
Information Available in These Sources: SATA 9

FLYNN, JACKSON
See Shirreffs, Gordon D(onald)

FLYNN, JAMES JOSEPH
Birthdate: 9/1/1911
Birthplace: Brooklyn, NY
Information Available in These Sources: ABYP 4

FLYNN, MARY
See Welsh, Mary Flynn

FODOR, RONALD V(ICTOR)
Birthdate: 6/10/1944
Birthplace: Cleveland, OH
Information Available in These Sources: SATA 25

FOLEY, ANNA BERNICE WILLIAMS
(Bernice Williams Foley)
Birthdate: 11/20/1902
Birthplace: Wigginsville, OH
Information Available in These Sources: SATA 28

FOLEY, ANNE LINDBERGH
See Sapieyevski, Anne Lindbergh

FOLEY, BERNICE WILLIAMS
See Foley, Anna Bernice Williams

FOLEY, DANIEL JOSEPH
Birthdate: 1/19/1913
Birthplace: Salem, MA
Information Available in These Sources: ABYP 2, ABYP 3

FOLEY, JUNE
Birthdate: 6/6/1944
Birthplace: Trenton, NJ
Information Available in These Sources: SATA 44

FOLEY, LOUISE MUNRO
See Foley, Mary Louise Munro

FOLEY, MARY LOUISE MUNRO
(Louise Munro Foley)
Birthdate: 10/22/1933
Birthplace: Toronto, Ontario, Canada
Information Available in These Sources: ABYP 4, SATA 40, SATA 54

FOLEY, RAE
See Denniston, Elinore

FOLEY, SCOTT
See Dareff, Hal

FOLLEN, ELIZA LEE (CABOT)
Birthdate: 8/15/1787
Birthplace: Boston, MA
Deathdate: 1/26/1860
Information Available in These Sources: SVC 2, SVC 3

FOLLETT, HELEN (THOMAS)
Birthdate: 1884?
Deathdate: 4/21/1970
Information Available in These Sources: ABYP 2, ABYP 3, SATA 27

FOLSOM, FRANKLIN (BREWSTER)
(Benjamin Brewster, Samuel Cutler, Michael Gorham, Lyman Hopkins, Troy Nesbit)
Birthdate: 7/21/1907
Birthplace: Boulder, CO
Information Available in These Sources: ABYP 2, ABYP 3, SATA 5

FOLSOM, MICHAEL (BREWSTER)
Birthdate: 1938
Birthplace: New York, NY
Information Available in These Sources: ABYP 3, SATA 40

FON EISEN, ANTHONY T.
Birthdate: 5/20/1917
Birthplace: Avon, CT
Information Available in These Sources: DACF

FONTENOT, MARY ALICE
Birthdate: 4/16/1910
Birthplace: Eunice, LA
Information Available in These Sources: SATA 34

FOON, DENNIS
Birthdate: 11/18/1951
Birthplace: Detroit, MI
Information Available in These Sources: TCCW 3

FOONER, MICHAEL
Birthplace: London, England
Information Available in These Sources: ABYP 4, SATA 22

FOOTE, TIMOTHY (GILSON)
Birthdate: 5/3/1926
Birthplace: London, England
Information Available in These Sources: SATA 52

FORBERG, ATI
See Forberg, Beate Gropius

FORBERG, BEATE GROPIUS
(Ati Forberg)
Birthdate: 12/19/1925
Birthplace: Germany
Information Available in These Sources: ABYP 2, ABYP 3, ICB 3, JBA 4, SATA 22

FORBES, CABOT L.
See Hoyt, Edwin P(almer), Jr.

FORBES, ESTHER
Birthdate: 6/28/1891
Birthplace: Westborough, MA
Deathdate: 8/12/1967
Information Available in These Sources: ABYP 1, ABYP 3, DLB 22, MJA, SATA 2, TCCW 1, TCCW 2, TCCW 3

FORBES, GRAHAM B.
See Stratemeyer, Edward L.

FORBES, KATHERINE (RUSSELL)
Birthdate: 1956
Birthplace: NH
Information Available in These Sources: ABYP 2, ABYP 3

FORBES, KATHRYN
See McLean, Kathryn (Anderson)

FORD, BARBARA
Birthplace: St. Louis, MO
Information Available in These Sources: SATA 34, SATA 56

FORD, GEORGE (CEPHAS, JR.)
Birthdate: 1936
Birthplace: Brooklyn, NY
Information Available in These Sources: BAI, ICB 4, SATA 31

FORD, HILDEGARDE
See Morrison, Velma Ford

FORD, LAUREN
Birthdate: 1/23/1891
Birthplace: New York, NY
Information Available in These Sources: ABYP 2, ABYP 3, ICB 1, ICB 2

FORD, MARCIA
See Radford, Ruby L(orraine)

FORD, NANCY K(EFFER)
Birthdate: 4/1/1906
Birthplace: Camp Hill, PA
Deathdate: 5/??/1961
Information Available in These Sources: ABYP 2, ABYP 3, SATA 29

FORD, PAMELA BALDWIN
See Baldwin-Ford, Pamela

FORD, PAUL LEICESTER
Birthdate: 3/23/1865
Birthplace: Brooklyn, NY
Deathdate: 5/8/1902
Information Available in These Sources: JBA 1

FORESTER, C(ECIL) S(COTT)
Birthdate: 8/27/1899
Birthplace: Cairo, Egypt
Deathdate: 4/2/1966
Information Available in These Sources: SATA 13

FORMAN, BRENDA
Birthdate: 8/1/1936
Birthplace: Hollywood, CA
Information Available in These Sources: ABYP 2, ABYP 3, SATA 4

FORMAN, HARRISON
Birthdate: 6/15/1904
Birthplace: Milwaukee, WI
Information Available in These Sources: ABYP 2, ABYP 3

FORMAN, JAMES DOUGLAS
Birthdate: 11/12/1932
Birthplace: Mineola, Long Island, NY
Information Available in These Sources: ABYP 2, ABYP 3, DACF, JBA 3, SATA 8

FORREST, SYBIL
See Markun, Patricia M(aloney)

FORRESTER, FRANK H.
Birthdate: 1919?
Birthplace: New York, NY
Deathdate: 5/21/1986
Information Available in These Sources: ABYP, 1, ABYP 3, SATA 52

FORRESTER, MARIAN
See Schachtel, Roger (Bernard)

FORRESTER, VICTORIA
Birthdate: 3/18/1940
Birthplace: Pasadena, CA
Information Available in These Sources: SATA 35, SATA 40

FORSEE, AYLESA
See Forsee, Frances Aylesa

FORSEE, FRANCES AYLESA
(Aylesa Forsee)
Birthdate: 8/03
Birthplace: Kirksville, MO
Information Available in These Sources: ABYP 4, SATA 1

FORSHAY-LUNSFORD, CIN
Birthdate: 5/2/1965
Birthplace: Syosset, NY
Information Available in These Sources: SATA 60

FORSYTH, GLORIA
Birthdate: 12/23/1923
Birthplace: Riverside, CA
Information Available in These Sources: ABYP 1, ABYP 3

FORT, PAUL
See Stockton, Francis Richard

FOSDICK, CHARLES AUSTIN
(Harry Castlemon)
Birthdate: 9/16/1842
Birthplace: Randolph, NY
Deathdate: 8/22/1915
Information Available in These Sources: DLB 42

FOSDICK, HARRY EMERSON
Birthdate: 5/24/1878
Birthplace: Buffalo, NY
Deathdate: 10/5/1969
Information Available in These Sources: ABYP 2, ABYP 3

FOSS, WILLIAM O(TTO)
Birthdate: 10/2/1918
Birthplace: Boston, MA
Information Available in These Sources: ABYP 2, ABYP 3

FOSTER, BRAD W.
Birthdate: 4/26/1955
Birthplace: San Antonio, TX
Information Available in These Sources: SATA 34

FOSTER, DORIS VAN LIEW
Birthdate: 11/9/1899
Birthplace: Bellaire, MI
Information Available in These Sources: SATA 10

FOSTER, E(LIZABETH) C(ONNELL)
Birthdate: 1/11/1902
Birthplace: Chicago, IL
Information Available in These Sources: ABYP 4, SATA 9

FOSTER, ELIZABETH
Birthdate: 7/1/1905
Birthplace: Cleveland, OH
Information Available in These Sources: ABYP 4, SATA 10

FOSTER, ELIZABETH VINCENT
Birthdate: 6/18/1902
Birthplace: Wilkes-Barre, PA
Information Available in These Sources: SATA 12

FOSTER, F. BLANCHE
Birthdate: 1/6/1919
Birthplace: Centerville, TN
Information Available in These Sources: SATA 11

FOSTER, G(EORGE) ALLEN
Birthdate: 3/28/1907
Birthplace: Plymouth, NH
Information Available in These Sources: ABYP 2, ABYP 3, SATA 26

FOSTER, GENEVIEVE (STUMP)
Birthdate: 4/13/1893
Birthplace: Oswego, NY
Deathdate: 8/30/1979
Information Available in These Sources: ABYP 2, ABYP 3, AICB, DLB 61, ICB 2, ICB 3, ICB 4, JBA 2, MBMP, SATA 2, SATA 23

FOSTER, HAL
See Foster, Harold Rudolf

FOSTER, HAROLD RUDOLF
(Hal Foster)
Birthdate: 8/16/1892
Birthplace: Halifax, Nova Scotia, Canada
Deathdate: 7/27/1982
Information Available in These Sources: SATA 31

FOSTER, JOANNA
(Joanna Foster Dougherty)
Birthdate: 7/30/1928
Birthplace: Chicago, IL
Information Available in These Sources: ABYP 4

FOSTER, JOHN T(HOMAS)
Birthdate: 7/19/1925
Birthplace: Chicago, IL
Information Available in These Sources: ABYP 4, SATA 8

FOSTER, LAURA LOUISE (JAMES)
Birthdate: 1/25/1918
Birthplace: Chillicothe, OH
Information Available in These Sources: ABYP 4, SATA 6

FOSTER, MARGARET LESSER
Birthdate: 1899?
Birthplace: MT
Deathdate: 11/21/1979
Information Available in These Sources: SATA 21

FOSTER, MARIAN CURTIS
(Mariana)
Birthdate: 1909
Birthplace: Cleveland, OH
Deathdate: 10/27/1978
Information Available in These Sources: ABYP 2, ABYP 3, ICB 2, ICB 3, JBA 3, SATA 23

FOSTER, SALLY
Birthplace: Baltimore, MD
Information Available in These Sources: SATA 58

FOWLKES, BRYAN
See Fulks, Bryan

FOX, CHARLES PHILIP
Birthdate: 5/27/1913
Birthplace: Milwaukee, WI
Information Available in These Sources: SATA 12

FOX, DOROTHEA M.
Birthdate: 11/16/1904
Birthplace: LaCrosse, WI
Information Available in These Sources: ABYP 4

FOX, DOROTHY
Birthplace: Oak Park, IL
Information Available in These Sources: ABYP 2, ABYP 3

FOX, ELEANOR
See St. John, Wylly Folk

FOX, FONTAINE TALBOT, JR.
Birthdate: 6/4/1884
Birthplace: Louisville, KY
Deathdate: 8/9/1964
Information Available in These Sources: SATA 23

FOX, FRED
Birthdate: 1903?
Deathdate: 8/27/1981
Information Available in These Sources: SATA 27

FOX, GRACE
See Anderson, Grace Fox

FOX, JOHN (WILLIAM), JR.
Birthdate: 12/16/1863
Birthplace: Stony Point, KY
Deathdate: 7/8/1919
Information Available in These Sources: JBA 1

FOX, LARRY
Information Available in These Sources: ABYP 4, SATA 30

FOX, LORRAINE
Birthdate: 5/22/1922
Birthplace: Brooklyn, NY
Deathdate: 3/26/1976
Information Available in These Sources: SATA 11, SATA 27

FOX, MARY VIRGINIA
Birthdate: 11/17/1919
Birthplace: Richmond, VA
Information Available in These Sources: ABYP 1, ABYP 3, SATA 39, SATA 44

FOX, MICHAEL WILSON
Birthdate: 8/13/1937
Birthplace: Bolton, England
Information Available in These Sources: ABYP 4, SATA 15

FOX, PAULA
Birthdate: 4/22/1923
Birthplace: New York, NY
Information Available in These Sources: ABYP 4, DACF, JBA 4, SATA 17, SATA 60, TCCW 1, TCCW 2, TCCW 3

FOX, ROBERT J.
Birthdate: 12/24/1927
Birthplace: Watertown, SD
Information Available in These Sources: SATA 33

FOX, SONNY
Birthdate: 6/17/1925
Birthplace: Brooklyn, NY
Information Available in These Sources: ABYP 4

FOX, WILLIAM WELLINGTON
Birthdate: 7/20/1909
Birthplace: Ontario, OR
Information Available in These Sources: ABYP 1, ABYP 3

FRACE, CHARLES
Birthdate: 2/18/1926
Birthplace: Mauch Chunk, PA
Information Available in These Sources: IBYP 2

FRADIN, DENNIS BRINDELL
Birthdate: 12/20/1945
Birthplace: Chicago, IL
Information Available in These Sources: SATA 29

FRAME, PAUL
Birthdate: 5/4/1913
Birthplace: Riderwood, MD
Information Available in These Sources: IBYP 1, IBYP 2, ICB 3, ICB 4, SATA 33, SATA 60

FRANCES, MISS
See Horwich, Frances (Rappaport)

FRANCHERE, RUTH
Birthdate: 11/10/1906
Birthplace: Mason City, IA
Information Available in These Sources: JBA 4, SATA 18

FRANCIS, CHARLES
See Holme, Bryan

FRANCIS, DEE
See Haas, Dorothy F.

FRANCIS, DOROTHY BRENNER
Birthdate: 11/30/1926
Birthplace: Lawrence, KS
Information Available in These Sources: SATA 10

FRANCIS, HENRY S.
Birthdate: 1925
Birthplace: Cambridge, MA
Information Available in These Sources: ABYP 2, ABYP 3

FRANCO, MARJORIE
Birthplace: Chicago, IL
Information Available in These Sources: SATA 38

FRANCOISE
See Seignobosc, Francoise

FRANK, DANIEL B.
Birthdate: 1/4/1956
Birthplace: Washington, DC
Information Available in These Sources: SATA 55

FRANK, HELENE
See Vautier, Ghislaine

FRANK, JOSETTE
Birthdate: 3/27/1893
Birthplace: New York, NY
Information Available in These Sources: ABYP 2, ABYP 3, SATA 10

FRANK, MARY
Birthdate: 2/4/1933
Birthplace: London, England
Information Available in These Sources: SATA 34

FRANK, R., JR.
See Ross, Frank (Xavier), Jr.

FRANKEL, BERNICE
Birthplace: New York, NY
Information Available in These Sources: SATA 9

FRANKEL, EDWARD
Birthdate: 6/4/1910
Birthplace: New York, NY
Information Available in These Sources: ABYP 2, ABYP 3, SATA 44

FRANKEL, JULIE
Birthdate: 6/24/1947
Birthplace: Los Angeles, CA
Information Available in These Sources: SATA 34, SATA 40

FRANKENBERG, ROBERT (CLINTON)
Birthdate: 3/19/1911
Birthplace: Mount Vernon, NY
Information Available in These Sources: IBYP 2, ICB 2, ICB 3, SATA 22

FRANKLIN, GEORGE CORY
Birthdate: 3/24/1872
Birthplace: Oswego, KS
Information Available in These Sources: MJA

FRANKLIN, HAROLD
Birthdate: 8/4/1920
Birthplace: Detroit, MI
Information Available in These Sources: SATA 13

FRANKLIN, MADELEINE
See L'Engle, Madeleine

FRANKLIN, MAX
See Deming, Richard

FRANKLIN, STEVE
See Stevens, Franklin

FRASCINO, EDWARD
Birthdate: 11/15/1938
Birthplace: Bronx, NY
Information Available in These Sources: IBYP 1, IBYP 2, JBA 5, SATA 33SATA 48

FRASCONI, ANTONIO
Birthdate: 4/28/1919 or 4/29/1919
Birthplace: Buenos Aires, Argentina
Information Available in These Sources: ABYP 1, ABYP 3, CFB, ICB 2, ICB 3, ICB 4, JBA 3, SATA 6, SATA 53

FRASER, BEATRICE
Information Available in These Sources: ABYP 1, ABYP 3

FRASER, BETTY (M.)
See Fraser, Elizabeth Marr

FRASER, ELIZABETH MARR
(Betty (M.) Fraser)
Birthdate: 2/25/1928
Birthplace: Boston, MA
Information Available in These Sources: IBYP 2, ICB 3, ICB 4, SATA 31

FRASER, FERRIN
Information Available in These Sources: ABYP 1, ABYP 3

FRAZER, ANDREW
See Marlowe, Stephen

FRAZETTA, FRANK
(Fritz Frazetta)
Birthdate: 2/9/1928
Birthplace: Brooklyn, NY
Information Available in These Sources: SATA 58

FRAZETTA, FRITZ
See Frazetta, Frank

FRAZIER, CARL
Information Available in These Sources: ABYP 4

FRAZIER, NETA LOHNES
Birthdate: 1890
Birthplace: Owosso, MI
Information Available in These Sources: ABYP 1, ABYP 3, SATA 7

FRAZIER, ROSALIE
Information Available in These Sources: ABYP 4

FREAS, LEN(WOOD)
Information Available in These Sources: IBYP 2

FREDERIC, MIKE
See Cox, William R(obert)

FREDERICKS, ARNOLD
See Kummer, Frederic Arnold

FREED, ALVYN M.
Birthdate: 6/19/1913
Birthplace: Philadelphia, PA
Information Available in These Sources: SATA 22

FREEDMAN, BENEDICT
Birthdate: 12/19/1919
Birthplace: New York, NY
Information Available in These Sources: SATA 27

FREEDMAN, NANCY
Birthdate: 7/4/1920
Birthplace: Chicago, IL
Information Available in These Sources: SATA 27

FREEDMAN, RUSSELL (BRUCE)
Birthdate: 10/11/1929
Birthplace: San Francisco, CA
Information Available in These Sources: ABYP 2, ABYP 3, SATA 16, JBA 6

FREEMAN, DON
Birthdate: 8/11/1908
Birthplace: San Diego, CA
Deathdate: 2/1/1978
Information Available in These Sources: ABYP 2, ABYP 3, BABP, ICB 2, ICB 3, ICB 4, MJA, SATA 17, TCCW 1, TCCW 2

FREEMAN, EUGENE
Birthdate: 2/16/1906
Birthplace: New York, NY
Information Available in These Sources: ABYP 2, ABYP 3

FREEMAN, IRA M(AXIMILIAN)
Birthdate: 8/15/1905
Birthplace: Chicago, IL
Information Available in These Sources: ABYP 1, ABYP 3, MJA, SATA 21

FREEMAN, LUCY (GREENBAUM)
Birthdate: 12/13/1916
Birthplace: New York, NY
Information Available in These Sources: SATA 24

FREEMAN, LYDIA
Birthdate: 1/13/1907
Birthplace: Tacoma, WA
Information Available in These Sources: MJA

FREEMAN, MAE (BLACKER)
Birthdate: 1907
Birthplace: Chicago, IL
Information Available in These Sources: ABYP 2, ABYP 3, MJA, SATA 25

FREEMAN, MARGARET
Birthdate: 5/13/1893
Birthplace: Cornwall-on-Hudson, NY
Information Available in These Sources: ICB 1

FREEMAN, MARY ELEANOR WILKINS
Birthdate: 10/31/1852
Birthplace: Randolph, MA
Deathdate: 3/13/1930
Information Available in These Sources: JBA 1

FREEMAN, PETER J.
See Calvert, Patricia

FREEMAN, SERGE HERBERT
Birthdate: 1925
Birthplace: Los Angeles, CA
Information Available in These Sources: ABYP 2, ABYP 3

FREEMAN, TONY
Information Available in These Sources: SATA 44

FREGOSI, CLAUDIA (ANNE MARIE)
Birthdate: 12/30/1946
Birthplace: Middlebury, VT
Information Available in These Sources: ABYP 4, SATA 24

FRENCH, ALLEN
Birthdate: 11/28/1870
Birthplace: Boston, MA
Deathdate: 10/6/1946
Information Available in These Sources: JBA 1, JBA 2, YABC

FRENCH, DOROTHY KAYSER
Birthdate: 2/11/1926
Birthplace: Milwaukee, WI
Information Available in These Sources: ABYP 2, ABYP 3, SATA 5

FRENCH, KATHRYN
See Mosesson, Gloria R(ubin)

FRENCH, MARION FLOOD
Birthdate: 1920
Information Available in These Sources: ABYP 2, ABYP 3

FRENCH, MICHAEL
Birthdate: 12/2/1944
Birthplace: Los Angeles, CA
Information Available in These Sources: SATA 38, SATA 49

FRENCH, PAUL
See Asimov, Isaac

FRESCHET, BERNIECE LOUISE (SPECK)
Birthdate: 8/4/1927
Birthplace: Miles City, MT
Information Available in These Sources: ABYP 4, JBA 4

FREUCHEN, PETER
Birthdate: 2/20/1886
Birthplace: Nykobing Falster, Denmark
Deathdate: 9/2/1957
Information Available in These Sources: ABYP 2, ABYP 3

FREUND, RUDOLF
Birthdate: 4/8/1915
Birthplace: Philadelphia, PA
Information Available in These Sources: IBYP 2, IBYP 2, ICB 1, ICB 2, SATA 28

FREW, MARIAN LARIVIERE
(Marian Lariviere)
Information Available in These Sources: ABYP 4

FREY, SHANEY
Birthplace: Baltimore, MD
Information Available in These Sources: ABYP 2, ABYP 3

FRIBOURG, MARJORIE G.
Birthdate: 4/26/1920
Birthplace: Chappaqua, NY
Information Available in These Sources: ABYP 2, ABYP 3

FRICK, C. H.
See Irwin, Constance Frick

FRICK, CONSTANCE
See Irwin, Constance Frick

FRIEDLANDER, JOANNE K(OHN)
Birthdate: 8/22/1930
Birthplace: Chicago, IL
Information Available in These Sources: ABYP 4, SATA 9

FRIEDMAN, ESTELLE (EHRENWALD)
Birthdate: 1/, /1920
Birthplace: Nashville, TN
Information Available in These Sources: ABYP 2, ABYP 3, SATA 7

FRIEDMAN, FRIEDA
Birthdate: 1905
Birthplace: Syracuse, NY
Information Available in These Sources: MJA, SATA 43

FRIEDMAN, INA R(OSEN)
Birthdate: 1/6/1926
Birthplace: Chester, PA
Information Available in These Sources: ABYP 4, SATA 41, SATA 49

FRIEDMAN, JUDI
Birthdate: 11/13/1935
Birthplace: Milwaukee, WI
Information Available in These Sources: SATA 59

FRIEDMAN, MARVIN
Birthdate: 9/26/1930
Birthplace: Chester, PA
Information Available in These Sources: SATA 33, SATA 42

FRIEDRICH, OTTO (ALVA)
Birthdate: 2/3/1929
Birthplace: Boston, MA?
Information Available in These Sources: SATA 33

FRIEDRICH, PRISCILLA
Birthdate: 8/13/1927
Birthplace: Peru
Information Available in These Sources: SATA 39

FRIENDLICH, DICK
See Friendlich, Richard J.

FRIENDLICH, RICHARD J.
(Dick Friendlich)
Birthdate: 1/20/1909
Birthplace: San Francisco, CA
Information Available in These Sources: ABYP 2, ABYP 3, SATA 11

FRIERMOOD, ELISABETH HAMILTON
Birthdate: 12/30/1903
Birthplace: Marion, IN
Information Available in These Sources: ABYP 2, ABYP 3, MJA, SATA 5

FRIMMER, STEVEN
Birthdate: 6/29/1928
Birthplace: New York, NY
Information Available in These Sources: ABYP 4, SATA 31

FRISBEE, LUCY POST
Information Available in These Sources: ABYP 2, ABYP 3

FRISCH, ROSE E.
Birthdate: 7/7/1918
Birthplace: New York, NY
Information Available in These Sources: ABYP 4

FRISKEY, MARGARET RICHARDS
(Elizabeth Sherman)
Birthdate: 3/1/1901
Birthplace: Moline, IL
Information Available in These Sources: ABYP 2, ABYP 3, SATA 5

FRITH, MICHAEL (K.)
(Rosetta Stone)
Information Available in These Sources: IBYP 2

FRITZ, JEAN (GUTTERY)
(Ann Scott)
Birthdate: 11/16/1915
Birthplace: Hankow, China
Information Available in These Sources: ABYP 1, ABYP 3, BC, DACF, JBA 3, MBMP, SATA 1, SATA 29, TCCW 1, TCCW 2, TCCW 3

FROEHLICH, MARGARET WALDEN
Birthdate: 6/17/1930
Birthplace: New Kensington, PA
Information Available in These Sources: SATA 56

FROMAN, ELIZABETH HULL
Birthdate: 4/26/1920
Birthplace: Minneapolis, MN
Deathdate: 1/11/1975
Information Available in These Sources: SATA 10

FROMAN, ROBERT (WINSLOW)
Birthdate: 5/25/1917
Birthplace: Big Timber, MT
Information Available in These Sources: ABYP 2, ABYP 3, JBA 4, SATA 8

FROMMER, HARVEY
Birthdate: 10/10/1937
Birthplace: Brooklyn, NY
Information Available in These Sources: SATA 41

FROST, A(RTHUR) B(URDETT)
Birthdate: 1/17/1851
Birthplace: Philadelphia, PA
Deathdate: 6/22/1928
Information Available in These Sources: SATA 19, SVC 2, SVC 3

FROST, ERICA
See Supraner, Robyn

FROST, FRANCES
Birthdate: 8/3/1905
Birthplace: St. Albans, VT
Deathdate: 2/11/1959
Information Available in These Sources: MJA, SVC 2, SVC 3

FROST, LESLEY
(Lesley Frost Ballantine)
Birthdate: 4/28/1899
Birthplace: Lawrence, MA
Deathdate: 7/9/1983
Information Available in These Sources: SATA 14, SATA 34

FROST, ROBERT (LEE)
Birthdate: 3/26/1874
Birthplace: San Francisco, CA
Deathdate: 1/29/1963
Information Available in These Sources: JBA 1, SATA 14, SVC 2, SVC 3

FRY, EDWARD BERNARD
Birthdate: 4/4/1925
Birthplace: Los Angeles, CA
Information Available in These Sources: SATA 35

FRYATT, NORMA R.
Information Available in These Sources: ABYP 2, ABYP 3

FUCHS, LUCY
Birthdate: 4/13/1935
Birthplace: OH
Information Available in These Sources: SATA 52

FUFUKA, KARAMA
(Sharon Antonia Morgan)
Birthdate: 1/30/1951
Birthplace: Chicago, IL
Information Available in These Sources: BAI

FUJIKAWA, GYO
Birthdate: 11/3/1908
Birthplace: Berkeley, CA
Information Available in These Sources: IBYP 2, ICB 3, JBA 4, SATA 30 SATA 39

FUKA, VLADIMIR
Birthdate: 2/25/1926
Birthplace: Pisek, Czechoslovakia
Deathdate: 3/29/1977
Information Available in These Sources: SATA 27

FULKS, BRYAN
(Bryan Fowlkes)
Birthdate: 6/21/1897
Birthplace: Heber Springs, AR
Information Available in These Sources: ABYP 4

FULLER, ALICE COOK
Birthplace: SD
Information Available in These Sources: ABYP 2, ABYP 3

FULLER, CATHERINE L(EUTHOLD)
Birthdate: 12/31/1916
Birthplace: Bucyrus, OH
Information Available in These Sources: SATA 9

FULLER, EDMUND (MAYBANK)
(Amicus Curiae)
Birthdate: 3/3/1914
Birthplace: Wilmington, DE
Information Available in These Sources: ABYP 2, ABYP 3, SATA 21

FULLER, IOLA
See McCoy, Iola Fuller

FULLER, LOIS HAMILTON
Birthdate: 8/13/1915
Birthplace: Bayonne, NJ
Information Available in These Sources: ABYP 4, SATA 11

FULLER, MARGARET
See Ossoli, Sarah Margaret (Fuller) marchesa d'

FULLER, RAYMOND TIFFT
Birthdate: 1889
Deathdate: 1960
Information Available in These Sources: ABYP 2, ABYP 3

FULTS, JOHN LEE
Birthdate: 3/14/1932
Birthplace: Bell Buckle, TN
Information Available in These Sources: SATA 33

FUNAI, MAMORU (ROLLAND)
Birthdate: 6/7/1932
Birthplace: Kauai, HI
Information Available in These Sources: ICB 3, SATA 46

FUNK, THOMPSON
(Tom Funk)
Birthdate: 7/18/1911
Birthplace: Brooklyn, NY
Information Available in These Sources: IBYP 2, SATA 7

FUNK, TOM
See Funk, Thompson

FUNKE, LEWIS
Birthdate: 1/25/1912
Birthplace: New York, NY
Information Available in These Sources: SATA 11

FURCHGOTT, TERRY
Birthdate: 7/29/1948
Birthplace: New York, NY
Information Available in These Sources: SATA 29

G

GACKENBACH, DICK
Birthdate: 2/9/1927
Birthplace: Allentown, PA
Information Available in These Sources: ABYP 4, JBA 5, SATA 30, SATA 48

GADDIS, VINCENT H.
Birthdate: 12/28/1913
Information Available in These Sources: SATA 35

GADLER, STEVE J.
Birthdate: 10/6/1905
Birthplace: Lead, SD
Information Available in These Sources: SATA 36

GAEDDERT, LOU ANN (BIGGE)
Birthdate: 6/20/1931
Birthplace: Garden City, KS
Information Available in These Sources: BABP, SATA 20

GAER, JOSEPH
Birthdate: 3/16/1897
Birthplace: Bessarabia, Russia
Information Available in These Sources: ABYP 2, ABYP 3, MJA

GAG, FLAVIA
Birthdate: 5/24/1907
Birthplace: New Ulm, MN
Deathdate: 10/12/1979
Information Available in These Sources: ABYP 1, ABYP 3, ICB 1, ICB 2, MJA, SATA 24

GAG, WANDA (HAZEL)
Birthdate: 3/11/1893
Birthplace: New Ulm, MN
Deathdate: 6/27/1946
Information Available in These Sources: ABYP 2, ABYP 3, DLB 22, ICB 1 JBA 1, JBA 2, TCCW 1, TCCW 2, TCCW 3, WC, YABC

GAGE, WILSON
See Steele, Mary Q(uintard Govan)

GAGLIARDO, RUTH GARVER
Birthdate: 9/6/1895?
Birthplace: Hastings, NE
Deathdate: 1/5/1980
Information Available in These Sources: ABYP 1, ABYP 3, SATA 22

GAINES, ERNEST J.
Birthdate: 1/15/1933
Birthplace: Oscar, LA
Information Available in These Sources: ABYP 4

GALDONE, PAUL
Birthdate: 6/2/1914
Birthplace: Budapest, Hungary
Deathdate: 11/7/1986
Information Available in These Sources: ABYP 2, ABYP 3, BABP, ICB 2, ICB 3, ICB 4, JBA 3, SATA 17, SATA 49

GALE, ZONA
Birthdate: 8/26/1874
Birthplace: Portage, WI
Deathdate: 12/27/1938
Information Available in These Sources: JBA 1

GALINSKY, ELLEN
Birthdate: 4/24/1942
Birthplace: Pittsburgh, PA
Information Available in These Sources: SATA 23

GALL, ALICE CREW
Birthdate: 1879
Birthplace: McConnelsville, OH
Deathdate: 1949
Information Available in: ABYP 1, 3, JBA 2

GALLANT, ROY (ARTHUR)
Birthdate: 4/17/1924
Birthplace: Portland, ME
Information Available in These Sources: ABYP 2, ABYP 3, JBA 5, SATA 4

GALLICO, PAUL (WILLIAM)
Birthdate: 7/26/1897
Birthplace: New York, NY
Deathdate: 7/15/1976
Information Available in These Sources: ABYP 4, SATA 13

GALLOB, EDWARD
Birthplace: Camden, NJ
Information Available in These Sources: ABYP 4

GALSTER, ROBERT
Birthdate: 7/19/1928
Birthplace: Dollville, IL
Information Available in These Sources: IBYP 1, IBYP 2, ICB 3

GALT, THOMAS FRANKLIN, JR.
(Tom Galt)
Birthdate: 7/29/1908
Birthplace: MI
Information Available in These Sources: MJA, SATA 5

GALT, TOM
See Galt, Thomas Franklin, Jr.

GAMERMAN, MARTHA
Birthdate: 6/13/1941
Birthplace: New York, NY
Information Available in These Sources: SATA 15

GAMMELL, STEPHEN
Birthdate: 2/10/1943
Birthplace: Des Moines, IA
Information Available in These Sources: JBA 5, SATA 53

GANNETT, RUTH CHRISMAN (ARENS)
Birthdate: 12/16/1896
Birthplace: Santa Ana, CA
Deathdate: 12/8/1979
Information Available in These Sources: ICB 2, MJA, SATA 33

GANNETT, RUTH STILES
(Ruth Gannett Kahn)
Birthdate: 8/12/1923
Birthplace: New York, NY
Information Available in These Sources: ABYP 1, ABYP 3, JBA 4, SATA 3 TCCW 1, TCCW 2, TCCW 3

GANNON, ROBERT (HAINES)
Birthdate: 3/5/1931
Birthplace: White Plains, NY
Information Available in These Sources: SATA 8

GANS, ROMA
Birthdate: 2/23/1894 or 2/22/1894
Birthplace: St. Cloud, MN
Information Available in These Sources: ABYP 4, JBA 5, SATA 45

GANT, ELIZABETH
Information Available in These Sources: ABYP 4

GANT, KATHERINE
Information Available in These Sources: ABYP 4

GANTOS, JACK
See Gantos, John (Bryan), Jr.

GANTOS, JOHN (BRYAN), JR.
(Jack Gantos)
Birthdate: 7/2/1951
Birthplace: Mount Pleasant, PA
Information Available in These Sources: ABYP 4, JBA 5, SATA 20

GANZ, YAFFA
Birthdate: 3/26/1938
Birthplace: Chicago, IL
Information Available in These Sources: SATA 52

GARBUTT, BERNARD
Birthdate: 8/25/1900
Birthplace: Ontario, CA
Information Available in These Sources: ICB 2, SATA 31

GARD, JANICE
See Latham, Jean Lee

GARD, ROBERT EDWARD
Birthdate: 7/3/1910
Birthplace: Iola, KS
Information Available in These Sources: ABYP 2, ABYP 3, SATA 18

GARD, SANFORD WAYNE
(Wayne Gard)
Birthdate: 6/21/1899
Birthplace: Brockton, IL
Deathdate: 9/24/1986
Information Available in These Sources: SATA 49

GARD, WAYNE
See Gard, Sanford Wayne

GARDEN, NANCY
Birthdate: 5/15/1938
Birthplace: Boston, MA
Information Available in These Sources: ABYP 4, JBA 5, SATA 12

GARDINER, JOHN REYNOLDS
Birthdate: 12/6/1944
Information Available in These Sources: JBA 6

GARDNER, BEAU
Birthdate: 8/28/1941
Birthplace: Oceanside, NY
Information Available in These Sources: SATA 50, JBA 6

GARDNER, DIC
See Gardner, Richard (M.)

GARDNER, JEANNE LEMONNIER
Birthplace: Chicago, IL
Information Available in These Sources: SATA 5

GARDNER, JOHN (CHAMPLIN, JR.)
Birthdate: 7/21/1933
Birthplace: Batavia, NY
Deathdate: 9/14/1982
Information Available in These Sources: ABYP 4, JBA 5, SATA 31, SATA 40

GARDNER, LILLIAN SOSKIN
Birthdate: 1907
Information Available in These Sources: ABYP 2, ABYP 3

GARDNER, MARTIN
Birthdate: 10/21/1914
Birthplace: Tulsa, OK
Information Available in These Sources: ABYP 4, SATA 16

GARDNER, RICHARD (M.)
(Clifford Anderson, John Carver, Richard Cummings, Dic Gardner, Arthur Orrmont, Richard Orth)
Birthdate: 8/26/1931
Birthplace: Bremerton, WA
Information Available in These Sources: ABYP 2, ABYP 3, SATA 24

GARDNER, RICHARD A.
Birthdate: 4/28/1931
Birthplace: New York, NY
Information Available in These Sources: ABYP 4, SATA 13

GARDNER, ROBERT
Birthdate: 1929
Information Available in These Sources: ABYP 4, SATA 43

GARDNER, SHELDON
Birthdate: 4/20/1934
Birthplace: Chelsea, MA
Information Available in These Sources: SATA 33

GARELICK, MAY
(Garel Clark)
Birthdate: 1910
Birthplace: Vobruisk, Russia
Information Available in These Sources: ABYP 2, ABYP 3, BABP, SATA 19

GARFIELD, JAMES B.
Birthdate: 9/19/1881
Birthplace: Atlanta, GA
Deathdate: 5/23/1984
Information Available in These Sources: SATA 6, SATA 38

GARIS, HOWARD R(OGER)
(Victor Appleton, Marion Davidson, Clarence Young)
Birthdate: 4/25/1873
Birthplace: Binghamton, NY
Deathdate: 11/5/1962
Information Available in These Sources: DLB 22, SATA 13

GARLAND, HAMLIN
See Garland, Hannibal Hamlin

GARLAND, HANNIBAL HAMLIN
(Hamlin Garland)
Birthdate: 9/14/1860
Birthplace: West Salem, WI
Deathdate: 3/4/1940
Information Available in These Sources: JBA 1, SVC 2, SVC 3

GARNER, ELVIRA (CARTER)
Birthdate: 5/24/1895
Birthplace: Lebanon, TN
Information Available in These Sources: ICB 1

GARNET, A. H.
See Slote, Alfred

GARRATY, JOHN A.
Birthdate: 7/4/1920
Birthplace: Brooklyn, NY
Information Available in These Sources: SATA 23

GARRET, MAXWELL R.
Birthdate: 4/18/1917
Birthplace: New York, NY
Information Available in These Sources: SATA 39

GARRETSON, VICTORIA DIANE
(Victoria Cox)
Birthdate: 11/12/1945
Birthplace: Roswell, NM
Information Available in These Sources: SATA 44

GARRETT, HELEN
Birthdate: 1895
Information Available in These Sources: ABYP 2, ABYP 3, SATA 21

GARRETT, RANDALL
See Silverberg, Robert

GARRIGUE, SHEILA
Birthdate: 12/30/1931
Birthplace: England
Information Available in These Sources: ABYP 4, SATA 21

GARRISON, BARBARA
Birthdate: 8/22/1931
Birthplace: London, England
Information Available in These Sources: SATA 19

GARRISON, FREDERICK
See Sinclair, Upton (Beall)

GARRISON, THEODOSIA
Birthdate: 1874
Birthplace: NJ
Information Available in These Sources: SVC 2, SVC 3

GARRISON, WEBB B(LACK)
(Gary Webster)
Birthdate: 7/19/1919
Birthplace: Covington, GA
Information Available in These Sources: SATA 25

GARSON, EUGENIA
Information Available in These Sources: ABYP 4

GARST, DORIS (SHANNON)
(Shannon Garst)
Birthdate: 7/24/1894 or 7/24/1899
Birthplace: Ironwood, MI
Information Available in These Sources: ABYP 1, ABYP 3, JBA 2, SATA 1

GARST, SHANNON
See Garst, Doris (Shannon)

GARTEN, JAN
Information Available in These Sources: ABYP 2, ABYP 3

GARTHWAITE, MARION H(OOK)
Birthdate: 12/17/1893
Birthplace: Oakland, CA
Information Available in These Sources: ABYP 1, ABYP 3, SATA 7

GARTON, MALINDA D(EAN)
Birthplace: Gallatin, MO
Deathdate: 5/8/1976
Information Available in These Sources: SATA 26

GASPERINI, JIM
Birthdate: 10/21/1952
Birthplace: Glen Cove, NY
Information Available in These Sources: SATA 49, SATA 54

GATES, DORIS
Birthdate: 11/26/1901
Birthplace: Mountain View, CA
Deathdate: 9/3/1987
Information Available in These Sources: ABYP 2, ABYP 3, AICB, DACF, DLB 22, JBA 2, SATA 1, SATA 34SATA 54, TCCW 1, TCCW 2, TCCW 3

GATES, FRIEDA
Birthdate: 5/30/1933
Birthplace: New York, NY
Information Available in These Sources: SATA 26

GATTI, ATTILIO
Birthdate: 1896
Birthplace: Voghera, Italy
Information Available in These Sources: ABYP 2, ABYP 3, JBA 2

GATTI, ELLEN MORGAN (WADDELL)
Birthplace: Springfield, MO
Information Available in These Sources: ABYP 2, ABYP 3, JBA 2

GAUCH, PATRICIA LEE
Birthdate: 1/3/1934
Birthplace: Detroit, MI
Information Available in These Sources: BC, JBA 5, SATA 26

GAUL, ALBRO T.
Birthplace: Brooklyn, NY
Information Available in These Sources: ABYP 1, ABYP 3

GAULT, CLARE S.
Birthdate: 3/20/1925
Birthplace: Oak Park, IL
Information Available in These Sources: SATA 36

GAULT, FRANK
Birthdate: 8/14/1926
Birthplace: Cameroun, West Africa
Information Available in These Sources: SATA 30, SATA 36

GAULT, WILLIAM CAMPBELL
(Will Duke, Roney Scott)
Birthdate: 3/9/1910
Birthplace: Milwaukee, WI
Information Available in These Sources: ABYP 1, ABYP 3, SATA 8

GAVER, BECKY
See Gaver, Rebecca

GAVER, REBECCA
(Becky Gaver)
Birthdate: 10/11/1952
Birthplace: Oakland, CA
Information Available in These Sources: SATA 20

GAY, AMELIA
See Hogarth, Grace (Weston Allen)

GAY, KATHLYN (MCGARRAHAN)
Birthdate: 3/4/1930
Birthplace: Zion, IL
Information Available in These Sources: ABYP 4, SATA 9

GAY, ZHENYA
Birthdate: 9/16/1906
Birthplace: Norwood, MA
Deathdate: 8/3/1978
Information Available in These Sources: ABYP 2, ABYP 3, ICB 1, ICB 2, MJA, SATA 19

GAYLE, ADDISON
Birthdate: 1932
Birthplace: Newport News, VA
Information Available in These Sources: BAI

GEARY, CLIFFORD N.
Birthdate: 1916
Birthplace: Somerville, Long Island, NY
Information Available in These Sources: IBYP 1, IBYP 2, ICB 2

GEE, MAURINE H.
Birthplace: MO
Information Available in These Sources: ABYP 4

GEER, CHARLES
Birthdate: 8/25/1922
Birthplace: Long Island, NY
Information Available in These Sources: IBYP 1, IBYP 2, ICB 2, ICB 3, SATA 32, SATA 42

GEHR, MARY
Birthplace: Chicago, IL
Information Available in These Sources: SATA 32

GEIS, DARLENE (STERN)
(Ralph Kelly, Jane London, Peter Stevens)
Birthdate: 4/8/1917 or 4/8/1916
Birthplace: Chicago, IL
Information Available in These Sources: ABYP 2, ABYP 3, SATA 7

GEISEL, HELEN
(Helen Marion Palmer)
Birthdate: 1898
Birthplace: New York, NY
Deathdate: 10/23/1967
Information Available in These Sources: ABYP 1, ABYP 3, SATA 26

GEISEL, THEODOR SEUSS
(Theo LeSieg, Rosetta Stone, Dr. Seuss)
Birthdate: 3/2/1904
Birthplace: Springfield, MA
Information Available in These Sources: ABYP 1, ABYP 3, AICB, BABP, CFB, DLB 61, ICB 1, ICB 2, ICB 3, ICB 4, MJA, SATA 1, SATA 28, SVC 2, SVC 3, TCCW 1 TCCW 2, TCCW 3, WCL

GEISERT, ARTHUR (FREDERICK)
Birthdate: 9/20/1941
Birthplace: Dallas, TX
Information Available in These Sources: SATA 52, SATA 56

GEKIERE, MADELEINE
Birthdate: 5/15/1919
Birthplace: Zurich, Switzerland
Information Available in These Sources: IBYP 1, IBYP 2, ICB 2, ICB 3, JBA 3

GELINAS, PAUL J.
Birthdate: 7/17/1911
Birthplace: Woonsocket, RI
Information Available in These Sources: SATA 10

GELL, FRANK
See Kowet, Don

GELMAN, JAN
Birthdate: 11/14/1963
Birthplace: New York, NY
Information Available in These Sources: SATA 58

GELMAN, RITA GOLDEN
(R. G. Austin)
Birthdate: 7/2/1937
Birthplace: Bridgeport, CT
Information Available in These Sources: SATA 51

GELMAN, STEVE
Birthdate: 3/15/1934
Birthplace: New York, NY
Information Available in These Sources: ABYP 4, SATA 3

GEMMING, ELIZABETH
Birthdate: 12/27/1932
Birthplace: Glen Cove, NY
Information Available in These Sources: SATA 11

GENDEL, EVELYN W.
Birthdate: 1916
Deathdate: 12/18/1977
Information Available in These Sources: SATA 27

GENG, VERONICA
Information Available in These Sources: ABYP 4

GENIA
See Wennerstrom, Genia Katherine

GENNARO, JOSEPH F(RANCIS), JR.
Birthdate: 4/9/1924
Birthplace: Brooklyn, NY
Information Available in These Sources: SATA 53

GEORGE, JEAN CRAIGHEAD
Birthdate: 7/2/1919
Birthplace: Washington, DC
Information Available in These Sources: ABYP 1, ABYP 3, DACF, ICB 2, MBMP, MJA, SATA 2, TCCW 1, TCCW 2, TCCW 3

GEORGE, JOHN LOTHAR
Birthdate: 4/17/1916
Birthplace: Milwaukee, WI
Information Available in These Sources: ABYP 1, ABYP 3, MJA, SATA 2

GEORGE, RENEE
Birthdate: 1/18/1924
Birthplace: Berlin, Germany
Information Available in These Sources: ICB 2

GEORGE, W(ILLIAM) LLOYD
Birthdate: 1900
Deathdate: 1/16/1975
Information Available in These Sources: SATA 30

GEORGIOU, CONSTANTINE
Birthdate: 4/2/1927
Birthplace: Calcutta, India
Information Available in These Sources: SATA 7

GERASSI, JOHN
Birthdate: 7/12/1931
Birthplace: Paris, France
Information Available in These Sources: ABYP 4

GERGELY, TIBOR
Birthdate: 8/3/1900
Birthplace: Budapest, Hungary
Deathdate: 1/13/1978
Information Available in These Sources: IBYP 1, ICB 1, ICB 2, SATA 20 SATA 54

GERINGER, LAURA
Birthdate: 2/23/1948
Birthplace: New York, NY
Information Available in These Sources: SATA 29

GERLER, WILLIAM R(OBERT)
Birthdate: 2/16/1917
Birthplace: Forest Park, IL
Information Available in These Sources: ABYP 4, SATA 47

GERSON, CORINNE (SCHREIBERSTEIN)
Birthdate: 1/19/1927
Birthplace: Allentown, PA
Information Available in These Sources: DACF, SATA 37

GERSON, NOEL B(ERTRAM)
(Ann Marie Burgess, Michael Burgess, Samuel Edwards, Paul Lewis, Leon Phillips, Donald Clayton Porter, Dana Fuller Ross, Carter A. Vaughan)
Birthdate: 11/6/1914
Birthplace: Chicago, IL
Deathdate: 11/20/1988
Information Available in These Sources: ABYP 2, ABYP 3, SATA 22, SATA 60

GERSON, VIRGINIA
Birthdate: 1864?
Birthplace: New York, NY
Deathdate: 1951
Information Available in These Sources: ICB 1

GERSTEIN, MORDICAI
Birthdate: 11/24/1935
Birthplace: Los Angeles, CA
Information Available in These Sources: SATA 47, JBA 6

GERVASI, FRANK HENRY
Birthdate: 2/5/1908
Birthplace: Baltimore, MD
Information Available in These Sources: ABYP 4

GESNER, CLARK
(John Gordon)
Birthdate: 3/27/1938
Birthplace: Augusta, ME
Information Available in These Sources: SATA 40

GESSNER, LYNNE
(Merle Clark)
Birthdate: 6/10/1919
Birthplace: Preston, Cuba
Information Available in These Sources: SATA 16

GEVIRTZ, ELIEZER
Birthdate: 1/10/1950
Birthplace: New York, NY
Information Available in These Sources: SATA 49

GHIKAS, PANOS (GEORGE)
Birthdate: 1923
Birthplace: Malden, MA
Information Available in These Sources: ICB 2

GIANAKOULIS, THEODORE
Birthplace: Greece
Information Available in These Sources: ABYP 2, ABYP 3

GIBBONS, GAIL
Birthdate: 8/1/1944
Birthplace: Oak Park, IL
Information Available in These Sources: SATA 23, JBA 6

GIBBS, ALONZO (LAWRENCE)
Birthdate: 2/17/1915
Birthplace: Brooklyn, NY
Information Available in These Sources: ABYP 2, ABYP 3, SATA 5

GIBBS, TONY
See Gibbs, Wolcott, Jr.

GIBBS, WOLCOTT, JR.
(Tony Gibbs)
Birthdate: 4/5/1935
Birthplace: New York, NY
Information Available in These Sources: SATA 40

GIBLIN, JAMES CROSS
Birthdate: 7/8/1933
Birthplace: Cleveland, OH
Information Available in These Sources: SATA 33, JBA 6

GIBSON, JOSEPHINE
See Hine, Al and Joslin, Sesyle

GIBSON, KATHARINE
Birthdate: 1893
Birthplace: Indianapolis, IN
Information Available in These Sources: JBA 2, SVC 2, SVC 3

GIDAL, SONIA (EPSTEIN)
Birthdate: 9/23/1922
Birthplace: Berlin, Germany
Information Available in These Sources: ABYP 2, ABYP 3, SATA 2

GIDAL, TIM N(AHUM)
Birthdate: 5/18/1909
Birthplace: Munich, Germany
Information Available in These Sources: ABYP 2, ABYP 3, SATA 2

GIEGLING, JOHN A(LLAN)
Birthdate: 1/23/1935
Birthplace: Sioux Falls, SD
Information Available in These Sources: SATA 17

GIFF, PATRICIA REILLY
Birthdate: 4/26/1935
Birthplace: Brooklyn, NY
Information Available in These Sources: JBA 5, SATA 33

GILBERT, AGNES JOAN (SEWELL)
(Joan Gilbert)
Birthdate: 11/7/1931
Birthplace: Dixon, MO
Information Available in These Sources: SATA 10

GILBERT, HELEN EARLE
Birthdate: 1903?
Birthplace: Hebron, CT?
Information Available in These Sources: ABYP 2, ABYP 3

GILBERT, JOAN
See Gilbert, Agnes Joan (Sewell)

GILBERT, MIRIAM
See Presberg, Miriam Goldstein

GILBERT, NAN
See Gilbertson, Mildred Geiger

GILBERT, SARA (DULANEY)
Birthdate: 10/5/1943
Birthplace: Washington, DC
Information Available in These Sources: ABYP 4, SATA 11

GILBERTSON, MILDRED GEIGER
(Nan Gilbert)
Birthdate: 6/9/1908
Birthplace: Galena, IL
Information Available in These Sources: SATA 2

GILBREATH, ALICE (THOMPSON)
Birthdate: 4/8/1921
Birthplace: Montpelier, ID
Information Available in These Sources: SATA 12

GILBRETH, FRANK B(UNKER), JR.
Birthdate: 3/17/1911
Birthplace: Plainfield, NJ
Information Available in These Sources: SATA 2

GILES, GORDON A.
See Binder, Otto O(scar)

GILFOND, HENRY
Information Available in These Sources: SATA 2

GILGE, JEANETTE
Birthdate: 3/31/1924
Birthplace: Phillips, WI
Information Available in These Sources: SATA 22

GILL, DEREK L(EWIS) T(HEODORE)
Birthdate: 12/23/1919
Birthplace: Kampala, Uganda
Information Available in These Sources: SATA 9

GILL, RICHARD COCHRAN
Birthdate: 11/22/1901
Birthplace: Washington, DC
Deathdate: 7/7/1958
Information Available in These Sources: ABYP 1, ABYP 3

GILLELAN, GEORGE HOWARD
(Captain Jim Purdy)
Birthdate: 1/25/1917
Birthplace: Baltimore, MD
Information Available in These Sources: ABYP 2, ABYP 3

GILLETT, MARY (BLEDSOE)
Birthplace: Jefferson, NC
Information Available in These Sources: SATA 7

GILLETTE, HENRY SAMPSON
Birthdate: 1/29/1915
Birthplace: New York, NY
Information Available in These Sources: SATA 14

GILLIAM, STAN
Birthdate: 4/16/1946
Birthplace: Kannapolis, NC
Information Available in These Sources: SATA 35, SATA 39

GILMAN, DOROTHY
See Butters, Dorothy Gilman

GILMAN, ESTHER
Birthdate: 1925
Birthplace: Cleveland, OH
Information Available in These Sources: SATA 15

GILMAN, PHOEBE
Birthdate: 4/4/1940
Birthplace: New York, NY
Information Available in These Sources: SATA 58

GILMORE, HORACE HERMAN
Birthdate: 1903
Information Available in These Sources: ABYP 2, ABYP 3

GILMORE, IRIS
Birthdate: 9/4/1900
Birthplace: Cairo (near), IL
Information Available in These Sources: ABYP 2, ABYP 3, SATA 22

GILMORE, SUSAN
Birthdate: 9/17/1954
Birthplace: Phoenix, AZ
Information Available in These Sources: SATA 59

GILSON, JAMIE
Birthdate: 7/4/1933
Birthplace: Beardstown, IL
Information Available in These Sources: SATA 34, SATA 37, JBA 6

GINSBURG, MIRRA
Birthdate: 1919
Birthplace: Bobruisk, Minsk, USSR
Information Available in These Sources: ABYP 4, SATA 6, JBA 6

GIOVANNI, NIKKI
(Yolande C. Giovanni)
Birthdate: 6/7/1943
Birthplace: Knoxville, TN
Information Available in These Sources: ABYP 4, BAI, JBA 5, SATA 24, TCCW 1

GIOVANNI, YOLANDE C.
See Giovanni, Nikki

GIOVANOPOULOS, PAUL (ARTHUR)
Birthdate: 11/12/1939
Birthplace: Kastoria, Greece
Information Available in These Sources: IBYP 1, IBYP 2, JBA 4, SATA 7

GIPSON, FRED(ERICK BENJAMIN)
Birthdate: 2/7/1908
Birthplace: Mason, TX
Deathdate: 8/14/1973
Information Available in These Sources: ABYP 2, ABYP 3, JBA 3, SATA 2 SATA 24, TCCW 1, TCCW 2, TCCW 3

GIRARD, LINDA WALVOORD
Birthdate: 11/16/1942
Birthplace: Amsterdam, NY
Information Available in These Sources: SATA 41

GIRION, BARBARA
Birthdate: 11/20/1937 or 11/20/1938
Birthplace: New York, NY
Information Available in These Sources: SATA 26, JBA 6

GIRVAN, HELEN (MASTERMAN)
Birthdate: 1891
Birthplace: Minneapolis, MN
Information Available in These Sources: ABYP 1, ABYP 3, MJA

GIVENS, JANET E(ATON)
(Janet Eaton)
Birthdate: 7/5/1932
Birthplace: New York, NY
Information Available in These Sources: SATA 60

GLADSTONE, EVE
See Werner, Herma

GLADSTONE, GARY
Birthdate: 7/8/1935
Birthplace: Philadelphia, PA
Information Available in These Sources: SATA 12

GLADSTONE, M(YRON) J.
Birthdate: 5/4/1923
Information Available in These Sources: SATA 37

GLADWIN, WILLIAM ZACHARY
See Zollinger, Gulielma

GLANCKOFF, SAMUEL
Birthdate: 10/30/1894
Birthplace: New York, NY
Deathdate: 1982
Information Available in These Sources: ICB 1

GLANZMAN, LOUIS S.
Birthdate: 2/8/1922
Birthplace: Baltimore, MD
Information Available in These Sources: IBYP 1, IBYP 2, ICB 3, ICB 4, SATA 36

GLASER, DIANNE ELIZABETH
Birthdate: 8/29/1937
Birthplace: Bronx, NY
Information Available in These Sources: SATA 50

GLASER, MILTON
(Max Catz)
Birthdate: 6/26/1929
Birthplace: New York, NY
Information Available in These Sources: IBYP 1, IBYP 2, ICB 3, ICB 4, JBA 4, SATA 11

GLASPELL, SUSAN
Birthdate: 7/1/1882
Birthplace: Davenport, IA
Deathdate: 7/27/1948
Information Available in These Sources: YABC

GLASS, ANDREW
Birthplace: Pittsburgh, PA
Information Available in These Sources: SATA 46, JBA 6

GLATTAUER, NED
Information Available in These Sources: IBYP 2

GLAZER, TOM
Birthdate: 9/3/1914
Birthplace: Philadelphia, PA
Information Available in These Sources: ABYP 4, SATA 9

GLEASNER, DIANA (COTTLE)
Birthdate: 4/26/1936
Birthplace: NJ
Information Available in These Sources: SATA 29

GLEASON, JUDITH
Birthdate: 12/9/1929
Birthplace: Pasadena, CA
Information Available in These Sources: SATA 24

GLEICK, BETH YOUMAN
Birthplace: NY
Information Available in These Sources: ABYP 2, ABYP 3

GLENDINNING, RICHARD
Birthdate: 10/10/1917
Birthplace: Elizabeth, NJ
Information Available in These Sources: SATA 24

GLENDINNING, SALLY
See Glendinning, Sara W(ilson)

GLENDINNING, SARA W(ILSON)
(Sally Glendinning)
Birthdate: 9/17/1913
Birthplace: Birmingham, AL
Information Available in These Sources: SATA 24

GLENN, MEL
Birthdate: 5/10/1943
Birthplace: Zurich, Switzerland
Information Available in These Sources: SATA 45, SATA 51

GLES, MARGARET BREITMAIER
Birthdate: 12/7/1940
Birthplace: New York, NY
Information Available in These Sources: SATA 22

GLICK, CARL (CANNON)
(Captain Frank Cunningham, Peter Holbrook)
Birthdate: 9/11/1890
Birthplace: Marshalltown, IA
Deathdate: 3/7/1971
Information Available in These Sources: SATA 14

GLICK, VIRGINIA KIRKUS
(Virginia Kirkus)
Birthdate: 12/7/1893
Birthplace: Meadville, PA
Deathdate: 9/10/1980
Information Available in These Sources: SATA 23

GLIEWE, UNADA (GRACE)
(Unada)
Birthdate: 7/10/1927
Birthplace: Rochester, NY
Information Available in These Sources: SATA 3

GLINES, CARROLL V(ANE), JR.
Birthdate: 12/2/1920
Birthplace: Baltimore, MD
Information Available in These Sources: SATA 19

GLOBE, LEAH AIN
Birthdate: 3/14/1900
Birthplace: Narevke, Russia
Information Available in These Sources: SATA 41

GLOVACH, LINDA
Birthdate: 6/24/1947
Birthplace: Rockville Centre, NY
Information Available in These Sources: ABYP 4, SATA 7

GLUBOK, SHIRLEY (ASTOR)
Birthdate: 6/15/1933
Birthplace: St. Louis, MO
Information Available in These Sources: ABYP 2, ABYP 3, JBA 3, MBMP, SATA 6

GOBBATO, IMERO
Birthdate: 12/28/1923
Birthplace: Milan, Italy
Information Available in These Sources: IBYP 1, IBYP 2, ICB 3, ICB 4, SATA 39

GOBHAI, MEHLLI
Birthplace: Bombay, India
Information Available in These Sources: ABYP 4

GOBLE, PAUL
Birthdate: 9/17/1933
Birthplace: Surrey, England
Information Available in These Sources: JBA 4, SATA 25

GODE, ALEXANDER
See Gode von Aesch, Alexander (Gottfried Friedrich)

GODE VON AESCH, ALEXANDER (GOTTFRIED FRIEDRICH)
(Alexander Gode)
Birthdate: 10/30/1906
Birthplace: Bremen, Germany
Deathdate: 8/10/1970
Information Available in These Sources: SATA 14

GODFREY, JANE
See Bowden, Joan Chase

GODROG, JUDITH (ALLEN)
Birthdate: 12/16/1938
Birthplace: Madison, WI
Information Available in These Sources: SATA 39

GODWIN, EDWARD FELL
Birthdate: 2/21/1912
Birthplace: London, England
Information Available in These Sources: ICB 2

GODWIN, STEPHANIE MARY (ALLFREE)
Birthplace: London, England
Information Available in These Sources: ICB 2

GOETTEL, ELINOR
Birthdate: 8/14/1930
Birthplace: Bangkok, Thailand
Information Available in These Sources: SATA 12

GOETZ, DELIA
Birthdate: 6/??/1898
Birthplace: Wesley, IA
Information Available in These Sources: ABYP 1, ABYP 3, SATA 22

GOFFSTEIN, M(ARILYN) B(ROOKE)
Birthdate: 12/20/1940
Birthplace: St. Paul, MN
Information Available in These Sources: ABYP 4, DLB 61, ICB 4, JBA 4, SATA 8

GOLANN, CECIL PAIGE
Birthdate: 1/20/1921
Birthplace: New York, NY
Information Available in These Sources: SATA 11

GOLBIN, ANDREE
Birthdate: 6/4/1923
Birthplace: Leipzig, Germany
Information Available in These Sources: SATA 15

GOLD, PHYLLIS
Birthplace: Long Island, NY
Information Available in These Sources: SATA 21

GOLD, SHARLYA
Birthplace: Los Angeles, CA
Information Available in These Sources: SATA 9

GOLDBERG, HERBERT S.
Birthdate: 7/23/1926
Birthplace: New York, NY
Information Available in These Sources: SATA 25

GOLDBERG, MARTHA
Birthdate: 1907
Birthplace: New York, NY
Information Available in These Sources: ABYP 2, ABYP 3

GOLDBERG, STAN J.
Birthdate: 3/5/1939
Birthplace: Atlanta, GA
Information Available in These Sources: SATA 26

GOLDFEDER, CHERYL
See Pahz, Anne Cheryl Suzanne

GOLDFEDER, JIM
See Pahz, James Alon

GOLDFRANK, HELEN COLODNY
(Helen Kay)
Birthdate: 10/27/1912
Birthplace: New York, NY
Information Available in These Sources: ABYP 1, ABYP 3, SATA 6

GOLDIN, AUGUSTA
Birthdate: 10/28/1906
Birthplace: New York, NY
Information Available in These Sources: SATA 13

GOLDSBOROUGH, JUNE
Birthdate: 5/30/1923
Birthplace: Paragould, AR
Information Available in These Sources: SATA 19

GOLDSMITH, HOWARD
(Ward Smith)
Birthdate: 8/24/1943
Birthplace: New York, NY
Information Available in These Sources: SATA 24

GOLDSTEIN, ERNEST A.
Birthdate: 7/13/1933
Birthplace: Providence, RI
Information Available in These Sources: SATA 52

GOLDSTEIN, NATHAN
Birthdate: 3/26/1927
Birthplace: Chicago, IL
Information Available in These Sources: IBYP 1, IBYP 2, SATA 47

GOLDSTEIN, PHILIP
Birthdate: 5/3/1910
Birthplace: New York, NY
Information Available in These Sources: ABYP 4, SATA 23

GOLDSTON, ROBERT (CONROY)
(Robert Conroy, James Stark)
Birthdate: 7/9/1927
Birthplace: New York, NY
Information Available in These Sources: ABYP 4, JBA 4, SATA 6

GOLL, REINHOLD W(EIMAR)
Birthdate: 3/20/1897
Birthplace: Philadelphia, PA
Information Available in These Sources: ABYP 2, ABYP 3, SATA 26

GOLLOMB, JOSEPH
Birthdate: 11/15/1881
Birthplace: St. Petersburg, Russia
Deathdate: 5/23/1950
Information Available in These Sources: ABYP 1, ABYP 3, JBA 1, JBA 2

GONDOSCH, LINDA
Birthdate: 10/25/1944
Birthplace: Hinton, WV
Information Available in These Sources: SATA 58

GONZALEZ, GLORIA
Birthdate: 1/10/1940
Birthplace: New York, NY
Information Available in These Sources: SATA 23

GONZALEZ, XAVIER
Birthdate: 2/15/1898
Birthplace: Almeria, Spain
Information Available in These Sources: IBYP 1, IBYP 2

GOODBODY, SLIM
See Burstein, John

GOODE, DIANE (CAPUOZZO)
Birthdate: 9/14/1949
Birthplace: Brooklyn, NY
Information Available in These Sources: ICB 4, JBA 5, SATA 15

GOODE, STEPHEN
Birthdate: 3/5/1943
Birthplace: Elkins, WV
Information Available in These Sources: SATA 40, SATA 55

GOODENOW, EARLE
Birthdate: 7/13/1913
Birthplace: Chicago, IL
Information Available in These Sources: ICB 2, SATA 40

GOODENOW, GIRARD
Birthdate: 5/4/1912
Birthplace: Chicago, IL
Information Available in These Sources: IBYP 1, IBYP 2, ICB 2

GOODMAN, DEBORAH LERME
Birthdate: 10/31/1956
Birthplace: New York, NY
Information Available in These Sources: SATA 49, SATA 50

GOODMAN, ELAINE (EGAN)
Birthdate: 1/23/1930
Birthplace: New York, NY
Information Available in These Sources: ABYP 4, SATA 9

GOODMAN, ELIZABETH B.
Birthdate: 5/30/1912
Birthplace: Oakland, CA
Information Available in These Sources: ABYP 4

GOODMAN, JOAN ELIZABETH
Birthdate: 6/18/1950
Birthplace: Fairfield, CT
Information Available in These Sources: SATA 50

GOODMAN, WALTER
Birthdate: 8/22/1927
Birthplace: New York, NY
Information Available in These Sources: ABYP 4, SATA 9

GOODRICH, SAMUEL GRISWOLD
(Peter Parley)
Birthdate: 8/19/1793
Birthplace: Ridgefield, CT
Deathdate: 5/9/1860
Information Available in These Sources: DLB 42, SATA 23, WCL

GOODSELL, JANE NEUBERGER
Birthdate, 1921?
Birthplace: Portland, OR
Deathdate: 9/??/1988
Information Available in These Sources: SATA 56

GOODWIN, HAL
See Goodwin, Harold Leland

GOODWIN, HAROLD
Birthdate: 6/10/1919
Birthplace: New York, NY
Information Available in These Sources: IBYP 2

GOODWIN, HAROLD LELAND
(John Blaine, Hal Goodwin, Hal Gordon, Blake Savage)
Birthdate: 11/20/1914
Birthplace: Ellenburg, NY
Information Available in These Sources: SATA 13, SATA 51

GOOR, NANCY (RUTH MILLER)
Birthdate: 3/27/1944
Birthplace: Washington, DC
Information Available in These Sources: SATA 34, SATA 39

GOOR, RON(ALD STEPHEN)
Birthdate: 5/31/1940
Birthplace: Washington, DC
Information Available in These Sources: SATA 34, SATA 39

GORDON, BERNARD LUDWIG
Birthdate: 11/6/1931
Birthplace: Westerly, RI
Information Available in These Sources: SATA 27

GORDON, COLONEL H. R.
See Ellis, Edward S(ylvester)

GORDON, CYRUS HERZL
Birthdate: 6/29/1908
Birthplace: Philadelphia, PA
Information Available in These Sources: ABYP 4

GORDON, DOROTHY (LERNER)
Birthdate: 4/4/1893
Birthplace: Odessa, Russia
Deathdate: 5/11/1970
Information Available in These Sources: ABYP 2, ABYP 3, SATA 20

GORDON, ESTHER S(ARANGA)
Birthdate: 3/29/1935
Birthplace: Boston, MA
Information Available in These Sources: SATA 10

GORDON, FREDERICK
See Stratemeyer, Edward L.

GORDON, GARY
See Edmonds, I(vy) G(ordon)

GORDON, GORDON
(The Gordons)
Birthdate: 3/12/1912
Birthplace: Anderson, IN
Information Available in These Sources: ABYP 4

GORDON, H. R.
See Ellis, Edward S(ylvester)

GORDON, HAL
See Goodwin, Harold Leland

GORDON, JOHN
See Gesner, Clark

GORDON, LEW
See Baldwin, Gordon C.

GORDON, MILDRED (NIXON)
(The Gordons)
Birthdate: 7/24/1912
Birthplace: Eureka, KS
Deathdate: 2/3/1979
Information Available in These Sources: ABYP 4, SATA 24

GORDON, SELMA
See Lanes, Selma G(ordon)

GORDON, SHIRLEY
Birthdate: 12/29/1921
Birthplace: Geneva, IL
Information Available in These Sources: SATA 41, SATA 48

GORDON, SOL
Birthdate: 6/12/1923
Birthplace: Brooklyn, NY
Information Available in These Sources: ABYP 4, SATA 11

GORDON, STEWART
See Shirreffs, Gordon D(onald)

GORDONS, THE
See Gordon, Gordon and Gordon, Mildred (Nixon)

GORELICK, MOLLY C.
Birthdate: 9/19/1920
Birthplace: New York, NY
Information Available in These Sources: SATA 9

GOREY, EDWARD ST. JOHN
(Eduard Blutig, Mrs. Regera Dowdy, Redway Grode, O Mude, Ogdred Weary, Dreary Wodge)
Birthdate: 2/22/1925
Birthplace: Chicago, IL
Information Available in These Sources: DLB 61, IBYP 1, IBYP 2, ICB 3 ICB 4, JBA 4, SATA 27, SATA 29

GORHAM, CHARLES ORSON
Birthdate: 1911
Birthplace: Philadelphia, PA
Information Available in These Sources: SATA 36

GORHAM, MICHAEL
See Folsom, Franklin (Brewster)

GORMAN, TERRY
See Powers, Richard M.

GORMLEY, BEATRICE
Birthdate: 10/15/1942
Birthplace: Glendale, CA
Information Available in These Sources: SATA 35, SATA 39

GORODETZKY, CHARLES W.
Birthdate: 5/31/1937
Birthplace: Boston, MA
Information Available in These Sources: ABYP 4

GORSLINE, DOUGLAS (WARNER)
Birthdate: 5/24/1913
Birthplace: Rochester, NY
Deathdate: 6/25/1985 or 6/26/1985
Information Available in These Sources: IBYP 2, ICB 2, ICB 3, SATA 11 SATA 43

GORSLINE, MARIE
See Gorsline, S(ally) M(arie)

GORSLINE, S(ALLY) M(ARIE)
(S. M. Carson, Marie Gorsline)
Birthdate: 10/3/1928
Birthplace: Winchester, MA
Information Available in These Sources: SATA 28

GORYAN, SIRAK
See Saroyan, William

GOSSETT, MARGARET
Information Available in These Sources: ABYP 2, ABYP 3

GOTTLIEB, BILL
See Gottlieb, William P(aul)

GOTTLIEB, GERALD
Birthdate: 8/12/1923
Birthplace: New York, NY
Information Available in These Sources: ABYP 2, ABYP 3, SATA 7

GOTTLIEB, ROBIN (GROSSMAN)
Birthdate: 6/19/1928
Birthplace: New York, NY
Information Available in These Sources: ABYP 2, ABYP 3

GOTTLIEB, WILLIAM P(AUL)
(Bill Gottlieb)
Birthdate: 1/28/1917
Birthplace: New York, NY
Information Available in These Sources: ABYP 1, ABYP 3, SATA 24

GOUDEY, ALICE E(DWARDS)
Birthdate: 1/3/1898
Birthplace: Junction City, KS
Information Available in These Sources: ABYP 1, ABYP 3, JBA 3, SATA 20

GOULART, RON(ALD JOSEPH)
Birthdate: 1/13/1933
Birthplace: Berkley, CA
Information Available in These Sources: SATA 6

GOULD, CHESTER
Birthdate: 11/20/1900
Birthplace: Pawnee, OK
Deathdate: 5/11/1985
Information Available in These Sources: SATA 43, SATA 49

GOULD, GEORGE
Information Available in These Sources: ABYP 4

GOULD, JEAN R(OSALIND)
Birthdate: 5/25/1919 or 5/25/1909
Birthplace: Greenville, OH
Information Available in These Sources: ABYP 1, ABYP 3, SATA 11

GOULD, LILIAN
Birthdate: 4/19/1920
Birthplace: Philadelphia, PA
Information Available in These Sources: SATA 6

GOULD, MARILYN
Birthdate: 2/12/1928
Birthplace: Cleveland, OH
Information Available in These Sources: ABYP 4, SATA 15

GOULD, TONI S.
Information Available in These Sources: ABYP 4

GOVAN, CHRISTINE NOBLE
(Mary Allerton, J. N. Darby)
Birthdate: 1898
Birthplace: New York, NY
Information Available in These Sources: ABYP 2, ABYP 3, SATA 9

GOVERN, ELAINE
Birthdate: 3/27/1939
Birthplace: Jackson Junction, IA
Information Available in These Sources: SATA 26

GRABER, RICHARD (FREDERICK)
Birthdate: 4/23/1927
Birthplace: Minneapolis, MN
Information Available in These Sources: SATA 26

GRABOFF, ABNER
Birthdate: 6/28/1919
Birthplace: New York, NY
Information Available in These Sources: IBYP 1, IBYP 2, ICB 3, SATA 35

GRACE, F(RANCES JANE)
Birthdate: 1942
Birthplace: Santa Monica, CA
Information Available in These Sources: SATA 45

GRACZA, MARGARET YOUNG
Birthdate: 4/16/1928
Birthplace: St. Paul, MN
Information Available in These Sources: SATA 56

GRAEBER, CHARLOTTE TOWNER
Birthplace: Peoria, IL
Information Available in These Sources: SATA 44, 56

GRAFF, POLLY ANNE (COLVER)
See Colver, Anne

GRAFF, S. STEWART
(Stewart Graff)
Birthdate: 5/8/1908
Birthplace: Worthington, PA
Information Available in These Sources: ABYP 2, ABYP 3, SATA 9

GRAFF, STEWART
See Graff, S. Stewart

GRAHAM, ADA
Birthdate: 8/22/1931
Birthplace: Dayton, OH
Information Available in These Sources: SATA 11

GRAHAM, AL
Birthdate: 1897
Birthplace: Newburyport, MA
Information Available in These Sources: ABYP 1, ABYP 3

GRAHAM, ALBERTA (POWELL)
Birthdate, 1874?
Birthplace: Harrington, DE
Deathdate: 1955
Information Available in These Sources: ABYP 1, ABYP 3

GRAHAM, BRENDA KNIGHT
Birthdate: 9/17/1942
Birthplace: Clarkesville, GA
Information Available in These Sources: SATA 32

GRAHAM, CHARLOTTE
See Bowden, Joan Chase

GRAHAM, CLARENCE REGINALD
Birthdate: 2/28/1907
Birthplace: Louisville, KY
Information Available in These Sources: ABYP 1, ABYP 3

GRAHAM, FRANK, JR.
Birthdate: 3/31/1925
Birthplace: New York, NY
Information Available in These Sources: ABYP 2, ABYP 3, SATA 11

GRAHAM, GAIL B.
Information Available in These Sources: DACF

GRAHAM, HELEN HOLLAND
Birthplace: Springtown, AR
Information Available in These Sources: ABYP 2, ABYP 3

GRAHAM, HUGH
See Barrows, R(uth) M(arjorie)

GRAHAM, JOHN
Birthdate: 9/1/1926
Birthplace: Washington, DC
Information Available in These Sources: SATA 11

GRAHAM, KENNON
See Harrison, David Lee

GRAHAM, LORENZ (BELL)
Birthdate: 1/27/1902
Birthplace: New Orleans, LA
Information Available in These Sources: ABYP 4, BAI, DACF, JBA 3, MBMPSATA 2, TCCW 1, TCCW 2, TCCW 3

GRAHAM, MARGARET BLOY
Birthdate: 11/2/1920
Birthplace: Toronto, Ontario, Canada
Information Available in These Sources: IBYP 2, ICB 2, ICB 3, ICB 4, MJA, SATA 11

GRAHAM, ROBIN LEE
Birthdate: 3/5/1949
Birthplace: Santa Ana, CA
Information Available in These Sources: SATA 7

GRAHAM, SHIRLEY
See DuBois, Shirley Graham

GRAHAM-BARBER, LYNDA
(Linda Barber)
Birthdate: 12/12/1944
Birthplace: Pittsburgh, PA
Information Available in These Sources: SATA 42

GRAMATKY, HARDIE
Birthdate: 4/12/1907
Birthplace: Dallas, TX
Deathdate: 4/29/1979
Information Available in These Sources: ABYP 1, ABYP 3, AICB, BABP, DLB 22, ICB 1, ICB 2, ICB 3, ICB 4, JBA 2, SATA 1, SATA 23 SATA 30, SVC 2, SVC 3, TCCW 3

GRAMET, CHARLES
Information Available in These Sources: ABYP 2, ABYP 3

GRAMMER, JUNE AMOS
Birthdate: 2/10/1927
Birthplace: Woodbury, NJ
Information Available in These Sources: SATA 58

GRAND, SAMUEL
Birthdate: 8/28/1912
Birthplace: New York, NY
Information Available in These Sources: SATA 42

GRANDA, JULIO
Birthplace: New York, NY
Information Available in These Sources: IBYP 2

GRANDMA MOSES
See Moses, Anna Mary (Robertson)

GRANGER, DARIUS JOHN
See Marlow, Stephen

GRANGER, MARGARET JANE
(Peggy Granger)
Birthdate, 1925?
Birthplace: Vallejo, CA
Deathdate: 5/12/1977
Information Available in These Sources: SATA 27

GRANGER, PEGGY
See Granger, Margaret Jane

GRANSTAFF, BILL
Birthdate: 5/17/1925
Birthplace: Paducah, KY
Information Available in These Sources: SATA 10

GRANT, ALICE LEIGH
(Leigh Grant)
Birthdate: 9/22/1947
Birthplace: Greenwich, CT
Information Available in These Sources: IBYP 2, SATA 10

GRANT, BRUCE
Birthdate: 4/17/1893
Birthplace: Wichita Falls, TX
Deathdate: 4/9/1977 or 4/8/1977
Information Available in These Sources: ABYP 1, ABYP 3, SATA 5, SATA 25

GRANT, CYNTHIA D.
Birthdate: 11/23/1950
Birthplace: Brockton, MA
Information Available in These Sources: SATA 33

GRANT, EVA (COHEN)
Birthdate: 11/23/1907
Birthplace: New York, NY
Information Available in These Sources: ABYP 4, SATA 7

GRANT, EVVA H.
Birthdate: 2/22/1913
Birthplace: Rock Island, IL
Deathdate: 9/29/1977
Information Available in These Sources: SATA 27

GRANT, GORDON (HOPE)
Birthdate: 6/7/1875
Birthplace: San Francisco, CA
Deathdate: 5/6/1962
Information Available in These Sources: ICB 1, ICB 2, SATA 25

GRANT, LEIGH
See Grant, Alice Leigh

GRANT, MADELEINE PARKER
Birthdate: 3/1/1895
Birthplace: Dorchester, MA
Information Available in These Sources: ABYP 2, ABYP 3

GRANT, MATTHEW G.
See May, Julian

GRANT, MAXWELL
See Lynds, Dennis

GRANT, MYRNA (LOIS)
Birthdate: 3/9/1934
Birthplace: Hamilton, Ontario, Canada
Information Available in These Sources: SATA 21

GRAVEL, FERN
See Hall, James Norman

GRAVES, CHARLES PARLIN
(John Parlin)
Birthdate: 1/23/1911
Birthplace: Apalachicola, FL
Deathdate: 8/2/1972
Information Available in These Sources: ABYP 2, ABYP 3, SATA 4

GRAVES, WILLIAM
Information Available in These Sources: ABYP 4

GRAY, ALICE
Information Available in These Sources: ABYP 2, ABYP 3

GRAY, ELIZABETH JANET
(Elizabeth (Janet) Gray Vining)
Birthdate: 10/6/1902
Birthplace: Philadelphia, PA
Information Available in These Sources: ABYP 1, ABYP 3, DACF, JBA 1, JBA 2, SATA 6, TCCW 1, TCCW 2 TCCW 3

GRAY, GENEVIEVE S.
(Jenny Gray)
Birthdate: 8/6/1920
Birthplace: Jonesboro, AR
Information Available in These Sources: SATA 4

GRAY, HAROLD (LINCOLN)
Birthdate: 1/20/1894
Birthplace: Kankakee, IL
Deathdate: 5/9/1968
Information Available in These Sources: SATA 32, SATA 33

GRAY, JENNY
See Gray, Genevieve S.

GRAY, LEE LEARNER
Birthdate: 9/27/1924
Birthplace: New York, NY
Information Available in These Sources: ABYP 4

GRAY, MARIAN
See Pierce, Edith Gray

GRAY, PATRICIA (CLARK)
(Patsey Gray, Virginia Clark)
Birthplace: San Mateo, CA
Information Available in These Sources: ABYP 2, ABYP 3, SATA 7

GRAY, PATSEY
See Gray, Patricia (Clark)

GRAY, ROBERT
Birthdate: 1922
Birthplace: Butte, MT
Information Available in These Sources: ABYP 4

GRAYSON, DAVID
See Baker, Ray Stannard

GRAYSON, MARION (FORBOURG)
Birthdate: 9/1/1906
Birthplace: New York, NY
Deathdate: 8/28/1976
Information Available in These Sources: ABYP 2, ABYP 3

GRAZIA, THOMAS DI
See DiGrazia, Thomas

GREEN, ADAM
See Weisgard, Leonard (Joseph)

GREEN, BARBARA
Information Available in These Sources: ABYP 4

GREEN, D.
See Casewit, Curtis

GREEN, ELIZABETH SHIPPEN
See Elliott, Elizabeth Shippen Green

GREEN, HANNAH
See Greenberg, Joanne (Goldenberg)

GREEN, JANE
Birthdate: 6/27/1937
Birthplace: New York, NY
Information Available in These Sources: ABYP 4, SATA 9

GREEN, MARGARET
Birthdate: 1926
Birthplace: Lawrence, MA
Information Available in These Sources: ABYP 2, ABYP 3

GREEN, MARY MCBURNEY
Birthdate: 10/1/1896
Birthplace: Englewood, NJ
Information Available in These Sources: ABYP 2, ABYP 3

GREEN, MARY MOORE
Birthdate: 3/17/1906
Birthplace: Romulus, MI
Information Available in These Sources: SATA 11

GREEN, MORTON
Birthdate: 5/18/1937
Birthplace: Los Angeles, CA
Information Available in These Sources: SATA 8

GREEN, NORMA B(ERGER)
Birthdate: 9/15/1925
Birthplace: Providence, RI
Information Available in These Sources: ABYP 4, SATA 11

GREEN, PHYLLIS
Birthdate: 6/24/1932
Birthplace: Pittsburgh, PA
Information Available in These Sources: SATA 20

GREEN, SHEILA ELLEN
(Sheila Greenwald)
Birthdate: 5/26/1934
Birthplace: New York, NY
Information Available in These Sources: IBYP 1, IBYP 2, ICB 3, JBA 5, SATA 8

GREENBERG, HARVEY R.
Birthdate: 6/27/1935
Birthplace: Philadelphia, PA
Information Available in These Sources: SATA 5

GREENBERG, JAN (SCHONWALD)
Birthdate: 12/29/1942
Information Available in These Sources: JBA 6

GREENBERG, JOANNE (GOLDENBERG)
(Hannah Green)
Birthdate: 9/24/1932
Birthplace: Brooklyn, NY
Information Available in These Sources: SATA 25

GREENBERG, POLLY
Birthdate: 4/21/1932
Birthplace: Milwaukee, WI
Information Available in These Sources: ABYP 4, SATA 43, SATA 52

GREENE, BETTE
Birthdate: 6/28/1934
Birthplace: Memphis, TN
Information Available in These Sources: ABYP 4, BC, DACF, JBA 5, SATA 8, TCCW 1, TCCW 2, TCCW 3

GREENE, CARLA
Birthdate: 12/18/1916
Birthplace: Minneapolis, MN
Information Available in These Sources: ABYP 1, ABYP 3, SATA 1

GREENE, CAROL
Birthdate: 1906
Information Available in These Sources: SATA 44

GREENE, CONSTANCE C(LARKE)
Birthdate: 10/27/1924
Birthplace: New York, NY
Information Available in These Sources: ABYP 4, DACF, JBA 4, SATA 11, TCCW 1, TCCW 2, TCCW 3

GREENE, ELLIN
Birthdate: 9/18/1927
Birthplace: Elizabeth, NJ
Information Available in These Sources: ABYP 4, SATA 23

GREENE, LAURA
Birthdate: 7/21/1935
Birthplace: New York, NY
Information Available in These Sources: SATA 38

GREENE, WADE
Birthdate: 1/17/1933
Birthplace: Syracuse, NY
Information Available in These Sources: ABYP 4, SATA 11

GREENE, YVONNE
See Flesch, Yolande (Catarina)

GREENFELD, HOWARD
Birthplace: New York, NY
Information Available in These Sources: ABYP 4, SATA 19

GREENFIELD, ELOISE (LITTLE)
Birthdate: 5/17/1929
Birthplace: Parmele, NC
Information Available in These Sources: BAI, DACF, JBA 5, SATA 19, TCCW 2, TCCW 3

GREENHAUS, THELMA NURENBERG
(Thelma Nurenberg)
Birthdate: 12/25/1903
Birthplace: Warsaw, Poland
Deathdate: 8/8/1984
Information Available in These Sources: SATA 45

GREENIDGE, EDWIN
Birthdate: 4/17/1929
Birthplace: New York, NY
Information Available in These Sources: ABYP 4

GREENLEAF, BARBARA KAYE
Birthdate: 7/1/1942
Birthplace: New York, NY
Information Available in These Sources: SATA 6

GREENLEAF, MARGERY
Birthplace: Brookline, MA
Information Available in These Sources: ABYP 4

GREENLEAF, PETER
Birthdate: 7/29/1910
Birthplace: Brooklyn, NY
Information Available in These Sources: SATA 33

GREENWALD, SHEILA
See Green, Sheila Ellen

GREGG, WALTER H(AROLD)
Birthdate: 4/7/1919
Birthplace: Columbus, OH
Information Available in These Sources: SATA 20

GREGOR, ARTHUR
Birthdate: 11/18/1923
Birthplace: Vienna, Austria
Information Available in These Sources: SATA 36

GREGORI, LEON
Birthdate: 6/3/1919
Birthplace: Kiev, USSR
Information Available in These Sources: SATA 15

GREGORIAN, JOYCE BALLOU
Birthdate: 7/5/1946
Birthplace: Boston, MA
Information Available in These Sources: SATA 30

GREGORY, DIANA (JEAN)
Birthdate: 4/27/1933
Birthplace: Pasadena, CA
Information Available in These Sources: SATA 42, SATA 49

GREGORY, STEPHEN
See Penzler, Otto

GREISMAN, JOAN RUTH
Birthdate: 5/4/1937
Birthplace: New York, NY
Information Available in These Sources: SATA 31

GREMMELS, MARION (LOUISE) CHAPMAN
Birthdate: 6/8/1924
Birthplace: Waverly, IA
Information Available in These Sources: ABYP 4

GRENDON, STEPHEN
See Derleth, August (William)

GRENVILLE, PELHAM
See Wodehouse, P(elham) G(renville)

GRETZ, SUSANNA
Birthdate: 9/27/1937
Birthplace: New York, NY
Information Available in These Sources: SATA 7

GRETZER, JOHN
Birthplace: Council Bluffs, IA
Information Available in These Sources: IBYP 1, IBYP 2, SATA 18

GREY, JERRY
Birthdate: 10/25/1926
Birthplace: New York, NY
Information Available in These Sources: SATA 11

GRIDER, DOROTHY
(Dottig, Patti Fenwick)
Birthdate: 1/19/1915
Birthplace: Bowling Green, KY
Information Available in These Sources: ICB 2, SATA 31

GRIDLEY, MARION E(LEANOR)
Birthdate: 11/16/1906
Birthplace: White Plains, NY
Deathdate: 10/31/1974
Information Available in These Sources: ABYP 4, SATA 26, SATA 35

GRIESE, ARNOLD A(LFRED)
Birthdate: 4/13/1921
Birthplace: Lakota, IA
Information Available in These Sources: SATA 9

GRIFALCONI, ANN WEIK
Birthdate: 9/22/1929
Birthplace: New York, NY
Information Available in These Sources: BABP, IBYP 1, IBYP 2, ICB 3, ICB 4, JBA 3, MBMP, SATA 2

GRIFFEN, ELIZABETH L.
Information Available in These Sources: ABYP 4

GRIFFIN, ELLA
Information Available in These Sources: ABYP 2, ABYP 3

GRIFFIN, GILLETT GOOD
Birthdate: 6/22/1928
Birthplace: Brooklyn, NY
Information Available in These Sources: ABYP 1, ABYP 3, ICB 2, SATA 26

GRIFFIN, JUDITH BERRY
Information Available in These Sources: ABYP 4, BAI, SATA 34

GRIFFIN, VELMA
Information Available in These Sources: ABYP 2, ABYP 3

GRIFFITH, FIELD
Birthplace: Washington, DC
Information Available in These Sources: ABYP 4

GRIFFITH, HELEN V(IRGINIA)
Birthdate: 10/31/1934
Birthplace: Wilmington, DE
Information Available in These Sources: SATA 39, TCCW 3

GRIFFITH, JEANNETTE
See Eyerly, Jeannette Hyde

GRIMES, NIKKI
Birthdate: 1950
Information Available in These Sources: BAI

GRIMM, WILLIAM C(AREY)
Birthdate: 7/1/1907
Birthplace: Pittsburgh, PA
Information Available in These Sources: SATA 14

GRINGHUIS, DIRK
See Gringhuis, Richard H.

GRINGHUIS, RICHARD H.
(Dirk Gringhuis)
Birthdate: 9/22/1918
Birthplace: Grand Rapids, MI
Deathdate: 3/31/1974
Information Available in These Sources: ABYP 2, ABYP 3, SATA 6, SATA 25

GRINNELL, DAVID
See Wollheim, Donald A(llen)

GRINNELL, GEORGE BIRD
Birthdate: 9/20/1849
Birthplace: Brooklyn, NY
Deathdate: 4/11/1938
Information Available in These Sources: JBA 1, JBA 2, SATA 16, SVC 2, SVC 3

GRISHA
See Dotzenko, Grisha F.

GROCH, JUDITH (GOLDSTEIN)
Birthdate: 5/14/1929
Birthplace: New York, NY
Information Available in These Sources: ABYP 2, ABYP 3, SATA 25

GRODE, REDWAY
See Gorey, Edward St. John

GRODIN, ADAMS JOHN
Birthdate: 1913
Birthplace: New York, NY
Information Available in These Sources: ICB 1

GROHSKOPF, BERNICE (APPELBAUM)
Birthdate: 9/22/1922 or 9/22/1921
Birthplace: Troy, NY
Information Available in These Sources: ABYP 4, SATA 7

GROLLMAN, EARL A.
Birthdate: 7/4/1925
Birthplace: Baltimore, MD
Information Available in These Sources: SATA 22

GROPPER, WILLIAM
Birthdate: 12/3/1897
Birthplace: New York, NY
Deathdate: 1/6/1977
Information Available in These Sources: ICB 2

GROSE, HELEN MASON
Birthdate: 10/8/1880
Birthplace: Providence, RI
Information Available in These Sources: ICB 1

GROSS, ALAN
Birthdate: 6/29/1947
Birthplace: Chicago, IL
Information Available in These Sources: SATA 43, SATA 54

GROSS, RUTH BELOV
Birthdate: 3/1/1929
Birthplace: Philadelphia, PA
Information Available in These Sources: ABYP 4, SATA 33

GROSS, SARAH CHOKLA
Birthdate: 10/13/1906
Birthplace: New York, NY
Deathdate: 7/20/1976
Information Available in These Sources: SATA 9, SATA 26

GROSSMAN, NANCY (S.)
Birthdate: 4/28/1940
Birthplace: New York, NY
Information Available in These Sources: IBYP 1, IBYP 2, ICB 3, SATA 29

GROSSMAN, ROBERT
Birthdate: 3/1/1940
Birthplace: New York, NY
Information Available in These Sources: SATA 11

GROTE, WILLIAM
Information Available in These Sources: ABYP 4

GROTH, JOHN (AUGUST)
Birthdate: 2/26/1908 or 2/2/1908
Birthplace: Chicago, IL
Deathdate: 6/27/1988
Information Available in These Sources: SATA 21, 56

GROVER, EULALIE OSGOOD
Birthdate: 6/22/1873
Birthplace: Mantorville, MN
Deathdate: 1958
Information Available in These Sources: ABYP 2, ABYP 3

GRUELLE, JOHN (BARTON)
(Johnny Gruelle)
Birthdate: 12/24/1880
Birthplace: Arcola, IL
Deathdate: 1/9/1938
Information Available in These Sources: DLB 22, SATA 32, SATA 35, TCCW 2, TCCW 3

GRUELLE, JOHNNY
See Gruelle, John (Barton)

GRUENBERG, SIDONIE M(ATSNER)
Birthdate: 6/10/1881
Birthplace: Vienna, Austria
Deathdate: 3/11/1974
Information Available in These Sources: ABYP 1, ABYP 3, SATA 2, SATA 27

GRUMBINE, E. EVALYN
(E. Evalyn (Grumbine) McNally)
Birthdate: 1900
Birthplace: Chicago, IL
Information Available in These Sources: ABYP 1, ABYP 3

GRUMMER, ARNOLD EDWARD
Birthdate: 8/19/1923
Birthplace: Spencer, IA
Information Available in These Sources: SATA 49

GUCK, DOROTHY
Birthdate: 5/17/1913
Birthplace: Grand Rapids, MI
Information Available in These Sources: SATA 27

GUETTEL, MARY RODGERS
See Rodgers, Mary

GUGGENHEIM, HANS
Birthdate: 1924
Birthplace: Berlin, Germany
Information Available in These Sources: ICB 3

GUGLIOTTA, BOBETTE
Birthdate: 11/8/1918
Birthplace: Chicago, IL
Information Available in These Sources: SATA 7

GUILLAUME, JEANETTE G. (FLIERL)
Birthdate: 5/6/1899
Birthplace: Buffalo, NY
Information Available in These Sources: SATA 8

GUISEWITE, CATHY
Birthdate: 9/5/1950
Birthplace: Dayton, OH
Information Available in These Sources: SATA 57

GUITERMAN, ARTHUR
Birthdate: 11/20/1871
Birthplace: Vienna, Austria
Deathdate: 1/11/1943
Information Available in These Sources: SVC 3

GULICK, PEGGY
Birthdate: 1918
Information Available in These Sources: ABYP 2, ABYP 3

GULLAHORN, GENEVIEVE
Birthplace: Lithuania
Information Available in These Sources: ABYP 1, ABYP 3

GULLEY, JULIE
Birthdate: 6/7/1942
Birthplace: Minneapolis, MN
Information Available in These Sources: SATA 58

GUMPERTZ, BOB
Birthdate: 8/17/1925
Birthplace: CA
Information Available in These Sources: ABYP 4

GUNDERSHEIMER, KAREN
Birthdate: 10/16/1939
Birthplace: Boston, MA
Information Available in These Sources: SATA 44, JBA 6

GUNN, JAMES E(DWIN)
(Edwin James)
Birthdate: 7/12/1923
Birthplace: Kansas City, MO
Information Available in These Sources: SATA 35

GUNTERMAN, BERTHA LISETTE
Birthdate: 1886
Deathdate: 10/3/1975
Information Available in These Sources: SATA 27

GUNTHER, JOHN
Birthdate: 8/30/1901
Birthplace: Chicago, IL
Deathdate: 5/29/1970
Information Available in These Sources: ABYP 2, ABYP 3, SATA 2

GURKO, LEO
Birthdate: 1/4/1914
Birthplace: Warsaw, Poland
Information Available in These Sources: JBA 3, SATA 9

GURKO, MIRIAM (BERWITZ)
Birthdate: 1910
Birthplace: Union City, NJ
Deathdate: 7/3/1988
Information Available in These Sources: JBA 3, SATA 9, SATA 58

GURNEY, ANTOINETTE
See Chaffee, Allen

GUSTAFSON, ANITA
Birthdate: 12/29/1942
Birthplace: Hastings, NE
Information Available in These Sources: SATA 45

GUSTAFSON, ELTON T.
Information Available in These Sources: ABYP 2, ABYP 3

GUSTAFSON, MARJORIE
Information Available in These Sources: ABYP 4

GUSTAFSON, SARAH REGAL
See Riedman, Sarah R(egal)

GUSTAFSON, SCOTT
Birthdate: 12/7/1956
Birthplace: Belvidere, IL
Information Available in These Sources: SATA 34

GUSTKEY, EARL
Birthdate: 2/20/1940
Birthplace: Washington, PA
Information Available in These Sources: ABYP 4

GUTHRIE, ANNE
Birthdate: 6/25/1890
Birthplace: San Diego, CA
Deathdate: 2/22/1979
Information Available in These Sources: ABYP 1, ABYP 3, SATA 28

GUTMAN, BILL
See Gutman, William

GUTMAN, WILLIAM
(Bill Gutman)
Birthplace: New York, NY
Information Available in These Sources: ABYP 4, SATA 43

GUY, ROSA (CUTHBERT)
Birthdate: 9/1/1928
Birthplace: Trinidad, West Indies
Information Available in These Sources: BAI, JBA 5, SATA 14, TCCW 1, TCCW 2, TCCW 3

GWYNNE, FRED(ERICK HUBBARD)
Birthdate: 7/10/1926
Birthplace: New York, NY
Information Available in These Sources: IBYP 1, IBYP 2, SATA 27, SATA 41

GWYNNE, JOHN HAROLD
Birthdate: 1899
Birthplace: PA
Information Available in These Sources: ABYP 2, ABYP 3

H

H. H.
See Jackson, Helen (Maria Fiske) Hunt

HAAS, CAROLYN BUHAI
Birthdate: 1/1/1926
Birthplace: Chicago, IL
Information Available in These Sources: SATA 43

HAAS, DOROTHY F.
(Dee Francis, Dan McCune)
Birthdate: 6/17
Birthplace: Racine, WI
Information Available in These Sources: SATA 43, SATA 46, JBA 6

HAAS, IRENE
Birthdate: 6/5/1929
Birthplace: New York, NY
Information Available in These Sources: IBYP 1, IBYP 2, ICB 2, ICB 3, ICB 4, JBA 3, SATA 17

HAAS, JAMES E(DWARD)
Birthdate: 1/17/1943
Birthplace: New York, NY
Information Available in These Sources: SATA 40

HAAS, MERLE S.
Birthdate, 1896?
Birthplace: Portland, OR
Deathdate: 1/7/1985
Information Available in These Sources: SATA 41

HABBERTON, JOHN
Birthdate: 2/24/1842
Birthplace: Brooklyn, NY
Deathdate: 2/24/1921
Information Available in These Sources: WCL

HABBERTON, WILLIAM
Birthdate: 1899
Birthplace: IL
Information Available in These Sources: ABYP 2, ABYP 3

HABENSTREIT, BARBARA (ZEIGLER)
Birthdate: 2/17/1937
Birthplace: New York, NY
Information Available in These Sources: ABYP 4, SATA 5

HABER, HEINZ
Birthdate: 5/15/1913
Birthplace: Mannheim, Germany
Information Available in These Sources: ABYP 2, ABYP 3

HABER, LOUIS
Birthdate: 1/12/1910
Birthplace: New York, NY
Information Available in These Sources: SATA 12

HACKETT, ALBERT
Birthdate: 2/16/1900
Birthplace: New York, NY
Information Available in These Sources: ABYP 2, ABYP 3

HACKETT, FRANCES (GOODRICH)
Birthdate: 1891
Birthplace: Belleville, NJ
Information Available in These Sources: ABYP 2, ABYP 3

HADER, BERTA (HOERNER)
Birthdate: 1891?
Birthplace: San Pedro, Coahuila, Mexico
Deathdate: 2/6/1976
Information Available in These Sources: ABYP 1, ABYP 3, AICB, BABP, FLTYP, IBYP 1, IBYP 2, ICB 1, ICB 2, ICB 3, JBA 1, JBA 2, SATA 16, SVC 2, SVC 3, TCCW 1 TCCW 2, TCCW 3

HADER, ELMER (STANLEY)
Birthdate: 9/7/1889
Birthplace: Pajaro, CA
Deathdate: 9/7/1973
Information Available in These Sources: ABYP 1, ABYP 3, AICB, BABP, FLTYP, IBYP 1, IBYP 2, ICB 1, ICB 2, ICB 3, JBA 1, JBA 2, SATA 16, SVC 2, SVC 3, TCCW 1, 2, 3

HADLEY, FRANKLIN
See Winterbotham, R(ussell) R(obert)

HADLEY, LEE
(Hadley Irwin)
Birthdate: 10/10/1934
Birthplace: Earlham, IA
Information Available in These Sources: SATA 38, SATA 47, JBA 6

HADLEY, LEILA (BURTON)
Birthdate: 9/22/1926
Birthplace: New York, NY
Information Available in These Sources: ABYP 4

HAFNER, MARYLIN
Birthdate: 12/14/1925
Birthplace: Brooklyn, NY
Information Available in These Sources: IBYP 2, SATA 7, JBA 6

HAGER, ALICE ROGERS
Birthdate: 8/3/1894
Birthplace: Peoria, IL
Deathdate: 12/5/1969
Information Available in These Sources: ABYP 1, ABYP 3, SATA 26

HAGGERTY, JAMES J(OSEPH)
Birthdate: 2/1/1920
Birthplace: Orange, NJ
Information Available in These Sources: SATA 5

HAGUE, KATHLEEN
See Hague, Susan Kathleen

HAGUE, MICHAEL R(ILEY)
Birthdate: 9/8/1948
Birthplace: Los Angeles, CA
Information Available in These Sources: JBA 5, SATA 32, SATA 48

HAGUE, SUSAN KATHLEEN
(Kathleen Hague)
Birthdate: 3/6/1949
Birthplace: Ventura, CA
Information Available in These Sources: SATA 45, SATA 49

HAHN, EMILY
Birthdate: 1/14/1905
Birthplace: St. Louis, MO
Information Available in These Sources: ABYP 1, ABYP 3, SATA 3

HAHN, HANNELORE
Birthdate: 11/9/1926
Birthplace: Dresden, Germany
Information Available in These Sources: SATA 8

HAHN, JAMES (SAGE)
Birthdate: 5/24/1947
Birthplace: Chicago, IL
Information Available in These Sources: SATA 9

HAHN, LYNN
See Hahn, Mona Lynn

HAHN, MARY DOWNING
Birthdate: 12/9/1937
Birthplace: Washington, DC
Information Available in These Sources: SATA 44, SATA 50, JBA 6

HAHN, MONA LYNN
(Lynn Hahn)
Birthdate: 7/3/1949
Birthplace: Cleveland, OH
Information Available in These Sources: SATA 9

HAIGHT, ANNE LYON
Birthdate: 5/11/1895
Birthplace: St. Paul, MN
Deathdate: 8/8/1977
Information Available in These Sources: SATA 30

HAINES, CHARLES
Birthdate: 3/22/1928
Birthplace: New York, NY
Information Available in These Sources: ABYP 4

HAINES, GAIL KAY (BECKMAN)
Birthdate: 3/15/1943
Birthplace: Mt. Vernon, IL
Information Available in These Sources: ABYP 4, SATA 11

HALACY, D(ANIEL) S(TEPHEN, JR.)
Birthdate: 5/16/1919
Birthplace: Charleston, SC
Information Available in These Sources: ABYP 2, ABYP 3, JBA 5, SATA 36

HALE, ARLENE
(Louise Christopher, Gail Everett, Will Kirkland, Mary Anne Tate, Lynn Williams)
Birthdate: 6/16/1924
Birthplace: New London, IA
Deathdate: 1/26/1982
Information Available in These Sources: ABYP 2, ABYP 3, SATA 49

HALE, EDWARD EVERETT
(Colonel Frederic Ingham)
Birthdate: 4/3/1822
Birthplace: Boston, MA
Deathdate: 6/10/1909
Information Available in These Sources: DLB 42, JBA 1, SATA 16

HALE, HELEN
See Mulcahy, Lucille Burnett

HALE, JANET CAMPBELL
Birthdate: 1/11/1947
Birthplace: Plummer, ID
Information Available in These Sources: ABYP 4

HALE, LINDA (HOWE)
Birthdate: 1/8/1929
Birthplace: Providence, RI
Information Available in These Sources: SATA 6

HALE, LUCRETIA PEABODY
Birthdate: 9/2/1820
Birthplace: Boston, MA
Deathdate: 6/12/1900
Information Available in These Sources: DLB 42, FSYP, JBA 1, SATA 26, TCCW 1, TCCW 2, TCCW 3, WC, WCL

HALE, NANCY
Birthdate: 5/6/1908
Birthplace: Boston, MA
Deathdate: 9/24/1988
Information Available in These Sources: SATA 31, SATA 57

HALE, SARAH JOSEPHA
Birthdate: 10/24/1788
Birthplace: Newport, NH
Deathdate: 4/30/1879
Information Available in These Sources: DLB 42

HALEY, GAIL E(INHART)
Birthdate: 11/4/1939
Birthplace: Charlotte, NC
Information Available in These Sources: IBYP 1, IBYP 2, ICB 4, JBA 3, SATA 28, SATA 43, TCCW 1

HALEY, NEALE
Birthplace: Buffalo, NY
Information Available in These Sources: SATA 52

HALL, ADAM
See Trevor, Elleston

HALL, ADELE
Birthdate: 10/2/1910
Birthplace: Philadelphia, PA
Information Available in These Sources: ABYP 2, ABYP 3, SATA 7

HALL, ANNA GERTRUDE
Birthdate: 2/9/1882
Birthplace: West Bloomfield, NY
Deathdate: 2/8/1967
Information Available in These Sources: SATA 8

HALL, BORDEN
See Yates, Robert F(rancis)

HALL, BRIAN P(ATRICK)
Birthdate: 12/29/1935
Birthplace: London, England
Information Available in These Sources: SATA 31

HALL, CAROLYN VOSBURG
Birthdate: 7/22/1927
Birthplace: Fenton, MI
Information Available in These Sources: ABYP 4

HALL, CARYL
See Hansen, Caryl (Hall)

HALL, DONALD (ANDREW, JR.)
Birthdate: 9/29/1928
Birthplace: New Haven, CT
Information Available in These Sources: ABYP 2, ABYP 3, JBA 5, SATA 23

HALL, ELIZABETH
Birthdate: 9/17/1929
Birthplace: Bakersfield, CA
Information Available in These Sources: ABYP 4

HALL, ELVAJEAN
Birthdate: 5/30/1910
Birthplace: Hamilton, IL
Information Available in These Sources: ABYP 1, ABYP 3, SATA 6

HALL, ESTHER GREENACRE
Birthplace: CO
Information Available in These Sources: ABYP 1, ABYP 3

HALL, GORDON LANGLEY
See Simmons, Dawn Langley

HALL, JAMES NORMAN
(Fern Gravel)
Birthdate: 4/22/1887
Birthplace: Colfax, IA
Deathdate: 7/6/1951
Information Available in These Sources: ABYP 2, ABYP 3, JBA 1, SATA 21

HALL, JESSE
See Boesen, Victor

HALL, KATY
See McMullan, Kate (Hall)

HALL, LYNN
Birthdate: 11/9/1937
Birthplace: Lombard, IL
Information Available in These Sources: ABYP 4, DACF, JBA 5, SATA 2, SATA 47, TCCW 2, TCCW 3

HALL, MALCOLM
Birthdate: 6/6/1945
Birthplace: Chicago, IL
Information Available in These Sources: ABYP 4, SATA 7

HALL, MARJORY
See Yeakley, Marjory Hall

HALL, NATALIE WATSON
Birthdate: 8/21/1923
Birthplace: Pittsburgh, PA
Information Available in These Sources: ICB 3

HALL, ROSALYS HASKELL
Birthdate: 3/27/1914
Birthplace: New York, NY
Information Available in These Sources: ABYP 2, ABYP 3, MJA, SATA 7

HALL, WILLIAM NORMAN
Birthdate: 1915
Deathdate: 12/3/1974
Information Available in These Sources: ABYP 2, ABYP 3

HALL-QUEST, EDNA OLGA WILBOURNE
(Olga W(ilbourne) Hall-Quest)
Birthdate: 8/30/1899
Birthplace: Willis, TX
Deathdate: 2/1/1986
Information Available in These Sources: ABYP 2, ABYP 3, SATA 11, SATA 47

HALL-QUEST, OLGA W(ILBOURNE)
See Hall-Quest, Edna Olga Wilbourne

HALLAS, RICHARD
See Knight, Eric (Mowbray)

HALLER, DORCAS WOODBURY
Birthdate: 7/31/1946
Birthplace: Concord, NH
Information Available in These Sources: SATA 46

HALLIBURTON, RICHARD
Birthdate: 1/9/1900
Birthplace: Brownsville, TN
Deathdate: 3/23/1939 or 3/24/1939
Information Available in These Sources: JBA 1

HALLIBURTON, WARREN J.
Birthdate: 8/2/1924
Birthplace: New York, NY
Information Available in These Sources: SATA 19

HALLIDAY, WILLIAM R(OSS)
Birthdate: 5/9/1926
Birthplace: Atlanta, GA
Information Available in These Sources: SATA 52

HALLIN, EMILY WATSON
Birthdate: 10/4/1919
Birthplace: Fort Smith, AR
Information Available in These Sources: SATA 6

HALLINAN, P(ATRICK) K(ENNETH)
Birthdate: 11/1/1944
Birthplace: Los Angeles, CA
Information Available in These Sources: SATA 37, SATA 39

HALLMAN, RUTH
Birthdate: 6/30/1929
Birthplace: Hertford, NC
Information Available in These Sources: SATA 28, SATA 43

HALLSTEAD, WILLIAM F(INN) III
Birthdate: 4/20/1924
Birthplace: Scranton, PA
Information Available in These Sources: ABYP 4, SATA 11

HALLWARD, MICHAEL
Birthdate: 10/2/1889
Birthplace: London, England
Information Available in These Sources: SATA 12

HALSELL, GRACE
Birthdate: 5/7/1923
Birthplace: Lubbock, TX
Information Available in These Sources: ABYP 2, ABYP 3, SATA 13

HALSTED, ANNA ROOSEVELT
Birthdate: 5/3/1906
Birthplace: New York, NY
Deathdate: 12/1/1975
Information Available in These Sources: SATA 30

HALTER, JON C(HARLES)
Birthdate: 11/24/1941
Birthplace: Hamilton, OH
Information Available in These Sources: ABYP 4, SATA 22

HAMALIAN, LEO
Birthdate: 1/13/1920
Birthplace: New York, NY
Information Available in These Sources: SATA 41

HAMBERGER, JOHN (F.)
Birthdate: 8/17/1934
Birthplace: Jamaica, Long Island, NY
Information Available in These Sources: IBYP 1, IBYP 2, ICB 3, SATA 14

HAMBLIN, DORA JANE
Birthdate: 6/15/1920
Birthplace: Bedford, IA
Information Available in These Sources: ABYP 3, SATA 36

HAMERSTROM, FRANCES
(Claire Windsor)
Birthdate: 12/17/1907
Birthplace: Needham, MA
Information Available in These Sources: SATA 24

HAMIL, THOMAS ARTHUR
(Tom Hamil)
Birthdate: 1928
Information Available in These Sources: ABYP 2, ABYP 3, SATA 14

HAMIL, TOM
See Hamil, Thomas Arthur

HAMILL, ETHEL
See Webb, Jean Francis (III)

HAMILTON, ALICE
See Cromie, Alice Hamilton

HAMILTON, CHARLES
Birthdate: 12/24/1913
Birthplace: Ludington, MI
Information Available in These Sources: ABYP 4

HAMILTON, DIANE (BROOKS)
Information Available in These Sources: ABYP 4

HAMILTON, DOROTHY
Birthdate: 9/25/1906
Birthplace: Selma, IN
Deathdate: 9/14/1983
Information Available in These Sources: SATA 12, SATA 35

HAMILTON, EDITH
Birthdate: 8/12/1867
Birthplace: Dresden, Germany
Deathdate: 5/31/1963
Information Available in These Sources: SATA 20

HAMILTON, GAIL
See Corcoran, Barbara

HAMILTON, KAY
See DeLeeuw, Cateau (Wilhelmina)

HAMILTON, MORSE
Birthdate: 8/16/1943
Birthplace: Detroit, MI
Information Available in These Sources: SATA 35

HAMILTON, RUSSEL
Information Available in These Sources: ABYP 2, ABYP 3

HAMILTON, VIRGINIA (ESTHER)
(Virginia Hamilton Adoff)
Birthdate: 3/12/1936 or 3/12/1933
Birthplace: Yellow Springs, OH
Information Available in These Sources: ABYP 3, AICB, BAI, DACF, JBA 4MBMP, SATA 4, SATA 56, TCCW 1 TCCW 2, TCCW 3

HAMLET, OVA
See Lupoff, Richard A(llen)

HAMMER, CHARLES
Birthdate: 8/8/1934
Birthplace: Tulsa, OK
Information Available in These Sources: SATA 58

HAMMER, RICHARD
Birthdate: 3/22/1928
Birthplace: Hartford, CT
Information Available in These Sources: SATA 6

HAMMERMAN, GAY M(ORENUS)
Birthdate: 5/14/1926
Birthplace: Richmond, VA
Information Available in These Sources: SATA 9

HAMMOND, WINIFRED G(RAHAM)
Birthdate: 6/22/1899
Birthplace: Covington, IN
Information Available in These Sources: ABYP 4, SATA 29

HAMMONTREE, MARIE (GERTRUDE)
Birthdate: 6/19/1913
Birthplace: Jefferson County, IN
Information Available in These Sources: SATA 13

HAMPSON, DENMAN
See Hampson, Richard Denman

HAMPSON, RICHARD DENMAN
(Denman Hampson)
Birthdate: 3/5/1929
Birthplace: San Bernadino, CA
Information Available in These Sources: SATA 15

HAMSA, BOBBIE
Birthdate: 6/14/1944
Birthplace: Ord, NE
Information Available in These Sources: SATA 38, SATA 52

HANCOCK, DAVNEY
See Carter, Katharine J(ones)

HANCOCK, MARY A.
Birthdate: 3/21/1923
Birthplace: Berlin, WI
Information Available in These Sources: SATA 31

HANCOCK, SIBYL
Birthdate: 11/10/1940
Birthplace: Pasadena, TX
Information Available in These Sources: SATA 9

HANDFORTH, THOMAS (SCHOFIELD)
Birthdate: 9/16/1897
Birthplace: Tacoma, WA
Deathdate: 10/19/1948
Information Available in These Sources: ABYP 1, ABYP 3, IBYP 1, IBYP 2ICB 1, ICB 2, JBA 2, SATA 42

HANDVILLE, ROBERT (TOMPKINS)
Birthdate: 3/23/1924
Birthplace: Paterson, NJ
Information Available in These Sources: SATA 45

HANE, ROGER
Birthdate: 1940
Birthplace: Bradford, PA
Deathdate: 6/14/1974 or 1973 or 1975
Information Available in These Sources: SATA 20

HANEY, ERENE CHEKI
Birthplace: Russia
Information Available in These Sources: ABYP 4

HANEY, LYNN
Birthdate: 2/12/1941
Birthplace: Pittsburgh, PA
Information Available in These Sources: SATA 23

HANFF, HELENE
Birthplace: Philadelphia, PA
Information Available in These Sources: SATA 11

HANLON, EMILY
Birthdate: 4/26/1945
Birthplace: New York, NY
Information Available in These Sources: SATA 15, JBA 6

HANN, JACQUIE
Birthdate: 5/18/1951
Birthplace: New York, NY
Information Available in These Sources: SATA 19

HANNA, BILL
See Hanna, William

HANNA, GENEVA R(EGULA)
Birthdate: 11/25/1914
Birthplace: Paynesville, MN
Information Available in These Sources: ABYP 2, ABYP 3

HANNA, PAUL R(OBERT)
Birthdate: 6/21/1902
Birthplace: Sioux City, IA
Information Available in These Sources: SATA 9

HANNA, WILLIAM
(Bill Hanna)
Birthdate: 7/14/1910
Birthplace: Melrose, NM
Information Available in These Sources: SATA 51

HANNUM, SARA
Birthplace: Moundsville, WV
Information Available in These Sources: ABYP 2, ABYP 3

HANO, ARNOLD
Birthdate: 3/2/1922
Birthplace: New York, NY
Information Available in These Sources: ABYP 2, ABYP 3, SATA 12

HANSEN, CARYL (HALL)
(Caryl Hall)
Birthdate: 11/3/1929
Birthplace: Berkeley, CA
Information Available in These Sources: SATA 39

HANSEN, HARRY
Birthdate: 12/26/1884
Birthplace: Davenport, IA
Deathdate: 1/2/1977
Information Available in These Sources: ABYP 2, ABYP 3

HANSEN, JOYCE W.
Birthdate: 10/18/1942
Birthplace: New York, NY
Information Available in These Sources: BAI, SATA 39, SATA 46, TCCW 3

HANSEN, RON
Birthdate: 12/8/1947
Birthplace: Omaha, NE
Information Available in These Sources: SATA 56

HANSER, RICHARD (FREDERICK)
Birthdate: 12/15/1909
Birthplace: Buffalo, NY
Information Available in These Sources: ABYP 4, SATA 13

HANSON, JOAN
Birthdate: 6/25/1938
Birthplace: Appleton, WI
Information Available in These Sources: SATA 8

HANSON, JOSEPH E.
Birthdate, 1894?
Deathdate: 3/15/1971
Information Available in These Sources: SATA 27

HAOZOUS (PULLING ROOTS)
See Houser, Allan C.

HARALD, ERIC
See Boesen, Victor

HARCOURT, ELLEN KNOWLES
Birthdate, 1890?
Deathdate: 1/1/1984
Information Available in These Sources: SATA 36

HARDIN, J. D.
See Sheldon, Walt(er J.)

HARDING, CHARLOTTE
Birthdate: 8/31/1873
Birthplace: Newark, NJ
Deathdate: 1951
Information Available in These Sources: ICB 1

HARDWICK, RICHARD (HOLMES, JR.)
(Rick Holmes)
Birthdate: 6/28/1923
Birthplace: Atlanta, GA
Information Available in These Sources: SATA 12

HARDY, ALICE DALE
See Stratemeyer, Edward L.

HARDY, STUART
See Schisgall, Oscar

HARE, NORMA Q(UARLES)
Birthdate: 7/10/1924
Birthplace: Dadeville, MO
Information Available in These Sources: SATA 41, SATA 46

HARGIS, JOHN EDWIN
Birthdate: 10/10/1914
Birthplace: Hughes Springs, TX
Information Available in These Sources: ICB 1

HARGRAVE, LEONIE
See Disch, Thomas M(ichael)

HARGROVE, JAMES
(Jim Hargrove)
Birthdate: 5/7/1947
Birthplace: New York, NY
Information Available in These Sources: SATA 50, 57

HARGROVE, JIM
See Hargrove, James

HARK, MILDRED
See McQueen, Mildred Hark

HARKINS, PHILIP
(John Blaine)
Birthdate: 9/29/1912
Birthplace: Boston, MA
Information Available in These Sources: ABYP 1, ABYP 3, MJA, SATA 6

HARLAN, ELIZABETH
Birthdate: 11/11/1945
Birthplace: New York, NY
Information Available in These Sources: SATA 35, SATA 41

HARLAN, GLEN
See Cebulash, Mel

HARLOW, ALVIN FAY
Birthdate: 3/10/1875
Birthplace: Sedalia, MO
Deathdate: 11/17/1963
Information Available in These Sources: ABYP 2, ABYP 3

HARMAN, FRED
Birthdate, 1902?
Deathdate: 1/2/1982
Information Available in These Sources: SATA 30

HARMAN, HUGH
Birthdate, 1903?
Birthplace: Pagosa Springs, CO
Deathdate: 11/26/1982
Information Available in These Sources: SATA 33

HARMELINK, BARBARA (MARY)
Birthplace: Ningpo, China
Information Available in These Sources: SATA 9

HARMER, MABEL
Birthdate: 9/28/1894
Birthplace: Logan, UT
Information Available in These Sources: SATA 45

HARMON, MARGARET
Birthdate: 1/4/1906
Birthplace: Philadelphia, PA
Information Available in These Sources: SATA 20

HARNAN, TERRY
(Eric Traviss Hull)
Birthdate: 2/1/1920
Birthplace: New York, NY
Information Available in These Sources: SATA 12

HARNDEN, RUTH (PEABODY)
Birthplace: Boston, MA
Information Available in These Sources: ABYP 4, DACF

HARPER, MARY WOOD
See Dixon, Jeanne

HARPER, WILHELMINA
Birthdate: 4/21/1884
Birthplace: Farmington, ME
Deathdate: 12/23/1973
Information Available in These Sources: ABYP 1, ABYP 3, SATA 4, SATA 26

HARRAH, MICHAEL
Birthdate: 2/19/1940
Birthplace: Marion, IN
Information Available in These Sources: SATA 41

HARRAH, WENDY MCLEOD WATSON
See Watson, Wendy (McLeod)

HARRELL, SARA GORDON
See Banks, Sara (Jeanne Gordon Harrell)

HARRIES, JOAN
(Joan Harries Katsarakis)
Birthdate: 10/23/1922
Birthplace: Pembrok, Wales (South)
Information Available in These Sources: SATA 39

HARRIS, AGES (KUEHNER)
Information Available in These Sources: ABYP 4

HARRIS, AURAND
Birthdate: 7/4/1915
Birthplace: Jamesport, MO
Information Available in These Sources: SATA 37, TCCW 1, TCCW 2, TCCW 3

HARRIS, BENJAMIN
Birthplace: England
Deathdate: 1720
Information Available in These Sources: DLB 42

HARRIS, CATHERINE
See Ainsworth, Catherine Harris

HARRIS, CHRISTIE (LUCY IRWIN)
Birthdate: 11/21/1907
Birthplace: Newark, NJ
Information Available in These Sources: ABYP 4, JBA 4, SATA 6

HARRIS, COLVER
See Colver, Anne

HARRIS, JANET (UROVSKY)
Birthdate: 4/17/1932
Birthplace: Newark, NJ
Deathdate: 12/6/1979
Information Available in These Sources: ABYP 4, SATA 4, SATA 23

HARRIS, JOEL CHANDLER
Birthdate: 12/9/1848 or 12/9/1845
Birthplace: Eatonton, GA
Deathdate: 7/3/1908
Information Available in These Sources: ABYP 1, ABYP 3, DLB 42, JBA 1 SVC 2, SVC 3, TCCW 1, TCCW 2, TCCW 3, WC, WCL, YABC

HARRIS, JOHN
Birthdate: 1935
Information Available in These Sources: ABYP 4

HARRIS, JONATHAN
Birthdate: 11/13/1921
Birthplace: New York, NY
Information Available in These Sources: SATA 52

HARRIS, JULIE
Birthdate: 12/2/1925
Birthplace: Grosse Pointe Park, MI
Information Available in These Sources: ABYP 4

HARRIS, LAVINIA
See Johnston, Norma

HARRIS, LEON A., JR.
Birthdate: 6/20/1926
Birthplace: New York, NY
Information Available in These Sources: ABYP 2, ABYP 3, SATA 4

HARRIS, LORLE K(EMPE)
Birthdate: 1/9/1912
Birthplace: Hackensack, NJ
Information Available in These Sources: SATA 22

HARRIS, MARILYN
See Springer, Marilyn Harris

HARRIS, MARK JONATHAN
Birthdate: 10/28/1941
Birthplace: Scranton, PA
Information Available in These Sources: DACF, SATA 32

HARRIS, POLLY ANNE (COLVER)
See Colver, Anne

HARRIS, ROBIE H.
Information Available in These Sources: SATA 53

HARRIS, SHERWOOD
Birthdate: 11/26/1932
Birthplace: New York, NY
Information Available in These Sources: SATA 25

HARRIS, STEVEN MICHAEL
Birthdate: 8/31/1957
Birthplace: Fall River, MA
Information Available in These Sources: SATA 55

HARRISON, C. WILLIAM
(Will Hickok, Coe Williams)
Birthdate: 7/14/1913
Birthplace: Indianapolis, IN
Information Available in These Sources: ABYP 2, ABYP 3, SATA 35

HARRISON, DAVID LEE
(Kennon Graham)
Birthdate: 3/13/1937
Birthplace: Springfield, MO
Information Available in These Sources: SATA 26

HARRISON, DELORIS
Birthdate: 2/4/1938
Birthplace: Bedford, VA
Information Available in These Sources: SATA 9

HARRISON, HARRY (MAX)
Birthdate: 3/12/1925
Birthplace: Stamford, CT
Information Available in These Sources: ABYP 4, SATA 4

HARSHAW, RUTH H(ETZEL)
Birthdate, 1890?
Birthplace: Almond, WI
Deathdate: 1/18/1968
Information Available in These Sources: ABYP 1, ABYP 3, SATA 27

HART, BRUCE
Birthdate: 1/15/1938
Birthplace: New York, NY
Information Available in These Sources: SATA 39, SATA 57

HART, CAROLE
Birthdate: 4/30/1943
Birthplace: Paterson, NJ
Information Available in These Sources: SATA 39, SATA 57

HARTE, BRET
See Harte, Francis Bret(t)

HARTE, FRANCIS BRET(T)
(Bret Harte)
Birthdate: 8/25/1836?
Birthplace: Albany, NY
Deathdate: 5/5/1902
Information Available in These Sources: ABYP 2, ABYP 3, SATA 26

HARTELIUS, MARGARET A.
Birthplace: Reading, MA
Information Available in These Sources: ABYP 4

HARTLEY, ELLEN (RAPHAEL)
Birthdate: 1/1/1915
Birthplace: Dortmund, Germany
Information Available in These Sources: SATA 23

HARTLEY, FRED ALLAN III
Birthdate: 3/22/1953
Birthplace: Morristown, NJ
Information Available in These Sources: SATA 41

HARTLEY, WILLIAM B(ROWN)
Birthdate: 7/21/1913
Birthplace: South Norwalk, CT
Information Available in These Sources: SATA 23

HARTMAN, GERTRUDE
Birthdate: 1876
Birthplace: Philadelphia, PA
Deathdate: 5/12/1955
Information Available in These Sources: JBA 2

HARTMAN, JANE E(VANGELINE)
Birthdate: 2/17/1928
Birthplace: Long Branch, NJ
Information Available in These Sources: SATA 47

HARTMAN, LOUIS F(RANCIS)
Birthdate: 1/17/1901
Birthplace: New York, NY
Information Available in These Sources: SATA 22

HARTSHORN, RUTH M.
Birthdate: 4/4/1928
Birthplace: Boston, MA
Information Available in These Sources: SATA 11

HARTWELL, NANCY
See Callahan, Claire Wallis

HARVEY, BRETT
Birthdate: 4/28/1936
Birthplace: Chicago, IL
Information Available in These Sources: JBA 6

HARVEY, EDITH
Birthdate, 1908?
Deathdate: 2/12/1972
Information Available in These Sources: SATA 27

HARWIN, BRIAN
See Henderson, LeGrand

HARWOOD, PEARL AUGUSTA (BRAGDON)
Birthdate: 12/21/1903
Birthplace: Grafton, MA
Information Available in These Sources: ABYP 4, SATA 9

HASELEY, DENNIS
Birthdate: 6/28/1950
Birthplace: Cleveland, OH
Information Available in These Sources: SATA 44, SATA 57

HASKELL, HELEN (EGGLESTON)
Birthdate: 1871
Birthplace: Fairwater, WI
Information Available in These Sources: JBA 1, JBA 2

HASKINS, JAMES S.
(Jim Haskins)
Birthdate: 9/19/1941
Birthplace: Montgomery or Demopolis, AL
Information Available in These Sources: ABYP 4, BAI, SATA 9, JBA 6

HASKINS, JIM
See Haskins, James S.

HASSLER, JON (FRANCIS)
Birthdate: 3/30/1933
Birthplace: Minneapolis, MN
Information Available in These Sources: SATA 19

HASTINGS, BEVERLY
See Barkin, Carol and James, Elizabeth

HATCH, ALDEN
Birthdate: 9/26/1898
Birthplace: New York, NY
Deathdate: 2/1/1975
Information Available in These Sources: ABYP 2, ABYP 3

HATCH, MARY COTTAM
Birthdate, 1912?
Birthplace: Salt Lake City, UT
Deathdate: 6/3/1970
Information Available in These Sources: SATA 28, SVC 2, SVC 3

HATLO, JIMMY
Birthdate: 9/1/1898
Birthplace: Providence, RI
Deathdate: 11/30/1963
Information Available in These Sources: SATA 23

HAUFRECHT, HERBERT
Birthdate: 1909
Information Available in These Sources: ABYP 4

HAUGHEY, BETTY ELLEN
Information Available in These Sources: ABYP 4

HAUMAN, DORIS
Birthdate: 8/29/1897
Birthplace: West Somerville, MA
Information Available in These Sources: ICB 2, SATA 32

HAUMAN, GEORGE
Birthdate: 5/19/1890
Birthplace: Revere, MA
Information Available in These Sources: ICB 2, SATA 32

HAUPTLY, DENIS J(AMES)
Birthdate: 11/6/1945
Birthplace: Jersey City, NJ
Information Available in These Sources: SATA 57

HAUSER, MARGARET L(OUISE)
(Gay Head)
Birthdate: 5/13/1909
Birthplace: High Point, NC
Information Available in These Sources: SATA 10

HAUSMAN, GERALD
(Gerry Hausman)
Birthdate: 10/13/1945
Birthplace: Baltimore, MD
Information Available in These Sources: SATA 13

HAUSMAN, GERRY
See Hausman, Gerald

HAUTZIG, DEBORAH
Birthdate: 10/1/1956
Birthplace: New York, NY
Information Available in These Sources: JBA 5, SATA 31

HAUTZIG, ESTHER (RUDOMIN)
(Esther Rudomin)
Birthdate: 10/18/1930
Birthplace: Vilna, Poland
Information Available in These Sources: ABYP 2, ABYP 3, JBA 3, SATA 4

HAVERSTOCK, MARY SAYRE
Birthdate: 6/24/1932
Birthplace: Cambridge, MA
Information Available in These Sources: ABYP 4

HAVIGHURST, MARION (BOYD)
Birthplace: Marietta, OH
Deathdate: 2/24/1974
Information Available in These Sources: ABYP 3, MJA

HAVIGHURST, WALTER (EDWIN)
Birthdate: 11/28/1901
Birthplace: Appleton, WI
Information Available in These Sources: ABYP 1, ABYP 3, MJA, SATA 1

HAVILAND, VIRGINIA
Birthdate: 5/21/1911
Birthplace: Rochester, NY
Deathdate: 1/6/1988
Information Available in These Sources: ABYP 4, JBA 4, SATA 6, SATA 54

HAWES, CHARLES BOARDMAN
Birthdate: 1/24/1889
Birthplace: Clifton Springs, NY
Deathdate: 7/15/1923
Information Available in These Sources: ABYP 1, ABYP 3, JBA 1, TCCW 2 TCCW 3

HAWES, JUDY
Birthdate: 10/16/1913
Birthplace: New York, NY
Information Available in These Sources: SATA 4

HAWKES, HESTER
Birthdate: 1900
Information Available in These Sources: ABYP 1, ABYP 3

HAWKES, LOUISE
(Jamie Suzanne)
Birthdate: 6/21/1943
Birthplace: Boulder, CO
Information Available in These Sources: SATA 60

HAWKINS, ARTHUR
Birthdate: 4/9/1903
Birthplace: Cumberland, MD
Information Available in These Sources: IBYP 2, SATA 19

HAWKINS, HELENA ANN QUAIL
(Quail Hawkins)
Birthdate: 3/29/1905
Birthplace: Spokane, WA
Information Available in These Sources: ABYP 1, ABYP 3, SATA 6

HAWKINS, QUAIL
See Hawkins, Helena Ann Quail

HAWKINSON, JOHN (SAMUEL)
Birthdate: 11/8/1912
Birthplace: Chicago, IL
Information Available in These Sources: ABYP 2, ABYP 3, JBA 4, SATA 4

HAWKINSON, LUCY (OZONE)
Birthdate: 1924
Birthplace: CA
Deathdate: 12/6/1971
Information Available in These Sources: ABYP 2, ABYP 3, SATA 21

HAWLEY, MABEL C.
See Stratemeyer, Edward L.

HAWTHORNE, CAPTAIN R. M.
See Ellis, Edward S(ylvester)

HAWTHORNE, HILDEGARDE
Birthdate: 9/25/1871
Birthplace: New York, NY
Deathdate: 1952
Information Available in These Sources: ABYP 1, ABYP 3, JBA 1, JBA 2

HAWTHORNE, NATHANIEL
Birthdate: 7/4/1804
Birthplace: Salem, MA
Deathdate: 5/19/1864
Information Available in These Sources: ABYP 4, SVC 2, SVC 3, WC, WCL YABC

HAWTHORNE, R. M.
See Ellis, Edward S(ylvester)

HAY, JOHN
Birthdate: 8/31/1915
Birthplace: Ipswich, MA
Information Available in These Sources: SATA 13

HAY, TIMOTHY
See Brown, Margaret Wise

HAYCRAFT, HOWARD
Birthdate: 7/24/1905
Birthplace: Madelia, MN
Information Available in These Sources: ABYP 1, ABYP 3, SATA 6

HAYCRAFT, MOLLY COSTAIN
Birthdate: 12/6/1911
Birthplace: Toronto, Canada
Information Available in These Sources: SATA 6

HAYDEN, ANNA BRADFORD
See Agle, Nan Hayden

HAYDEN, GWENDOLEN LAMPSHIRE
Birthdate: 1904
Birthplace: Eugene, OR
Information Available in These Sources: SATA 35

HAYDEN, ROBERT C(ARTER), JR.
Birthdate: 8/21/1937
Birthplace: New Bedford, MA
Information Available in These Sources: SATA 28, 47

HAYDEN, ROBERT E(ARL)
Birthdate: 8/4/1913
Birthplace: Detroit, MI
Deathdate: 2/25/1980
Information Available in These Sources: ABYP 4, SATA 19, SATA 26

HAYES, CARLTON J. H.
Birthdate: 5/16/1882
Birthplace: Afton, NY
Deathdate: 9/3/1964
Information Available in These Sources: SATA 11

HAYES, FLORENCE (SOOY)
Birthdate: 1895
Information Available in These Sources: ABYP 1, ABYP 3

HAYES, GEOFFREY
Birthdate: 12/3/1947
Birthplace: Pasadena, CA
Information Available in These Sources: SATA 26

HAYES, JOHN F.
Birthdate: 8/5/1904
Birthplace: Dryden, Ontario, Canada
Information Available in These Sources: SATA 11

HAYES, SHEILA
Birthdate: 6/16/1937
Birthplace: New York, NY
Information Available in These Sources: SATA 50, SATA 51

HAYES, WILL
Birthplace: New York, NY
Information Available in These Sources: SATA 7

HAYES, WILLIAM D(IMITT)
Birthdate: 3/5/1913
Birthplace: Goliad, TX
Information Available in These Sources: ABYP 2, ABYP 3, SATA 8

HAYMAN, LEROY
Birthdate: 8/12/1916
Birthplace: Chicago, IL
Information Available in These Sources: ABYP 4

HAYNES, ANNE
See Madlee, Dorothy (Haynes)

HAYNES, BETSY
(James Betts)
Birthdate: 10/20/1937
Birthplace: Benton, IL
Information Available in These Sources: SATA 37, SATA 48

HAYNES, BOB
See Haynes, Robert

HAYNES, LINDA
See Swinford, Betty (June Wells)

HAYNES, NANDA WARD
See Ward, Nanda Weedon

HAYNES, NELMA
Birthplace: TX
Information Available in These Sources: ABYP 4

HAYNES, ROBERT
(Bob Haynes)
Birthplace: CO
Information Available in These Sources: IBYP 1, IBYP 2

HAYS, H(OFFMANN) R(EYNOLDS)
Birthdate: 3/25/1904
Birthplace: New York, NY
Deathdate: 10/16/1980
Information Available in These Sources: SATA 26

HAYS, HOBART VANCE
(Hobe Hays)
Information Available in These Sources: ABYP 2, ABYP 3

HAYS, HOBE
See Hays, Hobart Vance

HAYS, WILMA PITCHFORD
Birthdate: 11/22/1909
Birthplace: Fullerton, NE
Information Available in These Sources: ABYP 2, ABYP 3, JBA 3, SATA 1 SATA 28

HAYWARD, LINDA
Birthdate: 6/6/1943
Birthplace: Los Angeles, CA
Information Available in These Sources: SATA 39

HAYWOOD, CAROLYN
Birthdate: 1/3/1898
Birthplace: Philadelphia, PA
Information Available in These Sources: ABYP 1, ABYP 3, AICB, JBA 2, MBMP, SATA 1, SATA 29, TCCW 1 TCCW 2, TCCW 3

HAZELTINE, ALICE ISABEL
Birthdate: 4/15/1878
Birthplace: Warren, PA
Deathdate: 1959
Information Available in These Sources: ABYP 2, ABYP 3

HAZELTON, ELIZABETH BALDWIN
Information Available in These Sources: ABYP 4

HAZEN, BARBARA SHOOK
Birthdate: 2/4/1930
Birthplace: Dayton, OH
Information Available in These Sources: SATA 27, JBA 6

HAZLETT, EDWARD EVERETT
Birthdate: 1892
Birthplace: KS
Information Available in These Sources: ABYP 1, ABYP 3

HEAD, GAY
See Hauser, Margaret L(ouise)

HEADLEY, ELIZABETH
See Cavanna, Betty

HEADSTROM, BIRGER RICHARD
(Richard Headstrom)
Birthdate: 2/21/1902
Birthplace: Cambridge, MA
Information Available in These Sources: ABYP 2, ABYP 3, SATA 8

HEADSTROM, RICHARD
See Headstrom, Birger Richard

HEADY, ELEANOR B(UTLER)
Birthdate: 3/13/1917
Birthplace: Bliss, ID
Information Available in These Sources: ABYP 4, SATA 7, SATA 8

HEAL, EDITH
(Edith Heal Berrien, Eileen Page, Margaret Powers)
Birthdate: 8/23/1903
Information Available in These Sources: SATA 7

HEALEY, BROOKS
See Albert, Burton, Jr.

HEALEY, LARRY
Birthdate: 11/10/1927
Birthplace: Boston, MA
Information Available in These Sources: SATA 42, SATA 44

HEAPS, WILLARD (ALLISON)
Birthdate: 2/3/1908 or 2/3/1909
Birthplace: Whiting, IA
Information Available in These Sources: ABYP 2, ABYP 3, SATA 26

HEARNE, BETSY GOULD
Birthdate: 10/6/1942
Birthplace: Wilsonville, AL
Information Available in These Sources: SATA 38, JBA 6

HEATH, CHARLES D(ICKINSON)
Birthdate: 6/28/1941
Birthplace: Waterloo, IA
Information Available in These Sources: SATA 46

HEAVLIN, JAY
Birthplace: OH
Information Available in These Sources: ABYP 4

HECHT, GEORGE J(OSEPH)
Birthdate: 11/1/1895
Birthplace: New York, NY
Deathdate: 4/23/1980
Information Available in These Sources: SATA 22

HECK, BESSIE HOLLAND
Birthdate: 10/25/1911
Birthplace: Colgate, OK
Information Available in These Sources: SATA 26

HEFTER, RICHARD
Birthdate: 3/20/1942
Birthplace: New York, NY
Information Available in These Sources: SATA 31

HEGARTY, REGINALD BEATON
Birthdate: 8/5/1906
Birthplace: Somerset, MA
Deathdate: 1/18/1973
Information Available in These Sources: ABYP 2, ABYP 3, SATA 10

HEIDE, FLORENCE PARRY
(Alex B. Allen, Jamie McDonald)
Birthdate: 2/27/1919
Birthplace: Pittsburgh, PA
Information Available in These Sources: ABYP 4, JBA 4, SATA 32, TCCW 2TCCW 3

HEIDERSTADT, DOROTHY
Birthdate: 10/8/1907
Birthplace: Geneva, NE
Information Available in These Sources: ABYP 1, ABYP 3, SATA 6

HEILBRONER, JOAN KNAPP
Birthdate: 3/13/1922
Birthplace: Garden City, NY
Information Available in These Sources: ABYP 4

HEILBRUN, LOIS HUSSEY
Birthdate, 1922?
Birthplace: Norwich, CT
Deathdate: 10/21/1987
Information Available in These Sources: SATA 54

HEILMAN, JOAN RATTNER
Birthplace: New York, NY
Information Available in These Sources: SATA 50

HEIN, LUCILLE ELEANOR
Birthdate: 6/11/1915
Birthplace: Chicago, IL
Information Available in These Sources: ABYP 4, SATA 20

HEINEMANN, GEORGE ALFRED
Birthdate: 12/9/1918
Birthplace: Chicago, IL
Information Available in These Sources: SATA 31

HEINLEIN, ROBERT A(NSON)
(Anson MacDonald, Lyle Monroe, John Riverside, Caleb Saunders, Simon York)
Birthdate: 7/7/1907 or 10/21/1907
Birthplace: Butler, MO
Deathdate: 5/8/1988
Information Available in These Sources: ABYP 1, ABYP 3, MJA, SATA 9, SATA 56, TCCW 1, TCCW 2, TCCW 3

HEINLY, JOHN
Birthdate: 1932
Information Available in These Sources: IBYP 2

HEINS, PAUL
Birthdate: 2/15/1909
Birthplace: Boston, MA
Information Available in These Sources: SATA 13

HEINTZE, CARL
Birthdate: 6/18/1922
Birthplace: Sacramento, CA
Information Available in These Sources: SATA 26

HEINZ, W(ILFRED) C(HARLES)
Birthdate: 1/11/1915
Birthplace: Mount Vernon, NY
Information Available in These Sources: SATA 26

HEINZEN, MILDRED
See Masters, Mildred

HEIT, ROBERT
Birthplace: NY
Information Available in These Sources: ABYP 4

HELFMAN, ELIZABETH S(EAVER)
Birthdate: 8/1/1911
Birthplace: Pittsfield, MA
Information Available in These Sources: ABYP 2, ABYP 3, SATA 3

HELFMAN, HARRY
See Helfman, Henry

HELFMAN, HENRY
(Harry Helfman)
Birthdate: 4/21/1910
Birthplace: New York, NY
Information Available in These Sources: ABYP 2, ABYP 3, SATA 3

HELLER, LINDA
Birthdate: 9/14/1944
Birthplace: New York, NY
Information Available in These Sources: SATA 40, SATA 46

HELLMAN, HAL
See Hellman, Harold

HELLMAN, HAROLD
(Hal Hellman)
Birthdate: 9/15/1927
Birthplace: New York, NY
Information Available in These Sources: ABYP 4, SATA 4

HELMER, JEAN CASSELS
Birthplace: Nashville, TN
Information Available in These Sources: IBYP 2

HELWEG, HANS H.
Birthdate: 2/21/1917
Birthplace: Denmark
Information Available in These Sources: ICB 2, ICB 3, ICB 4, SATA 33, SATA 50

HEMMING, ROY
Birthdate: 5/27/1928
Birthplace: Hamden, CT
Information Available in These Sources: SATA 11

HEMPHILL, MARTHA LOCKE
Birthdate: 7/25/1904
Birthplace: Fort Dodge, IA
Information Available in These Sources: SATA 37

HEMPHILL, PAUL (JAMES)
Birthdate: 2/18/1936
Birthplace: Birmingham, AL
Information Available in These Sources: ABYP 4

HEMSCHEMEYER, JUDITH
Birthdate: 8/7/1935
Birthplace: Sheboygan, WI
Information Available in These Sources: ABYP 4

HENDERLEY, BROOKS
See Stratemeyer, Edward L.

HENDERSHOT, JUDITH
Birthdate: 5/19/1940
Information Available in These Sources: JBA 6

HENDERSON, LEGRAND
(Brian Harwin, LeGrand)
Birthdate: 5/24/1901
Birthplace: Torrington, CT
Deathdate: 1/25/1964
Information Available in These Sources: ABYP 1, ABYP 3, ICB 1, ICB 2, JBA 2, SATA 9

HENDERSON, NANCY WALLACE
Birthdate: 7/21/1916
Birthplace: Wilmington, NC
Information Available in These Sources: SATA 22

HENDERSON, ZENNA (CHLARSON)
Birthdate: 11/1/1917
Birthplace: Tucson, AZ
Information Available in These Sources: SATA 5

HENDRICK, JOE
See Hendrick, Joseph

HENDRICK, JOSEPH
(Joe Hendrick)
Birthdate: 1934
Information Available in These Sources: IBYP 2

HENDRICKSON, WALTER BROOKFIELD, JR.
Birthdate: 8/24/1936
Birthplace: Indianapolis, IN
Information Available in These Sources: SATA 9

HENKES, KEVIN
Birthdate: 11/27/1960
Birthplace: Racine, WI
Information Available in These Sources: SATA 43, JBA 6

HENKLE, HENRIETTA
See Stephens, Henrietta Henkle

HENNEBERGER, ROBERT G.
Birthdate: 3/8/1921
Birthplace: Baltimore, MD
Information Available in These Sources: IBYP 1, IBYP 2, ICB 2

HENRIOD, LORRAINE (STEPHENS)
Birthdate: 5/12/1925
Birthplace: Los Angeles, CA
Information Available in These Sources: ABYP 4, SATA 26

HENRY, JOANNE LANDERS
Birthdate: 2/24/1927
Birthplace: Indianapolis, IN
Information Available in These Sources: SATA 6

HENRY, MARGUERITE (BREITHAUPT)
Birthdate: 4/13/1902
Birthplace: Hamden, CT
Information Available in These Sources: ABYP 1, ABYP 3, AICB, DACF, DLB 22, JBA 2, SATA 11, TCCW 1

HENRY, O(LIVER)
See Porter, William Sydney

HENRY, WILL
See Allen, Henry Wilson

HENSON, JAMES MAURY
(Jim Henson)
Birthdate: 9/24/1936
Birthplace: Greenville, MS
Deathdate: 5/16/1990
Information Available in These Sources: SATA 43

HENSON, JIM
See Henson, James Maury

HENTOFF, NAT(HAN IRVING)
Birthdate: 6/10/1925
Birthplace: Boston, MA
Information Available in These Sources: ABYP 2, ABYP 3, DACF, JBA 3, SATA 27, SATA 42, TCCW 1, TCCW 2, TCCW 3

HERBERT, DON
(Mr. Wizard)
Birthdate: 7/10/1917
Birthplace: Waconia, MN
Information Available in These Sources: ABYP 2, ABYP 3, SATA 2

HERBERT, FRANK (PATRICK)
Birthdate: 10/8/1920
Birthplace: Tacoma, WA
Deathdate: 2/11/1986
Information Available in These Sources: SATA 9, SATA 37, SATA 47

HEREFORD, ROBERT A.
Birthdate: 1902
Birthplace: Philippines
Information Available in These Sources: ABYP 2, ABYP 3

HERFORD, OLIVER
Birthdate: 12/1/1863
Birthplace: Sheffield, England
Deathdate: 7/5/1935
Information Available in These Sources: ABYP 4

HERKIMER, L(AWRENCE) R(USSELL)
Birthdate: 10/25/1925
Information Available in These Sources: ABYP 4, SATA 42

HERMAN, CHARLOTTE
Birthdate: 6/10/1937
Birthplace: Chicago, IL
Information Available in These Sources: SATA 20

HERMANSON, DENNIS (EVERETT)
Birthdate: 1/1/1947
Birthplace: Enterprise, AL
Information Available in These Sources: SATA 10

HERMES, PATRICIA
Birthdate: 2/21/1936
Birthplace: Brooklyn, NY
Information Available in These Sources: SATA 31, JBA 6

HERRERA, VELINO
Birthdate, 1902?
Birthplace: Zia Pueblo, Bernalillo, NM
Information Available in These Sources: ICB 1

HERRICK, JEAN MELLIN
See Mellin, Jeanne

HERRON, EDWARD A(LBERT)
Birthdate: 6/5/1912
Birthplace: Philadelphia, PA
Information Available in These Sources: SATA 4

HERSEY, JOHN (RICHARD)
Birthdate: 6/17/1914
Birthplace: Tientsin, China
Information Available in These Sources: SATA 25

HESS, FJERIL
Birthdate: 8/27/1893
Birthplace: Omaha, NE
Information Available in These Sources: JBA 1, JBA 2

HESS, LILO
Birthdate: 1916
Birthplace: Erfurt, Germany
Information Available in These Sources: ABYP 4, JBA 5, SATA 4

HEST, AMY
Birthdate: 4/28/1950
Birthplace: New York, NY
Information Available in These Sources: SATA 55

HEUER, KENNETH JOHN
Birthdate: 1/30/1927
Birthplace: Yonkers, NY
Information Available in These Sources: SATA 44

HEUMAN, WILLIAM
(George Kramer)
Birthdate: 2/11/1912
Birthplace: Brooklyn, NY
Deathdate: 8/21/1971
Information Available in These Sources: ABYP 1, ABYP 2, ABYP 3, SATA 21

HEWES, AGNES DANFORTH
Birthdate: 3/30/1874
Birthplace: Tripoli, Syria
Deathdate: 9/30/1963
Information Available in These Sources: ABYP 2, ABYP 3, JBA 1, JBA 2, SATA 35

HEYLIGER, WILLIAM
(Hawley Williams)
Birthdate: 3/22/1884
Birthplace: Hoboken, NJ
Deathdate: 1/15/1955
Information Available in These Sources: ABYP 1, ABYP 3, JBA 1, JBA 2, YABC

HEYMAN, KEN(NETH LOUIS)
Birthdate: 10/6/1930
Birthplace: New York, NY
Information Available in These Sources: SATA 34

HEYNEMAN, ANNE
Birthdate: 7/22/1910 or 7/22/1909
Birthplace: San Francisco, CA
Information Available in These Sources: ICB 1, ICB 2

HEYWARD, DU BOSE
Birthdate: 8/31/1885
Birthplace: Charleston, SC
Deathdate: 6/16/1940
Information Available in These Sources: SATA 21

HICKMAN, JANET
Birthdate: 7/8/1940
Birthplace: Kilbourne, OH
Information Available in These Sources: SATA 12

HICKMAN, MARTHA WHITMORE
Birthdate: 12/9/1925
Birthplace: Holyoke, MA
Information Available in These Sources: SATA 26

HICKOCK, WILL
See Harrison, C. William

HICKOK, LORENA A.
Birthdate, 1892?
Birthplace: East Troy, WI
Deathdate: 5/3/1968
Information Available in These Sources: ABYP 1, ABYP 3, SATA 20

HICKS, CLIFFORD B.
Birthdate: 8/10/1920
Birthplace: Marshalltown, IA
Information Available in These Sources: ABYP 1, ABYP 3, SATA 50

HICKS, ELEANOR B.
See Coerr, Eleanor (Page)

HIEATT, CONSTANCE B(ARTLETT)
Birthdate: 2/11/1928
Birthplace: Boston, MA
Information Available in These Sources: SATA 4

HIEBERT, RAY ELDON
Birthdate: 5/21/1932
Birthplace: Freeman, SD
Information Available in These Sources: SATA 13

HIGDON, HAL
(Lafayette Smith)
Birthdate: 6/17/1931
Birthplace: Chicago, IL
Information Available in These Sources: ABYP 4, SATA 4

HIGGINBOTTOM, J(EFFREY) WINSLOW
Birthdate: 3/24/1945
Birthplace: Worcester, MA
Information Available in These Sources: SATA 29

HIGHET, HELEN
See MacInnes, Helen

HIGHTOWER, FLORENCE (COLE)
Birthdate: 6/9/1916
Birthplace: Boston, MA
Deathdate: 3/6/1981
Information Available in These Sources: ABYP 1, ABYP 3, DACF, JBA 3, SATA 4, SATA 27, TCCW 1, TCCW 3

HIGHWATER, JAMAKE
(J. Marks)
Birthdate: 2/14/1942
Birthplace: Glacier County, MT
Information Available in These Sources: JBA 5, SATA 30, SATA 32, TCCW 2, TCCW 3

HILDEBRANDT, GREG
(The Brothers Hildebrandt, The Hildebrants)
Birthdate: 1/23/1939
Birthplace: Detroit, MI
Information Available in These Sources: SATA 33, SATA 55

HILDEBRANDT, TIM(OTHY)
(The Brothers Hildebrandt, The Hildebrandts)
Birthdate: 1/23/1939
Birthplace: Detroit, MI
Information Available in These Sources: SATA 33, SATA 55

HILDEBRANDTS, THE
See Hildebrandt, Greg; Hildebrandt, Tim(othy)

HILDER, ROWLAND
Birthdate: 6/28/1905
Birthplace: Great Neck, Long Island, NY
Information Available in These Sources: ICB 1, SATA 36

HILGARTNER, BETH
Birthdate: 6/7/1957
Birthplace: Baltimore, MD
Information Available in These Sources: SATA 58

HILL, DONNA (MARIE)
Birthplace: Salt Lake City, UT
Information Available in These Sources: SATA 24

HILL, ELIZABETH STARR
Birthdate: 11/4/1925
Birthplace: Lynn Haven, FL
Information Available in These Sources: ABYP 4, SATA 24

HILL, FRANK ERNEST
Birthdate: 8/29/1888
Birthplace: San Jose, CA
Deathdate: 11/2/1969
Information Available in These Sources: ABYP 2, ABYP 3

HILL, GRACE LIVINGSTON
(Marcia Macdonald)
Birthdate: 4/16/1865
Birthplace: Wellsville, NY
Deathdate: 2/23/1947
Information Available in These Sources: YABC

HILL, HELEN M(OREY)
Birthdate: 3/26/1915
Birthplace: Brooklyn, NY
Information Available in These Sources: SATA 27

HILL, MARGARET (OHLER)
(Meg Hill, Rachel Bennett, Andrea Thomas)
Birthdate: 9/6/1915
Birthplace: Jefferson, CO
Information Available in These Sources: ABYP 2, ABYP 3, SATA 36

HILL, MEG
See Hill, Margaret (Ohler)

HILL, MONICA
See Watson, Jane Werner

HILL, RALPH NADING
Birthdate: 9/19/1917
Birthplace: Burlington, VT
Information Available in These Sources: ABYP 2, ABYP 3

HILL, ROBERT W(HITE)
Birthdate: 9/12/1919
Birthplace: Richmond, VA
Information Available in These Sources: ABYP 2, ABYP 3, SATA 12

HILL, RUTH A.
See Viguers, Ruth Hill

HILL, RUTH LIVINGSTON
See Munce, Ruth (Livingston) Hill

HILLCOURT, WILLIAM
(Vilhelm Hans Bjerregaard-Jensen)
Birthdate: 8/6/1900
Birthplace: Aarhus, Denmark
Information Available in These Sources: ABYP 1, ABYP 3, SATA 27

HILLER, CARL E.
Information Available in These Sources: ABYP 4

HILLER, ILO (ANN)
Birthdate: 7/28/1938
Birthplace: Alexandria, IN
Information Available in These Sources: SATA 59

HILLERMAN, TONY
Birthdate: 5/27/1925
Information Available in These Sources: SATA 6

HILLERT, MARGARET
Birthdate: 1/22/1920
Birthplace: Saginaw, MI
Information Available in These Sources: SATA 8

HILLES, HELEN (TRAIN)
Birthdate: 1905
Birthplace: NY
Information Available in These Sources: ABYP 2, ABYP 3

HILLMAN, MAY
See Hipshman, May

HILLMAN, PRISCILLA (HARTFORD)
Birthdate: 7/24/1940
Birthplace: Newton, MA
Information Available in These Sources: SATA 39, SATA 48

HILLYER, V(IRGIL) M(ORES)
Birthdate: 9/2/1875
Birthplace: Weymouth, MA
Deathdate: 12/21/1931
Information Available in These Sources: ABYP 2, ABYP 3, JBA 1, JBA 2

HILTON, JAMES
Birthdate: 9/9/1900
Birthplace: Lancashire, England
Deathdate: 12/20/1954
Information Available in These Sources: SATA 34

HILTON, RALPH
Birthdate: 9/10/1907
Birthplace: Mendenhall, MS
Information Available in These Sources: SATA 8

HILTON, SUZANNE (MCLEAN)
Birthdate: 9/3/1922
Birthplace: Pittsburgh, PA
Information Available in These Sources: ABYP 4, SATA 4

HIMLER, ANN
Birthdate: 5/1/1946
Birthplace: Camden, NJ
Information Available in These Sources: SATA 8

HIMLER, RONALD (NORBERT)
Birthdate: 10/16/1937
Birthplace: Cleveland, OH
Information Available in These Sources: IBYP 2, ICB 4, SATA 6, JBA 6

HIMMELMAN, JOHN (CARL)
Birthdate: 10/3/1959
Birthplace: Kittery, ME
Information Available in These Sources: SATA 47

HINCKLEY, HELEN
See Jones, Helen Hinckley

HINE, AL
(Josephine Gibson, G. B. Kirtland)
Birthdate: 12/11/1915
Birthplace: Pittsburgh, PA
Information Available in These Sources: ABYP 2, ABYP 3, JBA 3

HINE, SESYLE JOSLIN
See Joslin, Sesyle

HINES, ANNA G(ROSSNICKLE)
Birthdate: 7/13/1946
Birthplace: Cincinnati, OH
Information Available in These Sources: SATA 45, SATA 51, JBA 6

HINES, BOB
See Hines, Robert W.

HINES, ROBERT W.
(Bob Hines)
Information Available in These Sources: IBYP 1, IBYP 2

HINKINS, VIRGINIA
Information Available in These Sources: ABYP 1, ABYP 3

HINKLE, THOMAS CLARK
Birthdate: 6/12/1876
Birthplace: Laclede, IL
Deathdate: 5/13/1949
Information Available in These Sources: ABYP 1, ABYP 3

HINTON, CHARLES LOUIS
Birthdate: 10/18/1869
Birthplace: Ithaca, NY
Deathdate: 10/12/1950
Information Available in These Sources: ICB 1

HINTON, S(USAN) E(LOISE)
Birthdate: 1950 or 1949 or 1948
Birthplace: Tulsa, OK
Information Available in These Sources: ABYP 4, DACF, JBA 4, SATA 19, SATA 58, TCCW 1, TCCW 2, TCCW 3

HINTON, SAM
Birthdate: 3/21/1917
Birthplace: Tulsa, OK
Information Available in These Sources: SATA 43

HINTZ, LOREN MARTIN
(Martin Hintz)
Birthdate: 6/1/1945
Birthplace: New Hampton, IA
Information Available in These Sources: SATA 39, SATA 47

HINTZ, MARTIN
See Hintz, Loren Martin

HIPPEL, URSULA VON
See VonHippel, Ursula

HIPPOPOTAMUS, EUGENE H.
See Kraus, Robert

HIPSHMAN, MAY
(May Hillman)
Birthdate: 1919
Information Available in These Sources: ABYP 2, ABYP 3

HIRSCH, PHIL
(Norman Lemon Peel, Bob Vlasic)
Birthdate: 8/18/1926
Birthplace: New York, NY
Information Available in These Sources: SATA 35

HIRSCH, S. CARL
Birthdate: 11/29/1913
Birthplace: Chicago, IL
Information Available in These Sources: ABYP 4, JBA 3, SATA 2

HIRSCHFELD, BURT
Birthdate: 1923
Birthplace: New York, NY
Information Available in These Sources: ABYP 4

HIRSCHI, RON
Birthdate: 5/18/1948
Birthplace: Bremerton, WA
Information Available in These Sources: SATA 56

HIRSCHMANN, LINDA (ANN)
Birthdate: 9/14/1941
Birthplace: Charleston, SC
Information Available in These Sources: SATA 40

HIRSH, MARILYN (JOYCE)
Birthdate: 1/1/1944
Birthplace: Chicago, IL
Deathdate: 10/17/1988
Information Available in These Sources: ABYP 4, ICB 4, JBA 5, SATA 7, SATA 58

HIRSHBERG, AL(BERT SIMON)
Birthdate: 5/10/1909
Birthplace: Boston, MA
Deathdate: 4/11/1973
Information Available in These Sources: ABYP 1, ABYP 3, SATA 38

HISCOCK, BRUCE
Birthdate: 12/4/1940
Birthplace: San Diego, CA
Information Available in These Sources: SATA 57

HISER, IONA SEIBERT
Birthdate: 1/30/1901
Birthplace: Pemberville, OH
Information Available in These Sources: SATA 4

HITCHCOCK, ALFRED (JOSEPH)
Birthdate: 8/13/1899
Birthplace: London, England
Deathdate: 4/29/1980
Information Available in These Sources: SATA 27

HITCHCOCK, PATRICIA
Information Available in These Sources: ABYP 4

HITTE, KATHRYN
Birthdate: 11/23/1919
Birthplace: Pana, IL
Information Available in These Sources: ABYP 2, ABYP 3, SATA 16

HITZ, DEMI
See Hunt, Charlotte Dumaresq

HNIZDOVSKY, JACQUES
Birthdate: 1/27/1915
Birthplace: Pylypcze, Ukraine, Russia
Information Available in These Sources: IBYP 1, IBYP 2, SATA 32

HOAG, EDWIN
Birthdate: 1926
Birthplace: New York, NY
Information Available in These Sources: ABYP 2, ABYP 3

HOAGLAND, EDWARD
Birthdate: 12/21/1932
Birthplace: New York, NY
Information Available in These Sources: SATA 51

HOBAN, LILLIAN
Birthdate: 5/18/1925
Birthplace: Philadelphia, PA
Information Available in These Sources: ABYP 2, ABYP 3, ICB 3, ICB 4, JBA 3, SATA 22

HOBAN, RUSSELL (CONWELL)
Birthdate: 2/4/1925
Birthplace: Lansdale, PA
Information Available in These Sources: ABYP 2, ABYP 3, DACF, JBA 3, SATA 1, SATA 40, TCCW 1, TCCW 2, TCCW 3

HOBAN, TANA
Birthplace: Philadelphia, PA
Information Available in These Sources: ABYP 4, JBA 4, SATA 22

HOBART, LOIS (ELAINE)
Birthdate: 8/09
Birthplace: Minneapolis, MN
Information Available in These Sources: ABYP 1, ABYP 3, SATA 7

HOBERMAN, MARY ANN (FREEDMAN)
Birthdate: 8/12/1930
Birthplace: Stamford, CT
Information Available in These Sources: ABYP 4, SATA 5, JBA 6

HOBSON, BURTON (HAROLD)
Birthdate: 4/16/1933
Birthplace: Galesburg, IL
Information Available in These Sources: SATA 28

HOBSON, JULIUS W(ILSON)
Birthdate, 1922?
Birthplace: Birmingham, AL
Deathdate: 3/23/1977
Information Available in These Sources: ABYP 4

HOBSON, LAURA Z(AMETKIN)
(Peter Field)
Birthdate: 6/19/1900
Birthplace: New York, NY
Deathdate: 2/28/1986
Information Available in These Sources: SATA 52

HOCHSCHILD, ARLIE RUSSELL
Birthdate: 1/15/1940
Birthplace: Boston, MA
Information Available in These Sources: SATA 11

HOCKENBERRY, HOPE
See Newell, Hope (Hockenberry)

HODGE, JANE AIKEN
Birthdate: 12/4/1917
Birthplace: Watertown, ME
Information Available in These Sources: ABYP 2, ABYP 3

HODGE, P(AUL) W(ILLIAM)
Birthdate: 11/8/1934
Birthplace: Seattle, WA
Information Available in These Sources: SATA 12

HODGELL, P(ATRICIA) C(HRISTINE)
Birthdate: 3/16/1951
Birthplace: Des Moines, IA
Information Available in These Sources: SATA 42

HODGES, CARL G.
Birthdate: 9/11/1902
Birthplace: Quincy, IL
Deathdate: 11/25/1964
Information Available in These Sources: ABYP 2, ABYP 3, DACF, SATA 10

HODGES, DAVID
Birthplace: Brooklyn, NY
Information Available in These Sources: IBYP 1, IBYP 2

HODGES, ELIZABETH JAMISON
Birthplace: Atlanta, GA
Information Available in These Sources: ABYP 2, ABYP 3, SATA 1

HODGES, MARGARET MOORE
Birthdate: 7/26/1911
Birthplace: Indianapolis, IN
Information Available in These Sources: ABYP 4, JBA 4, SATA 1, SATA 33

HODGETTS, BLAKE CHRISTOPHER
Birthdate: 7/7/1967
Birthplace: New York, NY
Information Available in These Sources: SATA 43

HOEHLING, MARY (DUPREY)
Birthdate: 12/8/1914
Birthplace: Worcester, MA
Information Available in These Sources: ABYP 1, ABYP 3

HOEXTER, CORINNE K.
Birthdate: 11/3/1927
Birthplace: Scranton, PA
Information Available in These Sources: SATA 6

HOFF, CAROL
Birthdate: 2/24/1900
Birthplace: Tucson, AZ
Information Available in These Sources: SATA 11

HOFF, SYD(NEY)
Birthdate: 9/4/1912
Birthplace: New York, NY
Information Available in These Sources: ABYP 1, ABYP 3, ICB 3, ICB 4, JBA 3, SATA 9, TCCW 1, TCCW 2 TCCW 3

HOFFECKER, JOHN SAVIN
(Savin Hoffecker)
Birthdate: 11/22/1908
Birthplace: Pine Bluff, AR
Information Available in These Sources: ABYP 4

HOFFECKER, SAVIN
See Hoffecker, John Savin

HOFFMAN, EDWIN D.
Birthplace: New York, NY
Information Available in These Sources: SATA 49

HOFFMAN, GLORIA
Birthplace: St. Louis, MO
Information Available in These Sources: ABYP 2, ABYP 3

HOFFMAN, PHYLLIS M.
Birthdate: 9/7/1944
Birthplace: New York, NY
Information Available in These Sources: SATA 4

HOFFMAN, ROSEKRANS
Birthdate: 1/7/1926
Birthplace: Denton, NE
Information Available in These Sources: SATA 15

HOFFMANN, HILDE
Birthdate: 7/28/1927
Birthplace: Munich, Germany
Information Available in These Sources: IBYP 2

HOFFMANN, MARGARET JONES
(Peggy Hoffmann)
Birthdate: 8/25/1910
Birthplace: Delaware, OH
Information Available in These Sources: ABYP 1, ABYP 3, SATA 48

HOFFMANN, PEGGY
See Hoffmann, Margaret Jones

HOFSINDE, ROBERT
Birthdate: 12/10/1902
Birthplace: Odense, Denmark
Deathdate: 11/26/1973
Information Available in These Sources: ABYP 1, ABYP 3, ICB 2, JBA 3, SATA 21

HOGAN, BERNICE HARRIS
Birthdate: 1/24/1929
Birthplace: Philadelphia, PA
Information Available in These Sources: SATA 12

HOGAN, INEZ
Birthdate: 8/5/1895
Birthplace: Washington, DC
Information Available in These Sources: ABYP 1, ABYP 3, ICB 1, MJA, SATA 2

HOGARTH, GRACE (WESTON ALLEN)
(Grace Allen, Amelia Gay, Allen Weston)
Birthdate: 11/5/1905
Birthplace: Newton, MA
Information Available in These Sources: TCCW 1, TCCW 2, TCCW 3

HOGARTH, JR.
See Kent, Rockwell

HOGEBOOM, AMY
Birthdate: 1891
Birthplace: NY
Information Available in These Sources: ABYP 2, ABYP 3

HOGNER, DOROTHY CHILDS
Birthdate: 1893
Birthplace: New York, NY
Information Available in These Sources: ABYP 1, ABYP 3, JBA 2, SATA 4

HOGNER, NILS
Birthdate: 7/22/1893
Birthplace: Whitinsville, MA
Deathdate: 7/30/1970 or 8/1/1970
Information Available in These Sources: ABYP 1, ABYP 3, ICB 1, ICB 2, ICB 3, JBA 2, SATA 25

HOGROGIAN, NONNY
Birthdate: 5/7/1932
Birthplace: New York, NY
Information Available in These Sources: ABYP 2, ABYP 3, BABP, IBYP 1, IBYP 2, ICB 3, ICB 4, JBA 3, SATA 7

HOH, DIANE
Birthdate: 4/28/1937
Birthplace: Warren, PA
Information Available in These Sources: SATA 48, SATA 52

HOKE, HELEN (L.)
(Helen Sterling)
Birthdate: 1903
Information Available in These Sources: ABYP 2, ABYP 3, SATA 15

HOKE, JOHN (LINDSAY)
Birthdate: 6/26/1925
Birthplace: Pittsburgh, PA
Information Available in These Sources: SATA 7

HOLBERG, RICHARD A.
Birthdate: 3/11/1889
Birthplace: Milwaukee, WI
Deathdate: 1942
Information Available in These Sources: ABYP 2, 3, JBA 2

HOLBERG, RUTH (LANGLAND)
Birthdate: 2/2/1891 or 2/2/1889
Birthplace: Milwaukee, WI
Information Available in These Sources: ABYP 2, ABYP 3, JBA 2, SATA 1

HOLBROOK, PETER
See Glick, Carl (Cannon)

HOLBROOK, SABRA
See Erickson, Sabra R(ollins)

HOLBROOK, STEWART HALL
Birthdate: 8/22/1893
Birthplace: Newport, VT
Deathdate: 9/3/1964
Information Available in These Sources: ABYP 2, ABYP 3, JBA 3, SATA 2

HOLDEN, RAYMOND PECKHAM
(Richard Peckham)
Birthdate: 4/7/1894
Birthplace: New York, NY
Deathdate: 6/26/1972
Information Available in These Sources: ABYP 1, ABYP 3

HOLDER, GLENN
Birthdate: 10/9/1906
Birthplace: Lynnville, IN
Information Available in These Sources: ABYP 4

HOLDER, WILLIAM G.
Birthdate: 3/15/1937
Birthplace: Richmond, IN
Information Available in These Sources: ABYP 4

HOLDING, JAMES (CLARK CARLISLE, JR.)
(Clark Carlisle, Ellery Queen, Jr.)
Birthdate: 4/27/1907
Birthplace: Pittsburgh, PA
Information Available in These Sources: ABYP 2, ABYP 3, SATA 3

HOLDSWORTH, WILLIAM CURTIS
Birthplace: Stoughton, MA
Information Available in These Sources: IBYP 2

HOLISHER, DESIDER
Birthdate: 2/2/1901
Birthplace: Budapest, Hungary
Deathdate: 8/11/1972
Information Available in These Sources: SATA 6

HOLL, ADELAIDE (HINKLE)
Birthdate: 12/9/1910
Birthplace: Pittsburgh, PA
Information Available in These Sources: ABYP 4, SATA 8

HOLL, KRISTI D(IANE)
Birthdate: 12/8/1951
Birthplace: Guthrie Center, IA
Information Available in These Sources: SATA 51

HOLLAND, ISABELLE
(Francesca Hunt)
Birthdate: 6/16/1920
Birthplace: Basel, Switzerland
Information Available in These Sources: ABYP 4, BC, DACF, JBA 5, SATA 8, TCCW 1, TCCW 2, TCCW 3

HOLLAND, JANICE
Birthdate: 5/23/1913
Birthplace: Washington, DC
Deathdate: 9/??/1962
Information Available in These Sources: IBYP 2, ICB 2, ICB 3, SATA 18

HOLLAND, JOHN L(EWIS)
Birthdate: 10/21/1919
Birthplace: Omaha, NE
Information Available in These Sources: ABYP 4, SATA 20

HOLLAND, MARION
Birthdate: 7/7/1908
Birthplace: Washington, DC
Information Available in These Sources: ABYP 1, ABYP 3, SATA 6

HOLLAND, RUPERT SARGENT
Birthdate: 10/15/1878
Birthplace: Louisville, KY
Deathdate: 5/3/1952
Information Available in These Sources: JBA 1, JBA 2

HOLLANDER, JOHN
Birthdate: 10/28/1929
Birthplace: New York, NY
Information Available in These Sources: ABYP 2, ABYP 3, SATA 13

HOLLANDER, PAUL
Information Available in These Sources: ABYP 2, ABYP 3

HOLLANDER, PHYLLIS
Birthdate: 8/25/1928
Birthplace: New York, NY
Information Available in These Sources: ABYP 4, SATA 39

HOLLANDER, ZANDER
(Alexander Peters)
Birthdate: 3/24/1923
Birthplace: New York, NY
Information Available in These Sources: ABYP 4

HOLLING, HOLLING C(LANCY)
(Holling Allison Clancy)
Birthdate: 8/2/1900
Birthplace: Holling Corners, MI
Deathdate: 9/7/1973
Information Available in These Sources: ABYP 1, ABYP 3, AICB, IBYP 2, ICB 1, ICB 2, ICB 3, JBA 2, SATA 15, SATA 26, SVC 2, SVC 3, TCCW 1, TCCW 2, TCCW 3

HOLLING, LUCILLE WEBSTER
Birthdate: 12/8/1900
Birthplace: Valparaiso, IN
Information Available in These Sources: IBYP 1, IBYP 2, ICB 1, ICB 2, ICB 3, JBA 2

HOLLINGSWORTH, ALVIN C(ARL)
Birthdate: 2/25/1930
Birthplace: New York, NY
Information Available in These Sources: IBYP 2, SATA 39

HOLLOWAY, TERESA (BRAGUNIER)
(Elizabeth Beatty, Margaret Vail McLeod)
Birthdate: 1/17/1906
Birthplace: Apalachicola, FL
Information Available in These Sources: SATA 26

HOLM, SAXE
See Jackson, Helen (Maria Fiske) Hunt

HOLMAN, FELICE
(Felice Holman Valen)
Birthdate: 10/24/1919
Birthplace: New York, NY
Information Available in These Sources: ABYP 2, ABYP 3, DACF, JBA 4, SATA 7, TCCW 1, TCCW 2, TCCW 3

HOLME, BRYAN
(Charles Francis)
Birthdate: 6/25/1913
Birthplace: Church Crookham, England
Information Available in These Sources: ABYP 2, ABYP 3, SATA 26

HOLMES, MARJORIE (ROSE)
Birthdate: 9/22/1910
Birthplace: Storm Lake, IA
Information Available in These Sources: ABYP 2, ABYP 3, SATA 43

HOLMES, OLIVER WENDELL
Birthdate: 8/29/1809
Birthplace: Cambridge, MA
Deathdate: 10/7/1894
Information Available in These Sources: SATA 34, SVC 2, SVC 3

HOLMES, RICK
See Hardwick, Richard (Holmes, Jr.)

HOLMGREN, GEORGE ELLEN
See Holmgren, Helen Jean

HOLMGREN, HELEN JEAN
(George Ellen Holmgrem)
Birthdate: 6/2/1930
Birthplace: Chicago, IL
Information Available in These Sources: SATA 45

HOLMGREN, VIRGINIA C(UNNINGHAM)
(Virginia Cunningham)
Birthdate: 6/20/1909
Birthplace: Dayton, OH
Information Available in These Sources: ABYP 1, ABYP 3, SATA 26

HOLMQUIST, EVE
Birthdate: 1/29/1921
Birthplace: MN
Information Available in These Sources: SATA 11

HOLSAERT, EUNICE
Deathdate: 5/6/1974
Information Available in These Sources: ABYP 2, ABYP 3

HOLSINGER, JANE LUMLEY
Birthplace: Woodstock, NY
Information Available in These Sources: ABYP 2, ABYP 3

HOLT, MARGARET (CECILE)
(Margaret Holt Parish)
Birthdate: 8/22/1937
Birthplace: Buffalo, NY
Information Available in These Sources: ABYP 2, ABYP 3, SATA 4

HOLT, MARGARET VAN VECHTEN (SAUNDERS)
(Rackham Holt)
Birthdate: 3/5/1899
Birthplace: Denver, CO
Deathdate: 2/4/1963
Information Available in These Sources: SATA 32

HOLT, RACKHAM
See Holt, Margaret Van Vechten (Saunders)

HOLT, ROCHELLE LYNN
(Rochelle Holt DuBois)
Birthdate: 3/17/1946
Birthplace: Chicago, IL
Information Available in These Sources: SATA 41

HOLT, STEPHEN
See Thompson, Harlan H.

HOLTON, LEONARD
See Wibberley, Leonard (Patrick O'Connor)

HOLTZMAN, JEROME
Birthdate: 7/12/1926
Birthplace: Chicago, IL
Information Available in These Sources: SATA 57

HOLYER, ERNA MARIA
(Ernie Holyer)
Birthdate: 3/15/1925
Birthplace: Weilheim, Germany
Information Available in These Sources: SATA 22

HOLYER, ERNIE
See Holyer, Erna Maria

HOLZ, LORETTA (MARIE)
Birthdate: 6/4/1943
Birthplace: Holden, MA
Information Available in These Sources: SATA 17

HOLZMAN, ROBERT STUART
Birthdate: 11/18/1907
Birthplace: Paterson, NJ
Information Available in These Sources: ABYP 4

HOMZE, ALMA C.
Birthdate: 10/28/1932
Birthplace: Washington, DC
Information Available in These Sources: SATA 17

HONIG, DONALD
Birthdate: 8/17/1931
Birthplace: Maspeth, Long Island, NY
Information Available in These Sources: SATA 18

HONNESS, ELIZABETH (HOFFMAN)
Birthdate: 6/29/1904
Birthplace: Boonton, NJ
Information Available in These Sources: ABYP 1, ABYP 3, SATA 2

HONORE, PAUL
Birthdate: 5/30/1885
Birthplace: Crawford County, PA
Deathdate: 4/12/1956
Information Available in These Sources: ICB 1

HOOBLER, DOROTHY
Birthplace: Philadelphia, PA
Information Available in These Sources: SATA 28

HOOBLER, THOMAS
Birthplace: Cincinnati, OH
Information Available in These Sources: SATA 28

HOOD, JOSEPH F.
Birthdate: 8/12/1925
Birthplace: Philadelphia, PA
Information Available in These Sources: SATA 4

HOOD, ROBERT E(RIC)
Birthdate: 4/15/1926
Birthplace: Mildred, PA
Information Available in These Sources: ABYP 4, SATA 21

HOOK, FRANCES
Birthdate: 12/24/1912
Birthplace: Ambler, PA
Information Available in These Sources: SATA 27

HOOK, MARTHA
Birthdate: 2/15/1936
Birthplace: Dallas, TX
Information Available in These Sources: SATA 27

HOOKER, RUTH
Birthdate: 4/30/1920
Birthplace: Rockville Center, NY
Information Available in These Sources: ABYP 4, SATA 21

HOOKS, WILLIAM H(ARRIS)
Birthdate: 11/14/1921
Birthplace: Whiteville, NC
Information Available in These Sources: SATA 16, JBA 6

HOOPER, BYRD
See St. Clair, Byrd Hooper

HOOPES, LYN L(ITTLEFIELD)
Birthdate: 7/14/1953
Birthplace: New York, NY
Information Available in These Sources: SATA 44, SATA 48

HOOPES, NED E(DWARD)
Birthdate: 5/22/1932
Birthplace: Safford, AZ
Information Available in These Sources: SATA 21

HOOPES, ROY
Birthdate: 5/17/1922
Birthplace: Salt Lake City, UT
Information Available in These Sources: ABYP 4, SATA 11

HOOPLE, CHERYL G.
Information Available in These Sources: ABYP 4, SATA 32

HOOVER, H(ELEN) M(ARY)
Birthdate: 4/5/1935
Birthplace: Stark County, OH
Information Available in These Sources: JBA 5, SATA 33, SATA 44, TCCW 3

HOOVER, HELEN (DRUSILLA BLACKBURN)
(Jennifer Price)
Birthdate: 1/20/1910
Birthplace: Greenfield, OH
Deathdate: 6/30/1984
Information Available in These Sources: SATA 12, SATA 39

HOPE, LAURA LEE
See Adams, Harriet S(tratemeyer) and Stratemeyer, Edward L.

HOPF, ALICE
See Hopf, Alice (Martha) L(ightner)

HOPF, ALICE (MARTHA) L(IGHTNER)
(Alice Hopf, A. M. Lightner, Alice Lightner)
Birthdate: 10/11/1904
Birthplace: Detroit, MI
Deathdate: 2/3/1988
Information Available in These Sources: ABYP 4, SATA 5, SATA 55

HOPKINS, A. T.
See Turngren, Annette

HOPKINS, CLARK
(Roy Lee)
Birthdate: 9/16/1895
Birthplace: New York, NY
Deathdate: 5/21/1976
Information Available in These Sources: ABYP 2, ABYP 3, SATA 34

HOPKINS, JOSEPH G(ERARD) E(DWARD)
Birthdate: 9/12/1909
Birthplace: Brooklyn, NY
Information Available in These Sources: SATA 11

HOPKINS, LEE BENNETT
Birthdate: 4/13/1938
Birthplace: Scranton, PA
Information Available in These Sources: ABYP 4, BC, JBA 5, SATA 3

HOPKINS, LYMAN
See Folsom, Franklin (Brewster)

HOPKINS, MARJORIE
Birthdate: 5/19/1911
Information Available in These Sources: ABYP 4, SATA 9

HOPPE, JOANNE
Birthdate: 1/10/1932
Birthplace: Worcester, MA
Information Available in These Sources: SATA 42

HOPPER, NANCY J.
Birthdate: 7/25/1937
Birthplace: Lewistown, PA
Information Available in These Sources: SATA 35, SATA 38

HORGAN, PAUL
Birthdate: 8/1/1903
Birthplace: Buffalo, NY
Information Available in These Sources: ABYP 2, ABYP 3, ICB 2, SATA 13

HORNADAY, WILLIAM T(EMPLE)
Birthdate: 12/1/1854
Birthplace: Plainfield, IN
Deathdate: 3/6/1937 or 3/6/1936
Information Available in These Sources: JBA 1

HORNBLOW, ARTHUR (JR.)
Birthdate: 3/15/1893
Birthplace: New York, NY
Deathdate: 7/17/1976
Information Available in These Sources: SATA 15

HORNBLOW, LEONORA (SCHINASI)
Birthdate: 1920
Birthplace: New York, NY
Information Available in These Sources: ABYP 2, ABYP 3, SATA 18

HORNER, ALTHEA (JANE)
Birthdate: 1/13/1926
Birthplace: Hartford, CT
Information Available in These Sources: SATA 36

HORNER, DAVE
Birthdate: 12/13/1934
Birthplace: Lynchburg, VA
Information Available in These Sources: SATA 12

HORNOS, AXEL
Birthdate: 7/3/1907
Birthplace: Buenos Aires, Argentina
Information Available in These Sources: SATA 20

HORSFALL, ROBERT BRUCE
Birthdate: 10/21/1868
Birthplace: Clinton, IA
Deathdate: 1948
Information Available in These Sources: ICB 1

HORVATH, BETTY (FERGUSON)
Birthdate: 5/20/1927
Birthplace: Jefferson City, MO
Information Available in These Sources: ABYP 4, SATA 4

HORVATH, FERDINAND HUSZTI
Birthdate: 8/28/1891
Birthplace: Budapest, Hungary
Information Available in These Sources: ICB 1

HORWICH, FRANCES R(APPAPORT)
(Miss Frances)
Birthdate: 7/16/1908
Birthplace: Ottawa, OH
Information Available in These Sources: ABYP 4, SATA 11

HORWITZ, ELINOR LANDER
Birthplace: New Haven, CT
Information Available in These Sources: ABYP 4, SATA 33, SATA 45

HOSFORD, DOROTHY (GRANT)
Birthdate: 1900
Birthplace: Pittsburgh, PA
Deathdate: 6/28/1952
Information Available in These Sources: ABYP 4, MJA, SATA 22, SVC 2, SVC 3

HOSFORD, JESSIE
Birthdate: 8/19/1892
Birthplace: NE
Information Available in These Sources: DACF, SATA 5

HOUCK, CARTER
Birthdate: 5/2/1924
Birthplace: Washington, DC
Information Available in These Sources: SATA 22

HOUGH, EMERSON
Birthdate: 6/28/1857
Birthplace: Jasper County, IA
Deathdate: 4/30/1923
Information Available in These Sources: JBA 1

HOULEHEN, ROBERT J.
Birthdate: 6/2/1918
Birthplace: Milwaukee, WI
Information Available in These Sources: SATA 18

HOUSE, CHARLES ALBERT
Birthdate: 11/26/1916
Birthplace: Milwaukee, WI
Information Available in These Sources: ABYP 4

HOUSER, ALLAN C.
(Haozous (Pulling Roots))
Birthdate: 6/30/1914
Birthplace: Apache, OK
Information Available in These Sources: IBYP 2, ICB 1, ICB 2, ICB 3

HOUSER, NORMAN W.
Information Available in These Sources: ABYP 4

HOUSTON, JAMES A(RCHIBALD)
Birthdate: 6/12/1921
Birthplace: Toronto, Ontario, Canada
Information Available in These Sources: ABYP 4, ICB 3, ICB 4, JBA 4, SATA 13, TCCW 1, TCCW 2

HOUSTON, JOAN
Birthdate: 5/11/1928
Birthplace: New York, NY
Information Available in These Sources: ABYP 2, ABYP 3

HOUTON, KATHLEEN
See Kilgore, Kathleen

HOVELL, LUCY A. (PETERSON)
Birthdate: 7/23/1916
Birthplace: Grafton, IL
Information Available in These Sources: ABYP 2, ABYP 3

HOWARD, ALYSSA
See Buckholtz, Eileen (Garber)

HOWARD, ELIZABETH
See Mizner, Elizabeth Howard

HOWARD, MOSES LEON
(Musa Nagenda)
Birthdate: 1/4/1928
Birthplace: Copiah County, MS
Information Available in These Sources: BAI

HOWARD, ROB
Information Available in These Sources: IBYP 1, IBYP 2

HOWARD, ROBERT WEST
(Michael Case)
Birthdate: 4/7/1908
Birthplace: Addison, NY
Information Available in These Sources: SATA 5

HOWARD, VERNON (LINWOOD)
(Paul Castle, Don Jordan)
Birthdate: 1918
Information Available in These Sources: ABYP 2, ABYP 3, SATA 40

HOWE, DEBORAH
Birthdate: 8/12/1946
Birthplace: Boston, MA
Deathdate: 6/3/1978
Information Available in These Sources: SATA 29, JBA 6

HOWE, FANNY
Birthdate: 10/15/1940
Birthplace: Buffalo, NY
Information Available in These Sources: SATA 52

HOWE, GERTRUDE HERRICK
Birthdate: 8/6/1902
Birthplace: Mohawk Valley, NY
Information Available in These Sources: ICB 2

HOWE, JAMES
Birthdate: 8/2/1946
Birthplace: Oneida, NY
Information Available in These Sources: SATA 29, TCCW 3, JBA 6

HOWELL, PAT
Birthdate: 2/12/1947
Birthplace: Glendale, CA
Information Available in These Sources: SATA 15

HOWELL, VIRGINIA TIER
See Ellison, Virginia Howell

HOWES, BARBARA
Birthdate: 5/1/1914
Birthplace: New York, NY
Information Available in These Sources: SATA 5

HOY, NINA
See Roth, Arthur J(oseph)

HOYT, EDWIN P(ALMER), JR.
(Cabot L. Forbes, Christopher Martin, C. Pritchard Smith, David Stuart)
Birthdate: 8/5/1923
Birthplace: Portland, OR
Information Available in These Sources: ABYP 2, ABYP 3, SATA 28

HOYT, MARY FINCH
Birthdate, 1924?
Birthplace: Visalia, CA
Information Available in These Sources: ABYP 2, ABYP 3

HOYT, OLGA (GRUHZIT)
Birthdate: 11/16/1922
Birthplace: Columbus, GA
Information Available in These Sources: ABYP 4, SATA 16

HUBBELL, HARRIET WEED
Birthdate: 9/19/1909
Birthplace: Buffalo, NY
Information Available in These Sources: ABYP 2, ABYP 3

HUBBELL, PATRICIA
Birthdate: 7/10/1928
Birthplace: Bridgeport, CT
Information Available in These Sources: SATA 8

HUBER, CHARLOTTE
Information Available in These Sources: SVC 2, SVC 3

HUBLEY, FAITH (ELLIOT)
Birthdate: 9/16/1924
Birthplace: New York, NY
Information Available in These Sources: SATA 48

HUBLEY, JOHN
Birthdate: 5/21/1914
Birthplace: Marinette, WI
Deathdate: 2/21/1977
Information Available in These Sources: SATA 24, SATA 48

HUCK, CHARLOTTE S(TEPHENA)
Birthdate: 1922
Information Available in These Sources: ABYP 4

HUDSON, JEFFREY
See Crichton, J. Michael

HUFF, RODERICK REMMELE
Birthdate: 1920
Information Available in These Sources: ABYP 4

HUFF, VIVIAN
Birthdate: 3/5/1948
Birthplace: New York, NY
Information Available in These Sources: SATA 59

HUFFAKER, SANDY
Birthdate: 9/23/1943
Birthplace: Chattanooga, TN
Information Available in These Sources: SATA 10

HUFFMAN, TOM
Birthplace: Cincinnati, OH
Information Available in These Sources: SATA 24

HUGHES, DEAN
Birthdate: 8/24/1943
Birthplace: Ogden, UT
Information Available in These Sources: SATA 33, JBA 6

HUGHES, JAMES LANGSTON
(Langston Hughes)
Birthdate: 2/1/1902
Birthplace: Joplin, MO
Deathdate: 5/22/1967
Information Available in These Sources: ABYP 2, ABYP 3, BAI, JBA 4, SATA 4, SATA 33, SVC 2, SVC 3, WC

HUGHES, LANGSTON
See Hughes, James Langston

HUGHES, MATILDA
See MacLeod, Charlotte (Matilda Hughes)

HUGHES, SARA
See Saunders, Susan

HUGHES, VIRGINIA
See Campbell, Hope

HULL, ELEANOR (MEANS)
Birthdate: 8/19/1913
Birthplace: Denver, CO
Information Available in These Sources: SATA 21

HULL, ERIC TRAVISS
See Harnan, Terry

HULL, H. BRAXTON
See Jacobs, Helen Hull

HULL, JESSE REDDING
See Hull, Jessie Redding

HULL, JESSIE REDDING
(Jesse Redding Hull)
Birthdate: 7/27/1932
Birthplace: Urbana, OH
Information Available in These Sources: SATA 51

HULTS, DOROTHY NIEBRUGGE
Birthdate: 9/6/1898
Birthplace: Brooklyn, NY
Information Available in These Sources: SATA 6

HUME, LOTTA CARSWELL
Information Available in These Sources: SATA 7

HUME, RUTH (FOX)
(Alexander Irving)
Birthdate: 1922
Birthplace: New York, NY
Deathdate: 3/1/1980
Information Available in These Sources: ABYP 2, ABYP 3, SATA 22, SATA 26

HUMPHREY, HENRY (III)
Birthdate: 4/26/1930
Birthplace: Mineola, NY
Information Available in These Sources: SATA 16

HUNGERFORD, EDWARD BUELL
Birthdate: 1/19/1900
Birthplace: New Britain, CT
Information Available in These Sources: ABYP 1, ABYP 3

HUNT, BERNICE KOHN
See Kohn, Bernice (Herstein)

HUNT, CHARLOTTE DUMARESQ
(Demi, Demi Hitz)
Birthdate: 9/2/1942
Birthplace: Cambridge, MA
Information Available in These Sources: BC, JBA 6, SATA 11

HUNT, CLARA WHITEHILL
Birthdate: 1871
Birthplace: Utica, NY
Deathdate: 1/10/1958
Information Available in These Sources: JBA 1, JBA 2

HUNT, FRANCESCA
See Holland, Isabelle

HUNT, GEORGE PINNEY
Birthdate: 7/17/1918
Birthplace: Philadelphia, PA
Information Available in These Sources: ABYP 1, ABYP 3

HUNT, IRENE
Birthdate: 5/18/1907
Birthplace: Newton, IL
Information Available in These Sources: ABYP 2, ABYP 3, DACF, JBA 3, MBMP, SATA 2, TCCW 1, TCCW 2, TCCW 3

HUNT, JOYCE
Birthdate: 10/31/1927
Birthplace: New York, NY
Information Available in These Sources: SATA 31

HUNT, KARI
Birthdate: 1/29/1920
Birthplace: Orange, NJ
Information Available in These Sources: ABYP 2, ABYP 3

HUNT, LAWRENCE J.
Birthdate: 5/30/1920
Birthplace: Banks, OR
Information Available in These Sources: DACF

HUNT, LINDA LAWRENCE
(Linda Lawrence)
Birthdate: 9/3/1940
Birthplace: Spokane, WA
Information Available in These Sources: SATA 39

HUNT, MABEL LEIGH
Birthdate: 11/1/1892
Birthplace: Coatesville, IN
Deathdate: 9/3/1971
Information Available in These Sources: ABYP 1, ABYP 3, JBA 2, SATA 1 SATA 26, TCCW 1, TCCW 2, TCCW 3

HUNT, MORTON
Birthdate: 2/20/1920
Birthplace: Philadelphia, PA
Information Available in These Sources: SATA 22

HUNTER, CLINGHAM, M.D.
See Adams, William Taylor

HUNTER, DAWE
See Downie, Mary Alice (Dawe)

HUNTER, EDITH FISHER
Birthdate: 12/3/1919
Birthplace: Boston, MA
Information Available in These Sources: SATA 31

HUNTER, EVAN
(Hunt Collins, Richard Marsten, Ed McBain)
Birthdate: 10/15/1926
Birthplace: New York, NY
Information Available in These Sources: ABYP 2, ABYP 3, SATA 25

HUNTER, KRISTIN (ELAINE EGGLESTON)
(Kristin Lattany)
Birthdate: 9/12/1931
Birthplace: Philadelphia, PA
Information Available in These Sources: ABYP 3, AICB, BAI, DACF, JBA 4SATA 12, TCCW 1, TCCW 2, TCCW 3

HUNTER, LEIGH
See Etchison, Birdie L(ee)

HUNTER, MEL
Birthdate: 7/27/1927
Birthplace: Oak Park, IL
Information Available in These Sources: SATA 39

HUNTINGTON, HARRIET E(LIZABETH)
Birthdate: 1/31/1909
Birthplace: Ormond Beach, FL
Information Available in These Sources: ABYP 1, ABYP 3, MJA, SATA 1

HUNTSBERRY, WILLIAM E(MERY)
Birthdate: 12/13/1916
Birthplace: Cleveland, OH
Information Available in These Sources: SATA 5

HURD, CLEMENT
Birthdate: 1/12/1908
Birthplace: New York, NY
Deathdate: 2/5/1988
Information Available in These Sources: ABYP 1, ABYP 3, ICB 1, ICB 2, ICB 3, ICB 4, MJA, SATA 2, SATA 54

HURD, EDITH THACHER
(Juniper Sage, Edith Thacher)
Birthdate: 9/14/1910
Birthplace: Kansas City, MO
Information Available in These Sources: ABYP 1, ABYP 3, MJA, SATA 2

HURD, PETER
Birthdate: 2/22/1904
Birthplace: Roswell, NM
Deathdate: 7/9/1984
Information Available in These Sources: ICB 1

HURD, THACHER
Birthdate: 3/6/1949
Birthplace: Burlington, VT
Information Available in These Sources: SATA 45, SATA 46, JBA 6

HURLEY, LESLIE J(OHN)
Birthdate: 6/25/1911
Birthplace: Bangor, ME
Information Available in These Sources: ABYP 3

HURMENCE, BELINDA
Birthdate: 8/20/1921
Information Available in These Sources: JBA 6

HURWITZ, JOHANNA
Birthdate: 10/9/1937
Birthplace: New York, NY
Information Available in These Sources: SATA 20, TCCW 3, JBA 6

HURWOOD, BERNHARDT J.
(Mallory T. Knight, D. Gunther Wilde, Father Xavier)
Birthdate: 7/22/1926
Birthplace: New York, NY
Deathdate: 1/23/1987
Information Available in These Sources: SATA 12, SATA 50

HUTCHENS, PAUL
Birthdate: 4/7/1902
Birthplace: Thorntown, IN
Deathdate: 1/23/1977
Information Available in These Sources: SATA 31

HUTCHINS, CARLEEN MALEY
Birthdate: 5/24/1911
Birthplace: Springfield, MA
Information Available in These Sources: SATA 9

HUTCHINS, ROSS E(LLIOTT)
Birthdate: 4/30/1906
Birthplace: Ruby, MT
Deathdate: 10/14/1983
Information Available in These Sources: ABYP 2, ABYP 3, JBA 3, SATA 4

HUTCHINSON, WILLIAM M.
Birthdate: 6/22/1916
Birthplace: Norfolk, VA
Information Available in These Sources: IBYP 1, IBYP 2, ICB 3

HUTCHISON, PAULA A.
Birthdate: 12/19/1905
Birthplace: Helena, MT
Information Available in These Sources: IBYP 1, IBYP 2, ICB 2

HUTHMACHER, J. JOSEPH
Birthdate: 11/1/1929
Birthplace: Trenton, NJ
Information Available in These Sources: SATA 5

HUTTO, NELSON (ALLEN)
Birthdate: 12/12/1904
Birthplace: Nuevo Laredo, Mexico
Information Available in These Sources: SATA 20

HYDE, DAYTON O(GDEN)
(Hawk Hyde)
Birthdate: 1925
Birthplace: Marquette, MI
Information Available in These Sources: ABYP 4, SATA 9

HYDE, HAWK
See Hyde, Dayton O(gden)

HYDE, MARGARET OLDROYD
Birthdate: 2/18/1917
Birthplace: Philadelphia, PA
Information Available in These Sources: ABYP 2, ABYP 3, JBA 3, SATA 1 SATA 42

HYDE, SHELLEY
See Reed, Kit

HYDE, WAYNE F(REDERICK)
Birthdate: 7/31/1922
Birthplace: Clintonville, WI
Information Available in These Sources: SATA 7

HYLANDER, CLARENCE J(OHN)
Birthdate: 11/24/1897
Birthplace: Waterbury, CT
Deathdate: 10/8/1964
Information Available in These Sources: ABYP 1, ABYP 3, SATA 7

HYMAN, LINDA
Birthdate: 6/11/1940
Birthplace: Buffalo, NY
Information Available in These Sources: ABYP 4

HYMAN, TRINA SCHART
Birthdate: 4/8/1939
Birthplace: Philadelphia, PA
Information Available in These Sources: DLB 61, IBYP 1, IBYP 2, ICB 3 ICB 4, JBA 4, SATA 7, SATA 46

HYMES, LUCIA M(ANLEY)
Birthdate: 2/6/1907
Birthplace: Marietta, OH
Information Available in These Sources: SATA 7

HYNDMAN, JANE (LEE) ANDREWS
(Lee Wyndham)
Birthdate: 12/16/1912
Birthplace: Melitopol, Ukraine, Russia
Deathdate: 3/18/1978
Information Available in These Sources: ABYP 1, ABYP 3, MJA, SATA 1, SATA 23, SATA 46, TCCW 1

HYNDMAN, ROBERT (UTLEY)
(Robert Wyndham)
Birthdate, 1906?
Deathdate: 5/24/1973
Information Available in These Sources: SATA 18

I

IANNONE, JEANNE (KOPPEL)
(Gina Bell, Gina Bell-Zano)
Birthdate: 4/1/1912
Birthplace: Philadelphia, PA
Information Available in These Sources: SATA 7

ICENHOWER, JOSEPH BRYAN
Birthdate: 3/13/1913
Birthplace: Parkersburg, WV
Information Available in These Sources: ABYP 2, ABYP 3

ICKS, ROBERT J.
Birthdate: 9/11/1900
Birthplace: Kaukauna, WI
Information Available in These Sources: ABYP 4

ILES, BERT
See Ross, Z(ola) H(elen Girdey)

ILOWITE, SHELDON A.
Birthdate: 2/19/1931
Birthplace: Brooklyn, NY
Information Available in These Sources: SATA 27

ILSLEY, DENT
See Chapman, John Stanton Higham

ILSLEY, VELMA (ELIZABETH)
Birthdate: 8/6/1918
Birthplace: Edmonton, Alberta, Canada
Information Available in These Sources: IBYP 1, IBYP 2, ICB 2, SATA 12

IMMEL, MARY BLAIR
Birthdate: 12/8/1930
Birthplace: Wichita, KS
Information Available in These Sources: ABYP 3, SATA 28

INGALLS, LEONARD
Birthplace: Lowell, MA
Information Available in These Sources: ABYP 2, ABYP 3

INGHAM, COLONEL FREDERIC
See Hale, Edward Everett

INGRAHAM, LEONARD W(ILLIAM)
Birthdate: 6/6/1913
Birthplace: New York, NY
Information Available in These Sources: SATA 4

INYART, GENE
Birthdate: 7/11/1927
Birthplace: Olney, IL
Information Available in These Sources: SATA 6

IPCAR, DAHLOV ZORACH
Birthdate: 11/12/1917
Birthplace: Windsor, VT
Information Available in These Sources: ABYP 2, ABYP 3, BABP, ICB 2, ICB 3, ICB 4, JBA 3, SATA 1, SATA 49

IRVIN, FRED
Birthdate: 11/19/1914
Birthplace: Chillicothe, MO
Information Available in These Sources: SATA 15

IRVING, ALEXANDER
See Hume, Ruth (Fox)

IRVING, ROBERT
See Adler, Robert Irving

IRVING, WASHINGTON
(Fray Antonio Agapida, Geoffrey Crayon, Diedrich Knickerbocker, Launcelot Langstaff, Jonathan Oldstyle)
Birthdate: 4/3/1783
Birthplace: New York, NY
Deathdate: 11/28/1859
Information Available in These Sources: SVC 2, WC, WCL, YABC

IRWIN, ANN(ABELLE BOWEN)
(Hadley Irwin)
Birthdate: 10/8/1915
Birthplace: Peterson, IA
Information Available in These Sources: SATA 38, SATA 44, JBA 6

IRWIN, CONSTANCE FRICK
(C. H. Frick, Constance Frick)
Birthdate: 5/11/1913
Birthplace: Evansville, IN
Information Available in These Sources: SATA 6

IRWIN, HADLEY
See Hadley, Lee and Irwin, Ann(abelle Bowen)

IRWIN, KEITH GORDON
Birthdate: 3/13/1885
Birthplace: Galesburg, IL
Deathdate: 1964
Information Available in These Sources: SATA 11

IRWIN, WALLACE (ADMAH)
Birthdate: 3/15/1875 or 3/15/1876
Birthplace: Oneida, NY
Deathdate: 2/14/1959
Information Available in These Sources: SVC 2, SVC 3

ISAAC, JOANNE
Birthdate: 6/12/1934
Birthplace: New York, NY
Information Available in These Sources: SATA 21

ISAACS, JACOB
See Kranzler, George G(ershon)

ISADORA, RACHEL
Birthdate, 1953?
Birthplace: New York, NY
Information Available in These Sources: JBA 5, SATA 32, SATA 54

ISH-KISHOR, JUDITH
Birthdate: 3/26/1892
Birthplace: Boston, MA
Deathdate: 1972
Information Available in These Sources: SATA 11

ISH-KISHOR, SULAMITH
Birthdate: 11/??/1896
Birthplace: London, England
Deathdate: 6/23/1977
Information Available in These Sources: ABYP 2, ABYP 3, DACF, JBA 5, SATA 17, TCCW 1, TCCW 2, TCCW 3

ISHAM, CHARLOTTE H(ICKOX)
Birthdate: 5/17/1912
Birthplace: Waterbury, CT
Information Available in These Sources: SATA 21

ISHMAEL, WOODI
Birthdate: 2/1/1914
Birthplace: Lewis County, KY
Information Available in These Sources: ICB 1, ICB 2, SATA 31

ISRAEL, ELAINE
Birthdate: 1/24/1945
Birthplace: New York, NY
Information Available in These Sources: SATA 12

ISRAEL, MARION LOUISE
Birthdate: 1882
Birthplace: Peabody, MA
Deathdate: 1/7/1973
Information Available in These Sources: SATA 26

IVAN, GUSTAVE
(Gus Tavo)
Birthdate: 1894
Birthplace: Budapest, Hungary
Deathdate: 1964
Information Available in These Sources: ABYP 2, ABYP 3

IVAN, MARTHA MILLER PFAFF
(Martha Miller)
Birthplace: St. Louis, MO
Information Available in These Sources: ABYP 2, ABYP 3

IVERSON, GENIE
Birthdate: 11/10/1942
Birthplace: Newport News, VA
Information Available in These Sources: ABYP 4, SATA 52

IWAMATSU, JUN ATSUSHI
(Taro Yashima)
Birthdate: 9/21/1908
Birthplace: Kagoshima, Japan
Information Available in These Sources: ABYP 1, ABYP 3, BABP, CFB, FLTYP, IBYP 1, IBYP 2, ICB 2, ICB 3, ICB 4, MJA, SATA 14, TCCW 2, TCCW 3

IZENBERG, JERRY
Information Available in These Sources: ABYP 4

J

JABLONSKI, EDWARD
Birthdate: 3/1/1922
Birthplace: Bay City, MI
Information Available in These Sources: ABYP 3

JAC, LEE
See Morton, Lee Jack, Jr.

JACKER, CORINNE (LITVIN)
Birthdate: 6/29/1933
Birthplace: Chicago, IL
Information Available in These Sources: ABYP 3

JACKSON, ANNE
Birthdate, 1896?
Deathdate: 1/4/1984

JACKSON, C(AARY) PAUL
(Caary Jackson, O. B. Jackson, Colin Lochlons, Jack Paulson)
Birthdate: 1902
Birthplace: Urbana, IL
Information Available in These Sources: ABYP 1, ABYP 3, SATA 6

JACKSON, CAARY
See Jackson, C(aary) Paul

JACKSON, GENEVIEVE VAUGHAN
See Vaughan-Jackson, Genevieve

JACKSON, HELEN (MARIA FISKE) HUNT
(H. H., Saxe Holm, Marah, Rip VanWinkle)
Birthdate: 10/15/1830
Birthplace: Amherst, MA
Deathdate: 8/12/1885
Information Available in These Sources: DLB 42, JBA 1, SVC 3, TCCW ?

JACKSON, JACQUELINE (DOUGAN)
Birthdate: 5/3/1928
Birthplace: Beloit, WI
Information Available in These Sources: ABYP 4, DACF, JBA 4

JACKSON, JESSE
Birthdate: 1/1/1908
Birthplace: Columbus, OH
Deathdate: 4/14/1983
Information Available in These Sources: ABYP 2, ABYP 3, BAI, SATA 2, SATA 29, SATA 48, TCCW 1, TCCW 2, TCCW 3

JACKSON, MARY COLEMAN
Information Available in These Sources: ABYP 2, ABYP 3

JACKSON, O. B.
See Jackson, C(aary) Paul and Jackson, Orpha (Cook)

JACKSON, ORPHA (COOK)
(O. B. Jackson)
Information Available in These Sources: ABYP 2, ABYP 3

JACKSON, ROBERT B(LAKE)
Birthdate: 11/11/1926
Birthplace: Hartford, CT
Information Available in These Sources: ABYP 1, ABYP 3, SATA 8

JACKSON, SALLY
See Kellogg, Jean (Defrees)

JACKSON, SHIRLEY
Birthdate: 12/14/1919
Birthplace: San Francisco, CA
Deathdate: 8/8/1965
Information Available in These Sources: SATA 2

JACKSON, STEPHANIE
See Werner, Vivian

JACOB, HELEN PIERCE
Birthdate: 11/9/1927
Birthplace: Lakewood, OH
Information Available in These Sources: SATA 21

JACOBI, KATHY
Birthplace: New York, NY
Information Available in These Sources: SATA 42

JACOBS, BETH
Birthplace: North Platte, NE
Information Available in These Sources: ABYP 2, ABYP 3

JACOBS, FLORA GILL
Birthdate: 12/22/1918
Birthplace: Washington, DC
Information Available in These Sources: ABYP 2, ABYP 3, SATA 5

JACOBS, FRANCINE
Birthdate: 5/11/1935
Birthplace: New York, NY
Information Available in These Sources: SATA 42, SATA 43

JACOBS, FRANK
Birthdate: 5/30/1929
Birthplace: Lincoln, NE
Information Available in These Sources: ABYP 2, ABYP 3, SATA 30

JACOBS, HELEN HULL
(H. Braxton Hull)
Birthdate: 8/6/1908
Birthplace: Globe, AZ
Information Available in These Sources: ABYP 2, ABYP 3, SATA 12

JACOBS, JOSEPH
Birthdate: 8/29/1854
Birthplace: Sydney, New South Wales, Australia
Deathdate: 1/30/1916
Information Available in These Sources: JBA 1, SATA 25

JACOBS, LELAND BLAIR
Birthdate: 2/12/1907
Birthplace: Tawas City, MI
Information Available in These Sources: ABYP 2, ABYP 3, SATA 20

JACOBS, LINDA C.
(Tom Austin, Claire Blackburn)
Birthdate: 1/22/1943
Birthplace: Winston-Salem, NC
Information Available in These Sources: SATA 21

JACOBS, LOU(IS), JR.
Birthdate: 7/24/1921
Birthplace: Dayton, OH
Information Available in These Sources: ABYP 4, SATA 2

JACOBS, SUSAN
(Susan Quinn)
Birthdate: 3/6/1940
Birthplace: Chillicothe, OH
Information Available in These Sources: SATA 30

JACOBS, WILLIAM JAY
Birthdate: 8/23/1933
Birthplace: Cincinnati, OH
Information Available in These Sources: SATA 28

JACOBSON, DANIEL
Birthdate: 11/6/1923
Birthplace: Newark, NJ
Information Available in These Sources: ABYP 4, SATA 12

JACOBSON, MORRIS K(ARL)
Birthdate: 12/29/1906
Birthplace: Memel, Germany
Information Available in These Sources: SATA 21

JACOPETTI, ALEXANDRA
Birthdate: 8/1/1939
Birthplace: Preston, ID
Information Available in These Sources: SATA 14

JAFFEE, AL(LAN)
Birthdate: 3/13/1921
Birthplace: Savannah, GA
Information Available in These Sources: SATA 37

JAGENDORF, MORITZ (ADOLF)
Birthdate: 8/24/1888
Birthplace: Czernowitz, Austria
Deathdate: 1/9/1981
Information Available in These Sources: ABYP 2, ABYP 3, MJA, SATA 2, SATA 24

JAHN, JOSEPH MICHAEL
(Mike Jahn)
Birthdate: 8/4/1943
Birthplace: Cincinnati, OH
Information Available in These Sources: SATA 28

JAHN, MIKE
See Jahn, Joseph Michael

JAHSMANN, ALLAN HART
Birthdate: 11/3/1916
Birthplace: Wausau, WI
Information Available in These Sources: SATA 28

JAKES, JOHN (W.)
(Alan Payne, Jay Scotland)
Birthdate: 3/31/1932
Birthplace: Chicago, IL
Information Available in These Sources: ABYP 4

JAKUBOWSKI, CHARLES
Information Available in These Sources: IBYP 2

JAMES, EDWIN
See Gunn, James E(dwin)

JAMES, ELIZABETH
(Elizabeth Carroll, Katherine Duval, Beverly Hastings, E. James Lloyd, James Lloyd)
Birthdate: 11/5/1942
Birthplace: Pittsburgh, PA
Information Available in These Sources: SATA 39, SATA 45, SATA 52

JAMES, HAROLD (LAYMONT)
Birthdate: 1929
Birthplace: Fayetteville, NC
Information Available in These Sources: IBYP 2

JAMES, HARRY CLEBOURNE
Birthdate: 4/25/1896
Birthplace: Ottawa, Ontario, Canada
Deathdate: 5/28/1978
Information Available in These Sources: SATA 11

JAMES, JOSEPHINE
See Sterne, Emma Gelders

JAMES, NORMA WOOD
Information Available in These Sources: ABYP 2, ABYP 3

JAMES, ROBIN (IRENE)
Birthdate: 9/24/1953
Birthplace: Seattle, WA
Information Available in These Sources: SATA 50

JAMES, T. F.
See Fleming, Thomas J(ames)

JAMES, WALTER S.
See Sheldon, Walt(er J.)

JAMES, WILL(IAM RODERICK)
Birthdate: 6/6/1892
Birthplace: Great Falls (near), MT
Deathdate: 9/3/1942
Information Available in These Sources: ABYP 1, ABYP 3, JBA 1, JBA 2, SATA 19

JAMESON, CYNTHIA
Information Available in These Sources: ABYP 4

JAMESON, JOHNETTE H.
Birthplace: Filmore, UT
Information Available in These Sources: ABYP 4

JAMESON, MALCOLM
Birthdate: 1891
Birthplace: Waco, TX
Deathdate: 1945
Information Available in These Sources: ABYP 2, ABYP 3

JAMISON, JANE
See Trachsel, Myrtle Jamison

JANCE, J(UDITH) A(NN)
Birthdate: 10/27/1944
Birthplace: Watertown, SD
Information Available in These Sources: SATA 50

JANE, MARY CHILDS
Birthdate: 9/18/1909
Birthplace: Needham, MA
Information Available in These Sources: ABYP 2, ABYP 3, SATA 6

JANECZKO, PAUL B(RYAN)
(P. Wolny)
Birthdate: 7/27/1945
Birthplace: Passaic, NJ
Information Available in These Sources: SATA 53, JBA 6

JANES, EDWARD C.
Birthdate: 1908
Birthplace: Westfield, MA
Information Available in These Sources: ABYP 2, ABYP 3, SATA 25

JANEWAY, ELIZABETH (HALL)
Birthdate: 10/7/1913
Birthplace: Brooklyn, NY
Information Available in These Sources: ABYP 2, ABYP 3, DACF, SATA 19

JANICE
See Brustlein, Janice Tworkov

JANSEN, JARED
See Cebulash, Mel

JANSON, DORA JANE (HEINEBERG)
Birthdate: 1916
Information Available in These Sources: ABYP 2, ABYP 3, SATA 31

JANSON, H(ORST) W(OLDEMAR)
Birthdate: 10/4/1913
Birthplace: St. Petersburg, Russia
Information Available in These Sources: ABYP 2, ABYP 3, SATA 9

JAQUES, FRANCIS LEE
Birthdate: 9/28/1887
Birthplace: Genesco, IL
Deathdate: 7/24/1969
Information Available in These Sources: ICB 2, SATA 28

JAQUITH, PRISCILLA
Birthdate: 8/21/1908
Birthplace: Brooklyn, NY
Information Available in These Sources: SATA 51

JARRELL, MARY VON SCHRADER
Birthdate: 5/2/1914
Birthplace: St. Louis, MO
Information Available in These Sources: SATA 35

JARRELL, RANDALL
Birthdate: 5/6/1914
Birthplace: Nashville, TN
Deathdate: 10/14/1965
Information Available in These Sources: ABYP 2, ABYP 3, DACF, JBA 3, SATA 7, TCCW 1, TCCW 2, TCCW 3

JARRETT, ROXANNE
See Werner, Herma

JASNER, W. K.
See Watson, Jane Werner

JASZI, JEAN YOURD
Birthplace: PA
Information Available in These Sources: ABYP 2, ABYP 3

JAUSS, ANNE MARIE
Birthdate: 2/3/1907
Birthplace: Munich, Germany
Information Available in These Sources: ABYP 2, ABYP 3, ICB 2, ICB 3, ICB 4, JBA 4, SATA 10

JAWORSKI, IRENE D.
Birthplace: NY
Information Available in These Sources: ABYP 2, ABYP 3

JAYNE, LIEUTENANT R. H.
See Ellis, Edward S(ylvester)

JAYNE, R. H.
See Ellis, Edward S(ylvester)

JAYNES, CLARE
See Mayer, Jane Rothschild and Spiegel, Clara

JEAKE, SAMUEL, JR.
See Aiken, Conrad (Potter)

JEFFERDS, VINCENT HARRIS
Birthdate: 8/23/1916
Birthplace: Jersey City, NJ
Information Available in These Sources: SATA 49, SATA 59

JEFFERS, HARRY PAUL
Birthdate: 1934
Birthplace: Phoenixville, PA
Information Available in These Sources: ABYP 3

JEFFERS, SUSAN (JANE)
Birthdate: 10/7/1942
Birthplace: Oakland, NJ
Information Available in These Sources: IBYP 2, ICB 2, JBA 4, SATA 17

JEFFERSON, ROBERT LOUIS
Birthdate: 1929
Birthplace: PA
Information Available in These Sources: IBYP 1, IBYP 2

JEMNE, ELSA LAUBACH
Birthdate: 1888
Birthplace: St. Paul, MN
Deathdate: 1974
Information Available in These Sources: ICB 1

JENKINS, MARIE M(AGDALEN)
(Sister Mary Scholastica, W. S. Markins)
Birthdate: 9/26/1909
Birthplace: Eldorado, IL
Information Available in These Sources: ABYP 4, SATA 7

JENKINS, WILLIAM A(TWELL)
Birthdate: 11/18/1922
Birthplace: Scranton, PA
Information Available in These Sources: SATA 9

JENKYNS, CHRIS
Birthdate: 7/3/1924
Birthplace: North Hollywood, CA
Information Available in These Sources: IBYP 2, ICB 2, SATA 51

JENNINGS, GARY (GAYNE)
Birthdate: 9/20/1928
Birthplace: Buena Vista, VA
Information Available in These Sources: ABYP 2, ABYP 3, SATA 9

JENNINGS, GORDON
Birthplace: CA
Information Available in These Sources: ABYP 4

JENNINGS, JOHN EDWARD, JR.
Birthdate: 12/30/1906
Birthplace: Brooklyn, NY
Deathdate: 12/4/1973
Information Available in These Sources: ABYP 2, ABYP 3

JENNINGS, MICHAEL
(Waco Brazos, Wyatt E. Kinkaid)
Birthdate: 4/17/1931
Birthplace: Buena Vista, VA
Information Available in These Sources: ABYP 4

JENNINGS, S. M.
See Meyer, Jerome Sydney

JENNISON, C. S.
See Starbird, Kaye

JENNISON, KEITH WARREN
Birthdate: 1911
Birthplace: Canada
Information Available in These Sources: ABYP 2, ABYP 3, SATA 14

JENSEN, DAVID E(DWARD)
Birthdate: 6/25/1929
Birthplace: Penn Yan, NY
Information Available in These Sources: ABYP 2, ABYP 3

JENSEN, VIRGINIA ALLEN
Birthdate: 9/21/1927
Birthplace: Des Moines, IA
Information Available in These Sources: SATA 8

JEPPSON, J(ANET) O(PAL)
(Janet Asimov)
Birthdate: 8/6/1926
Birthplace: Ashland, PA
Information Available in These Sources: SATA 46, SATA 54

JERR, WILLIAM A.
Birthplace: MA
Information Available in These Sources: ABYP 1, ABYP 3

JESCHKE, SUSAN
Birthdate: 10/18/1942
Birthplace: Cleveland, OH
Information Available in These Sources: ICB 4, JBA 5, SATA 27, SATA 42

JESSEY, CORNELIA
See Sussman, Cornelia (Silver)

JEWELL, NANCY
Birthdate: 8/12/1940
Birthplace: Washington, DC
Information Available in These Sources: SATA 41

JEWETT, ELEANORE MYERS
Birthdate: 4/4/1890
Birthplace: New York, NY
Deathdate: 3/30/1967
Information Available in These Sources: MJA, SATA 5

JEWETT, SARAH ORNE
Birthdate: 9/3/1849
Birthplace: South Berwick, ME
Deathdate: 6/24/1909
Information Available in These Sources: ABYP 2, ABYP 3, JBA 1, SATA 15

JILER, JOHN
Birthdate: 4/4/1946
Birthplace: New York, NY
Information Available in These Sources: SATA 35, SATA 42

JOBB, JAMIE
(Osh Kabibble)
Birthdate: 11/29/1945
Birthplace: Gallipolis, OH
Information Available in These Sources: SATA 29

JOERNS, CONSUELO
Information Available in These Sources: IBYP 2, SATA 33, SATA 44

JOHANSEN, MARGARET (ALISON)
Birthdate: 1896
Birthplace: AL
Information Available in These Sources: ABYP 2, ABYP 3

JOHN, JOYCE
Birthplace: New York, NY
Information Available in These Sources: SATA 59

JOHN, NAOMI
See Flack, Naomi (John White)

174 JOHNS

JOHNS, AVERY
See Cousins, Margaret

JOHNSON, A.
See Johnson, Annabel (Jones)

JOHNSON, A. E.
See Johnson, Annabel (Jones) and Johnson, Edgar (Raymond)

JOHNSON, ANNABEL (JONES)
(A. Johnson, A. E. Johnson)
Birthdate: 6/18/1921
Birthplace: Kansas City, MO
Information Available in These Sources: ABYP 2, ABYP 3, DACF, JBA 3, SATA 2, TCCW 1, TCCW 2, TCCW 3

JOHNSON, AVERY F.
Birthdate: 4/3/1906
Birthplace: Wheaton, IL
Information Available in These Sources: ICB 1, ICB 2

JOHNSON, B(URDETTA) F(AYE)
(B(urdetta) F(aye) Beebe)
Birthdate: 2/4/1920
Birthplace: Marshall, OK
Information Available in These Sources: ABYP 4, SATA 1

JOHNSON, BENJ. F., OF BOONE
See Riley, James Whitcomb

JOHNSON, CHARLES FREDERICK
Information Available in These Sources: ABYP 2, ABYP 3

JOHNSON, CHARLES R.
(Chuck Johnson)
Birthdate: 9/16/1925
Birthplace: Williston, ND
Information Available in These Sources: SATA 11

JOHNSON, CHARLOTTE BUEL
Birthdate: 7/21/1918
Birthplace: Syracuse, NY
Deathdate: 2/11/1982
Information Available in These Sources: SATA 46

JOHNSON, CHUCK
See Johnson, Charles R.

JOHNSON, CORINNE B.
Birthplace: MA
Information Available in These Sources: ABYP 4

JOHNSON, CROCKETT
See Leisk, David (Johnson)

JOHNSON, D(ANA) WILLIAM
Birthdate: 5/30/1945
Birthplace: Helena, MT
Information Available in These Sources: SATA 23

JOHNSON, DORIS
Birthdate: 1922
Information Available in These Sources: ABYP 4

JOHNSON, DOROTHY M(ARIE)
Birthdate: 12/19/1905
Birthplace: McGregor, IA
Deathdate: 11/11/1984
Information Available in These Sources: SATA 6, SATA 40

JOHNSON, E(UGENE) HARPER
Birthplace: Birmingham, AL
Information Available in These Sources: IBYP 2, ICB 2, ICB 3, SATA 44

JOHNSON, E. NED
See Johnson, Enid

JOHNSON, EDGAR (RAYMOND)
(A. E. Johnson)
Birthdate: 10/24/1912
Birthplace: Washoe, MT
Information Available in These Sources: ABYP 2, ABYP 3, DACF, JBA 3, SATA 2, TCCW 1, TCCW 2, TCCW 3

JOHNSON, ELEANOR (MURDOCK)
Birthdate: 12/10/1892
Birthplace: Washington County, MD
Deathdate: 10/8/1987 or 10/7/1987
Information Available in These Sources: SATA 54

JOHNSON, ELIZABETH
Birthdate: 10/10/1911
Birthplace: Swampscott, MA
Information Available in These Sources: ABYP 4, SATA 7, SATA 39

JOHNSON, ENID
(E. Ned Johnson)
Birthdate: 1892
Birthplace: IN
Information Available in These Sources: ABYP 2, ABYP 3, JBA 1

JOHNSON, ERIC W(ARNER)
Birthdate: 3/22/1918
Birthplace: Philadelphia, PA
Information Available in These Sources: ABYP 4, SATA 8

JOHNSON, EVELYNE
Birthdate: 1/20/1932
Birthplace: New York, NY
Information Available in These Sources: SATA 20

JOHNSON, GAYLORD
Birthdate: 2/8/1884
Birthplace: Adrian, MI
Information Available in These Sources: SATA 7

JOHNSON, GERALD WHITE
Birthdate: 8/6/1890
Birthplace: Riverton, NJ
Deathdate: 3/23/1980
Information Available in These Sources: ABYP 1, ABYP 3, JBA 3, SATA 19SATA 28

JOHNSON, HARPER
See Johnson, E(ugene) Harper

JOHNSON, HARRIETT
Birthdate: 8/31/1908
Birthplace: Minneapolis, MN
Deathdate: 6/26/1987
Information Available in These Sources: SATA 53

JOHNSON, JAMES RALPH
Birthdate: 5/20/1922
Birthplace: Fort Payne, AL
Information Available in These Sources: ABYP 2, ABYP 3, SATA 1

JOHNSON, JAMES WELDON
See Johnson, James William

JOHNSON, JAMES WILLIAM
(James Weldon Johnson)
Birthdate: 6/17/1871
Birthplace: Jacksonville, FL
Deathdate: 6/26/1938
Information Available in These Sources: BAI, JBA 4, SATA 31

JOHNSON, JOAN J.
Birthdate: 9/8/1942
Birthplace: Norwalk, CT
Information Available in These Sources: SATA 59

JOHNSON, JOHN E(MIL)
Birthdate: 5/14/1929
Birthplace: Worcester, MA
Information Available in These Sources: IBYP 1, IBYP 2, ICB 3, SATA 34

JOHNSON, LA VERNE B(RAVO)
Birthdate: 5/23/1925
Birthplace: Stockton, CA
Information Available in These Sources: SATA 13

JOHNSON, LOIS S(MITH)
Birthdate: 7/26/1894
Birthplace: Parkersburg, WV
Information Available in These Sources: SATA 6

JOHNSON, LOIS W(ALFRID)
Birthdate: 11/23/1936
Birthplace: Starbuck, MN
Information Available in These Sources: SATA 22

JOHNSON, MARGARET S(WEET)
Birthdate: 11/1/1893
Birthplace: Brooklyn, NY
Deathdate: 1964
Information Available in These Sources: ABYP 2, ABYP 3, JBA 2, SATA 35

JOHNSON, MARTHA
See Lansing, Elisabeth Carleton (Hubbard)

JOHNSON, MARY FRANCES K.
Birthdate, 1929?
Deathdate: 7/11/1979
Information Available in These Sources: SATA 27

JOHNSON, MAUD BATTLE
Birthdate, 1918?
Birthplace: Richmond, VA
Deathdate: 9/5/1985
Information Available in These Sources: SATA 46

JOHNSON, MILTON
Birthdate: 8/16/1932
Birthplace: Milwaukee, WI
Information Available in These Sources: ICB 3, SATA 31

JOHNSON, NATALIE
See Robison, Nancy L(ouise)

JOHNSON, OSA HELEN (LEIGHTY)
Birthdate: 3/14/1894
Birthplace: Chanute, KS
Deathdate: 1/7/1953
Information Available in These Sources: ABYP 2, ABYP 3

JOHNSON, OWEN (MCMAHON)
Birthdate: 1898
Deathdate: 1952
Information Available in These Sources: JBA 1

JOHNSON, ROBERT E.
Birthdate: 1907
Birthplace: Yakima, WA
Information Available in These Sources: ABYP 2, ABYP 3

JOHNSON, RYERSON
See Johnson, Walter Ryerson

JOHNSON, SHIRLEY K(ING)
Birthdate: 3/18/1927
Birthplace: Adair County, IA
Information Available in These Sources: SATA 10

JOHNSON, SIDDIE JOE
Birthdate: 8/20/1905
Birthplace: Dallas, TX
Deathdate: 7/27/1977
Information Available in These Sources: ABYP 1, ABYP 3, JBA 2, SATA 20

JOHNSON, SPENCER
Birthdate: 11/24/1938
Birthplace: Watertown, SD
Information Available in These Sources: SATA 38

JOHNSON, SYLVIA A.
Birthplace: Indianapolis, IN
Information Available in These Sources: SATA 52

JOHNSON, WALTER RYERSON
(Ryerson Johnson)
Birthdate: 10/19/1901
Birthplace: Divernon, IL
Information Available in These Sources: ABYP 4, SATA 10

JOHNSON, WILLIAM R.
Birthplace: Minneapolis, MN
Information Available in These Sources: SATA 38

JOHNSON, WILLIAM WEBER
Birthdate: 12/18/1909
Birthplace: Mattoon, IL
Information Available in These Sources: ABYP 2, ABYP 3, SATA 7

JOHNSTON, AGNES CHRISTINE
See Dazey, Agnes J(ohnston)

JOHNSTON, ANNIE FELLOWS
Birthdate: 5/15/1863
Birthplace: Evansville, IN
Deathdate: 10/5/1931
Information Available in These Sources: DLB 42, JBA 1, SATA 37

JOHNSTON, DOROTHY GRUNBOCK
Birthdate: 7/30/1915
Birthplace: Seattle, WA
Information Available in These Sources: SATA 54

JOHNSTON, EDITH CONSTANCE FARRINGTON
Birthdate: 5/2/1890 or 5/3/1890
Birthplace: Waucoma, IA
Information Available in These Sources: ICB 1, ICB 2

JOHNSTON, GINNY
Birthdate: 5/18/1946
Birthplace: Salem, NJ
Information Available in These Sources: SATA 60

JOHNSTON, JOHANNA (VOIGT)
Birthdate, 1914?
Birthplace: Chicago, IL
Deathdate: 12/14/1982
Information Available in These Sources: ABYP 2, ABYP 3, JBA 4, SATA 12, SATA 33

JOHNSTON, LAURIE
Birthplace: Pueblo, CO
Information Available in These Sources: ABYP 2, ABYP 3

JOHNSTON, LOUISA MAE
Birthdate: 1925
Information Available in These Sources: ABYP 2, ABYP 3

JOHNSTON, MARY
Birthdate: 1870
Deathdate: 1936
Information Available in These Sources: JBA 1

JOHNSTON, NORMA
(Elizabeth Bolton, Catherine E. Chambers, Pamela Dryden, Lavinia Harris, Nicole St. John)
Birthplace: Ridgewood, NJ
Information Available in These Sources: JBA 5, SATA 29

JOHNSTON, PORTIA
See Takakjian, Portia

JOHNSTON, RALPH E.
Birthdate: 1902
Information Available in These Sources: ABYP 2, ABYP 3

JOHNSTON, TONY
Birthdate: 1/30/1942
Birthplace: Los Angeles, CA
Information Available in These Sources: ABYP 4, SATA 8, JBA 6

JONAS, ANN
Birthdate: 1/28/1932
Birthplace: Flushing, Long Island, NY
Information Available in These Sources: SATA 42, SATA 50

JONES, ADRIENNE
Birthdate: 7/28/1915
Birthplace: Atlanta, GA
Information Available in These Sources: JBA 5, SATA 7

JONES, BETTY MILLSAPS
Birthdate: 6/23/1940
Birthplace: Chattanooga, TN
Information Available in These Sources: SATA 54

JONES, CHARLES M(ARTIN)
(Chuck Jones)
Birthdate: 9/21/1912
Birthplace: Spokane, WA
Information Available in These Sources: SATA 53

JONES, CHUCK
See Jones, Charles M(artin)

JONES, DOUGLAS C(LYDE)
Birthdate: 12/6/1924
Birthplace: Winslow, AR
Information Available in These Sources: SATA 52

JONES, ELIZABETH ORTON
Birthdate: 6/25/1910
Birthplace: Highland Park, IL
Information Available in These Sources: ABYP 1, ABYP 3, IBYP 1, IBYP 2ICB 1, ICB 2, ICB 3, JBA 2, SATA 18, SVC 2, SVC 3

JONES, EVAN
Birthdate: 5/6/1915
Birthplace: Le Sueur, MN
Information Available in These Sources: SATA 3

JONES, HELEN HINCKLEY
(Helen Hinckley)
Birthdate: 4/12/1903
Birthplace: Provo, UT
Information Available in These Sources: ABYP 2, ABYP 3, SATA 26

JONES, HELEN L(OUISE)
Birthdate: 1904
Birthplace: Billerica, MA
Deathdate: 1/6/1973
Information Available in These Sources: SATA 22

JONES, HETTIE
Birthdate: 7/16/1934
Birthplace: Brooklyn, NY
Information Available in These Sources: ABYP 4, SATA 27, SATA 42

JONES, HORTENSE P.
Birthdate: 1/10/1918
Birthplace: Franklin, VA
Information Available in These Sources: SATA 9

JONES, JESSIE MAE ORTON
Birthdate: 1887 or 1886
Birthplace: Lacon, IL
Deathdate: 10/6/1983
Information Available in These Sources: JBA 5, SATA 37

JONES, JUANITA NUTTALL
Birthdate: 1912
Information Available in These Sources: ABYP 2, ABYP 3

JONES, KATHARINE MARY
See Carter, Katharine J(ones)

JONES, LLOID
Birthdate: 1908
Information Available in These Sources: ABYP 2, ABYP 3

JONES, MARGARET BOONE
See Zarif, Margaret Min'imah

JONES, MARY ALICE
Birthdate: 1898
Birthplace: Dallas, TX
Information Available in These Sources: ABYP 1, ABYP 3, MJA, SATA 6

JONES, MCCLURE
Information Available in These Sources: SATA 34

JONES, PENELOPE
Birthdate: 2/17/1938
Birthplace: Rochester, NY
Information Available in These Sources: SATA 31

JONES, REBECCA C(ASTALDI)
Birthdate: 9/10/1947
Birthplace: Evergreen Park, IL
Information Available in These Sources: SATA 33

JONES, RICHARD C.
Birthdate: 12/13/1910
Birthplace: Chicago, IL
Information Available in These Sources: ICB 1, ICB 2

JONES, SANFORD W.
See Thorn, John

JONES, WEYMAN (B.)
Birthdate: 2/6/1928
Birthplace: Lima, OH
Information Available in These Sources: ABYP 2, ABYP 3, DACF, JBA 4, SATA 4

JONES, WILFRED J.
Birthdate: 1/20/1888
Birthplace: Philadelphia, PA
Information Available in These Sources: CICB, ICB 1

JONK, CLARENCE
Birthdate: 7/16/1906
Birthplace: Raymond (near), MN
Information Available in These Sources: SATA 10

JOOSSE, BARBARA M(ONNOT)
Birthdate: 2/18/1949
Birthplace: Grafton, WI
Information Available in These Sources: SATA 52

JORDAN, DON
See Howard, Vernon (Linwood)

JORDAN, E(MIL) L(EOPOLD)
Birthdate: 10/2/1900
Birthplace: Russ, Germany
Information Available in These Sources: SATA 31

JORDAN, HOPE (DAHLE)
Birthdate: 12/9/1905
Birthplace: Mt Horeb, WI
Information Available in These Sources: SATA 15

JORDAN, JUNE (MEYER)
(June (Jordan) Meyer)
Birthdate: 7/9/1936
Birthplace: New York, NY
Information Available in These Sources: ABYP 4, BAI, DACF, JBA 4, SATA 4, TCCW 1, TCCW 2, TCCW 3

JORDAN, MILDRED
Birthdate: 3/18/1901
Birthplace: Chicago, IL
Information Available in These Sources: SATA 5

JORDAN, PHILIP DILLON
Birthdate: 11/7/1903
Birthplace: Burlington, IA
Information Available in These Sources: ABYP 2, ABYP 3

JORGENSEN, MARY VENN
(Mary Adrian, Mary Eleanor Venn)
Birthdate: 1908
Birthplace: Sewickley, PA
Information Available in These Sources: ABYP 2, ABYP 3, SATA 36

JORGENSON, IVAR
See Silverberg, Robert

JOSEPH, ALEXANDER
Birthdate: 5/17/1907
Birthplace: Paris, France
Deathdate: 1976
Information Available in These Sources: ABYP 2, ABYP 3

JOSEPH, JAMES (HERZ)
(Lowell Adams, Walter Perez, Juan Sanchez Alzada)
Birthdate: 5/12/1924
Birthplace: Terre Haute, IN
Information Available in These Sources: SATA 53

JOSEPH, JOAN
Birthdate: 7/13/1939
Birthplace: Tel Aviv, Israel
Information Available in These Sources: SATA 34

JOSEPH, JOSEPH M(ARON)
Birthdate: 8/1/1903
Birthplace: Philadelphia, PA
Deathdate: 5/22/1979
Information Available in These Sources: SATA 22

JOSLIN, SESYLE
(Josephine Gibson, G. B. Kirtland)
Birthdate: 8/30/1929
Birthplace: Providence, RI
Information Available in These Sources: ABYP 2, ABYP 3, JBA 3, SATA 2 TCCW 1

JOY, CHARLES RHIND
Birthdate: 12/5/1885
Birthplace: Boston, MA
Information Available in These Sources: ABYP 2, ABYP 3

JOYCE, WILLIAM
Birthdate: 12/11/1957 or 12/11/1959
Information Available in These Sources: SATA 46, JBA 6

JOYNER, JERRY
Birthdate: 12/5/1938
Birthplace: Kilgore, TX
Information Available in These Sources: IBYP 2, SATA 34

JUDD, FRANCES K.
See Stratemeyer, Edward L.

JUDSON, CLARA INGRAM
Birthdate: 5/4/1897
Birthplace: Logansport, IN
Deathdate: 5/24/1960
Information Available in These Sources: ABYP 1, ABYP 3, AICB, JBA 2, SATA 27, SATA 38

JUDY, STEPHEN
See Tchudi, Stephen N.

JUDY, STEPHEN N.
See Tchudi, Stephen N.

JUKES, MAVIS
Birthdate: 5/3/1947
Birthplace: Nyack, NY
Information Available in These Sources: SATA 43, JBA 6

JULIAN, NANCY R.
Birthdate: 1923
Birthplace: TN
Information Available in These Sources: ABYP 1, ABYP 3

JUMPP, HUGO
See MacPeek, Walter G.

JUPO, FRANK J.
Birthdate: 2/28/1904
Birthplace: Dessau, Germany
Information Available in These Sources: ABYP 2, ABYP 3, ICB 2, SATA 7

JUSTER, NORTON
Birthdate: 6/2/1929
Birthplace: Brooklyn, NY
Information Available in These Sources: ABYP 2, ABYP 3, DACF, JBA 4, SATA 3, TCCW 1, TCCW 2, TCCW 3, WCL

JUSTUS, MAY
Birthdate: 5/12/1898
Birthplace: Del Rio, TN
Information Available in These Sources: ABYP 1, ABYP 3, JBA 2, SATA 1

K

K. O. S.
See Dombrowski, Kathe Schonberger von

KABIBBLE, OSH
See Jobb, Jamie

KADESCH, ROBERT R(UDSTONE)
Birthdate: 5/14/1922
Birthplace: Cedar Falls, IA
Information Available in These Sources: ABYP 4, SATA 31

KAHL, M(ARVIN) P(HILIP)
Birthdate: 9/28/1934
Birthplace: Indianapolis, IN
Information Available in These Sources: SATA 37

KAHL, VIRGINIA (CAROLINE)
Birthdate: 2/18/1919
Birthplace: Milwaukee, WI
Information Available in These Sources: ABYP 1, ABYP 3, BABP, ICB 2, ICB 3, MJA, SATA 38, SATA 48, TCCW 1, TCCW 2, TCCW 3

KAHN, JOAN
Birthdate: 4/13/1914
Birthplace: New York, NY
Information Available in These Sources: ABYP 4, SATA 48

KAHN, ROGER
Birthdate: 10/31/1927
Birthplace: Brooklyn, NY
Information Available in These Sources: ABYP 2, ABYP 3, SATA 37

KAHN, RUTH GANNETT
See Gannett, Ruth Stiles

KAKACEK, GEN
Birthplace: Naperville, IL
Information Available in These Sources: ABYP 2, ABYP 3

KALAB, THERESA
See Smith, Theresa Kalab

KALASHNIKOFF, NICHOLAS
Birthdate: 5/17/1888
Birthplace: Minusinsk, Siberia, Russia
Deathdate: 8/17/1961
Information Available in These Sources: MJA, SATA 16

KALB, JONAH
Birthdate: 9/17/1926
Birthplace: New York, NY
Information Available in These Sources: ABYP 4, SATA 23

KALER, JAMES OTIS
(James Otis)
Birthdate: 3/19/1848
Birthplace: Frankfort (Winterport), ME
Deathdate: 12/11/1912
Information Available in These Sources: DLB 42, JBA 1, JBA 2, SATA 15 TCCW 2, TCCW 3

KALINA, SIGMUND
Birthdate: 7/28/1911
Birthplace: Brooklyn, NY
Information Available in These Sources: ABYP 4

KALMENOFF, MATTHEW
Birthdate: 2/11/1905
Birthplace: New York, NY
Information Available in These Sources: IBYP 1, IBYP 2

KALNAY, FRANCIS
Birthdate: 7/18/1899
Birthplace: Budapest, Hungary
Information Available in These Sources: ABYP 2, ABYP 3, SATA 7

KALUSKY, REBECCA
Birthplace: New York, NY
Information Available in These Sources: ABYP 2, ABYP 3

KAMEN, GLORIA
Birthdate: 4/9/1923
Birthplace: New York, NY
Information Available in These Sources: IBYP 2, SATA 9

KAMERMAN, SYLVIA E.
See Burack, Sylvia K.

KAMPEN, OWEN
Birthplace: Madison, WI
Information Available in These Sources: IBYP 2

KANDELL, ALICE S.
Birthdate: 11/6/1938
Birthplace: New York, NY
Information Available in These Sources: SATA 35

KANE, HENRY BUGBEE
Birthdate: 1/8/1902
Birthplace: Cambridge, MA
Deathdate: 2/16/1971
Information Available in These Sources: ABYP 2, ABYP 3, ICB 1, ICB 2, ICB 3, ICB 4, SATA 14

KANE, L. A.
See Mannetti, Lisa

KANE, ROBERT W(ILLIAM)
Birthdate: 8/17/1910
Birthplace: New York, NY
Information Available in These Sources: ICB 2, SATA 18

KANETZKE, HOWARD W(ILLIAM)
Birthdate: 2/25/1932
Birthplace: Racine, WI
Information Available in These Sources: SATA 38

KANGAROO, CAPTAIN
See Keeshan, Robert J.

KANTOR, MACKINLAY
Birthdate: 2/4/1904
Birthplace: Webster City, IA
Deathdate: 10/11/1977
Information Available in These Sources: ABYP 2, ABYP 3

KAPLAN, ALBERT A.
Information Available in These Sources: ABYP 2, ABYP 3

KAPLAN, ANNE BERNAYS
(Anne Bernays)
Birthdate: 9/14/1930
Birthplace: New York, NY
Information Available in These Sources: SATA 32

KAPLAN, BOCHE
(A. K. Roche)
Birthdate: 12/7/1926
Birthplace: Oceanside, NY
Information Available in These Sources: IBYP 2, ICB 4, SATA 24

KAPLAN, JEAN CARYL KORN
(Jean Caryl)
Birthdate: 3/28/1926
Birthplace: Mount Vernon, NY
Information Available in These Sources: ABYP 2, ABYP 3, SATA 10

KAPLAN, MARGARET (DEMILLE)
Information Available in These Sources: ABYP 2, ABYP 3

KAPP, PAUL
Birthdate: 1907
Birthplace: Chicago, IL
Information Available in These Sources: ABYP 2, ABYP 3

KARAGEORGE, MICHAEL
See Anderson, Poul (William)

KARASZ, ILONKA
Birthdate: 7/13/1896
Birthplace: Budapest, Hungary
Deathdate: 5/26/1981
Information Available in These Sources: IBYP 2, ICB 2, SATA 29

KAREN, RUTH
Birthdate: 2/18/1922
Birthplace: Germany
Deathdate: 7/11/1987
Information Available in These Sources: SATA 9, SATA 54

KARL, JEAN E(DNA)
Birthdate: 7/29/1927
Birthplace: Chicago, IL
Information Available in These Sources: ABYP 4, JBA 5, SATA 34

KARLIN, EUGENE
Birthdate: 12/15/1918
Birthplace: Kenosha, WI
Information Available in These Sources: IBYP 2, ICB 3, SATA 10

KARP, NAOMI J.
Birthdate: 10/17/1926
Birthplace: New York, NY
Information Available in These Sources: ABYP 4, SATA 16

KARP, WALTER
Information Available in These Sources: ABYP 4

KASHIWAGI, ISAMI
(Sam Kashiwagi)
Birthdate: 7/17/1925
Birthplace: Onomea, HI
Information Available in These Sources: IBYP 1, IBYP 2, ICB 2, SATA 10

KASHIWAGI, SAM
See Kashiwagi, Isami

KASSEM, LOU
Birthplace: TN
Information Available in These Sources: SATA 51

KASSIRER, NORMA
Birthplace: Buffalo, NY
Information Available in These Sources: ABYP 2, ABYP 3

KATCHAMAKOFF, ATANAS
Birthdate: 1/31/1898
Birthplace: Leskovitz, Bulgaria
Information Available in These Sources: ICB 1

KATCHEN, CAROLE
Birthdate: 1/30/1944
Birthplace: Denver, CO
Information Available in These Sources: SATA 9

KATONA, ROBERT
Birthdate: 3/16/1949
Birthplace: Athens, OH
Information Available in These Sources: SATA 21

KATSARAKIS, JOAN HARRIES
See Harries, Joan

KATZ, BOBBI
Birthdate: 5/2/1933
Birthplace: Newburgh, NJ
Information Available in These Sources: SATA 12

KATZ, FRED(ERIC PHILLIP)
Birthdate: 9/23/1938
Birthplace: Rochester, NY
Information Available in These Sources: SATA 6

KATZ, HERBERT (MELVIN)
Birthdate: 11/13/1930
Birthplace: New York, NY
Information Available in These Sources: ABYP 4

KATZ, JACQUELINE HUNT
Birthplace: Portsmouth, England
Information Available in These Sources: ABYP 4

KATZ, JANE (BRESLER)
Birthdate: 12/18/1934
Birthplace: New York, NY
Information Available in These Sources: SATA 33

KATZ, MARJORIE P.
See Weiser, Marjorie P(hillis) K(atz)

KATZ, WILLIAM LOREN
Birthdate: 6/2/1927
Birthplace: Brooklyn, NY
Information Available in These Sources: ABYP 4, SATA 13

KAUFMAN, BEL
Birthplace: Berlin, Germany
Information Available in These Sources: SATA 57

KAUFMAN, JOE
Birthdate: 5/21/1911
Birthplace: Bridgeport, CT
Information Available in These Sources: SATA 33

KAUFMAN, MERVYN D.
Birthdate: 11/30/1932
Birthplace: Los Angeles, CA
Information Available in These Sources: SATA 4

KAUFMANN, HELEN (LOEB)
Birthdate: 2/2/1887
Birthplace: New York, NY
Information Available in These Sources: ABYP 4

KAUFMANN, JOHN
(David Swift)
Birthdate: 1931
Birthplace: New York, NY
Information Available in These Sources: IBYP 1, IBYP 2, ICB 3, SATA 18

KAULA, EDNA MASON
Birthdate: 1906
Birthplace: Sydney, Australia
Information Available in These Sources: SATA 13

KAVALER, LUCY
Birthdate: 8/29/1930
Birthplace: New York, NY
Information Available in These Sources: ABYP 2, ABYP 3, SATA 23

KAY, HELEN
See Goldfrank, Helen Colodny

KAY, MARA
Birthplace: Europe
Information Available in These Sources: SATA 13

KAYE, CASSANDRA
See Disch, Thomas M(ichael)

KAYE, DANNY
(David Daniel Kominski)
Birthdate: 1/18/1913
Birthplace: New York, NY
Deathdate: 3/3/1987
Information Available in These Sources: SATA 50

KAYE, MARILYN
(Shannon Blair)
Birthdate: 7/19/1949
Birthplace: New Britain, CT
Information Available in These Sources: SATA 56

KEANE, BIL
Birthdate: 10/5/1922
Birthplace: Philadelphia, PA
Information Available in These Sources: SATA 4

KEATING, BERN
See Keating, Leo Bernard

KEATING, LAWRENCE A(LFRED)
(John Keith Bassett, H. C. Thomas)
Birthdate: 1/21/1903
Birthplace: Chicago, IL
Deathdate: 6/16/1966
Information Available in These Sources: ABYP 1, ABYP 3, SATA 23

KEATING, LEO BERNARD
(Bern Keating)
Birthdate: 5/14/1915
Birthplace: Fassett, Quebec, Canada
Information Available in These Sources: SATA 10

KEATING, NORMA
Information Available in These Sources: ABYP 2, ABYP 3

KEATS, EZRA JACK
Birthdate: 3/11/1916
Birthplace: Brooklyn, NY
Deathdate: 5/6/1983
Information Available in These Sources: ABYP 1, ABYP 3, AICB, BABP, DLB 61, IBYP 1, IBYP 2, ICB 2 ICB 3, ICB 4, MJA, SATA 14, SATA 34, SATA 57, TCCW 1, 2, 3

KEEGAN, MARCIA
Birthdate: 5/23/1943
Birthplace: Tulsa, OK
Information Available in These Sources: SATA 9

KEEL, FRANK
See Keeler, Ronald F(ranklin)

KEELER, KATHERINE (SOUTHWICK)
See Southwick, Katherine

KEELER, RONALD F(RANKLIN)
(Frank Keel)
Birthdate: 1/29/1913
Birthplace: Bloomsburg, PA
Information Available in These Sources: SATA 47

KEEN, MARTIN L.
Birthdate: 2/14/1913
Birthplace: Atlantic City, NJ
Information Available in These Sources: ABYP 4, SATA 4

KEENE, CAROLYN
See Adams, Harriet S(tratemeyer)

KEENEN, GEORGE
Birthplace: NJ
Information Available in These Sources: ABYP 4

KEESHAN, ROBERT J.
(Captain Kangaroo)
Birthdate: 6/27/1927
Birthplace: Lynbrook, Long Island, NY
Information Available in These Sources: SATA 32

KEILLOR, GARRISON
Birthdate: 8/7/1942
Birthplace: Anoka, MN
Information Available in These Sources: SATA 58

KEITH, CARLTON
See Robertson, Keith (Carlton)

KEITH, EROS
Birthdate: 6/24/1942
Birthplace: Fulton, MO
Information Available in These Sources: IBYP 1, IBYP 2, ICB 4, JBA 4, SATA 52

KEITH, HAL
Birthdate: 1/24/1934
Birthplace: NY
Information Available in These Sources: SATA 36

KEITH, HAROLD (VERNE)
Birthdate: 4/8/1903
Birthplace: Lambert, OK
Information Available in These Sources: ABYP 1, ABYP 3, DACF, MBMP, MJA, SATA 2, TCCW 1, TCCW 2, TCCW 3

KEITH, JOSEPH JOEL
Birthdate: 1908
Birthplace: Pittsburgh (near), PA
Information Available in These Sources: SVC 2

KEITH, ROBERT
See Applebaum, Stan

KELEN, EMERY
Birthdate: 12/22/1896
Birthplace: Gyor, Hungary
Deathdate: 10/9/1978
Information Available in These Sources: ABYP 4, ICB 1, SATA 13, SATA 26

KELLEAM, JOSEPH E(VERIDGE)
Birthdate: 2/11/1913
Birthplace: Boswell, OK
Deathdate: 6/15/1975
Information Available in These Sources: SATA 31

KELLER, BEVERLY L(OU HARWICK)
Birthplace: San Francisco, CA
Information Available in These Sources: ABYP 4, SATA 13

KELLER, CHARLES
Birthdate: 3/30/1942
Birthplace: NY
Information Available in These Sources: ABYP 4, SATA 8

KELLER, DICK
Birthdate: 3/8/1923
Birthplace: Chicago, IL
Information Available in These Sources: SATA 36

KELLER, FRANCES RUTH
Birthdate: 1911
Birthplace: Moab, UT
Information Available in These Sources: ABYP 2, ABYP 3

KELLER, GAIL FAITHFULL
See Faithfull, Gail

KELLER, HOLLY
Birthplace: New York, NY
Information Available in These Sources: SATA 42

KELLER, IRENE (BARRON)
Birthdate: 1/13/1927
Birthplace: Falkirk, Scotland
Information Available in These Sources: SATA 36

KELLER, MOLLIE
Birthplace: Brooklyn, NY
Information Available in These Sources: SATA 50

KELLEY, LEO P(ATRICK)
Birthdate: 9/10/1928
Birthplace: Wilkes-Barre, PA
Information Available in These Sources: SATA 31, SATA 32

KELLEY, TRUE ADELAIDE
Birthdate: 2/25/1946
Birthplace: Cambridge, MA
Information Available in These Sources: SATA 39, SATA 41

KELLIN, SALLY MOFFET
Birthdate: 4/21/1932
Birthplace: New York, NY
Information Available in These Sources: SATA 9

KELLING, FURN L.
Birthdate: 9/11/1914
Birthplace: Shawnee, OK
Information Available in These Sources: SATA 37

KELLOGG, GENE
See Kellogg, Jean (Defrees)

KELLOGG, JEAN (DEFREES)
(Sally Jackson, Gene Kellogg)
Birthdate: 12/28/1916
Birthplace: Chicago, IL
Deathdate: 3/12/1978
Information Available in These Sources: ABYP 2, ABYP 3, SATA 10

KELLOGG, STEVEN (CASTLE)
Birthdate: 10/26/1941
Birthplace: Norwalk, CT
Information Available in These Sources: DLB 61, IBYP 2, ICB 4, JBA 4, SATA 8, SATA 57, TCCW 3

KELLY, ERIC P(HILBROOK)
Birthdate: 3/16/1884
Birthplace: Amesbury, MA
Deathdate: 1/3/1960
Information Available in These Sources: ABYP 1, ABYP 3, JBA 1, JBA 2, TCCW 1, TCCW 2, TCCW 3, YABC

KELLY, GEORGE ANTHONY
Birthdate: 9/17/1916
Birthplace: New York, NY
Information Available in These Sources: ABYP 4

KELLY, MARTHA ROSE
(Marty Kelly)
Birthdate: 11/14/1914
Birthplace: Fort Benton, MT
Information Available in These Sources: SATA 37

KELLY, MARTY
See Kelly, Martha Rose

KELLY, RALPH
See Geis, Darlene (Stern)

KELLY, REGINA Z(IMMERMAN)
Birthplace: New Orleans, LA
Information Available in These Sources: SATA 5

KELLY, ROSALIE (RUTH)
Birthplace: Grand Rapids, MI
Information Available in These Sources: SATA 43

KELLY, WALT(ER CRAWFORD)
Birthdate: 8/25/1913
Birthplace: Philadelphia, PA
Deathdate: 10/18/1973
Information Available in These Sources: IBYP 1, IBYP 2, SATA 18

KELSEY, ALICE GEER
Birthdate: 9/21/1896
Birthplace: Danvers, MA
Information Available in These Sources: ABYP 1, ABYP 3, MJA, SATA 1

KEMPNER, MARY JEAN
Birthdate: 1913
Birthplace: Galveston, TX
Deathdate: 9/11/1969
Information Available in These Sources: SATA 10

KEMPTON, JEAN WELCH
(Jean-Louise Welch)
Birthdate: 4/3/1914
Birthplace: Vineland, NJ
Information Available in These Sources: SATA 10

KENDALL, CAROL (SEEGER)
Birthdate: 9/13/1917
Birthplace: Bucyrus, OH
Information Available in These Sources: ABYP 1, ABYP 3, DACF, JBA 3, SATA 11, TCCW 1, TCCW 2, TCCW 3

KENDALL, LACE
See Stoutenberg, Adrien (Pearl)

KENEALY, JAMES P.
(Jim Kenealy)
Birthdate: 6/4/1927
Birthplace: Dorchester, MA
Information Available in These Sources: SATA 29, SATA 52

KENEALY, JIM
See Kenealy, James P.

KENNEDY, BRENDAN
Birthdate: 7/3/1970
Birthplace: Albany, NY
Information Available in These Sources: SATA 57

KENNEDY, DOROTHY M(INTZLAFF)
Birthdate: 3/8/1931
Birthplace: Milwaukee, WI
Information Available in These Sources: SATA 53

KENNEDY, JEROME RICHARD
(Richard Kennedy)
Birthdate: 12/23/1932
Birthplace: Jefferson City, MO
Information Available in These Sources: JBA 5, SATA 22, TCCW 2, TCCW 3

KENNEDY, JOHN FITZGERALD
Birthdate: 5/29/1917
Birthplace: Brookline, MA
Deathdate: 11/22/1963
Information Available in These Sources: SATA 11

KENNEDY, JOSEPH CHARLES
(X. J. Kennedy)
Birthdate: 8/21/1929
Birthplace: Dover, NJ
Information Available in These Sources: SATA 14, TCCW 3, JBA 6

KENNEDY, PAUL E(DWARD)
Birthdate: 10/7/1929
Birthplace: IN
Information Available in These Sources: ICB 3, SATA 33

KENNEDY, RICHARD
See Kennedy, Jerome Richard

KENNEDY, T(ERESA) A.
(Kate Vickery)
Birthdate: 6/12/1953
Birthplace: WI
Information Available in These Sources: SATA 35, SATA 42

KENNEDY, WILLIAM
Birthdate: 1/16/1928
Birthplace: Albany, NY
Information Available in These Sources: SATA 57

KENNEDY, X. J.
See Kennedy, Joseph Charles

KENNELL, RUTH E(PPERSON)
Birthdate: 9/21/1893
Birthplace: Oklahoma City, OK
Deathdate: 3/5/1977
Information Available in These Sources: SATA 6, SATA 25

KENNY, ELLSWORTH NEWCOMB
(Ellsworth Newcomb)
Birthdate: 12/16/1909
Birthplace: Washington, DC
Deathdate: 11/15/1971
Information Available in These Sources: ABYP 2, ABYP 3, SATA 26

KENNY, HERBERT A(NDREW)
Birthdate: 12/22/1912
Birthplace: Boston, MA
Information Available in These Sources: SATA 13

KENNY, HUGH
Information Available in These Sources: ABYP 2, ABYP 3

KENNY, KATHRYN
See Bowden, Joan Chase and Krull, Kathleen

KENNY, KEVIN
See Krull, Kathleen

KENT, DEBORAH ANN
Birthdate: 10/11/1948
Birthplace: Little Falls, NJ
Information Available in These Sources: SATA 41, SATA 47

KENT, JACK
See Kent, John Wellington

KENT, JOHN WELLINGTON
(Jack Kent)
Birthdate: 3/10/1920
Birthplace: Burlington, IA
Deathdate: 10/8/1985
Information Available in These Sources: ICB 4, JBA 5, SATA 24, SATA 45

KENT, LOUISE (ANDREWS)
Birthdate: 5/25/1886
Birthplace: Brookline, MA
Deathdate: 8/6/1969
Information Available in These Sources: ABYP 2, ABYP 3, JBA 2

KENT, ROCKWELL
(Hogarth, Jr.)
Birthdate: 6/21/1882
Birthplace: Tarrytown Heights, NY
Deathdate: 3/13/1971
Information Available in These Sources: IBYP 1, IBYP 2, ICB 1, SATA 6

KENT, SHERMAN
Birthdate: 12/1/1903
Birthplace: Chicago, IL
Deathdate: 3/11/1986
Information Available in These Sources: SATA 20, SATA 47

KENWORTHY, LEONARD S.
Birthdate: 3/26/1912
Information Available in These Sources: SATA 6

KENYON, KATE
See Ransom, Candice F.

KENYON, RAYMOND G.
Birthdate: 1922
Birthplace: Gloversville, NY
Information Available in These Sources: ABYP 1, ABYP 3

KEPES, JULIET A(PPLEBY)
Birthdate: 6/29/1919
Birthplace: London, England
Information Available in These Sources: ABYP 2, ABYP 3, ICB 2, ICB 3, ICB 4, JBA 3, SATA 13

KERIGAN, FLORENCE
(Frances Kerry)
Birthdate: 12/4/1896
Birthplace: Haverford, PA
Information Available in These Sources: SATA 12

KERMAN, GERTRUDE LERNER
Birthdate: 8/29/1909
Birthplace: Quebec City, Quebec, Canada
Information Available in These Sources: SATA 21

KERNER, BEN
Birthdate, 1917?
Birthplace: New York, NY
Information Available in These Sources: ABYP 2, ABYP 3

KERR, JESSICA (GORDON)
Birthdate: 2/2/1901
Birthplace: Dublin, Ireland
Information Available in These Sources: ABYP 4, SATA 13

KERR, LAURA (NOWAK)
Birthdate: 1904
Birthplace: Chicago, IL
Information Available in These Sources: ABYP 1, ABYP 3

KERR, M. E.
See Meaker, Marijane

KERR, MARIJANE MEAKER
See Meaker, Marijane

KERRY, FRANCES
See Kerigan, Florence

KERRY, LOIS
See Duncan, Lois S(teinmetz)

KESSEL, JOYCE KAREN
Birthdate: 1/27/1937
Birthplace: Kulm, ND
Information Available in These Sources: SATA 41

KESSLER, ETHEL
Birthdate: 1/7/1922
Birthplace: Pittsburgh, PA
Information Available in These Sources: JBA 5, SATA 37, SATA 44

KESSLER, LEONARD P.
Birthdate: 10/28/1921
Birthplace: Akron, OH
Information Available in These Sources: ABYP 2, ABYP 3, ICB 2, ICB 3, ICB 4, JBA 5, SATA 14

KETCHAM, HANK
See Ketcham, Henry King

KETCHAM, HENRY KING
(Hank Ketcham)
Birthdate: 3/14/1920
Birthplace: Seattle, WA
Information Available in These Sources: SATA 27, SATA 28

KETTELKAMP, LARRY DALE
Birthdate: 4/25/1933
Birthplace: Harvey, IL
Information Available in These Sources: ABYP 2, ABYP 3, ICB 3, ICB 4, JBA 3, SATA 2

KEVLES, BETTYANN
Birthdate: 8/20/1938
Birthplace: New York, NY
Information Available in These Sources: SATA 23

KEY, ALEXANDER (HILL)
Birthdate: 9/21/1904
Birthplace: La Plata, MD
Deathdate: 7/25/1979
Information Available in These Sources: ABYP 2, ABYP 3, DACF, SATA 8, SATA 23

KEYES, DANIEL
Birthdate: 8/9/1927
Birthplace: Brooklyn, NY
Information Available in These Sources: SATA 37

KEYES, FENTON
Birthdate: 1/26/1915
Birthplace: New York, NY
Information Available in These Sources: SATA 34

KEYES, NELSON BEECHER
Birthdate: 1894
Deathdate: 1958
Information Available in These Sources: ABYP 2, ABYP 3

KEYSER, MARCIA
Birthdate: 10/17/1933
Birthplace: Minneapolis, MN
Information Available in These Sources: SATA 42

KEYSER, SARAH
See McGuire, Leslie (Sarah)

KHANSHENDEL, CHIRON
See Rose, Wendy

KHERDIAN, DAVID
Birthdate: 12/17/1931
Birthplace: Racine, WI
Information Available in These Sources: JBA 5, SATA 16

KIBBE, PAT (HOSLEY)
Information Available in These Sources: SATA 60

KIDD, RONALD
Birthdate: 4/29/1948
Birthplace: St. Louis, MO
Information Available in These Sources: SATA 42

KIDWELL, CARL
Birthdate: 8/8/1910
Birthplace: Washington, IN
Information Available in These Sources: IBYP 2, SATA 43

KIEFER, IRENE
Birthdate: 11/1/1926
Birthplace: Red Lodge, MT
Information Available in These Sources: SATA 21

KIELTY, BERNARDINE
(Bernardine Kielty Scherman)
Birthdate, 189?
Birthplace: Fitchburg, MA?
Information Available in These Sources: ABYP 2, ABYP 3

KIENE, JULIA
Information Available in These Sources: ABYP 2, ABYP 3

KIERAN, JOHN (FRANCIS)
Birthdate: 8/2/1892
Birthplace: New York, NY
Deathdate: 12/10/1981
Information Available in These Sources: ABYP 4

KIESEL, STANLEY
Birthdate: 7/16/1925
Birthplace: Los Angeles, CA
Information Available in These Sources: SATA 35

KIKUKAWA, CECILY H(ARDER)
Birthdate: 10/23/1919
Birthplace: West Haven, CT
Information Available in These Sources: SATA 35, SATA 44

KILGORE, KATHLEEN
(Kathleen Houton)
Birthdate: 7/11/1946
Birthplace: Washington, DC
Information Available in These Sources: SATA 42

KILIAN, CRAWFORD
Birthdate: 2/7/1941
Birthplace: New York, NY
Information Available in These Sources: SATA 35

KILLILEA, MARIE (LYONS)
Birthdate: 6/28/1913
Birthplace: New York, NY
Information Available in These Sources: SATA 2

KILMER, ALFRED JOYCE
(Joyce Kilmer)
Birthdate: 12/6/1886
Birthplace: New Brunswick, NJ
Deathdate: 7/30/1918
Information Available in These Sources: SVC 2, SVC 3

KILMER, JOYCE
See Kilmer, Alfred Joyce

KILREON, BETH
See Walker, Barbara K(erlin)

KIMBALL, DEAN
Birthdate: 4/26/1912
Birthplace: Smith Center, KS
Information Available in These Sources: ABYP 4

KIMBALL, YEFFE
Birthdate: 3/30/1914
Birthplace: Mountain Park, OK
Deathdate: 4/10/1978
Information Available in These Sources: ICB 3, SATA 37

KIMBROUGH, EMILY
Birthdate: 10/23/1899
Birthplace: Muncie, IN
Deathdate: 2/11/1989
Information Available in These Sources: SATA 2, SATA 59

KIMMEL, ERIC A.
Birthdate: 10/30/1946
Birthplace: Brooklyn, NY
Information Available in These Sources: SATA 13

KIMMEL, MARGARET MARY
Birthdate: 5/12/1938
Birthplace: Gary, IN
Information Available in These Sources: SATA 33, SATA 43

KINDRED, WENDY (GOOD)
Birthdate: 12/19/1937
Birthplace: Detroit, MI
Information Available in These Sources: SATA 7

KINERT, REED CHARLES
Birthdate: 8/31/1912
Birthplace: Richmond, IN
Information Available in These Sources: ABYP 1, ABYP 3

KINES, PAT DECKER
(Pat Decker Tapio)
Birthdate: 12/22/1937
Birthplace: Grangeville, ID
Information Available in These Sources: SATA 12

KING, ARTHUR
See Cain, Arthur H(omer)

KING, BILLIE JEAN
Birthdate: 11/22/1943
Birthplace: Long Beach, CA
Information Available in These Sources: SATA 12

KING, CYNTHIA
Birthdate: 8/27/1925
Birthplace: New York, NY
Information Available in These Sources: SATA 7

KING, FRANK O.
Birthdate: 4/9/1883
Birthplace: Cashton, WI
Deathdate: 6/23/1969
Information Available in These Sources: SATA 22

KING, MARIAN
Birthdate, 1900?
Birthplace: Washington, DC
Deathdate: 3/12/1986
Information Available in These Sources: SATA 23, SATA 47

KING, MARTHA BENNETT
Information Available in These Sources: ABYP 1, ABYP 3

KING, MARTIN LUTHER, JR.
Birthdate: 1/15/1929
Birthplace: Atlanta, GA
Deathdate: 4/4/1968
Information Available in These Sources: SATA 14

KING, REEFE
See Barker, Albert W.

KING, ROBIN
Birthdate: 8/31/1919
Birthplace: Syracuse, NY
Information Available in These Sources: ICB 2

KING, SETH S.
Birthplace: Okmulgee, OK
Information Available in These Sources: ABYP 2, ABYP 3

KING, STEPHEN (EDWIN)
(Richard Bachman)
Birthdate: 9/21/1947
Birthplace: Portland, ME
Information Available in These Sources: SATA 9, SATA 55

KINGMAN, DONG (MOY SHU)
Birthdate: 3/31/1911 or 4/1/1911
Birthplace: Oakland, CA
Information Available in These Sources: ICB 2, SATA 44, 4/1/1911

KINGMAN, LEE
See Kingman, Mary Lee

KINGMAN, MARY LEE
(Lee Kingman)
Birthdate: 10/6/1919
Birthplace: Reading, MA
Information Available in These Sources: ABYP 2, ABYP 3, DACF, MJA, SATA 1, TCCW 1, TCCW 2, TCCW 3

KINGSLEY, EMILY PERL
Birthdate: 2/28/1940
Birthplace: New York, NY
Information Available in These Sources: SATA 33

KINGSTON, MAXINE (TING TING) HONG
Birthdate: 10/27/1940
Birthplace: Stockton, CA
Information Available in These Sources: SATA 53

KINKAID, WYATT E.
See Jennings, Michael

KINNEY, C. CLE(LAND)
(Cle Kinney)
Birthdate: 12/15/1915
Birthplace: Victoria, British Columbia, Canada
Information Available in These Sources: ABYP 4, SATA 6

KINNEY, CLE
See Kinney, C. Cle(land)

KINNEY, HARRISON
Birthdate: 8/16/1921
Birthplace: Mars Hill, ME
Information Available in These Sources: SATA 13

KINNEY, JEAN STOUT
Birthdate: 3/17/1912
Birthplace: Waukon, IA
Information Available in These Sources: ABYP 4, SATA 12

KINSER, CHARLEEN
Information Available in These Sources: ABYP 4

KINSEY, ELIZABETH
See Clymer, Eleanor (Lowenton)

KINZEL, DOROTHY
(Dottie Kinzel)
Birthdate: 7/26/1950
Birthplace: Schenectady, NY
Information Available in These Sources: SATA 57

KIPNISS, ROBERT
Birthdate: 2/1/1931
Birthplace: New York, NY
Information Available in These Sources: IBYP 2

KIRBY, JEAN
See McDonnell, Virginia (Bleecker)

KIRK, RHINA
Information Available in These Sources: ABYP 4

KIRK, RUTH (ELEANOR KRATZ)
Birthdate: 5/7/1925
Birthplace: Los Angeles, CA
Information Available in These Sources: ABYP 2, ABYP 3, SATA 5

KIRKLAND, WILL
See Hale, Arlene

KIRKPATRICK, OLIVER AUSTIN
(John Canoe)
Birthdate: 6/12/1911
Birthplace: Jamaica, West Indies
Information Available in These Sources: BAI

KIRKUS, VIRGINIA
See Glick, Virginia Kirkus

KIRMSE, MARGUERITE
Birthdate: 12/14/1885
Birthplace: Bournemouth, England
Deathdate: 1954
Information Available in These Sources: CICB, IBYP 1, IBYP 2, ICB 1, ICB 2

KIRN, ANN MINETTE
Birthdate: 4/4/1910
Birthplace: Montgomery City, MO
Information Available in These Sources: ABYP 2, 3, ICB 3

KIRTLAND, G. B.
See Hine, Al and Joslin, Sesyle

KISER, MARTHA GWINN
Birthplace: Bloomfield, IN
Information Available in These Sources: ABYP 2, ABYP 3

KISINGER, GRACE GELVIN (MAZE)
Birthdate: 5/14/1913
Birthplace: Ridgway, PA
Deathdate: 12/7/1965
Information Available in These Sources: ABYP 2, ABYP 3, SATA 10

KISSIN, EVA H.
Birthdate: 2/12/1923
Birthplace: New York, NY
Information Available in These Sources: SATA 10

KITT, TAMARA
See DeRegniers, Beatrice Schenk

KJELGAARD, JAMES ARTHUR
(Jim Kjelgaard)
Birthdate: 12/6/1910
Birthplace: New York, NY
Deathdate: 7/12/1959
Information Available in These Sources: ABYP 1, ABYP 3, JBA 2, SATA 17SVC 3, TCCW 1, TCCW 2, TCCW 3

KJELGAARD, JIM
See Kjelgaard, James Arthur

KLAGSBRUN, FRANCINE (LIFTON)
Birthplace: Brooklyn, NY
Information Available in These Sources: SATA 36

KLAITS, BARRIE
Birthdate: 7/2/1944
Birthplace: Biloxi, MS
Information Available in These Sources: SATA 52

KLAPERMAN, GILBERT
Birthdate: 2/25/1921
Birthplace: New York, NY
Information Available in These Sources: SATA 33

KLAPERMAN, LIBBY MINDLIN
Birthdate: 12/28/1921
Birthplace: Petrikow, USSR
Deathdate: 6/18/1982
Information Available in These Sources: SATA 31, SATA 33

KLASS, MORTON
Birthdate: 6/24/1927
Birthplace: Brooklyn, NY
Information Available in These Sources: ABYP 4, SATA 11

KLASS, SHEILA SOLOMON
Birthdate: 11/6/1927
Birthplace: Brooklyn, NY
Information Available in These Sources: SATA 45

KLAVENESS, JAN O'DONNELL
Birthdate: 1939
Birthplace: York, PA
Information Available in These Sources: DACF

KLEEBERG, IRENE (FLITNER) CUMMING
Birthdate: 4/21/1932
Birthplace: Chicago, IL
Information Available in These Sources: ABYP 4

KLEIN, AARON E.
(A. Edward Little)
Birthdate: 7/8/1930
Birthplace: Atlanta, GA
Information Available in These Sources: ABYP 4, SATA 28, SATA 45

KLEIN, DAVID
Birthdate: 3/30/1919
Birthplace: New York, NY
Information Available in These Sources: ABYP 2, ABYP 3, SATA 59

KLEIN, GERDA WEISSMANN
Birthdate: 5/8/1924
Birthplace: Bielsko, Poland
Information Available in These Sources: SATA 44

KLEIN, H(ERBERT) ARTHUR
Birthplace: NY
Information Available in These Sources: ABYP 2, ABYP 3, SATA 8

KLEIN, LEONORE (GLOTZER)
Birthdate: 9/4/1916
Birthplace: New York, NY
Information Available in These Sources: ABYP 2, ABYP 3, SATA 6

KLEIN, MINA C(OOPER)
Birthplace: England
Information Available in These Sources: SATA 8

KLEIN, NORMA
Birthdate: 5/13/1938
Birthplace: New York, NY
Deathdate: 5/13/1989
Information Available in These Sources: ABYP 4, DACF, JBA 5, SATA 7, SATA 57, TCCW 1, TCCW 2, TCCW 3

KLEMIN, DIANA
Birthplace: New York, NY
Information Available in These Sources: ABYP 4

KLEMM, EDWARD G., JR.
Birthdate: 6/6/1910
Birthplace: Louisville, KY
Information Available in These Sources: SATA 30

KLEMM, ROBERTA K(OHNHORST)
Birthdate: 11/29/1884
Birthplace: Louisville, KY
Information Available in These Sources: SATA 30

KLEVER, ANITA
Information Available in These Sources: ABYP 4

KLEVIN, JILL ROSS
Birthdate: 9/7/1935
Birthplace: Brooklyn, NY
Information Available in These Sources: SATA 38, SATA 39

KLIBAN, B.
Birthdate: 1/1/1935
Birthplace: Norwalk, CT
Information Available in These Sources: SATA 35

KLIMOWICZ, BARBARA (TINGLEY)
Birthdate: 9/11/1927
Birthplace: Mansfield, OH
Information Available in These Sources: ABYP 4, SATA 10

KLINE, SUZY
Birthdate: 8/27/1943
Birthplace: Berkeley, CA
Information Available in These Sources: SATA 48

KLOPP, VAHRAH VON
See Malvern, Gladys

KLUG, RON(ALD)
Birthdate: 6/26/1939
Birthplace: Milwaukee, WI
Information Available in These Sources: SATA 31

KNAPP, RON
Birthdate: 2/11/1952
Birthplace: Battle Creek, MI
Information Available in These Sources: SATA 34

KNEBEL, FLETCHER
Birthdate: 10/1/1911
Birthplace: Dayton, OH
Information Available in These Sources: SATA 36

KNICKERBOCKER, DIEDRICH
See Irving, Washington

KNIGGE, ROBERT (R.)
Birthdate, 1921?
Birthplace: St. Louis, MO
Deathdate: 1/4/1987
Information Available in These Sources: SATA 50

KNIGHT, CHARLES ROBERT
Birthdate: 10/21/1874
Birthplace: Brooklyn, NY
Deathdate: 4/15/1953
Information Available in These Sources: ICB 2

KNIGHT, CLAYTON
Birthdate: 3/30/1891
Birthplace: Rochester, NY
Deathdate: 7/17/1969
Information Available in These Sources: ABYP 1, ABYP 3

KNIGHT, DAMON
Birthdate: 9/19/1922
Birthplace: Baker, OR
Information Available in These Sources: SATA 9

KNIGHT, DAVID C(ARPENTER)
Birthdate: 8/6/1925
Birthplace: Glens Falls, NY
Information Available in These Sources: ABYP 2, ABYP 3, SATA 14

KNIGHT, ERIC (MOWBRAY)
(Richard Hallas)
Birthdate: 4/10/1897
Birthplace: Menston, Yorkshire, England
Deathdate: 1/15/1943
Information Available in These Sources: SATA 18

KNIGHT, HILARY
Birthdate: 11/1/1926
Birthplace: Hempstead, Long Island, NY
Information Available in These Sources: ABYP 2, ABYP 3, ICB 3, JBA 4, SATA 15

KNIGHT, MALLORY T.
See Hurwood, Bernhardt J.

KNIGHT, MAX
(Peter Fabrizius)
Birthdate: 6/8/1909
Birthplace: Austria
Information Available in These Sources: ABYP 4

KNIGHT, RUTH ADAMS (YINGLING)
Birthdate: 10/5/1898
Birthplace: Defiance, OH
Deathdate: 7/4/1974
Information Available in These Sources: ABYP 2, ABYP 3, MJA, SATA 20

KNIPE, ALDEN ARTHUR
Birthdate: 6/26/1870
Birthplace: Philadelphia, PA
Deathdate: 5/22/1950
Information Available in These Sources: JBA 1, JBA 2

KNIPE, EMILIE BENSON
Birthdate: 6/12/1870
Birthplace: Philadelphia, PA
Deathdate: 10/25/1958
Information Available in These Sources: JBA 1, JBA 2

KNOEPFLE, JOHN
Birthdate: 2/4/1923
Birthplace: Cincinnati, OH
Information Available in These Sources: ABYP 4

KNOTT, BILL
See Knott, William Cecil, Jr.

KNOTT, WILLIAM CECIL, JR.
(Bill J. Carol, Bill Knott)
Birthdate: 8/7/1927
Birthplace: Boston, MA
Information Available in These Sources: ABYP 4, SATA 3

KNOTTS, HOWARD (CLAYTON, JR.)
Birthdate: 10/13/1922
Birthplace: Springfield, IL
Information Available in These Sources: ICB 4, SATA 25

KNOWLES, JOHN
Birthdate: 9/16/1926
Birthplace: Fairmont, WV
Information Available in These Sources: SATA 8

KNOX, CALVIN M.
See Silverberg, Robert

KNOX, JAMES
See Brittain, William

KNOX, ROSE B(ELL)
Birthdate: 12/16/1879
Birthplace: Talladega, AL
Information Available in These Sources: JBA 1, JBA 2

KNUDSEN, JAMES
Birthdate: 12/7/1950
Birthplace: Geneva, IL
Information Available in These Sources: SATA 42

KNUDSON, R. R.
See Knudson, Rozanne

KNUDSON, RICHARD L(EWIS)
Birthdate: 6/4/1930
Birthplace: Newton, MA
Information Available in These Sources: SATA 34

KNUDSON, ROZANNE
(R. R. Knudson)
Birthdate: 6/1/1932
Birthplace: Washington, DC
Information Available in These Sources: SATA 7, JBA 6

KOCH, DOROTHY (CLARKE)
Birthdate: 10/8/1924
Birthplace: Ahoskie, NC
Information Available in These Sources: ABYP 1, ABYP 3, SATA 6

KOCK, CARL
Birthdate, 1935?
Information Available in These Sources: ABYP 4

KOCSIS, J(AMES) C.
See Paul, James

KOEHN, ILSE
See VanZwienin, Ilse (Charlotte Koehn)

KOERING, URSULA
Birthdate: 12/22/1921
Birthplace: Vineland, NJ
Information Available in These Sources: IBYP 2, ICB 2, MJA

KOERNER, W(ILLIAM) H(ENRY) D(AVID)
Birthdate: 11/19/1878
Birthplace: Lunden, Schleswig-Holstein, Germany
Deathdate: 8/1/1938
Information Available in These Sources: SATA 21

KOERTGE, RONALD
Birthdate: 4/22/1940
Birthplace: Olney, IL
Information Available in These Sources: SATA 53

KOFFLER, CAMILLA
(Ylla)
Birthplace: Austria
Deathdate: 3/30/1955
Information Available in These Sources: ABYP 1, ABYP 3, MJA

KOGAN, DEBORAH
See Ray, Deborah (Kogan)

KOGAN, HERMAN
Birthdate: 11/6/1914
Birthplace: Chicago, IL
Information Available in These Sources: ABYP 4

KOHL, HERBERT
Birthdate: 8/22/1937
Birthplace: Bronx, NY
Information Available in These Sources: SATA 47

KOHL, MARGUERITE
Birthdate: 1918
Information Available in These Sources: ABYP 2, ABYP 3

KOHLER, JULILLY H(OUSE)
Birthdate: 10/18/1908
Birthplace: Cincinnati, OH
Deathdate: 12/24/1976
Information Available in These Sources: SATA 20

KOHN, BERNICE (HERSTEIN)
(Bernice Kohn Hunt)
Birthdate: 6/15/1920
Birthplace: Philadelphia, PA
Information Available in These Sources: ABYP 2, ABYP 3, SATA 4

KOHNER, FREDERICK
Birthdate: 9/25/1905
Birthplace: Trnovany or Teplitz-Schoenau, Czechoslovakia
Deathdate: 7/6/1986
Information Available in These Sources: SATA 10, SATA 48

KOLBA, TAMARA
(St. Tamara)
Birthplace: Byelorussia
Information Available in These Sources: SATA 22

KOMINSKI, DAVID DANIEL
See Kaye, Danny

KOMISAR, LUCY
Birthdate: 4/8/1942
Birthplace: New York, NY
Information Available in These Sources: ABYP 4, SATA 9

KOMODA, BEVERLY
Birthdate: 11/26/1939
Birthplace: Seattle, WA
Information Available in These Sources: SATA 25

KOMODA, KIYO(AKI)
Birthdate: 3/3/1937
Birthplace: Saijo-Shi, Ehime, Japan
Information Available in These Sources: ICB 3, SATA 9

KOMROFF, MANUEL
Birthdate: 9/7/1890
Birthplace: New York, NY
Deathdate: 12/10/1974
Information Available in These Sources: ABYP 1, ABYP 3, SATA 2, SATA 20

KONIGSBURG, E(LAINE) L(OBL)
Birthdate: 2/10/1930
Birthplace: New York, NY
Information Available in These Sources: ABYP 3, AICB, DACF, JBA 3, MBMP, SATA 4, SATA 48, TCCW 1 TCCW 2, TCCW 3

KONING, HANS
See Koningsberger, Hans

KONINGSBERGER, HANS
(Hans Koning)
Birthdate: 7/12/1921
Birthplace: Amsterdam, Holland
Information Available in These Sources: SATA 5

KONKLE, JANET EVEREST
Birthdate: 11/5/1917
Birthplace: Grand Rapids, MI
Information Available in These Sources: SATA 12

KOOB, THEODORA (JOHANNA FOTH)
Birthdate: 9/16/1918
Birthplace: Jersey City, NJ
Information Available in These Sources: ABYP 2, ABYP 3, SATA 23

KOPPER, LISA (ESTHER)
Birthdate: 8/8/1950
Birthplace: Chicago, IL
Information Available in These Sources: SATA 51

KORACH, MIMI
Birthdate: 4/25/1922
Birthplace: New York, NY
Information Available in These Sources: SATA 9

KOREN, ED(WARD)
Birthdate: 12/13/1935
Birthplace: New York, NY
Information Available in These Sources: SATA 5

KORTY, CAROL
Birthdate: 1/4/1937
Birthplace: Albany, NY
Information Available in These Sources: SATA 15

KOSSIN, SANDY (SANFORD)
Birthdate: 6/4/1926
Birthplace: Los Angeles, CA
Information Available in These Sources: SATA 10

KOSTICH, DRAGOS D.
Birthdate: 7/16/1921
Birthplace: Belgrade, Yugoslavia
Information Available in These Sources: ABYP 2, ABYP 3

KOTZWINKLE, WILLIAM
Birthdate: 1938
Information Available in These Sources: SATA 24

KOUTOUKAS, H. M.
See Rivoli, Mario

KOUTS, ANNE
Birthdate: 7/3/1945
Birthplace: Washington, DC
Information Available in These Sources: SATA 8

KOVALIK, NADA
Birthdate: 12/19/1926
Birthplace: St. Catharines, Ontario, Canada
Information Available in These Sources: ABYP 3

KOVALSKI, MARYANN
Birthdate: 6/4/1951
Birthplace: New York, NY
Information Available in These Sources: SATA 58

KOWET, DON
(Frank Gell)
Birthdate: 3/29/1937
Birthplace: Boston, MA
Information Available in These Sources: ABYP 4

KRAMER, ANTHONY
(Tony Kramer)
Information Available in These Sources: SATA 42

KRAMER, GEORGE
See Heuman, William

KRAMER, NORA
Birthdate, 1896?
Birthplace: Pendleton, England
Deathdate: 7/4/1984
Information Available in These Sources: ABYP 2, ABYP 3, SATA 26, SATA 39

KRAMER, TONY
See Kramer, Anthony

KRANTZ, HAZEL (NEWMAN)
Birthdate: 1/29/1920
Birthplace: Brooklyn, NY
Information Available in These Sources: SATA 12

KRANTZ, LUCRETIA
Birthplace: Saint Michaels, MD
Information Available in These Sources: ABYP 4

KRANZLER, GEORGE G(ERSHON)
(Gershon Kranzler, Jacob Isaacs)
Birthdate: 1/27/1916
Birthplace: Stuttgart, Germany
Information Available in These Sources: SATA 28

KRANZLER, GERSHON
See Kranzler, George G(ershon)

KRASILOVSKY, PHYLLIS (MANNING)
Birthdate: 8/28/1926
Birthplace: Brooklyn or Chappaqua, NY
Information Available in These Sources: ABYP 1, ABYP 3, MJA, SATA 1, SATA 38, TCCW 1, TCCW 2, TCCW 3

KRASKE, ROBERT
Birthplace: Detroit, MI
Information Available in These Sources: SATA 36

KRASNE, BETTY
See Levine, Betty K(rasne)

KRAUS, JOANNA HALPERT
Birthdate: 12/7/1937
Birthplace: Portland, ME
Information Available in These Sources: TCCW 1, TCCW 2, TCCW 3

KRAUS, ROBERT
(Eugene H. Hippopotamus, E. S. Silly, I. M. Tubby)
Birthdate: 6/21/1925
Birthplace: Milwaukee, WI
Information Available in These Sources: ABYP 2, ABYP 3, ICB 3, ICB 4, JBA 3, SATA 4, TCCW 1, TCCW 2 TCCW 3

KRAUSS, OSCAR
Information Available in These Sources: IBYP 1, IBYP 2

KRAUSS, RUTH (IDA)
Birthdate: 7/25/1911
Birthplace: Baltimore, MD
Information Available in These Sources: ABYP 2, ABYP 3, AICB, BABP, MJA, SATA 1, SATA 30, TCCW 1, TCCW 2, TCCW 3

KRAUTTER, ELISA (BIALK)
(Elisa Bialk)
Birthdate: 10/4/1912
Birthplace: Chicago, IL
Information Available in These Sources: ABYP 4, MJA, SATA 1

KREDEL, FRITZ
Birthdate: 2/8/1900
Birthplace: Michelstadt, Odenwald, Germany
Deathdate: 6/10/1973
Information Available in These Sources: IBYP 1, IBYP 2, ICB 1, ICB 2, ICB 3, MJA, SATA 17

KREDENSER, GAIL
Birthdate: 12/6/1936
Birthplace: Everett, MA
Information Available in These Sources: ABYP 4

KREMENTZ, JILL
Birthdate: 2/19/1940
Birthplace: New York, NY
Information Available in These Sources: JBA 5, SATA 17

KRENSKY, STEPHEN (ALAN)
Birthdate: 11/25/1953
Birthplace: Boston, MA
Information Available in These Sources: SATA 41, SATA 47, JBA 6

KRIPKE, DOROTHY KARP
Birthplace: Highland Falls, NY
Information Available in These Sources: SATA 30

KRISTOF, JANE
Birthdate: 5/25/1932
Birthplace: Chicago, IL
Information Available in These Sources: SATA 8

KRISTOFFERSON, EVA M(ARGARET STIEGELMEYER)
Birthdate: 1901
Birthplace: Denmark
Information Available in These Sources: ABYP 1, ABYP 3

KROEBER, THEODORA (KRACAW BROWN)
(Theodora Kroeber-Quinn)
Birthdate: 3/24/1897
Birthplace: Denver, CO
Deathdate: 7/4/1979
Information Available in These Sources: SATA 1

KROEBER-QUINN, THEODORA
See Kroeber, Theodora (Kracaw Brown)

KROLL, FRANCIS LYNDE
Birthdate: 11/9/1904
Birthplace: Fairbury, NE
Deathdate: 11/12/1973
Information Available in These Sources: SATA 10

KROLL, STEVEN
Birthdate: 8/11/1941
Birthplace: New York, NY
Information Available in These Sources: ABYP 4, BC, JBA 5, SATA 19

KROPP, PAUL (STEPHAN)
Birthdate: 2/22/1948
Birthplace: Buffalo, NY
Information Available in These Sources: SATA 34, SATA 38

KRUIF, PAUL DE
See DeKruif, Paul (Henry)

KRULL, KATHLEEN
(Kathleen Cowles, Kathryn Kenny, Kevin Kenny)
Birthdate: 7/29/1952
Birthplace: Fort Leonard Wood, MO
Information Available in These Sources: SATA 39, SATA 52

KRUM, CHARLOTTE
Birthdate: 1886
Birthplace: Bloomington, IL
Information Available in These Sources: ABYP 1, ABYP 3

KRUMGOLD, JOSEPH (QUINCY)
Birthdate: 4/9/1908
Birthplace: Jersey City, NJ
Deathdate: 7/10/1980
Information Available in These Sources: ABYP 1, ABYP 3, DACF, MJA, SATA 1, SATA 23, SATA 48, TCCW 1, TCCW 2, TCCW 3

KRUPP, E(DWIN) C(HARLES)
Birthdate: 11/18/1944
Birthplace: Chicago, IL
Information Available in These Sources: SATA 53

KRUPP, ROBIN RECTOR
Birthdate: 3/29/1946
Birthplace: Brooklyn, NY
Information Available in These Sources: SATA 53

KRUSH, BETH
Birthdate: 3/31/1918
Birthplace: Washington, DC
Information Available in These Sources: IBYP 1, IBYP 2, ICB 2, ICB 3, MJA, SATA 18

KRUSH, JOE
Birthdate: 5/18/1918
Birthplace: Camden, NJ
Information Available in These Sources: IBYP 1, IBYP 2, ICB 2, ICB 3, MJA, SATA 18

KUBIE, NORA (GOTTHEIL) BENJAMIN
(Nora Benjamin)
Birthdate: 1/4/1899
Birthplace: New York, NY
Deathdate: 9/4/1988
Information Available in These Sources: ABYP 2, ABYP 3, SATA 39, SATA 59

KUBINYI, KALMAN
Birthdate: 7/29/1906
Birthplace: Cleveland (Lakewood), OH
Information Available in These Sources: CICB, ICB 1

KUBINYI, LASZLO (KALMAN)
Birthdate: 12/20/1937
Information Available in These Sources: IBYP 1, IBYP 2, ICB 4, SATA 17

KUBLIN, HYMAN
Birthdate: 12/29/1919
Birthplace: Boston, MA
Information Available in These Sources: ABYP 4

KUEHNER, LOUIS C.
Information Available in These Sources: ABYP 4

KUGELMASS, JOSEPH ALVIN
Birthdate: 9/25/1910
Birthplace: New York, NY
Deathdate: 3/11/1972
Information Available in These Sources: ABYP 2, ABYP 3

KUH, CHARLOTTE
Birthdate: 1892
Deathdate: 3/4/1985
Information Available in These Sources: SATA 43

KUHN, DORIS (YOUNG)
Birthdate, 1920?
Information Available in These Sources: ABYP 4

KUJOTH, JEAN SPEALMAN
Birthdate: 4/20/1935
Birthplace: Champaign, IL
Deathdate: 9/27/1975 9/27/1976
Information Available in These Sources: ABYP 4, SATA 30

KULA, ELSA
Information Available in These Sources: ABYP 4

KUMIN, MAXINE (WINOKUR)
Birthdate: 6/6/1925
Birthplace: Philadelphia, PA
Information Available in These Sources: ABYP 2, ABYP 3, SATA 12

KUMMER, FREDERIC ARNOLD
(Arnold Fredericks)
Birthdate: 8/5/1873
Birthplace: Cantonsville, MD
Deathdate: 11/22/1943
Information Available in These Sources: ABYP 2, ABYP 3

KUNHARDT, DOROTHY MESERVE
Birthdate: 1901
Birthplace: New York, NY
Deathdate: 12/23/1979
Information Available in These Sources: ABYP 4, SATA 22, SATA 53

KUNHARDT, PHILIP B(RADISH), JR.
Birthdate: 2/5/1928
Birthplace: New York, NY
Information Available in These Sources: ABYP 4

KUNSTLER, MORTON
(Mutz)
Birthdate: 8/28/1927
Birthplace: Brooklyn, NY
Information Available in These Sources: SATA 10

KUNZ, ROXANE (BROWN)
Birthdate: 7/29/1932
Birthplace: Jamestown, NY
Information Available in These Sources: SATA 53

KUPFERBERG, HERBERT
Birthdate: 1/20/1918
Birthplace: New York, NY
Information Available in These Sources: SATA 19

KURLAND, GERALD
Birthdate: 7/24/1942
Birthplace: Brooklyn, NY
Information Available in These Sources: SATA 13

KURLAND, MICHAEL (JOSEPH)
(Jennifer Plum)
Birthdate: 3/1/1938
Birthplace: New York, NY
Information Available in These Sources: SATA 48

KUSHNER, DONN
Birthdate: 3/29/1927
Birthplace: Lake Charles, LA
Information Available in These Sources: SATA 52

KUSKIN, KARLA (SEIDMAN)
(Nicholas Charles)
Birthdate: 7/17/1932
Birthplace: New York, NY
Information Available in These Sources: ABYP 1, ABYP 3, ICB 3, ICB 4, JBA 3, SATA 2, TCCW 1, 2, 3

KUTCHER, BEN
Birthdate: 8/15/1895
Birthplace: Kiev, Russia
Deathdate: 1967
Information Available in These Sources: CICB, ICB 1, ICB 2

KUTTNER, PAUL
Birthdate: 9/20/1931
Birthplace: Berlin, Germany
Information Available in These Sources: SATA 18

KUUMBA
See Briggs, Barbara A.

KUZMA, KAY
Birthdate: 4/25/1941
Birthplace: Ogallala, NE
Information Available in These Sources: SATA 39

KVALE, VELMA R(UTH)
Birthdate: 5/12/1898
Birthplace: Hastings, NE
Information Available in These Sources: SATA 8

KYLE, ANNE D.
Birthdate: 10/18/1896
Birthplace: Frankford, PA
Information Available in These Sources: JBA 1, JBA 2

KYTE, KATHY S.
Birthdate: 6/5/1946
Birthplace: Reno, NV
Information Available in These Sources: SATA 44, SATA 50

L

L'ENGLE, MADELEINE
(Madeleine L'Engle Camp, Madeleine Franklin)
Birthdate: 11/29/1918
Birthplace: New York, NY
Information Available in These Sources: ABYP 1, ABYP 3, DACF, MBMP, MJA, SATA 1, SATA 27, TCCW 1, TCCW 2, TCCW 3

L'HOMMEDIEU, DOROTHY K(EASLEY)
Birthdate: 1885
Deathdate: 3/16/1961
Information Available in These Sources: ABYP 1, ABYP 3, SATA 29

LACHER, GISELLA LOEFFLER
(Gisella Loeffler)
Birthdate: 9/24/1900
Birthplace: Graz, Austria or VarGraz, Vienna, Austria
Information Available in These Sources: ICB 1

LACY, LESLIE ALEXANDER
Birthdate: 1937
Birthplace: Franklin, LA
Information Available in These Sources: SATA 6

LADD, VERONICA
See Miner, Jane Claypool

LADER, LAWRENCE
Birthdate: 8/6/1919
Birthplace: New York, NY
Information Available in These Sources: SATA 6

LAFARGE, OLIVER (HAZARD PERRY)
Birthdate: 12/19/1901
Birthplace: New York, NY
Deathdate: 8/2/1963
Information Available in These Sources: ABYP 2, ABYP 3, SATA 19

LAFARGE, PHYLLIS
Birthdate: 6/10/1933
Birthplace: New York, NY
Information Available in These Sources: ABYP 2, ABYP 3, SATA 44

LAGER, MARILYN
Birthdate: 6/29/1939
Birthplace: Bronx, NY
Information Available in These Sources: SATA 52

LAIKEN, DEIRDRE S(USAN)
Birthdate: 1/21/1948
Birthplace: New York, NY
Information Available in These Sources: SATA 40, SATA 48

LAING, MARTHA
See Celestino, Martha Laing

LAIRD, JEAN E(LOUISE)
(J. E. Drial, Marcia McKeever, Jean L. Wakefield)
Birthdate: 1/18/1930
Birthplace: Wakefield, MI
Information Available in These Sources: SATA 38

LAITE, GORDON
Birthdate: 7/11/1925
Birthplace: New York, NY
Information Available in These Sources: IBYP 1, IBYP 2, ICB 3, SATA 31

LAKE, HARRIET
See Taylor, Paula (Wright)

LAKLAN, CARLI (LAUGHLIN AIELLO)
(John Clarke, Virginia Carli Laughlin)
Birthdate: 12/4/1907
Birthplace: Paoli, OK
Information Available in These Sources: ABYP 4, DACF, SATA 5

LAMB, BEATRICE PITNEY
Birthdate: 5/12/1904
Information Available in These Sources: SATA 21

LAMB, ELIZABETH SEARLE
Birthdate: 1/22/1917
Birthplace: Topeka, KS
Information Available in These Sources: SATA 31

LAMB, HAROLD (ALBERT)
Birthdate: 9/1/1892
Birthplace: Alpine, NJ
Deathdate: 4/9/1962
Information Available in These Sources: ABYP 1, ABYP 3, JBA 1, JBA 2, SATA 53

LAMB, ROBERT (BOYDEN)
Birthdate: 6/19/1941
Birthplace: Washington, DC
Information Available in These Sources: SATA 13

LAMBERT, JANET (SNYDER)
Birthdate: 12/17/1894
Birthplace: Crawfordsville, IN
Deathdate: 3/16/1973
Information Available in These Sources: ABYP 1, ABYP 3, JBA 3, SATA 25

LAMBERT, SAUL
Birthdate: 3/12/1928
Birthplace: New York, NY
Information Available in These Sources: IBYP 2, SATA 23

LAMBO, DON(ALD W.)
Birthdate: 1903
Information Available in These Sources: IBYP 1, IBYP 2

LAMPERT, EMILY
Birthdate: 4/26/1951
Birthplace: Boston, MA
Information Available in These Sources: SATA 49, SATA 52

LAMPMAN, EVELYN (SIBLEY)
(Lynn Bronson)
Birthdate: 4/18/1907
Birthplace: Dallas, OR
Deathdate: 6/13/1980
Information Available in These Sources: ABYP 1, ABYP 3, DACF, MJA, SATA 4, SATA 23, TCCW 1, TCCW 2, TCCW 3

LAMPREY, LOUISE
Birthdate: 4/17/1869
Birthplace: Alexandria, NH
Deathdate: 1/15/1951
Information Available in These Sources: JBA 1, JBA 2, YABC

LAMPTON, CHRIS(TOPHER)
Information Available in These Sources: SATA 47

LANCASTER, ANNE FLEUR
See Fleur, Anne (Elizabeth)

LANCASTER, BRUCE
Birthdate: 8/22/1896
Birthplace: Worcester, MA
Deathdate: 6/20/1963
Information Available in These Sources: SATA 9

LANCASTER, MATTHEW
Birthdate, 1973?
Deathdate: 3/00/1983
Information Available in These Sources: SATA 45

LAND, BARBARA (NEBLETT)
Birthdate: 7/11/1923
Birthplace: Hopkinsville, KY
Information Available in These Sources: SATA 16

LAND, JANE
See Borland, Kathryn Kilby and Speicher, Helen Ross (Smith)

LAND, MYRICK (EBBEN)
Birthdate: 2/25/1922
Birthplace: Shreveport, LA
Information Available in These Sources: SATA 15

LAND, ROSS
See Borland, Kathryn Kilby and Speicher, Helen Ross (Smith)

LANDAU, ELAINE (GARMIZA)
Birthdate: 2/15/1948
Birthplace: Lakewood, NJ
Information Available in These Sources: ABYP 4, SATA 10

LANDAU, JACOB
Birthdate: 12/17/1917
Birthplace: Philadelphia, PA
Information Available in These Sources: IBYP 1, IBYP 2, ICB 2, ICB 3, ICB 4, SATA 38

LANDECK, BEATRICE
Birthdate: 4/27/1904
Birthplace: New York, NY
Information Available in These Sources: ABYP 1, ABYP 3, SATA 15

LANDIN, LES(LIE)
Birthdate: 8/24/1923
Birthplace: Los Angeles, CA
Information Available in These Sources: SATA 2

LANDIS, J(AMES) D(AVID)
Birthdate: 6/30/1942
Birthplace: Springfield, MA
Information Available in These Sources: SATA 52, SATA 60

LANDON, LUCINDA
Birthdate: 8/15/1950
Birthplace: Galesburg, IL
Information Available in These Sources: SATA 51, SATA 56

LANDON, MARGARET (DOROTHEA MORTENSON)
Birthdate: 9/7/1903
Birthplace: Somers, WI
Information Available in These Sources: SATA 50

LANDSHOFF, URSULA
Birthdate: 5/17/1908
Birthplace: Berlin, Germany
Information Available in These Sources: SATA 13

LANE, CARL DANIEL
Birthdate: 10/10/1901 or 10/10/1899
Birthplace: New York, NY
Information Available in These Sources: ABYP 1, ABYP 3

LANE, CAROLYN (BLOCKER)
Birthdate: 6/4/1926
Birthplace: Providence, RI
Information Available in These Sources: ABYP 4, SATA 10

LANE, JERRY
See Martin, Patricia Miles

LANE, JOHN
Birthdate: 8/12/1932
Birthplace: Jefferson City, MO
Information Available in These Sources: SATA 15

LANE, NEOLA TRACY
Information Available in These Sources: ABYP 1, ABYP 3

LANE, ROSE WILDER
Birthdate: 12/5/1886 or 12/5/1887
Birthplace: De Smet, SD
Deathdate: 10/30/1968
Information Available in These Sources: ABYP 4, SATA 28, SATA 29

LANES, SELMA G(ORDON)
(Selma Gordon)
Birthdate: 3/13/1929
Birthplace: Boston, MA
Information Available in These Sources: ABYP 4, SATA 3

LANGE, JOHN
See Crichton, J. Michael

LANGE, SUZANNE
Birthdate: 4/30/1945
Birthplace: Dallas, TX
Information Available in These Sources: SATA 5

LANGLEY, NOEL
Birthdate: 12/25/1911
Birthplace: Durban, South Africa
Deathdate: 11/4/1980
Information Available in These Sources: SATA 25

LANGNER, NOLA
Birthdate: 9/24/1930
Birthplace: New York, NY
Information Available in These Sources: IBYP 1, IBYP 2, ICB 3, ICB 4, SATA 8

LANGONE, JOHN (MICHAEL)
Birthdate: 12/23/1929 or 12/2/1929
Birthplace: Cambridge, MA
Information Available in These Sources: SATA 38, SATA 46

LANGSTAFF, JOHN (MEREDITH)
Birthdate: 12/24/1920
Birthplace: New York, NY
Information Available in These Sources: ABYP 4, JBA 3, SATA 6

LANGSTAFF, LAUNCELOT
See Irving, Washington

LANGTON, JANE (GILLSON)
Birthdate: 12/30/1922
Birthplace: Boston, MA
Information Available in These Sources: ABYP 1, ABYP 3, DACF, JBA 5, SATA 3, TCCW 1, TCCW 2, TCCW 3

LANIER, SIDNEY
Birthdate: 2/3/1842
Birthplace: Macon, GA
Deathdate: 9/7/1881
Information Available in These Sources: SATA 18, SVC 2

LANIER, STERLING E.
Birthdate: 12/18/1927
Birthplace: New York, NY
Information Available in These Sources: ABYP 3

LANKES, JULIUS J.
Birthdate: 8/31/1884
Birthplace: Buffalo, NY
Deathdate: 4/22/1960
Information Available in These Sources: ICB 1

LANSING, ALFRED
Birthdate: 7/21/1921
Birthplace: Chicago, IL
Deathdate: 8/27/1975
Information Available in These Sources: SATA 35

LANSING, ELISABETH CARLETON (HUBBARD)
(Martha Johnson)
Birthdate: 5/4/1911
Birthplace: Providence, RI
Information Available in These Sources: ABYP1, ABYP 3

LANSING, MARION FLORENCE
Birthdate: 6/10/1883
Birthplace: Waverley, MA
Information Available in These Sources: JBA 1, JBA 2

LANTZ, PAUL
Birthdate: 2/14/1908
Birthplace: Stromberg, NE
Information Available in These Sources: ICB 1, ICB 2, SATA 45

LANTZ, WALTER
Birthdate: 4/27/1900
Birthplace: New Rochelle, NY
Information Available in These Sources: SATA 37

LAPP, ELEANOR J.
Birthdate: 1/7/1936
Birthplace: Wausau, WI
Information Available in These Sources: ABYP 4

LAPPIN, PETER
Birthdate: 4/29/1911
Birthplace: Ireland
Information Available in These Sources: SATA 32

LARDNER, REX
Birthdate: 9/3/1881
Birthplace: Niles, MI
Deathdate: 6/23/1941
Information Available in These Sources: ABYP 4

LARIVIERE, MARIAN
See Frew, Marian Lariviere

LAROM, HENRY V.
Birthdate, 1903?
Deathdate: 12/7/1975
Information Available in These Sources: ABYP 2, ABYP 3, SATA 30

LARRECQ, JOHN M(AURICE)
Birthdate: 4/10/1926
Birthplace: Santa Rosa, CA
Deathdate: 10/4/1980
Information Available in These Sources: IBYP 2, ICB 4, SATA 25, SATA 44

LARRICK, NANCY G(RAY)
Birthdate: 12/28/1910
Birthplace: Winchester, VA
Information Available in These Sources: ABYP 1, ABYP 3, DLB 61, MBMP, SATA 4

LARRIS, ANN
Information Available in These Sources: ABYP 4

LARSEN, REBECCA
Birthdate: 8/19/1944
Birthplace: Milwaukee, WI
Information Available in These Sources: SATA 54

LARSEN, SUZANNE KESTELOO
Birthdate: 10/30/1930
Birthplace: Richmond, VA
Information Available in These Sources: ICB 3

LARSON, EVE
See St. John, Wylly Folk

LARSON, GARY
Birthdate: 8/14/1950
Birthplace: Tacoma, WA
Information Available in These Sources: SATA 57

LARSON, JEAN RUSSELL
Birthdate: 7/25/1930
Birthplace: Marshalltown, IA
Information Available in These Sources: ABYP 4, DACF

LARSON, NORITA D.
Birthdate: 4/26/1944
Birthplace: St. Paul, MN
Information Available in These Sources: SATA 29

LARSON, WILLIAM H.
Birthdate: 6/3/1938
Birthplace: La Crosse, WI
Information Available in These Sources: SATA 10

LASCHEVER, BARNETT D.
(L. David Barnett)
Birthdate: 3/13/1924
Birthplace: Hartford, CT
Information Available in These Sources: ABYP 2, ABYP 3

LASELL, ELINOR H.
(Fen H(egemann) Lasell)
Birthdate: 5/15/1929
Birthplace: Berlin, Germany
Information Available in These Sources: ABYP 2, ABYP 3, ICB 3, SATA 19

LASELL, FEN H(EGEMANN)
See Lasell, Elinor H.

LASH, JOSEPH P.
Birthdate: 12/2/1909
Birthplace: New York, NY
Information Available in These Sources: SATA 43

LASHER, FAITH B.
Birthdate: 1/26/1921
Birthplace: Lincoln County, MT
Information Available in These Sources: SATA 12

LASKER, DAVID
Birthdate: 4/21/1950
Birthplace: New York, NY
Information Available in These Sources: SATA 38

LASKER, JOE
See Lasker, Joseph Leon

LASKER, JOSEPH LEON
(Joe Lasker)
Birthdate: 6/26/1919
Birthplace: Brooklyn, NY
Information Available in These Sources: IBYP 2, ICB 3, JBA 5, SATA 9

LASKOWSKI, JANINA DOMANSKA
See Domanska, Janina

LASKOWSKI, JERZY
Birthdate: 4/12/1919
Birthplace: Krakow, Poland
Information Available in These Sources: JBA 3

LASKY, KATHRYN
Birthdate: 6/24/1944
Birthplace: Indianapolis, IN
Information Available in These Sources: SATA 13, JBA 6

LASSALLE, C. E.
See Ellis, Edward S(ylvester)

LASSON, ROBERT
Birthdate: 1922
Information Available in These Sources: ABYP 2, ABYP 3

LATHAM, BARBARA
Birthdate: 6/6/1896
Birthplace: Walpole, MA
Information Available in These Sources: ICB 1, ICB 2, SATA 16

LATHAM, DONALD CRAWFORD
Birthdate: 12/22/1932
Birthplace: Sayre, PA
Information Available in These Sources: ABYP 4

LATHAM, FRANK B(ROWN)
Birthdate: 10/20/1910
Birthplace: Belington, WV
Information Available in These Sources: ABYP 4, SATA 6

LATHAM, JEAN LEE
(Janice Gard, Julian Lee)
Birthdate: 4/19/1902
Birthplace: Buckhannon, WV
Information Available in These Sources: ABYP 1, ABYP 3, MBMP, MJA, SATA 2, SVC 3, TCCW 1, TCCW 2 TCCW 3

LATHAM, PHILIP
See Richardson, Robert S(hirley)

LATHROP, DOROTHY P(ULIS)
Birthdate: 4/16/1891
Birthplace: Albany, NY
Deathdate: 12/30/1980
Information Available in These Sources: ABYP 1, ABYP 3, BABP, DLB 22, IBYP 1, IBYP 2, ICB 1, ICB 2, ICB 3, JBA 1, JBA 2, SATA 14, SATA 24, SVC 2, SVC 3

LATHROP, FRANCIS
See Leiber, Fritz

LATROBE, ARCHER
See Carroll, Archer Latrobe

LATTANY, KRISTIN
See Hunter, Kristin (Elaine Eggleston)

LATTIMORE, ELEANOR FRANCES
Birthdate: 6/30/1904
Birthplace: Shanghai, China
Deathdate: 5/12/1986
Information Available in These Sources: ABYP 1, ABYP 3, ICB 1, ICB 2, ICB 3, JBA 1, JBA 2, SATA 5, SATA 7, SATA 48, TCCW 1, TCCW 2, TCCW 3

LATTIN, HARRIET (PRATT)
Birthdate: 11/29/1898
Birthplace: Corning, NY
Information Available in These Sources: ABYP 1, ABYP 3

LAUBER, PATRICIA (GRACE)
Birthdate: 2/5/1924
Birthplace: New York, NY
Information Available in These Sources: ABYP 1, ABYP 3, JBA 3, SATA 1, SATA 33

LAUGESEN, MARY E(AKIN)
Birthdate: 5/4/1906
Birthplace: Bangkok, Thailand
Information Available in These Sources: SATA 5

LAUGHBAUM, STEVE
Birthdate: 8/24/1945
Birthplace: Nashville, TN
Information Available in These Sources: SATA 12

LAUGHLIN, FLORENCE (YOUNG)
Birthdate: 6/1/1910
Birthplace: Crosby, ND
Information Available in These Sources: SATA 3

LAUGHLIN, RUTH
Birthdate: 1889
Information Available in These Sources: ABYP 1, ABYP 3

LAUGHLIN, VIRGINIA CARLI
See Laklan, Carli (Laughlin Aiello)

LAURE, JASON
Birthdate: 10/15/1940
Birthplace: Chehalis, WA
Information Available in These Sources: SATA 44, SATA 50

LAURENCE, ESTER HAUSER
Birthdate: 7/27/1935
Birthplace: Charleston, NY
Information Available in These Sources: SATA 7

LAURIN, ANNE
See McLaurin, Anne

LAURITZEN, JONREED
Birthdate: 7/22/1902
Birthplace: Richfield, UT
Information Available in These Sources: SATA 13

LAUT, AGNES C(HRISTINA)
Birthdate: 2/11/1871
Birthplace: Ontario, Canada
Deathdate: 11/15/1936
Information Available in These Sources: JBA 1, JBA 2

LAUX, DOROTHY
Birthdate: 8/25/1920
Birthplace: Waco, TX
Information Available in These Sources: SATA 49

LAVENDER, DAVID (SIEVERT)
Birthdate: 2/4/1910
Birthplace: Telluride, CO
Information Available in These Sources: ABYP 2, ABYP 3

LAVIN, MARY
Birthdate: 6/11/1912
Birthplace: East Walpole, MA
Information Available in These Sources: ABYP 4

LAVINE, DAVID
Birthdate: 11/11/1928 or 11/11/1929
Birthplace: New York, NY
Information Available in These Sources: ABYP 2, ABYP 3, SATA 31

LAVINE, SIGMUND A(RNOLD)
Birthdate: 3/18/1908
Birthplace: Boston, MA
Information Available in These Sources: ABYP 1, ABYP 3, SATA 3

LAWRENCE, ISABELLE (WENTWORTH)
Birthdate: 1892
Birthplace: Cambridge, MA
Information Available in These Sources: ABYP 2, ABYP 3, SATA 29

LAWRENCE, JACOB
Birthdate: 9/7/1917
Birthplace: Atlantic City, NJ
Information Available in These Sources: BAI, IBYP 1, IBYP 2, JBA 4

LAWRENCE, JAMES D(UNCAN)
Birthdate: 11/22/1918
Birthplace: Detroit, MI
Information Available in These Sources: ABYP 4

LAWRENCE, JOSEPHINE
Birthdate, 1890?
Birthplace: Newark, NJ
Deathdate: 2/22/1978
Information Available in These Sources: SATA 24

LAWRENCE, LINDA
See Hunt, Linda Lawrence

LAWRENCE, MILDRED (ELWOOD)
Birthdate: 11/10/1907
Birthplace: Charleston, IL
Information Available in These Sources: ABYP 2, ABYP 3, MJA, SATA 3, TCCW 1

LAWSON, DON(ALD ELMER)
Birthdate: 5/20/1917
Birthplace: Chicago, IL
Information Available in These Sources: ABYP 1, ABYP 3, SATA 9, JBA 6

LAWSON, JOHN (SHULTS)
Birthplace: New York, NY
Information Available in These Sources: DACF

LAWSON, MARIE ABRAMS
Birthdate: 1894
Birthplace: Atlanta, GA
Deathdate: 1956
Information Available in These Sources: ABYP 1, ABYP 3, ICB 2, JBA 2

LAWSON, MARION TUBBS
Birthdate: 8/8/1896
Birthplace: Elkhorn, WI
Information Available in These Sources: SATA 22

LAWSON, PATRICK
See Eby, Lois Christine

LAWSON, ROBERT
Birthdate: 10/4/1892
Birthplace: New York, NY
Deathdate: 5/26/1957
Information Available in These Sources: ABYP 1, ABYP 3, AICB, DLB 22, IBYP 1, IBYP 2, ICB 1, ICB 2, JBA 2, SVC 2, SVC 3, TCCW 1, TCCW 2, TCCW 3, WC, YABC

LAYCOCK, GEORGE (EDWIN)
Birthdate: 5/29/1921
Birthplace: Zanesville, OH
Information Available in These Sources: ABYP 2, ABYP 3, SATA 5

LAZARE, GERALD JOHN
(Jerry Lazare)
Birthdate: 9/25/1927
Birthplace: Toronto, Ontario, Canada
Information Available in These Sources: IBYP 2, ICB 3, SATA 44

LAZARE, JERRY
See Lazare, Gerald John

LAZAREVICH, MILA
Birthdate: 4/24/1942
Birthplace: Philadelphia, PA
Information Available in These Sources: SATA 17

LAZARUS, KEO FELKER
Birthdate: 10/22/1913
Birthplace: Callaway, NE
Information Available in These Sources: ABYP 4, SATA 21

LEACH, MARIA
Birthdate: 4/30/1892
Birthplace: Brooklyn, NY
Deathdate: 5/22/1977
Information Available in These Sources: ABYP 2, ABYP 3, SATA 28, SATA 39

LEAF, MARGARET P.
Birthdate, 1909?
Birthplace: East Orange, NJ
Deathdate: 2/24/1988
Information Available in These Sources: SATA 55

LEAF, MUNRO
See Leaf, Wilbur Munro

LEAF, VADONNA JEAN
Birthdate: 4/12/1929
Birthplace: Hamilton County, IA
Information Available in These Sources: SATA 26

LEAF, WILBUR MUNRO
(John Calvert, Munro Leaf, Mun)
Birthdate: 12/4/1905
Birthplace: Baltimore (Hamilton), MD
Deathdate: 12/21/1976
Information Available in These Sources: ABYP 1, ABYP 3, BABP, JBA 2, SATA 20, TCCW 1, TCCW 2, TCCW 3, WCL

LEAMY, EDMUND (STANISLAUS)
Birthdate: 1889
Birthplace: Dublin, Ireland
Deathdate: 1962
Information Available in These Sources: SVC 2

LEANDER, ED
See Richelson, Geraldine

LEAVITT, JEROME E(DWARD)
Birthdate: 8/1/1916
Birthplace: Verona, NJ
Information Available in These Sources: ABYP 1, ABYP 3, SATA 23

LEBAR, MARY E(VELYN)
Birthdate: 1/29/1910
Birthplace: Olean, NY
Deathdate: 1982
Information Available in These Sources: SATA 35

LEBLANC, L(EE)
Birthdate: 10/5/1913
Birthplace: Powers, MI
Information Available in These Sources: SATA 54

LECKIE, ROBERT (HUGH)
(Roger Barlow, Mark Porter)
Birthdate: 12/18/1920
Birthplace: Philadelphia, PA
Information Available in These Sources: ABYP 2, ABYP 3

LEDER, JANE MERSKY
Birthdate: 7/25/1945
Birthplace: Detroit, MI
Information Available in These Sources: SATA 51

LEDERER, MURIEL
Birthdate: 5/31/1929
Birthplace: Chicago, IL
Information Available in These Sources: SATA 48

LEE, AMANDA
See Buckholtz, Eileen (Garber)

LEE, ANNE S.
See Murphy, Mabel (Ansley)

LEE, BETSY
Birthdate: 6/4/1949
Birthplace: Bayshore, NY
Information Available in These Sources: SATA 37

LEE, CAROL
See Fletcher, Helen Jill

LEE, DORIS (EMRICK)
Birthdate: 2/1/1905
Birthplace: Aledo, IL
Deathdate: 6/16/1983
Information Available in These Sources: ICB 2, SATA 35, SATA 44

LEE, HARPER
See Lee, Nelle Harper

LEE, JOHN R(OBERT)
Birthdate: 12/26/1923
Birthplace: Petoskey, MI
Deathdate: 10/10/1976
Information Available in These Sources: SATA 27

LEE, JULIAN
See Latham, Jean Lee

LEE, MANNING DE V(ILLENEUVE)
Birthdate: 3/15/1894
Birthplace: Summerville, SC
Deathdate: 3/31/1980
Information Available in These Sources: IBYP 1, IBYP 2, ICB 1, ICB 2, MJA, SATA 22, SATA 37

LEE, MARIAN
See Clish, Lee Marian

LEE, MARY PRICE
Birthdate: 7/10/1934
Birthplace: Philadelphia, PA
Information Available in These Sources: ABYP 4, SATA 8

LEE, MILDRED
(Mildred Lee Scudder)
Birthdate: 2/19/1908
Birthplace: Blocton, AL
Information Available in These Sources: ABYP 4, DACF, JBA 3, SATA 6, TCCW 1, TCCW 2, TCCW 3

LEE, NELLE HARPER
(Harper Lee)
Birthdate: 4/28/1926
Birthplace: Monroeville, AL
Information Available in These Sources: SATA 11

LEE, NORMA E.
Birthdate: 8/28/1924
Birthplace: Ross County, OH
Information Available in These Sources: ABYP 4

LEE, ROBERT C.
Birthdate: 12/21/1931
Birthplace: Brooklyn, NY
Information Available in These Sources: ABYP 4, SATA 20

LEE, ROBERT J.
Birthdate: 12/26/1921
Birthplace: Oakland, CA
Information Available in These Sources: IBYP 2, SATA 10

LEE, ROY
See Hopkins, Clark

LEE, TAMMIE
See Townsend, Thomas L.

LEE, TINA SANDOVEL
Birthplace: St. Louis, MO
Information Available in These Sources: MJA

LEEDY, LOREEN (JANELLE)
Birthdate: 6/15/1959
Birthplace: Wilmington, DE
Information Available in These Sources: SATA 50, 54

LEEKLEY, THOMAS B(RIGGS)
Birthdate: 3/9/1910
Birthplace: Parker, SD
Information Available in These Sources: ABYP 2, ABYP 3, SATA 23

LEEMING, JO ANN
See Leeming, Joseph

LEEMING, JOSEPH
(Jo Ann Leeming, Merlin Swift, Professor Zingara)
Birthdate: 1897
Birthplace: Brooklyn, NY
Deathdate: 1968
Information Available in These Sources: ABYP 1, ABYP 3, JBA 2, SATA 26

LEFLER, IRENE (WHITNEY)
Birthdate: 5/29/1917
Birthplace: Hominy Falls, WV
Information Available in These Sources: SATA 12

LEGALLIENNE, EVA
Birthdate: 1/11/1899
Birthplace: London, England
Information Available in These Sources: ABYP 1, ABYP 3, SATA 9

LEGG, SARAH MARTHA ROSS BRUGGEMAN
Deathdate: 8/29/1982
Information Available in These Sources: SATA 40

LEGRAND
See Henderson, LeGrand

LEGUIN, URSULA K(ROEBER)
Birthdate: 10/21/1929
Birthplace: Berkeley, CA
Information Available in These Sources: ABYP 4, DACF, JBA 4, SATA 4, SATA 52, TCCW 1, TCCW 2, TCCW 3

LEHR, DELORES
Birthdate: 12/22/1920
Birthplace: Dallas, TX
Information Available in These Sources: SATA 10

LEIBER, FRITZ
(Francis Lathrop)
Birthdate: 12/25/1910
Birthplace: Chicago, IL
Information Available in These Sources: SATA 45

LEIBOLD, JAY
Birthdate: 10/15/1957
Birthplace: Denver, CO
Information Available in These Sources: SATA 52, 57

LEICHMAN, SEYMOUR
Birthdate: 4/26/1933
Birthplace: New York, NY
Information Available in These Sources: IBYP 1, IBYP 2, SATA 5

LEIGH, TOM
Birthdate: 2/14/1947
Birthplace: Princeton, NJ
Information Available in These Sources: SATA 46

LEIGHT, EDWARD
Information Available in These Sources: IBYP 1, IBYP 2

LEIGHTON, CLARE (VERONICA HOPE)
Birthdate: 4/12/1899 or 4/12/1900 or 4/12/1901
Birthplace: London, England
Information Available in These Sources: IBYP 2, ICB 2, ICB 3, SATA 37

LEIGHTON, LEE
See Overholser, Wayne D.

LEIGHTON, MARGARET (CARVER)
Birthdate: 12/20/1896
Birthplace: Oberlin, OH
Deathdate: 6/19/1987
Information Available in These Sources: ABYP 2, ABYP 3, SATA 1, SATA 52, SVC 2, SVC 3

LEIPOLD, L. EDMUND
Birthdate: 8/5/1902
Birthplace: MN
Information Available in These Sources: SATA 16

LEISK, DAVID (JOHNSON)
(Crockett Johnson)
Birthdate: 10/20/1906
Birthplace: New York, NY
Deathdate: 7/11/1975
Information Available in These Sources: ABYP 2, ABYP 3, BABP, ICB 2, ICB 3, ICB 4, JBA 3, SATA 1, SATA 26, SATA 30, TCCW 1, TCCW 2, TCCW 3

LEISTER, MARY
Birthdate: 10/4/1917
Birthplace: Brackenridge, PA
Information Available in These Sources: SATA 29

LEMMON, ROBERT STELL
Birthdate: 6/26/1885
Birthplace: Englewood, NJ
Deathdate: 3/3/1964
Information Available in These Sources: ABYP 1, ABYP 3

LENGYEL, CORNEL ADAM
(Cornel Adam)
Birthdate: 1915
Birthplace: Fairfield, CT
Information Available in These Sources: SATA 27

LENGYEL, EMIL
Birthdate: 4/26/1895
Birthplace: Budapest, Hungary
Deathdate: 2/12/1985
Information Available in These Sources: SATA 3, SATA 42

LENS, SIDNEY
Birthdate: 1/28/1912
Birthplace: Newark, NJ
Deathdate: 6/18/1986
Information Available in These Sources: ABYP 1, ABYP 3, SATA 13, SATA 48

LENSKI, LOIS (LENORE)
Birthdate: 10/14/1893
Birthplace: Springfield, OH
Deathdate: 9/11/1974
Information Available in These Sources: ABYP 1, ABYP 3, AICB, BABP, DLB 22, ICB 1, ICB 2, ICB 3, ICB 4, JBA 1, JBA 2, SATA 1, SATA 26, TCCW 1, TCCW 2

LENT, BLAIR
(Ernest Small)
Birthdate: 1/22/1930
Birthplace: Boston, MA
Information Available in These Sources: BABP, IBYP 1, IBYP 2, ICB 3, ICB 4, JBA 3, SATA 2

LENT, HENRY BOLLES
Birthdate: 11/1/1901
Birthplace: New Bedford, MA
Deathdate: 10/26/1973
Information Available in These Sources: ABYP 1, ABYP 3, JBA 1, JBA 2, SATA 17, SVC 2, SVC 3

LEOKUM, ARKADY
Birthdate: 1916 or 1915
Birthplace: Russia
Information Available in These Sources: SATA 45

LEONARD, A. BYRON
Birthdate: 1904
Birthplace: Manhattan, KS
Information Available in These Sources: ABYP 2, ABYP 3

LEONARD, CONSTANCE (BRINK)
Birthdate: 4/27/1923
Birthplace: Pottsville, PA
Information Available in These Sources: SATA 40, SATA 42

LEONARD, JONATHAN N(ORTON)
Birthdate: 5/25/1903
Birthplace: Somerville, MA
Deathdate: 5/15/1975
Information Available in These Sources: SATA 36

LERNER, AARON B(UNSEN)
Birthdate: 9/21/1920
Birthplace: Minneapolis, MN
Information Available in These Sources: SATA 35

LERNER, CAROL
Birthdate: 7/6/1927
Birthplace: Chicago, IL
Information Available in These Sources: SATA 33, JBA 6

LERNER, MARGUERITE RUSH
Birthdate: 5/17/1924
Birthplace: Minneapolis, MN
Deathdate: 3/3/1987
Information Available in These Sources: ABYP 2, ABYP 3, SATA 11, SATA 51

LERNER, SHARON (RUTH)
Birthdate: 11/9/1938
Birthplace: Chicago, IL
Deathdate: 3/8/1982
Information Available in These Sources: SATA 11, SATA 29

LEROE, ELLEN W(HITNEY)
Birthdate: 4/26/1949
Birthplace: Newark, NJ
Information Available in These Sources: SATA 51

LEROY, GEN
Birthplace: Highland Park, NJ
Information Available in These Sources: SATA 36, SATA 52

LERRIGO, MARION OLIVE
Birthdate: 10/27/1898
Birthplace: Topeka, KS
Deathdate: 9/29/1968
Information Available in These Sources: SATA 29

LESHAN, EDA J(OAN GROSSMAN)
Birthdate: 6/6/1922
Birthplace: New York, NY
Information Available in These Sources: ABYP 4, SATA 21

LESIEG, THEO
See Geisel, Theodor Seuss

LESLIE, ROBERT FRANKLIN
Birthdate: 10/21/1911
Birthplace: Dublin, TX
Information Available in These Sources: SATA 7

LESLIE, SARAH
See McGuire, Leslie (Sarah)

LESSER, MARGARET
Birthdate: 1899
Deathdate: 11/21/1979
Information Available in These Sources: SATA 22

LESSER, MILTON
See Marlowe, Stephen

LESSER, RIKA
Birthdate: 7/21/1953
Birthplace: Brooklyn, NY
Information Available in These Sources: SATA 53

LESSIN, ANDREW
Birthplace: Brooklyn, NY
Information Available in These Sources: ABYP 1, ABYP 3

LESTER, HELEN
Birthdate: 6/12/1936
Birthplace: Evanston, IL
Information Available in These Sources: SATA 46

LESTER, JOHN
See Werner, Vivian

LESTER, JULIUS B.
Birthdate: 1/27/1939
Birthplace: St. Louis, MO
Information Available in These Sources: AICB, BAI, JBA 4, SATA 12, TCCW 2, TCCW 3

LESUEUR, MERIDEL
Birthdate: 2/22/1900
Birthplace: Murray, IA
Information Available in These Sources: MJA, SATA 6

LETORD, BIJOU
Birthdate: 1/15/1945
Birthplace: St. Raphael, France
Information Available in These Sources: SATA 49

LEVAI, BLAISE
Birthdate: 4/17/1919
Birthplace: Passaic, NJ
Information Available in These Sources: SATA 39

LEVERT, WILLIAM JOHN
Birthdate: 6/14/1946
Birthplace: Brighton, MA
Information Available in These Sources: SATA 55

LEVIN, BETTY (LOWENTHAL)
Birthdate: 9/10/1927
Birthplace: New York, NY
Information Available in These Sources: SATA 19, TCCW 2, TCCW 3, JBA 6

LEVIN, MARCIA OBRASKY
(Jeremy Martin, Marcia Martin)
Birthdate: 10/29/1918
Birthplace: Philadelphia, PA
Information Available in These Sources: ABYP 2, ABYP 3, SATA 13

LEVIN, MEYER
Birthdate: 10/8/1905
Birthplace: Chicago, IL
Deathdate: 7/9/1981
Information Available in These Sources: SATA 21, SATA 27

LEVINE, ABBY
Birthdate: 9/27/1943
Birthplace: New York, NY
Information Available in These Sources: SATA 52, SATA 54

LEVINE, BETTY K(RASNE)
(Betty Krasne)
Birthdate: 5/25/1933
Birthplace: New York, NY
Information Available in These Sources: ABYP 4

LEVINE, DAVID
Birthdate: 12/20/1926
Birthplace: Brooklyn, NY
Information Available in These Sources: ICB 3, SATA 35, SATA 43

LEVINE, EDNA S(IMON)
Birthplace: New York, NY
Information Available in These Sources: SATA 35

LEVINE, I(SRAEL) E.
Birthdate: 8/30/1923
Birthplace: New York, NY
Information Available in These Sources: ABYP 1, ABYP 3, SATA 12

LEVINE, JOAN GOLDMAN
Birthplace: New York, NY
Information Available in These Sources: SATA 11

LEVINE, JOSEPH
Birthdate: 1910
Information Available in These Sources: ABYP 2, ABYP 3, BABP, SATA 33

LEVINE, RHODA
Birthplace: New York, NY
Information Available in These Sources: ABYP 2, ABYP 3, SATA 14

LEVINE, SARAH
Birthdate: 3/9/1970
Birthplace: Pittsburgh, PA
Information Available in These Sources: SATA 57

LEVINGER, ELMA (EHRLICH)
Birthdate: 10/6/1887
Birthplace: Chicago, IL
Deathdate: 1/27/1958
Information Available in These Sources: ABYP 1, ABYP 3

LEVINSON, NANCY SMILER
Birthdate: 11/5/1938
Birthplace: Minneapolis, MN
Information Available in These Sources: SATA 33

LEVINSON, RIKI (FRIEDBERG)
Birthplace: Brooklyn, NY
Information Available in These Sources: SATA 49, SATA 52, JBA 6

LEVITIN, SONIA (WOLFF)
(Sonia Wolff)
Birthdate: 8/18/1934
Birthplace: Berlin, Germany
Information Available in These Sources: ABYP 4, DACF, JBA 5, SATA 4, TCCW 3

LEVOY, MYRON
Birthdate: 1/30/1930
Birthplace: New York, NY
Information Available in These Sources: ABYP 4, DACF, JBA 5, SATA 37, SATA 49, TCCW 3

LEVY, ELIZABETH
Birthdate: 4/4/1942
Birthplace: Buffalo, NY
Information Available in These Sources: ABYP 4, JBA 5, SATA 31

LEWEES, JOHN
See Stockton, Francis Richard

LEWELLEN, JOHN BRYAN
Birthdate: 3/30/1910
Birthplace: Gaston, IN
Deathdate: 7/27/1956
Information Available in These Sources: ABYP 1, ABYP 3, MJA

LEWIN, BETSY
Birthdate: 5/12/1937
Birthplace: PA
Information Available in These Sources: SATA 32

LEWIN, TED
Birthdate: 5/6/1935
Birthplace: Buffalo, NY
Information Available in These Sources: IBYP 2, SATA 21

LEWIS, ALFRED E.
Birthdate: 1912
Birthplace: Boston, MA
Deathdate: 3/28/1968
Information Available in These Sources: ABYP 2, ABYP 3, SATA 32

LEWIS, ALICE C.
Birthdate: 10/7/1936
Birthplace: Walla Walla, WA
Information Available in These Sources: SATA 46

LEWIS, ALICE HUDSON
Birthdate, 1895?
Deathdate: 10/24/1971
Information Available in These Sources: ABYP 1, ABYP 3, SATA 29

LEWIS, ANNE
Birthplace: Boston, MA
Information Available in These Sources: IBYP 2

LEWIS, ANTHONY
See Lewis, Joseph Anthony

LEWIS, ARTHUR ALLEN
Birthdate: 4/7/1873
Birthplace: Mobile, AL
Deathdate: 3/20/1957
Information Available in These Sources: ICB 1, ICB 2

LEWIS, CLAUDIA (LOUISE)
Birthdate: 10/14/1907
Birthplace: Corvallis, OR
Information Available in These Sources: ABYP 4, SATA 5

LEWIS, ELIZABETH FOREMAN
Birthdate: 5/24/1892
Birthplace: Baltimore, MD
Deathdate: 8/7/1958
Information Available in These Sources: ABYP 1, ABYP 3, JBA 1, JBA 2, TCCW 3, YABC

LEWIS, FRANCINE
See Wells, Helen (Frances Weinstock)

LEWIS, JOSEPH ANTHONY
(Anthony Lewis)
Birthdate: 3/27/1927
Birthplace: New York, NY
Information Available in These Sources: SATA 27

LEWIS, LUCIA Z.
See Anderson, Lucia (Lewis)

LEWIS, MARJORIE
Birthdate: 5/3/1929
Birthplace: New York, NY
Information Available in These Sources: SATA 35, SATA 39

LEWIS, MILDRED
Birthplace: New York, NY
Information Available in These Sources: ABYP 1, ABYP 3

LEWIS, MILDRED D.
(James DeWitt)
Birthdate: 2/4/1912
Birthplace: Battle Creek, MI
Information Available in These Sources: ABYP 3

LEWIS, MILTON
Birthplace: New York, NY
Information Available in These Sources: ABYP 1, ABYP 3

LEWIS, PAUL
See Gerson, Noel B(ertram)

LEWIS, RICHARD
Birthdate: 5/15/1935
Birthplace: New York, NY
Information Available in These Sources: ABYP 2, ABYP 3, BABP, SATA 3

LEWIS, RICHARD WILLIAM
Birthdate: 7/11/1933
Birthplace: Avondale, PA
Deathdate: 8/16/1966
Information Available in These Sources: ICB 3

LEWIS, ROGER
See Zarchy, Harry

LEWIS, SHARI
Birthdate: 1/17/1934
Birthplace: New York, NY
Information Available in These Sources: ABYP 4, SATA 30, SATA 35

LEWIS, STEPHEN
Birthplace: Birmingham, AL
Information Available in These Sources: ABYP 4

LEWIS, THOMAS P(ARKER)
Birthdate: 7/1/1936
Birthplace: Mount Vernon, NY
Information Available in These Sources: SATA 27

LEWITON, MINA
(Mina Lewiton Simon)
Birthdate: 3/22/1904
Birthplace: New York, NY
Deathdate: 2/11/1970
Information Available in These Sources: ABYP 2, ABYP 3, MJA, SATA 2

LEXAU, JOAN M.
(Joan L. Nodset, Marie Seth)
Birthdate: 3/09/??
Birthplace: St. Paul, MN
Information Available in These Sources: ABYP 2, ABYP 3, BABP, DACF, JBA 4, SATA 1, SATA 36, TCCW 1TCCW 2, TCCW 3

LEY, WILLY
(Robert Willey)
Birthdate: 10/2/1906
Birthplace: Berlin, Germany
Deathdate: 6/24/1969
Information Available in These Sources: ABYP 1, ABYP 3, SATA 2

LEYDON, RITA (FLODEN)
Birthdate: 12/24/1949
Birthplace: Sweden
Information Available in These Sources: SATA 21

LEYSON, BURR WATKINS
Birthdate: 1898
Birthplace: Medical Lake, WA
Information Available in These Sources: ABYP 1, ABYP 3

LIANG, YEN
Birthdate: 4/17/1908
Birthplace: Peking, China
Information Available in These Sources: ICB 2

LIBBY, BILL
See Libby, William M.

LIBBY, WILLIAM M.
(Bill Libby)
Birthdate: 11/14/1927
Birthplace: Atlantic City, NJ
Deathdate: 6/16/1984
Information Available in These Sources: ABYP 4, SATA 5, SATA 39

LIBERTY, GENE
Birthdate: 6/3/1924
Birthplace: Bronx, NY
Information Available in These Sources: SATA 3

LICHELLO, ROBERT
Birthdate: 9/12/1926
Birthplace: Parkersburg, WV
Information Available in These Sources: ABYP 1, ABYP 3

LIDDELL, MARY
Birthdate: 12/27/1891
Birthplace: Lawrenceville, NJ
Information Available in These Sources: ICB 1

LIDE, ALICE (ALISON)
Birthdate: 2/7/1890
Birthplace: Richmond, AL
Information Available in These Sources: ABYP 2, ABYP 3

LIEB, FREDERICK GEORGE
Birthdate: 3/5/1888
Birthplace: Philadelphia, PA
Deathdate: 6/3/1980
Information Available in These Sources: ABYP 1, ABYP 3

LIEBERS, ARTHUR
Birthdate: 1/7/1913
Birthplace: New York, NY
Information Available in These Sources: SATA 12

LIEBLICH, IRENE
Birthdate: 4/20/1923
Birthplace: Zamosc, Poland
Information Available in These Sources: SATA 22

LIEBMAN, OSCAR
Birthdate: 11/4/1919
Birthplace: Brooklyn, NY
Information Available in These Sources: ICB 2

LIERS, EMIL E(RNEST)
Birthdate: 1890
Birthplace: Clayton, IA
Deathdate: 10/17/1975
Information Available in These Sources: ABYP 2, ABYP 3, SATA 37

LIETZ, GERALD S(YLVANE)
Birthdate: 8/9/1918
Birthplace: Bellwood, IL
Information Available in These Sources: ABYP 2, ABYP 3, SATA 11

LIFTON, BETTY JEAN (KIRSCHNER)
Birthdate: 6/11/1926
Birthplace: New York, NY
Information Available in These Sources: ABYP 2, ABYP 3, DCAF, JBA 3, SATA 6, TCCW 1, TCCW 2, TCCW 3

LIGHTNER, A. M.
See Hopf, Alice (Martha) L(ightner)

LIGHTNER, ALICE
See Hopf, Alice (Martha) L(ightner)

LIGNELL, LOIS
Birthdate: 6/4/1911
Birthplace: Duluth, MN
Information Available in These Sources: ICB 2, SATA 37

LILLIE, AMY MORRIS
Birthplace: Elizabeth, NJ
Information Available in These Sources: ABYP 1, ABYP 3

LILLY, CHARLES
Birthplace: NY
Information Available in These Sources: BAI, IBYP 1, SATA 33

LILLY, RAY
See Curtis, Richard (Alan)

LIMAN, ELLEN (FOGELSON)
Birthdate: 1/4/1936
Birthplace: New York, NY
Information Available in These Sources: ABYP 4, SATA 22

LIMBURG, PETER R(ICHARD)
Birthdate: 11/4/1929
Birthplace: New York, NY
Information Available in These Sources: SATA 13

LINCOLN, C(HARLES) ERIC
Birthdate: 6/23/1924
Birthplace: Athens, AL
Information Available in These Sources: SATA 5

LINDBERGH, ANNE
See Sapieyevski, Anne Lindbergh

LINDBERGH, ANNE MORROW (SPENCER)
(Anne Spencer Morrow)
Birthdate: 1906 or 1907
Birthplace: Englewood, NJ
Information Available in These Sources: SATA 33

LINDBERGH, CHARLES A(UGUSTUS, JR.)
Birthdate: 2/4/1902
Birthplace: Detroit, MI
Deathdate: 8/26/1974
Information Available in These Sources: SATA 33, SVC 2

LINDBLOM, STEVEN (WINTHER)
Birthdate: 3/29/1946
Birthplace: Minneapolis, MN
Information Available in These Sources: SATA 39, SATA 42

LINDEBURG, FRANKLIN A(LFRED)
Birthdate: 11/23/1918
Birthplace: San Francisco, CA
Information Available in These Sources: ABYP 4

LINDEMANN, EDWARD
Information Available in These Sources: ABYP 4

LINDERMAN, FRANK B(IRD)
Birthdate: 9/25/1869
Birthplace: Cleveland, OH
Deathdate: 5/12/1938
Information Available in These Sources: JBA 1, JBA 2

LINDOP, EDMUND
Birthdate: 8/31/1925
Birthplace: Chicago, IL
Information Available in These Sources: ABYP 4, SATA 5

LINDQUIST, JENNIE D(OROTHEA)
Birthdate: 1899
Birthplace: Manchester, NH
Deathdate: 2/8/1977
Information Available in These Sources: ABYP 1, ABYP 3, MJA, SATA 13

LINDQUIST, WILLIS
Birthdate: 6/5/1908
Birthplace: Winthrop, MN
Information Available in These Sources: ABYP 2, ABYP 3, MJA, SATA 20

LINDSAY, MAUD MCKNIGHT
Birthdate: 5/13/1874
Birthplace: Tuscumbia, AL
Deathdate: 5/30/1941
Information Available in These Sources: ABYP 2, ABYP 3

LINDSAY, NICHOLAS VACHEL
(Vachel Lindsay)
Birthdate: 11/10/1879
Birthplace: Springfield, IL
Deathdate: 12/5/1931
Information Available in These Sources: SATA 40, SVC 2, SVC 3

LINDSAY, VACHEL
See Lindsay, Nicholas Vachel

LINE, LES
Birthdate: 6/24/1935
Birthplace: Sparta, MI
Information Available in These Sources: SATA 27

LINFIELD, ESTHER
Birthplace: Cape Town, South Africa
Information Available in These Sources: SATA 40

LINK, MARTIN
Birthdate: 9/26/1934
Birthplace: Madison, WI
Information Available in These Sources: SATA 28

LINN, CHARLES F.
Birthdate: 8/19/1930
Birthplace: Beaver, PA
Information Available in These Sources: ABYP 4

LINQUIST, WILLIS
Birthdate: 1908
Birthplace: Winthrop, MN
Information Available in These Sources: ABYP 2, ABYP 3, MJA

LIONNI, LEO(NARD)
Birthdate: 5/5/1910
Birthplace: Amsterdam, Holland, Netherlands
Information Available in These Sources: ABYP 1, ABYP 3, AICB, BABP, CFB, DLB 61, ICB 3, ICB 4, JBA 3, SATA 8, TCCW 1, TCCW 2, TCCW 3

LIPINSKY DE ORLOV, LINO S(IGISMONDO)
Birthdate: 1/14/1908
Birthplace: Rome, Italy
Information Available in These Sources: ICB 3, SATA 22

LIPKIND, WILLIAM
(Will)
Birthdate: 12/17/1904
Birthplace: New York, NY
Deathdate: 10/2/1974
Information Available in These Sources: ABYP 1, ABYP 3, MJA, SATA 15, TCCW 1, TCCW 2, TCCW 3

LIPMAN, DAVID
Birthdate: 2/13/1931
Birthplace: Springfield, MO
Information Available in These Sources: ABYP 4, SATA 21

LIPMAN, MATTHEW
Birthdate: 8/24/1923
Birthplace: Vineland, NJ
Information Available in These Sources: SATA 14

LIPPINCOTT, BERTRAM
Birthdate: 11/18/1898 or 11/18/1897
Birthplace: Philadelphia, PA
Deathdate: 4/28/1985
Information Available in These Sources: SATA 42

LIPPINCOTT, JOSEPH WHARTON
Birthdate: 2/28/1887
Birthplace: Philadelphia, PA
Deathdate: 10/22/1976
Information Available in These Sources: ABYP 1, ABYP 3, MJA, SATA 17, TCCW 1, TCCW 2, TCCW 3

LIPPINCOTT, SARAH LEE
Birthdate: 10/26/1920
Birthplace: Philadelphia, PA
Information Available in These Sources: SATA 22

LIPPMAN, PETER J.
Birthdate: 5/19/1936
Birthplace: Flushing, Queens, NY
Information Available in These Sources: IBYP 1, IBYP 2, ICB 3, SATA 31

LIPSCOMB, GEORGE D(EWEY)
Birthdate: 1898
Information Available in These Sources: SVC 2, SVC 3

LIPSYTE, ROBERT (MICHAEL)
Birthdate: 1/16/1938
Birthplace: New York, NY
Information Available in These Sources: ABYP 4, DACF, JBA 5, SATA 5, TCCW 3

LISKER, SONIA O(LSON)
Birthdate: 3/22/1933
Birthplace: New York, NY
Information Available in These Sources: ABYP 4, SATA 44

LISLE, JANET TAYLOR
Birthdate: 2/13/1947
Birthplace: Englewood, NJ
Information Available in These Sources: SATA 47, SATA 59, JBA 6

LISLE, SEWARD D.
See Ellis, Edward S(ylvester)

LISS, HOWARD
Birthdate: 7/22/1922
Birthplace: Brooklyn, NY
Information Available in These Sources: ABYP 2, ABYP 3, SATA 4

LISSIM, SIMON
Birthdate: 10/24/1900
Birthplace: Kiev, Russia
Deathdate: 5/10/1981
Information Available in These Sources: ICB 2, SATA 28

LIST, ILKA KATHERINE
(Ilka List Maidoff)
Birthdate: 11/22/1935
Birthplace: Orange, NJ
Information Available in These Sources: SATA 6

LISTON, ROBERT A.
Birthdate: 8/23/1927
Birthplace: Youngstown, OH
Information Available in These Sources: ABYP 2, ABYP 3, SATA 5

LITCHFIELD, ADA B(ASSETT)
Birthdate: 4/1/1916
Birthplace: Harwich, MA
Information Available in These Sources: SATA 5

LITOWINSKY, OLGA (JEAN)
Birthdate: 2/9/1936
Birthplace: Newark, NJ
Information Available in These Sources: SATA 26

LITTELL, ROBERT
Birthdate: 1935
Information Available in These Sources: ABYP 4

LITTEN, FREDERIC NELSON
Birthdate: 5/26/1885
Birthplace: Chicago, IL
Deathdate: 7/26/1951
Information Available in These Sources: ABYP 2, ABYP 3

LITTKE, LAEL J.
Birthdate: 12/2/1929
Birthplace: Mink Creek, ID
Information Available in These Sources: SATA 51

LITTLE, A. EDWARD
See Klein, Aaron E.

LITTLE, LESSIE JONES
Birthdate: 10/1/1906
Birthplace: Parmele, NC
Deathdate: 11/4/1986
Information Available in These Sources: SATA 50, SATA 60

LITTLE, MARY E.
Birthdate: 7/29/1912
Birthplace: Englewood, KS
Information Available in These Sources: ABYP 2, ABYP 3, SATA 28

LITTLEDALE, FREYA (LOTA BROWN)
Birthdate: 1929
Birthplace: New York, NY
Information Available in These Sources: SATA 2

LIVESAY, JOHN
Information Available in These Sources: ABYP 4

LIVINGSTON, CAROLE
(J. Aphrodite)
Birthdate: 2/22/1941
Birthplace: New York, NY
Information Available in These Sources: SATA 42

LIVINGSTON, MYRA COHN
Birthdate: 8/17/1926
Birthplace: Omaha, NE
Information Available in These Sources: ABYP 4, BABP, DLB 61, JBA 4, SATA 5, TCCW 1, TCCW 2, TCCW 3

LIVINGSTON, PETER W.
Information Available in These Sources: ABYP 4

LIVINGSTON, RICHARD R(OLAND)
Birthdate: 9/1/1922
Birthplace: South Bend, IN
Information Available in These Sources: SATA 8

LLERENA-AGUIRRE, CARLOS ANTONIO
Birthdate: 3/31/1952
Birthplace: Arequipa, Peru
Information Available in These Sources: SATA 19

LLOYD, E. JAMES
See James, Elizabeth

LLOYD, JAMES
See James, Elizabeth

LLOYD, MARY NORRIS
(Norris Lloyd)
Birthdate: 9/1/1908
Birthplace: Greenwood, SC
Information Available in These Sources: SATA 10

LLOYD, NORMAN
Birthdate: 11/8/1909
Birthplace: Pottsville, PA
Deathdate: 7/31/1980
Information Available in These Sources: ABYP 4, SATA 23

LLOYD, NORRIS
See Lloyd, Mary Norris

LOB, JEFFREY
See Loeb, Jeffrey

LOBEL, ANITA (KEMPLER)
Birthdate: 6/3/1934
Birthplace: Krakow, Poland
Information Available in These Sources: BABP, IBYP 1, IBYP 2, ICB 3, ICB 4, JBA 3, SATA 6, SATA 55 TCCW 1, TCCW 2, TCCW 3

LOBEL, ARNOLD (STARK)
Birthdate: 5/22/1933
Birthplace: Los Angeles, CA
Deathdate: 12/4/1987
Information Available in These Sources: ABYP 1, ABYP 3, BABP, DLB 61, ICB 3, ICB 4, JBA 3, SATA 6, SATA 54, SATA 55, TCCW 2, TCCW 3

LOBSENZ, AMELIA (FREITAG)
Birthplace: Greensboro, NC
Information Available in These Sources: ABYP 1, ABYP 3, SATA 12

LOBSENZ, NORMAN M(ITCHELL)
Birthdate: 5/16/1919
Birthplace: New York, NY
Information Available in These Sources: SATA 6

LOCHLONS, COLIN
See Jackson C(aary) Paul

LOCKE, CLINTON W.
See Stratemeyer, Edward L.

LOCKE, LUCIE
(Lucie Locke Price)
Birthdate: 2/22/1904
Birthplace: Valdosta, GA
Information Available in These Sources: SATA 10

LOCKE, MARGO
Information Available in These Sources: IBYP 2

LOCKE, ROBERT
(Clayton Bess)
Birthdate: 12/30/1944
Birthplace: Vallejo, California
Information Available in These Sources: JBA 6

LOCKE, VANCE
Information Available in These Sources: IBYP 2

LOCKER, THOMAS
Birthdate: 6/26/1937
Birthplace: New York, NY
Information Available in These Sources: SATA 59, JBA 6

LOCKWOOD, MARY
See Spelman, Mary

LOCKWOOD, MYNA
Birthplace: Rome, IA
Information Available in These Sources: ABYP 1, ABYP 3

LOEB, JEFFREY
(Jeffrey Lob)
Birthdate: 6/6/1946
Birthplace: New York, NY
Information Available in These Sources: SATA 57

LOEB, ROBERT H., JR.
Birthdate: 11/1/1917
Birthplace: New York, NY
Information Available in These Sources: SATA 21

LOEBL, SUZANNE (BAMBERGER)
Birthplace: Hannover, Germany
Information Available in These Sources: ABYP 4

LOEFFLER, GISELLA
See Lacher, Gisella Loeffler

LOEPER, JOHN J(OSEPH)
(Jay Lowe, Jr.)
Birthdate: 7/9/1929
Birthplace: Ashland, PA
Information Available in These Sources: SATA 10

LOESCHER, ANN DULL
Birthdate: 11/11/1942
Birthplace: Rutherford, NJ
Information Available in These Sources: SATA 20

LOESCHER, GIL(BURT DAMIAN)
Birthdate: 3/7/1945
Birthplace: San Francisco, CA
Information Available in These Sources: SATA 20

LOEWENSTEIN, BERNICE
Birthplace: New York, NY
Information Available in These Sources: IBYP 1, IBYP 2, SATA 40

LOFTING, HUGH
Birthdate: 1/14/1886
Birthplace: Maidenhead, Berkshire, England
Deathdate: 9/26/1947
Information Available in These Sources: ABYP 1, ABYP 3, ICB 1, JBA 1, JBA 2, SATA 15, SVC 2, SVC 3, TCCW 3, WC

LOGSDON, LOIS IRENE (KUPFER)
Birthplace: Scio, OH
Information Available in These Sources: ABYP 2, ABYP 3

LOGSDON, RICHARD HENRY
Birthdate: 6/24/1912
Birthplace: Upper Sandusky, OH
Information Available in These Sources: ABYP 2, ABYP 3

LOKEN, NEWTON (CLAYTON)
Birthdate: 2/27/1919
Birthplace: Breckenridge, MN
Information Available in These Sources: SATA 26

LOMAS, STEVE
See Brennan, Joseph L(omas)

LOMASK, MILTON (NACHMAN)
Birthdate: 6/26/1909
Birthplace: Fairmont, WV
Information Available in These Sources: ABYP 2, ABYP 3, SATA 20

LOMAX, JOHN A.
Birthdate: 9/23/1872 or 9/23/1867
Birthplace: Goodman, MS
Deathdate: 1/26/1948
Information Available in These Sources: SVC 2, SVC 3

LOME, MIKE
See Pinkwater, Daniel Manus

LONDON, JACK
(John Griffith London)
Birthdate: 1/12/1876
Birthplace: San Francisco, CA
Deathdate: 11/22/1916
Information Available in These Sources: ABYP 2, ABYP 3, JBA 1, SATA 18SVC 2, SVC 3

LONDON, JANE
See Geis, Darlene (Stern)

LONDON, JOHN GRIFFITH
See London, Jack

LONERGAN, JOY
See Lonergan, Pauline Joy (MacLean)

LONERGAN, PAULINE JOY (MACLEAN)
(Joy Lonergan)
Birthdate: 12/5/1909
Birthplace: Toronto, Ontario, Canada
Information Available in These Sources: ABYP 1, ABYP 3, SATA 10

LONETTE, REISIE (DOMINEE)
Birthdate: 2/13/1924
Birthplace: New York, NY
Information Available in These Sources: IBYP 2, ICB 2, ICB 3, SATA 43

LONG, EARLENE (ROBERTA)
Birthdate: 10/4/1938
Birthplace: Ford County, IL
Information Available in These Sources: SATA 50

LONG, HELEN BEECHER
See Stratemeyer, Edward L.

LONG, JUDITH ELAINE
(Judy Long)
Birthdate: 4/20/1953
Birthplace: Norfolk, VA
Information Available in These Sources: SATA 20

LONG, JUDY
See Long, Judith Elaine

LONG, LAURA MOONEY
Birthdate: 8/4/1892
Birthplace: Columbus, IN
Deathdate: 3/28/1967
Information Available in These Sources: SATA 29

LONGFELLOW, HENRY WADSWORTH
Birthdate: 2/27/1807
Birthplace: Portland, ME
Deathdate: 3/24/1882
Information Available in These Sources: ABYP 2, ABYP 3, SATA 19, SVC 2SVC 3

LONGMAN, HAROLD S.
Birthdate: 1/18/1919
Birthplace: San Francisco, CA
Information Available in These Sources: SATA 5

LONGSTRETH, JOSEPH
Birthdate: 1920
Birthplace: IN
Information Available in These Sources: ABYP 1, ABYP 3

LONGSTRETH, T(HOMAS) MORRIS
Birthdate: 2/17/1886
Birthplace: Philadelphia, PA
Deathdate: 12/21/1975
Information Available in These Sources: ABYP 1, ABYP 3, MJA

LONGSWORTH, POLLY (ORMSBY)
Birthdate: 10/21/1933
Birthplace: Buffalo, NY
Information Available in These Sources: ABYP 2, ABYP 3, SATA 28

LONGTEMPS, KENNETH
Birthdate: 8/9/1933
Birthplace: Saranac Lake, NY
Information Available in These Sources: SATA 17

LOOMIS, J. PAUL
Birthplace: Juneau, AK
Information Available in These Sources: ABYP 1, ABYP 3

LOOMIS, ROBERT D.
Birthdate: 8/24/1926
Birthplace: Conneaut, OH
Information Available in These Sources: ABYP 1, ABYP 3, SATA 5

LOPSHIRE, ROBERT (MARTIN)
Birthdate: 4/14/1927
Birthplace: Sarasota, FL
Information Available in These Sources: ABYP 2, ABYP 3, SATA 6

LORD, ATHENA V.
Birthdate: 7/21/1932
Birthplace: Cohoes, NY
Information Available in These Sources: DACF, SATA 39

LORD, BEMAN
(Harold Beman Lord)
Birthdate: 11/22/1924
Birthplace: Delaware County, NY
Information Available in These Sources: ABYP 2, ABYP 3, JBA 4, SATA 5

LORD, BETTE BAO
Birthdate: 11/3/1938
Birthplace: Shanghai, China
Information Available in These Sources: SATA 58, JBA 6

LORD, HAROLD BEMAN
See Lord, Beman

LORD, NANCY
See Titus, Eve

LORD, PATRICIA C.
Birthdate: 3/8/1927
Birthplace: Attleboro, MA
Deathdate: 7/2/1988
Information Available in These Sources: SATA 58

LORD, WALTER
Birthdate: 10/8/1917
Birthplace: Baltimore, MD
Information Available in These Sources: SATA 3

LORENTOWICZ, IRENA
Birthdate: 1910
Birthplace: Warsaw, Poland
Information Available in These Sources: IBYP 2, ICB 1, ICB 2

LORENZ, LEE (SHARP)
Birthdate: 10/17/1932?
Birthplace: Hackensack, NJ
Information Available in These Sources: SATA 39

LORIMER, JANET
Birthdate: 12/31/1941
Birthplace: Los Angeles, CA
Information Available in These Sources: SATA 60

LORING, EMILIE (BAKER)
(Josephine Story)
Birthdate, 1864?
Birthplace: Boston, MA
Deathdate: 3/14/1951
Information Available in These Sources: SATA 51

LORING, SELDEN M(ELVILLE)
Information Available in These Sources: ABYP 2, ABYP 3

LORRAINE, WALTER (HENRY)
Birthdate: 2/3/1929
Birthplace: Worcester, MA
Information Available in These Sources: IBYP 1, IBYP 2, ICB 2, ICB 3, ICB 4, JBA 4, SATA 16

LOSS, JOAN
Birthdate: 8/10/1933
Birthplace: Baltimore, MD
Information Available in These Sources: SATA 11

LOTHROP, HARRIET MULFORD STONE
(Margaret Sidney)
Birthdate: 6/22/1844
Birthplace: New Haven, CT
Deathdate: 8/2/1924
Information Available in These Sources: ABYP 4, DLB 42, FSYP, JBA 1, SATA 20, TCCW 2, TCCW 3

LOUIE, AI-LING
Birthdate: 7/18/1949
Birthplace: New York, NY
Information Available in These Sources: SATA 34, SATA 40

LOVE, KATHERINE (ISABEL)
Birthdate: 6/22/1907
Birthplace: Orion, IL
Information Available in These Sources: SATA 3

LOVE, SANDRA (WELLER)
Birthdate: 3/28/1940
Birthplace: Louisville, KY
Information Available in These Sources: SATA 26

LOVEJOY, BAHIJA FATTOUHI
Birthdate: 5/7/1914
Birthplace: Mosul, Iraq
Information Available in These Sources: ABYP 2, ABYP 3

LOVELACE, DELOS WHEELER
Birthdate: 12/2/1894
Birthplace: Brainerd, MN
Deathdate: 1/17/1967
Information Available in These Sources: ABYP 1, ABYP 3, SATA 7

LOVELACE, MAUD HART (PALMER)
Birthdate: 4/25/1892
Birthplace: Mankato, MN
Deathdate: 3/11/1980
Information Available in These Sources: ABYP 1, ABYP 3, JBA 2, SATA 2 SATA 23, TCCW 2, TCCW 3

LOVELL, INGRAHAM
See Bacon, Josephine Dodge (Daskam)

LOVOOS, JANICE
Birthplace: IA
Information Available in These Sources: ABYP 4

LOW, ALICE
Birthdate: 6/5/1926
Birthplace: New York, NY
Information Available in These Sources: ABYP 4, SATA 11, JBA 6

LOW, ELIZABETH HAMMOND
Birthdate: 8/3/1898
Birthplace: Brooklyn, NY
Information Available in These Sources: ABYP 2, ABYP 3, SATA 5

LOW, JOSEPH
Birthdate: 8/11/1911
Birthplace: Coraopolis, PA
Information Available in These Sources: ABYP 1, ABYP 3, ICB 2, ICB 3, ICB 4, JBA 3, SATA 14

LOWE, JAY, JR.
See Loeper, John J(oseph)

LOWELL, AMY
Birthdate: 2/9/1874
Birthplace: Brookline, MA
Deathdate: 5/12/1925
Information Available in These Sources: SVC 2, SVC 3

LOWELL, JAMES RUSSELL
Birthdate: 2/22/1819
Birthplace: Cambridge, MA
Deathdate: 1891
Information Available in These Sources: SVC 2, SVC 3

LOWENFELS, WALTER
Birthdate: 5/10/1897
Birthplace: New York, NY
Deathdate: 7/7/1976
Information Available in These Sources: ABYP 4

LOWENSTEIN, DYNO
Birthdate: 11/29/1914
Birthplace: Berlin, Germany
Information Available in These Sources: SATA 6

LOWITZ, ANSON C.
Birthdate, 1901?
Deathdate: 1/22/1978
Information Available in These Sources: SATA 18

LOWITZ, SADYEBETH (HEATH)
Birthdate: 12/3/1901
Birthplace: Richmond, MI
Information Available in These Sources: SATA 17

LOWNSBERY, ELOISE
Birthdate: 4/16/1888
Birthplace: Pawpaw, IL
Information Available in These Sources: JBA 2

LOWREY, JANETTE SEBRING
Birthdate: 3/2/1892
Birthplace: Orange, TX
Information Available in These Sources: ABYP 1, ABYP 3, SATA 43

LOWRY, LOIS (HAMMBERSBERG)
Birthdate: 3/20/1937
Birthplace: Honolulu, HI
Information Available in These Sources: ABYP 4, DACF, JBA 5, SATA 23, TCCW 3

LOWRY, PETER
Birthdate: 3/6/1953
Birthplace: Berkeley, CA
Information Available in These Sources: ABYP 4, SATA 7

LOWTHER, GEORGE F.
Birthdate: 1913
Deathdate: 4/28/1975
Information Available in These Sources: SATA 30

LOZIER, HERBERT
Birthdate: 12/19/1915
Birthplace: New York, NY
Information Available in These Sources: SATA 26

LUBELL, CECIL
Birthdate: 6/6/1912
Birthplace: Leeds, England
Information Available in These Sources: ABYP 1, ABYP 3, BABP, JBA 4, SATA 6

LUBELL, WINIFRED (MILIUS)
Birthdate: 6/14/1914
Birthplace: New York, NY
Information Available in These Sources: ABYP 1, ABYP 3, BABP, ICB 2, ICB 3, ICB 4, SATA 6

LUBIN, LEONARD B.
Birthdate: 11/27/1943
Birthplace: Detroit, MI
Information Available in These Sources: ICB 4, SATA 37, SATA 45

LUCAS, GEORGE (WALTON)
Birthdate: 5/14/1944
Birthplace: Modesto, CA
Information Available in These Sources: SATA 56

LUCAS, JANETTE MAY
Birthdate: 1885
Birthplace: Washington, DC
Information Available in These Sources: JBA 2

LUCAS, JERRY
Birthdate: 3/30/1940
Birthplace: Middletown, OH
Information Available in These Sources: SATA 33

LUCE, CELIA (GENEVA LARSEN)
Birthdate: 12/3/1914
Birthplace: Provo, UT
Information Available in These Sources: SATA 38

LUCE, WILLARD (RAY)
Birthdate: 9/18/1914
Birthplace: Price, UT
Information Available in These Sources: SATA 38

LUCKHARDT, MILDRED (MADELEINE) CORELL
Birthdate: 11/20/1898
Birthplace: New York, NY
Information Available in These Sources: ABYP 4, SATA 5

LUDDEN, ALLEN (ELLSWORTH)
Birthdate: 10/5/1918?
Birthplace: Mineral Point, WI
Deathdate: 6/9/1981
Information Available in These Sources: SATA 27

LUDLUM, MABEL CLELAND
See Widdemer, Mabel Cleland

LUDWIG, HELEN
Birthplace: Tolland, CT
Information Available in These Sources: IBYP 1, IBYP 2, SATA 33

LUEDERS, EDWARD (GEORGE)
Birthdate: 2/14/1923
Birthplace: Chicago, IL
Information Available in These Sources: ABYP 4, SATA 14

LUENN, NANCY
Birthdate: 12/28/1954
Birthplace: Pasadena, CA
Information Available in These Sources: SATA 51

LUFKIN, RAYMOND H.
Birthdate: 1/29/1897
Birthplace: Salem, MA
Information Available in These Sources: IBYP 2, ICB 1, ICB 2, SATA 38

LUGER, HARRIETT M(ANDELAY)
Birthdate: 7/21/1914
Birthplace: Vancouver, B. C., Canada
Information Available in These Sources: SATA 23

LUGINBUHL, EDNA
Information Available in These Sources: ABYP 4

LUHRMANN, WINIFRED B(RUCE)
Birthdate: 11/19/1934
Birthplace: Greenfield, MA
Information Available in These Sources: SATA 11

LUIS, EARLENE W.
Birthdate: 10/21/1929
Birthplace: AL
Information Available in These Sources: SATA 11

LUKAS, J(AY) ANTHONY
Birthdate: 4/25/1933
Birthplace: New York, NY
Information Available in These Sources: ABYP 4

LUM(M), PETER
See Crowe, Bettina Lum

LUND, DORIS (HEROLD)
Birthdate: 1/14/1919
Birthplace: Indianapolis, IN
Information Available in These Sources: SATA 12

LUNN, JANET
Birthdate: 12/28/1928
Birthplace: Dallas, TX
Information Available in These Sources: SATA 4, JBA 6

LUPOFF, DICK
See Lupoff, Richard A(llen)

LUPOFF, RICHARD A(LLEN)
(Ova Hamlet, Dick Lupoff, Dick O'Donnell, Pascal Pascudniak, Addison Steele II)
Birthdate: 2/21/1935
Birthplace: Brooklyn, NY
Information Available in These Sources: SATA 60

LURIE, ALISON
Birthdate: 9/3/1926
Birthplace: Chicago, IL
Information Available in These Sources: SATA 46

LUSTIG, ARNOST
Birthdate: 12/21/1926
Birthplace: Prague, Czechoslovakia
Information Available in These Sources: SATA 56

LUSTIG, LORETTA
Birthdate: 4/9/1944
Birthplace: New York, NY
Information Available in These Sources: SATA 46

LUTHER, FRANK
(Francis Luther Crow)
Birthdate: 8/4/1905
Birthplace: Lakin (near), KS
Deathdate: 11/16/1980
Information Available in These Sources: SATA 25

LUTTRELL, GUY L.
Birthdate: 3/3/1938
Birthplace: Chicago, IL
Information Available in These Sources: SATA 22

LUTTRELL, IDA (ALLEENE)
Birthdate: 4/18/1934
Birthplace: Laredo, TX
Information Available in These Sources: SATA 35, SATA 40

LUTZKER, EDYTHE
Birthdate: 6/25/1904
Birthplace: Berlin, Germany
Information Available in These Sources: SATA 5

LYALL, DENNIS
Information Available in These Sources: IBYP 2

LYDON, MICHAEL
Birthdate: 9/14/1942
Birthplace: Boston, MA
Information Available in These Sources: SATA 11

LYFICK, WARREN
See Reeves, Lawrence F.

LYLE, KATIE LETCHER
Birthdate: 5/12/1938
Birthplace: Peking, China
Information Available in These Sources: SATA 8

LYMAN, SUSAN E(LIZABETH)
Birthdate: 1906
Deathdate: 9/13/1976
Information Available in These Sources: ABYP 2, ABYP 3

LYNCH, LORENZO
Birthdate: 5/27/1932
Information Available in These Sources: BAI, SATA 7

LYNCH, MARIETTA
Birthdate: 12/21/1947
Information Available in These Sources: SATA 29

LYNDS, DENNIS
(William Arden, Nick Carter, Michael Collins, John Crowe, Carl Dekker, Maxwell Grant, Mark Sadler)
Birthdate: 1/15/1924
Birthplace: St. Louis, MO
Information Available in These Sources: SATA 37, SATA 47

LYNN, MARY
See Brokamp, Marilyn

LYNN, PATRICIA
See Watts, Mabel Pizzey

LYON, JESSICA
See DeLeeuw, Cateau (Wilhelmina)

LYON, LYMAN R.
See DeCamp, L(yon) Sprague

LYONS, DOROTHY (MARAWEE)
Birthdate: 12/4/1907
Birthplace: Fenton, MI
Information Available in These Sources: SATA 3

LYONS, GRANT
Birthdate: 8/19/1941
Birthplace: Butler, PA
Information Available in These Sources: SATA 30

LYSTAD, MARY (HANEMANN)
Birthdate: 4/11/1928
Birthplace: New Orleans, LA
Information Available in These Sources: SATA 11

LYTTLE, RICHARD B(ARD)
Birthdate: 6/9/1927
Birthplace: Los Angeles, CA
Information Available in These Sources: ABYP 4, SATA 23

M

MAAR, LEONARD (F., JR.)
Birthdate: 4/27/1927
Birthplace: Poughkeepsie, NY
Information Available in These Sources: SATA 30

MAAS, JULIE
Birthplace: New York, NY
Information Available in These Sources: IBYP 1, IBYP 2

MAAS, SELVE
Birthplace: Estonia
Information Available in These Sources: SATA 14

MABERY, D. L.
Birthdate: 1/13/1953
Birthplace: Reading, CA
Information Available in These Sources: SATA 53

MAC
See MacManus, Seumas

MACAGY, DOUGLAS (GUERNSEY)
Birthdate: 7/8/1913
Birthplace: Winnipeg, Manitoba, Canada
Deathdate: 9/6/1973
Information Available in These Sources: ABYP 1, ABYP 3

MAC AODHAGAIN, EAMON
See Egan, E(dward) W(elstead)

MACAULAY, DAVID ALEXANDER
Birthdate: 12/2/1946
Birthplace: Burton-on-Trent, England
Information Available in These Sources: ABYP 4, DLB 61, ICB 4, JBA 5, SATA 27, SATA 46

MACBRIDE, ROGER LEA
Birthdate: 8/6/1929
Birthplace: New Rochelle, NY
Information Available in These Sources: ABYP 4

MACCLINTOCK, DORCAS
Birthdate: 7/16/1932
Birthplace: New York, NY
Information Available in These Sources: ABYP 4, SATA 8

MACCLOUD, MALCOLM
Information Available in These Sources: DACF

MACDONALD, ANSON
See Heinlein, Robert A(nson)

MACDONALD, BETTY (HESKETT BARD)
(Anne Elizabeth Campbell Bard)
Birthdate: 3/26/1908
Birthplace: Boulder, CO
Deathdate: 2/7/1958
Information Available in These Sources: ABYP 1, ABYP 3, YABC

MACDONALD, BLACKIE
See Emrich, Duncan (Black Macdonald)

MACDONALD, DWIGHT
Birthdate: 3/24/1906
Birthplace: New York, NY
Deathdate: 12/19/1982
Information Available in These Sources: SATA 29, SATA 33

MACDONALD, GOLDEN
See Brown, Margaret Wise

MACDONALD, JAMES
Birthplace: Scotland
Information Available in These Sources: IBYP 1, IBYP 2

MACDONALD, MARCIA
See Hill, Grace Livingston

MACDONALD, SUSE (SUSAN KELSEY)
Birthdate: 3/3/1940
Birthplace: Evanston, IL
Information Available in These Sources: SATA 52, SATA 54, JBA 6

MACDONALD, ZILLAH KATHERINE
(Zillah)
Birthdate: 1/15/1885
Birthplace: Halifax, Nova Scotia, Canada
Information Available in These Sources: ABYP 1, ABYP 3

MACE, KATHERINE (KEELER)
Birthdate: 1921
Birthplace: New York, NY
Information Available in These Sources: ABYP 1, ABYP 3

MACE, VARIAN
Birthdate: 6/12/1938
Birthplace: American Falls, ID
Information Available in These Sources: SATA 49

MACE, WYNN
Information Available in These Sources: ABYP 1, ABYP 3

MACFARLAN, ALLAN A.
Birthdate: 1892
Birthplace: Canada
Deathdate: 12/30/1982
Information Available in These Sources: ABYP 1, ABYP 3, SATA 35

MACGREGOR, ELLEN
Birthdate: 5/15/1906
Birthplace: Baltimore, MD
Deathdate: 3/29/1954
Information Available in These Sources: ABYP 1, ABYP 3, MJA, SATA 27, SATA 39, TCCW 1, TCCW 2, TCCW 3

MACHETANZ, FREDERICK
Birthdate: 2/20/1908
Birthplace: Kenton, OH
Information Available in These Sources: IBYP 2, ICB 1, ICB 2, SATA 34

MACINNES, HELEN
(Helen Highet)
Birthdate: 10/7/1907
Birthplace: Glasgow, Scotland
Deathdate: 9/30/1985
Information Available in These Sources: SATA 22, SATA 44

MACK, STAN(LEY)
Birthdate: 1935
Birthplace: Brooklyn, NY
Information Available in These Sources: IBYP 2, JBA 4, SATA 17

MACKAY, CONSTANCE D'ARCY
Birthplace: St. Paul, MN
Deathdate: 8/21/1966
Information Available in These Sources: JBA 1, JBA 2, TCCW 1, TCCW 2, TCCW 3

MACKAY, DONALD A.
Birthdate: 1895
Information Available in These Sources: IBYP 1, IBYP 2

MACKAYE, PERCY (WALLACE)
Birthdate: 3/16/1875
Birthplace: New York, NY
Deathdate: 8/31/1956
Information Available in These Sources: JBA 1, SATA 32, SVC 2, SVC 3

MACKELLAR, WILLIAM
Birthdate: 2/20/1914
Birthplace: Glasgow, Scotland
Information Available in These Sources: ABYP 1, ABYP 3, SATA 4

MACKENZIE, GARRY
Birthdate: 9/7/1921
Birthplace: Portage La Prairie, Canada (Manitoba)
Information Available in These Sources: IBYP 1, IBYP 2, ICB 2, ICB 3, SATA 31

MACKENZIE, JEANETTE BROWN
Information Available in These Sources: ABYP 2, ABYP 3

MACKIE, MARON
See McNeely, Jeannette

MACKINNON GROOMER, VERA
Birthdate: 8/5/1915
Birthplace: Corvallis, OR
Information Available in These Sources: SATA 57

MACKINSTRY, ELIZABETH
Birthdate: 3/31/1879
Birthplace: Scranton, PA
Deathdate: 5/13/1956
Information Available in These Sources: CICB, ICB 1, MJA, SATA 42

MACKNIGHT, NINON
(Ninon)
Birthdate: 4/5/1908
Birthplace: Sydney, Australia
Information Available in These Sources: IBYP 1, IBYP 2, ICB 2

MACLACHLAN, PATRICIA
Birthdate: 3/3/1938
Birthplace: Cheyenne, WY
Information Available in These Sources: DACF, TCCW 3, JBA 6

MACLEOD, BEATRICE (BEACH)
Birthdate: 1/15/1910
Birthplace: Brentwood, Long Island, NY
Information Available in These Sources: ABYP 1, ABYP 3, SATA 10

MACLEOD, CHARLOTTE (MATILDA HUGHES)
(Matilda Hughes, Alisa Craig)
Birthdate: 11/12/1922
Birthplace: Bath, New Brunswick, Canada
Information Available in These Sources: DACF, SATA 28

MACMANUS, JAMES
See MacManus, Seumas

MACMANUS, SEUMAS
(James MacManus, Mac)
Birthdate: 1869
Birthplace: Mountcharles, Cy. Donegal, Ireland
Deathdate: 10/23/1960
Information Available in These Sources: SATA 25

MACMASTER, EVE (RUTH) B(OWERS)
Birthdate: 9/24/1942
Birthplace: Baltimore, MD
Information Available in These Sources: SATA 46

MACMILLAN, ANNABELLE
See Quick, Annabelle (MacMillan)

MACPEEK, WALTER G.
(Hugo Jumpp)
Birthdate: 3/14/1902
Birthplace: Stockton, IL
Deathdate: 1/31/1973
Information Available in These Sources: ABYP 4, SATA 4, SATA 25

MACPHERSON, THOMAS GEORGE
(Tom Parsons)
Birthdate: 10/28/1915
Birthplace: Barrow-in-Furness, England
Deathdate: 5/7/1976
Information Available in These Sources: ABYP 2, ABYP 3, SATA 30

MACRAE, HAWK
See Barker, Albert W.

MACRAE, TRAVIS
See Feagles, Anita MacRae

MACUMBER, MARI
See Sandoz, Mari (Susette)

MADDEN, DON
Birthdate: 10/14/1927
Birthplace: Cleveland, OH
Information Available in These Sources: IBYP 2, SATA 3

MADIAN, JON
Birthdate: 4/10/1941
Birthplace: New York, NY
Information Available in These Sources: SATA 9

MADISON, ARNOLD
Birthdate: 11/28/1937
Birthplace: Bayport, Long Island, NY
Information Available in These Sources: ABYP 4, DACF, SATA 6

MADISON, STEVE
Birthplace: Brooklyn, NY
Information Available in These Sources: IBYP 2

MADISON, WINIFRED
Birthplace: Pawtucket, RI
Information Available in These Sources: SATA 5

MADLEE, DOROTHY (HAYNES)
(Anne Haynes, Wade Rogers)
Birthdate: 2/1/1917
Birthplace: Springfield, MO
Information Available in These Sources: ABYP 4

MAESTRO, BETSY (CRIPPEN)
Birthdate: 1/5/1944
Birthplace: New York, NY
Information Available in These Sources: ABYP 4, SATA 30, SATA 59, JBA 6

MAESTRO, GIULIO (MARCELLO)
Birthdate: 5/6/1942
Birthplace: New York, NY
Information Available in These Sources: ABYP 4, IBYP 2, ICB 4, SATA 8 SATA 59, JBA 6

MAGORIAN, JAMES
Birthdate: 4/24/1942
Birthplace: Palisade, NE
Information Available in These Sources: SATA 32

MAGUIRE, ANNE
See Nearing, Penny

MAGUIRE, GREGORY
Birthdate: 6/9/1954
Birthplace: Albany, NY
Information Available in These Sources: SATA 28, TCCW 3

MAHER, RAMONA
Birthdate: 10/25/1934
Birthplace: Phoenix, AZ
Information Available in These Sources: DACF, SATA 13

MAHLMANN, LEWIS
Information Available in These Sources: ABYP 4

MAHON, JULIA C(UNHA)
Birthdate: 2/20/1916
Birthplace: Phoenix City, AL
Information Available in These Sources: ABYP 4, SATA 11

MAHONY, ELIZABETH WINTHROP
(Elizabeth Winthrop)
Birthdate: 9/14/1948
Birthplace: Washington, DC
Information Available in These Sources: JBA 5, SATA 8

MAIDOFF, ILKA LIST
See List, Ilka Katherine

MAIORANO, ROBERT
Birthdate: 8/29/1946
Birthplace: Brooklyn, NY
Information Available in These Sources: SATA 43

MAJOR, CHARLES
Birthdate: 7/25/1856
Birthplace: Indianapolis, IN
Deathdate: 2/13/1913
Information Available in These Sources: SVC 2, SVC 3

MAKIE, PAM
Birthdate: 8/17/1943
Birthplace: Ithaca, NY
Information Available in These Sources: SATA 37

MALCOLMSON, ANNE (BURNETT)
(Anne Burnett Malcolmson VonStorch)
Birthdate: 12/6/1910
Birthplace: St. Louis, MO
Information Available in These Sources: ABYP 2, ABYP 3, MJA, SATA 1

MALCOLMSON, DAVID
Birthdate: 1/27/1899
Birthplace: El Paso, TX
Information Available in These Sources: SATA 6

MALI, JANE LAWRENCE
Birthdate: 6/2/1937
Birthplace: New York, NY
Information Available in These Sources: SATA 44, 51

MALKUS, ALIDA (WRIGHT) SIMS
Birthdate: 9/19/1895 or 9/19/1899
Birthplace: Crenessee Valley, NY
Information Available in These Sources: ABYP 1, ABYP 3, JBA 1, JBA 2

MALLOCH, DOUGLAS
Birthdate: 1877
Birthplace: Muskegon, MI
Deathdate: 1938
Information Available in These Sources: SVC 2, SVC 3

MALMBERG, CARL
(Timothy Trent)
Birthdate: 6/26/1904
Birthplace: Oshkosh, WI
Information Available in These Sources: SATA 9

MALO, JOHN
Birthdate: 4/11/1911
Birthplace: Ringo, KS
Information Available in These Sources: SATA 4

MALONE, MARY
Birthplace: Lambertville, NJ
Information Available in These Sources: ABYP 1, ABYP 3

MALTESE, MICHAEL
Birthdate, 1908?
Deathdate: 2/??/1981
Information Available in These Sources: SATA 24

MALVERN, CORINNE
Birthdate: 1905
Birthplace: Newark, NJ
Deathdate: 11/9/1956 or 10/??/1956
Information Available in These Sources: IBYP 1, IBYP 2, JBA 2, SATA 34

MALVERN, GLADYS
(Sabra Lee Corbin, Vahrah von Klopp, Vahrah VonKlopp)
Deathdate: 11/16/1962
Information Available in These Sources: ABYP 1, ABYP 3, JBA 2, SATA 23

MALZBERG, BARRY (N.)
(K. M. O'Donnell)
Birthdate: 7/24/1939
Birthplace: New York, NY
Information Available in These Sources: ABYP 4

MAMA G.
See Davis, Grania

MAMMEN, EDWARD WILLIAM
Birthdate: 1907
Birthplace: Brooklyn, NY
Information Available in These Sources: ABYP 1, ABYP 3

MANCHEL, FRANK
Birthdate: 7/22/1935
Birthplace: Detroit, MI
Information Available in These Sources: ABYP 4, SATA 10

MANDELKORN, EUGENIA MILLER
(Eugenia Miller)
Birthdate: 5/11/1916
Information Available in These Sources: ABYP 2, ABYP 3

MANDRY, KATHY
Birthplace: Utica, NY
Information Available in These Sources: ABYP 4

MANES, STEPHEN
(Mel Murch, Hans Pemsteen, Ward Starr, A. M. Stephensen)
Birthdate: 1/8/1949
Birthplace: Pittsburgh, PA
Information Available in These Sources: SATA 40, SATA 42

MANFRED, FREDERICK F(EIKEMA)
(Feike Feikema)
Birthdate: 1/6/1912
Birthplace: Rock Township, Doon, IA
Information Available in These Sources: SATA 30

MANGIONE, JERRE
Birthdate: 3/20/1909
Birthplace: Rochester, NY
Information Available in These Sources: SATA 6

MANGO, KARIN N.
Birthdate: 1/11/1936
Birthplace: Riga, Latvia
Information Available in These Sources: SATA 52

MANGURIAN, DAVID
Birthdate: 7/18/1938
Birthplace: Baltimore, MD
Information Available in These Sources: SATA 14

MANISCALCO, JOSEPH
Birthdate: 10/12/1926
Birthplace: San Francisco, CA
Information Available in These Sources: SATA 10

MANLEY, SEON
Birthplace: CT
Information Available in These Sources: ABYP 4, SATA 15

MANN, AVERY
See Breetveld, Jim Patrick

MANN, PEGGY
Birthplace: New York, NY
Information Available in These Sources: SATA 6

MANNETTI, LISA
(L.A. Kane)
Birthdate: 1/9/1953
Birthplace: White Plains, NY
Information Available in These Sources: SATA 51, SATA 57

MANNHEIM, GRETE (SALOMON)
Birthdate: 5/14/1909
Birthplace: Celle, West Germany
Information Available in These Sources: SATA 10

MANNIX, DANIEL P(RATT)
Birthdate: 1911
Information Available in These Sources: ABYP 4

MANTEL, S. G.
Birthplace: New York, NY
Information Available in These Sources: ABYP 2, ABYP 3

MANUSHKIN, FRAN(CES)
Birthdate: 11/2/1942
Birthplace: Chicago, IL
Information Available in These Sources: SATA 7, SATA 54

MAPES, MARY A.
See Ellison, Virginia Howell

MARA, BARNEY
See Roth, Arthur J(oseph)

MARA, JEANETTE
See Cebulash, Mel

MARABELLA, MADELINE
Information Available in These Sources: ABYP 2, ABYP 3

MARAH
See Jackson, Helen (Maria Fiske) Hunt

MARAIS, JOSEF
Birthdate: 11/17/1905
Birthplace: Sir Lowry Pass, South Africa
Deathdate: 4/27/1978
Information Available in These Sources: SATA 24

MARASMUS, SEYMOUR
See Rivoli, Mario

MARCELINO
See Agnew, Edith J(osephine)

MARCHER, MARION WALDEN
Birthdate: 12/16/1890
Birthplace: Racine, WI
Information Available in These Sources: SATA 10

MARCHETTE, KATHARINE E.
Birthdate: 5/30/1941
Birthplace: Corvallis, OR
Information Available in These Sources: SATA 38

MARCIARELLI, GARRY
See Marshall, Garry

MARCUS, REBECCA B(RIAN)
Birthdate: 11/26/1907
Birthplace: New York, NY
Information Available in These Sources: ABYP 1, ABYP 3, SATA 9

MAREK, GEORGE R(ICHARD)
Birthdate: 7/13/1902
Birthplace: Austria
Information Available in These Sources: ABYP 4

MAREK, MARGOT L.
Birthdate, 1934?
Deathdate: 9/29/1987
Information Available in These Sources: SATA 54

MARGARET, KARLA
See Andersdatter, Karla M(argaret)

MARGOLIS, RICHARD (J.)
Birthdate: 6/30/1929
Birthplace: St. Paul, MN
Information Available in These Sources: ABYP 4, SATA 4

MARGOLIS, VIVIENNE
(Vivienne Eisner)
Birthdate: 1/11/1922
Birthplace: Dayton, OH
Information Available in These Sources: SATA 46

MARIANA
See Foster, Marian Curtis

MARINO, DOROTHY BRONSON
Birthdate: 11/12/1912
Birthplace: Oakland, OR
Information Available in These Sources: ABYP 1, ABYP 3, ICB 2, ICB 3, SATA 14

MARK, PAULINE (DAHLIN)
(Polly Mark)
Birthdate: 8/11/1913
Birthplace: Mayville, NY
Information Available in These Sources: SATA 14

MARK, POLLY
See Mark, Pauline (Dahlin)

MARKHAM, EDWIN
Birthdate: 4/23/1852
Birthplace: Oregon City, OR
Deathdate: 3/7/1940
Information Available in These Sources: SVC 2

MARKHAM, MARION M.
Birthdate: 6/12/1929
Birthplace: Chicago, IL
Information Available in These Sources: SATA 60

MARKINS, W. S.
See Jenkins, Marie M(agdalen)

MARKLE, SANDRA L(EE)
Birthdate: 11/10/1946
Birthplace: Fostoria, OH
Information Available in These Sources: SATA 41, SATA 57

MARKO, KATHERINE D(OLORES)
Birthdate: 1913
Birthplace: Allentown, PA
Information Available in These Sources: SATA 28

MARKS, BURTON
Birthdate: 8/11/1930
Birthplace: Akron, OH
Information Available in These Sources: SATA 43, SATA 47

MARKS, GEOFFREY
Birthdate: 5/20/1906
Birthplace: Melbourne, Australia
Information Available in These Sources: ABYP 4

MARKS, HANNAH K.
See Trivelpiece, Laurel

MARKS, J.
See Highwater, Jamake

MARKS, MARGARET L.
Birthdate, 1911?
Birthplace: London, England
Deathdate: 6/30/1980
Information Available in These Sources: SATA 23

MARKS, MICKEY KLAR
Birthdate: 1/9/1914
Birthplace: Brooklyn, NY
Information Available in These Sources: ABYP 1, ABYP 2, ABYP 3, SATA 12

MARKS, PETER
See Smith, Robert Kimmel

MARKS, RITA (WEISS)
Birthdate: 8/14/1938
Birthplace: Akron, OH
Information Available in These Sources: SATA 47

MARKS-HIGHWATER, J.
See Highwater, Jamake

MARKUN, PATRICIA M(ALONEY)
(Sybil Forrest, Ryan O'Carroll)
Birthdate: 8/24/1924
Birthplace: Chisholm, MN
Information Available in These Sources: ABYP 1, ABYP 3, SATA 15

MARLEE
See Alex, Marlee

MARLOWE, STEPHEN
(Adam Chase, Andrew Frazer, Darius John Granger, Milton Lesser, Jason Ridgeway, C. H. Thames, Stephen Wilder)
Birthdate: 8/7/1928
Birthplace: Brooklyn, NY
Information Available in These Sources: ABYP 1, ABYP 3

MAROKVIA, ARTUR
Birthdate: 7/21/1909
Birthplace: Stuttgart, Germany
Information Available in These Sources: IBYP 2, ICB 2, ICB 3, SATA 31

MAROKVIA, MIREILLE (JOURNET)
Birthdate: 12/7/1918
Birthplace: France
Information Available in These Sources: ABYP 1, ABYP 3, SATA 5

MARQUIS, DON
Birthdate: 1878
Birthplace: IL
Deathdate: 1937
Information Available in These Sources: SVC 2, SVC 3

MARR, JOHN S(TUART)
Birthdate: 4/22/1940
Birthplace: New York, NY
Information Available in These Sources: SATA 48

MARRAN, RAY J.
Birthplace: New York, NY
Information Available in These Sources: ABYP 1, ABYP 3

MARRIN, ALBERT
Birthdate: 7/24/1936
Birthplace: New York, NY
Information Available in These Sources: SATA 43, SATA 53

MARRIOTT, ALICE LEE
Birthdate: 1/8/1910
Birthplace: Wilmette, IL
Information Available in These Sources: ABYP 1, ABYP 3, SATA 31

MARS, W(ITOLD) T(ADEUSZ, JR.)
Birthdate: 9/1/1912
Birthplace: Rzesna, Poland
Information Available in These Sources: IBYP 1, IBYP 2, ICB 2, ICB 3, SATA 3

MARSH, CORINNA
Birthplace: NY
Information Available in These Sources: ABYP 2, ABYP 3

MARSH, REGINALD
Birthdate: 3/14/1898
Birthplace: Paris, France
Deathdate: 7/3/1954
Information Available in These Sources: IBYP 1, 2, ICB 2

MARSHALL, ANTHONY D(RYDEN)
Birthdate: 5/30/1924
Birthplace: New York, NY
Information Available in These Sources: SATA 18

MARSHALL, CATHERINE
See Marshall, Sarah Catherine

MARSHALL, DEAN
Birthdate: 1900
Birthplace: Louisville, KY
Information Available in These Sources: ABYP 2, ABYP 3

MARSHALL, DOUGLAS
See McClintock, Marshall

MARSHALL, EDWARD
See Marshall, James (Edward)

MARSHALL, GARRY
(Garry Marciarelli)
Birthdate: 11/13/1934
Birthplace: New York, NY
Information Available in These Sources: SATA 60

MARSHALL, JAMES
Birthdate: 1933
Birthplace: Nova Scotia, Canada
Information Available in These Sources: ABYP 4

MARSHALL, JAMES (EDWARD)
(Edward Marshall)
Birthdate: 10/10/1942
Birthplace: San Antonio, TX
Information Available in These Sources: ABYP 4, DLB 61, ICB 4, JBA 4, SATA 6, SATA 51, TCCW 2, TCCW 3

MARSHALL, JIM
Birthdate: 1891
Birthplace: England
Deathdate: 1956
Information Available in These Sources: SVC 2, SVC 3

MARSHALL, KIM
See Marshall, Michael (Kimbrough)

MARSHALL, MICHAEL (KIMBROUGH)
(Kim Marshall)
Birthdate: 3/11/1948
Birthplace: Oakland, CA
Information Available in These Sources: SATA 37

MARSHALL, S(AMUEL) L(YMAN) A(TWOOD)
Birthdate: 7/18/1900
Birthplace: Catskill, NY
Deathdate: 12/17/1977
Information Available in These Sources: SATA 21

MARSHALL, SARAH CATHERINE
(Catherine Marshall)
Birthdate: 9/27/1914
Birthplace: Johnson City, TN
Deathdate: 3/18/1983
Information Available in: ABYP 1, 3, SATA 2, 34

MARSOLI, LISA ANN
Birthdate: 11/4/1958
Birthplace: Providence, RI
Information Available in These Sources: SATA 53

MARSTEN, RICHARD
See Hunter, Evan

MARSTON, HOPE IRVIN
Birthdate: 1/31/1935
Birthplace: Fishing Creek (Mill Hall), PA
Information Available in These Sources: SATA 31

MARTIGNONI, MARGARET E.
Birthdate: 7/12/1908
Birthplace: Dunkirk, NY
Deathdate: 2/11/1974
Information Available in These Sources: SATA 27

MARTIN, ANN M(ATTHEWS)
(Ann Matthews)
Birthdate: 8/12/1955
Birthplace: Princeton, NJ
Information Available in These Sources: SATA 41, SATA 44

MARTIN, BILL, JR.
See Martin, William Ivan

MARTIN, CHARLES MORRIS
(Chuck Martin)
Birthdate: 1891
Birthplace: OH
Information Available in These Sources: ABYP 1, ABYP 3

MARTIN, CHRISTOPHER
See Hoyt, Edwin P(almer), Jr.

MARTIN, CHUCK
See Martin, Charles Morris

MARTIN, DAVID STONE
Birthdate: 6/13/1913
Birthplace: Chicago, IL
Information Available in These Sources: IBYP 1, IBYP 2, ICB 2, SATA 39

MARTIN, DOROTHY
Birthdate: 3/19/1921
Birthplace: Chisholm, MN
Information Available in These Sources: SATA 47

MARTIN, EUGENE
See Stratemeyer, Edward L.

MARTIN, FRANCES M(CENTEE)
Birthdate: 10/25/1906
Birthplace: Montclair, NJ
Information Available in These Sources: SATA 36

MARTIN, FREDRIC
See Christopher, Matt(hew) F.

MARTIN, GEORGE
Birthdate: 1/25/1926
Birthplace: New York, NY
Information Available in These Sources: ABYP 1, ABYP 3

MARTIN, JEREMY
See Levin, Marcia Obrasky

MARTIN, JUDITH
Information Available in These Sources: ABYP 2, ABYP 3

MARTIN, LYNNE
Birthdate: 8/8/1923
Birthplace: Flushing, NY
Information Available in These Sources: ABYP 4, SATA 21

MARTIN, MARCIA
See Levin, Marcia Obrasky

MARTIN, PATRICIA MILES
(Patricia A. Miles, Miska Miles, Jerry Lane)
Birthdate: 11/14/1899
Birthplace: Cherokee, KS
Deathdate: 1/2/1986
Information Available in These Sources: ABYP 1, ABYP 3, JBA 4, SATA 1 SATA 43, SATA 48, TCCW 1, TCCW 2, TCCW 3

MARTIN, RALPH G.
Birthdate: 3/4/1920
Birthplace: Chicago, IL
Information Available in These Sources: ABYP 2, ABYP 3

MARTIN, RENE
Birthdate: 2/11/1891
Birthplace: Paris, France
Deathdate: 8/14/1977
Information Available in These Sources: IBYP 1, IBYP 2, SATA 20, SATA 42

MARTIN, STEFAN
Birthdate: 1/10/1936
Birthplace: Elgin, IL
Information Available in These Sources: IBYP 1, IBYP 2, ICB 3, SATA 32

MARTIN, SYLVIA PARSONS
Information Available in These Sources: ABYP 4

MARTIN, WILLIAM G.
Information Available in These Sources: ABYP 4

MARTIN, WILLIAM IVAN
(Bill Martin, Jr.)
Birthdate: 1916
Birthplace: KS
Information Available in These Sources: SATA 40, JBA 6

MARTINEZ, JOHN
Birthplace: New York, NY
Information Available in These Sources: IBYP 1, IBYP 2

MARTINI, TERI
Birthdate: 6/4/1930
Birthplace: Teaneck, NJ
Information Available in These Sources: ABYP 1, ABYP 3, SATA 3

MARX, ROBERT F(RANK)
Birthdate: 12/8/1936
Birthplace: Pittsburgh, PA
Information Available in These Sources: SATA 24

MARZANI, CARL (ALDO)
Birthdate: 3/4/1912
Birthplace: Rome, Italy
Information Available in These Sources: SATA 12

MARZOLLO, JEAN
Birthdate: 6/24/1942
Birthplace: Manchester, CT
Information Available in These Sources: SATA 29, JBA 6

MASEY, MARY LOU(ISE LEACH)
Birthdate: 4/8/1932
Birthplace: Philadelphia, PA
Information Available in These Sources: ABYP 4

MASHA
See Stern, Marie Simchow

MASON, EDWIN A.
Birthdate: 4/25/1905
Birthplace: Nottingham, England
Deathdate: 7/9/1979
Information Available in These Sources: SATA 32

MASON, F(RANCIS) VAN WYCK
(Geoffrey Coffin, Frank W. Mason, Van Wyck Mason, Ward Weaver)
Birthdate: 11/11/1901
Birthplace: Boston, MA
Deathdate: 8/28/1978
Information Available in These Sources: ABYP 1, ABYP 3, SATA 3, SATA 26

MASON, FRANK W.
See Mason, F(rancis) van Wyck

MASON, GEORGE FREDERICK
Birthdate: 10/18/1904
Birthplace: Princeton, MA
Information Available in These Sources: ABYP 1, ABYP 3, ICB 2, ICB 3, SATA 14

MASON, MIRIAM E(VANGELINE)
Birthdate: 1/23/1900
Birthplace: Goshen, IN
Deathdate: 2/20/1973
Information Available in These Sources: ABYP 1, ABYP 3, MJA, SATA 2, SATA 26

MASON, TALLY
See Derleth, August (William)

MASON, VAN WYCK
See Mason, F(rancis) van Wyck

MASSELMAN, GEORGE
Birthdate: 12/9/1897
Birthplace: Amsterdam, Netherlands
Deathdate: 10/8/1971
Information Available in These Sources: SATA 19

MASSIE, DIANE REDFIELD
Birthdate: 7/27/1930
Birthplace: Los Angeles, CA
Information Available in These Sources: ABYP 1, ABYP 3, ICB 3, SATA 16

MASTERS, KELLY RAY
(Zachary Ball)
Birthdate: 6/16/1899 or 6/16/1897
Birthplace: Princeton,Blackjack Hills, MO
Information Available in These Sources: ABYP 1, ABYP 3, DACF, JBA 4, DACF

MASTERS, MILDRED
(Mildred Heinzen)
Birthdate: 7/8/1932
Birthplace: Indianapolis, IN
Information Available in These Sources: SATA 42

MASTERS, WILLIAM
See Cousins, Margaret

MATH, IRWIN
Birthdate: 7/8/1940
Birthplace: New York, NY
Information Available in These Sources: SATA 42

MATHEWS, LOUISE
See Tooke, Louise Mathews

MATHIEU, JOE
See Mathieu, Joseph P.

MATHIEU, JOSEPH P.
(Joe Mathieu)
Birthdate: 1/23/1949
Birthplace: Springfield, VT
Information Available in These Sources: SATA 36, SATA 43

MATHIS, SHARON BELL
Birthdate: 2/26/1937
Birthplace: Atlantic City, NJ
Information Available in These Sources: ABYP 4, BAI, DACF, SATA 7, SATA 58, TCCW 1, TCCW 2, TCCW 3

MATSON, EMERSON N(ELS)
Birthdate: 5/23/1926
Birthplace: Seattle, WA
Information Available in These Sources: SATA 12

MATTE, ENCARNACION L'ENC
(L'Enc Matte)
Birthdate: 3/5/1936
Birthplace: Reus, Tarragona, Spain
Information Available in These Sources: SATA 22

MATTE, L'ENC
See Matte, Encarnacion L'Enc

MATTHEW, EUNICE S.
Birthplace: New York, NY
Information Available in These Sources: ABYP 2, ABYP 3

MATTHEWS, ANN
See Martin, Ann M(atthews)

MATTHEWS, ELLEN
Birthdate: 5/2/1950
Birthplace: Greencastle, IN
Information Available in These Sources: SATA 28

MATTHEWS, HERBERT L(IONEL)
Birthdate: 1/10/1900
Birthplace: New York, NY
Deathdate: 7/29/1977
Information Available in These Sources: ABYP 2, ABYP 3

MATTHEWS, JACKLYN MEEK
See Meek, Jacklyn O'Hanlon

MATTHEWS, PATRICIA
(Pat A. Brisco, Patty Brisco, Laura Wylie)
Birthdate: 7/1/1927
Birthplace: San Fernando, CA
Information Available in These Sources: SATA 28

MATTHEWS, WILLIAM HENRY III
Birthdate: 3/1/1919
Birthplace: Henrietta, OK
Information Available in These Sources: ABYP 4, SATA 28, SATA 45

MATTHIAS, CATHERINE
Birthdate: 2/2/1945
Birthplace: Philadelphia, PA
Information Available in These Sources: SATA 41

MATTHIESSEN, PETER
Birthdate: 5/22/1927
Birthplace: New York, NY
Information Available in These Sources: SATA 27

MATULAY, LAZLO
Birthdate: 1912
Birthplace: Vienna, Austria
Information Available in These Sources: IBYP 2, ICB 2, SATA 43

MATULKA, JAN
Birthdate: 11/7/1890
Birthplace: Vlachovo Brezi, Czechoslovakia
Deathdate: 6/25/1972
Information Available in These Sources: ICB 1, SATA 28

MATUS, GRETA
Birthdate: 11/13/1938
Birthplace: New York, NY
Information Available in These Sources: SATA 12

MAULE, HAMILTON BEE
(Tex Maule)
Birthdate: 3/19/1915
Birthplace: Ojus, FL
Information Available in These Sources: ABYP 1, ABYP 3

MAULE, TEX
See Maule, Hamilton Bee

MAUSER, PATRICIA RHOADS
Birthdate: 1/14/1943
Birthplace: Sacramento, CA
Information Available in These Sources: SATA 37

MAUZEY, MERRITT
Birthdate: 9/16/1897 or 9/16/1898
Birthplace: Clifton, TX
Information Available in These Sources: IBYP 2, ICB 2

MAVES, MARY CAROLYN
Birthdate: 4/30/1916
Birthplace: Hooker, OK
Information Available in These Sources: SATA 10

MAVES, PAUL B(ENJAMIN)
Birthdate: 4/21/1913
Birthplace: Burwell, NE
Information Available in These Sources: SATA 10

MAWICKE, TRAN
Birthdate: 9/20/1911
Birthplace: Chicago, IL
Information Available in These Sources: SATA 15

MAX, PETER
Birthdate: 10/19/1939
Birthplace: Berlin, Germany
Information Available in These Sources: IBYP 2, SATA 45

MAXEY, DALE
Birthdate: 3/7/1927
Birthplace: Anderson, IN
Information Available in These Sources: ICB 3

MAXON, ANNE
See Best, Evangel Allena Champlin

MAXWELL, ARTHUR S.
Birthdate: 1/14/1896
Birthplace: London, England
Deathdate: 11/13/1970
Information Available in These Sources: SATA 11

MAXWELL, EDITH (SMITH)
Birthdate: 3/12/1923
Birthplace: Newburgh, NY
Information Available in These Sources: ABYP 4, SATA 7

MAXWELL, WILLIAM
Birthdate: 8/16/1908
Birthplace: Lincoln, IL
Information Available in These Sources: ABYP 1, ABYP 3

MAY, CHARLES PAUL
Birthdate: 11/23/1920
Birthplace: Bedford, IA
Information Available in These Sources: ABYP 1, ABYP 2, ABYP 3, SATA 4

MAY, JULIAN
(John Feilen, Matthew G. Grant, Ian Thorne)
Birthdate: 7/10/1931
Birthplace: Chicago, IL
Information Available in These Sources: ABYP 1, ABYP 3, SATA 11

MAY, ROBERT LEWIS
Birthdate: 7/27/1905
Birthplace: Arverne, NY
Deathdate: 8/11/1976
Information Available in These Sources: SATA 27

MAY, SOPHIE
See Clarke, Rebecca Sophia

MAYBERRY, FLORENCE V(IRGINIA WILSON)
Birthplace: Sleeper, MO
Information Available in These Sources: SATA 10

MAYER, ALBERT IGNATIUS, JR.
Birthdate: 5/25/1906
Birthplace: Columbus, OH
Deathdate: 6/4/1960
Information Available in These Sources: SATA 29

MAYER, ANN M(ARGARET)
Birthdate: 8/5/1938
Birthplace: Schenectady, NY
Information Available in These Sources: SATA 14

MAYER, JANE ROTHSCHILD
(Clare Jaynes)
Birthdate: 12/30/1903
Birthplace: Kansas City, MO
Information Available in These Sources: ABYP 1, ABYP 3, SATA 38

MAYER, MARIANNA
Birthdate: 11/8/1945
Birthplace: Queens, NY
Information Available in These Sources: JBA 4, SATA 32

MAYER, MERCER
Birthdate: 12/30/1943
Birthplace: Little Rock, AR
Information Available in These Sources: DLB 61, IBYP 1, IBYP 2, ICB 4 JBA 4, SATA 16, SATA 32

MAYERSON, CHARLOTTE LEON
Birthplace: New York, NY
Information Available in These Sources: SATA 36

MAYERSON, EVELYN WHITE
Birthdate: 1/12/1935
Birthplace: New York, NY
Information Available in These Sources: SATA 55

MAYHAR, ARDATH
(Ravenna Cannon)
Birthdate: 2/20/1930
Birthplace: Timpson, TX
Information Available in These Sources: SATA 38

MAYNARD, OLGA
Birthdate: 1/16/1920
Birthplace: Belem, Brazil
Information Available in These Sources: SATA 40

MAYNES, DR. J. O. ROCKY
See Maynes, J. Oscar, Jr.

MAYNES, J. O. ROCKY
See Maynes, J. Oscar, Jr.

MAYNES, J. OSCAR, JR.
(Dr. J. O. Rocky Maynes, J. O. Rocky Maynes, Jr.)
Birthdate: 5/7/1929
Birthplace: El Paso, TX
Information Available in These Sources: SATA 38

MAYS, LEWIS VICTOR, JR.
(Victor Mays)
Birthdate: 7/2/1927
Birthplace: New York, NY
Information Available in These Sources: IBYP 2, JBA 4, ICB 2, ICB 3, SATA 5

MAYS, LUCINDA L(A BELLA)
Birthdate: 6/16/1924
Birthplace: Latrobe, PA
Information Available in These Sources: SATA 49

MAYS, VICTOR
See Mays, Lewis Victor, Jr.

MAZER, HARRY
Birthdate: 5/31/1925
Birthplace: New York, NY
Information Available in These Sources: JBA 5, SATA 31

MAZER, NORMA FOX
Birthdate: 5/15/1931
Birthplace: New York, NY
Information Available in These Sources: DACF, JBA 5, SATA 24, TCCW 3

MCALLISTER, MARIANA KENNEDY
Birthdate: 10/2/1910
Birthplace: Cincinnati, OH
Information Available in These Sources: ABYP 2, ABYP 3

MCBAIN, ED
See Hunter, Evan

MCBRIDE, MARY MARGARET
Birthdate: 11/16/1899
Birthplace: Paris, MO
Deathdate: 4/7/1976
Information Available in These Sources: ABYP 4

MCCAFFERY, JANET
Birthdate: 12/8/1936
Birthplace: Philadelphia, PA
Information Available in These Sources: IBYP 1, IBYP 2, ICB 4, SATA 38

MCCAFFREY, ANNE (INEZ)
Birthdate: 4/1/1926
Birthplace: Cambridge, MA
Information Available in These Sources: DACF, JBA 5, SATA 8, TCCW 3

MCCAHILL, WILLIAM P.
Birthdate: 6/29/1916
Birthplace: Marshalltown, IA
Information Available in These Sources: ABYP 1, ABYP 3

MCCAIN, MURRAY (DAVID, JR.)
Birthdate: 12/28/1926
Birthplace: Newport, NC
Deathdate: 11/19/1981
Information Available in These Sources: SATA 7, SATA 29

MCCALL, EDITH S(ANSUM)
Birthdate: 9/5/1911
Birthplace: Charles City, IA
Information Available in These Sources: SATA 6

MCCALL, VIRGINIA NIELSEN
(Virginia Nielsen)
Birthdate: 6/14/1909
Birthplace: Idaho Falls, ID
Information Available in These Sources: ABYP 4, SATA 13

MCCALLUM, PHYLLIS
Birthdate: 4/5/1911
Birthplace: Pacific Grove, CA
Information Available in These Sources: SATA 10

MCCANN, GERALD
Birthdate: 1916
Birthplace: Brooklyn, NY
Information Available in These Sources: IBYP 2, ICB 2, SATA 41

MCCANNON, DINDGA FATIMA
Birthdate: 1947
Birthplace: Harlem, NY
Information Available in These Sources: BAI, SATA 41

MCCARTER, NEELY DIXON
Birthdate: 10/4/1929
Birthplace: Gastonia, NC
Information Available in These Sources: SATA 47

MCCARTHY, AGNES
Birthdate: 6/20/1933
Birthplace: New York, NY
Information Available in These Sources: SATA 4

MCCARTY, REGA KRAMER
Birthdate: 1/8/1904
Birthplace: Batavia, IA
Information Available in These Sources: SATA 10

MCCASLIN, NELLIE
Birthdate: 8/20/1914
Birthplace: Cleveland, OH
Information Available in These Sources: SATA 12

MCCAY, WINSOR
(Silas)
Birthdate: 9/26/1871 or 9/26/1869
Birthplace: Spring Lake, MI
Deathdate: 7/26/1934
Information Available in These Sources: DLB 22, SATA 41

MCCLAIN, GEORGE
Birthdate, 1938?
Information Available in These Sources: IBYP 2

MCCLARY, JANE STEVENSON
(Jane (Stevenson) McIlvaine)
Birthdate: 2/19/1919
Birthplace: Pittsburgh, PA
Information Available in These Sources: ABYP 1, ABYP 3

MCCLINTOCK, BARBARA
Birthdate: 5/6/1955
Birthplace: Flemington, NJ
Information Available in These Sources: SATA 57

MCCLINTOCK, MARSHALL
(Gregory Duncan, Douglas Marshall, Mike McClintock, William Starret)
Birthdate: 8/21/1906
Birthplace: Topeka, KS
Information Available in These Sources: ABYP 1, ABYP 3, SATA 3

MCCLINTOCK, MIKE
See McClintock, Marshall

MCCLINTOCK, THEODORE
Birthdate: 1902
Deathdate: 11/21/1971
Information Available in These Sources: ABYP 2, ABYP 3, SATA 14

MCCLINTON, LEON
Birthdate: 1/29/1933
Birthplace: Des Moines, IA
Information Available in These Sources: SATA 11

MCCLOSKEY, JOHN ROBERT
(Balfour Dangerfield, Robert McCloskey)
Birthdate: 9/15/1914
Birthplace: Hamilton, OH
Information Available in These Sources: ABYP 1, ABYP 3, AICB, BABP, DLB 22, IBYP 1, IBYP 2, ICB 1 ICB 2, ICB 3, ICB 4, JBA 2, SATA 2, SATA 39, SVC 2, SVC 3, TCCW 1, TCCW 2, TCCW 3

MCCLOSKEY, ROBERT
See McCloskey, John Robert

MCCLOY, JAMES F(LOYD)
Birthdate: 2/13/1941
Birthplace: Collingswood, NJ
Information Available in These Sources: SATA 59

MCCLUNG, ROBERT MARSHALL
Birthdate: 9/10/1916
Birthplace: Butler, PA
Information Available in These Sources: ABYP 1, ABYP 3, ICB 3, ICB 4, MJA, SATA 2

MCCORD, DAVID (THOMPSON WATSON)
Birthdate: 11/15/1897
Birthplace: New York, NY
Information Available in These Sources: BABP, DLB 61, JBA 3, SATA 18, SVC 2, SVC 3, TCCW 1, TCCW 2, TCCW 3

MCCORD, JEAN
Birthdate: 3/21/1924
Birthplace: Hayward, WI
Information Available in These Sources: SATA 34

MCCORMICK, ALMA HEFLIN
Birthdate: 9/2/1910
Birthplace: Winona, MO
Information Available in These Sources: ABYP 1, ABYP 3

MCCORMICK, BILL
Information Available in These Sources: ABYP 4

MCCORMICK, BROOKS
See Adams, William Taylor

MCCORMICK, DELL J.
Birthdate: 1892
Deathdate: 1949
Information Available in These Sources: SATA 19

MCCORMICK, EDITH (JOAN)
Birthdate: 8/18/1934
Birthplace: Chicago, IL
Information Available in These Sources: SATA 30

MCCORMICK, WILFRED
(Rand Allison, Lon Dunlap)
Birthdate: 2/8/1903
Birthplace: Newland, IN
Information Available in These Sources: ABYP 1, ABYP 3

MCCOY, IOLA FULLER
(Iola Fuller)
Birthdate: 1906
Birthplace: Marcellus, MI
Information Available in These Sources: SATA 3

MCCOY, J(OSEPH) J(EROME)
Birthdate: 1/4/1917
Birthplace: Philadelphia, PA
Information Available in These Sources: ABYP 2, ABYP 3, SATA 8

MCCOY, LOIS (RICH)
Birthdate: 7/5/1941
Birthplace: Newark, NJ
Information Available in These Sources: SATA 38

MCCRACKEN, HAROLD
Birthdate: 8/31/1894
Birthplace: Colorado Springs, CO
Information Available in These Sources: ABYP 1, ABYP 3, JBA 2

MCCRADY, LADY
Birthdate: 10/13/1951
Birthplace: Indianapolis, IN
Information Available in These Sources: SATA 16

MCCREA, JAMES (CRAIG, JR.)
Birthdate: 9/12/1920
Birthplace: Peoria, IL
Information Available in These Sources: ICB 3, SATA 3

MCCREA, MARY
Information Available in These Sources: ABYP 4

MCCREA, RUTH (PIRMAN)
Birthdate: 5/28/1921
Birthplace: Jersey City, NJ
Information Available in These Sources: ICB 3, SATA 3

MCCUE, LILLIAN BUENO
(Lillian De La Torre, Lillian De La Torre-Bueno)
Birthdate: 3/15/1902
Birthplace: New York, NY
Information Available in These Sources: ABYP 1, ABYP 3

MCCULLERS, CARSON
See McCullers, Lula Carson

MCCULLERS, LULA CARSON
(Carson McCullers)
Birthdate: 2/19/1917
Birthplace: Columbus, GA
Deathdate: 9/29/1967
Information Available in These Sources: SATA 27

MCCULLOUGH, FRANCES MONSON
Birthdate: 10/23/1938
Birthplace: Quantico, VA
Information Available in These Sources: SATA 8

MCCULLY, EMILY ARNOLD
(Emily Arnold)
Birthdate: 7/1/1939
Birthplace: Galesburg, IL
Information Available in These Sources: IBYP 1, IBYP 2, ICB 3, ICB 4, JBA 4, SATA 5, SATA 50

MCCUNE, DAN
See Haas, Dorothy F.

MCCURDY, MICHAEL
Birthdate: 2/17/1942
Birthplace: New York, NY
Information Available in These Sources: SATA 13

MCDANIEL, J. W.
Information Available in These Sources: IBYP 2

MCDEARMON, KAY
Birthplace: San Francisco, CA
Information Available in These Sources: ABYP 4, SATA 20

MCDERMOTT, BEVERLY BRODSKY
(Beverly Brodsky)
Birthdate: 8/16/1941
Birthplace: Brooklyn, NY
Information Available in These Sources: ABYP 4, ICB 4, JBA 5, SATA 11

MCDERMOTT, GERALD
Birthdate: 1/31/1941
Birthplace: Detroit, MI
Information Available in These Sources: IBYP 2, ICB 4, JBA 5, SATA 16

MCDOLE, CAROL
See Farley, Carol (J. McDole)

MCDONALD, BARBARA GUTHRIE
Birthplace: Brooklyn, NY
Information Available in These Sources: ABYP 2, ABYP 3

MCDONALD, FORREST
Birthdate: 1/7/1927
Birthplace: Orange, TX
Information Available in These Sources: ABYP 4

MCDONALD, GERALD D(OAN)
Birthdate: 6/5/1905
Birthplace: Wilmington, OH
Deathdate: 5/6/1970
Information Available in These Sources: SATA 3

MCDONALD, JAMIE
See Heide, Florence Parry

MCDONALD, LUCILE SAUNDERS
Birthdate: 9/1/1898
Birthplace: Portland, OR
Information Available in These Sources: ABYP 1, ABYP 3, SATA 10

MCDONALD, RALPH J.
Information Available in These Sources: IBYP 2

MCDONNELL, CHRISTINE
Birthdate: 7/3/1949
Birthplace: Southampton, NY
Information Available in These Sources: SATA 34, JBA 6

MCDONNELL, JINNY
See McDonnell, Virginia (Bleecker)

MCDONNELL, LOIS EDDY
Birthdate: 6/20/1914
Birthplace: State College, PA
Information Available in These Sources: SATA 10

MCDONNELL, VIRGINIA (BLEECKER)
(Jean Kirby, Jinny McDonnell)
Birthdate: 11/24/1917
Birthplace: Short Hills, NJ
Information Available in These Sources: ABYP 4

MCELROY, CLIFFORD D., JR.
Birthplace: New York, NY
Information Available in These Sources: ABYP 4

MCENTEE, DOROTHY (LAYNG)
Birthdate: 9/21/1902
Birthplace: Brooklyn, NY
Information Available in These Sources: IBYP 2, ICB 2, SATA 37

MCENTEE, HOWARD GARRETT
Birthdate: 1905
Information Available in These Sources: ABYP 4

MCFADDEN, DOROTHY LOA (MAUSOLFF)
Birthdate: 6/11/1902
Birthplace: Frankfurt, Germany
Information Available in These Sources: ABYP 2, ABYP 3

MCFALL, CHRISTIE
Birthdate: 7/5/1918
Birthplace: Cincinnati, OH
Information Available in These Sources: SATA 12

MCFARLAND, KENTON D(EAN)
Birthdate: 10/11/1920
Birthplace: Branson, MO
Information Available in These Sources: ABYP 4, SATA 11

MCFARLAND, WILMA
Birthdate: 1/5/1890
Birthplace: Estherville, IA
Information Available in These Sources: ABYP 2, ABYP 3

MCGAVRAN, GRACE WINIFRED
Birthplace: India
Information Available in These Sources: ABYP 1, ABYP 3

MCGAW, JESSIE BREWER
Birthdate: 10/17/1913
Birthplace: Clarksville, TN
Information Available in These Sources: ICB 3, SATA 10

MCGEE, BARBARA
Birthdate: 2/1/1943
Birthplace: Greenbelt, MD
Information Available in These Sources: SATA 6

MCGEE, DOROTHY HORTON
Birthdate: 11/30/1913
Birthplace: West Point, NY
Information Available in These Sources: ABYP 1, ABYP 3

MCGIFFIN, LEE
See McGiffin, Lewis Lee Shaffer

MCGIFFIN, LEWIS LEE SHAFFER
(Lee McGiffin)
Birthdate: 10/1/1908
Birthplace: Delphi, IN
Information Available in These Sources: ABYP 4, SATA 1

MCGILL, MARCI
See Ridlon, Marci

MCGILLICUDDY, MR.
See Abisch, Roslyn Kroop

MCGINLEY, PHYLLIS (LOUISE)
Birthdate: 3/21/1905
Birthplace: Ontario, OR
Deathdate: 2/22/1978
Information Available in These Sources: ABYP 1, ABYP 3, BABP, JBA 2, SATA 2, SATA 24, SATA 44, TCCW 1, TCCW 2, TCCW 3

MCGINNIS, LILA S(PRAGUE)
Birthdate: 5/29/1924
Birthplace: Ashtabula Harbor, OH
Information Available in These Sources: SATA 44

MCGORWVEN, THOMAS E.
(Tom McGorwven)
Birthdate: 5/6/1927
Birthplace: Evanston, IL
Information Available in These Sources: ABYP 4, SATA 2

MCGORWVEN, TOM
See McGorwven, Thomas E.

MCGOUGH, ELIZABETH (HEMMES)
Birthdate: 11/15/1934
Birthplace: Oakmont, PA
Information Available in These Sources: SATA 33

MCGOVERN, ANN
(Ann McGovern Scheiner)
Birthplace: New York, NY
Information Available in These Sources: ABYP 1, ABYP 3, BABP, JBA 4, SATA 8

MCGRADY, MIKE
Birthdate: 10/4/1933
Birthplace: New York, NY
Information Available in These Sources: SATA 6

MCGRATH, THOMAS
Birthdate: 11/20/1916
Birthplace: Sheldon, ND
Information Available in These Sources: SATA 41

MCGRAW, ELOISE JARVIS
Birthdate: 12/9/1915
Birthplace: Houston, TX
Information Available in These Sources: ABYP 1, ABYP 3, DACF, MJA, SATA 1, TCCW 1, TCCW 2, TCCW 3

MCGRAW, WILLIAM CORBIN
(William Corbin)
Birthdate: 1/22/1916
Birthplace: Des Moines, IA
Information Available in These Sources: ABYP 2, ABYP 3, DACF, SATA 3

MCGUFFEY, ALEXANDER HAMILTON
Birthdate: 8/13/1816
Birthplace: Youngstown, OH
Deathdate: 6/3/1896
Information Available in These Sources: SATA 60

MCGUFFEY, WILLIAM HOLMES
Birthdate: 9/23/1800
Birthplace: Washington, PA
Deathdate: 5/4/1873
Information Available in These Sources: DLB 42, SATA 60

MCGUIRE, EDNA
(Edna McGuire Boyd)
Birthdate: 8/31/1899
Birthplace: Sweet Springs, MO
Information Available in These Sources: ABYP 2, ABYP 3, SATA 13

MCGUIRE, FRANCES (LYNCH)
Birthdate: 1869
Birthplace: Crawfordsville, IN
Deathdate: 1947
Information Available in These Sources: ABYP 1, ABYP 3

MCGUIRE, LESLIE (SARAH)
(Louisa Britton, Leslie Burton, Dorothy Eyre, Sarah Keyser, Sarah Leslie, Shari Robinson, David Strong)
Birthdate: 1/18/1945
Birthplace: New York, NY
Information Available in These Sources: SATA 45

MCGURK, SLATER
See Roth, Arthur J(oseph)

MCHARGUE, GEORGESS
(Alice (Elizabeth) Chase, Margo Scegge Usher)
Birthdate: 6/7/1941
Birthplace: Norwalk, CT
Information Available in These Sources: ABYP 4, JBA 5, SATA 4

MCHUGH, BERIT ELISABET
(Elisabet McHugh)
Birthdate: 1/26/1941
Birthplace: Stoede, Sweden
Information Available in These Sources: SATA 44, 55

MCHUGH, ELISABET
See McHugh, Berit Elisabet

MCILHANY, STERLING (FISHER)
Birthdate: 4/12/1930
Birthplace: San Gabriel, CA
Information Available in These Sources: ABYP 4

MCILVAINE, JANE (STEVENSON)
See McClary, Jane Stevenson

MCINERNEY, JUDITH W(HITELOCK)
Birthdate: 6/1/1945
Birthplace: Chicago, IL
Information Available in These Sources: SATA 46, SATA 49

MCINTOSH, FRANK
Birthdate: 1901
Birthplace: Portland, OR
Information Available in These Sources: ICB 1

MCINTYRE, KEVIN
Birthplace: New York, NY
Information Available in These Sources: IBYP 1 IBYP 2

MCKAY, DONALD
Birthdate: 1895
Birthplace: San Francisco, CA
Information Available in These Sources: ICB 2, SATA 45

MCKAY, ROBERT W.
Birthdate: 6/4/1921
Birthplace: Mayville, NY
Information Available in These Sources: ABYP 4, SATA 15

MCKEEVER, MARCIA
See Laird, Jean E(louise)

MCKELVEY, GERTRUDE DELLA
Birthdate: 1904
Information Available in These Sources: ABYP 1, ABYP 3

MCKENNY, MARGARET
Birthplace: Olympia, WA
Information Available in These Sources: ABYP 1, ABYP 3

MCKENZIE, DOROTHY CLAYTON
Birthdate: 11/2/1910
Birthplace: Garden City, KS
Deathdate: 10/??/1981
Information Available in These Sources: SATA 28

MCKILLIP, PATRICIA A(NNE)
Birthdate: 2/29/1948
Birthplace: Salem, OR
Information Available in These Sources: ABYP 4, JBA 5, SATA 30, TCCW 3

MCKINLEY, JENNIFER CAROLYN ROBIN
(Robin McKinley)
Birthdate: 11/16/1952
Birthplace: Warren, OH
Information Available in These Sources: DACF, JBA 5, SATA 32, TCCW 3

MCKINLEY, ROBIN
See McKinley, Jennifer Carolyn Robin

MCKINNEY, ROLAND JOSEPH
Birthdate: 11/4/1898
Birthplace: Niagara Falls, NY
Information Available in These Sources: ABYP 1, ABYP 3

MCKISSACK, FREDRICK L(EMUEL)
Birthdate: 8/12/1939
Birthplace: Nashville, TN
Information Available in These Sources: SATA 53

MCKISSACK, PATRICIA (L'ANN) C(ARWELL)
(L'Ann Carwell)
Birthdate: 8/9/1944
Birthplace: Nashville, TN
Information Available in These Sources: SATA 51

MCKOWN, ROBIN
Birthdate: 1906
Birthplace: Denver, CO
Information Available in These Sources: ABYP 1, ABYP 3, DACF, JBA 3, SATA 6

MCLACHLIN, STEVE
Information Available in These Sources: IBYP 1, IBYP 2

MCLANATHAN, RICHARD BARTON KENNEDY
Birthdate: 3/12/1916
Birthplace: Methuen, MA
Information Available in These Sources: ABYP 4

MCLAURIN, ANNE
(Anne Laurin)
Birthdate: 9/29/1953
Birthplace: St. Louis, MO
Information Available in These Sources: SATA 27

MCLEAN, KATHRYN (ANDERSON)
(Kathryn Forbes)
Birthdate: 3/10/1909
Birthplace: San Francisco, CA
Information Available in These Sources: SATA 9

MCLENIGHAN, VALJEAN
Birthdate: 12/28/1947
Birthplace: Chicago, IL
Information Available in These Sources: SATA 40, SATA 46

MCLEOD, EMILIE WARREN
Birthdate: 12/2/1926
Birthplace: Boston, MA
Deathdate: 10/2/1982
Information Available in These Sources: SATA 23, SATA 31

MCLEOD, MARGARET VAIL
See Holloway, Teresa (Bragunier)

MCLOUGHLIN, JOHN C.
Birthdate: 2/8/1949
Birthplace: Rye, NY
Information Available in These Sources: SATA 47

MCMAHAN, IAN
Information Available in These Sources: SATA 45

MCMANUS, PATRICK (FRANCIS)
Birthdate: 8/26/1933
Birthplace: Sandpoint, ID
Information Available in These Sources: SATA 46

MCMEEKIN, CLARK
See McMeekin, Isabel (McLennan)

MCMEEKIN, ISABEL (McLENNAN)
(Clark McMeekin)
Birthdate: 11/19/1895
Birthplace: Louisville, KY
Information Available in These Sources: ABYP 1, ABYP 3, MJA, SATA 3

MCMILLAN, BRUCE
Birthdate: 5/10/1947
Birthplace: Boston, MA
Information Available in These Sources: SATA 22, JBA 6

MCMILLEN, WHEELER
Birthdate: 1/27/1893
Birthplace: Ada, OH
Information Available in These Sources: ABYP 1, ABYP 3

MCMULLAN, JAMES
Birthdate: 6/14/1934
Birthplace: Tsintao, China
Information Available in These Sources: IBYP 1, IBYP 2, ICB 3

MCMULLAN, KATE (HALL)
(Katy Hall)
Birthdate: 1/16/1947
Birthplace: St. Louis, MO
Information Available in These Sources: SATA 48, SATA 52

MCMURTREY, MARTIN A(LOYSIUS)
Birthdate: 4/16/1921
Birthplace: East St. Louis, IL
Information Available in These Sources: SATA 21

MCNAIR, KATE (MALLORY)
Birthdate: 1911
Birthplace: IL
Information Available in These Sources: ABYP 4, SATA 3

MCNALLY, E. EVALYN (GRUMBINE)
See Grumbine, E. Evalyn

MCNAMARA, LOUISE (GREEP)
Birthplace: Boston, MA
Information Available in These Sources: ABYP 4

MCNAMARA, MARGARET (CRAIG)
Birthdate: 8/22/1915
Birthplace: Seattle, WA
Deathdate: 2/3/1981
Information Available in These Sources: SATA 24

MCNAMEE, JAMES
Birthdate: 2/26/1904
Birthplace: Port Townsend, WA
Information Available in These Sources: ABYP 2, ABYP 3

MCNAUGHT, HARRY
Birthdate: 1923
Birthplace: Scotland
Information Available in These Sources: IBYP 1, IBYP 2, SATA 32

MCNEELY, JEANNETTE
(Maron Mackie)
Birthdate: 12/12/1918
Birthplace: San Francisco, CA
Information Available in These Sources: SATA 25

MCNEELY, MARIAN HURD
Birthdate: 7/26/1877
Birthplace: Dubuque, IA
Deathdate: 12/18/1930
Information Available in These Sources: JBA 1, JBA 2

MCNEER, MAY YONGE
(Mary McNeer Ward)
Birthdate: 1902
Birthplace: Tampa, FL
Information Available in These Sources: ABYP 1, ABYP 3, AICB, BABP, FLTYP, JBA 1, JBA 2, SATA 1, SVC 2, SVC 3

MCNICKLE, D'ARCY
See McNickle, William D'Arcy

MCNICKLE, WILLIAM D'ARCY
Birthdate: 1/18/1904
Birthplace: St. Ignatius, MT
Deathdate: 12/??/1977
Information Available in These Sources: SATA 22

MCNULTY, FAITH
Birthdate: 11/28/1918
Birthplace: New York, NY
Information Available in These Sources: SATA 12

MCPHAIL, DAVID M(ICHAEL)
Birthdate: 6/30/1940
Birthplace: Newburyport, MA
Information Available in These Sources: ABYP 4, ICB 4, JBA 5, SATA 32 SATA 47

MCPHARLIN, PAUL
Birthdate: 12/22/1903
Birthplace: Detroit, MI
Deathdate: 9/28/1948
Information Available in These Sources: SATA 31

MCPHEE, RICHARD BYRON
Birthdate: 11/29/1934
Birthplace: New Rochelle, NY
Information Available in These Sources: SATA 41

MCPHERSON, JAMES M.
Birthdate: 10/11/1936
Birthplace: Valley City, ND
Information Available in These Sources: SATA 16

MCQUEEN, LUCINDA (EMILY)
Birthdate: 3/8/1950
Birthplace: Springfield, MA
Information Available in These Sources: SATA 48, SATA 58

MCQUEEN, MILDRED HARK
(Mildred Hark)
Birthdate: 10/19/1908
Birthplace: LaMoure, ND
Information Available in These Sources: SATA 12

MCSHEAN, GORDON
Birthdate: 10/7/1936
Birthplace: Glasgow, Scotland
Information Available in These Sources: SATA 41

MCSWIGAN, MARIE
Birthdate: 5/22/1907
Birthplace: Pittsburgh, PA
Deathdate: 7/16/1962
Information Available in These Sources: ABYP 1, ABYP 3, MJA, SATA 24

MCVICKER, CHARLES (TAGGART)
(Chuck McVicker)
Birthdate: 8/31/1930
Birthplace: Canonsburg, PA
Information Available in These Sources: SATA 39

MCVICKER, CHUCK
See McVicker, Charles (Taggart)

MCWEBB, ELIZABETH UPHAM
(Elizabeth Norine Upham)
Birthdate: 1904
Birthplace: MI
Information Available in These Sources: SVC 2, SVC 3

MEAD, MARGARET
Birthdate: 12/16/1901
Birthplace: Philadelphia, PA
Deathdate: 11/15/1978
Information Available in These Sources: ABYP 1, ABYP 3, SATA 20

MEAD, RUSSELL (M., JR.)
Birthdate: 1/1/1935
Birthplace: Pueblo, CO
Information Available in These Sources: SATA 10

MEAD, STELLA
Deathdate: 3/30/1981
Information Available in These Sources: SATA 27

MEADE, ELLEN (RODDICK)
Birthdate: 2/13/1936
Birthplace: Bronxville, NY
Information Available in These Sources: SATA 5

MEADE, MARION
Birthdate: 1/7/1934
Birthplace: Pittsburgh, PA
Information Available in These Sources: SATA 23

MEADER, STEPHEN W(ARREN)
Birthdate: 5/2/1892
Birthplace: Providence, RI
Deathdate: 7/18/1977
Information Available in These Sources: ABYP 1, ABYP 3, JBA 1, JBA 2, SATA 1, TCCW 1, TCCW 2, TCCW 3

MEADOW, CHARLES (TROUB)
Birthdate: 12/16/1929
Birthplace: Paterson, NJ
Information Available in These Sources: ABYP 4, SATA 23

MEADOWCROFT, ENID (LAMONTE)
(Enid Meadowcroft (LaMont) Wright)
Birthdate: 3/31/1898
Birthplace: New York, NY
Deathdate: 11/23/1966
Information Available in These Sources: ABYP 1, ABYP 3, JBA 2, SATA 3

MEAKER, M. J.
See Meaker, Marijane

MEAKER, MARIJANE
(M. J. Meaker, Ann Aldrich, M. E. Kerr, Vin Packer, Marijane Meaker Kerr)
Birthdate: 5/27/1927 or 5/27/1932
Birthplace: Auburn, NY
Information Available in These Sources: ABYP 4, DACF, JBA 4, SATA 20, TCCW 1, TCCW 2, TCCW 3

MEANS, ELLIOTT
Birthdate: 3/10/1905 or 3/10/1904
Birthplace: Stamford, TX
Information Available in These Sources: IBYP 2

MEANS, FLORENCE CRANNELL
Birthdate: 5/15/1891
Birthplace: Baldwinsville, NY
Deathdate: 11/19/1980
Information Available in These Sources: ABYP 1, ABYP 3, JBA 1, JBA 2, SATA 1, SATA 25, TCCW 1, TCCW 2, TCCW 3

MEARIAN, JUDY FRANK
Birthdate: 11/26/1936
Birthplace: Cincinnati, OH
Information Available in These Sources: SATA 49

MEDARY, MARJORIE
Birthdate: 7/24/1890
Birthplace: Waukon, IA
Information Available in These Sources: JBA 2, SATA 14

MEDDAUGH, SUSAN
Birthdate: 10/4/1944
Birthplace: Montclair, NJ
Information Available in These Sources: SATA 29

MEDEARIS, MARY
Birthdate: 5/31/1915
Birthplace: Little Rock, AR
Information Available in These Sources: SATA 5

MEE, CHARLES L., JR.
Birthdate: 9/15/1938
Birthplace: Evanston, IL
Information Available in These Sources: SATA 8

MEEK, JACKLYN O'HANLON
(Jacklyn Meek Matthews, Jacklyn O'Hanlon)
Birthdate: 12/5/1933
Birthplace: CA
Information Available in These Sources: SATA 34, SATA 51

MEEK, S(TERNER ST.) P(AUL)
Birthdate: 4/8/1894
Birthplace: Chicago, IL
Deathdate: 6/10/1972
Information Available in These Sources: SATA 28

MEEKER, ODEN
Birthdate: 1919 or 1918
Deathdate: 1/19/1976
Information Available in These Sources: ABYP 2, ABYP 3, SATA 14

MEEKS, ESTHER K. (MACBAIN)
Birthdate: 1909
Birthplace: Council Bluffs, IA
Information Available in These Sources: ABYP 1, ABYP 3, SATA 1

MEHDEVI, ALEXANDER (SINCLAIR)
Birthdate: 6/9/1947
Birthplace: Mazatlan, Mexico
Information Available in These Sources: SATA 7

MEHDEVI, ANNE (MARIE) SINCLAIR
Birthdate: 1922 or 1918
Birthplace: Manila, Philippines
Information Available in These Sources: ABYP 2, ABYP 3, JBA 4, SATA 8

MEIER, MINTA
Birthdate: 5/26/1906
Birthplace: Dayton, WA
Information Available in These Sources: SATA 55

MEIGHAN, DONALD CHARLES
(Donald Charles)
Birthdate: 3/15/1929
Birthplace: San Francisco, CA
Information Available in These Sources: IBYP 2, SATA 30

MEIGS, CORNELIA LYNDE
(Adair Aldon)
Birthdate: 12/6/1884
Birthplace: Rock Island, IL
Deathdate: 9/10/1973
Information Available in These Sources: ABYP 1, ABYP 3, JBA 1, JBA 2, SATA 6, SVC 2, SVC 3, TCCW 1, TCCW 2, TCCW 3, WC

MEIGS, ELIZABETH BLEECKER
Birthdate: 1923
Information Available in These Sources: ABYP 1, ABYP 3

MEILACH, DONA Z(WEIGORON)
(Sue Stanli)
Birthdate: 8/26/1926
Birthplace: Chicago, IL
Information Available in These Sources: ABYP 4, SATA 34

MELBO, IRVING ROBERT
Birthdate: 6/20/1908
Birthplace: Gully, MN
Information Available in These Sources: ABYP 2, ABYP 3

MELCHER, DANIEL
Birthdate: 7/10/1912
Birthplace: Newton Center, MA
Deathdate: 7/22/1985
Information Available in These Sources: SATA 43

MELCHER, FREDERIC GERSHOM
Birthdate: 4/12/1879
Birthplace: Malden, MA
Deathdate: 3/9/1963
Information Available in These Sources: SATA 22

MELCHER, MARGUERITE FELLOWS
Birthdate: 9/2/1879
Birthplace: Boston, MA
Deathdate: 1969
Information Available in These Sources: SATA 10

MELE, FRANK M(ICHAEL)
Birthdate: 8/15/1935
Birthplace: Englewood, NJ
Information Available in These Sources: ABYP 4

MELIN, GRACE HATHAWAY
Birthdate: 2/19/1892
Birthplace: Columbus, OH
Deathdate: 12/1/1973
Information Available in These Sources: SATA 10

MELLIN, JEANNE
(Jean Mellin Herrick)
Birthdate: 2/3/1929
Birthplace: Stamford, CT
Information Available in These Sources: ABYP 1, ABYP 3

MELLOR, WILLIAM BANCROFT
Birthdate: 3/31/1906
Birthplace: Philadelphia, PA
Information Available in These Sources: ABYP 4

MELTON, DAVID
Birthdate: 4/10/1934
Birthplace: Springfield, MO
Information Available in These Sources: ABYP 4

MELTZER, MILTON
Birthdate: 5/8/1915
Birthplace: Worcester, MA
Information Available in These Sources: ABYP 4, DLB 61, JBA 3, MBMP, SATA 1, SATA 50

MELVILLE, HERMAN
Birthdate: 8/1/1819
Birthplace: New York, NY
Deathdate: 8/28/1891
Information Available in These Sources: SATA 59

MEMLING, CARL
Birthdate: 1/18/1918
Birthplace: New York, NY
Deathdate: 10/16/1969
Information Available in These Sources: ABYP 1, ABYP 3, SATA 6

MENDEL, JO
See Bond, Gladys Baker

MENDONCA, SUSAN
See Smith, Susan Vernon

MENDOZA, GEORGE
Birthdate: 6/2/1934
Birthplace: New York, NY
Information Available in These Sources: ABYP 4, JBA 3, SATA 39, SATA 41

MENG, HEINZ (KARL)
Birthdate: 2/25/1924
Birthplace: Baden, Germany
Information Available in These Sources: SATA 13

MENOTTI, GIAN CARLO
Birthdate: 7/7/1911
Birthplace: Cadegliano, Italy
Information Available in These Sources: ABYP 4, SATA 29

MENUHIN, YEHUDI
Birthdate: 4/22/1916
Birthplace: New York, NY
Information Available in These Sources: SATA 40

MERCER, CHARLES (EDWARD)
Birthdate: 7/12/1917
Birthplace: Stouffville, Ontario, Canada
Information Available in These Sources: ABYP 4, SATA 16

MERCER, JESSIE
(Terry Shannon, Jessie Mercer Knechtel Payzant)
Birthplace: Bellingham, WA
Information Available in These Sources: ABYP 1, ABYP 2, SATA 21

MEREDITH, DAVID WILLIAM
See Miers, Earl Schenck

MEREDITH, NICOLETE
See Stack, Nicolete Meredith

MERINGOFF, LAURENE KRASNY
See Brown, Laurene Krasny

MERIWETHER, LOUISE
Birthdate: 5/8/1923
Birthplace: Haverstraw, NY
Information Available in These Sources: BAI, SATA 31, SATA 52

MERKLING, ERICA
Birthplace: Vienna, Austria
Information Available in These Sources: IBYP 2

MERRIAM, EVE
Birthdate: 7/19/1916
Birthplace: Philadelphia, PA
Information Available in These Sources: ABYP 2, ABYP 3, BABP, DLB 61, JBA 3, SATA 3, SATA 40, TCCW 1TCCW 2, TCCW 3

MERRILL, JANE
(Janie Filstrup, Jane Merrill Filstrup, Phil Merrill)
Birthdate: 10/26/1946
Birthplace: Oakland, CA
Information Available in These Sources: SATA 42

MERRILL, JEAN (FAIRBANKS)
Birthdate: 1/27/1923
Birthplace: Rochester, NY
Information Available in These Sources: ABYP 1, ABYP 3, DACF, JBA 3, MBMP, SATA 1, TCCW 1, TCCW 2, TCCW 3

MERRILL, PHIL
See Merrill, Jane

MERTINS, LOUIS
See Mertins, Marshall Louis

MERTINS, MARSHALL LOUIS
(Louis Mertins)
Birthdate: 12/7/1885
Birthplace: Jackson County, MO
Deathdate: 1/17/1973
Information Available in These Sources: SVC 2, SVC 3

MERTZ, BARBARA (GROSS)
(Barbara Michaels, Elizabeth Peters)
Birthdate: 9/29/1927
Birthplace: Canton, IL
Information Available in These Sources: SATA 49

MERWIN, DECIE
Birthdate: 10/20/1894
Birthplace: Middleboro, KY
Deathdate: 9/6/1961
Information Available in These Sources: IBYP 1, IBYP 2, ICB 2, SATA 32

MESSICK, DALE
Birthdate: 1906
Birthplace: South Bend, IN
Information Available in These Sources: SATA 48

MESSMER, OTTO
Birthdate: 1892 or 1894
Birthplace: West Hoboken, NJ
Deathdate: 10/28/1983
Information Available in These Sources: SATA 37

METCALF, SUZANNE
See Baum, L(yman) Frank

METCALFE, JUNE M.
Birthplace: Saskatchewan, Canada
Information Available in These Sources: ABYP 1, ABYP 3

METOS, THOMAS H(ARRY)
Birthdate: 6/14/1932
Birthplace: Salt Lake City, UT
Information Available in These Sources: SATA 37

METTER, BERT(RAM MILTON)
Birthdate: 8/14/1927
Birthplace: New York, NY
Information Available in These Sources: SATA 56

MEYER, CAROLYN (MAE)
Birthdate: 6/8/1935
Birthplace: Lewistown, PA
Information Available in These Sources: ABYP 4, JBA 5, SATA 9

MEYER, EDITH PATTERSON
Birthdate: 6/2/1895
Birthplace: Chatham, MA
Information Available in These Sources: ABYP 2, ABYP 3, DACF, SATA 5

MEYER, F(RANKLYN) E(DWARD)
Birthdate: 2/9/1932
Birthplace: St. Louis, MO
Information Available in These Sources: ABYP 1, ABYP 3, SATA 9

MEYER, GERARD PREVIN
Birthdate: 5/29/1907
Birthplace: NY
Information Available in These Sources: ABYP 1, ABYP 3

MEYER, JEAN SHEPHERD
(Jean Berwick)
Birthdate: 9/3/1929
Information Available in These Sources: SATA 11

MEYER, JEROME SYDNEY
(S. M. Jennings)
Birthdate: 1/14/1895
Birthplace: New York, NY
Deathdate: 2/26/1975
Information Available in These Sources: ABYP 1, ABYP 3, SATA 3, SATA 25

MEYER, JUNE (JORDAN)
See Jordan, June (Meyer)

MEYER, KATHLEEN ALLAN
Birthdate: 2/25/1918
Birthplace: Dunellen, NJ
Information Available in These Sources: SATA 46, SATA 51

MEYER, LOUIS A(LBERT)
Birthdate: 8/22/1942
Birthplace: Johnstown, PA
Information Available in These Sources: SATA 12

MEYERS, JOAN (SIMPSON)
Birthdate: 9/20/1927
Birthplace: Boulder, CO
Information Available in These Sources: ABYP 2, ABYP 3

MEYERS, ROBERT W.
Birthdate: 6/17/1919
Birthplace: New York, NY
Information Available in These Sources: IBYP 2, ICB 2

MEYERS, SUSAN (THOMPSON)
Birthdate: 11/5/1942
Birthplace: Brooklyn, NY
Information Available in These Sources: ABYP 4, SATA 19

MEZEY, ROBERT
Birthdate: 2/28/1935
Birthplace: Philadelphia, PA
Information Available in These Sources: SATA 33

MIAN, MARY (LAWRENCE SHIPMAN)
Birthdate: 9/9/1902
Birthplace: Andover, MA
Information Available in These Sources: SATA 47

MICALE, ALBERT
Birthdate: 12/8/1913
Birthplace: Punxytawney, PA
Information Available in These Sources: SATA 22

MICHAEL, MANFRED
See Winterfeld, Henry

MICHAELS, BARBARA
See Mertz, Barbara (Gross)

MICHAELS, JOANNE LOUISE
See Teitelbaum, Michael

MICHAELS, NEAL
See Teitelbaum, Michael

MICHAELS, SKI
See Pellowski, Michael J(oseph)

MICHEL, ANNA
Birthdate: 12/12/1943
Birthplace: Mishawaka, IN
Information Available in These Sources: SATA 40, SATA 49

MICHIE, ALLAN ANDREW
Birthdate: 7/4/1915
Birthplace: Aberdeen, Scotland
Deathdate: 11/11/1973
Information Available in These Sources: ABYP 2, ABYP 3

MICKLISH, RITA
Birthdate: 2/7/1931
Birthplace: Maywood, CA
Information Available in These Sources: SATA 12

MICOLEAU, TYLER
Information Available in These Sources: IBYP 1, IBYP 2

MIERS, EARL SCHENCK
(David William Meredith)
Birthdate: 5/27/1910
Birthplace: Brooklyn, NY
Deathdate: 11/18/1972
Information Available in These Sources: ABYP 1, ABYP 3, JBA 3, SATA 1 SATA 26

MIKLOWITZ, GLORIA D(UBOV)
Birthdate: 5/18/1927
Birthplace: New York, NY
Information Available in These Sources: ABYP 4, SATA 4, JBA 6

MIKOLAYCAK, CHARLES
Birthdate: 1/26/1937
Birthplace: Scranton, PA
Information Available in These Sources: BC, IBYP 2, ICB 4, JBA 5, SATA 9

MILD, WARREN (PAUL)
Birthdate: 3/22/1922
Birthplace: Minneapolis, MN
Information Available in These Sources: SATA 41

MILES, BETTY
Birthdate: 5/16/1928
Birthplace: Chicago, IL
Information Available in These Sources: ABYP 2, ABYP 3, JBA 5, SATA 8

MILES, MISKA
See Martin, Patricia Miles

MILES, PATRICIA A.
See Martin, Patricia Miles

MILGROM, HARRY
Birthdate: 2/29/1912
Birthplace: New York, NY
Information Available in These Sources: ABYP 4, SATA 25

MILHOUS, KATHERINE
Birthdate: 11/27/1894
Birthplace: Philadelphia, PA
Deathdate: 12/5/1977
Information Available in These Sources: ABYP 1, ABYP 3, AICB, BABP, IBYP 1, IBYP 2, ICB 1, ICB 2, ICB 3, JBA 2, SATA 15, SVC 2, SVC 3, TCCW 1

MILITANT
See Sandburg, Carl (August)

MILL, ELEANOR
Birthdate: 3/21/1927
Birthplace: Royal Oak, MI
Information Available in These Sources: IBYP 1, IBYP 2

MILLAR, BARBARA F.
Birthdate: 8/26/1924
Birthplace: Bay City, MI
Information Available in These Sources: SATA 12

MILLARD, REED
Information Available in These Sources: ABYP 4

MILLAY, EDNA ST. VINCENT
Birthdate: 2/22/1892
Birthplace: Rockland, ME
Deathdate: 10/19/1950
Information Available in These Sources: JBA 1, SVC 2, SVC 3

MILLBURN, CYNTHIA
See Brooks, Anne (Tedlock)

MILLENDER, DHARATHULA (HOOD)
Birthdate: 2/4/1920
Birthplace: Terre Haute, IN
Information Available in These Sources: ABYP 4, BAI

MILLER, ALBERT G(RIFFITH)
Birthdate: 12/28/1905
Birthplace: Philadelphia, PA
Deathdate: 6/25/1982
Information Available in These Sources: SATA 12, SATA 31

MILLER, ALICE P(ATRICIA MCCARTHY)
Birthplace: Lynn, MA
Information Available in These Sources: SATA 22

MILLER, ALLAN
Information Available in These Sources: ABYP 4

MILLER, CINCINNATUS HEINE
See Miller, Joaquin

MILLER, CINCINNATUS HINER
See Miller, Joaquin

MILLER, DON
Birthdate: 6/30/1923
Birthplace: Jamaica, West Indies
Information Available in These Sources: BAI, SATA 15

MILLER, DONALD G(EORGE)
Birthdate: 10/30/1909
Birthplace: Braddock, PA
Information Available in These Sources: ABYP 1, ABYP 3

MILLER, DORIS R.
See Mosesson, Gloria R(ubin)

MILLER, EDDIE
See Miller, Edward

MILLER, EDNA (ANITA)
Birthdate: 3/8/1920
Birthplace: Weehawken, NJ
Information Available in These Sources: ABYP 2, ABYP 3, ICB 3, SATA 29JBA 6

MILLER, EDWARD
(Eddie Miller)
Birthdate: 9/5/1905
Birthplace: De Soto, MO
Deathdate: 2/14/1974
Information Available in These Sources: SATA 8

MILLER, ELIZABETH
Birthdate: 5/25/1933
Birthplace: Istanbul, Turkey
Information Available in These Sources: SATA 41

MILLER, ELIZABETH CLEVELAND
Birthdate: 7/13/1889
Birthplace: Seymour, CT
Deathdate: 11/??/1936
Information Available in These Sources: JBA 1, JBA 2

MILLER, EUGENE
Birthdate: 10/6/1925
Birthplace: Chicago, IL
Information Available in These Sources: SATA 33

MILLER, EUGENIA
See Mandelkorn, Eugenia Miller

MILLER, FRANCES A.
Birthdate: 10/15/1937
Birthplace: New York, NY
Information Available in These Sources: SATA 46, SATA 52

MILLER, GRAMBS
Birthplace: Peking, China
Information Available in These Sources: IBYP 2

MILLER, HELEN KNAPP
See Miller, Helen M(arkley)

MILLER, HELEN LOUISE
Information Available in These Sources: ABYP 1, ABYP 3

MILLER, HELEN M(ARKLEY)
(Helen Knapp Miller)
Birthdate: 12/4/1899
Birthplace: Cedar Falls, IA
Information Available in These Sources: ABYP 1, ABYP 3, SATA 5

MILLER, HELEN TOPPING
Birthdate: 12/8/1884
Birthplace: Fenton, MI
Deathdate: 2/4/1960
Information Available in These Sources: ABYP 1, ABYP 3, SATA 29

MILLER, JOAQUIN
(Cincinnatus Heine Miller, Cincinnatus Hiner Miller)
Birthdate: 3/10/1839 or 3/10/1841
Birthplace: Liberty, IN
Deathdate: 2/17/1913
Information Available in These Sources: SVC 2, SVC 3

MILLER, JOHN
See Samachson, Joseph

MILLER, KATHERINE
Information Available in These Sources: ABYP 2, ABYP 3

MILLER, LISA
Information Available in These Sources: ABYP 2, ABYP 3

MILLER, MADGE
Birthdate: 5/31/1918
Birthplace: Pittsburgh, PA
Information Available in These Sources: TCCW 1, TCCW 2, TCCW 3

MILLER, MARILYN (JEAN)
Birthdate: 11/12/1925
Birthplace: San Francisco, CA
Information Available in These Sources: ICB 3, SATA 33

MILLER, MARK
Information Available in These Sources: ABYP 1, ABYP 3

MILLER, MARTHA
See Ivan, Martha Miller Pfaff

MILLER, MARY BETH
(Mary Beth)
Birthdate: 12/18/1942
Birthplace: Louisville, KY
Information Available in These Sources: SATA 9

MILLER, MARY BRITTON
(Isabel Bolton)
Birthdate: 8/6/1883
Birthplace: New London, CT
Deathdate: 4/3/1975
Information Available in These Sources: ABYP 1, ABYP 3, SVC 2, SVC 3

MILLER, MITCHELL (ALEXANDER)
Birthdate: 2/22/1947
Birthplace: New York, NY
Information Available in These Sources: IBYP 2, ICB 4, JBA 4

MILLER, NATALIE
Birthdate: 1917
Birthplace: Sanford, ME
Deathdate: 2/28/1976
Information Available in These Sources: SATA 35

MILLER, RUTH WHITE
See White, Ruth C.

MILLER, SANDY (PEDEN)
Birthdate: 12/25/1948
Birthplace: Horton, KS
Information Available in These Sources: SATA 35, SATA 41

MILLER, SHANE
Birthdate: 1/25/1907
Birthplace: Reading, PA
Information Available in These Sources: ICB 3

MILLS, CLAUDIA
Birthdate: 8/21/1954
Birthplace: New York, NY
Information Available in These Sources: SATA 41, SATA 44

MILLS, YAROSLAVA SURMACH
(Yaroslava)
Birthdate: 7/11/1925
Birthplace: New York, NY
Information Available in These Sources: ICB 3, SATA 35

MILLSTEAD, THOMAS EDWARD
Birthplace: Milwaukee, WI
Information Available in These Sources: SATA 30

MILNE, LORUS J(OHNSON)
Birthdate: 9/12/1910 or 9/12/1912
Birthplace: Toronto, Ontario, Canada
Information Available in These Sources: ABYP 1, ABYP 3, SATA 5

MILNE, MARGAREY (JOAN GREENE)
Birthdate: 1/18/1915 or 1/18/1914
Birthplace: New York, NY
Information Available in These Sources: ABYP 1, ABYP 3, SATA 5

MILONAS, ROLF
See Myller, Rolf

MILOTTE, ALFRED G(EORGE)
Birthdate: 11/24/1904
Birthplace: Appleton, WI
Information Available in These Sources: SATA 11

MILTON, HILARY (HERBERT)
Birthdate: 4/2/1920
Birthplace: Jasper, AL
Information Available in These Sources: SATA 23

MILTON, JOHN R(ONALD)
Birthdate: 5/24/1924
Birthplace: Anoka, MN
Information Available in These Sources: SATA 24

MILTON, JOYCE
Birthdate: 1/12/1946
Birthplace: McKeesport, PA
Information Available in These Sources: SATA 41, SATA 52

MILVERTON, CHARLES A.
See Penzler, Otto

MIMS, SAM (S.)
Birthdate: 1887
Birthplace: Webster Parish, LA
Information Available in These Sources: ABYP 1, ABYP 3

MINARIK, ELSE HOLMELUND
Birthdate: 9/13/1920
Birthplace: Aarhus, Denmark
Information Available in These Sources: ABYP 1, ABYP 3, BABP, JBA 3, SATA 15, TCCW 1, TCCW 2, TCCW 3

MINCIELI, ROSE LAURA
(Laura Ross)
Birthdate: 11/10/1912
Birthplace: New York, NY
Information Available in These Sources: ABYP 4

MINDLIN, HELEN MATHER-SMITH
Birthplace: Kansas City, MO
Information Available in These Sources: ABYP 4

MINER, IRENE SEVREY
See Miner, Opal Irene Sevrey (Frazine)

MINER, JANE CLAYPOOL
(Jane Claypool, Veronica Ladd)
Birthdate: 4/22/1933
Birthplace: McAllen, TX
Information Available in These Sources: SATA 37, SATA 38

MINER, LEWIS S.
Birthdate: 11/18/1909
Birthplace: Waterloo, IA
Information Available in These Sources: SATA 11

MINER, OPAL IRENE SEVREY (FRAZINE)
(Irene Sevrey Miner)
Birthdate: 9/3/1906
Birthplace: Kewadin, MI
Information Available in These Sources: ABYP 2, ABYP 3

MINIER, NELSON
See Stoutenburg, Adrien (Pearl)

MINJA, PARK
Birthplace: Korea
Information Available in These Sources: IBYP 2

MINTONYE, GRACE
Birthplace: Kansas City, MO
Information Available in These Sources: SATA 4

MINTZ, LORELIE MILLER
Birthplace: Toronto, Ontario, Canada
Information Available in These Sources: ABYP 4

MIRSKY, JEANNETTE
Birthdate: 9/3/1903
Birthplace: Bradley Beach, NJ
Deathdate: 3/10/1987
Information Available in These Sources: SATA 8, SATA 51

MIRSKY, REBA PAEFF
Birthdate: 5/25/1902
Birthplace: Boston, MA
Deathdate: 11/22/1966
Information Available in These Sources: ABYP 1, ABYP 3, SATA 1

MISKOVITS, CHRISTINE
Birthdate: 7/17/1939
Birthplace: Elizabeth, NJ
Information Available in These Sources: SATA 10

MISS FRANCES
See Horwich, Frances R(appaport)

MISTER ROGERS
See Rogers, Fred (McFeely)

MITCHELL, ISLA
Birthplace: New York, NY
Information Available in These Sources: ABYP 1, ABYP 3

MITCHELL, JOYCE SLAYTON
Birthdate: 8/13/1933
Birthplace: Hardwick, VT
Information Available in These Sources: SATA 43, 46

MITCHELL, KATHY
Birthdate: 7/27/1948
Birthplace: Cincinnati, OH
Information Available in These Sources: SATA 59

MITSUHASHI, YOKO
Birthplace: Tokyo, Japan
Information Available in These Sources: IBYP 1, IBYP 2, SATA 33, SATA 45

MIZNER, ELIZABETH HOWARD
(Elizabeth Howard)
Birthdate: 8/24/1907
Birthplace: Detroit, MI
Information Available in These Sources: ABYP 2, ABYP 3, MJA, SATA 27

MIZUMURA, KAZUE
Birthplace: Kawakeera, Japan
Information Available in These Sources: IBYP 1, IBYP 2, ICB 3, ICB 4, JBA 3, SATA 18

MOCHE, DINAH (RACHEL) L(EVINE)
Birthdate: 10/24/1936
Birthplace: New York, NY
Information Available in These Sources: SATA 40, SATA 44

MOCHI, UGO (A.)
Birthdate: 3/11/1889
Birthplace: Florence, Italy
Deathdate: 8/31/1977
Information Available in These Sources: SATA 38

MOCNIAK, GEORGE
Birthplace: Greensboro, PA
Information Available in These Sources: IBYP 1, IBYP 2

MODELL, FRANK B.
Birthdate: 9/6/1917
Birthplace: Philadelphia, PA
Information Available in These Sources: JBA 5, SATA 36, SATA 39

MODEROW, GERTRUDE
Birthdate: 1900
Deathdate: 1973
Information Available in These Sources: SVC 2, SVC 3

MOE, BARBARA
Birthdate: 10/10/1937
Birthplace: Cincinnati, OH
Information Available in These Sources: SATA 20

MOERI, LOUISE (HEALY)
Birthdate: 11/30/1924
Birthplace: Klamath Falls, OR
Information Available in These Sources: DACF, JBA 5, SATA 24

MOFFETT, MARTHA (LEATHERWOOD)
Birthdate: 1/3/1934
Birthplace: Pell City, AL
Information Available in These Sources: SATA 8

MOFFETT, ROBERT K(NIGHT)
Information Available in These Sources: ABYP 4

MOFSIE, LOUIS B.
Birthdate: 1936
Birthplace: New York, NY
Information Available in These Sources: IBYP 2, SATA 33

MOHAN, BEVERLY (MOFFET)
Birthdate: 7/16/1918
Birthplace: Chicago, IL
Information Available in These Sources: ABYP 4

MOHN, PETER B(URNET)
Birthdate: 5/17/1934
Birthplace: New York, NY
Information Available in These Sources: SATA 28

MOHN, VIOLA KOHL
Birthdate: 2/18/1914
Birthplace: Myerstown, PA
Information Available in These Sources: SATA 8

MOHR, NICHOLASA (GOLPE)
Birthdate: 11/1/1935
Birthplace: New York, NY
Information Available in These Sources: ABYP 4, DACF, JBA 5, SATA 8

MOLARSKY, OSMOND
Birthdate: 11/17/1909
Birthplace: Boston, MA
Information Available in These Sources: SATA 16

MOLLOY, ANNE (STEARNS) BAKER
Birthdate: 10/4/1907
Birthplace: Boston, MA
Information Available in These Sources: ABYP 1, ABYP 3, SATA 32

MOLLOY, PAUL
Birthdate: 7/4/1920
Birthplace: Winnipeg, Manitoba, Canada
Information Available in These Sources: SATA 5

MOMADAY, N(AVARRE) SCOTT
Birthdate: 2/27/1934
Birthplace: Lawton, OK
Information Available in These Sources: SATA 30, SATA 48

MOMADAY, NATACHEE SCOTT
Birthplace: Fairview, KY
Information Available in These Sources: DACF

MONCURE, JANE BELK
(Bruce Wannamaker)
Birthdate: 12/16/1926
Birthplace: Orlando, FL
Information Available in These Sources: SATA 23

MONJO, F(ERDINAND) N(ICHOLAS)
Birthdate: 8/28/1924
Birthplace: Stamford, CT
Deathdate: 10/9/1978
Information Available in These Sources: ABYP 4, JBA 5, SATA 16, TCCW 1TCCW 2, TCCW 3

MONK, MARVIN RANDOLPH
(Randy Monk)
Birthdate: 6/6/1921
Birthplace: Moultrie, GA
Information Available in These Sources: IBYP 2, ICB 2

MONK, RANDY
See Monk, Marvin Randolph

MONROE, LYLE
See Heinlein, Robert A(nson)

MONROE, MARION
Birthdate: 2/4/1898
Birthplace: Mount Vernon, NY
Deathdate: 6/25/1983
Information Available in These Sources: SATA 34

MONSELL, HELEN (ALBEE)
Birthdate: 2/24/1895
Birthplace: Richmond, VA
Deathdate: 9/15/1971
Information Available in These Sources: SATA 24

MONTANA, BOB
Birthdate: 10/23/1920
Birthplace: Stockton, CA
Deathdate: 1/4/1975
Information Available in These Sources: SATA 21

MONTGOMERY, CONSTANCE
See Cappel, Constance

MONTGOMERY, ELIZABETH RIDER
Birthdate: 7/12/1902
Birthplace: Huaras, Peru
Deathdate: 2/19/1985
Information Available in These Sources: ABYP 1, ABYP 3, SATA 3, SATA 34, SATA 41

MONTGOMERY, R(AYMOND) A. (,JR.)
(Robert Mountain)
Birthdate: 3/9/1936
Birthplace: CT
Information Available in These Sources: SATA 39

MONTGOMERY, RUTHERFORD (GEORGE)
(A. A. Avery, Al Avery, Everitt Proctor)
Birthdate: 4/12/1894 or 4/12/1894
Birthplace: Straubville, ND
Deathdate: 7/3/1985
Information Available in These Sources: ABYP 1, ABYP 3, DACF, MJA, SATA 3, TCCW 1, TCCW 2, TCCW 3

MONTGOMERY, VIVIAN
Birthplace: Chicago, IL
Information Available in These Sources: SATA 36

MONTRESOR, BENI
Birthdate: 3/31/1926
Birthplace: Bussolengo, Italy
Information Available in These Sources: ABYP 2, ABYP 3, BABP, IBYP 1, IBYP 2, ICB 3, SATA 3, SATA 38

MOODY, RALPH O(WEN)
Birthdate: 12/16/1898
Birthplace: East Rochester, NH
Information Available in These Sources: ABYP 1, ABYP 3, SATA 1

MOON, CARL
Birthdate: 10/5/1879
Birthplace: Wilmington, OH
Deathdate: 6/24/1948
Information Available in These Sources: ABYP 1, ABYP 3, ICB 1, JBA 1, JBA 2, SATA 25

MOON, GRACE (PURDIE)
Birthdate: 1877 or 1883
Birthplace: Indianapolis, IN
Deathdate: 9/6/1947
Information Available in These Sources: ABYP 1, ABYP 3, JBA 1, JBA 2, SATA 25

MOON, SHEILA (ELIZABETH)
Birthdate: 12/25/1910
Birthplace: Denver, CO
Information Available in These Sources: ABYP 4, DACF, SATA 5

MOONEY, ELIZABETH C(OMSTOCK)
Birthdate: 2/8/1918
Birthplace: Rome, NY
Deathdate: 5/20/1986
Information Available in These Sources: SATA 48

MOOR, EMILY
See Deming, Richard

MOORE, ANNE CARROLL
Birthdate: 7/12/1871
Birthplace: Limerick, ME
Deathdate: 1/20/1961
Information Available in These Sources: ABYP 1, ABYP 3, JBA 1, JBA 2, SATA 13

Moore, Carman Leroy
Birthdate: 10/8/1936
Birthplace: Lorain, OH
Information Available in These Sources: BAI

MOORE, CLEMENT CLARKE
(Columella)
Birthdate: 7/15/1779
Birthplace: New York, NY
Deathdate: 7/10/1863
Information Available in These Sources: DLB 42, SATA 18, SVC 2, SVC 3

MOORE, CLYDE B.
Birthdate: 1/13/1886
Birthplace: Albion, NE
Deathdate: 11/4/1973
Information Available in These Sources: ABYP 4

MOORE, DAVID WILLIAM
Birthdate: 1895
Birthplace: Highland, OH
Deathdate: 1954
Information Available in These Sources: ABYP 1, ABYP 3

MOORE, DON W.
Birthdate, 1905?
Deathdate: 4/7/1986
Information Available in These Sources: SATA 48

MOORE, EMILY R.
Birthdate: 1948
Birthplace: New York, NY
Information Available in These Sources: BAI

MOORE, EVA
Birthdate: 4/16/1942
Birthplace: Rome, NY
Information Available in These Sources: ABYP 4, SATA 20

MOORE, JACK (WILLIAM)
Birthdate: 11/14/1941
Birthplace: Macon, GA
Information Available in These Sources: SATA 32, 46

MOORE, JANET GAYLORD
Birthdate: 6/2/1905
Birthplace: Hanover, NH
Information Available in These Sources: IBYP 1, IBYP 2, SATA 18

MOORE, JIM
Birthdate: 5/9/1946
Birthplace: Glendale, CA
Information Available in These Sources: SATA 42

MOORE, JOHN TRAVERS
Birthdate: 8/24/1908
Birthplace: Wellston, OH
Information Available in These Sources: SATA 12

MOORE, LAMONT
Birthdate: 1909
Information Available in These Sources: ABYP 1, ABYP 3, SATA 29

MOORE, LILIAN (MOORE REAVIN)
Birthdate: 3/17/1909
Birthplace: New York, NY
Information Available in These Sources: ABYP 1, ABYP 3, BABP, JBA 4, SATA 52

MOORE, MARGARET R(UMBERGER)
Birthdate: 6/28/1903
Birthplace: DuBois, PA
Information Available in These Sources: SATA 12

MOORE, MARIANNE (CRAIG)
Birthdate: 11/15/1887
Birthplace: Kirkwood, MO
Deathdate: 2/6/1972
Information Available in These Sources: SATA 20

MOORE, NANCY
Information Available in These Sources: ABYP 1, ABYP 3

MOORE, RAY (S.)
Birthdate, 1905?
Birthplace: Montgomery City, MO
Deathdate: 1/13/1984
Information Available in These Sources: SATA 37

MOORE, REGINA
See Dunne, Mary Collins

MOORE, ROSALIE
See Brown, Rosalie (Gertrude) Moore

MOORE, RUTH (NULTON)
Birthdate: 6/19/1923
Birthplace: Easton, PA
Information Available in These Sources: SATA 23, SATA 38

MOORE, S(ARAH) E.
Birthplace: Berkeley, CA
Information Available in These Sources: SATA 23

MOORE, VARDINE (RUSSELL)
Birthdate: 9/25/1906
Birthplace: Uniontown, KY
Information Available in These Sources: ABYP 1, ABYP 3

MOORES, DICK
See Moores, Richard (Arnold)

MOORES, RICHARD (ARNOLD)
(Dick Moores)
Birthdate: 12/12/1909
Birthplace: Lincoln, NE
Deathdate: 4/22/1986 or 4/23/1986
Information Available in These Sources: SATA 48

MOOSER, STEPHEN
Birthdate: 7/4/1941
Birthplace: Fresno, CA
Information Available in These Sources: SATA 28

MORAN, CONNIE
Information Available in These Sources: IBYP 1, IBYP 2

MORAN, EUGENE FRANCIS
Birthdate: 3/24/1872
Birthplace: Brooklyn, NY
Deathdate: 4/13/1961
Information Available in These Sources: ABYP 1, ABYP 3

MORAN, TOM
Birthdate: 12/5/1943
Birthplace: Philadelphia, PA
Information Available in These Sources: SATA 60

MORDINOFF, NICOLAS
(Nicolas)
Birthdate: 9/27/1911
Birthplace: St. Petersburg, Russia
Deathdate: 5/5/1973
Information Available in These Sources: ABYP 1, ABYP 3, BABP, IBYP 1, IBYP 2, ICB 1, ICB 2, ICB 3, MJA, SATA 17

MORE, CAROLINE
See Cone, Molly (Lamken) and Strachan, Margaret Pitcairn

MORETON, JOHN
See Cohen, Morton N(orton)

MOREY, CHARLES
See Fletcher, Helen Jill

MOREY, WALT(ER NELSON)
Birthdate: 2/3/1907
Birthplace: Hoquiam, WA
Information Available in These Sources: ABYP 2, ABYP 3, DACF, JBA 3, SATA 3, SATA 51, TCCW 1, TCCW 2, TCCW 3

MORGAN, ALFRED P(OWELL)
(A. M. Powell)
Birthdate: 4/15/1889
Birthplace: Brooklyn, NY
Deathdate: 3/16/1972
Information Available in These Sources: ABYP 1, ABYP 3, MJA, SATA 33

MORGAN, ALLEN
Birthdate: 1908
Information Available in These Sources: ABYP 4

MORGAN, AVA
Information Available in These Sources: IBYP 2

MORGAN, JANE
See Cooper, James Fenimore

MORGAN, LENORE
Birthdate: 10/3/1908
Birthplace: Princeton, NJ
Information Available in These Sources: SATA 8

MORGAN, MARK
See Overholser, Wayne D.

MORGAN, SHARON ANTONIA
See Fufuka, Karama

MORGAN, SHIRLEY
Birthdate: 12/11/1933
Birthplace: Dorset, England
Information Available in These Sources: SATA 10

MORGAN, TOM
Birthdate: 6/20/1942
Birthplace: Syracuse, NY
Information Available in These Sources: SATA 42

MORGENROTH, BARBARA
Information Available in These Sources: SATA 36

MORISON, SAMUEL ELIOT
Birthdate: 7/9/1887
Birthplace: Boston, MA
Deathdate: 5/15/1976
Information Available in These Sources: ABYP 1, ABYP 3

MORLEY, CHRISTOPHER (DARLINGTON)
Birthdate: 5/5/1890
Birthplace: Haverford, PA
Deathdate: 3/28/1957
Information Available in These Sources: SVC 2, SVC 3

MORRAH, DAVE
See Morrah, David Wardlaw, Jr.

MORRAH, DAVID WARDLAW, JR.
(Dave Morrah)
Birthdate: 3/27/1914
Birthplace: Atlanta, GA
Information Available in These Sources: SATA 10

MORRESSY, JOHN
Birthdate: 12/8/1930
Birthplace: Brooklyn, NY
Information Available in These Sources: ABYP 4, SATA 23

MORRILL, LESLIE H(OLT)
Birthdate: 2/10/1934
Birthplace: Hudson, NH
Information Available in These Sources: IBYP 2, SATA 33, SATA 48

MORRIS, GREGGORY
Information Available in These Sources: ABYP 4

MORRIS, RICHARD BRANDON
Birthdate: 7/24/1904
Birthplace: New York, NY
Information Available in These Sources: ABYP 1, ABYP 3

MORRIS, ROBERT A(DA)
Birthdate: 11/15/1933
Birthplace: Charlottesville, VA
Information Available in These Sources: SATA 7

MORRIS, WILLIAM
Birthdate: 4/13/1913
Birthplace: Boston, MA
Information Available in These Sources: SATA 29

MORRIS, WILLIE
Birthdate: 11/29/1934
Birthplace: Jackson, MS
Information Available in These Sources: ABYP 4

MORRISON, BILL
Birthdate: 1935
Information Available in These Sources: SATA 37

MORRISON, DOROTHY NAFUS
Birthplace: Nashua, IA
Information Available in These Sources: SATA 29

MORRISON, LILLIAN
Birthdate: 10/27/1917
Birthplace: Jersey City, NJ
Information Available in These Sources: BABP, SATA 3, JBA 6

MORRISON, ROBERTA
See Webb, Jean Francis (III)

MORRISON, TONI (CHLOE ANTHONY WOFFORD)
Birthdate: 2/18/1931
Birthplace: Lorain, OH
Information Available in These Sources: SATA 57

MORRISON, VELMA FORD
(Hildegarde Ford)
Birthdate: 4/30/1909
Birthplace: Madrid, IA
Information Available in These Sources: SATA 21

MORRISON, WILLIAM
See Samachson, Joseph

MORRISS, JAMES E(DWARD)
Birthdate: 2/9/1932
Birthplace: Oklahoma City, OK
Information Available in These Sources: SATA 8

MORROW, ANNE SPENCER
See Lindbergh, Anne Morrow (Spencer)

MORROW, BARBARA
Information Available in These Sources: IBYP 1, IBYP 2

MORROW, BETTY
See Bacon, Elizabeth

MORROW, ELIZABETH (REEVE CUTTER)
Birthdate: 5/29/1873
Birthplace: Cleveland, OH
Deathdate: 1/23/1955
Information Available in These Sources: SVC 2, SVC 3

MORROW, HONORE WILLSIE
Birthdate, 1880?
Birthplace: Ottumwa, IA
Deathdate: 4/12/1940
Information Available in These Sources: JBA 1

MORROW, SUZANNE STARK
Birthplace: CA
Information Available in These Sources: ABYP 2, ABYP 3

MORSE, CAROL
See Yeakley, Marjory Hall

MORSE, DOROTHY B(AYLEY)
Birthdate: 1906
Birthplace: New York, NY
Deathdate: 3/13/1979
Information Available in These Sources: IBYP 2, ICB 2, SATA 24

MORSE, FLO
Birthdate: 6/21/1921
Birthplace: Yonkers, NY
Information Available in These Sources: SATA 30

MORT, VIVIAN
See Cromie, Alice Hamilton

MORTON, DAVID
Birthdate: 2/21/1886
Birthplace: Elkton, KY
Deathdate: 6/13/1957
Information Available in These Sources: SVC 2, SVC 3

MORTON, EVA JANE
(Jane Morton)
Birthdate: 11/13/1931
Birthplace: Colorado Springs, CO
Information Available in These Sources: SATA 50

MORTON, JANE
See Morton, Eva Jane

MORTON, LEE JACK, JR.
(Lee Jac)
Birthdate: 4/20/1928
Birthplace: Detroit, MI
Information Available in These Sources: SATA 32

MORTON, MARIAN
Information Available in These Sources: IBYP 1, IBYP 2

MORTON, MIRIAM (BIDNER)
Birthdate: 6/14/1918
Birthplace: Kishinev, Romania
Deathdate: 9/22/1985
Information Available in These Sources: ABYP 4, SATA 9, SATA 46

MOSCOW, ALVIN
Birthdate: 12/31/1925
Birthplace: New York, NY
Information Available in These Sources: ABYP 1, ABYP 3, SATA 3

MOSEL, ARLENE (TICHY)
Birthdate: 8/27/1921
Birthplace: Cleveland, OH
Information Available in These Sources: JBA 5, SATA 7

MOSER, BARRY
Birthdate: 10/15/1940
Birthplace: Chattanooga, TN
Information Available in These Sources: SATA 56, JBA 6

MOSER, DON(ALD BRUCE)
Birthdate: 10/19/1932
Birthplace: Cleveland, OH
Information Available in These Sources: SATA 31

MOSES, ANNA MARY (ROBERTSON)
(Grandma Moses)
Birthdate: 9/7/1860
Birthplace: Greenwich, NY
Deathdate: 12/13/1961
Information Available in These Sources: ABYP 2, ABYP 3

MOSES, GRANDMA
See Moses, Anna Mary (Robertson)

MOSESSON, GLORIA R(UBIN)
(Kathryn French, Doris R. Miller)
Birthplace: Brooklyn, NY
Information Available in These Sources: SATA 24

MOSKIN, MARIETTA D(UNSTON)
Birthdate: 4/30/1928
Birthplace: Vienna, Austria
Information Available in These Sources: SATA 23

MOSKOF, MARTIN STEPHEN
Birthdate: 5/18/1930
Birthplace: New York, NY
Information Available in These Sources: SATA 27

MOSLEY, ELIZABETH ROBARDS
Birthplace: Robards, KY
Information Available in These Sources: ABYP 4

MOSS, DON(ALD)
Birthdate: 1/20/1920
Birthplace: Somerville, MA
Information Available in These Sources: SATA 11

MOST, BERNARD
Birthdate: 9/2/1937
Birthplace: New York, NY
Information Available in These Sources: SATA 40, SATA 48

MOTZ, LLOYD
Birthdate: 6/5/1910 or 6/5/1909
Birthplace: Susquehanna, PA
Information Available in These Sources: SATA 20

MOUNTAIN, ROBERT
See Montgomery, R(aymond) A., (Jr.)

MOY, SEONG
Birthdate: 4/20/1921
Birthplace: Canton, China
Information Available in These Sources: IBYP 2, ICB 3

MOYERS, WILLIAM
Birthdate: 12/11/1916
Birthplace: Atlanta, GA
Information Available in These Sources: IBYP 1, IBYP 2, ICB 2

MOYLER, ALAN (FRANK POWELL)
Birthdate: 12/4/1926
Birthplace: Peking, China
Information Available in These Sources: SATA 36

MR. WIZARD
See Herbert, Don

MUDE, O
See Gorey, Edward St. John

MUELLER, HANS ALEXANDER
Birthdate: 3/12/1888
Birthplace: Nordhausen, Germany
Deathdate: 7/7/1962
Information Available in These Sources: IBYP 2, ICB 2

MUELLER, VIRGINIA
Birthdate: 3/22/1924
Birthplace: Sheboygan, WI
Information Available in These Sources: SATA 28

MUIR, JOHN
Birthdate: 4/21/1838
Birthplace: Dunbar, Scotland
Deathdate: 12/24/1914
Information Available in These Sources: JBA 1

MUKERJI, DHAN GOPAL
Birthdate: 7/6/1890
Birthplace: Calcutta, India
Deathdate: 7/14/1936
Information Available in These Sources: ABYP 1, ABYP 3, JBA 1, SATA 40

MULCAHY, LUCILLE BURNETT
(Helen Hale)
Birthdate: 11/10/1918
Birthplace: Albuquerque, NM
Information Available in These Sources: ABYP 1, ABYP 3, SATA 12

MULFORD, PHILIPPA GREENE
Birthdate: 5/29/1948
Birthplace: New York, NY
Information Available in These Sources: SATA 43

MULLER, BILLEX
See Ellis, Edward S(ylvester)

MULLER, CAROLYN
See Wolcott, Carolyn Muller

MULLINS, EDWARD S(WIFT)
Birthdate: 2/25/1922
Birthplace: Sanford, ME
Information Available in These Sources: IBYP 1, IBYP 2, SATA 10

MULVIHILL, WILLIAM PATRICK
Birthdate: 6/25/1923
Birthplace: Sag Harbor, Long Island, NY
Information Available in These Sources: SATA 8

MUN
See Leaf, Wilbur Munro

MUNCE, RUTH (LIVINGSTON) HILL
(Ruth Livingston Hill)
Birthdate: 1/24/1898
Birthplace: Philadelphia, PA
Information Available in These Sources: SATA 12

MUNN, MERYL LUCILE
See Nearing, Penny

MUNOWITZ, KEN
Birthdate: 5/2/1935
Birthplace: Bronx, NY
Deathdate: 12/20/1977
Information Available in These Sources: SATA 14

MUNOZ, WILLIAM
Birthdate: 1/12/1949
Birthplace: Chicago, IL
Information Available in These Sources: SATA 42

MUNRO, ELEANOR (C.)
Birthdate: 3/28/1928
Birthplace: Brooklyn, NY
Information Available in These Sources: ABYP 1, ABYP 3, SATA 37

MUNRO, ROXIE
Birthdate: 9/5/1945
Birthplace: Mineral Wells, TX
Information Available in These Sources: SATA 58, JBA 6

MUNROE, KIRK
Birthdate: 9/15/1850
Birthplace: Prairie du Chien (near), WI
Deathdate: 6/16/1930
Information Available in These Sources: DLB 42, JBA 1

MUNSCH, ROBERT N.
Birthdate: 6/11/1945
Birthplace: Pittsburgh, PA
Information Available in These Sources: SATA 48, SATA 50, TCCW 2

MUNSINGER, LYNN
Birthdate: 12/24/1951
Birthplace: Greenfield, MA
Information Available in These Sources: SATA 33

MUNSON, GORHAM (BERT)
Birthdate: 5/26/1896
Birthplace: Amityville, NY
Deathdate: 8/15/1969
Information Available in These Sources: ABYP 1, ABYP 3

MUNSON(-BENSON), TUNIE
Birthdate: 8/15/1946
Birthplace: Chicago, IL
Information Available in These Sources: SATA 15

MUNVES, JAMES (ALBERT)
Birthdate: 3/23/1922
Birthplace: New York, NY
Information Available in These Sources: SATA 30

MUNZER, MARTHA E(ISEMAN)
Birthdate: 9/22/1899
Birthplace: New York, NY
Information Available in These Sources: ABYP 4, SATA 4

MURCH, MEL
See Manes, Stephen

MURPHY, BARBARA BEASLEY
Birthdate: 2/4/1933
Birthplace: Springfield, OH
Information Available in These Sources: SATA 5

MURPHY, E(MMETT) JEFFERSON
(Pat Murphy)
Birthdate: 7/2/1926
Birthplace: Thomasville, GA
Information Available in These Sources: ABYP 4, SATA 4

MURPHY, JIM
Birthdate: 9/25/1947
Birthplace: Newark, NJ
Information Available in These Sources: SATA 32

MURPHY, MABEL (ANSLEY)
(Anne S. Lee)
Birthdate: 2/21/1870
Birthplace: Plumville, PA
Information Available in These Sources: ABYP 1, ABYP 3

MURPHY, PAT
See Murphy, E(mmett) Jefferson

MURPHY, ROBERT (WILLIAM)
Birthdate: 8/27/1902
Birthplace: Ridley Park, PA
Deathdate: 7/13/1971
Information Available in These Sources: ABYP 2, ABYP 3, JBA 4, SATA 10

MURPHY, SHIRLEY ROUSSEAU
Birthdate: 5/20/1928
Birthplace: Oakland, CA
Information Available in These Sources: SATA 36, TCCW 3, JBA 6

MURRAY, DON(ALD M.)
Birthdate: 9/16/1924
Birthplace: Boston, MA
Information Available in These Sources: ABYP 2, ABYP 3

MURRAY, GLADYS HALL
Information Available in These Sources: ABYP 2, ABYP 3

MURRAY, JOHN
(Robert Combs)
Birthdate: 7/8/1923
Birthplace: Yonkers, NY
Information Available in These Sources: SATA 39

MURRAY, JUDITH MICHELE (FREEDMAN)
(Michele Murray)
Birthdate: 4/25/1933
Birthplace: Brooklyn, NY
Deathdate: 3/14/1974
Information Available in These Sources: ABYP 4, SATA 7

MURRAY, MARIAN
Birthplace: Quincy, MA
Information Available in These Sources: SATA 5

MURRAY, MICHELE
See Murray, Judith Michele Freedman

MUSCIANO, WALTER A.
Birthplace: New York, NY
Information Available in These Sources: ABYP 1, ABYP 3

MUSGRAVE, FLORENCE
Birthdate: 7/21/1902
Birthplace: Mount Clare, WV
Information Available in These Sources: ABYP 1, ABYP 3, SATA 3

MUSGROVE, MARGARET W(YNKOOP)
Birthdate: 11/19/1943
Birthplace: New Britain, CT
Information Available in These Sources: ABYP 4, BAI, SATA 26

MUSSEY, VIRGINIA T. H.
See Ellison, Virginia Howell

MUTZ
See Kunstler, Morton

MYERS, ARTHUR
Birthdate: 10/24/1917
Birthplace: Buffalo, NY
Information Available in These Sources: SATA 35

MYERS, BERNICE
Birthplace: Bronx, NY
Information Available in These Sources: IBYP 2, SATA 9

MYERS, CAROLINE ELIZABETH (CLARK)
Birthdate: 7/14/1887
Birthplace: Morris, PA
Deathdate: 7/3/1980
Information Available in These Sources: SATA 28

MYERS, ELISABETH P(ERKINS)
Birthdate: 7/22/1918
Birthplace: Grand Rapids, MI
Information Available in These Sources: ABYP 4, SATA 36

MYERS, HORTENSE (POWNER)
Birthdate: 7/15/1913
Birthplace: Indianapolis, IN
Information Available in These Sources: SATA 10

MYERS, MADELEINE NEUBERGER
Birthdate: 1896
Information Available in These Sources: ABYP 1, ABYP 3

MYERS, WALTER DEAN
Birthdate: 8/12/1937
Birthplace: Martinsburg, WV
Information Available in These Sources: ABYP 4, BAI, DACF, JBA 5, SATA 27, SATA 41, TCCW 3

MYLLER, ROLF
(David Brown, Rolf Milonas)
Birthdate: 10/13/1926
Birthplace: Nuremburg, Germany
Information Available in These Sources: ABYP 1, ABYP 3, BC, SATA 27

MYRA, HAROLD L(AWRENCE)
Birthdate: 7/19/1939
Birthplace: Camden, NJ
Information Available in These Sources: SATA 42, SATA 46

MYRICK, MILDRED
Birthplace: FL
Information Available in These Sources: ABYP 4

MYRON, ROBERT
Birthdate: 3/15/1926
Birthplace: Brooklyn, NY
Information Available in These Sources: ABYP 4

MYRUS, DONALD (RICHARD)
Birthdate: 9/22/1927
Birthplace: Baldwin, NY
Information Available in These Sources: ABYP 2, ABYP 3, SATA 23

N

NADLER, ROBERT
Birthdate: 1934
Birthplace: Alexandria, Egypt
Information Available in These Sources: IBYP 1, IBYP 2

NAGENDA, MUSA
See Howard, Moses Leon

NAGY, AL
Birthplace: New York, NY
Information Available in These Sources: IBYP 1, IBYP 2

NAILOR, GERALD A.
Birthdate: 1/21/1917
Birthplace: Crown Point, NM
Information Available in These Sources: ICB 1

NAMIOKA, LENSEY (CHAO)
Birthdate: 6/14/1929
Birthplace: Peking, China
Information Available in These Sources: DACF, SATA 27

NANKIVEL, CLAUDINE
Information Available in These Sources: IBYP 1, IBYP 2

NASH, BRUCE M(ITCHELL)
Birthdate: 8/14/1947
Birthplace: Brooklyn, NY
Information Available in These Sources: SATA 34

NASH, FREDERIC OGDEN
(Ogden Nash)
Birthdate: 8/19/1902
Birthplace: Rye, NY
Deathdate: 5/19/1971
Information Available in These Sources: ABYP 1, ABYP 3, JBA 4, SATA 2 SATA 46

NASH, ISABEL
See Eberstadt, Isabel (Nash)

NASH, LINELL
See Smith, Linell Nash

NASH, MARY (HUGHES)
Birthdate: 7/7/1925
Birthplace: Milwaukee, WI
Information Available in These Sources: ABYP 2, ABYP 3, SATA 41

NASH, OGDEN
See Nash, Frederic Ogden

NAST, ELSA RUTH
See Watson, Jane Werner

NAST, THOMAS
Birthdate: 9/27/1840
Birthplace: Landau, Germany
Deathdate: 12/7/1902
Information Available in These Sources: SATA 33, SATA 51

NASTICK, SHARON
Birthdate: 7/30/1954
Birthplace: Washington, DC
Information Available in These Sources: SATA 41

NATHAN, ADELE (GUTMAN)
Birthdate: 1900
Birthplace: Baltimore, MD
Deathdate: 7/24/1986
Information Available in These Sources: ABYP 2, ABYP 3, SATA 48

NATHAN, DANIEL
See Dannay, Frederic

NATHAN, DOROTHY (GOLDEEN)
Birthplace: Portland, OR
Deathdate: 12/22/1966
Information Available in These Sources: SATA 15

NATHAN, ROBERT (GRUNTAL)
Birthdate: 1/2/1894
Birthplace: New York, NY
Deathdate: 5/25/1985
Information Available in These Sources: SATA 6, SATA 43

NATHANSON, LAURA WALTHER
(J. K. Thorpe)
Birthdate: 1/3/1941
Birthplace: Lakewood, OH
Information Available in These Sources: SATA 57

NATION, BOB
Information Available in These Sources: ABYP 4

NATION, KAY
Information Available in These Sources: ABYP 4

NATTI, SUSANNA
Birthdate: 10/19/1948
Birthplace: Gloucester, MA
Information Available in These Sources: SATA 32

NAVARRA, JOHN GABRIEL
Birthdate: 7/3/1927
Birthplace: Bayonne, NJ
Information Available in These Sources: ABYP 4, SATA 8

NAVARRA, TOBY
Information Available in These Sources: IBYP 2

NAYLOR, PENELOPE
Birthdate: 1/13/1941
Birthplace: New York, NY
Information Available in These Sources: IBYP 2, SATA 10

NAYLOR, PHYLLIS REYNOLDS
Birthdate: 1/4/1933
Birthplace: Anderson, IN
Information Available in These Sources: ABYP 4, DACF, JBA 5, SATA 12, TCCW 3

NAZAROFF, ALEXANDER I.
Birthdate: 2/21/1898
Birthplace: Kiev, Russia
Information Available in These Sources: ABYP 4, SATA 4

NEAL, HARRY EDWARD
Birthdate: 5/4/1906
Birthplace: Pittsfield, MA
Information Available in These Sources: ABYP 1, ABYP 3, SATA 5

NEAL, JEAN
Information Available in These Sources: ABYP 4

NEAL, MICHAEL
See Teitelbaum, Michael

NEARING, JOHN SCOTT
See Scott, John

NEARING, PENNY
(Anne Maguire, Meryl Lucile Munn)
Birthdate: 4/16/1916
Birthplace: Waterport, NY
Information Available in These Sources: SATA 42, SATA 47

NEBEL, GUSTAVE E.
(Mimouca Nebel)
Birthplace: Paris, France
Information Available in These Sources: IBYP 1, SATA 33, SATA 45

NEBEL, MIMOUCA
See Nebel, Gustave E.

NEE, KAY BONNER
Birthplace: Plummer, MN
Information Available in These Sources: SATA 10

NEEDLEMAN, JACOB
Birthdate: 10/6/1934
Birthplace: Philadelphia, PA
Information Available in These Sources: SATA 6

NEF, EVELYN STEFANSSON
(Evelyn (Schwartz) Baird Stefansson)
Birthdate: 7/24/1913
Birthplace: New York, NY
Information Available in These Sources: ABYP 2, ABYP 3

NEGRI, ROCCO (ANTONIO)
Birthdate: 6/26/1932
Birthplace: Reggio Calabria, Italy
Information Available in These Sources: IBYP 2, ICB 4, SATA 12

NEIER, ARYEH
Birthdate: 4/22/1937
Birthplace: Berlin, Germany
Information Available in These Sources: SATA 59

NEIGOFF, ANNE
Birthplace: Chicago, IL
Information Available in These Sources: SATA 13

NEIGOFF, MIKE
Birthdate: 12/26/1920
Birthplace: Chicago, IL
Information Available in These Sources: SATA 13

NEILSON, FRANCES FULLERTON (JONES)
Birthdate: 10/21/1912
Birthplace: Philadelphia, PA
Information Available in These Sources: ABYP 1, ABYP 3, SATA 14

NEIMARK, ANNE E.
Birthdate: 10/3/1935
Birthplace: Chicago, IL
Information Available in These Sources: SATA 4

NEIMARK, PAUL G.
Birthdate: 10/13/1934
Birthplace: Chicago, IL
Information Available in These Sources: ABYP 4, SATA 37

NELSON, CHOLMONDELEY M.
Birthdate: 7/24/1903
Birthplace: London, England
Information Available in These Sources: ABYP 1, ABYP 3

NELSON, CORDNER (BRUCE)
Birthdate: 8/6/1918
Birthplace: San Diego, CA
Information Available in These Sources: SATA 29, SATA 54

NELSON, ESTHER L.
Birthdate: 9/9/1928
Birthplace: New York, NY
Information Available in These Sources: SATA 13

NELSON, LAWRENCE E(RNEST)
Birthdate: 10/4/1928
Birthplace: Des Moines, IA
Deathdate: 12/17/1977
Information Available in These Sources: SATA 28

NELSON, MARG (RAIBLEY)
Birthdate: 7/10/1899
Birthplace: Los Angeles, CA
Information Available in These Sources: ABYP 2, ABYP 3

NELSON, MARY CARROLL
Birthdate: 4/24/1929
Birthplace: College Station, TX
Information Available in These Sources: SATA 23

NELSON, MARY E.
See Carter, Katharine J(ones)

NELSON, ROY PAUL
Birthdate: 6/17/1923
Birthplace: Portland, OR
Information Available in These Sources: SATA 59

NEPHEW, WILLIAM
Information Available in These Sources: ABYP 2, ABYP 3

NERLOVE, MIRIAM
Birthdate: 7/24/1959
Birthplace: Minneapolis, MN
Information Available in These Sources: SATA 49, SATA 53

NESBIT, TROY
See Folsom, Franklin (Brewster)

NESBITT, ESTA
Birthdate: 11/10/1918
Birthplace: New York, NY
Information Available in These Sources: ICB 3

NESPOJOHN, KATHERINE V(ERONICA)
Birthdate: 6/25/1912
Birthplace: Bridgeport, CT
Information Available in These Sources: SATA 7

NESS, EVALINE (MICHELOW)
(Evaline Boyd)
Birthdate: 4/24/1911
Birthplace: Union City, OH
Deathdate: 8/12/1986
Information Available in These Sources: BABP, DLB 61, IBYP 1, IBYP 2, ICB 3, ICB 4, JBA 3, SATA 1, SATA 26, SATA 49, TCCW 1, TCCW 2, TCCW 3

NESTOR, WILLIAM PRODROMAS
Birthdate: 7/29/1947
Birthplace: Atlantic City, NJ
Information Available in These Sources: SATA 49

NETAMUXWE
See Bock, William Sauts Netamux'we

NEUFELD, JOHN (ARTHUR)
Birthdate: 12/14/1938
Birthplace: Chicago, IL
Information Available in These Sources: DACF, SATA 6

NEUMEYER, PETER F(LORIAN)
Birthdate: 8/4/1929
Birthplace: Munich, Germany
Information Available in These Sources: SATA 13

NEUSNER, JACOB
Birthdate: 7/28/1932
Birthplace: Hartford, CT
Information Available in These Sources: SATA 38

NEVILLE, EMILY CHENEY
Birthdate: 12/28/1919
Birthplace: Manchester, CT
Information Available in These Sources: ABYP 1, ABYP 3, DACF, JBA 3, MBMP, SATA 1, TCCW 1, TCCW 2, TCCW 3

NEVILLE, MARY
See Woodrich, Mary Neville

NEVINS, ALBERT J.
Birthdate: 9/11/1915
Birthplace: Yonkers, NY
Information Available in These Sources: ABYP 1, ABYP 3, SATA 20

NEWBERRY, CLARE TURLAY
Birthdate: 4/10/1903
Birthplace: Enterprise, OR
Deathdate: 2/12/1970
Information Available in These Sources: ABYP 1, ABYP 3, ICB 1, ICB 2, ICB 4, JBA 2, SATA 1, SATA 26 TCCW 1

NEWCOMB, COVELLE
Birthdate: 9/7/1908
Birthplace: San Antonio, TX
Information Available in These Sources: ABYP 1, ABYP 3, JBA 2

NEWCOMB, ELLSWORTH
See Kenny, Ellsworth Newcomb

NEWCOMBE, JACK
Birthdate: 7/25/1924
Birthplace: Burlington, VT
Information Available in These Sources: ABYP 1, ABYP 3, SATA 33, SATA 45

NEWELL, CROSBY
See Bonsall, Crosby (Barbara Newell)

NEWELL, EDYTHE W.
Birthdate: 10/28/1910
Birthplace: Arlington, OR
Information Available in These Sources: SATA 11

NEWELL, HOMER EDWARD, JR.
Birthdate: 3/11/1915
Birthplace: Holyoke, MA
Deathdate: 7/18/1983
Information Available in These Sources: ABYP 1, ABYP 3

NEWELL, HOPE (HOCKENBERRY)
(Hope Hockenberry)
Birthdate: 1896
Birthplace: Bradford, PA
Deathdate: 1965
Information Available in These Sources: ABYP 1, ABYP 3, MJA, SATA 24

NEWELL, PETER
Birthdate: 3/5/1862
Birthplace: MacDonough County, IL
Deathdate: 1/15/1924
Information Available in These Sources: DLB 42

NEWLON, CLARKE
See Newlon, Frank Clarke

NEWLON, FRANK CLARKE
(Clarke Newlon, Michael Clarke)
Birthdate, 1905?
Birthplace: Griswold, IA
Deathdate: 12/15/1982
Information Available in These Sources: ABYP 4, SATA 6, SATA 33

NEWMAN, DAISY
Birthdate: 5/9/1904
Birthplace: Southport, Lancashire, England
Information Available in These Sources: ABYP 4, SATA 27

NEWMAN, GERALD
Birthdate: 5/3/1939
Birthplace: New York, NY
Information Available in These Sources: SATA 42, 46

NEWMAN, MATTHEW (HARRISON)
Birthdate: 7/22/1955
Birthplace: St. Petersburg, FL
Information Available in These Sources: SATA 56

NEWMAN, ROBERT (HOWARD)
Birthdate: 6/3/1909
Birthplace: New York, NY
Deathdate: 12/7/1988
Information Available in These Sources: ABYP 1, ABYP 3, DACF, SATA 4, SATA 60, TCCW 2, TCCW 3, JBA 6

NEWMAN, SHIRLEE PETKIN
Birthdate: 2/16/1924
Birthplace: Boston, MA
Information Available in These Sources: ABYP 4, SATA 10

NEWSOM, CAROL
Birthdate: 8/15/1948
Birthplace: Fort Worth, TX
Information Available in These Sources: SATA 40

NEWSOME, ARDEN J(EANNE BOKEENO)
(Jeanne Sebastian)
Birthdate: 7/27/1932
Birthplace: Philadelphia, PA
Information Available in These Sources: ABYP 4

NEWTON, JAMES R(OBERT)
Birthdate: 12/22/1935
Birthplace: Yakima, WA
Information Available in These Sources: SATA 23

NEWTON, SUZANNE (LATHAM)
Birthdate: 10/8/1936
Birthplace: Bunnlevel, NC
Information Available in These Sources: ABYP 4, SATA 5, JBA 6

NEY, JOHN
Birthdate: 5/3/1923
Birthplace: St. Paul, MN
Information Available in These Sources: ABYP 4, DACF, JBA 5, SATA 33, SATA 43

NEYHART, LOUISE (PAULINE) ALBRIGHT
Birthdate: 1/30/1905
Birthplace: Amboy, IL
Information Available in These Sources: ABYP 2, ABYP 3

NICHOLS, CECILIA FAWN
Birthdate: 3/6/1906
Birthplace: Bellevue, NE
Information Available in These Sources: SATA 12

NICHOLS, DALE
Birthdate: 7/13/1904
Birthplace: David City, NE
Information Available in These Sources: ICB 1

NICHOLS, MARIE C.
Birthdate: 4/15/1905
Birthplace: Brooklyn, NY
Information Available in These Sources: IBYP 2, ICB 2

NICHOLS, NELL B.
Information Available in These Sources: ABYP 4

NICHOLS, SPENCER BAIRD
Birthdate: 2/13/1875
Birthplace: Washington, DC
Deathdate: 8/27/1950
Information Available in These Sources: ICB 1

NICKELSBURG, JANET
Birthdate: 3/1/1893
Birthplace: San Francisco, CA
Information Available in These Sources: SATA 11

NICKERSON, BETTY
See Nickerson, Elizabeth

NICKERSON, ELIZABETH
(Betty Nickerson)
Birthdate: 6/26/1922
Birthplace: Fort Scott, KS
Information Available in These Sources: SATA 14

NICKERSON, JAN
(Mildred Nickerson Smith)
Birthplace: Somerville, MA
Information Available in These Sources: ABYP 1, ABYP 3

NICKLAUS, CAROL
Information Available in These Sources: IBYP 2, SATA 33

NICLEODHAS, SORCHE
See Alger, Leclaire (Gowans)

NICOLAS
See Mordvinoff, Nicolas

NICOLAY, HELEN
Birthdate: 3/9/1866
Birthplace: Paris, France
Deathdate: 9/12/1954
Information Available in These Sources: ABYP 1, ABYP 3, JBA 1, JBA 2, YABC

NIEHUIS, CHARLES C(ARROLL)
Birthdate: 1907
Birthplace: Buck Grove, IA
Information Available in These Sources: ABYP 1, ABYP 3

NIELSEN, KAY (RASMUS)
Birthdate: 3/12/1886
Birthplace: Copenhagen, Denmark
Deathdate: 6/??/1957
Information Available in These Sources: ICB 1, SATA 16

NIELSEN, VIRGINIA
See McCall, Virginia Nielson

NINON
See Macknight, Ninon

NISENSON, SAMUEL
Birthdate, 1905?
Information Available in These Sources: IBYP 1, IBYP 2

NIVOLA, CLAIRE (A.)
Birthplace: New York, NY
Information Available in These Sources: IBYP 2

NIXON, HERSHELL HOWARD
Birthdate: 8/4/1923
Birthplace: Duncan, OK
Information Available in These Sources: SATA 42

NIXON, JOAN LOWERY
Birthdate: 2/3/1927
Birthplace: Los Angeles, CA
Information Available in These Sources: ABYP 4, DACF, JBA 5, SATA 8, SATA 44

NOBLE, IRIS (DAVIS)
Birthdate: 2/22/1922
Birthplace: Calgary, Alberta, Canada
Deathdate: 6/30/1986
Information Available in These Sources: ABYP 1, ABYP 3, SATA 5, SATA 49

NOBLE, TRINKA HAKES
Information Available in These Sources: SATA 37, JBA 6

NODSET, JOAN L.
See Lexau, Joan M.

NOGUERE, SUZANNE
Birthdate: 12/1/1947
Birthplace: New York, NY
Information Available in These Sources: SATA 34

NOLAN, DENNIS
Birthdate: 10/19/1945
Birthplace: San Francisco, CA
Information Available in These Sources: SATA 34, SATA 42

NOLAN, JEANNETTE COVERT
(Caroline Tucker)
Birthdate: 3/31/1897 or 3/31/1896
Birthplace: Evansville, IN
Deathdate: 10/12/1974
Information Available in These Sources: ABYP 1, ABYP 3, JBA 2, SATA 2 SATA 27

NOLAN, PAUL T(HOMAS)
Birthdate: 4/4/1919
Birthplace: Rochester, NY
Information Available in These Sources: SATA 48

NOLAN, WILLIAM F(RANCIS)
Birthdate: 3/6/1928
Birthplace: Kansas City, MO
Information Available in These Sources: SATA 28

NONNAST, MARIE
Birthdate: 7/4/1924
Birthplace: Jenkintown, PA
Information Available in These Sources: IBYP 2, ICB 2, ICB 3

NOONAN, JULIA
Birthdate: 10/25/1946
Birthplace: Brooklyn, NY
Information Available in These Sources: IBYP 2, ICB 4, SATA 4

NORCROSS, JOHN
See Conroy, Jack (Wesley)

NORDHOFF, CHARLES (BERNARD)
Birthdate: 2/1/1887
Birthplace: London, England
Deathdate: 4/11/1947
Information Available in These Sources: ABYP 1, ABYP 3, JBA 1, JBA 2, SATA 23

NORDICUS
See Snyder, Louis Leo

NORDLICHT, LILLIAN
Birthplace: New York, NY
Information Available in These Sources: SATA 29

NORDSTROM, URSULA (LITCHFIELD)
Birthdate: 2/1/1910
Birthplace: New York, NY
Deathdate: 10/11/1988
Information Available in These Sources: ABYP 2, ABYP 3, DACF, SATA 3, SATA 57

NORLING, ERNEST RALPH
Birthdate: 9/26/1892
Birthplace: Pasco, WA
Information Available in These Sources: ABYP 1, ABYP 3

NORLING, JO(SEPHINE STEARNS)
Birthdate: 1895
Birthplace: Kalamo Township, MI
Information Available in These Sources: ABYP 1, ABYP 3

NORMAN, CHARLES
Birthdate: 5/9/1904
Birthplace: Russia
Information Available in These Sources: ABYP 1, ABYP 3, SATA 38

NORMAN, JAMES
See Schmidt, James Norman

NORMAN, STEVE
See Pashko, Stanley

NORRIS, FAITH (GRIGSBY)
Information Available in These Sources: ABYP 1, ABYP 3

NORRIS, GUNILLA B(RODDE)
Birthdate: 1939
Birthplace: Argentina
Information Available in These Sources: ABYP 4, SATA 20

NORRIS, MARGARET
Information Available in These Sources: SVC 2, SVC 3

NORRIS, MARIANNA
Information Available in These Sources: ABYP 4

NORTH, ANDREW
See Norton, Alice Mary

NORTH, ROBERT
See Withers, Carl A.

NORTH, STERLING
Birthdate: 11/4/1906
Birthplace: Edgerton, WI
Deathdate: 12/22/1974 or 12/21/1974
Information Available in These Sources: ABYP 1, ABYP 3, DACF, JBA 3, SATA 1, SATA 26, SATA 45, TCCW 1, TCCW 2, TCCW 3

NORTON, ALICE MARY
(Andre Norton, Andrew North, Allen Weston)
Birthdate: 2/17/1912
Birthplace: Cleveland, OH
Information Available in These Sources: MJA, SATA 1, SATA 43, TCCW 1, TCCW 2, TCCW 3

NORTON, ANDRE
See Norton, Alice Mary

NORTON, FRANK R(OWLAND) B(ROWNING)
(Browning Norton)
Birthdate: 3/5/1909
Birthplace: Parkman, OH
Information Available in These Sources: SATA 10

NOURSE, ALAN E(DWARD)
(Dr. X, Al Edwards)
Birthdate: 8/11/1928
Birthplace: Des Moines, IA
Information Available in These Sources: ABYP 1, ABYP 3, SATA 48

NOVAK, MATT
Birthdate: 10/23/1962
Birthplace: Trenton, NJ
Information Available in These Sources: SATA 52, SATA 60

NOWELL, ELIZABETH CAMERON
(Elizabeth Cameron, Elizabeth Clemons)
Information Available in These Sources: SATA 12

NUGENT, FRANCES ROBERTS
Birthdate: 1/28/1904
Birthplace: New York, NY
Information Available in These Sources: ABYP 1, ABYP 3

NUMEROFF, LAURA JOFFE
Birthdate: 7/14/1953
Birthplace: Brooklyn, NY
Information Available in These Sources: SATA 28

NUNN, JESSIE ALFORD
Birthplace: Sedan, KS
Information Available in These Sources: ABYP 4

NURA
See Ulreich, Nura Woodson

NURENBERG, THELMA
See Greenhaus, Thelma Nurenberg

NURNBERG, MAXWELL
Birthdate: 12/11/1897
Birthplace: Poland
Deathdate: 12/22/1984
Information Available in These Sources: SATA 27, 41

NYCE, HELENE VON STRECKER
(Nellie Nyce)
Birthdate: 6/11/1885
Birthplace: Warren County, NJ
Deathdate: 1969
Information Available in These Sources: SATA 19

NYCE, NELLIE
See Nyce, Helene Von Strecker

NYCE, VERA
Birthdate: 7/26/1862
Birthplace: Reading, PA
Deathdate: 1925
Information Available in These Sources: SATA 19

O

O'BRIEN, ANNE SIBLEY
Birthdate: 6/10/1952
Birthplace: Chicago, IL
Information Available in These Sources: SATA 48, SATA 53

O'BRIEN, DEAN D.
See Binder, Otto O(scar)

O'BRIEN, ESSE FORRESTER
Birthdate, 1895?
Birthplace: Waco, TX
Deathdate: 5/21/1975
Information Available in These Sources: SATA 30

O'BRIEN, JACK
See O'Brien, John Sherman

O'BRIEN, JOHN SHERMAN
(Jack O'Brien)
Birthdate: 8/18/1898
Birthplace: Duluth, MN
Deathdate: 12/6/1938
Information Available in These Sources: ABYP 1, ABYP 3, MJA

O'BRIEN, ROBERT C.
See Conly, Robert Leslie

O'BRIEN, THOMAS C(LEMENT)
Birthdate: 7/10/1938
Birthplace: New York, NY
Information Available in These Sources: SATA 29

O'CARROLL, RYAN
See Markun, Patricia M(aloney)

O'CONNELL, MARGARET F(ORSTER)
Birthdate: 1/7/1935
Birthplace: Wilmington, DE
Deathdate: 11/6/1977
Information Available in These Sources: SATA 30, SATA 49

O'CONNELL, PEG
See Ahern, Margaret McCrohan

O'CONNOR, JANE
Birthdate: 12/30/1947
Birthplace: New York, NY
Information Available in These Sources: SATA 47, SATA 59

O'CONNOR, KAREN
(Karen O'Connor Sweeney)
Birthdate: 4/8/1938
Birthplace: Chicago, IL
Information Available in These Sources: SATA 34

O'CONNOR, PATRICK
See Wibberley, Leonard (Patrick O'Connor)

O'CONNOR, RICHARD
(Frank Archer, John Burke, Patrick Wayland)
Birthdate: 3/10/1915
Birthplace: La Porte, IN
Deathdate: 2/15/1975
Information Available in These Sources: ABYP 4, SATA 21

O'DANIEL, JANET
Birthdate: 1/17/1921
Birthplace: Ithaca, NY
Information Available in These Sources: SATA 24

O'DELL, SCOTT
Birthdate: 5/23/1898 or 5/23/1902 or 5/23/1903
Birthplace: Los Angeles, CA
Deathdate: 10/15/1989
Information Available in These Sources: ABYP 1, ABYP 3, AICB, DACF, MJA, SATA 12, SATA 60, SVC 3, TCCW 1, TCCW 2, TCCW 3

O'DONNELL, DICK
See Lupoff, Richard A(llen)

O'DONNELL, K. M.
See Malzberg, Barry (N.)

O'HANLON, JACKLYN
See Meek, Jacklyn O'Hanlon

O'HARA, MARY
See Alsop, Mary O'Hara

O'KANE, DICK
Birthplace: Little Rock, AR
Information Available in These Sources: ABYP 4

O'KELLEY, MATTIE LOU
Birthdate: 3/30/1908
Birthplace: Banks County, GA
Information Available in These Sources: SATA 36

O'LEARY, BRIAN (TODD)
Birthdate: 1/27/1940
Birthplace: Boston, MA
Information Available in These Sources: SATA 6

O'LEARY, FRANK(LIN J.)
Birthdate: 2/1/1922
Birthplace: Marfa, TX
Information Available in These Sources: ABYP 4

O'MALLEY, PATRICIA
Birthdate: 1900
Birthplace: Manchester, NH
Information Available in These Sources: ABYP 1, ABYP 3

O'NEILL, EUGENE (GLADSTONE)
Birthdate: 10/6/1888
Birthplace: New York, NY
Deathdate: 11/27/1953
Information Available in These Sources: JBA 1

O'NEILL, HESTER (ADAMS)
Birthdate: 2/18/1908
Birthplace: Marseilles, IL
Information Available in These Sources: ABYP 1, ABYP 3

O'NEILL, MARY L(E DUC)
Birthdate: 2/16/1908
Birthplace: New York, NY
Information Available in These Sources: ABYP 1, ABYP 3, JBA 3, SATA 2

O'REILLY, JOHN
Birthdate: 1906 or 1907
Information Available in These Sources: ABYP 1, ABYP 3

O'REILLY, SEAN
See Deegan, Paul Joseph

OAKES, VANYA
(Virginia Armstrong Oakes)
Birthdate: 9/13/1909
Birthplace: Nutley, NJ
Deathdate: 11/2/1983
Information Available in These Sources: ABYP 1, ABYP 3, SATA 6, SATA 37

OAKES, VIRGINIA ARMSTRONG
See Oakes, Vanya

OAKLEY, DON(ALD G.)
Birthdate: 11/3/1927
Birthplace: Pittsburgh, PA
Information Available in These Sources: SATA 8

OAKLEY, HELEN (MCKELVEY)
Birthdate: 2/10/1906
Birthplace: New York, NY
Information Available in These Sources: SATA 10

OAKLEY, THORNTON
Birthdate: 3/27/1881
Birthplace: Pittsburgh, PA
Deathdate: 4/4/1953
Information Available in These Sources: ICB 1

OANA, KATHERINE D.
(Kay D. Oana)
Birthdate: 8/29/1929
Birthplace: Akron, OH
Information Available in These Sources: SATA 37, SATA 53

OANA, KAY D.
See Oana, Katherine D.

OATES, STEPHEN B.
Birthdate: 1/5/1936
Birthplace: Pampa, TX
Information Available in These Sources: SATA 59

OBLIGADO, LILIAN (ISABEL)
Birthdate: 4/12/1931
Birthplace: Buenos Aires, Argentina
Information Available in These Sources: ICB 3, SATA 45

OBRANT, SUSAN
Birthdate: 8/24/1946
Birthplace: Philadelphia, PA
Information Available in These Sources: IBYP 2, SATA 11

ODENWALD, ROBERT P(AUL)
Birthdate: 6/25/1899
Birthplace: Karlsruhe, Germany
Deathdate: 1965
Information Available in: ABYP 1, 3, SATA 11

ODOR, RUTH SHANNON
Birthdate: 9/22/1926
Birthplace: Corinth, KY
Information Available in These Sources: SATA 44

OECHSLI, KELLY
Birthdate: 2/23/1918
Birthplace: Butte, MT
Information Available in These Sources: IBYP 2, ICB 3, SATA 5

OFFIT, SIDNEY
Birthdate: 10/13/1928
Birthplace: Baltimore, MD
Information Available in These Sources: ABYP 4, SATA 10

OFFORD, LENORE (GLEN)
Birthdate: 10/24/1905
Birthplace: Spokane, WA
Information Available in These Sources: ABYP 1, ABYP 3

OGAN, GEORGE F.
(Lee Castle, M. G. Ogan)
Birthdate: 2/1/1912
Birthplace: St. Louis (Kirkwood), MO
Information Available in These Sources: ABYP 4, SATA 13

OGAN, M. G.
See Ogan, George F. and Ogan, Margaret E. (Nettles)

OGAN, MARGARET E. (NETTLES)
(Lee Castle, M. G. Ogan)
Birthdate: 4/27/1923
Birthplace: Columbia, LA
Deathdate: 4/15/1979
Information Available in These Sources: ABYP 4, SATA 13

OGBURN, CHARLTON, JR.
Birthdate: 3/15/1911
Birthplace: Atlanta, GA
Information Available in These Sources: SATA 3

OGILVIE, ELISABETH MAY
Birthdate: 5/20/1917
Birthplace: Boston, MA
Information Available in These Sources: ABYP 2, ABYP 3, SATA 29, SATA 40

OGLE, LUCILLE (EDITH)
Birthdate: 9/20/1904
Birthplace: Cleveland, OH
Deathdate: 12/17/1988
Information Available in These Sources: ABYP 4, SATA 59

OHIYESA
See Eastman, Charles A(lexander)

OHLSSON, IB
Birthdate: 8/9/1935
Birthplace: Copenhagen, Denmark
Information Available in These Sources: IBYP 1, IBYP 2, ICB 3, ICB 4, SATA 7

OKIMOTO, JEAN DAVIES
Birthdate: 12/14/1942
Birthplace: Cleveland, OH
Information Available in These Sources: SATA 34

OLCOTT, FRANCES JENKINS
Birthdate, 1872?
Birthplace: Paris, France
Deathdate: 3/29/1963
Information Available in These Sources: ABYP 4, JBA 1, JBA 2, SATA 19

OLCOTT, VIRGINIA
Birthplace: Albany, NY
Information Available in These Sources: JBA 1, JBA 2

OLDDEN, RICHARD
Information Available in These Sources: IBYP 2

OLDEN, SAM
Birthplace: Yazoo City (near), MS
Information Available in These Sources: ABYP 1, ABYP 3

OLDENBURG, E(GBERT) WILLIAM
Birthdate: 4/4/1936
Birthplace: Muskegon, MI
Deathdate: 9/7/1974
Information Available in These Sources: SATA 35

OLDFIELD, MARGARET J(EAN)
Birthdate: 9/23/1932
Birthplace: Waukegan, IL
Information Available in These Sources: SATA 56

OLDRIN, JOHN
Birthdate: 1901
Birthplace: CT
Information Available in These Sources: ABYP 1, ABYP 3

OLDS, ELIZABETH
Birthdate: 12/10/1896 or 12/10/1897
Birthplace: Minneapolis, MN
Information Available in These Sources: ABYP 1, ABYP 3, ICB 2, ICB 3, SATA 3

OLDS, HELEN DIEHL
Birthdate: 4/29/1895
Birthplace: Springfield, OH
Deathdate: 1/1/1981
Information Available in These Sources: ABYP 1, ABYP 3, SATA 9, SATA 25

OLDSTYLE, JONATHAN
See Irving, Washington

OLEKSY, WALTER
(Walter Olesky)
Birthdate: 6/24/1930
Birthplace: Chicago, IL
Information Available in These Sources: SATA 33

OLESKY, WALTER
See Oleksy, Walter

OLESON, CLAIRE
Birthplace: Chicago, IL
Information Available in These Sources: ABYP 4

OLIVER, JOHN EDWARD
Birthdate: 10/21/1933
Birthplace: Dover, Kent, England
Information Available in These Sources: SATA 21

OLMSTED, LORENA ANN
Birthdate: 8/26/1890
Birthplace: Coronado, CA
Information Available in These Sources: SATA 13

OLNEY, ROSS R.
Birthdate: 4/9/1929
Birthplace: Lima, OH
Information Available in These Sources: ABYP 2, ABYP 3, SATA 13

OLSCHEWSKI, ALFRED (ERICH)
Birthdate: 3/8/1920
Birthplace: Gumbinnen, Germany
Information Available in These Sources: SATA 7

OLSEN, VIOLET (MAE)
Birthdate: 5/8/1922
Birthplace: Spencer, IA
Information Available in These Sources: SATA 58

OLSON, GENE
Birthdate: 1922
Birthplace: Montevideo, MN
Information Available in These Sources: ABYP 1, ABYP 3, SATA 32

OLSON, HELEN KRONBERG
Birthplace: Mt. Angel, OR
Information Available in These Sources: SATA 48

OLUGEBEFOLA, ADEMOLE
Birthdate: 10/2/1941
Birthplace: St. Thomas, VI
Information Available in These Sources: IBYP 2, SATA 15

ONCKEN, CLARA
Birthplace: IL
Information Available in These Sources: ABYP 2, ABYP 3

ONEAL, ELIZABETH (BISGARD)
(Zibby Oneal)
Birthdate: 3/17/1934
Birthplace: Omaha, NE
Information Available in These Sources: DACF, SATA 30, TCCW 3, JBA 6

ONEAL, ZIBBY
See Oneal, Elizabeth (Bisgard)

OPPENHEIM, JOANNE
Birthdate: 5/11/1934
Birthplace: Middletown, NY
Information Available in These Sources: SATA 5

OPPENHEIMER, JOAN L(ETSON)
Birthdate: 1/25/1925
Birthplace: Ellendale, ND
Information Available in These Sources: SATA 28

OPPENHEIMER, LILLIAN
Information Available in These Sources: ABYP 2, ABYP 3

OPTIC, OLIVER
See Adams, William Taylor

ORBAAN, ALBERT F.
Birthdate: 3/17/1913
Birthplace: Rome, Italy
Information Available in These Sources: IBYP 1, IBYP 2, ICB 2

ORBACH, RUTH GARY
Birthdate: 1/16/1941
Birthplace: New York, NY
Information Available in These Sources: SATA 21

ORGEL, DORIS (ADELBERG)
(Doris Adelberg)
Birthdate: 2/15/1929
Birthplace: Vienna, Austria
Information Available in These Sources: ABYP 2, ABYP 3, DACF, JBA 4, SATA 7, TCCW 1, TCCW 2, TCCW 3

ORIOLO, JOE
See Oriolo, Joseph

ORIOLO, JOSEPH
(Joe Oriolo)
Birthdate: 2/21/1913
Birthplace: Union City, NJ
Deathdate: 12/25/1985
Information Available in These Sources: SATA 46

ORLEANS, ILO
Birthdate: 2/24/1897
Birthplace: London, England
Deathdate: 9/26/1962
Information Available in These Sources: SATA 10

ORLOB, HELEN SEABURG
Birthdate: 10/28/1908
Birthplace: Seattle, WA
Information Available in These Sources: ABYP 4

ORMAI, STELLA
Information Available in These Sources: SATA 48, SATA 57

ORMES, JACKIE
See Ormes, Zelda J.

ORMES, ZELDA J.
(Jackie Ormes)
Birthdate: 8/1/1914
Birthplace: Pittsburgh, PA
Deathdate: 1/2/1986
Information Available in These Sources: SATA 47

ORMONDROYD, EDWARD
Birthdate: 10/8/1925
Birthplace: Wilkinsburg, PA
Information Available in These Sources: ABYP 2, ABYP 3, DACF, JBA 3, SATA 14, TCCW 1, TCCW 2, TCCW 3

ORMSBY, VIRGINIA H(AIRE)
Birthplace: Atlanta, GA
Information Available in These Sources: SATA 11

ORR, JACK
Information Available in These Sources: ABYP 4

ORR, WILLIAM A.
Information Available in These Sources: IBYP 2

ORRMONT, ARTHUR
See Gardner, Richard (M.)

ORTH, RICHARD
See Gardner, Richard (M.)

ORTON, HELEN (FULLER)
Birthdate: 11/1/1872
Birthplace: Pekin, NY
Deathdate: 2/16/1955
Information Available in These Sources: ABYP 1, ABYP 3, JBA 1, JBA 2

OSBORN, ROBERT CHESLEY
Birthdate: 10/26/1904
Birthplace: Oshkosh, WI
Information Available in These Sources: IBYP 1, IBYP 2, ICB 3

OSBORNE, CHESTER G.
Birthdate: 9/18/1915
Birthplace: Portsmouth, NH
Information Available in These Sources: SATA 11

OSBORNE, DAVID
See Silverberg, Robert

OSBORNE, LEONE NEAL
Birthdate: 9/25/1914
Birthplace: Toledo, OH
Information Available in These Sources: SATA 2

OSBORNE, MARY POPE
Birthdate: 5/20/1949
Birthplace: Fort Sill, OK
Information Available in These Sources: SATA 41, SATA 55

OSGOOD, WILLIAM E(DWARD)
Birthdate: 3/24/1926
Birthplace: Nashua, NH
Information Available in These Sources: SATA 37

OSSOLI, SARAH MARGARET (FULLER) MARCHESA D'
(Margaret Fuller)
Birthdate: 5/23/1810
Birthplace: Cambridgeport, MA
Deathdate: 6/19/1850
Information Available in These Sources: SATA 25

OSTENDORF, ARTHUR LLOYD, JR.
(Lloyd Ostendorf, Jr.)
Birthdate: 6/23/1921
Birthplace: Dayton, OH
Information Available in These Sources: ABYP 2, ABYP 3

OSTENDORF, LLOYD, JR.
See Ostendorf, Arthur Lloyd, Jr.

OSTERRITTER, JOHN F(ERDINAND)
Birthdate: 2/1/1923
Birthplace: Millvale, PA
Information Available in These Sources: ABYP 4

OSTMAN, LEMPI
Birthdate: 7/7/1899
Birthplace: Brooklyn (Bay Ridge), NY
Information Available in These Sources: ICB 1

OTFINOSKI, STEVEN
Birthdate: 1/11/1949
Birthplace: Queens, NY
Information Available in These Sources: SATA 56

OTIS, JAMES
See Kaler, James Otis

OTTO, MARGARET GLOVER
Birthdate: 1909
Deathdate: 1/6/1976
Information Available in These Sources: ABYP 1, ABYP 3, SATA 30

OURSLER, CHARLES FULTON
(Fulton Oursler)
Birthdate: 1/22/1893
Birthplace: Baltimore, MD
Deathdate: 5/24/1952
Information Available in These Sources: ABYP 2, ABYP 3

OURSLER, FULTON
See Oursler, Charles Fulton

OUSLEY, ODILLE
Birthdate: 10/19/1896
Birthplace: Macon, GA
Information Available in These Sources: SATA 10

OVERHOLSER, WAYNE D.
(John S. Daniels, Lee Leighton, Mark Morgan, Wayne Roberts, Dan J. Stevens, Joseph Wayne)
Birthdate: 9/4/1906
Birthplace: Pomeroy, WA
Information Available in These Sources: DACF

OVINGTON, RAY(MOND W.)
Birthdate: 1917
Information Available in These Sources: ABYP 2, ABYP 3

OWEN, CAROLINE DALE
See Snedeker, Caroline Dale (Parke)

OWEN, RUSSELL
Birthdate: 1/8/1889
Birthplace: Chicago, IL
Deathdate: 4/3/1952
Information Available in These Sources: ABYP 1, ABYP 3

OWEN, RUTH (BRYAN)
(Ruth Bryan Owen Rohde)
Birthdate: 10/2/1885
Birthplace: Jacksonville, IL
Deathdate: 7/26/1954
Information Available in These Sources: ABYP 1, ABYP 3

OWENS, GAIL
Birthdate: 3/13/1939
Birthplace: Detroit, MI
Information Available in These Sources: ICB 4, SATA 54, JBA 6

OZ, FRANK (RICHARD)
Birthdate: 5/24/1944
Birthplace: Hereford, England
Information Available in These Sources: SATA 60

OZER, JEROME S.
Birthdate: 7/18/1927
Birthplace: New York, NY
Information Available in These Sources: SATA 59

P

PACE, MILDRED MASTIN
Birthdate: 6/8/1907
Birthplace: St. Louis, MO
Information Available in These Sources: ABYP 4, SATA 29, SATA 46

PACK, ROBERT
Birthdate: 5/19/1929
Birthplace: New York, NY
Information Available in These Sources: ABYP 2, ABYP 3

PACKARD, EDWARD
Birthdate: 2/16/1931
Birthplace: Huntington, NY
Information Available in These Sources: SATA 47

PACKER, VIN
See Meaker, Marijane

PAGE, EILEEN
See Heal, Edith

PAGE, ELEANOR
See Coerr, Eleanor (Page)

PAGE, LOU WILLIAMS
Birthdate: 10/23/1912
Birthplace: Belleville, NJ
Information Available in These Sources: SATA 38

PAGE, THOMAS NELSON
Birthdate: 4/23/1853
Birthplace: Oakland, VA
Deathdate: 11/1/1922
Information Available in These Sources: JBA 1, SVC 2, SVC 3

PAGET-FREDERICKS, JOSEPH E(DWARD) P(AGET) ROUS-MARTEN
Birthdate: 12/22/1903 or 12/22/1905 or 12/22/1908
Birthplace: San Francisco, CA
Information Available in These Sources: IBYP 2, ICB 2, SATA 30, SVC 2 SVC 3

PAHL, ALETA
Information Available in These Sources: ABYP 4

PAHZ, ANNE CHERYL SUZANNE
(Cheryl Goldfeder, Cheryl Suzanne Pahz, Zan Paz)
Birthdate: 1/29/1949
Birthplace: Ypsilanti, MI
Information Available in These Sources: SATA 11

PAHZ, CHERYL SUZANNE
See Pahz, Anne Cheryl Suzanne

PAHZ, JAMES ALON
(Jim Goldfeder, A. Paz)
Birthdate: 9/11/1943
Birthplace: Chattanooga, TN
Information Available in These Sources: SATA 11

PAIGE, HARRY W.
Birthdate: 9/25/1922
Birthplace: Syracuse, NY
Information Available in These Sources: SATA 35, SATA 41

PAINE, ALBERT BIGELOW
Birthdate: 7/10/1861
Birthplace: New Bedford, MA
Deathdate: 4/9/1937
Information Available in These Sources: ABYP 4, JBA 1

PAINE, RALPH D.
Birthdate: 8/28/1871
Birthplace: Lemont, IL
Deathdate: 4/29/1925
Information Available in These Sources: JBA 1

PAINE, ROBERTA M.
Birthdate: 10/2/1925
Birthplace: Los Angeles, CA
Information Available in These Sources: ABYP 4, SATA 13

PAISLEY, TOM
See Bethancourt, T(omas) Ernesto

PALAZZO, ANTHONY D.
(Tony Palazzo)
Birthdate: 4/7/1905
Birthplace: New York, NY
Deathdate: 9/10/1970
Information Available in These Sources: ABYP 1, ABYP 3, ICB 2, ICB 3, ICB 4, JBA 3, SATA 3

PALAZZO, TONY
See Palazzo, Anthony D.

PALDER, EDWARD L.
Birthdate: 12/5/1922
Birthplace: Boston, MA
Information Available in These Sources: SATA 5

PALFREY, SARAH
See Cooke, Sarah (Palfrey) Fabyan

PALLADINI, DAVID (MARIO)
Birthdate: 4/1/1946
Birthplace: Roteglia, Italy
Information Available in These Sources: ICB 4, SATA 32, SATA 40

PALLAS, NORVIN
Birthdate: 4/4/1918
Birthplace: Cleveland, OH
Information Available in These Sources: SATA 23

PALLISTER, JOHN C(LARE)
Birthdate: 6/12/1891
Birthplace: Cleveland, OH
Deathdate: 3/6/1980
Information Available in These Sources: SATA 26

PALMER, BERNARD
(John Runyan)
Birthdate: 11/ /1914
Birthplace: Central City, NE
Information Available in These Sources: SATA 26

PALMER, BRUCE HAMILTON
Birthdate: 12/26/1932
Birthplace: Norwood, MA
Information Available in These Sources: ABYP 4

PALMER, CANDIDA
See Palmer, Ruth Candida

PALMER, HEIDI
Birthdate: 9/28/1948
Birthplace: Geneva, Switzerland
Information Available in These Sources: SATA 15

PALMER, HELEN MARION
See Geisel, Helen

PALMER, ROBIN
Birthdate: 1911
Birthplace: New York, NY
Information Available in These Sources: ABYP 1, ABYP 3, SATA 43

PALMER, RUTH CANDIDA
(Candida Palmer)
Birthdate: 6/19/1926
Birthplace: Germany
Information Available in These Sources: SATA 11

PALOVIC, CLARA LORA
(Lora Palovic)
Birthdate: 2/24/1918
Birthplace: Rockland, MI
Information Available in These Sources: ABYP 4

PALOVIC, LORA
See Palovic, Clara Lora

PALTROWITZ, DONNA (MILMAN)
Birthdate: 4/12/1950
Birthplace: Brooklyn, NY
Information Available in These Sources: SATA 50

PALTROWITZ, STUART
Birthdate: 1/31/1946
Birthplace: Brooklyn, NY
Information Available in These Sources: SATA 50

PANESIS, NICHOLAS
Birthdate: 12/9/1913
Birthplace: Middleboro, MA
Information Available in These Sources: ICB 1

PANETTA, GEORGE
Birthdate: 8/6/1915
Birthplace: New York, NY
Information Available in These Sources: ABYP 4, SATA 15

PANOWSKI, EILEEN THOMPSON
(Eileen Thompson)
Birthdate: 3/17/1920
Birthplace: Lincoln, NE
Information Available in These Sources: ABYP 2, ABYP 3, DACF, SATA 49

PANSY
See Alden, Isabella (Macdonald)

PANTELL, DORA (FUCHS)
Birthdate: 12/25/1915
Birthplace: New York, NY
Information Available in These Sources: ABYP 4, SATA 39

PANTER, CAROL (YECKES)
Birthdate: 1/19/1936
Birthplace: New York, NY
Information Available in These Sources: ABYP 4, SATA 9

PAPASHVILY, GEORGE
Birthdate: 8/23/1898
Birthplace: Kobiantkari, Georgia, Russia
Deathdate: 3/29/1978
Information Available in These Sources: SATA 17

PAPASHVILY, HELEN (WAITE)
Birthdate: 12/19/1906
Birthplace: Stockton, CA
Information Available in These Sources: SATA 17

PAPE, D(ONNA) L(UGG)
Birthdate: 6/21/1930
Birthplace: Sheboygan, WI
Information Available in These Sources: SATA 2

PAPIN, JOSEPH
Birthplace: St. Louis, MO
Information Available in These Sources: IBYP 1, IBYP 2

PARADIS, ADRIAN ALEXIS
Birthdate: 11/3/1912
Birthplace: Brooklyn, NY
Information Available in These Sources: ABYP 1, ABYP 3, MJA, SATA 1

PARADIS, MARJORIE (BARTHOLOMEW)
Birthdate, 1886?
Birthplace: Montclair, NJ
Deathdate: 7/2/1970
Information Available in These Sources: ABYP 1, ABYP 3, SATA 17

PARENTEAU, SHIRLEY (LAUROLYN)
Birthdate: 1/22/1935
Birthplace: Garibaldi, OR
Information Available in These Sources: SATA 40, SATA 47

PARISH, AGNES SMITH
See Smith, Agnes

PARISH, MARGARET CECILE
(Peggy Parish)
Birthdate: 7/14/1927
Birthplace: Manning, SC
Deathdate: 11/19/1988
Information Available in These Sources: ABYP 1, ABYP 3, JBA 4, SATA 17, SATA 59, TCCW 1, TCCW 2, TCCW 3

PARISH, MARGARET HOLT
See Holt, Margaret (Cecile)

PARISH, PEGGY
See Parish, Margaret Cecile

PARK, BARBARA
Birthdate: 4/21/1947
Birthplace: Mt. Holly, NJ
Information Available in These Sources: SATA 35, SATA 40, JBA 6

PARK, BILL
See Park, W(illiam) B(ryan)

PARK, THOMAS CHOONBAI
Birthdate: 5/21/1919
Birthplace: Bookchong, Korea
Information Available in These Sources: ABYP 2, ABYP 3

PARK, W(ILLIAM) B(RYAN)
(Bill Park)
Birthdate: 6/12/1936
Birthplace: Sanford, FL
Information Available in These Sources: SATA 22

PARKE, MARGARET BITTNER
Birthdate: 1/6/1901
Birthplace: Jim Thorpe (Mauch Chunk), PA
Information Available in These Sources: ABYP 1, ABYP 3

PARKER, ALFRED EUSTACE
Birthdate: 1899
Information Available in These Sources: ABYP 1, ABYP 3

PARKER, ALLISON
See Clyne, Patricia Edwards

PARKER, BERTHA MORRIS
Birthdate: 2/7/1890
Birthplace: Rochester, IL
Deathdate: 11/14/1980
Information Available in These Sources: ABYP 1, ABYP 3, MJA

PARKER, DOROTHY (LANE) D(ANIELS)
Birthdate: 9/22/1927
Birthplace: Chicago, IL
Information Available in These Sources: JBA 4

PARKER, EDGAR
See Parker, James Edgar, Jr.

PARKER, ELINOR (MILNOR)
Birthdate: 3/20/1906
Birthplace: Jersey City, NJ
Information Available in These Sources: SATA 3

PARKER, FAN(IA M. POCKROSE)
Birthdate: 1908
Birthplace: Latvia
Information Available in These Sources: ABYP 1, ABYP 3

PARKER, JAMES EDGAR, JR.
(Edgar Parker)
Birthdate: 1925
Birthplace: Meridian, MS
Information Available in These Sources: ICB 3, JBA 3

PARKER, KAY PETERSON
Birthdate: 10/11/1901
Birthplace: Oak Hill, PA
Information Available in These Sources: ICB 2

PARKER, KRISTY (KETTELKAMP)
Birthdate: 5/3/1957
Birthplace: Decatur, IL
Information Available in These Sources: SATA 59

PARKER, LOIS M(ARY)
Birthdate: 4/18/1912
Birthplace: NE
Information Available in These Sources: SATA 30

PARKER, MARGOT M.
Birthdate: 4/22/1937
Birthplace: Vacaville, CA
Information Available in These Sources: SATA 52

PARKER, NANCY WINSLOW
Birthdate: 10/18/1930
Birthplace: Maplewood, NJ
Information Available in These Sources: IBYP 2, ICB 4, JBA 5, SATA 10

PARKER, ROBERT
See Boyd, Waldo T.

PARKER, ROBERT ANDREW
Birthdate: 5/14/1927
Birthplace: Norfolk, VA
Information Available in These Sources: IBYP 2, ICB 4, JBA 4

PARKHILL, JOHN
See Cox, William R(obert)

PARKINSON, ETHELYN M(INERVA)
Birthdate: 9/13/1906
Birthplace: Oconto County, WI
Information Available in These Sources: ABYP 4, SATA 11

PARKS, EDD WINFIELD
Birthdate: 2/25/1906
Birthplace: Newbern, TN
Information Available in These Sources: SATA 10

PARKS, GORDON (ALEXANDER BUCHANAN)
Birthdate: 11/30/1912
Birthplace: Fort Scott (near), KS
Information Available in These Sources: SATA 8

PARLEY, PETER
See Goodrich, Samuel Griswold

PARLIN, JOHN
See Graves, Charles Parlin

PARNALL, PETER
Birthdate: 5/23/1936
Birthplace: Syracuse, NY
Information Available in These Sources: IBYP 2, ICB 3, ICB 4, JBA 3, SATA 16

PARR, A(DOLPH) H(ENRY)
Birthdate: 1900
Information Available in These Sources: ABYP 2, ABYP 3

PARR, LUCY
(Laura Carroll)
Birthdate: 7/25/1924
Birthplace: Kanab, UT
Information Available in These Sources: SATA 10

PARRISH, ANNE
Birthdate: 11/12/1888
Birthplace: Colorado Springs, CO
Deathdate: 9/5/1957
Information Available in These Sources: IBYP 2, ICB 1, ICB 2, JBA 1, SATA 27, TCCW 2, TCCW 3

PARRISH, FREDERICK MAXFIELD
(Maxfield Parrish)
Birthdate: 7/25/1870
Birthplace: Philadelphia, PA
Deathdate: 3/30/1966
Information Available in These Sources: IBYP 2, ICB 1, JBA 1, JBA 2, SATA 14

PARRISH, MARY
See Cousins, Margaret

PARRISH, MAXFIELD
See Parrish, Frederick Maxfield

PARRY, MARIAN
Birthdate: 1/28/1924
Birthplace: San Francisco, CA
Information Available in These Sources: SATA 13

PARSONS, TOM
See MacPherson, Thomas George

PARSONS, VIRGINIA
Information Available in These Sources: IBYP 2

PARSONS, WILLIAM E(DWARD), JR.
Birthdate: 4/16/1936
Birthplace: Lynn, MA
Information Available in These Sources: ABYP 4

PARTCH, VIRGIL FRANKLIN II
(Vip)
Birthdate: 10/17/1916
Birthplace: St. Paul Island, AK
Deathdate: 8/10/1984
Information Available in These Sources: ABYP 4, SATA 39, SATA 45

PARTON, ETHEL
Birthdate: 12/1/1862
Birthplace: New York, NY
Deathdate: 2/27/1944
Information Available in These Sources: JBA 1, JBA 2

PARTRIDGE, BENJAMIN W(ARING), JR.
Birthdate: 3/9/1915
Birthplace: Huntington, WV
Information Available in These Sources: SATA 28

PASCAL, DAVID
Birthdate: 8/16/1918
Birthplace: New York, NY
Information Available in These Sources: ICB 3, SATA 14

PASCAL, FRANCINE
Birthdate: 5/13/1938
Birthplace: New York, NY
Information Available in These Sources: JBA 5, SATA 37, SATA 51

PASCHAL, NANCY
See Trotter, Grace V(iolet)

PASCUDNIAK, PASCAL
See Lupoff, Richard A(llen)

PASHKO, STANLEY
(Steve Norman, Tony Robbins)
Birthdate: 2/19/1913
Birthplace: New Haven, CT
Information Available in These Sources: SATA 29

PASSAILAIGUE, THOMAS E.
See Bethancourt, T(omas) Ernesto

PATCH, EDITH M(ARION)
Birthdate: 7/27/1876
Birthplace: Worcester, MA
Deathdate: 9/28/1954
Information Available in These Sources: JBA 1, JBA 2

PATENT, DOROTHY HINSHAW
Birthdate: 4/30/1940
Birthplace: Rochester, MN
Information Available in These Sources: ABYP 4, SATA 22, JBA 6

PATERSON, DIANE (R. COLE)
Birthdate: 7/23/1946
Birthplace: Brooklyn, NY
Information Available in These Sources: ABYP 4, ICB 4, SATA 33, SATA 59, JBA 6

PATERSON, KATHERINE (WOMELDORF)
Birthdate: 10/31/1932
Birthplace: Tsing-Tsiang pu, China
Information Available in These Sources: ABYP 4, JBA 5, SATA 13, SATA 53, TCCW 2, TCCW 3

PATON, ALAN (STEWART)
Birthdate: 1/11/1903
Birthplace: Peitermaritzburg, South Africa
Deathdate: 4/12/1988
Information Available in These Sources: ABYP 1, ABYP 3, SATA 11, SATA 56

PATTEN, LEWIS BYFORD
Birthdate: 1/13/1915
Birthplace: Denver, CO
Deathdate: 5/22/1981
Information Available in These Sources: DACF

PATTERSON, CHARLES
Birthdate: 8/5/1935
Birthplace: New Britain, CT
Information Available in These Sources: SATA 59

PATTERSON, LILLIE G.
Birthplace: Hilton Head Island, SC
Information Available in These Sources: ABYP 1, ABYP 3, BAI, SATA 14

PAUL, AILEEN (PHILLIPS)
Birthdate: 6/2/1917
Birthplace: Waycross, GA
Information Available in These Sources: ABYP 4, SATA 12

PAUL, DAVID (TYLER)
Birthdate: 11/18/1934
Birthplace: New York, NY
Deathdate: 3/28/1988
Information Available in These Sources: SATA 56

PAUL, ELIZABETH
See Crow, Donna Fletcher

PAUL, JAMES
(J(ames) C. Kocsis)
Birthdate: 4/27/1936
Birthplace: Buffalo, NY
Information Available in These Sources: IBYP 1, IBYP 2, ICB 3, SATA 23

PAUL, ROBERT
See Roberts, John G(aither)

PAULI, HERTHA (ERNESTINE)
Birthdate: 9/4/1909
Birthplace: Vienna, Austria
Deathdate: 2/9/1973
Information Available in These Sources: ABYP 1, ABYP 3, SATA 3, SATA 26

PAULL, GRACE A(LICE)
Birthdate: 10/7/1898
Birthplace: Cold Brook, NY
Information Available in These Sources: ABYP 1, ABYP 3, ICB 1, ICB 2, JBA 2, SATA 24

PAULSEN, GARY
Birthdate: 5/17/1939
Birthplace: Minneapolis, MN
Information Available in These Sources: SATA 22, SATA 50, SATA 54, TCCW 3, JBA 6

PAULSON, JACK
See Jackson, C(aary) Paul

PAVEL, FRANCES
Birthdate: 2/26/1907
Birthplace: Bethelehem, PA
Information Available in These Sources: SATA 10

PAYNE, ALAN
See Jakes, John (W.)

PAYNE, ALMA SMITH
See Ralston, Alma (Smith Payne)

PAYNE, BERNAL C., JR.
Birthdate: 7/11/1941
Birthplace: St. Louis, MO
Information Available in These Sources: SATA 60

PAYNE, EMMY
See West, Emily G(ovan)

PAYNE, JOAN BALFOUR
Birthdate: 12/2/1923
Birthplace: Natchez, MS
Information Available in These Sources: IBYP 1, IBYP 2, ICB 2, ICB 3

PAYSON, DALE
Birthdate: 6/3/1943
Birthplace: White Plains, NY
Information Available in These Sources: IBYP 1, IBYP 2, SATA 9

PAYZANT, CHARLES
Information Available in These Sources: IBYP 1, IBYP 2, SATA 18

PAYZANT, JESSIE MERCER KNECHTEL
See Mercer, Jessie

PAZ, A.
See Pahz, James Alon

PAZ, ZAN
See Pahz, Anne Cheryl Suzanne

PEABODY, JOSEPHINE PRESTON
Birthdate: 5/30/1874
Birthplace: Brooklyn, NY
Deathdate: 12/4/1922
Information Available in These Sources: JBA 1

PEALE, NORMAN VINCENT
Birthdate: 5/31/1898
Birthplace: Bowersville, OH
Information Available in These Sources: ABYP 2, ABYP 3, SATA 20

PEARE, CATHERINE OWENS
Birthdate: 2/4/1911
Birthplace: Perth Amboy, NJ
Information Available in These Sources: ABYP 1, ABYP 3, MJA, SATA 9

PEARL, RICHARD M(AXWELL)
Birthdate: 5/4/1913
Birthplace: New York, NY
Deathdate: 11/28/1980
Information Available in These Sources: ABYP 1, ABYP 3

PEARSON, GAYLE
Birthdate: 7/12/1947
Birthplace: Chicago, IL
Information Available in These Sources: SATA 53

PEARSON, SUSAN
Birthdate: 12/21/1946
Birthplace: Boston, MA
Information Available in These Sources: ABYP 4, SATA 27, SATA 39

PEASE, HOWARD
Birthdate: 9/6/1894
Birthplace: Stockton, CA
Deathdate: 4/14/1974
Information Available in These Sources: ABYP 1, ABYP 3, JBA 1, JBA 2, SATA 2, SATA 25, TCCW 1, TCCW 2, TCCW 3

PEASE, JOSEPHINE VAN DOLZEN
Birthplace: Au Sable, MI
Information Available in These Sources: ABYP 1, ABYP 3

PEATTIE, DONALD CULROSS
Birthdate: 6/21/1898
Birthplace: Chicago, IL
Deathdate: 11/16/1964
Information Available in These Sources: ABYP 1, ABYP 3

PEAVY, LINDA
Birthdate: 11/5/1943
Birthplace: Hattiesburg, MS
Information Available in These Sources: SATA 54

PECK, ANNE MERRIMAN
Birthdate: 7/21/1884
Birthplace: Piermont-on-Hudson, NY
Information Available in These Sources: ABYP 2, ABYP 3, ICB 1, ICB 2, JBA 1, JBA 2, SATA 18

PECK, GEORGE WILBUR
Birthdate: 9/28/1840
Birthplace: Henderson, NY
Deathdate: 4/16/1916
Information Available in These Sources: DLB 42, WCL

PECK, RICHARD (WAYNE)
Birthdate: 4/5/1934
Birthplace: Decatur, IL
Information Available in These Sources: DACF, JBA 5, SATA 18, SATA 55 TCCW 1, TCCW 2, TCCW 3

PECK, ROBERT NEWTON, III
Birthdate: 2/17/1928
Birthplace: VT
Information Available in These Sources: ABYP 4, DACF, JBA 5, SATA 21, TCCW 1, TCCW 2, TCCW 3

PECKHAM, RICHARD
See Holden, Raymond Peckham

PECKINPAH, BETTY
Information Available in These Sources: ABYP 2, ABYP 3

PEDERSEN, ELSA (KIENITZ)
Birthdate: 5/15/1915
Birthplace: Salt Lake City, UT
Information Available in These Sources: ABYP 2, ABYP 3

PEEK, MERLE
Birthdate: 5/23/1938
Birthplace: Denver, CO
Information Available in These Sources: SATA 39

PEEL, NORMAN LEMON
See Hirsch, Phil

PEEPLES, EDWIN A(UGUSTUS, JR.)
Birthdate: 3/2/1915
Birthplace: Atlanta, GA
Information Available in These Sources: SATA 6

PEET, BILL
See Peet, William Bartlett

PEET, CREIGHTON B.
Birthdate, 1899?
Birthplace: New York, NY
Deathdate: 5/16/1977
Information Available in These Sources: ABYP 1, ABYP 3, SATA 30

PEET, WILLIAM BARTLETT
(Bill Peet)
Birthdate: 1/29/1915
Birthplace: Grandview, IN
Information Available in These Sources: ABYP 1, ABYP 3, CFB, ICB 3, ICB 4, JBA 3, SATA 2, SATA 41 TCCW 1, TCCW 2, TCCW 3

PEIRCE, WALDO
Birthdate: 12/17/1884
Birthplace: Bangor, ME
Deathdate: 3/8/1970
Information Available in These Sources: ICB 1, SATA 28

PELAEZ, JILL
Birthdate: 4/24/1924
Birthplace: Santurce, PR
Information Available in These Sources: SATA 12

PELLOWSKI, ANNE
Birthdate: 6/28/1933
Birthplace: Pine Creek, WI
Information Available in These Sources: ABYP 4, JBA 5, SATA 20

PELLOWSKI, MICHAEL J(OSEPH)
(Ski Michaels)
Birthdate: 1/24/1949
Birthplace: New Brunswick, NJ
Information Available in These Sources: SATA 48

PELS, GERTRUDE JAECKEL
Information Available in These Sources: ABYP-1, ABYP 3

PELTA, KATHY
Birthdate: 10/18/1928
Birthplace: Madrid, IA
Information Available in These Sources: SATA 18

PELTIER, LESLIE C(OPUS)
Birthdate: 1/2/1900
Birthplace: Delphos, OH
Information Available in These Sources: SATA 13

PEMSTEEN, HANS
See Manes, Stephen

PENDERY, ROSEMARY (SCHMITZ)
Birthplace: Elgin, IL
Information Available in These Sources: SATA 7

PENDLE, ALEXY
Birthdate: 4/26/1943
Birthplace: Buenos Aires, Argentina
Information Available in These Sources: SATA 29

PENN, RUTH BONN
See Rosenberg, Ethel (Clifford)

PENNEY, GRACE JACKSON
Birthdate: 6/3/1904
Birthplace: Birmingham, AL
Information Available in These Sources: SATA 35

PENNINGTON, EUNICE
Birthdate: 2/16/1923
Birthplace: Fremont, MO
Information Available in These Sources: SATA 27

PENNINGTON, LILLIAN BOYER
Birthdate: 4/2/1904
Birthplace: Harrisburg, PA
Information Available in These Sources: SATA 45

PENZLER, OTTO
(Irene Adler, Lucy Ferrier, Stephen Gregory, Charles A. Milverton)
Birthdate: 7/8/1942
Birthplace: Hamburg, Germany
Information Available in These Sources: SATA 38

PEPE, PHIL(IP)
Birthdate: 3/21/1935
Birthplace: Brooklyn, NY
Information Available in These Sources: SATA 20

PERARD, VICTOR SEMON
Birthdate: 1/16/1870
Birthplace: Paris, France
Deathdate: 7/9/1957
Information Available in These Sources: ICB 1

PERCEVAL, DON
Birthdate: 1/8/1908
Birthplace: Woodford, Essex, England
Information Available in These Sources: IBYP 2, ICB 2

PERCY, CHARLES HARTING
Birthdate: 9/27/1919
Birthplace: Pensacola, FL
Information Available in These Sources: ABYP 4

PERERA, THOMAS BIDDLE
Birthdate: 11/20/1938
Birthplace: New York, NY
Information Available in These Sources: SATA 13

PEREZ, WALTER
See Joseph, James (Herz)

PERKINS, AL(BERT ROGERS)
Birthdate: 8/27/1904
Birthplace: New York, NY
Deathdate: 2/10/1975
Information Available in These Sources: SATA 30

PERKINS, LUCY FITCH
Birthdate: 7/12/1865
Birthplace: Maples, IN
Deathdate: 3/18/1937
Information Available in These Sources: JBA 1, JBA 2, TCCW 1, TCCW 2, TCCW 3

PERKINS, MARLIN
See Perkins, Richard Marlin

PERKINS, RICHARD MARLIN
(Marlin Perkins)
Birthdate: 3/28/1905
Birthplace: Carthage, MO
Deathdate: 6/14/1986
Information Available in These Sources: ABYP 1, ABYP 3, SATA 21, SATA 48

PERL, LILA
Birthplace: New York, NY
Information Available in These Sources: ABYP 2, ABYP 3, SATA 6, JBA 6

PERL, SUSAN
Birthdate: 9/8/1922
Birthplace: Vienna, Austria
Deathdate: 6/27/1983
Information Available in These Sources: IBYP 2, ICB 3, ICB 4, SATA 22 SATA 34

PERLMUTTER, O(SCAR) WILLIAM
(William Perlmutter)
Birthdate: 7/5/1920
Deathdate: 3/5/1975
Information Available in These Sources: ABYP 4, SATA 8

PERRINE, MARY (BUSH)
Birthdate: 5/5/1913
Birthplace: Moscow, ID
Information Available in These Sources: ABYP 4, SATA 2

PERROTT, JENNIFER
(Jennifer Emry-Perrott)
Information Available in These Sources: IBYP 2

PERRY, BARBARA FISHER
See Fisher, Barbara

PERRY, JOHN
Birthdate: 2/25/1914
Birthplace: Newark, NJ
Information Available in These Sources: ABYP 2, ABYP 3

PERRY, PATRICIA
Birthdate: 9/21/1949
Information Available in These Sources: SATA 30

PERRY, PHYLLIS J.
Birthdate: 10/23/1933
Birthplace: Nevada City, CA
Information Available in These Sources: SATA 60

PERSHING, MARIE
See Schultz, Pearle Henriksen

PERSKE, ROBERT
Birthdate: 10/16/1927
Birthplace: Denver, CO
Information Available in These Sources: SATA 57

PERSON, WILLIAM THOMAS
Birthdate: 1900
Birthplace: Mt. Pleasant, MS
Information Available in These Sources: ABYP 1, ABYP 3

PETERS, ALEXANDER
See Hollander, Zander

PETERS, CAROLINE
See Betz, Eva Kelly

PETERS, ELIZABETH
See Mertz, Barbara (Gross)

PETERS, S. H.
See Porter, William Sydney

PETERSEN, P(ETER) J(AMES)
Birthdate: 10/23/1941
Birthplace: Santa Rosa, CA
Information Available in These Sources: SATA 43, SATA 48, JBA 6

PETERSHAM, MAUD (SYLVIA FULLER)
Birthdate: 8/5/1890 or 8/5/1889
Birthplace: Kingston, NY
Deathdate: 11/29/1971
Information Available in These Sources: ABYP 1, ABYP 3, BABP, DLB 22, FLTYP, IBYP 1, IBYP 2, ICB 1, ICB 2, ICB 3, ICB 4, JBA 1, JBA 2, SATA 17, SVC 2, SVC 3, TCCW 1, TCCW 2, TCCW 3

PETERSHAM, MISKA
(Mikaly Petrezselyen)
Birthdate: 9/20/1888 or 9/20/1889
Birthplace: Toeroekszentmiklos, Hungary
Deathdate: 5/15/1960
Information Available in These Sources: ABYP 1, ABYP 3, BABP, DLB 22, FLTYP, IBYP 1, IBYP 2, ICB 1, ICB 2, ICB 3, JBA 1, JBA 2, SATA 17, SVC 2, SVC 3, TCCW 1 TCCW 2, TCCW 3

PETERSON, BETTY FERGUSON
Birthdate: 11/9/1917
Birthplace: London, England
Information Available in These Sources: ICB 3

PETERSON, ESTHER (ALLEN)
(Ruth Allen)
Birthdate: 3/9/1934
Birthplace: Carson, ND
Information Available in These Sources: SATA 35

PETERSON, HAROLD L(ESLIE)
Birthdate: 5/22/1922
Birthplace: Peekskill, NY
Information Available in These Sources: ABYP 4, SATA 8

PETERSON, HELEN STONE
Birthdate: 5/12/1910
Birthplace: Binghamton, NY
Information Available in These Sources: SATA 8

PETERSON, JEANNE WHITEHOUSE
See Whitehouse, Jeanne

PETERSON, JOHN LAWRENCE
Birthdate: 1924
Information Available in These Sources: ABYP 4

PETERSON, LORRAINE
Birthdate: 7/10/1940
Birthplace: Red Wing, MN
Information Available in These Sources: SATA 44, SATA 56

PETERSON, RUSSELL FRANCIS
Birthplace: Montclair, NJ
Information Available in These Sources: ABYP 1, ABYP 3, ICB 3

PETIE, HARIS
Birthdate: 6/26/1915
Birthplace: Boulder Creek, CA
Information Available in These Sources: IBYP 1, IBYP 2, SATA 10

PETREZSELYEN, MIKALY
See Petersham, Miska

PETRIE, CATHERINE
Birthdate: 10/22/1947
Birthplace: Elkhorn, WI
Information Available in These Sources: SATA 41, SATA 52

PETROSKI, CATHERINE (ANN GROOM)
Birthdate: 9/7/1939
Birthplace: St. Louis, MO
Information Available in These Sources: SATA 48

PETROVICH, MICHAEL B(ORO)
Birthdate: 10/18/1922
Birthplace: Cleveland, OH
Information Available in These Sources: SATA 40

PETROVSKAYA, KYRA
See Wayne, Kyra Petrovskaya

PETRY, ANN (LANE)
Birthdate: 10/12/1912 or 10/12/1911 or 10/12/1908
Birthplace: Old Saybrook, CT
Information Available in These Sources: ABYP 1, ABYP 3, BAI, DACF, JBA 3, SATA 5, TCCW 1, TCCW 2 TCCW 3

PETTIT, FLORENCE H.
Information Available in These Sources: ABYP 4

PETTIT, MARY P.
Information Available in These Sources: ABYP 2, ABYP 3

PEVSNER, STELLA
Birthplace: Lincoln, IL
Information Available in These Sources: JBA 5, SATA 8

PFEFFER, SUSAN BETH
Birthdate: 2/17/1948
Birthplace: New York, NY
Information Available in These Sources: SATA 4, JBA 6

PHELAN, JOSEPH
Information Available in These Sources: IBYP 2

PHELAN, MARY KAY (HARRIS)
Birthdate: 6/30/1914
Birthplace: Baldwin City, KS
Information Available in These Sources: ABYP 4, SATA 3

PHELAN, TERRY WOLFE
Birthdate: 5/26/1941
Birthplace: New York, NY
Information Available in These Sources: SATA 56

PHELPS, ETHEL JOHNSTON
Birthdate: 3/8/1914
Birthplace: Long Island, NY
Information Available in These Sources: SATA 35

PHELPS, MARGARET (NELSON)
Birthplace: VA
Information Available in These Sources: ABYP 2, ABYP 3

PHELPS, WILLIAM LYON
Birthdate: 1865
Deathdate: 1943
Information Available in These Sources: JBA 1

PHILBROOK, CLEM(ENT E.)
Birthdate: 10/30/1917
Birthplace: Old Town, ME
Information Available in These Sources: SATA 24

PHILLIPS, BETTY LOU
See Phillips, Elizabeth Louise

PHILLIPS, ELIZABETH LOUISE
(Betty Lou Phillips)
Birthplace: Cleveland, OH
Information Available in These Sources: SATA 48, 58

PHILLIPS, ETHEL CALVERT
Birthplace: Jersey City, NJ
Deathdate: 2/6/1947
Information Available in These Sources: JBA 1, JBA 2

PHILLIPS, IRV(ING W.)
(Sabuso)
Birthdate: 10/29/1908
Birthplace: Wilton, WI
Information Available in These Sources: SATA 11

PHILLIPS, JACK
See Sandburg, Carl (August)

PHILLIPS, LEON
See Gerson, Noel B(ertram)

PHILLIPS, LORETTA (HOSEY)
Birthdate: 4/17/1893
Birthplace: Southbridge, MA
Information Available in These Sources: SATA 10

PHILLIPS, LOUIS
Birthdate: 6/15/1942
Birthplace: Lowell, MA
Information Available in These Sources: SATA 8

PHILLIPS, MARY GEISLER
Birthdate: 5/13/1881
Birthplace: Philadelphia, PA
Deathdate: 1/25/1964
Information Available in These Sources: ABYP 1, ABYP 3, SATA 10

PHILLIPS, PRENTICE
Birthdate: 5/15/1894
Birthplace: Plainfield, CT
Information Available in These Sources: SATA 10

PHIN
See Thayer, Ernest Lawrence

PHLEGER, FRED B.
Birthdate: 7/31/1909
Birthplace: Kansas City, KS
Information Available in These Sources: ABYP 1, ABYP 3, SATA 34

PHLEGER, MARJORIE TEMPLE
Birthdate, 1908?
Birthplace: Glendale, CA
Deathdate: 2/15/1986
Information Available in These Sources: SATA 1, SATA 47

PICKERING, JAMES SAYRE
Birthdate: 10/28/1897
Birthplace: Newark, NJ
Deathdate: 2/14/1969
Information Available in These Sources: SATA 28, SATA 36

PIER, ARTHUR STANWOOD
Birthdate: 4/21/1874
Birthplace: Pittsburgh, PA
Deathdate: 8/14/1966
Information Available in These Sources: JBA 1, JBA 2

PIERCE, EDITH GRAY
(Marian Gray)
Birthdate: 12/22/1893
Birthplace: Columbus Junction, IA
Deathdate: 10/11/1977
Information Available in These Sources: SATA 45

PIERCE, KATHERINE
See St. John, Wylly Folk

PIERCE, MARY CUNNINGHAM (FITZGERALD)
(Mary Cunningham)
Birthdate: 1908
Birthplace: Chicago, IL
Information Available in These Sources: ABYP 2, ABYP 3

PIERCE, MEREDITH ANN
Birthdate: 7/5/1958
Birthplace: Seattle, WA
Information Available in These Sources: DACF, SATA 48, TCCW 3, JBA 6

PIERCE, PHILIP NASON
Birthdate: 1917
Information Available in These Sources: ABYP 1, ABYP 3

PIERCE, RUTH (IRELAND)
Birthdate: 9/14/1936
Birthplace: Cleveland, OH
Information Available in These Sources: SATA 5

PIERCE, TAMORA
Birthdate: 12/13/1954
Birthplace: Connellsville, PA
Information Available in These Sources: SATA 49, SATA 51

PIERIK, ROBERT
Birthdate: 12/29/1921
Information Available in These Sources: SATA 13

PIERSON, SHERLEIGH G.
Information Available in These Sources: ABYP 2, ABYP 3

PILARSKI, LAURA
Birthdate: 12/10/1926
Birthplace: Niagara Falls, NY
Information Available in These Sources: SATA 13

PINCHOT, DAVID
Birthdate, 1914?
Deathdate: 4/25/1983
Information Available in These Sources: SATA 34

PINCUS, HARRIET
Birthdate: 10/13/1938
Birthplace: Bronx, NY
Information Available in These Sources: IBYP 2, ICB 4, JBA 4, SATA 27

PINE, TILLIE S(CHLOSS)
Birthdate: 3/4/1896 or 3/4/1897
Birthplace: Pultusk, Poland
Information Available in These Sources: ABYP 2, ABYP 3, BABP, SATA 13

PINKERTON, KATHRENE SUTHERLAND (GEDNEY)
Birthdate: 6/9/1887
Birthplace: Minneapolis, MN
Deathdate: 9/6/1967
Information Available in These Sources: ABYP 1, ABYP 3, SATA 26

PINKNEY, JERRY
Birthdate: 12/22/1939
Birthplace: Philadelphia, PA
Information Available in These Sources: BAI, ICB 3, SATA 32, SATA 41, JBA 6

PINKWATER, DANIEL MANUS
(Captain Duck, Mike Lome, Manus Pinkwater, Arthur Tress)
Birthdate: 11/15/1941
Birthplace: Memphis, TN
Information Available in These Sources: ABYP 4, JBA 5, SATA 8, SATA 46TCCW 3

PINKWATER, MANUS
See Pinkwater, Daniel Manus

PINNER, JOMA
See Werner, Herma

PINTO, RALPH
Birthplace: Brooklyn, NY
Information Available in These Sources: IBYP 1, IBYP 2

PIONEER
See Yates, Raymond F(rancis)

PIOWATY, KIM KENNELLY
Birthdate: 9/7/1957
Birthplace: Spokane, WA
Information Available in These Sources: SATA 49

PIPER, WATTY
See Bragg, Mabel Caroline

PIRO, RICHARD
Birthdate: 7/18/1934
Birthplace: Somerville, MA
Information Available in These Sources: SATA 7

PIRSIG, ROBERT M.
Birthdate: 9/6/1928
Birthplace: Minneapolis, MN
Information Available in These Sources: SATA 39

PISTORIUS, ANNA
Information Available in These Sources: ABYP 1, ABYP 3

PITRONE, JEAN MADDERN
Birthdate: 12/20/1920
Birthplace: Ishpeming, MI
Information Available in These Sources: ABYP 4, SATA 4

PITZ, HENRY C(LARENCE)
Birthdate: 6/16/1895
Birthplace: Philadelphia, PA
Deathdate: 11/26/1976
Information Available in These Sources: IBYP 2, ICB 1, ICB 2, ICB 3, ICB 4, MJA, SATA 4, SATA 24

PIUSSI-CAMPBELL, JUDY
(Judy Piussi Campbell)
Birthplace: South Bend, IN
Information Available in These Sources: IBYP 1, IBYP 2

PIZER, VERNON
Birthdate: 2/20/1918
Birthplace: Boston, MA
Information Available in These Sources: ABYP 1, ABYP 3, SATA 21

PLACE, MARIAN T(EMPLETON)
(Dale White, R. D. Whitinger)
Birthdate: 10/14/1910
Birthplace: Gary, IN
Information Available in These Sources: ABYP 1, ABYP 3, SATA 3

PLAGEMANN, BENTZ
Birthdate: 7/27/1913
Birthplace: Springfield, OH
Information Available in These Sources: ABYP 4

PLAINE, ALFRED R.
Birthdate, 1898?
Deathdate: 12/19/1981
Information Available in These Sources: SATA 29

PLASENCIA, PETER P.
Information Available in These Sources: IBYP 2

PLATE, ROBERT
Birthdate: 7/31/1918
Birthplace: Brooklyn, NY
Information Available in These Sources: ABYP 1, ABYP 3

PLATH, SYLVIA
Birthdate: 10/27/1932
Birthplace: Boston, MA
Deathdate: 2/11/1963
Information Available in These Sources: ABYP 4

PLATT, KIN
Birthdate: 12/8/1911
Birthplace: New York, NY
Information Available in These Sources: ABYP 4, DACF, JBA 5, SATA 21

PLIMPTON, GEORGE (AMES)
Birthdate: 3/18/1927
Birthplace: New York, NY
Information Available in These Sources: SATA 10

PLISS, LOUISE
Birthplace: Gowanda, NY
Information Available in These Sources: ABYP 1, ABYP 3

PLOTZ, HELEN (RATNOFF)
Birthdate: 3/20/1913
Birthplace: New York, NY
Information Available in These Sources: SATA 38, JBA 6

PLOWDEN, DAVID
Birthdate: 10/9/1932
Birthplace: Boston, MA
Information Available in These Sources: SATA 52

PLOWHEAD, RUTH GIPSON
Birthdate: 12/11/1877
Birthplace: Greeley, CO
Deathdate: 1967
Information Available in These Sources: SATA 43

PLUFF, BARBARA (LITTLEFIELD)
(Barbara Clayton)
Birthdate: 11/12/1926
Birthplace: Cambridge, MA
Information Available in These Sources: ABYP 4

PLUM, J.
See Wodehouse, P(elham) G(renville)

PLUM, JENNIFER
See Kurland, Michael (Joseph)

PLUMB, CHARLES P.
Birthdate, 1900?
Deathdate: 1/19/1982
Information Available in These Sources: SATA 29

PLUME, ILSE
Birthplace: Dresden, Germany
Information Available in These Sources: JBA 5, SATA 43

PLUMMER, W(ILLIAM) KIRTMAN
Information Available in These Sources: IBYP 1, IBYP 2

PODENDORF, ILLA E.
Birthdate, 1903?
Deathdate: 6/22/1983
Information Available in These Sources: SATA 18, 35

POE, EDGAR ALLAN
Birthdate: 1/19/1809
Birthplace: Boston, MA
Deathdate: 10/7/1849
Information Available in These Sources: SATA 23, SVC 2, SVC 3

POGANY, WILLIAM ANDREW
(Willy Pogany)
Birthdate: 8/24/1882
Birthplace: Szeged, Hungary
Deathdate: 7/30/1955
Information Available in These Sources: IBYP 2, ICB 1, JBA 1, JBA 2, SATA, 30, SATA 44

POGANY, WILLY
See Pogany, William Andrew

POHL, FREDERIK
Birthdate: 11/26/1919
Birthplace: New York, NY
Information Available in These Sources: SATA 24

POHLMANN, LILLIAN (GRENFELL)
Birthdate: 3/31/1902
Birthplace: Grass Valley, CA
Information Available in These Sources: ABYP 2, ABYP 3, SATA 8, SATA 11

POLA
See Watson, Pauline

POLATNICK, FLORENCE T.
Birthdate: 3/30/1923
Birthplace: New York, NY
Information Available in These Sources: SATA 5

POLE, JAMES T.
Birthplace: England
Information Available in These Sources: ABYP 4

POLESE, CAROLYN
Birthdate: 12/26/1947
Birthplace: Berkeley, CA
Information Available in These Sources: SATA 58

POLETTE, NANCY (JANE)
Birthdate: 5/18/1930
Birthplace: Richmond Heights, MO
Information Available in These Sources: SATA 42

POLGREEN, JOHN
Information Available in These Sources: IBYP 2

POLHAMUS, JEAN BURT
Birthdate: 4/30/1928
Birthplace: MS
Information Available in These Sources: SATA 21

POLITI, LEO
Birthdate: 11/21/1908
Birthplace: Fresno, CA
Information Available in These Sources: ABYP 1, ABYP 3, AICB, BABP, IBYP 1, IBYP 2, ICB 1, ICB 2, ICB 3, ICB 4, JBA 2, SATA 1, SATA 47, SVC 2, SVC 3, TCCW 1

POLKING, KIRK
Birthdate: 12/21/1925
Birthplace: Covington, KY
Information Available in These Sources: SATA 5

POLLACK, MERRILL S.
Birthdate: 7/24/1924
Birthplace: Middle Village, Long Isl., NY
Deathdate: 2/14/1988
Information Available in These Sources: SATA 55

POLLACK, REGINALD MURRAY
Birthdate: 9/29/1924
Birthplace: Middle Village, Long Isl., NY
Information Available in These Sources: ICB 3, ICB 4

POLLAND, BARBARA K(AY)
Birthdate: 10/14/1939
Birthplace: Milwaukee, WI
Information Available in These Sources: SATA 44

POLLOCK, BRUCE
Birthdate: 7/24/1945
Birthplace: Brooklyn, NY
Information Available in These Sources: SATA 46

POLLOCK, PENNY
Birthdate: 5/24/1935
Birthplace: Cleveland, OH
Information Available in These Sources: SATA 42, SATA 44

POLLOWITZ, MELINDA (KILBORN)
Birthdate: 9/22/1944
Birthplace: Petoskey, MI
Information Available in These Sources: SATA 26

POLONSKY, ARTHUR
Birthdate: 6/6/1925
Birthplace: Lynn, MA
Information Available in These Sources: SATA 34

POLSENO, JO
Information Available in These Sources: IBYP 1, IBYP 2, SATA 17

POLUSHKIN, MARIA
(Robbins, Maria (Polushkin))
Birthplace: Russia
Information Available in These Sources: ABYP 4, JBA 6

POMERANTZ, CHARLOTTE
Birthdate: 7/24/1930
Birthplace: Brooklyn, NY
Information Available in These Sources: ABYP 4, SATA 20, JBA 6

POMEROY, PETE
See Roth, Arthur J(oseph)

POND, ALONZO W(ILLIAM)
Birthdate: 6/18/1894
Birthplace: Janesville, WI
Information Available in These Sources: SATA 5

POND, SEYMOUR GATES
Birthdate: 1896
Information Available in These Sources: ABYP 2, ABYP 3

PONTIFLET, TED
Birthdate: 6/19/1932
Birthplace: Oakland, CA
Information Available in These Sources: SATA 32

POOLE, ERNEST
Birthdate: 1/23/1880
Birthplace: Chicago, IL
Deathdate: 1/10/1950
Information Available in These Sources: JBA 1

POOLE, GRAY (JOHNSON)
Birthdate: 9/26/1906
Birthplace: Philadelphia, PA
Information Available in These Sources: ABYP 1, ABYP 3, ABYP 4, MJA, SATA 1

POOLE, LYNN D.
Birthdate: 8/11/1910
Birthplace: Eagle Grove, IA
Deathdate: 4/14/1969
Information Available in These Sources: ABYP 1, ABYP 3, ABYP 4, MJA, SATA 1

POPE, CLIFFORD HILLHOUSE
Birthdate: 4/11/1899
Birthplace: Washington, GA
Deathdate: 6/3/1974
Information Available in These Sources: ABYP 1, ABYP 3

POPE, ELIZABETH MARIE
Birthdate: 5/1/1917
Birthplace: Washington, DC
Information Available in These Sources: ABYP 4, DACF, JBA 5, SATA 36, SATA 38

PORTE, BARBARA ANN
(Barbara Ann Porte-Thomas)
Birthdate: 5/18/1943
Birthplace: New York, NY
Information Available in These Sources: SATA 45, SATA 57, JBA 6

PORTE-THOMAS, BARBARA ANN
See Porte, Barbara Ann

PORTER, DONALD CLAYTON
See Gerson, Noel B(ertram)

PORTER, ELEANOR H(ODGMAN)
(Eleanor Stuart)
Birthdate: 12/19/1868
Birthplace: Littleton, NH
Deathdate: 5/21/1920
Information Available in These Sources: TCCW 2, TCCW 3, WCL

PORTER, ELLA (BLODWEN) WILLIAMS
Birthplace: Williamsburg, IA
Information Available in These Sources: ABYP 1, ABYP 3

PORTER, GENE(VA GRACE) STRATTON
(Gene(va Grace) Stratton-Porter)
Birthdate: 8/17/1863
Birthplace: Wabash County, IN
Deathdate: 12/6/1924
Information Available in These Sources: SATA 15, TCCW 1, TCCW 2, TCCW 3, WCL

PORTER, GEORGE
Birthplace: Perry, FL
Information Available in These Sources: IBYP 1, IBYP 2

PORTER, JEAN MACDONALD
Birthdate: 3/11/1906
Birthplace: Ardmore, PA
Information Available in These Sources: IBYP 1, IBYP 2, ICB 2

PORTER, KATHERINE ANNE
Birthdate: 5/15/1890
Birthplace: Indian Creek, TX
Deathdate: 9/18/1980
Information Available in These Sources: SATA 23, SATA 39

PORTER, KATHRYN
See Swinford, Betty (June Wells)

PORTER, MARK
See Leckie, Robert (Hugh)

PORTER, WILLIAM SYDNEY
(O(liver) Henry, S. H. Peters)
Birthdate: 9/11/1862
Birthplace: Greensboro, NC
Deathdate: 6/5/1910
Information Available in These Sources: ABYP 4, JBA 1, YABC

PORTTEUS, ELEANORA MARIE MANTHEI
Birthplace: Rosendale, WI
Deathdate: 11/4/1983
Information Available in These Sources: SATA 36

POSELL, ELSA Z(EIGERMAN)
Birthplace: Russia
Information Available in These Sources: ABYP 4, SATA 3

POSTEN, MARGARET L(OIS)
Birthdate: 3/28/1915
Birthplace: Villisca, IA
Information Available in These Sources: SATA 10

POSTON, MARTHA LEE
Birthplace: Shanghai, China
Information Available in These Sources: ABYP 1, ABYP 3

POTOK, CHAIM
Birthdate: 2/17/1929
Birthplace: New York, NY
Information Available in These Sources: SATA 33

POTTER, BRONSON
Information Available in These Sources: ABYP 4, DACF

POTTER, MARIAN
Birthdate: 1/9/1915
Birthplace: Blackwell, MO
Information Available in These Sources: SATA 9

POTTER, MIRIAM S. (CLARK)
Birthdate: 5/2/1886
Birthplace: Minneapolis, MN
Deathdate: 1/??/1965
Information Available in These Sources: ABYP 1, ABYP 3, SATA 3

POTTER, ROBERT DUCHARME
Birthdate: 2/5/1905
Deathdate: 3/18/1978
Information Available in These Sources: ABYP 1, ABYP 3

POUGH, FREDERICK HARVEY
Birthdate: 6/26/1906
Birthplace: Brooklyn, NY
Information Available in These Sources: ABYP 1, ABYP 3

POULSSON, ANNE EMILIE
(Emilie Poulsson)
Birthdate: 9/8/1853
Birthplace: Cedar Grove, NJ
Deathdate: 3/18/1939
Information Available in These Sources: JBA 1, JBA 2

POULSSON, EMILIE
See Poulsson, Anne Emilie

POURNELLE, JERRY (EUGENE)
(Wade Curtis)
Birthdate: 8/7/1933
Birthplace: Shreveport, LA
Information Available in These Sources: SATA 26

POWELL, A. M.
See Morgan, Alfred P(owell)

POWELL, RICHARD STILLMAN
See Barbour, Ralph Henry

POWER, EFFIE LOUISE
Birthdate: 1873
Birthplace: Conneautville (near), PA
Information Available in These Sources: ABYP 1, ABYP 3

POWERS, ANNE
See Schwartz, Anne Powers

POWERS, BILL
Birthdate: 2/3/1931
Birthplace: Brooklyn, NY
Information Available in These Sources: SATA 31, SATA 52

POWERS, MARGARET
See Heal, Edith

POWERS, RICHARD M.
(Terry Gorman)
Birthdate: 2/24/1921
Birthplace: Chicago, IL
Information Available in These Sources: IBYP 1, IBYP 2, ICB 2, ICB 3

POWLEDGE, FRED
Birthdate: 2/23/1935
Birthplace: Nash County, NC
Information Available in These Sources: SATA 37

POYNTER, MARGARET
Birthdate: 5/30/1927
Birthplace: Long Beach, CA
Information Available in These Sources: SATA 27

PRAGER, ARTHUR
Birthplace: New York, NY
Information Available in These Sources: SATA 44

PRATHER, RAY
Information Available in These Sources: BAI

PRATT, AGNES EDWARDS ROTHERY
(Agnes Edwards, Agnes Edwards Rothery, Agnes Rothery)
Birthdate: 1/31/1888
Birthplace: Brookline, MA
Deathdate: 8/11/1954
Information Available in These Sources: ABYP 1, ABYP 3

PRATT, DAVIS
Information Available in These Sources: ABYP 4

PRATT, FLETCHER
Birthdate: 4/25/1897
Birthplace: Buffalo, NY
Deathdate: 6/10/1956
Information Available in These Sources: ABYP 1, ABYP 3

PRATT, JOHN LOWELL
Birthdate: 2/22/1906
Birthplace: Montclair, NJ
Deathdate: 12/25/1968
Information Available in These Sources: ABYP 4

PREISS, BYRON (CARY)
Birthdate: 4/11/1953
Birthplace: New York, NY
Information Available in These Sources: SATA 42, SATA 47

PRELUTSKY, JACK
Birthdate: 9/8/1940
Birthplace: Brooklyn, NY
Information Available in These Sources: ABYP 4, DLB 61, JBA 5, SATA 22TCCW 2, TCCW 3

PRESBERG, MIRIAM GOLDSTEIN
(Miriam Gilbert)
Birthdate: 12/1/1919
Birthplace: New York, NY
Deathdate: 6/13/1978
Information Available in These Sources: SATA 38

PRESCOTT, ORVILLE
Birthdate: 9/8/1906
Birthplace: Cleveland, OH
Information Available in These Sources: ABYP 2, ABYP 3

PRESTON, ALICE BOLAM
Birthdate: 3/6/1889
Birthplace: Malden, MA
Deathdate: 8/12/1958
Information Available in These Sources: ICB 1

PRESTON, CAROL
Information Available in These Sources: ABYP 4

PRESTON, EDNA MITCHELL
Information Available in These Sources: ABYP 4, SATA 40

PRESTON, LILLIAN ELVIRA
Birthdate: 1/16/1918
Birthplace: Battle Creek, IA
Information Available in These Sources: SATA 47

PRICE, CHRISTINE (HILDA)
Birthdate: 4/15/1928
Birthplace: London, England
Deathdate: 1/13/1980
Information Available in These Sources: ABYP 1, ABYP 3, ICB 2, ICB 4, MJA, SATA 3, SATA 23

PRICE, EDITH BALLINGER
Birthdate: 4/26/1897
Birthplace: New Brunswick, NJ
Information Available in These Sources: JBA 1, JBA 2

PRICE, GARRETT
Birthdate: 11/21/1896
Birthplace: Bucyrus, KS
Deathdate: 4/8/1979
Information Available in These Sources: IBYP 1, IBYP 2, ICB 3, SATA 22

PRICE, HAROLD
Birthdate: 10/13/1912
Birthplace: Portland, OR
Information Available in These Sources: IBYP 2, ICB 2

PRICE, HATTIE LONGSTREET
Birthdate: 7/17/1891
Birthplace: Germantown, PA
Information Available in These Sources: CICB, ICB 1

PRICE, JENNIFER
See Hoover, Helen (Drusilla Blackburn)

PRICE, JONATHAN (REEVE)
Birthdate: 10/19/1941
Birthplace: Boston, MA
Information Available in These Sources: SATA 46

PRICE, LUCIE LOCKE
See Locke, Lucie

PRICE, MARGARET (EVANS)
Birthdate: 3/20/1888
Birthplace: Chicago, IL
Deathdate: 11/20/1973
Information Available in These Sources: ICB 1, SATA 28

PRICE, NORMAN MILLS
Birthdate: 4/16/1877
Birthplace: Brampton, Ontario, Canada
Deathdate: 8/2/1951
Information Available in These Sources: IBYP 2, ICB 1, ICB 2

PRICE, OLIVE (M.)
(Anne Cherryholmes, Barbara West)
Birthdate: 9/21/1903
Birthplace: Pittsburgh, PA
Information Available in These Sources: ABYP 1, ABYP 3, SATA 8

PRICE, WILLADENE (ANTON)
Birthdate: 3/8/1914
Birthplace: Omaha, NE
Information Available in These Sources: ABYP 1, ABYP 3

PRICE, WILLARD (DEMILLE)
Birthdate: 7/28/1887
Birthplace: Peterborough, Ontario, Canada
Deathdate: 10/14/1983
Information Available in These Sources: ABYP 2, ABYP 3, SATA 38, SATA 48, TCCW 2, TCCW 3

PRIDDY, FRANCES (ROSALEEN)
Birthdate: 10/25/1931
Birthplace: Decatur, IL
Information Available in These Sources: ABYP 2, ABYP 3

PRIDEAUX, TOM
Birthdate: 5/9/1908
Birthplace: Hillsdale, MI
Information Available in These Sources: SATA 37

PRIESTLEY, LEE (SHORE)
Birthdate: 8/30/1904
Birthplace: Iola, KS
Information Available in These Sources: ABYP 2, ABYP 3, SATA 27

PRIETO, MARIANA B(EECHING)
Birthdate: 8/6/1912
Birthplace: Cincinnati, OH
Information Available in These Sources: ABYP 1, ABYP 3, AICB, BABP, SATA 8

PRIMAVERA, ELISE
Birthdate: 5/19/1954
Birthplace: West Long Branch, NJ
Information Available in These Sources: BC, SATA 48, SATA 58, JBA 6

PRINCE, LEONORE E.
Information Available in These Sources: IBYP 2

PRINGLE, LAURENCE P.
(Sean Edmund)
Birthdate: 11/26/1935
Birthplace: Rochester, NY
Information Available in These Sources: ABYP 4, JBA 4, SATA 4

PRITCHETT, ELAINE H(ILLYER)
Birthdate: 3/7/1920
Birthplace: Fort Worth, TX
Information Available in These Sources: SATA 36

PROCTOR, EVERITT
See Montgomery, Rutherford (George)

PROFESSOR ZINGARA
See Leeming, Joseph

PROSPER, JOHN
See Farrar, John C(hipman)

PROUDFIT, ISABEL (KATHERINE BOYD)
Birthdate: 1898
Birthplace: Evanston, IL
Information Available in These Sources: ABYP 1, ABYP 3, MJA

PROVENSEN, ALICE
Birthdate: 8/14/1918
Birthplace: Chicago, IL
Information Available in These Sources: IBYP 2, ICB 2, ICB 3, ICB 4, JBA 3, SATA 9, WCL

PROVENSEN, MARTIN (ELIAS)
Birthdate: 7/10/1916
Birthplace: Chicago, IL
Deathdate: 3/27/1987
Information Available in These Sources: IBYP 2, ICB 2, ICB 3, ICB 4, SATA 9, SATA 51, WCL

PRUD'HOMMEAUX, RENE
Birthplace: Egypt
Information Available in These Sources: ABYP 1, ABYP 3

PRYOR, HELEN BRENTON
Birthdate: 7/31/1897
Birthplace: Green Montain Falls(Near), CO
Deathdate: 7/7/1972
Information Available in These Sources: SATA 4

PUCCI, ALBERT JOHN
Birthdate: 3/11/1920
Birthplace: Cleveland, OH
Information Available in These Sources: SATA 44

PUGH, ELLEN T(IFFANY)
Birthdate: 6/2/1920
Birthplace: Cleveland, OH
Information Available in These Sources: ABYP 4, SATA 7

PUNDT, HELEN MARIE
Birthdate: 2/1/1903
Birthplace: Rochester, NY
Information Available in These Sources: ABYP 2, ABYP 3

PUNER, HELEN W(ALKER)
Birthdate: 6/18/1915
Birthplace: New York, NY
Information Available in These Sources: SATA 37

PURCELL, JOHN WALLACE
Information Available in These Sources: ABYP 2, ABYP 3

PURDY, CAPTAIN JIM
See Gillelan, George Howard

PURDY, CLAIRE LEE
Birthdate: 11/27/1906
Birthplace: Chihuahua, Mexico
Information Available in These Sources: ABYP 1, ABYP 3

PURDY, SUSAN GOLD
Birthdate: 5/17/1939
Birthplace: New York, NY
Information Available in These Sources: ICB 3, SATA 8

PURSCELL, PHYLLIS
Birthdate: 12/18/1934
Birthplace: Fort Dodge, IA
Information Available in These Sources: SATA 7

PURSELL, WEIMER
Information Available in These Sources: IBYP 1, IBYP 2

PURTILL, RICHARD L.
Birthdate: 3/12/1931
Birthplace: Chicago, IL
Information Available in These Sources: SATA 53

PUTNAM, ARTHUR LEE
See Alger, Horatio, Jr.

PUTNAM, PETER B(ROCK)
Birthdate: 6/11/1920
Birthplace: Fort Oglethorpe, GA
Information Available in These Sources: SATA 30

PYLE, HOWARD
Birthdate: 3/5/1853
Birthplace: Wilmington, DE
Deathdate: 11/9/1911
Information Available in These Sources: ABYP 2, ABYP 3, DLB 42, FSYP, IBYP 1, IBYP 2, JBA 1, SATA 16 TCCW 1, TCCW 2, TCCW 3, WC, WCL

PYLE, KATHARINE
Birthplace: Wilmington, DE
Information Available in These Sources: JBA 1, JBA 2

PYNE, MABLE MANDEVILLE
Birthdate: 1/15/1903
Birthplace: Mount Vernon, NY
Deathdate: 9/19/1969
Information Available in These Sources: ABYP 1, ABYP 3, ICB 1, ICB 2, SATA 9

PYRNELLE, LOUISE CLARKE
Birthdate: 6/19/1850
Birthplace: Uniontown (Ittabena), AL
Deathdate: 8/26/1907
Information Available in These Sources: DLB 42

QUARLES, BENJAMIN
Birthdate: 1/23/1904
Birthplace: Boston, MA
Information Available in These Sources: BAI, SATA 12

QUEEN, ELLERY
See Dannay, Frederic

QUEEN, ELLERY, JR.
See Holding, James (Clark Carlisle, Jr.)

QUICK, ANNABELLE (MACMILLAN)
(Annabelle MacMillan)
Birthdate: 10/16/1922
Birthplace: Greeley, CO
Information Available in These Sources: SATA 2

QUIGG, JANE (HULDA)
Birthplace: Marlborough, CT
Deathdate: 4/9/1986
Information Available in These Sources: SATA 49

QUIN-HARKIN, JANET
Birthdate: 9/24/1941
Birthplace: Bath, England
Information Available in These Sources: SATA 18

QUINN, ELISABETH
(Dale Adams, Vernon Quinn, Capini Vequin)
Birthdate: 1/5/1881
Birthplace: Waldorf, MD
Deathdate: 3/21/1962
Information Available in These Sources: SATA 22

QUINN, SUSAN
See Jacobs, Susan

QUINN, VERNON
See Quinn, Elisabeth

QUINTANILLA, LUIS
Birthdate: 6/13/1895
Birthplace: Santander, Spain
Information Available in These Sources: IBYP 2, ICB 2

Q

QUACKENBUSH, ROBERT M(EAD)
Birthdate: 7/23/1929
Birthplace: Hollywood, CA
Information Available in These Sources: IBYP 1, IBYP 2, ICB 3, ICB 4, JBA 4, SATA 7

QUAMMEN, DAVID
Birthdate: 2/24/1948
Birthplace: Cincinnati, OH
Information Available in These Sources: SATA 7

R

RABE, BERNIECE (LOUISE)
Birthdate: 1/11/1928
Birthplace: Parma, MO
Information Available in These Sources: JBA 5, SATA 7

RABE, OLIVE H(ANSON)
Birthdate: 4/6/1887
Birthplace: Chicago, IL
Deathdate: 12/11/1968
Information Available in These Sources: ABYP 2, ABYP 3, SATA 13

RABINOWICH, ELLEN
Birthdate: 10/21/1946
Birthplace: Brooklyn, NY
Information Available in These Sources: SATA 29

RABINOWITZ, SANDY
Birthdate: 10/25/1954
Birthplace: New Haven, CT
Information Available in These Sources: SATA 39, SATA 52

RABOFF, ERNEST LLOYD
Birthplace: Atlantic City, NJ
Information Available in These Sources: ABYP 4, SATA 37

RACHLIN, HARVEY (BRANT)
Birthdate: 6/23/1951
Birthplace: Philadelphia, PA
Information Available in These Sources: SATA 47

RACHLIS, EUGENE (JACOB)
Birthdate: 2/5/1920
Birthplace: Boston, MA
Deathdate: 11/10/1986
Information Available in These Sources: SATA 50

RADFORD, RUBY L(ORRAINE)
(Matilda Bailey, Marcia Ford)
Birthdate: 12/7/1891
Birthplace: Augusta, GA
Deathdate: 7/19/1971
Information Available in These Sources: SATA 6

RADIN, RUTH YAFFE
Birthdate: 10/8/1938
Birthplace: Hartford, CT
Information Available in These Sources: SATA 52, SATA 56

RADLAUER, DAVID
Birthdate: 1/3/1952
Birthplace: Los Angeles, CA
Information Available in These Sources: SATA 28

RADLAUER, EDWARD
Birthdate: 3/3/1921
Birthplace: KY
Information Available in These Sources: SATA 15

RADLAUER, RUTH (SHAW)
Birthdate: 8/18/1926
Birthplace: Midwest, WY
Information Available in These Sources: SATA 15

RADLEY, GAIL
Birthdate: 5/21/1951
Birthplace: Boston, MA
Information Available in These Sources: SATA 25

RAE, JOHN
Birthdate: 7/4/1882
Birthplace: Jersey City, NJ
Deathdate: 10/18/1963
Information Available in These Sources: ICB 1

RAEBECK, LOIS
Birthdate: 10/2/1921
Birthplace: West Chicago, IL
Information Available in These Sources: SATA 5

RAFTERY, GERALD (BRANSFIELD)
Birthdate: 10/30/1905
Birthplace: Elizabeth, NJ
Information Available in These Sources: SATA 11

RAHN, JOAN ELMA
Birthdate: 2/5/1929
Birthplace: Cleveland, OH
Information Available in These Sources: SATA 27, JBA 6

RAIBLE, ALTON (ROBERT)
Birthdate: 11/14/1918
Birthplace: Modesto, CA
Information Available in These Sources: IBYP 1, IBYP 2, ICB 3, SATA 35

RAIFF, STAN
Birthdate: 7/28/1930
Birthplace: New York, NY
Information Available in These Sources: SATA 11

RAINEY, W. B.
See Blassingame, Wyatt (Rainey)

RALSTON, ALMA (SMITH PAYNE)
(Alma Smith Payne)
Birthdate: 5/13/1900
Birthplace: Oakland, CA
Information Available in These Sources: ABYP 2, ABYP 3

RANADIVE, GAIL
Birthdate: 2/16/1944
Birthplace: Boston, MA
Information Available in These Sources: SATA 10

RAND, ADDISON
See Regli, Adolph Casper

RAND, ANN(E BINKLEY)
(Anne Binkley)
Birthplace: Chicago, IL
Information Available in These Sources: ABYP 1, ABYP 3, JBA 3, SATA 30

RAND, PAUL
Birthdate: 8/15/1914
Birthplace: Brooklyn, NY
Information Available in These Sources: ABYP 1, ABYP 3, ICB 2, ICB 3, JBA 3, SATA 6

RAND, TED
Birthdate: 12/27/1915
Birthplace: Mercer Island, WA
Information Available in These Sources: JBA 6

RANDALL, BLOSSOM E.
Birthdate: 1902
Information Available in These Sources: ABYP 1, ABYP 3

RANDALL, CHRISTINE
Information Available in These Sources: IBYP 2

RANDALL, FLORENCE ENGEL
Birthdate: 10/18/1917
Birthplace: Brooklyn, NY
Information Available in These Sources: ABYP 4, SATA 5, JBA 6

RANDALL, JAN(ET)
See Young, Jan(et Randall) and Young, Robert W(illiam)

RANDALL, KENNETH CHARLES
Information Available in These Sources: ABYP 1, ABYP 3

RANDALL, MARY
See Colver, Alice Mary (Ross)

RANDALL, ROBERT
See Silverberg, Robert

RANDALL, RUTH PAINTER
Birthdate: 11/1/1892
Birthplace: Salem, VA
Deathdate: 1/22/1971
Information Available in These Sources: ABYP 1, ABYP 3, SATA 3

RANDOLPH, J. H.
See Ellis, Edward S(ylvester)

RANDOLPH, LIEUTENANT J. H.
See Ellis, Edward S(ylvester)

RANKIN, LOUISE D.
Birthdate, 1897?
Birthplace: Baltimore, MD
Deathdate: 1951
Information Available in These Sources: MJA

RANKIN, ROBERT H(ARRY)
Birthdate: 5/31/1909
Birthplace: Martins Ferry, OH
Information Available in These Sources: ABYP 4

RANNEY, AGNES V.
(Ruth Ellen Reeves)
Birthdate: 5/14/1916
Birthplace: Council, ID
Information Available in These Sources: SATA 6

RANSOHOFF, DORIS
Birthplace: Cincinnati, OH
Information Available in These Sources: ABYP 1, ABYP 3

RANSOM, CANDICE F.
(Kate Kenyon)
Birthdate: 7/10/1952
Birthplace: Washington, DC
Information Available in These Sources: SATA 49, 52

RANUCCI, RENATO
(Renato Rascel)
Birthdate: 1921
Birthplace: Turin, Italy
Information Available in These Sources: ABYP 1, ABYP 3

RAPAPORT, STELLA F(READ)
Birthdate: 8/07
Birthplace: New York, NY
Information Available in These Sources: SATA 10

RAPHAEL, ELAINE
See Bolognese, Elaine Raphael (Chionchio)

RAPPAPORT, EVA
Birthdate: 4/7/1924
Information Available in These Sources: SATA 6

RARICK, CARRIE
Birthdate: 12/16/1911
Birthplace: Somerset, OH
Information Available in These Sources: SATA 41

RASCEL, RENATO
See Ranucci, Renato

RASKIN, EDITH LEFKOWITZ
Birthdate: 10/17/1908
Birthplace: New York, NY
Information Available in These Sources: ABYP 4, SATA 9

RASKIN, ELLEN
Birthdate: 3/13/1928 or 3/13/1925
Birthplace: Milwaukee, WI
Deathdate: 8/8/1984
Information Available in These Sources: BABP, BC, DACF, IBYP 1, IBYP 2ICB 3, ICB 4, JBA 3, SATA 2, SATA 38, TCCW 1, TCCW 2, TCCW 3

RASKIN, JOSEPH
Birthdate: 4/14/1897
Birthplace: Nogaisk, Russia
Deathdate: 1/26/1982
Information Available in These Sources: SATA 12, 29

RATHJEN, CARL H(ENRY)
(Charlotte Russell)
Birthdate: 8/28/1909
Birthplace: Jersey City, NJ
Information Available in These Sources: SATA 11

RATTRAY, SIMON
See Trevor, Elleston

RAU, MARGARET
Birthdate: 12/23/1913
Birthplace: Swatow, China
Information Available in These Sources: SATA 9

RAUCH, MABEL THOMPSON
Birthdate: 11/30/1888
Birthplace: Carbondale, IL
Deathdate: 1972
Information Available in These Sources: SATA 26

RAUCHER, HERMAN
Birthdate: 4/13/1928
Birthplace: New York, NY
Information Available in These Sources: SATA 8

RAVIELLI, ANTHONY
Birthdate: 7/1/1916
Birthplace: New York, NY
Information Available in These Sources: ABYP 1, ABYP 3, ICB 2, ICB 3, JBA 3, SATA 3

RAWLINGS, MARJORIE KINNAN
Birthdate: 8/8/1896
Birthplace: Washington, DC
Deathdate: 12/14/1953
Information Available in These Sources: DLB 22, JBA 3, TCCW 1, TCCW 2 TCCW 3, WC, YABC

RAWLS, WILSON
See Rawls, Woodrow Wilson

RAWLS, WOODROW WILSON
(Wilson Rawls)
Birthdate: 9/24/1913
Birthplace: Scraper, OK
Deathdate: 12/16/1984
Information Available in: ABYP 4, SATA 22, JBA 6

RAY, DEBORAH (KOGAN)
(Deborah Kogan)
Birthdate: 8/31/1940
Birthplace: Philadelphia, PA
Information Available in These Sources: IBYP 2, SATA 8, SATA 50, JBA 6

RAY, IRENE
See Sutton, Margaret (Beebe)

RAY, JOANNE
Birthdate: 6/19/1935
Birthplace: Duluth, MN
Information Available in These Sources: SATA 9

RAY, OPHELIA
Birthplace: TX
Information Available in These Sources: ABYP 2, ABYP 3

RAY, RALPH
Birthdate: 1920
Birthplace: Gastonia, NC
Deathdate: 1952
Information Available in These Sources: IBYP 2, ICB 2

RAYMOND, JAMES CROSSLEY
Birthdate: 2/25/1917
Birthplace: Riverside, CT
Deathdate: 10/14/1981
Information Available in These Sources: SATA 29

RAYMOND, JOHN F(RANCIS)
Birthdate: 1925
Birthplace: Findlay, OH
Information Available in These Sources: ABYP 2, ABYP 3

RAYMOND, MARGARET THOMSEN
Birthdate: 1900
Birthplace: Baltimore, MD
Information Available in These Sources: ABYP 1, ABYP 3

RAYMOND, ROBERT
See Alter, Robert Edmond

RAYNOR, DORKA
Birthplace: Warsaw, Poland
Information Available in These Sources: SATA 28

RAZZI, JAMES
Birthdate: 8/20/1931
Birthplace: New York, NY
Information Available in These Sources: SATA 10

READY, KIRK L.
Birthdate: 12/29/1943
Birthplace: Louisville, KY
Information Available in These Sources: SATA 39

RECHNITZER, FERDINAND EDSTED
Birthdate: 1894
Birthplace: Perth Amboy, NJ
Information Available in These Sources: ABYP 1, ABYP 3

RECK, ALMA KEHOE
Birthdate: 1/26/1901
Birthplace: Washington, IN
Information Available in These Sources: ABYP 1, ABYP 3

RECK, FRANKLIN MERING
Birthdate: 11/29/1896
Birthplace: Chicago, IL
Deathdate: 10/14/1965
Information Available in These Sources: SATA 30

REDDING, ROBERT HULL
Birthdate: 12/3/1919
Birthplace: Los Angeles, CA
Information Available in These Sources: ABYP 4, SATA 2

REDFORD, LORA BRYNING
Birthplace: Olympia, WA
Information Available in These Sources: ABYP 2, ABYP 3

REED, BETTY JANE
Birthdate: 8/6/1921
Birthplace: Pittsburgh, PA
Information Available in These Sources: SATA 4

REED, GWENDOLYN (ELIZABETH)
Birthdate: 6/27/1932
Birthplace: Louisville, KY
Information Available in These Sources: ABYP 2, ABYP 3, SATA 7, SATA 21

REED, KIT
(Shelley Hyde)
Birthdate: 6/7/1932
Birthplace: San Diego, CA
Information Available in These Sources: SATA 34

REED, PHILIP G.
Birthdate: 1/17/1908
Birthplace: Park Ridge, IL
Information Available in These Sources: IBYP 2, ICB 1, ICB 3, JBA 3, SATA 29

REED, THOMAS (JAMES)
Birthdate: 11/5/1947
Birthplace: New York, NY
Information Available in These Sources: SATA 34

REED, VERONICA
See Sherman, Theresa

REED, W(ILLIAM) MAXWELL
Birthdate: 1871
Birthplace: Bath, ME
Deathdate: 1962
Information Available in These Sources: JBA 2, SATA 15

REEDER, COLONEL RED
See Reeder, Russell P(otter), Jr.

REEDER, RUSSELL P(OTTER), JR.
(Colonel Red Reeder)
Birthdate: 3/4/1902
Birthplace: Fort Leavenworth, KS
Information Available in These Sources: ABYP 1, ABYP 3, SATA 4

REELY, MARY KATHARINE
Birthdate: 1881
Birthplace: Spring Green (near), WI
Deathdate: 1959
Information Available in These Sources: ABYP 1, ABYP 3

REES, ENNIS (SAMUEL, JR.)
Birthdate: 3/17/1925
Birthplace: Newport News, VA
Information Available in These Sources: ABYP 2, ABYP 3, SATA 3

REESE, BOB
See Reese, Robert A.

REESE, JOHN HENRY
Birthdate: 1910
Birthplace: Sweetwater, NE
Deathdate: 1981
Information Available in These Sources: ABYP 1, ABYP 3

REESE, ROBERT A.
(Bob Reese)
Birthdate: 8/15/1938
Birthplace: Hollywood, CA
Information Available in These Sources: SATA 53, SATA 60

REEVE, JOEL
See Cox, William R(obert)

REEVES, LAWRENCE F.
(Warren Lyfick, R. Seever)
Birthdate: 6/2/1926
Birthplace: Belmont, MA
Information Available in These Sources: SATA 29

REEVES, RUTH ELLEN
See Ranney, Agnes V.

REGEHR, LYDIA
Birthdate: 11/29/1903
Birthplace: Russia
Information Available in These Sources: SATA 37

REGLI, ADOLPH CASPER
(Addison Rand)
Birthdate: 1896
Birthplace: Eau Claire, WI
Information Available in These Sources: ABYP 1, ABYP 3

REICHERT, EDWIN C(LARK)
Birthdate: 4/4/1909
Birthplace: Duluth, MN
Deathdate: 7/7/1988
Information Available in These Sources: SATA 57

REID, BARBARA
Birthdate: 4/18/1922
Birthplace: New York, NY
Information Available in These Sources: SATA 21

REID, BILL
Birthdate: 1920
Information Available in These Sources: IBYP 1, IBYP 2

REID, EUGENIE CHAZAL
Birthdate: 12/21/1924
Birthplace: Woodbury, NJ
Information Available in These Sources: SATA 12

REID, JOHN CALVIN
Birthdate: 1901
Birthplace: Charlotte, NC
Information Available in These Sources: SATA 21

REID, MAYNE
See Reid, Thomas Mayne

REID, THOMAS MAYNE
(Charles Beach, Mayne Reid)
Birthdate: 4/4/1818
Birthplace: Ballyroney, County Down, Ireland
Deathdate: 10/22/1883
Information Available in These Sources: SATA 24

REIFF, STEPHANIE ANN
Birthdate: 9/14/1948
Birthplace: New York, NY
Information Available in These Sources: SATA 28, SATA 47

REIG, JUNE
Birthdate: 6/1/1933
Birthplace: Schenectady, NY
Information Available in These Sources: SATA 30

REIGOT, BETTY POLISAR
Birthdate: 3/9/1924
Birthplace: Brooklyn, NY
Information Available in These Sources: SATA 41, SATA 55

REILEY, CATHERINE CONWAY
Birthplace: Rumson, NJ
Information Available in These Sources: ABYP 1, ABYP 3

REINACH, JACQUELYN (KRASNE)
Birthdate: 9/17/1930
Birthplace: Omaha, NE
Information Available in These Sources: SATA 28

REINER, WILLIAM B(UCK)
Birthdate: 5/23/1910
Birthplace: New York, NY
Deathdate: 1/24/1976
Information Available in These Sources: SATA 30, SATA 46

REINFELD, FRED
(Edward Young)
Birthdate: 1/27/1910
Birthplace: New York, NY
Deathdate: 5/29/1964
Information Available in These Sources: ABYP 1, ABYP 3, SATA 3

REINGOLD, CARMEL BERMAN
(Karmel Berman Reingold)
Information Available in These Sources: ABYP 4

REINGOLD, KARMEL BERMAN
See Reingold, Carmel Berman

REISS, JOHANNA DE LEEUW
Birthdate: 4/4/1932
Birthplace: Winterswijk, Holland
Information Available in These Sources: ABYP 4, JBA 5, SATA 18, TCCW 1

REISS, JOHN (J.)
Birthplace: Milwaukee, WI
Information Available in These Sources: ABYP 4, ICB 4, SATA 23

REISS, MARILYN LEITNER
Information Available in These Sources: ABYP 4

REIT, SEYMOUR
(Sy Reit)
Birthdate: 11/11/1918
Birthplace: New York, NY
Information Available in These Sources: ABYP 4, SATA 21

REIT, SY
See Reit, Seymour

REITCI, RITA KROHNE
(Rita (Marie Krohne) Ritchie)
Birthdate: 5/9/1930
Birthplace: Milwaukee, WI
Information Available in These Sources: ABYP 1, ABYP 3

REMINGTON, FREDERIC (SACKRIDER)
Birthdate: 10/4/1861 or 10/1/1861
Birthplace: Canton, NY
Deathdate: 12/26/1909
Information Available in These Sources: SATA 41

RENDINA, LAURA (JONES) COOPER
Birthdate: 11/9/1902
Birthplace: Northhampton, MA
Information Available in These Sources: ABYP 1, ABYP 3, MJA, SATA 10

RENICK, MARION (LEWIS)
Birthdate: 1905
Birthplace: Springfield, OH
Information Available in These Sources: ABYP 1, ABYP 3, MJA, SATA 1

RENKEN, ALEDA
Birthdate: 6/21/1907
Birthplace: Jefferson City, MO
Information Available in These Sources: SATA 27

RENLIE, FRANK H.
Birthdate: 4/17/1936
Birthplace: Ketchikan, AK
Information Available in These Sources: SATA 11

RENSIE, WILLIS
See Eisner, Will(iam Erwin)

REPPLIER, AGNES
Birthdate: 4/1/1855
Birthplace: Philadelphia, PA
Deathdate: 12/15/1950
Information Available in These Sources: JBA 1

RESNICK, MICHAEL D(IAMOND)
(Mike Resnick)
Birthdate: 3/5/1942
Birthplace: Chicago, IL
Information Available in These Sources: SATA 38

RESNICK, MIKE
See Resnick, Michael D(iamond)

RESNICK, SEYMOUR
Birthdate: 1/15/1920
Birthplace: New York, NY
Information Available in: ABYP 2, 3, SATA 23

RESSLER, THEODORE WHITSON
Birthdate: 1926
Information Available in These Sources: ABYP 2, ABYP 3

RESSNER, PHIL(IP)
Birthdate: 10/29/1922
Birthplace: Brooklyn, NY
Information Available in These Sources: ABYP 2, ABYP 3

RETHI, LILI
Birthdate: 11/19/1894 or 11/19/1896
Birthplace: Vienna, Austria
Deathdate: 1969
Information Available in These Sources: IBYP 1, IBYP 2

RETLA, ROBERT
See Alter, Robert Edmond

REUTER, CAROL (JOAN)
Birthdate: 6/7/1931
Birthplace: Newark, NJ
Information Available in These Sources: SATA 2

REVENA
See Wright, Betty Ren

REY, H(ANS) A(UGUSTO)
(Uncle Gus)
Birthdate: 9/16/1898
Birthplace: Hamburg, Germany
Deathdate: 8/26/1977
Information Available in These Sources: ABYP 1, ABYP 3, AICB, BABP, CFB, DLB 22, ICB 1, ICB 2, ICB 3, ICB 4, JBA 2, SATA 1, SATA 26, TCCW 1, TCCW 2, TCCW 3

REY, LESTER DEL
See del Rey, Lester

REY, MARGRET (ELIZABETH WALDSTEIN)
Birthdate: 5/??/1906
Birthplace: Hamburg, Germany
Information Available in These Sources: ABYP 1, ABYP 3, AICB, BABP, JBA 2, SATA 26, TCCW 1, TCCW 2TCCW 3

REYHER, BECKY
See Reyher, Rebecca Hourwich

REYHER, REBECCA HOURWICH
(Becky Reyher)
Birthdate: 1/21/1897
Birthplace: New York, NY
Deathdate: 1/10/1987
Information Available in These Sources: SATA 18, SATA 50

REYNOLDS, BARBARA LEONARD
Birthdate: 1915
Information Available in These Sources: ABYP 4

REYNOLDS, DALLAS MCCORD
(Mack Reynolds)
Birthdate: 11/11/1917
Birthplace: Corcoran, CA
Information Available in These Sources: ABYP 4

REYNOLDS, MACK
See Reynolds, Dallas McCord

REYNOLDS, MALVINA
Birthdate: 8/23/1900
Birthplace: San Francisco, CA
Deathdate: 3/17/1978
Information Available in These Sources: SATA 24, SATA 44

REYNOLDS, MARJORIE (HARRIS)
Birthdate: 1/19/1903
Birthplace: Rochester, NY
Information Available in These Sources: ABYP 2, ABYP 3

REYNOLDS, PAMELA
Birthdate: 6/6/1923
Birthplace: New York, NY
Information Available in These Sources: SATA 34

REYNOLDS, QUENTIN JAMES
Birthdate: 4/11/1902
Birthplace: Brooklyn, NY
Deathdate: 3/17/1965
Information Available in These Sources: ABYP 1, ABYP 3

RHINE, RICHARD
See Silverstein, Virginia B(arbara Opshelor)

RHOADS, DOROTHY (MARY)
Birthdate: 3/19/1895
Birthplace: Pekin, IL
Information Available in These Sources: ABYP 1, ABYP 3

RHODES, BENNIE (LORAN)
Birthdate: 12/5/1927
Birthplace: Blytheville, AR
Information Available in These Sources: SATA 35

RHODES, FRANK H(AROLD TREVOR)
Birthdate: 10/29/1926
Birthplace: Warwickshire, England
Information Available in These Sources: SATA 37

RHUE, MORTON
See Strasser, Todd

RHYS, MEGAN
See Williams, J(eanne R.)

RICCIUTI, EDWARD R(APHAEL)
Birthdate: 5/27/1938
Birthplace: New York, NY
Information Available in These Sources: SATA 10

RICE, ALICE (CALDWELL) HEGAN
Birthdate: 1/11/1870
Birthplace: Shelbyville, KY
Deathdate: 2/10/1942
Information Available in These Sources: JBA 1, TCCW 2, TCCW 3

RICE, CHARLES D(UANE)
Birthdate: 1910
Birthplace: Cambridge, MA
Deathdate: 1/30/1971
Information Available in These Sources: ABYP 1, ABYP 3, SATA 27

RICE, DALE R(ICHARD)
Birthdate: 8/6/1948
Birthplace: New Castle, PA
Information Available in These Sources: SATA 42

RICE, EDWARD E.
Birthdate: 10/23/1918
Birthplace: New York, NY
Information Available in These Sources: ABYP 4, SATA 42, SATA 47

RICE, ELIZABETH
Birthdate: 5/28/1913
Birthplace: Marshall, TX
Information Available in These Sources: IBYP 1, IBYP 2, SATA 2

RICE, EVE (HART)
Birthdate: 2/2/1951
Birthplace: New York, NY
Information Available in These Sources: ABYP 4, ICB 4, JBA 5, SATA 34

RICE, INEZ
Birthdate: 9/16/1907
Birthplace: Portland, OR
Information Available in These Sources: ABYP 2, ABYP 3, SATA 13

RICE, JAMES
Birthdate: 2/10/1934
Birthplace: Coleman, TX
Information Available in These Sources: SATA 22

RICH, BARBARA
See Rinkoff, Barbara (Jean Rich)

RICH, ELAINE SOMMERS
Birthdate: 2/8/1926
Birthplace: Plevna, IN
Information Available in These Sources: ABYP 2, ABYP 3, SATA 6

RICH, JOSEPHINE (BOUCHARD)
Birthdate: 6/27/1912
Birthplace: Tamora, NE
Information Available in These Sources: ABYP 1, ABYP 3, SATA 10

RICH, LOUISE (DICKINSON)
Birthdate: 6/14/1903
Birthplace: Huntington, MA
Information Available in These Sources: ABYP 1, ABYP 3, DACF, SATA 54

RICH, MARK J.
Birthdate: 11/23/1948
Birthplace: Ray, AZ
Information Available in These Sources: SATA 53

RICHARD, ADRIENNE
Birthdate: 10/31/1921
Birthplace: Evanston, IL
Information Available in These Sources: ABYP 4, DACF, JBA 5, SATA 5

RICHARD, JAMES ROBERT
See Bowen, R(obert) Sydney

RICHARDS, CURTIS
See Curtis, Richard (Alan)

RICHARDS, GEORGE MATHER
Birthdate: 9/3/1880
Birthplace: Darien, CT
Information Available in These Sources: ICB 1

RICHARDS, JOHN PAUL
Birthplace: Houston, TX
Information Available in These Sources: IBYP 2

RICHARDS, LAURA E(LIZABETH HOWE)
Birthdate: 2/27/1850
Birthplace: Boston, MA
Deathdate: 1/14/1943
Information Available in These Sources: DLB 42, JBA 1, SVC 2, SVC 3, TCCW 1, TCCW 2, TCCW 3, WC, YABC

RICHARDS, NORMAN
Birthdate: 3/14/1932
Birthplace: Winchendon, MA
Information Available in These Sources: ABYP 4, SATA 48

RICHARDS, RUTH
Birthplace: New York, NY
Information Available in These Sources: ABYP 4

RICHARDSON, CAROL
Birthdate: 12/25/1932
Birthplace: Orlando, FL
Information Available in These Sources: SATA 58

RICHARDSON, FRANK HOWARD
Birthdate: 7/1/1882
Birthplace: Brooklyn, NY
Deathdate: 5/26/1970
Information Available in These Sources: ABYP 4, SATA 27

RICHARDSON, GRACE LEE
See Dickson, Naida

RICHARDSON, ROBERT S(HIRLEY)
(Philip Latham, Robert Shirley Robinson)
Birthdate: 4/22/1902
Birthplace: Kokomo, IN
Information Available in These Sources: ABYP 2, ABYP 3, SATA 8

RICHARDSON, WILLIS
Birthdate: 11/5/1889
Birthplace: Wilmington, NC
Deathdate: 11/8/1977
Information Available in These Sources: SATA 60

RICHELSON, GERALDINE
(Ed Leander)
Birthdate: 8/20/1922
Birthplace: New York, NY
Information Available in These Sources: SATA 29

RICHMOND, JULIUS B(ENJAMIN)
Birthdate: 9/26/1916
Birthplace: Chicago, IL
Information Available in These Sources: ABYP 4

RICHOUX, PAT(RICIA)
Birthdate: 11/1/1927
Birthplace: Omaha, NE
Information Available in These Sources: SATA 7

RICHTER, ALICE
Birthdate: 10/19/1941
Birthplace: Brooklyn, NY
Information Available in These Sources: SATA 30

RICHTER, CONRAD (MICHAEL)
Birthdate: 10/13/1890
Birthplace: Pine Grove, PA
Deathdate: 10/30/1968
Information Available in These Sources: ABYP 4, SATA 3

RICHTER, ED
Information Available in These Sources: ABYP 4

RICHTER, MISCHA
Birthdate: 8/12/1910
Birthplace: Russia
Information Available in These Sources: ABYP 4

RICO, DON(ATO)
Birthdate: 9/26/1917
Birthplace: Rochester, NY
Deathdate: 3/27/1985
Information Available in These Sources: SATA 43

RIDDLE, MAXWELL
Birthdate: 7/29/1907
Birthplace: Ravenna, OH
Information Available in These Sources: ABYP 4

RIDGE, MARTIN
Birthdate: 5/7/1923
Birthplace: Chicago, IL
Information Available in These Sources: SATA 43

RIDGEWAY, JASON
See Marlowe, Stephen

RIDLON, MARCI
(Marci Carafoli, Marci McGill)
Birthdate: 7/27/1942
Birthplace: Chicago, IL
Information Available in These Sources: SATA 22

RIEDMAN, SARAH R(EGAL)
(Sarah Regal Gustafson)
Birthdate: 4/20/1902
Birthplace: Kishinev, Romania
Information Available in These Sources: ABYP 2, ABYP 3, SATA 1

RIENOW, LEONA TRAIN
Birthdate, 1903?
Birthplace: Duluth, MN
Deathdate: 8/18/1983
Information Available in These Sources: ABYP 2, ABYP 3

RIESENBERG, FELIX, JR.
Birthdate: 8/5/1913
Birthplace: New York, NY
Deathdate: 3/22/1962
Information Available in These Sources: ABYP 1, ABYP 3, SATA 23

RIESSEN, CLARE
See Riessen, Martin Clare

RIESSEN, MARTIN CLARE
(Clare Riessen)
Birthdate: 12/4/1941
Birthplace: Hinsdale, IL
Information Available in These Sources: ABYP 4

RIETVELD, JANE KLATT
Birthdate: 1913
Birthplace: Algoma, WI
Information Available in These Sources: ABYP 2, ABYP 3

RIFKIN, LILLIAN
Birthplace: Wilkes-Barre, PA
Information Available in These Sources: ABYP 1, ABYP 3

RIGGS, IDA BERRY
Information Available in These Sources: ABYP 2, ABYP 3

RIGGS, SIDNEY NOYES
Birthdate: 4/14/1892
Birthplace: Newark, NJ
Deathdate: 6/00/1975
Information Available in These Sources: SATA 28

RIKHOFF, JEAN
Birthdate: 5/28/1928
Birthplace: Chicago, IL
Information Available in These Sources: ABYP 4, SATA 9

RILEY, JAMES WHITCOMB
(Benj. F. Johnson, of Boone)
Birthdate: 10/7/1849
Birthplace: Greenfield, IN
Deathdate: 7/22/1916
Information Available in These Sources: JBA 1, SATA 17, SVC 2, SVC 3

RILEY, JOCELYN (CAROL)
Birthdate: 3/6/1949
Birthplace: Minneapolis, MN
Information Available in These Sources: SATA 50, SATA 60

RINALDI, ANN
Birthdate: 8/27/1934
Birthplace: New York, NY
Information Available in These Sources: SATA 50, SATA 51

RINARD, JUDITH E(LLEN)
Birthdate: 8/15/1947
Birthplace: Mason City, IA
Information Available in These Sources: SATA 44

RINGI, KJELL ARNE SORENSEN
(Kjell S-Ringi)
Birthdate: 2/3/1939
Birthplace: Gothenburg, Sweden
Information Available in These Sources: IBYP 1, IBYP 2, JBA 4, SATA 12

RINK, PAUL
Birthdate: 1912
Birthplace: San Jose, CA
Information Available in These Sources: ABYP 1, ABYP 3

RINKOFF, BARBARA (JEAN RICH)
(Barbara Rich)
Birthdate: 1/25/1923
Birthplace: New York, NY
Deathdate: 2/18/1975
Information Available in These Sources: ABYP 2, ABYP 3, DACF, MBMP, SATA 4, SATA 27

RIOS, TERE
See Versace, Marie Teresa

RIPLEY, ELIZABETH BLAKE
Birthdate: 6/9/1906
Birthplace: New Haven, CT
Deathdate: 6/21/1969
Information Available in These Sources: ABYP 1, ABYP 3, SATA 5

RIPPER, CHARLES L(EWIS)
Birthdate: 10/28/1929
Birthplace: Pittsburgh, PA
Information Available in These Sources: IBYP 2, ICB 2, ICB 3, SATA 3

RIQ
See Atwater, Richard (Tupper)

RISKIND, MARY (JULIA LONGENBERGER)
Birthdate: 8/2/1944
Birthplace: Elmira, NY
Information Available in These Sources: SATA 60

RISSMAN, ART
See Sussman, Susan

RISSMAN, SUSAN
See Sussman, Susan

RISWOLD, GILBERT
Birthplace: Chicago, IL
Information Available in These Sources: IBYP 1, IBYP 2, ICB 3, ICB 4

RITCHIE, BARBARA (GIBBONS)
Birthplace: Bemidji, MN
Information Available in These Sources: ABYP 2, ABYP 3, SATA 14

RITCHIE, RITA (MARIE KROHNE)
See Reitci, Rita Krohne

RITTER, LAWRENCE S(TANLEY)
Birthdate: 5/23/1922
Birthplace: New York, NY
Information Available in These Sources: SATA 58

RITTS, PAUL
Birthdate, 1920?
Deathdate: 10/18/1980
Information Available in These Sources: SATA 25

RIVERA, EDITH BUCKET 'PIE' VONNEGUT
Information Available in These Sources: ABYP 4

RIVERA, GERALDO
Birthdate: 7/4/1943
Birthplace: New York, NY
Information Available in These Sources: ABYP 4, SATA 28, SATA 54

RIVERSIDE, JOHN
See Heinlein, Robert A(nson)

RIVOLI, MARIO
(Seymour Marasmus, H. M. Koutoukas)
Birthdate: 1/31/1943
Birthplace: New York, NY
Information Available in These Sources: IBYP 1, IBYP 2, ICB 3, SATA 10

ROACH, MARILYNNE K(ATHLEEN)
Birthdate: 7/15/1946
Birthplace: Cambridge, MA
Information Available in These Sources: SATA 9

ROACH, PORTIA
See Takakjian, Portia

ROBBINS, FRANK
Birthdate: 9/9/1917
Birthplace: Boston, MA
Information Available in These Sources: IBYP 2, SATA 32, SATA 42

ROBBINS, KEN
Information Available in These Sources: SATA 53

ROBBINS, MARIA (POLUSHKIN)
See Polushkin, Maria

ROBBINS, RUTH
(Ruth Robbins Schein)
Birthdate: 12/29/1917 or 12/29/1918
Birthplace: Newark, NJ
Information Available in These Sources: ABYP 2, ABYP 3, ICB 3, ICB 4, JBA 3, SATA 14

ROBBINS, TONY
See Pashko, Stanley

ROBBINS, WAYNE
See Cox, William R(obert)

ROBERSON, JOHN R(OYSTER)
Birthdate: 3/7/1930
Birthplace: Roanoke, VA
Information Available in These Sources: SATA 53

ROBERTS, BRUCE (STUART)
Birthdate: 2/4/1930
Birthplace: Mount Vernon, NY
Information Available in These Sources: SATA 39, SATA 47

ROBERTS, CATHERINE CHRISTOPHER
Birthdate: 1905
Information Available in These Sources: ABYP 2, ABYP 3

ROBERTS, ELIZABETH MADOX
Birthdate: 10/30/1886 or 10/30/1885
Birthplace: Perryville, KY
Deathdate: 3/13/1941
Information Available in These Sources: TCCW 1, TCCW 2, SATA 27, SATA 33, SVC 2, SVC 3, TCCW 3, WC

ROBERTS, JIM
See Bates, Barbara S(nedeker)

ROBERTS, JOHN G(AITHER)
(Robert Paul)
Birthdate: 1/14/1913
Birthplace: New Britain, CT
Information Available in These Sources: SATA 27

ROBERTS, NANCY CORRELL
Birthdate: 5/30/1924
Birthplace: South Milwaukee, WI
Information Available in These Sources: ABYP 4, SATA 28, SATA 52

ROBERTS, TERENCE
See Sanderson, Ivan T(erence)

ROBERTS, VIRGINIA
See Dean, Nell Marr

ROBERTS, WAYNE
See Overholser, Wayne D.

ROBERTS, WILLO DAVIS
Birthdate: 5/29/1928
Birthplace: Grand Rapids, MI
Information Available in These Sources: DACF, JBA 5, SATA 21

ROBERTSON, DON
Birthdate: 3/21/1929
Birthplace: Cleveland, OH
Information Available in These Sources: SATA 8

ROBERTSON, DOROTHY LEWIS
Birthdate: 8/31/1912
Birthplace: New York, NY
Information Available in These Sources: ABYP 4, SATA 12

ROBERTSON, KEITH (CARLTON)
(Carlton Keith)
Birthdate: 5/9/1914
Birthplace: Dows, IA
Information Available in These Sources: ABYP 1, ABYP 3, DACF, MBMP, MJA, SATA 1, TCCW 1, TCCW 2, TCCW 3

ROBINET, HARRIETTE GILLEM
Birthdate: 7/14/1931
Birthplace: Washington, DC
Information Available in These Sources: BAI, SATA 27

ROBINS, SEELIN
See Ellis, Edward S(ylvester)

ROBINSON, BARBARA (WEBB)
Birthdate: 10/24/1927
Birthplace: Portsmouth, OH
Information Available in These Sources: ABYP 2, ABYP 3, JBA 5, SATA 8

ROBINSON, BOARDMAN
Birthdate: 9/6/1876
Birthplace: Somerset, Nova Scotia, Canada
Information Available in These Sources: ICB 1

ROBINSON, C(HARLES) A(LEXANDER), JR.
Birthdate: 3/30/1900
Birthplace: Princeton, NJ
Deathdate: 2/23/1965
Information Available in These Sources: ABYP 1, ABYP 3, SATA 36

ROBINSON, CHARLES
Birthdate: 6/25/1931
Birthplace: Morristown, NJ
Information Available in These Sources: IBYP 2, ICB 4, SATA 6, JBA 6

ROBINSON, DOROTHY W.
Birthdate: 10/1/1929
Birthplace: Waycross, GA
Information Available in These Sources: SATA 54

ROBINSON, EDWIN ARLINGTON
Birthdate: 12/22/1869
Birthplace: Head Tide, ME
Deathdate: 4/6/1935
Information Available in These Sources: JBA 1

ROBINSON, IRENE BOWEN
(Irene Bowen)
Birthdate: 1891 or 1892
Birthplace: South Bend, WA
Information Available in These Sources: ABYP 2, ABYP 3, IBYP 2, ICB 1 ICB 2, JBA 2

ROBINSON, JAN M.
(Flash Flood)
Birthdate: 10/30/1933
Information Available in These Sources: ABYP 4, SATA 6

ROBINSON, JEAN O. (KRONER)
Birthdate: 8/19/1934
Birthplace: La Crosse, WI
Information Available in These Sources: ABYP 4, SATA 7

ROBINSON, JERRY
Birthdate: 1922
Birthplace: New York, NY
Information Available in These Sources: IBYP 2, SATA 34

ROBINSON, LLOYD
Birthdate: 1935
Information Available in These Sources: ABYP 4

ROBINSON, LOUIE, JR.
(James Wyatt)
Birthdate: 10/4/1926
Birthplace: Dallas, TX
Information Available in These Sources: ABYP 4, BAI

ROBINSON, MABEL LOUISE
Birthdate: 7/19/1874
Birthplace: Waltham, MA
Deathdate: 2/21/1962
Information Available in These Sources: DLB 22, JBA 2

ROBINSON, MARILETA
Birthdate: 12/26/1942
Birthplace: Kansas City, KS
Information Available in These Sources: SATA 32

ROBINSON, MAUDIE
See Robinson, Millian Oller

ROBINSON, MAURICE R.
Birthdate: 12/24/1895
Birthplace: Wilkinsburg, PA
Deathdate: 2/7/1982
Information Available in These Sources: SATA 29

ROBINSON, MILLIAN OLLER
(Maudie Robinson)
Birthdate: 8/4/1914
Birthplace: Norris, OK
Information Available in These Sources: SATA 11

ROBINSON, NANCY K(ONHEIM)
Birthdate: 8/12/1942
Birthplace: New York, NY
Information Available in These Sources: SATA 31, SATA 32

ROBINSON, RAY(MOND KENNETH)
Birthdate: 12/4/1920
Birthplace: New York, NY
Information Available in These Sources: ABYP 1, ABYP 3, SATA 23

ROBINSON, ROBERT SHIRLEY
See Richardson, Robert S(hirley)

ROBINSON, SHARI
See McGuire, Leslie (Sarah)

ROBINSON, THOMAS PENDLETON
(Tom Robinson)
Birthdate: 6/18/1878
Birthplace: Calais, ME
Deathdate: 11/21/1954
Information Available in These Sources: ABYP 2, ABYP 3, JBA 2, SVC 2, SVC 3

ROBINSON, TOM
See Robinson, Thomas Pendleton

ROBINSON, TOM D.
Birthplace: Bellingham, WA
Information Available in These Sources: ABYP 4

ROBINSON, W(ILLIAM) W(ILCOX)
Birthdate: 1891
Birthplace: CA
Information Available in These Sources: JBA 2, SVC 2, SVC 3

ROBISON, BONNIE
Birthdate: 8/4/1924
Birthplace: Mound City, KS
Information Available in These Sources: SATA 12

ROBISON, NANCY L(OUISE)
(Natalie Johnson)
Birthdate: 1/20/1934
Birthplace: Compton, CA
Information Available in These Sources: SATA 32

ROCHE, A. K.
See Abisch, Roslyn Kroop and Kaplan, Boche

ROCHE, P(ATRICIA) K.
Birthdate: 6/15/1935
Birthplace: Brooklyn, NY
Information Available in These Sources: SATA 34, 57

ROCK, GAIL
Information Available in These Sources: ABYP 4, SATA 32

ROCKER, FERMIN
Birthdate: 12/22/1907
Birthplace: London, England
Information Available in These Sources: ICB 3, SATA 40

ROCKWELL, ANNE (FOOTE)
Birthdate: 2/8/1934
Birthplace: Memphis, TN
Information Available in These Sources: IBYP 2, ICB 4, JBA 5, SATA 33 TCCW 3

ROCKWELL, GAIL
Birthdate: 1894
Birthplace: New York, NY
Deathdate: 1978
Information Available in These Sources: IBYP 2, ICB 4, SATA 33, SATA 36

ROCKWELL, HARLOW
Birthdate: 1910
Deathdate: 4/7/1988
Information Available in These Sources: IBYP 2, ICB 4, JBA 5, SATA 33,SATA 56

ROCKWELL, NORMAN (PERCEVEL)
Birthdate: 2/3/1894
Birthplace: New York, NY
Deathdate: 11/8/1978
Information Available in These Sources: IBYP 1, IBYP 2, ICB 1, SATA 23

ROCKWELL, THOMAS
Birthdate: 3/13/1933
Birthplace: New Rochelle, NY
Information Available in These Sources: JBA 5, SATA 7

ROCKWOOD, JOYCE
Birthdate: 6/1/1947
Birthplace: Ames, IA
Information Available in These Sources: DACF, SATA 39

ROCKWOOD, ROY
See Stratemeyer, Edward L.

RODDENBERRY, EUGENE WESLEY
(Gene Roddenberry)
Birthdate: 8/19/1921
Birthplace: El Paso, TX
Information Available in These Sources: SATA 45

RODDENBERRY, GENE
See Roddenberry, Eugene Wesley

RODDY, LEE
(Rachel Banner)
Birthdate: 8/22/1921
Birthplace: Marion County, IL
Information Available in These Sources: SATA 57

RODGERS, MARY
(Mary Rodgers Guettel)
Birthdate: 1/11/1931
Birthplace: New York, NY
Information Available in These Sources: ABYP 4, DACF, JBA 5, SATA 8, TCCW 1, TCCW 2, TCCW 3

RODMAN, BELLA (KASHIN)
Birthdate: 12/25/1903
Birthplace: Warsaw, Poland
Information Available in These Sources: ABYP 4

RODMAN, EMERSON
See Ellis, Edward S(ylvester)

RODMAN, MAIA
See Wojciechowska, Maia (Teresa Rodman)

RODMAN, SELDEN
Birthdate: 2/19/1909
Birthplace: New York, NY
Information Available in These Sources: ABYP 4, SATA 9

RODOWSKY, COLBY
Birthdate: 2/26/1932
Birthplace: Baltimore, MD
Information Available in These Sources: SATA 21, JBA 6

ROEVER, J(OAN) M(ARILYN)
Birthdate: 12/13/1935
Birthplace: Philadelphia, PA
Information Available in These Sources: ABYP 4, IBYP 2, SATA 26

ROFES, ERIC EDWARD
Birthdate: 8/31/1954
Birthplace: Manhasset, NY
Information Available in These Sources: SATA 52

ROGERS, CAROL
Birthplace: Waco, TX
Information Available in These Sources: IBYP 1, IBYP 2

ROGERS, CEDRIC
See Rogers, Grenville Cedric Harry

ROGERS, FRANCES
Birthdate: 1888
Birthplace: Grand Rapids, MI
Deathdate: 6/6/1974
Information Available in These Sources: SATA 10

ROGERS, FRED (MCFEELY)
(Mister Rogers, Mr. Rogers)
Birthdate: 3/20/1928
Birthplace: Latrobe, PA
Information Available in These Sources: SATA 33

ROGERS, GRENVILLE CEDRIC HARRY
(Cedric Rogers)
Birthdate: 5/29/1915
Birthplace: Schenectady, NY
Information Available in These Sources: ABYP 1, ABYP 3

ROGERS, JEAN
Birthdate: 10/1/1919
Birthplace: Wendell, ID
Information Available in These Sources: SATA 47, 55

ROGERS, MATILDA
Birthdate: 3/3/1894
Birthplace: Budapest, Hungary
Deathdate: 1976
Information Available in These Sources: SATA 5, SATA 34

ROGERS, MISTER
See Rogers, Fred (McFeely)

ROGERS, MR.
See Rogers, Fred (McFeely)

ROGERS, W(ILLIAM) G(ARLAND)
Birthdate: 2/29/1896
Birthplace: Chicopee Falls, MA
Deathdate: 3/1/1978
Information Available in These Sources: ABYP 2, ABYP 3, SATA 23

ROGERS, WADE
See Madlee, Dorothy (Haynes)

ROHDE, RUTH BRYAN OWEN
See Owen, Ruth (Bryan)

ROHMER, HARRIET
Birthdate: 5/19/1938
Birthplace: Washington, DC
Information Available in These Sources: SATA 56

ROJAN
See Rojankovsky, Feodor (Stephanovich)

ROJANKOVSKY, FEODOR (STEPHANOVICH)
(Rojan)
Birthdate: 12/24/1891
Birthplace: Mitava, Russia
Deathdate: 10/12/1970
Information Available in These Sources: ABYP 1, ABYP 3, BABP, IBYP 1, IBYP 2, ICB 1, ICB 2, ICB 3, ICB 4, JBA 2, SATA 21

ROLAND, ALBERT
Birthdate: 12/9/1925
Birthplace: Pinerolo, Italy
Information Available in These Sources: SATA 11

ROLERSON, DARRELL A(LLEN)
Birthdate: 2/21/1946
Birthplace: Camden, ME
Information Available in These Sources: SATA 8

ROLLINS, CHARLEMAE HILL
Birthdate: 6/20/1897
Birthplace: Yazoo City, MS
Deathdate: 2/3/1979
Information Available in These Sources: ABYP 1, ABYP 3, BAI, MBMP, SATA 3, SATA 26

ROMANO, CLARE
See Ross, Clare (Romano)

ROMANO, LOUIS G.
Birthdate: 1/1/1921
Birthplace: Milwaukee, WI
Information Available in These Sources: SATA 35

ROME, ANTHONY
See Albert, Marvin H.

ROOD, RONALD (N.)
Birthdate: 7/7/1920
Birthplace: Torrington, CT
Information Available in These Sources: SATA 12

ROOP, CONNIE
See Roop, Constance Betzer

ROOP, CONSTANCE BETZER
(Connie Roop)
Birthdate: 6/18/1951
Birthplace: Elkhorn, WI
Information Available in These Sources: SATA 49, SATA 54

ROOP, PETER
Birthdate: 3/8/1951
Birthplace: Winchester, MA
Information Available in These Sources: SATA 49, SATA 54

ROOS, ANN
Birthplace: Brooklyn, NY
Information Available in These Sources: ABYP 1, ABYP 3, MJA

ROOS, STEPHEN (KELLEY)
Birthdate: 2/9/1945
Birthplace: New York, NY
Information Available in These Sources: SATA 41, SATA 47, JBA 6

ROOSEVELT, ANNA ELEANOR (ROOSEVELT)
Birthdate: 10/11/1884
Birthplace: New York, NY
Deathdate: 11/7/1962
Information Available in These Sources: ABYP 2, ABYP 3, SATA 50

ROOT, PHYLLIS
Birthdate: 2/14/1949
Birthplace: Fort Wayne, IN
Information Available in These Sources: SATA 48, SATA 55

ROOT, SHELTON L., JR.
Birthdate: 8/1/1923
Birthplace: Berea, OH
Deathdate: 11/12/1986
Information Available in These Sources: SATA 51

ROOTE, MIKE
See Fleischer, Lenore

ROPER, LAURA WOOD
(Laura N(ewbold) Wood)
Birthdate: 3/15/1911
Birthplace: St. Louis, MO
Information Available in These Sources: ABYP 1, ABYP 3, SATA 34

ROSE, ANNA PERROT
See Wright, Anna (Maria Louisa Perrot) Rose

ROSE, ANNE K.
Birthplace: Antwerp, Belgium
Information Available in These Sources: SATA 8

ROSE, CARL
(Earl Cros)
Birthdate, 1903?
Birthplace: NY
Deathdate: 6/20/1971
Information Available in These Sources: SATA 31

ROSE, FLORELLA
See Carlson, Vada F.

ROSE, NANCY A.
See Sweetland, Nancy A(nn Rose)

ROSE, WENDY
(Bronwen Elizabeth Edwards, Chiron Khanshendel)
Birthdate: 5/7/1948
Birthplace: Oakland, CA
Information Available in These Sources: SATA 12

ROSELLI, LUCIANA
Birthplace: Alessandria, Italy
Information Available in These Sources: ABYP 2, ABYP 3

ROSEMAN, KENNETH DAVID
Birthdate: 5/10/1939
Birthplace: Washington, DC
Information Available in These Sources: SATA 52

ROSEN, SIDNEY
Birthdate: 6/5/1916
Birthplace: Boston, MA
Information Available in These Sources: SATA 1

ROSEN, WINIFRED
Birthdate: 10/16/1943
Birthplace: Columbia, SC
Information Available in These Sources: SATA 8

ROSENBAUM, EILEEN
Birthdate: 1/11/1936
Birthplace: Tarentum, PA
Information Available in These Sources: ABYP 4

ROSENBERG, DOROTHY
(Dorothy Young Croman)
Birthdate: 12/25/1906
Birthplace: Waverly, WA
Information Available in These Sources: SATA 40

ROSENBERG, ETHEL (CLIFFORD)
(Eth Clifford, Ruth Bonn Penn)
Birthdate: 12/25/1915
Birthplace: New York, NY
Information Available in These Sources: ABYP 4, JBA 6, SATA 3

ROSENBERG, JANE
Birthdate: 12/7/1949
Birthplace: New York, NY
Information Available in These Sources: SATA 58

ROSENBERG, MAXINE B(ERTA)
Birthdate: 8/6/1939
Birthplace: New York, NY
Information Available in These Sources: SATA 47, SATA 55

ROSENBERG, NANCY SHERMAN
(Nancy Sherman)
Birthdate: 6/21/1931
Birthplace: New York, NY
Information Available in These Sources: ABYP 4, SATA 4

ROSENBERG, SHARON
Birthdate: 12/14/1942
Birthplace: New York, NY
Information Available in These Sources: SATA 8

ROSENBLATT, ARTHUR S.
Birthdate: 4/21/1938
Birthplace: Boston, MA
Information Available in These Sources: SATA 45

ROSENBLOOM, JOSEPH
Birthdate: 6/28/1928
Birthplace: New York, NY
Information Available in These Sources: SATA 21

ROSENBLUM, RICHARD
Birthdate: 1/24/1928
Birthplace: Brooklyn, NY
Information Available in These Sources: IBYP 2, SATA 11

ROSENBURG, JOHN M.
Birthdate: 6/2/1918
Birthplace: Mountainhome, PA
Information Available in These Sources: ABYP 1, ABYP 3, SATA 6

ROSENFELD, SAM
Birthdate: 11/30/1920
Birthplace: New York, NY
Information Available in These Sources: ABYP 4

ROSENTHAL, HAROLD
Birthdate: 3/11/1914
Birthplace: New York, NY
Information Available in These Sources: SATA 35

ROSENTHAL, M(ACHA) L(OUIS)
Birthdate: 3/14/1917
Birthplace: Washington, DC
Information Available in These Sources: SATA 59

ROSS, ALEXANDER
Birthdate: 10/28/1909
Birthplace: Dumferline, Scotland
Information Available in These Sources: SATA 29

ROSS, BARNABY
See Dannay, Frederic

ROSS, CLARE (ROMANO)
(Clare Romano)
Birthdate: 8/24/1922
Birthplace: Palisade, NJ
Information Available in These Sources: ICB 3, ICB 4, SATA 48

ROSS, DANA FULLER
See Gerson, Noel B(ertram)

ROSS, DAVE
Birthdate: 4/2/1949
Birthplace: Scotia, NY
Information Available in These Sources: SATA 32

ROSS, DAVID
Birthdate: 7/7/1896
Birthplace: New York, NY
Deathdate: 11/12/1975
Information Available in These Sources: SATA 20, SATA 49

ROSS, FRANK (XAVIER), JR.
(R. Frank, Jr.)
Birthdate: 2/8/1914
Birthplace: New York, NY
Information Available in These Sources: ABYP 4, SATA 28

ROSS, JOHN
Birthdate: 9/25/1921
Birthplace: New York, NY
Information Available in These Sources: IBYP 1, IBYP 2, ICB 3, ICB 4, SATA 45

ROSS, LAURA
See Mincieli, Rose Laura

ROSS, PAT(RICIA KIENZIE)
Birthdate: 2/4/1943
Birthplace: Baltimore, MD
Information Available in These Sources: BC, SATA 53

ROSS, PATRICIA (FENT)
Birthdate: 1899 or 1901
Birthplace: KS
Information Available in These Sources: ABYP 2, ABYP 3

ROSS, WILDA (S.)
Birthdate: 10/23/1915
Birthplace: Santa Barbara, CA
Information Available in These Sources: ABYP 4, SATA 39, SATA 51

ROSS, Z(OLA) H(ELEN GIRDEY)
(Helen Arre, Bert Iles)
Birthdate: 5/9/1912
Birthplace: Dayton, IA
Information Available in These Sources: ABYP 1, ABYP 3

ROSSEL, SEYMOUR
Birthdate: 8/9/1945
Birthplace: Chicago, IL
Information Available in These Sources: SATA 28

ROSSEL-WAUGH, C. C.
See Waugh, Carol-Lynn Rossel

ROSTKOWSKI, MARGARET I.
Birthdate: 1/12/1945
Birthplace: Little Rock, AR
Information Available in These Sources: SATA 59, JBA 6

ROTH, ARNOLD
Birthdate: 2/25/1929
Birthplace: Philadelphia, PA
Information Available in These Sources: ABYP 4, IBYP 2, SATA 21

ROTH, ARTHUR J(OSEPH)
(Nina Hoy, Barney Mara, Slater McGurk, Pete Pomeroy)
Birthdate: 8/3/1925
Birthplace: New York, NY
Information Available in These Sources: ABYP 4, SATA 28, SATA 43

ROTH, BERNHARD A.
Information Available in These Sources: ABYP 4

ROTH, DAVID
Birthdate: 10/27/1940
Birthplace: New York, NY
Information Available in These Sources: SATA 36

ROTH, HAROLD
Birthplace: Austria
Information Available in These Sources: SATA 49

ROTHBERG, ABRAHAM
Birthdate: 1/14/1922
Birthplace: New York, NY
Information Available in These Sources: SATA 59

ROTHERY, AGNES
See Pratt, Agnes Edwards Rothery

ROTHERY, AGNES EDWARDS
See Pratt, Agnes Edwards Rothery

ROTHKOPF, CAROL Z.
Birthdate: 9/16/1929
Birthplace: New York, NY
Information Available in These Sources: SATA 4

ROTHMAN, JOEL
Birthdate: 4/6/1938
Birthplace: New York, NY
Information Available in These Sources: SATA 7

ROUECHE, BERTON
Birthdate: 4/16/1911
Birthplace: Kansas City, MO
Information Available in These Sources: SATA 28

ROUNDS, GLEN (HAROLD)
Birthdate: 4/4/1906
Birthplace: Wall (near), SD
Information Available in These Sources: ABYP 1, ABYP 3, ICB 1, ICB 2, ICB 3, ICB 4, JBA 2, SATA 8, TCCW 1, TCCW 2, TCCW 3

ROURKE, CONSTANCE (MAYFIELD)
Birthdate: 11/14/1885
Birthplace: Cleveland, OH
Deathdate: 3/23/1941
Information Available in These Sources: MJA, YABC

ROWAND, PHYLLIS
Birthdate: 1915
Birthplace: VT
Information Available in These Sources: IBYP 2, ICB 2

ROWE, DOROTHY
Birthdate: 6/20/1898
Birthplace: Rome, NY
Information Available in These Sources: JBA 1, JBA 2

ROWE, VIOLA CARSON
Birthdate: 1/28/1903
Birthplace: Melrose Park, IL
Deathdate: 12/4/1969
Information Available in These Sources: ABYP 1, ABYP 3, SATA 26

ROWLAND, FLORENCE WIGHTMAN
Birthdate: 1/2/1900
Birthplace: Newark, NJ
Information Available in These Sources: ABYP 4, SATA 8

ROWSOME, FRANK (HOWARD), JR.
Birthdate: 3/12/1914
Birthplace: Dedham, MA
Deathdate: 3/15/1983
Information Available in These Sources: SATA 36

ROY, JESSIE HAILSTALK
Birthdate: 10/29/1895
Birthplace: Warrenton, VA
Deathdate: 12/29/1986
Information Available in These Sources: SATA 51

ROY, LIAM
See Scarry, Patricia (Murphy)

ROY, RON(ALD)
Birthdate: 4/29/1940
Birthplace: Hartford, CT
Information Available in These Sources: SATA 35, SATA 40

RUBEL, NICOLE
Birthdate: 4/29/1953
Birthplace: Miami, FL
Information Available in These Sources: ICB 4, JBA 5, SATA 18

RUBICAM, HARRY COGSWELL, JR.
Birthdate: 2/27/1902
Birthplace: Denver, CO
Information Available in These Sources: ABYP 1, ABYP 3

RUBIN, BOB
See Rubin, Robert

RUBIN, ROBERT
(Bob Rubin)
Information Available in These Sources: ABYP 4

RUBINSTEIN, ROBERT E(DWARD)
Birthdate: 11/12/1943
Birthplace: Boston, MA
Information Available in These Sources: SATA 49

RUBLOWSKY, JOHN M(ARTIN)
Birthdate: 3/5/1928
Birthplace: Evansville, PA
Information Available in These Sources: ABYP 4

RUBY, LOIS
Birthdate: 9/11/1942
Birthplace: San Francisco, CA
Information Available in These Sources: SATA 34, SATA 35, JBA 6

RUCHLIS, HY(MAN)
Birthdate: 4/6/1913
Birthplace: Brooklyn, NY
Information Available in These Sources: ABYP 1, ABYP 3, SATA 3

RUCKMAN, IVY
Birthdate: 5/25/1931
Birthplace: Hastings, NE
Information Available in These Sources: SATA 37, JBA 6

RUDEEN, KENNETH
Information Available in These Sources: SATA 36

RUDLEY, STEPHEN
Birthdate: 4/29/1946
Birthplace: Los Angeles, CA
Information Available in These Sources: SATA 30

RUDOLPH, MARGUERITA
Birthdate: 3/14/1908
Birthplace: Chernigov, Russia
Information Available in These Sources: ABYP 2, ABYP 3, SATA 21

RUDOMIN, ESTHER
See Hautzig, Esther (Rudomin)

RUE, LEONARD LEE III
Birthdate: 2/20/1926
Birthplace: Paterson, NJ
Information Available in These Sources: ABYP 4, SATA 37

RUEDI, NORMA PAUL
See Ainsworth, Norma

RUFFINS, REYNOLD
Birthdate: 8/5/1930
Birthplace: New York, NY
Information Available in These Sources: BAI, JBA 5, SATA 41

RUGH, BELLE DORMAN
Birthdate: 6/8/1908
Birthplace: Beirut, Lebanon
Information Available in These Sources: ABYP 1, ABYP 3, JBA 3

RUGOFF, MILTON
Birthdate: 3/6/1913
Birthplace: New York, NY
Information Available in These Sources: SATA 30

RUKEYSER, MURIEL
Birthdate: 12/15/1913
Birthplace: New York, NY
Deathdate: 2/12/1980
Information Available in These Sources: ABYP 1, ABYP 3, SATA 22

RUMSEY, MARIAN (BARRITT)
Birthdate: 5/18/1928
Birthplace: Nebraska City, NE
Information Available in These Sources: SATA 16, SVC 3

RUNYON, JOHN
See Palmer, Bernard

RUSH, WILLIAM MARSHALL
Birthdate: 1887
Birthplace: WV
Deathdate: 1950
Information Available in These Sources: ABYP 1, ABYP 3

RUSHMORE, HELEN
Birthdate: 1/19/1898
Birthplace: Independence, KS
Information Available in: ABYP 2, 3, SATA 3

RUSHMORE, ROBERT (WILLIAM)
Birthdate: 7/7/1926 or 7/12/1926
Birthplace: Tuxedo Park, NY
Deathdate: 9/20/1986
Information Available in These Sources: SATA 8, SATA 49

RUSKIN, ARIANE
See Batterberry, Ariane Ruskin

RUSS, LAVINIA
(Lavinia Faxon)
Birthdate: 7/30/1904
Birthplace: Kansas City, MO
Information Available in These Sources: ABYP 4

RUSSELL, CHARLOTTE
See Rathjen, Carl H(enry)

RUSSELL, DON(ALD BERT)
Birthdate: 1899
Birthplace: Huntington, IN
Deathdate: 2/17/1986
Information Available in These Sources: SATA 47

RUSSELL, FRANKLIN (ALEXANDER)
Birthdate: 10/9/1926
Birthplace: Christchurch, Canterbury, New Zealand
Information Available in These Sources: ABYP 2, ABYP 3, SATA 11

RUSSELL, HELEN ROSS
Birthdate: 2/21/1915
Birthplace: Myerstown, PA
Information Available in These Sources: SATA 8

RUSSELL, PATRICK
See Sammis, John

RUSSELL, SOLVEIG PAULSON
Birthdate: 3/??/1904
Birthplace: Salt Lake City, UT
Information Available in These Sources: ABYP 1, ABYP 3, SATA 3

RUSSO, SUSAN
Birthdate: 12/21/1947
Birthplace: Chicago, IL
Information Available in These Sources: SATA 30

RUTH, ROD
Birthdate: 9/21/1912
Birthplace: Benton Harbor, MI
Information Available in These Sources: IBYP 2, SATA 9

RUTZ, VIOLA LARKIN
Birthdate: 3/14/1932
Birthplace: New York, NY
Information Available in These Sources: SATA 12

RUZICKA, RUDOLPH
Birthdate: 6/29/1883
Birthplace: Bohemia
Deathdate: 7/20/1978
Information Available in These Sources: ICB 1, ICB 2, SATA 24

RYAN, BETSY
See Ryan, Elizabeth (Anne)

RYAN, CHELI DURAN
Birthplace: New York, NY
Information Available in These Sources: ABYP 4, JBA 5, SATA 20

RYAN, ELIZABETH (ANNE)
(Betsy Ryan)
Birthdate: 11/13/1943
Birthplace: New York, NY
Information Available in These Sources: SATA 30

RYDBERG, ERNEST E(MIL)
Birthdate: 8/9/1901
Birthplace: Central City, NE
Information Available in These Sources: SATA 21

RYDBERG, LOU(ISA HAMPTON)
Birthdate: 8/24/1908
Birthplace: Long Beach, CA
Information Available in These Sources: SATA 27

RYDELL, WENDELL
(Wendy Rydell)
Birthdate: 12/9/1927
Birthplace: Perth Amboy, NJ
Information Available in These Sources: SATA 4

RYDELL, WENDY
See Rydell, Wendell

RYDEN, HOPE
Birthplace: St. Paul, MN
Information Available in These Sources: SATA 8

RYDER, JOANNE
Birthdate: 9/16/1946
Birthplace: Morristown, NJ
Information Available in These Sources: SATA 34, JBA 6

RYLANT, CYNTHIA
Birthdate: 6/6/1954
Birthplace: Hopewell, VA
Information Available in These Sources: JBA 6, SATA 44, SATA 50, TCCW 3

RYMER, ALTA MAY
Birthdate: 6/20/1925
Birthplace: San Diego, CA
Information Available in These Sources: SATA 34

S

S-RINGI, KJELL
See Ringi, Kjell Arne Sorensen

SAAL, JOCELYN
See Sachs, Judith

SABERHAGEN, FRED (THOMAS)
Birthdate: 5/18/1930
Birthplace: Chicago, IL
Information Available in These Sources: SATA 37

SABIN, EDWIN L(EGRAND)
Birthdate: 12/23/1870
Birthplace: Rockford, IL
Deathdate: 11/24/1952
Information Available in These Sources: JBA 1, JBA 2, YABC

SABIN, FRANCENE
Information Available in These Sources: SATA 27

SABIN, LOUIS
(Keith Brandt)
Birthdate: 6/25/1930
Birthplace: Salt Lake City, UT
Information Available in These Sources: SATA 27

SABUSO
See Phillips, Irv(ing W.)

SACHAR, LOUIS
Birthdate: 3/20/1954
Birthplace: East Meadow, NY
Information Available in These Sources: SATA 50

SACHS, ELIZABETH-ANN
Birthdate: 6/25/1946
Birthplace: New York, NY
Information Available in These Sources: SATA 48

SACHS, JUDITH
(Emily Chase, Petra Diamond, Rebecca Diamond, Jocelyn Saal, Jennifer Sarasin, Antonia Saxon)
Birthdate: 2/13/1947
Birthplace: New York, NY
Information Available in These Sources: SATA 51, SATA 52

SACHS, MARILYN (STICKLE)
Birthdate: 12/18/1927
Birthplace: New York, NY
Information Available in These Sources: DACF, JBA 4, SATA 3, SATA 52, TCCW 1, TCCW 2, TCCW 3

SACKETT, S(AMUEL) J(OHN)
Birthdate: 1928
Birthplace: Redlands, CA
Information Available in These Sources: SATA 12

SACKSON, SID
Birthdate: 2/4/1920
Birthplace: Chicago, IL
Information Available in These Sources: SATA 16

SADER, LILLIAN
Information Available in These Sources: IBYP 1, IBYP 2

SADLER, CATHERINE EDWARDS
Birthdate: 12/3/1952
Birthplace: Los Angeles, CA
Information Available in These Sources: SATA 45, SATA 60

SADLER, MARK
See Lynds, Dennis

SAGAN, CARL
Birthdate: 11/9/1934
Birthplace: New York, NY
Information Available in These Sources: SATA 58

SAGE, JUNIPER
See Brown, Margaret Wise and Hurd, Edith Thacher

SAGE, MICHAEL
Information Available in These Sources: ABYP 4

SAGSOORIAN, PAUL
Birthdate: 3/26/1923
Birthplace: New York, NY
Information Available in These Sources: IBYP 2, SATA 12

SALASSI, OTTO R(USSELL)
Birthdate: 10/2/1939
Birthplace: Vicksburg, MS
Information Available in These Sources: JBA 6, SATA 38

SALDUTH, DENISE
Birthdate: 7/24/1953
Birthplace: Newark, NJ
Information Available in These Sources: SATA 39

SALVADORI, MARIO (GEORGE)
Birthdate: 3/19/1907
Birthplace: Rome, Italy
Information Available in These Sources: SATA 40

SALZER, L. E.
See Wilson, Lionel

SALZMAN, YURI
Birthplace: USSR
Information Available in These Sources: SATA 42

SAMACHSON, DOROTHY (MIRKIN)
Birthdate: 8/22/1914
Birthplace: New York, NY
Information Available in These Sources: ABYP 1, ABYP 3, SATA 3

SAMACHSON, JOSEPH
(John Miller, William Morrison, Brett Sterling)
Birthdate: 10/13/1906
Birthplace: Trenton, NJ
Deathdate: 6/2/1980
Information Available in These Sources: ABYP 1, ABYP 3, SATA 3, SATA 52

SAMMIS, JOHN
(Patrick Russell)
Birthdate: 6/22/1942
Birthplace: New York, NY
Information Available in These Sources: SATA 4

SAMSON, ANNE S(TRINGER)
Birthdate: 6/6/1933
Birthplace: St. Paul, MN
Information Available in These Sources: SATA 2

SAMSON, JOAN
Birthdate: 9/9/1937
Birthplace: Erie, PA
Deathdate: 2/27/1976
Information Available in These Sources: SATA 13

SAMSTAG, NICHOLAS
Birthdate: 12/25/1903
Birthplace: New York, NY
Deathdate: 3/26/1968
Information Available in These Sources: ABYP 2, ABYP 3

SAMUELS, CHARLES
Birthdate: 9/15/1902
Information Available in These Sources: SATA 12

SAMUELS, GERTRUDE
Birthplace: Manchester, England
Information Available in These Sources: ABYP 1, ABYP 3, SATA 17

SAN SOUCI, ROBERT D.
Birthdate: 10/10/1946
Birthplace: San Francisco, CA
Information Available in These Sources: SATA 40

SANBERG, KARL C.
Birthdate: 3/7/1931
Birthplace: Salt Lake City, UT
Information Available in These Sources: SATA 35

SANBORN, DUANE
(Duane Bradley)
Birthdate: 6/13/1914
Birthplace: Clarinda, IA
Information Available in These Sources: SATA 38

SANCHEZ, SONIA
Birthdate: 9/9/1934
Birthplace: Birmingham, AL
Information Available in These Sources: SATA 22

SAND, GEORGE X.
Birthplace: NJ
Information Available in These Sources: ABYP 4, SATA 45

SANDAK, CASS R(OBERT)
Birthdate: 5/4/1950
Birthplace: Johnstown, PA
Information Available in These Sources: SATA 37, SATA 51

SANDBURG, CARL (AUGUST)
(Militant, Jack Phillips, Charles A. Sandburg)
Birthdate: 1/6/1878
Birthplace: Galesburg, IL
Deathdate: 7/22/1967
Information Available in These Sources: ABYP 2, ABYP 3, SATA 8, SVC 2 SVC 3, WC

SANDBURG, CHARLES A.
See Sandburg, Carl (August)

SANDBURG, HELGA
(Helga Sandburg Crile)
Birthdate: 11/24/1918
Birthplace: Maywood or Elmhurst, IL
Information Available in These Sources: ABYP 2, ABYP 3, JBA 3, SATA 3

SANDERLIN, GEORGE
Birthdate: 2/5/1915
Birthplace: Baltimore, MD
Information Available in These Sources: SATA 4

SANDERLIN, OWENITA (HARRAH)
Birthdate: 6/2/1916
Birthplace: Los Angeles, CA
Information Available in These Sources: SATA 11

SANDERS, SCOTT R(USSELL)
Birthdate: 10/26/1945
Birthplace: Memphis, TN
Information Available in These Sources: SATA 56

SANDERS, WINSTON P.
See Anderson, Poul (William)

SANDERSON, IVAN T(ERENCE)
(Terence Roberts)
Birthdate: 1/30/1911
Birthplace: Edinburgh, Scotland
Deathdate: 2/19/1973
Information Available in These Sources: ICB 1, ICB 2, ABYP 1, ABYP 3, SATA 6

SANDERSON, RUTH (L.)
Birthdate: 11/24/1951
Birthplace: Ware, MA
Information Available in These Sources: ICB 4, SATA 41

SANDIN, JOAN
Birthdate: 4/30/1942
Birthplace: Watertown, WI
Information Available in These Sources: IBYP 1, IBYP 2, ICB 4, JBA 6, SATA 12

SANDOZ, EDOUARD
Birthdate: 3/23/1918
Information Available in These Sources: IBYP 2, ICB 2

SANDOZ, MARI (SUSETTE)
(Mari Macumber, P. O. Sandoz)
Birthdate: 1901 or 1896 or 1907
Birthplace: Sheridan County, NE
Deathdate: 3/10/1966
Information Available in These Sources: ABYP 1, ABYP 3, DACF, JBA 3, SATA 5

SANDOZ, P. O.
See Sandoz, Mari (Susette)

SANDSTROM, GEORGE F.
Birthplace: Argentina
Information Available in These Sources: IBYP 2

SANDSTROM, MARITA
Information Available in These Sources: IBYP 2

SANGER, FRANCES ELLA (FITZ)
Birthplace: Summertown, TN
Information Available in These Sources: ABYP 1, ABYP 3

SANGER, MARJORY BARTLETT
Birthdate: 2/11/1920
Birthplace: Baltimore, MD
Information Available in These Sources: ABYP 4, SATA 8

SANKEY, ALICE (ANN-SUSAN)
Birthdate: 2/3/1910
Birthplace: Waukegan, IL
Information Available in These Sources: SATA 27

SANTALO, LOIS
Birthplace: Grand Rapids, MI
Information Available in These Sources: ABYP 2, ABYP 3

SANTESSON, HANS STEFAN
Birthdate: 1914
Birthplace: Sweden
Deathdate: 2/21/1975
Information Available in These Sources: SATA 30

SAPIEHA, CHRISTINE
Birthplace: Poland
Information Available in These Sources: IBYP 1, IBYP 2

SAPIEYEVSKI, ANNE LINDBERGH
(Anne Lindbergh, Anne Lindbergh Feydy, Anne Lindbergh Foley)
Birthdate: 10/2/1940
Birthplace: New York, NY
Information Available in These Sources: ABYP 4, JBA 6, SATA 32, SATA 35

SARAC, ROGER
See Caras, Roger A(ndrew)

SARASIN, JENNIFER
See Sachs, Judith

SARASY, PHYLLIS POWELL
Birthdate: 4/8/1930
Birthplace: Cleveland, OH
Information Available in These Sources: ABYP 1, ABYP 3

SARG, ANTHONY FREDERICK
See Sarg, Tony

SARG, TONY
(Anthony Frederick Sarg)
Birthdate: 4/24/1880
Birthplace: Guatemala
Deathdate: 3/7/1942
Information Available in These Sources: JBA 1, JBA 2, YABC

SARGENT, PAMELA
Birthdate: 3/20/1948
Birthplace: Ithaca, NY
Information Available in These Sources: JBA 6, SATA 29, TCCW 3

SARGENT, ROBERT EDWARD
Birthdate: 3/26/1933
Birthplace: Northfield, VT
Information Available in These Sources: ICB 3, SATA 2

SARGENT, SARAH
Birthdate: 3/15/1937
Birthplace: Roanoke, VA
Information Available in These Sources: JBA 6, SATA 41, SATA 44

SARGENT, SHIRLEY
Birthdate: 7/12/1927
Birthplace: Los Angeles, CA
Information Available in These Sources: ABYP 1, ABYP 3, SATA 11

SARI
See Fleur, Anne (Elizabeth)

SARNOFF, JANE
Birthdate: 6/25/1937
Birthplace: Brooklyn, NY
Information Available in These Sources: ABYP 4, JBA 5, SATA 10

SAROYAN, WILLIAM
(Sirak Goryan)
Birthdate: 8/31/1908
Birthplace: Fresno, CA
Deathdate: 5/18/1981
Information Available in These Sources: SATA 23, SATA 24

SARTON, ELEANOR MAY
(Eleanore Marie Sarton, May Sarton)
Birthdate: 5/3/1912
Birthplace: Wondelgem, Belgium
Information Available in These Sources: SATA 36

SARTON, ELEANORE MARIE
See Sarton, Eleanor May

SARTON, MAY
See Sarton, Eleanor May

SASEEN, SHARON (DILLON)
(Sharon Saseen Dillon)
Birthdate: 1/23/1949
Birthplace: Savannah, GA
Information Available in These Sources: SATA 59

SATTLER, HELEN RONEY
Birthdate: 3/2/1921
Birthplace: Newton, IA
Information Available in These Sources: ABYP 4, JBA 6, SATA 4

SAUER, JULIA (LINA)
Birthdate: 4/8/1891
Birthplace: Rochester, NY
Deathdate: 6/26/1983
Information Available in These Sources: MJA, SATA 32, SATA 36, TCCW 2 TCCW 3

SAUL, E. WENDY
(Wendy Saul)
Birthdate: 9/10/1946
Birthplace: Paterson, NJ
Information Available in These Sources: SATA 42

SAUL, WENDY
See Saul, E. Wendy

SAUNDERS, BLANCHE
Birthdate: 9/12/1906 or 9/12/1905
Birthplace: Easton, ME
Information Available in These Sources: ABYP 1, ABYP 3

SAUNDERS, CALEB
See Heinlein, Robert A(nson)

SAUNDERS, KEITH
Birthdate: 2/21/1910
Birthplace: Elizabeth City, NC
Information Available in These Sources: SATA 12

SAUNDERS, RUBIE (AGNES)
Birthdate: 1/31/1929
Birthplace: New York, NY
Information Available in These Sources: SATA 21

SAUNDERS, SUSAN
(Sara Hughes)
Birthdate: 4/14/1945
Birthplace: San Antonio, TX
Information Available in These Sources: SATA 41, SATA 46

SAVAGE, BLAKE
See Goodwin, Harold Leland

SAVAGE, STEELE
Birthdate: 1900
Birthplace: Detroit, MI
Information Available in These Sources: IBYP 1, IBYP 2, ICB 2

SAVIOZZI, ADRIANA
Birthdate: 4/8/1928
Birthplace: Florence, Italy
Information Available in These Sources: ICB 3

SAVITT, SAM
Birthdate: 3/22/1917
Birthplace: Wilkes-Barre, PA
Information Available in These Sources: ABYP 1, ABYP 3, SATA 8

SAVITZ, HARRIET MAY (BLATSTEIN)
Birthdate: 5/19/1933
Birthplace: Newark, NJ
Information Available in These Sources: ABYP 4, JBA 5, SATA 5

SAVOLDI, GLORIA ROOT
Birthplace: Birmingham, AL
Information Available in These Sources: ABYP 2, ABYP 3

SAWYER, RUTH
Birthdate: 8/5/1880
Birthplace: Boston, MA
Deathdate: 6/3/1970
Information Available in These Sources: ABYP 1, ABYP 3, DLB 22, JBA 2 SATA 17, TCCW 1, TCCW 2, TCCW 3, WC

SAXE, JOHN GODFREY
Birthdate: 6/2/1816
Birthplace: Highgate, VT
Deathdate: 3/31/1887
Information Available in These Sources: ABYP 1, ABYP 3

SAXON, ANTONIA
See Sachs, Judith

SAY, ALLEN
Birthdate: 8/28/1974
Birthplace: Yokohama, Japan
Information Available in These Sources: JBA 6, SATA 28

SAYERS, CHARLES MARSHALL
Birthdate: 1892
Birthplace: Kirkcudbright, Scotland
Deathdate: 5/10/1971
Information Available in These Sources: ABYP 1, ABYP 3

SAYERS, FRANCES (CLARKE)
Birthdate: 9/4/1897
Birthplace: Topeka, KS
Information Available in These Sources: ABYP 1, ABYP 3, JBA 2, SATA 3

SAYLES, THELMA
See Clifton, Lucille

SAZER, NINA
Birthdate: 3/2/1949
Birthplace: Houston, TX
Information Available in These Sources: SATA 13

SCABRINI, JANET
Birthdate: 10/11/1953
Birthplace: Buffalo, NY
Information Available in These Sources: SATA 13

SCAGNETTI, JACK
Birthdate: 12/24/1924
Birthplace: Piney Fork, OH
Information Available in These Sources: ABYP 4, SATA 7

SCANLON, MARION STEPHANY
Birthplace: Lanesboro, MN
Information Available in These Sources: SATA 11

SCARF, MAGGI(E)
Birthdate: 5/13/1932
Birthplace: Philadelphia, PA
Information Available in These Sources: SATA 5

SCARRY, HUCK
See Scarry, Richard, Jr.

SCARRY, PATRICIA (MURPHY)
(Patsy Scarry, Liam Roy)
Birthdate: 9/9/1924
Birthplace: Vancouver, B.C., Canada
Information Available in These Sources: ABYP 4, SATA 2

SCARRY, PATSY
See Scarry, Patricia (Murphy)

SCARRY, RICHARD (MCCLURE)
Birthdate: 6/5/1919
Birthplace: Boston, MA
Information Available in These Sources: ABYP 2, ABYP 3, DLB 61, ICB 3 ICB 4, JBA 3, SATA 2, SATA 35 TCCW 1, TCCW 2, TCCW 3

SCARRY, RICHARD, JR.
(Huck Scarry)
Birthdate: 1/21/1953
Birthplace: Norwalk, CT
Information Available in These Sources: SATA 35

SCHACHNER, ERWIN
Birthplace: Austria
Information Available in These Sources: IBYP 1, IBYP 2

SCHACHTEL, ROGER (BERNARD)
(Marian Forrester)
Birthdate: 11/21/1949
Birthplace: New York, NY
Information Available in These Sources: SATA 38

SCHAEFER, JACK (WARNER)
Birthdate: 11/19/1907
Birthplace: Cleveland, OH
Information Available in These Sources: ABYP 2, ABYP 3, DACF, JBA 3, SATA 3, TCCW 1, TCCW 2, TCCW 3

SCHAEFFER, MEAD
Birthdate: 7/15/1898
Birthplace: Freedom Plains, NY
Information Available in These Sources: ICB 1, SATA 21

SCHAFF, LOUISE E.
Birthplace: NV
Information Available in These Sources: ABYP 4

SCHALLER, GEORGE B(EALS)
Birthdate: 5/26/1933
Birthplace: Berlin, Germany
Information Available in These Sources: ABYP 4, SATA 30

SCHARL, JOSEF
Birthdate: 12/9/1896
Birthplace: Munich, Bavaria, Germany
Deathdate: 12/6/1954
Information Available in These Sources: ICB 1, ICB 2

SCHATELL, BRIAN
Information Available in These Sources: SATA 47

SCHATZ, PHILIP
See Sterling, Philip

SCHATZKI, WALTER
Birthdate: 8/26/1899
Birthplace: Klafeld, Westphalia, Germany
Information Available in These Sources: SATA 31

SCHEALER, JOHN M(ILTON)
Birthdate: 7/5/1920
Birthplace: Boyertown, PA
Information Available in These Sources: ABYP 1, ABYP 3

SCHECHTER, BETTY (GOODSTEIN)
Birthdate: 2/5/1921
Birthplace: New York, NY
Information Available in These Sources: ABYP 2, ABYP 3, JBA 4, SATA 5

SCHEELE, WILLIAM EARL
Birthdate: 4/14/1920
Birthplace: Cleveland, OH
Information Available in These Sources: ABYP 1, ABYP 3, ICB 2, ICB 3, JBA 3

SCHEER, GEORGE F(ABIAN)
Birthdate: 10/21/1917
Birthplace: Richmond, VA
Information Available in These Sources: ABYP 4

SCHEER, JULIAN (WEISEL)
Birthdate: 2/20/1926
Birthplace: Richmond, VA
Information Available in These Sources: ABYP 2, ABYP 3, SATA 8

SCHEFFER, VICTOR B(LANCHARD)
Birthdate: 11/27/1906
Birthplace: Manhattan, KS
Information Available in These Sources: SATA 6

SCHEIB, IDA
Birthplace: Brooklyn, NY
Information Available in These Sources: ABYP 1, ABYP 3

SCHEIER, MICHAEL
Birthdate: 5/1/1943
Birthplace: New York, NY
Information Available in These Sources: SATA 36, SATA 40

SCHEIN, RUTH ROBBINS
See Robbins, Ruth

SCHEINER, ANN MCGOVERN
See McGovern, Ann

SCHELL, MILDRED
Birthdate: 10/13/1922
Birthplace: Union Furnace, OH
Information Available in These Sources: SATA 41

SCHELL, ORVILLE H.
Birthdate: 5/20/1940
Birthplace: New York, NY
Information Available in These Sources: ABYP 4, SATA 10

SCHELLIE, DON
Birthdate: 3/8/1932
Birthplace: Chicago, IL
Information Available in These Sources: SATA 29

SCHEMM, MILDRED WALKER
(Mildred Walker)
Birthdate: 5/2/1905
Birthplace: Philadelphia, PA
Information Available in These Sources: SATA 21

SCHER, PAULA
Birthdate: 10/6/1948
Birthplace: Washington, DC
Information Available in These Sources: ABYP 4, SATA 47

SCHERF, MARGARET (LOUISE)
Birthdate: 4/1/1908
Birthplace: Fairmont, WV
Deathdate: 5/12/1979
Information Available in These Sources: ABYP 4, DACF, SATA 10

SCHERMAN, BERNARDINE KIELTY
See Kielty, Bernardine

SCHERMAN, KATHARINE
Birthdate: 10/7/1915
Birthplace: New York, NY
Information Available in These Sources: ABYP 1, ABYP 3

SCHERMER, JUDITH (DENISE)
Birthdate: 2/19/1941
Birthplace: Detroit, MI
Information Available in These Sources: SATA 30

SCHERTLE, ALICE
Birthdate: 4/7/1941
Birthplace: Los Angeles, CA
Information Available in These Sources: SATA 36

SCHICK, ALICE
Birthdate: 6/20/1946
Birthplace: New York, NY
Information Available in These Sources: ABYP 4, SATA 27

SCHICK, ELEANOR (GROSSMAN)
Birthdate: 4/15/1942
Birthplace: New York, NY
Information Available in These Sources: ABYP 4, ICB 3, ICB 4, JBA 5, SATA 9

SCHICK, JOEL
Birthdate: 5/27/1945
Birthplace: Chicago, IL
Information Available in These Sources: ICB 4, SATA 30, SATA 31

SCHIESEL, JANE
Information Available in These Sources: ABYP 4

SCHIFF, KEN(NETH ROY)
Birthdate: 8/3/1942
Birthplace: New York, NY
Information Available in These Sources: SATA 7

SCHIFFER, ROBERT L.
Information Available in These Sources: ABYP 4

SCHIFFLER, SELMA
Information Available in These Sources: ABYP 4

SCHILLER, ANDREW
Birthdate: 2/1/1919
Birthplace: Hlomovec, Czechoslovakia
Information Available in These Sources: SATA 21

SCHILLER, BARBARA (HEYMAN)
Birthdate: 4/14/1928
Birthplace: Chicago, IL
Information Available in These Sources: ABYP 2, ABYP 3, SATA 21

SCHILLER, JUSTIN G.
Birthdate: 1943
Information Available in These Sources: SATA 31

SCHILLING, BETTY
Birthdate: 4/3/1925
Birthplace: El Paso, TX
Information Available in These Sources: IBYP 2

SCHINDELMAN, JOSEPH
Birthdate: 7/4/1923
Birthplace: New York, NY
Information Available in These Sources: IBYP 1, IBYP 2, ICB 3, JBA 3, SATA 32

SCHINDLER, S(TEVEN) D.
Information Available in These Sources: SATA 50

SCHISGALL, OSCAR
(Jackson Cole, Stuart Hardy)
Birthdate: 2/23/1901
Birthplace: Antwerp, Belgium
Deathdate: 5/20/1984
Information Available in These Sources: SATA 12, SATA 38

SCHLEE, ANN
Birthdate: 5/26/1934
Birthplace: Greenwich, CT
Information Available in These Sources: JBA 5, SATA 36, SATA 44, TCCW 1, TCCW 2

SCHLEIN, MIRIAM
(Lavinia Stanhope)
Birthdate: 6/6/1926
Birthplace: Brooklyn, NY
Information Available in These Sources: ABYP 1, ABYP 3, MJA, SATA 2, TCCW 1, TCCW 2, TCCW 3

SCHLICHTING, HAROLD E(UGENE, JR.)
Birthdate: 3/19/1926
Birthplace: Detroit, MI
Information Available in These Sources: ABYP 4

SCHLICHTING, MARY SOUTHWORTH
Information Available in These Sources: ABYP 4

SCHLOAT, G. WARREN, JR.
Birthdate: 7/15/1914
Birthplace: Mexico, MO
Information Available in These Sources: SATA 4

SCHMIDERER, DOROTHY
Birthdate: 10/26/1940
Birthplace: New York, NY
Information Available in These Sources: SATA 19

SCHMIDT, ELIZABETH
Birthdate: 6/26/1915
Birthplace: Ubly, MI
Information Available in These Sources: SATA 15

SCHMIDT, JAMES NORMAN
(James Norman)
Birthdate: 1912
Birthplace: Chicago, IL
Information Available in These Sources: SATA 21

SCHNEIDER, HERMAN
Birthdate: 5/31/1905
Birthplace: Kreschov, Poland
Information Available in These Sources: ABYP 1, ABYP 3, MJA, SATA 7

SCHNEIDER, LAURIE
See Adams, Laurie

SCHNEIDER, NINA (ZIMET)
Birthdate: 1/29/1913
Birthplace: Antwerp, Belgium
Information Available in These Sources: ABYP 1, ABYP 3, MJA, SATA 2

SCHNEIDER, REX
Birthdate: 2/22/1937
Birthplace: Butler, PA
Information Available in These Sources: SATA 44

SCHNIREL, JAMES R(EINHOLD)
Birthdate: 10/26/1931
Birthplace: Geneva, NY
Information Available in These Sources: SATA 14

SCHOCK, PAULINE
(Pauline Boyd)
Birthdate: 7/30/1928
Birthplace: Chicago, IL
Information Available in These Sources: SATA 45

SCHOEN, BARBARA
Birthdate: 7/4/1924
Birthplace: New York, NY
Information Available in These Sources: SATA 13

SCHOENHERR, JOHN (CARL)
Birthdate: 7/5/1935
Birthplace: New York, NY
Information Available in These Sources: IBYP 1, IBYP 2, ICB 3, ICB 4, JBA 4, SATA 37

SCHOLASTICA, SISTER MARY
See Jenkins, Marie M(agdalen)

SCHOLEFIELD, EDMUND O.
See Butterworth, W(illiam) E(dmund III)

SCHOLZ, JACKSON (VOLNEY)
Birthdate: 3/15/1897
Birthplace: Buchanan, MI
Deathdate: 10/26/1986
Information Available in These Sources: ABYP 2, ABYP 3, MJA, SATA 49

SCHONBERG, HAROLD C(HARLES)
Birthdate: 11/29/1915
Birthplace: New York, NY
Information Available in These Sources: ABYP 4

SCHONBERGER, KATHE OLSHAUSEN
See Dombrowski, Kathe Schonberger von

SCHONE, VIRGINIA
Birthplace: McAlester, OK
Information Available in These Sources: SATA 22

SCHONGUT, EMANUEL
Birthdate: 5/19/1936
Birthplace: Monticello, NY
Information Available in These Sources: IBYP 1, IBYP 2, SATA 36, SATA 52

SCHOONOVER, FRANK (EARLE)
Birthdate: 8/19/1877
Birthplace: Oxford, NJ
Deathdate: 9/1/1972
Information Available in These Sources: ICB 1, MJA, SATA 24

SCHOOR, GENE
Birthdate: 7/26/1921
Birthplace: Passaic, NJ
Information Available in These Sources: ABYP 1, ABYP 3, SATA 3

SCHRAFF, ANNE E(LAINE)
Birthdate: 9/21/1939
Birthplace: Cleveland, OH
Information Available in These Sources: ABYP 4, SATA 27

SCHRANK, JOSEPH
Birthdate: 7/10/1900
Birthplace: New York, NY
Deathdate: 3/23/1984
Information Available in These Sources: ABYP 2, ABYP 3, SATA 38

SCHREIBER, ELIZABETH ANNE (FERGUSON)
Birthdate: 6/24/1947
Birthplace: Indianapolis, IN
Information Available in These Sources: SATA 13

SCHREIBER, GEORGES
Birthdate: 4/25/1904
Birthplace: Brussels, Belgium
Information Available in These Sources: IBYP 1, IBYP 2, ICB 2, SATA 29

SCHREIBER, RALPH W(ALTER)
Birthdate: 7/6/1942
Birthplace: Wooster, OH
Information Available in These Sources: SATA 13

SCHREITER, RICK
Birthdate: 2/16/1936
Birthplace: Boston, MA
Information Available in These Sources: IBYP 2, ICB 3

SCHROEDER, TED
Birthdate, 1931?
Birthplace: Peoria, IL
Deathdate: 8/9/1973
Information Available in These Sources: SATA 20

SCHUCKER, JAMES (W.)
Birthdate: 1903
Birthplace: Mt. Carmel, IL
Information Available in These Sources: IBYP 2

SCHULE, CLIFFORD H.
Information Available in These Sources: IBYP 2, ICB 2

SCHULKE, FLIP (PHILPS GRAEME)
Birthdate: 6/24/1930
Birthplace: St. Paul, MN
Information Available in These Sources: SATA 57

SCHULMAN, JANET
Birthdate: 9/16/1933
Birthplace: Pittsburgh, PA
Information Available in These Sources: SATA 22

SCHULMAN, L(ESTER) M(ARTIN)
Birthdate: 9/3/1934
Birthplace: Brooklyn, NY
Information Available in These Sources: SATA 13

SCHULTE, ELAINE L(OUISE)
(Elaine L. Young)
Birthdate: 11/18/1934
Birthplace: IN
Information Available in These Sources: SATA 36

SCHULTZ, GWENDOLYN
Birthplace: Milwaukee, WI
Information Available in These Sources: SATA 21

SCHULTZ, JAMES WILLARD
(Apikuni)
Birthdate: 8/26/1859
Birthplace: Boonville, NY
Deathdate: 6/11/1947
Information Available in These Sources: ABYP 1, ABYP 3, JBA 1, JBA 2, YABC

SCHULTZ, PEARLE HENRIKSEN
(Marie Pershing)
Birthdate: 9/10/1918
Birthplace: Havre, MT
Information Available in These Sources: SATA 21

SCHULZ, CHARLES M(ONROE)
Birthdate: 11/26/1922
Birthplace: Minneapolis, MN
Information Available in These Sources: ABYP 1, ABYP 3, JBA 3, SATA 10

SCHUON, KARL
Birthdate: 11/26/1913
Birthplace: Allentown, PA
Deathdate: 11/16/1984
Information Available in These Sources: ABYP 1, ABYP 3

SCHUR, MAXINE
Birthdate: 10/21/1948
Birthplace: San Francisco, CA
Information Available in These Sources: SATA 49, SATA 53

SCHURFRANZ, VIVIAN
Birthdate: 7/12/1925
Birthplace: Mason City, IA
Information Available in These Sources: SATA 13

SCHUTZER, A. I.
Birthdate: 1/3/1922
Birthplace: Bridgeport, CT
Information Available in These Sources: SATA 13

SCHUYLER, PAMELA R(ICKA)
Birthdate: 10/26/1948
Birthplace: Brooklyn, NY
Information Available in These Sources: SATA 30

SCHUYLER, REMINGTON
Birthdate: 7/8/1884
Birthplace: Buffalo, NY
Deathdate: 10/19/1955
Information Available in These Sources: IBYP 1, IBYP 2, ICB 1, ICB 2

SCHWALJE, EARL G(EORGE)
Birthdate: 1921
Birthplace: NY
Information Available in These Sources: ABYP 1, ABYP 3

SCHWALJE, MARJORY C.
Information Available in These Sources: ABYP 1, ABYP 3

SCHWARK, MARY BETH
Birthdate: 1/2/1954
Birthplace: Mt. Clemens, MI
Information Available in These Sources: SATA 51

SCHWARTZ, ALVIN
Birthdate: 4/25/1927
Birthplace: Brooklyn, NY
Information Available in These Sources: ABYP 4, JBA 5, SATA 4, SATA 56

SCHWARTZ, AMY
Birthdate: 4/2/1954
Birthplace: San Diego, CA
Information Available in These Sources: JBA 6, SATA 41, SATA 47

SCHWARTZ, ANNE POWERS
(Anne Powers)
Birthdate: 5/7/1913
Birthplace: Cloquet, MN
Information Available in These Sources: SATA 10

SCHWARTZ, CHARLES W(ALSH)
Birthdate: 6/2/1914
Birthplace: St. Louis, MO
Information Available in These Sources: ABYP 1, ABYP 3, SATA 8

SCHWARTZ, DANIEL (BENNET)
Birthdate: 2/16/1929
Birthplace: New York, NY
Information Available in These Sources: SATA 29

SCHWARTZ, DAVID M(ARTIN)
Birthdate: 11/29/1951
Birthplace: New York, NY
Information Available in These Sources: JBA 6, SATA 59

SCHWARTZ, ELIZABETH REEDER
Birthdate: 9/13/1912
Birthplace: Columbus, OH
Information Available in These Sources: ABYP 1, ABYP 3, SATA 8

SCHWARTZ, JOEL L.
Birthdate: 4/23/1940
Birthplace: Philadelphia, PA
Information Available in These Sources: SATA 51, SATA 54

SCHWARTZ, JULIUS
Birthdate: 1907
Information Available in These Sources: ABYP 1, ABYP 3, SATA 45

SCHWARTZ, SHEILA (RUTH)
Birthdate: 3/15/1929
Birthplace: New York, NY
Information Available in These Sources: SATA 27

SCHWARTZ, STEPHEN (LAWRENCE)
Birthdate: 3/6/1948
Birthplace: New York, NY
Information Available in These Sources: SATA 19

SCHWEITZER, BYRD BAYLOR
See Baylor, Byrd

SCHWEITZER, IRIS
Birthplace: Israel
Information Available in These Sources: SATA 36, SATA 59

SCHWENINGER, ANN
Birthdate: 8/1/1951
Birthplace: Boulder, CO
Information Available in These Sources: SATA 29

SCOGGIN, MARGARET C(LARA)
Birthdate: 4/14/1905
Birthplace: Columbia, MO
Deathdate: 7/11/1968
Information Available in These Sources: SATA 28, SATA 47

SCOPPETONE, SANDRA
Birthdate: 6/1/1936
Birthplace: Morristown, NJ
Information Available in These Sources: ABYP 4, JBA 5, SATA 9

SCOTLAND, JAY
See Jakes, John (W.)

SCOTT, ANN
See Fritz, Jean (Guttery)

SCOTT, ANN HERBERT
Birthdate: 11/19/1926
Birthplace: Philadelphia, PA
Information Available in These Sources: ABYP 4, BABP, JBA 4, SATA 29, SATA 56

SCOTT, BILL
Birthdate, 1920?
Deathdate: 11/29/1985
Information Available in These Sources: SATA 46

SCOTT, CORA ANNETT (PIPITONE)
(Cora Annett)
Birthdate: 4/15/1931
Birthplace: Boston, MA
Information Available in These Sources: ABYP 2, ABYP 3, DACF, SATA 11

SCOTT, DAN
See Barker, S(quire) Omar

SCOTT, ELAINE
Birthdate: 6/20/1940
Birthplace: Philadelphia, PA
Information Available in These Sources: SATA 36

SCOTT, ERIC
Information Available in These Sources: DACF

SCOTT, HENRY JOSEPH
(Joseph Scott)
Birthdate: 9/23/1917
Birthplace: New York, NY
Information Available in These Sources: ABYP 4

SCOTT, JACK DENTON
Birthdate: 1915
Information Available in These Sources: JBA 6, SATA 31

SCOTT, JANE (HARRINGTON)
Birthdate: 2/14/1931
Birthplace: New York, NY
Information Available in These Sources: SATA 55

SCOTT, JOHN
(John Scott Nearing)
Birthdate: 3/26/1912
Birthplace: Philadelphia, PA
Deathdate: 12/1/1976
Information Available in These Sources: SATA 14

SCOTT, JOHN ANTHONY
(Tony Scott)
Birthdate: 1/20/1916
Birthplace: London, England
Information Available in These Sources: ABYP 4, SATA 23

SCOTT, JOHN M(ARTIN)
Birthdate: 4/8/1913
Birthplace: Omaha, NE
Information Available in These Sources: SATA 12

SCOTT, JOSEPH
See Scott, Henry Joseph

SCOTT, LENORE (KURTZ)
Birthplace: New York, NY
Information Available in These Sources: ABYP 4

SCOTT, ROBERT LEE
Birthdate: 4/12/1908
Birthplace: Macon, GA
Information Available in These Sources: ABYP 1, ABYP 3

SCOTT, RONEY
See Gault, William Campbell

SCOTT, SALLY FISHER
Birthdate: 6/30/1909
Birthplace: Arlington, VT
Deathdate: 9/6/1978
Information Available in These Sources: SATA 43

SCOTT, TONY
See Scott, John Anthony

SCOTT, WARWICK
See Trevor, Elleston

SCOVILLE, SAMUEL, JR.
Birthdate: 6/9/1872
Birthplace: Norwich, NY
Deathdate: 12/4/1950
Information Available in These Sources: JBA 1, JBA 2

SCRIBNER, CHARLES, JR.
Birthdate: 7/13/1921
Birthplace: Quogue, NY
Information Available in These Sources: SATA 13

SCRIBNER, JOANNE L.
Birthdate: 8/6/1949
Birthplace: Spokane, WA
Information Available in These Sources: SATA 33

SCRIMSHER, LILA GRAVATT
Birthdate: 12/26/1897
Birthplace: Talmage, NE
Deathdate: 9/12/1974
Information Available in These Sources: ABYP 1, ABYP 3, SATA 28

SCUDDER, HORACE E(LISHA)
Birthdate: 10/16/1838
Birthplace: Boston, MA
Deathdate: 1/11/1902
Information Available in These Sources: DLB 42, JBA 1

SCUDDER, MILDRED LEE
See Lee, Mildred

SCURO, VINCENT
Birthdate: 9/28/1951
Birthplace: Jersey City, NJ
Information Available in These Sources: SATA 21

SEABROOKE, BRENDA
Birthdate: 5/23/1941
Birthplace: FL
Information Available in These Sources: SATA 30

SEAMAN, AUGUSTA HUIELL
Birthdate: 4/3/1879
Birthplace: New York, NY
Deathdate: 6/4/1950
Information Available in These Sources: ABYP 1, ABYP 3, JBA 1, JBA 2, SATA 31

SEAMAN, DAVID M.
Information Available in These Sources: ABYP 1, ABYP 3

SEAMANDS, RUTH (CHILDERS)
Birthdate: 12/15/1916
Birthplace: Herrin, IL
Information Available in These Sources: SATA 9

SEARCY, MARGARET ZEHMER
Birthdate: 10/26/1926
Birthplace: Raleigh, NC
Information Available in These Sources: SATA 39, SATA 54

SEARIGHT, MARY W(ILLIAMS)
Birthdate: 1/4/1918
Birthplace: Cordell, OK
Information Available in These Sources: SATA 17

SEARS, STEPHEN W.
Birthdate: 7/27/1942
Birthplace: Lakewood, OH
Information Available in These Sources: SATA 4

SEATON, IRENE
See Wicker, Ireene

SEBASTIAN, JEANNE
See Newsome, Arden J(eanne Bokeeno)

SEBASTIAN, LEE
See Silverberg, Robert

SEBESTYEN, IGEN
See Sebestyen, Ouida (Dockery)

SEBESTYEN, OUIDA (DOCKERY)
(Igen Sebestyen)
Birthdate: 2/13/1924 or 2/13/1923
Birthplace: Vernon, TX
Information Available in These Sources: DACF, JBA 5, SATA 39, TCCW 3

SECHRIST, ELIZABETH (HOUGH)
Birthdate: 8/31/1903
Birthplace: Media, PA
Information Available in These Sources: ABYP 1, ABYP 3, SATA 2

SEDGES, JOHN
See Buck, Pearl S(ydenstricker)

SEED, SHEILA TURNER
(Sheila R. Turner)
Birthdate, 1937?
Deathdate: 6/22/1979
Information Available in These Sources: SATA 23

SEED, SUZANNE (LIDDELL)
Birthdate: 3/8/1940
Birthplace: Gary, IN
Information Available in These Sources: ABYP 4

SEEGER, ELIZABETH
Birthdate: 1889
Deathdate: 11/2/1973
Information Available in These Sources: SATA 20

SEEGER, PETE(R)
Birthdate: 5/3/1919
Birthplace: New York, NY
Information Available in These Sources: SATA 13

SEEGER, RUTH PORTER (CRAWFORD)
(Ruth Porter Crawford-Seeger)
Birthdate: 7/3/1901
Birthplace: East Liverpool, OH
Deathdate: 11/18/1953
Information Available in These Sources: ABYP 1, ABYP 3

SEEVER, R.
See Reeves, Lawrence F.

SEGAL, JOYCE
Birthdate: 12/7/1940
Birthplace: Brooklyn, NY
Information Available in These Sources: SATA 35

SEGAL, LORE (GROSZMANN)
Birthdate: 3/8/1928
Birthplace: Vienna, Austria
Information Available in These Sources: ABYP 4, SATA 4

SEIDELMAN, JAMES EDWARD
Birthdate: 12/7/1926
Birthplace: Kansas City, MO
Information Available in These Sources: SATA 6

SEIDEN, ART(HUR)
Birthplace: Brooklyn, NY
Information Available in These Sources: SATA 42

SEIDLER, TOR
Birthdate: 6/26/1952
Birthplace: Littleton, NH
Information Available in These Sources: JBA 6, SATA 46, SATA 52

SEIDMAN, LAURENCE (IVAN)
Birthdate: 3/8/1925
Birthplace: New York, NY
Information Available in These Sources: SATA 15

SEIGEL, KALMAN
Birthdate: 10/17/1917
Birthplace: Brooklyn, NY
Information Available in These Sources: SATA 12

SEIGNOBOSC, FRANCOISE
(Francoise)
Birthdate: 11/??/1897
Birthplace: Lodeve, Herault, France
Deathdate: 1961
Information Available in These Sources: SATA 21

SEITZ, JACQUELINE
Birthdate: 11/10/1931
Birthplace: New York, NY
Information Available in These Sources: SATA 50

SEITZ, PATRICIA
Information Available in These Sources: IBYP 1, IBYP 2

SEIXAS, JUDITH S.
Birthdate: 8/7/1922
Birthplace: New York, NY
Information Available in These Sources: SATA 17

SELDEN, GEORGE
See Thompson, George Selden

SELDEN, SAMUEL
Birthdate: 1/2/1899
Birthplace: Canton, China
Deathdate: 4/27/1979
Information Available in These Sources: ABYP 1, ABYP 3

SELF, MARGARET CABELL
Birthdate: 2/12/1902
Birthplace: Cincinnati, OH
Information Available in These Sources: ABYP 1, ABYP 3, SATA 24

SELIGMAN, DOROTHY HALLE
Birthplace: Memphis, TN
Information Available in These Sources: ABYP 4

SELKIRK, JANE
See Chapman, John Stanton Higham

SELLERS, NAOMI (JOHN)
See Flack, Naomi (John White)

SELLEW, CATHARINE F.
Birthdate: 1922
Information Available in These Sources: ABYP 1, ABYP 3

SELMAN, LARUE W.
Birthdate: 8/27/1927
Birthplace: Scipio, UT
Information Available in These Sources: SATA 55

SELSAM, MILLICENT E(LLIS)
Birthdate: 5/30/1912
Birthplace: New York, NY
Information Available in These Sources: ABYP 1, ABYP 3, BABP, MJA, SATA 1, SATA 29

SELTZER, MEYER
Birthdate: 4/28/1932
Birthplace: Chicago, IL
Information Available in These Sources: SATA 17

SELTZER, RICHARD (WARREN, JR.)
Birthdate: 2/23/1946
Birthplace: Clarksville, TN
Information Available in These Sources: SATA 41

SENDAK, JACK
Birthplace: Brooklyn, NY
Information Available in These Sources: ABYP 2, ABYP 3, SATA 28

SENDAK, MAURICE (BERNARD)
Birthdate: 6/10/1928
Birthplace: Brooklyn, NY
Information Available in These Sources: ABYP 1, ABYP 3, AICB, BABP, CFB, DLB 61, IBYP 1, IBYP 2, ICB 2, ICB 3, ICB 4, MJA, SATA 1, SATA 27, SVC 3, TCCW 1, 2, 3

SENN, STEVE
Birthdate: 8/4/1950
Birthplace: Americus, GA
Information Available in These Sources: SATA 48, SATA 60

SENTMAN, GEORGE ARMOR
Birthdate: 1913
Birthplace: MD
Information Available in These Sources: ABYP 1, ABYP 3

SERAGE, NANCY
Birthdate: 3/24/1924
Birthplace: Columbus, OH
Information Available in These Sources: SATA 10

SEREDY, KATE
Birthdate: 11/10/1899 or 11/10/1896
Birthplace: Budapest, Hungary
Deathdate: 3/7/1975
Information Available in These Sources: ABYP 1, ABYP 3, AICB, DLB 22, ICB 1, ICB 2, JBA 2, SATA 1, SATA 24, SVC 2, SVC 3, TCCW 1 TCCW 2, TCCW 3, WC

SEROFF, VICTOR I(LYITCH)
Birthdate: 10/14/1902
Birthplace: Batoum, Russia
Deathdate: 5/10/1979
Information Available in These Sources: SATA 12, SATA 26

SERVELLO, JOE
Birthdate: 6/19/1932
Birthplace: Altoona, PA
Information Available in These Sources: ICB 4, SATA 10

SERWER, BLANCHE L.
Birthdate: 7/13/1910
Birthplace: New York, NY
Information Available in These Sources: SATA 10

SETH, MARIE
See Lexau, Joan M.

SETON, ANN
See Seton, Anya

SETON, ANYA
(Anya Seton Chase, Ann Seton)
Birthdate: 1916
Birthplace: New York, NY
Information Available in These Sources: SATA 3

SETON, ERNEST (EVAN) THOMPSON
(Ernest Evan Seton Thompson)
Birthdate: 8/14/1860
Birthplace: South Shields, Durham, England
Deathdate: 10/23/1946
Information Available in These Sources: ICB 1, JBA 1, SATA 18, TCCW 1 TCCW 2, TCCW 3

SEULING, BARBARA
Birthdate: 7/22/1937
Birthplace: Brooklyn, NY
Information Available in These Sources: SATA 10

SEUSS, DR.
See Geisel, Theodor Seuss

SEVERN, BILL
See Severn, William Irving

SEVERN, SUE
Birthdate: 12/8/1918
Birthplace: Baltimore, MD
Information Available in These Sources: ABYP 1, ABYP 3

SEVERN, WILLIAM IRVING
(Bill Severn)
Birthdate: 5/11/1914
Birthplace: Brooklyn, NY
Information Available in These Sources: ABYP 1, ABYP 3, SATA 1

SEWALL, MARCIA (OSGOOD)
Birthdate: 11/5/1935
Birthplace: Providence, RI
Information Available in These Sources: ICB 4, JBA 5, SATA 37

SEWELL, HELEN (MOORE)
Birthdate: 6/27/1896
Birthplace: Mare Island (Navy Yard), CA
Deathdate: 2/24/1957
Information Available in These Sources: ABYP 1, ABYP 3, ICB 1, ICB 2, JBA 2, SATA 38, SVC 2, SVC 3, TCCW 1, TCCW 2, TCCW 3

SEXTON, ANNE (HARVEY)
Birthdate: 11/9/1928
Birthplace: Newton, MA
Information Available in These Sources: SATA 10

SEYFERT, ELLA MAIE
Birthplace: Lancaster County, PA
Information Available in These Sources: ABYP 1, ABYP 3

SEYMOUR, ALTA HALVERSON
Birthplace: Deer Park, WI
Information Available in These Sources: SATA 10

SEYMOUR, MARASMUS
See Rivoli, Mario

SHACHTMAN, TOM
Birthdate: 2/15/1942
Birthplace: New York, NY
Information Available in These Sources: SATA 49

SHAFER, ROBERT E(UGENE)
Birthdate: 3/30/1925
Birthplace: Beloit, WI
Information Available in These Sources: SATA 9

SHAHN, BEN(JAMIN)
Birthdate: 9/12/1898
Birthplace: Kovno (Kaunas), Lithuania
Deathdate: 3/21/1969 or 3/15/1969 or 3/14/1969
Information Available in These Sources: ICB 3, ICB 4, SATA 21

SHAHN, BERNARDA BRYSON
See Bryson, Bernarda

SHANE, HAROLD GRAY
Birthdate: 8/11/1914
Birthplace: Milwaukee, WI
Information Available in These Sources: SATA 36

SHANKS, ANN ZANE (KUSHNER)
Birthplace: Brooklyn, NY
Information Available in These Sources: SATA 10

SHANNON, GEORGE (WILLIAM BONES)
Birthdate: 2/14/1952
Birthplace: Caldwell, KS
Information Available in These Sources: JBA 6, SATA 35

SHANNON, MONICA
Birthdate, 1905?
Birthplace: Belleville, Ontario, Canada
Deathdate: 8/13/1965
Information Available in These Sources: ABYP 1, ABYP 3, JBA 2, SATA 28SVC 2, SVC 3, TCCW 1, TCCW 2, TCCW 3

SHANNON, TERRY
See Mercer, Jessie

SHAPIRO, IRWIN
Birthdate: 5/19/1911
Birthplace: Pittsburgh, PA
Deathdate: 11/7/1981
Information Available in These Sources: ABYP 1, ABYP 3, JBA 2, SATA 32

SHAPIRO, MILTON J.
Birthdate: 1926
Birthplace: Brooklyn, NY
Information Available in These Sources: ABYP 1, ABYP 3, SATA 32

SHAPIRO, REBECCA
Information Available in These Sources: ABYP 2, ABYP 3

SHAPP, MARTHA (GLAUBER)
Birthdate: 1/16/1910
Birthplace: New York, NY
Information Available in These Sources: SATA 3

SHARFMAN, AMALIE
Birthplace: Baltimore, MD
Information Available in These Sources: ABYP 1, ABYP 3, SATA 14

SHARMAT, MARJORIE WEINMAN
Birthdate: 11/12/1928
Birthplace: Portland, ME
Information Available in These Sources: ABYP 4, JBA 5, SATA 4, SATA 33TCCW 1, TCCW 2, TCCW 3

SHARMAT, MITCHELL
Birthdate: 4/18/1927
Birthplace: Brookline, MA
Information Available in These Sources: JBA 6, SATA 33

SHARP, ADDA MAI (CUMMINGS)
Information Available in These Sources: ABYP 1, ABYP 3

SHARP, DALLAS LORE
Birthdate: 12/13/1870
Birthplace: Haleyville, NJ
Deathdate: 11/29/1929
Information Available in These Sources: JBA 1

SHARP, WILLIAM
Birthdate: 6/13/1900
Birthplace: Lemberg, Austria
Deathdate: 4/1/1961
Information Available in: IBYP 2, ICB 1, ICB 2

SHARP, ZERNA A.
Birthdate: 8/12/1889
Birthplace: Hillisburg, IN
Deathdate: 6/17/1981
Information Available in These Sources: SATA 27

SHARPE, MITCHELL R(AYMOND)
Birthdate: 12/22/1924
Birthplace: Knoxville, TN
Information Available in These Sources: SATA 12

SHATZ, PHILIP
See Sterling, Philip

SHAW, ARNOLD
Birthdate: 6/28/1909
Birthplace: New York, NY
Information Available in These Sources: SATA 4

SHAW, CHARLES (GREEN)
Birthdate: 5/1/1892
Birthplace: New York, NY
Deathdate: 4/2/1974
Information Available in: IBYP 1, IBYP 2, SATA 13

SHAW, EVELYN
Birthdate: 1/19/1927
Birthplace: Jersey City, NJ
Information Available in These Sources: SATA 28

SHAW, RAY
Information Available in These Sources: SATA 7

SHAW, RICHARD
Birthdate: 5/21/1923
Birthplace: Greensboro, NC
Information Available in These Sources: SATA 12

SHAY, ARTHUR
Birthdate: 3/31/1922
Birthplace: New York, NY
Information Available in These Sources: SATA 4

SHAY, FRANK
Birthdate: 4/8/1888
Birthplace: East Orange, NJ
Deathdate: 1/14/1954
Information Available in These Sources: SVC 2, SVC 3

SHAY, LACEY
See Shebar, Sharon Sigmond

SHEA, GEORGE
Birthdate: 6/12/1940
Birthplace: New York, NY
Information Available in These Sources: SATA 42, SATA 54

SHEAHAN, HENRY BESTON
See Beston, Henry B.

SHEARER, JOHN
Birthdate: 1947
Birthplace: New York, NY
Information Available in These Sources: BAI, SATA 27, SATA 43

SHEARER, TED
Birthdate: 11/1/1919
Birthplace: Maypen, Jamaica, West Indies
Information Available in These Sources: SATA 43

SHEBAR, SHARON SIGMOND
(Lacey Shay)
Birthdate: 7/24/1945
Birthplace: Brooklyn, NY
Information Available in These Sources: SATA 36

SHECTER, BEN
Birthdate: 4/28/1935
Birthplace: Brooklyn, NY
Information Available in These Sources: ABYP 2, ABYP 3, ICB 3, ICB 4, JBA 3, SATA 16

SHEEDY, ALEXANDRA (ELIZABETH)
(Ally Sheedy)
Birthdate: 6/13/1962
Birthplace: New York, NY
Information Available in These Sources: SATA 19, SATA 39

SHEEDY, ALLY
See Sheedy, Alexandra (Elizabeth)

SHEEHAN, ETHNA
Birthdate: 11/22/1908
Birthplace: Castletown Berehaven, Ireland
Information Available in These Sources: ABYP 2, ABYP 3, SATA 9

SHEFELMAN, JANICE (JORDAN)
Birthdate: 4/12/1930
Birthplace: Baytown, TX
Information Available in These Sources: SATA 58

SHEFFER, H. R.
See Abels, Harriette Sheffer

SHEFFIELD, JANET N.
Birthdate: 11/27/1926
Birthplace: Salt Lake City, UT
Information Available in These Sources: SATA 26

SHEFTS, JOELLE
Birthplace: San Antonio, TX
Information Available in These Sources: SATA 49

SHEKERJIAN, HAIG
Birthdate: 11/3/1922
Birthplace: Chicago, IL
Information Available in These Sources: IBYP 2

SHEKERJIAN, REGINA TOR
(Regina Tor)
Information Available in These Sources: ABYP 1, ABYP 3, IBYP 2, SATA 16

SHELDON, AURE
Birthdate: 10/12/1917
Birthplace: Peoria, IL
Deathdate: 3/23/1976
Information Available in These Sources: SATA 12

SHELDON, MURIEL
(Muriel Batherman)
Birthdate: 10/16/1926
Birthplace: New York, NY
Information Available in These Sources: ABYP 4, SATA 39, SATA 45

SHELDON, WALT(ER J.)
(J. D. Hardin, Walter S. James, Shel Walker, Shelly Walters)
Birthdate: 1/9/1917
Birthplace: Philadelphia, PA
Information Available in These Sources: ABYP 1, ABYP 3

SHELLEY, FRANCES
See Wees, Frances Shelley

SHELTON, WILLIAM ROY
Birthdate: 4/9/1919
Birthplace: Rutherfordton, NC
Information Available in These Sources: SATA 5

SHEMIN, MARGARETHA (HOENEVELD)
Birthdate: 11/23/1928
Birthplace: Alkmaar, Netherlands
Information Available in These Sources: DACF, SATA 4

SHENTON, EDWARD
Birthdate: 11/29/1895
Birthplace: Pottsdown, PA
Deathdate: 6/17/1977
Information Available in These Sources: IBYP 1, IBYP 2, ICB 1, ICB 2, SATA 45

SHEPHARD, ESTHER
Birthdate: 7/29/1891
Birthplace: Minneapolis, MN
Deathdate: 2/10/1975
Information Available in These Sources: SATA 5, SATA 26

SHEPHERD, ELIZABETH
Birthplace: Boston, MA
Information Available in These Sources: SATA 4

SHERBURNE, ZOA (MORIN)
Birthdate: 9/30/1912
Birthplace: Seattle, WA
Information Available in These Sources: ABYP 2, ABYP 3, JBA 4, SATA 3

SHERIN, RAY
Birthdate: 6/26/1926
Birthplace: Elroy, WI
Information Available in These Sources: ICB 3

SHERMAN, ALLAN
(Allan Copelon)
Birthdate: 11/30/1924
Birthplace: Chicago, IL
Deathdate: 11/20/1973
Information Available in These Sources: ABYP 2, ABYP 3

SHERMAN, DIANE (FINN)
Birthdate: 12/6/1928
Birthplace: Boston, MA
Information Available in These Sources: SATA 12

SHERMAN, ELIZABETH
See Friskey, Margaret Richards

SHERMAN, HAROLD (MORROW)
Birthdate: 7/13/1898
Birthplace: Traverse City, MI
Information Available in These Sources: SATA 37

SHERMAN, NANCY
See Rosenberg, Nancy Sherman

SHERMAN, THERESA
(Veronica Reed)
Birthdate: 2/7/1916
Birthplace: New York, NY
Information Available in These Sources: IBYP 1, IBYP 2, ICB 2

SHERROD, JANE
See Singer, Jane Sherrod

SHERWAN, EARL
Birthdate: 12/17/1917
Birthplace: Shorewood, WI
Information Available in These Sources: SATA 3

SHI, MAIMAI
See Sze, Mai-Mai

SHIEFMAN, VICKY
Birthplace: Detroit, MI
Information Available in These Sources: SATA 22

SHIELDS, CHARLES
Birthdate: 7/19/1944
Birthplace: KS
Information Available in These Sources: SATA 10

SHIELDS, KARENA
Birthplace: Isthmus of Tehuantepic, Chiapus
Information Available in These Sources: ABYP 1, ABYP 3

SHIELDS, RITA
Birthplace: San Francisco, CA
Information Available in These Sources: ABYP 1, ABYP 3

SHIH, YUAN-TSUNG
See Sze, Mai-Mai

SHILSTONE, ARTHUR
Birthdate, 1923?
Information Available in These Sources: IBYP 2

SHIMIN, SYMEON
Birthdate: 11/1/1902
Birthplace: Astrakhan, Russia
Information Available in These Sources: BABP, IBYP 1, IBYP 2, ICB 2, ICB 3, JBA 3, SATA 13

SHINN, EVERETT
Birthdate: 11/7/1876
Birthplace: Woodstown, NJ
Deathdate: 5/1/1953 or 5/3/1953
Information Available in These Sources: IBYP 2, ICB 1, ICB 2, SATA 21

SHIPPEN, KATHERINE B(INNEY)
Birthdate: 4/1/1892
Birthplace: Hoboken, NJ
Deathdate: 2/20/1980
Information Available in These Sources: ABYP 1, ABYP 3, MJA, SATA 1, SATA 23, SVC 2, SVC 3

SHIRER, WILLIAM L(AWRENCE)
Birthdate: 2/23/1904
Birthplace: Chicago, IL
Information Available in These Sources: ABYP 1, ABYP 3, SATA 45

SHIRK, JEANNETTE CAMPBELL
Birthdate: 4/16/1898
Birthplace: Middletown, PA
Information Available in These Sources: ABYP 1, ABYP 3

SHIRREFFS, GORDON D(ONALD)
(Gordon Donalds, Jackson Flynn, Stewart Gordon)
Birthdate: 1/15/1914
Birthplace: Chicago, IL
Information Available in These Sources: ABYP 1, ABYP 3, SATA 11

SHORE, JUNE LEWIS
Birthdate: 1930
Birthplace: Louisville, KY
Information Available in These Sources: ABYP 4, SATA 30

SHORE, ROBERT
Birthdate: 2/27/1924
Birthplace: New York, NY
Information Available in These Sources: IBYP 1, IBYP 2, ICB 3, SATA 39

SHORT, ROGER
See Arkin, Alan (Wolf)

SHORTALL, LEONARD W.
Birthplace: Seattle, WA
Information Available in These Sources: IBYP 1, IBYP 2, ICB 2, ICB 3, ICB 4, SATA 19

SHOTWELL, LOUISA R(OSSITER)
Birthdate: 5/1/1902
Birthplace: Chicago, IL
Information Available in These Sources: ABYP 4, DACF, JBA 3, MBMP, SATA 3, TCCW 1, TCCW 2, TCCW 3

SHOWALTER, JEAN B(RECKINRIDGE)
Birthdate: 1921
Birthplace: Roanoke, VA
Information Available in These Sources: ABYP 4, SATA 12

SHOWELL, ELLEN HARVEY
Birthdate: 10/26/1934
Birthplace: Kingsport, TN
Information Available in These Sources: SATA 33

SHOWERS, PAUL C.
Birthdate: 4/12/1910
Birthplace: Sunnyside, Yakima Valley, WA
Information Available in These Sources: JBA 4, SATA 21

SHREVE, SUSAN RICHARDS
Birthdate: 5/2/1939
Birthplace: Toledo, OH
Information Available in These Sources: JBA 6, SATA 41, SATA 46

SHTAINMETZ, LEON
(Leon Steinmetz)
Birthplace: Siberia, Russia
Information Available in These Sources: ICB 4, SATA 32

SHUB, ELIZABETH
Birthplace: Vilna, Poland
Information Available in These Sources: ABYP 4, JBA 5, SATA 5

SHULEVITZ, URI
Birthdate: 2/27/1935
Birthplace: Warsaw, Poland
Information Available in These Sources: ABYP 4, BABP, DLB 61, IBYP 1, IBYP 2, ICB 3, ICB 4, JBA 3, SATA 3, SATA 50

SHULMAN, ALIX KATES
Birthdate: 8/17/1932
Birthplace: Cleveland, OH
Information Available in These Sources: SATA 7

SHULMAN, IRVING
Birthdate: 5/21/1913
Birthplace: Brooklyn, NY
Information Available in These Sources: SATA 13

SHULMAN, MAX
Birthdate: 3/14/1919
Birthplace: St. Paul, MN
Deathdate: 8/28/1988
Information Available in These Sources: SATA 59

SHUMSKY, ZENA
See Collier, Zena

SHURA, MARY FRANCIS
(Mary Francis Craig)
Birthdate: 2/27/1923
Birthplace: Pratt, KS
Information Available in These Sources: JBA 3, SATA 6

SHUTTLESWORTH, DOROTHY (EDWARDS)
Birthdate: 10/10/1907
Birthplace: Brooklyn, NY
Information Available in These Sources: ABYP 1, ABYP 3, JBA 5, SATA 3

SHYER, MARLENE FANTA
Birthplace: Czechoslovakia
Information Available in These Sources: SATA 13

SIBAL, JOSEPH
Birthplace: Vienna, Austria
Information Available in These Sources: IBYP 1, IBYP 2

SIBERELL, ANN(E)
Birthplace: Los Angeles, CA
Information Available in These Sources: IBYP 1, IBYP 2, SATA 29

SIBLEY, DON
Birthdate: 3/16/1922
Birthplace: Hornell, NY
Information Available in These Sources: IBYP 1, IBYP 2, ICB 3, SATA 12

SICULAN, DANIEL
Birthdate: 12/30/1922
Birthplace: Martins Ferry, OH
Information Available in These Sources: SATA †2

SIDJAKOV, NICOLAS
Birthdate: 12/16/1924
Birthplace: Riga, Latvia
Information Available in These Sources: ABYP 1, ABYP 3, CFB, IBYP 1, IBYP 2, ICB 1, ICB 2, ICB 3, MJA, SATA 18

SIDNEY, MARGARET
See Lothrop, Harriet Mulford Stone

SIEBEL, FRITZ (FREDERICK)
Birthdate: 12/19/1913
Birthplace: Vienna, Austria
Information Available in These Sources: IBYP 2, ICB 3, SATA 44

SIEGAL, ARANKA
Birthdate: 6/10/1930
Birthplace: Beregszasz, Hungary
Information Available in These Sources: JBA 5

SIEGEL, BEATRICE
Birthplace: New York, NY
Information Available in These Sources: SATA 36

SIEGEL, HELEN
See Siegl, Helen

SIEGEL, ROBERT (HAROLD)
Birthdate: 8/18/1939
Birthplace: Oak Park, IL
Information Available in These Sources: SATA 39

SIEGEL, WILLIAM
Birthdate: 1905
Birthplace: Riga (near), Latvia
Information Available in These Sources: CICB, ICB 1

SIEGL, HELEN
(Helen Siegel)
Birthdate: 8/18/1924
Birthplace: Vienna, Austria
Information Available in These Sources: ICB 3, SATA 34

SIEGMEISTER, ELIE
Birthdate: 1/15/1909
Birthplace: New York, NY
Information Available in These Sources: ABYP 1, ABYP 3

SIGOURNEY, LYDIA HUNTLEY
Birthdate: 9/1/1791
Birthplace: Hartford, CT
Deathdate: 6/10/1865
Information Available in These Sources: DLB 42

SILAS
See McCay, Winsor

SILLIMAN, LELAND
Birthdate: 1906
Birthplace: NY
Information Available in These Sources: ABYP 1, ABYP 3

SILLY, E. S.
See Kraus, Robert

SILMAN, ROBERTA (KARPEL)
Birthdate: 12/29/1934
Birthplace: Brooklyn, NY
Information Available in These Sources: DACF

SILVER, RUTH
See Chew, Ruth

SILVERBERG, ROBERT
(Walker Chapman, Walter Drummond, Randall Garrett, Ivar Jorgenson, Calvin M. Knox, David Osborne, Robert Randall, Lee Sebastian)
Birthdate: 1/15/1935
Birthplace: New York, NY
Information Available in These Sources: ABYP 1, ABYP 3, JBA 3, SATA 13

SILVERMAN, AL
Birthdate: 4/12/1926
Birthplace: Lynn, MA
Information Available in These Sources: ABYP 1, ABYP 3

SILVERMAN, BURTON PHILIP
Birthdate: 6/11/1928
Birthplace: Brooklyn, NY
Information Available in These Sources: IBYP 1, IBYP 2, ICB 3

SILVERMAN, MEL(VYN FRANK)
Birthdate: 1/26/1931
Birthplace: Denver, CO
Deathdate: 9/16/1966
Information Available in These Sources: IBYP 1, IBYP 2, ICB 3, SATA 9

SILVERSTEIN, ALVIN
(Dr. A)
Birthdate: 12/30/1933
Birthplace: Brooklyn, NY
Information Available in These Sources: ABYP 4, JBA 5, SATA 8

SILVERSTEIN, SHEL(BY)
(Uncle Shelby)
Birthdate: 1932
Birthplace: Chicago, IL
Information Available in These Sources: JBA 5, SATA 27, SATA 33, TCCW 2, TCCW 3

SILVERSTEIN, VIRGINIA B(ARBARA OPSHELOR)
(Ralph Buxton, Richard Rhine)
Birthdate: 4/3/1937
Birthplace: Philadelphia, PA
Information Available in These Sources: ABYP 4, JBA 5, SATA 8

SILVERTHORNE, ELIZABETH
Birthdate: 7/18/1930
Birthplace: Hot Springs, AR
Information Available in These Sources: SATA 35

SIMAK, CLIFFORD D(ONALD)
Birthdate: 8/3/1904
Birthplace: Millville, WI
Deathdate: 4/25/1988
Information Available in These Sources: SATA 56

SIMMONS, DAWN LANGLEY
(Gordon Langley Hall)
Birthdate: 1937
Birthplace: Heathfield, Sussex, England
Information Available in These Sources: ABYP 2, ABYP 3

SIMMONS, ELLIE
Information Available in These Sources: ABYP 4

SIMON, CHARLIE MAY (HOGUE)
See Fletcher, Charlie May Hogue

SIMON, HENRY W(ILLIAM)
Birthdate: 10/9/1901
Birthplace: New York, NY
Deathdate: 10/1/1970
Information Available in These Sources: ABYP 4

SIMON, HILDA (RITA)
Birthdate: 11/22/1921
Birthplace: Santa Ana, CA
Information Available in These Sources: ABYP 2, ABYP 3, ICB 3, ICB 4, JBA 4, SATA 28

SIMON, HOWARD
Birthdate: 7/22/1903
Birthplace: New York, NY
Deathdate: 10/15/1979
Information Available in These Sources: ABYP 2, ABYP 3, IBYP 2, ICB 1 ICB 2, ICB 3, MJA, SATA 21, SATA 32

SIMON, JOE
See Simon, Joseph H.

SIMON, JOSEPH H.
(Joe Simon)
Birthdate: 10/11/1913
Birthplace: Rochester, NY
Information Available in These Sources: SATA 7

SIMON, MARTIN P(AUL WILLIAM)
Birthdate: 2/16/1903
Birthplace: Angelica, WI
Deathdate: 9/23/1969
Information Available in These Sources: SATA 12

SIMON, MINA LEWITON
See Lewiton, Mina

SIMON, NORMA (FELDSTEIN)
Birthdate: 12/24/1927
Birthplace: New York, NY
Information Available in These Sources: ABYP 1, ABYP 3, SATA 3

SIMON, PAUL
Birthdate: 11/29/1928
Birthplace: Eugene, OR
Information Available in These Sources: ABYP 4

SIMON, RUTH CORABEL (SHIMER)
Birthdate: 1918
Birthplace: Orosi, CA
Information Available in These Sources: ABYP 1, ABYP 3

SIMON, SEYMOUR
Birthdate: 8/9/1931
Birthplace: New York, NY
Information Available in These Sources: ABYP 4, JBA 5, SATA 4

SIMON, SHIRLEY (SCHWARTZ)
Birthdate: 3/21/1921
Birthplace: Cleveland, OH
Information Available in These Sources: SATA 11

SIMON, SOLOMON
Birthdate: 7/4/1895
Birthplace: Kolinkovich, Russia
Deathdate: 11/8/1970
Information Available in These Sources: SATA 40

SIMONETTA, LINDA
Birthdate: 1/26/1948
Birthplace: Ann Arbor, MI
Information Available in These Sources: SATA 14

SIMONETTA, SAM
Birthdate: 1/7/1936
Birthplace: Easton, PA
Information Available in These Sources: SATA 14

SIMONS, BARBARA B(ROOKS)
(Barbara Brooks)
Birthdate: 12/4/1934
Birthplace: Rockford, IL
Information Available in These Sources: SATA 41

SIMONT, MARC
Birthdate: 11/23/1915
Birthplace: Paris, France
Information Available in These Sources: ABYP 1, ABYP 3, BABP, IBYP 1, IBYP 2, ICB 2, ICB 3, MJA, SATA 9

SIMPSON, HARRIETTE
See Arnow, Harriette (Louisa) Simpson

SIMPSON, MAXWELL STEWART
Birthdate: 9/11/1896
Birthplace: Elizabeth, NJ
Information Available in These Sources: ICB 1

SIMS, LYDEL
Information Available in These Sources: ABYP 2, ABYP 3

SINCLAIR, UPTON (BEALL)
(Clarke Fitch, Frederick Garrison, Arthur Stirling)
Birthdate: 9/20/1878
Birthplace: Baltimore, MD
Deathdate: 11/25/1968
Information Available in These Sources: ABYP 2, ABYP 3, SATA 9

SINGER, DAVID (LIN)
Birthdate: 2/6/1937
Birthplace: New York, NY
Information Available in These Sources: ABYP 4

SINGER, ISAAC (BASHEVIS)
(Isaac Bashevis, Isaac Warshofsky)
Birthdate: 7/14/1904
Birthplace: Radzymin, Poland
Information Available in These Sources: JBA 3, MBMP, SATA 3, SATA 27, TCCW 1, TCCW 2, TCCW 3

SINGER, JANE SHERROD
(Jane Sherrod)
Birthdate: 5/26/1917
Birthplace: Wichita Falls, TX
Deathdate: 1/26/1985
Information Available in These Sources: SATA 4, SATA 42

SINGER, JULIA
Birthdate: 1/20/1917
Birthplace: New York, NY
Information Available in These Sources: SATA 28

SINGER, KURT D(EUTSCH)
Birthdate: 8/10/1911
Birthplace: Vienna, Austria
Information Available in These Sources: SATA 38

SINGER, MARILYN
Birthdate: 10/3/1948
Birthplace: New York, NY
Information Available in These Sources: BC, SATA 38, SATA 48

SINGER, SUSAN (MAHLER)
Birthdate: 7/30/1941
Birthplace: Brooklyn, NY
Information Available in These Sources: SATA 9

SINGMASTER, ELSIE
Birthdate: 8/29/1879
Birthplace: Schuylkill Haven, PA
Deathdate: 9/30/1958
Information Available in These Sources: JBA 1

SIROFF, HARRIET
Birthdate: 10/18/1930
Birthplace: New York, NY
Information Available in These Sources: SATA 37

SIS, PETER
Birthdate: 5/11/1949
Birthplace: Prague, Czechoslovakia
Information Available in These Sources: JBA 6

SISTER MARY SCHOLASTICA
See Jenkins, Marie M(agdalen)

SISTER NOEMI
See Weygant, Sister Noemi

SITOMER, HARRY
Birthdate: 12/31/1903
Birthplace: Russia
Information Available in These Sources: SATA 31

SITOMER, MINDEL
Birthdate: 5/5/1903
Birthplace: New York, NY
Information Available in These Sources: SATA 31

SIVE, HELEN R.
Birthdate: 10/31/1951
Birthplace: New York, NY
Information Available in These Sources: SATA 30

SIVULICH, SANDRA (JEANNE) STRONER
Birthdate: 4/8/1941
Birthplace: Berwyn, IL
Information Available in These Sources: ABYP 4, SATA 9

SKELLY, JAMES R(ICHARD)
Birthdate: 5/23/1927
Birthplace: Evansville, IN
Information Available in These Sources: ABYP 4, SATA 17

SKELTON, CHARLES L.
Birthplace: IL
Information Available in These Sources: SVC 2, SVC 3

SKELTON, RED
Birthdate: 7/18/1913
Birthplace: Vincennes, IN
Information Available in These Sources: ABYP 4

SKINNER, CONSTANCE LINDSAY
Birthdate: 12/7/1882 or 12/7/1879
Birthplace: Quesnel, British Columbia, Canada
Deathdate: 3/27/1939
Information Available in These Sources: JBA 1, MJA, SVC 2, SVC 3, YABC

SKINNER, CORNELIA OTIS
Birthdate: 5/30/1901
Birthplace: Chicago, IL
Deathdate: 7/9/1979
Information Available in These Sources: SATA 2

SKIPPER, G. C.
Birthdate: 3/22/1939
Birthplace: Ozark, AL
Information Available in These Sources: SATA 38, SATA 46

SKOFIELD, JAMES
Birthplace: Karachi, Pakistan
Information Available in These Sources: SATA 44

SKOLD, BETTY WESTROM
Birthdate: 8/27/1923
Birthplace: Braham, MN
Information Available in These Sources: SATA 41

SKORPEN, LIESEL (MOAK)
Birthdate: 7/1/1935
Birthplace: Berlin, Germany
Information Available in These Sources: SATA 3

SKURZYNSKI, GLORIA (JOAN)
Birthdate: 7/6/1930
Birthplace: Duquesne, PA
Information Available in These Sources: DACF, JBA 5, SATA 8

SLACKMAN, CHARLES B.
Birthdate: 6/10/1934
Birthplace: Brooklyn, NY
Information Available in These Sources: SATA 12

SLATE, JOSEPH (FRANK)
Birthdate: 1/19/1928
Birthplace: Hollidays Cove, WV
Information Available in These Sources: SATA 38

SLAUGHTER, JEAN
See Doty, Jean Slaughter

SLEATOR, WILLIAM (WARNER III)
Birthdate: 2/13/1945
Birthplace: Havre de Grace, MD
Information Available in These Sources: BC, JBA 5, SATA 3, TCCW 3

SLEPIAN, JAN(ICE B.)
Birthdate: 1/2/1921
Birthplace: New York, NY
Information Available in These Sources: DACF, JBA 5, SATA 45, SATA 51

SLICER, MARGARET O.
Birthdate: 1/5/1920
Birthplace: Baltimore, MD
Information Available in These Sources: SATA 4

SLOANE, ERIC
Birthdate: 2/27/1910 or 2/27/1905
Birthplace: New York, NY
Deathdate: 3/6/1985
Information Available in These Sources: ICB 3, SATA 42, SATA 52

SLOBODKIN, FLORENCE (GERSH)
Birthdate: 1/19/1905
Birthplace: New York, NY
Information Available in These Sources: SATA 5

SLOBODKIN, LOUIS
Birthdate: 2/19/1903
Birthplace: Albany, NY
Deathdate: 5/8/1975 or 5/9/1975
Information Available in These Sources: ABYP 1, ABYP 3, BABP, IBYP 1, IBYP 2, ICB 1, ICB 2, ICB 3, ICB 4, JBA 2, SATA 1, SATA 26 TCCW 1, TCCW 2, TCCW 3

SLOBODKINA, ESPHYR
(Esphyr Slobodkina Urquhart)
Birthdate: 9/22/1908 or 9/22/1909
Birthplace: Cheliabinsk, Siberia, Russia
Information Available in These Sources: ABYP 1, ABYP 3, ICB 2, JBA 3, SATA 1, TCCW 1, TCCW 2, TCCW 3

SLOCUM, ROSALIE
Birthdate: 12/17/1906
Birthplace: Providence, RI
Information Available in These Sources: ICB 1

SLOTE, ALFRED
(A. H. Garnet)
Birthdate: 9/11/1926
Birthplace: Brooklyn, NY
Information Available in These Sources: ABYP 4, DACF, JBA 5, SATA 8, TCCW 3

SMALL, DAVID
Birthdate: 2/12/1945
Birthplace: Detroit, MI
Information Available in These Sources: JBA 6, SATA 46, SATA 50

SMALL, ERNEST
See Lent, Blair

SMARIDGE, NORAH (ANTOINETTE)
Birthdate: 3/30/1903
Birthplace: England
Information Available in These Sources: ABYP 2, ABYP 3, SATA 6

SMILEY, VIRGINIA KESTER
Birthdate: 2/21/1923
Birthplace: Rochester, NY
Information Available in These Sources: SATA 2

SMITH, AGNES
(Agnes Smith Parish)
Birthplace: Clarksburg, WV
Information Available in These Sources: ABYP 1, ABYP 3

SMITH, ALISON (PORTER)
Birthdate: 6/10/1932
Information Available in These Sources: DACF

SMITH, ALVIN
Birthdate: 11/27/1933
Birthplace: Gary, IN
Information Available in These Sources: IBYP 1, IBYP 2, ICB 3

SMITH, ANNE WARREN
Birthdate: 7/3/1938
Birthplace: Ticonderoga, NY
Information Available in These Sources: SATA 34, SATA 41

SMITH, BEATRICE S(CHILLINGER)
Birthplace: Madison, WI
Information Available in These Sources: SATA 12

SMITH, BETSY COVINGTON
Birthdate: 7/29/1937
Birthplace: Omaha, NE
Information Available in These Sources: SATA 43, SATA 55

SMITH, BETTY (WEHNER)
Birthdate: 12/15/1896
Birthplace: Brooklyn, NY
Deathdate: 1/17/1972
Information Available in These Sources: SATA 6

SMITH, BRADFORD
Birthdate: 5/13/1909
Birthplace: North Adams, MA
Deathdate: 7/14/1964
Information Available in These Sources: SATA 5

SMITH, C. PRITCHARD
See Hoyt, Edwin P(almer), Jr.

SMITH, CAESAR
See Trevor, Elleston

SMITH, DATUS C(LIFFORD), JR.
Birthdate: 5/3/1907
Birthplace: Jackson, MI
Information Available in These Sources: ABYP 4, SATA 13

SMITH, DORIS BUCHANAN
Birthdate: 6/1/1934
Birthplace: Washington, DC
Information Available in These Sources: ABYP 4, DACF, JBA 5, SATA 28, TCCW 3

SMITH, E(DRIC) BROOKS
Birthdate: 4/23/1917
Birthplace: Brooklyn, NY
Information Available in These Sources: SATA 40

SMITH, ELVA S(OPHRONIA)
Birthdate: 4/28/1871
Birthplace: Burke Hollow, VT
Deathdate: 10/26/1965
Information Available in These Sources: SATA 31

SMITH, EUNICE YOUNG
Birthdate: 6/10/1902
Birthplace: LaSalle, IL
Information Available in These Sources: ABYP 1, ABYP 3, SATA 5

SMITH, FRANCES C(HRISTINE)
(Jean Smith)
Birthdate: 9/6/1904
Birthplace: Washington, KS
Information Available in These Sources: SATA 3

SMITH, FREDRIKA SHUMWAY
Birthdate: 7/30/1877
Birthplace: Chicago, IL
Deathdate: 3/7/1968
Information Available in These Sources: ABYP 2, ABYP 3, SATA 30

SMITH, GARRY (VANDORN)
Birthdate: 2/28/1933
Birthplace: Alamo, TX
Information Available in These Sources: ABYP 4

SMITH, GARY R(ICHARD)
Birthdate: 10/20/1932
Birthplace: Pocatello, ID
Information Available in These Sources: SATA 14

SMITH, GEORGE HARMON
Birthdate: 1/12/1920
Birthplace: Spearsville, LA
Information Available in These Sources: SATA 5

SMITH, H(ARRY) ALLEN
Birthdate: 12/19/1907
Birthplace: McLeansboro, IL
Deathdate: 2/24/1976
Information Available in These Sources: SATA 20

SMITH, HOWARD E(VERETT) JR.
Birthdate: 11/18/1927
Birthplace: Gloucester, MA
Information Available in These Sources: SATA 12

SMITH, HOWARD G.
Information Available in These Sources: ABYP 4

SMITH, HUGH L(ETCHER)
Birthdate: 6/20/1921
Birthplace: Dallas, TX
Information Available in These Sources: ABYP 4, SATA 5

SMITH, IMOGENE HENDERSON
Birthdate: 5/31/1922
Birthplace: Decatur, IL
Information Available in These Sources: ABYP 2, ABYP 3, SATA 12

SMITH, IRENE
Birthdate: 1903
Birthplace: Columbia, KY
Information Available in These Sources: ABYP 1, ABYP 3

SMITH, JACQUELINE B.
Birthdate: 9/15/1937
Birthplace: Abington, PA
Information Available in These Sources: SATA 39

SMITH, JANICE LEE
Birthdate: 5/12/1949
Birthplace: Fowler, KS
Information Available in These Sources: SATA 54

SMITH, JEAN
See Smith, Frances C(hristine)

SMITH, JEAN PAJOT
Birthdate: 11/14/1945
Birthplace: Saline, MI
Information Available in These Sources: SATA 10

SMITH, JESSIE WILLCOX
Birthdate: 9/??/1863
Birthplace: Philadelphia, PA
Deathdate: 5/3/1935
Information Available in These Sources: ABYP 2, ABYP 3, JBA 1, JBA 2, SATA 21

SMITH, JOHNSTON
See Crane, Stephen (Townley)

SMITH, LAWRENCE BEALL
Birthdate: 10/2/1909
Birthplace: Washington, DC
Information Available in These Sources: IBYP 1, IBYP 2, ICB 3

SMITH, LAYFAYETTE
See Higdon, Hal

SMITH, LEE
See Albion, Lee Smith

SMITH, LEROI
(Tex Smith, LeRoi Ugama, Charles Scott Welch)
Birthdate: 1/1/1934
Birthplace: Cleveland, OK
Information Available in These Sources: ABYP 4

SMITH, LILLIAN H(ELENA)
Birthdate: 1887
Birthplace: London, Ontario, Canada
Deathdate: 1/5/1983
Information Available in These Sources: SATA 32

SMITH, LINELL NASH
(Nell Chenault, Linell Nash)
Birthdate: 3/26/1932
Birthplace: New York, NY
Information Available in These Sources: ABYP 4, SATA 2

SMITH, LUCIA B.
Birthdate: 4/5/1943
Birthplace: New York, NY
Information Available in These Sources: SATA 30

SMITH, MARGARET CHASE
Birthdate: 12/14/1897
Birthplace: Skowhegan, ME
Information Available in These Sources: ABYP 4

SMITH, MARION HAGENS
Birthdate: 12/13/1913
Birthplace: Grand Rapids, MI
Information Available in These Sources: SATA 12

SMITH, MARION JAQUES
Birthdate: 11/16/1899
Birthplace: Haverhill, MA
Information Available in These Sources: SATA 13

SMITH, MARY ELLEN
(Mike Smith)
Birthplace: Melbourne, FL
Information Available in These Sources: SATA 10

SMITH, MIKE
See Smith, Mary Ellen

SMITH, MILDRED NICKERSON
See Nickerson, Jan

SMITH, MOYNE RICE
Birthplace: Oskaloosa, KS
Information Available in These Sources: ABYP 1, ABYP 3

SMITH, NANCY COVERT
Birthdate: 3/18/1935
Birthplace: Bascom, OH
Information Available in These Sources: SATA 12

SMITH, NED
Information Available in These Sources: IBYP 2

SMITH, NORA ARCHIBALD
Birthdate: 2/21/1859?
Birthplace: Philadelphia, PA
Deathdate: 2/1/1934
Information Available in These Sources: ABYP 4, JBA 1

SMITH, NORMAN F.
Birthdate: 7/18/1920
Birthplace: Waterbury, CT
Information Available in These Sources: SATA 5

SMITH, PAULINE C(OGGESHALL)
Birthdate: 12/14/1908
Birthplace: Randolph, IA
Information Available in These Sources: SATA 27

SMITH, PHILIP M.
Birthdate: 1927
Birthplace: Springfield, OH
Information Available in These Sources: ABYP 2, ABYP 3

SMITH, PHILIP WARREN
Birthdate: 11/18/1936
Birthplace: San Francisco, CA
Information Available in These Sources: SATA 46

SMITH, RALPH LEE
Birthdate: 11/6/1927
Birthplace: Philadelphia, PA
Information Available in These Sources: ABYP 2, ABYP 3

SMITH, ROBERT KIMMEL
(Peter Marks)
Birthdate: 7/31/1930
Birthplace: Brooklyn, NY
Information Available in These Sources: ABYP 4. JBA 6, SATA 12

SMITH, ROBERT PAUL
Birthdate: 4/16/1915
Birthplace: Brooklyn, NY
Deathdate: 1/30/1977
Information Available in These Sources: ABYP 2, ABYP 3, SATA 30, SATA 52

SMITH, ROBERT W(ILLIAM)
Birthdate: 12/27/1926
Birthplace: Richland, IA
Information Available in These Sources: ABYP 4

SMITH, RUTH LESLIE
Birthdate: 3/1/1902
Birthplace: Brooklyn, NY
Information Available in These Sources: SATA 2

SMITH, S. S.
See Williamson, T(hames) R(oss)

SMITH, SAMANTHA
Birthdate: 1972
Deathdate: 8/25/1985
Information Available in These Sources: SATA 45

SMITH, SUSAN CARLTON
Birthdate: 6/30/1923
Birthplace: Athens, GA
Information Available in These Sources: SATA 12

SMITH, SUSAN MATHIAS
Birthdate: 1/23/1950
Birthplace: Rockingham County, VA
Information Available in These Sources: SATA 35, SATA 43

SMITH, SUSAN VERNON
(Carrie Enfield, Susan Mendonca, Rosemary Vernon)
Birthdate: 6/6/1950
Birthplace: Harrow, England
Information Available in These Sources: SATA 45, SATA 48

SMITH, TEX
See Smith, LeRoi

SMITH, THERESA KALAB
(Theresa Kalab)
Birthplace: Vienna, Austria
Information Available in These Sources: ABYP 4

SMITH, URSULA
Birthdate: 1/3/1934
Birthplace: Santa Maria, CA
Information Available in These Sources: SATA 54

SMITH, VESTA (HENDERSON)
Birthdate: 10/3/1933
Birthplace: Weslaco, TX
Information Available in These Sources: ABYP 4

SMITH, WARD
See Goldsmith, Howard

SMITH, WILLIAM A(RTHUR)
Birthdate: 4/19/1918
Birthplace: Toledo, OH
Information Available in These Sources: IBYP 2, ICB 1, ICB 2, SATA 10

SMITH, WILLIAM JAY
Birthdate: 4/22/1918
Birthplace: Winnfield, LA
Information Available in These Sources: ABYP 2, ABYP 3, JBA 5, SATA 2 TCCW 1, TCCW 2, TCCW 3

SMITH, Z. Z.
See Westheimer, David

SMITS, TEO
See Smits, Theodore R(ichard)

SMITS, THEODORE R(ICHARD)
(Teo Smits)
Birthdate: 4/24/1905
Birthplace: Jackson, MI
Information Available in These Sources: SATA 28, SATA 45

SMUCKER, BARBARA (CLAASSEN)
Birthdate: 9/1/1915
Birthplace: Newton, KS
Information Available in These Sources: SATA 29, TCCW 2, TCCW 3

SNEDEKER, CAROLINE DALE (PARKE)
(Caroline Dale Owen)
Birthdate: 3/23/1871
Birthplace: New Harmony, IN
Deathdate: 1/22/1956
Information Available in These Sources: ABYP 2, ABYP 3, JBA 1, JBA 2, TCCW 1, TCCW 2, TCCW 3, YABC

SNEVE, VIRGINIA DRIVING HAWK
(Virginia Driving Hawk)
Birthdate: 2/21/1933
Birthplace: Rosebud, SD
Information Available in These Sources: SATA 8

SNIFF, MR.
See Abisch, Roslyn Kroop

SNOW, DONALD CLIFFORD
(Thomas Fall)
Birthdate: 8/14/1917
Birthplace: Ozark Mountains, AR
Information Available in These Sources: ABYP 2, ABYP 3, DACF, JBA 4, SATA 16

SNOW, DOROTHEA J(OHNSTON)
Birthdate: 4/17/1909
Birthplace: McMinnville, TN
Information Available in These Sources: SATA 9

SNOW, RICHARD F(OLGER)
Birthdate: 10/28/1947
Birthplace: New York, NY
Information Available in These Sources: DACF, SATA 37, SATA 52

SNYDER, ANNE
Birthdate: 10/3/1922
Birthplace: Boston, MA
Information Available in These Sources: SATA 4

SNYDER, CAROL
Birthdate: 8/11/1941
Birthplace: Brooklyn, NY
Information Available in These Sources: SATA 35

SNYDER, DICK
Information Available in These Sources: ABYP2, ABYP 3

SNYDER, GERALD S(EYMOUR)
Birthdate: 6/4/1933
Birthplace: New York, NY
Information Available in These Sources: SATA 34, SATA 48

SNYDER, JEROME
Birthdate: 4/20/1916
Birthplace: New York, NY
Deathdate: 5/2/1976
Information Available in These Sources: IBYP 1, IBYP 2, ICB 3, SATA 20

SNYDER, LOUIS LEO
(Nordicus)
Birthdate: 7/4/1907
Birthplace: Annapolis, MD
Information Available in These Sources: ABYP 2, ABYP 3

SNYDER, ZILPHA KEATLEY
Birthdate: 5/11/1927 or 5/11/1928
Birthplace: Lemoore, CA
Information Available in These Sources: ABYP 2, ABYP 3, DACF, JBA 3, MBMP, SATA 1, SATA 28, TCCW 1 TCCW 2, TCCW 3

SNYDERMAN, REUVEN K.
Birthdate: 7/6/1922
Birthplace: Philadelphia, PA
Information Available in These Sources: SATA 5

SOBLE, JENNIE
See Cavin, Ruth (Brodie)

SOBOL, DONALD J.
Birthdate: 10/4/1924
Birthplace: New York, NY
Information Available in These Sources: ABYP 2, ABYP 3, DACF, JBA 4, SATA 1, SATA 31, TCCW 1, TCCW 2, TCCW 3

SOBOL, HARRIET LANGSAM
Birthdate: 4/30/1936
Birthplace: New York, NY
Information Available in These Sources: SATA 34, SATA 47

SODERLIND, ARTHUR E(DWIN)
Birthdate: 8/15/1920
Birthplace: Brooklyn, NY
Information Available in These Sources: SATA 14

SOFIA
See Zeiger, Sophia

SOGLOW, OTTO
Birthdate: 12/23/1900
Birthplace: Yorkville, NY
Deathdate: 4/3/1975
Information Available in These Sources: SATA 30

SOHL, FREDERIC J(OHN)
Birthdate: 3/5/1916
Birthplace: Brooklyn, NY
Information Available in These Sources: SATA 10

SOKOL, BILL
See Sokol, William

SOKOL, WILLIAM
(Bill Sokol)
Birthdate: 11/21/1923 or 11/21/1925
Birthplace: Warsaw, Poland
Information Available in These Sources: ABYP 2, ABYP 3, CFB, ICB 3, SATA 37

SOLBERT, ROMAINE G.
(Ronni G. Solbert)
Birthdate: 9/7/1925
Birthplace: Washington, DC
Information Available in These Sources: IBYP 1, IBYP 2, ICB 2, ICB 3, ICB 4, SATA 2

SOLBERT, RONNI G.
See Solbert, Romaine G.

SOLOMON, LOUIS
Birthdate: 1945
Information Available in These Sources: ABYP 2, ABYP 3

SOLONEVICH, GEORGE
Birthdate: 10/15/1915
Birthplace: Moscow, Russia
Information Available in These Sources: SATA 15

SOLOT, MARY LYNN (MARX)
Birthdate: 5/7/1939
Birthplace: New York, NY
Information Available in These Sources: ABYP 4, SATA 12

SOMMER, ELYSE (VORCHHEIMER)
Birthdate: 1/26/1929
Birthplace: Frankfurt, Germany
Information Available in These Sources: ABYP 4, SATA 7

SOMMER, ROBERT
Birthdate: 4/26/1929
Birthplace: New York, NY
Information Available in These Sources: SATA 12

SOMMERSCHIELD, ROSE
Information Available in These Sources: IBYP 2

SONI, WELTHY H.
Birthplace: Ann Arbor, MI
Information Available in These Sources: ABYP 2, ABYP 3

SONNEBORN, RUTH (CANTOR) A.
Birthdate: 10/14/1899
Birthplace: New York, NY
Deathdate: 2/24/1974
Information Available in These Sources: BABP, SATA 4, SATA 27

SOOTIN, HARRY
Birthplace: NY
Information Available in These Sources: ABYP 1, ABYP 3

SOREL, EDWARD
Birthdate: 3/26/1929
Birthplace: New York, NY
Information Available in These Sources: IBYP 1, IBYP 2, ICB 3, SATA 37

SORENSEN, VIRGINIA (EGGERSTEN)
Birthdate: 2/17/1912
Birthplace: Provo, UT
Information Available in These Sources: ABYP 1, ABYP 3, DACF, MBMP, MJA, SATA 2, TCCW 1, TCCW 2, TCCW 3

SORRENTINO, JOSEPH N.
Birthdate: 5/16
Birthplace: Brooklyn, NY
Information Available in These Sources: SATA 6

SORTOR, JUNE ELIZABETH
(Toni Sorter)
Birthdate: 6/4/1939
Birthplace: Utica, NY
Information Available in These Sources: SATA 12

SORTOR, TONI
See Sortor, June Elizabeth

SOSKIN, V. H.
See Ellison, Virginia Howell

SOTOMAYOR, ANTONIO
Birthdate: 5/13/1902 or 5/13/1904
Birthplace: Chulumani, Bolivia
Information Available in These Sources: IBYP 2, ICB 2, SATA 11

SOUDLEY, HENRY
See Wood, James Playsted

SOULE, GARDNER (BOSWORTH)
Birthdate: 12/16/1913
Birthplace: Paris, TX
Information Available in These Sources: ABYP 4, SATA 14

SOULE, JEAN CONDER
Birthdate: 2/4/1919
Birthplace: Brookline, MA
Information Available in These Sources: SATA 10

SOUTHWICK, KATHERINE
(Katherine (Southwick) Keeler)
Birthdate: 1887
Birthplace: Buxton, ME
Information Available in These Sources: ABYP 1, ABYP 3

SOWERS, PHYLLIS (AYER)
Birthplace: Brooklyn, NY
Information Available in These Sources: ABYP 2, ABYP 3

SPACHE, GEORGE DANIEL
Birthdate: 2/22/1909
Birthplace: New York, NY
Information Available in These Sources: ABYP 2, ABYP 3

SPANFELLER, JAMES J(OHN)
(Jim Spanfeller)
Birthdate: 10/27/1930
Birthplace: Philadelphia, PA
Information Available in These Sources: ICB 3, SATA 19

SPANFELLER, JIM
See Spanfeller, James J(ohn)

SPANGENBERG, JUDITH DUNN
(Judy Dunn)
Birthdate: 10/6/1942
Birthplace: NJ
Information Available in These Sources: SATA 5

SPAR, JEROME
Birthdate: 10/7/1918
Birthplace: New York, NY
Information Available in These Sources: SATA 10

SPARKS, BEATRICE MATHEWS
Birthdate: 1/15/1918
Birthplace: Goldberg, ID
Information Available in These Sources: SATA 28, SATA 44

SPARKS, JAMES CALVIN, JR.
Birthplace: Birmingham, AL
Information Available in These Sources: ABYP 4

SPARKS, MARY W.
Birthdate: 8/27/1920
Birthplace: Brown Summit, NC
Information Available in These Sources: SATA 15

SPEARE, ELIZABETH GEORGE
Birthdate: 11/21/1908
Birthplace: Melrose, MA
Information Available in These Sources: ABYP 1, ABYP 3, DACF, MBMP, MJA, SATA 5, TCCW 1, TCCW 2, TCCW 3

SPEARING, JUDITH (MARY HARLOW)
Birthdate: 11/29/1922
Birthplace: Boston, MA
Information Available in These Sources: SATA 9

SPECKING, INEZ
Birthdate: 4/8/1890
Birthplace: Washington, MO
Information Available in These Sources: SATA 11

SPEEVACK, YETTA
Birthplace: Romania
Information Available in These Sources: ABYP 2, ABYP 3

SPEICHER, HELEN ROSS (SMITH)
(Alice Abbott, Jane Land, Ross Land)
Birthdate: 9/14/1915
Birthplace: Indianapolis, IN
Information Available in These Sources: SATA 8

SPELLMAN, ROGER G.
See Cox, William R(obert)

SPELMAN, MARY
(Mary Lockwood, Mary Towne)
Birthdate: 3/14/1934
Birthplace: Brooklyn, NY
Information Available in These Sources: ABYP 4, SATA 28

SPENCER, ANN
Birthdate: 6/13/1918
Birthplace: New Hope, PA
Information Available in These Sources: SATA 10

SPENCER, CORNELIA
See Yaukey, Grace S(ydenstricker)

SPENCER, DONALD D(EAN)
Birthdate: 3/28/1931
Birthplace: Louisa, KY
Information Available in These Sources: SATA 41

SPENCER, ELIZABETH
Birthdate: 7/19/1921
Birthplace: Carrollton, MS
Information Available in These Sources: SATA 14

SPENCER, LILA
Birthdate: 1928
Birthplace: Murpheysboro, IL
Information Available in These Sources: ABYP 4

SPENCER, WILLIAM
Birthdate: 6/1/1922
Birthplace: Erie, PA
Information Available in These Sources: ABYP 2, ABYP 3, SATA 9

SPENCER, ZANE A(NN)
Birthdate: 5/21/1935
Birthplace: Murray, KY
Information Available in These Sources: SATA 35

SPERRY, ARMSTRONG W.
Birthdate: 11/7/1897
Birthplace: New Haven, CT
Deathdate: 4/28/1976
Information Available in These Sources: ABYP 1, ABYP 3, ICB 1, ICB 2, JBA 2, SATA 1, SATA 27, SVC 2 SVC 3, TCCW 1, TCCW 2, TCCW 3

SPERRY, RAYMOND, JR.
See Stratemeyer, Edward L.

SPICER, DOROTHY (GLADYS)
Birthplace: New York, NY
Deathdate: 1/??/1975
Information Available in These Sources: ABYP 2, ABYP 3, SATA 32

SPIEGELMAN, JUDITH M.
Birthplace: New York, NY
Information Available in These Sources: SATA 5

SPIELBERG, STEVEN
Birthdate: 12/18/1947
Birthplace: Cincinnati, OH
Information Available in These Sources: SATA 32

SPIER, PETER (EDWARD)
Birthdate: 6/6/1927
Birthplace: Amsterdam, Netherlands
Information Available in These Sources: ABYP 4, BABP, DLB 61, IBYP 1, IBYP 2, ICB 2, ICB 3, ICB 4, JBA 3, SATA 4, SATA 54

SPILHAUS, ATHELSTAN
Birthdate: 11/25/1911
Birthplace: Cape Town, South Africa
Information Available in These Sources: SATA 13

SPILKA, ARNOLD
Birthdate: 11/13/1917
Birthplace: New York, NY
Information Available in These Sources: ABYP 2, ABYP 3, ICB 3, JBA 3, SATA 6

SPINELLI, EILEEN
Birthdate: 8/16/1942
Birthplace: Philadelphia, PA
Information Available in These Sources: SATA 38

SPINELLI, JERRY
Birthdate: 2/1/1941
Birthplace: Norristown, PA
Information Available in These Sources: JBA 6, SATA 39

SPINNER, STEPHANIE
Birthdate: 11/16/1943
Birthplace: Davenport, IA
Information Available in These Sources: SATA 38

SPINOSSIMUS
See White, William, Jr.

SPLAVER, SARAH
Birthdate: 1921
Birthplace: New York, NY
Information Available in These Sources: ABYP 4, SATA 28

SPOLLEN, CHRISTOPHER
Birthdate: 8/12/1952
Birthplace: Staten Island, NY
Information Available in These Sources: SATA 12

SPRAGUE, GRETCHEN (BURNHAM)
Birthdate: 3/26/1926
Birthplace: Lincoln, NE
Information Available in These Sources: ABYP 2, ABYP 3, DACF, SATA 27

SPRAGUE, ROSEMARY
Birthdate, 1922?
Birthplace: New York, NY
Information Available in These Sources: ABYP 2, ABYP 3

SPRINGER, MARILYN HARRIS
(Marilyn Harris)
Birthdate: 6/4/1931
Birthplace: Oklahoma City, OK
Information Available in These Sources: SATA 47

SPRINGSTUBB, TRICIA
Birthdate: 9/15/1950
Birthplace: New York, NY
Information Available in These Sources: JBA 6, SATA 40, SATA 46

SPYKMAN, E(LIZABETH) C(HOATE)
Birthdate: 7/17/1896
Birthplace: Southboro, MA
Deathdate: 8/7/1965
Information Available in These Sources: DACF, MJA, SATA 10, TCCW 1, TCCW 2, TCCW 3

SQUIRE, ROGER
Information Available in These Sources: ABYP 4

SQUIRES, PHIL
See Barker, S(quire) Omar

SRIVASTAVA, JANE JONAS
Information Available in These Sources: SATA 37

ST. BRIAVELS, JAMES
See Wood, James Playsted

ST. CLAIR, BYRD HOOPER
(Byrd Hooper)
Birthdate: 9/29/1905
Birthplace: Cerro Gordo, AR
Deathdate: 1/25/1976
Information Available in These Sources: SATA 28

ST. GEORGE, JUDITH
Birthdate: 2/26/1931
Birthplace: Westfield, NJ
Information Available in These Sources: JBA 6, SATA 13

ST. JOHN, NICOLE
See Johnston, Norma

ST. JOHN, PHILIP
See delRey, Lester

ST. JOHN, WYLLY FOLK
(Eleanor Fox, Eve Larson, Katherine Pierce, Mary Keith Vincent, Michael Williams)
Birthdate: 10/20/1908
Birthplace: Ehrhardt (near), SC
Deathdate: 8/16/1985
Information Available in These Sources: ABYP 4, DACF, SATA 10, SATA 45

STACK, NICOLETE MEREDITH
(Nicolete Meredith)
Birthdate: 2/22/1896
Birthplace: Des Moines, IA
Information Available in These Sources: ABYP 1, ABYP 3

STADTLER, BEA
Birthdate: 6/26/1921
Birthplace: Cleveland, OH
Information Available in These Sources: SATA 17

STAFFORD, JEAN
Birthdate: 7/1/1915
Birthplace: Covina, CA
Deathdate: 3/26/1979
Information Available in These Sources: SATA 22

STAHL, BEN(JAMIN ALBERT)
Birthdate: 9/7/1910
Birthplace: Chicago, IL
Deathdate: 10/19/1987
Information Available in These Sources: IBYP 2, ICB 3, ICB 4, SATA 5, SATA 54

STAHL, HILDA
Birthdate: 9/13/1938
Birthplace: Chadron, NE
Information Available in These Sources: SATA 48

STAIR, GOBIN (JOHN)
Birthdate: 7/30/1912
Birthplace: Staten Island, NY
Information Available in These Sources: SATA 35

STALL, DOROTHY
Birthplace: Thayer, KS
Information Available in These Sources: ABYP 2, ABYP 3

STAMATY, MARK ALAN
Birthdate: 8/1/1947
Birthplace: Brooklyn, NY
Information Available in These Sources: ICB 4, SATA 12

STAMBLER, IRWIN
Birthdate: 11/20/1924
Birthplace: Brooklyn, NY
Information Available in These Sources: ABYP 2, ABYP 3, SATA 5

STANEK, MURIEL (NOVELLA)
Birthdate: 1915
Birthplace: Chicago, IL
Information Available in These Sources: SATA 34

STANHOPE, LAVINIA
See Schlein, Miriam

STANKEVICH, BORIS
Birthdate: 8/19/1928
Birthplace: Los Angeles, CA
Information Available in These Sources: SATA 2

STANLEY, DIANE Z.
(Diane Zuromskis)
Birthdate: 12/27/1943
Birthplace: Abilene, TX
Information Available in These Sources: JBA 6, SATA 32, SATA 37

STANLEY, GEORGE EDWARD
(Stuart Symons)
Birthdate: 7/15/1942
Birthplace: Memphis, TX
Information Available in These Sources: SATA 53

STANLI, SUE
See Meilach, Dona Z(weigoron)

STANOVICH, BETTY JO
Birthdate: 7/13/1954
Birthplace: San Pedro, CA
Information Available in These Sources: SATA 51

STAPP, ARTHUR D(ONALD)
Birthdate: 12/26/1906
Birthplace: Seattle, WA
Deathdate: 1/10/1972
Information Available in These Sources: ABYP 2, ABYP 3, MJA, SATA 4

STARBIRD, KAYE
(C. S. Jennison)
Birthdate: 6/3/1916
Birthplace: Fort Sill, OK
Information Available in These Sources: SATA 6

STARK, JAMES
See Goldston, Robert (Conroy)

STARKEY, MARION L(ENA)
Birthdate: 4/13/1901
Birthplace: Worcester, MA
Information Available in These Sources: SATA 8

STARR, WARD
See Manes, Stephen

STARRET, WILLIAM
See McClintock, Marshall

STARRETT, CHARLES VINCENT EMERSON
(Vincent Starrett)
Birthdate: 1886
Birthplace: Toronto, Ontario, Canada
Deathdate: 1974
Information Available in These Sources: ABYP 2, ABYP 3

STARRETT, VINCENT
See Starrett, Charles Vincent Emerson

STASIAK, KRYSTYNA
Birthplace: Poland
Information Available in These Sources: SATA 49

STAUFFER, DON
See Berkebile, Fred D(onovan)

STAUFFER, DWIGHT G.
Birthplace: Shanghai, China
Information Available in These Sources: ABYP 4

STAUNTON, SCHUYLER
See Baum, L(yman) Frank

STEARNS, MONROE (MATHER)
Birthdate: 9/28/1913
Birthplace: New York, NY
Deathdate: 12/17/1987
Information Available in These Sources: ABYP 4, SATA 5, SATA 55

STEEDMAN, MARGUERITE COUTURIER
Birthdate: 1/4/1908
Birthplace: Atlanta, GA
Information Available in These Sources: ABYP 4

STEELE, ADDISON II
See Lupoff, Richard A(llen)

STEELE, HENRY MAX(WELL)
(Max Steele)
Birthdate: 3/30/1922
Birthplace: Greenville, SC
Information Available in These Sources: SATA 10

STEELE, MARY Q(UINTARD GOVAN)
(Wilson Gage)
Birthdate: 5/8/1922
Birthplace: Chattanooga, TN
Information Available in These Sources: ABYP 2, ABYP 3, DACF, JBA 3, SATA 3, SATA 51, TCCW 1, TCCW 2, TCCW 3

STEELE, MAX
See Steele, Henry Max(well)

STEELE, WILLIAM O(WEN)
Birthdate: 12/22/1917
Birthplace: Franklin, TN
Deathdate: 6/25/1979
Information Available in These Sources: ABYP 2, ABYP 3, MJA, SATA 1, SATA 27, SATA 51, TCCW 1, TCCW 3

STEFANIK, ALFRED T.
Birthdate: 7/5/1939
Birthplace: Copaigue, NY
Information Available in These Sources: SATA 55

STEFANSSON, EVELYN (SCHWARTZ) BAIRD
See Nef, Evelyn Stefansson

STEFFERUD, ALFRED DANIEL
Birthdate: 5/17/1903
Birthplace: Kenyon, MN
Information Available in These Sources: ABYP 2, ABYP 3

STEGEMAN, JANET ALLAIS
(Kate Britton)
Birthdate: 10/18/1923
Birthplace: Oak Park, IL
Information Available in These Sources: SATA 49, SATA 53

STEIG, WILLIAM
Birthdate: 11/14/1907
Birthplace: New York, NY
Information Available in These Sources: DACF, DLB 61, IBYP 1, IBYP 2, ICB 4, JBA 3, SATA 18, TCCW 1 TCCW 2, TCCW 3

STEIN, EVALEEN
Birthdate: 10/12/1863
Birthplace: Lafayette, IN
Deathdate: 12/11/1923
Information Available in These Sources: JBA 1, JBA 2

STEIN, HARVE
Birthdate: 4/23/1904
Birthplace: Chicago, IL
Information Available in These Sources: IBYP 1, IBYP 2, ICB 2, SATA 30

STEIN, M(EYER) L(EWIS)
Birthdate: 7/30/1920
Birthplace: Escanaba, MI
Information Available in These Sources: ABYP 2, ABYP 3, SATA 6

STEIN, MINI
Birthplace: Port Elizabeth, South Africa
Information Available in These Sources: SATA 2

STEIN, R(ICHARD) CONRAD
Birthdate: 4/22/1937
Birthplace: Chicago, IL
Information Available in These Sources: SATA 31

STEIN, SARA BONNETT
Information Available in These Sources: SATA 34

STEINBECK, JOHN (ERNST)
Birthdate: 2/27/1902
Birthplace: Salinas, CA
Deathdate: 12/20/1968
Information Available in These Sources: ABYP 4. SATA 9

STEINBERG, ALFRED
Birthdate: 12/8/1917
Birthplace: St. Paul, MN
Information Available in These Sources: ABYP 2, ABYP 3, SATA 9

STEINBERG, DAVID MICHAEL
Information Available in These Sources: IBYP 1, IBYP 2

STEINBERG, FANNIE
Birthdate: 4/6/1899
Birthplace: Russia
Information Available in These Sources: SATA 43

STEINBERG, FRED J.
Birthdate: 8/9/1933
Birthplace: New York, NY
Information Available in These Sources: SATA 4

STEINBERG, PHILLIP ORSO
Birthdate: 5/1/1921
Birthplace: Minneapolis, MN
Information Available in These Sources: SATA 34

STEINBERG, RAFAEL (MARK)
Birthdate: 6/2/1927
Birthplace: Newark, NJ
Information Available in These Sources: SATA 45

STEINER, BARBARA A(NNETTE)
(Annette Cole, Kate D'Andrea, Anne Daniel)
Birthdate: 11/3/1934
Birthplace: Dardanelle, AR
Information Available in These Sources: SATA 13

STEINER, CHARLOTTE
Birthdate: 1900
Birthplace: Vienna, Austria
Deathdate: 8/12/1981
Information Available in These Sources: ABYP 2, ABYP 3, SATA 45

STEINER, STAN(LEY)
Birthdate: 1/1/1925
Birthplace: Brooklyn, NY
Deathdate: 1/12/1987
Information Available in These Sources: SATA 14, SATA 50

STEINMETZ, LEON
See Shtainmetz, Leon

STEPHENS, CHARLES ASBURY
Birthdate: 10/21/1844
Birthplace: Norway, ME
Deathdate: 9/22/1931
Information Available in These Sources: DLB 42

STEPHENS, HENRIETTA HENKLE
(Henrietta Buckmaster, Henrietta Henkle)
Birthdate: 1909
Birthplace: Cleveland, OH
Deathdate: 4/26/1983
Information Available in These Sources: SATA 6

STEPHENS, MARGARET MCCURDY
(Peggy Stephens)
Information Available in These Sources: ABYP 4

STEPHENS, MARY JO
Birthdate: 3/10/1935
Birthplace: Harlan, KY
Information Available in These Sources: SATA 8

STEPHENS, PEGGY
See Stephens, Margaret McCurdy

STEPHENS, WILLIAM M(CLAIN)
Birthdate: 5/11/1925
Birthplace: Chattanooga, TN
Information Available in These Sources: ABYP 4, SATA 21

STEPHENSEN, A. M.
See Manes, Stephen

STEPP, ANN
Birthdate: 7/20/1935
Birthplace: Headrick, OK
Information Available in These Sources: ABYP 4, SATA 29

STEPTOE, JOHN (LEWIS)
Birthdate: 9/14/1950
Birthplace: Brooklyn, NY
Deathdate: 8/28/1989
Information Available in These Sources: BAI, IBYP 2, ICB 4, JBA 4, SATA 8, TCCW 1, TCCW 2, TCCW 3

STERLING, BRETT
See Samachson, Joseph

STERLING, DOROTHY
Birthdate: 11/23/1913
Birthplace: New York, NY
Information Available in These Sources: ABYP 2, ABYP 3, JBA 3, MBMP, SATA 1

STERLING, HELEN
See Hoke, Helen (L.)

STERLING, PHILIP
(Philip Shatz)
Birthdate: 7/12/1907
Birthplace: New Rochelle, NY
Information Available in These Sources: SATA 8

STERN, CATHERINE (BRIEGER)
Birthdate: 1/6/1894
Birthplace: Breslau, Germany
Deathdate: 1/8/1973
Information Available in These Sources: ABYP 4

STERN, ELLEN N(ORMAN)
Birthdate: 7/10/1927
Birthplace: Hanover, Germany
Information Available in These Sources: SATA 26

STERN, MADELEINE B(ETTINA)
Birthdate: 7/1/1912
Birthplace: New York, NY
Information Available in These Sources: ABYP 2, ABYP 3, SATA 14

STERN, MARIE SIMCHOW
(Masha)
Birthdate: 4/20/1909
Birthplace: New York, NY
Information Available in These Sources: ICB 1

STERN, PHILIP VAN DOREN
(Peter Storme)
Birthdate: 9/10/1900
Birthplace: Wyalusing, PA
Deathdate: 7/31/1984
Information Available in These Sources: ABYP 4, SATA 13, SATA 39

STERNE, EMMA GELDERS
(Emily Broun, Josephine James)
Birthdate: 5/13/1894
Birthplace: Birmingham, AL
Deathdate: 8/29/1971
Information Available in These Sources: MJA, SATA 6

STEURT, MARJORIE RANKIN
Birthdate: 10/8/1888
Birthplace: PA
Information Available in These Sources: SATA 10

STEVENS, ALDEN GIFFORD
Birthdate: 1886
Information Available in These Sources: ABYP 2, ABYP 3

STEVENS, CARLA M(CBRIDE)
Birthdate: 3/26/1928
Birthplace: New York, NY
Information Available in These Sources: ABYP 2, ABYP 3, SATA 13

STEVENS, DAN J.
See Overholser, Wayne D.

STEVENS, FRANKLIN
(Steve Franklin)
Birthdate: 10/31/1933
Birthplace: Camden, NJ
Information Available in These Sources: SATA 6

STEVENS, GWENDOLYN
Birthdate: 2/29/1944
Birthplace: Los Angeles, CA
Information Available in These Sources: SATA 33

STEVENS, JANET
Birthdate: 1953
Birthplace: Dallas, TX
Information Available in These Sources: JBA 6

STEVENS, KATHLEEN
Birthdate: 2/16/1936
Birthplace: Brooklyn, NY
Information Available in These Sources: SATA 49

STEVENS, LUCILE V(ERNON)
Birthdate: 3/7/1899
Birthplace: St. Paul, MN
Information Available in These Sources: SATA 59

STEVENS, LUCY BEATRICE
Birthdate: 9/4/1876
Birthplace: New York, NY
Information Available in These Sources: ICB 1

STEVENS, MARY E.
Birthdate: 9/9/1920
Birthplace: Bar Harbor, ME
Deathdate: 10/18/1966
Information Available in These Sources: IBYP 1, IBYP 2, ICB 2, ICB 3

STEVENS, PATRICIA BUNNING
Birthdate: 9/28/1931
Birthplace: Buenos Aires, Argentina
Information Available in These Sources: SATA 27

STEVENS, PETER
See Geis, Darlene (Stern)

STEVENS, WILLIAM OLIVER
Birthdate: 10/7/1878
Birthplace: Rangoon, Burma
Deathdate: 1/15/1955
Information Available in These Sources: ABYP 2, ABYP 3

STEVENSON, ANNA (M.)
Birthdate: 12/23/1905
Birthplace: Heber, UT
Information Available in These Sources: SATA 12

STEVENSON, ARTHUR LIONEL
See Stevenson, Lionel

STEVENSON, AUGUSTA
Birthdate, 1869?
Birthplace: Patriot, IN
Deathdate: 7/7/1976
Information Available in These Sources: ABYP 1, ABYP 3, MJA, SATA 2, SATA 26

STEVENSON, BURTON E(GBERT)
Birthdate: 11/9/1872
Birthplace: Chillicothe, OH
Deathdate: 5/13/1962
Information Available in These Sources: SATA 25

STEVENSON, DREW
Birthdate: 12/25/1947
Birthplace: Washington, PA
Information Available in These Sources: SATA 60

STEVENSON, JAMES
Birthdate: 7/11/1929
Birthplace: New York, NY
Information Available in These Sources: ABYP 4, ICB 4, JBA 5, SATA 34 SATA 42, TCCW 3

STEVENSON, JANET (MARSHALL)
Birthdate: 2/4/1913
Birthplace: Chicago, IL
Information Available in These Sources: ABYP 4, SATA 8

STEVENSON, LIONEL
(Arthur Lionel Stevenson)
Birthdate: 7/16/1902
Birthplace: Edinburgh, Scotland
Deathdate: 12/21/1973
Information Available in These Sources: SVC 2

STEWART, ANNA BIRD
Birthdate: 1880
Birthplace: Cincinnati, OH
Information Available in These Sources: ABYP 2, ABYP 3

STEWART, ARVIS L.
Birthplace: TX
Information Available in These Sources: IBYP 1, IBYP 2

STEWART, CHARLES
See Zurhorst, Charles (Stewart, Jr.)

STEWART, ELIZABETH LAING
Birthdate: 9/1/1907
Birthplace: Colorado Springs, CO
Information Available in These Sources: ABYP 2, ABYP 3, SATA 6

STEWART, GEORGE RIPPEY
Birthdate: 5/31/1895
Birthplace: Sewickley, PA
Deathdate: 8/22/1980
Information Available in These Sources: SATA 3, SATA 23

STEWART, JOHN (WILLIAM)
(Jack Cole)
Birthdate: 10/1/1920
Birthplace: Chicago, IL
Information Available in These Sources: SATA 14

STEWART, MARJABELLE YOUNG
See Young, Marjabelle

STEWART, SCOTT
See Zaffo, George J.

STEWIG, JOHN WARREN
Birthdate: 1/7/1937
Birthplace: Waukesha, WI
Information Available in These Sources: SATA 26

STILES, MARTHA BENNETT
Birthplace: Manila, Philippines
Information Available in These Sources: DACF, SATA 6

STILES, NORMAN B.
Birthdate: 12/4/1942
Birthplace: New York, NY
Information Available in These Sources: SATA 36

STILL, JAMES
Birthdate: 7/16/1906
Birthplace: LaFayette, AL
Information Available in These Sources: SATA 29

STILLERMAN, ROBBIE
Birthdate: 5/12/1947
Birthplace: New York, NY
Information Available in These Sources: SATA 12

STILLEY, FRANK
Birthdate: 4/18/1918
Birthplace: Wardville, OK
Information Available in These Sources: SATA 29

STILLMAN, MYRA (STEPHENS)
Birthdate: 3/7/1915
Birthplace: Albany, NY
Information Available in These Sources: ABYP 2, ABYP 3

STILWELL, ALISON
Birthdate: 2/5/1921
Birthplace: Peking, China
Information Available in These Sources: ICB 2

STINE, G(EORGE) HARRY
(Lee Correy)
Birthdate: 3/26/1928
Birthplace: Philadelphia, PA
Information Available in These Sources: ABYP 2, ABYP 3, SATA 10

STINE, JOVIAL BOB
See Stine, Robert Lawrence

STINE, ROBERT LAWRENCE
(Jovial Bob Stine)
Birthdate: 10/8/1943
Birthplace: Columbus, OH
Information Available in These Sources: BC, SATA 31

STINETORF, LOUISE (ALLENDER)
Birthdate: 2/4/1900
Birthplace: Ward Township, IN
Information Available in These Sources: SATA 10

STIRLING, ARTHUR
See Sinclair, Upton (Beall)

STIRLING, LILLA
Birthplace: Nova Scotia, Canada
Information Available in These Sources: ABYP 2, ABYP 3

STIRLING, NORA B(ROMLEY)
Birthdate: 1900
Birthplace: Atlanta, GA
Information Available in These Sources: ABYP 2, ABYP 3, SATA 3

STIRNWEIS, SHANNON
Birthdate: 2/26/1931
Birthplace: Portland, OR
Information Available in These Sources: IBYP 1, IBYP 2, SATA 10

STOCKTON, FRANCIS RICHARD
(Paul Fort, John Lewees, Frank R. Stockton)
Birthdate: 4/5/1834
Birthplace: Philadelphia (Blockley), PA
Deathdate: 4/20/1902 or 4/16/1902
Information Available in These Sources: ABYP 2, ABYP 3, DLB 42, FSYP, JBA 1, SATA 32, SATA 44, TCCW 1, TCCW 2, TCCW 3, WC

STOCKTON, FRANK R.
See Stockton, Francis Richard

STODDARD, EDWARD G.
Birthdate: 11/26/1923
Birthplace: Peking, China
Information Available in These Sources: ABYP 2, ABYP 3, SATA 10

STODDARD, HOPE
Birthdate: 3/31/1900
Birthplace: New Bedford, MA
Information Available in These Sources: ABYP 2, ABYP 3, SATA 6

STODDARD, SANDOL
See Warburg, Sandol Stoddard

STOIKO, MICHAEL
Birthdate: 4/10/1919
Birthplace: New York, NY
Information Available in These Sources: SATA 14

STOKES, JACK (TILDEN)
Birthdate: 8/26/1923
Birthplace: Sullivan, IN
Information Available in These Sources: SATA 13

STOKES, OLIVIA PEARL
Birthdate: 1/11/1916
Birthplace: Middlesex, NC
Information Available in These Sources: SATA 32

STOLPER, JOEL
Birthplace: Jersey City, NJ
Information Available in These Sources: ICB 1

STOLZ, MARY (SLATTERY)
Birthdate: 3/24/1920
Birthplace: Boston, MA
Information Available in These Sources: ABYP 1, ABYP 3, DACF, MBMP, MJA, SATA 10, TCCW 1, 2, 3

STONAKER, FRANCES BENSON
Birthplace: Boston, MA
Information Available in These Sources: ABYP 4

STONE, A. HARRIS
Birthdate: 12/11/1934
Birthplace: Philadelphia, PA
Information Available in These Sources: ABYP 4

STONE, ALAN
See Svenson, Andrew E. and Stratemeyer, Edward L.

STONE, D(AVID) K(ARL)
Birthdate: 3/24/1922
Birthplace: Reedsport, OR
Information Available in These Sources: IBYP 2, SATA 9

STONE, EUGENIA
(Gene Stone)
Birthdate: 5/11/1879
Birthplace: Gold Hill, NV
Deathdate: 1971
Information Available in These Sources: SATA 7

STONE, GENE
See Stone, Eugenia

STONE, GEORGE K.
Information Available in These Sources: ABYP 2, ABYP 3

STONE, HELEN
Birthdate: 10/31/1904
Birthplace: Englewood, NJ
Information Available in These Sources: IBYP 1, IBYP 2, ICB 1, ICB 2, ICB 3

STONE, HELEN (VIRGINIA)
Birthplace: Philadelphia, PA
Information Available in These Sources: SATA 6

STONE, IRVING
Birthdate: 7/14/1903
Birthplace: San Francisco, CA
Information Available in These Sources: SATA 3

STONE, JON
Birthdate: 4/13/1931
Birthplace: New Haven, CT
Information Available in These Sources: SATA 39

STONE, JOSEPHINE RECTOR
See Dixon, Jeanne

STONE, RAYMOND
See Stratemeyer, Edward L.

STONE, ROSETTA
See Frith, Michael (K.) and Geisel, Theodor Seuss

STONG, PHIL(IP DUFFIELD)
Birthdate: 1/27/1899
Birthplace: Keosauqua, IA
Deathdate: 4/26/1957
Information Available in These Sources: ABYP 1, ABYP 3, MJA, SATA 32, SVC 3, TCCW 1, TCCW 2TCCW 3

STORME, PETER
See Stern, Philip Van Doren

STORY, JOSEPHINE
See Loring, Emilie (Baker)

STORY LADY
See Faulkner, Georgene

STOUTENBURG, ADRIEN (PEARL)
(Barbi(e) Arden, Lace Kendall, Nelson Minier)
Birthdate: 12/1/1916
Birthplace: Darfur, MN
Information Available in These Sources: ABYP 2, ABYP 3, JBA 3, SATA 3

STOVER, ALLAN C(ARL)
Birthdate: 6/28/1938
Birthplace: Cleveland, OH
Information Available in These Sources: SATA 14

STOVER, JO ANN
Birthdate: 4/23/1931
Birthplace: Peterborough, NH
Information Available in These Sources: IBYP 1, IBYP 2

STOVER, MARJORIE FILLEY
Birthdate: 6/23/1914
Birthplace: Lincoln, NE
Information Available in These Sources: SATA 9

STOWE, HARRIET (ELIZABETH) BEECHER
(Christopher Crowfield)
Birthdate: 6/13/1811 or 6/14/1811
Birthplace: Litchfield, CT
Deathdate: 7/1/1896
Information Available in These Sources: ABYP 4, DLB 42, JBA 1, WCL, YABC

STOWE, LELAND
Birthdate: 11/10/1899
Birthplace: Southbury, CT
Information Available in These Sources: SATA 60

STRACHAN, MARGARET PITCAIRN
(Caroline More)
Birthdate: 11/13/1908
Birthplace: Philadelphia, PA
Information Available in These Sources: SATA 14

STRAIT, TREVA ADAMS
Birthdate: 6/27/1909
Birthplace: Papillion, NE
Information Available in These Sources: SATA 35

STRAND, MARK
Birthdate: 4/11/1934
Birthplace: Prince Edward Island, Canada (Summerside)
Information Available in These Sources: SATA 41

STRASSER, TODD
(Morton Rhue)
Birthdate: 5/5/1950
Birthplace: New York, NY
Information Available in These Sources: BC, JBA 6, SATA 41, SATA 45

STRATEMEYER, EDWARD L.
(Harrison Adams, Victor Appleton, Richard Barnum, Philip A. Bartlett, May Hollis Barton, Charles Amory Beach, Lester Chadwick, Allen Chapman, John E. Cooper, Elmer A. Dawson, Franklin W. Dixon, Alice B. Emerson, James Cody Ferris, Graham B. Forbes, Frederick Gordon, Alice Dale Hardy, Mabel C. Hawley, Brooks Henderley, Laura Lee Hope, Frances K. Judd, Clinton W. Locke, Helen Beecher Long, Eugene Martin, Roy Rockwood, Raymond Sperry, Jr., Alan Stone, Raymond Stone, Helen Louise Thorndyke, Frank A. Warner, Frank V. Webster, Janet D. Wheeler, Ramy Allison White, Clarence Young)
Birthdate: 10/4/1862
Birthplace: Elizabeth, NJ
Deathdate: 5/10/1930
Information Available in These Sources: DLB 42, SATA 1

STRATTON, LUCILLE (NEVILLE)
Information Available in These Sources: ABYP 2, ABYP 3

STRATTON, THOMAS
See DeWeese, Thomas Eugene

STRATTON, WILLIAM DAVID
Birthdate: 4/17/1896
Birthplace: Grand Rapids, MI
Information Available in These Sources: ABYP 2, ABYP 3

STRATTON-PORTER, GENE(VA GRACE)
See Porter, Gene(va Grace) Stratton

STRAUS, JACQUELINE HARRIS
Birthplace: New York, NY
Information Available in These Sources: ABYP 2, ABYP 3

STRAUSS, JOYCE
Birthdate: 8/12/1936
Birthplace: Los Angeles, CA
Information Available in These Sources: SATA 53

STREANO, VINCE(NT CATELLO)
Birthdate: 12/9/1945
Birthplace: Santa Barbara, CA
Information Available in These Sources: SATA 20

STREET, JULIA MONTGOMERY
Birthdate: 1/19/1898
Birthplace: Concord, NC
Information Available in These Sources: SATA 11

STRETE, CRAIG KEE
Birthdate: 1950
Birthplace: Fort Wayne, IN
Information Available in These Sources: SATA 44

STRETTON, BARBARA (HUMPHREY)
Birthdate: 6/23/1936
Birthplace: Salt Lake City, UT
Information Available in These Sources: SATA 35, 43

STRONG, CHARLES
See Epstein, Beryl (M. Williams) and Epstein, Samuel

STRONG, CHARLES STANLEY
Birthdate: 11/29/1906
Birthplace: Brooklyn, NY
Deathdate: 10/10/1962
Information Available in These Sources: ABYP 2, ABYP 3

STRONG, DAVID
See McGuire, Leslie (Sarah)

STUART, DAVID
See Hoyt, Edwin P(almer), Jr.

STUART, ELEANOR
See Porter, Eleanor H(odgman)

STUART, GENE S.
Birthdate: 10/22/1930
Information Available in These Sources: ABYP 4

STUART, GEORGE E.
Information Available in These Sources: ABYP 4

STUART, HILTON JESSE
(Jesse Stuart)
Birthdate: 8/8/1907
Birthplace: W-Hollow, Riverton, KY
Deathdate: 2/17/1984
Information Available in: ABYP 4, DACF, SATA 2, 36

STUART, JESSE
See Stuart, Hilton Jesse

STUBENRAUCH, BOB
See Stubenrauch, Robert

STUBENRAUCH, ROBERT
(Bob Stubenrauch)
Information Available in These Sources: ABYP 4

STUBIS, TALIVALDIS
Birthdate: 5/22/1926
Birthplace: Riga, Latvia
Information Available in These Sources: IBYP 1, IBYP 2, SATA 5

STULTIFER, MORTON
See Curtis, Richard (Alan)

STURE-VASA, MARY
See Alsop, Mary O'Hara

STURTZEL, HOWARD A(LLISON)
(Paul Annixter)
Birthdate: 6/25/1894
Birthplace: Minneapolis, MN
Information Available in These Sources: SATA 1

STURTZEL, JANE LEVINGTON
(Jane Annixter, Jane Levington Comfort)
Birthdate: 6/22/1903
Birthplace: Detroit, MI
Information Available in These Sources: ABYP 2, ABYP 3, SATA 1

SUBA, SUZANNE
Birthdate: 12/31/1913
Birthplace: Budapest, Hungary
Information Available in These Sources: IBYP 1, IBYP 2, ICB 1, ICB 2, ICB 3, ICB 4, MJA, SATA 4

SUBLETTE, C(LIFFORD) M(CCLELLAN)
Birthdate: 8/16/1887
Birthplace: Charleston, IL
Deathdate: 1939
Information Available in These Sources: JBA 1, JBA 2

SUGARMAN, TRACY
Birthdate: 11/14/1921
Birthplace: Syracuse, NY
Information Available in These Sources: SATA 37

SUGGS, ROBERT CARL
Birthdate: 2/24/1932
Birthplace: Portchester, NY
Information Available in These Sources: ABYP 2, ABYP 3

SUGIMOTO, ETSU INAGAKI
Birthdate: 1874
Birthplace: Echigo, Japan
Deathdate: 6/20/1950
Information Available in These Sources: JBA 1

SUHL, YURI
Birthdate: 7/30/1908
Birthplace: Podhajce, Poland
Deathdate: 11/8/1986
Information Available in These Sources: ABYP 4, SATA 8, SATA 50

SUID, MURRAY
Birthdate: 5/16/1942
Birthplace: Cleveland, OH
Information Available in These Sources: SATA 27

SULLIVAN, GEORGE E(DWARD)
Birthdate: 8/11/1927
Birthplace: Lowell, MA
Information Available in These Sources: ABYP 2, ABYP 3, SATA 4

SULLIVAN, MARY W(ILSON)
Birthdate: 12/25/1907
Birthplace: Grants Pass, OR
Information Available in These Sources: SATA 13

SULLIVAN, THOMAS JOSEPH, JR.
(Tom Sullivan)
Birthdate: 3/27/1947
Birthplace: Boston, MA
Information Available in These Sources: SATA 16

SULLIVAN, TOM
See Sullivan, Thomas Joseph, Jr.

SUMICHRAST, JOZEF
Birthdate: 7/26/1948
Birthplace: Hobart, IN
Information Available in These Sources: SATA 29

SUMMERS, JAMES L(EVINGSTON)
Birthdate: 9/11/1910
Birthplace: Oshkosh, WI
Deathdate: 10/26/2973
Information Available in These Sources: ABYP 2, ABYP 3, MJA, SATA 28, SATA 57

SUNDELL, ABNER
Information Available in These Sources: ABYP 4

SUNDERLIN, SYLVIA
Birthdate: 9/22/1911
Birthplace: Lakeside, MT
Information Available in These Sources: SATA 28

SUNG, BETTY LEE
Birthplace: Baltimore, MD
Information Available in These Sources: SATA 26

SUPRANER, ROBYN
(Olive Blake, Erica Frost, Elizabeth Warren)
Birthdate: 9/14/1930
Birthplace: New York, NY
Information Available in These Sources: SATA 20

SURANY, ANICO
Birthplace: Paris, France
Information Available in These Sources: ABYP 2, ABYP 3

SURGE, FRANK
Birthdate: 9/27/1931
Birthplace: Buhl, MN
Information Available in These Sources: SATA 13

SUSAC, ANDREW
Birthdate: 7/4/1929
Birthplace: Provident, OH
Information Available in These Sources: SATA 5

SUSSMAN, CORNELIA (SILVER)
(Cornelia Jessey)
Birthdate: 2/9/1914
Birthplace: Jeanette, PA
Information Available in These Sources: SATA 59

SUSSMAN, IRVING
Birthdate: 12/25/1908
Birthplace: New York, NY
Information Available in These Sources: SATA 59

SUSSMAN, SUSAN
(Art Rissman, Susan Rissman)
Birthdate: 4/22/1942
Birthplace: Chicago, IL
Information Available in These Sources: SATA 48

SUTHERLAND, ZENA B(AILEY)
Birthdate: 9/17/1915
Birthplace: Winthrop, MA
Information Available in These Sources: ABYP 4, SATA 37

SUTTLES, SHIRLEY (SMITH)
(Lesley Conger)
Birthdate: 3/25/1922
Birthplace: Seattle, WA
Information Available in These Sources: SATA 21

SUTTON, ANN (LIVESAY)
Birthdate: 9/5/1923
Birthplace: Ashley, IL
Information Available in These Sources: ABYP 2, ABYP 3, SATA 31

SUTTON, EUGENIA GENEVA (HANSEN)
(Jean Sutton)
Birthdate: 7/5/1917
Birthplace: Denmark, WI
Information Available in These Sources: ABYP 4

SUTTON, FELIX
Birthdate, 1910?
Birthplace: WV
Information Available in These Sources: ABYP 2, ABYP 3, SATA 31

SUTTON, JANE
Birthdate: 5/11/1950
Birthplace: New York, NY
Information Available in These Sources: SATA 43, SATA 52

SUTTON, JEAN
See Sutton, Eugenia Geneva (Hansen)

SUTTON, JEFF(ERSON H.)
Birthdate: 7/25/1913
Birthplace: Los Angeles, CA
Information Available in These Sources: ABYP 4

SUTTON, LARRY M(ATTHEW)
Birthdate: 2/24/1931
Birthplace: Winter Haven, FL
Information Available in These Sources: SATA 29

SUTTON, MARGARET (BEEBE)
(Rachel Irene Beebe, Irene Ray)
Birthdate: 1/22/1903
Birthplace: Odin, PA
Information Available in These Sources: ABYP 2, ABYP 3, SATA 1

SUTTON, MYRON DANIEL
Birthdate: 10/9/1925
Birthplace: Prescott, AZ
Information Available in These Sources: ABYP 2, ABYP 3, SATA 31

SUZANNE, JAMIE
See Hawkes, Louise

SVENSON, ANDREW E.
(Franklin W. Dixon, Alan Stone, Jerry West)
Birthdate: 5/8/1910
Birthplace: Belleville, NJ
Deathdate: 8/21/1975
Information Available in These Sources: SATA 2, SATA 26

SWADOS, HARVEY
Birthdate: 10/28/1920
Birthplace: Buffalo, NY
Deathdate: 12/11/1972
Information Available in These Sources: ABYP 4

SWAIN, SU ZAN (NOGUCHI)
Birthdate: 3/8/1916
Birthplace: Iliff, CO
Information Available in These Sources: ICB 3, SATA 21

SWAN, SUSAN
Birthdate: 9/13/1944
Birthplace: Coral Gables, FL
Information Available in These Sources: SATA 22

SWANSON, ANNE (SHERBOURNE)
Birthplace: Baltimore, MD
Information Available in These Sources: ABYP 2, ABYP 3

SWANSON, ARLENE COLLYER
Birthdate: 12/12/1913
Birthplace: Ossining, NY
Information Available in These Sources: ABYP 2, ABYP 3

SWANSON, NEIL HARMON
Birthdate: 6/30/1896
Birthplace: Minneapolis, MN
Deathdate: 2/5/1983
Information Available in These Sources: ABYP 2, ABYP 3

SWARTHOUT, GLENDON (FRED)
Birthdate: 4/8/1918
Birthplace: Pinckney, MI
Information Available in These Sources: DACF, JBA 4, SATA 26

SWARTHOUT, KATHRYN (BLAIR VAUGHN)
Birthdate: 1/8/1919
Birthplace: Columbus, MT
Information Available in These Sources: DACF, JBA 4, SATA 7

SWAYNE, SAM(UEL F.)
Birthdate: 12/22/1907
Birthplace: Paulding County, OH
Information Available in These Sources: SATA 53

SWAYNE, ZOA LOURANA (SHAW)
Birthdate: 12/23/1905
Birthplace: Torrington, WY
Information Available in These Sources: IBYP 2, ICB 2, SATA 53

SWEAT, LYNN
Birthdate: 5/27/1934
Birthplace: Alexandria, LA
Information Available in These Sources: IBYP 2, SATA 57

SWEENEY, JAMES B(ARTHOLOMEW)
Birthdate: 7/7/1910
Birthplace: Philadelphia, PA
Information Available in These Sources: SATA 21

SWEENEY, KAREN O'CONNOR
See O'Connor, Karen

SWEET, OSCAR COWAN
(Ozzie Sweet)
Birthdate: 9/10/1918
Birthplace: Stamford, CT
Information Available in These Sources: JBA 6

SWEET, OZZIE
See Sweet, Oscar Cowan

SWEETLAND, NANCY A(NN ROSE)
(Nancy A. Rose)
Birthdate: 5/6/1934
Birthplace: Chamberlain, SD
Information Available in These Sources: SATA 48

SWENEY, FREDERIC
Birthdate: 6/5/1912
Birthplace: Hollidaysburg, PA
Information Available in These Sources: IBYP 1, ICB 3

SWENSON, ALLAN A(RMSTRONG)
Birthdate: 12/26/1933
Birthplace: Passaic, NJ
Information Available in These Sources: SATA 21

SWENSON, MAY
Birthdate: 5/28/1919
Birthplace: Logan, UT
Information Available in These Sources: ABYP 4, SATA 15

SWIFT, DAVID
See Kaufmann, John

SWIFT, HELEN MILLER
Birthdate: 4/15/1914
Birthplace: Danvers, MA
Information Available in These Sources: ABYP 2, ABYP 3

SWIFT, HILDEGARDE HOYT
Birthdate, 1890?
Birthplace: Clinton, NY
Deathdate: 1/10/1977
Information Available in These Sources: ABYP 1, ABYP 3, JBA 2, SATA 20

SWIFT, MERLIN
See Leeming, Joseph

SWIGER, ELINOR PORTER
Birthdate: 8/1/1927
Birthplace: Cleveland, OH
Information Available in These Sources: ABYP 4, SATA 8

SWINBURNE, LAURENCE
Birthdate: 7/2/1924
Birthplace: New York, NY
Information Available in These Sources: SATA 9

SWINFORD, BETTY (JUNE WELLS)
(Linda Haynes, Kathryn Porter, Bob Swinford, June Wells)
Birthdate: 6/21/1927
Birthplace: Cartersburg, IN
Information Available in These Sources: SATA 58

SWINFORD, BOB
See Swinford, Betty (June Wells)

SWITZER, ELLEN
Birthdate: 10/18/1923
Birthplace: Germany
Information Available in These Sources: SATA 48

SYKES, JO
Birthdate: 1928
Birthplace: American Falls, ID
Information Available in These Sources: ABYP 2, ABYP 3

SYLVESTER, NATALIE G(ABRY)
Birthdate: 9/30/1922
Birthplace: Newark, NJ
Information Available in These Sources: SATA 22

SYMONS, STUART
See Stanley, George Edward

SYPHER, LUCY JOHNSTON
Birthdate: 8/6/1907
Birthplace: Wales, ND
Information Available in These Sources: SATA 7

SZASZ, SUZANNE SHORR
Birthdate: 10/20/1919
Birthplace: Budapest, Hungary
Information Available in These Sources: ABYP 2, ABYP 3, SATA 13

SZE, MAI-MAI
(Yuan-tsung Shih, Yuen-tsung Sze, Maimai Shi)
Birthdate: 1909
Birthplace: Tientsin, China
Information Available in These Sources: ABYP 1, ABYP 3

SZE, YUEN-TSUNG
See Sze, Mai-Mai

SZEKERES, CYNDY
Birthdate: 10/31/1933
Birthplace: Bridgeport, CT
Information Available in These Sources: IBYP 1, IBYP 2, ICB 4, SATA 5 SATA 60

SZULC, TAD
Birthdate: 7/25/1926
Birthplace: Warsaw, Poland
Information Available in These Sources: SATA 26

SZYK, ARTHUR
Birthdate: 6/3/1894
Birthplace: Lodz, Poland
Deathdate: 9/13/1951
Information Available in These Sources: IBYP 1, IBYP 2, ICB 2

T

TABACK, SIMMS
Birthdate: 2/13/1932
Birthplace: New York, NY
Information Available in These Sources: SATA 36, SATA 40

TABER, GLADYS (BAGG)
Birthdate: 4/2/1899
Birthplace: Colorado Springs, CO
Deathdate: 3/11/1980
Information Available in These Sources: SATA 22

TABRAH, RUTH (MILANDER)
Birthdate: 2/28/1921
Birthplace: Buffalo, NY
Information Available in These Sources: SATA 14

TAFURI, NANCY
Birthdate: 11/14/1946
Birthplace: New York, NY
Information Available in These Sources: JBA 6, SATA 39

TAIT, AGNES
Birthdate: 6/14/1897 or 6/14/1894
Birthplace: New York, NY
Deathdate: 1981
Information Available in These Sources: IBYP 2, ICB 2

TAKAKJIAN, PORTIA
(Portia Johnston, Portia Roach, Portia Wiesner)
Birthdate: 12/10/1930
Birthplace: Los Angeles, CA
Information Available in These Sources: SATA 15

TALBERT, ANSEL EDWARD MCLAURINE
Birthdate: 1/6/1912 or 1/6/1915
Birthplace: Washington, DC
Information Available in These Sources: ABYP 2, ABYP 3

TALBOT, CHARLENE JOY
Birthdate: 11/14/1928
Birthplace: Frankfort, KS
Information Available in These Sources: ABYP 4, SATA 10

TALBOT, TOBY (TOLPEN)
Birthdate: 11/29/1928
Birthplace: New York, NY
Information Available in These Sources: ABYP 4, SATA 14

TALIAFERRO, BOOKER
See Washington, Booker T(aliaferro)

TALLANT, ROBERT
Birthdate: 4/20/1909
Birthplace: New Orleans, LA
Deathdate: 4/1/1957
Information Available in These Sources: ABYP 2, ABYP 3

TALLCOTT, EMOGENE
Birthplace: Parish, NY
Information Available in These Sources: SATA 10

TALLON, ROBERT
Birthdate: 9/21/1940
Birthplace: New York, NY
Information Available in These Sources: ABYP 4, SATA 28, SATA 43

TALMADGE, MARIAN
Information Available in These Sources: ABYP 2, ABYP 3, SATA 14

TAMARA, ST.
See Kolba, Tamara

TAMARIN, ALFRED
Birthdate: 5/31/1913
Birthplace: Hudson, NY
Deathdate: 8/19/1980
Information Available in These Sources: JBA 5, MBMP, SATA 13

TAMBURINE, JEAN
Birthdate: 2/20/1930
Birthplace: Meriden, CT
Information Available in These Sources: ABYP 2, ABYP 3, SATA 12

TANG, YOU-SHAN
Birthdate: 1/10/1946
Birthplace: China
Information Available in These Sources: SATA 53

TANNEHILL, IVAN RAY
Birthdate: 1890
Deathdate: 1959
Information Available in These Sources: ABYP 2, ABYP 3

TANNEN, MARY
Birthdate: 6/2/1943
Birthplace: New London, CT
Information Available in These Sources: SATA 37

TANNENBAUM, BEULAH (GOLDSTEIN)
Birthdate: 4/14/1916
Birthplace: New York, NY
Information Available in These Sources: ABYP 2, ABYP 3, SATA 3

TANNENBAUM, D(ONALD) LEB
Birthdate: 4/8/1948
Birthplace: Orange, NJ
Information Available in These Sources: SATA 42

TANNER, LOUISE S(TICKNEY)
Birthdate: 2/16/1922
Birthplace: New York, NY
Information Available in These Sources: ABYP 4, SATA 9

TANOUS, HELEN NICOL
Birthdate: 1917
Birthplace: Minneapolis, MN
Information Available in These Sources: ABYP 2, ABYP 3

TAPIO, PAT DECKER
See Kines, Pat Decker

TAPP, KATHY KENNEDY
Birthdate: 1/1/1949
Birthplace: Long Beach, CA
Information Available in These Sources: SATA 50

TAPPAN, EVA MARCH
Birthdate: 12/26/1854
Birthplace: Blackstone, MA
Deathdate: 1/30/1930
Information Available in These Sources: JBA 1

TARKINGTON, BOOTH
See Tarkington, Newton Booth

TARKINGTON, NEWTON BOOTH
(Booth Tarkington)
Birthdate: 7/29/1869
Birthplace: Indianapolis, IN
Deathdate: 5/19/1946
Information Available in These Sources: JBA 1, SATA 17, TCCW 3, WCL

TARRY, ELLEN
Birthdate: 9/26/1906
Birthplace: Birmingham, AL
Information Available in These Sources: ABYP 2, ABYP 3, BABP, BAI, SATA 16

TARSHIS, BARRY
Birthdate: 1/24/1939
Information Available in These Sources: ABYP 4

TARSHIS, JEROME
Birthdate: 6/27/1936
Birthplace: New York, NY
Information Available in These Sources: SATA 9

TARSKY, SUE
Birthdate: 7/26/1946
Birthplace: New York, NY
Information Available in These Sources: SATA 41

TASHJIAN, VIRGINIA A.
Birthdate: 9/20/1921
Birthplace: Brockton, MA
Information Available in These Sources: ABYP 4, JBA 5, SATA 3

TATE, ELEANORA E(LAINE)
Birthdate: 4/16/1948
Birthplace: Canton, MO
Information Available in These Sources: BAI, SATA 38

TATE, ELIZABETH
Information Available in These Sources: ABYP 2, ABYP 3

TATE, MARY ANNE
See Hale, Arlene

TATHAM, CAMPBELL
See Elting, Mary

TAVES, ISABELLA
Birthdate: 9/20/1915
Birthplace: Lincoln, NE
Information Available in These Sources: SATA 27

TAVO, GUS
See Ivan, Gustave

TAYLOR, ARTHUR (RAYMOND)
Birthdate: 1936
Information Available in These Sources: ABYP 2, ABYP 3

TAYLOR, AUDILEE BOYD
Birthdate: 12/2/1931
Birthplace: Sylvania, GA
Information Available in These Sources: SATA 59

TAYLOR, BARBARA J.
Birthdate: 6/27/1927
Birthplace: Provo, UT
Information Available in These Sources: SATA 10

TAYLOR, CARL
Birthdate: 1/3/1937
Birthplace: New York, NY
Information Available in These Sources: ABYP 2, ABYP 3, SATA 14

TAYLOR, DAVID
Birthdate: 11/11/1900
Birthplace: Aberdeen, Scotland
Deathdate: 7/1/1905
Information Available in These Sources: SATA 10

TAYLOR, FLORANCE WALTON
Birthplace: Danville, IL
Information Available in These Sources: SATA 9

TAYLOR, FLORENCE M(ARIAN TOMPKINS)
Birthdate: 3/4/1892
Birthplace: Brooklyn, NY
Information Available in These Sources: SATA 9

TAYLOR, HERB(ERT NORMAN, JR.)
Birthdate: 6/11/1942
Birthplace: Brooklyn, NY
Deathdate: 7/14/1987
Information Available in These Sources: SATA 22, SATA 54

TAYLOR, JERRY DUNCAN
Birthdate: 6/5/1938
Birthplace: Plumerville, AR
Information Available in These Sources: SATA 47

TAYLOR, KENNETH N(ATHANIEL)
Birthdate: 5/8/1917
Birthplace: Portland, OR
Information Available in These Sources: SATA 26

TAYLOR, L(ESTER) B(ARBOUR), JR.
Birthdate: 11/9/1932
Birthplace: Lynchburg, VA
Information Available in These Sources: SATA 27

TAYLOR, LOUISE TODD
Birthdate: 2/6/1939
Birthplace: Mt. Vernon, OH
Information Available in These Sources: SATA 47

TAYLOR, MARGARET
See Burroughs, Margaret Taylor G.

TAYLOR, MARK
Birthdate: 8/15/1927
Birthplace: Linden, MI
Information Available in These Sources: ABYP 4, SATA 28, SATA 32

TAYLOR, MILDRED D(ELOIS)
Birthdate: 1943
Birthplace: Jackson, MS
Information Available in These Sources: ABYP 4, BAI, DACF, JBA 5, SATA 15, TCCW 2, TCCW 3

TAYLOR, PAULA (WRIGHT)
(Harriet Lake)
Birthdate: 5/24/1942
Birthplace: Fond du Lac, WI
Information Available in These Sources: SATA 33, SATA 48

TAYLOR, ROBERT LEWIS
Birthdate: 9/24/1912
Birthplace: Carbondale, IL
Information Available in These Sources: SATA 10

TAYLOR, SYDNEY (BRENNER)
Birthdate: 10/31/1904
Birthplace: New York, NY
Deathdate: 2/12/1978
Information Available in These Sources: ABYP 2, ABYP 3, MBMP, MJA, SATA 1, SATA 26, SATA 28, TCCW 1, TCCW 2, TCCW 3

TAYLOR, THEODORE (LANGHANS)
Birthdate: 6/23/1921 or 6/23/1924
Birthplace: Statesville, NC
Information Available in These Sources: ABYP 4, DACF, JBA 4, SATA 5, SATA 54, TCCW 1, TCCW 2, TCCW 3

TCHUDI, STEPHEN N.
(Stephen Judy, Stephen N. Judy)
Birthdate: 1/31/1942
Birthplace: Waterbury, CT
Information Available in These Sources: SATA 55

TEAGUE, BOB
See Teague, Robert

TEAGUE, DONALD
Birthdate: 11/27/1897
Birthplace: Brooklyn, NY
Information Available in These Sources: ICB 1

TEAGUE, ROBERT
(Bob Teague)
Birthdate: 1/2/1929
Birthplace: Milwaukee, WI
Information Available in These Sources: ABYP 4, SATA 31, SATA 32

TEAL, VAL(ENTINE M.)
Birthdate: 2/14/1903
Birthplace: Bottineau, ND
Information Available in These Sources: SATA 10

TEALE, EDWIN WAY
Birthdate: 6/2/1899 or 6/2/1890
Birthplace: Joliet, IL
Deathdate: 10/18/1980
Information Available in These Sources: ABYP 2, ABYP 3, JBA 3, SATA 7 SATA 25, SVC 2, SVC 3

TEASDALE, SARA
Birthdate: 8/8/1884
Birthplace: St. Louis, MO
Deathdate: 1/29/1933
Information Available in These Sources: JBA 1, SATA 32, SVC 2, SVC 3

TEBBEL, JOHN (WILLIAM)
Birthdate: 11/16/1912
Birthplace: Boyne City, MI
Information Available in These Sources: SATA 26

TEE-VAN, HELEN DAMROSCH
(Helen Therese Damrosch)
Birthdate: 5/26/1893
Birthplace: New York, NY
Deathdate: 7/29/1976
Information Available in These Sources: IBYP 1, IBYP 2, SATA 10, SATA 27

TEITELBAUM, MICHAEL
(Joanne Louise Michaels, Neal Michaels, Michael Neal, B.S. Watson)
Birthdate: 4/23/1953
Birthplace: Brooklyn, NY
Information Available in These Sources: SATA 59

TELEKI, GEZA
Birthdate: 12/7/1943
Birthplace: Kolozsvar, Hungary
Information Available in These Sources: SATA 45

TELEMAQUE, ELEANOR WONG
Birthdate: 1/1/1934
Birthplace: Albert Lea, MN
Information Available in These Sources: SATA 43

TELTSCH, KATHLEEN
Birthplace: New York, NY
Information Available in These Sources: ABYP 4

TEMKIN, SARA ANNE (SCHLOSSBERG)
Birthdate: 10/1/1913
Birthplace: Hoboken, NJ
Information Available in These Sources: ABYP 2, ABYP 3, SATA 26

TEMKO, FLORENCE
Birthdate: 10/20/1927
Information Available in These Sources: ABYP 4, SATA 13

TEMPLE, HERBERT
Birthdate: 7/6/1919
Birthplace: Gary, IN
Information Available in These Sources: SATA 45

TENGGREN, GUSTAF (ADOLF)
Birthdate: 11/2/1896
Birthplace: Magra, Sweden
Deathdate: 4/6/1970
Information Available in These Sources: IBYP 1, IBYP 2, ICB 1, ICB 2, ICB 4, MJA, SATA 18, SATA 26

TENSEN, RUTH MARJORIE
Birthdate: 1905
Birthplace: Rochester, NY
Information Available in These Sources: ABYP 1, ABYP 3

TERBAN, MARVIN
Birthdate: 4/28/1940
Birthplace: Chelsea, MA
Information Available in These Sources: SATA 45, SATA 54

TERHUNE, ALBERT PAYSON
Birthdate: 12/21/1872
Birthplace: Newark, NJ
Deathdate: 2/18/1942
Information Available in These Sources: ABYP 1, ABYP 3, JBA 1, SATA 15TCCW 2, TCCW 3

TERKEL, SUSAN N(EIBURG)
Birthdate: 4/7/1948
Birthplace: Philadelphia, PA
Information Available in These Sources: SATA 59

TERRELL, JOHN UPTON
Birthdate: 12/9/1900
Birthplace: Chicago, IL
Deathdate: 12/1/1988
Information Available in These Sources: ABYP 2, ABYP 3, SATA 60

TERRIS, SUSAN (DUBINSKY)
Birthdate: 5/6/1937
Birthplace: St. Louis, MO
Information Available in These Sources: ABYP 4, JBA 5, SATA 3

TERRY, LUTHER L(EONIDAS)
Birthdate: 9/15/1911
Birthplace: Red Level, AL
Deathdate: 3/29/1985
Information Available in These Sources: SATA 11, SATA 42

TERRY, WALTER
Birthdate: 5/14/1913
Birthplace: Brooklyn, NY
Deathdate: 10/5/1982
Information Available in These Sources: ABYP 2, ABYP 3, SATA 14

TERZIAN, JAMES P.
Birthdate: 10/12/1915
Birthplace: Adana, Turkey
Information Available in These Sources: ABYP 4, SATA 14

TESTER, SYLVIA ROOT
Birthdate: 10/6/1939
Information Available in These Sources: SATA 37

TETHER, CYNTHIA GRAHAM
(Graham Tether)
Birthdate: 9/14/1950
Birthplace: White Plains, NY
Information Available in These Sources: SATA 36, SATA 46

TETHER, GRAHAM
See Tether, Cynthia Graham

THACHER, EDITH
See Hurd, Edith Thacher

THACHER, MARY MCGRATH
Birthdate: 12/20/1933
Birthplace: New York, NY
Information Available in These Sources: SATA 9

THALER, MICHAEL C.
(Mike Thaler)
Birthdate: 1936
Birthplace: Los Angeles, CA
Information Available in These Sources: SATA 47, SATA 56

THALER, MIKE
See Thaler, Michael C.

THAMER, KATIE
Birthdate: 3/27/1955
Birthplace: Los Angeles, CA
Information Available in These Sources: SATA 42

THAMES, C. H.
See Marlowe, Stephen

THANE, ADELE
See Thane, Lillian Adele

THANE, ELSWYTH
Birthdate: 5/16/1900
Birthplace: Burlington, IA
Information Available in These Sources: SATA 32

THANE, LILLIAN ADELE
(Adele Thane)
Birthdate: 4/5/1904
Birthplace: Worcester, MA
Information Available in These Sources: ABYP 4

THARP, LOUISE HALL
Birthdate: 6/19/1898
Birthplace: Oneonta, NY
Information Available in These Sources: ABYP 2, ABYP 3, MJA, SATA 3

THAYER, ERNEST LAWRENCE
(Phin)
Birthdate: 8/14/1863
Birthplace: Lawrence, MA
Deathdate: 8/21/1940
Information Available in These Sources: ABYP 2, ABYP 3, SATA 60

THAYER, JANE
See Woolley, Catherine

THAYER, MARJORIE
Information Available in These Sources: SATA 37

THAYER, PETER
See Wyler, Rose

THEISS, LEWIS EDWIN
Birthdate: 7/29/1878
Birthplace: Birmingham (Derby), CT
Deathdate: 5/22/1963
Information Available in These Sources: ABYP 2, ABYP 3

THEROUX, PAUL
Birthdate: 4/10/1941
Birthplace: Medford, MA
Information Available in These Sources: SATA 44

THIEDA, SHIRLEY ANN
Birthdate: 5/31/1943
Birthplace: IL
Information Available in These Sources: SATA 13

THIRY, JOAN (MARIE)
Birthdate: 10/27/1926
Birthplace: Chicago, IL
Information Available in These Sources: SATA 45

THOBURN, TINA
Information Available in These Sources: ABYP 4

THOLLANDER, EARL (GUSTAVE)
Birthdate: 4/13/1922
Birthplace: Kingsburg, CA
Information Available in These Sources: IBYP 1, IBYP 2, ICB 3, SATA 22

THOMAS, ALLISON
See Fleischer, Lenore

THOMAS, ANDREA
See Hill, Margaret (Ohler)

THOMAS, ART(HUR LAWRENCE)
Birthdate: 7/8/1952
Birthplace: Cleveland, OH
Information Available in These Sources: SATA 48

THOMAS, BENJAMIN PLATT
Birthdate: 2/22/1902
Birthplace: Pemberton, NJ
Deathdate: 11/29/1956
Information Available in These Sources: ABYP 2, ABYP 3

THOMAS, DAWN C.
Information Available in These Sources: BAI

THOMAS, ESTELLE WEBB
Birthdate: 1/11/1899
Birthplace: Woodruff, AZ
Information Available in These Sources: SATA 26

THOMAS, GLEN
Birthplace: Sterling, IL
Information Available in These Sources: IBYP 1, IBYP 2

THOMAS, H. C.
See Keating, Lawrence A(lfred)

THOMAS, IANTHE
Birthdate: 1951
Information Available in These Sources: SATA 42

THOMAS, J. F.
See Fleming, Thomas J(ames)

THOMAS, JANE RESH
Birthdate: 8/15/1936
Birthplace: Kalamazoo, MI
Information Available in These Sources: SATA 38

THOMAS, JOYCE CAROL
Birthdate: 5/25/1938
Birthplace: Ponca City, OK
Information Available in These Sources: BAI, SATA 40

THOMAS, LOWELL (JACKSON)
Birthdate: 4/6/1892
Birthplace: Woodington, OH
Deathdate: 8/29/1981
Information Available in These Sources: ABYP 2, ABYP 3, JBA 1

THOMAS, LOWELL (JACKSON), JR.
Birthdate: 10/6/1923
Birthplace: London, England
Information Available in These Sources: ABYP 2, ABYP 3, SATA 15

THOMAS, PATRICIA J(ACK)
Birthdate: 1/26/1934
Birthplace: Sandy Lake, PA
Information Available in These Sources: ABYP 4, SATA 51

THOMAS, RUTH (H.)
Information Available in These Sources: ABYP 2, ABYP 3

THOMAS, VICTORIA
See DeWeese, Thomas Eugene

THOMPSON, BLANCHE JENNINGS
Birthdate: 3/16/1887
Birthplace: Genesco, NY
Information Available in These Sources: ABYP 4, BABP

THOMPSON, DAVID H(UGH)
Birthplace: New Haven, CT
Information Available in These Sources: SATA 17

THOMPSON, DONNIS (STARK)
Birthdate: 9/28/1928
Birthplace: Stockton, IL
Information Available in These Sources: ABYP 4

THOMPSON, EILEEN
See Panowski, Eileen Thompson

THOMPSON, ERNEST EVAN SETON
See Seton, Ernest (Evan) Thompson

THOMPSON, GEORGE SELDEN
(George Selden)
Birthdate: 5/14/1929
Birthplace: Hartford, CT
Information Available in These Sources: ABYP 2, ABYP 3, DACF, JBA 4, MBMP, SATA 4, TCCW 1, TCCW 2, TCCW 3

THOMPSON, HARLAN H.
(Stephen Holt)
Birthdate: 12/25/1894
Birthplace: Brewster, KS
Information Available in These Sources: ABYP 1, ABYP 3, SATA 10, SATA 53, SVC 2, SVC 3

THOMPSON, HILDEGARD (STEERSTEDTER)
Birthdate: 1/13/1901
Birthplace: De Pauw, IN
Information Available in These Sources: ABYP 2, ABYP 3

THOMPSON, JULIAN F(RANCIS)
Birthdate: 11/16/1927
Birthplace: New York, NY
Information Available in These Sources: SATA 40, SATA 55

THOMPSON, KAY
Birthdate: 11/9/1912 or 11/9/1913
Birthplace: St. Louis, MO
Information Available in These Sources: JBA 4, SATA 16

THOMPSON, MARY (WOLFE)
Birthdate: 12/7/1886
Birthplace: Winsted, CT
Information Available in These Sources: ABYP 2, ABYP 3

THOMPSON, MOZELLE
Birthplace: Pittsburgh, PA
Information Available in These Sources: IBYP 1, IBYP 2

THOMPSON, RUTH PLUMLY
Birthdate: 7/27/1891
Birthplace: Philadelphia, PA
Deathdate: 4/6/1976
Information Available in These Sources: DLB 22, WCL

THOMPSON, STITH
Birthdate: 3/7/1885
Birthplace: Bloomfield, KY
Deathdate: 1/10/1976
Information Available in These Sources: SATA 20, SATA 57

THOMPSON, VIVIAN L(AUBACH)
Birthdate: 1911
Birthplace: Jersey City, NJ
Information Available in These Sources: ABYP 2, ABYP 3, SATA 3

THOMSON, ARLINE K.
Birthdate: 9/12/1912
Birthplace: Lawrence, MA
Information Available in These Sources: IBYP 2, ICB 2

THOMSON, PEGGY (BEBIE)
Birthdate: 11/6/1922
Birthplace: St. Louis, MO
Information Available in These Sources: JBA 6, SATA 31

THOMSON, PETER
Birthdate: 2/27/1913
Birthplace: Iloilo, Philippines
Information Available in These Sources: ABYP 2, ABYP 3

THORN, JOHN
(Sanford W. Jones)
Birthdate: 4/17/1947
Birthplace: Stuttgart, Germany
Information Available in These Sources: SATA 59

THORNDYKE, HELEN LOUISE
See Adams, Harriet S(tratemeyer) and Stratemeyer, Edward L.

THORNE, DIANA
Birthdate: 10/7/1894 or 10/7/1895
Birthplace: Winnipeg, Manitoba, Canada
Information Available in These Sources: IBYP 2, ICB 1, 2

THORNE, IAN
See May, Julian

THORNE-THOMSEN, GUDRUN
Birthdate: 1873
Birthplace: Norway
Deathdate: 1956
Information Available in These Sources: JBA 1, JBA 2

THORNTON, W. B.
See Burgess, Thornton W(aldo)

THORPE, J. K.
See Nathanson, Laura Walther

THRASHER, CRYSTAL (FAYE)
Birthdate: 12/5/1921
Birthplace: Oolitic, IN
Information Available in These Sources: JBA 6, SATA 27

THROCKMORTON, PETER
Birthdate: 7/30/1928
Birthplace: NY
Information Available in These Sources: ABYP 2, ABYP 3

THRONEBURG, JAMES
Birthplace: Maiden, NC
Information Available in These Sources: ABYP 2, ABYP 3

THUM, GLADYS
Birthdate: 11/9/1920
Birthplace: St. Louis, MO
Information Available in These Sources: SATA 26

THUM, MARCELLA
Birthdate: 1924
Birthplace: St. Louis, MO
Information Available in These Sources: ABYP 4, DACF, SATA 3, SATA 28

THUNDERCLOUD, KATHERINE
See Witt, Shirley Hill

THURBER, JAMES (GROVER)
Birthdate: 12/8/1894
Birthplace: Columbus, OH
Deathdate: 11/2/1961
Information Available in These Sources: ABYP 1, ABYP 3, DLB 22, MJA, SATA 13, TCCW 1, TCCW 2, TCCW 3

THURMAN, JUDITH
Birthdate: 10/28/1946
Birthplace: New York, NY
Information Available in These Sources: JBA 6, SATA 33

TIBBETS, ALBERT B.
Birthdate: 12/9/1888
Birthplace: Hastings, NE
Information Available in These Sources: ABYP 4

TICHENOR, TOM
Birthdate: 2/10/1923
Birthplace: Decatur, AL
Information Available in These Sources: ABYP 4, SATA 14

TICHY, WILLIAM
Birthdate: 1/17/1924
Birthplace: Timisoura, Romania
Information Available in These Sources: SATA 31

TIEGREEN, ALAN F.
Birthdate: 7/6/1935
Birthplace: Boise, ID
Information Available in These Sources: JBA 5, SATA 36

TIETJENS, EUNICE HAMMOND
Birthdate: 7/29/1884
Birthplace: Chicago, IL
Deathdate: 9/6/1944
Information Available in These Sources: JBA 1

TILTON, MADONNA ELAINE
(Rafael Tilton)
Birthdate: 10/4/1929
Birthplace: Laurin, MT
Information Available in These Sources: SATA 41

TILTON, RAFAEL
See Tilton, Madonna Elaine

TIMMINS, WILLIAM F(REDERICK)
Birthplace: Chicago, IL
Information Available in These Sources: SATA 10

TINER, JOHN HUDSON
Birthdate: 10/8/1944
Birthplace: Pocahontas, AR
Information Available in These Sources: SATA 32

TINKELMAN, MURRAY
Birthdate: 4/2/1933
Birthplace: Brooklyn, NY
Information Available in These Sources: SATA 12

TINKLE, JULIEN LON
(Lon Tinkle)
Birthdate: 3/20/1906
Birthplace: Dallas, TX
Deathdate: 1/11/1980
Information Available in These Sources: SATA 36

TINKLE, LON
See Tinkle, Julien Lon

TIPPETT, JAMES S(TERLING)
Birthdate: 9/7/1885
Birthplace: Memphis, MO
Deathdate: 2/20/1958
Information Available in These Sources: SVC 2, SVC 3

TITHERINGTON, JEANNE
Birthdate: 5/23/1951
Birthplace: New York, NY
Information Available in These Sources: JBA 6

TITLER, DALE MILTON
Birthdate: 8/25/1926
Birthplace: Altoona, PA
Information Available in These Sources: ABYP 4, SATA 28, SATA 35

TITUS, EVE
(Nancy Lord)
Birthdate: 7/16/1922
Birthplace: New York, NY
Information Available in These Sources: ABYP 2, ABYP 3, JBA 3, SATA 2 TCCW 1, TCCW 2, TCCW 3

TOBIAS, TOBI
Birthdate: 9/12/1938
Birthplace: New York, NY
Information Available in These Sources: SATA 5

TODARO, JOHN
Information Available in These Sources: ABYP 2, ABYP 3

TODD, ANNE OPHELIA
See Dowden, Anne Ophelia (Todd)

TODD, BARBARA K(EITH)
Birthdate: 9/11/1917
Birthplace: Durango, CO
Information Available in These Sources: SATA 10

TODD, MARY FIDELIS
Birthplace: Detroit, MI
Information Available in These Sources: ABYP 1, ABYP 3

TODD, RUTHVEN
Birthdate: 6/14/1914
Birthplace: Edinburgh, Scotland
Information Available in These Sources: ABYP 1, ABYP 3, MJA

TOLAN, STEPHANIE S.
Birthdate: 10/25/1942
Birthplace: Canton, OH
Information Available in These Sources: JBA 6, SATA 38

TOLAND, JOHN (WILLARD)
Birthdate: 6/29/1912
Birthplace: La Crosse, WI
Information Available in These Sources: SATA 38

TOLFORD, JOSHUA
Birthdate: 5/22/1909
Birthplace: Thorp, WI
Information Available in These Sources: IBYP 1, IBYP 2, ICB 2

TOLLES, MARTHA
Birthdate: 9/7/1921
Birthplace: Oklahoma City, OK
Information Available in These Sources: SATA 8

TOLLIVER, RUBY C(HANGOS)
Birthdate: 5/29/1922
Birthplace: Fort Worth, TX
Information Available in These Sources: SATA 41, SATA 55

TOMERLIN, JOHN
Birthdate: 1930
Birthplace: Los Angeles, CA
Information Available in These Sources: ABYP 4

TOMES, MARGOT (LADD)
Birthdate: 8/10/1917
Birthplace: Yonkers, NY
Information Available in These Sources: IBYP 1, IBYP 2, ICB 3, ICB 4, JBA 5, SATA 27, SATA 36

TOMKINS, TOM JASPER
See Batey, Tom

TOMPERT, ANN
Birthdate: 1/11/1918
Birthplace: Detroit, MI
Information Available in These Sources: JBA 6, SATA 14

TOMPKINS, JANE
Birthdate: 1898
Information Available in These Sources: ABYP 1, ABYP 3

TOMPKINS, WALKER ALLISON
Birthdate: 7/10/1909
Birthplace: Prosser, WA
Information Available in These Sources: ABYP 1, ABYP 3

TONER, RAYMOND JOHN
Birthdate: 6/8/1908
Birthplace: Chicago, IL
Information Available in These Sources: SATA 10

TOOKE, LOUISE MATHEWS
(Louise Mathews)
Birthdate: 6/15/1950
Birthplace: New York, NY
Information Available in These Sources: SATA 38

TOOTHAKER, ROY EUGENE
Birthdate: 7/30/1928
Birthplace: Van Buren, AR
Information Available in These Sources: SATA 18

TOOZE, RUTH (ANDERSON)
Birthdate: 6/29/1892
Birthplace: Chicago, IL
Deathdate: 6/15/1972
Information Available in These Sources: ABYP 1, ABYP 3, SATA 4

TOR, REGINA
See Shekerjian, Regina Tor

TORBERT, FLOYD JAMES
Birthdate: 2/7/1922
Birthplace: Jacksonville, FL
Information Available in These Sources: SATA 22

TORGERSEN, DON ARTHUR
Birthdate: 9/27/1934
Birthplace: Chicago, IL
Information Available in These Sources: SATA 41, SATA 55

TORREY, HELEN
Birthdate: 2/19/1901
Birthplace: Cambridge, MA
Information Available in These Sources: IBYP 2, ICB 2

TORREY, MARJORIE
Birthdate: 1899
Birthplace: New York, NY
Information Available in These Sources: IBYP 2, ICB 2, MJA

TOSCHIK, LARRY
Birthdate: 7/17/1922
Birthplace: Milwaukee, WI
Information Available in These Sources: IBYP 2, ICB 2

TOTO, JOE
Birthplace: Brooklyn, NY
Information Available in These Sources: IBYP 2

TOTTLE, JOHN
Information Available in These Sources: ABYP 1, ABYP 3

TOUSEY, SANFORD
See Tousey, Thomas Sanford

TOUSEY, THOMAS SANFORD
(Sanford Tousey)
Birthplace: Clay Center, KS
Information Available in These Sources: ABYP 1, ABYP 3, JBA 2

TOUSTER, IRWIN
Birthdate: 1921
Information Available in These Sources: ABYP 4

TOWNE, MARY
See Spelman, Mary

TOWNSEND, LEE
Birthdate: 8/7/1895
Birthplace: Wyoming, IL
Deathdate: 1/21/1965
Information Available in These Sources: IBYP 2, ICB 2

TOWNSEND, RICHARD F.
Information Available in These Sources: IBYP 2

TOWNSEND, THOMAS L.
(Tammie Lee, Tom Townsend)
Birthdate: 1/6/1944
Birthplace: Waukegan, IL
Information Available in These Sources: SATA 59

TOWNSEND, TOM
See Townsend, Thomas L.

TOYE, CLIVE
Birthdate: 1933
Information Available in These Sources: SATA 30

TRACHSEL, MYRTLE JAMISON
(Jane Jamison)
Birthplace: Gower, MO
Information Available in These Sources: ABYP 1, ABYP 3

TRADER VIC
See Bergeron, Victor (Jules, Jr.)

TRAHEY, JANE
(Baba Erlanger)
Birthdate: 11/19/1923
Birthplace: Chicago, IL
Information Available in These Sources: SATA 36

TRAPP, MARIA (AUGUSTA) VON
Birthdate: 1/26/1905
Birthplace: Vienna, Austria
Information Available in These Sources: SATA 16

TRAVELLER BIRD
See Tsisghwanai, Traveller Bird

TREADWAY, RUBY PEEPLES
Birthplace: MS
Information Available in These Sources: ABYP 4

TREAT, LAWRENCE
Birthdate: 12/21/1903
Birthplace: New York, NY
Information Available in These Sources: SATA 59

TREAT, ROGER L.
Birthdate: 1905
Deathdate: 1969
Information Available in These Sources: ABYP 1, ABYP 3

TREGASKIS, RICHARD (WILLIAM)
Birthdate: 11/28/1916
Birthplace: Elizabeth, NJ
Deathdate: 8/15/1973
Information Available in These Sources: ABYP 1, ABYP 3, SATA 3, SATA 26

TREICHLER, JESSIE C(AMBRON)
Birthdate, 1906?
Deathdate: 7/11/1972
Information Available in These Sources: ABYP 1, ABYP 3

TRELEASE, ALLEN W(ILLIAM)
Birthdate: 1/31/1928
Birthplace: Boulder, CO
Information Available in These Sources: ABYP 4

TRELL, MAX
Birthdate: 9/6/1900
Birthplace: New York, NY
Information Available in These Sources: SATA 14

TREMAIN, RUTHVEN
Birthdate: 6/13/1922
Birthplace: New York, NY
Information Available in These Sources: SATA 17

TRENT, ROBBIE
Birthdate: 2/15/1894
Birthplace: Wolf Creek, KY
Information Available in These Sources: ABYP 1, ABYP 3, SATA 26

TRENT, TIMOTHY
See Malmberg, Carl

TRESS, ARTHUR
See Pinkwater, Daniel Manus

TRESSELT, ALVIN (R.)
Birthdate: 9/30/1916
Birthplace: Passaic, NJ
Information Available in These Sources: ABYP 1, ABYP 3, BABP, MJA, SATA 7, TCCW 1, TCCW 2, TCCW 3

TREVINO, ELIZABETH B(ORTON) DE
See Borton, Elizabeth

TREVOR, ELLESTON
(Mansell Black, Trevor Burgess, Roger Fitzalan, Adam Hall, Simon Rattray, Warwick Scott, Caesar Smith)
Birthdate: 2/17/1920
Birthplace: England
Information Available in These Sources: SATA 28

TRIMBLE, JOE
Birthplace: Brooklyn, NY
Information Available in These Sources: ABYP 1, ABYP 3

TRIPP, ELEANOR B(ALDWIN)
Birthdate: 5/27/1936
Birthplace: Boston, MA
Information Available in These Sources: SATA 4

TRIPP, PAUL
Birthdate: 2/20/1916 or 2/20/1911
Birthplace: New York, NY
Information Available in These Sources: ABYP 4, SATA 8

TRIPP, WALLACE (WHITNEY)
Birthdate: 6/26/1940
Birthplace: Boston, MA
Information Available in These Sources: IBYP 2, ICB 4, JBA 5, SATA 31

TRIVELPIECE, LAUREL
(Hannah K. Marks)
Birthdate: 1/18/1926
Birthplace: Curtis, NE
Information Available in These Sources: SATA 46, SATA 56

TRIVETT, DAPHNE (HARWOOD)
Birthdate: 7/7/1940
Birthplace: Boston, MA
Information Available in These Sources: SATA 22

TROST, LUCILLE WOOD
Birthdate: 11/4/1938
Birthplace: Candor, NY
Information Available in These Sources: SATA 12

TROTTER, GRACE V(IOLET)
(Nancy Paschal)
Birthdate: 11/23/1900
Birthplace: Dallas, TX
Information Available in These Sources: ABYP 1, ABYP 3, SATA 10

TROWBRIDGE, LESLIE W(ALTER)
Birthdate: 5/21/1920
Birthplace: Curtiss, WI
Information Available in These Sources: ABYP 4

TROY, HUGH
Birthdate: 4/28/1906
Birthplace: Ithaca, NY
Deathdate: 7/7/1964
Information Available in These Sources: IBYP 2, ICB 1, ICB 2, ICB 3

TRUDEAU, G(ARRETSON) B(EEKMAN)
(Garry B. Trudeau)
Birthdate: 1948
Birthplace: New York, NY
Information Available in These Sources: SATA 35

TRUDEAU, GARRY B.
See Trudeau, G(arretson) B(eekman)

TRUESDELL, SUE
See Truesdell, Susan G.

TRUESDELL, SUSAN G.
(Sue Truesdell)
Information Available in These Sources: SATA 45

TRUMBULL, JOHN
Birthdate: 6/6/1756
Birthplace: Lebanon, CT
Deathdate: 11/10/1843
Information Available in These Sources: IBYP 1

TSISGHWANAI, TRAVELLER BIRD
(Traveller Bird)
Birthdate: 1930
Birthplace: Eastern Cherokee Reservation, NC
Information Available in These Sources: ABYP 4

TUBBY, I. M.
See Kraus, Robert

TUCKER, CAROLINE
See Nolan, Jeannette Covert

TUCKER, ERNEST EDWARD
Birthdate: 11/18/1916
Birthplace: Chicago, IL
Deathdate: 1/26/1969
Information Available in These Sources: ABYP 1, ABYP 3

TUDOR, BETHANY
Information Available in These Sources: ABYP 2, ABYP 3

TUDOR, TASHA
(Starling Burgess)
Birthdate: 8/28/1915
Birthplace: Boston, MA
Information Available in These Sources: ABYP 1, ABYP 3, ICB 1, ICB 2, ICB 3, ICB 4, JBA 2, SATA 20, TCCW 1

TUFTS, ANNE
Birthplace: Boston, MA
Information Available in These Sources: ABYP 1, ABYP 3

TUFTS, GEORGIA
Information Available in These Sources: ABYP 1, ABYP 3

TUNIS, EDWIN (BURDETT)
Birthdate: 12/8/1897
Birthplace: Cold Spring Harbor, NY
Deathdate: 8/7/1973 or 8/9/1973
Information Available in These Sources: ABYP 2, ABYP 3, ICB 2, ICB 3, ICB 4, MJA, SATA 1, SATA 24, SATA 28

TUNIS, JOHN R(OBERTS)
Birthdate: 12/7/1889
Birthplace: Boston, MA
Deathdate: 2/4/1975
Information Available in These Sources: AICB, ABYP 1, ABYP 3, DACF, DLB 22, MJA, SATA 30, SATA 37 TCCW 1, TCCW 2, TCCW 3

TURKLE, BRINTON (CASSADY)
Birthdate: 8/15/1915
Birthplace: Alliance, OH
Information Available in These Sources: BABP, IBYP 1, IBYP 2, ICB 3, ICB 4, JBA 3, SATA 2, TCCW 1, TCCW 2

TURLINGTON, BAYLY
Birthdate: 9/14/1919
Birthplace: Norfolk, VA
Deathdate: 11/??/1977
Information Available in These Sources: SATA 5, SATA 52

TURNBULL, AGNES SLIGH
Birthdate: 10/14/1888
Birthplace: New Alexandria, PA
Deathdate: 1/31/1982
Information Available in These Sources: ABYP 1, ABYP 3, SATA 14

TURNER, ALICE K.
Birthdate: 5/29/1940
Birthplace: China
Information Available in These Sources: SATA 10

TURNER, ANN W(ARREN)
Birthdate: 12/10/1945
Birthplace: Northampton, MA
Information Available in These Sources: JBA 6, SATA 14

TURNER, ELOISE FAIN
Birthdate: 7/11/1906
Birthplace: Shepherd, TX
Information Available in These Sources: ABYP 2, ABYP 3

TURNER, GERRY ALAIN
Information Available in These Sources: ABYP 4

TURNER, JOSIE
See Crawford, Phyllis

TURNER, NANCY BYRD
Birthdate: 7/29/1880
Birthplace: Boydton, VA
Information Available in These Sources: SVC 2, SVC 3

TURNER, SHEILA R.
See Seed, Sheila Turner

TURNGREN, ANNETTE
(A. T. Hopkins)
Birthdate, 1902?
Birthplace: Montrose, MN
Deathdate: 5/14/1980
Information Available in These Sources: ABYP 1, ABYP 3, MJA, SATA 3, SATA 23

TURNGREN, ELLEN
Birthplace: Montrose, MN
Deathdate: 7/??/1964
Information Available in These Sources: ABYP 1, ABYP 3, SATA 3

TUSAN, STAN
Birthdate: 8/6/1936
Birthplace: Fresno, CA
Information Available in These Sources: SATA 22

TUSIANI, JOSEPH
Birthdate: 1/14/1924
Birthplace: Foggia, Italy
Information Available in These Sources: ABYP 2, ABYP 3, SATA 45

TUTT, KAY CUNNINGHAM
Information Available in These Sources: ABYP 2, ABYP 3

TWAIN, MARK
(Samuel Langhorne Clemens)
Birthdate: 11/30/1835
Birthplace: Florida, MO
Deathdate: 4/21/1910
Information Available in These Sources: ABYP 1, ABYP 2, ABYP 3, JBA 1 SVC 2, SVC 3, TCCW 1, TCCW 3, WC, WCL, YABC

TWETON, D. JEROME
Birthdate: 5/8/1933
Birthplace: Grand Forks, ND
Information Available in These Sources: SATA 48

TWORKOV, JACK
Birthdate: 8/15/1900
Birthplace: Biala, Poland
Deathdate: 9/4/1982
Information Available in These Sources: SATA 31, SATA 47

TYLER, ANNE
Birthdate: 10/25/1941
Birthplace: Minneapolis, MN
Information Available in These Sources: SATA 7

TYLL, AL
Birthdate: 1932
Birthplace: Troy, NY
Information Available in These Sources: ABYP 4

U

UBELL, EARL
Birthdate: 6/21/1926
Birthplace: Brooklyn, NY
Information Available in These Sources: SATA 4

UCHIDA, YOSHIKO
Birthdate: 11/24/1921
Birthplace: Alameda, CA
Information Available in These Sources: ABYP 1, ABYP 3, MJA, SATA 1, SATA 53, TCCW 1, TCCW 2, TCCW 3

UDRY, JANICE (MAY)
Birthdate: 6/14/1928
Birthplace: Jacksonville, IL
Information Available in These Sources: ABYP 1, ABYP 3, BABP, JBA 3, MJA, SATA 4, TCCW 1, TCCW 2

UGAMA, LEROI
See Smith, LeRoi

ULAM, S(TANISLAW) M(ARCIN)
Birthdate: 4/13/1909
Birthplace: Lvov, Poland
Deathdate: 5/13/1984
Information Available in These Sources: SATA 51

ULLMAN, JAMES RAMSEY
Birthdate: 11/24/1907
Birthplace: New York, NY
Deathdate: 6/20/1971
Information Available in These Sources: ABYP 1, ABYP 3, JBA 4, SATA 7

ULM, ROBERT
Birthdate: 4/30/1934
Birthplace: Chicago, IL
Deathdate: 10/17/1977
Information Available in These Sources: SATA 17

ULMER, LOUISE
Birthdate: 1/11/1943
Birthplace: Fayetteville, AR
Information Available in These Sources: SATA 53

ULREICH, NURA WOODSON
(Nura)
Birthdate: 12/, /1899
Birthplace: Kansas City, MO
Deathdate: 10/25/1950
Information Available in These Sources: IBYP 2, ICB 1, ICB 2

ULRICH, HOMER
Birthdate: 3/27/1906
Birthplace: Chicago, IL
Information Available in These Sources: ABYP 1, ABYP 3

UNADA
See Gliewe, Unada (Grace)

UNCLE GUS
See Rey, H(ans) A(ugusto)

UNCLE NOAH
See Brooks, Noah

UNCLE RAY
See Coffman, Ramon Peyton

UNCLE SHELBY
See Silverstein, Shel(by)

UNDERHILL, ALICE MERTIE (WATERMAN)
Birthdate: 9/14/1900
Birthplace: Watertown, SD
Deathdate: 9/6/1971
Information Available in These Sources: SATA 10

UNDERWOOD, BETTY
See Underwood, Mary Betty Anderson

UNDERWOOD, MARY BETTY ANDERSON
Birthdate: 7/4/1921
Birthplace: Rockford, IL
Information Available in These Sources: ABYP 4, DACF

UNKELBACH, KURT
Birthdate: 11/21/1913
Birthplace: New Britain, CT
Information Available in These Sources: ABYP 4, SATA 4

UNRAU, RUTH
Birthdate: 2/28/1922
Birthplace: Kouts, IN
Information Available in These Sources: SATA 9

UNTERECKER, JOHN
Birthdate: 12/14/1922
Birthplace: Buffalo, NY
Information Available in These Sources: ABYP 2, ABYP 3

UNTERMEYER, LOUIS
Birthdate: 10/1/1885
Birthplace: New York, NY
Deathdate: 12/18/1977
Information Available in These Sources: ABYP 2, ABYP 3, JBA 1, SATA 2 SATA 26, SATA 37

UNWIN, NORA S(PICER)
Birthdate: 2/22/1907
Birthplace: Surbiton, Surrey, England
Deathdate: 1/5/1982
Information Available in These Sources: ABYP 1, ABYP 3, ICB 2, ICB 3, ICB 4, SATA 3, SATA 49

UPDIKE, JOHN (HOYER)
Birthdate: 3/18/1932
Birthplace: Shillington, PA
Information Available in These Sources: ABYP 1, ABYP 3

UPHAM, ELIZABETH NORINE
See McWebb, Elizabeth Upham

UPINGTON, MARION
Birthplace: OR
Information Available in These Sources: ABYP 2, ABYP 3

UPTON, BERTHA (HUDSON)
Birthdate: 1849
Deathdate: 1912
Information Available in These Sources: TCCW 1, TCCW 2, TCCW 3

URIS, LEON (MARCUS)
Birthdate: 8/3/1924
Birthplace: Baltimore, MD
Information Available in These Sources: SATA 49

URMSTON, MARY
Birthdate: 8/27/1891
Birthplace: Tullahoma, TN
Information Available in These Sources: MJA

URQUHART, ESPHYR SLOBODKINA
See Slobodkina, Esphyr

USCHOLD, MAUD E.
Birthplace: IL
Information Available in These Sources: SVC 2, SVC 3

USHER, MARGO SCEGGE
See McHargue, Georgess

UTZ, LOIS (MARIE)
Birthdate: 1/4/1932
Birthplace: Paterson, NJ
Deathdate: 11/12/1986
Information Available in These Sources: SATA 5, SATA 50

V

VAETH, J(OSEPH) GORDON
Birthdate: 2/12/1921
Birthplace: New York, NY
Information Available in These Sources: SATA 17

VALEN, FELICE HOLMAN
See Holman, Felice

VALEN, NANINE
Birthdate: 11/7/1950
Birthplace: New York, NY
Information Available in These Sources: SATA 21

VALENS, EVANS G., JR.
Birthdate: 4/17/1920
Birthplace: State College, PA
Information Available in These Sources: ABYP 1, ABYP 3, SATA 1

VALLI
See VandeBovencamp, Valli

VANALLSBURG, CHRIS
Birthdate: 6/18/1949
Birthplace: Grand Rapids, MI
Information Available in These Sources: DLB 61, JBA 5, SATA 37, SATA 53, TCCW 3

VANCE, ELEANOR GRAHAM
Birthdate: 10/16/1908
Birthplace: Pittsburgh, PA
Information Available in These Sources: SATA 11

VANCE, MARGUERITE
Birthdate: 11/27/1889
Birthplace: Chicago, IL
Deathdate: 5/22/1965
Information Available in These Sources: ABYP 1, ABYP 3, MJA, SATA 29

VANCOEVERING, JACK
See VanCoevering, Jan Adrian

VANCOEVERING, JAN ADRIAN
(Jack VanCoevering)
Birthdate: 3/12/1900
Birthplace: Herwynen, Netherlands
Information Available in These Sources: ABYP 1, ABYP 3

VANDEBOVENCAMP, VALLI
(Valli)
Birthplace: Bucharest, Romania
Information Available in These Sources: IBYP 1, IBYP 2

VANDENBURG, MARY LOU
Birthdate: 12/18/1943
Birthplace: Passaic, NJ
Information Available in These Sources: SATA 17

VANDER ELS, BETTY
Birthdate: 10/3/1936
Birthplace: Chengtu, China
Information Available in These Sources: JBA 6

VANDERBOOM, MAE M.
Birthplace: SD
Information Available in These Sources: ABYP 2, ABYP 3, SATA 14

VANDERHAAS, HENRIETTA
Birthplace: The Hague, Netherlands
Information Available in These Sources: ABYP 2, ABYP 3

VANDERVEER, JUDY
Birthdate: 10/17/1912
Birthplace: Oil City, PA
Deathdate: 11/22/1982
Information Available in These Sources: SATA 4, SATA 33

VANDOREN, MARGARET
Birthdate: 10/21/1917
Birthplace: New York, NY
Information Available in These Sources: ICB 1

VANDUYN, JANET
Birthdate: 9/23/1910
Birthplace: Auburn, NY
Information Available in These Sources: SATA 18

VANDYKE, HENRY JACKSON, JR.
Birthdate: 11/10/1852
Birthplace: Germantown, PA
Deathdate: 4/10/1933
Information Available in These Sources: JBA 1, SVC 2, SVC 3

VANDYNE, EDITH
See Baum, L(yman) Frank

VANEVEREN, JAY
Information Available in These Sources: CICB, ICB 1

VANGELDER, RICHARD G(EORGE)
Birthdate: 12/17/1928
Birthplace: New York, NY
Information Available in These Sources: ABYP 4

VANHORN, GRACE
Information Available in These Sources: ABYP 1, ABYP 3

VANHORN, WILLIAM
Birthdate: 2/15/1939
Birthplace: Oakland, CA
Information Available in These Sources: SATA 43

VANLEEUWEN, JEAN
Birthdate: 12/26/1937
Birthplace: Glen Ridge, NJ
Information Available in These Sources: JBA 5, SATA 6

VANLHIN, ERIK
See del Rey, Lester

VANLOON, HENDRIK WILLEM
Birthdate: 1/14/1882
Birthplace: Rotterdam, Holland
Deathdate: 3/11/1944
Information Available in These Sources: ABYP 1, ABYP 3, JBA 1, SATA 18

VANORDEN, M(ERTON) D(ICK)
Birthdate: 2/24/1921
Birthplace: Austin, TX
Information Available in These Sources: ABYP 4, SATA 4

VANRENSSELAER, ALEXANDER (TAYLOR MASON)
Birthdate: 1892
Deathdate: 8/20/1962
Information Available in These Sources: ABYP 2, ABYP 3, SATA 14

VANRIPER, GUERNSEY, JR.
Birthdate: 7/5/1909
Birthplace: Indianapolis, IN
Information Available in These Sources: ABYP 4, SATA 3

VANSTEENWYK, ELIZABETH ANN
Birthdate: 7/1/1928
Birthplace: Galesburg, IL
Information Available in These Sources: ABYP 4, SATA 34

VANSTOCKUM, HILDA (GERARDA)
Birthdate: 2/9/1908
Birthplace: Rotterdam, Netherlands
Information Available in These Sources: ABYP 1, ABYP 3, DACF, ICB 2, ICB 3, JBA 2, TCCW 2, TCCW 3

VANTUYL, BARBARA
Birthdate: 11/26/1940
Birthplace: Brooklyn, NY
Information Available in These Sources: SATA 11

VANWINKLE, RIP
See Jackson, Helen (Maria Fiske) Hunt

VANWOERKOM, DOROTHY (O'BRIEN)
Birthdate: 6/26/1924
Birthplace: Buffalo, NY
Information Available in These Sources: ABYP 4, JBA 5, SATA 21

VANWORMER, JOE
See VanWormer, Joseph Edward

VANWORMER, JOSEPH EDWARD
(Joe VanWormer)
Birthdate: 6/15/1913
Birthplace: West Plains, MO
Information Available in These Sources: SATA 35

VANZWIENEN, ILSE (CHARLOTTE KOEHN)
(Ilse Koehn)
Birthdate: 8/6/1929
Birthplace: Berlin, Germany
Information Available in These Sources: JBA 5, SATA 28, SATA 34

VARLEY, DIMITRY V.
Birthdate: 2/10/1906
Birthplace: Russia
Information Available in These Sources: SATA 10

VASILIU, MIRCEA
Birthdate: 7/16/1920
Birthplace: Bucharest, Romania
Information Available in These Sources: IBYP 1, IBYP 2, ICB 2, ICB 3, SATA 2

VASS, GEORGE
Birthdate: 3/27/1927
Birthplace: Leipzig, Germany
Information Available in These Sources: SATA 31, SATA 57

VAUGHAN, ANNE
Birthdate: 10/2/1913
Birthplace: Worcester, MA
Information Available in These Sources: IBYP 2, ICB 1, ICB 2

VAUGHAN, CARTER A.
See Gerson, Noel B(ertram)

VAUGHAN, HAROLD CECIL
Birthdate: 10/26/1923
Birthplace: New York, NY
Information Available in These Sources: SATA 14

VAUGHAN, MARCIA
Birthdate: 4/6/1951
Birthplace: Tacoma, WA
Information Available in These Sources: SATA 60

VAUGHAN, SAM(UEL) S.
Birthdate: 8/3/1928
Birthplace: Philadelphia, PA
Information Available in These Sources: SATA 14

VAUGHAN-JACKSON, GENEVIEVE
(Genevieve Vaughan Jackson)
Birthdate: 5/17/1913
Birthplace: London, England
Information Available in These Sources: IBYP 2, ICB 2

VAUGHN, RUTH
Birthdate: 8/31/1935
Birthplace: Wellington, TX
Information Available in These Sources: SATA 14

VAUTIER, GHISLAINE
(Helene Frank)
Birthdate: 12/28/1932
Birthplace: New York, NY
Information Available in These Sources: SATA 53

VAVRA, ROBERT JAMES
Birthdate: 3/9/1935
Birthplace: Los Angeles, CA
Information Available in These Sources: SATA 8

VECSEY, GEORGE
Birthdate: 7/4/1939
Birthplace: Jamaica, Long Island, NY
Information Available in These Sources: SATA 9

VEGLAHN, NANCY (CRARY)
Birthdate: 7/17/1937
Birthplace: Sioux City, IA
Information Available in These Sources: ABYP 2, ABYP 3, SATA 5

VENABLE, ALAN (HUDSON)
Birthdate: 10/26/1944
Birthplace: Pittsburgh, PA
Information Available in These Sources: SATA 8

VENN, ELEANOR
See Jorgensen, Mary Venn

VENN, MARY ELEANOR
See Jorgensen, Mary Venn

VENTURO, BETTY LOU BAKER
See Baker, Betty (Lou)

VEQUIN, CAPINI
See Quinn, Elisabeth

VERMEER, JACKIE
Information Available in These Sources: ABYP 4

VERMES, HAL G.
Information Available in These Sources: ABYP 1, ABYP 3

VERMES, JEAN C(AMPBELL PATTISON)
Birthdate: 11/15/1907 or 11/15/1909
Birthplace: Ottawa, Ontario, Canada
Information Available in These Sources: ABYP 2, ABYP 3

VERNON, ELDA LOUISE A(NDERSON)
(Louise A. Vernon)
Birthdate: 3/6/1914
Birthplace: Coquille, OR
Information Available in These Sources: SATA 14

VERNON, LOUISE A.
See Vernon, Elda Louise A(nderson)

VERNON, ROSEMARY
See Smith, Susan Vernon

VERNOR, D.
See Casewit, Curtis

VERRAL, CHARLES SPAIN
(George L. Eaton)
Birthdate: 11/7/1904
Birthplace: Highfield, Ontario, Canada
Information Available in These Sources: ABYP 1, ABYP 3, SATA 11

VERRONE, ROBERT J.
Birthdate, 1935?
Deathdate: 8/4/1984
Information Available in These Sources: SATA 39

VERSACE, MARIE TERESA
(Tere Rios)
Birthdate: 11/9/1917
Birthplace: Brooklyn, NY
Information Available in These Sources: SATA 2

VESEY, PAUL
See Allen, Samuel (Washington)

VESTAL, HERMAN B.
Information Available in These Sources: IBYP 2

VIC, TRADER
See Bergeron, Victor (Jules, Jr.)

VICKER, ANGUS
See Felsen, Henry Gregor

VICKERY, KATE
See Kennedy, T(eresa) A.

VICTOR, EDWARD
Birthdate: 3/4/1914
Birthplace: Boston, MA
Information Available in These Sources: SATA 3

VICTOR, JOAN BERG
(Joan Berg)
Birthdate: 7/11/1937
Birthplace: Chicago, IL
Information Available in These Sources: IBYP 1, IBYP 2, ICB 3, SATA 30

VIERECK, ELLEN R.
Birthdate: 5/4/1928
Birthplace: Brookline, MA
Information Available in These Sources: ABYP 1, ABYP 3, SATA 14

VIERECK, PHILLIP R.
Birthdate: 6/2/1925
Birthplace: New Bedford, MA
Information Available in These Sources: ABYP 1, ABYP 3, DACF, SATA 3

VIERTEL, JANET
Birthdate: 8/4/1915
Birthplace: Newark, NJ
Information Available in These Sources: SATA 10

VIGNA, JUDITH
Birthdate: 4/27/1936
Birthplace: Gedney, England
Information Available in These Sources: SATA 15

VIGUERS, RUTH HILL
(Ruth A. Hill)
Birthdate: 7/24/1903
Birthplace: Oakland, CA
Deathdate: 2/2/1971
Information Available in These Sources: ABYP 2, ABYP 3, SATA 6

VILLIARD, PAUL
(J. H. DeGros)
Birthdate: 1/16/1910
Birthplace: Spokane, WA
Deathdate: 8/18/1974
Information Available in These Sources: ABYP 4, SATA 20, SATA 51

VINCENT, ERIC DOUGLAS
Birthdate: 6/4/1953
Birthplace: Gainesville, FL
Information Available in These Sources: SATA 40

VINCENT, MARY KEITH
See St. John, Wylly Folk

VINCIGUERRA, FRANCESCA
See Winwar, Frances

VINGE, JOAN D(ENNISON)
Birthdate: 4/2/1948
Birthplace: Baltimore, MD
Information Available in These Sources: SATA 36

VINING, ELIZABETH (JANET) GRAY
See Gray, Elizabeth Janet

VINSON, KATHRYN
Birthdate: 3/23/1911
Birthplace: Cordele, GA
Information Available in These Sources: SATA 21

VINTON, IRIS
Birthdate: 3/3/1905 or 3/3/1906
Birthplace: West Point, MS
Deathdate: 2/6/1988
Information Available in These Sources: ABYP 1, ABYP 3, SATA 24, SATA 55

VIORST, JUDITH (STAHL)
Birthdate: 2/2/1931
Birthplace: Newark, NJ
Information Available in These Sources: ABYP 4, JBA 4, SATA 7, TCCW 1 TCCW 2, TCCW 3

VIP
See Partch, Virgil Franklin II

VITTENGL, MORGAN J(OHN)
Birthdate: 12/2/1928
Birthplace: Wilmington, DE
Information Available in These Sources: ABYP 1, ABYP 3

VLAHOS, OLIVIA
Birthdate: 1/8/1924
Birthplace: Houston, TX
Information Available in These Sources: SATA 31

VLASIC, BOB
See Hirsch, Phil

VO-DINH, MAI
Birthdate: 11/14/1933
Birthplace: Hue, Vietnam
Information Available in These Sources: SATA 16

VOGEL, ILSE-MARGRET
Birthdate: 6/5/1914
Birthplace: Breslau, Germany
Information Available in These Sources: SATA 14

VOGEL, JOHN H(OLLISTER), JR.
Birthdate: 4/16/1950
Birthplace: New York, NY
Information Available in These Sources: SATA 18

VOGEL, RAY
Birthdate: 10/20/1943
Birthplace: Brooklyn, NY
Information Available in These Sources: ABYP 4

VOGT, ESTHER LOEWEN
Birthdate: 11/19/1915
Birthplace: Collinsville, OK
Information Available in These Sources: SATA 14

VOGT, GREGORY
Information Available in These Sources: SATA 45

VOGT, MARIE BOLLINGER
Birthdate: 3/9/1921
Birthplace: Toledo, OH
Information Available in These Sources: SATA 45

VOIGHT, VIRGINIA FRANCES
Birthdate: 3/30/1909
Birthplace: New Britain, CT
Information Available in These Sources: APYP 2, APYP 3, MJA, SATA 8

VOIGT, CYNTHIA
Birthdate: 2/25/1942
Birthplace: Boston, MA
Information Available in These Sources: DACF, JBA 5, SATA 33, SATA 48 TCCW 3

VOJTECH, ANNA
Birthdate: 2/6/1946
Birthplace: Prague, Czechoslovakia
Information Available in These Sources: SATA 42

VONHAGEN, CHRISTINE SHEILDS
Birthdate: 1912
Information Available in These Sources: ABYP 1, ABYP 3

VONHAGEN, VICTOR WOLFGANG
Birthdate: 2/29/1908
Birthplace: St. Louis, MO
Information Available in These Sources: ABYP 2, ABYP 3, SATA 29

VON HIPPEL, URSULA
(Ursula von Hippel)
Birthplace: Germany
Information Available in These Sources: ABYP 1, ABYP 3

VONKLOPP, VAHRAH
See Malvern, Gladys

VONROEDER-BOSTELMANN, ELSE W.
See Bostelmann, Else W. von Roeder

VONSCHMIDT, ERIC
Birthdate: 5/28/1931
Birthplace: Bridgeport, CT
Information Available in These Sources: ABYP 2, ABYP 3, ICB 3, ICB 4, SATA 36, SATA 50

VONSTORCH, ANNE BURNETT MALCOLMSON
See Malcolmson, Anne (Burnett)

VORWALD, ALAN
Information Available in These Sources: ABYP 2, ABYP 3

VOSBURGH, LEONARD (W.)
Birthdate: 9/23/1912
Birthplace: Yonkers, NY
Information Available in These Sources: IBYP 1, IBYP 2, SATA 15

VOUTE, KATHLEEN
Birthdate: 1892
Birthplace: Montclair, NJ
Information Available in These Sources: IBYP 2, ICB 2

VUGTEVEEN, VERNA AARDEMA
See Aardema, Verna (Norberg)

VUONG, LYNETTE (DYER)
Birthdate: 6/20/1938
Birthplace: Owosso, MI
Information Available in These Sources: SATA 60

W

WABBES, MARIA
(Florence)
Information Available in These Sources: IBYP 2

WABER, BERNARD
Birthdate: 9/27/1924
Birthplace: Philadelphia, PA
Information Available in These Sources: ABYP 1, ABYP 3, ICB 3, ICB 4, JBA 3, SATA 40, SATA 47, TCCW 1, TCCW 2, TCCW 3

WACHTER, ORALEE ROBERTS
Birthdate: 4/16/1935
Birthplace: Los Angeles, CA
Information Available in These Sources: SATA 51

WACKER, CHARLES H(ENRY), JR.
Birthdate: 8/19/1925
Birthplace: Newark, NJ
Information Available in These Sources: ABYP 4

WADE, JENNIFER
See Wehen, Joy DeWeese

WADE, THEODORE E., JR.
Birthdate: 6/28/1936
Birthplace: Pueblo, CO
Information Available in These Sources: SATA 37

WADOWSKI-BAK, ALICE
Birthdate: 1936
Birthplace: Buffalo (near), NY
Information Available in These Sources: IBYP 1, IBYP 2

WADSWORTH, WALLACE (CARTER)
Birthdate: 9/19/1894
Birthplace: Odon, IN
Deathdate: 2/9/1933
Information Available in These Sources: SVC 2, SVC 3

WAGENHEIM, KAL
Birthdate: 4/21/1935
Birthplace: Newark, NJ
Information Available in These Sources: SATA 21

WAGNER, FREDERICK (REESE, JR.)
Birthdate: 4/15/1928
Birthplace: Philadelphia, PA
Information Available in These Sources: ABYP 1, ABYP 3

WAGNER, GLENN A.
Birthplace: Buffalo, NY
Information Available in These Sources: ABYP 1, ABYP 3

WAGNER, JANE
Birthdate: 2/26
Birthplace: Morristown, TN
Information Available in These Sources: ABYP 4, DACF, SATA 33

WAGNER, SHARON B.
Birthdate: 12/16/1936
Birthplace: Wallace, ID
Information Available in These Sources: SATA 4

WAGONER, DAVID (RUSSELL)
Birthdate: 6/5/1926
Birthplace: Massillon, OH
Information Available in These Sources: SATA 14

WAHL, JAN (BOYER)
Birthdate: 4/1/1933
Birthplace: Columbus, OH
Information Available in These Sources: ABYP 2, ABYP 3, JBA 3, SATA 2 SATA 34, TCCW 1, TCCW 2, TCCW 3

WAIDE, JAN
Birthdate: 6/7/1952
Birthplace: Wichita Falls, TX
Information Available in These Sources: SATA 29

WAITLEY, DOUGLAS
Birthdate: 11/28/1927
Birthplace: Evanston, IL
Information Available in These Sources: SATA 30

WAKEFIELD, JEAN L.
See Laird, Jean E(louise)

WAKEMAN, MARION FREEMAN
Birthdate: 12/5/1891
Birthplace: Montclair, NJ
Deathdate: 9/22/1953
Information Available in These Sources: IBYP 2, ICB 2

WAKIN, EDWARD
Birthdate: 12/13/1927
Birthplace: Brooklyn, NY
Information Available in These Sources: SATA 37

WALCK, HENRY Z(EIGLER)
Birthdate: 3/30/1908
Birthplace: Greencastle, PA
Deathdate: 12/24/1984
Information Available in These Sources: SATA 40

WALDECK, JO BESSE MCELVEEN
Birthplace: Kingstree, SC
Information Available in These Sources: JBA 2

WALDECK, THEODORE J.
Birthdate: 1894
Birthplace: Brooklyn, NY
Information Available in These Sources: ABYP 2, ABYP 3, JBA 2

WALDEN, AMELIA ELIZABETH
Birthdate: 1/16/1909
Birthplace: New York, NY
Information Available in These Sources: ABYP 1, ABYP 3, MJA, SATA 3

WALDMAN, BRUCE
Birthdate: 11/14/1949
Birthplace: Bronx, NY
Information Available in These Sources: SATA 15

WALDMAN, FRANK
(Joe Webster)
Birthdate: 1919
Birthplace: Chicago, IL
Information Available in These Sources: ABYP 1, ABYP 3

WALDMAN, NEIL
Birthdate: 10/22/1947
Birthplace: Bronx, NY
Information Available in These Sources: SATA 51

WALDRON, ANN WOOD
Birthdate: 12/14/1924
Birthplace: Birmingham, AL
Information Available in These Sources: SATA 16

WALKER, ADDISON MORT
(Mort Walker)
Birthdate: 9/3/1923
Birthplace: El Dorado, KS
Information Available in These Sources: SATA 8

WALKER, ALICE
Birthdate: 2/9/1944
Birthplace: Eatonton, GA
Information Available in These Sources: BAI, SATA 31

WALKER, BARBARA K(ERLIN)
(Beth Kilreon)
Birthdate: 10/13/1921
Birthplace: Ann Arbor, MI
Information Available in These Sources: ABYP 4, SATA 4

WALKER, BARBARA M(UHS)
Birthdate: 1928
Birthplace: Reading, PA
Information Available in These Sources: SATA 57

WALKER, BRAZ
See Walker, James Brazelton

WALKER, CHARLES W.
Birthplace: Hempstead, Long Island, NY
Information Available in These Sources: IBYP 1, IBYP 2

WALKER, DAVID G(ORDON)
Birthdate: 12/16/1926
Birthplace: Glen Ridge, NJ
Information Available in These Sources: SATA 60

WALKER, HOLLY BETH
See Bond, Gladys Baker

WALKER, JAMES BRAZELTON
(Braz Walker)
Birthdate: 5/29/1934
Birthplace: Waco, TX
Deathdate: 3/27/1983
Information Available in These Sources: SATA 45

WALKER, LOU ANN
Birthdate: 12/9/1952
Birthplace: Blackwood County, IN
Information Available in These Sources: SATA 53

WALKER, LOUISE JEAN
Birthdate: 2/10/1891
Birthplace: Jackson, MI
Information Available in These Sources: SATA 35

WALKER, MILDRED
See Schemm, Mildred Walker

WALKER, MORT
See Walker, Addison Mort

WALKER, NEDDA
Birthplace: Canada
Information Available in These Sources: IBYP 1, IBYP 2, ICB 2

WALKER, PAMELA
Birthdate: 4/28/1948
Birthplace: Burlington, IA
Information Available in These Sources: SATA 24

WALKER, SHEL
See Sheldon, Walt(er J.)

WALKER, STEPHEN J.
Birthdate: 5/5/1951
Birthplace: Seattle, WA
Information Available in These Sources: SATA 12

WALKER, STUART (ARMSTRONG)
Birthdate: 3/4/1880
Birthplace: Augusta, KY
Deathdate: 3/13/1941
Information Available in These Sources: TCCW 1, TCCW 2, TCCW 3

WALL, GERTRUDE WALLACE
Information Available in These Sources: ABYP 1, ABYP 3

WALLACE, BARBARA BROOKS
Birthdate: 12/3/1922
Birthplace: Soochow, China
Information Available in These Sources: JBA 6, SATA 4

WALLACE, BEVERLY DOBRIN
Birthdate: 3/16/1921
Birthplace: Chattanooga, TN
Information Available in These Sources: SATA 19

WALLACE, BILL
Birthdate: 1947
Information Available in These Sources: SATA 47

WALLACE, DAISY
See Cuyler, Margery Stuyvesant

WALLACE, DILLON
Birthdate: 6/24/1863
Birthplace: Craigville, NY
Deathdate: 9/29/1939
Information Available in These Sources: JBA 1, JBA 2

WALLACE, JOHN A(DAM)
Birthdate: 8/12/1915
Birthplace: Lansdowne, PA
Information Available in These Sources: ABYP 1, ABYP 3, SATA 3

WALLACE, LEW(IS)
Birthdate: 4/10/1827
Birthplace: Brookville, IN
Deathdate: 2/15/1905
Information Available in These Sources: JBA 1

WALLACE, MAY NICKERSON
Birthdate: 6/11/1902
Birthplace: Willimantic, CT
Information Available in These Sources: ABYP 1, ABYP 3

WALLACE, ROBERT A.
Birthdate: 1/10/1932
Birthplace: Springfield, MO
Information Available in These Sources: SATA 37, SATA 47

WALLACE-BRODEUR, RUTH
Birthdate: 8/25/1941
Birthplace: Springfield, MA
Information Available in These Sources: SATA 41, SATA 51

WALLER, LESLIE
Birthdate: 4/1/1923
Birthplace: Chicago, IL
Information Available in These Sources: ABYP 4, SATA 20

WALLERSTEDT, DON
Information Available in These Sources: IBYP 2

WALLIS, G. MCDONALD
See Campbell, Hope

WALLNER, ALEXANDRA
Birthdate: 2/28/1946
Birthplace: Germany
Information Available in These Sources: SATA 41, SATA 51

WALLNER, JOHN C(HARLES)
Birthdate: 2/3/1945
Birthplace: St. Louis, MO
Information Available in These Sources: ICB 4, JBA 5, SATA 10, SATA 51

WALLOWER, LUCILLE
Birthdate: 7/27/1910
Birthplace: Waynesboro, PA
Information Available in These Sources: ABYP 1, ABYP 3, SATA 11

WALSH, ELLEN STOLL
Birthdate: 9/2/1942
Birthplace: Baltimore, MD
Information Available in These Sources: SATA 49

WALSH, FRANCES (WAGGENER)
Birthplace: Clark County, MO
Information Available in These Sources: ABYP 1, ABYP 3

WALSH, PEGGY ADLER
See Adler, Peggy

WALSH, RICHARD JOHN
Birthdate: 11/20/1886
Birthplace: Lyons, KS
Deathdate: 5/28/1960
Information Available in These Sources: ABYP 1, ABYP 3

WALSH, WILLIAM B(ERTALAN)
Birthdate: 4/26/1920
Birthplace: Brooklyn, NY
Information Available in These Sources: ABYP 4

WALTER, FRANCES
Birthplace: San Diego, CA
Information Available in These Sources: IBYP 2

WALTER, MARION
Information Available in These Sources: ABYP 4

WALTER, MILDRED PITTS
Birthdate: 1922
Birthplace: De Ridder, LA
Information Available in These Sources: ABYP 4, BAI, JBA 6, SATA 45, TCCW 3

WALTERS, AUDREY
Birthdate: 7/10/1929
Birthplace: Philadelphia, PA
Information Available in These Sources: IBYP 1, IBYP 2, SATA 18

WALTERS, HELEN B.
Birthplace: WI
Deathdate: 1/26/1987
Information Available in These Sources: SATA 50

WALTERS, MARGUERITE
Birthplace: Bridgewater, MA
Information Available in These Sources: ABYP 1, ABYP 3

WALTERS, SHELLY
See Sheldon, Walt(er J.)

WALTHER, THOMAS A.
(Tom Walther)
Birthdate: 2/20/1950
Birthplace: Elko, NV
Information Available in These Sources: SATA 31

WALTHER, TOM
See Walther, Thomas A.

WALTNER, ELMA
Birthdate: 11/30/1912
Birthplace: Yankton, SD
Information Available in These Sources: ABYP 1, ABYP 3, SATA 40

WALTNER, WILLARD H.
Birthdate: 9/10/1909
Birthplace: Freeman, SD
Information Available in These Sources: ABYP 1, ABYP 3, SATA 40

WALTON, RICHARD J.
Birthdate: 5/24/1928
Birthplace: Saratoga Springs, NY
Information Available in These Sources: SATA 4

WALTRIP, LELA (KINGSTON)
Birthdate: 2/2/1904
Birthplace: Coleman, TX
Information Available in These Sources: SATA 9

WALTRIP, MILDRED
Birthdate: 10/4/1911
Birthplace: Nebo, KY
Information Available in These Sources: IBYP 1, IBYP 2, SATA 37

WALTRIP, RUFUS (CHARLES)
Birthdate: 9/26/1898
Birthplace: Rosenburg, TX
Information Available in These Sources: SATA 9

WALWORTH, JANE (ARMSTRONG)
Birthplace: Evanston, IL
Information Available in These Sources: IBYP 2

WALWORTH, NANCY ZINSSER
Birthdate: 10/29/1917
Birthplace: New York, NY
Information Available in These Sources: SATA 14

WANGERIN, WALTER, JR.
Birthdate: 2/13/1944
Birthplace: Portland, OR
Information Available in These Sources: SATA 37, SATA 45

WANIEK, MARILYN (NELSON)
Birthdate: 4/26/1946
Birthplace: Cleveland, OH
Information Available in These Sources: SATA 60

WANNAMAKER, BRUCE
See Moncure, Jane Belk

WARBURG, SANDOL STODDARD
(Sandol Stoddard)
Birthdate: 12/16/1927
Birthplace: Birmingham, AL
Information Available in These Sources: ABYP 2, ABYP 3, BABP, JBA 4, SATA 14

WARD, JONAS
See Cox, William R(obert)

WARD, LYND (KENDALL)
Birthdate: 6/26/1905
Birthplace: Chicago, IL
Deathdate: 6/28/1985
Information Available in These Sources: ABYP 1, ABYP 3, AICB, BABP, DLB 22, FLTYP, IBYP 1, IBYP 2 ICB 1, ICB 2, ICB 3, JBA 1, JBA 2, JBA 4, SATA 2, SATA 36 SATA 42, SVC 2, SVC 3

WARD, MARTHA (EADS)
Birthdate: 7/21/1921
Birthplace: Quincy, IL
Information Available in These Sources: SATA 5

WARD, MARY MCNEER
See McNeer, May Yonge

WARD, MELANIE
See Curtis, Richard (Alan)

WARD, NANDA WEEDON
(Nanda Ward Haynes)
Birthdate: 1932
Information Available in These Sources: ABYP 1, ABYP 3

WARD, RALPH T.
Birthdate: 7/18/1927
Birthplace: New York, NY
Information Available in These Sources: ABYP 4

WARE, LEON (VERNON)
Birthdate: 2/21/1909
Birthplace: Plainview, MN
Deathdate: 9/1/1976
Information Available in These Sources: ABYP 1, ABYP 3, DACF, SATA 4

WARNER, EDYTHE RECORDS
Birthdate: 10/26/1916
Birthplace: St. Paul, MN
Information Available in These Sources: ICB 3

WARNER, FRANK A.
See Stratemeyer, Edward L.

WARNER, GERTRUDE CHANDLER
Birthdate: 4/16/1890
Birthplace: Putnam, CT
Deathdate: 8/30/1979
Information Available in These Sources: ABYP 1, ABYP 3, SATA 9

WARNER, LUCILLE SCHULBERG
Birthplace: Mount Vernon, NY
Information Available in These Sources: SATA 30

WARNER, MATT
See Fichter, George S.

WARNER, SUSAN BOGERT
(Elizabeth Wetherell)
Birthdate: 7/11/1819
Birthplace: New York, NY
Deathdate: 3/17/1885
Information Available in These Sources: DLB 42, TCCW 3, WCL, WWCL

WARREN, BETSY
See Warren, Elizabeth Avery

WARREN, BILLY
See Warren, William Stephen

WARREN, CATHY
Information Available in These Sources: SATA 46

WARREN, ELIZABETH
See Supraner, Robyn

WARREN, ELIZABETH AVERY
(Betsy Warren)
Birthdate: 1/27/1916
Birthplace: St. Louis, MO
Information Available in These Sources: SATA 38, SATA 46

WARREN, FRED
Birthdate: 1921
Information Available in These Sources: ABYP 4

WARREN, JOYCE W(ILLIAMS)
Birthdate: 6/16/1935
Birthplace: Springfield, MA
Information Available in These Sources: SATA 18

WARREN, MARY PHRANER
Birthdate: 3/27/1929
Birthplace: New York, NY
Information Available in These Sources: ABYP 4, SATA 10

WARREN, ROBERT PENN
Birthdate: 4/24/1905
Birthplace: Guthrie, KY
Information Available in These Sources: SATA 46

WARREN, WILLIAM STEPHEN
(Billy Warren)
Birthdate: 9/6/1882
Birthplace: Carrollton, AR
Deathdate: 10/18/1968
Information Available in These Sources: ABYP 1, ABYP 3, SATA 9

WARRICK, PATRICIA SCOTT
Birthdate: 2/6/1925
Birthplace: La Grange, IN
Information Available in These Sources: SATA 35

WARRINER, JOHN
Birthdate: 1907
Deathdate: 7/29/1987
Information Available in These Sources: SATA 53

WARSH
See Warshaw, Jerry

WARSHAW, JERRY
(Warsh)
Birthdate: 6/12/1929
Birthplace: Chicago, IL
Information Available in These Sources: SATA 30

WARSHOFSKY, FRED
Birthdate: 2/14/1931
Birthplace: Brooklyn, NY
Information Available in These Sources: SATA 24

WARSHOFSKY, ISAAC
See Singer, Isaac (Bashevis)

WARTSKI, MAUREEN (ANN CRANE)
(M. A. Crane)
Birthdate: 1/25/1940
Birthplace: Ashiya, Japan
Information Available in These Sources: DACF, SATA 37, SATA 50

WASHBURN, BRADFORD
See Washburn, Henry Bradford, Jr.

WASHBURN, HENRY BRADFORD, JR.
(Bradford Washburn)
Birthdate: 6/7/1910
Birthplace: Cambridge, MA
Information Available in These Sources: SATA 38

WASHBURNE, HELUIZ CHANDLER
Birthdate: 1/25/1892
Birthplace: Cincinnati, OH
Deathdate: 9/23/1970
Information Available in These Sources: ABYP 1, ABYP 3, SATA 10, SATA 26

WASHINGTON, BOOKER T(ALIAFERRO)
(Booker Taliaferro)
Birthdate: 4/5/1858
Birthplace: Hale's Ford, Franklin Cty, VA
Deathdate: 11/14/1915
Information Available in These Sources: SATA 28

WASSERSUG, JOSEPH D(AVID)
(Adam Bradford, M.D.)
Birthdate: 10/19/1912
Birthplace: Boston, MA
Information Available in These Sources: ABYP 1, ABYP 3

WATANABE, SHIGEO
Birthdate: 3/20/1928
Birthplace: Shizuoka, Japan
Information Available in These Sources: JBA 6

WATERS, JOHN F(REDERICK)
Birthdate: 10/27/1930
Birthplace: Somerville, MA
Information Available in These Sources: ABYP 4, SATA 4

WATSON, ALDREN A(ULD)
Birthdate: 5/10/1917
Birthplace: Brooklyn, NY
Information Available in These Sources: IBYP 1, IBYP 2, ICB 1, ICB 2, ICB 3, ICB 4, SATA 36, SATA 42

WATSON, B.S.
See Teitelbaum, Michael

WATSON, CLYDE (DINGMAN)
Birthdate: 7/25/1947
Birthplace: New York, NY
Information Available in These Sources: ABYP 4, JBA 4, SATA 5, TCCW 1 TCCW 2, TCCW 3

WATSON, EMILY
Birthplace: Cleveland, OH
Information Available in These Sources: ABYP 1, ABYP 3

WATSON, HELEN ORR
Birthdate: 12/1/1892
Birthplace: Pipestone, MN
Deathdate: 2/1/1978
Information Available in These Sources: ABYP 1, ABYP 3, SATA 24

WATSON, HOWARD N.
Information Available in These Sources: IBYP 1, IBYP 2

WATSON, JANE WERNER
(A(nnie) N(orth) Bedford, Monica Hill, W.K. Jasner, Elsa Ruth Nast, Elsa Jane Werner, Jane Werner)
Birthdate: 7/11/1915
Birthplace: Fond du Lac, WI
Information Available in These Sources: ABYP 4, SATA 3, SATA 54

WATSON, NANCY DINGMAN
Birthplace: Paterson, NJ
Information Available in These Sources: ABYP 4, SATA 32

WATSON, PAULINE
(Pola)
Birthdate: 7/24/1925
Birthplace: New Iberia, LA
Information Available in These Sources: SATA 14

WATSON, SALLY (LOU)
Birthdate: 1/28/1924
Birthplace: Seattle, WA
Information Available in These Sources: ABYP 4, DACF, JBA 4, SATA 3

WATSON, SARA RUTH
Birthdate: 1/7/1907 or 1/7/1909
Birthplace: Cleveland, OH
Information Available in These Sources: ABYP 1, ABYP 3

WATSON, WENDY (MCLEOD)
(Wendy McLeod Watson Harrah)
Birthdate: 7/7/1942
Birthplace: Paterson, NJ
Information Available in These Sources: IBYP 1, IBYP 2, ICB 4, JBA 4, SATA 5

WATTS, FRANKLIN (MOWRY)
Birthdate: 6/11/1904
Birthplace: Sioux City, IA
Deathdate: 5/21/1978
Information Available in These Sources: SATA 21, SATA 46

WATTS, JAMES K(ENNEDY) M(OFFITT)
Birthdate: 3/20/1955
Birthplace: San Francisco, CA
Information Available in These Sources: SATA 59

WATTS, MABEL PIZZEY
(Patricia Lynn)
Birthdate: 5/20/1906
Birthplace: London, England
Information Available in These Sources: ABYP 2, ABYP 3, SATA 11

WAUGH, CAROL-LYNN ROSSEL
(C. C. Rossel-Waugh)
Birthdate: 1/5/1947
Birthplace: Staten Island, NY
Information Available in These Sources: SATA 41

WAUGH, DOROTHY
Birthdate: 9/23/1896
Birthplace: Burlington, VT
Information Available in These Sources: ICB 1, ICB 2, SATA 11

WAYLAND, PATRICK
See O'Connor, Richard

WAYNE, JOSEPH
See Overholser, Wayne D.

WAYNE, KYRA PETROVSKAYA
(Kyra Petrovskaya)
Birthdate: 12/31/1918
Birthplace: Crimea, USSR
Information Available in These Sources: SATA 8

WAYNE, RICHARD
See Decker, Duane (Walter)

WEALES, GERALD (CLIFFORD)
Birthdate: 6/12/1925
Birthplace: Connersville, IN
Information Available in These Sources: SATA 11

WEART, EDITH LUCIE
Birthdate: 1898 or 1897
Information Available in These Sources: ABYP 1, ABYP 3

WEARY, OGDRED
See Gorey, Edward St. John

WEAVER, JACK
Birthdate: 1/31/1925
Birthplace: Philadelphia, PA
Information Available in These Sources: IBYP 2, ICB 2

WEAVER, JOHN D(OWNING)
Birthdate: 2/4/1912
Birthplace: Washington, DC
Information Available in These Sources: ABYP 1, ABYP 3

WEAVER, JOHN L.
Birthdate: 5/5/1949
Birthplace: Waco, TX
Information Available in These Sources: SATA 42

WEAVER, ROBERT (GLENN)
Birthdate: 1920
Information Available in These Sources: IBYP 2

WEAVER, WARD
See Mason, F(rancis) van Wyck

WEBB, CHRISTOPHER
See Wibberley, Leonard (Patrick O'Connor)

WEBB, FRANCOISE
Birthplace: Brussels, Belgium
Information Available in These Sources: IBYP 2

WEBB, JEAN FRANCIS (III)
(Roswell Brown, Ethel Hamill, Roberta Morrison)
Birthdate: 10/1/1910
Birthplace: White Plains, NY
Information Available in These Sources: SATA 35

WEBB, ROBERT N.
Birthdate: 1906
Birthplace: Dayton, OH
Information Available in These Sources: ABYP 2, ABYP 3

WEBB, SHARON
Birthdate: 2/29/1936
Birthplace: Tampa, FL
Information Available in These Sources: SATA 41

WEBBER, IRMA E(LEANOR SCHMIDT)
Birthdate: 8/16/1904
Birthplace: San Diego, CA
Information Available in These Sources: IBYP 2, ICB 1, ICB 2, SATA 14

WEBER, DEVORA
Birthdate: 3/21/1935
Birthplace: Cleveland, OH
Information Available in These Sources: SATA 58

WEBER, LENORA MATTINGLY
Birthdate: 10/1/1895
Birthplace: Dawn, MO
Deathdate: 1/29/1971
Information Available in These Sources: ABYP 2, ABYP 3, MJA, SATA 2, SATA 26

WEBER, WALTER ALOIS
Birthdate: 5/23/1906
Birthplace: Chicago, IL
Information Available in These Sources: ICB 1

WEBER, WILLIAM JOHN
Birthdate: 9/8/1927
Birthplace: Cleveland, OH
Information Available in These Sources: SATA 14

WEBSTER, ALICE (JEAN CHANDLER)
(Jean Webster)
Birthdate: 7/24/1876
Birthplace: Fredonia, NY
Deathdate: 6/11/1916
Information Available in These Sources: JBA 1, SATA 17, TCCW 2, TCCW 3

WEBSTER, DAVID
Birthdate: 4/14/1930
Birthplace: Philadelphia, PA
Information Available in These Sources: ABYP 4, SATA 11

WEBSTER, FRANK V.
See Stratemeyer, Edward L.

WEBSTER, GARY
See Garrison, Webb B(lack)

WEBSTER, JEAN
See Webster, Alice (Jane Chandler)

WEBSTER, JOE
See Waldman, Frank

WEBSTER, NOAH
Birthdate: 10/16/1758
Birthplace: Hartford, CT
Deathdate: 5/28/1843
Information Available in These Sources: DLB 42

WECHSLER, HERMAN
Birthdate: 8/21/1904
Birthplace: New York, NY
Deathdate: 1/13/1976
Information Available in These Sources: SATA 20

WECHTERR, NELL WISE
Birthdate: 8/6/1913
Birthplace: Stumpy Point, NC
Information Available in These Sources: SATA 60

WEDDLE, ETHEL H(ARSHBARGER)
Birthdate: 9/6/1897
Birthplace: Girard, IL
Information Available in These Sources: ABYP 2, ABYP 3, SATA 11

WEEMS, MASON LOCKE
Birthdate: 10/11/1759
Birthplace: Anne Arundel County, MD
Deathdate: 5/23/1825
Information Available in These Sources: DLB 42

WEES, FRANCES SHELLEY
(Frances Shelley)
Birthdate: 4/29/1902
Birthplace: Gresham, OR
Information Available in These Sources: ABYP 2, ABYP 3, SATA 58

WEGEN, RON(ALD)
(Sebastian Fleuret)
Birthplace: NJ
Information Available in These Sources: SATA 44

WEHEN, JOY DEWEESE
(Jennifer Wade)
Birthdate: 1936 or 1926
Birthplace: Penang, Malaya
Information Available in These Sources: ABYP 2, ABYP 3

WEIDHORN, MANFRED
Birthdate: 10/10/1931
Birthplace: Vienna, Austria
Information Available in These Sources: SATA 60

WEIHS, ERIKA
Birthdate: 11/4/1917
Birthplace: Vienna, Austria
Information Available in These Sources: SATA 15

WEIK, MARY HAYS
Birthdate, 1898?
Birthplace: Greencastle, IN
Deathdate: 12/25/1979
Information Available in These Sources: ABYP 4, MBMP, SATA 3, SATA 23

WEIL, ANN YEZNER
Birthdate: 8/31/1908
Birthplace: Harrisburg, IL
Information Available in These Sources: SATA 9

WEIL, LISL
Birthdate: 6/22/1910
Birthplace: Vienna, Austria
Information Available in These Sources: IBYP 1, IBYP 2, ICB 2, ICB 3, ICB 4, SATA 7

WEILERSTEIN, SADIE ROSE
Birthdate: 7/28/1894
Birthplace: Rochester, NY
Information Available in These Sources: SATA 3

WEINBERG, LARRY
See Weinberg, Lawrence (E.)

WEINBERG, LAWRENCE (E.)
(Larry Weinberg)
Information Available in These Sources: SATA 48

WEINER, SANDRA (SMITH)
Birthdate: 9/14/1922
Birthplace: Poland
Information Available in These Sources: ABYP 4, SATA 14

WEINGARTEN, VIOLET (BROWN)
Birthdate: 2/23/1915
Birthplace: San Francisco, CA
Deathdate: 7/17/1976
Information Available in These Sources: SATA 3, SATA 27

WEINGARTNER, CHARLES
Birthdate: 5/30/1922
Birthplace: New York, NY
Information Available in These Sources: SATA 5

WEINGAST, DAVID E(LLIOTT)
Birthdate: 5/5/1912
Birthplace: Newark, NJ
Information Available in These Sources: ABYP 2, ABYP 3

WEINHEIMER, GEORGE
Information Available in These Sources: IBYP 1, IBYP 2

WEINSTOCK, HERBERT
Birthdate: 11/16/1905
Birthplace: Milwaukee, WI
Deathdate: 10/21/1971
Information Available in These Sources: ABYP 2, ABYP 3

WEIR, LA VADA
Birthdate: 11/23/1918
Birthplace: Kansas City, MO
Information Available in These Sources: SATA 2

WEIS, MARGARET (EDITH)
(Margaret Baldwin)
Birthdate: 3/16/1948
Birthplace: Independence, MO
Information Available in These Sources: SATA 38

WEISBERG, JOSEPH S(IMPSON)
Birthdate: 6/7/1937
Birthplace: Jersey City, NJ
Information Available in These Sources: ABYP 4

WEISBERGER, BERNARD A(LLEN)
Birthdate: 8/15/1922
Birthplace: Hudson, NY
Information Available in These Sources: SATA 21

WEISER, MARJORIE P(HILLIS) K(ATZ)
(Marjorie P. Katz)
Birthdate: 2/2/1934
Birthplace: New York, NY
Information Available in These Sources: ABYP 4, SATA 33

WEISGARD, LEONARD (JOSEPH)
(Adam Green)
Birthdate: 12/13/1916
Birthplace: New Haven, CT
Information Available in These Sources: ABYP 1, ABYP 3, BABP, IBYP 1, IBYP 2, ICB 1, ICB 2, ICB 3, ICB 4, JBA 2, SATA 2, SATA 30

WEISS, ADELLE
Birthdate: 7/30/1920
Birthplace: New York, NY
Information Available in These Sources: SATA 18

WEISS, ANN E(DWARDS)
Birthdate: 3/21/1943
Birthplace: Newton, MA
Information Available in These Sources: JBA 6, SATA 30

WEISS, CAROL
Information Available in These Sources: ABYP 4

WEISS, DAVID ANSEL
Information Available in These Sources: ABYP 4

WEISS, EDNA
See Barth, Edna (Smith)

WEISS, ELLEN
Birthdate: 12/7/1953
Birthplace: New York, NY
Information Available in These Sources: SATA 44

WEISS, EMIL
Birthdate: 8/14/1896
Birthplace: Olmutz, Moravia, Austria
Deathdate: 1/6/1965
Information Available in These Sources: IBYP 2, ICB 3

WEISS, HARVEY
Birthdate: 4/10/1922
Birthplace: New York, NY
Information Available in These Sources: ABYP 2, ABYP 3, ICB 2, ICB 3, ICB 4, JBA 3, SATA 1, SATA 27

WEISS, LEATIE
Birthdate: 5/8/1928
Birthplace: New York, NY
Information Available in These Sources: SATA 50

WEISS, MALCOLM E.
Birthdate: 1/22/1928
Birthplace: Philadelphia, PA
Information Available in These Sources: SATA 3

WEISS, NICKI
Birthdate: 1/25/1954
Birthplace: New York, NY
Information Available in These Sources: JBA 6, SATA 33

WEISS, PETER
Birthdate: 1945
Information Available in These Sources: ABYP 4

WEISS, RENEE KAROL
Birthdate: 9/11/1923
Birthplace: Allentown, PA
Information Available in These Sources: ABYP 4, SATA 5

WELBER, ROBERT
Birthplace: Paterson, NJ
Information Available in These Sources: ABYP 4, SATA 26

WELCH, CHARLES SCOTT
See Smith, LeRoi

WELCH, D'ALTE ALDRIDGE
Birthdate: 1907
Deathdate: 1/4/1970
Information Available in These Sources: SATA 27

WELCH, JEAN-LOUISE
See Kempton, Jean Welch

WELCH, MARTHA McKEEN
Birthdate: 5/17/1914
Birthplace: Easton, PA
Information Available in These Sources: SATA 45

WELDON, MARTIN
Birthdate: 1913
Birthplace: Brooklyn, NY
Information Available in These Sources: ABYP 2, ABYP 3

WELLER, GEORGE (ANTHONY)
(Michael Wharf)
Birthdate: 7/13/1907
Birthplace: Boston, MA
Information Available in These Sources: SATA 31

WELLES, WINIFRED
Birthdate: 1/26/1893
Birthplace: Norwichtown, CT
Deathdate: 11/22/1939
Information Available in These Sources: SATA 27, SVC 2, SVC 3

WELLMAN, ALICE
Birthdate: 5/11/1900
Birthplace: Salt Lake City, UT
Deathdate: 3/12/1984
Information Available in These Sources: SATA 36, SATA 51

WELLMAN, MANLY WADE
(Gans T. Field)
Birthdate: 5/21/1903 or 5/21/1905
Birthplace: Kamundongo, Angola, Portugese West Africa
Deathdate: 4/5/1986
Information Available in These Sources: ABYP 2, ABYP 3, MJA, SATA 6, SATA 47

WELLMAN, PAUL I(SELIN)
Birthdate: 10/14/1898
Birthplace: Enid, OK
Deathdate: 9/16/1966
Information Available in These Sources: ABYP 2, ABYP 3, SATA 3

WELLS, HELEN
See Campbell, Hope

WELLS, HELEN (FRANCES WEINSTOCK)
(Francine Lewis)
Birthdate: 3/29/1910
Birthplace: Danville, IL
Deathdate: 2/10/1986
Information Available in These Sources: ABYP 2, ABYP 3, SATA 2, SATA 49

WELLS, J. WELLINGTON
See DeCamp, L(yon) Sprague

WELLS, JUNE
See Swinford, Betty (June Wells)

WELLS, MAIE LOUNSBURY
Birthplace: Fergus Falls, MN
Information Available in These Sources: ABYP 2, ABYP 3

WELLS, PETER
Birthdate: 1/8/1912
Birthplace: Port Clinton, OH
Information Available in These Sources: ICB 1

WELLS, RHEA
Birthdate: 9/24/1891
Birthplace: Jonesboro, TN
Information Available in These Sources: ICB 1, JBA 1, JBA 2

WELLS, ROBERT L.
Birthdate: 1913
Birthplace: IL
Information Available in These Sources: ABYP 1, ABYP 3

WELLS, ROSEMARY
Birthdate: 1/29/1943
Birthplace: New York, NY
Information Available in These Sources: DACF, IBYP 2, ICB 4, JBA 4, SATA 18, TCCW 2, TCCW 3

WELS, BYRON G(ERALD)
Birthdate: 4/20/1924
Birthplace: New York, NY
Information Available in These Sources: SATA 9

WELSH, MARY FLYNN
(Mary Flynn)
Birthdate, 1910?
Birthplace: County Longford, Ireland
Deathdate: 2/13/1984
Information Available in These Sources: SATA 38

WELTNER, LINDA R(IVERLY)
Birthdate: 10/13/1938
Birthplace: Worcester, MA
Information Available in These Sources: SATA 38

WELTY, S(USAN) F(ULTON)
Birthdate: 1/20/1905
Birthplace: Fairfield, IA
Information Available in These Sources: SATA 9

WENDE, PHILIP
Birthdate: 1/9/1939
Birthplace: Ogdensburg, NY
Information Available in These Sources: IBYP 2

WENDELIN, RUDOLPH
Birthdate: 2/27/1910
Birthplace: Herndon, KS
Information Available in These Sources: SATA 23

WENDT, LLOYD
Birthdate: 5/16/1908
Birthplace: Spencer, SD
Information Available in These Sources: ABYP 4

WENNERSTROM, GENIA KATHERINE
(Genia)
Birthdate: 8/9/1930
Birthplace: New York, NY
Information Available in These Sources: IBYP 1, IBYP 2, ICB 3

WENNING, ELISABETH
(Elisabeth Wenning Davidson)
Information Available in These Sources: ABYP 1, ABYP 3

WERNECKE, HERBERT HENRY
Birthdate: 7/24/1895
Birthplace: Newton, WI
Information Available in These Sources: ABYP 2, ABYP 3

WERNER, ELSA JANE
See Watson, Jane Werner

WERNER, HERMA
(Eve Cowen, Eve Gladstone, Roxanne Jarrett, Joma Pinner)
Birthdate: 11/12/1926
Birthplace: New York, NY
Information Available in These Sources: SATA 41, SATA 47

WERNER, JANE
See Watson, Jane Werner

WERNER, K.
See Casewit, Curtis

WERNER, PAT
Information Available in These Sources: ABYP 2, ABYP 3

WERNER, VIVIAN
(Stephanie Jackson, John Lester)
Birthdate: 9/5/1921
Birthplace: Bellingham, WA
Information Available in These Sources: ABYP 4

WERSBA, BARBARA
Birthdate: 8/19/1932
Birthplace: Chicago, IL
Information Available in These Sources: ABYP 2, ABYP 3, DACF, JBA 3, SATA 1, SATA 58, TCCW 1, TCCW 2, TCCW 3

WERSTEIN, IRVING
Birthdate: 5/22/1914
Birthplace: Brooklyn, NY
Deathdate: 4/7/1971
Information Available in These Sources: ABYP 1, ABYP 3, JBA 4, SATA 14

WERTH, KURT
Birthdate: 9/21/1896
Birthplace: Leipzig, Germany
Information Available in These Sources: IBYP 1, IBYP 2, ICB 2, ICB 3, ICB 4, MJA, SATA 20

WEST, ANNA
Birthdate: 4/5/1938
Birthplace: Crete, IL
Information Available in These Sources: SATA 40

WEST, BARBARA
See Price, Olive (M.)

WEST, BETTY
(Betty Morgan Bowen)
Birthdate: 8/9/1921
Birthplace: Chicago, IL
Information Available in These Sources: ABYP 2, ABYP 3, SATA 11

WEST, C. P.
See Wodehouse, P(elham) G(renville)

WEST, EMILY G(OVAN)
(Emmy Payne, Emmy West)
Birthdate: 1919
Information Available in These Sources: ABYP 2, ABYP 3, SATA 38

WEST, EMMY
See West, Emily G(ovan)

WEST, JAMES
See Withers, Carl A.

WEST, JERRY
See Svenson, Andrew E.

WEST, JESSAMYN
See West, Mary Jessamyn

WEST, MARY JESSAMYN
(Jessamyn West)
Birthdate: 7/18/1902
Birthplace: North Vernon, IN
Deathdate: 2/23/1984
Information Available in These Sources: SATA 37

WEST, WALTER RICHARD
Birthdate: 9/8/1912
Birthplace: Darlington, OK
Information Available in These Sources: IBYP 2, ICB 2

WEST, WARD
See Borland, Harold Glen

WESTCOTT, NADINE BERN
Birthdate: 6/24/1949
Information Available in These Sources: JBA 6

WESTERBERG, CHRISTINE
Birthdate: 9/26/1950
Birthplace: Glen Cove, NY
Information Available in These Sources: SATA 29

WESTERVELT, VIRGINIA (VEEDER)
Birthdate: 9/19/1914
Birthplace: Schenectady, NY
Information Available in These Sources: SATA 10

WESTHEIMER, DAVID
(Z. Z. Smith)
Birthdate: 4/11/1917
Birthplace: Houston, TX
Information Available in These Sources: SATA 14

WESTMAN, PAUL (WENDELL)
Birthdate: 10/27/1956
Birthplace: Minneapolis, MN
Information Available in These Sources: SATA 39

WESTON, ALLEN
See Hogarth, Grace (Weston Allen) and Norton, Alice Mary

WESTON, JOHN (HARRISON)
Birthdate: 5/17/1932
Birthplace: Prescott, AZ
Information Available in These Sources: SATA 21

WESTON, MARTHA
Birthdate: 1/16/1947
Birthplace: Asheville, NC
Information Available in These Sources: SATA 53

WESTPHAL, ARNOLD CARL
(The Children's Shepherd)
Birthdate: 6/23/1897
Birthplace: Michigan City, IN
Information Available in These Sources: SATA 57

WETHERELL, ELIZABETH
See Warner, Susan Bogert

WETTERER, MARGARET K.
Information Available in These Sources: ABYP 4

WEXLER, JEROME (LEROY)
(Roy Delmar)
Birthdate: 2/6/1923
Birthplace: New York, NY
Information Available in These Sources: SATA 14

WEYGANT, SISTER NOEMI
Birthplace: Ada, MN
Information Available in These Sources: MBMP

WHARF, MICHAEL
See Weller, George (Anthony)

WHARTON, EDITH
Birthdate: 1/24/1862
Birthplace: New York, NY
Deathdate: 8/11/1937
Information Available in These Sources: JBA 1

WHEATLEY, ARABELLE
Birthdate: 3/28/1921
Birthplace: Washington, PA
Information Available in These Sources: SATA 16

WHEELER, BUCK
See Wheeler, Sessions S(amuel)

WHEELER, CAPTAIN
See Ellis, Edward S(ylvester)

WHEELER, CINDY
Birthdate: 5/17/1955
Birthplace: Montgomery, AL
Information Available in These Sources: SATA 40, SATA 49

WHEELER, JANET D.
See Stratemeyer, Edward L.

WHEELER, OPAL
Birthdate: 10/??/1898
Birthplace: Superior, WI
Information Available in These Sources: MJA, SATA 23

WHEELER, POST
Birthdate: 8/6/1869
Birthplace: Oswego, NY
Deathdate: 12/23/1956
Information Available in These Sources: ABYP 1, ABYP 3

WHEELER, SESSIONS S(AMUEL)
(Buck Wheeler)
Birthdate: 4/27/1911
Birthplace: Fernley (near), NV
Information Available in These Sources: ABYP 2, ABYP 3

WHEELING, LYNN
Birthplace: PA
Information Available in These Sources: ABYP 2, ABYP 3

WHEELWRIGHT, JERE HUNGERFORD, JR.
Birthdate: 9/8/1905
Birthplace: Baltimore, MD
Deathdate: 1/21/1961
Information Available in These Sources: ABYP 2, ABYP 3

WHELAN, ELIZABETH M(URPHY)
Birthdate: 12/4/1943
Birthplace: New York, NY
Information Available in These Sources: SATA 14

WHITAKER, GEORGE O.
Birthplace: Valdosta, GA
Information Available in These Sources: ABYP 2, ABYP 3

WHITCOMB, JON
Birthdate: 6/9/1906
Birthplace: Weatherford, OK
Information Available in These Sources: SATA 10

WHITE, ANNE (WILSON) HITCHCOCK
Birthdate: 2/22/1902
Birthplace: St. Louis, MO
Deathdate: 6/30/1970
Information Available in These Sources: JBA 4, SATA 33

WHITE, ANNE TERRY
Birthdate: 2/19/1896
Birthplace: Ukraine, Russia
Information Available in These Sources: ABYP 1, ABYP 3, MJA, SATA 2

WHITE, BESSIE (FEISTINER)
Birthdate, 1892?
Birthplace: Buchach, Austria-Hungary
Deathdate: 12/30/1986
Information Available in These Sources: ABYP 1, ABYP 3, SATA 50

WHITE, DALE
See Place, Marian T(empleton)

WHITE, DAVID OMAR
Birthdate: 5/28/1927
Birthplace: Appleton, WI
Information Available in These Sources: IBYP 1, IBYP 2

WHITE, DORI
Birthdate: 7/13/1919
Birthplace: Portland, OR
Information Available in These Sources: SATA 10

WHITE, E(LWYN) B(ROOKS)
Birthdate: 7/11/1899
Birthplace: Mount Vernon, NY
Deathdate: 10/1/1985 or 9/30/1985
Information Available in These Sources: ABYP 1, ABYP 3, AICB, DACF, DLB 22, MBMP, MJA, SATA 2, SATA 29, SATA 44, TCCW 1, TCCW 2, WCL

WHITE, EDGAR B.
Birthdate: 1947
Birthplace: British West Indies
Information Available in These Sources: BAI

WHITE, EDWARD LUCAS
Birthdate: 5/18/1866
Birthplace: Bergen, NJ
Deathdate: 3/30/1934
Information Available in These Sources: JBA 1

WHITE, ELIZA ORNE
Birthdate: 8/2/1856
Birthplace: Keene, NH
Deathdate: 1/23/1947
Information Available in These Sources: JBA 1, JBA 2, TCCW 1, TCCW 2, TCCW 3, YABC

WHITE, FLORENCE M(EIMAN)
Birthdate: 12/26/1910
Birthplace: New York, NY
Information Available in These Sources: SATA 14

WHITE, LAURENCE B(ARTON), JR.
Birthdate: 9/21/1935
Birthplace: Norwood, MA
Information Available in These Sources: SATA 10

WHITE, NANCY BEAN
Birthdate: 9/8/1922
Birthplace: Hartford, CT
Information Available in These Sources: ABYP 2, ABYP 3

WHITE, PAULINE (ARNOLD)
Information Available in These Sources: ABYP 1, ABYP 3

WHITE, PERCIVAL
Birthdate: 1/8/1887
Birthplace: Winchendon, MA
Deathdate: 6/4/1970
Information Available in These Sources: ABYP 1, ABYP 3

WHITE, PURA BELPRE
See Belpre, Pura

WHITE, RAMY ALLISON
See Stratemeyer, Edward L.

WHITE, ROBB
Birthdate: 6/20/1909
Birthplace: Baquiro, Luzon, Philippines
Information Available in These Sources: ABYP 1, ABYP 3, DACF, JBA 2, SATA 1

WHITE, RUTH C.
(Ruth White Miller)
Birthdate: 3/15/1942
Birthplace: Whitewood, VA
Information Available in These Sources: SATA 39

WHITE, STEWART EDWARD
Birthdate: 3/12/1873
Birthplace: Grand Rapids, MI
Deathdate: 9/18/1946
Information Available in These Sources: JBA 1

WHITE, TIMOTHY (THOMAS ANTHONY)
Birthdate: 1/25/1952
Birthplace: Paterson, NJ
Information Available in These Sources: SATA 60

WHITE, WILLIAM, JR.
(Spinossimus)
Birthdate: 6/8/1934
Birthplace: Philadelphia, PA
Information Available in These Sources: SATA 16

WHITEBEAD, BAIDA
Birthplace: OK
Information Available in These Sources: IBYP 2

WHITEHEAD, DON(ALD) F.
Birthdate: 4/8/1908
Birthplace: Inman, VA
Information Available in These Sources: SATA 4

WHITEHEAD, RUTH
Birthplace: TX
Information Available in These Sources: ABYP 4

WHITEHOUSE, ARCH
See Whitehouse, Arthur George

WHITEHOUSE, ARTHUR GEORGE
(Arch Whitehouse)
Birthdate: 12/11/1895
Birthplace: Northampton, England
Deathdate: 11/15/1979
Information Available in These Sources: ABYP 2, ABYP 3, SATA 14

WHITEHOUSE, ELIZABETH S(COTT)
Birthdate: 7/15/1893
Birthplace: Springfield, MA
Deathdate: 10/31/1968
Information Available in These Sources: SATA 35

WHITEHOUSE, JEANNE
(Jeanne Whitehouse Peterson)
Birthdate: 5/8/1939
Birthplace: Walla Walla, WA
Information Available in These Sources: SATA 29

WHITINGER, R. D.
See Place, Marian T(empleton)

WHITMAN, WALT(ER)
Birthdate: 5/31/1819
Birthplace: West Hills, Long Island, NY
Deathdate: 3/26/1892
Information Available in These Sources: SATA 20, SVC 2, SVC 3

WHITNEY, ALEX(ANDRA)
Birthdate: 10/8/1922
Birthplace: Flushing, NY
Information Available in These Sources: SATA 14

WHITNEY, DAVID C(HARLES)
Birthdate: 3/8/1921
Birthplace: Salina, KS
Information Available in These Sources: SATA 29, SATA 48

WHITNEY, ELINOR
Birthdate: 12/27/1889
Birthplace: Dorcester, MA
Information Available in These Sources: JBA 1, JBA 2

WHITNEY, LEON FRADLEY
Birthdate: 1894
Information Available in These Sources: ABYP 1, ABYP 3

WHITNEY, PHYLLIS A(YAME)
Birthdate: 9/9/1903
Birthplace: Yokohama, Japan
Information Available in These Sources: ABYP 1, ABYP 3, DACF, JBA 2, SATA 1, SATA 30, TCCW 1, TCCW 2, TCCW 3

WHITNEY, THOMAS P(ORTER)
Birthdate: 1/26/1917
Birthplace: Toledo, OH
Information Available in These Sources: ABYP 4, SATA 25

WHITTIER, JOHN GREENLEAF
Birthdate: 12/17/1807
Birthplace: Haverhill, MA
Deathdate: 9/7/1892
Information Available in These Sources: SVC 2, SVC 3

WHITTLESEY, SUSAN
Birthdate: 10/25/1938
Birthplace: Pittsfield, MA
Information Available in These Sources: ABYP 4

WIBBELSMAN, CHARLES J(OSEPH)
Birthdate: 2/5/1945
Birthplace: Cincinnati, OH
Information Available in These Sources: SATA 59

WIBBERLEY, LEONARD (PATRICK O'CONNOR)
(Leonard Holton, Patrick O'Connor, Christopher Webb)
Birthdate: 4/9/1915
Birthplace: Dublin, Ireland
Deathdate: 11/23/1983 or 11/22/1983
Information Available in These Sources: ABYP 1, ABYP 3, DACF, MJA, SATA 2, SATA 36, SATA 45, TCCW 1, TCCW 2, TCCW 3

WICKER, IREENE (SEATON)
(Irene Seaton)
Birthdate: 11/24/1905 or 11/24/1900 or 11/24/1901
Birthplace: Quincy, IL
Deathdate: 11/17/1987 or 11/16/1987
Information Available in These Sources: ABYP 4, SATA 55

WIDDEMER, MABEL CLELAND
(Mabel Cleland, Mabel Cleland Ludlum)
Birthdate: 6/27/1902
Birthplace: New York, NY
Deathdate: 8/5/1964
Information Available in These Sources: ABYP 2, ABYP 3, SATA 5

WIER, ESTER (ALBERTI)
Birthdate: 10/17/1910
Birthplace: Seattle, WA
Information Available in These Sources: ABYP 1, ABYP 3, DACF, JBA 3, SATA 3, TCCW 1, TCCW 2, TCCW 3

WIESE, KURT
Birthdate: 4/22/1887
Birthplace: Minden, Germany
Deathdate: 5/27/1974 or 5/29/1974
Information Available in These Sources: ABYP 1, ABYP 3, ICB 1, ICB 3, ICB 4, JBA 1, JBA 2, SATA 3, SATA 24, SATA 36, TCCW 1

WIESEL, ELIE(ZER)
Birthdate: 9/30/1928
Birthplace: Sighet, Romania
Information Available in These Sources: SATA 56

WIESNER, PORTIA
See Takakjian, Portia

WIESNER, WILLIAM
Birthdate: 4/28/1899
Birthplace: Vienna, Austria
Information Available in These Sources: IBYP 1, IBYP 2, ICB 2, ICB 3, ICB 4, SATA 5

WIGGIN, KATE DOUGLAS (SMITH)
Birthdate: 9/28/1856
Birthplace: Philadelphia, PA
Deathdate: 8/24/1923
Information Available in These Sources: ABYP 4, DLB 42, FSYP, JBA 1, TCCW 1, TCCW 2, TCCW 3, WC, WCL, YABC

WILBER, DONALD N(EWTON)
Birthdate: 11/14/1907
Birthplace: Madison, WI
Information Available in These Sources: ABYP 1, ABYP 3, SATA 35

WILBUR, C. KEITH
Birthdate: 6/21/1923
Birthplace: Providence, RI
Information Available in These Sources: SATA 27

WILBUR, RICHARD (PURDY)
Birthdate: 3/1/1921
Birthplace: New York, NY
Information Available in These Sources: ABYP 4, SATA 9

WILCOX, DON
Birthplace: Lucas, KS
Information Available in These Sources: ABYP 1, ABYP 3

WILCOX, R(UTH) TURNER
Birthdate: 4/29/1888
Birthplace: New York, NY
Deathdate: 6/3/1970
Information Available in These Sources: SATA 36

WILDE, D. GUNTHER
See Hurwood, Bernhardt J.

WILDE, PERCIVAL
Information Available in These Sources: JBA 1

WILDER, ALEC
Birthdate: 2/16/1907
Birthplace: Rochester, NY
Deathdate: 1980
Information Available in These Sources: ABYP 2, ABYP 3

WILDER, LAURA (ELIZABETH) INGALLS
Birthdate: 2/7/1867
Birthplace: Lake Pepin, WI
Deathdate: 1/10/1957
Information Available in These Sources: ABYP 1, ABYP 3, DLB 22, JBA 2 SATA 15, SATA 29, SVC 3, TCCW 1, TCCW 2, TCCW 3, WC, WCL

WILDER, STEPHEN
See Marlowe, Stephen

WILEY, KARLA H(UMMEL)
Birthdate: 7/20/1918
Birthplace: Brooklyn, NY
Information Available in These Sources: ABYP 2, ABYP 3

WILFORD, JOHN NOBLE, JR.
Birthdate: 10/4/1933
Birthplace: Camden, TN
Information Available in These Sources: ABYP 4

WILHELM, HANS
Birthdate: 9/21/1945
Birthplace: Bremen, West Germany
Information Available in These Sources: SATA 58

WILKIE, KATHERINE E(LLIOTT)
Birthdate: 2/6/1904
Birthplace: Lexington, KY
Deathdate: 4/5/1980
Information Available in These Sources: ABYP 1, ABYP 3, SATA 31

WILKIN, ELOISE (BURNS)
Birthdate: 3/30/1904
Birthplace: Rochester, NY
Deathdate: 10/4/1987
Information Available in These Sources: IBYP 1, IBYP 2, ICB 1, ICB 2, SATA 49, SATA 54

WILKINS, MARY HUISKAMP CALHOUN
See Calhoun, Mary Huiskamp

WILKINSON, BRENDA
Birthdate: 1/1/1946
Birthplace: Moultrie, GA
Information Available in These Sources: BAI, DACF, JBA 5, SATA 14

WILKINSON, BURKE
See Wilkinson, John Burke

WILKINSON, JOHN BURKE
(Burke Wilkinson)
Birthdate: 8/24/1913
Birthplace: New York, NY
Information Available in These Sources: ABYP 2, ABYP 3, SATA 4

WILKINSON, SYLVIA (J.)
Birthdate: 4/3/1940
Birthplace: Durham, NC
Information Available in These Sources: SATA 39, SATA 56

WILL
See Lipkind, William

WILLARD, MILDRED WILDS
Birthdate: 10/11/1911
Birthplace: New Kensington, PA
Information Available in These Sources: SATA 14

WILLARD, NANCY (MARGARET)
Birthdate: 6/26/1936
Birthplace: Ann Arbor, MI
Information Available in These Sources: DACF, JBA 5, SATA 30, SATA 37 TCCW 2, TCCW 3

WILLCOX, ISOBEL
Birthdate: 7/27/1907
Birthplace: Long Branch, NJ
Information Available in These Sources: SATA 42

WILLCOX, SANDRA
Information Available in These Sources: IBYP 1, IBYP 2

WILLEY, ROBERT
See Ley, Willy

WILLIAMS, BARBARA (WRIGHT)
Birthdate: 1/1/1925
Birthplace: Salt Lake City, UT
Information Available in These Sources: ABYP 4, JBA 6, SATA 11

WILLIAMS, BERYL
See Epstein, Beryl (M. Williams)

WILLIAMS, CAROL
See Fenner, Carol (Elizabeth)

WILLIAMS, CHARLES
See Collier, James Lincoln

WILLIAMS, CLYDE C.
(Slim Williams)
Birthdate: 1/14/1881
Birthplace: Fresno, CA
Deathdate: 10/9/1974
Information Available in These Sources: ABYP 4, SATA 8, SATA 27

WILLIAMS, COE
See Harrison, C. William

WILLIAMS, EDGAR
Birthplace: Lansdale, PA
Information Available in These Sources: ABYP 1, ABYP 3

WILLIAMS, EDWARD G.
Birthdate: 11/3/1929
Birthplace: Fayetteville, NC
Information Available in These Sources: ABYP 4

WILLIAMS, FRANCES B.
See Browin, Frances Williams

WILLIAMS, GARTH (MONTGOMERY)
Birthdate: 4/16/1912
Birthplace: New York, NY
Information Available in These Sources: ABYP 1, ABYP 3, DLB 22, ICB 1 ICB 2, ICB 3, ICB 4, MJA, SATA 18, SVC 3

WILLIAMS, HAWLEY
See Heyliger, William

WILLIAMS, J(EANNE R.)
(Jeanne Crecy, Megan Rhys)
Birthdate: 4/10/1930
Birthplace: Elkhart, KS
Information Available in These Sources: DACF, SATA 5

WILLIAMS, J. WALKER
See Wodehouse, P(elham) G(renville)

WILLIAMS, JAY
(Michael Delving)
Birthdate: 5/31/1914
Birthplace: Buffalo, NY
Deathdate: 7/12/1978
Information Available in These Sources: ABYP 1, ABYP 3, ABYP 4, DACF, JBA 4, SATA 3, SATA 24, SATA 41, TCCW 1, TCCW 2, TCCW 3

WILLIAMS, LESLIE
Birthdate: 12/15/1941
Birthplace: Allentown, PA
Information Available in These Sources: SATA 42

WILLIAMS, LINDA
Birthdate: 1/6/1948
Birthplace: Honolulu, HI
Information Available in These Sources: SATA 59

WILLIAMS, LOU(ISE BONINO)
Birthdate, 1904?
Deathdate: 9/11/1984
Information Available in These Sources: ABYP 1, ABYP 3, SATA 39

WILLIAMS, LYNN
See Hale, Arlene

WILLIAMS, MICHAEL
See St. John, Wylly Folk

WILLIAMS, PATRICK J.
See Butterworth, W(illiam) E(dmund, III)

WILLIAMS, SELMA R(UTH)
Birthdate: 10/26/1925
Birthplace: Malden, MA
Information Available in These Sources: SATA 14

WILLIAMS, SLIM
See Williams, Clyde C.

WILLIAMS, VERA B.
Birthdate: 1/28/1927
Birthplace: Hollywood, CA or New York, NY
Information Available in These Sources: JBA 5, SATA 33, SATA 53, TCCW 3

WILLIAMSON, JOANNE S(MALL)
Birthdate: 5/13/1926
Birthplace: Arlington, MA
Information Available in These Sources: ABYP 2, ABYP 3, DACF, JBA 3, SATA 3

WILLIAMSON, MARGARET
Birthdate: 1924
Birthplace: Quebec, Canada
Information Available in These Sources: ABYP 1, ABYP 3

WILLIAMSON, T(HAMES) R(OSS)
(S. S. Smith)
Birthdate: 2/7/1894
Birthplace: Genesee (near), ID
Information Available in These Sources: JBA 1

WILLIS, CORINNE (DENNEY)
(Patricia Denning)
Birthplace: Buffalo, NY
Information Available in These Sources: ABYP 4

WILLIS, PRISCILLA D.
Information Available in These Sources: ABYP 1, ABYP 3

WILLIS, ROBERT J.
Birthplace: NY
Information Available in These Sources: ABYP 1, ABYP 3

WILLSON, DIXIE
Birthplace: Mason City, IA
Information Available in These Sources: ABYP 1, ABYP 3

WILMA, DANA
See Faralla, Dana

WILSON, AUGUSTA JANE EVANS
Birthdate: 5/8/1835
Birthplace: Columbus, GA
Deathdate: 5/9/1909
Information Available in These Sources: DLB 42

WILSON, BETH P(IERRE)
Birthplace: Tacoma, WA
Information Available in These Sources: ABYP 4, BAI, SATA 8

WILSON, CARTER
Birthdate: 12/27/1941
Birthplace: Washington, DC
Information Available in These Sources: ABYP 4, SATA 6

WILSON, CHARLES BANKS
Birthdate: 8/6/1918
Birthplace: Springdale, OK
Information Available in These Sources: IBYP 2, ICB 2

WILSON, CHARLES MORROW
Birthdate: 6/16/1905
Birthplace: Fayetteville, AR
Deathdate: 3/2/1977
Information Available in These Sources: ABYP 2, ABYP 3, SATA 30

WILSON, CHRISTOPHER B.
Birthdate: 1910
Birthplace: England
Deathdate: 10/3/1985
Information Available in These Sources: SATA 46

WILSON, DAGMAR
Birthdate: 1/25/1916
Birthplace: New York, NY
Information Available in These Sources: SATA 31

WILSON, DOROTHY CLARKE
Birthdate: 5/9/1904
Birthplace: Gardiner, ME
Information Available in These Sources: SATA 16

WILSON, EDWARD A(RTHUR)
Birthdate: 3/4/1886
Birthplace: Glasgow, Scotland
Deathdate: 10/2/1970
Information Available in These Sources: IBYP 2, ICB 1, ICB 2, SATA 38

WILSON, ELEANORE (HUBBARD)
Birthplace: Baltimore, MD
Information Available in These Sources: ABYP 1, ABYP 3

WILSON, ELLEN (JANET CAMERON)
Birthplace: Pittsburgh, PA
Deathdate: 12/17/1976
Information Available in These Sources: ABYP 4, SATA 9, SATA 26

WILSON, ERICA
Birthplace: England
Information Available in These Sources: SATA 51

WILSON, FORREST
Birthdate: 4/21/1918
Birthplace: San Francisco, CA
Information Available in These Sources: SATA 27

WILSON, GAHAN
Birthdate: 2/18/1930
Birthplace: Evanston, IL
Information Available in These Sources: IBYP 2, SATA 27, SATA 35

WILSON, HAZEL (HUTCHINS)
Birthdate: 4/8/1898
Birthplace: Portland, ME
Information Available in These Sources: ABYP 1, ABYP 3, SATA 3

WILSON, HOLLY
Birthplace: Duluth, MN
Information Available in These Sources: ABYP 1, ABYP 3

WILSON, JOHN
Birthdate: 4/14/1922
Birthplace: Boston, MA
Information Available in These Sources: IBYP 1, IBYP 2, BABP, SATA 22

WILSON, JULIA
Birthdate: 4/26/1927
Birthplace: Chicago, IL
Information Available in These Sources: BABP

WILSON, LIONEL
(Peter Blackton, Herbert Ellis, L. E. Salzer)
Birthdate: 3/22/1924
Birthplace: New York, NY
Information Available in These Sources: SATA 31, SATA 33

WILSON, PEGGY
Birthplace: Galveston, TX
Information Available in These Sources: IBYP 2, ICB 3

WILSON, RUTH
Birthdate: 1899
Birthplace: Philadelphia, PA?
Information Available in These Sources: ABYP 1, ABYP 3

WILSON, SARAH
Birthdate: 10/18/1934
Birthplace: Syracuse, NY
Information Available in These Sources: SATA 50

WILSON, TOM
Birthdate: 8/1/1931
Birthplace: Grant Town, WV
Information Available in These Sources: SATA 30, SATA 33

WILSON, WALT(ER N.)
Birthdate: 3/26/1939
Birthplace: TX
Information Available in These Sources: SATA 14

WILT, JOY
See Berry, Joy Wilt

WILWERDING, WALTER JOSEPH
Birthdate: 2/13/1891
Birthplace: Winona, MN
Deathdate: 9/19/1966
Information Available in These Sources: ICB 1, SATA 9

WIMMER, HELMUT KARL
Birthdate: 12/8/1925
Birthplace: Munich, Germany
Information Available in These Sources: ICB 3

WINCHESTER, JAMES H(UGH)
Birthdate: 6/27/1917
Birthplace: Midlothian, TX
Deathdate: 11/20/1985
Information Available in These Sources: SATA 30, SATA 45

WINDER, VIOLA HITTI
Birthplace: NY
Information Available in These Sources: ABYP 2, ABYP 3

WINDERS, GERTRUDE HECKER
Birthplace: Indianapolis, IN
Information Available in These Sources: SATA 3

WINDHAM, BASIL
See Wodehouse, P(elham) G(renville)

WINDHAM, KATHRYN T(UCKER)
Birthdate: 6/2/1918
Birthplace: Selma, AL
Information Available in These Sources: SATA 14

WINDSOR, CLAIRE
See Hamerstrom, Frances

WINDSOR, PATRICIA
Birthdate: 9/21/1938
Birthplace: New York, NY
Information Available in These Sources: JBA 5, SATA 30

WINN, JANET BRUCE
Birthdate: 5/21/1928
Birthplace: Orange, NJ
Information Available in These Sources: SATA 43

WINN, MARIE
Birthdate: 10/21/1936
Birthplace: Prague, Czechoslovakia
Information Available in These Sources: ABYP 4, SATA 38

WINNICK, KAREN B(ETH) B(INKOFF)
Birthdate: 6/28/1946
Birthplace: New York, NY
Information Available in These Sources: SATA 51

WINSOR, ROBERT
Birthplace: MI
Information Available in These Sources: ABYP 4

WINSTON, CLARA
Birthdate: 12/6/1921
Birthplace: New York, NY
Deathdate: 11/7/1983
Information Available in These Sources: SATA 39, SATA 54

WINSTON, LENA
See Chaffin, Lillie D(orton)

WINSTON, RICHARD
Birthdate: 7/21/1917
Birthplace: New York, NY
Deathdate: 12/22/1979
Information Available in These Sources: ABYP 4, SATA 54

WINTER, GINNY LINVILLE
Birthdate: 12/11/1925
Birthplace: West Lafayette, IN
Information Available in These Sources: ABYP 1, ABYP 3

WINTER, MILO (KENDALL)
Birthdate: 8/7/1888
Birthplace: Princeton, IL
Deathdate: 8/15/1956
Information Available in These Sources: IBYP 2, ICB 1, ICB 2, SATA 21

WINTER, PAULA (CECELIA)
Birthdate: 10/26/1929
Birthplace: New York, NY
Information Available in These Sources: ICB 4, JBA 6, SATA 48

WINTER, R. R.
See Winterbotham, R(ussell) R(obert)

WINTER, WILLIAM (JOHN)
Birthdate: 1912
Information Available in These Sources: ABYP 1, ABYP 3

WINTERBOTHAM, R(USSELL) R(OBERT)
(Ted Addy, J. Harvey Bond, Franklin Hadley, R. R. Winter)
Birthdate: 8/1/1904
Birthplace: Salina, KS
Deathdate: 6/9/1971
Information Available in These Sources: SATA 10

WINTERFELD, HENRY
(Manfred Michael)
Birthdate: 4/9/1901
Birthplace: Hamburg, Germany
Information Available in These Sources: JBA 3, SATA 55

WINTERTON, GAYLE
See Adams, William Taylor

WINTHROP, ELIZABETH
See Mahony, Elizabeth Winthrop

WINWAR, FRANCES
(Francesca Vinciguerra)
Birthdate: 5/3/1900
Birthplace: Taormina, Sicily
Information Available in These Sources: ABYP 1, ABYP 3

WIRT, MILDRED (AUGUSTINE)
Birthdate: 1905
Information Available in These Sources: ABYP 1, ABYP 3

WIRTENBERG, PATRICIA Z(ARRELLA)
Birthdate: 5/21/1932
Birthplace: Arlington, MA
Information Available in These Sources: SATA 10

WISE, WILLIAM
Birthdate: 7/21/1923
Birthplace: New York, NY
Information Available in These Sources: ABYP 1, ABYP 3, SATA 4

WISE, WINIFRED E.
Birthplace: Fond du Lac, WI
Information Available in These Sources: ABYP 1, ABYP 3, SATA 2

WISEMAN, ANN (SAYRE)
(Ann Wiseman Denzer)
Birthdate: 7/20/1926
Birthplace: New York, NY
Information Available in These Sources: SATA 31

WISEMAN, B(ERNARD)
Birthdate: 8/26/1922
Birthplace: Brooklyn, NY
Information Available in These Sources: ABYP 4, SATA 4

WISKUR, DARRELL D.
Information Available in These Sources: IBYP 2

WISLER, G(ARY) CLIFTON
(G. Clifton)
Birthdate: 5/15/1950
Birthplace: Oklahoma City, OK
Information Available in These Sources: DACF, SATA 46, SATA 58

WISMER, DONALD (RICHARD)
Birthdate: 12/27/1946
Birthplace: Chicago, IL
Information Available in These Sources: SATA 59

WISNER, BILL
See Wisner, William L.

WISNER, WILLIAM L.
(Bill Wisner)
Birthdate, 1914?
Birthplace: Brightwaters, Long Island, NY
Deathdate: 8/3/1983
Information Available in These Sources: ABYP 2, ABYP 3, SATA 42

WISSMANN, RUTH H(ELEN LESLIE)
Birthdate: 5/29/1914
Birthplace: Lima, OH
Information Available in These Sources: ABYP 1, ABYP 3

WISTER, OWEN
Birthdate: 7/14/1860
Birthplace: Philadelphia, PA
Deathdate: 7/21/1938
Information Available in These Sources: JBA 1

WITHAM, PHILLIP ROSS
(Ross Witham)
Birthdate: 4/11/1917
Birthplace: Stuart, FL
Information Available in These Sources: SATA 37

WITHAM, ROSS
See Witham, Phillip Ross

WITHERIDGE, ELIZABETH P(LUMB)
Birthdate: 9/27/1907
Birthplace: Saginaw, MI
Information Available in These Sources: ABYP 4

WITHERS, CARL A.
(Robert North, James West)
Birthdate: 3/20/1900
Birthplace: Sheldon (near), MO
Deathdate: 1/5/1970
Information Available in These Sources: ABYP 1, ABYP 3, SATA 14

WITKER, JIM
Birthplace: Pasadena, CA
Information Available in These Sources: ABYP 2, ABYP 3

WITT, SHIRLEY HILL
(Katherine Thundercloud)
Birthdate: 4/17/1934
Birthplace: Whittier, CA
Information Available in These Sources: SATA 17

WITTANEN, ETOLIN
Birthdate: 8/11/1907
Birthplace: Wrangell, AL
Information Available in These Sources: SATA 55

WITTE, BETTY J.
Information Available in These Sources: ABYP 2, ABYP 3

WITTELS, HARRIET JOAN
Birthdate: 4/6/1938
Birthplace: New York, NY
Information Available in These Sources: SATA 31

WITTMAN, SALLY (ANNE CHRISTENSEN)
Birthdate: 9/25/1941
Birthplace: Portland, OR
Information Available in These Sources: SATA 30

WITTON, DOROTHY
Birthplace: MI
Information Available in These Sources: ABYP 1, ABYP 3

WITTY, PAUL A(NDREW)
Birthdate: 7/23/1898
Birthplace: Terre Haute, IN
Deathdate: 2/11/1976
Information Available in These Sources: ABYP 1, ABYP 3, SATA 30, SATA 50

WIZARD, MR.
See Herbert, Don

WODEHOUSE, P(ELHAM) G(RENVILLE)
(P. Brooke-Haven, Pelham Grenville, J. Plum, C. P. West, J. Walker Williams, Basil Windham)
Birthdate: 10/15/1881
Birthplace: Guildford, Surrey, England
Deathdate: 2/14/1975
Information Available in These Sources: SATA 22

WODGE, DREARY
See Gorey, Edward St. John

WOHLBERG, MEG
Birthdate: 2/6/1905
Birthplace: New York, NY
Information Available in These Sources: ICB 3, SATA 41

WOHLRABE, RAYMOND A(DOLPH)
Birthdate: 4/25/1900 or 4/5/1900
Birthplace: Superior, WI
Deathdate: 6/23/1977
Information Available in These Sources: ABYP 1, ABYP 3, SATA 4

WOJCIECHOWSKA, MAIA (TERESA RODMAN)
(Maia Rodman)
Birthdate: 8/7/1927
Birthplace: Warsaw, Poland
Information Available in These Sources: ABYP 2, ABYP 3, AICB, JBA 3, MBMP, SATA 1, SATA 28, TCCW 1 TCCW 2, TCCW 3

WOLCOTT, CAROLYN MULLER
(Carolyn Muller)
Information Available in These Sources: ABYP 1, ABYP 3

WOLCOTT, PATTY
Birthdate: 9/26/1929
Birthplace: Lowell, MA
Information Available in These Sources: SATA 14

WOLD, JO ANNE
Birthdate: 4/20/1938
Birthplace: Fairbanks, AK
Information Available in These Sources: SATA 30

WOLDIN, BETH WEINER
Birthdate: 4/18/1955
Birthplace: Philadelphia, PA
Information Available in These Sources: SATA 34

WOLF, BERNARD
Birthdate: 2/26/1930
Birthplace: New York, NY
Information Available in These Sources: JBA 5, SATA 37

WOLFE, BURTON H.
Birthdate: 9/2/1932
Birthplace: Washington, DC
Information Available in These Sources: SATA 5

WOLFE, LOUIS
Birthdate: 6/29/1905
Birthplace: Bound Brook, NJ
Information Available in These Sources: ABYP 1, ABYP 3. SATA 8

WOLFE, RINNA (EVELYN)
Birthdate: 5/2/1925
Birthplace: Brooklyn, NY
Information Available in These Sources: SATA 38

WOLFERT, JERRY
Information Available in These Sources: ABYP 1, ABYP 3

WOLFF, ASHLEY
See Wolff, Jenifer Ashley

WOLFF, DIANE
Birthdate: 10/12/1945
Birthplace: New York, NY
Information Available in These Sources: SATA 27

WOLFF, JENIFER ASHLEY
(Ashley Wolff)
Birthdate: 1/26/1956
Birthplace: Boston, MA
Information Available in These Sources: JBA 6, SATA 50

WOLFF, ROBERT JAY
Birthdate: 7/27/1905
Birthplace: Chicago, IL
Information Available in These Sources: SATA 10

WOLFF, SONIA
See Levitin, Sonia (Wolff)

WOLITZER, HILMA
Birthdate: 1/25/1930
Birthplace: Brooklyn, NY
Information Available in These Sources: JBA 5, SATA 31

WOLKOFF, JUDIE (EDWARDS)
Birthplace: MT
Information Available in These Sources: SATA 37

WOLKSTEIN, DIANE
Birthdate: 11/11/1942
Birthplace: New York, NY
Information Available in These Sources: JBA 5, SATA 7

WOLLHEIM, DONALD A(LLEN)
(David Grinnell)
Birthdate: 10/1/1914
Birthplace: New York, NY
Information Available in These Sources: ABYP 1, ABYP 3

WOLNY, P.
See Janeczko, Paul B(ryan)

WOLTERS, RICHARD A.
Birthdate: 2/8/1920
Birthplace: Philadelphia, PA
Information Available in These Sources: SATA 35

WONDRISKA, WILLIAM ALLEN
Birthdate: 6/29/1931
Birthplace: Chicago, IL
Information Available in These Sources: ABYP 2, ABYP 3, ICB 3, JBA 3, SATA 6

WONG, JEANYEE
Birthdate: 5/8/1920
Birthplace: San Francisco, CA
Information Available in These Sources: IBYP 1, 2, ICB 2

WONSETLER, JOHN CHARLES
Birthdate: 8/25/1900
Birthplace: Camden, NJ
Information Available in These Sources: IBYP 2, ICB 1, 2

WOOD, AUDREY
Birthdate: 1948
Birthplace: Little Rock, AR
Information Available in These Sources: JBA 6, SATA 44, SATA 50

WOOD, CATHERINE
See Etchison, Birdie L(ee)

WOOD, DON
Birthdate: 5/4/1945
Birthplace: Atwater, CA
Information Available in These Sources: JBA 6, SATA 44, SATA 50

WOOD, EDGAR A(LLARDYCE)
(Kerry Wood)
Birthdate: 6/2/1907
Birthplace: New York, NY
Information Available in These Sources: SATA 14, TCCW 2

WOOD, ESTHER
See Brady, Esther Wood

WOOD, FRANCES ELIZABETH
Birthplace: CO
Information Available in These Sources: SATA 34

WOOD, HARRIE
Birthdate: 4/28/1902
Birthplace: Rushford, NY
Information Available in These Sources: CICB, ICB 1

WOOD, JAMES PLAYSTED
(Henry Soudley, James St. Briavels)
Birthdate: 12/11/1905
Birthplace: Brooklyn, NY
Information Available in These Sources: ABYP 2, ABYP 3, JBA 4, SATA 1

WOOD, KERRY
See Wood, Edgar A(llardyce)

WOOD, LAURA N(EWBOLD)
See Roper, Laura Wood

WOOD, LINDA C(AROL)
Birthdate: 9/4/1945
Birthplace: Smyrna, TN
Information Available in These Sources: SATA 59

WOOD, NANCY
Birthdate: 6/20/1936
Birthplace: Trenton, NJ
Information Available in These Sources: SATA 6

WOOD, PHYLLIS ANDERSON
Birthdate: 10/24/1923
Birthplace: Palo Alto, CA
Information Available in These Sources: ABYP 4, SATA 30, SATA 33

WOOD, RUTH C.
Birthplace: CO
Information Available in These Sources: ABYP 4

WOOD, WALLACE
Birthdate: 6/17/1927
Birthplace: Menahga, MN
Deathdate: 11/2/1981
Information Available in These Sources: SATA 33

WOODARD, CAROL
Birthdate: 1/19/1929
Birthplace: Buffalo, NY
Information Available in These Sources: SATA 14

WOODBURN, JOHN HENRY
Birthdate: 7/17/1914
Birthplace: Marietta, OH
Information Available in These Sources: ABYP 4, SATA 11

WOODBURY, DAVID O(AKES)
Birthdate: 1896
Birthplace: ME
Information Available in These Sources: ABYP 4

WOODRICH, MARY NEVILLE
(Mary Neville)
Birthdate: 7/29/1915
Birthplace: Winchester, VA
Information Available in These Sources: SATA 2

WOODS, GEORGE A(LLAN)
Birthdate: 1/26/1926
Birthplace: Lake Placid, NY
Deathdate: 8/11/1988
Information Available in These Sources: ABYP 4, DACF, SATA 30, SATA 57

WOODS, GERALDINE
Birthdate: 9/30/1948
Birthplace: New York, NY
Information Available in These Sources: SATA 42, SATA 56

WOODS, HAROLD
Birthdate: 9/4/1945
Birthplace: New York, NY
Information Available in These Sources: SATA 42, SATA 56

WOODSON, CARTER GOODWIN
Birthdate: 1875
Birthplace: Canton, VA
Deathdate: 1950
Information Available in These Sources: BAI

WOODSON, JACK
See Woodson, John Waddie, Jr.

WOODSON, JOHN WADDIE, JR.
(Jack Woodson)
Birthdate: 1/23/1913
Birthplace: Richmond, VA
Information Available in These Sources: SATA 10

WOODWARD, CLEVELAND
See Woodward, Landon Cleveland

WOODWARD, HILDEGARD
Birthdate: 2/10/1898
Birthplace: Worcester, MA
Information Available in These Sources: ABYP 1, ABYP 3, ICB 1, ICB 2

WOODWARD, LANDON CLEVELAND
(Cleveland Woodward)
Birthdate: 6/25/1900
Birthplace: Glendale, OH
Information Available in These Sources: SATA 10, SATA 48

WOODY, REGINA (LLEWELLYN) JONES
Birthdate: 1/4/1894
Birthplace: Boston (Chestnut Hill), MA
Information Available in These Sources: ABYP 1, ABYP 3, MJA, SATA 3

WOOLDRIDGE, RHODA
Birthdate: 5/25/1906
Birthplace: Buckner, MO
Information Available in These Sources: ABYP 2, ABYP 3, SATA 22

WOOLLEY, CATHERINE
(Jane Thayer)
Birthdate: 8/11/1904
Birthplace: Chicago, IL
Information Available in These Sources: ABYP 1, ABYP 3, MJA, SATA 3

WOOLSEY, JANETTE
Birthdate: 12/11/1904
Birthplace: Livingston Manor, NY
Information Available in These Sources: ABYP 1, ABYP 3, SATA 3

WOOLSEY, SARAH CHAUNCY
(Susan Coolidge)
Birthdate: 1/29/1835
Birthplace: Cleveland, OH
Deathdate: 4/9/1905
Information Available in These Sources: DLB 42, JBA 1, TCCW 1, TCCW 2 TCCW 3, WCL

WORCESTER, DONALD EMMET
Birthdate: 4/29/1915
Birthplace: Tempe, AZ
Information Available in These Sources: ABYP 1, ABYP 3, SATA 18

WORCESTER, GURDON SALTONSTALL
Birthdate: 12/7/1897
Birthplace: Philadelphia, PA
Information Available in These Sources: DACF

WORK, VIRGINIA
Birthdate: 9/26/1946
Birthplace: Moscow, ID
Information Available in These Sources: SATA 45, SATA 57

WORLINE, BONNIE BESS
Birthdate: 8/3/1914
Birthplace: El Dorado, KS
Information Available in These Sources: ABYP 1, ABYP 3, SATA 14

WORMSER, RICHARD EDWARD
Birthdate: 1908
Birthplace: New York, NY
Information Available in These Sources: DACF

WORMSER, SOPHIE
Birthdate: 10/21/1897
Birthplace: Astoria, NY
Information Available in These Sources: SATA 22

WORRELL, ESTELLE (ANSLEY)
Birthdate: 1929
Information Available in These Sources: ABYP 4

WORTH, KATHRYN
Birthdate: 1898
Birthplace: Wilmington, NC
Information Available in These Sources: ABYP 2, ABYP 3, JBA 2

WORTH, RICHARD
Birthdate: 11/13/1945
Birthplace: Hartford, CT
Information Available in These Sources: SATA 46, SATA 59

WORTH, VALERIE
(Valerie Worth Bahlke)
Birthdate: 10/29/1933
Birthplace: Philadelphia, PA
Information Available in These Sources: JBA 5, SATA 8, TCCW 3

WORTIS, AVI
(Avi)
Birthdate: 12/23/1937
Birthplace: New York, NY
Information Available in These Sources: BC, DACF, JBA 5, SATA 14, TCCW 3

WOSMEK, FRANCES
Birthdate: 12/16/1917
Birthplace: Popple, MN
Information Available in These Sources: DACF, SATA 29

WRIGGINS, SALLEY HOVEY
Birthdate: 5/6/1922
Birthplace: Seattle, WA
Information Available in These Sources: SATA 17

WRIGHT, ANNA (MARIA LOUISA PERROT) ROSE
(Anna Perrot Rose)
Birthdate: 10/13/1890
Birthplace: New York, NY
Deathdate: 9/4/1968
Information Available in These Sources: SATA 35

WRIGHT, BETTY REN
(Revena)
Birthdate: 6/15/1927
Birthplace: Wakefield, MI
Information Available in These Sources: DACF, JBA 6, SATA 48

WRIGHT, DARE
Birthdate, 1926?
Birthplace: Ontario, Canada
Information Available in These Sources: ABYP 1, ABYP 3, SATA 21

WRIGHT, ENID MEADOWCROFT (LAMONT)
See Meadowcroft, Enid (La Monte)

WRIGHT, FRANCES FITZPATRICK
Birthdate: 6/26/1897
Information Available in These Sources: ABYP 2, ABYP 3, SATA 10

WRIGHT, KENNETH
See del Rey, Lester

WRIGHT, MILDRED WHEATLEY
Information Available in These Sources: ABYP 4

WRIGHT, NANCY MEANS
Birthplace: Glen Ridge, NJ
Information Available in These Sources: SATA 38

WRIGHT-FRIERSON, VIRGINIA
(Wrightfrierson)
Birthdate: 10/8/1949
Birthplace: Washington, DC
Information Available in These Sources: SATA 58

WRIGHTFRIERSON
See Wright-Frierson, Virginia

WRONKER, LILI (CASSEL)
(Lili Cassel)
Birthdate: 5/5/1924
Birthplace: Berlin, Germany
Information Available in These Sources: IBYP 2, ICB 3, SATA 10

WULFF, EDGUN VALDEMAR
(Edgun)
Birthdate: 12/13/1913
Birthplace: New York, NY
Information Available in These Sources: IBYP 2, ICB 2

WULFFSON, DON L.
Birthdate: 8/21/1943
Birthplace: Los Angeles, CA
Information Available in These Sources: SATA 32

WUNSCH, JOSEPHINE (MCLEAN)
Birthdate: 2/3/1914
Birthplace: Detroit, MI
Information Available in These Sources: ABYP 2, ABYP 3

WYATT, EDGAR
Information Available in These Sources: ABYP 1, ABYP 3

WYATT, GERALDINE (TOLMAN)
Birthdate: 1907
Birthplace: Hope, KS
Information Available in These Sources: ABYP 1, ABYP 3

WYATT, JAMES
See Robinson, Louie, Jr.

WYATT, JANE
See Bradbury, Bianca

WYATT, MOLLY
See Bradbury, Bianca

WYCKOFF, JAMES (M.)
Birthdate: 2/24/1918
Birthplace: New York, NY
Information Available in These Sources: ABYP 2, ABYP 3

WYETH, BETSY JAMES
Birthdate: 9/26/1921
Birthplace: East Aurora, NY
Information Available in These Sources: SATA 41

WYETH, N(EWELL) C(ONVERS)
Birthdate: 10/22/1882
Birthplace: Needham, MA
Deathdate: 10/19/1945
Information Available in These Sources: IBYP 1, IBYP 2, JBA 1, JBA 2, SATA 17

WYLER, ROSE
(Rose Wyler Ames, Peter Thayer)
Birthdate: 10/29/1909
Birthplace: Bronx, NY
Information Available in These Sources: ABYP 1, ABYP 3, BABP, JBA 3, SATA 18

WYLIE, ELINOR HOYT
Birthdate: 9/7/1885
Birthplace: Somerville, NJ
Deathdate: 12/16/1928
Information Available in These Sources: SVC 2, SVC 3

WYLIE, LAURA
See Matthews, Patricia

WYMARK, OLWEN (MARGARET BUCK)
Birthdate: 2/14/1932
Birthplace: Oakland, CA
Information Available in These Sources: TCCW 1, TCCW 2, TCCW 3

WYNDHAM, LEE
See Hyndman, Jane (Lee) Andrews

WYNDHAM, ROBERT
See Hyndman, Robert (Utley)

WYNNE, ANNETTE
Birthdate: 1885
Birthplace: Brooklyn, NY
Information Available in These Sources: SVC 2, SVC 3

WYSS, THELMA HATCH
Birthdate: 11/17/1934
Birthplace: Bancroft, ID
Information Available in These Sources: SATA 10

X

X, DR.
See Nourse, Alan E(dward)

XAVIER, FATHER
See Hurwood, Bernhardt J.

Y

YAFFE, ALAN
See Yorinks, Arthur

YAKOVETIC, (JOSEPH SANDY)
(Joe Yakovetic)
Birthdate: 12/12/1952
Birthplace: Bridgeport, CT
Information Available in These Sources: SATA 59

YAKOVETIC, JOE
See Yakovetic, (Joseph Sandy)

YAMAGUCHI, JOHN TOHR
(Tohr Yamaguchi)
Birthdate: 10/22/1932
Birthplace: Toyko, Japan
Information Available in These Sources: JBA 3

YAMAGUCHI, MARIANNE ILLENBERGER
Birthdate: 1/10/1936
Birthplace: Cuyahoga Falls, OH
Information Available in These Sources: IBYP 1, IBYP 2, ICB 3, JBA 3, SATA 7

YAMAGUCHI, TOHR
See Yamaguchi, John Tohr

YANG, JAY
Birthdate: 1/15/1941
Birthplace: Taiwan
Information Available in These Sources: IBYP 2, SATA 12

YAP, WEDA
(Louise Drew Cook)
Birthdate: 12/11/1894
Birthplace: Philadelphia, PA
Information Available in These Sources: IBYP 1, IBYP 2, ICB 2

YARBROUGH, CAMILLE
Birthdate: 1948
Birthplace: Chicago, IL
Information Available in These Sources: BAI

YARBROUGH, IRA
Birthdate, 1910?
Deathdate: 2/28/1983
Information Available in These Sources: SATA 35

YAROSLAVA
See Mills, Yaroslava Surmach

YASHIMA, MITSU
Information Available in These Sources: FLTYP

YASHIMA, TARO
See Iwamatsu, Jun Atsushi

YATES, BROCK W(ENDEL)
Birthdate: 10/21/1933
Birthplace: Buffalo, NY
Information Available in These Sources: ABYP 1, ABYP 3

YATES, ELIZABETH
Birthdate: 12/6/1905
Birthplace: Buffalo, NY
Information Available in These Sources: ABYP 1, ABYP 3, AICB, JBA 2, MBMP, SATA 4, TCCW 1, TCCW 2, TCCW 3

YATES, RAYMOND F(RANCIS)
(Borden Hall, Pioneer)
Birthdate: 9/1/1895
Birthplace: Lockport, NY
Deathdate: 9/23/1966
Information Available in These Sources: ABYP 1, ABYP 3, MJA, SATA 31

YAUKEY, GRACE S(YDENSTRICKER)
(Cornelia Spencer)
Birthdate: 5/12/1899
Birthplace: Chinkiang, China
Information Available in These Sources: ABYP 2, ABYP 3, JBA 2, SATA 5

YEAKLEY, MARJORY HALL
(Marjory Hall, Carol Morse)
Birthdate: 5/16/1908
Birthplace: Pittsfield, MA
Information Available in These Sources: ABYP 2, ABYP 3, SATA 21

YENSID, RETLAW
See Disney, Walt(er Elias)

YEO, WILMA (LETHEM)
Birthdate: 12/23/1918
Birthplace: Republican City, NE
Information Available in These Sources: SATA 24

YEP, LAURENCE M(ICHAEL)
Birthdate: 6/14/1948
Birthplace: San Francisco, CA
Information Available in These Sources: DACF, JBA 5, SATA 7, TCCW 2, TCCW 3

YEPSEN, ROGER B(ENNET) JR.
Birthdate: 11/5/1947
Birthplace: Schenectady, NY
Information Available in These Sources: SATA 59

YERIAN, CAMERON JOHN
Birthplace: MI
Information Available in These Sources: SATA 21

YERKOW, CHARLES
Birthdate: 1912
Birthplace: NY
Information Available in These Sources: ABYP 4

YLLA
See Koffler, Camilla

YOLEN, JANE H(YATT)
Birthdate: 2/11/1939
Birthplace: New York, NY
Information Available in These Sources: ABYP 2, ABYP 3, BC, JBA 4, SATA 4, SATA 40, TCCW 1, TCCW 2, TCCW 3

YORINKS, ARTHUR
(Alan Yaffe)
Birthdate: 8/21/1953
Birthplace: Roslyn, NY
Information Available in These Sources: JBA 6, SATA 33, SATA 49

YORK, CAROL BEACH
Birthdate: 1/21/1928
Birthplace: Chicago, IL
Information Available in These Sources: ABYP 4, JBA 5, SATA 6

YORK, REBECCA
See Buckholtz, Eileen (Garber)

YORK, SIMON
See Heinlein, Robert A(nson)

YOST, EDNA
Birthdate: 11/16/1889
Birthplace: Clearfield County, PA
Deathdate: 9/10/1971
Information Available in These Sources: ABYP 1, ABYP 3, SATA 26

YOUNG, A(NDREW) S(TURGEON NASH)
(Doc Young)
Birthdate: 1924
Information Available in These Sources: BAI

YOUNG, BERNICE ELIZABETH
Birthdate: 10/7/1931
Birthplace: Cleveland, OH
Information Available in These Sources: ABYP 4, BAI

YOUNG, BOB
See Young, Robert W(illiam)

YOUNG, CLARENCE
See Garis, Howard R(oger) and Stratemeyer, Edward L.

YOUNG, DOC
See Young, A(ndrew) S(turgeon Nash)

YOUNG, ED
Birthdate: 11/28/1931
Birthplace: Tientsin, China
Information Available in These Sources: IBYP 1, IBYP 2, ICB 4, JBA 3, SATA 10

YOUNG, EDWARD
See Reinfeld, Fred

YOUNG, ELAINE L.
See Schulte, Elaine L(ouise)

YOUNG, FREDERICA
Information Available in These Sources: ABYP 2, ABYP 3

YOUNG, JAN(ET RANDALL)
(Janet Randall)
Birthdate: 3/6/1919
Birthplace: Lancaster, CA
Information Available in These Sources: ABYP 1, ABYP 3, SATA 3

YOUNG, JOHN RICHARD
Information Available in These Sources: ABYP 1, ABYP 3

YOUNG, LOIS HORTON
Birthdate: 4/2/1911
Birthplace: Hamburg, NY
Deathdate: 3/1/1981
Information Available in These Sources: ABYP 4, SATA 26

YOUNG, MARGARET B(UCKNER)
Birthdate: 3/20/1922
Birthplace: Campbellsville, KY
Information Available in These Sources: BABP, BAI, SATA 2

YOUNG, MARJABELLE
(Stewart, Marjabelle Young)
Birthdate: 1930
Information Available in These Sources: ABYP 4

YOUNG, MIRIAM
Birthdate: 2/26/1913
Birthplace: New York, NY
Deathdate: 9/12/1974
Information Available in These Sources: ABYP 1, ABYP 3, SATA 7

YOUNG, PATRICK
See Young, Rodney Lee Patrick (, Jr.)

YOUNG, ROBERT W(ILLIAM)
(Janet Randall, Bob Young)
Birthdate: 11/6/1916
Birthplace: Chico, CA
Deathdate: 7/??/1969
Information Available in These Sources: ABYP 1, ABYP 3, SATA 3

YOUNG, RODNEY LEE PATRICK (, JR.)
(Patrick Young)
Birthdate: 10/19/1937
Birthplace: Ladysmith, WI
Information Available in These Sources: ABYP 2, ABYP 3, SATA 22

YOUNG, STANLEY (PRESTON)
Birthdate: 2/3/1906
Birthplace: Greencastle, IN
Deathdate: 3/22/1975
Information Available in These Sources: ABYP 1, ABYP 3

YOUNG, STARK
Birthdate: 10/11/1881
Birthplace: Como, MS
Deathdate: 1/6/1963
Information Available in These Sources: JBA 1

YUNG, LEONG GOR
See Ellison, Virginia Howell

YURCHENCO, HENRIETTA (WEISS)
Birthdate: 3/22/1916
Birthplace: New Haven, CT
Information Available in These Sources: ABYP 4

Z

ZACH, CHERYL (BYRD)
(Jennifer Cole)
Birthdate: 6/9/1947
Birthplace: Clarksville, TN
Information Available in These Sources: SATA 51, SATA 58

ZACKS, IRENE
Birthplace: Paris, France
Information Available in These Sources: ABYP 2, ABYP 3

ZAFFO, GEORGE J.
(Scott Stewart)
Birthplace: Bridgeport, CT
Information Available in These Sources: ABYP 1, ABYP 3, SATA 42

ZAID, BARRY
Birthdate: 6/8/1938
Birthplace: Toronto, Ontario, Canada
Information Available in These Sources: SATA 51

ZAIDENBERG, ARTHUR
(Azaid)
Birthdate: 8/15/1908
Birthplace: Brooklyn, NY
Information Available in These Sources: ABYP 1, ABYP 3, ABYP 4, SATA 34

ZALBEN, JANE BRESKIN
Birthdate: 4/21/1950
Birthplace: New York, NY
Information Available in These Sources: ICB 4, JBA 5, SATA 7

ZALLINGER, JEAN (DAY)
Birthdate: 2/15/1918
Birthplace: Boston, MA
Information Available in These Sources: IBYP 1, IBYP 2, ICB 2, ICB 3, ICB 4, SATA 14

ZALLINGER, PETER FRANZ
Birthdate: 11/29/1943
Birthplace: New Haven, CT
Information Available in These Sources: SATA 49

ZAPPLER, LISBETH (MOSES)
Birthdate: 9/30/1930
Birthplace: Geneva, NY
Information Available in These Sources: ABYP 4, SATA 10

ZAPUN, SIMONE
Information Available in These Sources: ABYP 4

ZARCHY, HARRY
(Roger Lewis)
Birthdate: 4/28/1912
Birthplace: New York, NY
Information Available in These Sources: ABYP 1, ABYP 3, MJA, SATA 34

ZAREM, LEWIS
Information Available in These Sources: ABYP 1, ABYP 3

ZARIF, MARGARET MIN'IMAH
(Margaret Boone Jones)
Birthplace: Detroit, MI
Deathdate: 8/31/1983 ?
Information Available in These Sources: SATA 33

ZARING, JANE (THOMAS)
Birthdate: 12/26/1936
Birthplace: Nelson, Glamorgan, Wales
Information Available in These Sources: SATA 40, SATA 51

ZARINS, JOYCE AUDY
(Joyce Audy dos Santos)
Birthdate: 1/14/1949
Birthplace: Methuen, MA
Information Available in These Sources: SATA 42, SATA 57

ZASLAVSKY, CLAUDIA
Birthdate: 1/12/1917
Birthplace: New York, NY
Information Available in These Sources: SATA 36

ZECK, GERALD ANTHONY
(Gerry Zeck, G. Anthony Zupa)
Birthdate: 12/29/1939
Birthplace: Minneapolis, MN
Information Available in These Sources: SATA 40

ZECK, GERRY
See Zeck, Gerald Anthony

ZEIGER, SOPHIA
(Sofia)
Birthdate: 8/29/1926
Birthplace: New York, NY
Information Available in These Sources: IBYP 2, ICB 2, ICB 3

ZELAZNY, ROGER (JOSEPH CHRISTOPHER)
(Harrison Denmark)
Birthdate: 5/13/1937
Birthplace: Cleveland, OH
Information Available in These Sources: SATA 39, SATA 57

ZELINSKY, PAUL O.
Birthdate: 2/14/1953
Birthplace: Evanston, IL
Information Available in These Sources: JBA 6, SATA 33, SATA 49

ZELLAN, AUDREY PENN
Birthdate: 5/4/1950
Birthplace: Tacoma Park, MD
Information Available in These Sources: SATA 22

ZEMACH, HARVE
(Harvey Fischstrom)
Birthdate: 12/5/1933
Birthplace: Newark, NJ
Deathdate: 11/2/1974
Information Available in These Sources: ABYP 4, JBA 3, SATA 3

ZEMACH, KAETHE
Birthdate: 3/18/1958
Birthplace: Boston, MA
Information Available in These Sources: SATA 39, SATA 49

ZEMACH, MARGOT
(Margot Zemach Fischstrom)
Birthdate: 11/30/1931
Birthplace: Los Angeles, CA
Deathdate: 5/21/1989
Information Available in These Sources: IBYP 1, IBYP 2, ICB 3, ICB 4, JBA 3, SATA 21, SATA 59

ZENS, PATRICIA MARTIN
Birthdate: 8/27/1926
Birthplace: Chicago, IL
Deathdate: 12/8/1972
Information Available in These Sources: SATA 50

ZERMAN, MELVYN BERNARD
Birthdate: 7/10/1930
Birthplace: New York, NY
Information Available in These Sources: SATA 46

ZIEGLER, JACK (DENMORE)
Birthdate: 7/13/1942
Birthplace: New York, NY
Information Available in These Sources: SATA 60

ZIEMIENSKI, DENNIS (THEODORE)
Birthdate: 5/6/1947
Birthplace: San Francisco, CA
Information Available in These Sources: SATA 10

ZILLAH
See MacDonald, Zillah Katherine

ZIM, HERBERT S(PENCER)
Birthdate: 7/12/1909
Birthplace: New York, NY
Information Available in These Sources: ABYP 1, ABYP 3, BABP, JBA 2, SATA 1, SATA 30

ZIM, SONIA BLEEKER
See Bleeker, Sonia

ZIMELMAN, NATHAN
Information Available in These Sources: ABYP 3, SATA 37

ZIMMER, DIRK
Birthdate: 10/2/1943
Birthplace: Austria
Information Available in These Sources: JBA 6

ZIMMERMAN, NAOMA
Birthdate: 8/2/1914
Birthplace: St. Louis, MO
Information Available in These Sources: SATA 10

ZIMMERMANN, ARNOLD E(RNST ALFRED)
Birthdate: 8/25/1909
Birthplace: Munich, Germany
Information Available in These Sources: SATA 58

ZINDEL, BONNIE
Birthdate: 5/3/1943
Birthplace: New York, NY
Information Available in These Sources: SATA 34

ZINDEL, PAUL
Birthdate: 5/15/1936
Birthplace: Staten Island, NY
Information Available in These Sources: DACF, JBA 5, SATA 16, SATA 58, TCCW 1, TCCW 2, TCCW 3

ZINER, FEENIE
See Ziner, Florence Feenie

ZINER, FLORENCE FEENIE
(Feenie Ziner)
Birthdate: 3/22/1921
Birthplace: Brooklyn, NY
Information Available in These Sources: ABYP 1, ABYP 3, SATA 5

ZINGARA, PROFESSOR
See Leeming, Joseph

ZINKOFF, DAVE
Information Available in These Sources: ABYP 1, ABYP 3

ZION, EUGENE
(Gene Zion)
Birthdate: 10/5/1913
Birthplace: New York, NY
Deathdate: 12/5/1975
Information Available in These Sources: ABYP 1, ABYP 3, MJA, SATA 18, TCCW 1, TCCW 2, TCCW 3

ZION, GENE
See Zion, Eugene

ZIRBES, LAURA
Birthdate: 4/26/1884
Birthplace: Buffalo, NY
Information Available in These Sources: ABYP 1, ABYP 3

ZOLLINGER, GULIELMA
(William Zachary Gladwin)
Birthdate: 1856
Birthplace: IL
Deathdate: 8/24/1917
Information Available in These Sources: JBA 1, JBA 2, SATA 27

ZOLOTOW, CHARLOTTE S(HAPIRO)
(Sarah Abbott, Charlotte Bookman)
Birthdate: 6/26/1915
Birthplace: Norfolk, VA
Information Available in These Sources: ABYP 1, ABYP 3, ABYP 4, BABP, MJA, SATA 1, SATA 35, TCCW 1, TCCW 2, TCCW 3

ZONIA, DHIMITRI
Birthdate: 6/12/1921
Birthplace: St. Louis, MO
Information Available in These Sources: SATA 20

ZUBROWSKI, BERNARD
Birthdate: 2/22/1939
Birthplace: Baltimore, MD
Information Available in These Sources: SATA 35

ZUPA, G. ANTHONY
See Zeck, Gerald Anthony

ZURHORST, CHARLES (STEWART, JR.)
(Charles Stewart)
Birthdate: 12/3/1913
Birthplace: Washington, DC
Information Available in These Sources: SATA 12

ZUROMSKIS, DIANE Z.
See Stanley, Diane

ZWEIFEL, FRANCES
Birthdate: 5/26/1931
Birthplace: Hampton, VA
Information Available in These Sources: SATA 14

ZWINGER, ANN
Birthdate: 3/12/1925
Birthplace: Muncie, IN
Information Available in These Sources: SATA 46

Birth Month Index

JANUARY

Day Year
01, 1888 Ackerman, Eugene (Francis)
01, 1897 Bowen, Catherine Drinker
01, 1899 Cottam, Clarence
01, 1908 Jackson, Jesse
01, 1915 Hartley, Ellen (Raphael)
01, 1921 Romano, Louis G.
01, 1922 Brick, John
01, 1925 Steiner, Stan(ley)
01, 1925 Williams, Barbara (Wright)
01, 1926 Haas, Carolyn Buhai
01, 1928 Cheney, Theodore Albert
01, 1932 Chwast, Jacqueline (Weiner)
01, 1934 Smith, LeRoi
01, 1934 Telemaque, Eleanor Wong
01, 1935 Kliban, B.
01, 1935 Mead, Russell (M., Jr.)
01, 1940 Choate, Judith (Newkirk)
01, 1944 Hirsh, Marilyn (Joyce)
01, 1946 Wilkinson, Brenda
01, 1947 Hermanson, Dennis (Everett)
01, 1949 Tapp, Kathy Kennedy
02, 1894 Albrecht, Lillie (Vanderveer)
02, 1894 Nathan, Robert (Gruntal)
02, 1899 Evans, Katherine (Floyd)
02, 1899 Selden, Samuel
02, 1900 Peltier, Leslie C(opus)
02, 1900 Rowland, Florence Wightman
02, 1920 Asimov, Isaac
02, 1921 Bonsall, Crosby (Barbara Newell)
02, 1921 Slepian, Jan(ice B.)
02, 1925 Carona, Philip B(en)
02, 1929 Teague, Robert
02, 1954 Schwark, Mary Beth
03, 1872 Chorpenning, Charlotte (Lee Barrows)
03, 1898 Goudey, Alice E(dwards)
03, 1898 Haywood, Carolyn
03, 1913 Butler, Hal
03, 1913 Chute, B(eatrice) J(oy)
03, 1916 Bate, Norman (Arthur)
03, 1922 Schutzer, A. I.
03, 1925 Barnett, Leo
03, 1926 Anglund, Joan Walsh
03, 1929 Chen, Anthony (Young)
03, 1929 Clark, Patricia (Finrow)
03, 1931 Elwood, Ann
03, 1932 Fenten, D(onald) X.
03, 1934 Gauch, Patricia Lee
03, 1934 Moffett, Martha (Leatherwood)
03, 1934 Smith, Ursula
03, 1937 Taylor, Carl
03, 1938 Ada, Alma Flor
03, 1941 Nathanson, Laura Walther
03, 1949 Flitner, David P(erkins)
03, 1952 Radlauer, David
04, 1892 Best, Evangel Allena Champlin
04, 1894 Woody, Regina (Llewellyn) Jones
04, 1896 Dirksen, Everett McKinley
04, 1899 Carr, Harriett H(elen)
04, 1899 Kubie, Nora (Gottheil) Benjamin
04, 1906 Harmon, Margaret
04, 1908 Steedman, Marguerite Couturier
04, 1914 Gurko, Leo
04, 1916 Duff, Margaret K.
04, 1917 McCoy, J(oseph) J(erome)
04, 1918 Searight, Mary W(illiams)
04, 1928 Howard, Moses Leon
04, 1932 Utz, Lois (Marie)
04, 1933 Naylor, Phyllis Reynolds
04, 1936 Burleigh, Robert
04, 1936 Liman, Ellen (Fogelson)
04, 1937 Korty, Carol
04, 1941 Delessert, Etienne
04, 1956 Frank, Daniel B.
05, 1881 Quinn, Elisabeth
05, 1890 McFarland, Wilma
05, 1894 Carroll, Archer Latrobe
05, 1895 Breckenfeld, Vivian Gurney
05, 1909 Bloch, Lucienne
05, 1920 Slicer, Margaret O.
05, 1936 Oates, Stephen B.
05, 1939 Cole, Sheila R(otenberg)
05, 1944 Maestro, Betsy (Crippen)
05, 1947 Waugh, Carol-Lynn Rossel
05, 1952 Cherry, Lynne
06, 1878 Sandburg, Carl (August)
06, 1889 Craven, Thomas
06, 1894 Stern, Catherine (Brieger)
06, 1901 Parke, Margaret Bittner
06, 1912 Manfred, Frederick F(eikema)
06, 1912 Talbert, Ansel Edward McLaurine
06, 1919 Angell, Madeline
06, 1919 Cleaver, Vera (Allen)
06, 1919 Foster, F. Blanche
06, 1926 Friedman, Ina R(osen)
06, 1934 Bolognese, Don(ald Alan)
06, 1944 Townsend, Thomas L.
06, 1948 Williams, Linda

06, 1949	D'Ignazio, Fred(erick)
06, 1951	Fleisher, Robbin
07, 1898	DeGering, Etta (Fowler)
07, 1906	Clymer, Eleanor (Lowenton)
07, 1907	Watson, Sara Ruth
07, 1911	Baker, Laura Nelson
07, 1912	Addams, Charles (Samuel)
07, 1913	Liebers, Arthur
07, 1914	Brooks, Anita
07, 1922	Kessler, Ethel
07, 1926	Hoffman, Rosekrans
07, 1927	McDonald, Forrest
07, 1934	Meade, Marion
07, 1935	O'Connell, Margaret F(orster)
07, 1936	Chorao, Ann McKay (Sproat)
07, 1936	Lapp, Eleanor J.
07, 1936	Simonetta, Sam
07, 1937	Stewig, John Warren
07, 1956	Detwiler, Susan Dill
08, 1887	White, Percival
08, 1889	Owen, Russell
08, 1902	Kane, Henry Bugbee
08, 1904	Choron, Jacques
08, 1904	McCarty, Rega Kramer
08, 1906	Faulkner, Nancy (Anne Irvin)
08, 1908	Perceval, Don
08, 1910	Marriott, Alice Lee
08, 1912	Wells, Peter
08, 1919	Swarthout, Kathryn (Blair Vaughn)
08, 1921	Ames, Lee J(udah)
08, 1924	Vlahos, Olivia
08, 1925	Burroughs, Polly
08, 1927	Brommer, Gerald F(rederick)
08, 1929	Hale, Linda (Howe)
08, 1944	Brooks, Terry
08, 1945	Bond, Nancy (Barbara)
08, 1949	Manes, Stephen
09, 1886	Brooks, Walter R(ollin)
09, 1900	Halliburton, Richard
09, 1912	Harris, Lorle K(empe)
09, 1914	Bulla, Clyde Robert
09, 1914	Marks, Mickey Klar
09, 1915	Potter, Marian
09, 1917	Sheldon, Walt(er J.)
09, 1939	Wende, Philip
09, 1953	Mannetti, Lisa
10, 1873	Christy, Howard Chandler
10, 1888	Fergusson, Erna
10, 1900	Matthews, Herbert L(ionel)
10, 1902	Durant, John
10, 1915	Austin, Mary C(arrington)
10, 1918	Jones, Hortense P.
10, 1926	Bolton, Carole (Roberts)
10, 1929	Charlip, Remy
10, 1930	Buck, William Ray
10, 1932	Hoppe, Joanne
10, 1932	Wallace, Robert A.
10, 1936	Ambrose, Stephen E(dward)
10, 1936	Martin, Stefan
10, 1936	Yamaguchi, Marianne Illenberger
10, 1940	Gonzalez, Gloria
10, 1946	Tang, You-Shan
10, 1947	Bloom, Lloyd
10, 1950	Gevirtz, Eliezer
11, 1870	Rice, Alice (Caldwell) Hegan
11, 1899	LeGallienne, Eva
11, 1899	Thomas, Estelle Webb
11, 1902	Cormack, Maribelle B.
11, 1902	Foster, E(lizabeth) C(onnell)
11, 1903	Paton, Alan (Stewart)
11, 1914	Andrist, Ralph K.
11, 1915	Heinz, W(ilfred) C(harles)
11, 1916	Stokes, Olivia Pearl
11, 1918	Conly, Robert Leslie
11, 1918	Tompert, Ann
11, 1922	Margolis, Vivienne
11, 1928	Rabe, Berniece (Louise)
11, 1931	Rodgers, Mary
11, 1936	Mango, Karin N.
11, 1936	Rosenbaum, Eileen
11, 1941	Billings, Charlene W(interer)
11, 1942	Byrd, Robert (John)
11, 1943	Ulmer, Louise
11, 1947	Hale, Janet Campbell
11, 1949	Otfinoski, Steven
11, 1950	Casey, Brigid
12, 1874	Armer, Laura (Adams)
12, 1876	London, Jack
12, 1908	Hurd, Clement
12, 1910	Haber, Louis
12, 1915	Allen, Lee
12, 1917	Zaslavsky, Claudia
12, 1920	Smith, George Harmon
12, 1925	Fehrenbach, T(heodore) R(eed, Jr.)
12, 1935	Mayerson, Evelyn White
12, 1936	Cadwallader, Sharon
12, 1945	Rostkowski, Margaret I.
12, 1946	Milton, Joyce
12, 1949	Munoz, William
13, 1832	Alger, Horatio, Jr.
13, 1886	Moore, Clyde B.
13, 1901	Thompson, Hildegard (Steerstedter)
13, 1907	Freeman, Lydia
13, 1908	Flexner, James Thomas
13, 1915	English, James W(ilson)
13, 1915	Patten, Lewis Byford
13, 1920	Hamalian, Leo
13, 1922	Bodecker, N(iels) M(ogens)
13, 1923	Elgin, Kathleen
13, 1926	Horner, Althea (Jane)
13, 1927	Keller, Irene (Barron)
13, 1933	Goulart, Ron(ald Joseph)
13, 1937	Arbeiter, Jean S(onkin)
13, 1940	Fitzgerald, F(rancis) A(nthony)
13, 1941	Naylor, Penelope
13, 1943	Elwood, Roger
13, 1948	Booher, Dianna Daniels
13, 1953	Mabery, D. L.
14, 1874	Burgess, Thornton W(aldo)
14, 1881	Williams, Clyde C.
14, 1882	VanLoon, Hendrik Willem
14, 1886	Lofting, Hugh
14, 1895	Meyer, Jerome Sydney
14, 1896	Maxwell, Arthur S.
14, 1905	Hahn, Emily
14, 1907	Alberts, Frances Jacobs
14, 1908	Lipinsky de Orlov, Lino S(igismondo)
14, 1913	Roberts, John G(aither)
14, 1919	Lund, Doris (Herold)
14, 1922	Rothberg, Abraham
14, 1924	Tusiani, Joseph
14, 1931	Connolly, Jerome P(atrick)
14, 1943	Mauser, Patricia Rhoads
14, 1949	Zarins, Joyce Audy
15, 1873	Benda, Wladyslaw Theodore
15, 1885	MacDonald, Zillah Katherine
15, 1886	Buff, Conrad
15, 1901	Child, Charles Jesse
15, 1903	Pyne, Mable Mandeville
15, 1909	Siegmeister, Elie
15, 1910	MacLeod, Beatrice (Beach)
15, 1914	Dunne, Mary Collins
15, 1914	Shirreffs, Gordon D(onald)
15, 1917	Denzel, Justin F(rancis)
15, 1918	Sparks, Beatrice Mathews
15, 1920	Resnick, Seymour
15, 1924	Lynds, Dennis
15, 1929	King, Martin Luther, Jr.
15, 1933	Gaines, Ernest J.
15, 1935	Silverberg, Robert
15, 1938	Hart, Bruce
15, 1940	Hochschild, Arlie Russell
15, 1941	Edwards, Page L., Jr.
15, 1941	Yang, Jay
15, 1945	LeTord, Bijou
16, 1870	Perard, Victor Semon
16, 1909	Walden, Amelia Elizabeth
16, 1910	Shapp, Martha (Glauber)
16, 1910	Villiard, Paul
16, 1911	Craig, Margaret Maze

16, 1918 Preston, Lillian Elvira
16, 1920 Maynard, Olga
16, 1922 Crawford, Deborah
16, 1928 Kennedy, William
16, 1932 Berry, James
16, 1938 Lipsyte, Robert (Michael)
16, 1941 Orbach, Ruth Gary
16, 1947 McMullan, Kate (Hall)
16, 1947 Weston, Martha
16, 1948 Carpenter, John
17, 1851 Frost, A(rthur) B(urdett)
17, 1901 Hartman, Louis F(rancis)
17, 1906 Holloway, Teresa (Bragunier)
17, 1908 Reed, Philip G.
17, 1921 O'Daniel, Janet
17, 1924 Tichy, William
17, 1925 Cormier, Robert (Edmund)
17, 1933 Greene, Wade
17, 1934 Lewis, Shari
17, 1938 Bellairs, John
17, 1943 Haas, James E(dward)
18, 1880 Bowman, James Cloyd
18, 1904 McNickle, William D'Arcy
18, 1908 Bronowski, Jacob
18, 1913 Kaye, Danny
18, 1915 Milne, Margarey (Joan Greene)
18, 1918 Memling, Carl
18, 1919 Longman, Harold S.
18, 1924 George, Renee
18, 1926 Trivelpiece, Laurel
18, 1930 Laird, Jean E(louise)
18, 1945 McGuire, Leslie (Sarah)
19, 1809 Poe, Edgar Allan
19, 1898 Rushmore, Helen
19, 1898 Street, Julia Montgomery
19, 1900 Hungerford, Edward Buell
19, 1903 Reynolds, Marjorie (Harris)
19, 1905 Slobodkin, Florence (Gersh)
19, 1913 Foley, Daniel Joseph
19, 1915 Grider, Dorothy
19, 1925 Darling, Richard L(ewis)
19, 1927 Gerson, Corinne (Schreiberstein)
19, 1927 Shaw, Evelyn
19, 1928 Slate, Joseph (Frank)
19, 1929 Woodard, Carol
19, 1936 Panter, Carol (Yeckes)
19, 1937 Batten, Mary
19, 1940 DePauw, Linda Grant
19, 1941 Dodson, Susan
19, 1942 Blocksma, Mary
19, 1946 Bell, Neill
20, 1888 Jones, Wilfred J.
20, 1890 Daniel, Hawthorne
20, 1894 Gray, Harold (Lincoln)
20, 1898 Boyce, George A(rthur)
20, 1905 Welty, S(usan) F(ulton)

20, 1909 Friendlich, Richard J.
20, 1910 Hoover, Helen (Drusilla Blackburn)
20, 1916 Scott, John Anthony
20, 1917 Singer, Julia
20, 1918 Kupferberg, Herbert
20, 1919 Cooper, Lester (Irving)
20, 1920 Moss, Don(ald)
20, 1921 Golann, Cecil Paige
20, 1932 Johnson, Evelyne
20, 1934 Robison, Nancy L(ouise)
20, 1939 Anderson, Mary (Quirk)
21, 1893 Barnaby, Ralph S(tanton)
21, 1897 Reyher, Rebecca Hourwich
21, 1903 Keating, Lawrence A(lfred)
21, 1904 Crawford, John E(dmund)
21, 1914 Delear, Frank J.
21, 1916 Antonacci, Robert Joseph
21, 1916 Boyle, Ann (Peters)
21, 1917 Nailor, Gerald A.
21, 1926 Collier, Zena
21, 1928 York, Carol Beach
21, 1948 Laiken, Deirdre S(usan)
21, 1953 Blair, Jay
21, 1953 Scarry, Richard, Jr.
22, 1893 Oursler, Charles Fulton
22, 1903 Sutton, Margaret (Beebe)
22, 1916 McGraw, William Corbin
22, 1917 Lamb, Elizabeth Searle
22, 1920 Hillert, Margaret
22, 1928 Weiss, Malcolm E.
22, 1930 Carlisle, Olga A(ndreyev)
22, 1930 Lent, Blair
22, 1935 Parenteau, Shirley (Laurolyn)
22, 1943 Jacobs, Linda C.
23, 1880 Poole, Ernest
23, 1891 Ford, Lauren
23, 1900 Mason, Miriam E(vangeline)
23, 1904 Quarles, Benjamin
23, 1905 Brandt, Catharine
23, 1907 Austin, Elizabeth S(chling)
23, 1910 Arbuckle, Dorothy Fry
23, 1911 Eifert, Virginia (Louise) S(nider)
23, 1911 Graves, Charles Parlin
23, 1913 Woodson, John Waddie, Jr.
23, 1930 Goodman, Elaine (Egan)
23, 1935 Giegling, John A(llan)
23, 1939 Hildebrandt, Greg
23, 1939 Hildebrandt, Tim(othy)
23, 1945 Crawford, Charles P.
23, 1949 Mathieu, Joseph P.
23, 1949 Saseen, Sharon (Dillon)

23, 1950 Smith, Susan Mathias
24, 1862 Wharton, Edith
24, 1889 Hawes, Charles Boardman
24, 1898 Munce, Ruth (Livingston) Hill
24, 1920 Cable, Mary
24, 1922 Beatty, John (Louis)
24, 1928 Rosenblum, Richard
24, 1929 Hogan, Bernice Harris
24, 1934 Keith, Hal
24, 1939 Ferris, Jean
24, 1939 Tarshis, Barry
24, 1945 Israel, Elaine
24, 1949 Bachman, Fred
24, 1949 Pellowski, Michael J(oseph)
25, 1892 Washburne, Heluiz Chandler
25, 1907 Miller, Shane
25, 1912 Funke, Lewis
25, 1914 Flora, James (Royer)
25, 1915 Deiss, Joseph Jay
25, 1916 Wilson, Dagmar
25, 1917 Gillelan, George Howard
25, 1918 Foster, Laura Louise (James)
25, 1923 Rinkoff, Barbara (Jean Rich)
25, 1925 Oppenheimer, Joan L(etson)
25, 1926 Martin, George
25, 1930 Wolitzer, Hilma
25, 1940 Wartski, Maureen (Ann Crane)
25, 1952 White, Timothy (Thomas Anthony)
25, 1954 Weiss, Nicki
26, 1831 Dodge, Mary (Elizabeth) Mapes
26, 1871 Adams, Samuel Hopkins
26, 1884 Andrews, Roy Chapman
26, 1893 Welles, Winifred
26, 1901 Reck, Alma Kehoe
26, 1902 Andrews, F(rank) Emerson
26, 1905 Cousins, Margaret
26, 1905 Trapp, Maria (Augusta) von
26, 1915 Keyes, Fenton
26, 1917 Whitney, Thomas P(orter)
26, 1921 Lasher, Faith B.
26, 1924 Eisenberg, Phyllis Rose
26, 1926 Woods, George A(llan)
26, 1929 Feiffer, Jules
26, 1929 Sommer, Elyse (Vorchheimer)
26, 1930 DeMessieres, Nicole
26, 1931 Silverman, Mel(vyn Frank)
26, 1934 Thomas, Patricia J(ack)
26, 1937 Mikolaycak, Charles
26, 1938 Figueroa, Pablo

26, 1941 McHugh, Berit Elisabet
26, 1948 Simonetta, Linda
26, 1954 Callan, Jamie
26, 1956 Wolff, Jenifer Ashley
27, 1893 McMillen, Wheeler
27, 1899 Malcolmson, David
27, 1899 Stong, Phil(ip Duffield)
27, 1901 Bridges, William (Andrew)
27, 1902 Graham, Lorenz (Bell)
27, 1910 Austin, Phil
27, 1910 Reinfeld, Fred
27, 1915 Archer, Jules
27, 1915 Hnizdovsky, Jacques
27, 1916 Kranzler, George G(ershon)
27, 1916 Warren, Elizabeth Avery
27, 1923 Merrill, Jean (Fairbanks)
27, 1928 Allard, Harry G(rover), Jr.
27, 1937 Kessel, Joyce Karen
27, 1939 Lester, Julius B.
27, 1940 O'Leary, Brian (Todd)
28, ???? Estep, Irene (Compton)
28, 1843 Bolton, Henry Carrington
28, 1899 Aiken, Clarissa (Lorenz)
28, 1903 Rowe, Viola Carson
28, 1904 Nugent, Frances Roberts
28, 1911 Bell, Gertrude (Wood)
28, 1912 Lens, Sidney
28, 1917 Gottlieb, William P(aul)
28, 1924 Parry, Marian
28, 1924 Watson, Sally (Lou)
28, 1925 Conn, Frances (Goldberg)
28, 1927 Williams, Vera B.
28, 1932 Jonas, Ann
29, 1835 Woolsey, Sarah Chauncy
29, 1897 Lufkin, Raymond H.
29, 1906 Bratton, Karl H(enry)
29, 1910 LeBar, Mary E(velyn)
29, 1913 Keeler, Ronald F(ranklin)
29, 1913 Schneider, Nina (Zimet)
29, 1915 Gillette, Henry Sampson
29, 1915 Peet, William Bartlett
29, 1918 Fleischman, Seymour
29, 1920 Hunt, Kari
29, 1920 Krantz, Hazel (Newman)
29, 1921 Holmquist, Eve
29, 1924 Faber, Doris (Greenberg)
29, 1928 Anderson, Norman (Dean)
29, 1930 Cassedy, Sylvia
29, 1930 Collier, Christopher
29, 1933 McClinton, Leon
29, 1943 Wells, Rosemary
29, 1949 Pahz, Anne Cheryl Suzanne

30, 1866 Burgess, F(rank) Gelett
30, 1901 Hiser, Iona Seibert
30, 1905 Neyhart, Louise (Pauline) Albright
30, 1911 Sanderson, Ivan T(erence)
30, 1921 Augelli, John P(at)
30, 1924 Alexander, Lloyd (Chudley)
30, 1925 Breetveld, Jim Patrick
30, 1925 Campbell, Ann R.
30, 1927 Heuer, Kenneth John
30, 1930 Levoy, Myron
30, 1931 Eckert, Allan W.
30, 1935 Brautigan, Richard (Gary)
30, 1942 Johnston, Tony
30, 1944 Katchen, Carole
30, 1951 Fufuka, Karama
31, 1888 Pratt, Agnes Edwards Rothery
31, 1898 Katchamakoff, Atanas
31, 1909 Huntington, Harriet E(lizabeth)
31, 1916 Bliven, Bruce, Jr.
31, 1925 Weaver, Jack
31, 1928 Trelease, Allen W(illiam)
31, 1929 Saunders, Rubie (Agnes)
31, 1932 Brown, Irene Bennett
31, 1933 Chittenden, Margaret
31, 1934 DeWeese, Thomas Eugene
31, 1935 Marston, Hope Irvin
31, 1941 McDermott, Gerald
31, 1942 Tchudi, Stephen N.
31, 1943 Rivoli, Mario
31, 1944 Carmichael, Harriet
31, 1946 Paltrowitz, Stuart

FEBRUARY

Day Year
??, 1817 Douglass, Frederick
01, 1887 Nordhoff, Charles (Bernard)
01, 1900 Busoni, Rafaello
01, 1902 Hughes, James Langston
01, 1903 Pundt, Helen Marie
01, 1905 Lee, Doris (Emrick)
01, 1910 Nordstrom, Ursula (Litchfield)
01, 1912 Ogan, George F.
01, 1914 Ishmael, Woodi
01, 1917 Madlee, Dorothy (Haynes)
01, 1919 Abodaher, David J. (Naiph)
01, 1919 Carswell, Evelyn M(edicus)
01, 1919 Schiller, Andrew
01, 1920 Haggerty, James J(oseph)

01, 1920 Harnan, Terry
01, 1922 O'Leary, Frank(lin J.)
01, 1923 Osterritter, John F(erdinand)
01, 1925 Chaffin, Lillie D(orton)
01, 1931 Kipniss, Robert
01, 1941 Spinelli, Jerry
01, 1943 McGee, Barbara
01, 1949 Buckholtz, Eileen (Garber)
02, 1819 Lowell, James Russell
02, 1887 Kaufmann, Helen (Loeb)
02, 1891 Holberg, Ruth (Langland)
02, 1899 Belpre, Pura
02, 1899 Caudill, Rebecca
02, 1901 Holisher, Desider
02, 1901 Kerr, Jessica (Gordon)
02, 1904 Waltrip, Lela (Kingston)
02, 1931 Baker, Jeffrey J(ohn) W(heeler)
02, 1931 Viorst, Judith (Stahl)
02, 1934 Weiser, Marjorie P(hillis) K(atz)
02, 1940 Bitter, Gary G(len)
02, 1940 Disch, Thomas M(ichael)
02, 1945 Matthias, Catherine
02, 1951 Rice, Eve (Hart)
03, 1842 Lanier, Sidney
03, 1894 Rockwell, Norman (Percevel)
03, 1906 Young, Stanley
03, 1907 Carter, William Hodding
03, 1907 Jauss, Anne Marie
03, 1907 Morey, Walt(er Nelson)
03, 1908 Heaps, Willard (Allison)
03, 1910 Sankey, Alice (Ann-Susan)
03, 1914 Wunsch, Josephine (McLean)
03, 1927 Nixon, Joan Lowery
03, 1929 Friedrich, Otto (Alva)
03, 1929 Lorraine, Walter (Henry)
03, 1929 Mellin, Jeanne
03, 1931 Powers, Bill
03, 1936 Brown, Buck
03, 1939 Ringi, Kjell Arne Sorensen
03, 1945 Wallner, John C(harles)
04, 1898 Monroe, Marion
04, 1900 Stinetorf, Louise (Allender)
04, 1902 Lindbergh, Charles A(ugustus, Jr.)
04, 1904 Kantor, MacKinlay
04, 1910 Ellison, Virginia Howell
04, 1910 Lavender, David (Sievert)
04, 1911 Peare, Catherine Owens
04, 1912 Lewis, Mildred D.
04, 1912 Weaver, John D(owning)

04,	1913	Stevenson, Janet (Marshall)	07,	1908	Gipson, Fred(erick Benjamin)	10,	1943	Gammell, Stephen
04,	1914	Blair, Anne Denton	07,	1909	Davis, Lavinia (Riker)	11,	1802	Child, Lydia Maria
04,	1918	Boyd, Waldo T.	07,	1913	Adamson, George Worsley	11,	1871	Laut, Agnes C(hristina)
04,	1919	D'Amato, Alex				11,	1891	Martin, Rene
04,	1919	Soule, Jean Conder	07,	1916	Sherman, Theresa	11,	1900	Brett, Grace N(eff)
04,	1920	Johnson, B(urdetta) F(aye)	07,	1920	Brand, Oscar	11,	1904	Armer, Alberta (Roller)
			07,	1922	Torbert, Floyd James	11,	1905	Kalmenoff, Matthew
04,	1920	Millender, Dharathula (Hood)	07,	1931	Micklish, Rita	11,	1912	Heuman, William
			07,	1933	Chandler, David Porter	11,	1913	Kelleam, Joseph E(veridge)
04,	1920	Sackson, Sid	07,	1940	Berelson, Howard			
04,	1922	Chambers, Bradford	07,	1941	Kilian, Crawford	11,	1920	Sanger, Marjory Bartlett
04,	1923	Knoepfle, John	08,	1884	Johnson, Gaylord	11,	1926	Edens, Bishop David
04,	1925	Hoban, Russell (Conwell)	08,	1899	Crawford, Phyllis	11,	1926	French, Dorothy Kayser
			08,	1900	Kredel, Fritz	11,	1928	Hieatt, Constance B(artlett)
04,	1929	Chandler, Linda S(mith)	08,	1903	McCormick, Wilfred			
04,	1930	Hazen, Barbara Shook	08,	1906	Adams, Adrienne	11,	1939	Yolen, Jane H(yatt)
04,	1930	Roberts, Bruce (Stuart)	08,	1907	Conrad, Arthur S.	11,	1952	Knapp, Ron
04,	1933	Frank, Mary	08,	1911	Bishop, Elizabeth	12,	1883	Brown, George Earl
04,	1933	Murphy, Barbara Beasley	08,	1912	Elbert, Virginia Fowler	12,	1888	Alexander, Frances (Laura)
			08,	1914	Ross, Frank (Xavier), Jr.			
04,	1935	Alexander, Linda				12,	1900	Fenton, Carroll Lane
04,	1938	Harrison, Deloris	08,	1915	Evarts, Hal G. (Jr.)	12,	1902	Self, Margaret Cabell
04,	1943	Ross, Pat(ricia Kienzie)	08,	1917	Bendick, Robert L(ouis)	12,	1907	Jacobs, Leland Blair
04,	1948	Fatigati, Frances Evelyn de Buhr	08,	1918	Mooney, Elizabeth C(omstock)	12,	1909	Barnett, Lincoln (Kinnear)
05,	1890	Dahl, Borghild	08,	1920	Wolters, Richard A.	12,	1912	Erickson, Sabra R(ollins)
05,	1905	Potter, Robert Ducharme	08,	1922	Glanzman, Louis S.			
			08,	1926	Rich, Elaine Sommers	12,	1913	Atwood, Ann (Margaret)
05,	1908	Gervasi, Frank Henry	08,	1934	Rockwell, Anne (Foote)	12,	1921	Vaeth, J(oseph) Gordon
05,	1911	Dubkin, Lois (Knudson)	08,	1949	McLoughlin, John C.	12,	1922	Bethell, Jean (Frankenberry)
05,	1915	Sanderlin, George	09,	1874	Lowell, Amy			
05,	1920	Rachlis, Eugene (Jacob)	09,	1882	Hall, Anna Gertrude	12,	1923	Kissin, Eva H.
			09,	1908	VanStockum, Hilda (Gerarda)	12,	1928	Gould, Marilyn
05,	1921	Schechter, Betty (Goodstein)				12,	1934	Downie, Mary Alice (Dawe)
			09,	1914	Sussman, Cornelia (Silver)			
05,	1921	Stilwell, Alison				12,	1938	Blume, Judy (Sussman)
05,	1924	Lauber, Patricia (Grace)	09,	1917	Archer, Marion Fuller	12,	1939	Dorin, Patrick C(arberry)
05,	1928	Kunhardt, Philip B(radish), Jr.	09,	1927	Epple, Anne Orth			
			09,	1927	Gackenbach, Dick	12,	1941	Haney, Lynn
05,	1929	Rahn, Joan Elma	09,	1928	Frazetta, Frank	12,	1945	Small, David
05,	1945	Wibbelsman, Charles J(oseph)	09,	1932	Meyer, F(ranklyn) E(dward)	12,	1947	Howell, Pat
						12,	1950	Conover, Chris
06,	1904	Wilkie, Katherine E(lliott)	09,	1932	Morriss, James E(dward)	13,	1875	Nichols, Spencer Baird
						13,	1882	Davis, Mary Gould
06,	1905	Wohlberg, Meg	09,	1936	Litowinsky, Olga (Jean)	13,	1891	Wilwerding, Walter Joseph
06,	1907	Hymes, Lucia M(anley)	09,	1944	Walker, Alice			
06,	1909	Blassingame, Wyatt (Rainey)	09,	1945	Roos, Stephen (Kelley)	13,	1903	Colorado (Capella), Antonio Julio
			10,	1889	Davis, Marguerite			
06,	1914	Bloom, Freddy	10,	1891	Walker, Louise Jean	13,	1910	Edey, Maitland A(rmstrong)
06,	1923	Wexler, Jerome (LeRoy)	10,	1898	Woodward, Hildegard			
			10,	1906	Oakley, Helen (McKelvey)	13,	1924	Lonette, Reisie (Dominee)
06,	1925	Warrick, Patricia Scott						
06,	1928	Jones, Weyman (B.)	10,	1906	Varley, Dimitry V.	13,	1924	Sebestyen, Ouida (Dockery)
06,	1937	Singer, David (Lin)	10,	1917	Crout, George C(lement)			
06,	1939	Taylor, Louise Todd				13,	1931	Lipman, David
06,	1946	Vojtech, Anna	10,	1923	Tichenor, Tom	13,	1932	Taback, Simms
07,	1867	Wilder, Laura (Elizabeth) Ingalls	10,	1924	Dolan, Edward F(rancis), Jr.	13,	1936	Meade, Ellen (Roddick)
						13,	1941	McCloy, James F(loyd)
07,	1890	Lide, Alice (Alison)	10,	1927	Grammer, June Amos	13,	1944	Wangerin, Walter, Jr.
07,	1890	Parker, Bertha Morris	10,	1930	Konigsburg, E(laine) L(obl)	13,	1945	Sleator, William (Warner III)
07,	1894	Williamson, T(hames) R(oss)						
			10,	1932	Brandenberg, Franz	13,	1946	Balducci, Carolyn Feleppa
07,	1898	Charlot, Jean	10,	1934	Morrill, Leslie H(olt)			
07,	1901	Botkin, B(enjamin) A(lbert)	10,	1934	Rice, James	13,	1947	Lisle, Janet Taylor
			10,	1935	Alcorn, John	13,	1947	Sachs, Judith
			10,	1940	Cosner, Shaaron	14,	1872	Berger, William Merritt
						14,	1884	Avinoff, Andrey

14, 1903 Teal, Val(entine M.)
14, 1908 Lantz, Paul
14, 1913 Allen, Mel
14, 1913 Keen, Martin L.
14, 1923 Lueders, Edward (George)
14, 1931 Scott, Jane (Harrington)
14, 1931 Warshofsky, Fred
14, 1932 Wymark, Olwen (Margaret Buck)
14, 1942 Highwater, Jamake
14, 1947 Leigh, Tom
14, 1949 Root, Phyllis
14, 1952 Shannon, George (William Bones)
14, 1953 Zelinsky, Paul O.
15, 1894 Trent, Robbie
15, 1898 Gonzalez, Xavier
15, 1904 Chase, Richard
15, 1909 Heins, Paul
15, 1917 Edmonds, I(vy) G(ordon)
15, 1918 Zallinger, Jean (Day)
15, 1926 Adams, Hazard
15, 1928 Bridwell, Norman
15, 1929 Orgel, Doris (Adelberg)
15, 1936 Hook, Martha
15, 1939 VanHorn, William
15, 1942 Shachtman, Tom
15, 1948 Landau, Elaine (Garmiza)
16, 1882 Cronbach, Abraham
16, 1884 Flaherty, Robert Joseph
16, 1893 Boyd, Frank
16, 1900 Hackett, Albert
16, 1903 Simon, Martin P(aul William)
16, 1906 Freeman, Eugene
16, 1907 Wilder, Alec
16, 1908 O'Neill, Mary L(e Duc)
16, 1916 Cooper, Elizabeth Keyser
16, 1917 Gerler, William R(obert)
16, 1921 Ahern, Margaret McCrohan
16, 1922 Tanner, Louise S(tickney)
16, 1923 Pennington, Eunice
16, 1924 Newman, Shirlee Petkin
16, 1925 Buck, Lewis
16, 1929 Schwartz, Daniel (Bennet)
16, 1931 Beiser, Arthur
16, 1931 Packard, Edward
16, 1933 Burkert, Nancy Ekholm
16, 1936 Schreiter, Rick
16, 1936 Stevens, Kathleen
16, 1944 Ranadive, Gail
17, 1875 Fitch, Florence Mary
17, 1876 Bacon, Josephine Dodge (Daskam)
17, 1879 Fisher, Dorothy (Frances) Canfield
17, 1881 Aldrich, Bess Streeter
17, 1886 Longstreth, T(homas) Morris
17, 1889 Barnhart, Nancy

17, 1900 Blochman, Lawrence G(oldtree)
17, 1912 Norton, Alice Mary
17, 1912 Sorensen, Virginia (Eggersten)
17, 1914 Campbell, Virginia
17, 1915 Gibbs, Alonzo (Lawrence)
17, 1920 Trevor, Elleston
17, 1928 Hartman, Jane E(vangeline)
17, 1928 Peck, Robert Newton, III
17, 1929 Potok, Chaim
17, 1930 Batson, Larry
17, 1937 Berry, B(arbara) J.
17, 1937 Habenstreit, Barbara (Zeigler)
17, 1938 Jones, Penelope
17, 1942 McCurdy, Michael
17, 1948 Pfeffer, Susan Beth
17, 1953 Black, Susan Adams
18, 1907 Bancroft, Griffing
18, 1908 O'Neill, Hester (Adams)
18, 1914 Mohn, Viola Kohl
18, 1917 Hyde, Margaret Oldroyd
18, 1918 Fijan, Carol
18, 1919 Kahl, Virginia (Caroline)
18, 1922 Karen, Ruth
18, 1926 Frace, Charles
18, 1930 Wilson, Gahan
18, 1931 Morrison, Toni (Chloe Anthony Wofford)
18, 1936 Hemphill, Paul (James)
18, 1949 Joosse, Barbara M(onnot)
19, 1892 Melin, Grace Hathaway
19, 1896 White, Anne Terry
19, 1901 Torrey, Helen
19, 1903 Slobodkin, Louis
19, 1908 Lee, Mildred
19, 1909 Rodman, Selden
19, 1913 Pashko, Stanley
19, 1917 McCullers, Lula Carson
19, 1919 McClary, Jane Stevenson
19, 1924 Cook, Joseph J(ay)
19, 1931 Ilowite, Sheldon A.
19, 1940 Harrah, Michael
19, 1940 Krementz, Jill
19, 1941 Schermer, Judith (Denise)
19, 1943 Callaway, Kathy
19, 1952 Etchemendy, Nancy
20, 1886 Freuchen, Peter
20, 1893 Crouse, Russell M.
20, 1903 Egypt, Ophelia Settle
20, 1907 Cruickshank, Helen Gere
20, 1908 Machetanz, Frederick
20, 1914 MacKellar, William
20, 1916 Mahon, Julia C(unha)
20, 1916 Tripp, Paul
20, 1918 Pizer, Vernon
20, 1920 Hunt, Morton
20, 1926 Rue, Leonard Lee III
20, 1926 Scheer, Julian (Weisel)

20, 1930 Mayhar, Ardath
20, 1930 Tamburine, Jean
20, 1933 Christian, Mary Blount
20, 1940 Gustkey, Earl
20, 1950 Walther, Thomas A.
21, 1859 Smith, Nora Archibald
21, 1870 Murphy, Mabel (Ansley)
21, 1886 Morton, David
21, 1898 Nazaroff, Alexander I.
21, 1902 Headstrom, Birger Richard
21, 1909 Ware, Leon (Vernon)
21, 1910 Saunders, Keith
21, 1912 Ellis, Mel(vin Richard)
21, 1912 Godwin, Edward Fell
21, 1913 Oriolo, Joseph
21, 1915 Russell, Helen Ross
21, 1917 Helweg, Hans H.
21, 1918 Carlsen, Ruth C(hristoffer)
21, 1923 Smiley, Virginia Kester
21, 1931 Angeles, Peter A.
21, 1933 Sneve, Virginia Driving Hawk
21, 1935 Lupoff, Richard A(llen)
21, 1936 Hermes, Patricia
21, 1941 Case, Marshal T(aylor)
21, 1943 Aylesworth, Jim
21, 1946 Rolerson, Darrell A(llen)
22, 1833 Clarke, Rebecca Sophia
22, 1892 Millay, Edna St. Vincent
22, 1896 Stack, Nicolete Meredith
22, 1900 LeSueur, Meridel
22, 1902 Thomas, Benjamin Platt
22, 1902 White, Anne (Wilson) Hitchcock
22, 1904 Hurd, Peter
22, 1904 Locke, Lucie
22, 1906 Pratt, John Lowell
22, 1907 Unwin, Nora S(picer)
22, 1909 Spache, George Daniel
22, 1913 Grant, Evva H.
22, 1922 Noble, Iris (Davis)
22, 1925 Coen, Rena Neumann
22, 1925 Gorey, Edward St. John
22, 1931 Brookins, Dana (Martin)
22, 1937 Schneider, Rex
22, 1939 Zubrowski, Bernard
22, 1941 Livingston, Carole
22, 1947 Miller, Mitchell (Alexander)
22, 1948 Kropp, Paul (Stephan)
23, 1868 DuBois, W(illiam) E(dward) B(urghardt)
23, 1879 DeForest, Charlotte B(urgis)
23, 1882 Fischer, Anton Otto
23, 1894 Gans, Roma
23, 1901 Schisgall, Oscar
23, 1904 Shirer, William L(awrence)
23, 1909 Fleischmann, Glen Harvey
23, 1915 Weingarten, Violet (Brown)

Day	Year	Name
23,	1918	Oechsli, Kelly
23,	1932	Adler, C(arole) S(chwerdtfeger)
23,	1935	Powledge, Fred
23,	1945	Bly, Janet (Chester)
23,	1946	Seltzer, Richard (Warren, Jr.)
23,	1948	Geringer, Laura
24,	1842	Habberton, John
24,	1887	Chase, Mary Ellen
24,	1895	Monsell, Helen (Albee)
24,	1897	Orleans, Ilo
24,	1900	Hoff, Carol
24,	1909	Derleth, August (William)
24,	1918	Palovic, Clara Lora
24,	1918	Wyckoff, James (M.)
24,	1921	Powers, Richard M.
24,	1921	VanOrden, M(erton) D(ick)
24,	1925	Bunin, Sherry
24,	1927	Henry, Joanne Landers
24,	1931	Sutton, Larry M(atthew)
24,	1932	Suggs, Robert Carl
24,	1948	Quammen, David
24,	1967	Bunin, Catherine
25,	1831	Austin, Mary Jane Goodwin
25,	1896	Farrar, John C(hipman)
25,	1905	Carter, Katharine J(ones)
25,	1906	Parks, Edd Winfield
25,	1907	Chase, Mary (Coyle)
25,	1911	Fletcher, Helen Jill
25,	1914	Bonham, Frank
25,	1914	Perry, John
25,	1917	Raymond, James Crossley
25,	1918	Meyer, Kathleen Allan
25,	1919	Bendick, Jeanne
25,	1921	Klaperman, Gilbert
25,	1922	Land, Myrick (Ebben)
25,	1922	Mullins, Edward S(wift)
25,	1924	Meng, Heinz (Karl)
25,	1926	Fuka, Vladimir
25,	1928	Fraser, Elizabeth Marr
25,	1929	Roth, Arnold
25,	1930	Hollingsworth, Alvin C(arl)
25,	1932	Kanetzke, Howard W(illiam)
25,	1942	Voigt, Cynthia
25,	1946	Kelley, True Adelaide
26,	????	Wagner, Jane
26,	1877	Dirks, Rudolph
26,	1880	Dunlap, Hope
26,	1904	McNamee, James
26,	1907	Pavel, Frances
26,	1908	Groth, John (August)
26,	1913	Young, Miriam
26,	1930	Wolf, Bernard
26,	1931	St. George, Judith
26,	1931	Stirnweis, Shannon
26,	1932	Rodowsky, Colby
26,	1937	Mathis, Sharon Bell
27,	1807	Longfellow, Henry Wadsworth
27,	1850	Richards, Laura E(lizabeth Howe)
27,	1891	Dennis, Morgan
27,	1897	Carlson, Vada F.
27,	1902	Rubicam, Harry Cogswell, Jr.
27,	1902	Steinbeck, John (Ernst)
27,	1910	Sloane, Eric
27,	1910	Wendelin, Rudolph
27,	1913	Duchacek, Ivo D(uka)
27,	1913	Thomson, Peter
27,	1919	Heide, Florence Parry
27,	1919	Loken, Newton (Clayton)
27,	1921	Cohen, Morton N(orton)
27,	1923	Shura, Mary Francis
27,	1924	Shore, Robert
27,	1933	Di Certo, Joseph John
27,	1934	Momaday, N(avarre) Scott
27,	1935	Shulevitz, Uri
28,	1887	Lippincott, Joseph Wharton
28,	1893	Bacmeister, Rhoda W(arner)
28,	1904	Jupo, Frank J.
28,	1907	Caniff, Milton (Arthur)
28,	1907	Graham, Clarence Reginald
28,	1908	Brown, Dee (Alexander)
28,	1921	Tabrah, Ruth (Milander)
28,	1922	Unrau, Ruth
28,	1933	Smith, Garry (VanDorn)
28,	1935	Mezey, Robert
28,	1940	Kingsley, Emily Perl
28,	1946	Wallner, Alexandra
29,	1896	Rogers, W(illiam) G(arland)
29,	1908	VonHagen, Victor Wolfgang
29,	1912	Milgrom, Harry
29,	1936	Webb, Sharon
29,	1940	Collins, David (Raymond)
29,	1944	Stevens, Gwendolyn
29,	1948	McKillip, Patricia A(nne)

MARCH

Day	Year	Name
??,	1904	Russell, Solveig Paulson
01,	1893	Nickelsburg, Janet
01,	1895	Grant, Madeleine Parker
01,	1901	Friskey, Margaret Richards
01,	1902	Smith, Ruth Leslie
01,	1904	Baker, Rachel (Mininberg)
01,	1905	Anderson, John Lonzo
01,	1905	Bobbe, Dorothie (de Bear)
01,	1914	Brussel-Smith, Bernard
01,	1919	Matthews, William Henry III
01,	1921	Burchard, Peter D(uncan)
01,	1921	Wilbur, Richard (Purdy)
01,	1922	Jablonski, Edward
01,	1929	Applebaum, Stan
01,	1929	Gross, Ruth Belov
01,	1934	Felts, Shirley
01,	1937	Elmer, Irene (Elizabeth)
01,	1938	Kurland, Michael (Joseph)
01,	1940	Grossman, Robert
01,	1944	Abrams, Lawrence F.
01,	1945	Berger, Barbara Helen
01,	1945	DeKruif, Paul (Henry)
02,	1890	DeKruif, Paul (Henry)
02,	1892	Lowrey, Janette Sebring
02,	1900	Bee, Clair (Francis)
02,	1904	Geisel, Theodor Seuss
02,	1909	Bischoff, Julia Bristol
02,	1915	Peeples, Edwin A(ugustus, Jr.)
02,	1921	Sattler, Helen Roney
02,	1922	Hano, Arnold
02,	1925	Cuffari, Richard
02,	1931	Beiser, Germaine (Bousquet)
02,	1933	Dillon, Leo
02,	1940	Eaton, Tom
02,	1949	Sazer, Nina
03,	1894	Rogers, Matilda
03,	1905	Vinton, Iris
03,	1907	Blanton, Martha Catherine
03,	1909	Doob, Leonard W(illiam)
03,	1914	Drury, Roger W(olcott)
03,	1914	Fuller, Edmund (Maybank)
03,	1920	Bileck, Marvin
03,	1921	Radlauer, Edward
03,	1923	Blegvad, Erik
03,	1927	Anderson, Gunnar (Donald)
03,	1937	Erikson, Mel
03,	1937	Komoda, Kiyo(aki)
03,	1938	Luttrell, Guy L.
03,	1938	MacLachlan, Patricia
03,	1940	MacDonald, Suse (Susan Kelsey)
04,	1880	Walker, Stuart (Armstrong)
04,	1886	Wilson, Edward A(rthur)
04,	1892	Taylor, Florence M(arian Tompkins)
04,	1896	Pine, Tillie S(chloss)
04,	1902	Reeder, Russell P(otter), Jr.
04,	1906	DeJong, Meindert
04,	1912	Marzani, Carl (Aldo)
04,	1914	Victor, Edward
04,	1917	Clarke, Clorinda
04,	1920	Martin, Ralph G.
04,	1930	Gay, Kathlyn (McGarrahan)

04, 1931	Bourne, Miriam Anne (Young)	
04, 1938	Daves, Michael	
05, 1853	Pyle, Howard	
05, 1862	Newell, Peter	
05, 1888	Lieb, Frederick George	
05, 1899	Holt, Margaret Van Vechten (Saunders)	
05, 1907	Baity, Elizabeth Chesley	
05, 1909	Norton, Frank R(owland) B(rowning)	
05, 1913	Hayes, William D(imitt)	
05, 1916	Sohl, Frederic J(ohn)	
05, 1919	Boles, Paul Darcy	
05, 1928	Rublowsky, John M(artin)	
05, 1929	Hampson, Richard Denman	
05, 1931	Bohlen, Nina	
05, 1931	Gannon, Robert (Haines)	
05, 1936	Matte, Encarnacion L'Enc	
05, 1939	Goldberg, Stan J.	
05, 1942	Resnick, Michael D(iamond)	
05, 1943	Goode, Stephen	
05, 1948	Huff, Vivian	
05, 1949	Graham, Robin Lee	
06, 1889	Preston, Alice Bolam	
06, 1906	Nichols, Cecilia Fawn	
06, 1913	Rugoff, Milton	
06, 1914	Vernon, Elda Louise A(nderson)	
06, 1919	Young, Jan(et Randall)	
06, 1921	Bealer, Alex W(inkler III)	
06, 1928	Nolan, William F(rancis)	
06, 1930	Elliott, Sarah M(cCarn)	
06, 1936	Braude, Michael	
06, 1939	Drescher, Joan E(lizabeth)	
06, 1940	Jacobs, Susan	
06, 1948	Schwartz, Stephen (Lawrence)	
06, 1949	Hague, Susan Kathleen	
06, 1949	Hurd, Thacher	
06, 1949	Riley, Jocelyn (Carol)	
06, 1953	Lowry, Peter	
07, 1875	Brown, Edna Adelaide	
07, 1885	Thompson, Stith	
07, 1892	Cason, Emille Mabel Earp	
07, 1899	Stevens, Lucile V(ernon)	
07, 1905	Bryson, Bernarda	
07, 1910	Erlich, Lillian (Feldman)	
07, 1913	Clark, Margaret Goff	
07, 1915	Stillman, Myra (Stephens)	
07, 1920	Pritchett, Elaine H(illyer)	
07, 1924	Beitler, Stanley (Samuel)	
07, 1927	Maxey, Dale	
07, 1930	Roberson, John R(oyster)
07, 1931	Sanberg, Karl C.
07, 1940	Christesen, Barbara
07, 1945	Loescher, Gil(burt Damian)
08, 1813	Cranch, Christopher Pearse
08, 1884	Dunn, Harvey T(homas)
08, 1911	Cook, Fred J(ames)
08, 1914	Phelps, Ethel Johnston
08, 1914	Price, Willadene (Anton)
08, 1915	Fetz, Ingrid
08, 1916	Swain, Su Zan (Noguchi)
08, 1920	Miller, Edna (Anita)
08, 1920	Olschewski, Alfred (Erich)
08, 1921	Henneberger, Robert G.
08, 1921	Whitney, David C(harles)
08, 1923	Keller, Dick
08, 1925	Seidman, Laurence (Ivan)
08, 1927	Lord, Patricia C.
08, 1928	Clancy, Joseph P(atrick)
08, 1928	Segal, Lore (Groszmann)
08, 1931	Kennedy, Dorothy M(intzlaff)
08, 1932	Schellie, Don
08, 1940	Seed, Suzanne (Liddell)
08, 1950	McQueen, Lucinda (Emily)
08, 1951	Roop, Peter
09, ????	Lexau, Joan M.
09, 1866	Nicolay, Helen
09, 1910	Gault, William Campbell
09, 1910	Leekley, Thomas B(riggs)
09, 1912	Darby, Ray(mond) K.
09, 1915	Partridge, Benjamin W(aring), Jr.
09, 1921	Vogt, Marie Bollinger
09, 1924	Reigot, Betty Polisar
09, 1934	Grant, Myrna (Lois)
09, 1934	Peterson, Esther (Allen)
09, 1935	Vavra, Robert James
09, 1936	Montgomery, R(aymond) A. (,Jr.)
09, 1970	Levine, Sarah
10, 1839	Miller, Joaquin
10, 1875	Harlow, Alvin Fay
10, 1904	Antolini, Margaret Fishback
10, 1905	Means, Elliott
10, 1909	McLean, Kathryn (Anderson)
10, 1915	O'Connor, Richard
10, 1920	Kent, John Wellington
10, 1931	Baum, Willi
10, 1935	Stephens, Mary Jo
11, 1889	Holberg, Richard A.
11, 1889	Mochi, Ugo (A.)
11, 1893	Gag, Wanda (Hazel)
11, 1897	Betz, Eva Kelly
11, 1906	Porter, Jean Macdonald
11, 1914	Rosenthal, Harold
11, 1915	Newell, Homer Edward, Jr.
11, 1916	Keats, Ezra Jack
11, 1920	Pucci, Albert John
11, 1921	Barrer-Russell, Gertrude
11, 1937	Ezzell, Marilyn
11, 1938	Chaconas, D(oris) J.
11, 1948	Marshall, Michael (Kimbrough)
12, 1873	White, Stewart Edward
12, 1886	Nielsen, Kay (Rasmus)
12, 1888	Mueller, Hans Alexander
12, 1893	Camp, Charles Lewis
12, 1900	VanCoevering, Jan Adrian
12, 1912	Gordon, Gordon
12, 1914	Rowsome, Frank (Howard), Jr.
12, 1916	Dorson, Richard M(ercer)
12, 1916	McLanathan, Richard Barton Kennedy
12, 1923	Maxwell, Edith (Smith)
12, 1925	Harrison, Harry (Max)
12, 1925	Zwinger, Ann
12, 1927	Brennan, Gale Patrick
12, 1928	Lambert, Saul
12, 1930	Cromie, William J(oseph)
12, 1931	Purtill, Richard L.
12, 1933	Alda, Arlene
12, 1936	Cohen, Daniel
12, 1936	Hamilton, Virginia (Esther)
13, 1885	Irwin, Keith Gordon
13, 1896	Aldis, Dorothy (Keeley)
13, 1913	Floethe, Louise Lee
13, 1913	Icenhower, Joseph Bryan
13, 1914	Barth, Edna (Smith)
13, 1915	Cary, Louis F(avreau)
13, 1917	Heady, Eleanor B(utler)
13, 1921	Jaffee, Al(lan)
13, 1922	Heilbroner, Joan Knapp
13, 1924	Laschever, Barnett D.
13, 1928	Raskin, Ellen
13, 1929	Lanes, Selma G(ordon)
13, 1931	Ferguson, Cecil
13, 1933	Dillon, Diane (C.)
13, 1933	Rockwell, Thomas
13, 1937	Harrison, David Lee
13, 1939	Owens, Gail
13, 1944	Fiarotta, Noel
13, 1957	Ernst, Lisa Campbell
14, 1869	Edwards, George Wharton
14, 1889	DeAngeli, Marguerite (Lofft)
14, 1891	Emerson, Caroline D(wight)

14, 1894 Johnson, Osa Helen (Leighty)
14, 1898 Marsh, Reginald
14, 1900 Globe, Leah Ain
14, 1902 MacPeek, Walter G.
14, 1908 Rudolph, Marguerita
14, 1917 Rosenthal, M(acha) L(ouis)
14, 1919 Shulman, Max
14, 1920 Ketcham, Henry King
14, 1922 Fletcher, Colin
14, 1932 Fults, John Lee
14, 1932 Richards, Norman
14, 1932 Rutz, Viola Larkin
14, 1933 Bolognese, Elaine Raphael (Chionchio)
14, 1934 Spelman, Mary
14, 1945 Drucker, Malka
14, 1947 Batiuk, Thomas M(artin)
15, 1875 Irwin, Wallace (Admah)
15, 1893 Hornblow, Arthur (, Jr.)
15, 1894 Lee, Manning de V(illeneuve)
15, 1897 Scholz, Jackson (Volney)
15, 1902 McCue, Lillian Bueno
15, 1907 Domjan, Joseph
15, 1911 Ogburn, Charlton, Jr.
15, 1911 Roper, Laura Wood
15, 1921 Daly, Maureen (McGivern)
15, 1925 Holyer, Erna Maria
15, 1926 Devaney, John
15, 1926 Myron, Robert
15, 1929 Meighan, Donald Charles
15, 1929 Schwartz, Sheila (Ruth)
15, 1932 Cohen, Barbara (Kauder)
15, 1934 Gelman, Steve
15, 1937 Holder, William G.
15, 1937 Sargent, Sarah
15, 1942 White, Ruth C.
15, 1943 Haines, Gail Kay (Beckman)
16, 1875 MacKaye, Percy (Wallace)
16, 1884 Kelly, Eric P(hilbrook)
16, 1887 Thompson, Blanche Jennings
16, 1897 Gaer, Joseph
16, 1904 Bourgeois, Florence
16, 1917 Eisner, Will(iam Erwin)
16, 1920 Fleischman, Albert Sid(ney)
16, 1921 Bruck, Lorraine
16, 1921 Wallace, Beverly Dobrin
16, 1922 Sibley, Don
16, 1923 Caswell, Helen (Rayburn)
16, 1927 Chalmers, Mary (Eileen)
16, 1948 Demuth, Patricia Brennan
16, 1948 Weis, Margaret (Edith)
16, 1949 Katona, Robert

16, 1951 Hodgell, P(atricia) C(hristine)
17, 1890 Collins, Ruth Philpott
17, 1906 Green, Mary Moore
17, 1909 Moore, Lilian (Moore Reavin)
17, 1911 Gilbreth, Frank B(unker), Jr.
17, 1912 Kinney, Jean Stout
17, 1913 Orbaan, Albert F.
17, 1920 Panowski, Eileen Thompson
17, 1925 Rees, Ennis (Samuel, Jr.)
17, 1934 Oneal, Elizabeth (Bisgard)
17, 1941 Abrams, Joy
17, 1946 Holt, Rochelle Lynn
18, 1892 Coffin, Robert P. Tristram
18, 1901 Jordan, Mildred
18, 1908 Lavine, Sigmund A(rnold)
18, 1920 Candy, William Robert
18, 1927 Johnson, Shirley K(ing)
18, 1927 Plimpton, George (Ames)
18, 1932 Updike, John (Hoyer)
18, 1935 Smith, Nancy Covert
18, 1940 Forrester, Victoria
18, 1950 Florian, Douglas
18, 1958 Zemach, Kaethe
19, 1848 Kaler, James Otis
19, 1895 Rhoads, Dorothy (Mary)
19, 1907 Salvadori, Mario (George)
19, 1911 Colonius, Lillian
19, 1911 Frankenberg, Robert (Clinton)
19, 1915 Maule, Hamilton Bee
19, 1921 Martin, Dorothy
19, 1926 Schlichting, Harold E(ugene, Jr.)
19, 1929 Doty, Jean Slaughter
19, 1936 Brancato, Robin F(idler)
19, 1937 Deegan, Paul Joseph
19, 1939 Bate, Lucy
19, 1946 Coalson, Glo
20, 1888 Price, Margaret (Evans)
20, 1897 Goll, Reinhold W(eimar)
20, 1900 Withers, Carl A.
20, 1903 Brier, Howard M(axwell)
20, 1906 Parker, Elinor (Milnor)
20, 1906 Tinkle, Julien Lon
20, 1909 Mangione, Jerre
20, 1913 Plotz, Helen (Ratnoff)
20, 1922 Young, Margaret B(uckner)
20, 1925 Gault, Clare S.
20, 1928 Rogers, Fred (McFeely)
20, 1928 Watanabe, Shigeo
20, 1929 Allen, Thomas B(enton)
20, 1937 Lowry, Lois (Hammbersberg)
20, 1942 Conford, Ellen (Schaffer)
20, 1942 Hefter, Richard

20, 1948 Sargent, Pamela
20, 1954 Sachar, Louis
20, 1955 Watts, James K(ennedy) M(offitt)
21, 1905 McGinley, Phyllis (Louise)
21, 1907 Bell, Raymond Martin
21, 1911 Braymer, Marjorie (Elizabeth)
21, 1917 Hinton, Sam
21, 1921 Simon, Shirley (Schwartz)
21, 1922 Casewit, Curtis
21, 1923 Hancock, Mary A.
21, 1924 McCord, Jean
21, 1927 Mill, Eleanor
21, 1929 Robertson, Don
21, 1935 Davis, Mary L(ee)
21, 1935 Pepe, Phil(ip)
21, 1935 Weber, Devora
21, 1943 Weiss, Ann E(dwards)
22, 1884 Heyliger, William
22, 1904 Lewiton, Mina
22, 1916 Yurchenco, Henrietta (Weiss)
22, 1917 Savitt, Sam
22, 1918 Devlin, Harry
22, 1918 Johnson, Eric W(arner)
22, 1921 Carter, Dorothy Sharp
22, 1921 Ziner, Florence Feenie
22, 1922 Mild, Warren (Paul)
22, 1924 Mueller, Virginia
22, 1924 Wilson, Lionel
22, 1928 Haines, Charles
22, 1928 Hammer, Richard
22, 1933 Lisker, Sonia O(lson)
22, 1938 Cazet, Denys
22, 1939 Skipper, G. C.
22, 1953 Hartley, Fred Allan III
23, 1865 Ford, Paul Leicester
23, 1871 Snedeker, Caroline Dale (Parke)
23, 1902 Dodge, Bertha S(anford)
23, 1911 Vinson, Kathryn
23, 1912 Braun, Wernher von
23, 1912 Cameron, Eleanor Frances (Butler)
23, 1916 Dias, Earl Joseph
23, 1918 Sandoz, Edouard
23, 1922 Munves, James (Albert)
23, 1924 Handville, Robert (Tompkins)
23, 1925 Bergaust, Erik
24, 1872 Franklin, George Cory
24, 1872 Moran, Eugene Francis
24, 1897 Kroeber, Theodora (Kracaw Brown)
24, 1906 MacDonald, Dwight
24, 1911 Barbera, Joseph Roland
24, 1911 Douty, Esther M(orris)
24, 1920 Cleaver, William Joseph
24, 1920 Stolz, Mary (Slattery)
24, 1922 Stone, D(avid) K(arl)

Day	Year	Name
24,	1923	Broekel, Rainer Lothar
24,	1923	Hollander, Zander
24,	1924	Serage, Nancy
24,	1926	Osgood, William E(dward)
24,	1945	Higginbottom, J(effrey) Winslow
25,	1894	Best, Oswald Herbert
25,	1904	Hays, H(offmann) R(eynolds)
25,	1908	Barker, Will
25,	1922	Suttles, Shirley (Smith)
25,	1925	Finlayson, Ann
25,	1927	Beck, Barbara L.
25,	1934	Bergey, Alyce (Mae)
25,	1937	Chevalier, Christa
25,	1938	Baldwin, Anne Norris
26,	1874	Frost, Robert (Lee)
26,	1892	Ish-Kishor, Judith
26,	1908	MacDonald, Betty (Heskett Bard)
26,	1912	Kenworthy, Leonard S.
26,	1912	Scott, John
26,	1915	Hill, Helen M(orey)
26,	1922	Egan, E(dward) W(elstead)
26,	1923	Beeby, Betty
26,	1923	Sagsoorian, Paul
26,	1926	Ahl, Anna Maria
26,	1926	Sprague, Gretchen (Burnham)
26,	1927	Goldstein, Nathan
26,	1928	Stevens, Carla M(cBride)
26,	1928	Stine, G(eorge) Harry
26,	1929	Sorel, Edward
26,	1932	Smith, Linell Nash
26,	1933	Deloria, Vine (Victor), Jr.
26,	1933	Sargent, Robert Edward
26,	1934	Arkin, Alan (Wolf)
26,	1938	Ganz, Yaffa
26,	1939	Wilson, Walt(er N.)
27,	1881	Oakley, Thornton
27,	1893	Frank, Josette
27,	1901	Barks, Carl
27,	1906	Ulrich, Homer
27,	1914	Hall, Rosalys Haskell
27,	1914	Morrah, David Wardlaw, Jr.
27,	1927	Lewis, Joseph Anthony
27,	1927	Vass, George
27,	1929	Warren, Mary Phraner
27,	1938	Gesner, Clark
27,	1939	Govern, Elaine
27,	1944	Goor, Nancy (Ruth Miller)
27,	1947	Carrier, Lark
27,	1947	Sullivan, Thomas Joseph, Jr.
27,	1955	Thamer, Katie
28,	1905	Perkins, Richard Marlin
28,	1907	Foster, G(eorge) Allen
28,	1910	Crowell, Pers
28,	1915	Posten, Margaret L(ois)
28,	1920	Betz, Betty
28,	1921	Wheatley, Arabelle
28,	1924	Baylor, Byrd
28,	1926	Kaplan, Jean Caryl Korn
28,	1928	Munro, Eleanor (C.)
28,	1930	Byfield, Barbara Ninde
28,	1931	Spencer, Donald D(ean)
28,	1940	Love, Sandra (Weller)
28,	1948	Begley, Kathleen A(nne)
29,	1903	Calapai, Letterio
29,	1905	Hawkins, Helena Ann Quail
29,	1910	Wells, Helen (Frances Weinstock)
29,	1921	Battles, Roxy Edith (Baker)
29,	1922	Cahn, Rhoda
29,	1927	Kushner, Donn
29,	1935	Gordon, Esther S(aranga)
29,	1937	Kowet, Don
29,	1938	Delulio, John
29,	1946	Krupp, Robin Rector
29,	1946	Lindblom, Steven (Winther)
30,	1874	Hewes, Agnes Danforth
30,	1891	Knight, Clayton
30,	1900	Robinson, C(harles) A(lexander), Jr.
30,	1903	Smaridge, Norah (Antoinette)
30,	1904	Wilkin, Eloise (Burns)
30,	1908	O'Kelley, Mattie Lou
30,	1908	Walck, Henry Z(eigler)
30,	1909	Voight, Virginia Frances
30,	1910	Lewellen, John Bryan
30,	1914	Kimball, Yeffe
30,	1919	Klein, David
30,	1922	Steele, Henry Max(well)
30,	1923	Polatnick, Florence T.
30,	1925	Shafer, Robert E(ugene)
30,	1927	Demas, Vida
30,	1933	Hassler, Jon (Francis)
30,	1934	Bauer, Fred
30,	1935	DeWaard, E(lliott) John
30,	1940	Lucas, Jerry
30,	1942	Davies, Bettilu D(onna)
30,	1942	Keller, Charles
31,	1879	MacKinstry, Elizabeth
31,	1897	Nolan, Jeannette Covert
31,	1898	Meadowcroft, Enid (LaMonte)
31,	1900	Stoddard, Hope
31,	1902	Pohlmann, Lillian (Grenfell)
31,	1906	Mellor, William Bancroft
31,	1911	Kingman, Dong (Moy Shu)
31,	1918	Krush, Beth
31,	1922	Daugherty, Richard D(eo)
31,	1922	Shay, Arthur
31,	1924	Gilge, Jeanette
31,	1925	Graham, Frank, Jr.
31,	1926	Montresor, Beni
31,	1932	Edwards, Jane Campbell
31,	1932	Jakes, John (W.)
31,	1936	Barry, Katharina (Maria Watjen)
31,	1952	Llerena-Aguirre, Carlos Antonio

APRIL

Day	Year	Name
01,	1855	Repplier, Agnes
01,	1892	Shippen, Katherine B(inney)
01,	1902	Felton, Harold W(illiam)
01,	1905	Bock, Vera
01,	1906	Ford, Nancy K(effer)
01,	1908	Scherf, Margaret (Louise)
01,	1911	Baker, Augusta (Braxston)
01,	1912	Iannone, Jeanne (Koppel)
01,	1916	Litchfield, Ada B(assett)
01,	1917	Block, Irvin
01,	1923	Waller, Leslie
01,	1926	McCaffrey, Anne (Inez)
01,	1933	Wahl, Jan (Boyer)
01,	1942	Berger, Phil
01,	1946	Palladini, David (Mario)
02,	1899	Taber, Gladys (Bagg)
02,	1904	Pennington, Lillian Boyer
02,	1911	Young, Lois Horton
02,	1917	Bacon, Martha Sherman
02,	1920	Milton, Hilary (Herbert)
02,	1921	Benezra, Barbara (Beardsley)
02,	1927	Abisch, Roslyn Kroop
02,	1927	Georgiou, Constantine
02,	1933	Tinkelman, Murray
02,	1948	Vinge, Joan D(ennison)
02,	1949	Ross, Dave
02,	1954	Schwartz, Amy
03,	1783	Irving, Washington
03,	1822	Hale, Edward Everett
03,	1837	Burroughs, John
03,	1879	Seaman, Augusta Huiell
03,	1886	Dickerson, Roy Ernest
03,	1906	Johnson, Avery F.
03,	1911	Bird, E(lzy) J(ay)
03,	1914	Kempton, Jean Welch
03,	1916	Caen, Herb (Eugene)
03,	1925	Schilling, Betty
03,	1927	Callen, Lawrence Willard, Jr.
03,	1928	Dinnerstein, Harvey
03,	1937	Silverstein, Virginia B(arbara Opshelor)

03, 1940 Wilkinson, Sylvia (J.)
03, 1953 Boynton, Sandra (Keith)
04, 1818 Reid, Thomas Mayne
04, 1890 Jewett, Eleanore Myers
04, 1893 Gordon, Dorothy (Lerner)
04, 1895 Boylston, Helen (Dore)
04, 1906 Rounds, Glen (Harold)
04, 1909 Reichert, Edwin C(lark)
04, 1910 Kirn, Ann Minette
04, 1914 Crockett, Lucy Herndon
04, 1918 Pallas, Norvin
04, 1919 Nolan, Paul T(homas)
04, 1920 Brenner, Fred
04, 1921 Eager, George B.
04, 1925 Fry, Edward Bernard
04, 1928 Angelou, Maya
04, 1928 Hartshorn, Ruth M.
04, 1932 Reiss, Johanna de Leeuw
04, 1936 Oldenburg, E(gbert) William
04, 1940 Gilman, Phoebe
04, 1942 Levy, Elizabeth
04, 1946 Jiler, John
05, 1834 Stockton, Francis Richard
05, 1858 Washington, Booker T(aliaferro)
05, 1904 Thane, Lillian Adele
05, 1908 Carey, Ernestine (Moller) Gilbreth
05, 1908 Macknight, Ninon
05, 1910 Beeler, Nelson F(rederick)
05, 1910 Brown, William Louis
05, 1911 McCallum, Phyllis
05, 1917 Bloch, Robert
05, 1934 Peck, Richard (Wayne)
05, 1935 Gibbs, Wolcott, Jr.
05, 1935 Hoover, H(elen) M(ary)
05, 1938 West, Anna
05, 1943 Smith, Lucia B.
06, 1887 Rabe, Olive H(anson)
06, 1892 Thomas, Lowell (Jackson)
06, 1899 Steinberg, Fannie
06, 1908 Bryant, Bernice (Morgan)
06, 1913 Ruchlis, Hy(man)
06, 1916 Clagett, John (Henry)
06, 1917 Earle, Vana
06, 1918 Chittum, Ida (Hoover)
06, 1930 Crompton, Anne Eliot
06, 1938 Rothman, Joel
06, 1938 Wittels, Harriet Joan
06, 1939 Abercrombie, Barbara (Mattes)
06, 1942 Bach, Alice (Hendricks)
06, 1948 Edler, Timothy
06, 1951 Vaughan, Marcia
07, 1859 Camp, Walter (Chauncey)
07, 1873 Lewis, Arthur Allen
07, 1890 Douglas, Marjory Stoneman

07, 1894 Holden, Raymond Peckham
07, 1895 Brecht, Edith
07, 1902 Hutchens, Paul
07, 1905 Palazzo, Anthony D.
07, 1908 Howard, Robert West
07, 1919 Gregg, Walter H(arold)
07, 1921 Bacon, Margaret Hope
07, 1924 Rappaport, Eva
07, 1929 Carrick, Donald
07, 1931 Barthelme, Donald
07, 1941 Clemens, Virginia Phelps
07, 1941 Schertle, Alice
07, 1948 Terkel, Susan N(eiburg)
08, 1888 Shay, Frank
08, 1890 Specking, Inez
08, 1891 Sauer, Julia (Lina)
08, 1894 Meek, S(terner St.) P(aul)
08, 1898 Wilson, Hazel (Hutchins)
08, 1903 Keith, Harold (Verne)
08, 1908 Whitehead, Don(ald) F.
08, 1911 Arntson, Herbert E(dward)
08, 1913 Scott, John M(artin)
08, 1915 Freund, Rudolf
08, 1917 Geis, Darlene (Stern)
08, 1918 Swarthout, Glendon (Fred)
08, 1920 Chew, Ruth
08, 1921 Gilbreath, Alice (Thompson)
08, 1928 Saviozzi, Adriana
08, 1930 Sarasy, Phyllis Powell
08, 1932 Batterberry, Michael (Carver)
08, 1932 Masey, Mary Lou(ise Leach)
08, 1938 O'Connor, Karen
08, 1939 Hyman, Trina Schart
08, 1941 Sivulich, Sandra (Jeanne) Stroner
08, 1942 Komisar, Lucy
08, 1945 Bentley, Judith (McBride)
08, 1947 Bonners, Susan
08, 1947 Clay, Patrice
08, 1948 Tannenbaum, D(onald) Leb
09, 1827 Cummins, Maria Susanna
09, 1883 King, Frank O.
09, 1901 Winterfeld, Henry
09, 1903 Hawkins, Arthur
09, 1908 Krumgold, Joseph (Quincy)
09, 1915 Wibberley, Leonard (Patrick O'Connor)
09, 1919 Shelton, William Roy
09, 1922 Evslin, Bernard
09, 1923 Kamen, Gloria
09, 1924 Gennaro, Joseph F(rancis), Jr.
09, 1929 Olney, Ross R.

09, 1938 Andersdatter, Karla M(argaret)
09, 1944 Lustig, Loretta
10, 1827 Wallace, Lew(is)
10, 1890 Buff, Mary Marsh
10, 1890 Callahan, Claire Wallis
10, 1897 Knight, Eric (Mowbray)
10, 1903 Newberry, Clare Turlay
10, 1919 Stoiko, Michael
10, 1922 Weiss, Harvey
10, 1923 Chenery, Janet (Dai)
10, 1924 Acuff, Selma Boyd
10, 1926 Caulfield, Peggy F.
10, 1926 Larrecq, John M(aurice)
10, 1927 Brandon, Brumsic, Jr.
10, 1930 Williams, J(eanne R.)
10, 1934 Melton, David
10, 1941 Madian, Jon
10, 1941 Theroux, Paul
10, 1947 Adler, David A.
11, 1840 Ellis, Edward S(ylvester)
11, 1899 Pope, Clifford Hillhouse
11, 1902 Reynolds, Quentin James
11, 1906 Doane, Pelage
11, 1908 Emrich, Duncan (Black Macdonald)
11, 1911 Malo, John
11, 1917 Westheimer, David
11, 1917 Witham, Phillip Ross
11, 1928 Lystad, Mary (Hanemann)
11, 1934 Strand, Mark
11, 1935 Fairman, Joan A(lexandra)
11, 1953 Preiss, Byron (Cary)
12, 1879 Melcher, Frederic Gershom
12, 1891 Anderson, C(larence) W(illiam)
12, 1894 Montgomery, Rutherford (George)
12, 1899 Leighton, Clare (Veronica Hope)
12, 1903 Jones, Helen Hinckley
12, 1907 Gramatky, Hardie
12, 1908 Scott, Robert Lee
12, 1910 Showers, Paul C.
12, 1911 Corcoran, Barbara
12, 1916 Cleary, Beverly (Bunn)
12, 1919 Laskowski, Jerzy
12, 1921 Ewing, Kathryn
12, 1923 Engle, Eloise Katherine
12, 1926 Silverman, Al
12, 1929 Leaf, VaDonna Jean
12, 1930 McIlhany, Sterling (Fisher)
12, 1930 Shefelman, Janice (Jordan)
12, 1931 Obligado, Lilian (Isabel)
12, 1950 Paltrowitz, Donna (Milman)
13, 1893 Foster, Genevieve (Stump)
13, 1901 Starkey, Marion L(ena)

13, 1902 Henry, Marguerite (Breithaupt)
13, 1905 Agle, Nan Hayden
13, 1909 Ulam, S(tanislaw) M(arcin)
13, 1913 Morris, William
13, 1914 Kahn, Joan
13, 1921 Griese, Arnold A(lfred)
13, 1922 Thollander, Earl (Gustave)
13, 1928 Raucher, Herman
13, 1931 Stone, Jon
13, 1935 Fuchs, Lucy
13, 1938 Hopkins, Lee Bennett
14, 1846 Brooks, Elbridge Streeter
14, 1892 Riggs, Sidney Noyes
14, 1897 Raskin, Joseph
14, 1901 Cox, William R(obert)
14, 1905 Scoggin, Margaret C(lara)
14, 1916 Tannenbaum, Beulah (Goldstein)
14, 1920 Scheele, William Earl
14, 1921 Alegria, Ricardo E.
14, 1922 Wilson, John
14, 1923 Eckblad, Edith Berven
14, 1927 Lopshire, Robert (Martin)
14, 1928 Schiller, Barbara (Heyman)
14, 1930 Webster, David
14, 1945 Saunders, Susan
14, 1949 Claflin, Edward
15, 1757 Bingham, Caleb
15, 1878 Hazeltine, Alice Isabel
15, 1889 Benedict, Dorothy Potter
15, 1889 Benton, Thomas Hart
15, 1889 Morgan, Alfred P(owell)
15, 1905 Campbell, Camilla
15, 1905 Nichols, Marie C.
15, 1907 Anderson, LaVere (Francis Shoenfelt)
15, 1914 Swift, Helen Miller
15, 1915 Ashley, Robert P(aul) Jr.
15, 1917 Carlsen, G(eorge) Robert
15, 1921 Briggs, Peter
15, 1926 Hood, Robert E(ric)
15, 1928 Price, Christine (Hilda)
15, 1928 Wagner, Frederick (Reese, Jr.)
15, 1931 Scott, Cora Annett (Pipitone)
15, 1942 Schick, Eleanor (Grossman)
15, 1944 Berry, Joy Wilt
16, 1865 Hill, Grace Livingston
16, 1877 Price, Norman Mills
16, 1888 Lownsbery, Eloise
16, 1890 Warner, Gertrude Chandler
16, 1891 Lathrop, Dorothy P(ulis)
16, 1898 Shirk, Jeannette Campbell

16, 1910 Fontenot, Mary Alice
16, 1911 Roueche, Berton
16, 1912 Williams, Garth (Montgomery)
16, 1915 Barnwell, D. Robinson
16, 1915 Smith, Robert Paul
16, 1916 Nearing, Penny
16, 1921 Cox, Donald William
16, 1921 McMurtrey, Martin A(loysius)
16, 1928 Gracza, Margaret Young
16, 1933 Hobson, Burton (Harold)
16, 1935 Wachter, Oralee Roberts
16, 1936 Parsons, William E(dward), Jr.
16, 1942 Moore, Eva
16, 1946 Gilliam, Stan
16, 1948 Tate, Eleanora E(laine)
16, 1950 Vogel, John H(ollister), Jr.
17, 1869 Lamprey, Louise
17, 1870 Baker, Ray Stannard
17, 1893 Grant, Bruce
17, 1893 Phillips, Loretta (Hosey)
17, 1896 Stratton, William David
17, 1908 Liang, Yen
17, 1909 Snow, Dorothea J(ohnston)
17, 1911 Elisofon, Eliot
17, 1916 George, John Lothar
17, 1919 Anderson, Ruth I(rene)
17, 1919 Levai, Blaise
17, 1920 Valens, Evans G., Jr.
17, 1924 Gallant, Roy (Arthur)
17, 1929 Greenidge, Edwin
17, 1931 Jennings, Michael
17, 1932 Harris, Janet (Urovsky)
17, 1934 Witt, Shirley Hill
17, 1936 Renlie, Frank H.
17, 1947 Thorn, John
18, 1864 Davis, Richard Harding
18, 1907 Lampman, Evelyn (Sibley)
18, 1908 Alcock, Gudrun
18, 1912 Parker, Lois M(ary)
18, 1916 Dickson, Naida
18, 1917 Garret, Maxwell R.
18, 1918 Stilley, Frank
18, 1922 Reid, Barbara
18, 1923 Davis, Bette J.
18, 1927 Sharmat, Mitchell
18, 1934 Luttrell, Ida (Alleene)
18, 1951 Demarest, Chris(topher) L(ynn)
18, 1955 Woldin, Beth Weiner
19, 1899 Douglas, Emily (Taft)
19, 1902 Latham, Jean Lee
19, 1918 Smith, William A(rthur)
19, 1920 Gould, Lilian
19, 1941 Barkley, James Edward
19, 1943 Ducornet, Erica
19, 1949 Eisenberg, Lisa
20, 1890 Call, Hughie Florence

20, 1902 Riedman, Sarah R(egal)
20, 1909 Stern, Marie Simchow
20, 1909 Tallant, Robert
20, 1914 Devereux, Frederick L(eonard), Jr.
20, 1915 Adler, Ruth
20, 1916 Snyder, Jerome
20, 1918 Beach, Edward L(atimer)
20, 1921 Boyd, Mildred Worthy
20, 1921 Moy, Seong
20, 1923 Lieblich, Irene
20, 1924 Hallstead, William F(inn) III
20, 1924 Wels, Byron G(erald)
20, 1928 Morton, Lee Jack, Jr.
20, 1934 Gardner, Sheldon
20, 1935 Davidson, Sandra Calder
20, 1935 Kujoth, Jean Spealman
20, 1938 Wold, Jo Anne
20, 1939 Beagle, Peter S.
20, 1953 Long, Judith Elaine
21, 1838 Muir, John
21, 1874 Pier, Arthur Stanwood
21, 1884 Harper, Wilhelmina
21, 1900 Blair, Walter
21, 1906 Dowling, Victor J.
21, 1907 Alexander, David
21, 1910 Helfman, Henry
21, 1913 Maves, Paul B(enjamin)
21, 1918 Wilson, Forrest
21, 1924 Burns, Ray(mond Howard)
21, 1932 Greenberg, Polly
21, 1932 Kellin, Sally Moffet
21, 1932 Kleeberg, Irene (Flitner) Cumming
21, 1935 Wagenheim, Kal
21, 1938 Rosenblatt, Arthur S.
21, 1943 Bernstein, Joanne E(ckstein)
21, 1947 Edwards, Audrey
21, 1947 Park, Barbara
21, 1950 Lasker, David
21, 1950 Zalben, Jane Breskin
22, 1882 Brawley, Benjamin Griffith
22, 1887 Hall, James Norman
22, 1887 Wiese, Kurt
22, 1902 Richardson, Robert S(hirley)
22, 1916 Dillard, Polly (Hargis)
22, 1916 Menuhin, Yehudi
22, 1918 Smith, William Jay
22, 1923 Baird, Thomas (P.)
22, 1923 Deyrup, Astrith Johnson
22, 1923 Fox, Paula
22, 1933 Miner, Jane Claypool
22, 1937 Bible, Charles
22, 1937 Neier, Aryeh
22, 1937 Parker, Margot M.
22, 1937 Stein, R(ichard) Conrad
22, 1940 Koertge, Ronald
22, 1940 Marr, John S(tuart)
22, 1942 Ault, Rosalie Sain

22, 1942 Sussman, Susan
22, 1943 Christelow, Eileen
23, 1852 Markham, Edwin
23, 1853 Page, Thomas Nelson
23, 1899 Carr, Mary Jane
23, 1904 Stein, Harve
23, 1913 Brown, Sevellon III
23, 1915 Arnstein, Helen S(olomon)
23, 1917 Smith, E(dric) Brooks
23, 1920 Copeland, Helen
23, 1927 Graber, Richard (Frederick)
23, 1930 Cutchen, Billye Walker
23, 1931 Burland, Brian (Berkeley)
23, 1931 Stover, Jo Ann
23, 1940 Schwartz, Joel L.
23, 1950 Baker, Gayle C(unningham)
23, 1953 Teitelbaum, Michael
24, 1880 Sarg, Tony
24, 1905 Smits, Theodore R(ichard)
24, 1905 Warren, Robert Penn
24, 1911 Ness, Evaline (Michelow)
24, 1920 Edsall, Marian S(tickney)
24, 1922 Atene, Rita Anna
24, 1923 Burn, Doris
24, 1924 Pelaez, Jill
24, 1926 DuBose, LaRocque (Russ)
24, 1929 Nelson, Mary Carroll
24, 1942 Galinsky, Ellen
24, 1942 Lazarevich, Mila
24, 1942 Magorian, James
25, 1873 Garis, Howard R(oger)
25, 1892 Lovelace, Maud Hart (Palmer)
25, 1894 Fischbach, Julius
25, 1896 James, Harry Clebourne
25, 1897 Pratt, Fletcher
25, 1900 Wohlrabe, Raymond A(dolph)
25, 1902 Bethers, Ray
25, 1904 Schreiber, Georges
25, 1905 Mason, Edwin A.
25, 1915 Deming, Richard
25, 1922 Korach, Mimi
25, 1925 Behrens, June York
25, 1925 Brooks, Thomas R(eed)
25, 1927 Schwartz, Alvin
25, 1933 Dollar, Diane (Hills)
25, 1933 Kettelkamp, Larry Dale
25, 1933 Lukas, J(ay) Anthony
25, 1933 Murray, Judith Michele (Freedman)
25, 1941 Kuzma, Kay
25, 1950 Brinckloe, Julie (Lorraine)
26, 1828 Finley, Martha
26, 1884 Zirbes, Laura
26, 1895 Lengyel, Emil
26, 1897 Price, Edith Ballinger

26, 1902 Daniels, Jonathan
26, 1912 Kimball, Dean
26, 1914 Ault, Phillip H(alliday)
26, 1916 Darling, Louis, Jr.
26, 1916 Earle, Eyvind
26, 1920 Fribourg, Marjorie G.
26, 1920 Froman, Elizabeth Hull
26, 1920 Walsh, William B(ertalan)
26, 1927 Wilson, Julia
26, 1929 Sommer, Robert
26, 1930 Humphrey, Henry (III)
26, 1933 Leichman, Seymour
26, 1935 Giff, Patricia Reilly
26, 1936 Gleasner, Diana (Cottle)
26, 1942 Eagle, Mike
26, 1943 Pendle, Alexy
26, 1944 Larson, Norita D.
26, 1945 Hanlon, Emily
26, 1946 Waniek, Marilyn (Nelson)
26, 1949 Leroe, Ellen W(hitney)
26, 1951 Lampert, Emily
26, 1955 Foster, Brad W.
27, 1853 Earle, Mary Alice Morse
27, 1898 Bemelmans, Ludwig
27, 1900 Lantz, Walter
27, 1904 Landeck, Beatrice
27, 1907 Holding, James (Clark Carlisle, Jr.)
27, 1911 Crowe, Bettina Lum
27, 1911 Wheeler, Sessions S(amuel)
27, 1913 Adler, Robert Irving
27, 1918 Devlin, Dorothy Wende
27, 1923 Leonard, Constance (Brink)
27, 1923 Ogan, Margaret E. (Nettles)
27, 1927 Maar, Leonard (F., Jr.)
27, 1930 Douglass, Barbara
27, 1933 Gregory, Diana (Jean)
27, 1936 Paul, James
27, 1936 Vigna, Judith
28, 1840 Cox, Palmer
28, 1871 Armer, Sidney
28, 1871 Smith, Elva S(ophronia)
28, 1882 Floherty, John Joseph
28, 1899 Frost, Lesley
28, 1899 Wiesner, William
28, 1902 Wood, Harrie
28, 1906 Troy, Hugh
28, 1912 Zarchy, Harry
28, 1919 Bates, Barbara S(nedeker)
28, 1919 Frasconi, Antonio
28, 1926 Lee, Nelle Harper
28, 1927 Bornstein, Ruth
28, 1931 Buell, Harold G.
28, 1931 Gardner, Richard A.
28, 1932 Seltzer, Meyer
28, 1934 Duncan, Lois S(teinmetz)
28, 1935 Shecter, Ben
28, 1936 Harvey, Brett
28, 1937 Hoh, Diane

28, 1940 Boorman, Linda (Kay)
28, 1940 Grossman, Nancy (S.)
28, 1940 Terban, Marvin
28, 1948 Walker, Pamela
28, 1950 Hest, Amy
29, 1862 Altsheler, Joseph A(lexander)
29, 1888 Wilcox, R(uth) Turner
29, 1895 Olds, Helen Diehl
29, 1897 Canfield, Jane White
29, 1902 Wees, Frances Shelley
29, 1904 Day, A(rthur) Grove
29, 1911 Lappin, Peter
29, 1912 Borden, Charles A.
29, 1915 Worcester, Donald Emmet
29, 1927 Carter, William E(arl)
29, 1934 Britt, Dell
29, 1940 Roy, Ron(ald)
29, 1946 Rudley, Stephen
29, 1948 Kidd, Ronald
29, 1953 Rubel, Nicole
30, 1877 Davis, William Stearns
30, 1890 Carpenter, Frances
30, 1892 Leach, Maria
30, 1904 Bryan, Joseph (III)
30, 1904 Davis, Hubert J(ackson)
30, 1906 Hutchins, Ross E(lliott)
30, 1909 Morrison, Velma Ford
30, 1916 Maves, Mary Carolyn
30, 1920 Hooker, Ruth
30, 1922 Corrigan, Barbara
30, 1928 Moskin, Marietta D(unston)
30, 1928 Polhamus, Jean Burt
30, 1934 Ulm, Robert
30, 1936 Sobol, Harriet Langsam
30, 1940 Patent, Dorothy Hinshaw
30, 1942 Sandin, Joan
30, 1943 Hart, Carole
30, 1945 Dillard, Annie
30, 1945 Lange, Suzanne

MAY

Day Year
??, 1906 Rey, Margret (Elizabeth Waldstein)
01, 1868 Baynes, Ernest Harold
01, 1892 Shaw, Charles (Green)
01, 1902 Shotwell, Louisa R(ossiter)
01, 1908 Dobkin, Alexander
01, 1909 Falstein, Louis
01, 1914 Howes, Barbara
01, 1917 Pope, Elizabeth Marie
01, 1921 Steinberg, Phillip Orso
01, 1922 Dougherty, Charles
01, 1925 Bowden, Joan Chase
01, 1925 Emerson, William K(eith)

01,	1932	Bradford, Richard (Roark)	04,	1932	Butler, Beverly (Kathleen)	07,	1923	Ridge, Martin
01,	1943	Scheier, Michael	04,	1937	Greisman, Joan Ruth	07,	1925	Davis, Paxton
01,	1946	Himler, Ann	04,	1945	Wood, Don	07,	1925	Kirk, Ruth (Eleanor Kratz)
02,	1856	Birch, Reginald B(athurst)	04,	1950	Sandak, Cass R(obert)	07,	1929	Maynes, J. Oscar, Jr.
02,	1886	Potter, Miriam S. (Clark)	04,	1950	Zellan, Audrey Penn	07,	1932	Hogrogian, Nonny
02,	1890	Johnston, Edith Constance Farrington	05,	1856	Denslow, W(illiam) W(allace)	07,	1939	Solot, Mary Lynn (Marx)
02,	1892	Meader, Stephen W(arren)	05,	1879	Bill, Alfred Hoyt	07,	1942	Auth, William Anthony, Jr.
02,	1895	Bacon, Margaret Frances	05,	1890	Morley, Christopher (Darlington)	07,	1947	Hargrove, James
02,	1898	Eshmeyer, R(einhart) E(rnst)	05,	1900	Dorian, Edith M(cEwen)	07,	1948	Rose, Wendy
02,	1905	Schemm, Mildred Walker	05,	1903	Sitomer, Mindel	08,	1835	Wilson, Augusta Jane Evans
02,	1914	Jarrell, Mary von Schrader	05,	1905	Creekmore, Raymond (L.)	08,	1881	Eaton, Anne T(haxter)
02,	1916	Chafetz, Henry	05,	1907	Brown, Lloyd Arnold	08,	1885	Costain, Thomas B(ertram)
02,	1924	Houck, Carter	05,	1910	Dowdell, Dorothy (Florence) Karns	08,	1908	Graff, S. Stewart
02,	1925	Wolfe, Rinna (Evelyn)	05,	1910	Lionni, Leo(nard)	08,	1909	Chernoff, Goldie Taub
02,	1930	Ayer, Jacqueline (Brandford)	05,	1912	Dolbier, Maurice (Wyman)	08,	1910	Svenson, Andrew E.
02,	1932	Allen, Maury	05,	1912	Weingast, David E(lliott)	08,	1911	Aymar, Brandt
02,	1933	Katz, Bobbi	05,	1913	Perrine, Mary (Bush)	08,	1914	Clampett, Robert
02,	1935	Clyne, Patricia Edwards	05,	1921	Bernard, Jacqueline (de Sieyes)	08,	1915	Meltzer, Milton
02,	1935	Munowitz, Ken	05,	1921	Brin, Ruth F(irestone)	08,	1917	Taylor, Kenneth N(athaniel)
02,	1939	Shreve, Susan Richards	05,	1924	Wronker, Lili (Cassel)	08,	1920	Dareff, Hal
02,	1950	Matthews, Ellen	05,	1949	Weaver, John L.	08,	1920	Wong, Jeanyee
02,	1965	Forshay-Lunsford, Cin	05,	1950	Strasser, Todd	08,	1922	Olsen, Violet (Mae)
03,	1859	Adams, Andy	05,	1951	Walker, Stephen J.	08,	1922	Steele, Mary Q(uintard Govan)
03,	1900	Winwar, Frances	05,	1953	Bograd, Larry	08,	1923	Meriwether, Louise
03,	1906	Halsted, Anna Roosevelt	06,	1885	Avison, George (Alfred)	08,	1924	Klein, Gerda Weissmann
03,	1907	Smith, Datus C(lifford), Jr.	06,	1897	Bragdon, Elspeth (MacDuffie)	08,	1926	Blegvad, Lenore (Hochman)
03,	1910	Goldstein, Philip	06,	1899	Guillaume, Jeanette G. (Flierl)	08,	1928	Weiss, Leatie
03,	1912	Sarton, Eleanor May	06,	1908	Hale, Nancy	08,	1933	Comins, Jeremy
03,	1916	Dupuy, T(revor) N(evitt)	06,	1914	Jarrell, Randall	08,	1933	Tweton, D. Jerome
03,	1919	Seeger, Pete(r)	06,	1915	Jones, Evan	08,	1939	Whitehouse, Jeanne
03,	1923	Ney, John	06,	1922	Wriggins, Salley Hovey	08,	1940	Benchley, Peter B(radford)
03,	1926	Foote, Timothy (Gilson)	06,	1927	McGorwven, Thomas E.	09,	1904	Newman, Daisy
03,	1928	Jackson, Jacqueline (Dougan)	06,	1928	Beers, V(ictor) Gilbert	09,	1904	Norman, Charles
03,	1929	Lewis, Marjorie	06,	1929	Anderson, David Poole	09,	1904	Wilson, Dorothy Clarke
03,	1939	Newman, Gerald	06,	1931	Delton, Judy	09,	1906	Estes, Eleanor (Ruth)
03,	1943	Zindel, Bonnie	06,	1933	Bosse, Malcolm J(oseph)	09,	1908	Prideaux, Tom
03,	1947	Jukes, Mavis	06,	1934	Sweetland, Nancy A(nn Rose)	09,	1912	Ross, Z(ola) H(elen Girdey)
03,	1957	Parker, Kristy (Kettelkamp)	06,	1935	Lewin, Ted	09,	1914	Robertson, Keith (Carlton)
04,	1897	Judson, Clara Ingram	06,	1937	Terris, Susan (Dubinsky)	09,	1916	DuBois, William (Sherman) Pene
04,	1906	Laugesen, Mary E(akin)	06,	1942	Maestro, Giulio (Marcello)	09,	1923	Aaron, Chester
04,	1906	Neal, Harry Edward	06,	1947	Ziemienski, Dennis (Theodore)	09,	1926	Halliday, William R(oss)
04,	1909	Campbell, R(osemae) W(ells)	06,	1955	McClintock, Barbara	09,	1930	Reitci, Rita Krohne
04,	1911	Lansing, Elisabeth Carleton (Hubbard)	07,	1889	Burlingame, William Roger	09,	1942	Filstrup, E(dward) Christian
04,	1912	Goodenow, Girard	07,	1904	Farrington, S(elwyn) Kip, Jr.	09,	1946	Moore, Jim
04,	1913	Frame, Paul	07,	1907	Barnes, Frank Eric Wollencott	10,	1897	Beers, Lorna
04,	1913	Pearl, Richard M(axwell)	07,	1912	Bond, Gladys Baker	10,	1897	Lowenfels, Walter
04,	1923	Gladstone, M(yron) J.	07,	1913	Schwartz, Anne Powers	10,	1909	Hirshberg, Al(bert Simon)
04,	1928	Viereck, Ellen R.	07,	1914	Lovejoy, Bahija Fattouhi	10,	1915	Dickens, Monica (Enid)
			07,	1923	Halsell, Grace	10,	1917	Watson, Aldren A(uld)
						10,	1919	Brown, Palmer
						10,	1929	Edwards, Harvey

10,	1939	Roseman, Kenneth David	13,	1921	Burchardt, Nellie	16,	????	Sorrentino, Joseph N.
10,	1943	Glenn, Mel	13,	1926	Williamson, Joanne S(mall)	16,	1882	Hayes, Carlton J. H.
10,	1947	Cooney, Caroline B.	13,	1927	Anderson, Eloise Adell	16,	1900	Thane, Elswyth
10,	1947	McMillan, Bruce	13,	1932	Scarf, Maggi(e)	16,	1901	Comins, Ethel M(ae)
10,	1949	Blake, Robert	13,	1937	Zelazny, Roger (Joseph Christopher)	16,	1903	Dennis, Wesley
11,	1879	Stone, Eugenia	13,	1938	Allmendinger, David F(rederick), Jr.	16,	1905	Douglas, John Scott
11,	1895	Haight, Anne Lyon	13,	1938	Klein, Norma	16,	1908	Wendt, Lloyd
11,	1900	Wellman, Alice	13,	1938	Pascal, Francine	16,	1908	Yeakley, Marjory Hall
11,	1901	Davis, Mary Octavia	13,	1941	Fleming, Ronald Lee	16,	1919	Halacy, D(aniel) S(tephen, Jr.)
11,	1903	Candell, Victor	13,	1947	Allington, Richard L(loyd)	16,	1919	Lobsenz, Norman M(itchell)
11,	1913	Irwin, Constance Frick	14,	1897	Buehr, Walter Franklin	16,	1928	Miles, Betty
11,	1914	Severn, William Irving	14,	1900	Borland, Harold Glen	16,	1942	Suid, Murray
11,	1916	Fink, William B(ertrand)	14,	1902	Chidsey, Donald Barr	16,	1944	Arnold, Caroline
11,	1916	Mandelkorn, Eugenia Miller	14,	1905	Dudley, Ruth H(ubbell)	16,	1950	Coville, Bruce
11,	1917	Carpenter, John Allan	14,	1909	Mannheim, Grete (Salomon)	17,	1865	Bennett, John
11,	1919	Daniels, Guy	14,	1913	Kisinger, Grace Gelvin (Maze)	17,	1888	Kalashnikoff, Nicholas
11,	1925	Stephens, William M(cLain)	14,	1913	Terry, Walter	17,	1901	D'Harnoncourt, Rene
11,	1927	Snyder, Zilpha Keatley	14,	1915	Keating, Leo Bernard	17,	1903	Stefferud, Alfred Daniel
11,	1928	Houston, Joan	14,	1916	Bailey, Jane H(orton)	17,	1907	Joseph, Alexander
11,	1934	Fisher, Laura Harrison	14,	1916	Ranney, Agnes V.	17,	1908	Landshoff, Ursula
11,	1934	Oppenheim, Joanne	14,	1922	Kadesch, Robert R(udstone)	17,	1909	Baerg, Harry J(ohn)
11,	1935	Jacobs, Francine	14,	1924	Anderson, Bradley Jay	17,	1910	Clark, Electa
11,	1939	Bock, Harold I.	14,	1926	Hammerman, Gay M(orenus)	17,	1912	Isham, Charlotte H(ickox)
11,	1949	Sis, Peter	14,	1927	Parker, Robert Andrew	17,	1913	Guck, Dorothy
11,	1950	Sutton, Jane	14,	1929	Groch, Judith (Goldstein)	17,	1913	Vaughan-Jackson, Genevieve
12,	1898	Justus, May	14,	1929	Johnson, John E(mil)	17,	1914	Welch, Martha McKeen
12,	1898	Kvale, Velma R(uth)	14,	1929	Thompson, George Selden	17,	1922	Hoopes, Roy
12,	1899	Yaukey, Grace S(ydenstricker)	14,	1932	Anderson, Grace Fox	17,	1924	Lerner, Marguerite Rush
12,	1903	Berger, Josef	14,	1936	Davidson, Margaret (Compere)	17,	1925	Granstaff, Bill
12,	1904	Lamb, Beatrice Pitney	14,	1939	Dickmeyer, Lowell A.	17,	1929	Greenfield, Eloise (Little)
12,	1908	Dietz, Elisabeth H.	14,	1944	Lucas, George (Walton)	17,	1932	Weston, John (Harrison)
12,	1910	Peterson, Helen Stone	14,	1947	Bliss, Corinne D(emas)	17,	1934	Mohn, Peter B(urnet)
12,	1912	Cahn, William	15,	1856	Baum, L(yman) Frank	17,	1939	Paulsen, Gary
12,	1915	Brown, Joe David	15,	1863	Johnston, Annie Fellows	17,	1939	Purdy, Susan Gold
12,	1922	Feravolo, Rocco Vincent	15,	1874	Courtis, Stuart Appleton	17,	1955	Wheeler, Cindy
12,	1924	Joseph, James (Herz)	15,	1890	Porter, Katherine Anne	18,	1866	White, Edward Lucas
12,	1925	Henriod, Lorraine (Stephens)	15,	1891	Means, Florence Crannell	18,	1898	Cram, L. D.
12,	1935	Bauer, Caroline Feller	15,	1893	Burnett, Constance Buel	18,	1907	Hunt, Irene
12,	1937	Lewin, Betsy	15,	1894	Phillips, Prentice	18,	1909	Gidal, Tim N(ahum)
12,	1938	Kimmel, Margaret Mary	15,	1904	Fadiman, Clifton (Paul)	18,	1915	Coates, Ruth Allison
12,	1938	Lyle, Katie Letcher	15,	1906	MacGregor, Ellen	18,	1918	Krush, Joe
12,	1947	Stillerman, Robbie	15,	1913	Haber, Heinz	18,	1925	Hoban, Lillian
12,	1949	Smith, Janice Lee	15,	1915	Pedersen, Elsa (Kienitz)	18,	1927	Miklowitz, Gloria D(ubov)
12,	1952	DeBruyn, Monica	15,	1919	Atkin, Flora B(lumenthal)	18,	1928	Rumsey, Marian (Barritt)
13,	1874	Lindsay, Maud McKnight	15,	1919	Gekiere, Madeleine	18,	1930	Moskof, Martin Stephen
13,	1881	Phillips, Mary Geisler	15,	1929	Lasell, Elinor H.	18,	1930	Polette, Nancy (Jane)
13,	1883	Chambers, C. Bosseron	15,	1931	Mazer, Norma Fox	18,	1930	Saberhagen, Fred (Thomas)
13,	1890	Dawson, Mitchell	15,	1935	Lewis, Richard	18,	1935	Cober, Alan E(dwin)
13,	1892	Finney, Gertrude E. (Bridgeman)	15,	1936	Zindel, Paul	18,	1937	Green, Morton
13,	1893	Freeman, Margaret	15,	1938	Garden, Nancy	18,	1942	Crary, Elizabeth (Ann)
13,	1894	Sterne, Emma Gelders	15,	1950	Wisler, G(ary) Clifton	18,	1943	DeJonge, Joanne E.
13,	1898	Bobritsky, Vladimir				18,	1943	Porte, Barbara Ann
13,	1900	Ralston, Alma (Smith Payne)				18,	1946	Johnston, Ginny
13,	1902	Sotomayor, Antonio				18,	1948	Hirschi, Ron
13,	1909	Hauser, Margaret L(ouise)				18,	1951	Hann, Jacquie
13,	1909	Smith, Bradford				18,	1952	Duane-Smyth, Diane (Elizabeth)
13,	1910	Angier, Bradford						

19,	1890	Hauman, George	22,	1943	Fabe, Maxene	25,	1920	Alexander, Martha
19,	1903	Chiang, Yee	23,	1810	Ossoli, Sarah Margaret (Fuller) marchesa d'	25,	1924	Day, Beth (Feagles)
19,	1911	Hopkins, Marjorie				25,	1928	Eitzen, Allan
19,	1911	Shapiro, Irwin	23,	1897	Butler, Mildred Allen	25,	1931	Ruckman, Ivy
19,	1925	Carey, M(ary) V(irginia)	23,	1898	O'Dell, Scott	25,	1932	Kristof, Jane
19,	1928	Fletcher, Alan Mark	23,	1906	Weber, Walter Alois	25,	1933	Levine, Betty K(rasne)
19,	1929	Pack, Robert	23,	1910	Brown, Margaret Wise	25,	1933	Miller, Elizabeth
19,	1933	Feelings, Thomas	23,	1910	Reiner, William B(uck)	25,	1937	Churchill, E. Richard
19,	1933	Savitz, Harriet May (Blatstein)	23,	1913	Holland, Janice	25,	1938	Thomas, Joyce Carol
			23,	1915	Butterworth, Oliver	25,	1943	Bottner, Barbara
19,	1936	Lippman, Peter J.	23,	1922	Ritter, Lawrence S(tanley)	25,	1948	Berman, Linda
19,	1936	Schongut, Emanuel				26,	1885	Litten, Frederic Nelson
19,	1938	Rohmer, Harriet	23,	1925	Johnson, La Verne B(ravo)	26,	1893	Tee-Van, Helen Damrosch
19,	1940	Hendershot, Judith						
19,	1942	Arehart-Treichel, Joan	23,	1926	Matson, Emerson N(els)	26,	1894	Burt, Olive Woolley
19,	1954	Primavera, Elise				26,	1896	Munson, Gorham (Bert)
20,	1898	Alger, Leclaire (Gowans)	23,	1927	Skelly, James R(ichard)	26,	1903	Brennan, Joseph L(omas)
			23,	1936	Parnall, Peter			
20,	1906	Marks, Geoffrey	23,	1938	Peek, Merle	26,	1904	Dow, Emily R.
20,	1906	Watts, Mabel Pizzey	23,	1941	Seabrooke, Brenda	26,	1906	Meier, Minta
20,	1917	Fon Eisen, Anthony T.	23,	1943	Keegan, Marcia	26,	1917	Singer, Jane Sherrod
20,	1917	Lawson, Don(ald Elmer)	23,	1951	Titherington, Jeanne	26,	1927	Armstrong, George D.
			24,	1878	Fosdick, Harry Emerson	26,	1931	Zweifel, Frances
20,	1917	Ogilvie, Elisabeth May				26,	1933	Schaller, George B(eals)
20,	1922	Johnson, James Ralph	24,	1892	Lewis, Elizabeth Foreman			
20,	1926	Berry, William D(avid)				26,	1934	Green, Sheila Ellen
20,	1927	Horvath, Betty (Ferguson)	24,	1895	Garner, Elvira (Carter)	26,	1934	Schlee, Ann
			24,	1901	Henderson, LeGrand	26,	1941	Phelan, Terry Wolfe
20,	1928	Murphy, Shirley Rousseau	24,	1903	Austin, Oliver L(uther) Jr.	27,	1889	Baldridge, Cyrus LeRoy
						27,	1899	Chalmers, Audrey
20,	1935	Carrick, Carol (Hatfield)	24,	1905	Crawford, Thelmar Wyche	27,	1907	Carson, Rachel (Louise)
20,	1940	Schell, Orville H.						
20,	1945	Croll, Carolyn	24,	1907	Gag, Flavia	27,	1910	Miers, Earl Schenck
20,	1949	Osborne, Mary Pope	24,	1911	Hutchins, Carleen Maley	27,	1913	Fox, Charles Philip
21,	1891	Chapman, John Stanton Higham				27,	1923	Carini, Edward
			24,	1912	Andriola, Alfred J.	27,	1925	Hillerman, Tony
21,	1893	Clifford, Harold B(urton)	24,	1913	Gorsline, Douglas (Warner)	27,	1927	Meaker, Marijane
21,	1903	Wellman, Manly Wade				27,	1928	Hemming, Roy
21,	1911	Haviland, Virginia	24,	1915	Dean, Anabel	27,	1932	Cunningham, Dale S(peers)
21,	1911	Kaufman, Joe	24,	1916	DeWit, Dorothy (May Knowles)			
21,	1913	Shulman, Irving				27,	1932	Lynch, Lorenzo
21,	1914	Hubley, John	24,	1924	Acheson, Patricia Castles	27,	1934	Sweat, Lynn
21,	1919	Park, Thomas Choonbai				27,	1936	Tripp, Eleanor B(aldwin)
			24,	1924	Milton, John R(onald)			
21,	1920	Trowbridge, Leslie W(alter)	24,	1928	Caras, Roger A(ndrew)	27,	1938	Ricciuti, Edward R(aphael)
			24,	1928	Walton, Richard J.			
21,	1923	Shaw, Richard	24,	1935	Carlson, Dale Bick	27,	1945	Schick, Joel
21,	1928	Winn, Janet Bruce	24,	1935	Pollock, Penny	28,	1908	Brown, Eleanor Frances
21,	1932	Hiebert, Ray Eldon	24,	1942	Taylor, Paula (Wright)			
21,	1932	Wirtenberg, Patricia Z(arrella)	24,	1944	Oz, Frank (Richard)	28,	1913	Rice, Elizabeth
			24,	1947	DeGroat, Diane L.	28,	1919	Swenson, May
21,	1934	Cleaver, Carole	24,	1947	Hahn, James (Sage)	28,	1920	Feaser, Daniel David
21,	1935	Spencer, Zane A(nn)	25,	1803	Emerson, Ralph Waldo	28,	1921	McCrea, Ruth (Pirman)
21,	1951	Radley, Gail	25,	1886	Kent, Louise (Andrews)	28,	1923	Brown, Robert Fletch
22,	1907	Dietz, Lew	25,	1898	Cerf, Bennett (Alfred)	28,	1927	White, David Omar
22,	1907	McSwigan, Marie	25,	1899	Artzybasheff, Boris (Miklailovich)	28,	1928	Rikhoff, Jean
22,	1909	Tolford, Joshua				28,	1931	VonSchmidt, Eric
22,	1914	Werstein, Irving	25,	1902	Mirsky, Reba Paeff	28,	1933	Bergere, Thea Lindgren
22,	1920	Carpenter, Patricia (Healy Evans)	25,	1903	Leonard, Jonathan N(orton)	29,	1873	Morrow, Elizabeth (Reeve Cutter)
22,	1922	Fox, Lorraine	25,	1906	Mayer, Albert Ignatius, Jr.	29,	1889	Dick, Trella Lamson
22,	1922	Peterson, Harold L(eslie)				29,	1907	Meyer, Gerard Previn
			25,	1906	Wooldridge, Rhoda	29,	1914	Cromie, Alice Hamilton
22,	1926	Stubis, Talivaldis	25,	1915	Barnouw, Victor	29,	1914	Wissmann, Ruth H(elen Leslie)
22,	1927	Matthiessen, Peter	25,	1917	Froman, Robert (Winslow)			
22,	1932	Hoopes, Ned E(dward)				29,	1915	Rogers, Grenville Cedric Harry
22,	1933	Lobel, Arnold (Stark)	25,	1919	Gould, Jean R(osalind)			

THE BIRTHDAY BOOK   BIRTH MONTH INDEX   387

29, 1917 Kennedy, John Fitzgerald
29, 1917 Lefler, Irene (Whitney)
29, 1921 Laycock, George (Edwin)
29, 1922 Coerr, Eleanor (Page)
29, 1922 Tolliver, Ruby C(hangos)
29, 1923 Ervin, Janet Halliday
29, 1924 McGinnis, Lila S(prague)
29, 1928 Roberts, Willo Davis
29, 1934 Walker, James Brazelton
29, 1936 Bradford, Lois J(ean)
29, 1938 Cole, Brock
29, 1940 Turner, Alice K.
29, 1948 Mulford, Philippa Greene
30, 1874 Peabody, Josephine Preston
30, 1885 Honore, Paul
30, 1901 Skinner, Cornelia Otis
30, 1903 Conklin, Gladys (Plemon)
30, 1903 Cullen, Countee Porter
30, 1910 Hall, Elvajean
30, 1912 Goodman, Elizabeth B.
30, 1912 Selsam, Millicent E(llis)
30, 1913 Berg, Jean Horton
30, 1915 Feague, Mildred H.
30, 1919 Coit, Margaret Louise
30, 1920 Hunt, Lawrence J.
30, 1922 Weingartner, Charles
30, 1923 Goldsborough, June
30, 1924 Marshall, Anthony D(ryden)
30, 1924 Roberts, Nancy Correll
30, 1927 Poynter, Margaret
30, 1929 Jacobs, Frank
30, 1931 Bowman, John S(tewart)
30, 1933 Gates, Frieda
30, 1941 Marchette, Katharine E.
30, 1943 Davis, Maggie S.
30, 1945 Johnson, D(ana) William
31, 1819 Whitman, Walt(er)
31, 1893 Coatsworth, Elizabeth (Jane)
31, 1895 Stewart, George Rippey
31, 1898 Peale, Norman Vincent
31, 1905 Schneider, Herman
31, 1909 Corrigan, Helen Adeline
31, 1909 Rankin, Robert H(arry)
31, 1913 Tamarin, Alfred
31, 1914 Williams, Jay
31, 1915 Medearis, Mary
31, 1918 Miller, Madge
31, 1922 Smith, Imogene Henderson
31, 1923 Borja, Robert
31, 1925 Mazer, Harry
31, 1929 Lederer, Muriel
31, 1937 Gorodetzky, Charles W.
31, 1940 Goor, Ron(ald Stephen)
31, 1943 Burr, Lonnie

31, 1943 Thieda, Shirley Ann

JUNE

Day Year
??, 1898 Goetz, Delia
01, 1888 Beston, Henry B.
01, 1889 Daugherty, James (Henry)
01, 1895 Burbank, Addison (Buswell)
01, 1910 Laughlin, Florence (Young)
01, 1914 Cushman, Jerome
01, 1922 Spencer, William
01, 1932 Knudson, Rozanne
01, 1933 Reig, June
01, 1934 Boone, Pat
01, 1934 Smith, Doris Buchanan
01, 1935 Corwin, June Atkin
01, 1936 Scoppetone, Sandra
01, 1938 Feinberg, Barbara Jane
01, 1945 Hintz, Loren Martin
01, 1945 McInerney, Judith W(hitelock)
01, 1947 Rockwood, Joyce
02, 1816 Saxe, John Godfrey
02, 1890 Allee, Marjorie Hill
02, 1895 Meyer, Edith Patterson
02, 1899 Teale, Edwin Way
02, 1905 Moore, Janet Gaylord
02, 1907 Wood, Edgar A(llardyce)
02, 1914 Galdone, Paul
02, 1914 Schwartz, Charles W(alsh)
02, 1915 del Rey, Lester
02, 1916 Sanderlin, Owenita (Harrah)
02, 1917 Paul, Aileen (Phillips)
02, 1918 Houlehen, Robert J.
02, 1918 Rosenburg, John M.
02, 1918 Windham, Kathryn T(ucker)
02, 1920 Pugh, Ellen T(iffany)
02, 1925 Viereck, Phillip R.
02, 1926 Reeves, Lawrence F.
02, 1927 Katz, William Loren
02, 1927 Steinberg, Rafael (Mark)
02, 1929 Juster, Norton
02, 1930 Holmgren, Helen Jean
02, 1932 Fava, Rita F.
02, 1934 Crane, Barbara J.
02, 1934 Mendoza, George
02, 1937 Mali, Jane Lawrence
02, 1943 Tannen, Mary
02, 1960 Emberley, Michael
03, 1894 Szyk, Arthur
03, 1904 Penney, Grace Jackson
03, 1909 Newman, Robert (Howard)
03, 1910 Buck, Margaret Waring

03, 1913 Doremus, Robert
03, 1916 Starbird, Kaye
03, 1919 Gregori, Leon
03, 1924 Liberty, Gene
03, 1926 Cosgrove, Margaret (Leota)
03, 1930 Arora, Shirley Lease
03, 1933 Angrist, Stanley W(olff)
03, 1934 Lobel, Anita (Kempler)
03, 1938 Larson, William H.
03, 1943 Payson, Dale
04, 1884 Fox, Fontaine Talbot, Jr.
04, 1902 Brockman, C(hristian) Frank
04, 1910 Frankel, Edward
04, 1911 Lignell, Lois
04, 1921 McKay, Robert W.
04, 1923 Golbin, Andree
04, 1926 Kossin, Sandy (Sanford)
04, 1926 Lane, Carolyn (Blocker)
04, 1927 Kenealy, James P.
04, 1930 Knudson, Richard L(ewis)
04, 1930 Martini, Teri
04, 1931 Springer, Marilyn Harris
04, 1933 Snyder, Gerald S(eymour)
04, 1939 Sortor, June Elizabeth
04, 1943 Holz, Loretta (Marie)
04, 1949 Lee, Betsy
04, 1951 Kovalski, Maryann
04, 1953 Vincent, Eric Douglas
05, 1905 McDonald, Gerald D(oan)
05, 1908 Baldwin, Gordon C.
05, 1908 Lindquist, Willis
05, 1910 Motz, Lloyd
05, 1912 Herron, Edward A(lbert)
05, 1912 Sweney, Frederic
05, 1914 Vogel, Ilse-Margret
05, 1915 Branley, Franklyn M(ansfield)
05, 1916 Rosen, Sidney
05, 1918 Brooks, Charlotte K.
05, 1919 Brindel, June (Rachuy)
05, 1919 Scarry, Richard (McClure)
05, 1925 D'Amato, Janet (Potter)
05, 1926 Low, Alice
05, 1926 Wagoner, David (Russell)
05, 1929 Haas, Irene
05, 1938 Taylor, Jerry Duncan
05, 1946 Kyte, Kathy S.
06, 1756 Trumbull, John
06, 1809 Arthur, Timothy Shay
06, 1892 James, Will(iam Roderick)
06, 1896 Latham, Barbara
06, 1905 DeWitt, Cornelius Hugh
06, 1906 Black, Irma S(imonton)
06, 1906 Donovan, Frank (Robert)
06, 1910 Klemm, Edward G., Jr.

06,	1911	Aardema, Verna (Norberg)	09,	1905	Ducas, Dorothy	12,	1920	Berg, David
06,	1912	Lubell, Cecil	09,	1906	Ripley, Elizabeth Blake	12,	1921	Houston, James A(rchibald)
06,	1913	Ingraham, Leonard W(illiam)	09,	1906	Whitcomb, Jon	12,	1921	Zonia, Dhimitri
06,	1916	Evernden, Margery	09,	1908	Gilbertson, Mildred Geiger	12,	1923	Gordon, So!
06,	1918	Barnes, Catherine J.	09,	1912	Blair, Ruth Van Ness	12,	1925	Weales, Gerald (Clifford)
06,	1918	Buckley, Helen E(lizabeth)	09,	1912	Clapp, Patricia	12,	1929	Markham, Marion M.
06,	1921	Monk, Marvin Randolph	09,	1916	Hightower, Florence (Cole)	12,	1929	Warshaw, Jerry
06,	1922	LeShan, Eda J(oan Grossman)	09,	1927	Lyttle, Richard B(ard)	12,	1932	Fleming, Susan
06,	1923	Reynolds, Pamela	09,	1941	Carey, Bonnie	12,	1934	Isaac, Joanne
06,	1924	Andrews, Virginia Cleo	09,	1947	Mehdevi, Alexander (Sinclair)	12,	1936	Lester, Helen
06,	1925	Kumin, Maxine (Winokur)	09,	1947	Zach, Cheryl (Byrd)	12,	1936	Park, W(illiam) B(ryan)
06,	1925	Polonsky, Arthur	09,	1954	Maguire, Gregory	12,	1938	Mace, Varian
06,	1926	Schlein, Miriam	10,	1881	Gruenberg, Sidonie M(atsner)	12,	1940	Shea, George
06,	1927	Spier, Peter (Edward)	10,	1883	Lansing, Marion Florence	12,	1953	Kennedy, T(eresa) A.
06,	1928	Dobrin, Arnold (Jack)	10,	1902	Smith, Eunice Young	13,	1811	Stowe, Harriet (Elizabeth) Beecher
06,	1932	Chermayeff, Ivan	10,	1906	Crosby, Alexander L.	13,	1884	Benet, Laura
06,	1933	Samson, Anne S(tringer)	10,	1910	Barlow, Genevieve	13,	1895	Quintanilla, Luis
06,	1943	Hayward, Linda	10,	1919	Gessner, Lynne	13,	1900	Sharp, William
06,	1944	Foley, June	10,	1919	Goodwin, Harold	13,	1908	Adelson, Leone
06,	1945	Hall, Malcolm	10,	1925	Hentoff, Nat(han Irving)	13,	1913	Martin, David Stone
06,	1946	Loeb, Jeffrey	10,	1928	Sendak, Maurice (Bernard)	13,	1914	Sanborn, Duane
06,	1950	Smith, Susan Vernon	10,	1930	Siegal, Aranka	13,	1918	Bamman, Henry A.
06,	1954	Rylant, Cynthia	10,	1932	Smith, Alison (Porter)	13,	1918	Spencer, Ann
07,	1875	Grant, Gordon (Hope)	10,	1933	LaFarge, Phyllis	13,	1922	Tremain, Ruthven
07,	1908	Eyerly, Jeanette Hyde	10,	1934	Slackman, Charles B.	13,	1924	Cellini, Joseph
07,	1910	Washburn, Henry Bradford, Jr.	10,	1937	Herman, Charlotte	13,	1941	Gamerman, Martha
07,	1917	Brooks, Gwendolyn	10,	1944	Fodor, Ronald V(ictor)	13,	1944	Farquharson, Alexander
07,	1917	Cooke, David Coxe	10,	1952	O'Brien, Anne Sibley	13,	1962	Sheedy, Alexandra (Elizabeth)
07,	1924	Field, Edward	11,	1881	Dombrowski, Kathe Schonberger von	14,	1897	Tait, Agnes
07,	1931	Crump, Fred H., Jr.	11,	1885	Nyce, Helene von Strecker	14,	1903	Rich, Louise (Dickinson)
07,	1931	Reuter, Carol (Joan)	11,	1886	Brock, Emma L(illian)	14,	1904	Carmer, Elizabeth Black
07,	1932	Funai, Mamoru (Rolland)	11,	1902	McFadden, Dorothy Loa (Mausolff)	14,	1909	DeGrazia, Ted
07,	1932	Reed, Kit	11,	1902	Wallace, May Nickerson	14,	1909	McCall, Virginia Nielsen
07,	1937	Weisberg, Joseph S(impson)	11,	1904	Watts, Franklin (Mowry)	14,	1914	Lubell, Winifred (Milius)
07,	1941	McHargue, Georgess	11,	1912	Lavin, Mary	14,	1914	Todd, Ruthven
07,	1942	Gulley, Julie	11,	1915	Hein, Lucille Eleanor	14,	1918	Morton, Miriam (Bidner)
07,	1943	Giovanni, Nikki	11,	1920	Putnam, Peter B(rock)	14,	1920	Erhard, Walter
07,	1952	Waide, Jan	11,	1922	Capps, Benjamin (Franklin)	14,	1928	Udry, Janice (May)
07,	1957	Hilgartner, Beth	11,	1926	Lifton, Betty Jean (Kirschner)	14,	1929	Namioka, Lensey (Chao)
08,	1893	Deming, Dorothy	11,	1928	Silverman, Burton Philip	14,	1932	Degen, Bruce N.
08,	1907	Pace, Mildred Mastin	11,	1933	Chu, Daniel	14,	1932	Metos, Thomas H(arry)
08,	1908	Rugh, Belle Dorman	11,	1934	Belair, Richard L.	14,	1934	McMullan, James
08,	1908	Toner, Raymond John	11,	1940	Hyman, Linda	14,	1944	Hamsa, Bobbie
08,	1909	Knight, Max	11,	1942	Bender, Lucy Ellen	14,	1946	LeVert, William John
08,	1924	Gremmels, Marion (Louise) Chapman	11,	1942	Taylor, Herb(ert Norman, Jr.)	14,	1948	Yep, Laurence M(ichael)
08,	1934	White, William, Jr.	11,	1945	Munsch, Robert N.	15,	1904	Forman, Harrison
08,	1935	Meyer, Carolyn (Mae)	12,	1864	Chapman, Frank Michler	15,	1913	VanWormer, Joseph Edward
08,	1938	Zaid, Barry	12,	1870	Knipe, Emilie Benson	15,	1920	Bixby, William (Courtney)
08,	1939	Dengler, Sandy	12,	1876	Hinkle, Thomas Clark	15,	1920	Hamblin, Dora Jane
08,	1940	Blauer, Ettagale Laure	12,	1881	Finta, Alexander	15,	1920	Kohn, Bernice (Herstein)
09,	1872	Scoville, Samuel, Jr.	12,	1891	Pallister, John C(lare)	15,	1927	Wright, Betty Ren
09,	1887	Pinkerton, Kathrene Sutherland (Gedney)	12,	1911	Kirkpatrick, Oliver Austin	15,	1933	Glubok, Shirley (Astor)
09,	1903	Davenport, Marcia (Gluck)				15,	1935	Roche, P(atricia) K.
09,	1905	Buell, Ellen Lewis				15,	1942	Phillips, Louis
09,	1905	DeJong, David C(ornel)				15,	1950	Tooke, Louise Mathews
						15,	1959	Leedy, Loreen (Janelle)

16, 1894	Barker, S(quire) Omar	
16, 1895	Pitz, Henry C(larence)	
16, 1899	Masters, Kelly Ray	
16, 1900	Brooks, Maurice (Graham)	
16, 1905	Wilson, Charles Morrow	
16, 1907	Fermi, Laura (Capon)	
16, 1916	Brandt, Sue R(eading)	
16, 1920	Holland, Isabelle	
16, 1921	Conrad, Sybil	
16, 1924	Hale, Arlene	
16, 1924	Mays, Lucinda L(a Bella)	
16, 1930	Alexander, Jocelyn (Anne Arundel)	
16, 1935	Warren, Joyce W(illiams)	
16, 1937	Hayes, Sheila	
16, 1948	Babcock, Dennis Arthur	
16, 1948	Edwards, Linda Strauss	
17, ????	Haas, Dorothy F.	
17, 1871	Johnson, James William	
17, 1914	Hersey, John (Richard)	
17, 1917	Beers, Dorothy Sands	
17, 1919	Meyers, Robert W.	
17, 1923	Nelson, Roy Paul	
17, 1925	Campbell, Hope	
17, 1925	Fox, Sonny	
17, 1927	Wood, Wallace	
17, 1930	Froehlich, Margaret Walden	
17, 1931	Higdon, Hal	
17, 1937	Branscum, Robbie	
18, 1878	Robinson, Thomas Pendleton	
18, 1888	Burger, Carl (Victor)	
18, 1894	Pond, Alonzo W(illiam)	
18, 1902	Foster, Elizabeth Vincent	
18, 1914	Case, Elinor Rutt	
18, 1915	Puner, Helen W(alker)	
18, 1921	Johnson, Annabel (Jones)	
18, 1922	Heintze, Carl	
18, 1941	Baker, Janice E(dla)	
18, 1947	Conrad, Pam(ela)	
18, 1949	VanAllsburg, Chris	
18, 1950	Goodman, Joan Elizabeth	
18, 1951	Roop, Constance Betzer	
19, 1850	Pyrnelle, Louise Clarke	
19, 1880	Dwiggins, William Addison	
19, 1881	Barney, Maginel Wright	
19, 1898	Tharp, Louise Hall	
19, 1900	Hobson, Laura Z(ametkin)	
19, 1913	Freed, Alvyn M.	
19, 1913	Hammontree, Marie (Gertrude)	
19, 1914	Crichlow, Ernest T.	
19, 1923	Moore, Ruth (Nulton)	
19, 1924	Engelhart, Margaret S(tevens)	
19, 1926	Palmer, Ruth Candida	
19, 1928	Gottlieb, Robin (Grossman)	
19, 1932	Pontiflet, Ted	
19, 1932	Servello, Joe	
19, 1935	Ray, JoAnne	
19, 1941	Lamb, Robert (Boyden)	
20, 1876	Ditmars, Raymond Lee	
20, 1897	Rollins, Charlemae Hill	
20, 1898	Rowe, Dorothy	
20, 1908	Colver, Anne	
20, 1908	Melbo, Irving Robert	
20, 1909	Holmgren, Virginia C(unningham)	
20, 1909	White, Robb	
20, 1914	McDonnell, Lois Eddy	
20, 1920	Bare, Arnold Edwin	
20, 1921	Smith, Hugh L(etcher)	
20, 1925	Rymer, Alta May	
20, 1926	Harris, Leon A., Jr.	
20, 1928	Baker, Betty (Lou)	
20, 1930	Borten, Helen Jacobson	
20, 1931	Gaeddert, Lou Ann (Bigge)	
20, 1933	McCarthy, Agnes	
20, 1936	Wood, Nancy	
20, 1938	Vuong, Lynette (Dyer)	
20, 1940	Scott, Elaine	
20, 1942	Morgan, Tom	
20, 1946	Schick, Alice	
21, 1850	Beard, Dan(iel Carter)	
21, 1882	Kent, Rockwell	
21, 1897	Fulks, Bryan	
21, 1898	Peattie, Donald Culross	
21, 1899	Gard, Sanford Wayne	
21, 1901	Chamberlain, Elinor	
21, 1902	Hanna, Paul R(obert)	
21, 1906	Elting, Mary	
21, 1907	Renken, Aleda	
21, 1921	Morse, Flo	
21, 1923	Wilbur, C. Keith	
21, 1925	Coughlan, Margaret N(ourse)	
21, 1925	Kraus, Robert	
21, 1926	Ubell, Earl	
21, 1927	Swinford, Betty (June Wells)	
21, 1930	Pape, D(onna) L(ugg)	
21, 1931	Rosenberg, Nancy Sherman	
21, 1943	Hawkes, Louise	
22, 1844	Lothrop, Harriet Mulford Stone	
22, 1873	Grover, Eulalie Osgood	
22, 1899	Hammond, Winifred G(raham)	
22, 1902	Beecroft, John William Richard	
22, 1903	Sturtzel, Jane Levington	
22, 1907	Love, Katherine (Isabel)	
22, 1910	Weil, Lisl	
22, 1916	Hutchinson, William M.	
22, 1928	Griffin, Gillett Good	
22, 1936	Cappel, Constance	
22, 1937	Etchison, Birdie L(ee)	
22, 1942	Sammis, John	
23, 1822	Darley, F(elix) O(ctavius) C(arr)	
23, 1897	Angelo, Valenti	
23, 1897	Westphal, Arnold Carl	
23, 1914	Stover, Marjorie Filley	
23, 1915	Fitz-Randolph, Jane (Currens)	
23, 1921	Ostendorf, Arthur Lloyd, Jr.	
23, 1921	Taylor, Theodore (Langhans)	
23, 1924	Lincoln, C(harles) Eric	
23, 1926	Bahti, Tom	
23, 1929	Broderick, Dorothy M.	
23, 1936	Bach, Richard David	
23, 1936	Stretton, Barbara (Humphrey)	
23, 1937	Curtis, Richard (Alan)	
23, 1940	Jones, Betty Millsaps	
23, 1951	Rachlin, Harvey (Brant)	
24, 1863	Wallace, Dillon	
24, 1892	Daringer, Helen Fern	
24, 1909	Cavanna, Betty	
24, 1912	Logsdon, Richard Henry	
24, 1916	Ciardi, John (Anthony)	
24, 1916	Edwards, Cecile (Pepin)	
24, 1919	Crone, Ruth	
24, 1924	Baker, James W.	
24, 1924	Fisher, Leonard Everett	
24, 1927	Klass, Morton	
24, 1930	Oleksy, Walter	
24, 1930	Schulke, Flip (Philps Graeme)	
24, 1932	Green, Phyllis	
24, 1932	Haverstock, Mary Sayre	
24, 1935	Line, Les	
24, 1942	Keith, Eros	
24, 1942	Marzollo, Jean	
24, 1944	Lasky, Kathryn	
24, 1947	Frankel, Julie	
24, 1947	Glovach, Linda	
24, 1947	Schreiber, Elizabeth Anne (Ferguson)	
24, 1949	Westcott, Nadine Bern	
25, 1890	Guthrie, Anne	
25, 1894	Sturtzel, Howard A(llison)	
25, 1899	Odenwald, Robert P(aul)	
25, 1900	Woodward, Landon Cleveland	
25, 1904	Lutzker, Edythe	
25, 1910	Jones, Elizabeth Orton	
25, 1911	Hurley, Leslie J(ohn)	
25, 1912	Nespojohn, Katherine V(eronica)	
25, 1913	Holme, Bryan	
25, 1923	Butters, Dorothy Gilman	
25, 1923	Mulvihill, William Patrick	
25, 1929	Carle, Eric	
25, 1929	Jensen, David E(dward)	
25, 1930	Baker, Liva	
25, 1930	Sabin, Louis	
25, 1931	Robinson, Charles	
25, 1937	Sarnoff, Jane	

25,	1938	Hanson, Joan	28,	1903	Moore, Margaret R(umberger)	01,	1882	Richardson, Frank Howard
25,	1942	Adamson, Wendy Wriston	28,	1905	Hilder, Rowland	01,	1905	Foster, Elizabeth
25,	1946	Sachs, Elizabeth-Ann	28,	1909	Shaw, Arnold	01,	1907	Grimm, William C(arey)
26,	1870	Knipe, Alden Arthur	28,	1913	Killilea, Marie (Lyons)	01,	1912	Stern, Madeleine B(ettina)
26,	1885	Lemmon, Robert Stell	28,	1919	Graboff, Abner	01,	1915	Stafford, Jean
26,	1897	Wright, Frances Fitzpatrick	28,	1921	Boatner, Mark Mayo III	01,	1916	Barss, William
26,	1904	Malmberg, Carl	28,	1923	Hardwick, Richard (Holmes, Jr.)	01,	1916	Ravielli, Anthony
26,	1905	Ward, Lynd (Kendall)	28,	1928	Rosenbloom, Joseph	01,	1927	Matthews, Patricia
26,	1906	Pough, Frederick	28,	1933	Pellowski, Anne	01,	1928	VanSteenwyk, Elizabeth Ann
26,	1908	Ames, Evelyn	28,	1934	Greene, Bette	01,	1932	FitzGerald, Cathleen
26,	1909	Lomask, Milton (Nachman)	28,	1936	Wade, Theodore E., Jr.	01,	1935	Skorpen, Liesel (Moak)
26,	1915	Farley, Walter (Lorimer)	28,	1938	Stover, Allan C(arl)	01,	1936	Lewis, Thomas P(arker)
26,	1915	Petie, Haris	28,	1941	Heath, Charles D(ickinson)	01,	1939	McCully, Emily Arnold
26,	1915	Schmidt, Elizabeth	28,	1946	Winnick, Karen B(eth) B(inkoff)	01,	1942	Greenleaf, Barbara Kaye
26,	1915	Zolotow, Charlotte S(hapiro)	28,	1950	Haseley, Dennis	02,	1871	Duncan, Norman
26,	1919	Lasker, Joseph Leon	29,	1883	Ruzicka, Rudolph	02,	1892	Allen, Merritt Parmalee
26,	1921	Stadtler, Bea	29,	1892	Tooze, Ruth (Anderson)	02,	1892	Day, Maurice
26,	1922	Nickerson, Elizabeth	29,	1894	Bechtel, Louise Seaman	02,	1909	D'Attilio, Anthony
26,	1924	VanWoerkom, Dorothy (O'Brien)	29,	1902	Benedict, Lois Trimble	02,	1919	George, Jean Craighead
26,	1925	Brenner, Barbara (Johnes)	29,	1904	Honness, Elizabeth (Hoffman)	02,	1924	Swinburne, Laurence
26,	1925	Burch, Robert (Joseph)	29,	1905	Wolfe, Louis	02,	1926	Murphy, E(mmett) Jefferson
26,	1925	Hoke, John (Lindsay)	29,	1908	Gordon, Cyrus Herzl	02,	1927	Mays, Lewis Victor, Jr.
26,	1926	Bruner, Richard W(allace)	29,	1910	Cauman, Samuel	02,	1931	Balow, Tom
26,	1926	Craz, Albert G.	29,	1912	Toland, John (Willard)	02,	1937	Gelman, Rita Golden
26,	1926	Sherin, Ray	29,	1916	McCahill, William P.	02,	1944	Klaits, Barrie
26,	1929	Glaser, Milton	29,	1917	Flory, Jane Trescott	02,	1951	Cauley, Lorinda Bryan
26,	1932	Negri, Rocco (Antonio)	29,	1919	Kepes, Juliet A(ppleby)	02,	1951	Gantos, John (Bryan), Jr.
26,	1936	Willard, Nancy (Margaret)	29,	1928	Frimmer, Steven	03,	1896	Bell, Thelma Harrington
26,	1937	Locker, Thomas	29,	1931	Wondriska, William Allen	03,	1901	Seeger, Ruth Porter (Crawford)
26,	1939	Klug, Ron(ald)	29,	1933	Jacker, Corinne (Litvin)	03,	1907	Hornos, Axel
26,	1940	Tripp, Wallace (Whitney)	29,	1934	Dauer, Rosamond	03,	1910	Dobler, Lavinia G.
26,	1950	Briggs, Carole S(uzanne)	29,	1935	Briscoe, Jill (Pauline)	03,	1910	Gard, Robert Edward
26,	1952	Seidler, Tor	29,	1939	Lager, Marilyn	03,	1924	Jenkyns, Chris
27,	1872	Dunbar, Paul Laurence	29,	1942	Feil, Hila	03,	1927	Navarra, John Gabriel
27,	1896	Sewell, Helen (Moore)	29,	1947	Gross, Alan	03,	1930	Berliner, Don
27,	1902	Widdemer, Mabel Cleland	30,	1896	Swanson, Neil Harmon	03,	1938	Smith, Anne Warren
27,	1909	Strait, Treva Adams	30,	1904	Lattimore, Eleanor Frances	03,	1939	Arenella, Roy
27,	1912	Rich, Josephine (Bouchard)	30,	1909	Scott, Sally Fisher	03,	1945	Kouts, Anne
27,	1914	Coombs, Charles I(ra)	30,	1914	Houser, Allan C.	03,	1949	Hahn, Mona Lynn
27,	1917	Campion, Nardi Reeder	30,	1914	Phelan, Mary Kay (Harris)	03,	1949	McDonnell, Christine
27,	1917	Winchester, James H(ugh)	30,	1923	Miller, Don	03,	1970	Kennedy, Brendan
27,	1920	Benedict, Rex (Arthur)	30,	1923	Smith, Susan Carlton	04,	1804	Hawthorne, Nathaniel
27,	1927	Keeshan, Robert J.	30,	1929	Hallman, Ruth	04,	1882	Rae, John
27,	1927	Taylor, Barbara J.	30,	1929	Margolis, Richard (J.)	04,	1888	Fanning, Leonard M(ulliken)
27,	1928	Collier, James Lincoln	30,	1933	Cruz, Ray(mond)	04,	1895	Simon, Solomon
27,	1932	Reed, Gwendolyn (Elizabeth)	30,	1940	McPhail, David M(ichael)	04,	1907	Snyder, Louis Leo
27,	1935	Greenberg, Harvey R.	30,	1942	Landis, J(ames) D(avid)	04,	1915	Harris, Aurand
27,	1936	Clifton, Lucille				04,	1915	Michie, Allan Andrew
27,	1936	Tarshis, Jerome				04,	1920	Freedman, Nancy
27,	1937	Green, Jane				04,	1920	Garraty, John A.
27,	1941	Bollen, Roger				04,	1920	Molloy, Paul
28,	1857	Hough, Emerson				04,	1921	Bell, Joseph N.
28,	1891	Forbes, Esther				04,	1921	Underwood, Mary Betty Anderson

JULY

Day Year
01, 1882 Glaspell, Susan

04,	1923	Schindelman, Joseph
04,	1924	Nonnast, Marie
04,	1924	Schoen, Barbara

04,	1925	Grollman, Earl A.	08,	1911	Ball, John (Dudley), Jr.	11,	1933	Lewis, Richard William
04,	1929	Susac, Andrew	08,	1913	MacAgy, Douglas (Guernsey)	11,	1937	Victor, Joan Berg
04,	1933	Gilson, Jamie				11,	1941	Payne, Bernal C., Jr.
04,	1939	Vecsey, George	08,	1923	Murray, John	11,	1946	Kilgore, Kathleen
04,	1941	Mooser, Stephen	08,	1930	Klein, Aaron E.	12,	1865	Perkins, Lucy Fitch
04,	1943	Rivera, Geraldo	08,	1932	Erickson, Russell E(verett)	12,	1871	Moore, Anne Carroll
05,	1900	Fabres, Oscar				12,	1885	Alsop, Mary O'Hara
05,	1909	VanRiper, Guernsey, Jr.	08,	1932	Masters, Mildred	12,	1902	Montgomery, Elizabeth Rider
			08,	1933	Giblin, James Cross			
05,	1917	Sutton, Eugenia Geneva (Hansen)	08,	1935	Gladstone, Gary	12,	1907	Sterling, Philip
			08,	1940	Hickman, Janet	12,	1908	Martignoni, Margaret E.
05,	1918	McFall, Christie	08,	1940	Math, Irwin	12,	1909	Zim, Herbert S(pencer)
05,	1920	Perlmutter, O(scar) William	08,	1942	Penzler, Otto	12,	1912	Fisher, Calvin C(argill)
			08,	1952	Thomas, Art(hur Lawrence)	12,	1917	Mercer, Charles (Edward)
05,	1920	Schealer, John M(ilton)						
05,	1922	Cunliffe, Marcus (Falkner)	09,	1887	Morison, Samuel Eliot	12,	1918	Cummings, Betty Sue
			09,	1902	Carse, Robert	12,	1921	Koningsberger, Hans
05,	1927	Fleming, Thomas J(ames)	09,	1904	Chappell, Warren	12,	1923	Gunn, James E(dwin)
			09,	1912	Bang, Betsy (Garrett)	12,	1925	Schurfranz, Vivian
05,	1931	Baron, Virginia Olsen	09,	1927	Goldston, Robert (Conroy)	12,	1926	Holtzman, Jerome
05,	1932	Givens, Janet E(aton)				12,	1927	Dorman, N. B.
05,	1935	Schoenherr, John (Carl)	09,	1929	Loeper, John J(oseph)	12,	1927	Sargent, Shirley
05,	1939	Stefanik, Alfred T.	09,	1936	Jordan, June (Meyer)	12,	1931	Gerassi, John
05,	1941	McCoy, Lois (Rich)	09,	1951	Celestino, Martha Laing	12,	1944	Ephron, Delia
05,	1946	Gregorian, Joyce Ballou	10,	1861	Paine, Albert Bigelow	12,	1947	Pearson, Gayle
05,	1958	Pierce, Meredith Ann	10,	1868	Bradley, Will(iam H.)	13,	1889	Miller, Elizabeth Cleveland
06,	1890	Mukerji, Dhan Gopal	10,	1899	Nelson, Marg (Raibley)			
06,	1919	Temple, Herbert	10,	1900	Schrank, Joseph	13,	1896	Karasz, Ilonka
06,	1922	Chetin, Helen	10,	1909	Tompkins, Walker Allison	13,	1898	Sherman, Harold (Morrow)
06,	1922	Snyderman, Reuven K.						
06,	1927	Lerner, Carol	10,	1911	Coggins, Jack Banham	13,	1901	Billings, Henry
06,	1930	Skurzynski, Gloria (Joan)	10,	1912	Melcher, Daniel	13,	1902	Marek, George R(ichard)
			10,	1916	Provensen, Martin (Elias)			
06,	1935	Tiegreen, Alan F.				13,	1904	Nichols, Dale
06,	1942	Schreiber, Ralph W(alter)	10,	1917	Herbert, Don	13,	1907	Weller, George (Anthony)
			10,	1918	Docktor, Irv			
06,	1951	Delaney, Ned	10,	1924	Hare, Norma Q(uarles)	13,	1910	Serwer, Blanche L.
07,	1896	Ross, David	10,	1926	Gwynne, Fred(erick Hubbard)	13,	1912	Allen, Leroy
07,	1899	Ostman, Lempi				13,	1913	Goodenow, Earle
07,	1900	Falkner, Leonard	10,	1927	Gliewe, Unada (Grace)	13,	1918	Brown, Marcia (Joan)
07,	1907	Heinlein, Robert A(nson)	10,	1927	Stern, Ellen N(orman)	13,	1919	Asinof, Eliot
			10,	1928	Doren, Marion (Walker)	13,	1919	White, Dori
07,	1908	Arnow, Harriette (Louisa) Simpson	10,	1928	Hubbell, Patricia	13,	1921	Scribner, Charles, Jr.
			10,	1929	Walters, Audrey	13,	1923	Bryan, Ashley F.
07,	1908	Holland, Marion	10,	1930	Zerman, Melvyn Bernard	13,	1924	Andre, Evelyn M(arie)
07,	1910	Sweeney, James B(artholomew)				13,	1933	Goldstein, Ernest A.
			10,	1931	May, Julian	13,	1939	Joseph, Joan
07,	1911	Menotti, Gian Carlo	10,	1934	Lee, Mary Price	13,	1942	Ziegler, Jack (Denmore)
07,	1912	Erdoes, Richard	10,	1937	Angell, Judie			
07,	1917	Fenton, Edward	10,	1938	O'Brien, Thomas C(lement)	13,	1946	Hines, Anna G(rossnickle)
07,	1918	Frisch, Rose E.						
07,	1920	Rood, Ronald (N.)	10,	1939	Adler, Larry	13,	1954	Stanovich, Betty Jo
07,	1925	Nash, Mary (Hughes)	10,	1940	Peterson, Lorraine	14,	1860	Wister, Owen
07,	1926	Rushmore, Robert (William)	10,	1941	Boulet, Susan Seddon	14,	1887	Myers, Caroline Elizabeth (Clark)
			10,	1952	Ransom, Candice F.			
07,	1940	Trivett, Daphne (Harwood)	11,	1819	Warner, Susan Bogert	14,	1903	Stone, Irving
			11,	1899	White, E(lwyn) B(rooks)	14,	1904	Singer, Isaac (Bashevis)
07,	1941	Billout, Guy Rene	11,	1901	Culp, Louanna McNary			
07,	1942	Watson, Wendy (McLeod)	11,	1906	Turner, Eloise Fain	14,	1910	Hanna, William
			11,	1915	Belting, Natalia Maree	14,	1913	Harrison, C. William
07,	1943	Deyneka, Anita	11,	1915	Watson, Jane Werner	14,	1927	Parish, Margaret Cecile
07,	1947	Brimberg, Stanlee	11,	1923	Land, Barbara (Neblett)	14,	1928	Ellis, Ella Thorp
07,	1948	Allison, Linda	11,	1925	Laite, Gordon	14,	1930	Ferguson, Walter (W.)
07,	1953	Aaseng, Nathan	11,	1925	Mills, Yaroslava Surmach	14,	1931	Robinet, Harriette Gillem
07,	1967	Hodgetts, Blake Christopher						
			11,	1927	Inyart, Gene	14,	1943	Bode, Janet
08,	1884	Schuyler, Remington	11,	1929	Stevenson, James	14,	1953	Hoopes, Lyn L(ittlefield)

14, 1953	Numeroff, Laura Joffe
15, 1779	Moore, Clement Clarke
15, 1796	Bulfinch, Thomas
15, 1893	Whitehouse, Elizabeth S(cott)
15, 1898	Schaeffer, Mead
15, 1903	Edmonds, Walter D(umaux)
15, 1913	Myers, Hortense (Powner)
15, 1914	Schloat, G. Warren, Jr.
15, 1942	Stanley, George Edward
15, 1946	Roach, Marilynne K(athleen)
16, 1894	Bell, Corydon Whitten
16, 1899	Chrisman, Arthur Bowie
16, 1901	Cook, Howard Norton
16, 1902	Stevenson, Lionel
16, 1906	Jonk, Clarence
16, 1906	Still, James
16, 1908	Horwich, Frances R(appaport)
16, 1913	Arno, Enrico
16, 1913	Bjorklund, Lorence F.
16, 1918	DeLage, Ida
16, 1918	Mohan, Beverly (Moffet)
16, 1920	Elam, Richard M(ace, Jr.)
16, 1920	Vasiliu, Mircea
16, 1921	Kostich, Dragos D.
16, 1922	Titus, Eve
16, 1923	Evans, Mari
16, 1925	Kiesel, Stanley
16, 1932	MacClintock, Dorcas
16, 1934	Jones, Hettie
16, 1935	Adoff, Arnold
16, 1952	Egielski, Richard
17, 1889	Fleischer, Max
17, 1891	Price, Hattie Longstreet
17, 1894	Chandler, Ruth Forbes
17, 1896	Spykman, E(lizabeth) C(hoate)
17, 1899	Bratton, Helen
17, 1909	Castor, Henry
17, 1911	Gelinas, Paul J.
17, 1914	Woodburn, John Henry
17, 1918	Hunt, George Pinney
17, 1922	Toschik, Larry
17, 1925	Kashiwagi, Isami
17, 1931	Brooks, Jerome
17, 1932	Alkema, Chester Jay
17, 1932	Kuskin, Karla (Seidman)
17, 1937	Veglahn, Nancy (Crary)
17, 1939	Miskovits, Christine
17, 1943	Davis, Grania
17, 1946	Crutcher, Chris(topher C.)
18, 1888	Allen, Gertrude E(lizabeth)
18, 1899	Kalnay, Francis
18, 1900	Marshall, S(amuel) L(yman) A(twood)
18, 1902	West, Mary Jessamyn
18, 1911	Funk, Thompson
18, 1913	Skelton, Red
18, 1920	Smith, Norman F.
18, 1927	Ozer, Jerome S.
18, 1927	Ward, Ralph T.
18, 1930	Silverthorne, Elizabeth
18, 1934	Piro, Richard
18, 1936	Dixon, Jeanne
18, 1938	Mangurian, David
18, 1949	Louie, Ai-Ling
18, 1954	Bond, Felicia
19, 1874	Robinson, Mabel Louise
19, 1916	Aitken, Dorothy (Lockwood)
19, 1916	Merriam, Eve
19, 1919	Garrison, Webb B(lack)
19, 1921	Spencer, Elizabeth
19, 1925	Foster, John T(homas)
19, 1928	Galster, Robert
19, 1929	Borja, Corinne
19, 1931	Cartey, Wilfred George Onslow
19, 1939	Feldman, Anne (Rodgers)
19, 1939	Myra, Harold L(awrence)
19, 1944	Shields, Charles
19, 1949	Kaye, Marilyn
19, 1956	Blumberg, Leda
20, 1900	Arnold, Oren
20, 1902	Dodds, John W(endell)
20, 1909	Fox, William Wellington
20, 1913	Balet, Jan (Bernard)
20, 1918	Wiley, Karla H(ummel)
20, 1924	Eitzen, Ruth (Carper)
20, 1926	Wiseman, Ann (Sayre)
20, 1935	Stepp, Ann
21, 1884	Peck, Anne Merriman
21, 1897	Budd, Lillian (Peterson)
21, 1902	Musgrave, Florence
21, 1907	Folsom, Franklin (Brewster)
21, 1909	Marokvia, Artur
21, 1910	Carlson, Bernice Wells
21, 1913	Hartley, William B(rown)
21, 1914	Luger, Harriett M(andelay)
21, 1916	Henderson, Nancy Wallace
21, 1917	Winston, Richard
21, 1918	Johnson, Charlotte Buel
21, 1921	Lansing, Alfred
21, 1921	Ward, Martha (Eads)
21, 1923	Wise, William
21, 1929	Almquist, Don
21, 1932	Lord, Athena V.
21, 1933	Gardner, John (Champlin, Jr.)
21, 1935	Greene, Laura
21, 1953	Lesser, Rika
21, 1957	Bly, Robert W(ayne)
22, 1881	Bianco, Margery (Williams)
22, 1893	Hogner, Nils
22, 1898	Benet, Stephen Vincent
22, 1899	Bennett, Richard
22, 1902	DuJardin, Rosamond Neal
22, 1902	Lauritzen, Jonreed
22, 1903	Simon, Howard
22, 1907	Fenderson, Lewis H.
22, 1908	Brown, Marion Marsh
22, 1910	Heyneman, Anne
22, 1918	Myers, Elisabeth P(erkins)
22, 1922	Liss, Howard
22, 1926	Hurwood, Bernhardt J.
22, 1927	Hall, Carolyn Vosburg
22, 1928	Anderson, Joy
22, 1931	Calvert, Patricia
22, 1935	Manchel, Frank
22, 1937	Seuling, Barbara
22, 1938	Alter, Judith (MacBain)
22, 1941	Brady, Maxine L.
22, 1941	Byard, Carole (Marie)
22, 1955	Newman, Matthew (Harrison)
23, 1898	Witty, Paul A(ndrew)
23, 1904	Adams, Julia Davis
23, 1916	Hovell, Lucy A. (Peterson)
23, 1926	Coombs, Patricia
23, 1926	Goldberg, Herbert S.
23, 1929	Quackenbush, Robert M(ead)
23, 1934	Brow, Thea
23, 1946	Paterson, Diane (R. Cole)
24, 1876	Webster, Alice (Jean Chandler)
24, 1887	Chapman, Frederick Trench
24, 1890	Medary, Marjorie
24, 1894	Garst, Doris (Shannon)
24, 1895	Wernecke, Herbert Henry
24, 1896	Coffman, Ramon Peyton
24, 1902	Averill, Esther (Holden)
24, 1903	Collier, Ethel
24, 1903	Nelson, Cholmondeley M.
24, 1903	Viguers, Ruth Hill
24, 1904	Morris, Richard Brandon
24, 1905	Haycraft, Howard
24, 1912	Gordon, Mildred (Nixon)
24, 1913	Davis, Burke
24, 1913	Nef, Evelyn Stefansson
24, 1921	Jacobs, Lou(is), Jr.
24, 1924	Pollack, Merrill S.
24, 1925	Watson, Pauline
24, 1930	Pomerantz, Charlotte
24, 1935	Booth, Graham (Charles)
24, 1936	Marrin, Albert
24, 1939	Malzberg, Barry (N.)
24, 1940	Hillman, Priscilla (Hartford)
24, 1942	Ehrlich, Amy
24, 1942	Kurland, Gerald
24, 1945	Pollock, Bruce

THE BIRTHDAY BOOK   BIRTH MONTH INDEX   393

24, 1945 Shebar, Sharon Sigmond
24, 1953 Salduth, Denise
24, 1959 Nerlove, Miriam
25, 1856 Major, Charles
25, 1870 Parrish, Frederick Maxfield
25, 1904 Buba, Joy Flinsch
25, 1904 Hemphill, Martha Locke
25, 1906 Armour, Richard (Willard)
25, 1911 Krauss, Ruth (Ida)
25, 1913 Sutton, Jeff(erson H.)
25, 1918 Eggenberger, David
25, 1921 Davidson, Rosalie
25, 1924 Newcombe, Jack
25, 1924 Parr, Lucy
25, 1926 Szulc, Tad
25, 1929 Farb, Peter
25, 1930 Larson, Jean Russell
25, 1937 Barrett, Ron
25, 1937 Hopper, Nancy J.
25, 1945 Leder, Jane Mersky
25, 1947 Watson, Clyde (Dingman)
26, 1862 Nyce, Vera
26, 1877 McNeely, Marian Hurd
26, 1885 Bransom, John Paul
26, 1892 Buck, Pearl S(ydenstricker)
26, 1894 Johnson, Lois S(mith)
26, 1897 Gallico, Paul (William)
26, 1899 Bell, Norman (Edward)
26, 1907 Bennett, Rainey
26, 1909 Colby, Jean Poindexter
26, 1911 Hodges, Margaret Moore
26, 1921 Schoor, Gene
26, 1923 Berenstain, Jan(ice Grant)
26, 1941 Cooper, Kay
26, 1945 Cosgrove, Stephen E(dward)
26, 1946 Tarsky, Sue
26, 1948 Sumichrast, Jozef
26, 1950 Kinzel, Dorothy
27, 1876 Patch, Edith M(arion)
27, 1889 Bliven, Bruce
27, 1891 Thompson, Ruth Plumly
27, 1905 May, Robert Lewis
27, 1905 Wolff, Robert Jay
27, 1907 Willcox, Isobel
27, 1910 Wallower, Lucille
27, 1913 Corbett, Scott
27, 1913 Plagemann, Bentz
27, 1927 Hunter, Mel
27, 1930 Massie, Diane Redfield
27, 1932 Hull, Jessie Redding
27, 1932 Newsome, Arden J(eanne Bokeeno)
27, 1935 Laurence, Ester Hauser
27, 1942 Ridlon, Marci
27, 1942 Sears, Stephen W.
27, 1945 Janeczko, Paul B(ryan)
27, 1948 Mitchell, Kathy
28, 1881 Davis, Robert
28, 1887 Price, Willard (DeMille)

28, 1894 Weilerstein, Sadie Rose
28, 1900 Cohen, Jene Barr
28, 1906 Duvall, Evelyn Millis
28, 1910 Decker, Duane (Walter)
28, 1911 Boardman, Fon Wyman, Jr.
28, 1911 Kalina, Sigmund
28, 1912 Bandel, Betty
28, 1915 Jones, Adrienne
28, 1927 Hoffmann, Hilde
28, 1929 Edwards, Sally (Cary)
28, 1930 Raiff, Stan
28, 1932 Babbitt, Natalie (Moore)
28, 1932 Neusner, Jacob
28, 1938 Hiller, Ilo (Ann)
28, 1945 Davis, James Robert
29, 1869 Tarkington, Newton Booth
29, 1877 Beebe, Charles William
29, 1878 Theiss, Lewis Edwin
29, 1880 Turner, Nancy Byrd
29, 1884 Tietjens, Eunice Hammond
29, 1891 Shephard, Esther
29, 1906 Kubinyi, Kalman
29, 1907 Riddle, Maxwell
29, 1908 Galt, Thomas Franklin, Jr.
29, 1909 Baker, Samm S(inclair)
29, 1910 Greenleaf, Peter
29, 1912 Little, Mary E.
29, 1915 Woodrich, Mary Neville
29, 1925 Bloome, Enid P.
29, 1927 Karl, Jean E(dna)
29, 1930 Catlin, Wynelle
29, 1932 Kunz, Roxane (Brown)
29, 1937 Smith, Betsy Covington
29, 1947 Nestor, William Prodromas
29, 1948 Furchgott, Terry
29, 1952 Krull, Kathleen
30, 1822 Adams, William Taylor
30, 1877 Smith, Fredrika Shumway
30, 1904 Russ, Lavinia
30, 1908 Suhl, Yuri
30, 1912 Stair, Gobin (John)
30, 1913 Cain, Arthur H(omer)
30, 1915 Johnston, Dorothy Grunbock
30, 1920 Stein, M(eyer) L(ewis)
30, 1920 Weiss, Adelle
30, 1928 Foster, Joanna
30, 1928 Schock, Pauline
30, 1928 Throckmorton, Peter
30, 1928 Toothaker, Roy Eugene
30, 1941 Singer, Susan (Mahler)
30, 1954 Nastick, Sharon
31, 1831 DuChaillu, Paul (Belloni)
31, 1897 Pryor, Helen Brenton
31, 1909 Phleger, Fred B.
31, 1910 Brasier, Virginia
31, 1918 Plate, Robert
31, 1921 Curtis, Patricia
31, 1922 Hyde, Wayne F(rederick)

31, 1930 Apfel, Necia H(alpern)
31, 1930 Smith, Robert Kimmel
31, 1938 Feelings, Muriel (Grey)
31, 1946 Haller, Dorcas Woodbury
??, 1877 Cady, Walter Harrison

AUGUST

Day Year
01, 1815 Dana, Richard Henry, Jr.
01, 1819 Melville, Herman
01, 1877 Diller, Angela
01, 1903 Horgan, Paul
01, 1903 Joseph, Joseph M(aron)
01, 1904 Winterbotham, R(ussell) R(obert)
01, 1911 Helfman, Elizabeth S(eaver)
01, 1914 Ormes, Zelda J.
01, 1916 Leavitt, Jerome E(dward)
01, 1923 Root, Shelton L., Jr.
01, 1927 Swiger, Elinor Porter
01, 1931 Wilson, Tom
01, 1936 Forman, Brenda
01, 1938 Bouchard, Lois Kalb
01, 1939 Jacopetti, Alexandra
01, 1944 Gibbons, Gail
01, 1945 Cusack, Margaret
01, 1947 Stamaty, Mark Alan
01, 1951 Schweninger, Ann
01, 1954 Brahm, Sumishta
02, 1856 White, Eliza Orne
02, 1892 Kieran, John (Francis)
02, 1900 Holling, Holling C(lancy)
02, 1903 Borski, Lucia Merecka
02, 1908 Benasutti, Marion
02, 1914 Zimmerman, Naoma
02, 1920 Carson, J(ohn) Franklin
02, 1921 Barr, Donald
02, 1923 Dowdey, Landon Gerald
02, 1924 Baldwin, James (Arthur)
02, 1924 Halliburton, Warren J.
02, 1944 Riskind, Mary (Julia Longenberger)
02, 1946 Howe, James
03, ???? Forsee, Frances Aylesa
03, 1894 Hager, Alice Rogers
03, 1898 Low, Elizabeth Hammond
03, 1900 Gergely, Tibor
03, 1904 Simak, Clifford D(onald)
03, 1905 Frost, Frances
03, 1909 Clark, Walter Van Tilburg
03, 1914 Worline, Bonnie Bess
03, 1921 Carruth, Hayden
03, 1924 Uris, Leon (Marcus)
03, 1925 Roth, Arthur J(oseph)

03, 1926 Calhoun, Mary Huiskamp
03, 1928 Vaughan, Sam(uel) S.
03, 1929 Boyer, Robert E(rnst)
03, 1942 Schiff, Ken(neth Roy)
04, 1889 Dolch, Edward William
04, 1892 Long, Laura Mooney
04, 1895 Anthony, Edward
04, 1905 Luther, Frank
04, 1909 Faralla, Dana
04, 1913 Hayden, Robert E(arl)
04, 1914 Robinson, Millian Oller
04, 1915 Ahnstrom, D(oris) N.
04, 1915 Viertel, Janet
04, 1920 Franklin, Harold
04, 1922 Clark, Frank J(ames)
04, 1923 Nixon, Hershell Howard
04, 1924 Robison, Bonnie
04, 1927 Freschet, Berniece Louise (Speck)
04, 1929 Neumeyer, Peter F(lorian)
04, 1943 Jahn, Joseph Michael
04, 1948 Carlstrom, Nancy White
04, 1950 Senn, Steve
05, 1873 Kummer, Frederic Arnold
05, 1880 Sawyer, Ruth
05, 1890 Petersham, Maud (Sylvia Fuller)
05, 1894 Bro, Margueritte (Harmon)
05, 1895 Hogan, Inez
05, 1899 Aiken, Conrad (Potter)
05, 1899 Bacharach, Herman Ilfeld
05, 1899 Baruch, Dorothy W(alter)
05, 1902 Alderman, Clifford Lindsey
05, 1902 Bright, Robert
05, 1902 Leipold, L. Edmund
05, 1904 Hayes, John F.
05, 1906 Hegarty, Reginald Beaton
05, 1913 Riesenberg, Felix, Jr.
05, 1915 MacKinnon Groomer, Vera
05, 1916 Cooke, Donald Ewin
05, 1923 Hoyt, Edwin P(almer), Jr.
05, 1930 Ruffins, Reynold
05, 1935 Patterson, Charles
05, 1938 Mayer, Ann M(argaret)
06, 1869 Wheeler, Post
06, 1883 Miller, Mary Britton
06, 1890 Johnson, Gerald White
06, 1900 Hillcourt, William
06, 1902 Howe, Gertrude Herrick
06, 1907 Sypher, Lucy Johnston
06, 1908 Jacobs, Helen Hull
06, 1909 Farber, Norma
06, 1912 Prieto, Mariana B(eeching)
06, 1913 Castellanos, Jane Mollie (Robinson)
06, 1913 Wechterr, Nell Wise

06, 1915 Panetta, George
06, 1917 Cooney, Barbara
06, 1918 Ilsley, Velma (Elizabeth)
06, 1918 Nelson, Cordner (Bruce)
06, 1918 Wilson, Charles Banks
06, 1919 Lader, Lawrence
06, 1920 Gray, Genevieve S.
06, 1921 Reed, Betty Jane
06, 1925 Knight, David C(arpenter)
06, 1926 Jeppson, J(anet) O(pal)
06, 1929 MacBride, Roger Lea
06, 1929 VanZwienen, Ilse (Charlotte Koehn)
06, 1936 Tusan, Stan
06, 1939 Rosenberg, Maxine B(erta)
06, 1946 Asch, Frank
06, 1948 Rice, Dale R(ichard)
06, 1949 Carey, Valerie Scho
06, 1949 Scribner, Joanne L.
07, ???? Rapaport, Stella F(read)
07, 1888 Winter, Milo (Kendall)
07, 1895 Townsend, Lee
07, 1922 Seixas, Judith S.
07, 1926 Davidson, R(aymond)
07, 1927 Knott, William Cecil, Jr.
07, 1927 Wojciechowska, Maia (Teresa Rodman)
07, 1928 Byars, Betsy (Cromer)
07, 1928 Marlowe, Stephen
07, 1933 Pournelle, Jerry (Eugene)
07, 1935 Hemschemeyer, Judith
07, 1942 Keillor, Garrison
07, 1948 Appel, Martin E(liot)
08, 1884 Teasdale, Sara
08, 1896 Lawson, Marion Tubbs
08, 1896 Rawlings, Marjorie Kinnan
08, 1907 Stuart, Hilton Jesse
08, 1910 Kidwell, Carl
08, 1923 Martin, Lynne
08, 1934 Hammer, Charles
08, 1939 Caraway, Caren
08, 1950 Kopper, Lisa (Esther)
09, ???? Hobart, Lois (Elaine)
09, 1899 Coffin, Joseph (John)
09, 1901 Rydberg, Ernest E(mil)
09, 1918 Doss, Helen (Grigsby)
09, 1918 Lietz, Gerald S(ylvane)
09, 1921 West, Betty
09, 1922 Anderson, Lucia (Lewis)
09, 1927 Keyes, Daniel
09, 1930 Wennerstrom, Genia Katherine
09, 1931 Simon, Seymour
09, 1932 Aruego, Jose
09, 1933 Longtemps, Kenneth
09, 1933 Steinberg, Fred J.
09, 1935 Ohlsson, Ib

09, 1944 McKissack, Patricia (L'Ann) C(arwell)
09, 1945 Rossel, Seymour
10, 1904 Dean, Graham M.
10, 1911 Elkin, Benjamin
10, 1911 Singer, Kurt D(eutsch)
10, 1917 Tomes, Margot (Ladd)
10, 1920 Hicks, Clifford B.
10, 1931 Dygard, Thomas J.
10, 1933 Loss, Joan
11, 1897 Bogan, Louise
11, 1904 Woolley, Catherine
11, 1907 Wittanen, Etolin
11, 1908 Freeman, Don
11, 1910 Poole, Lynn D.
11, 1911 Low, Joseph
11, 1912 Brooks, Polly Schoyer
11, 1913 Mark, Pauline (Dahlin)
11, 1914 Shane, Harold Gray
11, 1917 Browne, Richard
11, 1925 Coopersmith, Jerome
11, 1927 Sullivan, George E(dward)
11, 1928 Nourse, Alan E(dward)
11, 1930 Marks, Burton
11, 1933 Berger, Terry
11, 1941 Kroll, Steven
11, 1941 Snyder, Carol
11, 1944 Cole, Joanna
12, 1859 Bates, Katharine Lee
12, 1867 Hamilton, Edith
12, 1889 Sharp, Zerna A.
12, 1899 DeLeeuw, Adele (Louise)
12, 1910 Richter, Mischa
12, 1914 Beckman, Delores
12, 1915 Wallace, John A(dam)
12, 1916 Hayman, LeRoy
12, 1918 Bartenbach, Jean
12, 1923 Anderson, Leone Castell
12, 1923 Gannett, Ruth Stiles
12, 1923 Gottlieb, Gerald
12, 1925 Hood, Joseph F.
12, 1930 Hoberman, Mary Ann (Freedman)
12, 1932 Lane, John
12, 1936 Strauss, Joyce
12, 1937 Myers, Walter Dean
12, 1939 McKissack, Fredrick L(emuel)
12, 1940 Jewell, Nancy
12, 1942 Bliss, Ronald G(ene)
12, 1942 Robinson, Nancy K(onheim)
12, 1946 Howe, Deborah
12, 1952 Spollen, Christopher
12, 1955 Martin, Ann M(atthews)
13, 1816 McGuffey, Alexander Hamilton
13, 1899 Hitchcock, Alfred (Joseph)
13, 1908 Allen, T(erril) D(iener)
13, 1915 Fuller, Lois Hamilton
13, 1927 Friedrich, Priscilla
13, 1933 Mitchell, Joyce Slayton
13, 1937 Fox, Michael Wilson

14, 1860 Seton, Ernest (Evan) Thompson
14, 1863 Thayer, Ernest Lawrence
14, 1889 Davis, Verne T(heodore)
14, 1896 Weiss, Emil
14, 1900 Bauer, Helen
14, 1904 Baird, Bil
14, 1906 Carley, V(an Ness) Royal
14, 1916 Borland, Kathryn Kilby
14, 1917 Snow, Donald Clifford
14, 1918 Provensen, Alice
14, 1921 Dahlstedt, Marden (Armstrong)
14, 1926 Gault, Frank
14, 1927 Metter, Bert(ram Milton)
14, 1930 Goettel, Elinor
14, 1938 Marks, Rita (Weiss)
14, 1947 Nash, Bruce M(itchell)
14, 1950 Larson, Gary
15, 1787 Follen, Eliza Lee (Cabot)
15, 1887 Ferber, Edna
15, 1895 Kutcher, Ben
15, 1900 Tworkov, Jack
15, 1904 Eunson, Dale
15, 1905 Freeman, Ira M(aximilian)
15, 1908 Zaidenberg, Arthur
15, 1914 Rand, Paul
15, 1915 Turkle, Brinton (Cassady)
15, 1917 Darling, Lois (MacIntyre)
15, 1920 Soderlind, Arthur E(dwin)
15, 1921 Clement, Clarles
15, 1922 Baskin, Leonard
15, 1922 Weisberger, Bernard A(llen)
15, 1925 Dolim, Mary N(uzum)
15, 1926 Clifford, Mary Louise (Beneway)
15, 1927 Taylor, Mark
15, 1935 Arneson, Don Jon
15, 1935 Mele, Frank M(ichael)
15, 1936 Thomas, Jane Resh
15, 1938 Reese, Robert A.
15, 1946 Munson(-Benson), Tunie
15, 1947 Rinard, Judith E(llen)
15, 1948 Newsom, Carol
15, 1950 Landon, Lucinda
16, 1887 Sublette, C(lifford) M(cClellan)
16, 1892 Foster, Harold Rudolf
16, 1899 Carleton, R(eginal) Milton
16, 1904 Webber, Irma E(leanor Schmidt)
16, 1908 Maxwell, William
16, 1909 Chute, Marchette (Gaylord)
16, 1914 DeRegniers, Beatrice Schenk

16, 1916 Felsen, Henry Gregor
16, 1917 Christopher, Matt(hew) F.
16, 1918 Pascal, David
16, 1921 Kinney, Harrison
16, 1932 Johnson, Milton
16, 1941 McDermott, Beverly Brodsky
16, 1942 Beamer, George Charles, Jr.
16, 1942 Spinelli, Eileen
16, 1943 Hamilton, Morse
17, 1863 Porter, Gene(va Grace) Stratton
17, 1897 Fletcher, Charlie May Hogue
17, 1903 Chasins, Abram
17, 1905 Evans, Eva Knox
17, 1910 Kane, Robert W(illiam)
17, 1917 Carleton, Barbee Oliver
17, 1918 Cross, Wilbur Lucius III
17, 1920 Cornell, Jean Gay
17, 1923 Deedy, John
17, 1925 Gumpertz, Bob
17, 1926 Livingston, Myra Cohn
17, 1931 Honig, Donald
17, 1932 Shulman, Alix Kates
17, 1934 Adorjan, Carol (Madden)
17, 1934 Hamberger, John (F.)
17, 1937 Dewey, Ariane
17, 1943 Makie, Pam
17, 1944 Bly, Stephen A(rthur)
18, 1898 O'Brien, John Sherman
18, 1902 Credle, Ellis
18, 1904 Fatio, Louise
18, 1924 Siegl, Helen
18, 1926 Hirsch, Phil
18, 1926 Radlauer, Ruth (Shaw)
18, 1930 Dunn, Mary Lois
18, 1931 Chwast, Seymour
18, 1934 Levitin, Sonia (Wolff)
18, 1934 McCormick, Edith (Joan)
18, 1938 Carris, Joan Davenport
18, 1939 Siegel, Robert (Harold)
18, 1944 Danziger, Paula
19, 1793 Goodrich, Samuel Griswold
19, 1877 Schoonover, Frank (Earle)
19, 1892 Hosford, Jessie
19, 1902 Nash, Frederic Ogden
19, 1907 Brown, Robert Joseph
19, 1913 Hull, Eleanor (Means)
19, 1921 Roddenberry, Eugene Wesley
19, 1923 Grummer, Arnold Edward
19, 1925 Wacker, Charles H(enry), Jr.
19, 1928 Stankevich, Boris
19, 1930 Linn, Charles F.
19, 1931 Dixon, Peter L.
19, 1932 Cohen, Joan Lebold
19, 1932 Wersba, Barbara

19, 1934 Robinson, Jean O. (Kroner)
19, 1938 Cobb, Vicki (Wolf)
19, 1941 Cerf, Christopher (Bennett)
19, 1941 Lyons, Grant
19, 1944 Larsen, Rebecca
19, 1947 Dyer, T(homas) A(llan)
19, 1951 Espeland, Pamela (Lee)
19, 1952 Blackburn, John(ny) Brewton
20, 1905 Johnson, Siddie Joe
20, 1914 McCaslin, Nellie
20, 1921 Hurmence, Belinda
20, 1922 Richelson, Geraldine
20, 1927 Edwards, Anne
20, 1931 Razzi, James
20, 1933 Alexander, Sue
20, 1938 Kevles, Bettyann
20, 1950 Flesch, Yolande (Catarina)
21, 1904 Wechsler, Herman
21, 1906 McClintock, Marshall
21, 1908 Jaquith, Priscilla
21, 1923 Hall, Natalie Watson
21, 1929 Kennedy, Joseph Charles
21, 1937 Hayden, Robert C(arter), Jr.
21, 1938 Epstein, Perle S(herry)
21, 1942 Fiarotta, Phyllis
21, 1943 Wulffson, Don L.
21, 1953 Yorinks, Arthur
21, 1954 Mills, Claudia
22, 1893 Holbrook, Stewart Hall
22, 1896 Lancaster, Bruce
22, 1909 Darrow, Whitney, Jr.
22, 1911 DeMejo, Oscar
22, 1914 Samachson, Dorothy (Mirkin)
22, 1915 McNamara, Margaret (Craig)
22, 1920 Bradbury, Ray (Douglas)
22, 1921 Roddy, Lee
22, 1922 Doss, Margot Patterson
22, 1927 Goodman, Walter
22, 1930 Friedlander, Joanne K(ohn)
22, 1931 Garrison, Barbara
22, 1931 Graham, Ada
22, 1937 Holt, Margaret (Cecile)
22, 1937 Kohl, Herbert
22, 1942 Meyer, Louis A(lbert)
23, 1898 Papashvily, George
23, 1899 Coe, Lloyd
23, 1900 Reynolds, Malvina
23, 1903 Heal, Edith
23, 1905 Bushmiller, Ernie
23, 1916 Jefferds, Vincent Harris
23, 1924 Birmingham, Lloyd
23, 1927 Berger, Melvin H.
23, 1927 Liston, Robert A.
23, 1933 Jacobs, William Jay
24, 1882 Pogany, William Andrew

Day, Year	Name	Day, Year	Name	Day, Year	Name
24, 1888	Jagendorf, Moritz (Adolf)	26, 1933	McManus, Patrick (Francis)	30, 1938	Crews, Donald
24, 1898	Brandhorst, Carl T(heodore)	27, 1884	Arbuthnot, May Hill	30, 1942	Buchan, Stuart
24, 1901	Becker, Beril	27, 1891	Urmston, Mary	31, 1873	Harding, Charlotte
24, 1905	Brady, Esther Wood	27, 1893	Hess, Fjeril	31, 1884	Lankes, Julius J.
24, 1907	Mizner, Elizabeth Howard	27, 1899	Forester, C(ecil) S(cott)	31, 1885	Heyward, Du Bose
24, 1908	Moore, John Travers	27, 1902	Murphy, Robert (William)	31, 1890	Childs, Halla Fay (Cochrane)
24, 1908	Rydberg, Lou(isa Hampton)	27, 1903	Bunce, William Harvey	31, 1894	McCracken, Harold
24, 1910	Fife, Dale (Odile)	27, 1904	Perkins, Al(bert Rogers)	31, 1899	McGuire, Edna
24, 1913	Wilkinson, John Burke	27, 1920	Sparks, Mary W.	31, 1903	Sechrist, Elizabeth (Hough)
24, 1922	Ross, Clare (Romano)	27, 1921	Mosel, Arlene (Tichy)	31, 1907	Christensen, Gardell Dano
24, 1923	Clark, Champ	27, 1923	Skold, Betty Westrom	31, 1908	Dolson, Hildegarde
24, 1923	Landin, Les(lie)	27, 1925	King, Cynthia	31, 1908	Johnson, Harriett
24, 1923	Lipman, Matthew	27, 1926	Zens, Patricia Martin	31, 1908	Saroyan, William
24, 1924	Markun, Patricia M(aloney)	27, 1927	Elwart, Joan Potter	31, 1908	Weil, Ann Yezner
24, 1925	Behrman, Carol (Helen)	27, 1927	Selman, LaRue W.	31, 1910	Baker, Charlotte
24, 1926	Loomis, Robert D.	27, 1934	Rinaldi, Ann	31, 1912	Kinert, Reed Charles
24, 1936	Hendrickson, Walter Brookfield, Jr.	27, 1936	Becker, Joyce	31, 1912	Robertson, Dorothy Lewis
24, 1937	Cebulash, Mel	27, 1943	Kline, Suzy	31, 1915	Hay, John
24, 1943	Adams, Barbara Johnston	27, 1944	Bellville, Cheryl Walsh	31, 1919	King, Robin
24, 1943	Bishop, Bonnie	28, 1871	Paine, Ralph D.	31, 1923	Brock, Betty (Carter)
24, 1943	Goldsmith, Howard	28, 1891	Horvath, Ferdinand Huszti	31, 1925	Lindop, Edmund
24, 1943	Hughes, Dean	28, 1892	Colver, Alice Mary (Ross)	31, 1930	McVicker, Charles (Taggart)
24, 1945	Laughbaum, Steve	28, 1904	Duvoisin, Roger (Antoine)	31, 1935	Vaughn, Ruth
24, 1946	Obrant, Susan	28, 1909	Rathjen, Carl H(enry)	31, 1940	Ray, Deborah (Kogan)
25, 1836	Harte, Francis Bret(t)	28, 1912	Grand, Samuel	31, 1954	Rofes, Eric Edward
25, 1900	Crespi, Pachita	28, 1915	Derman, Sarah Audrey	31, 1957	Harris, Steven Michael
25, 1900	Garbutt, Bernard	28, 1915	Tudor, Tasha		
25, 1900	Wonsetler, John Charles	28, 1919	Embry, Margaret (Jacob)		

SEPTEMBER

Day, Year	Name
25, 1909	Zimmermann, Arnold E(rnst Alfred)
28, 1924	Lee, Norma E.
25, 1910	Hoffmann, Margaret Jones
28, 1924	Monjo, F(erdinand) N(icholas)
25, 1913	Kelly, Walt(er Crawford)
28, 1926	Krasilovsky, Phyllis (Manning)

Day	Year	Name
??,	1863	Smith, Jessie Willcox
25, 1920	Laux, Dorothy	28, 1927	Kunstler, Morton	01,	1791	Sigourney, Lydia Huntley
25, 1922	Geer, Charles	28, 1941	Gardner, Beau	01,	1875	Burroughs, Edgar Rice
25, 1926	Titler, Dale Milton	28, 1974	Say, Allen	01,	1892	Lamb, Harold (Albert)
25, 1928	Hollander, Phyllis	29, 1809	Holmes, Oliver Wendell	01,	1895	Yates, Raymond F(rancis)
25, 1929	Brown, Walter R(eed)	29, 1854	Jacobs, Joseph	01,	1898	Hatlo, Jimmy
25, 1935	Fenten, Barbara D(oris)	29, 1879	Singmaster, Elsie	01,	1898	McDonald, Lucile Saunders
25, 1941	Wallace-Brodeur, Ruth	29, 1888	Hill, Frank Ernest	01,	1904	Costello, David (Francis)
26, 1859	Schultz, James Willard	29, 1897	Hauman, Doris	01,	1905	Cameron, Edna M.
26, 1873	Becker, May Lamberton	29, 1903	Eisenberg, Azriel	01,	1906	Grayson, Marion (Forbourg)
26, 1874	Gale, Zona	29, 1909	Kerman, Gertrude Lerner	01,	1907	Emery, Anne (Eleanor McGuigan)
26, 1890	Olmsted, Lorena Ann	29, 1921	Burt, Jesse Clifton	01,	1907	Stewart, Elizabeth Laing
26, 1892	Cook, Olive Rambo	29, 1923	Callahan, Philip S(erna)	01,	1908	Lloyd, Mary Norris
26, 1899	Schatzki, Walter	29, 1926	Zeiger, Sophia	01,	1911	Flynn, James Joseph
26, 1911	Binder, Otto O(scar)	29, 1929	Oana, Katherine D.	01,	1912	Mars, W(itold) T(adeusz, Jr.)
26, 1913	Broadhead, Helen Cross	29, 1930	Kavaler, Lucy			
26, 1922	Beatty, Patricia (Robbins)	29, 1937	Glaser, Dianne Elizabeth	01,	1915	Smucker, Barbara (Claassen)
26, 1922	Wiseman, B(ernard)	29, 1945	DiFranco, Anthony (Mario)	01,	1922	Livingston, Richard R(oland)
26, 1923	Stokes, Jack (Tilden)	29, 1946	Maiorano, Robert			
26, 1924	Millar, Barbara F.	30, 1899	Hall-Quest, Edna Olga Wilbourne			
26, 1926	Meilach, Dona Z(weigoron)	30, 1901	Gunther, John			
26, 1931	Gardner, Richard (M.)	30, 1904	Priestley, Lee (Shore)			
26, 1933	Bossom, Naomi	30, 1909	Burton, Virginia Lee			
		30, 1923	Levine, I(srael) E.			
		30, 1929	Joslin, Sesyle	01,	1926	Graham, John

01, 1928 Guy, Rosa (Cuthbert)
01, 1940 Ernst, Lyman John
01, 1946 Arnosky, Jim
02, 1820 Hale, Lucretia Peabody
02, 1875 Hillyer, V(irgil) M(ores)
02, 1879 Melcher, Marguerite Fellows
02, 1881 Beals, Frank Lee
02, 1898 Archibald, Joseph S(topford)
02, 1901 Eliot, Frances
02, 1901 Floethe, Richard
02, 1904 Borton, Elizabeth
02, 1910 McCormick, Alma Heflin
02, 1912 Bearden, Romare (Howard)
02, 1915 Edelman, Lily (Judith)
02, 1920 Fishler, Mary (Shiverick)
02, 1927 Dillon, Barbara
02, 1932 Wolfe, Burton H.
02, 1936 Bierhorst, John (William)
02, 1937 Most, Bernard
02, 1942 Hunt, Charlotte Dumaresq
02, 1942 Walsh, Ellen Stoll
03, 1849 Jewett, Sarah Orne
03, 1850 Field, Eugene
03, 1880 Richards, George Mather
03, 1881 Lardner, Rex
03, 1900 Benson, Sally
03, 1903 Mirsky, Jeannette
03, 1906 Miner, Opal Irene Sevrey (Frazine)
03, 1913 Beckett, Sheila
03, 1914 Glazer, Tom
03, 1922 Hilton, Suzanne (McLean)
03, 1923 Walker, Addison Mort
03, 1926 Lurie, Alison
03, 1929 Brandenberg, Aliki (Liacouras)
03, 1929 Meyer, Jean Shepherd
03, 1934 Schulman, L(ester) M(artin)
03, 1940 Hunt, Linda Lawrence
03, 1948 Allen, Jeffrey (Yale)
04, 1876 Stevens, Lucy Beatrice
04, 1897 Sayers, Frances (Clarke)
04, 1900 Gilmore, Iris
04, 1906 Overholser, Wayne D.
04, 1909 Pauli, Hertha (Ernestine)
04, 1912 Hoff, Syd(ney)
04, 1916 Comfort, Barbara
04, 1916 Klein, Leonore (Glotzer)
04, 1931 Evans, Shirlee
04, 1945 Wood, Linda C(arol)
04, 1945 Woods, Harold
05, 1875 Aylward, William James
05, 1895 Bonner, Mary Graham
05, 1905 Miller, Edward

05, 1907 Blough, Glenn O(rlando)
05, 1911 McCall, Edith S(ansum)
05, 1921 Werner, Vivian
05, 1923 Sutton, Ann (Livesay)
05, 1928 Butterworth, Emma Macalik
05, 1945 Munro, Roxie
05, 1947 Daniel, Becky
05, 1950 Guisewite, Cathy
05, 1952 Fleischman, Paul (Taylor)
06, 1876 Robinson, Boardman
06, 1882 Warren, William Stephen
06, 1894 Pease, Howard
06, 1895 Gagliardo, Ruth Garver
06, 1897 Weddle, Ethel H(arshbarger)
06, 1898 Hults, Dorothy Niebrugge
06, 1900 Trell, Max
06, 1904 Smith, Frances C(hristine)
06, 1915 Hill, Margaret (Ohler)
06, 1917 Modell, Frank B.
06, 1919 Behnke, Frances L. (Berry)
06, 1924 Cook, Bernadine
06, 1926 Faulhaber, Martha
06, 1927 Facklam, Margery Metz
06, 1928 Pirsig, Robert M.
06, 1935 Buchwald, Emilie
06, 1937 Aragones, Sergio
07, 1860 Moses, Anna Mary (Robertson)
07, 1885 Tippett, James S(terling)
07, 1885 Wylie, Elinor Hoyt
07, 1888 DeMuth, Flora Nash
07, 1889 Hader, Elmer (Stanley)
07, 1890 Komroff, Manuel
07, 1903 Landon, Margaret (Dorothea Mortenson)
07, 1904 Colby, C(arroll) B(urleigh)
07, 1908 Boesen, Victor
07, 1908 Newcomb, Covelle
07, 1910 Stahl, Ben(jamin Albert)
07, 1917 Lawrence, Jacob
07, 1921 Davis, Louise Littleton
07, 1921 MacKenzie, Garry
07, 1921 Tolles, Martha
07, 1925 Solbert, Romaine G.
07, 1932 Andersen, Yvonne
07, 1935 Klevin, Jill Ross
07, 1939 Petroski, Catherine (Ann Groom)
07, 1944 Hoffman, Phyllis M.
07, 1957 Piowaty, Kim Kennelly
08, 1853 Poulsson, Anne Emilie
08, 1905 Wheelwright, Jere Hungerford, Jr.
08, 1906 Prescott, Orville
08, 1912 West, Walter Richard
08, 1913 Condit, Martha Olson

08, 1920 Calvert, James
08, 1922 Perl, Susan
08, 1922 White, Nancy Bean
08, 1927 Weber, William John
08, 1930 Barton, Byron (Theodore Vartanian)
08, 1940 Prelutsky, Jack
08, 1942 Johnson, Joan J.
08, 1943 Darling, Mary Kathleen
08, 1948 Hague, Michael R(iley)
09, 1868 Austin, Mary (Hunter)
09, 1900 Hilton, James
09, 1902 Mian, Mary (Lawrence Shipman)
09, 1903 Whitney, Phyllis A(yame)
09, 1906 Fisher, Aileen (Lucia)
09, 1917 Robbins, Frank
09, 1920 Brokamp, Marilyn
09, 1920 Stevens, Mary E.
09, 1924 Scarry, Patricia (Murphy)
09, 1928 Nelson, Esther L.
09, 1932 Cooney, Nancy Evans
09, 1934 Sanchez, Sonia
09, 1937 Samson, Joan
10, 1895 Chapman, Mary Hamilton Illsley
10, 1900 Stern, Philip Van Doren
10, 1903 DeMartelly, John Stockton
10, 1907 Hilton, Ralph
10, 1909 Waltner, Willard H.
10, 1916 McClung, Robert Marshall
10, 1918 Schultz, Pearle Henriksen
10, 1918 Sweet, Oscar Cowan
10, 1919 Fitzgerald, Edward Earl
10, 1922 Doty, Roy
10, 1925 Crawford, Mel
10, 1927 Levin, Betty (Lowenthal)
10, 1928 Kelley, Leo P(atrick)
10, 1932 Edelson, Edward
10, 1946 Saul, E. Wendy
10, 1947 Jones, Rebecca C(astaldi)
10, 1948 Agard, Nadema
11, 1862 Porter, William Sydney
11, 1890 Glick, Carl (Cannon)
11, 1896 Simpson, Maxwell Stewart
11, 1900 Icks, Robert J.
11, 1902 Hodges, Carl G.
11, 1904 Brustlein, Daniel
11, 1910 Summers, James L(evingston)
11, 1911 Amerman, Lockhart
11, 1914 Kelling, Furn L.
11, 1915 Nevins, Albert J.
11, 1917 Todd, Barbara K(eith)
11, 1923 Weiss, Renee Karol
11, 1926 Slote, Alfred
11, 1927 Klimowicz, Barbara (Tingley)
11, 1940 Alderson, Sue Ann

11, 1942 Ruby, Lois
11, 1943 Pahz, James Alon
12, 1898 Shahn, Ben(jamin)
12, 1906 Crayder, Dorothy
12, 1906 Saunders, Blanche
12, 1909 Hopkins, Joseph G(erard) E(dward)
12, 1910 Milne, Lorus J(ohnson)
12, 1912 Thomson, Arline K.
12, 1917 Bearman, Jane (Ruth)
12, 1919 Faber, Harold
12, 1919 Hill, Robert W(hite)
12, 1920 Dank, Milton
12, 1920 McCrea, James (Craig, Jr.)
12, 1926 Lichello, Robert
12, 1927 Bruce, Mary
12, 1931 Hunter, Kristin (Elaine Eggleston)
12, 1938 Tobias, Tobi
12, 1939 Boring, Mel
13, 1898 Browin, Frances Williams
13, 1906 Parkinson, Ethelyn M(inerva)
13, 1907 Appel, Benjamin
13, 1909 Oakes, Vanya
13, 1912 Arnold, Elliott
13, 1912 Schwartz, Elizabeth Reeder
13, 1917 Kendall, Carol (Seeger)
13, 1920 Minarik, Else Holmelund
13, 1938 Stahl, Hilda
13, 1944 Swan, Susan
14, 1860 Garland, Hannibal Hamlin
14, 1890 DuBois, Theodora (McCormick)
14, 1900 Underhill, Alice Mertie (Waterman)
14, 1904 Brevannes, Maurice
14, 1909 Cabral, O(lga) M(arie)
14, 1910 Hurd, Edith Thacher
14, 1914 Armstrong, William H(oward)
14, 1914 Castellon, Federico
14, 1915 Speicher, Helen Ross (Smith)
14, 1919 Turlington, Bayly
14, 1922 Weiner, Sandra (Smith)
14, 1930 Kaplan, Anne Bernays
14, 1930 Supraner, Robyn
14, 1936 Pierce, Ruth (Ireland)
14, 1939 Anticaglia, Elizabeth
14, 1941 Hirschmann, Linda (Ann)
14, 1942 Lydon, Michael
14, 1944 Heller, Linda
14, 1948 Mahony, Elizabeth Winthrop
14, 1948 Reiff, Stephanie Ann
14, 1949 Goode, Diane (Capuozzo)
14, 1950 Steptoe, John (Lewis)
14, 1950 Tether, Cynthia Graham

15, 1789 Cooper, James Fenimore
15, 1850 Munroe, Kirk
15, 1870 Bragg, Mabel Caroline
15, 1902 Samuels, Charles
15, 1911 Terry, Luther L(eonidas)
15, 1913 Boegehold, Betty (Doyle)
15, 1914 Bacon, Elizabeth
15, 1914 McCloskey, John Robert
15, 1925 Green, Norma B(erger)
15, 1927 Hellman, Harold
15, 1934 DePaola, Thomas Anthony
15, 1936 Davis, Daniel S(heldon)
15, 1937 Smith, Jacqueline B.
15, 1938 Mee, Charles L., Jr.
15, 1950 Springstubb, Tricia
16, 1842 Fosdick, Charles Austin
16, 1895 Hopkins, Clark
16, 1897 Handforth, Thomas (Schofield)
16, 1897 Mauzey, Merritt
16, 1898 Rey, H(ans) A(ugusto)
16, 1906 Gay, Zhenya
16, 1907 Rice, Inez
16, 1908 Constant, Alberta Wilson
16, 1918 Koob, Theodora (Johanna Foth)
16, 1924 Hubley, Faith (Elliot)
16, 1924 Murray, Don(ald M.)
16, 1925 Johnson, Charles R.
16, 1926 Knowles, John
16, 1929 Rothkopf, Carol Z.
16, 1933 Schulman, Janet
16, 1946 Ryder, Joanne
17, 1907 Dowden, Anne Ophelia (Todd)
17, 1909 Enright, Elizabeth (Wright)
17, 1913 Glendinning, Sara W(ilson)
17, 1915 Sutherland, Zena B(ailey)
17, 1916 Kelly, George Anthony
17, 1922 Fichter, George S.
17, 1923 Berg, Bjorn
17, 1926 Kalb, Jonah
17, 1929 Hall, Elizabeth
17, 1930 Reinach, Jacquelyn (Krasne)
17, 1933 Goble, Paul
17, 1935 Allen, Nina (Stromgren)
17, 1942 Graham, Brenda Knight
17, 1954 Gilmore, Susan
18, 1908 Courlander, Harold
18, 1909 Jane, Mary Childs
18, 1914 Luce, Willard (Ray)
18, 1915 Osborne, Chester G.
18, 1927 Greene, Ellin
18, 1935 Batterberry, Ariane Ruskin
18, 1939 Bock, William Sauts Netamux'we

19, 1881 Garfield, James B.
19, 1894 Field, Rachel (Lyman)
19, 1894 Wadsworth, Wallace (Carter)
19, 1895 Malkus, Alida (Wright) Sims
19, 1897 Desmond, Alice Curtis
19, 1909 Brodin, Pierre Eugene
19, 1909 Hubbell, Harriet Weed
19, 1911 Abel, Raymond
19, 1914 Westervelt, Virginia (Veeder)
19, 1917 Hill, Ralph Nading
19, 1920 Gorelick, Molly C.
19, 1922 Knight, Damon
19, 1929 Dukert, Joseph M(ichael)
19, 1941 Haskins, James S.
19, 1945 Crowley, Arthur M(cBlair)
20, 1849 Grinnell, George Bird
20, 1878 Sinclair, Upton (Beall)
20, 1888 Petersham, Miska
20, 1900 Denniston, Elinore
20, 1904 Ogle, Lucille (Edith)
20, 1911 Mawicke, Tran
20, 1915 Taves, Isabella
20, 1921 Tashjian, Virginia A.
20, 1924 Dain, Martin J.
20, 1925 Bolian, Polly
20, 1927 Meyers, Joan (Simpson)
20, 1928 Jennings, Gary (Gayne)
20, 1929 Clifford, M(argaret) C(ort)
20, 1930 Durell, Ann
20, 1931 Kuttner, Paul
20, 1941 Geisert, Arthur (Frederick)
20, 1942 Bridgers, Sue Ellen
21, 1878 Fillmore, Parker H(oysted)
21, 1893 Kennell, Ruth E(pperson)
21, 1896 Kelsey, Alice Geer
21, 1896 Werth, Kurt
21, 1902 McEntee, Dorothy (Layng)
21, 1903 Price, Olive (M.)
21, 1904 Key, Alexander (Hill)
21, 1908 Corcos, Lucille
21, 1908 Iwamatsu, Jun Atsushi
21, 1912 Jones, Charles M(artin)
21, 1912 Ruth, Rod
21, 1914 Cohn, Angelo
21, 1920 Lerner, Aaron B(unsen)
21, 1927 Jensen, Virginia Allen
21, 1935 White, Laurence B(arton), Jr.
21, 1936 Burroway, Janet (Gay)
21, 1937 Bozzo, Frank
21, 1938 Windsor, Patricia
21, 1939 Schraff, Anne E(laine)
21, 1940 Tallon, Robert
21, 1945 Wilhelm, Hans
21, 1947 King, Stephen (Edwin)
21, 1949 Perry, Patricia

21, 1953 Davidson, Judith
22, 1876 Donahey, Mary
(Augusta) Dickerson
22, 1895 Deutsch, Babette
22, 1899 Munzer, Martha
E(iseman)
22, 1903 DeLeeuw, Cateau
(Wilhelmina)
22, 1908 Slobodkina, Esphyr
22, 1910 Holmes, Marjorie
(Rose)
22, 1911 Sunderlin, Sylvia
22, 1918 Gringhuis, Richard H.
22, 1922 Grohskopf, Bernice
(Appelbaum)
22, 1924 Bradfield, Roger
22, 1926 Hadley, Leila (Burton)
22, 1926 Odor, Ruth Shannon
22, 1927 Myrus, Donald
(Richard)
22, 1927 Parker, Dorothy (Lane)
D(aniels)
22, 1929 Grifalconi, Ann Weik
22, 1932 Davidson, Alice Joyce
22, 1944 Pollowitz, Melinda
(Kilborn)
22, 1945 Cornell, J(effrey)
22, 1947 Grant, Alice Leigh
22, 1953 Dunrea, Olivier
23, 1800 McGuffey, William
Holmes
23, 1848 Boyesen, Hjalmar
Hjorth
23, 1872 Lomax, John A.
23, 1896 Waugh, Dorothy
23, 1901 Eyre, Katherine
Wigmore
23, 1910 VanDuyn, Janet
23, 1912 Vosburgh, Leonard (W.)
23, 1917 Scott, Henry Joseph
23, 1922 Gidal, Sonia (Epstein)
23, 1926 Chaneles, Sol
23, 1931 Fassler, Joan (Grace)
23, 1932 Oldfield, Margaret
J(ean)
23, 1938 Katz, Fred(eric Phillip)
23, 1943 Huffaker, Sandy
24, 1891 Wells, Rhea
24, 1893 Bailey, Ralph Edgar
24, 1898 Behn, Harry
24, 1899 Carroll, Ruth
(Robinson)
24, 1900 Lacher, Gisella Loeffler
24, 1902 Coy, Harold
24, 1903 Benet, Sula
24, 1905 Abrahams, Robert
D(avid)
24, 1912 Taylor, Robert Lewis
24, 1913 Rawls, Woodrow
Wilson
24, 1925 Carew, Jan (Rynveld)
24, 1930 Cohen, Robert Carl
24, 1930 Langner, Nola
24, 1932 Curry, Jane L(ouise)
24, 1932 Greenberg, Joanne
(Goldenberg)
24, 1936 Henson, James Maury

24, 1939 Brown, Drollene P.
24, 1941 Quin-Harkin, Janet
24, 1942 MacMaster, Eve (Ruth)
B(owers)
24, 1948 Deveaux, Alexis
24, 1953 James, Robin (Irene)
25, 1869 Linderman, Frank B(ird)
25, 1871 Hawthorne, Hildegarde
25, 1905 Kohner, Frederick
25, 1906 Hamilton, Dorothy
25, 1906 Moore, Vardine
(Russell)
25, 1910 Kugelmass, Joseph
Alvin
25, 1914 Osborne, Leone Neal
25, 1921 Ross, John
25, 1922 Paige, Harry W.
25, 1927 Lazare, Gerald John
25, 1936 Albert, Burton, Jr.
25, 1938 Coleman, William
L(eroy)
25, 1938 Cornell, James
(Clayton, Jr.)
25, 1941 Wittman, Sally (Anne
Christensen)
25, 1945 Edens, Cooper
25, 1947 Murphy, Jim
25, 1955 Cheng, Judith
26, 1859 Bacheller, Irving
(Addison)
26, 1871 McCay, Winsor
26, 1888 Dobie, J(ames) Frank
26, 1892 Norling, Ernest Ralph
26, 1898 Hatch, Alden
26, 1898 Waltrip, Rufus (Charles)
26, 1899 Cavanah, Frances
26, 1906 Poole, Gray (Johnson)
26, 1906 Tarry, Ellen
26, 1909 Jenkins, Marie
M(agdalen)
26, 1916 Richmond, Julius
B(enjamin)
26, 1917 Rico, Don(ato)
26, 1918 Cagle, Malcolm
W(infield)
26, 1921 Wyeth, Betsy James
26, 1925 Amoss, Berthe (Marks)
26, 1929 Wolcott, Patty
26, 1930 Friedman, Marvin
26, 1934 Link, Martin
26, 1946 Work, Virginia
26, 1950 Westerberg, Christine
27, 1840 Nast, Thomas
27, 1906 Crary, Margaret
(Coleman)
27, 1907 Witheridge, Elizabeth
P(lumb)
27, 1911 Mordinoff, Nicolas
27, 1914 Coburn, John Bowen
27, 1914 Marshall, Sarah
Catherine
27, 1919 Percy, Charles Harting
27, 1924 Gray, Lee Learner
27, 1924 Waber, Bernard
27, 1926 Bonham, Barbara
(Thomas)
27, 1927 Feagles, Anita MacRae

27, 1931 Surge, Frank
27, 1934 Torgersen, Don Arthur
27, 1937 Gretz, Susanna
27, 1943 Levine, Abby
27, 1946 Clish, Lee Marian
28, 1840 Peck, George Wilbur
28, 1856 Wiggin, Kate Douglas
(Smith)
28, 1887 Jaques, Francis Lee
28, 1894 Harmer, Mabel
28, 1909 Caplin, Alfred Gerald
28, 1910 Dean, Nell Marr
28, 1913 Stearns, Monroe
(Mather)
28, 1919 Abbott, Robert Tucker
28, 1927 Brightfield, Richard
28, 1928 Thompson, Donnis
(Stark)
28, 1931 Stevens, Patricia
Bunning
28, 1934 Kahl, M(arvin) P(hilip)
28, 1935 Berkey, Barry Robert
28, 1948 Palmer, Heidi
28, 1951 Scuro, Vincent
29, 1905 St. Clair, Byrd Hooper
29, 1908 Avery, Kay
29, 1912 Harkins, Philip
29, 1919 Fern, Eugene A.
29, 1923 Berenstain, Stan(ley)
29, 1924 Pollack, Reginald
Murray
29, 1927 Mertz, Barbara (Gross)
29, 1928 Hall, Donald (Andrew,
Jr.)
29, 1929 Fiammenghi, Gioia
29, 1933 Chambers, John W.
29, 1941 Adams, Laurie
29, 1953 McLaurin, Anne
30, 1898 D'Aulaire, Edgar Parin
30, 1912 Sherburne, Zoa (Morin)
30, 1916 Tresselt, Alvin (R.)
30, 1922 Sylvester, Natalie
G(abry)
30, 1928 Wiesel, Elie(zer)
30, 1929 Fenner, Carol
(Elizabeth)
30, 1930 Zappler, Lisbeth
(Moses)
30, 1948 Woods, Geraldine

OCTOBER

Day Year
??, 1898 Wheeler, Opal
01, 1885 Untermeyer, Louis
01, 1895 Weber, Lenora
Mattingly
01, 1896 Green, Mary McBurney
01, 1901 DeVeyrac, Robert
01, 1906 Little, Lessie Jones

01,	1908	McGiffin, Lewis Lee Shaffer	04,	1907	Molloy, Anne (Stearns) Baker	06,	1942	Spangenberg, Judith Dunn
01,	1910	Webb, Jean Francis (III)	04,	1911	Waltrip, Mildred	06,	1948	Scher, Paula
01,	1911	Knebel, Fletcher	04,	1912	Krautter, Elisa (Bialk)	07,	1849	Riley, James Whitcomb
01,	1913	Temkin, Sara Anne (Schlossberg)	04,	1913	Janson, H(orst) W(oldemar)	07,	1878	Stevens, William Oliver
						07,	1893	Dalgliesh, Alice
01,	1914	Boorstin, Daniel J(oseph)	04,	1916	Caroselli, Remus F(rancis)	07,	1894	Thorne, Diana
						07,	1898	Paull, Grace A(lice)
01,	1914	Wollheim, Donald A(llen)	04,	1916	Cunningham, Julia W(oolfolk)	07,	1900	Berkebile, Fred D(onovan)
01,	1919	Rogers, Jean	04,	1917	Leister, Mary	07,	1907	MacInnes, Helen
01,	1920	Stewart, John (William)	04,	1918	Curley, Daniel	07,	1909	Burns, William A(loysius)
01,	1929	Robinson, Dorothy W.	04,	1919	Hallin, Emily Watson			
01,	1935	Edwards, Julie (Andrews)	04,	1924	Sobol, Donald J.	07,	1913	Janeway, Elizabeth (Hall)
			04,	1926	Robinson, Louie, Jr.	07,	1915	Scherman, Katharine
01,	1956	Hautzig, Deborah	04,	1928	Nelson, Lawrence E(rnest)	07,	1918	Spar, Jerome
02,	1885	Owen, Ruth (Bryan)				07,	1929	Kennedy, Paul E(dward)
02,	1889	Hallward, Michael	04,	1929	McCarter, Neely Dixon			
02,	1900	Jordan, E(mil) L(eopold)	04,	1929	Tilton, Madonna Elaine	07,	1931	Barry, Robert (Everett)
			04,	1933	McGrady, Mike	07,	1931	Young, Bernice Elizabeth
02,	1906	Ley, Willy	04,	1933	Wilford, John Noble, Jr.			
02,	1909	Smith, Lawrence Beall	04,	1938	Long, Earlene (Roberta)	07,	1936	Lewis, Alice C.
02,	1910	Hall, Adele				07,	1936	McShean, Gordon
02,	1910	McAllister, Mariana Kennedy	04,	1944	Meddaugh, Susan	07,	1942	Jeffers, Susan (Jane)
			05,	1879	Moon, Carl	08,	1880	Grose, Helen Mason
02,	1913	Vaughan, Anne	05,	1898	Knight, Ruth Adams (Yingling)	08,	1888	Steurt, Marjorie Rankin
02,	1918	Foss, William O(tto)				08,	1902	Cummings, Parke
02,	1921	Raebeck, Lois	05,	1910	Ainsworth, Catherine Harris	08,	1905	Levin, Meyer
02,	1923	Altschuler, Franz				08,	1907	Beatty, Hetty Burlingame
02,	1925	Paine, Roberta M.	05,	1913	LeBlanc, L(ee)			
02,	1930	Alvarez, Joseph A.	05,	1913	Zion, Eugene	08,	1907	Heiderstadt, Dorothy
02,	1932	Bethancourt, T(omas) Ernesto	05,	1918	Ludden, Allen (Ellsworth)	08,	1910	Brown, Rosalie (Gertrude) Moore
02,	1935	Antell, Will D.	05,	1920	DeLaurentis, Louise Budde	08,	1910	Conkling, Hilda
02,	1937	Bladow, Suzanne Wilson				08,	1915	Booth, Ernest Sheldon
			05,	1921	Bates, Betty	08,	1915	Irwin, Ann(abelle Bowen)
02,	1939	Salassi, Otto R(ussell)	05,	1922	Keane, Bil			
02,	1940	Sapieyevski, Anne Lindbergh	05,	1928	Fitzhugh, Louise (Perkins)	08,	1917	Lord, Walter
						08,	1920	DeClements, Barthe
02,	1941	Betancourt, Jeanne	05,	1940	Dewey, Ken(neth Francis)	08,	1920	Herbert, Frank (Patrick)
02,	1941	Dewey, Jennifer (Owings)				08,	1922	Whitney, Alex(andra)
			05,	1943	Gilbert, Sara (Dulaney)	08,	1924	Koch, Dorothy (Clarke)
02,	1941	Olugebefola, Ademole	05,	1955	Dank, Gloria Rand	08,	1925	Ormondroyd, Edward
02,	1943	Zimmer, Dirk	06,	1873	Faulkner, Georgene	08,	1927	Ferry, Charles
03,	1906	Carlson, Natalie Savage	06,	1887	Levinger, Elma (Ehrlich)	08,	1930	Caudell, Marian
			06,	1888	O'Neill, Eugene (Gladstone)	08,	1936	Moore, Carman Leroy
03,	1908	Morgan, Lenore				08,	1936	Newton, Suzanne (Latham)
03,	1915	Davidson, Jessica	06,	1897	Dietz, David H(enry)			
03,	1918	Cone, Molly (Lamken)	06,	1902	Gray, Elizabeth Janet	08,	1938	Radin, Ruth Yaffe
03,	1922	Snyder, Anne	06,	1904	Carter, Samuel III	08,	1943	Stine, Robert Lawrence
03,	1928	Gorsline, S(ally) M(arie)	06,	1905	Farquhar, Margaret C(utting)	08,	1944	Tiner, John Hudson
03,	1931	Epstein, Anne Merrick				08,	1949	Wright-Frierson, Virginia
03,	1932	Chesler, Bernice	06,	1905	Gadler, Steve J.			
03,	1933	Smith, Vesta (Henderson)	06,	1909	Busch, Phyllis S.	09,	1877	Barnouw, Adriaan Jacob
			06,	1913	Alexander, Anna B(arbara Cooke)			
03,	1935	Neimark, Anne E.				09,	1890	Burton, William H(enry)
03,	1936	Vander els, Betty	06,	1919	Kingman, Mary Lee	09,	1899	Catton, Charles Bruce
03,	1948	Singer, Marilyn	06,	1923	Thomas, Lowell (Jackson), Jr.	09,	1901	Simon, Henry W(illiam)
03,	1954	Disalvo-Ryan, DyAnne				09,	1906	Holder, Glenn
03,	1959	Himmelman, John (Carl)	06,	1925	Miller, Eugene	09,	1909	Fax, Elton Clay
			06,	1930	Heyman, Ken(neth Louis)	09,	1921	Cone, Ferne Geller
04,	1861	Remington, Frederic (Sackrider)				09,	1925	Sutton, Myron Daniel
			06,	1932	Collins, Pat Lowery	09,	1926	Russell, Franklin (Alexander)
04,	1862	Stratemeyer, Edward L.	06,	1934	Needleman, Jacob			
04,	1892	Lawson, Robert	06,	1939	Tester, Sylvia Root	09,	1932	Dorman, Michael
			06,	1942	Hearne, Betsy Gould	09,	1932	Plowden, David

09, 1937 Hurwitz, Johanna
09, 1941 Anastasio, Dina
09, 1943 Blumenthal, Shirley
10, 1901 Lane, Carl Daniel
10, 1907 Shuttlesworth, Dorothy (Edwards)
10, 1908 Cosgrave, John O'Hara, II
10, 1911 DeJong, Dola
10, 1911 Johnson, Elizabeth
10, 1914 Hargis, John Edwin
10, 1917 Glendinning, Richard
10, 1926 Einsel, Walter
10, 1931 Weidhorn, Manfred
10, 1934 Hadley, Lee
10, 1937 Benagh, Jim
10, 1937 Frommer, Harvey
10, 1937 Moe, Barbara
10, 1938 Chapian, Marie
10, 1942 Marshall, James (Edward)
10, 1946 San Souci, Robert D.
10, 1953 Carlson, Nancy Lee
11, 1759 Weems, Mason Locke
11, 1881 Young, Stark
11, 1884 Roosevelt, Anna Eleanor (Roosevelt)
11, 1897 Auslander, Joseph
11, 1901 Parker, Kay Peterson
11, 1904 Hopf, Alice (Martha) L(ightner)
11, 1907 Dodson, Kenneth M(acKenzie)
11, 1910 Berkowitz, Freda Pastor
11, 1911 Willard, Mildred Wilds
11, 1913 Simon, Joseph H.
11, 1920 McFarland, Kenton D(ean)
11, 1929 Freedman, Russell (Bruce)
11, 1936 McPherson, James M.
11, 1948 Kent, Deborah Ann
11, 1951 Arnold, Susan (Riser)
11, 1952 Gaver, Rebecca
11, 1953 Scabrini, Janet
12, 1863 Stein, Evaleen
12, 1912 Petry, Ann (Lane)
12, 1914 Bonnell, Dorothy Haworth
12, 1915 Terzian, James P.
12, 1917 Sheldon, Aure
12, 1920 Childress, Alice
12, 1926 Maniscalco, Joseph
12, 1928 Flynn, Barbara
12, 1929 Coles, Robert (Martin)
12, 1931 Anderson, Helen Jean
12, 1944 Emmens, Carol Ann
12, 1945 Wolff, Diane
13, 1890 Richter, Conrad (Michael)
13, 1890 Wright, Anna (Maria Louisa Perrot) Rose
13, 1897 Agnew, Edith J(osephine)
13, 1898 Alexander, Raymond Pace

13, 1902 Bontemps, Arna(ud Wendell)
13, 1906 Gross, Sarah Chokla
13, 1906 Samachson, Joseph
13, 1912 Price, Harold
13, 1921 Walker, Barbara K(erlin)
13, 1922 Knotts, Howard (Clayton, Jr.)
13, 1922 Schell, Mildred
13, 1926 Myller, Rolf
13, 1928 Offit, Sidney
13, 1934 Neimark, Paul G.
13, 1937 Fitschen, Dale
13, 1938 Pincus, Harriet
13, 1938 Weltner, Linda R(iverly)
13, 1945 Hausman, Gerald
13, 1951 McCrady, Lady
14, 1888 Turnbull, Agnes Sligh
14, 1893 Lenski, Lois (Lenore)
14, 1894 Cummings, E(dward) E(stlin)
14, 1898 Wellman, Paul I(selin)
14, 1899 Sonneborn, Ruth (Cantor) A.
14, 1902 Seroff, Victor I(ilyitch)
14, 1907 Lewis, Claudia (Louise)
14, 1910 Place, Marian T(empleton)
14, 1925 Belden, Wilanne Schneider
14, 1926 Cohen, Miriam
14, 1927 Madden, Don
14, 1928 Cameron, Polly (McQuiston)
14, 1939 Polland, Barbara K(ay)
15, 1830 Jackson, Helen (Maria Fiske) Hunt
15, 1878 Holland, Rupert Sargent
15, 1881 Wodehouse, P(elham) G(renville)
15, 1903 Bettmann, Otto Ludwig
15, 1915 Solonevich, George
15, 1918 Cavin, Ruth (Brodie)
15, 1926 Hunter, Evan
15, 1928 Amon, Aline
15, 1933 Brown, Judith Gwyn
15, 1934 Bourdon, David
15, 1937 Miller, Frances A.
15, 1940 Howe, Fanny
15, 1940 Laure, Jason
15, 1940 Moser, Barry
15, 1942 Gormley, Beatrice
15, 1957 Leibold, Jay
16, 1758 Webster, Noah
16, 1838 Scudder, Horace E(lisha)
16, 1893 Carmer, Carl (Lamson)
16, 1895 Bracker, Charles Eugene
16, 1898 Douglas, William O(rville)
16, 1908 Coolidge, Olivia E(nsor)
16, 1908 Vance, Eleanor Graham

16, 1913 Hawes, Judy
16, 1922 Quick, Annabelle (MacMillan)
16, 1926 Sheldon, Muriel
16, 1927 Danska, Herbert
16, 1927 Perske, Robert
16, 1937 Himler, Ronald (Norbert)
16, 1939 Arrowood, McKendrick Lee Clinton
16, 1939 Gundersheimer, Karen
16, 1942 Asher, Sandy (Fenichel)
16, 1942 Bruchac, Joseph III
16, 1943 Rosen, Winifred
17, 1906 Ames, Gerald
17, 1908 Cathon, Laura E(lizabeth)
17, 1908 Raskin, Edith Lefkowitz
17, 1910 Wier, Ester (Alberti)
17, 1911 Coleman, Pauline (Hodgkinson)
17, 1912 VanderVeer, Judy
17, 1913 Bason, Lillian
17, 1913 McGaw, Jessie Brewer
17, 1916 Partch, Virgil Franklin II
17, 1917 Seigel, Kalman
17, 1926 Arnov, Boris, Jr.
17, 1926 Karp, Naomi J.
17, 1932 Lorenz, Lee (Sharp)
17, 1933 Keyser, Marcia
17, 1951 Caseley, Judith
18, 1869 Hinton, Charles Louis
18, 1880 Fargo, Lucile Foster
18, 1896 Kyle, Anne D.
18, 1904 Mason, George Frederick
18, 1908 Kohler, Julilly H(ouse)
18, 1917 Randall, Florence Engel
18, 1922 Petrovich, Michael B(oro)
18, 1923 Stegeman, Janet Allais
18, 1923 Switzer, Ellen
18, 1928 Pelta, Kathy
18, 1930 Hautzig, Esther (Rudomin)
18, 1930 Parker, Nancy Winslow
18, 1930 Siroff, Harriet
18, 1934 Wilson, Sarah
18, 1942 Hansen, Joyce W.
18, 1942 Jeschke, Susan
18, 1955 Ackley, Peggy Jo
19, 1884 Donahey, William
19, 1896 Ousley, Odille
19, 1901 Johnson, Walter Ryerson
19, 1907 Barish, Matthew
19, 1908 McQueen, Mildred Hark
19, 1912 Wassersug, Joseph D(avid)
19, 1914 Davis, Clive E(dward)
19, 1929 Caffrey, Nancy
19, 1931 Emberley, Ed(ward Randolph)
19, 1932 Moser, Don(ald Bruce)
19, 1937 Young, Rodney Lee Patrick (Jr.)

19,	1939	Max, Peter	23,	1902	Edwards, Margaret (Alexander)	26,	1926	Searcy, Margaret Zehmer
19,	1941	Price, Jonathan (Reeve)	23,	1910	Espenshade, Edward Bowman, Jr.	26,	1929	Winter, Paula (Cecelia)
19,	1941	Richter, Alice	23,	1912	Page, Lou Williams	26,	1931	Schnirel, James R(einhold)
19,	1945	Nolan, Dennis	23,	1915	Ross, Wilda (S.)	26,	1934	Showell, Ellen Harvey
19,	1948	Natti, Susanna	23,	1918	Barry, James P(otvin)	26,	1940	Schmiderer, Dorothy
19,	1950	Diamond, Donna	23,	1918	Rice, Edward E.	26,	1941	Kellogg, Steven (Castle)
19,	1952	Aitken, Amy	23,	1919	Kikukawa, Cecily H(arder)	26,	1944	Venable, Alan (Hudson)
20,	1894	Merwin, Decie	23,	1920	Montana, Bob	26,	1945	Sanders, Scott R(ussell)
20,	1905	Dannay, Frederic	23,	1922	Harries, Joan			
20,	1906	Leisk, David (Johnson)	23,	1928	Davis, Christopher	26,	1946	Merrill, Jane
20,	1908	St. John, Wylly Folk	23,	1933	Perry, Phyllis J.	26,	1948	Schuyler, Pamela R(icka)
20,	1910	Latham, Frank B(rown)	23,	1938	McCullough, Frances Monson	26,	1952	Brewster, Patience
20,	1919	Szasz, Suzanne Shorr				27,	1898	Lerrigo, Marion Olive
20,	1921	Arkhurst, Joyce (Cooper)	23,	1941	Petersen, P(eter) J(ames)	27,	1912	Goldfrank, Helen Colodny
20,	1925	Buchwald, Art(hur)	23,	1942	Crichton, J. Michael	27,	1917	Morrison, Lillian
20,	1927	Temko, Florence	23,	1962	Novak, Matt	27,	1918	Brown, Myra Berry
20,	1932	Smith, Gary R(ichard)	24,	1788	Hale, Sarah Josepha	27,	1924	Chambers, Robert Warner
20,	1937	Haynes, Betsy	24,	1830	Brooks, Noah			
20,	1943	Vogel, Ray	24,	1894	Bronson, Wilfrid Swancourt	27,	1924	Greene, Constance C(larke)
20,	1960	Carlson, Daniel	24,	1899	Fenner, Phyllis Reid			
21,	1844	Stephens, Charles Asbury	24,	1900	Lissim, Simon	27,	1926	Thiry, Joan (Marie)
21,	1868	Horsfall, Robert Bruce	24,	1901	Eichenberg, Fritz	27,	1928	Breisky, William J(ohn)
21,	1874	Knight, Charles Robert	24,	1905	Offord, Lenore (Glen)	27,	1930	Spanfeller, James J(ohn)
21,	1897	Wormser, Sophie	24,	1912	Johnson, Edgar (Raymond)	27,	1930	Waters, John F(rederick)
21,	1904	Atwater, Montgomery Meigs	24,	1917	Myers, Arthur			
21,	1911	Blair, Mary Robinson	24,	1919	Holman, Felice	27,	1931	Cohen, Peter Zachary
21,	1911	Leslie, Robert Franklin	24,	1923	Wood, Phyllis Anderson	27,	1932	Plath, Sylvia
21,	1912	Neilson, Frances Fullerton (Jones)	24,	1927	Robinson, Barbara (Webb)	27,	1940	Kingston, Maxine (Ting Ting) Hong
21,	1914	Gardner, Martin	24,	1929	Brosnan, James Patrick	27,	1940	Roth, David
21,	1917	Scheer, George F(abian)	24,	1936	Moche, Dinah (Rachel) L(evine)	27,	1944	Jance, J(udith) A(nn)
21,	1917	VanDoren, Margaret	24,	1942	Chiefari, Janet D.	27,	1956	Westman, Paul (Wendell)
21,	1919	Holland, John L(ewis)	25,	1875	Bailey, Carolyn Sherwin	28,	1897	Pickering, James Sayre
21,	1929	LeGuin, Ursula K(roeber)	25,	1902	Commager, Henry Steele	28,	1906	Goldin, Augusta
21,	1929	Luis, Earlene W.	25,	1906	Martin, Frances M(cEntee)	28,	1908	Orlob, Helen Seaburg
21,	1933	Longsworth, Polly (Ormsby)	25,	1911	Heck, Bessie Holland	28,	1909	Ross, Alexander
21,	1933	Oliver, John Edward	25,	1925	Herkimer, L(awrence) R(ussell)	28,	1910	Newell, Edythe W.
21,	1933	Yates, Brock W(endel)				28,	1915	MacPherson, Thomas George
21,	1936	Winn, Marie	25,	1926	Grey, Jerry			
21,	1941	Dresang, Eliza (Carolyn Timberlake)	25,	1931	Priddy, Frances (Rosaleen)	28,	1920	Swados, Harvey
21,	1943	Cameron, Ann	25,	1934	Maher, Ramona	28,	1921	Kessler, Leonard P.
21,	1946	Rabinowich, Ellen	25,	1938	Whittlesey, Susan	28,	1929	Armstrong, Gerry (Breen)
21,	1948	Schur, Maxine	25,	1941	Tyler, Anne	28,	1929	Hollander, John
21,	1952	Gasperini, Jim	25,	1942	Tolan, Stephanie S.	28,	1929	Ripper, Charles L(ewis)
22,	1882	Wyeth, N(ewell) C(onvers)	25,	1944	Gondosch, Linda	28,	1932	Homze, Alma C.
22,	1913	Lazarus, Keo Felker	25,	1946	Brown, Rich(ard Eric)	28,	1941	Harris, Mark Jonathan
22,	1924	Baum, Allyn Z(elton)	25,	1946	Noonan, Julia	28,	1946	Thurman, Judith
22,	1930	Stuart, Gene S.	25,	1954	Rabinowitz, Sandy	28,	1947	Snow, Richard F(olger)
22,	1932	Yamaguchi, John Tohr	26,	1867	Crownfield, Gertrude	29,	1895	Roy, Jessie Hailstalk
22,	1933	Foley, Mary Louise Munro	26,	1899	Cottler, Joseph	29,	1908	Phillips, Irv(ing W.)
			26,	1904	Osborn, Robert Chesley	29,	1909	Wyler, Rose
22,	1947	Petrie, Catherine				29,	1911	DiValentin, Maria (Messuri)
22,	1947	Waldman, Neil	26,	1916	Warner, Edythe Records			
23,	1887	Collings, Ellsworth				29,	1917	Walworth, Nancy Zinsser
23,	1897	Flack, Marjorie	26,	1920	Lippincott, Sarah Lee	29,	1918	Levin, Marcia Obrasky
23,	1899	Kimbrough, Emily	26,	1923	Vaughan, Harold Cecil	29,	1922	Davis, Russell G(erard)
23,	1901	Bentel, Pearl B(ucklen)	26,	1925	Williams, Selma R(uth)	29,	1922	Ressner, Phil(ip)
						29,	1924	Flender, Harold

29, 1926	Rhodes, Frank H(arold Trevor)	
29, 1927	Dreves, Veronica R.	
29, 1933	Worth, Valerie	
29, 1934	Ballard, Mignon Franklin	
29, 1940	Bahr, Robert	
30, 1886	Roberts, Elizabeth Madox	
30, 1894	Glanckoff, Samuel	
30, 1905	Raftery, Gerald (Bransfield)	
30, 1906	Gode von Aesch, Alexander (Gottfried Friedrich)	
30, 1909	Miller, Donald G(eorge)	
30, 1917	Philbrook, Clem(ent E.)	
30, 1926	Barbe, Walter Burke	
30, 1930	Crane, Caroline	
30, 1930	Larsen, Suzanne Kesteloo	
30, 1933	Robinson, Jan M.	
30, 1946	Kimmel, Eric A.	
31, 1852	Freeman, Mary Eleanor Wilkins	
31, 1877	Crowell, Grace Noll	
31, 1904	Stone, Helen	
31, 1904	Taylor, Sydney (Brenner)	
31, 1917	Boesch, Mark J(oseph)	
31, 1921	Richard, Adrienne	
31, 1924	Dunning, Arthur Stephen, Jr.	
31, 1927	Hunt, Joyce	
31, 1927	Kahn, Roger	
31, 1930	Collins, Michael	
31, 1932	Paterson, Katherine (Womeldorf)	
31, 1933	Stevens, Franklin	
31, 1933	Szekeres, Cyndy	
31, 1934	Griffith, Helen V(irginia)	
31, 1951	Sive, Helen R.	
31, 1956	Goodman, Deborah Lerme	

NOVEMBER

Day Year

??, 1892	DuSoe, Robert C(oleman)
??, 1896	Ish-Kishor, Sulamith
??, 1897	Seignobosc, Francoise
??, 1914	Palmer, Bernard
01, 1871	Crane, Stephen (Townley)
01, 1872	Orton, Helen (Fuller)
01, 1892	Hunt, Mabel Leigh
01, 1892	Randall, Ruth Painter
01, 1893	Johnson, Margaret S(weet)
01, 1895	Hecht, George J(oseph)
01, 1901	Lent, Henry Bolles
01, 1902	Shimin, Symeon
01, 1909	Feder, Robert Arthur
01, 1917	Burroughs, Margaret Taylor G.
01, 1917	Henderson, Zenna (Chlarson)
01, 1917	Loeb, Robert H., Jr.
01, 1919	Shearer, Ted
01, 1920	Blackburn, Joyce Knight
01, 1926	Kiefer, Irene
01, 1926	Knight, Hilary
01, 1927	Richoux, Pat(ricia)
01, 1929	Huthmacher, J. Joseph
01, 1935	Mohr, Nicholasa (Golpe)
01, 1944	Hallinan, P(atrick) K(enneth)
02, 1896	Tenggren, Gustaf (Adolf)
02, 1910	Brennan, Joseph Gerard
02, 1910	McKenzie, Dorothy Clayton
02, 1912	Burleson, Elizabeth
02, 1919	Ames, Mildred
02, 1920	Graham, Margaret Bloy
02, 1925	Eiseman, Alberta
02, 1938	Allen, Rodney F.
02, 1942	Manushkin, Fran(ces)
03, 1841	Alden, Isabella (Macdonald)
03, 1908	Fujikawa, Gyo
03, 1912	Paradis, Adrian Alexis
03, 1916	Jahsmann, Allan Hart
03, 1918	Feller, Robert William Andrew
03, 1921	Ashabranner, Brent (Kenneth)
03, 1922	Shekerjian, Haig
03, 1927	Hoexter, Corinne K.
03, 1927	Oakley, Don(ald G.)
03, 1929	Hansen, Caryl (Hall)
03, 1929	Williams, Edward G.
03, 1931	Cavallo, Diana
03, 1934	Steiner, Barbara A(nnette)
03, 1938	Lord, Bette Bao
04, 1898	McKinney, Roland Joseph
04, 1903	Chittenden, Elizabeth F.
04, 1906	North, Sterling
04, 1917	Weihs, Erika
04, 1919	Liebman, Oscar
04, 1925	Alexander, Vincent Arthur
04, 1925	Elfman, Blossom
04, 1925	Hill, Elizabeth Starr
04, 1926	Cooper, Lee (Pelham)
04, 1929	Limburg, Peter R(ichard)
04, 1938	Trost, Lucille Wood
04, 1939	Haley, Gail E(inhart)
04, 1949	Cochran, Bobbye A.
04, 1958	Marsoli, Lisa Ann
05, 1889	Richardson, Willis
05, 1905	Berrill, Jacquelyn (Batsel)
05, 1905	Hogarth, Grace (Weston Allen)
05, 1917	Konkle, Janet Everest
05, 1927	Abernethy, Robert G(ordon)
05, 1927	Aylesworth, Thomas G(ibbons)
05, 1935	Feder, Paula (Kurzband)
05, 1935	Sewall, Marcia (Osgood)
05, 1938	Levinson, Nancy Smiler
05, 1942	James, Elizabeth
05, 1942	Meyers, Susan (Thompson)
05, 1943	Peavy, Linda
05, 1947	Reed, Thomas (James)
05, 1947	Yepsen, Roger B(ennet) Jr.
06, 1907	DeCamp, Catherine C(rook)
06, 1914	Gerson, Noel B(ertram)
06, 1914	Kogan, Herman
06, 1916	Burgess, Mary Wyche
06, 1916	Young, Robert W(illiam)
06, 1922	Thomson, Peggy (Bebie)
06, 1923	Jacobson, Daniel
06, 1927	Klass, Sheila Solomon
06, 1927	Smith, Ralph Lee
06, 1931	Gordon, Bernard Ludwig
06, 1938	Kandell, Alice S.
06, 1945	Hauptly, Denis J(ames)
07, 1876	Shinn, Everett
07, 1890	Matulka, Jan
07, 1897	Sperry, Armstrong W.
07, 1901	Cook, Gladys Emerson
07, 1902	Dodd, Ed(ward Benton)
07, 1903	Jordan, Philip Dillon
07, 1904	Verral, Charles Spain
07, 1929	Abdul, Raoul
07, 1931	Gilbert, Agnes Joan (Sewell)
07, 1937	Banks, Sara (Jeanne Gordon Harrell)
07, 1944	Adkins, Jan
07, 1950	Valen, Nanine
08, 1909	Lloyd, Norman
08, 1912	Hawkinson, John (Samuel)
08, 1918	Gugliotta, Bobette
08, 1924	Brooks, Lester
08, 1932	Bova, Ben(jamin William)
08, 1934	Hodge, P(aul) W(illiam)
08, 1937	Feig, Barbara Krane
08, 1945	Mayer, Marianna
09, 1872	Stevenson, Burton E(gbert)
09, 1899	Foster, Doris Van Liew
09, 1902	Rendina, Laura (Jones) Cooper
09, 1904	Kroll, Francis Lynde
09, 1906	Charosh, Mannis
09, 1912	Bailey-Jones, Beryl
09, 1912	Thompson, Kay

09,	1917	Bradford, Ann (Liddell)	12,	1917	Ipcar, Dahlov Zorach	14,	1933	Vo-Dinh, Mai
09,	1917	Peterson, Betty Ferguson	12,	1922	MacLeod, Charlotte (Matilda Hughes)	14,	1941	Moore, Jack (William)
09,	1917	Versace, Marie Teresa	12,	1925	Donze, Sara Lee (Hathaway)	14,	1945	Smith, Jean Pajot
09,	1920	Boeckman, Charles				14,	1946	Corwin, Judith Hoffman
09,	1920	Thum, Gladys	12,	1925	Miller, Marilyn (Jean)	14,	1946	Tafuri, Nancy
09,	1926	Hahn, Hannelore	12,	1926	Pluff, Barbara (Littlefield)	14,	1947	Brewer, Sally King
09,	1927	Jacob, Helen Pierce				14,	1949	Waldman, Bruce
09,	1928	Sexton, Anne (Harvey)	12,	1926	Werner, Herma	14,	1950	Erlanger, Ellen (Louise)
09,	1932	Taylor, L(ester) B(arbour), Jr.	12,	1928	Sharmat, Marjorie Weinman	14,	1951	Baker, Alan
			12,	1930	Chardiet, Bernice (Kroll)	14,	1963	Gelman, Jan
09,	1934	Ehlert, Lois (Jane)	12,	1932	Forman, James Douglas	15,	1881	Gollomb, Joseph
09,	1934	Sagan, Carl				15,	1887	Moore, Marianne (Craig)
09,	1936	Davis, Lou Ellen	12,	1939	Giovanopoulos, Paul (Arthur)			
09,	1937	Hall, Lynn				15,	1897	McCord, David (Thompson Watson)
09,	1938	Lerner, Sharon (Ruth)	12,	1942	Ernst, Kathryn (Fitzgerald)			
09,	1940	Bales, Carol Ann				15,	1902	Christgau, Alice Erickson
09,	1950	Cummings, Pat (Marie)	12,	1943	Rubinstein, Robert E(dward)			
10,	1852	VanDyke, Henry Jackson, Jr.				15,	1907	Vermes, Jean C(ampbell Pattison)
			12,	1945	Garretson, Victoria Diane			
10,	1879	Lindsay, Nicholas Vachel				15,	1910	Epstein, Beryl (M. Williams)
			13,	1803	Abbott, Jacob			
10,	1899	Seredy, Kate	13,	1870	Barbour, Ralph Henry	15,	1913	Dwiggins, Don
10,	1899	Stowe, Leland	13,	1893	Beals, Carleton	15,	1925	Charmatz, Bill
10,	1906	Franchere, Ruth	13,	1907	Apsler, Alfred	15,	1926	Borhegyi, Suzanne Catherine Sims de
10,	1907	Lawrence, Mildred (Elwood)	13,	1908	Strachan, Margaret Pitcairn			
						15,	1933	Morris, Robert A(da)
10,	1912	Bishop, Curtis (Kent)	13,	1913	Crane, Irving (Donald)	15,	1934	McGough, Elizabeth (Hemmes)
10,	1912	Mincieli, Rose Laura	13,	1915	Benchley, Nathaniel (Goddard)			
10,	1917	Farrar, Susan Clement				15,	1938	Frascino, Edward
10,	1918	Mulcahy, Lucille Burnett	13,	1917	Spilka, Arnold	15,	1941	Crow, Donna Fletcher
10,	1918	Nesbitt, Esta	13,	1921	Harris, Jonathan	15,	1941	Pinkwater, Daniel Manus
10,	1927	Healey, Larry	13,	1922	Cannon, Bettie (Waddell)			
10,	1929	Butterworth, W(illiam) E(dmund III)				16,	1889	Yost, Edna
			13,	1924	Castillo, Edmund Luis	16,	1899	McBride, Mary Margaret
10,	1931	Seitz, Jacqueline	13,	1927	Barnstone, Willis			
10,	1940	Hancock, Sibyl	13,	1930	Andrews, Benny	16,	1899	Smith, Marion Jaques
10,	1942	Iverson, Genie	13,	1930	Katz, Herbert (Melvin)	16,	1900	Barrett, William E(dmund)
10,	1946	Markle, Sandra L(ee)	13,	1931	Morton, Eva Jane			
11,	1836	Aldrich, Thomas Bailey	13,	1934	Densen-Gerber, Judianne	16,	1904	Fox, Dorothea M.
11,	1896	Coates, Belle				16,	1905	Weinstock, Herbert
11,	1898	Eberle, Irmengarde	13,	1934	Marshall, Garry	16,	1906	Gridley, Marion E(leanor)
11,	1900	Taylor, David	13,	1935	Friedman, Judi			
11,	1901	Mason, F(rancis) van Wyck	13,	1938	Matus, Greta	16,	1908	Chandler, Edna Walker
			13,	1943	Ryan, Elizabeth (Anne)	16,	1912	Tebbel, John (William)
11,	1907	Barr, George	13,	1945	Cohen, Paul S.	16,	1915	Fritz, Jean (Guttery)
11,	1907	DuBois, Shirley Graham	13,	1945	Worth, Richard	16,	1922	Hoyt, Olga (Gruhzit)
			14,	1873	Dickson, Marguerite (Stockman)	16,	1924	Boardman, Gwenn R.
11,	1914	Fast, Howard (Melvin)				16,	1927	Thompson, Julian F(rancis)
11,	1917	Reynolds, Dallas McCord	14,	1885	Rourke, Constance (Mayfield)			
						16,	1932	Coskey, Evelyn
11,	1918	Reit, Seymour	14,	1897	Curry, John Steuart	16,	1939	Chess, Victoria (Dickerson)
11,	1921	Cretan, Gladys (Yessayan)	14,	1899	Martin, Patricia Miles			
			14,	1901	Crane, Alan (Horton)	16,	1942	Girard, Linda Walvoord
11,	1926	Ditzel, Paul C(alvin)	14,	1907	Steig, William	16,	1943	Spinner, Stephanie
11,	1926	Jackson, Robert B(lake)	14,	1907	Wilber, Donald N(ewton)	16,	1952	McKinley, Jennifer Carolyn Robin
11,	1928	Lavine, David						
11,	1933	Dotts, Maryann J.	14,	1914	Kelly, Martha Rose	16,	1953	Davis, Gibbs
11,	1942	Loescher, Ann Dull	14,	1918	Raible, Alton (Robert)	17,	1876	Cannon, Cornelia (James)
11,	1942	Wolkstein, Diane	14,	1921	Hooks, William H(arris)			
11,	1945	Harlan, Elizabeth	14,	1921	Sugarman, Tracy	17,	1894	Anderson, Bernice G(oudy)
11,	1947	Barner, Bob	14,	1923	Baker, Mary Elizabeth (Gillette)			
12,	1888	Parrish, Anne				17,	1898	Ayars, James S(terling)
12,	1894	Bufano, Remo	14,	1927	Ebel, Alex	17,	1901	Boggs, Ralph Steele
12,	1912	Marino, Dorothy Bronson	14,	1927	Libby, William M.	17,	1904	Bernstein, Theodore M(enline)
			14,	1928	Talbot, Charlene Joy			
12,	1916	Beyer, Audrey White				17,	1905	Marais, Josef
						17,	1909	Molarsky, Osmond

17, 1914	Daugherty, Charles Michael	
17, 1919	Fox, Mary Virginia	
17, 1934	Wyss, Thelma Hatch	
18, 1898	Lippincott, Bertram	
18, 1900	Alajalov, Constantin	
18, 1907	Holzman, Robert Stuart	
18, 1909	Miner, Lewis S.	
18, 1916	Tucker, Ernest Edward	
18, 1922	Jenkins, William A(twell)	
18, 1923	Gregor, Arthur	
18, 1925	Addona, Angelo F.	
18, 1927	Smith, Howard E(verett) Jr.	
18, 1934	Paul, David (Tyler)	
18, 1934	Schulte, Elaine L(ouise)	
18, 1936	Smith, Philip Warren	
18, 1942	Cornelius, Carol	
18, 1944	Krupp, E(dwin) C(harles)	
18, 1951	Foon, Dennis	
19, 1878	Koerner, W(illiam) H(enry) D(avid)	
19, 1890	Ferris, Helen Josephine	
19, 1894	Rethi, Lili	
19, 1895	McMeekin, Isabel (McLennan)	
19, 1900	Black, Algernon David	
19, 1907	Schaefer, Jack (Warner)	
19, 1914	Irvin, Fred	
19, 1915	Vogt, Esther Loewen	
19, 1923	Trahey, Jane	
19, 1925	Dines, Harry Glen	
19, 1926	Bauernschmidt, Marjorie	
19, 1926	Scott, Ann Herbert	
19, 1934	Luhrmann, Winifred B(ruce)	
19, 1943	Musgrove, Margaret W(ynkoop)	
20, 1871	Guiterman, Arthur	
20, 1886	Walsh, Richard John	
20, 1898	Luckhardt, Mildred (Madeleine) Corell	
20, 1899	Byrne, Donn	
20, 1900	Gould, Chester	
20, 1902	Foley, Anna Bernice Williams	
20, 1914	Goodwin, Harold Leland	
20, 1916	McGrath, Thomas	
20, 1919	Cole, William (Rossa)	
20, 1924	Costabel, Eva Deutsch	
20, 1924	Stambler, Irwin	
20, 1925	Barris, George	
20, 1930	Campbell, Patricia J(ean)	
20, 1936	Faithfull, Gail	
20, 1937	Girion, Barbara	
20, 1938	Bauer, Marion Dane	
20, 1938	Perera, Thomas Biddle	
21, 1891	Ellsberg, Edward	
21, 1896	Price, Garrett	
21, 1901	Bischoff, Ilse Marthe	
21, 1907	Harris, Christie (Lucy Irwin)	
21, 1908	Politi, Leo	
21, 1908	Speare, Elizabeth George	
21, 1913	Burt, Nathaniel	
21, 1913	Unkelbach, Kurt	
21, 1923	Sokol, William	
21, 1926	Berson, Harold	
21, 1933	DeLarrea, Victoria	
21, 1933	Elmore, Carolyn Patricia	
21, 1949	Schachtel, Roger (Bernard)	
22, 1901	Crane, Roy(ston Campbell)	
22, 1901	Gill, Richard Cochran	
22, 1908	Hoffecker, John Savin	
22, 1908	Sheehan, Ethna	
22, 1909	Epstein, Samuel	
22, 1909	Hays, Wilma Pitchford	
22, 1913	Berlitz, Charles L. (Frambach)	
22, 1918	Lawrence, James D(uncan)	
22, 1921	Simon, Hilda (Rita)	
22, 1924	Lord, Beman	
22, 1929	Bethel, Dell	
22, 1935	List, Ilka Katherine	
22, 1943	King, Billie Jean	
23, 1897	Baner, Skulda V(anadis)	
23, 1900	Trotter, Grace V(iolet)	
23, 1907	Erickson, Phoebe	
23, 1907	Grant, Eva (Cohen)	
23, 1913	Sterling, Dorothy	
23, 1915	Simont, Marc	
23, 1918	Lindeburg, Franklin A(lfred)	
23, 1918	Weir, La Vada	
23, 1919	Hitte, Kathryn	
23, 1920	May, Charles Paul	
23, 1928	Chester, Michael (Arthur)	
23, 1928	Shemin, Margaretha (Hoeneveld)	
23, 1936	Johnson, Lois W(alfrid)	
23, 1937	Burchard, Sue (Huston)	
23, 1948	Rich, Mark J.	
23, 1950	Grant, Cynthia D.	
24, 1849	Burnett, Frances (Eliza) Hodgson	
24, 1897	Hylander, Clarence J(ohn)	
24, 1904	Milotte, Alfred G(eorge)	
24, 1905	Wicker, Ireene (Seaton)	
24, 1907	Barker, Melvern (J.)	
24, 1907	Ullman, James Ramsey	
24, 1909	Childs, John Farnsworth	
24, 1917	McDonnell, Virginia (Bleecker)	
24, 1918	Sandburg, Helga	
24, 1921	Uchida, Yoshiko	
24, 1923	Dean, Karen Strickler	
24, 1926	Dunbar, Robert E(verett)	
24, 1933	Engdahl, Sylvia Louise	
24, 1935	Gerstein, Mordicai	
24, 1938	Johnson, Spencer	
24, 1941	Halter, Jon C(harles)	
24, 1951	Sanderson, Ruth (L.)	
25, 1894	Carbonnier, Jeanne	
25, 1909	Eastman, P(hilip) D(ey)	
25, 1911	Spilhaus, Athelstan	
25, 1914	Hanna, Geneva R(egula)	
25, 1915	Criner, Beatrice (Hall)	
25, 1923	Cartwright, Sally	
25, 1926	Anderson, Poul (William)	
25, 1928	Climo, Shirley	
25, 1931	Clements, Bruce	
25, 1942	Bortstein, Larry	
25, 1946	Brown, Marc (Tolon)	
25, 1952	Dragonwagon, Crescent (Zolotow)	
25, 1953	Krensky, Stephen (Alan)	
26, 1874	Britt, Albert	
26, 1887	DeSchweinitz, Karl	
26, 1891	Cole, Walter	
26, 1901	Gates, Doris	
26, 1906	Cleven, Kathryn Seward	
26, 1907	Ewen, David	
26, 1907	Marcus, Rebecca B(rian)	
26, 1913	Schuon, Karl	
26, 1916	House, Charles Albert	
26, 1919	Pohl, Frederik	
26, 1922	Schulz, Charles M(onroe)	
26, 1923	Stoddard, Edward G.	
26, 1932	Harris, Sherwood	
26, 1935	Pringle, Laurence P.	
26, 1936	Mearian, Judy Frank	
26, 1939	Komoda, Beverly	
26, 1940	VanTuyl, Barbara	
26, 1941	Enderle, Judith (Ann)	
27, 1874	Beard, Charles Austin	
27, 1889	Vance, Marguerite	
27, 1893	Brown, Paul	
27, 1894	Milhous, Katherine	
27, 1897	Teague, Donald	
27, 1906	Purdy, Claire Lee	
27, 1906	Scheffer, Victor B(lanchard)	
27, 1907	DeCamp, L(yon) Sprague	
27, 1913	Caldwell, John C(ope)	
27, 1926	Sheffield, Janet N.	
27, 1933	Smith, Alvin	
27, 1943	Lubin, Leonard B.	
27, 1960	Henkes, Kevin	
28, 1870	French, Allen	
28, 1893	Downey, Fairfax D(avis)	
28, 1901	Havighurst, Walter (Edwin)	
28, 1909	Bleeker, Sonia	
28, 1916	Tregaskis, Richard (William)	
28, 1918	McNulty, Faith	
28, 1922	Boshinski, Blanche	

Day	Year	Name
28,	1927	Waitley, Douglas
28,	1931	Young, Ed
28,	1937	Madison, Arnold
28,	1952	Calmenson, Stephanie
28,	1957	Bunting, Glenn (Davison)
29,	1832	Alcott, Louisa May
29,	1884	Klemm, Roberta K(ohnhorst)
29,	1895	Shenton, Edward
29,	1896	Reck, Franklin Mering
29,	1898	Lattin, Harriet (Pratt)
29,	1903	Regehr, Lydia
29,	1906	Strong, Charles Stanley
29,	1913	Hirsch, S. Carl
29,	1914	Lowenstein, Dyno
29,	1915	Schonberg, Harold C(harles)
29,	1918	L'Engle, Madeleine
29,	1922	Spearing, Judith (Mary Harlow)
29,	1928	Simon, Paul
29,	1928	Talbot, Toby (Tolpen)
29,	1934	McPhee, Richard Byron
29,	1934	Morris, Willie
29,	1943	Zallinger, Peter Franz
29,	1945	Jobb, Jamie
29,	1946	Coontz, Otto
29,	1951	Schwartz, David M(artin)
30,	1835	Twain, Mark
30,	1884	Boyton, Neil
30,	1886	Eaton, Jeanette
30,	1888	Rauch, Mabel Thompson
30,	1896	Bennett, Russell H(oradley)
30,	1912	Parks, Gordon (Alexander Buchanan)
30,	1912	Waltner, Elma
30,	1913	McGee, Dorothy Horton
30,	1920	Rosenfeld, Sam
30,	1924	Moeri, Louise (Healy)
30,	1924	Sherman, Allan
30,	1926	Francis, Dorothy Brenner
30,	1927	Burgess, Robert F(orrest)
30,	1927	Eichner, James A.
30,	1931	Belton, John Raynor
30,	1931	Zemach, Margot
30,	1932	Kaufman, Mervyn D.

DECEMBER

Day	Year	Name
??,	1899	Ulreich, Nura Woodson
01,	1854	Hornaday, William T(emple)
01,	1862	Parton, Ethel
01,	1863	Herford, Oliver
01,	1892	Watson, Helen Orr
01,	1903	Kent, Sherman
01,	1910	Bloch, Marie Halun
01,	1913	Antoncich, Betty (Kennedy)
01,	1916	Stoutenburg, Adrien (Pearl)
01,	1919	Presberg, Miriam Goldstein
01,	1926	Abels, Harriette Sheffer
01,	1939	Berends, Polly Berrien
01,	1947	Noguere, Suzanne
01,	1949	Brett, Jan (Churchill)
01,	1952	Barry, Scott
02,	1889	Benary-Isbert, Margot
02,	1894	Lovelace, Delos Wheeler
02,	1909	Lash, Joseph P.
02,	1912	Bradley, Virginia
02,	1920	Glines, Carroll V(ane), Jr.
02,	1923	Payne, Joan Balfour
02,	1925	Bodie, Idella F(allaw)
02,	1925	Harris, Julie
02,	1926	McLeod, Emilie Warren
02,	1928	Vittengl, Morgan J(ohn)
02,	1929	Littke, Lael J.
02,	1931	Taylor, Audilee Boyd
02,	1944	French, Michael
02,	1946	Macaulay, David Alexander
03,	1897	Gropper, William
03,	1901	Lowitz, Sadyebeth (Heath)
03,	1909	Brigham, Grace A.
03,	1913	Zurhorst, Charles (Stewart, Jr.)
03,	1914	Luce, Celia (Geneva Larsen)
03,	1919	Hunter, Edith Fisher
03,	1919	Redding, Robert Hull
03,	1920	Carlson, Esther Elisabeth
03,	1922	Wallace, Barbara Brooks
03,	1931	Blue, Rose
03,	1947	Hayes, Geoffrey
03,	1952	Sadler, Catherine Edwards
04,	1896	Kerigan, Florence
04,	1899	Miller, Helen M(arkley)
04,	1905	Leaf, Wilbur Munro
04,	1907	Laklan, Carli (Laughlin Aiello)
04,	1907	Lyons, Dorothy (Marawee)
04,	1908	Bradbury, Bianca
04,	1908	Burroughs, Jean Mitchell
04,	1917	Hodge, Jane Aiken
04,	1920	Robinson, Ray(mond Kenneth)
04,	1926	Moyler, Alan (Frank Powell)
04,	1929	Ancona, George
04,	1934	Simons, Barbara B(rooks)
04,	1937	Christian, Samuel T(erry)
04,	1939	Cavanagh, Helen (Carol)
04,	1940	Hiscock, Bruce
04,	1941	Riessen, Martin Clare
04,	1942	Stiles, Norman B.
04,	1943	Whelan, Elizabeth M(urphy)
05,	1857	Brown, Alice
05,	1869	Butler, Ellis Parker
05,	1885	Joy, Charles Rhind
05,	1886	Lane, Rose Wilder
05,	1891	Wakeman, Marion Freeman
05,	1895	Bakeless, Katherine Little
05,	1896	Clark, Ann Nolan
05,	1899	Conroy, Jack (Wesley)
05,	1901	Disney, Walt(er Elias)
05,	1909	Lonergan, Pauline Joy (MacLean)
05,	1921	Thrasher, Crystal (Faye)
05,	1922	Palder, Edward L.
05,	1927	Rhodes, Bennie (Loran)
05,	1933	Meek, Jacklyn O'Hanlon
05,	1933	Zemach, Harve
05,	1938	Joyner, Jerry
05,	1943	Moran, Tom
05,	1948	Bram, Elizabeth
06,	1884	Meigs, Cornelia Lynde
06,	1886	Kilmer, Alfred Joyce
06,	1892	Crane, William D(wight)
06,	1894	Adams, Harriet S(tratemeyer)
06,	1905	Yates, Elizabeth
06,	1910	Kjelgaard, James Arthur
06,	1910	Malcolmson, Anne (Burnett)
06,	1911	Haycraft, Molly Costain
06,	1921	Winston, Clara
06,	1924	Cox, Wallace Maynard
06,	1924	Jones, Douglas C(lyde)
06,	1928	Sherman, Diane (Finn)
06,	1936	Kredenser, Gail
06,	1940	Anton, Michael J(ames)
06,	1944	Gardiner, John Reynolds
06,	1947	Cutchens, Judy
06,	1950	Dubanevich, Arlene
07,	1873	Cather, Willa (Sibert)
07,	1882	Skinner, Constance Lindsay
07,	1885	Mertins, Marshall Louis
07,	1886	Thompson, Mary (Wolfe)
07,	1887	Crump, J(ames) Irving
07,	1888	Broun, Heywood Campbell
07,	1889	Tunis, John R(oberts)
07,	1891	Radford, Ruby L(orraine)
07,	1893	Glick, Virginia Kirkus

07, 1897	Worcester, Gurdon Saltonstall	
07, 1906	Chandler, Caroline A(ugusta)	
07, 1912	Brown, Vinson	
07, 1918	Marokvia, Mireille (Journet)	
07, 1924	Felt, Sue	
07, 1926	Kaplan, Boche	
07, 1926	Seidelman, James Edward	
07, 1937	Elkins, Dov Peretz	
07, 1937	Kraus, Joanna Halpert	
07, 1940	Gles, Margaret Breitmaier	
07, 1940	Segal, Joyce	
07, 1943	Teleki, Geza	
07, 1949	Rosenberg, Jane	
07, 1950	Knudsen, James	
07, 1953	Weiss, Ellen	
07, 1956	Gustafson, Scott	
08, 1866	Crew, Helen (Cecilia) Coale	
08, 1881	Colum, Padraic	
08, 1884	Miller, Helen Topping	
08, 1894	Thurber, James (Grover)	
08, 1897	Tunis, Edwin (Burdett)	
08, 1899	Adams, Charlotte	
08, 1900	Holling, Lucille Webster	
08, 1911	Platt, Kin	
08, 1912	Byrd, Elizabeth	
08, 1913	Micale, Albert	
08, 1914	Hoehling, Mary (Duprey)	
08, 1917	Steinberg, Alfred	
08, 1918	Severn, Sue	
08, 1925	Wimmer, Helmut Karl	
08, 1927	Dunnahoo, Terry	
08, 1928	Chaikin, Miriam	
08, 1930	Immel, Mary Blair	
08, 1930	Morressy, John	
08, 1931	Allen, Marjorie	
08, 1934	Beame, Rona	
08, 1936	Marx, Robert F(rank)	
08, 1936	McCaffery, Janet	
08, 1947	Hansen, Ron	
08, 1948	Fisher, Lois I.	
08, 1951	Holl, Kristi D(iane)	
09, 1848	Harris, Joel Chandler	
09, 1888	Tibbets, Albert B.	
09, 1890	Bailey, Alice Cooper	
09, 1896	Scharl, Josef	
09, 1897	Masselman, George	
09, 1900	Terrell, John Upton	
09, 1905	Jordan, Hope (Dahle)	
09, 1910	Holl, Adelaide (Hinkle)	
09, 1913	Brondfield, Jerome	
09, 1913	Panesis, Nicholas	
09, 1915	McGraw, Eloise Jarvis	
09, 1917	Allen, Samuel (Washington)	
09, 1918	Beatty, Jerome, Jr.	
09, 1918	Heinemann, George Alfred	
09, 1921	Ellis, Harry Bearse	
09, 1925	Hickman, Martha Whitmore	
09, 1925	Roland, Albert	
09, 1927	Rydell, Wendell	
09, 1928	Blos, Joan W(insor)	
09, 1928	Cunningham, Chet	
09, 1929	Brower, Pauline (York)	
09, 1929	Gleason, Judith	
09, 1937	Hahn, Mary Downing	
09, 1945	Streano, Vince(nt Catello)	
09, 1946	Chin, Richard (M.)	
09, 1948	Bromley, Dudley	
09, 1952	Walker, Lou Ann	
10, 1830	Dickinson, Emily (Elizabeth)	
10, 1837	Eggleston, Edward	
10, 1874	Falls, C(harles) B(uckles)	
10, 1892	Johnson, Eleanor (Murdock)	
10, 1896	Olds, Elizabeth	
10, 1902	Bergeron, Victor (Jules, Jr.)	
10, 1902	Hofsinde, Robert	
10, 1903	Banning, Evelyn I.	
10, 1914	Burgwyn, Mebane H(oloman)	
10, 1925	Alter, Robert Edmond	
10, 1926	Pilarski, Laura	
10, 1930	Takakjian, Portia	
10, 1932	Auerbach, Marjorie (Hoffberg)	
10, 1940	Fisher, Barbara	
10, 1945	Turner, Ann W(arren)	
11, 1877	Plowhead, Ruth Gipson	
11, 1886	Comfort, Mildred Houghton	
11, 1894	Yap, Weda	
11, 1895	Whitehouse, Arthur George	
11, 1897	Nurnberg, Maxwell	
11, 1902	Balch, Glenn	
11, 1904	Woolsey, Janette	
11, 1905	Wood, James Playsted	
11, 1910	Espy, Willard R(ichardson)	
11, 1915	Hine, Al	
11, 1916	Moyers, William	
11, 1925	Winter, Ginny Linville	
11, 1933	Morgan, Shirley	
11, 1934	Stone, A. Harris	
11, 1957	Joyce, William	
12, 1884	Beaty, John Yocum	
12, 1895	Burman, Ben Lucien	
12, 1901	Becker, John (Leonard)	
12, 1904	Hutto, Nelson (Allen)	
12, 1906	Evanoff, Vlad	
12, 1909	Moores, Richard (Arnold)	
12, 1913	Swanson, Arlene Collyer	
12, 1918	Burdick, Eugene (Leonard)	
12, 1918	McNeely, Jeannette	
12, 1932	Emberley, Barbara A(nne Collins)	
12, 1943	Michel, Anna	
12, 1944	Graham-Barber, Lynda	
12, 1952	Yakovetic, (Joseph Sandy)	
13, 1870	Sharp, Dallas Lore	
13, 1880	Brett, Harold M.	
13, 1890	Connelly, Marc(us Cook)	
13, 1910	Jones, Richard C.	
13, 1913	Smith, Marion Hagens	
13, 1913	Wulff, Edgun Valdemar	
13, 1916	Freeman, Lucy (Greenbaum)	
13, 1916	Huntsberry, William E(mery)	
13, 1916	Weisgard, Leonard (Joseph)	
13, 1927	Wakin, Edward	
13, 1934	Horner, Dave	
13, 1935	Koren, Ed(ward)	
13, 1935	Roever, J(oan) M(arilyn)	
13, 1954	Pierce, Tamora	
14, 1885	Kirmse, Marguerite	
14, 1897	Smith, Margaret Chase	
14, 1908	Smith, Pauline C(oggeshall)	
14, 1917	Blumberg, Rhoda	
14, 1919	Jackson, Shirley	
14, 1922	Unterecker, John	
14, 1924	Waldron, Ann Wood	
14, 1925	Hafner, Marylin	
14, 1927	Barnett, Naomi	
14, 1929	Balian, Lorna (Kohl)	
14, 1929	Brown, Joseph E(dward)	
14, 1933	Delano, Hugh	
14, 1934	Crofut, William E. III	
14, 1938	Neufeld, John (Arthur)	
14, 1942	Okimoto, Jean Davies	
14, 1942	Rosenberg, Sharon	
14, 1945	Artis, Vicki Kimmel	
15, 1841	Baldwin, James	
15, 1896	Smith, Betty (Wehner)	
15, 1908	Chastain, Madye Lee	
15, 1909	Hanser, Richard (Frederick)	
15, 1913	Rukeyser, Muriel	
15, 1915	Kinney, C. Cle(land)	
15, 1916	Seamands, Ruth (Childers)	
15, 1918	Karlin, Eugene	
15, 1921	Cetin, Frank Stanley	
15, 1941	Dockery, Wallene T.	
15, 1941	Williams, Leslie	
15, 1955	Drescher, Henrik	
16, 1847	Catherwood, Mary Hartwell	
16, 1863	Fox, John (William), Jr.	
16, 1879	Knox, Rose B(ell)	
16, 1890	Marcher, Marion Walden	
16, 1891	Dolch, Marguerite Pierce	
16, 1893	Ets, Marie Hall	
16, 1896	Gannett, Ruth Chrisman (Arens)	

16, 1898 Moody, Ralph O(wen)
16, 1901 Mead, Margaret
16, 1909 Kenny, Ellsworth Newcomb
16, 1911 Rarick, Carrie
16, 1912 Biemiller, Carl Ludwig
16, 1912 Hyndman, Jane (Lee) Andrews
16, 1913 Soule, Gardner (Bosworth)
16, 1916 Burack, Sylvia K.
16, 1917 Wosmek, Frances
16, 1924 Sidjakov, Nicolas
16, 1926 Moncure, Jane Belk
16, 1926 Walker, David G(ordon)
16, 1927 Warburg, Sandol Stoddard
16, 1929 Meadow, Charles (Troub)
16, 1930 Brittain, William
16, 1936 Wagner, Sharon B.
16, 1938 Godrog, Judith (Allen)
16, 1945 Brown, Laurene Krasny
17, 1807 Whittier, John Greenleaf
17, 1884 Peirce, Waldo
17, 1893 Garthwaite, Marion H(ook)
17, 1894 Lambert, Janet (Snyder)
17, 1899 Beach, Stewart Taft
17, 1904 Lipkind, William
17, 1906 Slocum, Rosalie
17, 1907 Hamerstrom, Frances
17, 1917 Landau, Jacob
17, 1917 Sherwan, Earl
17, 1923 DeKay, Ormonde, Jr.
17, 1928 VanGelder, Richard G(eorge)
17, 1929 Baldwin, Stan(ley C.)
17, 1931 Kherdian, David
18, 1909 Johnson, William Weber
18, 1916 Greene, Carla
18, 1920 Leckie, Robert (Hugh)
18, 1927 Lanier, Sterling E.
18, 1927 Sachs, Marilyn (Stickle)
18, 1929 Behr, Joyce
18, 1934 Katz, Jane (Bresler)
18, 1934 Purscell, Phyllis
18, 1942 Miller, Mary Beth
18, 1943 Vandenburg, Mary Lou
18, 1947 Spielberg, Steven
19, 1868 Porter, Eleanor H(odgman)
19, 1898 Brewton, John E(dmund)
19, 1901 LaFarge, Oliver (Hazard Perry)
19, 1905 Hutchison, Paula A.
19, 1905 Johnson, Dorothy M(arie)
19, 1906 Arkin, David
19, 1906 Papashvily, Helen (Waite)
19, 1907 Crouse, William H(arry)
19, 1907 Smith, H(arry) Allen

19, 1913 Siebel, Fritz (Frederick)
19, 1915 Lozier, Herbert
19, 1919 Freedman, Benedict
19, 1925 Forberg, Beate Gropius
19, 1926 Kovalik, Nada
19, 1928 Bunting, A(nne) E(velyn Bolton)
19, 1937 Kindred, Wendy (Good)
19, 1938 Ellen, Barbara
19, 1942 Bowman, Kathleen (Gill)
19, 1946 Batey, Tom
20, 1885 Davidson, Mary R.
20, 1896 Leighton, Margaret (Carver)
20, 1916 Cheney, Cora
20, 1920 Pitrone, Jean Maddern
20, 1926 Levine, David
20, 1933 Thacher, Mary McGrath
20, 1936 Farley, Carol (J. McDole)
20, 1937 Blaine, Marge(ry Kay)
20, 1937 Kubinyi, Laszlo (Kalman)
20, 1940 Goffstein, M(arilyn) B(rooke)
20, 1945 Fradin, Dennis Brindell
20, 1957 Delacre, Lulu
21, 1872 Terhune, Albert Payson
21, 1903 Harwood, Pearl Augusta (Bragdon)
21, 1903 Treat, Lawrence
21, 1908 DeMiskey, Julian
21, 1924 Reid, Eugenie Chazal
21, 1925 Polking, Kirk
21, 1926 Lustig, Arnost
21, 1928 Fleming, Alice Mulcahey
21, 1929 Dank, Leonard Dewey
21, 1931 Lee, Robert C.
21, 1932 Hoagland, Edward
21, 1944 Curtis, Bruce (Richard)
21, 1946 Pearson, Susan
21, 1947 Lynch, Marietta
21, 1947 Russo, Susan
21, 1951 Berenstain, Michael
22, 1839 Butterworth, Hezekiah
22, 1869 Robinson, Edwin Arlington
22, 1893 Pierce, Edith Gray
22, 1896 Kelen, Emery
22, 1903 McPharlin, Paul
22, 1903 Paget-Fredericks, Joseph E(dward) P(aget) Rous-Marten
22, 1907 Rocker, Fermin
22, 1907 Swayne, Sam(uel F.)
22, 1912 Kenny, Herbert A(ndrew)
22, 1917 Steele, William O(wen)
22, 1918 Jacobs, Flora Gill
22, 1920 Lehr, Delores
22, 1921 Koering, Ursula
22, 1924 Sharpe, Mitchell R(aymond)
22, 1932 Latham, Donald Crawford

22, 1935 Cornish, Sam(uel James)
22, 1935 Newton, James R(obert)
22, 1937 Kines, Pat Decker
22, 1939 Pinkney, Jerry
22, 1944 Barkin, Carol
23, 1870 Sabin, Edwin L(egrand)
23, 1899 Bartlett, Robert Merrill
23, 1900 Soglow, Otto
23, 1905 Stevenson, Anna (M.)
23, 1905 Swayne, Zoa Lourana (Shaw)
23, 1913 Rau, Margaret
23, 1914 Dilson, Jesse
23, 1918 Brown, Fern G.
23, 1918 Yeo, Wilma (Lethem)
23, 1919 Gill, Derek L(ewis) T(heodore)
23, 1923 Forsyth, Gloria
23, 1929 Langone, John (Michael)
23, 1932 Kennedy, Jerome Richard
23, 1937 Wortis, Avi
24, 1880 Gruelle, John (Barton)
24, 1891 Rojankovsky, Feodor (Stephanovich)
24, 1895 Robinson, Maurice R.
24, 1912 Bennett, Jay
24, 1912 Hook, Frances
24, 1913 Hamilton, Charles
24, 1920 Langstaff, John (Meredith)
24, 1922 Finke, Blythe F(oote)
24, 1924 Scagnetti, Jack
24, 1927 Fox, Robert J.
24, 1927 Simon, Norma (Feldstein)
24, 1929 Blood, Charles Lewis
24, 1929 Clark, Mary Higgins
24, 1931 Anderson, Margaret J(ean)
24, 1934 Callahan, Dorothy M(onahan)
24, 1942 Cott, Jonathan
24, 1949 Leydon, Rita (Floden)
24, 1951 Munsinger, Lynn
25, 1869 Finger, Charles J(oseph)
25, 1876 Dix, Beulah Marie
25, 1894 Thompson, Harlan H.
25, 1900 Angle, Paul M(cClelland)
25, 1903 Greenhaus, Thelma Nurenberg
25, 1903 Rodman, Bella (Kashin)
25, 1903 Samstag, Nicholas
25, 1906 Rosenberg, Dorothy
25, 1907 Sullivan, Mary W(ilson)
25, 1908 Sussman, Irving
25, 1910 Leiber, Fritz
25, 1910 Moon, Sheila (Elizabeth)
25, 1911 Langley, Noel
25, 1915 Pantell, Dora (Fuchs)

25,	1915	Rosenberg, Ethel (Clifford)	27,	1950	Burton, Marilee Robin	29,	1943	Ready, Kirk L.
25,	1932	Richardson, Carol	28,	1895	Brink, Carol Ryrie	29,	1948	Alex, Marlee
25,	1934	Donna, Natalie	28,	1905	Miller, Albert G(riffith)	30,	1841	Carryl, Charles E(dward)
25,	1947	Stevenson, Drew	28,	1910	Larrick, Nancy G(ray)	30,	1894	Bakeless, John (Edwin)
25,	1948	Miller, Sandy (Peden)	28,	1913	Gaddis, Vincent H.	30,	1900	Barnhart, Clarence L(ewis)
25,	1949	Burstein, John	28,	1914	Esherick, Joseph	30,	1903	Friermood, Elisabeth Hamilton
26,	1854	Tappan, Eva March	28,	1916	Kellogg, Jean (Defrees)	30,	1903	Mayer, Jane Rothschild
26,	1884	Hansen, Harry	28,	1919	Neville, Emily Cheney	30,	1906	Jennings, John Edward, Jr.
26,	1897	Scrimsher, Lila Gravatt	28,	1921	Klaperman, Libby Mindlin	30,	1908	Davis, D(elbert) Dwight
26,	1906	Stapp, Arthur D(onald)	28,	1923	Gobbato, Imero	30,	1911	Curry, Peggy Simson
26,	1909	Clark, Van D(eusen)	28,	1926	McCain, Murray (David, Jr.)	30,	1922	Langton, Jane (Gillson)
26,	1910	White, Florence M(eiman)	28,	1928	Lunn, Janet	30,	1922	Siculan, Daniel
26,	1920	Neigoff, Mike	28,	1932	Vautier, Ghislaine	30,	1927	Ferguson, Robert Bruce
26,	1921	Allen, Stephen Valentine Patrick William	28,	1940	Dana, Barbara	30,	1931	Garrigue, Sheila
26,	1921	Lee, Robert J.	28,	1947	McLenighan, Valjean	30,	1933	Silverstein, Alvin
26,	1923	Lee, John R(obert)	28,	1954	Luenn, Nancy	30,	1943	Mayer, Mercer
26,	1932	Palmer, Bruce Hamilton	29,	1892	Atwater, Richard (Tupper)	30,	1944	Locke, Robert
26,	1933	Swenson, Allan A(rmstrong)	29,	1895	Douglass, Ralph	30,	1946	Fregosi, Claudia (Anne Marie)
26,	1936	Zaring, Jane (Thomas)	29,	1898	Bell, Margaret E(lizabeth)	30,	1947	O'Connor, Jane
26,	1937	VanLeeuwen, Jean	29,	1904	Ballard, Lowell Clyne	31,	1883	Darby, Ada Claire
26,	1942	Robinson, Marileta	29,	1906	Jacobson, Morris K(arl)	31,	1888	Baker, Nina (Brown)
26,	1947	Polese, Carolyn	29,	1910	Blair, Helen	31,	1903	Sitomer, Harry
27,	1889	Whitney, Elinor	29,	1917	Robbins, Ruth	31,	1904	Farr, Finis (King)
27,	1891	Liddell, Mary	29,	1919	Kublin, Hyman	31,	1906	Bianco, Pamela
27,	1904	D'Aulaire, Ingri (Maartenson)	29,	1921	Gordon, Shirley	31,	1913	Suba, Suzanne
27,	1911	Clarke, Mary Stetson	29,	1921	Pierik, Robert	31,	1915	Brown, Elizabeth M(yers)
27,	1915	Rand, Ted	29,	1929	Bienenfeld, Florence L(ucille)	31,	1915	Carmichael, Joel
27,	1924	Benedict, Stewart H(urd)	29,	1934	Silman, Roberta (Karpel)	31,	1916	Fuller, Catherine L(euthold)
27,	1926	Smith, Robert W(illiam)	29,	1935	Hall, Brian P(atrick)	31,	1918	Wayne, Kyra Petrovskaya
27,	1930	Allred, Gordon T.	29,	1939	Zeck, Gerald Anthony	31,	1925	Moscow, Alvin
27,	1932	Gemming, Elizabeth	29,	1942	Greenberg, Jan (Schonwald)	31,	1941	Lorimer, Janet
27,	1941	Wilson, Carter	29,	1942	Gustafson, Anita	31,	1948	Cuyler, Margery Stuyvesant
27,	1943	Stanley, Diane Z.	29,	1943	Bang, Molly Garrett			
27,	1946	Wismer, Donald (Richard)	29,	1943	Brady, Irene			

Birth Year Index

Please note that the first number indicates the month of birth, and it is followed by the day of the month.

1756
06/06 Trumbull, John

1757
04/15 Bingham, Caleb

1758
10/16 Webster, Noah

1759
10/11 Weems, Mason Locke

1779
07/15 Moore, Clement Clarke

1783
04/03 Irving, Washington

1787
08/15 Follen, Eliza Lee (Cabot)

1788
10/24 Hale, Sarah Josepha

1789
09/15 Cooper, James Fenimore

1791
09/01 Sigourney, Lydia Huntley

1793
08/19 Goodrich, Samuel Griswold

1794
??/?? Bryant, William Cullen

1796
07/15 Bulfinch, Thomas

1800
09/23 McGuffey, William Holmes

1802
02/11 Child, Lydia Maria

1803
05/25 Emerson, Ralph Waldo
11/13 Abbott, Jacob

1804
07/04 Hawthorne, Nathaniel

1807
02/27 Longfellow, Henry Wadsworth
12/17 Whittier, John Greenleaf

1809
01/19 Poe, Edgar Allan
06/06 Arthur, Timothy Shay
08/29 Holmes, Oliver Wendell

1810
05/23 Ossoli, Sarah Margaret (Fuller) marchesa d'

1811
06/13 Stowe, Harriet (Elizabeth) Beecher

1813
03/08 Cranch, Christopher Pearse

1815
08/01 Dana, Richard Henry, Jr.

1816
06/02 Saxe, John Godfrey
08/13 McGuffey, Alexander Hamilton

1817
02/?? Douglass, Frederick

1818
04/04 Reid, Thomas Mayne

1819
02/22 Lowell, James Russell

05/31 Whitman, Walt(er)
07/11 Warner, Susan Bogert
08/01 Melville, Herman

1820
09/02 Hale, Lucretia Peabody

1822
04/03 Hale, Edward Everett
06/23 Darley, F(elix) O(ctavius) C(arr)
07/30 Adams, William Taylor

1827
04/09 Cummins, Maria Susanna
04/10 Wallace, Lew(is)

1828
04/26 Finley, Martha

1830
10/15 Jackson, Helen (Maria Fiske) Hunt
10/24 Brooks, Noah
12/10 Dickinson, Emily (Elizabeth)

1831
01/26 Dodge, Mary (Elizabeth) Mapes
02/25 Austin, Mary Jane Goodwin
07/31 DuChaillu, Paul (Belloni)

1832
01/13 Alger, Horatio, Jr.
11/29 Alcott, Louisa May

1833
02/22 Clarke, Rebecca Sophia

1834
04/05 Stockton, Francis Richard

411

1835
01/29　Woolsey, Sarah Chauncy
05/08　Wilson, Augusta Jane Evans
11/30　Twain, Mark

1836
08/25　Harte, Francis Bret(t)
11/11　Aldrich, Thomas Bailey

1837
04/03　Burroughs, John
12/10　Eggleston, Edward

1838
04/21　Muir, John
10/16　Scudder, Horace E(lisha)

1839
03/10　Miller, Joaquin
12/22　Butterworth, Hezekiah

1840
04/11　Ellis, Edward S(ylvester)
04/28　Cox, Palmer
09/27　Nast, Thomas
09/28　Peck, George Wilbur

1841
11/03　Alden, Isabella (Macdonald)
12/15　Baldwin, James
12/30　Carryl, Charles E(dward)

1842
02/03　Lanier, Sidney
02/24　Habberton, John
09/16　Fosdick, Charles Austin

1843
01/28　Bolton, Henry Carrington

1844
06/22　Lothrop, Harriet Mulford Stone
10/21　Stephens, Charles Asbury

1846
04/14　Brooks, Elbridge Streeter

1847
12/16　Catherwood, Mary Hartwell

1848
03/19　Kaler, James Otis
09/23　Boyesen, Hjalmar Hjorth
12/09　Harris, Joel Chandler

1849
??/??　Upton, Bertha (Hudson)
09/03　Jewett, Sarah Orne
09/20　Grinnell, George Bird
10/07　Riley, James Whitcomb
11/24　Burnett, Frances (Eliza) Hodgson

1850
02/27　Richards, Laura E(lizabeth Howe)
06/19　Pyrnelle, Louise Clarke
06/21　Beard, Dan(iel Carter)
09/03　Field, Eugene
09/15　Munroe, Kirk

1851
01/17　Frost, A(rthur) B(urdett)

1852
04/23　Markham, Edwin
10/31　Freeman, Mary Eleanor Wilkins
11/10　VanDyke, Henry Jackson, Jr.

1853
03/05　Pyle, Howard
04/23　Page, Thomas Nelson
04/27　Earle, Mary Alice Morse
09/08　Poulsson, Anne Emilie

1854
08/29　Jacobs, Joseph
12/01　Hornaday, William T(emple)
12/26　Tappan, Eva March

1855
04/01　Repplier, Agnes

1856
??/??　Zollinger, Gulielma
05/02　Birch, Reginald B(athurst)
05/05　Denslow, W(illiam) W(allace)
05/15　Baum, L(yman) Frank
07/25　Major, Charles
08/02　White, Eliza Orne
09/28　Wiggin, Kate Douglas (Smith)

1857
06/28　Hough, Emerson
12/05　Brown, Alice

1858
??/??　Chesnutt, Charles Waddell
??/??　Eastman, Charles A(lexander)
04/05　Washington, Booker T(aliaferro)

1859
02/21　Smith, Nora Archibald
04/07　Camp, Walter (Chauncey)
05/03　Adams, Andy
08/12　Bates, Katharine Lee
08/26　Schultz, James Willard
09/26　Bacheller, Irving (Addison)

1860
??/??　Andrews, Mary Raymond Shipman

??/??　Curtis, Alice (Turner)
07/14　Wister, Owen
08/14　Seton, Ernest (Evan) Thompson
09/07　Moses, Anna Mary (Robertson)
09/14　Garland, Hannibal Hamlin

1861
07/10　Paine, Albert Bigelow
10/04　Remington, Frederic (Sackrider)

1862
01/24　Wharton, Edith
03/05　Newell, Peter
04/29　Altsheler, Joseph A(lexander)
07/26　Nyce, Vera
09/11　Porter, William Sydney
10/04　Stratemeyer, Edward L.
12/01　Parton, Ethel

1863
??/??　Atkinson, Eleanor (Stackhouse)
05/15　Johnston, Annie Fellows
06/24　Wallace, Dillon
08/14　Thayer, Ernest Lawrence
08/17　Porter, Gene(va Grace) Stratton
09/??　Smith, Jessie Willcox
10/12　Stein, Evaleen
12/01　Herford, Oliver
12/16　Fox, John (William), Jr.

1864
??/??　Gerson, Virginia
??/??　Loring, Emilie (Baker)
04/18　Davis, Richard Harding
06/12　Chapman, Frank Michler

1865
??/??　Phelps, William Lyon
03/23　Ford, Paul Leicester
04/16　Hill, Grace Livingston
05/17　Bennett, John
07/12　Perkins, Lucy Fitch

1866
01/30　Burgess, F(rank) Gelett
03/09　Nicolay, Helen
05/18　White, Edward Lucas
12/08　Crew, Helen (Cecilia) Coale

1867
02/07　Wilder, Laura (Elizabeth) Ingalls
08/12　Hamilton, Edith
10/26　Crownfield, Gertrude

1868
02/23　DuBois, W(illiam) E(dward) B(urghardt)
05/01　Baynes, Ernest Harold
07/10　Bradley, Will(iam H.)

09/09	Austin, Mary (Hunter)
10/21	Horsfall, Robert Bruce
12/19	Porter, Eleanor H(odgman)

1869
??/??	Crawford, Will
??/??	MacManus, Seumas
??/??	McGuire, Frances (Lynch)
??/??	Stevenson, Augusta
03/14	Edwards, George Wharton
04/17	Lamprey, Louise
07/29	Tarkington, Newton Booth
08/06	Wheeler, Post
09/25	Linderman, Frank B(ird)
10/18	Hinton, Charles Louis
12/05	Butler, Ellis Parker
12/22	Robinson, Edwin Arlington
12/25	Finger, Charles J(oseph)

1870
??/??	Johnston, Mary
01/11	Rice, Alice (Caldwell) Hegan
01/16	Perard, Victor Semon
02/21	Murphy, Mabel (Ansley)
04/17	Baker, Ray Stannard
06/12	Knipe, Emilie Benson
06/26	Knipe, Alden Arthur
07/25	Parrish, Frederick Maxfield
09/15	Bragg, Mabel Caroline
11/13	Barbour, Ralph Henry
11/28	French, Allen
12/13	Sharp, Dallas Lore
12/23	Sabin, Edwin L(egrand)

1871
??/??	Elliott, Elizabeth Shippen Green
??/??	Haskell, Helen (Eggleston)
??/??	Hunt, Clara Whitehill
??/??	Reed, W(illiam) Maxwell
01/26	Adams, Samuel Hopkins
02/11	Laut, Agnes C(hristina)
03/23	Snedeker, Caroline Dale (Parke)
04/28	Armer, Sidney
04/28	Smith, Elva S(ophronia)
06/17	Johnson, James William
07/02	Duncan, Norman
07/12	Moore, Anne Carroll
08/28	Paine, Ralph D.
09/25	Hawthorne, Hildegarde
09/26	McCay, Winsor
11/01	Crane, Stephen (Townley)
11/20	Guiterman, Arthur

1872
??/??	Brown, Abbie Farwell
??/??	Olcott, Frances Jenkins
01/03	Chorpenning, Charlotte (Lee Barrows)
02/14	Berger, William Merritt
03/24	Franklin, George Cory
03/24	Moran, Eugene Francis
06/09	Scoville, Samuel, Jr.
06/27	Dunbar, Paul Laurence
09/23	Lomax, John A.
11/01	Orton, Helen (Fuller)
11/09	Stevenson, Burton E(gbert)
12/21	Terhune, Albert Payson

1873
??/??	Power, Effie Louise
??/??	Thorne-Thomsen, Gudrun
01/10	Christy, Howard Chandler
01/15	Benda, Wladyslaw Theodore
03/12	White, Stewart Edward
04/07	Lewis, Arthur Allen
04/25	Garis, Howard R(oger)
05/29	Morrow, Elizabeth (Reeve Cutter)
06/22	Grover, Eulalie Osgood
08/05	Kummer, Frederic Arnold
08/26	Becker, May Lamberton
08/31	Harding, Charlotte
10/06	Faulkner, Georgene
11/14	Dickson, Marguerite (Stockman)
12/07	Cather, Willa (Sibert)

1874
??/??	Bull, Charles Livingston
??/??	Garrison, Theodosia
??/??	Graham, Alberta (Powell)
??/??	Sugimoto, Etsu Inagaki
01/12	Armer, Laura (Adams)
01/14	Burgess, Thornton W(aldo)
02/09	Lowell, Amy
03/26	Frost, Robert (Lee)
03/30	Hewes, Agnes Danforth
04/21	Pier, Arthur Stanwood
05/13	Lindsay, Maud McKnight
05/15	Courtis, Stuart Appleton
05/30	Peabody, Josephine Preston
07/19	Robinson, Mabel Louise
08/26	Gale, Zona
10/21	Knight, Charles Robert
11/26	Britt, Albert
11/27	Beard, Charles Austin
12/10	Falls, C(harles) B(uckles)

1875
??/??	Ashmun, Margaret Eliza
??/??	Woodson, Carter Goodwin
02/13	Nichols, Spencer Baird
02/17	Fitch, Florence Mary
03/07	Brown, Edna Adelaide
03/10	Harlow, Alvin Fay
03/15	Irwin, Wallace (Admah)
03/16	MacKaye, Percy (Wallace)
06/07	Grant, Gordon (Hope)
09/01	Burroughs, Edgar Rice
09/02	Hillyer, V(irgil) M(ores)
09/05	Aylward, William James
10/25	Bailey, Carolyn Sherwin

1876
??/??	Hartman, Gertrude
01/12	London, Jack
02/17	Bacon, Josephine Dodge (Daskam)
06/12	Hinkle, Thomas Clark
06/20	Ditmars, Raymond Lee
07/24	Webster, Alice (Jean Chandler)
07/27	Patch, Edith M(arion)
09/04	Stevens, Lucy Beatrice
09/06	Robinson, Boardman
09/22	Donahey, Mary (Augusta) Dickerson
11/07	Shinn, Everett
11/17	Cannon, Cornelia (James)
12/25	Dix, Beulah Marie

1877
??/??	Malloch, Douglas
??/??	Moon, Grace (Purdie)
02/26	Dirks, Rudolph
04/16	Price, Norman Mills
04/30	Davis, William Stearns
07/26	McNeely, Marian Hurd
07/29	Beebe, Charles William
07/30	Smith, Fredrika Shumway
07/??	Cady, Walter Harrison
08/01	Diller, Angela
08/19	Schoonover, Frank (Earle)
10/09	Barnouw, Adriaan Jacob
10/31	Crowell, Grace Noll
12/11	Plowhead, Ruth Gipson

1878
??/??	Eaton, Walter Pritchard
??/??	Marquis, Don
01/06	Sandburg, Carl (August)
04/15	Hazeltine, Alice Isabel
05/24	Fosdick, Harry Emerson
06/18	Robinson, Thomas Pendleton
07/29	Theiss, Lewis Edwin
09/20	Sinclair, Upton (Beall)
09/21	Fillmore, Parker H(oysted)
10/07	Stevens, William Oliver
10/15	Holland, Rupert Sargent
11/19	Koerner, W(illiam) H(enry) D(avid)

1879
??/??	Bolton, Ivy May
??/??	Gall, Alice Crew
02/17	Fisher, Dorothy (Frances) Canfield
02/23	DeForest, Charlotte B(urgis)
03/31	MacKinstry, Elizabeth
04/03	Seaman, Augusta Huiell
04/12	Melcher, Frederic Gershom
05/05	Bill, Alfred Hoyt
05/11	Stone, Eugenia
08/29	Singmaster, Elsie
09/02	Melcher, Marguerite Fellows
10/05	Moon, Carl
11/10	Lindsay, Nicholas Vachel
12/16	Knox, Rose B(ell)

1880
| ??/?? | Morrow, Honore Willsie |

??/?? Stewart, Anna Bird
01/18 Bowman, James Cloyd
01/23 Poole, Ernest
02/26 Dunlap, Hope
03/04 Walker, Stuart (Armstrong)
04/24 Sarg, Tony
06/19 Dwiggins, William Addison
07/29 Turner, Nancy Byrd
08/05 Sawyer, Ruth
09/03 Richards, George Mather
10/08 Grose, Helen Mason
10/18 Fargo, Lucile Foster
12/13 Brett, Harold M.

1881
??/?? Almond, Linda Stevens
??/?? Reely, Mary Katharine
01/05 Quinn, Elisabeth
01/14 Williams, Clyde C.
02/17 Aldrich, Bess Streeter
03/27 Oakley, Thornton
05/08 Eaton, Anne T(haxter)
05/13 Phillips, Mary Geisler
06/10 Gruenberg, Sidonie M(atsner)
06/11 Dombrowski, Kathe Schonberger von
06/12 Finta, Alexander
06/19 Barney, Maginel Wright
07/22 Bianco, Margery (Williams)
07/28 Davis, Robert
09/02 Beals, Frank Lee
09/03 Lardner, Rex
09/19 Garfield, James B.
10/11 Young, Stark
10/15 Wodehouse, P(elham) G(renville)
11/15 Gollomb, Joseph
12/08 Colum, Padraic

1882
??/?? Bostelmann, Else W. von Roeder
??/?? Crew, Fleming H.
??/?? Israel, Marion Louise
01/14 VanLoon, Hendrik Willem
02/09 Hall, Anna Gertrude
02/13 Davis, Mary Gould
02/16 Cronbach, Abraham
02/23 Fischer, Anton Otto
04/22 Brawley, Benjamin Griffith
04/28 Floherty, John Joseph
05/16 Hayes, Carlton J. H.
06/21 Kent, Rockwell
07/01 Glaspell, Susan
07/01 Richardson, Frank Howard
07/04 Rae, John
08/24 Pogany, William Andrew
09/06 Warren, William Stephen
10/22 Wyeth, N(ewell) C(onvers)
12/07 Skinner, Constance Lindsay

1883
??/?? Daugherty, Harry R.
02/12 Brown, George Earl
04/09 King, Frank O.

05/13 Chambers, C. Bosseron
06/10 Lansing, Marion Florence
06/29 Ruzicka, Rudolph
08/06 Miller, Mary Britton
12/31 Darby, Ada Claire

1884
??/?? Fauset, Jessie (Redmon)
??/?? Follett, Helen (Thomas)
01/26 Andrews, Roy Chapman
02/08 Johnson, Gaylord
02/14 Avinoff, Andrey
02/16 Flaherty, Robert Joseph
03/08 Dunn, Harvey T(homas)
03/16 Kelly, Eric P(hilbrook)
03/22 Heyliger, William
04/21 Harper, Wilhelmina
04/26 Zirbes, Laura
06/04 Fox, Fontaine Talbot, Jr.
06/13 Benet, Laura
07/08 Schuyler, Remington
07/21 Peck, Anne Merriman
07/29 Tietjens, Eunice Hammond
08/08 Teasdale, Sara
08/27 Arbuthnot, May Hill
08/31 Lankes, Julius J.
10/11 Roosevelt, Anna Eleanor (Roosevelt)
10/19 Donahey, William
11/29 Klemm, Roberta K(ohnhorst)
11/30 Boyton, Neil
12/06 Meigs, Cornelia Lynde
12/08 Miller, Helen Topping
12/12 Beaty, John Yocum
12/17 Peirce, Waldo
12/26 Hansen, Harry

1885
??/?? L'Hommedieu, Dorothy K(easley)
??/?? Lucas, Janette May
??/?? Wynne, Annette
01/15 MacDonald, Zillah Katherine
03/07 Thompson, Stith
03/13 Irwin, Keith Gordon
05/06 Avison, George (Alfred)
05/08 Costain, Thomas B(ertram)
05/26 Litten, Frederic Nelson
05/30 Honore, Paul
06/11 Nyce, Helene von Strecker
06/26 Lemmon, Robert Stell
07/12 Alsop, Mary O'Hara
07/26 Bransom, John Paul
08/31 Heyward, Du Bose
09/07 Tippett, James S(terling)
09/07 Wylie, Elinor Hoyt
10/01 Untermeyer, Louis
10/02 Owen, Ruth (Bryan)
11/14 Rourke, Constance (Mayfield)
12/05 Joy, Charles Rhind
12/07 Mertins, Marshall Louis
12/14 Kirmse, Marguerite
12/20 Davidson, Mary R.

1886
??/?? Gunterman, Bertha Lisette
??/?? Krum, Charlotte
??/?? Paradis, Marjorie (Bartholomew)
??/?? Starrett, Charles Vincent Emerson
??/?? Stevens, Alden Gifford
01/09 Brooks, Walter R(ollin)
01/13 Moore, Clyde B.
01/14 Lofting, Hugh
01/15 Buff, Conrad
02/17 Longstreth, T(homas) Morris
02/20 Freuchen, Peter
02/21 Morton, David
03/04 Wilson, Edward A(rthur)
03/12 Nielsen, Kay (Rasmus)
04/03 Dickerson, Roy Ernest
05/02 Potter, Miriam S. (Clark)
05/25 Kent, Louise (Andrews)
06/11 Brock, Emma L(illian)
10/30 Roberts, Elizabeth Madox
11/20 Walsh, Richard John
11/30 Eaton, Jeanette
12/05 Lane, Rose Wilder
12/06 Kilmer, Alfred Joyce
12/07 Thompson, Mary (Wolfe)
12/11 Comfort, Mildred Houghton

1887
??/?? Barksdale, Lena
??/?? Carter, Helene
??/?? Jones, Jessie Mae Orton
??/?? Mims, Sam (S.)
??/?? Rush, William Marshall
??/?? Smith, Lillian H(elena)
??/?? Southwick, Katherine
01/08 White, Percival
02/01 Nordhoff, Charles (Bernard)
02/02 Kaufmann, Helen (Loeb)
02/24 Chase, Mary Ellen
02/28 Lippincott, Joseph Wharton
03/16 Thompson, Blanche Jennings
04/06 Rabe, Olive H(anson)
04/22 Hall, James Norman
04/22 Wiese, Kurt
06/09 Pinkerton, Kathrene Sutherland (Gedney)
07/09 Morison, Samuel Eliot
07/14 Myers, Caroline Elizabeth (Clark)
07/24 Chapman, Frederick Trench
07/28 Price, Willard (DeMille)
08/15 Ferber, Edna
08/16 Sublette, C(lifford) M(cClellan)
09/28 Jaques, Francis Lee
10/06 Levinger, Elma (Ehrlich)
10/23 Collings, Ellsworth
11/15 Moore, Marianne (Craig)
11/26 DeSchweinitz, Karl
12/07 Crump, J(ames) Irving

1888
??/??	Barnum, Jay Hyde
??/??	Bonestell, Chesley
??/??	Bugbee, Emma
??/??	Earle, Olive (Lydia)
??/??	Fleming, Elizabeth P.
??/??	Jemne, Elsa Laubach
??/??	Rogers, Frances
01/01	Ackerman, Eugene (Francis)
01/10	Fergusson, Erna
01/20	Jones, Wilfred J.
01/31	Pratt, Agnes Edwards Rothery
02/12	Alexander, Frances (Laura)
03/05	Lieb, Frederick George
03/12	Mueller, Hans Alexander
03/20	Price, Margaret (Evans)
04/08	Shay, Frank
04/16	Lownsbery, Eloise
04/29	Wilcox, R(uth) Turner
05/17	Kalashnikoff, Nicholas
06/01	Beston, Henry B.
06/18	Burger, Carl (Victor)
07/04	Fanning, Leonard M(ulliken)
07/18	Allen, Gertrude E(lizabeth)
08/07	Winter, Milo (Kendall)
08/24	Jagendorf, Moritz (Adolf)
08/29	Hill, Frank Ernest
09/07	DeMuth, Flora Nash
09/20	Petersham, Miska
09/26	Dobie, J(ames) Frank
10/06	O'Neill, Eugene (Gladstone)
10/08	Steurt, Marjorie Rankin
10/14	Turnbull, Agnes Sligh
11/12	Parrish, Anne
11/30	Rauch, Mabel Thompson
12/07	Broun, Heywood Campbell
12/09	Tibbets, Albert B.
12/31	Baker, Nina (Brown)

1889
??/??	Field, Elinor Whitney
??/??	Fuller, Raymond Tifft
??/??	Laughlin, Ruth
??/??	Leamy, Edmund (Stanislaus)
??/??	Seeger, Elizabeth
01/06	Craven, Thomas
01/08	Owen, Russell
01/24	Hawes, Charles Boardman
02/10	Davis, Marguerite
02/17	Barnhart, Nancy
03/06	Preston, Alice Bolam
03/11	Holberg, Richard A.
03/11	Mochi, Ugo (A.)
03/14	DeAngeli, Marguerite (Lofft)
04/15	Benedict, Dorothy Potter
04/15	Benton, Thomas Hart
04/15	Morgan, Alfred P(owell)
05/07	Burlingame, William Roger
05/27	Baldridge, Cyrus LeRoy
05/29	Dick, Trella Lamson
06/01	Daugherty, James (Henry)
07/13	Miller, Elizabeth Cleveland
07/17	Fleischer, Max
07/27	Bliven, Bruce
08/04	Dolch, Edward William
08/12	Sharp, Zerna A.
08/14	Davis, Verne T(heodore)
09/07	Hader, Elmer (Stanley)
10/02	Hallward, Michael
11/05	Richardson, Willis
11/16	Yost, Edna
11/27	Vance, Marguerite
12/02	Benary-Isbert, Margot
12/07	Tunis, John R(oberts)
12/27	Whitney, Elinor

1890
??/??	Burton, Katherine (Kurz)
??/??	Criss, Mildred
??/??	Frazier, Neta Lohnes
??/??	Harcourt, Ellen Knowles
??/??	Harshaw, Ruth H(etzel)
??/??	Lawrence, Josephine
??/??	Liers, Emil E(rnest)
??/??	Swift, Hildegarde Hoyt
??/??	Tannehill, Ivan Ray
01/05	McFarland, Wilma
01/20	Daniel, Hawthorne
02/05	Dahl, Borghild
02/07	Lide, Alice (Alison)
02/07	Parker, Bertha Morris
03/02	DeKruif, Paul (Henry)
03/17	Collins, Ruth Philpott
04/04	Jewett, Eleanore Myers
04/07	Douglas, Marjory Stoneman
04/08	Specking, Inez
04/10	Buff, Mary Marsh
04/10	Callahan, Claire Wallis
04/16	Warner, Gertrude Chandler
04/20	Call, Hughie Florence
04/30	Carpenter, Frances
05/02	Johnston, Edith Constance Farrington
05/05	Morley, Christopher (Darlington)
05/13	Dawson, Mitchell
05/15	Porter, Katherine Anne
05/19	Hauman, George
06/02	Allee, Marjorie Hill
06/25	Guthrie, Anne
07/06	Mukerji, Dhan Gopal
07/24	Medary, Marjorie
08/05	Petersham, Maud (Sylvia Fuller)
08/06	Johnson, Gerald White
08/26	Olmsted, Lorena Ann
08/31	Childs, Halla Fay (Cochrane)
09/07	Komroff, Manuel
09/11	Glick, Carl (Cannon)
09/14	DuBois, Theodora (McCormick)
10/09	Burton, William H(enry)
10/13	Richter, Conrad (Michael)
10/13	Wright, Anna (Maria Louisa Perrot) Rose
11/07	Matulka, Jan
11/19	Ferris, Helen Josephine
12/09	Bailey, Alice Cooper
12/13	Connelly, Marc(us Cook)
12/16	Marcher, Marion Walden

1891
??/??	Baker, William C.
??/??	Girvan, Helen (Masterman)
??/??	Hackett, Frances (Goodrich)
??/??	Hader, Berta (Hoerner)
??/??	Hogeboom, Amy
??/??	Jameson, Malcolm
??/??	Marshall, Jim
??/??	Martin, Charles Morris
??/??	Robinson, Irene Bowen
??/??	Robinson, W(illiam) W(ilcox)
01/23	Ford, Lauren
02/02	Holberg, Ruth (Langland)
02/10	Walker, Louise Jean
02/11	Martin, Rene
02/13	Wilwerding, Walter Joseph
02/27	Dennis, Morgan
03/14	Emerson, Caroline D(wight)
03/30	Knight, Clayton
04/08	Sauer, Julia (Lina)
04/12	Anderson, C(larence) W(illiam)
04/16	Lathrop, Dorothy P(ulis)
05/15	Means, Florence Crannell
05/21	Chapman, John Stanton Higham
06/12	Pallister, John C(lare)
06/28	Forbes, Esther
07/17	Price, Hattie Longstreet
07/27	Thompson, Ruth Plumly
07/29	Shephard, Esther
08/27	Urmston, Mary
08/28	Horvath, Ferdinand Huszti
09/24	Wells, Rhea
11/21	Ellsberg, Edward
11/26	Cole, Walter
12/05	Wakeman, Marion Freeman
12/07	Radford, Ruby L(orraine)
12/16	Dolch, Marguerite Pierce
12/24	Rojankovsky, Feodor (Stephanovich)
12/27	Liddell, Mary

1892
??/??	Barrows, R(uth) M(ajorie)
??/??	Downer, Marion
??/??	Eppenstein, Louise (Kohn)
??/??	Hazlett, Edward Everett
??/??	Hickok, Lorena A.
??/??	Johnson, Enid
??/??	Kuh, Charlotte
??/??	Lawrence, Isabelle (Wentworth)
??/??	MacFarlan, Allan A.

??/??	McCormick, Dell J.
??/??	Messmer, Otto
??/??	Sayers, Charles Marshall
??/??	VanRensselaer, Alexander (Taylor Mason)
??/??	Voute, Kathleen
??/??	White, Bessie (Feistiner)
01/04	Best, Evangel Allena Champlin
01/25	Washburne, Heluiz Chandler
02/19	Melin, Grace Hathaway
02/22	Millay, Edna St. Vincent
03/02	Lowrey, Janette Sebring
03/04	Taylor, Florence M(arian Tompkins)
03/07	Cason, Emille Mabel Earp
03/18	Coffin, Robert P. Tristram
03/26	Ish-Kishor, Judith
04/01	Shippen, Katherine B(inney)
04/06	Thomas, Lowell (Jackson)
04/14	Riggs, Sidney Noyes
04/25	Lovelace, Maud Hart (Palmer)
04/30	Leach, Maria
05/01	Shaw, Charles (Green)
05/02	Meader, Stephen W(arren)
05/13	Finney, Gertrude E. (Bridgeman)
05/24	Lewis, Elizabeth Foreman
06/06	James, Will(iam Roderick)
06/24	Daringer, Helen Fern
06/29	Tooze, Ruth (Anderson)
07/02	Allen, Merritt Parmalee
07/02	Day, Maurice
07/26	Buck, Pearl S(ydenstricker)
08/02	Kieran, John (Francis)
08/04	Long, Laura Mooney
08/16	Foster, Harold Rudolf
08/19	Hosford, Jessie
08/26	Cook, Olive Rambo
08/28	Colver, Alice Mary (Ross)
09/01	Lamb, Harold (Albert)
09/26	Norling, Ernest Ralph
10/04	Lawson, Robert
11/??	DuSoe, Robert C(oleman)
11/01	Hunt, Mabel Leigh
11/01	Randall, Ruth Painter
12/01	Watson, Helen Orr
12/06	Crane, William D(wight)
12/10	Johnson, Eleanor (Murdock)
12/29	Atwater, Richard (Tupper)

1893
??/??	Boni, Margaret Bradford
??/??	Chapin, Henry
??/??	Daniel, Anita
??/??	Gibson, Katharine
??/??	Hogner, Dorothy Childs
01/21	Barnaby, Ralph S(tanton)
01/22	Oursler, Charles Fulton
01/26	Welles, Winifred
01/27	McMillen, Wheeler
02/16	Boyd, Frank
02/20	Crouse, Russell M.
02/28	Bacmeister, Rhoda W(arner)
03/01	Nickelsburg, Janet
03/11	Gag, Wanda (Hazel)
03/12	Camp, Charles Lewis
03/15	Hornblow, Arthur (, Jr.)
03/27	Frank, Josette
04/04	Gordon, Dorothy (Lerner)
04/13	Foster, Genevieve (Stump)
04/17	Grant, Bruce
04/17	Phillips, Loretta (Hosey)
05/13	Freeman, Margaret
05/15	Burnett, Constance Buel
05/21	Clifford, Harold B(urton)
05/26	Tee-Van, Helen Damrosch
05/31	Coatsworth, Elizabeth (Jane)
06/08	Deming, Dorothy
07/15	Whitehouse, Elizabeth S(cott)
07/22	Hogner, Nils
08/22	Holbrook, Stewart Hall
08/27	Hess, Fjeril
09/21	Kennell, Ruth E(pperson)
09/24	Bailey, Ralph Edgar
10/07	Dalgliesh, Alice
10/14	Lenski, Lois (Lenore)
10/16	Carmer, Carl (Lamson)
11/01	Johnson, Margaret S(weet)
11/13	Beals, Carleton
11/27	Brown, Paul
11/28	Downey, Fairfax D(avis)
12/07	Glick, Virginia Kirkus
12/16	Ets, Marie Hall
12/17	Garthwaite, Marion H(ook)
12/22	Pierce, Edith Gray

1894
??/??	Braddy, Nella
??/??	Hanson, Joseph E.
??/??	Ivan, Gustave
??/??	Keyes, Nelson Beecher
??/??	Lawson, Marie Abrams
??/??	Rechnitzer, Ferdinand Edsted
??/??	Rockwell, Gail
??/??	Waldeck, Theodore J.
??/??	Whitney, Leon Fradley
01/02	Albrecht, Lillie (Vanderveer)
01/02	Nathan, Robert (Gruntal)
01/04	Woody, Regina (Llewellyn) Jones
01/05	Carroll, Archer Latrobe
01/06	Stern, Catherine (Brieger)
01/20	Gray, Harold (Lincoln)
02/03	Rockwell, Norman (Percevel)
02/07	Williamson, T(hames) R(oss)
02/15	Trent, Robbie
02/23	Gans, Roma
03/03	Rogers, Matilda
03/14	Johnson, Osa Helen (Leighty)
03/15	Lee, Manning de V(illeneuve)
03/25	Best, Oswald Herbert
04/07	Holden, Raymond Peckham
04/08	Meek, S(terner St.) P(aul)
04/12	Montgomery, Rutherford (George)
04/25	Fischbach, Julius
05/13	Sterne, Emma Gelders
05/15	Phillips, Prentice
05/26	Burt, Olive Woolley
06/03	Szyk, Arthur
06/16	Barker, S(quire) Omar
06/18	Pond, Alonzo W(illiam)
06/25	Sturtzel, Howard A(llison)
06/29	Bechtel, Louise Seaman
07/16	Bell, Corydon Whitten
07/17	Chandler, Ruth Forbes
07/24	Garst, Doris (Shannon)
07/26	Johnson, Lois S(mith)
07/28	Weilerstein, Sadie Rose
08/03	Hager, Alice Rogers
08/05	Bro, Margueritte (Harmon)
08/31	McCracken, Harold
09/06	Pease, Howard
09/19	Field, Rachel (Lyman)
09/19	Wadsworth, Wallace (Carter)
09/28	Harmer, Mabel
10/07	Thorne, Diana
10/14	Cummings, E(dward) E(stlin)
10/20	Merwin, Decie
10/24	Bronson, Wilfrid Swancourt
10/30	Glanckoff, Samuel
11/12	Bufano, Remo
11/17	Anderson, Bernice G(oudy)
11/19	Rethi, Lili
11/25	Carbonnier, Jeanne
11/27	Milhous, Katherine
12/02	Lovelace, Delos Wheeler
12/06	Adams, Harriet S(tratemeyer)
12/08	Thurber, James (Grover)
12/11	Yap, Weda
12/17	Lambert, Janet (Snyder)
12/25	Thompson, Harlan H.
12/30	Bakeless, John (Edwin)

1895
??/??	Emerson, Sybil (Davis)
??/??	Garrett, Helen
??/??	Hayes, Florence (Sooy)
??/??	Lewis, Alice Hudson
??/??	MacKay, Donald A.
??/??	McKay, Donald
??/??	Moore, David William
??/??	Norling, Jo(sephine Stearns)
??/??	O'Brien, Esse Forrester
01/05	Breckenfeld, Vivian Gurney

01/14 Meyer, Jerome Sydney
02/24 Monsell, Helen (Albee)
03/01 Grant, Madeleine Parker
03/19 Rhoads, Dorothy (Mary)
04/04 Boylston, Helen (Dore)
04/07 Brecht, Edith
04/26 Lengyel, Emil
04/29 Olds, Helen Diehl
05/02 Bacon, Margaret Frances
05/11 Haight, Anne Lyon
05/24 Garner, Elvira (Carter)
05/31 Stewart, George Rippey
06/01 Burbank, Addison (Buswell)
06/02 Meyer, Edith Patterson
06/13 Quintanilla, Luis
06/16 Pitz, Henry C(larence)
07/04 Simon, Solomon
07/24 Wernecke, Herbert Henry
08/04 Anthony, Edward
08/05 Hogan, Inez
08/07 Townsend, Lee
08/15 Kutcher, Ben
09/01 Yates, Raymond F(rancis)
09/05 Bonner, Mary Graham
09/06 Gagliardo, Ruth Garver
09/10 Chapman, Mary Hamilton Illsley
09/16 Hopkins, Clark
09/19 Malkus, Alida (Wright) Sims
09/22 Deutsch, Babette
10/01 Weber, Lenora Mattingly
10/16 Bracker, Charles Eugene
10/29 Roy, Jessie Hailstalk
11/01 Hecht, George J(oseph)
11/19 McMeekin, Isabel (McLennan)
11/29 Shenton, Edward
12/05 Bakeless, Katherine Little
12/11 Whitehouse, Arthur George
12/12 Burman, Ben Lucien
12/24 Robinson, Maurice R.
12/28 Brink, Carol Ryrie
12/29 Douglass, Ralph

1896
??/?? Bryan, Dorothy M(arie)
??/?? Burglon, Nora
??/?? Burman, Alice Caddy
??/?? Bush-Brown, Louise
??/?? Gatti, Attilio
??/?? Haas, Merle S.
??/?? Jackson, Anne
??/?? Johansen, Margaret (Alison)
??/?? Kramer, Nora
??/?? Myers, Madeleine Neuberger
??/?? Newell, Hope (Hockenberry)
??/?? Pond, Seymour Gates
??/?? Regli, Adolph Casper
??/?? Woodbury, David O(akes)
01/04 Dirksen, Everett McKinley
01/14 Maxwell, Arthur S.

02/19 White, Anne Terry
02/22 Stack, Nicolete Meredith
02/25 Farrar, John C(hipman)
02/29 Rogers, W(illiam) G(arland)
03/04 Pine, Tillie S(chloss)
03/13 Aldis, Dorothy (Keeley)
04/17 Stratton, William David
04/25 James, Harry Clebourne
05/26 Munson, Gorham (Bert)
06/06 Latham, Barbara
06/27 Sewell, Helen (Moore)
06/30 Swanson, Neil Harmon
07/03 Bell, Thelma Harrington
07/07 Ross, David
07/13 Karasz, Ilonka
07/17 Spykman, E(lizabeth) C(hoate)
07/24 Coffman, Ramon Peyton
08/08 Lawson, Marion Tubbs
08/08 Rawlings, Marjorie Kinnan
08/14 Weiss, Emil
08/22 Lancaster, Bruce
09/11 Simpson, Maxwell Stewart
09/21 Kelsey, Alice Geer
09/21 Werth, Kurt
09/23 Waugh, Dorothy
10/01 Green, Mary McBurney
10/18 Kyle, Anne D.
10/19 Ousley, Odille
11/?? Ish-Kishor, Sulamith
11/02 Tenggren, Gustaf (Adolf)
11/11 Coates, Belle
11/21 Price, Garrett
11/29 Reck, Franklin Mering
11/30 Bennett, Russell H(oradley)
12/04 Kerigan, Florence
12/05 Clark, Ann Nolan
12/09 Scharl, Josef
12/10 Olds, Elizabeth
12/15 Smith, Betty (Wehner)
12/16 Gannett, Ruth Chrisman (Arens)
12/20 Leighton, Margaret (Carver)
12/22 Kelen, Emery

1897
??/?? Adams, Pauline Batchelder
??/?? Brother Ernest,
??/?? Coblentz, Catherine Cate
??/?? Denman, Frank
??/?? Eggenhofer, Nicholas
??/?? Graham, Al
??/?? Leeming, Joseph
??/?? Rankin, Louise D.
01/01 Bowen, Catherine Drinker
01/21 Reyher, Rebecca Hourwich
01/29 Lufkin, Raymond H.
02/24 Orleans, Ilo
02/27 Carlson, Vada F.
03/11 Betz, Eva Kelly
03/15 Scholz, Jackson (Volney)
03/16 Gaer, Joseph

03/20 Goll, Reinhold W(eimar)
03/24 Kroeber, Theodora (Kracaw Brown)
03/31 Nolan, Jeannette Covert
04/10 Knight, Eric (Mowbray)
04/14 Raskin, Joseph
04/25 Pratt, Fletcher
04/26 Price, Edith Ballinger
04/29 Canfield, Jane White
05/04 Judson, Clara Ingram
05/06 Bragdon, Elspeth (MacDuffie)
05/10 Beers, Lorna
05/10 Lowenfels, Walter
05/14 Buehr, Walter Franklin
05/23 Butler, Mildred Allen
06/14 Tait, Agnes
06/20 Rollins, Charlemae Hill
06/21 Fulks, Bryan
06/23 Angelo, Valenti
06/23 Westphal, Arnold Carl
06/26 Wright, Frances Fitzpatrick
07/21 Budd, Lillian (Peterson)
07/26 Gallico, Paul (William)
07/31 Pryor, Helen Brenton
08/11 Bogan, Louise
08/17 Fletcher, Charlie May Hogue
08/29 Hauman, Doris
09/04 Sayers, Frances (Clarke)
09/06 Weddle, Ethel H(arshbarger)
09/16 Handforth, Thomas (Schofield)
09/16 Mauzey, Merritt
09/19 Desmond, Alice Curtis
10/06 Dietz, David H(enry)
10/11 Auslander, Joseph
10/13 Agnew, Edith J(osephine)
10/21 Wormser, Sophie
10/23 Flack, Marjorie
10/28 Pickering, James Sayre
11/?? Seignobosc, Francoise
11/07 Sperry, Armstrong W.
11/14 Curry, John Steuart
11/15 McCord, David (Thompson Watson)
11/23 Baner, Skulda V(anadis)
11/24 Hylander, Clarence J(ohn)
11/27 Teague, Donald
12/03 Gropper, William
12/07 Worcester, Gurdon Saltonstall
12/08 Tunis, Edwin (Burdett)
12/09 Masselman, George
12/11 Nurnberg, Maxwell
12/14 Smith, Margaret Chase
12/26 Scrimsher, Lila Gravatt

1898
??/?? Geisel, Helen
??/?? Govan, Christine Noble
??/?? Johnson, Owen (McMahon)
??/?? Jones, Mary Alice

??/??	Leyson, Burr Watkins	09/30	D'Aulaire, Edgar Parin	05/12	Yaukey, Grace S(ydenstricker)
??/??	Lipscomb, George D(ewey)	10/??	Wheeler, Opal	05/25	Artzybasheff, Boris (Miklailovich)
??/??	Plaine, Alfred R.	10/05	Knight, Ruth Adams (Yingling)	05/27	Chalmers, Audrey
??/??	Proudfit, Isabel (Katherine Boyd)	10/07	Paull, Grace A(lice)	06/02	Teale, Edwin Way
		10/13	Alexander, Raymond Pace	06/16	Masters, Kelly Ray
??/??	Tompkins, Jane	10/14	Wellman, Paul I(selin)	06/21	Gard, Sanford Wayne
??/??	Weart, Edith Lucie	10/16	Douglas, William O(rville)	06/22	Hammond, Winifred G(raham)
??/??	Weik, Mary Hays	10/27	Lerrigo, Marion Olive		
??/??	Worth, Kathryn	11/04	McKinney, Roland Joseph	06/25	Odenwald, Robert P(aul)
01/03	Goudey, Alice E(dwards)	11/11	Eberle, Irmengarde	07/07	Ostman, Lempi
01/03	Haywood, Carolyn	11/17	Ayars, James S(terling)	07/10	Nelson, Marg (Raibley)
01/07	DeGering, Etta (Fowler)	11/18	Lippincott, Bertram	07/11	White, E(lwyn) B(rooks)
01/19	Rushmore, Helen	11/20	Luckhardt, Mildred (Madeleine) Corell	07/16	Chrisman, Arthur Bowie
01/19	Street, Julia Montgomery			07/17	Bratton, Helen
01/20	Boyce, George A(rthur)	11/29	Lattin, Harriet (Pratt)	07/18	Kalnay, Francis
01/24	Munce, Ruth (Livingston) Hill	12/16	Moody, Ralph O(wen)	07/22	Bennett, Richard
		12/19	Brewton, John E(dmund)	07/26	Bell, Norman (Edward)
01/31	Katchamakoff, Atanas	12/29	Bell, Margaret E(lizabeth)	08/05	Aiken, Conrad (Potter)
02/04	Monroe, Marion			08/05	Bacharach, Herman Ilfeld
02/07	Charlot, Jean			08/05	Baruch, Dorothy W(alter)
02/10	Woodward, Hildegard	**1899**		08/09	Coffin, Joseph (John)
02/15	Gonzalez, Xavier	??/??	Burch, Gladys	08/12	DeLeeuw, Adele (Louise)
02/21	Nazaroff, Alexander I.	??/??	Carson, Julia Margaret (Hicks)	08/13	Hitchcock, Alfred (Joseph)
03/14	Marsh, Reginald			08/16	Carleton, R(eginal) Milton
03/31	Meadowcroft, Enid (LaMonte)	??/??	Colman, Morris	08/23	Coe, Lloyd
		??/??	Fenton, Mildred Adams	08/26	Schatzki, Walter
04/08	Wilson, Hazel (Hutchins)	??/??	Foster, Margaret Lesser	08/27	Forester, C(ecil) S(cott)
04/16	Shirk, Jeannette Campbell	??/??	Gwynne, John Harold	08/30	Hall-Quest, Edna Olga Wilbourne
04/27	Bemelmans, Ludwig	??/??	Habberton, William		
05/02	Eshmeyer, R(einhart) E(rnst)	??/??	Lesser, Margaret	08/31	McGuire, Edna
		??/??	Lindquist, Jennie D(orothea)	09/22	Munzer, Martha E(iseman)
05/12	Justus, May			09/24	Carroll, Ruth (Robinson)
05/12	Kvale, Velma R(uth)	??/??	Parker, Alfred Eustace	09/26	Cavanah, Frances
05/13	Bobritsky, Vladimir	??/??	Peet, Creighton B.	10/09	Catton, Charles Bruce
05/18	Cram, L. D.	??/??	Ross, Patricia (Fent)	10/14	Sonneborn, Ruth (Cantor) A.
05/20	Alger, Leclaire (Gowans)	??/??	Russell, Don(ald Bert)		
05/23	O'Dell, Scott	??/??	Torrey, Marjorie	10/23	Kimbrough, Emily
05/25	Cerf, Bennett (Alfred)	??/??	Wilson, Ruth	10/24	Fenner, Phyllis Reid
05/31	Peale, Norman Vincent	01/01	Cottam, Clarence	10/26	Cottler, Joseph
06/??	Goetz, Delia	01/02	Evans, Katherine (Floyd)	11/09	Foster, Doris Van Liew
06/19	Tharp, Louise Hall	01/02	Selden, Samuel	11/10	Seredy, Kate
06/20	Rowe, Dorothy	01/04	Carr, Harriett H(elen)	11/10	Stowe, Leland
06/21	Peattie, Donald Culross	01/04	Kubie, Nora (Gottheil) Benjamin	11/14	Martin, Patricia Miles
07/13	Sherman, Harold (Morrow)			11/16	McBride, Mary Margaret
		01/11	LeGallienne, Eva	11/16	Smith, Marion Jaques
07/15	Schaeffer, Mead	01/11	Thomas, Estelle Webb	11/20	Byrne, Donn
07/22	Benet, Stephen Vincent	01/27	Malcolmson, David	12/??	Ulreich, Nura Woodson
07/23	Witty, Paul A(ndrew)	01/27	Stong, Phil(ip Duffield)	12/04	Miller, Helen M(arkley)
08/03	Low, Elizabeth Hammond	01/28	Aiken, Clarissa (Lorenz)	12/05	Conroy, Jack (Wesley)
08/18	O'Brien, John Sherman	02/02	Belpre, Pura	12/08	Adams, Charlotte
08/23	Papashvily, George	02/02	Caudill, Rebecca	12/17	Beach, Stewart Taft
08/24	Brandhorst, Carl T(heodore)	02/08	Crawford, Phyllis	12/23	Bartlett, Robert Merrill
		03/05	Holt, Margaret Van Vechten (Saunders)		
09/01	Hatlo, Jimmy			**189?**	
09/01	McDonald, Lucile Saunders	03/07	Stevens, Lucile V(ernon)	??/??	Kielty, Bernardine
		04/02	Taber, Gladys (Bagg)		
09/02	Archibald, Joseph S(topford)	04/06	Steinberg, Fannie	**1900**	
		04/11	Pope, Clifford Hillhouse	??/??	Barker, Albert W.
09/06	Hults, Dorothy Niebrugge	04/12	Leighton, Clare (Veronica Hope)	??/??	Barringer, Daniel Moreau, Jr.
09/12	Shahn, Ben(jamin)				
09/13	Browin, Frances Williams	04/19	Douglas, Emily (Taft)	??/??	Bowen, R(obert) Sydney
09/16	Rey, H(ans) A(ugusto)	04/23	Carr, Mary Jane	??/??	George, W(illiam) Lloyd
09/24	Behn, Harry	04/28	Frost, Lesley	??/??	Grumbine, E. Evalyn
09/26	Hatch, Alden	04/28	Wiesner, William	??/??	Hawkes, Hester
09/26	Waltrip, Rufus (Charles)	05/06	Guillaume, Jeanette G. (Flierl)	??/??	Hosford, Dorothy (Grant)

??/??	King, Marian	08/25	Crespi, Pachita	06/21	Chamberlain, Elinor
??/??	Marshall, Dean	08/25	Garbutt, Bernard	07/03	Seeger, Ruth Porter (Crawford)
??/??	Moderow, Gertrude	08/25	Wonsetler, John Charles	07/11	Culp, Louanna McNary
??/??	Nathan, Adele (Gutman)	09/03	Benson, Sally	07/13	Billings, Henry
??/??	O'Malley, Patricia	09/04	Gilmore, Iris	07/16	Cook, Howard Norton
??/??	Parr, A(dolph) H(enry)	09/06	Trell, Max	08/09	Rydberg, Ernest E(mil)
??/??	Person, William Thomas	09/09	Hilton, James	08/24	Becker, Beril
??/??	Plumb, Charles P.	09/10	Stern, Philip Van Doren	08/30	Gunther, John
??/??	Raymond, Margaret Thomsen	09/11	Icks, Robert J.	09/02	Eliot, Frances
??/??	Savage, Steele	09/14	Underhill, Alice Mertie (Waterman)	09/02	Floethe, Richard
??/??	Steiner, Charlotte	09/20	Denniston, Elinore	09/23	Eyre, Katherine Wigmore
??/??	Stirling, Nora B(romley)	09/24	Lacher, Gisella Loeffler	10/01	DeVeyrac, Robert
01/02	Peltier, Leslie C(opus)	10/02	Jordan, E(mil) L(eopold)	10/09	Simon, Henry W(illiam)
01/02	Rowland, Florence Wightman	10/07	Berkebile, Fred D(onovan)	10/10	Lane, Carl Daniel
01/09	Halliburton, Richard	10/24	Lissim, Simon	10/11	Parker, Kay Peterson
01/10	Matthews, Herbert L(ionel)	11/11	Taylor, David	10/19	Johnson, Walter Ryerson
01/19	Hungerford, Edward Buell	11/16	Barrett, William E(dmund)	10/23	Bentel, Pearl B(ucklen)
01/23	Mason, Miriam E(vangeline)	11/18	Alajalov, Constantin	10/24	Eichenberg, Fritz
02/01	Busoni, Rafaello	11/19	Black, Algernon David	11/01	Lent, Henry Bolles
02/04	Stinetorf, Louise (Allender)	11/20	Gould, Chester	11/07	Cook, Gladys Emerson
02/08	Kredel, Fritz	11/23	Trotter, Grace V(iolet)	11/11	Mason, F(rancis) van Wyck
02/11	Brett, Grace N(eff)	12/08	Holling, Lucille Webster	11/14	Crane, Alan (Horton)
02/12	Fenton, Carroll Lane	12/09	Terrell, John Upton	11/17	Boggs, Ralph Steele
02/16	Hackett, Albert	12/23	Soglow, Otto	11/21	Bischoff, Ilse Marthe
02/17	Blochman, Lawrence G(oldtree)	12/25	Angle, Paul M(cClelland)	11/22	Crane, Roy(ston Campbell)
02/22	LeSueur, Meridel	12/30	Barnhart, Clarence L(ewis)	11/22	Gill, Richard Cochran
02/24	Hoff, Carol			11/26	Gates, Doris
03/02	Bee, Clair (Francis)	**1901**		11/28	Havighurst, Walter (Edwin)
03/12	VanCoevering, Jan Adrian	??/??	Bailey, Bernadine Freeman	12/03	Lowitz, Sadyebeth (Heath)
03/14	Globe, Leah Ain	??/??	Engeman, John T.	12/05	Disney, Walt(er Elias)
03/20	Withers, Carl A.	??/??	Fleur, Anne (Elizabeth)	12/12	Becker, John (Leonard)
03/30	Robinson, C(harles) A(lexander), Jr.	??/??	Kristofferson, Eva M(argaret Stiegelmeyer)	12/16	Mead, Margaret
03/31	Stoddard, Hope	??/??	Kunhardt, Dorothy Meserve	12/19	LaFarge, Oliver (Hazard Perry)
04/21	Blair, Walter	??/??	Lowitz, Anson C.		
04/25	Wohlrabe, Raymond A(dolph)	??/??	McIntosh, Frank	**1902**	
04/27	Lantz, Walter	??/??	Oldrin, John	??/??	Brady, Lillian
05/03	Winwar, Frances	??/??	Reid, John Calvin	??/??	Dobias, Frank
05/05	Dorian, Edith M(cEwen)	??/??	Sandoz, Mari (Susette)	??/??	Harman, Fred
05/11	Wellman, Alice	01/06	Parke, Margaret Bittner	??/??	Hereford, Robert A.
05/13	Ralston, Alma (Smith Payne)	01/13	Thompson, Hildegard (Steerstedter)	??/??	Herrera, Velino
05/14	Borland, Harold Glen	01/15	Child, Charles Jesse	??/??	Jackson, C(aary) Paul
05/16	Thane, Elswyth	01/17	Hartman, Louis F(rancis)	??/??	Johnston, Ralph E.
06/13	Sharp, William	01/26	Reck, Alma Kehoe	??/??	McClintock, Theodore
06/16	Brooks, Maurice (Graham)	01/27	Bridges, William (Andrew)	??/??	McNeer, May Yonge
06/19	Hobson, Laura Z(ametkin)	01/30	Hiser, Iona Seibert	??/??	Randall, Blossom E.
06/25	Woodward, Landon Cleveland	02/02	Holisher, Desider	??/??	Turngren, Annette
07/05	Fabres, Oscar	02/02	Kerr, Jessica (Gordon)	01/08	Kane, Henry Bugbee
07/07	Falkner, Leonard	02/07	Botkin, B(enjamin) A(lbert)	01/10	Durant, John
07/10	Schrank, Joseph	02/19	Torrey, Helen	01/11	Cormack, Maribelle B.
07/18	Marshall, S(amuel) L(yman) A(twood)	02/23	Schisgall, Oscar	01/11	Foster, E(lizabeth) C(onnell)
07/20	Arnold, Oren	03/01	Friskey, Margaret Richards	01/26	Andrews, F(rank) Emerson
07/28	Cohen, Jene Barr	03/18	Jordan, Mildred	01/27	Graham, Lorenz (Bell)
08/02	Holling, Holling C(lancy)	03/27	Barks, Carl	02/01	Hughes, James Langston
08/03	Gergely, Tibor	04/09	Winterfeld, Henry	02/04	Lindbergh, Charles A(ugustus, Jr.)
08/06	Hillcourt, William	04/13	Starkey, Marion L(ena)	02/12	Self, Margaret Cabell
08/14	Bauer, Helen	04/14	Cox, William R(obert)	02/21	Headstrom, Birger Richard
08/15	Tworkov, Jack	05/11	Davis, Mary Octavia	02/22	Thomas, Benjamin Platt
08/23	Reynolds, Malvina	05/16	Comins, Ethel M(ae)	02/22	White, Anne (Wilson) Hitchcock
		05/17	D'Harnoncourt, Rene		
		05/24	Henderson, LeGrand		
		05/30	Skinner, Cornelia Otis		

02/27	Rubicam, Harry Cogswell, Jr.	10/13	Bontemps, Arna(ud Wendell)	05/25	Leonard, Jonathan N(orton)
02/27	Steinbeck, John (Ernst)	10/14	Seroff, Victor I(ilyitch)	05/26	Brennan, Joseph L(omas)
03/01	Smith, Ruth Leslie	10/23	Edwards, Margaret (Alexander)	05/30	Conklin, Gladys (Plemon)
03/04	Reeder, Russell P(otter), Jr.	10/25	Commager, Henry Steele	05/30	Cullen, Countee Porter
03/14	MacPeek, Walter G.	11/01	Shimin, Symeon	06/09	Davenport, Marcia (Gluck)
03/15	McCue, Lillian Bueno	11/07	Dodd, Ed(ward Benton)	06/14	Rich, Louise (Dickinson)
03/23	Dodge, Bertha S(anford)	11/09	Rendina, Laura (Jones) Cooper	06/22	Sturtzel, Jane Levington
03/31	Pohlmann, Lillian (Grenfell)	11/15	Christgau, Alice Erickson	06/28	Moore, Margaret R(umberger)
04/01	Felton, Harold W(illiam)	11/20	Foley, Anna Bernice Williams	07/14	Stone, Irving
04/07	Hutchens, Paul	12/10	Bergeron, Victor (Jules, Jr.)	07/15	Edmonds, Walter D(umaux)
04/11	Reynolds, Quentin James	12/10	Hofsinde, Robert	07/22	Simon, Howard
04/13	Henry, Marguerite (Breithaupt)	12/11	Balch, Glenn	07/24	Collier, Ethel
04/19	Latham, Jean Lee			07/24	Nelson, Cholmondeley M.
04/20	Riedman, Sarah R(egal)	**1903**		07/24	Viguers, Ruth Hill
04/22	Richardson, Robert S(hirley)	??/??	Ayer, Margaret	08/01	Horgan, Paul
04/25	Bethers, Ray	??/??	Brindze, Ruth	08/01	Joseph, Joseph M(aron)
04/26	Daniels, Jonathan	??/??	Cleveland, George	08/02	Borski, Lucia Merecka
04/28	Wood, Harrie	??/??	Cole, Lois Dwight	08/17	Chasins, Abram
04/29	Wees, Frances Shelley	??/??	Fox, Fred	08/23	Heal, Edith
05/01	Shotwell, Louisa R(ossiter)	??/??	Gilbert, Helen Earle	08/27	Bunce, William Harvey
05/13	Sotomayor, Antonio	??/??	Gilmore, Horace Herman	08/29	Eisenberg, Azriel
05/14	Chidsey, Donald Barr	??/??	Harman, Hugh	08/31	Sechrist, Elizabeth (Hough)
05/25	Mirsky, Reba Paeff	??/??	Hoke, Helen (L.)	09/03	Mirsky, Jeannette
06/04	Brockman, C(hristian) Frank	??/??	Lambo, Don(ald W.)	09/07	Landon, Margaret (Dorothea Mortenson)
06/10	Smith, Eunice Young	??/??	Larom, Henry V.	09/09	Whitney, Phyllis A(yame)
06/11	McFadden, Dorothy Loa (Mausolff)	??/??	Podendorf, Illa E.	09/10	DeMartelly, John Stockton
06/11	Wallace, May Nickerson	??/??	Rienow, Leona Train	09/21	Price, Olive (M.)
06/18	Foster, Elizabeth Vincent	??/??	Rose, Carl	09/22	DeLeeuw, Cateau (Wilhelmina)
06/21	Hanna, Paul R(obert)	??/??	Schucker, James (W.)	09/24	Benet, Sula
06/22	Beecroft, John William Richard	??/??	Smith, Irene	10/15	Bettmann, Otto Ludwig
06/27	Widdemer, Mabel Cleland	01/11	Paton, Alan (Stewart)	11/04	Chittenden, Elizabeth F.
06/29	Benedict, Lois Trimble	01/15	Pyne, Mable Mandeville	11/07	Jordan, Philip Dillon
07/09	Carse, Robert	01/19	Reynolds, Marjorie (Harris)	11/29	Regehr, Lydia
07/12	Montgomery, Elizabeth Rider	01/21	Keating, Lawrence A(lfred)	12/01	Kent, Sherman
07/13	Marek, George R(ichard)	01/22	Sutton, Margaret (Beebe)	12/10	Banning, Evelyn I.
07/16	Stevenson, Lionel	01/28	Rowe, Viola Carson	12/21	Harwood, Pearl Augusta (Bragdon)
07/18	West, Mary Jessamyn	02/01	Pundt, Helen Marie	12/21	Treat, Lawrence
07/20	Dodds, John W(endell)	02/08	McCormick, Wilfred	12/22	McPharlin, Paul
07/21	Musgrave, Florence	02/13	Colorado (Capella), Antonio Julio	12/22	Paget-Fredericks, Joseph E(dward) P(aget) Rous-Marten
07/22	DuJardin, Rosamond Neal	02/14	Teal, Val(entine M.)	12/25	Greenhaus, Thelma Nurenberg
07/22	Lauritzen, Jonreed	02/16	Simon, Martin P(aul William)	12/25	Rodman, Bella (Kashin)
07/24	Averill, Esther (Holden)	02/19	Slobodkin, Louis	12/25	Samstag, Nicholas
08/05	Alderman, Clifford Lindsey	02/20	Egypt, Ophelia Settle	12/30	Friermood, Elisabeth Hamilton
08/05	Bright, Robert	03/20	Brier, Howard M(axwell)	12/30	Mayer, Jane Rothschild
08/05	Leipold, L. Edmund	03/29	Calapai, Letterio	12/31	Sitomer, Harry
08/06	Howe, Gertrude Herrick	03/30	Smaridge, Norah (Antoinette)		
08/18	Credle, Ellis	04/08	Keith, Harold (Verne)	**1904**	
08/19	Nash, Frederic Ogden	04/09	Hawkins, Arthur	??/??	Aronin, Ben
08/27	Murphy, Robert (William)	04/10	Newberry, Clare Turlay	??/??	Blaisdell, Elinore
09/09	Mian, Mary (Lawrence Shipman)	04/12	Jones, Helen Hinckley	??/??	Brown, Helen (Evans)
09/11	Hodges, Carl G.	05/05	Sitomer, Mindel	??/??	Chrystie, Frances Nicholson
09/15	Samuels, Charles	05/11	Candell, Victor		
09/21	McEntee, Dorothy (Layng)	05/12	Berger, Josef	??/??	Cooke, Charles Harris
09/24	Coy, Harold	05/16	Dennis, Wesley	??/??	Covarrubias, Miguel
10/06	Gray, Elizabeth Janet	05/17	Stefferud, Alfred Daniel	??/??	DeArmand, Frances Ullmann
10/08	Cummings, Parke	05/19	Chiang, Yee		
		05/21	Wellman, Manly Wade		
		05/24	Austin, Oliver L(uther) Jr.		

??/??	Duff, Annis (James)	07/25	Buba, Joy Flinsch	??/??	Treat, Roger L.
??/??	Hayden, Gwendolen Lampshire	07/25	Hemphill, Martha Locke	??/??	Wirt, Mildred (Augustine)
??/??	Jones, Helen L(ouise)	07/30	Russ, Lavinia	01/14	Hahn, Emily
??/??	Kerr, Laura (Nowak)	08/01	Winterbotham, R(ussell) R(obert)	01/19	Slobodkin, Florence (Gersh)
??/??	Leonard, A. Byron	08/03	Simak, Clifford D(onald)	01/20	Welty, S(usan) F(ulton)
??/??	McKelvey, Gertrude Della	08/05	Hayes, John F.	01/23	Brandt, Catharine
??/??	McWebb, Elizabeth Upham	08/10	Dean, Graham M.	01/26	Cousins, Margaret
??/??	Williams, Lou(ise Bonino)	08/11	Woolley, Catherine	01/26	Trapp, Maria (Augusta) von
01/08	Choron, Jacques	08/14	Baird, Bil	01/30	Neyhart, Louise (Pauline) Albright
01/08	McCarty, Rega Kramer	08/15	Eunson, Dale	02/01	Lee, Doris (Emrick)
01/18	McNickle, William D'Arcy	08/16	Webber, Irma E(leanor Schmidt)	02/05	Potter, Robert Ducharme
01/21	Crawford, John E(dmund)	08/18	Fatio, Louise	02/06	Wohlberg, Meg
01/23	Quarles, Benjamin	08/21	Wechsler, Herman	02/11	Kalmenoff, Matthew
01/28	Nugent, Frances Roberts	08/27	Perkins, Al(bert Rogers)	02/25	Carter, Katharine J(ones)
02/02	Waltrip, Lela (Kingston)	08/28	Duvoisin, Roger (Antoine)	03/01	Anderson, John Lonzo
02/04	Kantor, MacKinlay	08/30	Priestley, Lee (Shore)	03/01	Bobbe, Dorothie (de Bear)
02/06	Wilkie, Katherine E(lliott)	09/01	Costello, David (Francis)	03/03	Vinton, Iris
02/11	Armer, Alberta (Roller)	09/02	Borton, Elizabeth	03/07	Bryson, Bernarda
02/15	Chase, Richard	09/06	Smith, Frances C(hristine)	03/10	Means, Elliott
02/22	Hurd, Peter	09/07	Colby, C(arroll) B(urleigh)	03/21	McGinley, Phyllis (Louise)
02/22	Locke, Lucie	09/11	Brustlein, Daniel	03/28	Perkins, Richard Marlin
02/23	Shirer, William L(awrence)	09/14	Brevannes, Maurice	03/29	Hawkins, Helena Ann Quail
02/26	McNamee, James	09/20	Ogle, Lucille (Edith)	04/01	Bock, Vera
02/28	Jupo, Frank J.	09/21	Key, Alexander (Hill)	04/07	Palazzo, Anthony D.
03/??	Russell, Solveig Paulson	10/06	Carter, Samuel III	04/13	Agle, Nan Hayden
03/01	Baker, Rachel (Mininberg)	10/11	Hopf, Alice (Martha) L(ightner)	04/14	Scoggin, Margaret C(lara)
03/02	Geisel, Theodor Seuss	10/18	Mason, George Frederick	04/15	Campbell, Camilla
03/10	Antolini, Margaret Fishback	10/21	Atwater, Montgomery Meigs	04/15	Nichols, Marie C.
03/16	Bourgeois, Florence	10/26	Osborn, Robert Chesley	04/24	Smits, Theodore R(ichard)
03/22	Lewiton, Mina	10/31	Stone, Helen	04/24	Warren, Robert Penn
03/25	Hays, H(offmann) R(eynolds)	10/31	Taylor, Sydney (Brenner)	04/25	Mason, Edwin A.
03/30	Wilkin, Eloise (Burns)	11/07	Verral, Charles Spain	05/02	Schemm, Mildred Walker
04/02	Pennington, Lillian Boyer	11/09	Kroll, Francis Lynde	05/05	Creekmore, Raymond (L.)
04/05	Thane, Lillian Adele	11/16	Fox, Dorothea M.	05/14	Dudley, Ruth H(ubbell)
04/23	Stein, Harve	11/17	Bernstein, Theodore M(enline)	05/16	Douglas, John Scott
04/25	Schreiber, Georges	11/24	Milotte, Alfred G(eorge)	05/24	Crawford, Thelmar Wyche
04/27	Landeck, Beatrice	12/11	Woolsey, Janette	05/31	Schneider, Herman
04/29	Day, A(rthur) Grove	12/12	Hutto, Nelson (Allen)	06/02	Moore, Janet Gaylord
04/30	Bryan, Joseph (III)	12/17	Lipkind, William	06/05	McDonald, Gerald D(oan)
04/30	Davis, Hubert J(ackson)	12/27	D'Aulaire, Ingri (Maartenson)	06/06	DeWitt, Cornelius Hugh
05/07	Farrington, S(elwyn) Kip, Jr.	12/29	Ballard, Lowell Clyne	06/09	Buell, Ellen Lewis
05/09	Newman, Daisy	12/31	Farr, Finis (King)	06/09	DeJong, David C(ornel)
05/09	Norman, Charles			06/09	Ducas, Dorothy
05/09	Wilson, Dorothy Clarke	**1905**		06/16	Wilson, Charles Morrow
05/12	Lamb, Beatrice Pitney	??/??	Brooks, Anne (Tedlock)	06/26	Ward, Lynd (Kendall)
05/15	Fadiman, Clifton (Paul)	??/??	Crosscup, Richard	06/28	Hilder, Rowland
05/26	Dow, Emily R.	??/??	Evers, Alf	06/29	Wolfe, Louis
06/03	Penney, Grace Jackson	??/??	Friedman, Frieda	07/01	Foster, Elizabeth
06/11	Watts, Franklin (Mowry)	??/??	Hilles, Helen (Train)	07/24	Haycraft, Howard
06/14	Carmer, Elizabeth Black	??/??	Malvern, Corinne	07/27	May, Robert Lewis
06/15	Forman, Harrison	??/??	McEntee, Howard Garrett	07/27	Wolff, Robert Jay
06/25	Lutzker, Edythe	??/??	Moore, Don W.	08/03	Frost, Frances
06/26	Malmberg, Carl	??/??	Moore, Ray (S.)	08/04	Luther, Frank
06/29	Honness, Elizabeth (Hoffman)	??/??	Newlon, Frank Clarke	08/15	Freeman, Ira M(aximilian)
06/30	Lattimore, Eleanor Frances	??/??	Nisenson, Samuel	08/17	Evans, Eva Knox
07/09	Chappell, Warren	??/??	Renick, Marion (Lewis)	08/20	Johnson, Siddie Joe
07/13	Nichols, Dale	??/??	Roberts, Catherine Christopher	08/23	Bushmiller, Ernie
07/14	Singer, Isaac (Bashevis)	??/??	Shannon, Monica	08/24	Brady, Esther Wood
07/23	Adams, Julia Davis	??/??	Siegel, William	09/01	Cameron, Edna M.
07/24	Morris, Richard Brandon	??/??	Tensen, Ruth Marjorie	09/05	Miller, Edward
				09/08	Wheelwright, Jere Hungerford, Jr.
				09/24	Abrahams, Robert D(avid)

09/25	Kohner, Frederick	03/27	Ulrich, Homer	10/30	Gode von Aesch, Alexander (Gottfried Friedrich)
09/29	St. Clair, Byrd Hooper	03/31	Mellor, William Bancroft		
10/06	Farquhar, Margaret C(utting)	04/01	Ford, Nancy K(effer)		
		04/03	Johnson, Avery F.	11/04	North, Sterling
10/06	Gadler, Steve J.	04/04	Rounds, Glen (Harold)	11/09	Charosh, Mannis
10/08	Levin, Meyer	04/11	Doane, Pelage	11/10	Franchere, Ruth
10/20	Dannay, Frederic	04/21	Dowling, Victor J.	11/16	Gridley, Marion E(leanor)
10/24	Offord, Lenore (Glen)	04/28	Troy, Hugh	11/26	Cleven, Kathryn Seward
10/30	Raftery, Gerald (Bransfield)	04/30	Hutchins, Ross E(lliott)	11/27	Purdy, Claire Lee
		05/??	Rey, Margret (Elizabeth Waldstein)	11/27	Scheffer, Victor B(lanchard)
11/05	Berrill, Jacquelyn (Batsel)				
11/05	Hogarth, Grace (Weston Allen)	05/03	Halsted, Anna Roosevelt	11/29	Strong, Charles Stanley
		05/04	Laugesen, Mary E(akin)	12/07	Chandler, Caroline A(ugusta)
11/16	Weinstock, Herbert	05/04	Neal, Harry Edward		
11/17	Marais, Josef	05/09	Estes, Eleanor (Ruth)	12/12	Evanoff, Vlad
11/24	Wicker, Ireene (Seaton)	05/15	MacGregor, Ellen	12/17	Slocum, Rosalie
12/04	Leaf, Wilbur Munro	05/20	Marks, Geoffrey	12/19	Arkin, David
12/06	Yates, Elizabeth	05/20	Watts, Mabel Pizzey	12/19	Papashvily, Helen (Waite)
12/09	Jordan, Hope (Dahle)	05/23	Weber, Walter Alois	12/25	Rosenberg, Dorothy
12/11	Wood, James Playsted	05/25	Mayer, Albert Ignatius, Jr.	12/26	Stapp, Arthur D(onald)
12/19	Hutchison, Paula A.			12/29	Jacobson, Morris K(arl)
12/19	Johnson, Dorothy M(arie)	05/25	Wooldridge, Rhoda	12/30	Jennings, John Edward, Jr.
12/23	Stevenson, Anna (M.)	05/26	Meier, Minta		
12/23	Swayne, Zoa Lourana (Shaw)	06/06	Black, Irma S(imonton)	12/31	Bianco, Pamela
		06/06	Donovan, Frank (Robert)		
12/28	Miller, Albert G(riffith)	06/09	Ripley, Elizabeth Blake	**1907**	
		06/09	Whitcomb, Jon	??/??	Bailey, John (Swartwout)
1906		06/10	Crosby, Alexander L.	??/??	Bell, Kensil
??/??	Coppock, Charles	06/21	Elting, Mary	??/??	Blumenthal, Gertrude
??/??	Greene, Carol	06/26	Pough, Frederick Harvey	??/??	Collins, Henry Hill
??/??	Hyndman, Robert (Utley)	07/11	Turner, Eloise Fain	??/??	Ellison, Lucile Watkins
??/??	Kaula, Edna Mason	07/16	Jonk, Clarence	??/??	Fitzgerald, John D(ennis)
??/??	Lindbergh, Anne Morrow (Spencer)	07/16	Still, James	??/??	Freeman, Mae (Blacker)
		07/25	Armour, Richard (Willard)	??/??	Gardner, Lillian Soskin
??/??	Lyman, Susan E(lizabeth)	07/28	Duvall, Evelyn Millis	??/??	Goldberg, Martha
??/??	McCoy, Iola Fuller	07/29	Kubinyi, Kalman	??/??	Johnson, Robert E.
??/??	McKown, Robin	08/05	Hegarty, Reginald Beaton	??/??	Kapp, Paul
??/??	Messick, Dale	08/14	Carley, V(an Ness) Royal	??/??	Mammen, Edward William
??/??	Morse, Dorothy B(ayley)	08/21	McClintock, Marshall	??/??	Niehuis, Charles C(arroll)
??/??	O'Reilly, John	09/01	Grayson, Marion (Forbourg)	??/??	Schwartz, Julius
??/??	Silliman, Leland			??/??	Warriner, John
??/??	Treichler, Jessie C(ambron)	09/03	Miner, Opal Irene Sevrey (Frazine)	??/??	Welch, D'Alte Aldridge
				??/??	Wyatt, Geraldine (Tolman)
??/??	Webb, Robert N.	09/04	Overholser, Wayne D.	01/07	Watson, Sara Ruth
01/04	Harmon, Margaret	09/08	Prescott, Orville	01/13	Freeman, Lydia
01/07	Clymer, Eleanor (Lowenton)	09/09	Fisher, Aileen (Lucia)	01/14	Alberts, Frances Jacobs
		09/12	Crayder, Dorothy	01/23	Austin, Elizabeth S(chling)
01/08	Faulkner, Nancy (Anne Irvin)	09/12	Saunders, Blanche		
		09/13	Parkinson, Ethelyn M(inerva)	01/25	Miller, Shane
01/17	Holloway, Teresa (Bragunier)			02/03	Carter, William Hodding
		09/16	Gay, Zhenya	02/03	Jauss, Anne Marie
01/29	Bratton, Karl H(enry)	09/25	Hamilton, Dorothy	02/03	Morey, Walt(er Nelson)
02/03	Young, Stanley (Preston)	09/25	Moore, Vardine (Russell)	02/06	Hymes, Lucia M(anley)
02/08	Adams, Adrienne	09/26	Poole, Gray (Johnson)	02/08	Conrad, Arthur S.
02/10	Oakley, Helen (McKelvey)	09/26	Tarry, Ellen	02/12	Jacobs, Leland Blair
		09/27	Crary, Margaret (Coleman)	02/16	Wilder, Alec
02/10	Varley, Dimitry V.			02/18	Bancroft, Griffing
02/16	Freeman, Eugene	10/01	Little, Lessie Jones	02/20	Cruickshank, Helen Gere
02/22	Pratt, John Lowell	10/02	Ley, Willy	02/22	Unwin, Nora S(picer)
02/25	Parks, Edd Winfield	10/03	Carlson, Natalie Savage	02/25	Chase, Mary (Coyle)
03/04	DeJong, Meindert	10/09	Holder, Glenn	02/26	Pavel, Frances
03/06	Nichols, Cecilia Fawn	10/13	Gross, Sarah Chokla	02/28	Caniff, Milton (Arthur)
03/11	Porter, Jean Macdonald	10/13	Samachson, Joseph	02/28	Graham, Clarence Reginald
03/17	Green, Mary Moore	10/17	Ames, Gerald		
03/20	Parker, Elinor (Milnor)	10/20	Leisk, David (Johnson)	03/03	Blanton, Martha Catherine
03/20	Tinkle, Julien Lon	10/25	Martin, Frances M(cEntee)	03/05	Baity, Elizabeth Chesley
03/24	MacDonald, Dwight	10/28	Goldin, Augusta	03/15	Domjan, Joseph

03/19	Salvadori, Mario (George)	11/06	DeCamp, Catherine C(rook)	02/14	Lantz, Paul
03/21	Bell, Raymond Martin	11/10	Lawrence, Mildred (Elwood)	02/16	O'Neill, Mary L(e Duc)
03/28	Foster, G(eorge) Allen			02/18	O'Neill, Hester (Adams)
04/12	Gramatky, Hardie	11/11	Barr, George	02/19	Lee, Mildred
04/15	Anderson, LaVere (Francis Shoenfelt)	11/11	DuBois, Shirley Graham	02/20	Machetanz, Frederick
		11/13	Apsler, Alfred	02/26	Groth, John (August)
04/18	Lampman, Evelyn (Sibley)	11/14	Steig, William	02/28	Brown, Dee (Alexander)
04/21	Alexander, David	11/14	Wilber, Donald N(ewton)	02/29	VonHagen, Victor Wolfgang
04/27	Holding, James (Clark Carlisle, Jr.)	11/15	Vermes, Jean C(ampbell Pattison)		
				03/14	Rudolph, Marguerita
05/03	Smith, Datus C(lifford), Jr.	11/18	Holzman, Robert Stuart	03/18	Lavine, Sigmund A(rnold)
05/05	Brown, Lloyd Arnold	11/19	Schaefer, Jack (Warner)	03/25	Barker, Will
05/07	Barnes, Frank Eric Wollencott	11/21	Harris, Christie (Lucy Irwin)	03/26	MacDonald, Betty (Heskett Bard)
05/17	Joseph, Alexander	11/23	Erickson, Phoebe	03/30	O'Kelley, Mattie Lou
05/18	Hunt, Irene	11/23	Grant, Eva (Cohen)	03/30	Walck, Henry Z(eigler)
05/22	Dietz, Lew	11/24	Barker, Melvern (J.)	04/01	Scherf, Margaret (Louise)
05/22	McSwigan, Marie	11/24	Ullman, James Ramsey	04/05	Carey, Ernestine (Moller) Gilbreth
05/24	Gag, Flavia	11/26	Ewen, David		
05/27	Carson, Rachel (Louise)	11/26	Marcus, Rebecca B(rian)	04/05	Macknight, Ninon
05/29	Meyer, Gerard Previn	11/27	DeCamp, L(yon) Sprague	04/06	Bryant, Bernice (Morgan)
06/02	Wood, Edgar A(llardyce)	12/04	Laklan, Carli (Laughlin Aiello)	04/07	Howard, Robert West
06/08	Pace, Mildred Mastin			04/08	Whitehead, Don(ald) F.
06/16	Fermi, Laura (Capon)	12/04	Lyons, Dorothy (Marawee)	04/09	Krumgold, Joseph (Quincy)
06/21	Renken, Aleda	12/17	Hamerstrom, Frances		
06/22	Love, Katherine (Isabel)	12/19	Crouse, William H(arry)	04/11	Emrich, Duncan (Black Macdonald)
07/01	Grimm, William C(arey)	12/19	Smith, H(arry) Allen		
07/03	Hornos, Axel	12/22	Rocker, Fermin	04/12	Scott, Robert Lee
07/04	Snyder, Louis Leo	12/22	Swayne, Sam(uel F.)	04/17	Liang, Yen
07/07	Heinlein, Robert A(nson)	12/25	Sullivan, Mary W(ilson)	04/18	Alcock, Gudrun
07/12	Sterling, Philip			05/01	Dobkin, Alexander
07/13	Weller, George (Anthony)	**1908**		05/06	Hale, Nancy
07/21	Folsom, Franklin (Brewster)	??/??	Banks, Laura Stockton Voorhees	05/08	Graff, S. Stewart
				05/09	Prideaux, Tom
07/22	Fenderson, Lewis H.	??/??	Eby, Lois Christine	05/12	Dietz, Elisabeth H.
07/26	Bennett, Rainey	??/??	Emery, Russell Guy	05/16	Wendt, Lloyd
07/27	Willcox, Isobel	??/??	Harvey, Edith	05/16	Yeakley, Marjory Hall
07/29	Riddle, Maxwell	??/??	Janes, Edward C.	05/17	Landshoff, Ursula
08/06	Sypher, Lucy Johnston	??/??	Jones, Lloid	05/28	Brown, Eleanor Frances
08/08	Stuart, Hilton Jesse	??/??	Jorgensen, Mary Venn	06/05	Baldwin, Gordon C.
08/11	Wittanen, Etolin	??/??	Keith, Joseph Joel	06/05	Lindquist, Willis
08/19	Brown, Robert Joseph	??/??	Linquist, Willis	06/07	Eyerly, Jeanette Hyde
08/24	Mizner, Elizabeth Howard	??/??	Maltese, Michael	06/08	Rugh, Belle Dorman
08/31	Christensen, Gardell Dano	??/??	Morgan, Allen	06/08	Toner, Raymond John
09/01	Emery, Anne (Eleanor McGuigan)	??/??	Parker, Fan(ia M. Pockrose)	06/09	Gilbertson, Mildred Geiger
09/01	Stewart, Elizabeth Laing	??/??	Phleger, Marjorie Temple	06/13	Adelson, Leone
09/05	Blough, Glenn O(rlando)	??/??	Pierce, Mary Cunningham (Fitzgerald)	06/20	Colver, Anne
09/10	Hilton, Ralph			06/20	Melbo, Irving Robert
09/13	Appel, Benjamin	??/??	Wormser, Richard Edward	06/26	Ames, Evelyn
09/16	Rice, Inez	01/01	Jackson, Jesse	06/29	Gordon, Cyrus Herzl
09/17	Dowden, Anne Ophelia (Todd)	01/04	Steedman, Marguerite Couturier	07/07	Arnow, Harriette (Louisa) Simpson
09/27	Witheridge, Elizabeth P(lumb)	01/08	Perceval, Don	07/07	Holland, Marion
		01/12	Hurd, Clement	07/12	Martignoni, Margaret E.
10/04	Molloy, Anne (Stearns) Baker	01/13	Flexner, James Thomas	07/16	Horwich, Frances R(appaport)
		01/14	Lipinsky de Orlov, Lino S(igismondo)		
10/07	MacInnes, Helen			07/22	Brown, Marion Marsh
10/08	Beatty, Hetty Burlingame	01/17	Reed, Philip G.	07/29	Galt, Thomas Franklin, Jr.
10/08	Heiderstadt, Dorothy	01/18	Bronowski, Jacob	07/30	Suhl, Yuri
10/10	Shuttlesworth, Dorothy (Edwards)	02/03	Heaps, Willard (Allison)	08/02	Benasutti, Marion
		02/05	Gervasi, Frank Henry	08/06	Jacobs, Helen Hull
10/11	Dodson, Kenneth M(acKenzie)	02/07	Gipson, Fred(erick Benjamin)	08/11	Freeman, Don
				08/13	Allen, T(erril) D(iener)
10/14	Lewis, Claudia (Louise)	02/09	VanStockum, Hilda (Gerarda)	08/15	Zaidenberg, Arthur
10/19	Barish, Matthew			08/16	Maxwell, William
				08/21	Jaquith, Priscilla

08/24	Moore, John Travers	01/31	Huntington, Harriet E(lizabeth)	08/04	Faralla, Dana
08/24	Rydberg, Lou(isa Hampton)	02/06	Blassingame, Wyatt (Rainey)	08/06	Farber, Norma
08/31	Dolson, Hildegarde			08/16	Chute, Marchette (Gaylord)
08/31	Johnson, Harriett	02/07	Davis, Lavinia (Riker)	08/22	Darrow, Whitney, Jr.
08/31	Saroyan, William	02/12	Barnett, Lincoln (Kinnear)	08/25	Zimmermann, Arnold E(rnst Alfred)
08/31	Weil, Ann Yezner				
09/01	Lloyd, Mary Norris	02/15	Heins, Paul	08/28	Rathjen, Carl H(enry)
09/07	Boesen, Victor	02/19	Rodman, Selden	08/29	Kerman, Gertrude Lerner
09/07	Newcomb, Covelle	02/21	Ware, Leon (Vernon)	08/30	Burton, Virginia Lee
09/16	Constant, Alberta Wilson	02/22	Spache, George Daniel	09/04	Pauli, Hertha (Ernestine)
		02/23	Fleischmann, Glen Harvey	09/10	Waltner, Willard H.
09/18	Courlander, Harold	02/24	Derleth, August (William)	09/12	Hopkins, Joseph G(erard) E(dward)
09/21	Corcos, Lucille	03/02	Bischoff, Julia Bristol		
09/21	Iwamatsu, Jun Atsushi	03/03	Doob, Leonard W(illiam)	09/13	Oakes, Vanya
09/22	Slobodkina, Esphyr	03/05	Norton, Frank R(owland) B(rowning)	09/14	Cabral, O(lga) M(arie)
09/29	Avery, Kay			09/17	Enright, Elizabeth (Wright)
10/01	McGiffin, Lewis Lee Shaffer	03/10	McLean, Kathryn (Anderson)	09/18	Jane, Mary Childs
				09/19	Brodin, Pierre Eugene
10/03	Morgan, Lenore	03/17	Moore, Lilian (Moore Reavin)	09/19	Hubbell, Harriet Weed
10/10	Cosgrave, John O'Hara II			09/26	Jenkins, Marie M(agdalen)
10/16	Coolidge, Olivia E(nsor)	03/20	Mangione, Jerre	09/28	Caplin, Alfred Gerald
10/16	Vance, Eleanor Graham	03/30	Voight, Virginia Frances	10/02	Smith, Lawrence Beall
10/17	Cathon, Laura E(lizabeth)	04/04	Reichert, Edwin C(lark)	10/06	Busch, Phyllis S.
10/17	Raskin, Edith Lefkowitz	04/13	Ulam, S(tanislaw) M(arcin)	10/07	Burns, William A(loysius)
10/18	Kohler, Julilly H(ouse)	04/17	Snow, Dorothea J(ohnston)	10/09	Fax, Elton Clay
10/19	McQueen, Mildred Hark			10/28	Ross, Alexander
10/20	St. John, Wylly Folk	04/20	Stern, Marie Simchow	10/29	Wyler, Rose
10/28	Orlob, Helen Seaburg	04/20	Tallant, Robert	10/30	Miller, Donald G(eorge)
10/29	Phillips, Irv(ing W.)	04/30	Morrison, Velma Ford	11/01	Feder, Robert Arthur
11/03	Fujikawa, Gyo	05/01	Falstein, Louis	11/08	Lloyd, Norman
11/13	Strachan, Margaret Pitcairn	05/04	Campbell, R(osemae) W(ells)	11/17	Molarsky, Osmond
				11/18	Miner, Lewis S.
11/16	Chandler, Edna Walker	05/08	Chernoff, Goldie Taub	11/22	Epstein, Samuel
11/21	Politi, Leo	05/10	Hirshberg, Al(bert Simon)	11/22	Hays, Wilma Pitchford
11/21	Speare, Elizabeth George	05/13	Hauser, Margaret L(ouise)	11/24	Childs, John Farnsworth
11/22	Hoffecker, John Savin	05/13	Smith, Bradford	11/25	Eastman, P(hilip) D(ey)
11/22	Sheehan, Ethna	05/14	Mannheim, Grete (Salomon)	11/28	Bleeker, Sonia
12/04	Bradbury, Bianca			12/02	Lash, Joseph P.
12/04	Burroughs, Jean Mitchell	05/17	Baerg, Harry J(ohn)	12/03	Brigham, Grace A.
12/14	Smith, Pauline C(oggeshall)	05/18	Gidal, Tim N(ahum)	12/05	Lonergan, Pauline Joy (MacLean)
		05/22	Tolford, Joshua		
12/15	Chastain, Madye Lee	05/31	Corrigan, Helen Adeline	12/12	Moores, Richard (Arnold)
12/21	DeMiskey, Julian	05/31	Rankin, Robert H(arry)	12/15	Hanser, Richard (Frederick)
12/25	Sussman, Irving	06/03	Newman, Robert (Howard)		
12/30	Davis, D(elbert) Dwight	06/08	Knight, Max	12/16	Kenny, Ellsworth Newcomb
		06/14	DeGrazia, Ted		
1909		06/14	McCall, Virginia Nielsen	12/18	Johnson, William Weber
??/??	Beim, Lorraine Levy	06/20	Holmgren, Virginia C(unningham)	12/26	Clark, Van D(eusen)
??/??	Crist, Eda (Szecskay)				
??/??	Crist, Richard Harrison	06/20	White, Robb	**1910**	
??/??	Dudley, Martha Ward	06/24	Cavanna, Betty	??/??	Beim, Jerrold
??/??	Foster, Marian Curtis	06/26	Lomask, Milton (Nachman)	??/??	Garelick, May
??/??	Haufrecht, Herbert	06/27	Strait, Treva Adams	??/??	Gurko, Miriam (Berwitz)
??/??	Leaf, Margaret P.	06/28	Shaw, Arnold	??/??	Levine, Joseph
??/??	Meeks, Esther K. (MacBain)	06/30	Scott, Sally Fisher	??/??	Lorentowicz, Irena
		07/02	D'Attilio, Anthony	??/??	Reese, John Henry
??/??	Moore, Lamont	07/05	VanRiper, Guernsey, Jr.	??/??	Rice, Charles D(uane)
??/??	Otto, Margaret Glover	07/10	Tompkins, Walker Allison	??/??	Rockwell, Harlow
??/??	Stephens, Henrietta Henkle	07/12	Zim, Herbert S(pencer)	??/??	Sutton, Felix
		07/17	Castor, Henry	??/??	Welsh, Mary Flynn
??/??	Sze, Mai-Mai	07/20	Fox, William Wellington	??/??	Wilson, Christopher B.
01/05	Bloch, Lucienne	07/21	Marokvia, Artur	??/??	Yarbrough, Ira
01/15	Siegmeister, Elie	07/26	Colby, Jean Poindexter	01/08	Marriott, Alice Lee
01/16	Walden, Amelia Elizabeth	07/29	Baker, Samm S(inclair)	01/12	Haber, Louis
01/20	Friendlich, Richard J.	07/31	Phleger, Fred B.	01/15	MacLeod, Beatrice (Beach)
		08/03	Clark, Walter Van Tilburg		

01/16	Shapp, Martha (Glauber)	07/31	Brasier, Virginia	01/23	Eifert, Virginia (Louise) S(nider)
01/16	Villiard, Paul	08/08	Kidwell, Carl	01/23	Graves, Charles Parlin
01/20	Hoover, Helen (Drusilla Blackburn)	08/11	Poole, Lynn D.	01/28	Bell, Gertrude (Wood)
01/23	Arbuckle, Dorothy Fry	08/12	Richter, Mischa	01/30	Sanderson, Ivan T(erence)
01/27	Austin, Phil	08/17	Kane, Robert W(illiam)	02/04	Peare, Catherine Owens
01/27	Reinfeld, Fred	08/24	Fife, Dale (Odile)	02/05	Dubkin, Lois (Knudson)
01/29	LeBar, Mary E(velyn)	08/25	Hoffmann, Margaret Jones	02/08	Bishop, Elizabeth
02/01	Nordstrom, Ursula (Litchfield)	08/31	Baker, Charlotte	02/25	Fletcher, Helen Jill
02/03	Sankey, Alice (Ann-Susan)	09/02	McCormick, Alma Heflin	03/08	Cook, Fred J(ames)
02/04	Ellison, Virginia Howell	09/07	Stahl, Ben(jamin Albert)	03/15	Ogburn, Charlton, Jr.
02/04	Lavender, David (Sievert)	09/11	Summers, James L(evingston)	03/15	Roper, Laura Wood
02/13	Edey, Maitland A(rmstrong)	09/12	Milne, Lorus J(ohnson)	03/17	Gilbreth, Frank B(unker), Jr.
02/21	Saunders, Keith	09/14	Hurd, Edith Thacher	03/19	Colonius, Lillian
02/27	Sloane, Eric	09/22	Holmes, Marjorie (Rose)	03/19	Frankenberg, Robert (Clinton)
02/27	Wendelin, Rudolph	09/23	VanDuyn, Janet	03/21	Braymer, Marjorie (Elizabeth)
03/07	Erlich, Lillian (Feldman)	09/25	Kugelmass, Joseph Alvin	03/23	Vinson, Kathryn
03/09	Gault, William Campbell	09/28	Dean, Nell Marr	03/24	Barbera, Joseph Roland
03/09	Leekley, Thomas B(riggs)	10/01	Webb, Jean Francis (III)	03/24	Douty, Esther M(orris)
03/28	Crowell, Pers	10/02	Hall, Adele	03/31	Kingman, Dong (Moy Shu)
03/29	Wells, Helen (Frances Weinstock)	10/02	McAllister, Mariana Kennedy	04/01	Baker, Augusta (Braxston)
03/30	Lewellen, John Bryan	10/05	Ainsworth, Catherine Harris	04/02	Young, Lois Horton
04/04	Kirn, Ann Minette	10/08	Brown, Rosalie (Gertrude) Moore	04/03	Bird, E(lzy) J(ay)
04/05	Beeler, Nelson F(rederick)	10/08	Conkling, Hilda	04/05	McCallum, Phyllis
04/05	Brown, William Louis	10/11	Berkowitz, Freda Pastor	04/08	Arntson, Herbert E(dward)
04/12	Showers, Paul C.	10/14	Place, Marian T(empleton)	04/11	Malo, John
04/16	Fontenot, Mary Alice	10/17	Wier, Ester (Alberti)	04/12	Corcoran, Barbara
04/21	Helfman, Henry	10/20	Latham, Frank B(rown)	04/16	Roueche, Berton
05/03	Goldstein, Philip	10/23	Espenshade, Edward Bowman, Jr.	04/17	Elisofon, Eliot
05/05	Dowdell, Dorothy (Florence) Karns	10/28	Newell, Edythe W.	04/24	Ness, Evaline (Michelow)
05/05	Lionni, Leo(nard)	11/02	Brennan, Joseph Gerard	04/27	Crowe, Bettina Lum
05/08	Svenson, Andrew E.	11/02	McKenzie, Dorothy Clayton	04/27	Wheeler, Sessions S(amuel)
05/12	Peterson, Helen Stone	11/15	Epstein, Beryl (M. Williams)	04/29	Lappin, Peter
05/13	Angier, Bradford	12/01	Bloch, Marie Halun	05/04	Lansing, Elisabeth Carleton (Hubbard)
05/17	Clark, Electa	12/06	Kjelgaard, James Arthur	05/08	Aymar, Brandt
05/23	Brown, Margaret Wise	12/06	Malcolmson, Anne (Burnett)	05/19	Hopkins, Marjorie
05/23	Reiner, William B(uck)	12/09	Holl, Adelaide (Hinkle)	05/19	Shapiro, Irwin
05/27	Miers, Earl Schenck	12/11	Espy, Willard R(ichardson)	05/21	Haviland, Virginia
05/30	Hall, Elvajean	12/13	Jones, Richard C.	05/21	Kaufman, Joe
06/01	Laughlin, Florence (Young)	12/25	Leiber, Fritz	05/24	Hutchins, Carleen Maley
06/03	Buck, Margaret Waring	12/25	Moon, Sheila (Elizabeth)	06/04	Lignell, Lois
06/04	Frankel, Edward	12/26	White, Florence M(eiman)	06/06	Aardema, Verna (Norberg)
06/05	Motz, Lloyd	12/28	Larrick, Nancy G(ray)	06/12	Kirkpatrick, Oliver Austin
06/06	Klemm, Edward G., Jr.	12/29	Blair, Helen	06/25	Hurley, Leslie J(ohn)
06/07	Washburn, Henry Bradford, Jr.			07/07	Menotti, Gian Carlo
06/10	Barlow, Genevieve	**1911**		07/08	Ball, John (Dudley), Jr.
06/22	Weil, Lisl	??/??	Abrashkin, Raymond	07/10	Coggins, Jack Banham
06/25	Jones, Elizabeth Orton	??/??	Chandler, Thomas	07/17	Gelinas, Paul J.
06/29	Cauman, Samuel	??/??	Eager, Edward (McMaken)	07/18	Funk, Thompson
07/03	Dobler, Lavinia G.	??/??	Gorham, Charles Orson	07/25	Krauss, Ruth (Ida)
07/03	Gard, Robert Edward	??/??	Jennison, Keith Warren	07/26	Hodges, Margaret Moore
07/07	Sweeney, James B(artholomew)	??/??	Keller, Frances Ruth	07/28	Boardman, Fon Wyman, Jr.
07/13	Serwer, Blanche L.	??/??	Mannix, Daniel P(ratt)	07/28	Kalina, Sigmund
07/14	Hanna, William	??/??	Marks, Margaret L.	08/01	Helfman, Elizabeth S(eaver)
07/21	Carlson, Bernice Wells	??/??	McNair, Kate (Mallory)	08/10	Elkin, Benjamin
07/22	Heyneman, Anne	??/??	Palmer, Robin	08/10	Singer, Kurt D(eutsch)
07/27	Wallower, Lucille	??/??	Thompson, Vivian L(aubach)	08/11	Low, Joseph
07/28	Decker, Duane (Walter)	01/07	Baker, Laura Nelson	08/22	DeMejo, Oscar
07/29	Greenleaf, Peter	01/16	Craig, Margaret Maze	08/26	Binder, Otto O(scar)
				09/01	Flynn, James Joseph

09/05	McCall, Edith S(ansum)	03/23	Cameron, Eleanor Frances (Butler)	10/13	Price, Harold
09/11	Amerman, Lockhart	03/26	Kenworthy, Leonard S.	10/17	VanderVeer, Judy
09/15	Terry, Luther L(eonidas)	03/26	Scott, John	10/19	Wassersug, Joseph D(avid)
09/19	Abel, Raymond	04/01	Iannone, Jeanne (Koppel)	10/21	Neilson, Frances Fullerton (Jones)
09/20	Mawicke, Tran	04/16	Williams, Garth (Montgomery)		
09/22	Sunderlin, Sylvia	04/18	Parker, Lois M(ary)	10/23	Page, Lou Williams
09/27	Mordinoff, Nicolas	04/26	Kimball, Dean	10/24	Johnson, Edgar (Raymond)
10/01	Knebel, Fletcher	04/28	Zarchy, Harry		
10/04	Waltrip, Mildred	04/29	Borden, Charles A.	10/27	Goldfrank, Helen Colodny
10/10	DeJong, Dola	05/03	Sarton, Eleanor May	11/02	Burleson, Elizabeth
10/10	Johnson, Elizabeth	05/04	Goodenow, Girard	11/03	Paradis, Adrian Alexis
10/11	Willard, Mildred Wilds	05/05	Dolbier, Maurice (Wyman)	11/08	Hawkinson, John (Samuel)
10/17	Coleman, Pauline (Hodgkinson)	05/05	Weingast, David E(lliott)	11/09	Bailey-Jones, Beryl
		05/07	Bond, Gladys Baker	11/09	Thompson, Kay
10/21	Blair, Mary Robinson	05/09	Ross, Z(ola) H(elen) Girdey)	11/10	Bishop, Curtis (Kent)
10/21	Leslie, Robert Franklin			11/10	Mincieli, Rose Laura
10/25	Heck, Bessie Holland	05/12	Cahn, William	11/12	Marino, Dorothy Bronson
10/29	DiValentin, Maria (Messuri)	05/17	Isham, Charlotte H(ickox)	11/16	Tebbel, John (William)
		05/24	Andriola, Alfred J.	11/30	Parks, Gordon (Alexander Buchanan)
11/25	Spilhaus, Athelstan	05/30	Goodman, Elizabeth B.		
12/06	Haycraft, Molly Costain	05/30	Selsam, Millicent E(llis)	11/30	Waltner, Elma
12/08	Platt, Kin	06/05	Herron, Edward A(lbert)	12/02	Bradley, Virginia
12/16	Rarick, Carrie	06/05	Sweney, Frederic	12/07	Brown, Vinson
12/25	Langley, Noel	06/06	Lubell, Cecil	12/08	Byrd, Elizabeth
12/27	Clarke, Mary Stetson	06/09	Blair, Ruth Van Ness	12/16	Biemiller, Carl Ludwig
12/30	Curry, Peggy Simson	06/09	Clapp, Patricia	12/16	Hyndman, Jane (Lee) Andrews
		06/11	Lavin, Mary		
1912		06/24	Logsdon, Richard Henry	12/22	Kenny, Herbert A(ndrew)
??/??	Allen, Henry Wilson	06/25	Nespojohn, Katherine V(eronica)	12/24	Bennett, Jay
??/??	Cary, Barbara Knapp			12/24	Hook, Frances
??/??	Hatch, Mary Cottam	06/27	Rich, Josephine (Bouchard)		
??/??	Jones, Juanita Nuttall			**1913**	
??/??	Lewis, Alfred E.	06/29	Toland, John (Willard)	??/??	Alsop, Reese Fell
??/??	Matulay, Lazlo	07/01	Stern, Madeleine B(ettina)	??/??	Bacon, Paul
??/??	Rink, Paul	07/07	Erdoes, Richard	??/??	Cooke, Sarah (Palfrey) Fabyan
??/??	Schmidt, James Norman	07/09	Bang, Betsy (Garrett)		
??/??	VonHagen, Christine Sheilds	07/10	Melcher, Daniel	??/??	Evans, Edna Hoffman
		07/12	Fisher, Calvin C(argill)	??/??	Grodin, Adams John
??/??	Winter, William (John)	07/13	Allen, Leroy	??/??	Kempner, Mary Jean
??/??	Yerkow, Charles	07/24	Gordon, Mildred (Nixon)	??/??	Lowther, George F.
01/06	Manfred, Frederick F(eikema)	07/28	Bandel, Betty	??/??	Marko, Katherine D(olores)
		07/29	Little, Mary E.	??/??	Rietveld, Jane Klatt
01/06	Talbert, Ansel Edward McLaurine	07/30	Stair, Gobin (John)	??/??	Sentman, George Armor
		08/06	Prieto, Mariana B(eeching)	??/??	Weldon, Martin
01/07	Addams, Charles (Samuel)	08/11	Brooks, Polly Schoyer	??/??	Wells, Robert L.
01/08	Wells, Peter	08/28	Grand, Samuel	01/03	Butler, Hal
01/09	Harris, Lorle K(empe)	08/31	Kinert, Reed Charles	01/03	Chute, B(eatrice) J(oy)
01/25	Funke, Lewis	08/31	Robertson, Dorothy Lewis	01/07	Liebers, Arthur
01/28	Lens, Sidney	09/01	Mars, W(itold) T(adeusz, Jr.)	01/14	Roberts, John G(aither)
02/01	Ogan, George F.			01/18	Kaye, Danny
02/04	Lewis, Mildred D.	09/02	Bearden, Romare (Howard)	01/19	Foley, Daniel Joseph
02/04	Weaver, John D(owning)			01/23	Woodson, John Waddie, Jr.
02/08	Elbert, Virginia Fowler	09/04	Hoff, Syd(ney)	01/29	Keeler, Ronald F(ranklin)
02/11	Heuman, William	09/08	West, Walter Richard	01/29	Schneider, Nina (Zimet)
02/12	Erickson, Sabra R(ollins)	09/12	Thomson, Arline K.	02/04	Stevenson, Janet (Marshall)
02/17	Norton, Alice Mary	09/13	Arnold, Elliott		
02/17	Sorensen, Virginia (Eggersten)	09/13	Schwartz, Elizabeth Reeder	02/07	Adamson, George Worsley
				02/11	Kelleam, Joseph E(veridge)
02/21	Ellis, Mel(vin Richard)	09/21	Jones, Charles M(artin)		
02/21	Godwin, Edward Fell	09/21	Ruth, Rod	02/12	Atwood, Ann (Margaret)
02/29	Milgrom, Harry	09/23	Vosburgh, Leonard (W.)	02/14	Allen, Mel
03/04	Marzani, Carl (Aldo)	09/24	Taylor, Robert Lewis	02/14	Keen, Martin L.
03/09	Darby, Ray(mond) K.	09/29	Harkins, Philip	02/19	Pashko, Stanley
03/12	Gordon, Gordon	09/30	Sherburne, Zoa (Morin)	02/21	Oriolo, Joseph
03/17	Kinney, Jean Stout	10/04	Krautter, Elisa (Bialk)	02/22	Grant, Evva H.
03/23	Braun, Wernher von	10/12	Petry, Ann (Lane)	02/26	Young, Miriam

02/27	Duchacek, Ivo D(uka)	08/06	Wechterr, Nell Wise	01/09	Bulla, Clyde Robert
02/27	Thomson, Peter	08/11	Mark, Pauline (Dahlin)	01/09	Marks, Mickey Klar
03/05	Hayes, William D(imitt)	08/19	Hull, Eleanor (Means)	01/11	Andrist, Ralph K.
03/06	Rugoff, Milton	08/24	Wilkinson, John Burke	01/15	Dunne, Mary Collins
03/07	Clark, Margaret Goff	08/25	Kelly, Walt(er Crawford)	01/15	Shirreffs, Gordon D(onald)
03/13	Floethe, Louise Lee	08/26	Broadhead, Helen Cross	01/21	Delear, Frank J.
03/13	Icenhower, Joseph Bryan	09/03	Beckett, Sheila	01/25	Flora, James (Royer)
03/17	Orbaan, Albert F.	09/08	Condit, Martha Olson	02/01	Ishmael, Woodi
03/20	Plotz, Helen (Ratnoff)	09/15	Boegehold, Betty (Doyle)	02/03	Wunsch, Josephine (McLean)
04/06	Ruchlis, Hy(man)	09/17	Glendinning, Sara W(ilson)	02/04	Blair, Anne Denton
04/08	Scott, John M(artin)	09/24	Rawls, Woodrow Wilson	02/06	Bloom, Freddy
04/13	Morris, William	09/28	Stearns, Monroe (Mather)	02/08	Ross, Frank (Xavier), Jr.
04/21	Maves, Paul B(enjamin)	10/01	Temkin, Sara Anne (Schlossberg)	02/09	Sussman, Cornelia (Silver)
04/23	Brown, Sevellon III			02/17	Campbell, Virginia
04/27	Adler, Robert Irving	10/02	Vaughan, Anne	02/18	Mohn, Viola Kohl
05/04	Frame, Paul	10/04	Janson, H(orst) W(oldemar)	02/20	MacKellar, William
05/04	Pearl, Richard M(axwell)			02/25	Bonham, Frank
05/05	Perrine, Mary (Bush)	10/05	LeBlanc, L(ee)	02/25	Perry, John
05/07	Schwartz, Anne Powers	10/05	Zion, Eugene	03/01	Brussel-Smith, Bernard
05/11	Irwin, Constance Frick	10/06	Alexander, Anna B(arbara Cooke)	03/03	Drury, Roger W(olcott)
05/14	Kisinger, Grace Gelvin (Maze)			03/03	Fuller, Edmund (Maybank)
		10/07	Janeway, Elizabeth (Hall)	03/04	Victor, Edward
05/14	Terry, Walter	10/11	Simon, Joseph H.	03/06	Vernon, Elda Louise A(nderson)
05/15	Haber, Heinz	10/16	Hawes, Judy		
05/17	Guck, Dorothy	10/17	Bason, Lillian	03/08	Phelps, Ethel Johnston
05/17	Vaughan-Jackson, Genevieve	10/17	McGaw, Jessie Brewer	03/08	Price, Willadene (Anton)
		10/22	Lazarus, Keo Felker	03/11	Rosenthal, Harold
05/21	Shulman, Irving	11/13	Crane, Irving (Donald)	03/12	Rowsome, Frank (Howard), Jr.
05/23	Holland, Janice	11/15	Dwiggins, Don		
05/24	Gorsline, Douglas (Warner)	11/21	Burt, Nathaniel	03/13	Barth, Edna (Smith)
		11/21	Unkelbach, Kurt	03/27	Hall, Rosalys Haskell
05/27	Fox, Charles Philip	11/22	Berlitz, Charles L. (Frambach)	03/27	Morrah, David Wardlaw, Jr.
05/28	Rice, Elizabeth				
05/30	Berg, Jean Horton	11/23	Sterling, Dorothy	03/30	Kimball, Yeffe
05/31	Tamarin, Alfred	11/26	Schuon, Karl	04/03	Kempton, Jean Welch
06/03	Doremus, Robert	11/27	Caldwell, John C(ope)	04/04	Crockett, Lucy Herndon
06/06	Ingraham, Leonard W(illiam)	11/29	Hirsch, S. Carl	04/13	Kahn, Joan
		11/30	McGee, Dorothy Horton	04/15	Swift, Helen Miller
06/13	Martin, David Stone	12/01	Antoncich, Betty (Kennedy)	04/20	Devereux, Frederick L(eonard), Jr.
06/15	VanWormer, Joseph Edward				
		12/03	Zurhorst, Charles (Stewart, Jr.)	04/26	Ault, Phillip H(alliday)
06/19	Freed, Alvyn M.			05/01	Howes, Barbara
06/19	Hammontree, Marie (Gertrude)	12/08	Micale, Albert	05/02	Jarrell, Mary von Schrader
		12/09	Brondfield, Jerome	05/06	Jarrell, Randall
06/25	Holme, Bryan	12/09	Panesis, Nicholas	05/07	Lovejoy, Bahija Fattouhi
06/28	Killilea, Marie (Lyons)	12/12	Swanson, Arlene Collyer	05/08	Clampett, Robert
07/08	MacAgy, Douglas (Guernsey)	12/13	Smith, Marion Hagens	05/09	Robertson, Keith (Carlton)
		12/13	Wulff, Edgun Valdemar	05/11	Severn, William Irving
07/13	Goodenow, Earle	12/15	Rukeyser, Muriel	05/17	Welch, Martha McKeen
07/14	Harrison, C. William	12/16	Soule, Gardner (Bosworth)	05/21	Hubley, John
07/15	Myers, Hortense (Powner)	12/19	Siebel, Fritz (Frederick)	05/22	Werstein, Irving
07/16	Arno, Enrico	12/23	Rau, Margaret	05/29	Cromie, Alice Hamilton
07/16	Bjorklund, Lorence F.	12/24	Hamilton, Charles	05/29	Wissmann, Ruth H(elen Leslie)
07/18	Skelton, Red	12/28	Gaddis, Vincent H.		
07/20	Balet, Jan (Bernard)	12/31	Suba, Suzanne	05/31	Williams, Jay
07/21	Hartley, William B(rown)			06/01	Cushman, Jerome
07/24	Davis, Burke	**1914**		06/02	Galdone, Paul
07/24	Nef, Evelyn Stefansson	??/??	Barrett, Ethel	06/02	Schwartz, Charles W(alsh)
07/25	Sutton, Jeff(erson H.)	??/??	Christopher, Milbourne	06/05	Vogel, Ilse-Margret
07/27	Corbett, Scott	??/??	Eberstadt, Charles F.	06/13	Sanborn, Duane
07/27	Plagemann, Bentz	??/??	Johnston, Johanna (Voigt)	06/14	Lubell, Winifred (Milius)
07/30	Cain, Arthur H(omer)	??/??	Pinchot, David	06/14	Todd, Ruthven
08/04	Hayden, Robert E(arl)	??/??	Santesson, Hans Stefan	06/17	Hersey, John (Richard)
08/05	Riesenberg, Felix, Jr.	??/??	Wisner, William L.	06/18	Case, Elinor Rutt
08/06	Castellanos, Jane Mollie (Robinson)	01/04	Gurko, Leo	06/19	Crichlow, Ernest T.
		01/07	Brooks, Anita	06/20	McDonnell, Lois Eddy

06/23 Stover, Marjorie Filley
06/27 Coombs, Charles I(ra)
06/30 Houser, Allan C.
06/30 Phelan, Mary Kay (Harris)
07/15 Schloat, G. Warren, Jr.
07/17 Woodburn, John Henry
07/21 Luger, Harriett M(andelay)
08/01 Ormes, Zelda J.
08/02 Zimmerman, Naoma
08/03 Worline, Bonnie Bess
08/04 Robinson, Millian Oller
08/11 Shane, Harold Gray
08/12 Beckman, Delores
08/15 Rand, Paul
08/16 DeRegniers, Beatrice Schenk
08/20 McCaslin, Nellie
08/22 Samachson, Dorothy (Mirkin)
09/03 Glazer, Tom
09/11 Kelling, Furn L.
09/14 Armstrong, William H(oward)
09/14 Castellon, Federico
09/15 Bacon, Elizabeth
09/15 McCloskey, John Robert
09/18 Luce, Willard (Ray)
09/19 Westervelt, Virginia (Veeder)
09/21 Cohn, Angelo
09/25 Osborne, Leone Neal
09/27 Coburn, John Bowen
09/27 Marshall, Sarah Catherine
10/01 Boorstin, Daniel J(oseph)
10/01 Wollheim, Donald A(llen)
10/10 Hargis, John Edwin
10/12 Bonnell, Dorothy Haworth
10/19 Davis, Clive E(dward)
10/21 Gardner, Martin
11/?? Palmer, Bernard
11/06 Gerson, Noel B(ertram)
11/06 Kogan, Herman
11/11 Fast, Howard (Melvin)
11/14 Kelly, Martha Rose
11/17 Daugherty, Charles Michael
11/19 Irvin, Fred
11/20 Goodwin, Harold Leland
11/25 Hanna, Geneva R(egula)
11/29 Lowenstein, Dyno
12/03 Luce, Celia (Geneva Larsen)
12/08 Hoehling, Mary (Duprey)
12/10 Burgwyn, Mebane H(oloman)
12/23 Dilson, Jesse
12/28 Esherick, Joseph

1915

??/?? Berry, Jane Cobb
??/?? Chapin, Alene Olsen Dalton
??/?? Conger, Marion
??/?? Craig, M. Jean
??/?? Hall, William Norman
??/?? Lengyel, Cornel Adam

??/?? Reynolds, Barbara Leonard
??/?? Rowand, Phyllis
??/?? Scott, Jack Denton
??/?? Stanek, Muriel (Novella)
01/01 Hartley, Ellen (Raphael)
01/09 Potter, Marian
01/10 Austin, Mary C(arrington)
01/11 Heinz, W(ilfred) C(harles)
01/12 Allen, Lee
01/13 English, James W(ilson)
01/13 Patten, Lewis Byford
01/18 Milne, Margarey (Joan Greene)
01/19 Grider, Dorothy
01/25 Deiss, Joseph Jay
01/26 Keyes, Fenton
01/27 Archer, Jules
01/27 Hnizdovsky, Jacques
01/29 Gillette, Henry Sampson
01/29 Peet, William Bartlett
02/05 Sanderlin, George
02/08 Evarts, Hal G. (,Jr.)
02/17 Gibbs, Alonzo (Lawrence)
02/21 Russell, Helen Ross
02/23 Weingarten, Violet (Brown)
03/02 Peeples, Edwin A(ugustus, Jr.)
03/07 Stillman, Myra (Stephens)
03/08 Fetz, Ingrid
03/09 Partridge, Benjamin W(aring), Jr.
03/10 O'Connor, Richard
03/11 Newell, Homer Edward, Jr.
03/13 Cary, Louis F(avreau)
03/19 Maule, Hamilton Bee
03/26 Hill, Helen M(orey)
03/28 Posten, Margaret L(ois)
04/08 Freund, Rudolf
04/09 Wibberley, Leonard (Patrick O'Connor)
04/15 Ashley, Robert P(aul) Jr.
04/16 Barnwell, D. Robinson
04/16 Smith, Robert Paul
04/20 Adler, Ruth
04/23 Arnstein, Helen S(olomon)
04/25 Deming, Richard
04/29 Worcester, Donald Emmet
05/06 Jones, Evan
05/08 Meltzer, Milton
05/10 Dickens, Monica (Enid)
05/12 Brown, Joe David
05/14 Keating, Leo Bernard
05/15 Pedersen, Elsa (Kienitz)
05/18 Coates, Ruth Allison
05/23 Butterworth, Oliver
05/24 Dean, Anabel
05/25 Barnouw, Victor
05/29 Rogers, Grenville Cedric Harry
05/30 Feague, Mildred H.
05/31 Medearis, Mary
06/02 del Rey, Lester
06/05 Branley, Franklyn M(ansfield)
06/11 Hein, Lucille Eleanor
06/18 Puner, Helen W(alker)

06/23 Fitz-Randolph, Jane (Currens)
06/26 Farley, Walter (Lorimer)
06/26 Petie, Haris
06/26 Schmidt, Elizabeth
06/26 Zolotow, Charlotte S(hapiro)
07/01 Stafford, Jean
07/04 Harris, Aurand
07/04 Michie, Allan Andrew
07/11 Belting, Natalia Maree
07/11 Watson, Jane Werner
07/28 Jones, Adrienne
07/29 Woodrich, Mary Neville
07/30 Johnston, Dorothy Grunbock
08/04 Ahnstrom, D(oris) N.
08/04 Viertel, Janet
08/05 MacKinnon Groomer, Vera
08/06 Panetta, George
08/12 Wallace, John A(dam)
08/13 Fuller, Lois Hamilton
08/15 Turkle, Brinton (Cassady)
08/22 McNamara, Margaret (Craig)
08/28 Derman, Sarah Audrey
08/28 Tudor, Tasha
08/31 Hay, John
09/01 Smucker, Barbara (Claassen)
09/02 Edelman, Lily (Judith)
09/06 Hill, Margaret (Ohler)
09/11 Nevins, Albert J.
09/14 Speicher, Helen Ross (Smith)
09/17 Sutherland, Zena B(ailey)
09/18 Osborne, Chester G.
09/20 Taves, Isabella
10/03 Davidson, Jessica
10/07 Scherman, Katharine
10/08 Booth, Ernest Sheldon
10/08 Irwin, Ann(abelle Bowen)
10/12 Terzian, James P.
10/15 Solonevich, George
10/23 Ross, Wilda (S.)
10/28 MacPherson, Thomas George
11/13 Benchley, Nathaniel (Goddard)
11/16 Fritz, Jean (Guttery)
11/19 Vogt, Esther Loewen
11/23 Simont, Marc
11/25 Criner, Beatrice (Hall)
11/29 Schonberg, Harold C(harles)
12/09 McGraw, Eloise Jarvis
12/11 Hine, Al
12/15 Kinney, C. Cle(land)
12/19 Lozier, Herbert
12/25 Pantell, Dora (Fuchs)
12/25 Rosenberg, Ethel (Clifford)
12/27 Rand, Ted
12/31 Brown, Elizabeth M(yers)
12/31 Carmichael, Joel

1916

??/?? Burgoyne, Leon E.

??/??	Darwin, Leonard
??/??	Draper, Nancy
??/??	Geary, Clifford N.
??/??	Gendel, Evelyn W.
??/??	Hess, Lilo
??/??	Janson, Dora Jane (Heineberg)
??/??	Leokum, Arkady
??/??	Martin, William Ivan
??/??	McCann, Gerald
??/??	Seton, Anya
01/03	Bate, Norman (Arthur)
01/04	Duff, Margaret K.
01/11	Stokes, Olivia Pearl
01/20	Scott, John Anthony
01/21	Antonacci, Robert Joseph
01/21	Boyle, Ann (Peters)
01/22	McGraw, William Corbin
01/25	Wilson, Dagmar
01/27	Kranzler, George G(ershon)
01/27	Warren, Elizabeth Avery
01/31	Bliven, Bruce, Jr.
02/07	Sherman, Theresa
02/16	Cooper, Elizabeth Keyser
02/20	Mahon, Julia C(unha)
02/20	Tripp, Paul
03/05	Sohl, Frederic J(ohn)
03/08	Swain, Su Zan (Noguchi)
03/11	Keats, Ezra Jack
03/12	Dorson, Richard M(ercer)
03/12	McLanathan, Richard Barton Kennedy
03/22	Yurchenco, Henrietta (Weiss)
03/23	Dias, Earl Joseph
04/01	Litchfield, Ada B(assett)
04/03	Caen, Herb (Eugene)
04/06	Clagett, John (Henry)
04/12	Cleary, Beverly (Bunn)
04/14	Tannenbaum, Beulah (Goldstein)
04/16	Nearing, Penny
04/17	George, John Lothar
04/18	Dickson, Naida
04/20	Snyder, Jerome
04/22	Dillard, Polly (Hargis)
04/22	Menuhin, Yehudi
04/26	Darling, Louis, Jr.
04/26	Earle, Eyvind
04/30	Maves, Mary Carolyn
05/02	Chafetz, Henry
05/03	Dupuy, T(revor) N(evitt)
05/09	DuBois, William (Sherman) Pene
05/11	Fink, William B(ertrand)
05/11	Mandelkorn, Eugenia Miller
05/14	Bailey, Jane H(orton)
05/14	Ranney, Agnes V.
05/24	DeWit, Dorothy (May Knowles)
06/02	Sanderlin, Owenita (Harrah)
06/03	Starbird, Kaye
06/05	Rosen, Sidney
06/06	Evernden, Margery
06/09	Hightower, Florence (Cole)
06/16	Brandt, Sue R(eading)
06/22	Hutchinson, William M.
06/24	Ciardi, John (Anthony)
06/24	Edwards, Cecile (Pepin)
06/29	McCahill, William P.
07/01	Barss, William
07/01	Ravielli, Anthony
07/10	Provensen, Martin (Elias)
07/19	Aitken, Dorothy (Lockwood)
07/19	Merriam, Eve
07/21	Henderson, Nancy Wallace
07/23	Hovell, Lucy A. (Peterson)
08/01	Leavitt, Jerome E(dward)
08/05	Cooke, Donald Ewin
08/12	Hayman, LeRoy
08/14	Borland, Kathryn Kilby
08/16	Felsen, Henry Gregor
08/23	Jefferds, Vincent Harris
09/04	Comfort, Barbara
09/04	Klein, Leonore (Glotzer)
09/10	McClung, Robert Marshall
09/17	Kelly, George Anthony
09/26	Richmond, Julius B(enjamin)
09/30	Tresselt, Alvin (R.)
10/04	Caroselli, Remus F(rancis)
10/04	Cunningham, Julia W(oolfolk)
10/17	Partch, Virgil Franklin II
10/26	Warner, Edythe Records
11/03	Jahsmann, Allan Hart
11/06	Burgess, Mary Wyche
11/06	Young, Robert W(illiam)
11/12	Beyer, Audrey White
11/18	Tucker, Ernest Edward
11/20	McGrath, Thomas
11/26	House, Charles Albert
11/28	Tregaskis, Richard (William)
12/01	Stoutenburg, Adrien (Pearl)
12/11	Moyers, William
12/13	Freeman, Lucy (Greenbaum)
12/13	Huntsberry, William E(mery)
12/13	Weisgard, Leonard (Joseph)
12/15	Seamands, Ruth (Childers)
12/16	Burack, Sylvia K.
12/18	Greene, Carla
12/20	Cheney, Cora
12/28	Kellogg, Jean (Defrees)
12/31	Fuller, Catherine L(euthold)

1917

??/??	Begay, Harrison
??/??	Bevans, Margaret (Van Doren)
??/??	Davis, Ossie
??/??	Fletcher, Richard E.
??/??	Kerner, Ben
??/??	Miller, Natalie
??/??	Ovington, Ray(mond W.)
??/??	Pierce, Philip Nason
??/??	Tanous, Helen Nicol
01/04	McCoy, J(oseph) J(erome)
01/09	Sheldon, Walt(er J.)
01/12	Zaslavsky, Claudia
01/15	Denzel, Justin F(rancis)
01/20	Singer, Julia
01/21	Nailor, Gerald A.
01/22	Lamb, Elizabeth Searle
01/25	Gillelan, George Howard
01/26	Whitney, Thomas P(orter)
01/28	Gottlieb, William P(aul)
02/01	Madlee, Dorothy (Haynes)
02/08	Bendick, Robert L(ouis)
02/09	Archer, Marion Fuller
02/10	Crout, George C(lement)
02/15	Edmonds, I(vy) G(ordon)
02/16	Gerler, William R(obert)
02/18	Hyde, Margaret Oldroyd
02/19	McCullers, Lula Carson
02/21	Helweg, Hans H.
02/25	Raymond, James Crossley
03/04	Clarke, Clorinda
03/13	Heady, Eleanor B(utler)
03/14	Rosenthal, M(acha) L(ouis)
03/16	Eisner, Will(iam Erwin)
03/21	Hinton, Sam
03/22	Savitt, Sam
04/01	Block, Irvin
04/02	Bacon, Martha Sherman
04/05	Bloch, Robert
04/06	Earle, Vana
04/08	Geis, Darlene (Stern)
04/11	Westheimer, David
04/11	Witham, Phillip Ross
04/15	Carlsen, G(eorge) Robert
04/18	Garret, Maxwell R.
04/23	Smith, E(dric) Brooks
05/01	Pope, Elizabeth Marie
05/08	Taylor, Kenneth N(athaniel)
05/10	Watson, Aldren A(uld)
05/11	Carpenter, John Allan
05/20	Fon Eisen, Anthony T.
05/20	Lawson, Don(ald Elmer)
05/20	Ogilvie, Elisabeth May
05/25	Froman, Robert (Winslow)
05/26	Singer, Jane Sherrod
05/29	Kennedy, John Fitzgerald
05/29	Lefler, Irene (Whitney)
06/02	Paul, Aileen (Phillips)
06/07	Brooks, Gwendolyn
06/07	Cooke, David Coxe
06/17	Beers, Dorothy Sands
06/27	Campion, Nardi Reeder
06/27	Winchester, James H(ugh)
06/29	Flory, Jane Trescott
07/05	Sutton, Eugenia Geneva (Hansen)
07/07	Fenton, Edward
07/10	Herbert, Don
07/12	Mercer, Charles (Edward)
07/21	Winston, Richard

08/06	Cooney, Barbara		01/11	Conly, Robert Leslie	09/10	Schultz, Pearle Henriksen
08/10	Tomes, Margot (Ladd)		01/11	Tompert, Ann	09/10	Sweet, Oscar Cowan
08/11	Browne, Richard		01/15	Sparks, Beatrice Mathews	09/16	Koob, Theodora (Johanna Foth)
08/14	Snow, Donald Clifford		01/16	Preston, Lillian Elvira	09/22	Gringhuis, Richard H.
08/15	Darling, Lois (MacIntyre)		01/18	Memling, Carl	09/26	Cagle, Malcolm W(infield)
08/16	Christopher, Matt(hew) F.		01/20	Kupferberg, Herbert	10/02	Foss, William O(tto)
08/17	Carleton, Barbee Oliver		01/25	Foster, Laura Louise (James)	10/03	Cone, Molly (Lamken)
09/06	Modell, Frank B.		01/29	Fleischman, Seymour	10/04	Curley, Daniel
09/07	Lawrence, Jacob		02/04	Boyd, Waldo T.	10/05	Ludden, Allen (Ellsworth)
09/09	Robbins, Frank		02/08	Mooney, Elizabeth C(omstock)	10/07	Spar, Jerome
09/11	Todd, Barbara K(eith)		02/15	Zallinger, Jean (Day)	10/15	Cavin, Ruth (Brodie)
09/12	Bearman, Jane (Ruth)		02/18	Fijan, Carol	10/23	Barry, James P(otvin)
09/13	Kendall, Carol (Seeger)		02/20	Pizer, Vernon	10/23	Rice, Edward E.
09/19	Hill, Ralph Nading		02/21	Carlsen, Ruth C(hristoffer)	10/27	Brown, Myra Berry
09/23	Scott, Henry Joseph		02/23	Oechsli, Kelly	10/29	Levin, Marcia Obrasky
09/26	Rico, Don(ato)		02/24	Palovic, Clara Lora	11/03	Feller, Robert William Andrew
10/04	Leister, Mary		02/24	Wyckoff, James (M.)	11/08	Gugliotta, Bobette
10/08	Lord, Walter		02/25	Meyer, Kathleen Allan	11/10	Mulcahy, Lucille Burnett
10/10	Glendinning, Richard		03/22	Devlin, Harry	11/10	Nesbitt, Esta
10/12	Sheldon, Aure		03/22	Johnson, Eric W(arner)	11/11	Reit, Seymour
10/17	Seigel, Kalman		03/23	Sandoz, Edouard	11/14	Raible, Alton (Robert)
10/18	Randall, Florence Engel		03/31	Krush, Beth	11/22	Lawrence, James D(uncan)
10/21	Scheer, George F(abian)		04/04	Pallas, Norvin	11/23	Lindeburg, Franklin A(lfred)
10/21	VanDoren, Margaret		04/06	Chittum, Ida (Hoover)	11/23	Weir, La Vada
10/24	Myers, Arthur		04/08	Swarthout, Glendon (Fred)	11/24	Sandburg, Helga
10/27	Morrison, Lillian		04/18	Stilley, Frank	11/28	McNulty, Faith
10/29	Walworth, Nancy Zinsser		04/19	Smith, William A(rthur)	11/29	L'Engle, Madeleine
10/30	Philbrook, Clem(ent E.)		04/20	Beach, Edward L(atimer)	12/07	Marokvia, Mireille (Journet)
10/31	Boesch, Mark J(oseph)		04/21	Wilson, Forrest	12/08	Severn, Sue
11/01	Burroughs, Margaret Taylor G.		04/22	Smith, William Jay	12/09	Beatty, Jerome, Jr.
11/01	Henderson, Zenna (Chlarson)		04/27	Devlin, Dorothy Wende	12/09	Heinemann, George Alfred
11/01	Loeb, Robert H., Jr.		05/18	Krush, Joe	12/12	Burdick, Eugene (Leonard)
11/04	Weihs, Erika		05/31	Miller, Madge	12/12	McNeely, Jeannette
11/05	Konkle, Janet Everest		06/02	Houlehen, Robert J.	12/15	Karlin, Eugene
11/09	Bradford, Ann (Liddell)		06/02	Rosenburg, John M.	12/22	Jacobs, Flora Gill
11/09	Peterson, Betty Ferguson		06/02	Windham, Kathryn T(ucker)	12/23	Brown, Fern G.
11/09	Versace, Marie Teresa		06/05	Brooks, Charlotte K.	12/23	Yeo, Wilma (Lethem)
11/10	Farrar, Susan Clement		06/06	Barnes, Catherine J.	12/31	Wayne, Kyra Petrovskaya
11/11	Reynolds, Dallas McCord		06/06	Buckley, Helen E(lizabeth)		
11/12	Ipcar, Dahlov Zorach		06/13	Bamman, Henry A.	**1919**	
11/13	Spilka, Arnold		06/13	Spencer, Ann	??/??	Chaffee, Allen
11/24	McDonnell, Virginia (Bleecker)		06/14	Morton, Miriam (Bidner)	??/??	Forrester, Frank H.
12/04	Hodge, Jane Aiken		07/05	McFall, Christie	??/??	Ginsburg, Mirra
12/08	Steinberg, Alfred		07/07	Frisch, Rose E.	??/??	Hipshman, May
12/09	Allen, Samuel (Washington)		07/10	Docktor, Irv	??/??	Meeker, Oden
12/14	Blumberg, Rhoda		07/12	Cummings, Betty Sue	??/??	Waldman, Frank
12/16	Wosmek, Frances		07/13	Brown, Marcia (Joan)	??/??	West, Emily G(ovan)
12/17	Landau, Jacob		07/16	DeLage, Ida	01/06	Angell, Madeline
12/17	Sherwan, Earl		07/16	Mohan, Beverly (Moffet)	01/06	Cleaver, Vera (Allen)
12/22	Steele, William O(wen)		07/17	Hunt, George Pinney	01/06	Foster, F. Blanche
12/29	Robbins, Ruth		07/20	Wiley, Karla H(ummel)	01/08	Swarthout, Kathryn (Blair Vaughn)
			07/21	Johnson, Charlotte Buel	01/14	Lund, Doris (Herold)
1918			07/22	Myers, Elisabeth P(erkins)	01/18	Longman, Harold S.
??/??	Ball, Robert		07/25	Eggenberger, David	01/20	Cooper, Lester (Irving)
??/??	Davidson, William		07/31	Plate, Robert	02/01	Abodaher, David J. (Naiph)
??/??	Gulick, Peggy		08/06	Ilsley, Velma (Elizabeth)		
??/??	Howard, Vernon (Linwood)		08/06	Nelson, Cordner (Bruce)	02/01	Carswell, Evelyn M(edicus)
??/??	Johnson, Maud Battle		08/06	Wilson, Charles Banks		
??/??	Kohl, Marguerite		08/09	Doss, Helen (Grigsby)	02/01	Schiller, Andrew
??/??	Simon, Ruth Corabel (Shimer)		08/09	Lietz, Gerald S(ylvane)	02/04	D'Amato, Alex
01/04	Searight, Mary W(illiams)		08/12	Bartenbach, Jean	02/04	Soule, Jean Conder
01/10	Jones, Hortense P.		08/14	Provensen, Alice		
			08/16	Pascal, David		
			08/17	Cross, Wilbur Lucius III		

02/18	Kahl, Virginia (Caroline)	11/01	Shearer, Ted	03/18	Candy, William Robert
02/19	McClary, Jane Stevenson	11/02	Ames, Mildred	03/24	Cleaver, William Joseph
02/25	Bendick, Jeanne	11/04	Liebman, Oscar	03/24	Stolz, Mary (Slattery)
02/27	Heide, Florence Parry	11/17	Fox, Mary Virginia	03/28	Betz, Betty
02/27	Loken, Newton (Clayton)	11/20	Cole, William (Rossa)	04/02	Milton, Hilary (Herbert)
03/01	Matthews, William Henry III	11/23	Hitte, Kathryn	04/04	Brenner, Fred
03/05	Boles, Paul Darcy	11/26	Pohl, Frederik	04/08	Chew, Ruth
03/06	Young, Jan(et Randall)	12/01	Presberg, Miriam Goldstein	04/14	Scheele, William Earl
03/14	Shulman, Max	12/03	Hunter, Edith Fisher	04/17	Valens, Evans G., Jr.
03/30	Klein, David	12/03	Redding, Robert Hull	04/19	Gould, Lilian
04/04	Nolan, Paul T(homas)	12/14	Jackson, Shirley	04/23	Copeland, Helen
04/07	Gregg, Walter H(arold)	12/19	Freedman, Benedict	04/24	Edsall, Marian S(tickney)
04/09	Shelton, William Roy	12/23	Gill, Derek L(ewis) T(heodore)	04/26	Fribourg, Marjorie G.
04/10	Stoiko, Michael	12/28	Neville, Emily Cheney	04/26	Froman, Elizabeth Hull
04/12	Laskowski, Jerzy	12/29	Kublin, Hyman	04/26	Walsh, William B(ertalan)
04/17	Anderson, Ruth I(rene)			04/30	Hooker, Ruth
04/17	Levai, Blaise	**1920**		05/08	Dareff, Hal
04/28	Bates, Barbara S(nedeker)	??/??	French, Marion Flood	05/08	Wong, Jeanyee
04/28	Frasconi, Antonio	??/??	Hornblow, Leonora (Schinasi)	05/21	Trowbridge, Leslie W(alter)
05/03	Seeger, Pete(r)	??/??	Huff, Roderick Remmele	05/22	Carpenter, Patricia (Healy Evans)
05/10	Brown, Palmer	??/??	Kuhn, Doris (Young)	05/25	Alexander, Martha
05/11	Daniels, Guy	??/??	Longstreth, Joseph	05/28	Feaser, Daniel David
05/15	Atkin, Flora B(lumenthal)	??/??	Ray, Ralph	05/30	Hunt, Lawrence J.
05/15	Gekiere, Madeleine	??/??	Reid, Bill	06/02	Pugh, Ellen T(iffany)
05/16	Halacy, D(aniel) S(tephen, Jr.)	??/??	Ritts, Paul	06/11	Putnam, Peter B(rock)
05/16	Lobsenz, Norman M(itchell)	??/??	Scott, Bill	06/12	Berg, David
05/21	Park, Thomas Choonbai	??/??	Weaver, Robert (Glenn)	06/14	Erhard, Walter
05/25	Gould, Jean R(osalind)	01/??	Friedman, Estelle (Ehrenwald)	06/15	Bixby, William (Courtney)
05/28	Swenson, May	01/02	Asimov, Isaac	06/15	Hamblin, Dora Jane
05/30	Coit, Margaret Louise	01/05	Slicer, Margaret O.	06/15	Kohn, Bernice (Herstein)
06/03	Gregori, Leon	01/12	Smith, George Harmon	06/16	Holland, Isabelle
06/05	Brindel, June (Rachuy)	01/13	Hamalian, Leo	06/20	Bare, Arnold Edwin
06/05	Scarry, Richard (McClure)	01/15	Resnick, Seymour	06/27	Benedict, Rex (Arthur)
06/10	Gessner, Lynne	01/16	Maynard, Olga	07/04	Freedman, Nancy
06/10	Goodwin, Harold	01/20	Moss, Don(ald)	07/04	Garraty, John A.
06/17	Meyers, Robert W.	01/22	Hillert, Margaret	07/04	Molloy, Paul
06/24	Crone, Ruth	01/24	Cable, Mary	07/05	Perlmutter, O(scar) William
06/26	Lasker, Joseph Leon	01/29	Hunt, Kari	07/05	Schealer, John M(ilton)
06/28	Graboff, Abner	01/29	Krantz, Hazel (Newman)	07/07	Rood, Ronald (N.)
06/29	Kepes, Juliet A(ppleby)	02/01	Haggerty, James J(oseph)	07/16	Elam, Richard M(ace, Jr.)
07/02	George, Jean Craighead	02/01	Harnan, Terry	07/16	Vasiliu, Mircea
07/06	Temple, Herbert	02/04	Johnson, B(urdetta) F(aye)	07/18	Smith, Norman F.
07/13	Asinof, Eliot	02/04	Millender, Dharathula (Hood)	07/30	Stein, M(eyer) L(ewis)
07/13	White, Dori	02/04	Sackson, Sid	07/30	Weiss, Adelle
07/19	Garrison, Webb B(lack)	02/05	Rachlis, Eugene (Jacob)	08/02	Carson, J(ohn) Franklin
08/06	Lader, Lawrence	02/07	Brand, Oscar	08/04	Franklin, Harold
08/28	Embry, Margaret (Jacob)	02/08	Wolters, Richard A.	08/06	Gray, Genevieve S.
08/31	King, Robin	02/11	Sanger, Marjory Bartlett	08/10	Hicks, Clifford B.
09/06	Behnke, Frances L. (Berry)	02/17	Trevor, Elleston	08/15	Soderlind, Arthur E(dwin)
09/10	Fitzgerald, Edward Earl	02/20	Hunt, Morton	08/17	Cornell, Jean Gay
09/12	Faber, Harold	03/03	Bileck, Marvin	08/22	Bradbury, Ray (Douglas)
09/12	Hill, Robert W(hite)	03/04	Martin, Ralph G.	08/25	Laux, Dorothy
09/14	Turlington, Bayly	03/07	Pritchett, Elaine H(illyer)	08/27	Sparks, Mary W.
09/27	Percy, Charles Harting	03/08	Miller, Edna (Anita)	09/02	Fishler, Mary (Shiverick)
09/28	Abbott, Robert Tucker	03/08	Olschewski, Alfred (Erich)	09/08	Calvert, James
09/29	Fern, Eugene A.	03/10	Kent, John Wellington	09/09	Brokamp, Marilyn
10/01	Rogers, Jean	03/11	Pucci, Albert John	09/09	Stevens, Mary E.
10/04	Hallin, Emily Watson	03/14	Ketcham, Henry King	09/12	Dank, Milton
10/06	Kingman, Mary Lee	03/16	Fleischman, Albert Sid(ney)	09/12	McCrea, James (Craig, Jr.)
10/20	Szasz, Suzanne Shorr	03/17	Panowski, Eileen Thompson	09/13	Minarik, Else Holmelund
10/21	Holland, John L(ewis)			09/19	Gorelick, Molly C.
10/23	Kikukawa, Cecily H(arder)			09/21	Lerner, Aaron B(unsen)
10/24	Holman, Felice			10/01	Stewart, John (William)
				10/05	DeLaurentis, Louise Budde

10/08	DeClements, Barthe	03/08	Whitney, David C(harles)	08/09	West, Betty
10/08	Herbert, Frank (Patrick)	03/09	Vogt, Marie Bollinger	08/14	Dahlstedt, Marden (Armstrong)
10/11	McFarland, Kenton D(ean)	03/11	Barrer-Russell, Gertrude		
10/12	Childress, Alice	03/13	Jaffee, Al(lan)	08/15	Clement, Clarles
10/23	Montana, Bob	03/15	Daly, Maureen (McGivern)	08/16	Kinney, Harrison
10/26	Lippincott, Sarah Lee	03/16	Bruck, Lorraine	08/19	Roddenberry, Eugene Wesley
10/28	Swados, Harvey	03/16	Wallace, Beverly Dobrin		
11/01	Blackburn, Joyce Knight	03/19	Martin, Dorothy	08/20	Hurmence, Belinda
11/02	Graham, Margaret Bloy	03/21	Simon, Shirley (Schwartz)	08/22	Roddy, Lee
11/09	Boeckman, Charles	03/22	Carter, Dorothy Sharp	08/27	Mosel, Arlene (Tichy)
11/09	Thum, Gladys	03/22	Ziner, Florence Feenie	08/29	Burt, Jesse Clifton
11/23	May, Charles Paul	03/28	Wheatley, Arabelle	09/05	Werner, Vivian
11/30	Rosenfeld, Sam	03/29	Battles, Roxy Edith (Baker)	09/07	Davis, Louise Littleton
12/02	Glines, Carroll V(ane), Jr.			09/07	MacKenzie, Garry
12/03	Carlson, Esther Elisabeth	04/02	Benezra, Barbara (Beardsley)	09/07	Tolles, Martha
12/04	Robinson, Ray(mond Kenneth)			09/20	Tashjian, Virginia A.
		04/04	Eager, George B.	09/25	Ross, John
12/18	Leckie, Robert (Hugh)	04/07	Bacon, Margaret Hope	09/26	Wyeth, Betsy James
12/20	Pitrone, Jean Maddern	04/08	Gilbreath, Alice (Thompson)	10/02	Raebeck, Lois
12/22	Lehr, Delores			10/05	Bates, Betty
12/24	Langstaff, John (Meredith)	04/12	Ewing, Kathryn	10/09	Cone, Ferne Geller
12/26	Neigoff, Mike	04/13	Griese, Arnold A(lfred)	10/13	Walker, Barbara K(erlin)
		04/14	Alegria, Ricardo E.	10/20	Arkhurst, Joyce (Cooper)
1921		04/15	Briggs, Peter	10/28	Kessler, Leonard P.
??/??	Agnew, Seth Marshall	04/16	Cox, Donald William	10/31	Richard, Adrienne
??/??	Bernstein, Ralph	04/16	McMurtrey, Martin A(loysius)	11/03	Ashabranner, Brent (Kenneth)
??/??	Carr, Rachel (Elizabeth)				
??/??	Chessare, Michele	04/20	Boyd, Mildred Worthy	11/11	Cretan, Gladys (Yessayan)
??/??	Clokey, Art	04/20	Moy, Seong	11/13	Harris, Jonathan
??/??	Goodsell, Jane Neuberger	05/01	Steinberg, Phillip Orso	11/14	Hooks, William H(arris)
??/??	Knigge, Robert (R.)	05/05	Bernard, Jacqueline (de Sieyes)	11/14	Sugarman, Tracy
??/??	Mace, Katherine (Keeler)			11/22	Simon, Hilda (Rita)
??/??	Ranucci, Renato	05/05	Brin, Ruth F(irestone)	11/24	Uchida, Yoshiko
??/??	Schwalje, Earl G(eorge)	05/13	Burchardt, Nellie	12/05	Thrasher, Crystal (Faye)
??/??	Showalter, Jean B(reckinridge)	05/28	McCrea, Ruth (Pirman)	12/06	Winston, Clara
		05/29	Laycock, George (Edwin)	12/09	Ellis, Harry Bearse
??/??	Splaver, Sarah	06/04	McKay, Robert W.	12/15	Cetin, Frank Stanley
??/??	Touster, Irwin	06/06	Monk, Marvin Randolph	12/22	Koering, Ursula
??/??	Warren, Fred	06/12	Houston, James A(rchibald)	12/26	Allen, Stephen Valentine Patrick William
01/01	Romano, Louis G.				
01/02	Bonsall, Crosby (Barbara Newell)	06/12	Zonia, Dhimitri	12/26	Lee, Robert J.
		06/16	Conrad, Sybil	12/28	Klaperman, Libby Mindlin
01/02	Slepian, Jan(ice B.)	06/18	Johnson, Annabel (Jones)	12/29	Gordon, Shirley
01/08	Ames, Lee J(udah)	06/20	Smith, Hugh L(etcher)	12/29	Pierik, Robert
01/17	O'Daniel, Janet	06/21	Morse, Flo		
01/20	Golann, Cecil Paige	06/23	Ostendorf, Arthur Lloyd, Jr.	**1922**	
01/26	Lasher, Faith B.			??/??	Barnett, Moneta
01/29	Holmquist, Eve	06/23	Taylor, Theodore (Langhans)	??/??	Brown, Conrad
01/30	Augelli, John P(at)			??/??	Carpenter, Edmund Snow
02/05	Schechter, Betty (Goodstein)	06/26	Stadtler, Bea	??/??	Curtis, Robert H.
		06/28	Boatner, Mark Mayo III	??/??	Faulkner, John
02/05	Stilwell, Alison	07/04	Bell, Joseph N.	??/??	Gray, Robert
02/12	Vaeth, J(oseph) Gordon	07/04	Underwood, Mary Betty Anderson	??/??	Heilbrun, Lois Hussey
02/16	Ahern, Margaret McCrohan			??/??	Hobson, Julius W(ilson)
		07/12	Koningsberger, Hans	??/??	Huck, Charlotte S(tephena)
02/24	Powers, Richard M.	07/13	Scribner, Charles, Jr.		
02/24	VanOrden, M(erton) D(ick)	07/16	Kostich, Dragos D.	??/??	Hume, Ruth (Fox)
02/25	Klaperman, Gilbert	07/19	Spencer, Elizabeth	??/??	Johnson, Doris
02/27	Cohen, Morton N(orton)	07/21	Lansing, Alfred	??/??	Kenyon, Raymond G.
02/28	Tabrah, Ruth (Milander)	07/21	Ward, Martha (Eads)	??/??	Lasson, Robert
03/01	Burchard, Peter D(uncan)	07/24	Jacobs, Lou(is), Jr.	??/??	Mehdevi, Anne (Marie) Sinclair
03/01	Wilbur, Richard (Purdy)	07/25	Davidson, Rosalie		
03/02	Sattler, Helen Roney	07/26	Schoor, Gene	??/??	Olson, Gene
03/03	Radlauer, Edward	07/31	Curtis, Patricia	??/??	Robinson, Jerry
03/06	Bealer, Alex W(inkler III)	08/02	Barr, Donald	??/??	Sellew, Catharine F.
03/08	Henneberger, Robert G.	08/03	Carruth, Hayden	??/??	Sprague, Rosemary
		08/06	Reed, Betty Jane	??/??	Walter, Mildred Pitts

01/01 Brick, John
01/03 Schutzer, A. I.
01/07 Kessler, Ethel
01/11 Margolis, Vivienne
01/13 Bodecker, N(iels) M(ogens)
01/14 Rothberg, Abraham
01/16 Crawford, Deborah
01/24 Beatty, John (Louis)
02/01 O'Leary, Frank(lin J.)
02/04 Chambers, Bradford
02/07 Torbert, Floyd James
02/08 Glanzman, Louis S.
02/12 Bethell, Jean (Frankenberry)
02/16 Tanner, Louise S(tickney)
02/18 Karen, Ruth
02/22 Noble, Iris (Davis)
02/25 Land, Myrick (Ebben)
02/25 Mullins, Edward S(wift)
02/28 Unrau, Ruth
03/01 Jablonski, Edward
03/02 Hano, Arnold
03/13 Heilbroner, Joan Knapp
03/14 Fletcher, Colin
03/16 Sibley, Don
03/20 Young, Margaret B(uckner)
03/21 Casewit, Curtis
03/22 Mild, Warren (Paul)
03/23 Munves, James (Albert)
03/24 Stone, D(avid) K(arl)
03/25 Suttles, Shirley (Smith)
03/26 Egan, E(dward) W(elstead)
03/29 Cahn, Rhoda
03/30 Steele, Henry Max(well)
03/31 Daugherty, Richard D(eo)
03/31 Shay, Arthur
04/09 Evslin, Bernard
04/10 Weiss, Harvey
04/13 Thollander, Earl (Gustave)
04/14 Wilson, John
04/18 Reid, Barbara
04/24 Atene, Rita Anna
04/25 Korach, Mimi
04/30 Corrigan, Barbara
05/01 Dougherty, Charles
05/06 Wriggins, Salley Hovey
05/08 Olsen, Violet (Mae)
05/08 Steele, Mary Q(uintard Govan)
05/12 Feravolo, Rocco Vincent
05/14 Kadesch, Robert R(udstone)
05/17 Hoopes, Roy
05/20 Johnson, James Ralph
05/22 Fox, Lorraine
05/22 Peterson, Harold L(eslie)
05/23 Ritter, Lawrence S(tanley)
05/29 Coerr, Eleanor (Page)
05/29 Tolliver, Ruby C(hangos)
05/30 Weingartner, Charles
05/31 Smith, Imogene Henderson
06/01 Spencer, William
06/06 LeShan, Eda J(oan Grossman)

06/11 Capps, Benjamin (Franklin)
06/13 Tremain, Ruthven
06/18 Heintze, Carl
06/26 Nickerson, Elizabeth
07/05 Cunliffe, Marcus (Falkner)
07/06 Chetin, Helen
07/06 Snyderman, Reuven K.
07/16 Titus, Eve
07/17 Toschik, Larry
07/22 Liss, Howard
07/31 Hyde, Wayne F(rederick)
08/04 Clark, Frank J(ames)
08/07 Seixas, Judith S.
08/09 Anderson, Lucia (Lewis)
08/15 Baskin, Leonard
08/15 Weisberger, Bernard A(llen)
08/20 Richelson, Geraldine
08/22 Doss, Margot Patterson
08/24 Ross, Clare (Romano)
08/25 Geer, Charles
08/26 Beatty, Patricia (Robbins)
08/26 Wiseman, B(ernard)
09/01 Livingston, Richard R(oland)
09/03 Hilton, Suzanne (McLean)
09/08 Perl, Susan
09/08 White, Nancy Bean
09/10 Doty, Roy
09/14 Weiner, Sandra (Smith)
09/17 Fichter, George S.
09/19 Knight, Damon
09/22 Grohskopf, Bernice (Appelbaum)
09/23 Gidal, Sonia (Epstein)
09/25 Paige, Harry W.
09/30 Sylvester, Natalie G(abry)
10/03 Snyder, Anne
10/05 Keane, Bil
10/08 Whitney, Alex(andra)
10/13 Knotts, Howard (Clayton, Jr.)
10/13 Schell, Mildred
10/16 Quick, Annabelle (MacMillan)
10/18 Petrovich, Michael B(oro)
10/23 Harries, Joan
10/29 Davis, Russell G(erard)
10/29 Ressner, Phil(ip)
11/03 Shekerjian, Haig
11/06 Thomson, Peggy (Bebie)
11/12 MacLeod, Charlotte (Matilda Hughes)
11/13 Cannon, Bettie (Waddell)
11/16 Hoyt, Olga (Gruhzit)
11/18 Jenkins, William A(twell)
11/26 Schulz, Charles M(onroe)
11/28 Boshinski, Blanche
11/29 Spearing, Judith (Mary Harlow)
12/03 Wallace, Barbara Brooks
12/05 Palder, Edward L.
12/14 Unterecker, John
12/24 Finke, Blythe F(oote)
12/30 Langton, Jane (Gillson)
12/30 Siculan, Daniel

1923
??/?? Ayres, Patricia Miller
??/?? Burns, Paul C(lay)
??/?? Fiedler, Jean(nette Feldman)
??/?? Ghikas, Panos (George)
??/?? Hirschfeld, Burt
??/?? Julian, Nancy R.
??/?? McNaught, Harry
??/?? Meigs, Elizabeth Bleecker
??/?? Shilstone, Arthur
01/13 Elgin, Kathleen
01/25 Rinkoff, Barbara (Jean Rich)
01/27 Merrill, Jean (Fairbanks)
02/01 Osterritter, John F(erdinand)
02/04 Knoepfle, John
02/06 Wexler, Jerome (LeRoy)
02/10 Tichenor, Tom
02/12 Kissin, Eva H.
02/14 Lueders, Edward (George)
02/16 Pennington, Eunice
02/21 Smiley, Virginia Kester
02/27 Shura, Mary Francis
03/03 Blegvad, Erik
03/08 Keller, Dick
03/12 Maxwell, Edith (Smith)
03/16 Caswell, Helen (Rayburn)
03/21 Hancock, Mary A.
03/24 Broekel, Rainer Lothar
03/24 Hollander, Zander
03/26 Beeby, Betty
03/26 Sagsoorian, Paul
03/30 Polatnick, Florence T.
04/01 Waller, Leslie
04/09 Kamen, Gloria
04/10 Chenery, Janet (Dai)
04/12 Engle, Eloise Katherine
04/14 Eckblad, Edith Berven
04/18 Davis, Bette J.
04/20 Lieblich, Irene
04/22 Baird, Thomas (P.)
04/22 Deyrup, Astrith Johnson
04/22 Fox, Paula
04/24 Burn, Doris
04/27 Leonard, Constance (Brink)
04/27 Ogan, Margaret E. (Nettles)
05/03 Ney, John
05/04 Gladstone, M(yron) J.
05/07 Halsell, Grace
05/07 Ridge, Martin
05/08 Meriwether, Louise
05/09 Aaron, Chester
05/21 Shaw, Richard
05/27 Carini, Edward
05/28 Brown, Robert Fletch
05/29 Ervin, Janet Halliday
05/30 Goldsborough, June
05/31 Borja, Robert
06/04 Golbin, Andree
06/06 Reynolds, Pamela
06/12 Gordon, Sol
06/17 Nelson, Roy Paul
06/19 Moore, Ruth (Nulton)

06/21	Wilbur, C. Keith	??/??	Hawkinson, Lucy (Ozone)	06/16	Hale, Arlene
06/25	Butters, Dorothy Gilman	??/??	Hoyt, Mary Finch	06/16	Mays, Lucinda L(a Bella)
06/25	Mulvihill, William Patrick	??/??	Peterson, John Lawrence	06/19	Engelhart, Margaret S(tevens)
06/28	Hardwick, Richard (Holmes, Jr.)	??/??	Thum, Marcella	06/23	Lincoln, C(harles) Eric
06/30	Miller, Don	??/??	Williamson, Margaret	06/24	Baker, James W.
06/30	Smith, Susan Carlton	??/??	Young, A(ndrew) S(turgeon Nash)	06/24	Fisher, Leonard Everett
07/04	Schindelman, Joseph	01/08	Vlahos, Olivia	06/26	VanWoerkom, Dorothy (O'Brien)
07/08	Murray, John	01/14	Tusiani, Joseph	07/02	Swinburne, Laurence
07/11	Land, Barbara (Neblett)	01/15	Lynds, Dennis	07/03	Jenkyns, Chris
07/12	Gunn, James E(dwin)	01/17	Tichy, William	07/04	Nonnast, Marie
07/13	Bryan, Ashley F.	01/18	George, Renee	07/04	Schoen, Barbara
07/16	Evans, Mari	01/26	Eisenberg, Phyllis Rose	07/10	Hare, Norma Q(uarles)
07/21	Wise, William	01/28	Parry, Marian	07/13	Andre, Evelyn M(arie)
07/26	Berenstain, Jan(ice Grant)	01/28	Watson, Sally (Lou)	07/20	Eitzen, Ruth (Carper)
08/01	Root, Shelton L., Jr.	01/29	Faber, Doris (Greenberg)	07/24	Pollack, Merrill S.
08/02	Dowdey, Landon Gerald	01/30	Alexander, Lloyd (Chudley)	07/25	Newcombe, Jack
08/04	Nixon, Hershell Howard	02/05	Lauber, Patricia (Grace)	07/25	Parr, Lucy
08/05	Hoyt, Edwin P(almer), Jr.	02/10	Dolan, Edward F(rancis), Jr.	08/02	Baldwin, James (Arthur)
08/08	Martin, Lynne	02/13	Lonette, Reisie (Dominee)	08/02	Halliburton, Warren J.
08/12	Anderson, Leone Castell	02/13	Sebestyen, Ouida (Dockery)	08/03	Uris, Leon (Marcus)
08/12	Gannett, Ruth Stiles	02/16	Newman, Shirlee Petkin	08/04	Robison, Bonnie
08/12	Gottlieb, Gerald	02/19	Cook, Joseph J(ay)	08/18	Siegl, Helen
08/17	Deedy, John	02/25	Meng, Heinz (Karl)	08/23	Birmingham, Lloyd
08/19	Grummer, Arnold Edward	02/27	Shore, Robert	08/24	Markun, Patricia M(aloney)
08/21	Hall, Natalie Watson	03/07	Beitler, Stanley (Samuel)	08/26	Millar, Barbara F.
08/24	Clark, Champ	03/09	Reigot, Betty Polisar	08/28	Lee, Norma E.
08/24	Landin, Les(lie)	03/13	Laschever, Barnett D.	08/28	Monjo, F(erdinand) N(icholas)
08/24	Lipman, Matthew	03/21	McCord, Jean	09/06	Cook, Bernadine
08/26	Stokes, Jack (Tilden)	03/22	Mueller, Virginia	09/09	Scarry, Patricia (Murphy)
08/27	Skold, Betty Westrom	03/22	Wilson, Lionel	09/16	Hubley, Faith (Elliot)
08/29	Callahan, Philip S(erna)	03/23	Handville, Robert (Tompkins)	09/16	Murray, Don(ald M.)
08/30	Levine, I(srael) E.	03/24	Serage, Nancy	09/20	Dain, Martin J.
08/31	Brock, Betty (Carter)	03/28	Baylor, Byrd	09/22	Bradfield, Roger
09/03	Walker, Addison Mort	03/31	Gilge, Jeanette	09/27	Gray, Lee Learner
09/05	Sutton, Ann (Livesay)	04/07	Rappaport, Eva	09/27	Waber, Bernard
09/11	Weiss, Renee Karol	04/09	Gennaro, Joseph F(rancis), Jr.	09/29	Pollack, Reginald Murray
09/17	Berg, Bjorn	04/10	Acuff, Selma Boyd	10/04	Sobol, Donald J.
09/29	Berenstain, Stan(ley)	04/17	Gallant, Roy (Arthur)	10/08	Koch, Dorothy (Clarke)
10/02	Altschuler, Franz	04/20	Hallstead, William F(inn) III	10/22	Baum, Allyn Z(elton)
10/06	Thomas, Lowell (Jackson), Jr.	04/20	Wels, Byron G(erald)	10/27	Chambers, Robert Warner
10/18	Stegeman, Janet Allais	04/21	Burns, Ray(mond Howard)	10/27	Greene, Constance C(larke)
10/18	Switzer, Ellen	04/24	Pelaez, Jill	10/29	Flender, Harold
10/24	Wood, Phyllis Anderson	05/02	Houck, Carter	10/31	Dunning, Arthur Stephen, Jr.
10/26	Vaughan, Harold Cecil	05/05	Wronker, Lili (Cassel)	11/08	Brooks, Lester
11/06	Jacobson, Daniel	05/08	Klein, Gerda Weissmann	11/13	Castillo, Edmund Luis
11/14	Baker, Mary Elizabeth (Gillette)	05/12	Joseph, James (Herz)	11/16	Boardman, Gwenn R.
11/18	Gregor, Arthur	05/14	Anderson, Bradley Jay	11/20	Costabel, Eva Deutsch
11/19	Trahey, Jane	05/17	Lerner, Marguerite Rush	11/20	Stambler, Irwin
11/21	Sokol, William	05/24	Acheson, Patricia Castles	11/22	Lord, Beman
11/24	Dean, Karen Strickler	05/24	Milton, John R(onald)	11/30	Moeri, Louise (Healy)
11/25	Cartwright, Sally	05/25	Day, Beth (Feagles)	11/30	Sherman, Allan
11/26	Stoddard, Edward G.	05/29	McGinnis, Lila S(prague)	12/06	Cox, Wallace Maynard
12/02	Payne, Joan Balfour	05/30	Marshall, Anthony D(ryden)	12/06	Jones, Douglas C(lyde)
12/17	DeKay, Ormonde, Jr.	05/30	Roberts, Nancy Correll	12/07	Felt, Sue
12/23	Forsyth, Gloria	06/03	Liberty, Gene	12/14	Waldron, Ann Wood
12/26	Lee, John R(obert)	06/06	Andrews, Virginia Cleo	12/16	Sidjakov, Nicolas
12/28	Gobbato, Imero	06/07	Field, Edward	12/21	Reid, Eugenie Chazal
		06/08	Gremmels, Marion (Louise) Chapman	12/22	Sharpe, Mitchell R(aymond)
1924				12/24	Scagnetti, Jack
??/??	Albert, Marvin H.				
??/??	Brown, Virginia Suggs				
??/??	Delaune, Jewel Lynn (de Grummond)	06/13	Cellini, Joseph	12/27	Benedict, Stewart H(urd)
??/??	Guggenheim, Hans				

1925

??/??	Bosworth, J. Allan
??/??	Francis, Henry S.
??/??	Freeman, Serge Herbert
??/??	Gilman, Esther
??/??	Granger, Margaret Jane
??/??	Hyde, Dayton O(gden)
??/??	Johnston, Louisa Mae
??/??	Parker, James Edgar, Jr.
??/??	Raymond, John F(rancis)
01/01	Steiner, Stan(ley)
01/01	Williams, Barbara (Wright)
01/02	Carona, Philip B(en)
01/03	Barnett, Leo
01/08	Burroughs, Polly
01/12	Fehrenbach, T(heodore) R(eed, Jr.)
01/17	Cormier, Robert (Edmund)
01/19	Darling, Richard L(ewis)
01/25	Oppenheimer, Joan L(etson)
01/28	Conn, Frances (Goldberg)
01/30	Breetveld, Jim Patrick
01/30	Campbell, Ann R.
01/31	Weaver, Jack
02/01	Chaffin, Lillie D(orton)
02/04	Hoban, Russell (Conwell)
02/06	Warrick, Patricia Scott
02/16	Buck, Lewis
02/22	Coen, Rena Neumann
02/22	Gorey, Edward St. John
02/24	Bunin, Sherry
03/02	Cuffari, Richard
03/08	Seidman, Laurence (Ivan)
03/12	Harrison, Harry (Max)
03/12	Zwinger, Ann
03/15	Holyer, Erna Maria
03/17	Rees, Ennis (Samuel, Jr.)
03/20	Gault, Clare S.
03/23	Bergaust, Erik
03/25	Finlayson, Ann
03/30	Shafer, Robert E(ugene)
03/31	Graham, Frank, Jr.
04/03	Schilling, Betty
04/04	Fry, Edward Bernard
04/25	Behrens, June York
04/25	Brooks, Thomas R(eed)
05/01	Bowden, Joan Chase
05/01	Emerson, William K(eith)
05/02	Wolfe, Rinna (Evelyn)
05/07	Davis, Paxton
05/07	Kirk, Ruth (Eleanor Kratz)
05/11	Stephens, William M(cLain)
05/12	Henriod, Lorraine (Stephens)
05/17	Granstaff, Bill
05/18	Hoban, Lillian
05/19	Carey, M(ary) V(irginia)
05/23	Johnson, La Verne B(ravo)
05/27	Hillerman, Tony
05/31	Mazer, Harry
06/02	Viereck, Phillip R.
06/05	D'Amato, Janet (Potter)
06/06	Kumin, Maxine (Winokur)
06/06	Polonsky, Arthur
06/10	Hentoff, Nat(han Irving)
06/12	Weales, Gerald (Clifford)
06/17	Campbell, Hope
06/17	Fox, Sonny
06/20	Rymer, Alta May
06/21	Coughlan, Margaret N(ourse)
06/21	Kraus, Robert
06/26	Brenner, Barbara (Johnes)
06/26	Burch, Robert (Joseph)
06/26	Hoke, John (Lindsay)
07/04	Grollman, Earl A.
07/07	Nash, Mary (Hughes)
07/11	Laite, Gordon
07/11	Mills, Yaroslava Surmach
07/12	Schurfranz, Vivian
07/16	Kiesel, Stanley
07/17	Kashiwagi, Isami
07/19	Foster, John T(homas)
07/24	Watson, Pauline
07/29	Bloome, Enid P.
08/03	Roth, Arthur J(oseph)
08/06	Knight, David C(arpenter)
08/11	Coopersmith, Jerome
08/12	Hood, Joseph F.
08/15	Dolim, Mary N(uzum)
08/17	Gumpertz, Bob
08/19	Wacker, Charles H(enry), Jr.
08/24	Behrman, Carol (Helen)
08/27	King, Cynthia
08/31	Lindop, Edmund
09/07	Solbert, Romaine G.
09/10	Crawford, Mel
09/15	Green, Norma B(erger)
09/16	Johnson, Charles R.
09/20	Bolian, Polly
09/24	Carew, Jan (Rynveld)
09/26	Amoss, Berthe (Marks)
10/02	Paine, Roberta M.
10/06	Miller, Eugene
10/08	Ormondroyd, Edward
10/09	Sutton, Myron Daniel
10/14	Belden, Wilanne Schneider
10/20	Buchwald, Art(hur)
10/25	Herkimer, L(awrence) R(ussell)
10/26	Williams, Selma R(uth)
11/02	Eiseman, Alberta
11/04	Alexander, Vincent Arthur
11/04	Elfman, Blossom
11/04	Hill, Elizabeth Starr
11/12	Donze, Sara Lee (Hathaway)
11/12	Miller, Marilyn (Jean)
11/15	Charmatz, Bill
11/18	Addona, Angelo F.
11/19	Dines, Harry Glen
11/20	Barris, George
12/02	Bodie, Idella F(allaw)
12/02	Harris, Julie
12/08	Wimmer, Helmut Karl
12/09	Hickman, Martha Whitmore
12/09	Roland, Albert
12/10	Alter, Robert Edmond
12/11	Winter, Ginny Linville
12/14	Hafner, Marylin
12/19	Forberg, Beate Gropius
12/21	Polking, Kirk
12/31	Moscow, Alvin

1926

??/??	Green, Margaret
??/??	Hoag, Edwin
??/??	Ressler, Theodore Whitson
??/??	Shapiro, Milton J.
??/??	Wright, Dare
01/01	Haas, Carolyn Buhai
01/03	Anglund, Joan Walsh
01/06	Friedman, Ina R(osen)
01/07	Hoffman, Rosekrans
01/10	Bolton, Carole (Roberts)
01/13	Horner, Althea (Jane)
01/18	Trivelpiece, Laurel
01/21	Collier, Zena
01/25	Martin, George
01/26	Woods, George A(llan)
02/08	Rich, Elaine Sommers
02/11	Edens, Bishop David
02/11	French, Dorothy Kayser
02/15	Adams, Hazard
02/18	Frace, Charles
02/20	Rue, Leonard Lee III
02/20	Scheer, Julian (Weisel)
02/25	Fuka, Vladimir
03/15	Devaney, John
03/15	Myron, Robert
03/19	Schlichting, Harold E(ugene, Jr.)
03/24	Osgood, William E(dward)
03/26	Ahl, Anna Maria
03/26	Sprague, Gretchen (Burnham)
03/28	Kaplan, Jean Caryl Korn
03/31	Montresor, Beni
04/01	McCaffrey, Anne (Inez)
04/10	Caulfield, Peggy F.
04/10	Larrecq, John M(aurice)
04/12	Silverman, Al
04/15	Hood, Robert E(ric)
04/24	DuBose, LaRocque (Russ)
04/28	Lee, Nelle Harper
05/03	Foote, Timothy (Gilson)
05/08	Blegvad, Lenore (Hochman)
05/09	Halliday, William R(oss)
05/13	Williamson, Joanne S(mall)
05/14	Hammerman, Gay M(orenus)
05/20	Berry, William D(avid)
05/22	Stubis, Talivaldis
05/23	Matson, Emerson N(els)
06/02	Reeves, Lawrence F.
06/03	Cosgrove, Margaret (Leota)
06/04	Kossin, Sandy (Sanford)
06/04	Lane, Carolyn (Blocker)
06/05	Low, Alice
06/05	Wagoner, David (Russell)
06/06	Schlein, Miriam

06/11	Lifton, Betty Jean (Kirschner)	11/01	Knight, Hilary	04/02	Georgiou, Constantine
06/19	Palmer, Ruth Candida	11/04	Cooper, Lee (Pelham)	04/03	Callen, Lawrence Willard, Jr.
06/20	Harris, Leon A., Jr.	11/09	Hahn, Hannelore	04/10	Brandon, Brumsic, Jr.
06/21	Ubell, Earl	11/11	Ditzel, Paul C(alvin)	04/14	Lopshire, Robert (Martin)
06/23	Bahti, Tom	11/11	Jackson, Robert B(lake)	04/18	Sharmat, Mitchell
06/26	Bruner, Richard W(allace)	11/12	Pluff, Barbara (Littlefield)	04/23	Graber, Richard (Frederick)
06/26	Craz, Albert G.	11/12	Werner, Herma	04/25	Schwartz, Alvin
06/26	Sherin, Ray	11/15	Borhegyi, Suzanne Catherine Sims de	04/26	Wilson, Julia
07/02	Murphy, E(mmett) Jefferson	11/19	Bauernschmidt, Marjorie	04/27	Maar, Leonard (F., Jr.)
07/07	Rushmore, Robert (William)	11/19	Scott, Ann Herbert	04/28	Bornstein, Ruth
07/10	Gwynne, Fred(erick Hubbard)	11/21	Berson, Harold	04/29	Carter, William E(arl)
07/12	Holtzman, Jerome	11/24	Dunbar, Robert E(verett)	05/06	McGorwven, Thomas E.
07/20	Wiseman, Ann (Sayre)	11/25	Anderson, Poul (William)	05/11	Snyder, Zilpha Keatley
07/22	Hurwood, Bernhardt J.	11/27	Sheffield, Janet N.	05/13	Anderson, Eloise Adell
07/23	Coombs, Patricia	11/30	Francis, Dorothy Brenner	05/14	Parker, Robert Andrew
07/23	Goldberg, Herbert S.	12/01	Abels, Harriette Sheffer	05/18	Miklowitz, Gloria D(ubov)
07/25	Szulc, Tad	12/02	McLeod, Emilie Warren	05/20	Horvath, Betty (Ferguson)
08/03	Calhoun, Mary Huiskamp	12/04	Moyler, Alan (Frank Powell)	05/22	Matthiessen, Peter
08/06	Jeppson, J(anet) O(pal)	12/07	Kaplan, Boche	05/23	Skelly, James R(ichard)
08/07	Davidson, R(aymond)	12/07	Seidelman, James Edward	05/26	Armstrong, George D.
08/14	Gault, Frank	12/10	Pilarski, Laura	05/27	Meaker, Marijane
08/15	Clifford, Mary Louise (Beneway)	12/16	Moncure, Jane Belk	05/28	White, David Omar
08/17	Livingston, Myra Cohn	12/16	Walker, David G(ordon)	05/30	Poynter, Margaret
08/18	Hirsch, Phil	12/19	Kovalik, Nada	06/02	Katz, William Loren
08/18	Radlauer, Ruth (Shaw)	12/20	Levine, David	06/02	Steinberg, Rafael (Mark)
08/24	Loomis, Robert D.	12/21	Lustig, Arnost	06/04	Kenealy, James P.
08/25	Titler, Dale Milton	12/27	Smith, Robert W(illiam)	06/06	Spier, Peter (Edward)
08/26	Meilach, Dona Z(weigoron)	12/28	McCain, Murray (David, Jr.)	06/09	Lyttle, Richard B(ard)
08/27	Zens, Patricia Martin			06/15	Wright, Betty Ren
08/28	Krasilovsky, Phyllis (Manning)	**1927**		06/17	Wood, Wallace
08/29	Zeiger, Sophia	??/??	Carter, Forrest	06/21	Swinford, Betty (June Wells)
09/01	Graham, John	??/??	Coconis, Ted	06/24	Klass, Morton
09/03	Lurie, Alison	??/??	Drummond, A. H.	06/27	Keeshan, Robert J.
09/06	Faulhaber, Martha	??/??	Smith, Philip M.	06/27	Taylor, Barbara J.
09/11	Slote, Alfred	01/07	McDonald, Forrest	07/01	Matthews, Patricia
09/12	Lichello, Robert	01/08	Brommer, Gerald F(rederick)	07/02	Mays, Lewis Victor, Jr.
09/16	Knowles, John	01/13	Keller, Irene (Barron)	07/03	Navarra, John Gabriel
09/17	Kalb, Jonah	01/19	Gerson, Corinne (Schreiberstein)	07/05	Fleming, Thomas J(ames)
09/22	Hadley, Leila (Burton)	01/19	Shaw, Evelyn	07/06	Lerner, Carol
09/22	Odor, Ruth Shannon	01/28	Williams, Vera B.	07/09	Goldston, Robert (Conroy)
09/23	Chaneles, Sol	01/30	Heuer, Kenneth John	07/10	Gliewe, Unada (Grace)
09/27	Bonham, Barbara (Thomas)	02/03	Nixon, Joan Lowery	07/10	Stern, Ellen N(orman)
10/04	Robinson, Louie, Jr.	02/09	Epple, Anne Orth	07/11	Inyart, Gene
10/09	Russell, Franklin (Alexander)	02/09	Gackenbach, Dick	07/12	Dorman, N. B.
10/10	Einsel, Walter	02/10	Grammer, June Amos	07/12	Sargent, Shirley
10/12	Maniscalco, Joseph	02/24	Henry, Joanne Landers	07/14	Parish, Margaret Cecile
10/13	Myller, Rolf	03/03	Anderson, Gunnar (Donald)	07/18	Ozer, Jerome S.
10/14	Cohen, Miriam	03/07	Maxey, Dale	07/18	Ward, Ralph T.
10/15	Hunter, Evan	03/08	Lord, Patricia C.	07/22	Hall, Carolyn Vosburg
10/16	Sheldon, Muriel	03/12	Brennan, Gale Patrick	07/27	Hunter, Mel
10/17	Arnov, Boris, Jr.	03/16	Chalmers, Mary (Eileen)	07/28	Hoffmann, Hilde
10/17	Karp, Naomi J.	03/18	Johnson, Shirley K(ing)	07/29	Karl, Jean E(dna)
10/25	Grey, Jerry	03/18	Plimpton, George (Ames)	08/01	Swiger, Elinor Porter
10/26	Searcy, Margaret Zehmer	03/21	Mill, Eleanor	08/04	Freschet, Berniece Louise (Speck)
10/27	Thiry, Joan (Marie)	03/25	Beck, Barbara L.	08/07	Knott, William Cecil, Jr.
10/29	Rhodes, Frank H(arold Trevor)	03/26	Goldstein, Nathan	08/07	Wojciechowska, Maia (Teresa Rodman)
10/30	Barbe, Walter Burke	03/27	Lewis, Joseph Anthony	08/09	Keyes, Daniel
11/01	Kiefer, Irene	03/27	Vass, George	08/11	Sullivan, George E(dward)
		03/29	Kushner, Donn	08/13	Friedrich, Priscilla
		03/30	Demas, Vida	08/14	Metter, Bert(ram Milton)
		04/02	Abisch, Roslyn Kroop	08/15	Taylor, Mark

08/20	Edwards, Anne	12/24	Simon, Norma (Feldstein)	05/08	Weiss, Leatie
08/22	Goodman, Walter	12/30	Ferguson, Robert Bruce	05/11	Houston, Joan
08/23	Berger, Melvin H.			05/16	Miles, Betty
08/23	Liston, Robert A.	**1928**		05/18	Rumsey, Marian (Barritt)
08/27	Elwart, Joan Potter	??/??	Bell, Frederic	05/19	Fletcher, Alan Mark
08/27	Selman, LaRue W.	??/??	Bennett, Lerone, Jr.	05/20	Murphy, Shirley Rousseau
08/28	Kunstler, Morton	??/??	Donovan, John	05/21	Winn, Janet Bruce
09/02	Dillon, Barbara	??/??	Hamil, Thomas Arthur	05/24	Caras, Roger A(ndrew)
09/06	Facklam, Margery Metz	??/??	Sackett, S(amuel) J(ohn)	05/24	Walton, Richard J.
09/08	Weber, William John	??/??	Spencer, Lila	05/25	Eitzen, Allan
09/10	Levin, Betty (Lowenthal)	??/??	Sykes, Jo	05/27	Hemming, Roy
09/11	Klimowicz, Barbara (Tingley)	??/??	Walker, Barbara M(uhs)	05/28	Rikhoff, Jean
09/12	Bruce, Mary	01/01	Cheney, Theodore Albert	05/29	Roberts, Willo Davis
09/15	Hellman, Harold	01/04	Howard, Moses Leon	06/06	Dobrin, Arnold (Jack)
09/18	Greene, Ellin	01/11	Rabe, Berniece (Louise)	06/10	Sendak, Maurice (Bernard)
09/20	Meyers, Joan (Simpson)	01/16	Kennedy, William	06/11	Silverman, Burton Philip
09/21	Jensen, Virginia Allen	01/19	Slate, Joseph (Frank)	06/14	Udry, Janice (May)
09/22	Myrus, Donald (Richard)	01/21	York, Carol Beach	06/19	Gottlieb, Robin (Grossman)
09/22	Parker, Dorothy (Lane) D(aniels)	01/22	Weiss, Malcolm E.	06/20	Baker, Betty (Lou)
09/25	Lazare, Gerald John	01/24	Rosenblum, Richard	06/22	Griffin, Gillett Good
09/27	Feagles, Anita MacRae	01/27	Allard, Harry G(rover), Jr.	06/27	Collier, James Lincoln
09/28	Brightfield, Richard	01/29	Anderson, Norman (Dean)	06/28	Rosenbloom, Joseph
09/29	Mertz, Barbara (Gross)	01/31	Trelease, Allen W(illiam)	06/29	Frimmer, Steven
10/08	Ferry, Charles	02/05	Kunhardt, Philip B(radish), Jr.	07/01	VanSteenwyk, Elizabeth Ann
10/14	Madden, Don	02/06	Jones, Weyman (B.)	07/10	Doren, Marion (Walker)
10/16	Danska, Herbert	02/09	Frazetta, Frank	07/10	Hubbell, Patricia
10/16	Perske, Robert	02/11	Hieatt, Constance B(artlett)	07/14	Ellis, Ella Thorp
10/20	Temko, Florence	02/12	Gould, Marilyn	07/19	Galster, Robert
10/24	Robinson, Barbara (Webb)	02/15	Bridwell, Norman	07/22	Anderson, Joy
10/29	Dreves, Veronica R.	02/17	Hartman, Jane E(vangeline)	07/30	Foster, Joanna
10/31	Hunt, Joyce	02/17	Peck, Robert Newton, III	07/30	Schock, Pauline
10/31	Kahn, Roger	02/25	Fraser, Elizabeth Marr	07/30	Throckmorton, Peter
11/01	Richoux, Pat(ricia)	03/05	Rublowsky, John M(artin)	07/30	Toothaker, Roy Eugene
11/03	Hoexter, Corinne K.	03/06	Nolan, William F(rancis)	08/03	Vaughan, Sam(uel) S.
11/03	Oakley, Don(ald G.)	03/08	Clancy, Joseph P(atrick)	08/07	Byars, Betsy (Cromer)
11/05	Abernethy, Robert G(ordon)	03/08	Segal, Lore (Groszmann)	08/07	Marlowe, Stephen
11/05	Aylesworth, Thomas G(ibbons)	03/12	Lambert, Saul	08/11	Nourse, Alan E(dward)
11/06	Klass, Sheila Solomon	03/13	Raskin, Ellen	08/19	Stankevich, Boris
11/06	Smith, Ralph Lee	03/20	Rogers, Fred (McFeely)	08/25	Hollander, Phyllis
11/09	Jacob, Helen Pierce	03/20	Watanabe, Shigeo	09/01	Guy, Rosa (Cuthbert)
11/10	Healey, Larry	03/22	Haines, Charles	09/05	Butterworth, Emma Macalik
11/13	Barnstone, Willis	03/22	Hammer, Richard	09/06	Pirsig, Robert M.
11/14	Ebel, Alex	03/26	Stevens, Carla M(cBride)	09/09	Nelson, Esther L.
11/14	Libby, William M.	03/26	Stine, G(eorge) Harry	09/10	Kelley, Leo P(atrick)
11/16	Thompson, Julian F(rancis)	03/28	Munro, Eleanor (C.)	09/20	Jennings, Gary (Gayne)
11/18	Smith, Howard E(verett) Jr.	04/03	Dinnerstein, Harvey	09/28	Thompson, Donnis (Stark)
11/28	Waitley, Douglas	04/04	Angelou, Maya	09/29	Hall, Donald (Andrew, Jr.)
11/30	Burgess, Robert F(orrest)	04/04	Hartshorn, Ruth M.	09/30	Wiesel, Elie(zer)
11/30	Eichner, James A.	04/08	Saviozzi, Adriana	10/03	Gorsline, S(ally) M(arie)
12/05	Rhodes, Bennie (Loran)	04/11	Lystad, Mary (Hanemann)	10/04	Nelson, Lawrence E(rnest)
12/08	Dunnahoo, Terry	04/13	Raucher, Herman	10/05	Fitzhugh, Louise (Perkins)
12/09	Rydell, Wendell	04/14	Schiller, Barbara (Heyman)	10/12	Flynn, Barbara
12/13	Wakin, Edward	04/15	Price, Christine (Hilda)	10/13	Offit, Sidney
12/14	Barnett, Naomi	04/15	Wagner, Frederick (Reese, Jr.)	10/14	Cameron, Polly (McQuiston)
12/16	Warburg, Sandol Stoddard	04/16	Gracza, Margaret Young	10/15	Amon, Aline
12/18	Lanier, Sterling E.	04/20	Morton, Lee Jack, Jr.	10/18	Pelta, Kathy
12/18	Sachs, Marilyn (Stickle)	04/30	Moskin, Marietta D(unston)	10/23	Davis, Christopher
12/24	Fox, Robert J.	04/30	Polhamus, Jean Burt	10/27	Breisky, William J(ohn)
		05/03	Jackson, Jacqueline (Dougan)	11/09	Sexton, Anne (Harvey)
		05/04	Viereck, Ellen R.	11/11	Lavine, David
		05/06	Beers, V(ictor) Gilbert	11/12	Sharmat, Marjorie Weinman
				11/14	Talbot, Charlene Joy

11/23	Chester, Michael (Arthur)	05/03	Lewis, Marjorie	11/01	Huthmacher, J. Joseph
11/23	Shemin, Margaretha (Hoeneveld)	05/06	Anderson, David Poole	11/03	Hansen, Caryl (Hall)
11/25	Climo, Shirley	05/07	Maynes, J. Oscar, Jr.	11/03	Williams, Edward G.
11/29	Simon, Paul	05/10	Edwards, Harvey	11/04	Limburg, Peter R(ichard)
11/29	Talbot, Toby (Tolpen)	05/14	Groch, Judith (Goldstein)	11/07	Abdul, Raoul
12/02	Vittengl, Morgan J(ohn)	05/14	Johnson, John E(mil)	11/10	Butterworth, W(illiam) E(dmund III)
12/06	Sherman, Diane (Finn)	05/14	Thompson, George Selden	11/22	Bethel, Dell
12/08	Chaikin, Miriam	05/15	Lasell, Elinor H.	12/02	Littke, Lael J.
12/09	Blos, Joan W(insor)	05/17	Greenfield, Eloise (Little)	12/04	Ancona, George
12/09	Cunningham, Chet	05/19	Pack, Robert	12/09	Brower, Pauline (York)
12/17	VanGelder, Richard G(eorge)	05/30	Jacobs, Frank	12/09	Gleason, Judith
12/19	Bunting, A(nne) E(velyn Bolton)	05/31	Lederer, Muriel	12/14	Balian, Lorna (Kohl)
12/21	Fleming, Alice Mulcahey	06/02	Juster, Norton	12/14	Brown, Joseph E(dward)
12/28	Lunn, Janet	06/05	Haas, Irene	12/16	Meadow, Charles (Troub)
		06/12	Markham, Marion M.	12/17	Baldwin, Stan(ley C.)
1929		06/12	Warshaw, Jerry	12/18	Behr, Joyce
??/??	Butler, William	06/14	Namioka, Lensey (Chao)	12/21	Dank, Leonard Dewey
??/??	Daly, Sheila John	06/23	Broderick, Dorothy M.	12/23	Langone, John (Michael)
??/??	Gardner, Robert	06/25	Carle, Eric	12/24	Blood, Charles Lewis
??/??	James, Harold (Laymont)	06/25	Jensen, David E(dward)	12/24	Clark, Mary Higgins
??/??	Jefferson, Robert Louis	06/26	Glaser, Milton	12/29	Bienenfeld, Florence L(ucille)
??/??	Johnson, Mary Frances K.	06/30	Hallman, Ruth		
??/??	Littledale, Freya (Lota Brown)	06/30	Margolis, Richard (J.)		
		07/04	Susac, Andrew		
??/??	Worrell, Estelle (Ansley)	07/09	Loeper, John J(oseph)	**1930**	
01/02	Teague, Robert	07/10	Walters, Audrey	??/??	Bowen, Joshua David
01/03	Chen, Anthony (Young)	07/11	Stevenson, James	??/??	Shore, June Lewis
01/03	Clark, Patricia (Finrow)	07/19	Borja, Corinne	??/??	Tomerlin, John
01/08	Hale, Linda (Howe)	07/21	Almquist, Don	??/??	Tsisghwanai, Traveller Bird
01/10	Charlip, Remy	07/23	Quackenbush, Robert M(ead)	??/??	Young, Marjabelle
01/15	King, Martin Luther, Jr.	07/25	Farb, Peter	01/10	Buck, William Ray
01/19	Woodard, Carol	07/28	Edwards, Sally (Cary)	01/18	Laird, Jean E(louise)
01/24	Hogan, Bernice Harris	08/03	Boyer, Robert E(rnst)	01/22	Carlisle, Olga A(ndreyev)
01/26	Feiffer, Jules	08/04	Neumeyer, Peter F(lorian)	01/22	Lent, Blair
01/26	Sommer, Elyse (Vorchheimer)	08/06	MacBride, Roger Lea	01/23	Goodman, Elaine (Egan)
01/31	Saunders, Rubie (Agnes)	08/06	VanZwienen, Ilse (Charlotte Koehn)	01/25	Wolitzer, Hilma
02/03	Friedrich, Otto (Alva)	08/21	Kennedy, Joseph Charles	01/26	DeMessieres, Nicole
02/03	Lorraine, Walter (Henry)	08/25	Brown, Walter R(eed)	01/29	Cassedy, Sylvia
02/03	Mellin, Jeanne	08/29	Oana, Katherine D.	01/29	Collier, Christopher
02/04	Chandler, Linda S(mith)	08/30	Joslin, Sesyle	01/30	Levoy, Myron
02/05	Rahn, Joan Elma	09/03	Brandenberg, Aliki (Liacouras)	02/04	Hazen, Barbara Shook
02/15	Orgel, Doris (Adelberg)	09/03	Meyer, Jean Shepherd	02/04	Roberts, Bruce (Stuart)
02/16	Schwartz, Daniel (Bennet)	09/16	Rothkopf, Carol Z.	02/10	Konigsburg, E(laine) L(obl)
02/17	Potok, Chaim	09/17	Hall, Elizabeth	02/17	Batson, Larry
02/25	Roth, Arnold	09/19	Dukert, Joseph M(ichael)	02/18	Wilson, Gahan
03/01	Applebaum, Stan	09/20	Clifford, M(argaret) C(ort)	02/20	Mayhar, Ardath
03/01	Gross, Ruth Belov	09/22	Grifalconi, Ann Weik	02/20	Tamburine, Jean
03/05	Hampson, Richard Denman	09/26	Wolcott, Patty	02/25	Hollingsworth, Alvin C(arl)
03/13	Lanes, Selma G(ordon)	09/29	Fiammenghi, Gioia	02/26	Wolf, Bernard
03/15	Meighan, Donald Charles	09/30	Fenner, Carol (Elizabeth)	03/04	Gay, Kathlyn (McGarrahan)
03/15	Schwartz, Sheila (Ruth)	10/01	Robinson, Dorothy W.	03/06	Elliott, Sarah M(cCarn)
03/19	Doty, Jean Slaughter	10/04	McCarter, Neely Dixon	03/07	Roberson, John R(oyster)
03/20	Allen, Thomas B(enton)	10/04	Tilton, Madonna Elaine	03/12	Cromie, William J(oseph)
03/21	Robertson, Don	10/07	Kennedy, Paul E(dward)	03/28	Byfield, Barbara Ninde
03/26	Sorel, Edward	10/11	Freedman, Russell (Bruce)	04/06	Crompton, Anne Eliot
03/27	Warren, Mary Phraner	10/12	Coles, Robert (Martin)	04/08	Sarasy, Phyllis Powell
04/07	Carrick, Donald	10/19	Caffrey, Nancy	04/10	Williams, J(eanne R.)
04/09	Olney, Ross R.	10/21	LeGuin, Ursula K(roeber)	04/12	McIlhany, Sterling (Fisher)
04/12	Leaf, VaDonna Jean	10/21	Luis, Earlene W.	04/12	Shefelman, Janice (Jordan)
04/17	Greenidge, Edwin	10/24	Brosnan, James Patrick		
04/24	Nelson, Mary Carroll	10/26	Winter, Paula (Cecelia)	04/14	Webster, David
04/26	Sommer, Robert	10/28	Armstrong, Gerry (Breen)	04/23	Cutchen, Billye Walker
		10/28	Hollander, John	04/26	Humphrey, Henry (III)
		10/28	Ripper, Charles L(ewis)	04/27	Douglass, Barbara

05/02 Ayer, Jacqueline (Brandford)
05/09 Reitci, Rita Krohne
05/18 Moskof, Martin Stephen
05/18 Polette, Nancy (Jane)
05/18 Saberhagen, Fred (Thomas)
06/02 Holmgren, Helen Jean
06/03 Arora, Shirley Lease
06/04 Knudson, Richard L(ewis)
06/04 Martini, Teri
06/10 Siegal, Aranka
06/16 Alexander, Jocelyn (Anne Arundel)
06/17 Froehlich, Margaret Walden
06/20 Borten, Helen Jacobson
06/21 Pape, D(onna) L(ugg)
06/24 Oleksy, Walter
06/24 Schulke, Flip (Philps Graeme)
06/25 Baker, Liva
06/25 Sabin, Louis
07/03 Berliner, Don
07/06 Skurzynski, Gloria (Joan)
07/08 Klein, Aaron E.
07/10 Zerman, Melvyn Bernard
07/14 Ferguson, Walter (W.)
07/18 Silverthorne, Elizabeth
07/24 Pomerantz, Charlotte
07/25 Larson, Jean Russell
07/27 Massie, Diane Redfield
07/28 Raiff, Stan
07/29 Catlin, Wynelle
07/31 Apfel, Necia H(alpern)
07/31 Smith, Robert Kimmel
08/05 Ruffins, Reynold
08/09 Wennerstrom, Genia Katherine
08/11 Marks, Burton
08/12 Hoberman, Mary Ann (Freedman)
08/14 Goettel, Elinor
08/18 Dunn, Mary Lois
08/19 Linn, Charles F.
08/22 Friedlander, Joanne K(ohn)
08/29 Kavaler, Lucy
08/31 McVicker, Charles (Taggart)
09/08 Barton, Byron (Theodore Vartanian)
09/14 Kaplan, Anne Bernays
09/14 Supraner, Robyn
09/17 Reinach, Jacquelyn (Krasne)
09/20 Durell, Ann
09/24 Cohen, Robert Carl
09/24 Langner, Nola
09/26 Friedman, Marvin
09/30 Zappler, Lisbeth (Moses)
10/02 Alvarez, Joseph A.
10/06 Heyman, Ken(neth Louis)
10/08 Caudell, Marian
10/18 Hautzig, Esther (Rudomin)
10/18 Parker, Nancy Winslow
10/18 Siroff, Harriet

10/22 Stuart, Gene S.
10/27 Spanfeller, James J(ohn)
10/27 Waters, John F(rederick)
10/30 Crane, Caroline
10/30 Larsen, Suzanne Kesteloo
10/31 Collins, Michael
11/12 Chardiet, Bernice (Kroll)
11/13 Andrews, Benny
11/13 Katz, Herbert (Melvin)
11/20 Campbell, Patricia J(ean)
12/08 Immel, Mary Blair
12/08 Morressy, John
12/10 Takakjian, Portia
12/16 Brittain, William
12/27 Allred, Gordon T.

1931
??/?? Bragg, Charles
??/?? Carty, Leo
??/?? Chan, Plato
??/?? Kaufmann, John
??/?? Schroeder, Ted
01/03 Elwood, Ann
01/11 Rodgers, Mary
01/14 Connolly, Jerome P(atrick)
01/26 Silverman, Mel(vyn Frank)
01/30 Eckert, Allan W.
02/01 Kipniss, Robert
02/02 Baker, Jeffrey J(ohn) W(heeler)
02/02 Viorst, Judith (Stahl)
02/03 Powers, Bill
02/07 Micklish, Rita
02/13 Lipman, David
02/14 Scott, Jane (Harrington)
02/14 Warshofsky, Fred
02/16 Beiser, Arthur
02/16 Packard, Edward
02/18 Morrison, Toni (Chloe Anthony Wofford)
02/19 Ilowite, Sheldon A.
02/21 Angeles, Peter A.
02/22 Brookins, Dana (Martin)
02/24 Sutton, Larry M(atthew)
02/26 St. George, Judith
02/26 Stirnweis, Shannon
03/02 Beiser, Germaine (Bousquet)
03/04 Bourne, Miriam Anne (Young)
03/05 Bohlen, Nina
03/05 Gannon, Robert (Haines)
03/07 Sanberg, Karl C.
03/08 Kennedy, Dorothy M(intzlaff)
03/10 Baum, Willi
03/12 Purtill, Richard L.
03/13 Ferguson, Cecil
03/28 Spencer, Donald D(ean)
04/07 Barthelme, Donald
04/12 Obligado, Lilian (Isabel)
04/13 Stone, Jon
04/15 Scott, Cora Annett (Pipitone)
04/17 Jennings, Michael
04/23 Burland, Brian (Berkeley)
04/23 Stover, Jo Ann

04/28 Buell, Harold G.
04/28 Gardner, Richard A.
05/06 Delton, Judy
05/15 Mazer, Norma Fox
05/25 Ruckman, Ivy
05/26 Zweifel, Frances
05/28 VonSchmidt, Eric
05/30 Bowman, John S(tewart)
06/04 Springer, Marilyn Harris
06/07 Crump, Fred H., Jr.
06/07 Reuter, Carol (Joan)
06/17 Higdon, Hal
06/20 Gaeddert, Lou Ann (Bigge)
06/21 Rosenberg, Nancy Sherman
06/25 Robinson, Charles
06/29 Wondriska, William Allen
07/02 Balow, Tom
07/05 Baron, Virginia Olsen
07/10 May, Julian
07/12 Gerassi, John
07/14 Robinet, Harriette Gillem
07/17 Brooks, Jerome
07/19 Cartey, Wilfred George Onslow
07/22 Calvert, Patricia
08/01 Wilson, Tom
08/09 Simon, Seymour
08/10 Dygard, Thomas J.
08/17 Honig, Donald
08/18 Chwast, Seymour
08/19 Dixon, Peter L.
08/20 Razzi, James
08/22 Garrison, Barbara
08/22 Graham, Ada
08/26 Gardner, Richard (M.)
09/04 Evans, Shirlee
09/12 Hunter, Kristin (Elaine Eggleston)
09/20 Kuttner, Paul
09/23 Fassler, Joan (Grace)
09/27 Surge, Frank
09/28 Stevens, Patricia Bunning
10/03 Epstein, Anne Merrick
10/07 Barry, Robert (Everett)
10/07 Young, Bernice Elizabeth
10/10 Weidhorn, Manfred
10/12 Anderson, Helen Jean
10/19 Emberley, Ed(ward Randolph)
10/25 Priddy, Frances (Rosaleen)
10/26 Schnirel, James R(einhold)
10/27 Cohen, Peter Zachary
11/03 Cavallo, Diana
11/06 Gordon, Bernard Ludwig
11/07 Gilbert, Agnes Joan (Sewell)
11/10 Seitz, Jacqueline
11/13 Morton, Eva Jane
11/25 Clements, Bruce
11/28 Young, Ed
11/30 Belton, John Raynor
11/30 Zemach, Margot
12/02 Taylor, Audilee Boyd
12/03 Blue, Rose
12/08 Allen, Marjorie

12/17	Kherdian, David	05/27	Cunningham, Dale S(peers)	11/26	Harris, Sherwood
12/21	Lee, Robert C.			11/30	Kaufman, Mervyn D.
12/24	Anderson, Margaret J(ean)	05/27	Lynch, Lorenzo	12/10	Auerbach, Marjorie (Hoffberg)
12/30	Garrigue, Sheila	06/01	Knudson, Rozanne		
		06/02	Fava, Rita F.	12/12	Emberley, Barbara A(nne Collins)

1932

??/??	Fischler, Stan(ley I.)	06/06	Chermayeff, Ivan	12/21	Hoagland, Edward
??/??	Gayle, Addison	06/07	Funai, Mamoru (Rolland)	12/22	Latham, Donald Crawford
??/??	Heinly, John	06/07	Reed, Kit	12/23	Kennedy, Jerome Richard
??/??	Silverstein, Shel(by)	06/10	Smith, Alison (Porter)	12/25	Richardson, Carol
??/??	Tyll, Al	06/12	Fleming, Susan	12/26	Palmer, Bruce Hamilton
??/??	Ward, Nanda Weedon	06/14	Degen, Bruce N.	12/27	Gemming, Elizabeth
01/01	Chwast, Jacqueline (Weiner)	06/14	Metos, Thomas H(arry)	12/28	Vautier, Ghislaine
		06/19	Pontiflet, Ted		
01/03	Fenten, D(onald) X.	06/19	Servello, Joe		
01/04	Utz, Lois (Marie)	06/24	Green, Phyllis	**1933**	
01/10	Hoppe, Joanne	06/24	Haverstock, Mary Sayre	??/??	Cardwell, Paul, Jr.
01/10	Wallace, Robert A.	06/26	Negri, Rocco (Antonio)	??/??	Marshall, James
01/16	Berry, James	06/27	Reed, Gwendolyn (Elizabeth)	??/??	Toye, Clive
01/20	Johnson, Evelyne			01/04	Naylor, Phyllis Reynolds
01/28	Jonas, Ann	07/01	FitzGerald, Cathleen	01/13	Goulart, Ron(ald Joseph)
01/31	Brown, Irene Bennett	07/05	Givens, Janet E(aton)	01/15	Gaines, Ernest J.
02/09	Meyer, F(ranklyn) E(dward)	07/08	Erickson, Russell E(verett)	01/17	Greene, Wade
		07/08	Masters, Mildred	01/29	McClinton, Leon
02/09	Morriss, James E(dward)	07/16	MacClintock, Dorcas	01/31	Chittenden, Margaret
02/10	Brandenberg, Franz	07/17	Alkema, Chester Jay	02/04	Frank, Mary
02/13	Taback, Simms	07/17	Kuskin, Karla (Seidman)	02/04	Murphy, Barbara Beasley
02/14	Wymark, Olwen (Margaret Buck)	07/21	Lord, Athena V.	02/07	Chandler, David Porter
		07/27	Hull, Jessie Redding	02/16	Burkert, Nancy Ekholm
02/23	Adler, C(arole) S(chwerdtfeger)	07/27	Newsome, Arden J(eanne Bokeeno)	02/20	Christian, Mary Blount
				02/21	Sneve, Virginia Driving Hawk
02/24	Suggs, Robert Carl	07/28	Babbitt, Natalie (Moore)		
02/25	Kanetzke, Howard W(illiam)	07/28	Neusner, Jacob	02/27	Di Certo, Joseph John
		07/29	Kunz, Roxane (Brown)	02/28	Smith, Garry (VanDorn)
02/26	Rodowsky, Colby	08/09	Aruego, Jose	03/02	Dillon, Leo
03/08	Schellie, Don	08/12	Lane, John	03/12	Alda, Arlene
03/14	Fults, John Lee	08/16	Johnson, Milton	03/13	Dillon, Diane (C.)
03/14	Richards, Norman	08/17	Shulman, Alix Kates	03/13	Rockwell, Thomas
03/14	Rutz, Viola Larkin	08/19	Cohen, Joan Lebold	03/14	Bolognese, Elaine Raphael (Chionchio)
03/15	Cohen, Barbara (Kauder)	08/19	Wersba, Barbara		
03/18	Updike, John (Hoyer)	09/02	Wolfe, Burton H.	03/22	Lisker, Sonia O(lson)
03/26	Smith, Linell Nash	09/07	Andersen, Yvonne	03/26	Deloria, Vine (Victor), Jr.
03/31	Edwards, Jane Campbell	09/09	Cooney, Nancy Evans	03/26	Sargent, Robert Edward
03/31	Jakes, John (W.)	09/10	Edelson, Edward	03/30	Hassler, Jon (Francis)
04/04	Reiss, Johanna de Leeuw	09/22	Davidson, Alice Joyce	04/01	Wahl, Jan (Boyer)
04/08	Batterberry, Michael (Carver)	09/23	Oldfield, Margaret J(ean)	04/02	Tinkelman, Murray
		09/24	Curry, Jane L(ouise)	04/16	Hobson, Burton (Harold)
04/08	Masey, Mary Lou(ise Leach)	09/24	Greenberg, Joanne (Goldenberg)	04/22	Miner, Jane Claypool
				04/25	Dollar, Diane (Hills)
04/17	Harris, Janet (Urovsky)	10/02	Bethancourt, T(omas) Ernesto	04/25	Kettelkamp, Larry Dale
04/21	Greenberg, Polly			04/25	Lukas, J(ay) Anthony
04/21	Kellin, Sally Moffet	10/03	Chesler, Bernice	04/25	Murray, Judith Michele (Freedman)
04/21	Kleeberg, Irene (Flitner) Cumming	10/06	Collins, Pat Lowery		
		10/09	Dorman, Michael	04/26	Leichman, Seymour
04/28	Seltzer, Meyer	10/09	Plowden, David	04/27	Gregory, Diana (Jean)
05/01	Bradford, Richard (Roark)	10/17	Lorenz, Lee (Sharp)	05/02	Katz, Bobbi
05/02	Allen, Maury	10/19	Moser, Don(ald Bruce)	05/06	Bosse, Malcolm J(oseph)
05/04	Butler, Beverly (Kathleen)	10/20	Smith, Gary R(ichard)	05/08	Comins, Jeremy
05/07	Hogrogian, Nonny	10/22	Yamaguchi, John Tohr	05/08	Tweton, D. Jerome
05/13	Scarf, Maggi(e)	10/27	Plath, Sylvia	05/19	Feelings, Thomas
05/14	Anderson, Grace Fox	10/28	Homze, Alma C.	05/19	Savitz, Harriet May (Blatstein)
05/17	Weston, John (Harrison)	10/31	Paterson, Katherine (Womeldorf)		
05/21	Hiebert, Ray Eldon			05/22	Lobel, Arnold (Stark)
05/21	Wirtenberg, Patricia Z(arrella)	11/08	Bova, Ben(jamin William)	05/25	Levine, Betty K(rasne)
		11/09	Taylor, L(ester) B(arbour), Jr.	05/25	Miller, Elizabeth
05/22	Hoopes, Ned E(dward)			05/26	Schaller, George B(eals)
05/25	Kristof, Jane	11/12	Forman, James Douglas	05/28	Bergere, Thea Lindgren
		11/16	Coskey, Evelyn	05/30	Gates, Frieda

06/01	Reig, June	??/??	Jeffers, Harry Paul	07/18	Piro, Richard
06/03	Angrist, Stanley W(olff)	??/??	Marek, Margot L.	07/23	Brow, Thea
06/04	Snyder, Gerald S(eymour)	??/??	Nadler, Robert	08/08	Hammer, Charles
06/06	Samson, Anne S(tringer)	01/01	Smith, LeRoi	08/17	Adorjan, Carol (Madden)
06/10	LaFarge, Phyllis	01/01	Telemaque, Eleanor Wong	08/17	Hamberger, John (F.)
06/11	Chu, Daniel	01/03	Gauch, Patricia Lee	08/18	Levitin, Sonia (Wolff)
06/15	Glubok, Shirley (Astor)	01/03	Moffett, Martha (Leatherwood)	08/18	McCormick, Edith (Joan)
06/20	McCarthy, Agnes	01/03	Smith, Ursula	08/19	Robinson, Jean O. (Kroner)
06/28	Pellowski, Anne	01/06	Bolognese, Don(ald Alan)	08/27	Rinaldi, Ann
06/29	Jacker, Corinne (Litvin)	01/07	Meade, Marion	09/03	Schulman, L(ester) M(artin)
06/30	Cruz, Ray(mond)	01/17	Lewis, Shari	09/09	Sanchez, Sonia
07/04	Gilson, Jamie	01/20	Robison, Nancy L(ouise)	09/15	DePaola, Thomas Anthony
07/08	Giblin, James Cross	01/24	Keith, Hal	09/26	Link, Martin
07/11	Lewis, Richard William	01/26	Thomas, Patricia J(ack)	09/27	Torgersen, Don Arthur
07/13	Goldstein, Ernest A.	01/31	DeWeese, Thomas Eugene	09/28	Kahl, M(arvin) P(hilip)
07/21	Gardner, John (Champlin, Jr.)	02/02	Weiser, Marjorie P(hillis) K(atz)	10/06	Needleman, Jacob
08/07	Pournelle, Jerry (Eugene)	02/08	Rockwell, Anne (Foote)	10/10	Hadley, Lee
08/09	Longtemps, Kenneth	02/10	Morrill, Leslie H(olt)	10/13	Neimark, Paul G.
08/09	Steinberg, Fred J.	02/10	Rice, James	10/15	Bourdon, David
08/10	Loss, Joan	02/12	Downie, Mary Alice (Dawe)	10/18	Wilson, Sarah
08/11	Berger, Terry	02/27	Momaday, N(avarre) Scott	10/25	Maher, Ramona
08/13	Mitchell, Joyce Slayton	03/01	Felts, Shirley	10/26	Showell, Ellen Harvey
08/20	Alexander, Sue	03/09	Grant, Myrna (Lois)	10/29	Ballard, Mignon Franklin
08/23	Jacobs, William Jay	03/09	Peterson, Esther (Allen)	10/31	Griffith, Helen V(irginia)
08/26	Bossom, Naomi	03/14	Spelman, Mary	11/03	Steiner, Barbara A(nnette)
08/26	McManus, Patrick (Francis)	03/15	Gelman, Steve	11/08	Hodge, P(aul) W(illiam)
09/16	Schulman, Janet	03/17	Oneal, Elizabeth (Bisgard)	11/09	Ehlert, Lois (Jane)
09/17	Goble, Paul	03/25	Bergey, Alyce (Mae)	11/09	Sagan, Carl
09/29	Chambers, John W.	03/26	Arkin, Alan (Wolf)	11/13	Densen-Gerber, Judianne
10/03	Smith, Vesta (Henderson)	03/30	Bauer, Fred	11/13	Marshall, Garry
10/04	McGrady, Mike	04/05	Peck, Richard (Wayne)	11/15	McGough, Elizabeth (Hemmes)
10/04	Wilford, John Noble, Jr.	04/10	Melton, David	11/17	Wyss, Thelma Hatch
10/15	Brown, Judith Gwyn	04/11	Strand, Mark	11/18	Paul, David (Tyler)
10/17	Keyser, Marcia	04/17	Witt, Shirley Hill	11/18	Schulte, Elaine L(ouise)
10/21	Longsworth, Polly (Ormsby)	04/18	Luttrell, Ida (Alleene)	11/19	Luhrmann, Winifred B(ruce)
10/21	Oliver, John Edward	04/20	Gardner, Sheldon	11/29	McPhee, Richard Byron
10/21	Yates, Brock W(endel)	04/28	Duncan, Lois S(teinmetz)	11/29	Morris, Willie
10/22	Foley, Mary Louise Munro	04/29	Britt, Dell	12/04	Simons, Barbara B(rooks)
10/23	Perry, Phyllis J.	04/30	Ulm, Robert	12/08	Beame, Rona
10/29	Worth, Valerie	05/06	Sweetland, Nancy A(nn Rose)	12/11	Stone, A. Harris
10/30	Robinson, Jan M.	05/11	Fisher, Laura Harrison	12/13	Horner, Dave
10/31	Stevens, Franklin	05/11	Oppenheim, Joanne	12/14	Crofut, William E. III
10/31	Szekeres, Cyndy	05/17	Mohn, Peter B(urnet)	12/18	Katz, Jane (Bresler)
11/11	Dotts, Maryann J.	05/21	Cleaver, Carole	12/18	Purscell, Phyllis
11/14	Vo-Dinh, Mai	05/26	Green, Sheila Ellen	12/24	Callahan, Dorothy M(onahan)
11/15	Morris, Robert A(da)	05/26	Schlee, Ann	12/25	Donna, Natalie
11/21	DeLarrea, Victoria	05/27	Sweat, Lynn	12/29	Silman, Roberta (Karpel)
11/21	Elmore, Carolyn Patricia	05/29	Walker, James Brazelton		
11/24	Engdahl, Sylvia Louise	06/01	Boone, Pat	**1935**	
11/27	Smith, Alvin	06/01	Smith, Doris Buchanan	??/??	Armstrong, Thomas E.
12/05	Meek, Jacklyn O'Hanlon	06/02	Crane, Barbara J.	??/??	Brent, Hope
12/05	Zemach, Harve	06/02	Mendoza, George	??/??	Harris, John
12/11	Morgan, Shirley	06/03	Lobel, Anita (Kempler)	??/??	Kock, Carl
12/14	Delano, Hugh	06/08	White, William, Jr.	??/??	Littell, Robert
12/20	Thacher, Mary McGrath	06/10	Slackman, Charles B.	??/??	Mack, Stan(ley)
12/26	Swenson, Allan A(rmstrong)	06/11	Belair, Richard L.	??/??	Morrison, Bill
12/30	Silverstein, Alvin	06/12	Isaac, Joanne	??/??	Robinson, Lloyd
		06/14	McMullan, James	??/??	Verrone, Robert J.
1934		06/28	Greene, Bette	01/01	Kliban, B.
??/??	Carter, Mary Kennedy	06/29	Dauer, Rosamond	01/01	Mead, Russell (M., Jr.)
??/??	Eberstadt, Isabel (Nash)	07/10	Lee, Mary Price	01/07	O'Connell, Margaret F(orster)
??/??	Fleischer, Lenore	07/16	Jones, Hettie		
??/??	Hendrick, Joseph				

01/12	Mayerson, Evelyn White	08/31	Vaughn, Ruth	04/04	Oldenburg, E(gbert) William
01/15	Silverberg, Robert	09/06	Buchwald, Emilie		
01/22	Parenteau, Shirley (Laurolyn)	09/07	Klevin, Jill Ross	04/16	Parsons, William E(dward), Jr.
		09/17	Allen, Nina (Stromgren)		
01/23	Giegling, John A(llan)	09/18	Batterberry, Ariane Ruskin	04/17	Renlie, Frank H.
01/30	Brautigan, Richard (Gary)	09/21	White, Laurence B(arton), Jr.	04/26	Gleasner, Diana (Cottle)
01/31	Marston, Hope Irvin			04/27	Paul, James
02/04	Alexander, Linda	09/28	Berkey, Barry Robert	04/27	Vigna, Judith
02/10	Alcorn, John	10/01	Edwards, Julie (Andrews)	04/28	Harvey, Brett
02/21	Lupoff, Richard A(llen)	10/02	Antell, Will D.	04/30	Sobol, Harriet Langsam
02/23	Powledge, Fred	10/03	Neimark, Anne E.		
02/27	Shulevitz, Uri	11/01	Mohr, Nicholasa (Golpe)	05/14	Davidson, Margaret (Compere)
02/28	Mezey, Robert	11/05	Feder, Paula (Kurzband)		
03/09	Vavra, Robert James	11/05	Sewall, Marcia (Osgood)	05/15	Zindel, Paul
03/10	Stephens, Mary Jo	11/13	Friedman, Judi	05/19	Lippman, Peter J.
03/18	Smith, Nancy Covert	11/22	List, Ilka Katherine	05/19	Schongut, Emanuel
03/21	Davis, Mary L(ee)	11/24	Gerstein, Mordicai	05/23	Parnall, Peter
03/21	Pepe, Phil(ip)	11/26	Pringle, Laurence P.	05/27	Tripp, Eleanor B(aldwin)
03/21	Weber, Devora	12/13	Koren, Ed(ward)	05/29	Bradford, Lois J(ean)
03/29	Gordon, Esther S(aranga)	12/13	Roever, J(oan) M(arilyn)	06/01	Scoppetone, Sandra
03/30	DeWaard, E(lliott) John	12/22	Cornish, Sam(uel James)	06/12	Lester, Helen
04/05	Gibbs, Wolcott, Jr.	12/22	Newton, James R(obert)	06/12	Park, W(illiam) B(ryan)
04/05	Hoover, H(elen) M(ary)	12/29	Hall, Brian P(atrick)	06/20	Wood, Nancy
04/11	Fairman, Joan A(lexandra)			06/22	Cappel, Constance
04/13	Fuchs, Lucy	**1936**		06/23	Bach, Richard David
04/16	Wachter, Oralee Roberts	??/??	Ford, George (Cephas, Jr.)	06/23	Stretton, Barbara (Humphrey)
04/20	Davidson, Sandra Calder				
04/20	Kujoth, Jean Spealman	??/??	Mofsie, Louis B.	06/26	Willard, Nancy (Margaret)
04/21	Wagenheim, Kal	??/??	Taylor, Arthur (Raymond)	06/27	Clifton, Lucille
04/26	Giff, Patricia Reilly	??/??	Thaler, Michael C.	06/27	Tarshis, Jerome
04/28	Shecter, Ben	??/??	Wadowski-Bak, Alice	06/28	Wade, Theodore E., Jr.
05/02	Clyne, Patricia Edwards	??/??	Wehen, Joy DeWeese	07/01	Lewis, Thomas P(arker)
05/02	Munowitz, Ken	01/04	Burleigh, Robert	07/09	Jordan, June (Meyer)
05/06	Lewin, Ted	01/04	Liman, Ellen (Fogelson)	07/18	Dixon, Jeanne
05/11	Jacobs, Francine	01/05	Oates, Stephen B.	07/24	Marrin, Albert
05/12	Bauer, Caroline Feller	01/07	Chorao, Ann McKay (Sproat)	08/01	Forman, Brenda
05/15	Lewis, Richard			08/06	Tusan, Stan
05/18	Cober, Alan E(dwin)	01/07	Lapp, Eleanor J.	08/12	Strauss, Joyce
05/20	Carrick, Carol (Hatfield)	01/07	Simonetta, Sam	08/15	Thomas, Jane Resh
05/21	Spencer, Zane A(nn)	01/10	Ambrose, Stephen E(dward)	08/24	Hendrickson, Walter Brookfield, Jr.
05/24	Carlson, Dale Bick				
05/24	Pollock, Penny	01/10	Martin, Stefan	08/27	Becker, Joyce
06/01	Corwin, June Atkin	01/10	Yamaguchi, Marianne Illenberger	09/02	Bierhorst, John (William)
06/08	Meyer, Carolyn (Mae)			09/14	Pierce, Ruth (Ireland)
06/15	Roche, P(atricia) K.	01/11	Mango, Karin N.	09/15	Davis, Daniel S(heldon)
06/16	Warren, Joyce W(illiams)	01/11	Rosenbaum, Eileen	09/21	Burroway, Janet (Gay)
		01/12	Cadwallader, Sharon	09/24	Henson, James Maury
06/19	Ray, JoAnne	01/19	Panter, Carol (Yeckes)	09/25	Albert, Burton, Jr.
06/24	Line, Les	02/03	Brown, Buck	10/03	Vander els, Betty
06/27	Greenberg, Harvey R.	02/09	Litowinsky, Olga (Jean)	10/07	Lewis, Alice C.
06/29	Briscoe, Jill (Pauline)	02/13	Meade, Ellen (Roddick)	10/07	McShean, Gordon
07/01	Skorpen, Liesel (Moak)	02/15	Hook, Martha	10/08	Moore, Carman Leroy
07/05	Schoenherr, John (Carl)	02/16	Schreiter, Rick	10/08	Newton, Suzanne (Latham)
07/06	Tiegreen, Alan F.	02/16	Stevens, Kathleen		
07/08	Gladstone, Gary	02/18	Hemphill, Paul (James)	10/11	McPherson, James M.
07/16	Adoff, Arnold	02/21	Hermes, Patricia	10/21	Winn, Marie
07/20	Stepp, Ann	02/29	Webb, Sharon	10/24	Moche, Dinah (Rachel) L(evine)
07/21	Greene, Laura	03/05	Matte, Encarnacion L'Enc		
07/22	Manchel, Frank	03/06	Braude, Michael	11/09	Davis, Lou Ellen
07/24	Booth, Graham (Charles)	03/09	Montgomery, R(aymond) A. (,Jr.)	11/18	Smith, Philip Warren
07/27	Laurence, Ester Hauser			11/20	Faithfull, Gail
08/05	Patterson, Charles	03/12	Cohen, Daniel	11/23	Johnson, Lois W(alfrid)
08/07	Hemschemeyer, Judith	03/12	Hamilton, Virginia (Esther)	11/26	Mearian, Judy Frank
08/09	Ohlsson, Ib			12/06	Kredenser, Gail
08/15	Arneson, Don Jon	03/19	Brancato, Robin F(idler)	12/08	Marx, Robert F(rank)
08/15	Mele, Frank M(ichael)	03/31	Barry, Katharina (Maria Watjen)	12/08	McCaffery, Janet
08/25	Fenten, Barbara D(oris)			12/16	Wagner, Sharon B.

| 12/20 | Farley, Carol (J. McDole) |
| 12/26 | Zaring, Jane (Thomas) |

1937

??/??	Lacy, Leslie Alexander
??/??	Seed, Sheila Turner
??/??	Simmons, Dawn Langley
01/03	Taylor, Carl
01/04	Korty, Carol
01/07	Stewig, John Warren
01/13	Arbeiter, Jean S(onkin)
01/19	Batten, Mary
01/26	Mikolaycak, Charles
01/27	Kessel, Joyce Karen
02/06	Singer, David (Lin)
02/17	Berry, B(arbara) J.
02/17	Habenstreit, Barbara (Zeigler)
02/22	Schneider, Rex
02/26	Mathis, Sharon Bell
03/01	Elmer, Irene (Elizabeth)
03/03	Erikson, Mel
03/03	Komoda, Kiyo(aki)
03/11	Ezzell, Marilyn
03/13	Harrison, David Lee
03/15	Holder, William G.
03/15	Sargent, Sarah
03/19	Deegan, Paul Joseph
03/20	Lowry, Lois (Hammbersberg)
03/25	Chevalier, Christa
03/29	Kowet, Don
04/03	Silverstein, Virginia B(arbara Opshelor)
04/22	Bible, Charles
04/22	Neier, Aryeh
04/22	Parker, Margot M.
04/22	Stein, R(ichard) Conrad
04/28	Hoh, Diane
05/04	Greisman, Joan Ruth
05/06	Terris, Susan (Dubinsky)
05/12	Lewin, Betsy
05/13	Zelazny, Roger (Joseph Christopher)
05/18	Green, Morton
05/25	Churchill, E. Richard
05/31	Gorodetzky, Charles W.
06/02	Mali, Jane Lawrence
06/07	Weisberg, Joseph S(impson)
06/10	Herman, Charlotte
06/16	Hayes, Sheila
06/17	Branscum, Robbie
06/22	Etchison, Birdie L(ee)
06/23	Curtis, Richard (Alan)
06/25	Sarnoff, Jane
06/26	Locker, Thomas
06/27	Green, Jane
07/02	Gelman, Rita Golden
07/10	Angell, Judie
07/11	Victor, Joan Berg
07/17	Veglahn, Nancy (Crary)
07/22	Seuling, Barbara
07/25	Barrett, Ron
07/25	Hopper, Nancy J.
07/29	Smith, Betsy Covington
08/12	Myers, Walter Dean
08/13	Fox, Michael Wilson
08/17	Dewey, Ariane
08/21	Hayden, Robert C(arter), Jr.
08/22	Holt, Margaret (Cecile)
08/22	Kohl, Herbert
08/24	Cebulash, Mel
08/29	Glaser, Dianne Elizabeth
09/02	Most, Bernard
09/06	Aragones, Sergio
09/09	Samson, Joan
09/15	Smith, Jacqueline B.
09/21	Bozzo, Frank
09/27	Gretz, Susanna
10/02	Bladow, Suzanne Wilson
10/09	Hurwitz, Johanna
10/10	Benagh, Jim
10/10	Frommer, Harvey
10/10	Moe, Barbara
10/13	Fitschen, Dale
10/15	Miller, Frances A.
10/16	Himler, Ronald (Norbert)
10/19	Young, Rodney Lee Patrick (, Jr.)
10/20	Haynes, Betsy
11/07	Banks, Sara (Jeanne Gordon Harrell)
11/08	Feig, Barbara Krane
11/09	Hall, Lynn
11/20	Girion, Barbara
11/23	Burchard, Sue (Huston)
11/28	Madison, Arnold
12/04	Christian, Samuel T(erry)
12/07	Elkins, Dov Peretz
12/07	Kraus, Joanna Halpert
12/09	Hahn, Mary Downing
12/19	Kindred, Wendy (Good)
12/20	Blaine, Marge(ry Kay)
12/20	Kubinyi, Laszlo (Kalman)
12/22	Kines, Pat Decker
12/23	Wortis, Avi
12/26	VanLeeuwen, Jean

1938

??/??	Caines, Jeannette (Franklin)
??/??	Folsom, Michael (Brewster)
??/??	Kotzwinkle, William
??/??	McClain, George
01/03	Ada, Alma Flor
01/15	Hart, Bruce
01/16	Lipsyte, Robert (Michael)
01/17	Bellairs, John
01/26	Figueroa, Pablo
02/04	Harrison, Deloris
02/12	Blume, Judy (Sussman)
02/17	Jones, Penelope
03/01	Kurland, Michael (Joseph)
03/03	Luttrell, Guy L.
03/03	MacLachlan, Patricia
03/04	Daves, Michael
03/11	Chaconas, D(oris) J.
03/22	Cazet, Denys
03/25	Baldwin, Anne Norris
03/26	Ganz, Yaffa
03/27	Gesner, Clark
03/29	Delulio, John
04/05	West, Anna
04/06	Rothman, Joel
04/06	Wittels, Harriet Joan
04/08	O'Connor, Karen
04/09	Andersdatter, Karla M(argaret)
04/13	Hopkins, Lee Bennett
04/20	Wold, Jo Anne
04/21	Rosenblatt, Arthur S.
05/12	Kimmel, Margaret Mary
05/12	Lyle, Katie Letcher
05/13	Allmendinger, David F(rederick), Jr.
05/13	Klein, Norma
05/13	Pascal, Francine
05/15	Garden, Nancy
05/19	Rohmer, Harriet
05/23	Peek, Merle
05/25	Thomas, Joyce Carol
05/27	Ricciuti, Edward R(aphael)
05/29	Cole, Brock
06/01	Feinberg, Barbara Jane
06/03	Larson, William H.
06/05	Taylor, Jerry Duncan
06/08	Zaid, Barry
06/12	Mace, Varian
06/20	Vuong, Lynette (Dyer)
06/25	Hanson, Joan
06/28	Stover, Allan C(arl)
07/03	Smith, Anne Warren
07/10	O'Brien, Thomas C(lement)
07/18	Mangurian, David
07/22	Alter, Judith (MacBain)
07/28	Hiller, Ilo (Ann)
07/31	Feelings, Muriel (Grey)
08/01	Bouchard, Lois Kalb
08/05	Mayer, Ann M(argaret)
08/14	Marks, Rita (Weiss)
08/15	Reese, Robert A.
08/18	Carris, Joan Davenport
08/19	Cobb, Vicki (Wolf)
08/20	Kevles, Bettyann
08/21	Epstein, Perle S(herry)
08/30	Crews, Donald
09/12	Tobias, Tobi
09/13	Stahl, Hilda
09/15	Mee, Charles L., Jr.
09/21	Windsor, Patricia
09/23	Katz, Fred(eric Phillip)
09/25	Coleman, William L(eroy)
09/25	Cornell, James (Clayton, Jr.)
10/04	Long, Earlene (Roberta)
10/08	Radin, Ruth Yaffe
10/10	Chapian, Marie
10/13	Pincus, Harriet
10/13	Weltner, Linda R(iverly)
10/23	McCullough, Frances Monson
10/25	Whittlesey, Susan
11/02	Allen, Rodney F.
11/03	Lord, Bette Bao
11/04	Trost, Lucille Wood
11/05	Levinson, Nancy Smiler
11/06	Kandell, Alice S.

11/09 Lerner, Sharon (Ruth)
11/13 Matus, Greta
11/15 Frascino, Edward
11/20 Bauer, Marion Dane
11/20 Perera, Thomas Biddle
11/24 Johnson, Spencer
12/05 Joyner, Jerry
12/14 Neufeld, John (Arthur)
12/16 Godrog, Judith (Allen)
12/19 Ellen, Barbara

1939
??/?? Basilevsky, Helen
??/?? Campbell, Barbara
??/?? Klaveness, Jan O'Donnell
??/?? Norris, Gunilla B(rodde)
01/05 Cole, Sheila R(otenberg)
01/09 Wende, Philip
01/20 Anderson, Mary (Quirk)
01/23 Hildebrandt, Greg
01/23 Hildebrandt, Tim(othy)
01/24 Ferris, Jean
01/24 Tarshis, Barry
01/27 Lester, Julius B.
02/03 Ringi, Kjell Arne Sorensen
02/06 Taylor, Louise Todd
02/11 Yolen, Jane H(yatt)
02/12 Dorin, Patrick C(arberry)
02/15 VanHorn, William
02/22 Zubrowski, Bernard
03/05 Goldberg, Stan J.
03/06 Drescher, Joan E(lizabeth)
03/13 Owens, Gail
03/19 Bate, Lucy
03/22 Skipper, G. C.
03/26 Wilson, Walt(er N.)
03/27 Govern, Elaine
04/06 Abercrombie, Barbara (Mattes)
04/08 Hyman, Trina Schart
04/20 Beagle, Peter S.
05/02 Shreve, Susan Richards
05/03 Newman, Gerald
05/07 Solot, Mary Lynn (Marx)
05/08 Whitehouse, Jeanne
05/10 Roseman, Kenneth David
05/11 Bock, Harold I.
05/14 Dickmeyer, Lowell A.
05/17 Paulsen, Gary
05/17 Purdy, Susan Gold
06/04 Sortor, June Elizabeth
06/08 Dengler, Sandy
06/26 Klug, Ron(ald)
06/29 Lager, Marilyn
07/01 McCully, Emily Arnold
07/03 Arenella, Roy
07/04 Vecsey, George
07/05 Stefanik, Alfred T.
07/10 Adler, Larry
07/13 Joseph, Joan
07/17 Miskovits, Christine
07/19 Feldman, Anne (Rodgers)
07/19 Myra, Harold L(awrence)
07/24 Malzberg, Barry (N.)
08/01 Jacopetti, Alexandra
08/06 Rosenberg, Maxine B(erta)
08/08 Caraway, Caren

08/12 McKissack, Fredrick L(emuel)
08/18 Siegel, Robert (Harold)
09/07 Petroski, Catherine (Ann Groom)
09/12 Boring, Mel
09/14 Anticaglia, Elizabeth
09/18 Bock, William Sauts Netamux'we
09/21 Schraff, Anne E(laine)
09/24 Brown, Drollene P.
10/02 Salassi, Otto R(ussell)
10/06 Tester, Sylvia Root
10/14 Polland, Barbara K(ay)
10/16 Arrowood, McKendrick Lee Clinton
10/16 Gundersheimer, Karen
10/19 Max, Peter
11/04 Haley, Gail E(inhart)
11/12 Giovanopoulos, Paul (Arthur)
11/16 Chess, Victoria (Dickerson)
11/26 Komoda, Beverly
12/01 Berends, Polly Berrien
12/04 Cavanagh, Helen (Carol)
12/22 Pinkney, Jerry
12/29 Zeck, Gerald Anthony

1940
??/?? Hane, Roger
01/01 Choate, Judith (Newkirk)
01/10 Gonzalez, Gloria
01/13 Fitzgerald, F(rancis) A(nthony)
01/15 Hochschild, Arlie Russell
01/19 DePauw, Linda Grant
01/25 Wartski, Maureen (Ann Crane)
01/27 O'Leary, Brian (Todd)
02/02 Bitter, Gary G(len)
02/02 Disch, Thomas M(ichael)
02/07 Berelson, Howard
02/10 Cosner, Shaaron
02/19 Harrah, Michael
02/19 Krementz, Jill
02/20 Gustkey, Earl
02/28 Kingsley, Emily Perl
02/29 Collins, David (Raymond)
03/01 Grossman, Robert
03/02 Eaton, Tom
03/03 MacDonald, Suse (Susan Kelsey)
03/06 Jacobs, Susan
03/07 Christesen, Barbara
03/08 Seed, Suzanne (Liddell)
03/18 Forrester, Victoria
03/28 Love, Sandra (Weller)
03/30 Lucas, Jerry
04/03 Wilkinson, Sylvia (J.)
04/04 Gilman, Phoebe
04/22 Koertge, Ronald
04/22 Marr, John S(tuart)
04/23 Schwartz, Joel L.
04/28 Boorman, Linda (Kay)
04/28 Grossman, Nancy (S.)
04/28 Terban, Marvin

04/29 Roy, Ron(ald)
04/30 Patent, Dorothy Hinshaw
05/08 Benchley, Peter B(radford)
05/19 Hendershot, Judith
05/20 Schell, Orville H.
05/29 Turner, Alice K.
05/31 Goor, Ron(ald Stephen)
06/08 Blauer, Ettagale Laure
06/11 Hyman, Linda
06/12 Shea, George
06/20 Scott, Elaine
06/23 Jones, Betty Millsaps
06/26 Tripp, Wallace (Whitney)
06/30 McPhail, David M(ichael)
07/07 Trivett, Daphne (Harwood)
07/08 Hickman, Janet
07/08 Math, Irwin
07/10 Peterson, Lorraine
07/24 Hillman, Priscilla (Hartford)
08/12 Jewell, Nancy
08/31 Ray, Deborah (Kogan)
09/01 Ernst, Lyman John
09/03 Hunt, Linda Lawrence
09/08 Prelutsky, Jack
09/11 Alderson, Sue Ann
09/21 Tallon, Robert
10/02 Sapieyevski, Anne Lindbergh
10/05 Dewey, Ken(neth Francis)
10/15 Howe, Fanny
10/15 Laure, Jason
10/15 Moser, Barry
10/26 Schmiderer, Dorothy
10/27 Kingston, Maxine (Ting Ting) Hong
10/27 Roth, David
10/29 Bahr, Robert
11/09 Bales, Carol Ann
11/10 Hancock, Sibyl
11/26 VanTuyl, Barbara
12/04 Hiscock, Bruce
12/06 Anton, Michael J(ames)
12/07 Gles, Margaret Breitmaier
12/07 Segal, Joyce
12/10 Fisher, Barbara
12/20 Goffstein, M(arilyn) B(rooke)
12/28 Dana, Barbara

1941
??/?? Barrett, Judi(th)
??/?? Bartholomew, Barbara (G.)
01/03 Nathanson, Laura Walther
01/04 Delessert, Etienne
01/11 Billings, Charlene W(interer)
01/13 Naylor, Penelope
01/15 Edwards, Page L., Jr.
01/15 Yang, Jay
01/16 Orbach, Ruth Gary
01/19 Dodson, Susan
01/26 McHugh, Berit Elisabet
01/31 McDermott, Gerald
02/01 Spinelli, Jerry
02/07 Kilian, Crawford
02/12 Haney, Lynn
02/13 McCloy, James F(loyd)

02/19	Schermer, Judith (Denise)	12/27	Wilson, Carter	08/12	Robinson, Nancy K(onheim)
02/21	Case, Marshal T(aylor)	12/31	Lorimer, Janet	08/16	Beamer, George Charles, Jr.
02/22	Livingston, Carole				
03/17	Abrams, Joy	**1942**		08/16	Spinelli, Eileen
04/07	Clemens, Virginia Phelps	??/??	Grace, F(rances Jane)	08/21	Fiarotta, Phyllis
04/07	Schertle, Alice	01/11	Byrd, Robert (John)	08/22	Meyer, Louis A(lbert)
04/08	Sivulich, Sandra (Jeanne) Stroner	01/19	Blocksma, Mary	08/30	Buchan, Stuart
		01/30	Johnston, Tony	09/02	Hunt, Charlotte Dumaresq
04/10	Madian, Jon	01/31	Tchudi, Stephen N.	09/02	Walsh, Ellen Stoll
04/10	Theroux, Paul	02/14	Highwater, Jamake	09/08	Johnson, Joan J.
04/19	Barkley, James Edward	02/15	Shachtman, Tom	09/11	Ruby, Lois
04/25	Kuzma, Kay	02/17	McCurdy, Michael	09/14	Lydon, Michael
05/13	Fleming, Ronald Lee	02/25	Voigt, Cynthia	09/17	Graham, Brenda Knight
05/23	Seabrooke, Brenda	03/05	Resnick, Michael D(iamond)	09/20	Bridgers, Sue Ellen
05/26	Phelan, Terry Wolfe			09/24	MacMaster, Eve (Ruth) B(owers)
05/30	Marchette, Katharine E.	03/15	White, Ruth C.		
06/07	McHargue, Georgess	03/20	Conford, Ellen (Schaffer)	10/06	Hearne, Betsy Gould
06/09	Carey, Bonnie	03/20	Hefter, Richard	10/06	Spangenberg, Judith Dunn
06/13	Gamerman, Martha	03/30	Davies, Bettilu D(onna)	10/07	Jeffers, Susan (Jane)
06/18	Baker, Janice E(dla)	03/30	Keller, Charles	10/10	Marshall, James (Edward)
06/19	Lamb, Robert (Boyden)	04/01	Berger, Phil	10/15	Gormley, Beatrice
06/27	Bollen, Roger	04/04	Levy, Elizabeth	10/16	Asher, Sandy (Fenichel)
06/28	Heath, Charles D(ickinson)	04/06	Bach, Alice (Hendricks)	10/16	Bruchac, Joseph III
07/04	Mooser, Stephen	04/08	Komisar, Lucy	10/18	Hansen, Joyce W.
07/05	McCoy, Lois (Rich)	04/15	Schick, Eleanor (Grossman)	10/18	Jeschke, Susan
07/07	Billout, Guy Rene			10/23	Crichton, J. Michael
07/10	Boulet, Susan Seddon	04/16	Moore, Eva	10/24	Chiefari, Janet D.
07/11	Payne, Bernal C., Jr.	04/22	Ault, Rosalie Sain	10/25	Tolan, Stephanie S.
07/22	Brady, Maxine L.	04/22	Sussman, Susan	11/02	Manushkin, Fran(ces)
07/22	Byard, Carole (Marie)	04/24	Galinsky, Ellen	11/05	James, Elizabeth
07/26	Cooper, Kay	04/24	Lazarevich, Mila	11/05	Meyers, Susan (Thompson)
07/30	Singer, Susan (Mahler)	04/24	Magorian, James		
08/11	Kroll, Steven	04/26	Eagle, Mike	11/10	Iverson, Genie
08/11	Snyder, Carol	04/30	Sandin, Joan	11/11	Loescher, Ann Dull
08/16	McDermott, Beverly Brodsky	05/06	Maestro, Giulio (Marcello)	11/11	Wolkstein, Diane
		05/07	Auth, William Anthony, Jr.	11/12	Ernst, Kathryn (Fitzgerald)
08/19	Cerf, Christopher (Bennett)	05/09	Filstrup, E(dward) Christian	11/16	Girard, Linda Walvoord
08/19	Lyons, Grant			11/18	Cornelius, Carol
08/25	Wallace-Brodeur, Ruth	05/16	Suid, Murray	11/25	Bortstein, Larry
08/28	Gardner, Beau	05/18	Crary, Elizabeth (Ann)	12/04	Stiles, Norman B.
09/14	Hirschmann, Linda (Ann)	05/19	Arehart-Treichel, Joan	12/14	Okimoto, Jean Davies
09/19	Haskins, James S.	05/24	Taylor, Paula (Wright)	12/14	Rosenberg, Sharon
09/20	Geisert, Arthur (Frederick)	06/07	Gulley, Julie	12/18	Miller, Mary Beth
09/24	Quin-Harkin, Janet	06/11	Bender, Lucy Ellen	12/19	Bowman, Kathleen (Gill)
09/25	Wittman, Sally (Anne Christensen)	06/11	Taylor, Herb(ert Norman, Jr.)	12/24	Cott, Jonathan
				12/26	Robinson, Marileta
09/29	Adams, Laurie	06/15	Phillips, Louis	12/29	Greenberg, Jan (Schonwald)
10/02	Betancourt, Jeanne	06/20	Morgan, Tom		
10/02	Dewey, Jennifer (Owings)	06/22	Sammis, John	12/29	Gustafson, Anita
10/02	Olugebefola, Ademole	06/24	Keith, Eros		
10/09	Anastasio, Dina	06/24	Marzollo, Jean	**1943**	
10/19	Price, Jonathan (Reeve)	06/25	Adamson, Wendy Wriston	??/??	Burke, Lynn
10/19	Richter, Alice	06/29	Feil, Hila	??/??	Schiller, Justin G.
10/21	Dresang, Eliza (Carolyn Timberlake)	06/30	Landis, J(ames) D(avid)	??/??	Taylor, Mildred D(elois)
		07/01	Greenleaf, Barbara Kaye	01/11	Ulmer, Louise
10/23	Petersen, P(eter) J(ames)	07/06	Schreiber, Ralph W(alter)	01/13	Elwood, Roger
10/25	Tyler, Anne	07/07	Watson, Wendy (McLeod)	01/14	Mauser, Patricia Rhoads
10/26	Kellogg, Steven (Castle)	07/08	Penzler, Otto	01/17	Haas, James E(dward)
10/28	Harris, Mark Jonathan	07/13	Ziegler, Jack (Denmore)	01/22	Jacobs, Linda C.
11/14	Moore, Jack (William)	07/15	Stanley, George Edward	01/29	Wells, Rosemary
11/15	Crow, Donna Fletcher	07/24	Ehrlich, Amy	01/31	Rivoli, Mario
11/15	Pinkwater, Daniel Manus	07/24	Kurland, Gerald	02/01	McGee, Barbara
11/24	Halter, Jon C(harles)	07/27	Ridlon, Marci	02/04	Ross, Pat(ricia Kienzie)
11/26	Enderle, Judith (Ann)	07/27	Sears, Stephen W.	02/10	Gammell, Stephen
12/04	Riessen, Martin Clare	08/03	Schiff, Ken(neth Roy)	02/19	Callaway, Kathy
12/15	Dockery, Wallene T.	08/07	Keillor, Garrison	02/21	Aylesworth, Jim
12/15	Williams, Leslie	08/12	Bliss, Ronald G(ene)		

03/05	Goode, Stephen	12/18	Vandenburg, Mary Lou	**1945**	
03/15	Haines, Gail Kay (Beckman)	12/27	Stanley, Diane Z.	??/??	Solomon, Louis
		12/29	Bang, Molly Garrett	??/??	Weiss, Peter
03/21	Weiss, Ann E(dwards)	12/29	Brady, Irene	01/08	Bond, Nancy (Barbara)
04/05	Smith, Lucia B.	12/29	Ready, Kirk L.	01/12	Rostkowski, Margaret I.
04/19	Ducornet, Erica	12/30	Mayer, Mercer	01/15	LeTord, Bijou
04/21	Bernstein, Joanne E(ckstein)			01/18	McGuire, Leslie (Sarah)
		1944		01/23	Crawford, Charles P.
04/22	Christelow, Eileen	??/??	Connor, James	01/24	Israel, Elaine
04/26	Pendle, Alexy	01/01	Hirsh, Marilyn (Joyce)	02/02	Matthias, Catherine
04/30	Hart, Carole	01/05	Maestro, Betsy (Crippen)	02/03	Wallner, John C(harles)
05/01	Scheier, Michael	01/06	Townsend, Thomas L.	02/05	Wibbelsman, Charles J(oseph)
05/03	Zindel, Bonnie	01/08	Brooks, Terry		
05/10	Glenn, Mel	01/30	Katchen, Carole	02/09	Roos, Stephen (Kelley)
05/18	DeJonge, Joanne E.	01/31	Carmichael, Harriet	02/12	Small, David
05/18	Porte, Barbara Ann	02/09	Walker, Alice	02/13	Sleator, William (Warner III)
05/22	Fabe, Maxene	02/13	Wangerin, Walter, Jr.		
05/23	Keegan, Marcia	02/16	Ranadive, Gail	02/23	Bly, Janet (Chester)
05/25	Bottner, Barbara	02/29	Stevens, Gwendolyn	03/01	Berger, Barbara Helen
05/30	Davis, Maggie S.	03/01	Abrams, Lawrence F.	03/07	Loescher, Gil(burt Damian)
05/31	Burr, Lonnie	03/13	Fiarotta, Noel	03/14	Drucker, Malka
05/31	Thieda, Shirley Ann	03/27	Goor, Nancy (Ruth Miller)	03/24	Higginbottom, J(effrey) Winslow
06/02	Tannen, Mary	04/09	Lustig, Loretta		
06/03	Payson, Dale	04/15	Berry, Joy Wilt	04/08	Bentley, Judith (McBride)
06/04	Holz, Loretta (Marie)	04/26	Larson, Norita D.	04/14	Saunders, Susan
06/06	Hayward, Linda	05/14	Lucas, George (Walton)	04/26	Hanlon, Emily
06/07	Giovanni, Nikki	05/16	Arnold, Caroline	04/30	Dillard, Annie
06/21	Hawkes, Louise	05/24	Oz, Frank (Richard)	04/30	Lange, Suzanne
07/04	Rivera, Geraldo	06/06	Foley, June	05/04	Wood, Don
07/07	Deyneka, Anita	06/10	Fodor, Ronald V(ictor)	05/20	Croll, Carolyn
07/14	Bode, Janet	06/13	Farquharson, Alexander	05/27	Schick, Joel
07/17	Davis, Grania	06/14	Hamsa, Bobbie	05/30	Johnson, D(ana) William
08/04	Jahn, Joseph Michael	06/24	Lasky, Kathryn	06/01	Hintz, Loren Martin
08/16	Hamilton, Morse	07/02	Klaits, Barrie	06/01	McInerney, Judith W(hitelock)
08/17	Makie, Pam	07/12	Ephron, Delia		
08/21	Wulffson, Don L.	07/19	Shields, Charles	06/06	Hall, Malcolm
08/24	Adams, Barbara Johnston	08/01	Gibbons, Gail	06/11	Munsch, Robert N.
08/24	Bishop, Bonnie	08/02	Riskind, Mary (Julia Longenberger)	07/03	Kouts, Anne
08/24	Goldsmith, Howard			07/24	Pollock, Bruce
08/24	Hughes, Dean	08/09	McKissack, Patricia (L'Ann) C(arwell)	07/24	Shebar, Sharon Sigmond
08/27	Kline, Suzy			07/25	Leder, Jane Mersky
09/08	Darling, Mary Kathleen	08/11	Cole, Joanna	07/26	Cosgrove, Stephen E(dward)
09/11	Pahz, James Alon	08/17	Bly, Stephen A(rthur)		
09/23	Huffaker, Sandy	08/18	Danziger, Paula	07/27	Janeczko, Paul B(ryan)
09/27	Levine, Abby	08/19	Larsen, Rebecca	07/28	Davis, James Robert
10/02	Zimmer, Dirk	08/27	Bellville, Cheryl Walsh	08/01	Cusack, Margaret
10/05	Gilbert, Sara (Dulaney)	09/07	Hoffman, Phyllis M.	08/09	Rossel, Seymour
10/08	Stine, Robert Lawrence	09/13	Swan, Susan	08/24	Laughbaum, Steve
10/09	Blumenthal, Shirley	09/14	Heller, Linda	08/29	DiFranco, Anthony (Mario)
10/16	Rosen, Winifred	09/22	Pollowitz, Melinda (Kilborn)		
10/20	Vogel, Ray			09/04	Wood, Linda C(arol)
10/21	Cameron, Ann	10/04	Meddaugh, Susan	09/04	Woods, Harold
11/05	Peavy, Linda	10/08	Tiner, John Hudson	09/05	Munro, Roxie
11/12	Rubinstein, Robert E(dward)	10/12	Emmens, Carol Ann	09/19	Crowley, Arthur M(cBlair)
		10/25	Gondosch, Linda	09/21	Wilhelm, Hans
11/13	Ryan, Elizabeth (Anne)	10/26	Venable, Alan (Hudson)	09/22	Cornell, J(effrey)
11/16	Spinner, Stephanie	10/27	Jance, J(udith) A(nn)	09/25	Edens, Cooper
11/19	Musgrove, Margaret W(ynkoop)	11/01	Hallinan, P(atrick) K(enneth)	10/12	Wolff, Diane
				10/13	Hausman, Gerald
11/22	King, Billie Jean	11/07	Adkins, Jan	10/19	Nolan, Dennis
11/27	Lubin, Leonard B.	11/18	Krupp, E(dwin) C(harles)	10/26	Sanders, Scott R(ussell)
11/29	Zallinger, Peter Franz	12/02	French, Michael	11/06	Hauptly, Denis J(ames)
12/04	Whelan, Elizabeth M(urphy)	12/06	Gardiner, John Reynolds	11/08	Mayer, Marianna
		12/12	Graham-Barber, Lynda	11/11	Harlan, Elizabeth
12/05	Moran, Tom	12/21	Curtis, Bruce (Richard)	11/12	Garretson, Victoria Diane
12/07	Teleki, Geza	12/22	Barkin, Carol	11/13	Cohen, Paul S.
12/12	Michel, Anna	12/30	Locke, Robert	11/13	Worth, Richard

11/14	Smith, Jean Pajot	10/28	Thurman, Judith	07/25	Watson, Clyde (Dingman)
11/29	Jobb, Jamie	10/30	Kimmel, Eric A.	07/29	Nestor, William Prodromas
12/09	Streano, Vince(nt Catello)	11/10	Markle, Sandra L(ee)	08/01	Stamaty, Mark Alan
12/10	Turner, Ann W(arren)	11/14	Corwin, Judith Hoffman	08/14	Nash, Bruce M(itchell)
12/14	Artis, Vicki Kimmel	11/14	Tafuri, Nancy	08/15	Rinard, Judith E(llen)
12/16	Brown, Laurene Krasny	11/25	Brown, Marc (Tolon)	08/19	Dyer, T(homas) A(llan)
12/20	Fradin, Dennis Brindell	11/29	Coontz, Otto	09/05	Daniel, Becky
		12/02	Macaulay, David Alexander	09/10	Jones, Rebecca C(astaldi)
1946		12/09	Chin, Richard (M.)	09/21	King, Stephen (Edwin)
??/??	Boyd, Candy Dawson	12/19	Batey, Tom	09/22	Grant, Alice Leigh
01/01	Wilkinson, Brenda	12/21	Pearson, Susan	09/25	Murphy, Jim
01/10	Tang, You-Shan	12/27	Wismer, Donald (Richard)	10/22	Petrie, Catherine
01/12	Milton, Joyce	12/30	Fregosi, Claudia (Anne Marie)	10/22	Waldman, Neil
01/19	Bell, Neill			10/28	Snow, Richard F(olger)
01/31	Paltrowitz, Stuart			11/05	Reed, Thomas (James)
02/06	Vojtech, Anna	**1947**		11/05	Yepsen, Roger B(ennet) Jr.
02/13	Balducci, Carolyn Feleppa	??/??	McCannon, Dindga Fatima		
02/21	Rolerson, Darrell A(llen)	??/??	Shearer, John	11/11	Barner, Bob
02/23	Seltzer, Richard (Warren, Jr.)	??/??	Wallace, Bill	11/14	Brewer, Sally King
		??/??	White, Edgar B.	12/01	Noguere, Suzanne
02/25	Kelley, True Adelaide	01/01	Hermanson, Dennis (Everett)	12/03	Hayes, Geoffrey
02/28	Wallner, Alexandra			12/06	Cutchens, Judy
03/17	Holt, Rochelle Lynn	01/05	Waugh, Carol-Lynn Rossel	12/08	Hansen, Ron
03/19	Coalson, Glo			12/18	Spielberg, Steven
03/29	Krupp, Robin Rector	01/10	Bloom, Lloyd	12/21	Lynch, Marietta
03/29	Lindblom, Steven (Winther)	01/11	Hale, Janet Campbell	12/21	Russo, Susan
		01/16	McMullan, Kate (Hall)	12/25	Stevenson, Drew
04/01	Palladini, David (Mario)	01/16	Weston, Martha	12/26	Polese, Carolyn
04/04	Jiler, John	02/12	Howell, Pat	12/28	McLenighan, Valjean
04/16	Gilliam, Stan	02/13	Lisle, Janet Taylor	12/30	O'Connor, Jane
04/26	Waniek, Marilyn (Nelson)	02/13	Sachs, Judith		
04/29	Rudley, Stephen	02/14	Leigh, Tom	**1948**	
05/01	Himler, Ann	02/22	Miller, Mitchell (Alexander)	??/??	Moore, Emily R.
05/09	Moore, Jim	03/14	Batiuk, Thomas M(artin)	??/??	Trudeau, G(arretson) B(eekman)
05/18	Johnston, Ginny	03/27	Carrier, Lark		
06/05	Kyte, Kathy S.	03/27	Sullivan, Thomas Joseph, Jr.	??/??	Wood, Audrey
06/06	Loeb, Jeffrey			??/??	Yarbrough, Camille
06/14	LeVert, William John	04/08	Bonners, Susan	01/06	Williams, Linda
06/20	Schick, Alice	04/08	Clay, Patrice	01/13	Booher, Dianna Daniels
06/25	Sachs, Elizabeth-Ann	04/10	Adler, David A.	01/16	Carpenter, John
06/28	Winnick, Karen B(eth) B(inkoff)	04/17	Thorn, John	01/21	Laiken, Deirdre S(usan)
		04/21	Edwards, Audrey	01/26	Simonetta, Linda
07/05	Gregorian, Joyce Ballou	04/21	Park, Barbara	02/04	Fatigati, Frances Evelyn de Buhr
07/11	Kilgore, Kathleen	05/03	Jukes, Mavis		
07/13	Hines, Anna G(rossnickle)	05/06	Ziemienski, Dennis (Theodore)	02/15	Landau, Elaine (Garmiza)
07/15	Roach, Marilynne K(athleen)			02/17	Pfeffer, Susan Beth
		05/07	Hargrove, James	02/22	Kropp, Paul (Stephan)
07/17	Crutcher, Chris(topher C.)	05/10	Cooney, Caroline B.	02/23	Geringer, Laura
07/23	Paterson, Diane (R. Cole)	05/10	McMillan, Bruce	02/24	Quammen, David
07/26	Tarsky, Sue	05/12	Stillerman, Robbie	02/29	McKillip, Patricia A(nne)
07/31	Haller, Dorcas Woodbury	05/13	Allington, Richard L(loyd)	03/05	Huff, Vivian
08/02	Howe, James	05/14	Bliss, Corinne D(emas)	03/06	Schwartz, Stephen (Lawrence)
08/06	Asch, Frank	05/24	DeGroat, Diane L.		
08/12	Howe, Deborah	05/24	Hahn, James (Sage)	03/11	Marshall, Michael (Kimbrough)
08/15	Munson(-Benson), Tunie	06/01	Rockwood, Joyce		
08/24	Obrant, Susan	06/09	Mehdevi, Alexander (Sinclair)	03/16	Demuth, Patricia Brennan
08/29	Maiorano, Robert			03/16	Weis, Margaret (Edith)
09/01	Arnosky, Jim	06/09	Zach, Cheryl (Byrd)	03/20	Sargent, Pamela
09/10	Saul, E. Wendy	06/18	Conrad, Pam(ela)	03/28	Begley, Kathleen A(nne)
09/16	Ryder, Joanne	06/24	Frankel, Julie	04/02	Vinge, Joan D(ennison)
09/26	Work, Virginia	06/24	Glovach, Linda	04/06	Edler, Timothy
09/27	Clish, Lee Marian	06/24	Schreiber, Elizabeth Anne (Ferguson)	04/07	Terkel, Susan N(eiburg)
10/10	San Souci, Robert D.			04/08	Tannenbaum, D(onald) Leb
10/21	Rabinowich, Ellen	06/29	Gross, Alan		
10/25	Brown, Rich(ard Eric)	07/07	Brimberg, Stanlee	04/16	Tate, Eleanora E(laine)
10/25	Noonan, Julia	07/12	Pearson, Gayle	04/28	Walker, Pamela
10/26	Merrill, Jane			04/29	Kidd, Ronald

05/07	Rose, Wendy	04/26	Leroe, Ellen W(hitney)	09/14	Steptoe, John (Lewis)
05/18	Hirschi, Ron	05/05	Weaver, John L.	09/14	Tether, Cynthia Graham
05/25	Berman, Linda	05/10	Blake, Robert	09/15	Springstubb, Tricia
05/29	Mulford, Philippa Greene	05/11	Sis, Peter	09/26	Westerberg, Christine
06/14	Yep, Laurence M(ichael)	05/12	Smith, Janice Lee	10/19	Diamond, Donna
06/16	Babcock, Dennis Arthur	05/20	Osborne, Mary Pope	11/07	Valen, Nanine
06/16	Edwards, Linda Strauss	06/04	Lee, Betsy	11/09	Cummings, Pat (Marie)
07/07	Allison, Linda	06/18	VanAllsburg, Chris	11/14	Erlanger, Ellen (Louise)
07/26	Sumichrast, Jozef	06/24	Westcott, Nadine Bern	11/23	Grant, Cynthia D.
07/27	Mitchell, Kathy	07/03	Hahn, Mona Lynn	12/06	Dubanevich, Arlene
07/29	Furchgott, Terry	07/03	McDonnell, Christine	12/07	Knudsen, James
08/04	Carlstrom, Nancy White	07/18	Louie, Ai-Ling	12/27	Burton, Marilee Robin
08/06	Rice, Dale R(ichard)	07/19	Kaye, Marilyn		
08/07	Appel, Martin E(liot)	08/06	Carey, Valerie Scho	**1951**	
08/15	Newsom, Carol	08/06	Scribner, Joanne L.	??/??	Thomas, Ianthe
09/03	Allen, Jeffrey (Yale)	09/14	Goode, Diane (Capuozzo)	01/06	Fleisher, Robbin
09/08	Hague, Michael R(iley)	09/21	Perry, Patricia	01/30	Fufuka, Karama
09/10	Agard, Nadema	10/08	Wright-Frierson, Virginia	02/02	Rice, Eve (Hart)
09/14	Mahony, Elizabeth Winthrop	11/04	Cochran, Bobbye A.	03/08	Roop, Peter
		11/14	Waldman, Bruce	03/16	Hodgell, P(atricia) C(hristine)
09/14	Reiff, Stephanie Ann	11/21	Schachtel, Roger (Bernard)	04/06	Vaughan, Marcia
09/24	Deveaux, Alexis	12/01	Brett, Jan (Churchill)	04/18	Demarest, Chris(topher) L(ynn)
09/28	Palmer, Heidi	12/07	Rosenberg, Jane	04/26	Lampert, Emily
09/30	Woods, Geraldine	12/24	Leydon, Rita (Floden)	05/05	Walker, Stephen J.
10/03	Singer, Marilyn	12/25	Burstein, John	05/18	Hann, Jacquie
10/06	Scher, Paula			05/21	Radley, Gail
10/11	Kent, Deborah Ann	**1950**		05/23	Titherington, Jeanne
10/19	Natti, Susanna	??/??	Brooks, Bruce	06/04	Kovalski, Maryann
10/21	Schur, Maxine	??/??	Grimes, Nikki	06/18	Roop, Constance Betzer
10/26	Schuyler, Pamela R(icka)	??/??	Hinton, S(usan) E(loise)	06/23	Rachlin, Harvey (Brant)
11/23	Rich, Mark J.	??/??	Strete, Craig Kee	07/02	Cauley, Lorinda Bryan
12/05	Bram, Elizabeth	01/10	Gevirtz, Eliezer	07/02	Gantos, John (Bryan), Jr.
12/08	Fisher, Lois I.	01/11	Casey, Brigid	07/06	Delaney, Ned
12/09	Bromley, Dudley	01/23	Smith, Susan Mathias	07/09	Celestino, Martha Laing
12/25	Miller, Sandy (Peden)	02/12	Conover, Chris	08/01	Schweninger, Ann
12/29	Alex, Marlee	02/20	Walther, Thomas A.	08/19	Espeland, Pamela (Lee)
12/31	Cuyler, Margery Stuyvesant	03/08	McQueen, Lucinda (Emily)	09/28	Scuro, Vincent
		03/18	Florian, Douglas	10/11	Arnold, Susan (Riser)
1949		04/12	Paltrowitz, Donna (Milman)	10/13	McCrady, Lady
01/01	Tapp, Kathy Kennedy	04/16	Vogel, John H(ollister), Jr.	10/17	Caseley, Judith
01/03	Flitner, David P(erkins)	04/21	Lasker, David	10/31	Sive, Helen R.
01/06	D'Ignazio, Fred(erick)	04/21	Zalben, Jane Breskin	11/14	Baker, Alan
01/08	Manes, Stephen	04/23	Baker, Gayle C(unningham)	11/18	Foon, Dennis
01/11	Otfinoski, Steven	04/25	Brinckloe, Julie (Lorraine)	11/24	Sanderson, Ruth (L.)
01/12	Munoz, William	04/28	Hest, Amy	11/29	Schwartz, David M(artin)
01/14	Zarins, Joyce Audy	05/02	Matthews, Ellen	12/08	Holl, Kristi D(iane)
01/23	Mathieu, Joseph P.	05/04	Sandak, Cass R(obert)	12/21	Berenstain, Michael
01/23	Saseen, Sharon (Dillon)	05/04	Zellan, Audrey Penn	12/24	Munsinger, Lynn
01/24	Bachman, Fred	05/05	Strasser, Todd		
01/24	Pellowski, Michael J(oseph)	05/11	Sutton, Jane	**1952**	
		05/15	Wisler, G(ary) Clifton	??/??	Bell, Clare
01/29	Pahz, Anne Cheryl Suzanne	05/16	Coville, Bruce	??/??	Flournoy, Valerie R.
02/01	Buckholtz, Eileen (Garber)	06/06	Smith, Susan Vernon	01/03	Radlauer, David
02/08	McLoughlin, John C.	06/15	Tooke, Louise Mathews	01/05	Cherry, Lynne
02/14	Root, Phyllis	06/18	Goodman, Joan Elizabeth	01/25	White, Timothy (Thomas Anthony)
02/18	Joosse, Barbara M(onnot)	06/26	Briggs, Carole S(uzanne)	02/11	Knapp, Ron
03/02	Sazer, Nina	06/28	Haseley, Dennis	02/14	Shannon, George (William Bones)
03/05	Graham, Robin Lee	07/26	Kinzel, Dorothy		
03/06	Hague, Susan Kathleen	08/04	Senn, Steve	02/19	Etchemendy, Nancy
03/06	Hurd, Thacher	08/08	Kopper, Lisa (Esther)	03/31	Llerena-Aguirre, Carlos Antonio
03/06	Riley, Jocelyn (Carol)	08/14	Larson, Gary		
03/16	Katona, Robert	08/15	Landon, Lucinda	05/12	DeBruyn, Monica
04/02	Ross, Dave	08/20	Flesch, Yolande (Catarina)		
04/14	Claflin, Edward	09/05	Guisewite, Cathy		
04/19	Eisenberg, Lisa				

05/18	Duane-Smyth, Diane (Elizabeth)	09/29	McLaurin, Anne	05/03	Parker, Kristy (Kettelkamp)
06/07	Waide, Jan	10/10	Carlson, Nancy Lee	06/07	Hilgartner, Beth
06/10	O'Brien, Anne Sibley	10/11	Scabrini, Janet	07/21	Bly, Robert W(ayne)
06/26	Seidler, Tor	11/16	Davis, Gibbs	08/31	Harris, Steven Michael
07/08	Thomas, Art(hur Lawrence)	11/25	Krensky, Stephen (Alan)	09/07	Piowaty, Kim Kennelly
		12/07	Weiss, Ellen	10/15	Leibold, Jay
07/10	Ransom, Candice F.			11/28	Bunting, Glenn (Davison)
07/16	Egielski, Richard			12/11	Joyce, William
07/29	Krull, Kathleen			12/20	Delacre, Lulu

1954

01/02	Schwark, Mary Beth
01/25	Weiss, Nicki
01/26	Callan, Jamie
03/20	Sachar, Louis
04/02	Schwartz, Amy
05/19	Primavera, Elise
06/06	Rylant, Cynthia
06/09	Maguire, Gregory
07/13	Stanovich, Betty Jo
07/18	Bond, Felicia
07/30	Nastick, Sharon
08/01	Brahm, Sumishta
08/21	Mills, Claudia
08/31	Rofes, Eric Edward
09/17	Gilmore, Susan
10/03	Disalvo-Ryan, DyAnne
10/25	Rabinowitz, Sandy
12/13	Pierce, Tamora
12/28	Luenn, Nancy

1958
03/18 Zemach, Kaethe
07/05 Pierce, Meredith Ann
11/04 Marsoli, Lisa Ann

1959
06/15 Leedy, Loreen (Janelle)
07/24 Nerlove, Miriam
10/03 Himmelman, John (Carl)

1960
??/?? Bassett, Jeni (Crisler)
06/02 Emberley, Michael
10/20 Carlson, Daniel
11/27 Henkes, Kevin

1962
06/13 Sheedy, Alexandra (Elizabeth)
10/23 Novak, Matt

1963
11/14 Gelman, Jan

1964
??/?? Clarke, Fred G.

1965
05/02 Forshay-Lunsford, Cin

1967
02/24 Bunin, Catherine
07/07 Hodgetts, Blake Christopher

1970
03/09 Levine, Sarah
07/03 Kennedy, Brendan

1972
??/?? Smith, Samantha

1973
??/?? Lancaster, Matthew

1974
08/28 Say, Allen

08/12 Spollen, Christopher
08/19 Blackburn, John(ny) Brewton
09/05 Fleischman, Paul (Taylor)
10/11 Gaver, Rebecca
10/19 Aitken, Amy
10/21 Gasperini, Jim
10/26 Brewster, Patience
11/16 McKinley, Jennifer Carolyn Robin
11/25 Dragonwagon, Crescent (Zolotow)
11/28 Calmenson, Stephanie
12/01 Barry, Scott
12/03 Sadler, Catherine Edwards
12/09 Walker, Lou Ann
12/12 Yakovetic, (Joseph Sandy)

1953
??/?? Atkinson, Allen
??/?? Isadora, Rachel
??/?? Stevens, Janet
01/09 Mannetti, Lisa
01/13 Mabery, D. L.
01/21 Blair, Jay
01/21 Scarry, Richard, Jr.
02/14 Zelinsky, Paul O.
02/17 Black, Susan Adams
03/06 Lowry, Peter
03/22 Hartley, Fred Allan III
04/03 Boynton, Sandra (Keith)
04/11 Preiss, Byron (Cary)
04/20 Long, Judith Elaine
04/23 Teitelbaum, Michael
04/29 Rubel, Nicole
05/05 Bograd, Larry
06/04 Vincent, Eric Douglas
06/12 Kennedy, T(eresa) A.
07/07 Aaseng, Nathan
07/14 Hoopes, Lyn L(ittlefield)
07/14 Numeroff, Laura Joffe
07/21 Lesser, Rika
07/24 Salduth, Denise
08/21 Yorinks, Arthur
09/21 Davidson, Judith
09/22 Dunrea, Olivier
09/24 James, Robin (Irene)

1955
03/20 Watts, James K(ennedy) M(offitt)
03/27 Thamer, Katie
04/18 Woldin, Beth Weiner
04/26 Foster, Brad W.
05/06 McClintock, Barbara
05/17 Wheeler, Cindy
07/22 Newman, Matthew (Harrison)
08/12 Martin, Ann M(atthews)
09/25 Cheng, Judith
10/05 Dank, Gloria Rand
10/18 Ackley, Peggy Jo
12/15 Drescher, Henrik

1956
??/?? Forbes, Katherine (Russell)
01/04 Frank, Daniel B.
01/07 Detwiler, Susan Dill
01/26 Wolff, Jenifer Ashley
07/19 Blumberg, Leda
10/01 Hautzig, Deborah
10/27 Westman, Paul (Wendell)
10/31 Goodman, Deborah Lerme
12/07 Gustafson, Scott

1957
03/13 Ernst, Lisa Campbell

Geographical Index

UNITED STATES

ALABAMA
  Johansen, Margaret (Alison)
  Luis, Earlene W.
Athens
  Lincoln, C(harles) Eric
Birmingham
  Allen, Mel
  Boni, Margaret Bradford
  Cheney, Cora
  Dank, Leonard Dewey
  Glendinning, Sara W(ilson)
  Hemphill, Paul (James)
  Hobson, Julius W(ilson)
  Johnson, E(ugene) Harper
  Lewis, Stephen
  Penney, Grace Jackson
  Sanchez, Sonia
  Savoldi, Gloria Root
  Sparks, James Calvin, Jr.
  Sterne, Emma Gelders
  Tarry, Ellen
  Waldron, Ann Wood
  Warburg, Sandol Stoddard
Blocton
  Lee, Mildred
Brewton
  Brewton, John E(dmund)
Decatur
  Tichenor, Tom
Demopolis
  Blassingame, Wyatt (Rainey)
East Lake
  Brown, Joe David
Enterprise
  Hermanson, Dennis (Everett)
Fayette
  Behnke, Frances L. (Berry)
Fort Payne
  Johnson, James Ralph
Huntsville
  Chase, Richard
Jasper
  Milton, Hilary (Herbert)
LaFayette
  Still, James
Lineville
  Dockery, Wallene T.
Mobile
  Andrews, Mary Raymond Shipman
  Lewis, Arthur Allen
Monroeville
  Lee, Nelle Harper
Montgomery
  Wheeler, Cindy
Montgomery or Demopolis
  Haskins, James S.
Ozark
  Skipper, G. C.
Pell City
  Moffett, Martha (Leatherwood)
Pennington
  Ellison, Lucile Watkins
Phoenix City
  Mahon, Julia C(unha)
Red Level
  Terry, Luther L(eonidas)
Richmond
  Lide, Alice (Alison)
Selma
  Windham, Kathryn T(ucker)
Talladega
  Knox, Rose B(ell)
Tuscaloosa
  Banks, Sara (Jeanne Gordon Harrell)
Tuscumbia
  Lindsay, Maud McKnight
Uniontown (Ittabena)
  Pyrnelle, Louise Clarke
Wilsonville
  Hearne, Betsy Gould
Wrangell
  Wittanen, Etolin

ALASKA
Fairbanks
  Wold, Jo Anne
Juneau
  Loomis, J. Paul
Ketchikan
  Renlie, Frank H.
St. Michael
  Blair, Ruth Van Ness
St. Paul Island
  Partch, Virgil Franklin II
Thorn Bay
  Bell, Margaret E(lizabeth)

ARIZONA
Bisbee
  Ballard, Lowell Clyne
Globe
  Eunson, Roby
  Jacobs, Helen Hull
Morenci
  DeGrazia, Ted
Phoenix
  English, James W(ilson)
  Gilmore, Susan
  Maher, Ramona
Prescott
  Sutton, Myron Daniel
  Weston, John (Harrison)
Prescott(McCabe)
  Behn, Harry
Ray
  Rich, Mark J.
Safford
  Hoopes, Ned E(dward)
Tempe
  Worcester, Donald Emmet
Thatcher
  Dickson, Naida
Tucson
  Alexander, Sue
  Burroway, Janet (Gay)
  Drucker, Malka
  Henderson, Zenna (Chlarson)
  Hoff, Carol
White Cone
  Begay, Harrison

451

Woodruff
   Thomas, Estelle Webb

ARKANSAS
   Campbell, Barbara
Arkadelphia
   Britt, Dell
Berryville
   Bond, Gladys Baker
Big Flats
   Branscum, Robbie
Blytheville
   Rhodes, Bennie (Loran)
Carrollton
   Warren, William Stephen
Cerro Gordo
   St. Clair, Byrd Hooper
Dardanelle
   Steiner, Barbara A(nnette)
DeQueen
   Bauer, Helen
Fayetteville
   Ulmer, Louise
   Wilson, Charles Morrow
Fort Smith
   Adams, Adrienne
   Hallin, Emily Watson
Heber Springs
   Fulks, Bryan
Hot Springs
   Silverthorne, Elizabeth
Jonesboro
   Gray, Genevieve S.
Little Rock
   Barnes, Frank Eric Wollencott
   Crawford, Phyllis
   Dygard, Thomas J.
   Mayer, Mercer
   Medearis, Mary
   O'Kane, Dick
   Rostkowski, Margaret I.
   Wood, Audrey
Monticello
   Fletcher, Charlie May Hogue
Ozark Mountains
   Snow, Donald Clifford
Paragould
   Goldsborough, June
Pine Bluff
   Hoffecker, John Savin
Plumerville
   Taylor, Jerry Duncan
Pocahontas
   Tiner, John Hudson
Springtown
   Graham, Helen Holland
Tuckerman
   Barner, Bob
Van Buren
   Toothaker, Roy Eugene
Winslow
   Jones, Douglas C(lyde)

CALIFORNIA
   Bosworth, J. Allan
   Brock, Virginia
   Burckmyer, Elizabeth
   Gumpertz, Bob
   Hawkinson, Lucy (Ozone)
   Jennings, Gordon
   Meek, Jacklyn O'Hanlon
   Morrow, Suzanne Stark
   Robinson, W(illiam) W(ilcox)
Alameda
   Uchida, Yoshiko
Atwater
   Wood, Don
Bakersfield
   Borton, Elizabeth
   Hall, Elizabeth
Berkeley
   Anderson, Gunnar (Donald)
   Babcock, Dennis Arthur
   Bacon, Martha Sherman
   Brommer, Gerald F(rederick)
   Fujikawa, Gyo
   Hansen, Caryl (Hall)
   Kline, Suzy
   LeGuin, Ursula K(roeber)
   Lowry, Peter
   Moore, S(arah) E.
   Polese, Carolyn
Berkley
   Goulart, Ron(ald Joseph)
Boulder Creek
   Petie, Haris
Chico
   Young, Robert W(illiam)
Compton
   Robison, Nancy L(ouise)
Corcoran
   Reynolds, Dallas McCord
Coronado
   Olmsted, Lorena Ann
Covina
   Stafford, Jean
Culver City
   Flynn, Barbara
Fresno
   Mooser, Stephen
   Politi, Leo
   Saroyan, William
   Tusan, Stan
   Williams, Clyde C.
Gardena
   Barlow, Genevieve
Glendale
   Bourdon, David
   Dillon, Diane (C.)
   Gormley, Beatrice
   Howell, Pat
   Moore, Jim
   Phleger, Marjorie Temple
Grass Valley
   Pohlmann, Lillian (Grenfell)
Heber
   Atwood, Ann (Margaret)
Hollywood
   Campbell, Patricia J(ean)
   Filstrup, E(dward) Christian
   Forman, Brenda
   Quackenbush, Robert M(ead)
   Reese, Robert A.
   Williams, Vera B.
Irvine
   Colonius, Lillian
Kingsburg
   Thollander, Earl (Gustave)
La Habra
   Coy, Harold
Laguna Beach
   Cohen, Robert Carl
Lancaster
   Berger, Barbara Helen
   Young, Jan(et Randall)
Lemoore
   Snyder, Zilpha Keatley
Long Beach
   Andersen, Yvonne
   Brower, Pauline (York)
   Caswell, Helen (Rayburn)
   Coleman, Pauline (Hodgkinson)
   King, Billie Jean
   Poynter, Margaret
   Rydberg, Lou(isa Hampton)
   Tapp, Kathy Kennedy
Los Angeles
   Anderson, Joy
   Anderson, Leone Castell
   Arnov, Boris, Jr.
   Bacon, Elizabeth
   Berson, Harold
   Bienenfeld, Florence L(ucille)
   Bliven, Bruce, Jr.
   Bonham, Frank
   Burbank, Addison (Buswell)
   Burton, Marilee Robin
   Chandler, Thomas
   Collins, Pat Lowery
   Coombs, Charles I(ra)
   Coombs, Patricia
   Dean, Karen Strickler
   DuSoe, Robert C(oleman)
   Ellis, Ella Thorp
   Engdahl, Sylvia Louise
   Ephron, Delia
   Eyre, Katherine Wigmore
   Fleming, Ronald Lee
   Frankel, Julie
   Freeman, Serge Herbert
   French, Michael
   Fry, Edward Bernard
   Gerstein, Mordicai
   Gold, Sharlya
   Green, Morton
   Hague, Michael R(iley)
   Hallinan, P(atrick) K(enneth)
   Hayward, Linda
   Henriod, Lorraine (Stephens)
   Johnston, Tony
   Kaufman, Mervyn D.
   Kiesel, Stanley
   Kirk, Ruth (Eleanor Kratz)
   Kossin, Sandy (Sanford)
   Landin, Les(lie)
   Lobel, Arnold (Stark)
   Lorimer, Janet
   Lyttle, Richard B(ard)
   Massie, Diane Redfield
   Nelson, Marg (Raibley)
   Nixon, Joan Lowery

O'Dell, Scott
Paine, Roberta M.
Radlauer, David
Redding, Robert Hull
Rudley, Stephen
Sadler, Catherine Edwards
Sanderlin, Owenita (Harrah)
Sargent, Shirley
Schertle, Alice
Siberell, Ann(e)
Stankevich, Boris
Stevens, Gwendolyn
Strauss, Joyce
Sutton, Jeff(erson H.)
Takakjian, Portia
Thaler, Michael C.
Thamer, Katie
Tomerlin, John
Vavra, Robert James
Wachter, Oralee Roberts
Wulffson, Don L.
Zemach, Margot
Mare Island
Brinckloe, Julie (Lorraine)
Mare Island (Navy Yard)
Sewell, Helen (Moore)
Maricopa
Behrens, June York
Maywood
Micklish, Rita
Modesto
Lucas, George (Walton)
Raible, Alton (Robert)
Monterey
Fleischman, Paul (Taylor)
Mountain View
Gates, Doris
Nevada City
Perry, Phyllis J.
North Hollywood
Jenkyns, Chris
Oakland
Bare, Colleen Stanley
Borden, Charles A.
Brown, Rosalie (Gertrude) Moore
Cazet, Denys
Chambers, Robert Warner
Dolan, Edward F(rancis), Jr.
Engvick, William
Felt, Sue
Garthwaite, Marion H(ook)
Gaver, Rebecca
Goodman, Elizabeth B.
Kingman, Dong (Moy Shu)
Lee, Robert J.
Marshall, Michael (Kimbrough)
Merrill, Jane
Murphy, Shirley Rousseau
Pontiflet, Ted
Ralston, Alma (Smith Payne)
Rose, Wendy
VanHorn, William
Viguers, Ruth Hill
Wymark, Olwen (Margaret Buck)
Ontario
Garbutt, Bernard

Orosi
Simon, Ruth Corabel (Shimer)
Pacific Grove
McCallum, Phyllis
Pajaro
Hader, Elmer (Stanley)
Palo Alto
Wood, Phyllis Anderson
Pasadena
Archambault, John
Eames, Genevieve Torrey
Finke, Blythe F(oote)
Forrester, Victoria
Gleason, Judith
Gregory, Diana (Jean)
Hayes, Geoffrey
Luenn, Nancy
Witker, Jim
Reading
Mabery, D. L.
Redlands
Sackett, S(amuel) J(ohn)
Reedley
Cretan, Gladys (Yessayan)
Riverside
Forsyth, Gloria
Sacramento
Ackley, Peggy Jo
Armer, Laura (Adams)
Caen, Herb (Eugene)
Heintze, Carl
Mauser, Patricia Rhoads
Salinas
Steinbeck, John (Ernst)
San Bernadino
Hampson, Richard Denman
San Bernardino
Allison, Linda
San Diego
Bailey, Alice Cooper
Bancroft, Griffing
Bixby, William (Courtney)
Blochman, Lawrence G(oldtree)
Clampett, Robert
Emerson, William K(eith)
Etchison, Birdie L(ee)
Freeman, Don
Guthrie, Anne
Hiscock, Bruce
Nelson, Cordner (Bruce)
Reed, Kit
Rymer, Alta May
Schwartz, Amy
Walter, Frances
Webber, Irma E(leanor Schmidt)
San Fernando
Matthews, Patricia
San Francisco
Alter, Robert Edmond
Andersdatter, Karla M(argaret)
Armer, Sidney
Baruch, Dorothy W(alter)
Bergeron, Victor (Jules, Jr.)
Bonestell, Chesley
Breckenfeld, Vivian Gurney
Brown, Joseph E(dward)
Cosgrave, John O'Hara II

Davis, Reda
Economakis, Olga
Edelman, Lily (Judith)
Freedman, Russell (Bruce)
Friendlich, Richard J.
Frost, Robert (Lee)
Grant, Gordon (Hope)
Heyneman, Anne
Jackson, Shirley
Keller, Beverly L(ou Harwick)
Lindeburg, Franklin A(lfred)
Loescher, Gil(burt Damian)
London, Jack
Longman, Harold S.
Maniscalco, Joseph
McDearmon, Kay
McKay, Donald
McLean, Kathryn (Anderson)
McNeely, Jeannette
Meighan, Donald Charles
Miller, Marilyn (Jean)
Nickelsburg, Janet
Nolan, Dennis
Paget-Fredericks, Joseph E(dward) P(aget) Rous-Marten
Parry, Marian
Reynolds, Malvina
Ruby, Lois
San Souci, Robert D.
Schur, Maxine
Shields, Rita
Smith, Philip Warren
Stone, Irving
Watts, James K(ennedy) M(offitt)
Weingarten, Violet (Brown)
Wilson, Forrest
Wong, Jeanyee
Yep, Laurence M(ichael)
Ziemienski, Dennis (Theodore)
San Gabriel
McIlhany, Sterling (Fisher)
San Jose
Hill, Frank Ernest
Rink, Paul
San Leandro
Bradford, Ann (Liddell)
San Mateo
Berry, William D(avid)
Gray, Patricia (Clark)
San Pedro
Armour, Richard (Willard)
Stanovich, Betty Jo
Santa Ana
Gannett, Ruth Chrisman (Arens)
Graham, Robin Lee
Simon, Hilda (Rita)
Santa Barbara
Ross, Wilda (S.)
Streano, Vince(nt Catello)
Santa Maria
Smith, Ursula
Santa Monica
Grace, F(rances Jane)
Santa Rosa
Larrecq, John M(aurice)
Petersen, P(eter) J(ames)
Southgate

Berry, Joy Wilt
Stockton
   Johnson, La Verne B(ravo)
   Kingston, Maxine (Ting Ting) Hong
   Montana, Bob
   Papashvily, Helen (Waite)
   Pease, Howard
Vacaville
   Parker, Margot M.
Vallejo
   Granger, Margaret Jane
   Locke, Robert
Ventura
   Hague, Susan Kathleen
Visalia
   Bly, Janet (Chester)
   Bly, Stephen A(rthur)
   Hoyt, Mary Finch
Walnut Creek
   Cameron, Polly (McQuiston)
Whittier
   Witt, Shirley Hill
Wilmar
   Douglass, Barbara
Windsor
   Chapman, Frederick Trench

COLORADO
   Aitken, Dorothy (Lockwood)
   Hall, Esther Greenacre
   Haynes, Robert
   Wood, Frances Elizabeth
   Wood, Ruth C.
Aguilar
   Batson, Larry
Boulder
   Fitz-Randolph, Jane (Currens)
   Folsom, Franklin (Brewster)
   Hawkes, Louise
   MacDonald, Betty (Heskett Bard)
   Meyers, Joan (Simpson)
   Schweninger, Ann
   Trelease, Allen W(illiam)
Colorado Springs
   McCracken, Harold
   Morton, Eva Jane
   Parrish, Anne
   Stewart, Elizabeth Laing
   Taber, Gladys (Bagg)
Creede
   Elting, Mary
Denver
   Agnew, Edith J(osephine)
   Berger, Josef
   Blackburn, Edith H.
   Bograd, Larry
   Chase, Mary (Coyle)
   Dowden, Anne Ophelia (Todd)
   Holt, Margaret Van Vechten (Saunders)
   Hull, Eleanor (Means)
   Katchen, Carole
   Kroeber, Theodora (Kracaw Brown)
   Leibold, Jay
   McKown, Robin

Moon, Sheila (Elizabeth)
Patten, Lewis Byford
Peek, Merle
Perske, Robert
Rubicam, Harry Cogswell, Jr.
Silverman, Mel(vyn Frank)
Durango
   Todd, Barbara K(eith)
Fort Morgan
   Boshinski, Blanche
Grand Junction
   Cagle, Malcolm W(infield)
Greeley
   Churchill, E. Richard
   Plowhead, Ruth Gipson
   Quick, Annabelle (MacMillan)
Green Montain Falls(Near)
   Pryor, Helen Brenton
Iliff
   Swain, Su Zan (Noguchi)
Jefferson
   Hill, Margaret (Ohler)
La Junta
   Choate, Judith (Newkirk)
Pagosa Springs
   Harman, Hugh
Pueblo
   Johnston, Laurie
   Mead, Russell (M., Jr.)
   Wade, Theodore E., Jr.
Sterling
   Burkert, Nancy Ekholm
Telluride
   Lavender, David (Sievert)
Woodman
   Benezra, Barbara (Beardsley)

CONNECTICUT
   Addona, Angelo F.
   Manley, Seon
   Montgomery, R(aymond) A. (Jr.)
   Oldrin, John
Avon
   Fon Eisen, Anthony T.
Birmingham (Derby)
   Theiss, Lewis Edwin
Bridgeport
   Allen, Thomas B(enton)
   Ames, Mildred
   Averill, Esther (Holden)
   Broderick, Dorothy M.
   Carley, V(an Ness) Royal
   Cornell, J(effrey)
   Decker, Duane (Walter)
   Gelman, Rita Golden
   Hubbell, Patricia
   Kaufman, Joe
   Nespojohn, Katherine V(eronica)
   Schutzer, A. I.
   Szekeres, Cyndy
   VonSchmidt, Eric
   Yakovetic, (Joseph Sandy)
   Zaffo, George J.
Danbury
   Coburn, John Bowen
Darien
   Richards, George Mather

Fairfield
   Goodman, Joan Elizabeth
   Lengyel, Cornel Adam
Fairhaven
   Edwards, George Wharton
Glastonbury
   Carini, Edward
Greenwich
   Grant, Alice Leigh
   Schlee, Ann
Hamden
   Ames, Evelyn
   Hemming, Roy
   Henry, Marguerite (Breithaupt)
Hartford
   Almquist, Don
   Burack, Sylvia K.
   Butterworth, Oliver
   Caulfield, Peggy F.
   Davis, Maggie S.
   Demarest, Chris(topher) L(ynn)
   Erickson, Russell E(verett)
   Hammer, Richard
   Horner, Althea (Jane)
   Jackson, Robert B(lake)
   Laschever, Barnett D.
   Neusner, Jacob
   Radin, Ruth Yaffe
   Roy, Ron(ald)
   Sigourney, Lydia Huntley
   Thompson, George Selden
   Webster, Noah
   White, Nancy Bean
   Worth, Richard
Hebron
   Gilbert, Helen Earle
Lebanon
   Trumbull, John
Litchfield
   Stowe, Harriet (Elizabeth) Beecher
Manchester
   Marzollo, Jean
   Neville, Emily Cheney
Marlborough
   Quigg, Jane (Hulda)
Meriden
   Bishop, Bonnie
   DePaola, Thomas Anthony
   Fiarotta, Noel
   Fiarotta, Phyllis
   Tamburine, Jean
Mystic
   Bradbury, Bianca
New Britain
   Camp, Walter (Chauncey)
   Hungerford, Edward Buell
   Kaye, Marilyn
   Musgrove, Margaret W(ynkoop)
   Patterson, Charles
   Roberts, John G(aither)
   Unkelbach, Kurt
   Voight, Virginia Frances
New Canaan
   Beatty, Hetty Burlingame
New Haven
   Caplin, Alfred Gerald

Deming, Dorothy
Ellsberg, Edward
Fleming, Alice Mulcahey
Hall, Donald (Andrew, Jr.)
Horwitz, Elinor Lander
Lothrop, Harriet Mulford Stone
Pashko, Stanley
Rabinowitz, Sandy
Ripley, Elizabeth Blake
Sperry, Armstrong W.
Stone, Jon
Thompson, David H(ugh)
Weisgard, Leonard (Joseph)
Yurchenco, Henrietta (Weiss)
Zallinger, Peter Franz
New London
Dolezal, Carroll
Miller, Mary Britton
Tannen, Mary
Norwalk
Atkinson, Allen
Avison, George (Alfred)
Johnson, Joan J.
Kellogg, Steven (Castle)
Kliban, B.
McHargue, Georgess
Scarry, Richard, Jr.
Norwich
Coit, Margaret Louise
Heilbrun, Lois Hussey
Norwichtown
Welles, Winifred
Old Saybrook
Petry, Ann (Lane)
Pine Orchard
Colby, Jean Poindexter
Plainfield
Phillips, Prentice
Putnam
Warner, Gertrude Chandler
Ridgefield
Bacon, Margaret Frances
Goodrich, Samuel Griswold
Riverside
Raymond, James Crossley
Salisbury
Bingham, Caleb
Seymour
Miller, Elizabeth Cleveland
South Norwalk
Hartley, William B(rown)
Southbury
Stowe, Leland
Southport
Desmond, Alice Curtis
Stamford
Bacon, Josephine Dodge (Daskam)
Caffrey, Nancy
Claflin, Edward
Darling, Louis, Jr.
Harrison, Harry (Max)
Hoberman, Mary Ann (Freedman)
Mellin, Jeanne
Monjo, F(erdinand) N(icholas)
Sweet, Oscar Cowan

Stratford
Fitch, Florence Mary
Tolland
Ludwig, Helen
Torrington
Henderson, LeGrand
Rood, Ronald (N.)
Waterbury
Burroughs, Polly
Carruth, Hayden
Durant, John
Hylander, Clarence J(ohn)
Isham, Charlotte H(ickox)
Smith, Norman F.
Tchudi, Stephen N.
West Haven
Estes, Eleanor (Ruth)
Kikukawa, Cecily H(arder)
Willimantic
Wallace, May Nickerson
Winsted
Thompson, Mary (Wolfe)

DELAWARE
Harrington
Graham, Alberta (Powell)
Seaford
Almond, Linda Stevens
Wilmington
Allen, Rodney F.
Cooke, David Coxe
Fuller, Edmund (Maybank)
Griffith, Helen V(irginia)
Leedy, Loreen (Janelle)
O'Connell, Margaret F(orster)
Pyle, Howard
Pyle, Katharine
Vittengl, Morgan J(ohn)

DISTRICT OF COLUMBIA
Washington
Alexander, Jocelyn (Anne Arundel)
Antolini, Margaret Fishback
Atkinson, Margaret Fleming
Bandel, Betty
Banks, Laura Stockton Voorhees
Bate, Lucy
Bauer, Caroline Feller
Bell, Neill
Brandon, Brumsic, Jr.
Bransom, John Paul
Brooks, Charlotte K.
Brown, Sevellon III
Bryan, Dorothy M(arie)
Burchard, Peter D(uncan)
Carpenter, Frances
Carroll, Archer Latrobe
Cauley, Lorinda Bryan
Christelow, Eileen
Cranch, Christopher Pearse
Crawford, Will
Danziger, Paula
Dowdey, Landon Gerald
Edens, Cooper
Frank, Daniel B.
George, Jean Craighead

Gilbert, Sara (Dulaney)
Gill, Richard Cochran
Goor, Nancy (Ruth Miller)
Goor, Ron(ald Stephen)
Graham, John
Griffith, Field
Hahn, Mary Downing
Hogan, Inez
Holland, Janice
Holland, Marion
Homze, Alma C.
Houck, Carter
Jacobs, Flora Gill
Jewell, Nancy
Kenny, Ellsworth Newcomb
Kilgore, Kathleen
King, Marian
Knudson, Rozanne
Kouts, Anne
Krush, Beth
Lamb, Robert (Boyden)
Lucas, Janette May
Mahony, Elizabeth Winthrop
Nastick, Sharon
Nichols, Spencer Baird
Pope, Elizabeth Marie
Ransom, Candice F.
Rawlings, Marjorie Kinnan
Robinet, Harriette Gillem
Rohmer, Harriet
Roseman, Kenneth David
Rosenthal, M(acha) L(ouis)
Scher, Paula
Smith, Doris Buchanan
Smith, Lawrence Beall
Solbert, Romaine G.
Talbert, Ansel Edward McLaurine
Weaver, John D(owning)
Wilson, Carter
Wolfe, Burton H.
Wright-Frierson, Virginia
Zurhorst, Charles (Stewart, Jr.)

FLORIDA
Myrick, Mildred
Seabrooke, Brenda
Apalachicola
Graves, Charles Parlin
Holloway, Teresa (Bragunier)
Coral Gables
Swan, Susan
Gainesville
Vincent, Eric Douglas
Jacksonville
Boone, Pat
Johnson, James William
Torbert, Floyd James
Lynn Haven
Hill, Elizabeth Starr
Melbourne
Smith, Mary Ellen
Miami
Barbe, Walter Burke
Elmore, Carolyn Patricia
Rubel, Nicole
Ojus
Maule, Hamilton Bee

Okeechobee
  Evernden, Margery
Orlando
  Moncure, Jane Belk
  Richardson, Carol
Ormond Beach
  Huntington, Harriet E(lizabeth)
Pensacola
  Percy, Charles Harting
Perry
  Porter, George
Sanford
  Park, W(illiam) B(ryan)
Sarasota
  Lopshire, Robert (Martin)
St. Petersburg
  Newman, Matthew (Harrison)
Stuart
  Witham, Phillip Ross
Tampa
  McNeer, May Yonge
  Webb, Sharon
Winter Haven
  Sutton, Larry M(atthew)

GEORGIA
  Braddy, Nella
Americus
  Senn, Steve
Athens
  Smith, Susan Carlton
Atlanta
  Boorstin, Daniel J(oseph)
  Buckholtz, Eileen (Garber)
  Cain, Arthur H(omer)
  Dresang, Eliza (Carolyn Timberlake)
  Fabe, Maxene
  Garfield, James B.
  Goldberg, Stan J.
  Halliday, William R(oss)
  Hardwick, Richard (Holmes, Jr.)
  Hodges, Elizabeth Jamison
  Jones, Adrienne
  King, Martin Luther, Jr.
  Klein, Aaron E.
  Lawson, Marie Abrams
  Morrah, David Wardlaw, Jr.
  Moyers, William
  Ogburn, Charlton, Jr.
  Ormsby, Virginia H(aire)
  Peeples, Edwin A(ugustus, Jr.)
  Steedman, Marguerite Couturier
  Stirling, Nora B(romley)
Augusta
  Alexander, Martha
  Radford, Ruby L(orraine)
Banks County
  O'Kelley, Mattie Lou
Calhoun
  Ballard, Mignon Franklin
Clarkesville
  Graham, Brenda Knight
Cogdell
  Davis, Ossie
Columbus
  Hoyt, Olga (Gruhzit)

McCullers, Lula Carson
Wilson, Augusta Jane Evans
Cordele
  Vinson, Kathryn
Covington
  Garrison, Webb B(lack)
Eatonton
  Harris, Joel Chandler
  Walker, Alice
Ellijay
  Anderson, John Lonzo
Fort Benning
  Callahan, Philip S(erna)
Fort Oglethorpe
  Putnam, Peter B(rock)
Inman
  Burch, Robert (Joseph)
LaFayette
  Dodd, Ed(ward Benton)
Macon
  Lanier, Sidney
  Moore, Jack (William)
  Ousley, Odille
  Scott, Robert Lee
Madison
  Andrews, Benny
Moultrie
  Monk, Marvin Randolph
  Wilkinson, Brenda
Savannah
  Aiken, Conrad (Potter)
  Jaffee, Al(lan)
  Saseen, Sharon (Dillon)
Sylvania
  Taylor, Audilee Boyd
Thomasville
  Murphy, E(mmett) Jefferson
Valdosta
  Bealer, Alex W(inkler III)
  Eager, George B.
  Locke, Lucie
  Whitaker, George O.
Washington
  Pope, Clifford Hillhouse
Waycross
  Paul, Aileen (Phillips)
  Robinson, Dorothy W.

HAWAII
  Apilado, Tony
Honolulu
  Campion, Nardi Reeder
  Crockett, Lucy Herndon
  Lowry, Lois (Hammbersberg)
  Williams, Linda
Kauai
  Funai, Mamoru (Rolland)
Onomea
  Kashiwagi, Isami

IDAHO
American Falls
  Mace, Varian
  Sykes, Jo
Bancroft
  Wyss, Thelma Hatch
Bliss

Heady, Eleanor B(utler)
Boise
  Tiegreen, Alan F.
Cascade
  Crutcher, Chris(topher C.)
Council
  Ranney, Agnes V.
Genesee (near)
  Williamson, T(hames) R(oss)
Goldberg
  Sparks, Beatrice Mathews
Gooding
  Edwards, Page L., Jr.
Grangeville
  Kines, Pat Decker
Harpster
  Conklin, Gladys (Plemon)
Idaho Falls
  McCall, Virginia Nielsen
Malad
  Fisher, Laura Harrison
Mink Creek
  Littke, Lael J.
Montpelier
  Gilbreath, Alice (Thompson)
Moscow
  Brink, Carol Ryrie
  Perrine, Mary (Bush)
  Work, Virginia
Nampa
  Crow, Donna Fletcher
Plummer
  Hale, Janet Campbell
Pocatello
  Smith, Gary R(ichard)
Preston
  Jacopetti, Alexandra
Sandpoint
  McManus, Patrick (Francis)
Shelley
  Christensen, Gardell Dano
Twin Falls
  Deiss, Joseph Jay
Wallace
  Wagner, Sharon B.
Wendell
  Rogers, Jean

ILLINOIS
  Habberton, William
  Marquis, Don
  McNair, Kate (Mallory)
  Oncken, Clara
  Skelton, Charles L.
  Thieda, Shirley Ann
  Uschold, Maud E.
  Wells, Robert L.
  Zollinger, Gulielma
Aledo
  Lee, Doris (Emrick)
Alton
  Barry, James P(otvin)
  Downie, Mary Alice (Dawe)
Amboy
  Neyhart, Louise (Pauline) Albright
Arcola

Gruelle, John (Barton)
Ashley
  Sutton, Ann (Livesay)
Beardstown
  Gilson, Jamie
Bellwood
  Lietz, Gerald S(ylvane)
Belvidere
  Gustafson, Scott
Benton
  Haynes, Betsy
Berwyn
  Sivulich, Sandra (Jeanne) Stroner
Bloomington
  Buck, William Ray
  Krum, Charlotte
Brockton
  Gard, Sanford Wayne
Cairo (near)
  Gilmore, Iris
Canton
  Mertz, Barbara (Gross)
Carbondale
  Rauch, Mabel Thompson
  Taylor, Robert Lewis
Carlinville
  Austin, Mary (Hunter)
Champaign
  Kujoth, Jean Spealman
Charleston
  Lawrence, Mildred (Elwood)
  Sublette, C(lifford) M(cClellan)
Chicago
  Abel, Raymond
  Acuff, Selma Boyd
  Adorjan, Carol (Madden)
  Ahl, Anna Maria
  Aldis, Dorothy (Keeley)
  Alter, Judith (MacBain)
  Armstrong, George D.
  Atwater, Richard (Tupper)
  Axeman, Lois
  Bailey, Jane H(orton)
  Barris, George
  Barrows, R(uth) M(ajorie)
  Baum, Allyn Z(elton)
  Becker, John (Leonard)
  Benedict, Dorothy Potter
  Berends, Polly Berrien
  Bethel, Dell
  Betz, Betty
  Bloch, Robert
  Bonners, Susan
  Borja, Corinne
  Borja, Robert
  Boyd, Candy Dawson
  Bozzo, Frank
  Bradford, Richard (Roark)
  Braude, Michael
  Braymer, Marjorie (Elizabeth)
  Brent, Stuart
  Brett, Grace N(eff)
  Brooks, Jerome
  Brown, Fern G.
  Brown, Palmer
  Budd, Lillian (Peterson)
  Buehr, Walter Franklin
  Buell, Harold G.
  Buntain, Ruth Jaeger
  Burleigh, Robert
  Burroughs, Edgar Rice
  Carleton, R(eginal) Milton
  Carter, Dorothy Sharp
  Ceder, Georgiana Dorcas
  Chess, Victoria (Dickerson)
  Clark, Electa
  Coconis, Ted
  Cohen, Daniel
  Conrad, Arthur S.
  Crane, Caroline
  Crichton, J. Michael
  Cummings, Pat (Marie)
  Cusack, Margaret
  Cushman, Jerome
  Dawson, Mitchell
  DeBruyn, Monica
  Dewey, Ariane
  Dewey, Jennifer (Owings)
  Dietz, Elisabeth H.
  Disney, Walt(er Elias)
  Dorin, Patrick C(arberry)
  Doty, Roy
  Dougherty, Charles
  Douglas, Emily (Taft)
  Dubkin, Lois (Knudson)
  Edsall, Marian S(tickney)
  Eisenberg, Phyllis Rose
  Elliott, Sarah M(cCarn)
  Emberley, Barbara A(nne Collins)
  Espenshade, Edward Bowman, Jr.
  Faulkner, Georgene
  Ferguson, Cecil
  Ferry, Charles
  Fishler, Mary (Shiverick)
  Fleischman, Seymour
  Foster, E(lizabeth) C(onnell)
  Foster, Joanna
  Foster, John T(homas)
  Fradin, Dennis Brindell
  Franco, Marjorie
  Freedman, Nancy
  Freeman, Ira M(aximilian)
  Freeman, Mae (Blacker)
  Friedlander, Joanne K(ohn)
  Fufuka, Karama
  Ganz, Yaffa
  Gardner, Jeanne LeMonnier
  Gehr, Mary
  Geis, Darlene (Stern)
  Gerson, Noel B(ertram)
  Goldstein, Nathan
  Goodenow, Earle
  Goodenow, Girard
  Gorey, Edward St. John
  Gross, Alan
  Groth, John (August)
  Grumbine, E. Evalyn
  Gugliotta, Bobette
  Gunther, John
  Haas, Carolyn Buhai
  Hahn, James (Sage)
  Hall, Malcolm
  Harvey, Brett
  Hawkinson, John (Samuel)
  Hayman, LeRoy
  Hein, Lucille Eleanor
  Heinemann, George Alfred
  Herman, Charlotte
  Higdon, Hal
  Hirsch, S. Carl
  Hirsh, Marilyn (Joyce)
  Holmgren, Helen Jean
  Holt, Rochelle Lynn
  Holtzman, Jerome
  Jacker, Corinne (Litvin)
  Jakes, John (W.)
  Johnston, Johanna (Voigt)
  Jones, Richard C.
  Jordan, Mildred
  Kapp, Paul
  Karl, Jean E(dna)
  Keating, Lawrence A(lfred)
  Keller, Dick
  Kellogg, Jean (Defrees)
  Kent, Sherman
  Kerr, Laura (Nowak)
  Kleeberg, Irene (Flitner) Cumming
  Kogan, Herman
  Kopper, Lisa (Esther)
  Krautter, Elisa (Bialk)
  Kristof, Jane
  Krupp, E(dwin) C(harles)
  Lansing, Alfred
  Lawson, Don(ald Elmer)
  Lederer, Muriel
  Leiber, Fritz
  Lerner, Carol
  Lerner, Sharon (Ruth)
  Levin, Meyer
  Levinger, Elma (Ehrlich)
  Lindop, Edmund
  Litten, Frederic Nelson
  Lueders, Edward (George)
  Lurie, Alison
  Luttrell, Guy L.
  Manushkin, Fran(ces)
  Markham, Marion M.
  Martin, David Stone
  Martin, Ralph G.
  Mawicke, Tran
  May, Julian
  McCormick, Edith (Joan)
  McInerney, Judith W(hitelock)
  McLenighan, Valjean
  Meek, S(terner St.) P(aul)
  Meilach, Dona Z(weigoron)
  Miles, Betty
  Miller, Eugene
  Mohan, Beverly (Moffet)
  Montgomery, Vivian
  Munoz, William
  Munson(-Benson), Tunie
  Neigoff, Anne
  Neigoff, Mike
  Neimark, Anne E.
  Neimark, Paul G.
  Neufeld, John (Arthur)

O'Brien, Anne Sibley
O'Connor, Karen
Oleksy, Walter
Oleson, Claire
Owen, Russell
Parker, Dorothy (Lane) D(aniels)
Pearson, Gayle
Peattie, Donald Culross
Pierce, Mary Cunningham (Fitzgerald)
Poole, Ernest
Powers, Richard M.
Price, Margaret (Evans)
Provensen, Alice
Provensen, Martin (Elias)
Purtill, Richard L.
Rabe, Olive H(anson)
Rand, Ann(e Binkley)
Reck, Franklin Mering
Resnick, Michael D(iamond)
Richmond, Julius B(enjamin)
Ridge, Martin
Ridlon, Marci
Rikhoff, Jean
Riswold, Gilbert
Rossel, Seymour
Russo, Susan
Saberhagen, Fred (Thomas)
Sackson, Sid
Schellie, Don
Schick, Joel
Schiller, Barbara (Heyman)
Schmidt, James Norman
Schock, Pauline
Seltzer, Meyer
Shekerjian, Haig
Sherman, Allan
Shirer, William L(awrence)
Shirreffs, Gordon D(onald)
Shotwell, Louisa R(ossiter)
Silverstein, Shel(by)
Skinner, Cornelia Otis
Smith, Fredrika Shumway
Stahl, Ben(jamin Albert)
Stanek, Muriel (Novella)
Stein, Harve
Stein, R(ichard) Conrad
Stevenson, Janet (Marshall)
Stewart, John (William)
Sussman, Susan
Terrell, John Upton
Thiry, Joan (Marie)
Tietjens, Eunice Hammond
Timmins, William F(rederick)
Toner, Raymond John
Tooze, Ruth (Anderson)
Torgersen, Don Arthur
Trahey, Jane
Tucker, Ernest Edward
Ulm, Robert
Ulrich, Homer
Vance, Marguerite
Victor, Joan Berg
Waldman, Frank
Waller, Leslie
Ward, Lynd (Kendall)
Warshaw, Jerry

Weber, Walter Alois
Wersba, Barbara
West, Betty
Wilson, Julia
Wismer, Donald (Richard)
Wolff, Robert Jay
Wondriska, William Allen
Woolley, Catherine
Yarbrough, Camille
York, Carol Beach
Zens, Patricia Martin
Chicago (Galesburg)
Feagles, Anita MacRae
Chicago (Morgan Park)
Bronson, Wilfrid Swancourt
Crete
West, Anna
Danville
Taylor, Florance Walton
Wells, Helen (Frances Weinstock)
Decatur
Ambrose, Stephen E(dward)
Parker, Kristy (Kettelkamp)
Peck, Richard (Wayne)
Priddy, Frances (Rosaleen)
Smith, Imogene Henderson
Divernon
Johnson, Walter Ryerson
Dollville
Galster, Robert
East St. Louis
McMurtrey, Martin A(loysius)
Eldorado
Jenkins, Marie M(agdalen)
Eldred
Arbuckle, Dorothy Fry
Elgin
Martin, Stefan
Pendery, Rosemary (Schmitz)
Elmhurst
Baker, Gayle C(unningham)
Evanston
Abercrombie, Barbara (Mattes)
Allard, Harry G(rover), Jr.
Bates, Betty
Lester, Helen
MacDonald, Suse (Susan Kelsey)
McGorwven, Thomas E.
Mee, Charles L., Jr.
Proudfit, Isabel (Katherine Boyd)
Richard, Adrienne
Waitley, Douglas
Walworth, Jane (Armstrong)
Wilson, Gahan
Zelinsky, Paul O.
Evergreen Park
Jones, Rebecca C(astaldi)
Fairland
DuJardin, Rosamond Neal
Ford County
Long, Earlene (Roberta)
Forest Park
Gerler, William R(obert)
Galena
Gilbertson, Mildred Geiger

Galesburg
Hobson, Burton (Harold)
Irwin, Keith Gordon
Landon, Lucinda
McCully, Emily Arnold
Sandburg, Carl (August)
VanSteenwyk, Elizabeth Ann
Genesco
Jaques, Francis Lee
Geneva
Gordon, Shirley
Knudsen, James
Girard
Weddle, Ethel H(arshbarger)
Grafton
Hovell, Lucy A. (Peterson)
Hamilton
Criner, Beatrice (Hall)
Hall, Elvajean
Harrisburg
Weil, Ann Yezner
Harvey
Kettelkamp, Larry Dale
Herrin
Seamands, Ruth (Childers)
Highland Park
Cohen, Joan Lebold
Jones, Elizabeth Orton
Hinsdale
Anglund, Joan Walsh
Riessen, Martin Clare
Jacksonville
Brandt, Catharine
Owen, Ruth (Bryan)
Udry, Janice (May)
Joliet
Teale, Edwin Way
Kankakee
Gray, Harold (Lincoln)
Laclede
Hinkle, Thomas Clark
Lacon
Jones, Jessie Mae Orton
LaSalle
Smith, Eunice Young
Lemont
Paine, Ralph D.
Lincoln
Maxwell, William
Pevsner, Stella
Lockport
Brennan, Dennis
Lombard
Hall, Lynn
MacDonough County
Newell, Peter
Marion County
Roddy, Lee
Marseilles
O'Neill, Hester (Adams)
Mattoon
Bailey, Bernadine Freeman
Daringer, Helen Fern
Johnson, William Weber
Maywood
Ault, Phillip H(alliday)
Sandburg, Helga

McLeansboro
　Allen, Leroy
　Smith, H(arry) Allen
Melrose Park
　Anderson, Grace Fox
　Rowe, Viola Carson
Moline
　Friskey, Margaret Richards
Mt. Carmel
　Coates, Ruth Allison
　Schucker, James (W.)
Mt. Vernon
　Haines, Gail Kay (Beckman)
Murpheysboro
　Spencer, Lila
Naperville
　Kakacek, Gen
Newton
　Hunt, Irene
Oak Park
　Bach, Richard David
　Berry, James
　Burchard, Sue (Huston)
　Enright, Elizabeth (Wright)
　Espeland, Pamela (Lee)
　Fox, Dorothy
　Gault, Clare S.
　Gibbons, Gail
　Hunter, Mel
　Siegel, Robert (Harold)
　Stegeman, Janet Allais
Oglesby
　Bauer, Marion Dane
Olney
　Inyart, Gene
　Koertge, Ronald
Orion
　Love, Katherine (Isabel)
Pana
　Hitte, Kathryn
Park Ridge
　Reed, Philip G.
Pawpaw
　Lownsbery, Eloise
Pekin
　Dirksen, Everett McKinley
　Rhoads, Dorothy (Mary)
Peoria
　Cleveland, George
　Fischer, Ann A.
　Graeber, Charlotte Towner
　Hager, Alice Rogers
　McCrea, James (Craig, Jr.)
　Schroeder, Ted
　Sheldon, Aure
Pontiac
　Eggenberger, David
Princeton
　Winter, Milo (Kendall)
Quincy
　Dazey, Frank M.
　Hodges, Carl G.
　Ward, Martha (Eads)
　Wicker, Ireene (Seaton)
Rochester
　Parker, Bertha Morris
Rock Island
　Derman, Sarah Audrey
　Grant, Evva H.
　Meigs, Cornelia Lynde
Rockford
　Davis, D(elbert) Dwight
　Sabin, Edwin L(egrand)
　Simons, Barbara B(rooks)
　Underwood, Mary Betty Anderson
Sidell
　Beers, V(ictor) Gilbert
Springfield
　Eifert, Virginia (Louise) S(nider)
　Knotts, Howard (Clayton, Jr.)
　Lindsay, Nicholas Vachel
Sterling
　Brooks, Terry
　Thomas, Glen
Stockton
　MacPeek, Walter G.
　Thompson, Donnis (Stark)
Streator
　Abodaher, David J. (Naiph)
　Cornell, Jean Gay
Toluca
　Antonacci, Robert Joseph
Urbana
　Jackson, C(aary) Paul
Utah
　Britt, Albert
Waukegan
　Austin, Phil
　Bradbury, Ray (Douglas)
　Oldfield, Margaret J(ean)
　Sankey, Alice (Ann-Susan)
　Townsend, Thomas L.
West Chicago
　Raebeck, Lois
Wheaton
　Johnson, Avery F.
Wilmette
　Ayars, James S(terling)
　Marriott, Alice Lee
Wyoming
　Townsend, Lee
Zion
　Gay, Kathlyn (McGarrahan)

INDIANA
　Conger, Marion
　Johnson, Enid
　Kennedy, Paul E(dward)
　Longstreth, Joseph
　Schulte, Elaine L(ouise)
Alexandria
　Hiller, Ilo (Ann)
Anderson
　Crouse, William H(arry)
　Gordon, Gordon
　Maxey, Dale
　Naylor, Phyllis Reynolds
Auburn
　Boles, Paul Darcy
Blackwood County
　Walker, Lou Ann
Bloomfield
　Kiser, Martha Gwinn
Bluffton
　Bell, Joseph N.
Brookville
　Wallace, Lew(is)
Cartersburg
　Swinford, Betty (June Wells)
Carthage
　Allee, Marjorie Hill
Coatesville
　Hunt, Mabel Leigh
Columbus
　Long, Laura Mooney
Connersville
　Weales, Gerald (Clifford)
Covington
　Hammond, Winifred G(raham)
Crawfordsville
　Lambert, Janet (Snyder)
　McGuire, Frances (Lynch)
De Pauw
　Thompson, Hildegard (Steerstedter)
Delphi
　McGiffin, Lewis Lee Shaffer
Elkhart
　Chorao, Ann McKay (Sproat)
Evansville
　Irwin, Constance Frick
　Johnston, Annie Fellows
　Nolan, Jeannette Covert
　Skelly, James R(ichard)
Fort Wayne
　Day, Beth (Feagles)
　Dickmeyer, Lowell A.
　Falls, C(harles) B(uckles)
　Root, Phyllis
　Strete, Craig Kee
Franklin
　Bridges, William (Andrew)
Gary
　Kimmel, Margaret Mary
　Place, Marian T(empleton)
　Seed, Suzanne (Liddell)
　Smith, Alvin
　Temple, Herbert
Gaston
　Lewellen, John Bryan
Goshen
　Mason, Miriam E(vangeline)
Grandview
　Peet, William Bartlett
Greencastle
　Matthews, Ellen
　Weik, Mary Hays
　Young, Stanley (Preston)
Greenfield
　Riley, James Whitcomb
Hamilton County
　Baldwin, James
Hillisburg
　Sharp, Zerna A.
Hobart
　Sumichrast, Jozef
Huntingburg
　Armer, Alberta (Roller)
Huntington
　Ackerman, Eugene (Francis)

Russell, Don(ald Bert)
Indianapolis
Bentley, Judith (McBride)
Carson, J(ohn) Franklin
Coffman, Ramon Peyton
Courlander, Harold
Cronbach, Abraham
DuBois, Shirley Graham
Gibson, Katharine
Harrison, C. William
Hendrickson, Walter Brookfield, Jr.
Henry, Joanne Landers
Hodges, Margaret Moore
Johnson, Sylvia A.
Kahl, M(arvin) P(hilip)
Lasky, Kathryn
Lund, Doris (Herold)
Major, Charles
Masters, Mildred
McCrady, Lady
Moon, Grace (Purdie)
Myers, Hortense (Powner)
Schreiber, Elizabeth Anne (Ferguson)
Speicher, Helen Ross (Smith)
Tarkington, Newton Booth
VanRiper, Guernsey, Jr.
Winders, Gertrude Hecker
Jefferson County
Hammontree, Marie (Gertrude)
Kingston
Bartlett, Robert Merrill
Knightstown
Beard, Charles Austin
Kokomo
Bridwell, Norman
Richardson, Robert S(hirley)
Kouts
Unrau, Ruth
La Grange
Warrick, Patricia Scott
La Porte
O'Connor, Richard
Lafayette
DeRegniers, Beatrice Schenk
Stein, Evaleen
Liberty
Miller, Joaquin
Logansport
Judson, Clara Ingram
Lynnville
Holder, Glenn
Maples
Perkins, Lucy Fitch
Marion
Bennett, Rainey
Davis, James Robert
Friermood, Elisabeth Hamilton
Harrah, Michael
Michigan City
Balow, Tom
Westphal, Arnold Carl
Mishawaka
Michel, Anna
Mitchell

Caudell, Marian
Morocco
Finney, Gertrude E. (Bridgeman)
Mount Vernon
Blackburn, Joyce Knight
Muncie
Ervin, Janet Halliday
Kimbrough, Emily
Zwinger, Ann
New Albany
Cochran, Bobbye A.
New Harmony
Snedeker, Caroline Dale (Parke)
Newland
McCormick, Wilfred
North Vernon
West, Mary Jessamyn
Odon
Wadsworth, Wallace (Carter)
Oolitic
Thrasher, Crystal (Faye)
Paoli
Davidson, Rosalie
Patriot
Stevenson, Augusta
Plainfield
Boesen, Victor
Hornaday, William T(emple)
Plevna
Rich, Elaine Sommers
Princeton
Cavanah, Frances
Rensselaer
Atkinson, Eleanor (Stackhouse)
Richmond
Holder, William G.
Kinert, Reed Charles
Rochester
DeWeese, Thomas Eugene
Selma
Hamilton, Dorothy
South Bend
Campbell, M. Rudolph
Livingston, Richard R(oland)
Messick, Dale
Piussi-Campbell, Judy
Sullivan
Stokes, Jack (Tilden)
Terre Haute
Boggs, Ralph Steele
Busby, Edith (A. Lake)
Joseph, James (Herz)
Millender, Dharathula (Hood)
Witty, Paul A(ndrew)
Thorntown
Hutchens, Paul
Valparaiso
Aylesworth, Thomas G(ibbons)
Holling, Lucille Webster
Versailles
Dickerson, Roy Ernest
Vevay
Eggleston, Edward
Vincennes
Skelton, Red
Wabash
Eby, Lois Christine

Wabash County
Porter, Gene(va Grace) Stratton
Walton
Duff, Margaret K.
Ward Township
Stinetorf, Louise (Allender)
Washington
Kidwell, Carl
Reck, Alma Kehoe
West Lafayette
Winter, Ginny Linville
Whitley County
Adams, Andy

IOWA
Curtis, Alice Bertha
Dorman, N. B.
Lovoos, Janice
Adair County
Johnson, Shirley K(ing)
Ames
Rockwood, Joyce
Batavia
McCarty, Rega Kramer
Battle Creek
Preston, Lillian Elvira
Bedford
Hamblin, Dora Jane
May, Charles Paul
Buck Grove
Niehuis, Charles C(arroll)
Burlington
Bruner, Richard W(allace)
Jordan, Philip Dillon
Kent, John Wellington
Thane, Elswyth
Walker, Pamela
Cedar Falls
Aldrich, Bess Streeter
Kadesch, Robert R(udstone)
Miller, Helen M(arkley)
Chariton
Cromie, Alice Hamilton
Charles City
McCall, Edith S(ansum)
Clarinda
Sanborn, Duane
Clayton
Liers, Emil E(rnest)
Clinton
Horsfall, Robert Bruce
Colfax
Hall, James Norman
Columbus Junction
Pierce, Edith Gray
Council Bluffs
Gretzer, John
Meeks, Esther K. (MacBain)
Davenport
Glaspell, Susan
Hansen, Harry
Spinner, Stephanie
Dayton
Ross, Z(ola) H(elen Girdey)
Des Moines
Anastasio, Dina
Batey, Tom

Bladow, Suzanne Wilson
Brooks, Lester
Deming, Richard
Disch, Thomas M(ichael)
Gammell, Stephen
Hodgell, P(atricia) C(hristine)
Jensen, Virginia Allen
McClinton, Leon
McGraw, William Corbin
Nelson, Lawrence E(rnest)
Nourse, Alan E(dward)
Stack, Nicolete Meredith
Dickens
Anderson, Norman (Dean)
Dows
Robertson, Keith (Carlton)
Dubuque
McNeely, Marian Hurd
Eagle Grove
Brady, Lillian
Poole, Lynn D.
Earlham
Hadley, Lee
Emmetsburg
Bliven, Bruce
Estherville
McFarland, Wilma
Fairfield
Welty, S(usan) F(ulton)
Farragut
Chaffee, Allen
Finchford
Beaty, John Yocum
Fort Dodge
Hemphill, Martha Locke
Purscell, Phyllis
Gilmore City
Daniels, Guy
Griswold
Bradford, Lois J(ean)
Newlon, Frank Clarke
Guthrie Center
Holl, Kristi D(iane)
Hamilton County
Leaf, VaDonna Jean
Humboldt
Baker, Laura Nelson
Inland
Crowell, Grace Noll
Iowa City
Allred, Gordon T.
Brewer, Sally King
Jackson Junction
Govern, Elaine
Jasper County
Hough, Emerson
Keokuk
Calhoun, Mary Huiskamp
Keosauqua
Stong, Phil(ip Duffield)
Ladora
Benson, Mildred W.
Lake View
Dean, Graham M.
Lakota
Griese, Arnold A(lfred)
Little Rock (near)
Brindel, June (Rachuy)
Madrid
Morrison, Velma Ford
Pelta, Kathy
Marshalltown
Collins, David (Raymond)
Glick, Carl (Cannon)
Hicks, Clifford B.
Larson, Jean Russell
McCahill, William P.
Mason City
Arbuthnot, May Hill
Franchere, Ruth
Rinard, Judith E(llen)
Schurfranz, Vivian
Willson, Dixie
McGregor
Johnson, Dorothy M(arie)
Murray
LeSueur, Meridel
Muscatine
Butler, Ellis Parker
Nashua
Morrison, Dorothy Nafus
Neola
Felton, Harold W(illiam)
New Hampton
Hintz, Loren Martin
New London
Hale, Arlene
Newton
Sattler, Helen Roney
Oskaloosa
Belting, Natalia Maree
Ottumwa
Daniel, Becky
Morrow, Honore Willsie
Parkersburg
Fenton, Carroll Lane
Peterson
Irwin, Ann(abelle Bowen)
Randolph
Smith, Pauline C(oggeshall)
Richland
Smith, Robert W(illiam)
Rock Township, Doon
Manfred, Frederick F(eikema)
Rome
Lockwood, Myna
Sharpsburg
Case, Elinor Rutt
Sheldon
Burdick, Eugene (Leonard)
Sioux City
Demuth, Patricia Brennan
Dreves, Veronica R.
Hanna, Paul R(obert)
Veglahn, Nancy (Crary)
Watts, Franklin (Mowry)
Spencer
Grummer, Arnold Edward
Olsen, Violet (Mae)
Storm Lake
Holmes, Marjorie (Rose)
Van Meter
Feller, Robert William Andrew
Victor
Coates, Belle
Villisca
Posten, Margaret L(ois)
Waterloo
Carpenter, John Allan
Heath, Charles D(ickinson)
Miner, Lewis S.
Waucoma
Johnston, Edith Constance Farrington
Waukon
Kinney, Jean Stout
Medary, Marjorie
Waverly
Gremmels, Marion (Louise) Chapman
Webster City
Kantor, MacKinlay
Wesley
Goetz, Delia
West Branch (Near)
Fenton, Mildred Adams
Whiting
Heaps, Willard (Allison)
Williamsburg
Porter, Ella (Blodwen) Williams

KANSAS
Hazlett, Edward Everett
Martin, William Ivan
Ross, Patricia (Fent)
Shields, Charles
Atwood
Bliss, Ronald G(ene)
Baldwin City
Phelan, Mary Kay (Harris)
Brewster
Thompson, Harlan H.
Bucyrus
Price, Garrett
Caldwell
Shannon, George (William Bones)
Chanute
Johnson, Osa Helen (Leighty)
Cherokee
Martin, Patricia Miles
Clay Center
Tousey, Thomas Sanford
Dunavant
Curry, John Steuart
El Dorado
Walker, Addison Mort
Worline, Bonnie Bess
Elkhart
Williams, J(eanne R.)
Englewood
Little, Mary E.
Eureka
Gordon, Mildred (Nixon)
Fort Leavenworth
Ferris, Jean
Reeder, Russell P(otter), Jr.
Fort Scott
Nickerson, Elizabeth
Fort Scott (near)

Parks, Gordon (Alexander Buchanan)
Fowler
Smith, Janice Lee
Frankfort
Talbot, Charlene Joy
Galena
Baker, Nina (Brown)
Garden City
Gaeddert, Lou Ann (Bigge)
McKenzie, Dorothy Clayton
Herndon
Wendelin, Rudolph
Hoisington
Bitter, Gary G(len)
Hope
Wyatt, Geraldine (Tolman)
Horton
Miller, Sandy (Peden)
Hutchinson
Evarts, Hal G. (,Jr.)
Independence
Rushmore, Helen
Iola
Gard, Robert Edward
Priestley, Lee (Shore)
Junction City
Goudey, Alice E(dwards)
Kansas City
Phleger, Fred B.
Robinson, Marileta
Lakin (near)
Luther, Frank
Lawrence
Anderson, Bernice G(oudy)
Bratton, Karl H(enry)
Fisher, Dorothy (Frances) Canfield
Francis, Dorothy Brenner
Lucas
Wilcox, Don
Lyons
Walsh, Richard John
Macksville
Chandler, Edna Walker
Manhattan
Leonard, A. Byron
Scheffer, Victor B(lanchard)
Medicine Lodge
Beals, Carleton
Mound City
Robison, Bonnie
Newton
Smucker, Barbara (Claassen)
Oskaloosa
Smith, Moyne Rice
Oswego
Franklin, George Cory
Pratt
Alex, Marlee
Shura, Mary Francis
Ringo
Malo, John
Salina
Craven, Thomas
Whitney, David C(harles)
Winterbotham, R(ussell) R(obert)

Sedan
Nunn, Jessie Alford
Smith Center
Kimball, Dean
Stafford
DeLaurentis, Louise Budde
Thayer
Stall, Dorothy
Timberhill
Dolim, Mary N(uzum)
Topeka
Brooks, Gwendolyn
Brown, Irene Bennett
Dunlap, Hope
Eyerly, Jeanette Hyde
Lamb, Elizabeth Searle
Lerrigo, Marion Olive
McClintock, Marshall
Sayers, Frances (Clarke)
Toronto
Brown, George Earl
Washington
Smith, Frances C(hristine)
Wichita
Eaton, Tom
Immel, Mary Blair

KENTUCKY
Radlauer, Edward
(Poor Fork) Cumberland
Caudill, Rebecca
Augusta
Walker, Stuart (Armstrong)
Bloomfield
Thompson, Stith
Bowling Green
Clagett, John (Henry)
Grider, Dorothy
Campbellsville
Young, Margaret B(uckner)
Catlettsburg
Burns, Paul C(lay)
Columbia
Smith, Irene
Corinth
Odor, Ruth Shannon
Covington
Brokamp, Marilyn
Burman, Ben Lucien
Polking, Kirk
Dayton
Burr, Lonnie
Elkton
Morton, David
Fairview
Momaday, Natachee Scott
Fort Knox
Detwiler, Susan Dill
Guthrie
Warren, Robert Penn
Harlan
Stephens, Mary Jo
Hopkinsville
Land, Barbara (Neblett)
Lewis County
Ishmael, Woodi
Lexington

Wilkie, Katherine E(lliott)
Louisa
Spencer, Donald D(ean)
Louisville
Arehart-Treichel, Joan
Conklin, Paul (S.)
Dillon, Corinne Boyd
Fox, Fontaine Talbot, Jr.
Graham, Clarence Reginald
Holland, Rupert Sargent
Klemm, Edward G., Jr.
Klemm, Roberta K(ohnhorst)
Love, Sandra (Weller)
Marshall, Dean
McMeekin, Isabel (McLennan)
Miller, Mary Beth
Ready, Kirk L.
Reed, Gwendolyn (Elizabeth)
Shore, June Lewis
Middleboro
Merwin, Decie
Murray
Spencer, Zane A(nn)
Nebo
Waltrip, Mildred
Owensboro
Baker, James W.
Paducah
Granstaff, Bill
Perryville
Roberts, Elizabeth Madox
Robards
Mosley, Elizabeth Robards
Shelbyville
Alexander, David
Rice, Alice (Caldwell) Hegan
Somerset
Dillard, Polly (Hargis)
South Carrollton
Berrill, Jacquelyn (Batsel)
Stony Point
Fox, John (William), Jr.
Three Springs
Altsheler, Joseph A(lexander)
Uniontown
Moore, Vardine (Russell)
Varney
Chaffin, Lillie D(orton)
W-Hollow, Riverton
Stuart, Hilton Jesse
Wayne County
Arnow, Harriette (Louisa) Simpson
Wolf Creek
Trent, Robbie

LOUISIANA
Brown, Dee (Alexander)
Alexandria
Bontemps, Arna(ud Wendell)
Sweat, Lynn
Canterville
Delaune, Jewel Lynn (de Grummond)
Centerville
DeGrummond, Lena Young
Columbia

Ogan, Margaret E. (Nettles)
De Ridder
  Walter, Mildred Pitts
Eunice
  Fontenot, Mary Alice
Franklin
  Lacy, Leslie Alexander
Hammond
  Carter, William Hodding
Lake Charles
  Kushner, Donn
New Iberia
  Edler, Timothy
  Watson, Pauline
New Orleans
  Amoss, Berthe (Marks)
  Callen, Lawrence Willard, Jr.
  Campbell, Virginia
  Carmer, Elizabeth Black
  Crary, Elizabeth (Ann)
  Cutchens, Judy
  Graham, Lorenz (Bell)
  Kelly, Regina Z(immerman)
  Lystad, Mary (Hanemann)
  Tallant, Robert
Oscar
  Gaines, Ernest J.
Shreveport
  Baker, Janice E(dla)
  Land, Myrick (Ebben)
  Pournelle, Jerry (Eugene)
Spearsville
  Smith, George Harmon
St. Rose
  Burroughs, Margaret Taylor G.
Webster Parish
  Mims, Sam (S.)
Winnfield
  Smith, William Jay

MAINE
  Woodbury, David O(akes)
Augusta
  Gesner, Clark
Bangor
  Davis, Mary Gould
  Hurley, Leslie J(ohn)
  Peirce, Waldo
Bar Harbor
  Stevens, Mary E.
Bath
  Reed, W(illiam) Maxwell
Bluehill
  Chase, Mary Ellen
Brunswick
  Coffin, Robert P. Tristram
Buxton
  Southwick, Katherine
Calais
  Robinson, Thomas Pendleton
Camden
  Rolerson, Darrell A(llen)
Castine
  Brooks, Noah
Damariscotta
  Day, Maurice
East Oreland

  Clark, Walter Van Tilburg
Easton
  Saunders, Blanche
Eliot
  Fleming, Susan
Farmington
  Harper, Wilhelmina
Frankfort (Winterport)
  Kaler, James Otis
Gardiner
  Wilson, Dorothy Clarke
Hallowell
  Abbott, Jacob
Head Tide
  Robinson, Edwin Arlington
Kittery
  Himmelman, John (Carl)
Lewiston
  Barnstone, Willis
Limerick
  Moore, Anne Carroll
Livermore Falls
  Bogan, Louise
Mars Hill
  Kinney, Harrison
Mt. Desert
  Eliot, Frances
Norridgewock
  Clarke, Rebecca Sophia
Norway
  Stephens, Charles Asbury
Old Town
  Philbrook, Clem(ent E.)
Portland
  Beyer, Audrey White
  Dickson, Marguerite (Stockman)
  Gallant, Roy (Arthur)
  King, Stephen (Edwin)
  Kraus, Joanna Halpert
  Longfellow, Henry Wadsworth
  Sharmat, Marjorie Weinman
  Wilson, Hazel (Hutchins)
Rockland
  Millay, Edna St. Vincent
Sanford
  Miller, Natalie
  Mullins, Edward S(wift)
Skowhegan
  Dolbier, Maurice (Wyman)
  Smith, Margaret Chase
South Berwick
  Jewett, Sarah Orne
Sullivan
  Curtis, Alice (Turner)
Thomaston
  Carleton, Barbee Oliver
Watertown
  Hodge, Jane Aiken
Winthrop
  Clifford, Harold B(urton)

MARYLAND
  Bacon, Paul
  Sentman, George Armor
Annapolis
  Snyder, Louis Leo
Anne Arundel County

  Weems, Mason Locke
Baltimore
  Agle, Nan Hayden
  Ashley, Robert P(aul) Jr.
  Atkin, Flora B(lumenthal)
  Baker, Augusta (Braxston)
  Bauernschmidt, Marjorie
  Brightfield, Richard
  Carswell, Evelyn M(edicus)
  Christopher, Milbourne
  Cornish, Sam(uel James)
  Coughlan, Margaret N(ourse)
  Crew, Helen (Cecilia) Coale
  Crook, Beverly Courtney
  Crownfield, Gertrude
  Dukert, Joseph M(ichael)
  Elkin, Benjamin
  Fax, Elton Clay
  Fenderson, Lewis H.
  Foster, Sally
  Frey, Shaney
  Gervasi, Frank Henry
  Gillelan, George Howard
  Glanzman, Louis S.
  Glines, Carroll V(ane), Jr.
  Grollman, Earl A.
  Hausman, Gerald
  Henneberger, Robert G.
  Hilgartner, Beth
  Krauss, Ruth (Ida)
  Lewis, Elizabeth Foreman
  Lord, Walter
  Loss, Joan
  MacGregor, Ellen
  MacMaster, Eve (Ruth) B(owers)
  Mangurian, David
  Nathan, Adele (Gutman)
  Offit, Sidney
  Oursler, Charles Fulton
  Rankin, Louise D.
  Raymond, Margaret Thomsen
  Rodowsky, Colby
  Ross, Pat(ricia Kienzie)
  Sanderlin, George
  Sanger, Marjory Bartlett
  Severn, Sue
  Sharfman, Amalie
  Sinclair, Upton (Beall)
  Slicer, Margaret O.
  Sung, Betty Lee
  Swanson, Anne (Sherbourne)
  Uris, Leon (Marcus)
  Vinge, Joan D(ennison)
  Walsh, Ellen Stoll
  Wheelwright, Jere Hungerford, Jr.
  Wilson, Eleanore (Hubbard)
  Zubrowski, Bernard
Baltimore (Hamilton)
  Leaf, Wilbur Munro
Barkhill
  Coleman, William L(eroy)
Bethesda
  Bond, Nancy (Barbara)
Cantonsville
  Kummer, Frederic Arnold
Catonsville

Crosby, Alexander L.
Cumberland
    Hawkins, Arthur
Grantsville
    Bender, Lucy Ellen
Greenbelt
    McGee, Barbara
Havre de Grace
    Sleator, William (Warner III)
La Plata
    Key, Alexander (Hill)
Riderwood
    Frame, Paul
Saint Michaels
    Krantz, Lucretia
Tacoma Park
    Zellan, Audrey Penn
Tuckahoe
    Douglass, Frederick
Waldorf
    Quinn, Elisabeth
Washington County
    Johnson, Eleanor (Murdock)

MASSACHUSETTS
    Jerr, William A.
    Johnson, Corinne B.
Adams
    Beeler, Nelson F(rederick)
Amesbury
    Kelly, Eric P(hilbrook)
Amherst
    Davis, William Stearns
    Dickinson, Emily (Elizabeth)
    Eastman, P(hilip) D(ey)
    Emerson, Caroline D(wight)
    Jackson, Helen (Maria Fiske) Hunt
Andover
    Mian, Mary (Lawrence Shipman)
Arlington
    Williamson, Joanne S(mall)
    Wirtenberg, Patricia Z(arrella)
Attleboro
    Corrigan, Barbara
    Lord, Patricia C.
Auburndale
    Davidson, Mary R.
Bellingham (Medway)
    Adams, William Taylor
Belmont
    Carlson, Esther Elisabeth
    Reeves, Lawrence F.
Beverly
    Davis, Robert
Beverly Farms
    Eaton, Anne T(haxter)
Billerica
    Farrar, Susan Clement
    Jones, Helen L(ouise)
Blackstone
    Tappan, Eva March
Boston
    Angier, Bradford
    Beck, Barbara L.
    Bierhorst, John (William)
    Bohlen, Nina

Boorman, Linda (Kay)
Botkin, B(enjamin) A(lbert)
Bowen, R(obert) Sydney
Bradley, Will(iam H.)
Brennan, Joseph Gerard
Brown, Abbie Farwell
Burgess, F(rank) Gelett
Burns, Irene
Calapai, Letterio
Campbell, Ann R.
Carden, Priscilla
Cauman, Samuel
Ciardi, John (Anthony)
Clapp, Patricia
Coles, Robert (Martin)
Crosscup, Richard
Darwin, Beatrice
Davis, Russell G(erard)
Delear, Frank J.
Dennis, Morgan
Drury, Roger W(olcott)
Emberley, Michael
Emerson, Ralph Waldo
Epstein, Samuel
Farber, Norma
Farquharson, Alexander
Flitner, David P(erkins)
Follen, Eliza Lee (Cabot)
Foss, William O(tto)
Fraser, Elizabeth Marr
French, Allen
Friedrich, Otto (Alva)
Garden, Nancy
Gordon, Esther S(aranga)
Gorodetzky, Charles W.
Gregorian, Joyce Ballou
Gundersheimer, Karen
Hale, Edward Everett
Hale, Lucretia Peabody
Hale, Nancy
Harkins, Philip
Harnden, Ruth (Peabody)
Hartshorn, Ruth M.
Healey, Larry
Heins, Paul
Hentoff, Nat(han Irving)
Hieatt, Constance B(artlett)
Hightower, Florence (Cole)
Hirshberg, Al(bert Simon)
Hochschild, Arlie Russell
Howe, Deborah
Hunter, Edith Fisher
Ish-Kishor, Judith
Joy, Charles Rhind
Kenny, Herbert A(ndrew)
Knott, William Cecil, Jr.
Kowet, Don
Krensky, Stephen (Alan)
Kublin, Hyman
Lampert, Emily
Lanes, Selma G(ordon)
Langton, Jane (Gillson)
Lavine, Sigmund A(rnold)
Lent, Blair
Lewis, Alfred E.
Lewis, Anne
Loring, Emilie (Baker)

Lydon, Michael
Mason, F(rancis) van Wyck
McLeod, Emilie Warren
McMillan, Bruce
McNamara, Louise (Greep)
Melcher, Marguerite Fellows
Mirsky, Reba Paeff
Molarsky, Osmond
Molloy, Anne (Stearns) Baker
Morison, Samuel Eliot
Morris, William
Murray, Don(ald M.)
Newman, Shirlee Petkin
O'Leary, Brian (Todd)
Ogilvie, Elisabeth May
Palder, Edward L.
Pearson, Susan
Pizer, Vernon
Plath, Sylvia
Plowden, David
Poe, Edgar Allan
Price, Jonathan (Reeve)
Quarles, Benjamin
Rachlis, Eugene (Jacob)
Radley, Gail
Ranadive, Gail
Richards, Laura E(lizabeth Howe)
Robbins, Frank
Rosen, Sidney
Rosenblatt, Arthur S.
Rubinstein, Robert E(dward)
Sawyer, Ruth
Scarry, Richard (McClure)
Schreiter, Rick
Scott, Cora Annett (Pipitone)
Scudder, Horace E(lisha)
Shepherd, Elizabeth
Sherman, Diane (Finn)
Snyder, Anne
Spearing, Judith (Mary Harlow)
Stolz, Mary (Slattery)
Stonaker, Frances Benson
Sullivan, Thomas Joseph, Jr.
Tripp, Eleanor B(aldwin)
Tripp, Wallace (Whitney)
Trivett, Daphne (Harwood)
Tudor, Tasha
Tufts, Anne
Tunis, John R(oberts)
Victor, Edward
Voigt, Cynthia
Wassersug, Joseph D(avid)
Weller, George (Anthony)
Wilson, John
Wolff, Jenifer Ashley
Zallinger, Jean (Day)
Zemach, Kaethe
Boston (Chestnut Hill)
    Woody, Regina (Llewellyn) Jones
Bridgewater
    Walters, Marguerite
Brighton
    LeVert, William John
Brockton
    Cary, Louis F(avreau)

Grant, Cynthia D.
Tashjian, Virginia A.
Brookline
Greenleaf, Margery
Kennedy, John Fitzgerald
Kent, Louise (Andrews)
Lowell, Amy
Pratt, Agnes Edwards Rothery
Sharmat, Mitchell
Soule, Jean Conder
Viereck, Ellen R.
Cambridge
Barbour, Ralph Henry
Beiser, Germaine (Bousquet)
Bowman, John S(tewart)
Cummings, E(dward) E(stlin)
Dain, Martin J.
Dana, Richard Henry, Jr.
Dodge, Bertha S(anford)
Francis, Henry S.
Haverstock, Mary Sayre
Headstrom, Birger Richard
Holmes, Oliver Wendell
Hunt, Charlotte Dumaresq
Kane, Henry Bugbee
Kelley, True Adelaide
Langone, John (Michael)
Lawrence, Isabelle (Wentworth)
Lowell, James Russell
McCaffrey, Anne (Inez)
Pluff, Barbara (Littlefield)
Rice, Charles D(uane)
Roach, Marilynne K(athleen)
Torrey, Helen
Washburn, Henry Bradford, Jr.
Cambridgeport
Ossoli, Sarah Margaret (Fuller) marchesa d'
Chatham
Meyer, Edith Patterson
Chelsea
Gardner, Sheldon
Terban, Marvin
Chicopee
Callaway, Kathy
Chicopee Falls
Rogers, W(illiam) G(arland)
Concord
Davidson, Sandra Calder
Danvers
Kelsey, Alice Geer
Swift, Helen Miller
Dedham
Rowsome, Frank (Howard), Jr.
Dorcester
Whitney, Elinor
Dorchester
Grant, Madeleine Parker
Kenealy, James P.
East Bridgewater
Curley, Daniel
East Walpole
Lavin, Mary
Edgartown
Coe, Lloyd
Everett
Kredenser, Gail

Fall River
Betz, Eva Kelly
Dunnahoo, Terry
Harris, Steven Michael
Falmouth
Bates, Katharine Lee
Dennis, Wesley
Fitchburg
Kielty, Bernardine
Gardner
Cady, Walter Harrison
Gloucester
Natti, Susanna
Smith, Howard E(verett) Jr.
Grafton
Harwood, Pearl Augusta (Bragdon)
Great Barrington
DuBois, W(illiam) E(dward) B(urghardt)
Greenfield
Luhrmann, Winifred B(ruce)
Munsinger, Lynn
Hamilton
Corcoran, Barbara
Harwich
Litchfield, Ada B(assett)
Haverhill
Cook, Gladys Emerson
Smith, Marion Jaques
Whittier, John Greenleaf
Hingham
Brett, Jan (Churchill)
Holden
Holz, Loretta (Marie)
Holyoke
Hickman, Martha Whitmore
Newell, Homer Edward, Jr.
Huntington
Rich, Louise (Dickinson)
Ipswich
Hay, John
Kingston
Dix, Beulah Marie
Lawrence
Frost, Lesley
Green, Margaret
Thayer, Ernest Lawrence
Thomson, Arline K.
Leominster
Cormier, Robert (Edmund)
Lowell
Brooks, Elbridge Streeter
Ingalls, Leonard
Phillips, Louis
Sullivan, George E(dward)
Wolcott, Patty
Lynn
Miller, Alice P(atricia McCarthy)
Parsons, William E(dward), Jr.
Polonsky, Arthur
Silverman, Al
Malden
Emberley, Ed(ward Randolph)
Ghikas, Panos (George)
Melcher, Frederic Gershom
Preston, Alice Bolam

Williams, Selma R(uth)
Marblehead
Barth, Edna (Smith)
Medfield
Edwards, Cecile (Pepin)
Medford
Child, Lydia Maria
Theroux, Paul
Melrose
Clarke, Mary Stetson
Speare, Elizabeth George
Methuen
Caras, Roger A(ndrew)
McLanathan, Richard Barton Kennedy
Zarins, Joyce Audy
Middleboro
Brett, Harold M.
Panesis, Nicholas
Milford
Bragg, Mabel Caroline
Milton
Candy, William Robert
Cheney, Theodore Albert
Needham
Hamerstrom, Frances
Jane, Mary Childs
Wyeth, N(ewell) C(onvers)
New Bedford
Best, Evangel Allena Champlin
Chandler, Ruth Forbes
Chesler, Bernice
Dias, Earl Joseph
Hayden, Robert C(arter), Jr.
Lent, Henry Bolles
Paine, Albert Bigelow
Stoddard, Hope
Viereck, Phillip R.
Newburyport
Graham, Al
McPhail, David M(ichael)
Newton
Benchley, Nathaniel (Goddard)
Bulfinch, Thomas
Butler, Mildred Allen
Hillman, Priscilla (Hartford)
Hogarth, Grace (Weston Allen)
Knudson, Richard L(ewis)
Sexton, Anne (Harvey)
Weiss, Ann E(dwards)
Newton Center
Burton, Virginia Lee
Melcher, Daniel
North Adams
Smith, Bradford
Northampton
Bacmeister, Rhoda W(arner)
Turner, Ann W(arren)
Northhampton
Crompton, Anne Eliot
Rendina, Laura (Jones) Cooper
Norwood
Gay, Zhenya
Palmer, Bruce Hamilton
White, Laurence B(arton), Jr.
Oakdale
Banning, Evelyn I.

Peabody
  Israel, Marion Louise
Pittsfield
  Albert, Burton, Jr.
  Helfman, Elizabeth S(eaver)
  Neal, Harry Edward
  Whittlesey, Susan
  Yeakley, Marjory Hall
Plymouth
  Brewster, Patience
Princeton
  Mason, George Frederick
Quincy
  Beston, Henry B.
  Cavanagh, Helen (Carol)
  Davis, Marguerite
  Dunbar, Robert E(verett)
  Murray, Marian
Randolph
  Freeman, Mary Eleanor Wilkins
Reading
  Hartelius, Margaret A.
  Kingman, Mary Lee
Revere
  Alger, Horatio, Jr.
  Hauman, George
Roxbury
  Conway, Helene
Salem
  Cummins, Maria Susanna
  Foley, Daniel Joseph
  Hawthorne, Nathaniel
  Lufkin, Raymond H.
Sandwich
  Bright, Robert
  Burgess, Thornton W(aldo)
Sharon
  Cooke, Sarah (Palfrey) Fabyan
Shrewsbury
  Brooks, Thomas R(eed)
Somerset
  Hegarty, Reginald Beaton
Somerville
  Leonard, Jonathan N(orton)
  Moss, Don(ald)
  Nickerson, Jan
  Piro, Richard
  Waters, John F(rederick)
South Orleans
  Brooks, Polly Schoyer
Southboro
  Spykman, E(lizabeth) C(hoate)
Southbridge
  Phillips, Loretta (Hosey)
Springfield
  Alderman, Clifford Lindsey
  Bragdon, Elspeth (MacDuffie)
  Cook, Howard Norton
  Ellis, Harry Bearse
  Geisel, Theodor Seuss
  Hutchins, Carleen Maley
  Landis, J(ames) D(avid)
  McQueen, Lucinda (Emily)
  Wallace-Brodeur, Ruth
  Warren, Joyce W(illiams)
  Whitehouse, Elizabeth S(cott)
Stoughton
  Holdsworth, William Curtis
Swampscott
  Johnson, Elizabeth
Walpole
  Latham, Barbara
Waltham
  Robinson, Mabel Louise
Ware
  Sanderson, Ruth (L.)
Watertown
  Abbott, Robert Tucker
Waverley
  Lansing, Marion Florence
West Medford
  Cummings, Parke
West Somerville
  Hauman, Doris
Westborough
  Forbes, Esther
Westfield
  Janes, Edward C.
Weymouth
  Barney, Maginel Wright
  Hillyer, V(irgil) M(ores)
Whitinsville
  Hogner, Nils
Winchendon
  Richards, Norman
  White, Percival
Winchester
  Gorsline, S(ally) M(arie)
  Roop, Peter
Winthrop
  Sutherland, Zena B(ailey)
Worcester
  Austin, Mary Jane Goodwin
  Bishop, Elizabeth
  Coontz, Otto
  Deedy, John
  Earle, Mary Alice Morse
  Emerson, Sybil (Davis)
  Erickson, Sabra R(ollins)
  Farquhar, Margaret C(utting)
  Higginbottom, J(effrey) Winslow
  Hoehling, Mary (Duprey)
  Hoppe, Joanne
  Johnson, John E(mil)
  Lancaster, Bruce
  Lorraine, Walter (Henry)
  Meltzer, Milton
  Patch, Edith M(arion)
  Starkey, Marion L(ena)
  Thane, Lillian Adele
  Vaughan, Anne
  Weltner, Linda R(iverly)
  Woodward, Hildegard

MICHIGAN
  Davis, Verne T(heodore)
  Galt, Thomas Franklin, Jr.
  McWebb, Elizabeth Upham
  Winsor, Robert
  Witton, Dorothy
  Yerian, Cameron John
Acme
  Bannon, Laura (May)
Adrian
  Johnson, Gaylord
Almont
  Bischoff, Julia Bristol
Ann Arbor
  Burt, Olive Woolley
  Carr, Harriett H(elen)
  Simonetta, Linda
  Soni, Welthy H.
  Walker, Barbara K(erlin)
  Willard, Nancy (Margaret)
Au Sable
  Pease, Josephine Van Dolzen
Battle Creek
  Knapp, Ron
  Lewis, Mildred D.
Bay City
  Jablonski, Edward
  Millar, Barbara F.
Bellaire
  Foster, Doris Van Liew
Benton Harbor
  Ruth, Rod
Bessemer
  Binder, Otto O(scar)
Boyne City
  Tebbel, John (William)
Buchanan
  Scholz, Jackson (Volney)
Charlotte
  Cole, Brock
Clare
  Carlson, Bernice Wells
Dearborn
  Carrick, Donald
Detroit
  Abrams, Lawrence F.
  Allen, Gertrude E(lizabeth)
  Allen, Jeffrey (Yale)
  Apple, Margot
  Armstrong, Gerry (Breen)
  Beeby, Betty
  Bell, Thelma Harrington
  Bosse, Malcolm J(oseph)
  Cannon, Bettie (Waddell)
  Clokey, Art
  Elwart, Joan Potter
  Enderle, Judith (Ann)
  Fern, Eugene A.
  Foon, Dennis
  Franklin, Harold
  Gauch, Patricia Lee
  Hamilton, Morse
  Hayden, Robert E(arl)
  Hildebrandt, Greg
  Hildebrandt, Tim(othy)
  Hopf, Alice (Martha) L(ightner)
  Kindred, Wendy (Good)
  Kraske, Robert
  Lawrence, James D(uncan)
  Leder, Jane Mersky
  Lindbergh, Charles A(ugustus, Jr.)
  Lubin, Leonard B.
  Manchel, Frank
  McDermott, Gerald
  McPharlin, Paul

Mizner, Elizabeth Howard
Morton, Lee Jack, Jr.
Owens, Gail
Savage, Steele
Schermer, Judith (Denise)
Schlichting, Harold E(ugene, Jr.)
Shiefman, Vicky
Small, David
Sturtzel, Jane Levington
Todd, Mary Fidelis
Tompert, Ann
Wunsch, Josephine (McLean)
Zarif, Margaret Min'imah
Edmore
Blough, Glenn O(rlando)
Escanaba
Stein, M(eyer) L(ewis)
Fenton
Hall, Carolyn Vosburg
Lyons, Dorothy (Marawee)
Miller, Helen Topping
Flint
Benagh, Jim
Engelhart, Margaret S(tevens)
Grand Rapids
Allington, Richard L(loyd)
Burgess, Robert F(orrest)
Gringhuis, Richard H.
Guck, Dorothy
Kelly, Rosalie (Ruth)
Konkle, Janet Everest
Myers, Elisabeth P(erkins)
Roberts, Willo Davis
Rogers, Frances
Santalo, Lois
Smith, Marion Hagens
Stratton, William David
VanAllsburg, Chris
White, Stewart Edward
Grosse Pointe Park
Harris, Julie
Hillsdale
Prideaux, Tom
Holling Corners
Holling, Holling C(lancy)
Iron Mountain
Flaherty, Robert Joseph
Iron River
Fisher, Aileen (Lucia)
Ironwood
Baner, Skulda V(anadis)
Garst, Doris (Shannon)
Ishpeming
Pitrone, Jean Maddern
Jackson
Smith, Datus C(lifford), Jr.
Smits, Theodore R(ichard)
Walker, Louise Jean
Kalamazoo
Ferber, Edna
Thomas, Jane Resh
Kalamo Township
Norling, Jo(sephine Stearns)
Kewadin
Miner, Opal Irene Sevrey
 (Frazine)
Lansing

Baker, Ray Stannard
Castellanos, Jane Mollie
 (Robinson)
Lapeer
DeAngeli, Marguerite (Lofft)
Linden
Taylor, Mark
Ludington
Farley, Carol (J. McDole)
Hamilton, Charles
Marcellus
McCoy, Iola Fuller
Marquette
Hyde, Dayton O(gden)
Marshall
Bellairs, John
Martin
Alkema, Chester Jay
Mt. Clemens
Schwark, Mary Beth
Muskegon
Ahnstrom, D(oris) N.
Chamberlain, Elinor
Malloch, Douglas
Oldenburg, E(gbert) William
New Era
Aardema, Verna (Norberg)
Niles
Bachman, Fred
Lardner, Rex
Owosso
Frazier, Neta Lohnes
Vuong, Lynette (Dyer)
Petoskey
Catton, Charles Bruce
Lee, John R(obert)
Pollowitz, Melinda (Kilborn)
Pinckney
Swarthout, Glendon (Fred)
Pontiac
Beach, Stewart Taft
Davies, Bettilu D(onna)
Powers
LeBlanc, L(ee)
Pullman
Borland, Kathryn Kilby
Richmond
Lowitz, Sadyebeth (Heath)
Rockland
Palovic, Clara Lora
Romulus
Green, Mary Moore
Royal Oak
Cox, Wallace Maynard
Mill, Eleanor
Saginaw
Cook, Bernadine
Hillert, Margaret
Witheridge, Elizabeth P(lumb)
Saline
Smith, Jean Pajot
Sault Ste. Marie
DeWaard, E(lliott) John
South Range
Bahti, Tom
Sparta
Line, Les

Spring Lake
McCay, Winsor
St. Clair Shores
Boring, Mel
Tawas City
Jacobs, Leland Blair
Traverse City
Sherman, Harold (Morrow)
Ubly
Schmidt, Elizabeth
Wakefield
Laird, Jean E(louise)
Wright, Betty Ren
Wyandotte
Courtis, Stuart Appleton
Ypsilanti
Pahz, Anne Cheryl Suzanne
Zeeland
DeKruif, Paul (Henry)

MINNESOTA
Bennett, Susan
Burglon, Nora
Emery, Russell Guy
Holmquist, Eve
Leipold, L. Edmund
Ada
Weygant, Sister Noemi
Albert Lea
Telemaque, Eleanor Wong
Anoka
Keillor, Garrison
Milton, John R(onald)
Bemidji
Ritchie, Barbara (Gibbons)
Braham
Skold, Betty Westrom
Brainerd
Lovelace, Delos Wheeler
Breckenridge
Loken, Newton (Clayton)
Buhl
Surge, Frank
Chisholm
Markun, Patricia M(aloney)
Martin, Dorothy
Cloquet
Schwartz, Anne Powers
Clydesdale
del Rey, Lester
Crookston
Andrist, Ralph K.
Darfur
Stoutenburg, Adrien (Pearl)
Duluth
Dunning, Arthur Stephen, Jr.
Lignell, Lois
O'Brien, John Sherman
Ray, JoAnne
Reichert, Edwin C(lark)
Rienow, Leona Train
Wilson, Holly
Fergus Falls
Wells, Maie Lounsbury
Gully
Melbo, Irving Robert
Hibbing

Blair, Helen
Kenyon
  Stefferud, Alfred Daniel
Lanesboro
  Bergey, Alyce (Mae)
  Scanlon, Marion Stephany
Le Sueur
  Jones, Evan
Madelia
  Haycraft, Howard
Maine
  Douglas, William O(rville)
Mankato
  Deegan, Paul Joseph
  Lovelace, Maud Hart (Palmer)
Mantorville
  Grover, Eulalie Osgood
Maple Plain
  Beers, Lorna
Mapleton
  Brown, Paul
Menahga
  Wood, Wallace
Minneapolis
  Bearman, Jane (Ruth)
  Bennett, Russell H(oradley)
  Bowman, Kathleen (Gill)
  Brown, Myra Berry
  Carlson, Nancy Lee
  Chapian, Marie
  Chew, Ruth
  Chute, B(eatrice) J(oy)
  Connolly, Jerome P(atrick)
  Crowe, Bettina Lum
  Dahl, Borghild
  Douglas, Marjory Stoneman
  Edelman, Elaine
  Froman, Elizabeth Hull
  Girvan, Helen (Masterman)
  Graber, Richard (Frederick)
  Greene, Carla
  Gulley, Julie
  Hassler, Jon (Francis)
  Hobart, Lois (Elaine)
  Johnson, Harriett
  Johnson, William R.
  Keyser, Marcia
  Lerner, Aaron B(unsen)
  Lerner, Marguerite Rush
  Levinson, Nancy Smiler
  Lindblom, Steven (Winther)
  Mild, Warren (Paul)
  Nerlove, Miriam
  Olds, Elizabeth
  Paulsen, Gary
  Pinkerton, Kathrene Sutherland
    (Gedney)
  Pirsig, Robert M.
  Potter, Miriam S. (Clark)
  Riley, Jocelyn (Carol)
  Schulz, Charles M(onroe)
  Shephard, Esther
  Steinberg, Phillip Orso
  Sturtzel, Howard A(llison)
  Swanson, Neil Harmon
  Tanous, Helen Nicol
  Tyler, Anne

  Westman, Paul (Wendell)
  Zeck, Gerald Anthony
Montevideo
  Arneson, Don Jon
  Olson, Gene
Montrose
  Turngren, Annette
  Turngren, Ellen
Mountain Lake
  Eitzen, Allan
New Ulm
  Gag, Flavia
  Gag, Wanda (Hazel)
Northfield
  DeSchweinitz, Karl
Park Rapids
  Aaseng, Nathan
Paynesville
  Hanna, Geneva R(egula)
Pipestone
  Watson, Helen Orr
Plainview
  Ware, Leon (Vernon)
Plummer
  Nee, Kay Bonner
Popple
  Wosmek, Frances
Raymond (near)
  Jonk, Clarence
Red Wing
  Peterson, Lorraine
Redwood Falls
  Eastman, Charles A(lexander)
Renville
  Faralla, Dana
Rochester
  Copeland, Helen
  Patent, Dorothy Hinshaw
Scandia
  Christgau, Alice Erickson
St. Cloud
  Gans, Roma
St. Paul
  Bjorklund, Lorence F.
  Briggs, Peter
  Brin, Ruth F(irestone)
  Cannon, Cornelia (James)
  Delton, Judy
  Doss, Margot Patterson
  Goffstein, M(arilyn) B(rooke)
  Gracza, Margaret Young
  Haight, Anne Lyon
  Jemne, Elsa Laubach
  Larson, Norita D.
  Lexau, Joan M.
  Mackay, Constance D'Arcy
  Margolis, Richard (J.)
  Ney, John
  Ryden, Hope
  Samson, Anne S(tringer)
  Schulke, Flip (Philps Graeme)
  Shulman, Max
  Steinberg, Alfred
  Stevens, Lucile V(ernon)
  Warner, Edythe Records
Starbuck
  Johnson, Lois W(alfrid)

Waconia
  Herbert, Don
Warren
  Anderson, Eloise Adell
Wayzata
  Chute, Marchette (Gaylord)
White Bear
  Bradfield, Roger
White Earth
  Antell, Will D.
Winona
  Comfort, Mildred Houghton
  Wilwerding, Walter Joseph
Winthrop
  Lindquist, Willis
  Linquist, Willis
Worthington
  Davis, Mary L(ee)

MISSISSIPPI
  Bolian, Polly
  Polhamus, Jean Burt
  Treadway, Ruby Peeples
Biloxi
  Klaits, Barrie
Carrollton
  Spencer, Elizabeth
Clarksdale
  Bennett, Lerone, Jr.
Como
  Young, Stark
Copiah County
  Howard, Moses Leon
Goodman
  Lomax, John A.
Greenville
  Henson, James Maury
Hattiesburg
  Peavy, Linda
Jackson
  Morris, Willie
  Taylor, Mildred D(elois)
Mendenhall
  Hilton, Ralph
Meridian
  Parker, James Edgar, Jr.
Mt. Pleasant
  Person, William Thomas
Natchez
  Payne, Joan Balfour
Vicksburg
  Salassi, Otto R(ussell)
West Point
  Vinton, Iris
Yazoo City
  Rollins, Charlemae Hill
Yazoo City (near)
  Olden, Sam

MISSOURI
  Coomer, Anne
  Gee, Maurine H.
Alma
  Erdman, Loula Grace
Avalon
  Cook, Olive Rambo
Blackwell

Potter, Marian
Branson
McFarland, Kenton D(ean)
Buckner
Wooldridge, Rhoda
Butler
Heinlein, Robert A(nson)
Canton
Tate, Eleanora E(laine)
Carthage
Alexander, Linda
Perkins, Richard Marlin
Chillicothe
Irvin, Fred
Clark County
Walsh, Frances (Waggener)
Clinton
Ainsworth, Norma
Columbia
Scoggin, Margaret C(lara)
Curryville
Brandt, Sue R(eading)
Dadeville
Hare, Norma Q(uarles)
Dawn
Weber, Lenora Mattingly
De Soto
Miller, Edward
Dixon
Gilbert, Agnes Joan (Sewell)
Florida
Twain, Mark
Fort Leonard Wood
Krull, Kathleen
Fremont
Pennington, Eunice
Fulton
Keith, Eros
Gallatin
Garton, Malinda D(ean)
Gower
Trachsel, Myrtle Jamison
Independence
Boyle, Ann (Peters)
Weis, Margaret (Edith)
Ironton
Baldwin, Clara
Jackson County
Mertins, Marshall Louis
Jamesport
Harris, Aurand
Jefferson City
Horvath, Betty (Ferguson)
Kennedy, Jerome Richard
Lane, John
Renken, Aleda
Joplin
Davis, Bette J.
Hughes, James Langston
Kansas City
Allen, Henry Wilson
Beamer, George Charles, Jr.
Brey, Charles
Corbett, Scott
Denison, Carol (Hamilton)
Dollar, Diane (Hills)
Gunn, James E(dwin)

Hurd, Edith Thacher
Johnson, Annabel (Jones)
Mayer, Jane Rothschild
Mindlin, Helen Mather-Smith
Mintonye, Grace
Nolan, William F(rancis)
Roueche, Berton
Russ, Lavinia
Seidelman, James Edward
Ulreich, Nura Woodson
Weir, La Vada
King City
Bulla, Clyde Robert
Kirksville
Forsee, Frances Aylesa
Kirkwood
Moore, Marianne (Craig)
Liberty
Bell, Gertrude (Wood)
Macon
Bamman, Henry A.
McDonald County
Collings, Ellsworth
Memphis
Tippett, James S(terling)
Mexico
Schloat, G. Warren, Jr.
Moberly (near)
Conroy, Jack (Wesley)
Montgomery City
Kirn, Ann Minette
Moore, Ray (S.)
Neosho
Benton, Thomas Hart
Paris
McBride, Mary Margaret
Parma
Rabe, Berniece (Louise)
Plattsburg
Barnhart, Clarence L(ewis)
Princeton, Blackjack Hills
Masters, Kelly Ray
Richmond Heights
Polette, Nancy (Jane)
Sedalia
Evans, Katherine (Floyd)
Harlow, Alvin Fay
Sheldon (near)
Withers, Carl A.
Sleeper
Mayberry, Florence V(irginia) Wilson)
Springfield
DeArmand, Frances Ullmann
Gatti, Ellen Morgan (Waddell)
Harrison, David Lee
Lipman, David
Madlee, Dorothy (Haynes)
Melton, David
Wallace, Robert A.
St. Joseph
Cornelius, Carol
Darby, Ada Claire
St. Louis
Angelou, Maya
Bales, Carol Ann
Barnhart, Nancy

Benson, Sally
Brookins, Dana (Martin)
Bryant, Bernice (Morgan)
Butler, Hal
Byrd, Elizabeth
Chambers, C. Bosseron
Clark, Champ
Dolch, Edward William
Dolch, Marguerite Pierce
Douglass, Ralph
Evans, Mark
Field, Eugene
Fitschen, Dale
Ford, Barbara
Glubok, Shirley (Astor)
Hahn, Emily
Hoffman, Gloria
Ivan, Martha Miller Pfaff
Jarrell, Mary von Schrader
Kidd, Ronald
Knigge, Robert (R.)
Lee, Tina Sandovel
Lester, Julius B.
Lynds, Dennis
Malcolmson, Anne (Burnett)
McLaurin, Anne
McMullan, Kate (Hall)
Meyer, F(ranklyn) E(dward)
Pace, Mildred Mastin
Papin, Joseph
Payne, Bernal C., Jr.
Petroski, Catherine (Ann Groom)
Roper, Laura Wood
Schwartz, Charles W(alsh)
Teasdale, Sara
Terris, Susan (Dubinsky)
Thompson, Kay
Thomson, Peggy (Bebie)
Thum, Gladys
Thum, Marcella
VonHagen, Victor Wolfgang
Wallner, John C(harles)
Warren, Elizabeth Avery
White, Anne (Wilson) Hitchcock
Zimmerman, Naoma
Zonia, Dhmitri
St. Louis (Kirkwood)
Ogan, George F.
Sweet Springs
McGuire, Edna
Washington
Fatigati, Frances Evelyn de Buhr
Specking, Inez
West Plains
VanWormer, Joseph Edward
Willow Springs
Ferguson, Robert Bruce
Winona
McCormick, Alma Heflin

MONTANA
Carrier, Lark
Foster, Margaret Lesser
Wolkoff, Judie (Edwards)
Big Timber
Froman, Robert (Winslow)
Bozeman

Carlsen, G(eorge) Robert
Butte
  Gray, Robert
  Oechsli, Kelly
Columbus
  Swarthout, Kathryn (Blair Vaughn)
Fort Benton
  Kelly, Martha Rose
Fort Shaw
  Brock, Emma L(illian)
Glacier County
  Highwater, Jamake
Great Falls
  Calvert, Patricia
  Darling, Richard L(ewis)
Great Falls (near)
  James, Will(iam Roderick)
Havre
  Schultz, Pearle Henriksen
Helena
  Hutchison, Paula A.
  Johnson, D(ana) William
Lakeside
  Sunderlin, Sylvia
Laurin
  Tilton, Madonna Elaine
Lincoln County
  Lasher, Faith B.
Miles City
  Edwards, Jane Campbell
  Freschet, Berniece Louise (Speck)
Red Lodge
  Kiefer, Irene
Ruby
  Hutchins, Ross E(lliott)
St. Ignatius
  McNickle, William D'Arcy
Two Medicine
  Dixon, Jeanne
Washoe
  Johnson, Edgar (Raymond)

NEBRASKA
  Appleyard, Dev
  Costello, David (Francis)
  Hosford, Jessie
  Parker, Lois M(ary)
Albion
  Moore, Clyde B.
Arcadia
  DeGering, Etta (Fowler)
Bellevue
  Nichols, Cecilia Fawn
Brownville
  Brown, Marion Marsh
Burwell
  Maves, Paul B(enjamin)
Callaway
  Lazarus, Keo Felker
Central City
  Palmer, Bernard
  Rydberg, Ernest E(mil)
Chadron
  Stahl, Hilda
Chambers

Childs, Halla Fay (Cochrane)
Cody
  Carlson, Vada F.
Curtis
  Trivelpiece, Laurel
David City
  Bro, Margueritte (Harmon)
  Nichols, Dale
Denton
  Hoffman, Rosekrans
Fairbury
  Kroll, Francis Lynde
Franklin
  Bonham, Barbara (Thomas)
Fullerton
  Hays, Wilma Pitchford
Geneva
  Heiderstadt, Dorothy
Grand Island
  Baird, Bil
Hastings
  Ferris, Helen Josephine
  Gagliardo, Ruth Garver
  Gustafson, Anita
  Kvale, Velma R(uth)
  Ruckman, Ivy
  Tibbets, Albert B.
Lincoln
  Brandhorst, Carl T(heodore)
  Crone, Ruth
  Jacobs, Frank
  Moores, Richard (Arnold)
  Panowski, Eileen Thompson
  Sprague, Gretchen (Burnham)
  Stover, Marjorie Filley
  Taves, Isabella
Manley
  Fleischmann, Glen Harvey
Nebraska City
  Rumsey, Marian (Barritt)
Neligh
  Bennett, Eve
Norfolk
  Daniel, Hawthorne
North Platte
  Jacobs, Beth
Ogallala
  Kuzma, Kay
Omaha
  Baird, Thomas (P.)
  Blair, Jay
  Bradley, Virginia
  Bruck, Lorraine
  Dobrin, Arnold (Jack)
  Hansen, Ron
  Hess, Fjeril
  Holland, John L(ewis)
  Livingston, Myra Cohn
  Oneal, Elizabeth (Bisgard)
  Price, Willadene (Anton)
  Reinach, Jacquelyn (Krasne)
  Richoux, Pat(ricia)
  Scott, John M(artin)
  Smith, Betsy Covington
Ord
  Hamsa, Bobbie
Orleans

Dick, Trella Lamson
Palisade
  Magorian, James
Papillion
  Strait, Treva Adams
Republican City
  Yeo, Wilma (Lethem)
Shelby
  Cunningham, Chet
Sheridan County
  Sandoz, Mari (Susette)
Sterling
  Borland, Harold Glen
Stromberg
  Lantz, Paul
Sweetwater
  Reese, John Henry
Talmage
  Scrimsher, Lila Gravatt
Tamora
  Rich, Josephine (Bouchard)
Wahoo
  Anderson, C(larence) W(illiam)
Winside
  Bothwell, Jean
Wood River
  Estep, Irene (Compton)

NEVADA
  Schaff, Louise E.
Elko
  Walther, Thomas A.
Fernley (near)
  Wheeler, Sessions S(amuel)
Gold Hill
  Stone, Eugenia
Las Vegas
  Bacharach, Herman Ilfeld
Reno
  Brown, Vinson
  Dowdell, Dorothy (Florence) Karns
  Etchemendy, Nancy
  Kyte, Kathy S.
Winnemucca
  Bell, Norman (Edward)

NEW HAMPSHIRE
  Forbes, Katherine (Russell)
Alexandria
  Lamprey, Louise
Claremont
  Colby, C(arroll) B(urleigh)
Concord
  Carey, Bonnie
  Haller, Dorcas Woodbury
East Rochester
  Moody, Ralph O(wen)
Exeter
  Dow, Emily R.
Hampton Falls
  Brown, Alice
Hanover
  Moore, Janet Gaylord
Hudson
  Morrill, Leslie H(olt)
Keene

White, Eliza Orne
Littleton
　Porter, Eleanor H(odgman)
　Seidler, Tor
Manchester
　Allen, Marjorie
　Billings, Charlene W(interer)
　Lindquist, Jennie D(orothea)
　O'Malley, Patricia
Nashua
　Osgood, William E(dward)
Newington
　Archibald, Joseph S(topford)
Newport
　Hale, Sarah Josepha
Peterborough
　Stover, Jo Ann
Plymouth
　Foster, G(eorge) Allen
Portsmouth
　Aldrich, Thomas Bailey
　Boylston, Helen (Dore)
　Osborne, Chester G.

NEW JERSEY
　Binzen, William
　Blood, Charles Lewis
　Bragdon, Lillian (Jacot)
　DiGrazia, Thomas
　Garrison, Theodosia
　Gleasner, Diana (Cottle)
　Keenen, George
　Sand, George X.
　Spangenberg, Judith Dunn
　Wegen, Ron(ald)
Alpine
　Lamb, Harold (Albert)
Arlington
　Fisher, Calvin C(argill)
Asbury Park
　Cohen, Barbara (Kauder)
Atlantic City
　Byard, Carole (Marie)
　Byrd, Robert (John)
　Elwood, Roger
　Keen, Martin L.
　Lawrence, Jacob
　Libby, William M.
　Mathis, Sharon Bell
　Nestor, William Prodromas
　Raboff, Ernest Lloyd
Bayonne
　Fuller, Lois Hamilton
　Navarra, John Gabriel
Belleplain
　Durell, Ann
Belleville
　Hackett, Frances (Goodrich)
　Page, Lou Williams
　Svenson, Andrew E.
Bergen
　White, Edward Lucas
Boonton
　Honness, Elizabeth (Hoffman)
Bound Brook
　Wolfe, Louis
Bradley Beach
　Mirsky, Jeannette
Burlington
　Cooper, James Fenimore
Camden
　Bell, Kensil
　Cavanna, Betty
　Chalmers, Mary (Eileen)
　Gallob, Edward
　Himler, Ann
　Krush, Joe
　Myra, Harold L(awrence)
　Stevens, Franklin
　Wonsetler, John Charles
Cape May Point
　Alsop, Mary O'Hara
Cedar Grove
　Poulsson, Anne Emilie
Clifton
　Denzel, Justin F(rancis)
Collingswood
　Allen, Laura Jean
　McCloy, James F(loyd)
Cranford
　Delano, Hugh
Dover
　Kennedy, Joseph Charles
Dunellen
　Meyer, Kathleen Allan
East Orange
　Bryant, Gertrude Thomson
　Condit, Martha Olson
　Leaf, Margaret P.
　Shay, Frank
Elizabeth
　Blume, Judy (Sussman)
　Chidsey, Donald Barr
　Crawford, Deborah
　Glendinning, Richard
　Greene, Ellin
　Lillie, Amy Morris
　Miskovits, Christine
　Raftery, Gerald (Bransfield)
　Simpson, Maxwell Stewart
　Stratemeyer, Edward L.
　Tregaskis, Richard (William)
Englewood
　Chapman, Frank Michler
　Green, Mary McBurney
　Lemmon, Robert Stell
　Lindbergh, Anne Morrow
　　(Spencer)
　Lisle, Janet Taylor
　Mele, Frank M(ichael)
　Stone, Helen
Flemington
　McClintock, Barbara
Florence
　Choate, Florence
Glen Ridge
　Doren, Marion (Walker)
　VanLeeuwen, Jean
　Walker, David G(ordon)
　Wright, Nancy Means
　Delaney, Ned

Hackensack
　Harris, Lorle K(empe)
　Lorenz, Lee (Sharp)
Haddonfield
　Biemiller, Carl Ludwig
Haleyville
　Sharp, Dallas Lore
Highland Park
　LeRoy, Gen
Hoboken
　Heyliger, William
　Shippen, Katherine B(inney)
　Temkin, Sara Anne
　　(Schlossberg)
Jersey City
　Barish, Matthew
　Brower, Millicent
　Cebulash, Mel
　Coskey, Evelyn
　Davidson, William
　Devlin, Harry
　Fleming, Thomas J(ames)
　Hauptly, Denis J(ames)
　Jefferds, Vincent Harris
　Koob, Theodora (Johanna Foth)
　Krumgold, Joseph (Quincy)
　McCrea, Ruth (Pirman)
　Morrison, Lillian
　Parker, Elinor (Milnor)
　Phillips, Ethel Calvert
　Rae, John
　Rathjen, Carl H(enry)
　Scuro, Vincent
　Shaw, Evelyn
　Stolper, Joel
　Thompson, Vivian L(aubach)
　Weisberg, Joseph S(impson)
Lakewood
　Landau, Elaine (Garmiza)
Lambertville
　Malone, Mary
Lawrenceville
　Liddell, Mary
Little Falls
　Kent, Deborah Ann
Long Branch
　Hartman, Jane E(vangeline)
　Willcox, Isobel
Maplewood
　Parker, Nancy Winslow
Montclair
　Baker, Jeffrey J(ohn) W(heeler)
　Child, Charles Jesse
　Dillon, Barbara
　Eicke, Edna
　Martin, Frances M(cEntee)
　Meddaugh, Susan
　Paradis, Marjorie (Bartholomew)
　Peterson, Russell Francis
　Pratt, John Lowell
　Voute, Kathleen
　Wakeman, Marion Freeman
Morristown
　Hartley, Fred Allan III
　Robinson, Charles
　Ryder, Joanne
　Scoppetone, Sandra
Mt. Holly
　Park, Barbara

New Brunswick
  Baskin, Leonard
  Butters, Dorothy Gilman
  Kilmer, Alfred Joyce
  Pellowski, Michael J(oseph)
  Price, Edith Ballinger
Newark
  Adams, Harriet S(tratemeyer)
  Applebaum, Stan
  Bahr, Robert
  Beim, Jerrold
  Berkowitz, Freda Pastor
  Brenner, Fred
  Butterworth, W(illiam) E(dmund III)
  Chasek, Judith
  Chwast, Jacqueline (Weiner)
  Cole, Joanna
  Crane, Stephen (Townley)
  Crews, Donald
  Ditmars, Raymond Lee
  Dorian, Edith M(cEwen)
  Emmens, Carol Ann
  Feravolo, Rocco Vincent
  Fitzsimmons, Robert
  Harding, Charlotte
  Harris, Christie (Lucy Irwin)
  Harris, Janet (Urovsky)
  Jacobson, Daniel
  Lawrence, Josephine
  Lens, Sidney
  Leroe, Ellen W(hitney)
  Litowinsky, Olga (Jean)
  Malvern, Corinne
  McCoy, Lois (Rich)
  Murphy, Jim
  Perry, John
  Pickering, James Sayre
  Reuter, Carol (Joan)
  Riggs, Sidney Noyes
  Robbins, Ruth
  Rowland, Florence Wightman
  Salduth, Denise
  Savitz, Harriet May (Blatstein)
  Steinberg, Rafael (Mark)
  Sylvester, Natalie G(abry)
  Terhune, Albert Payson
  Viertel, Janet
  Viorst, Judith (Stahl)
  Wacker, Charles H(enry), Jr.
  Wagenheim, Kal
  Weingast, David E(lliott)
  Zemach, Harve
Newburgh
  Katz, Bobbi
Newton
  DeGroat, Diane L.
Nutley
  DuBois, William (Sherman) Pene
  Oakes, Vanya
Oakland
  Jeffers, Susan (Jane)
Orange
  Boynton, Sandra (Keith)
  Criss, Mildred
  Curtis, Patricia
  Farrington, S(elwyn) Kip, Jr.

  Haggerty, James J(oseph)
  Hunt, Kari
  List, Ilka Katherine
  Tannenbaum, D(onald) Leb
  Winn, Janet Bruce
Oxford
  Schoonover, Frank (Earle)
Palisade
  Ross, Clare (Romano)
Palmyra
  Doane, Pelage
  Flournoy, Valerie R.
Passaic
  Bileck, Marvin
  Janeczko, Paul B(ryan)
  Levai, Blaise
  Schoor, Gene
  Swenson, Allan A(rmstrong)
  Tresselt, Alvin (R.)
  Vandenburg, Mary Lou
Paterson
  Baker, Samm S(inclair)
  Black, Irma S(imonton)
  Blake, Robert
  Bly, Robert W(ayne)
  DeJonge, Joanne E.
  Handville, Robert (Tompkins)
  Hart, Carole
  Holzman, Robert Stuart
  Meadow, Charles (Troub)
  Rue, Leonard Lee III
  Saul, E. Wendy
  Utz, Lois (Marie)
  Watson, Nancy Dingman
  Watson, Wendy (McLeod)
  Welber, Robert
  White, Timothy (Thomas Anthony)
Peapack
  Cox, William R(obert)
Pemberton
  Thomas, Benjamin Platt
Perth Amboy
  Peare, Catherine Owens
  Rechnitzer, Ferdinand Edsted
  Rydell, Wendell
Plainfield
  Carmichael, Harriet
  Colver, Alice Mary (Ross)
  Dwiggins, Don
  Gilbreth, Frank B(unker), Jr.
Point Pleasant
  Cook, Fred J(ames)
Princeton
  Bang, Molly Garrett
  Cuyler, Margery Stuyvesant
  Darrow, Whitney, Jr.
  Leigh, Tom
  Martin, Ann M(atthews)
  Morgan, Lenore
  Robinson, C(harles) A(lexander), Jr.
Rahway
  Caseley, Judith
Ridgewood
  Adams, Charlotte
  Cleaver, Carole

  Elwood, Ann
  Johnston, Norma
Riverton
  Johnson, Gerald White
Rumson
  Reiley, Catherine Conway
Rutherford
  Cox, Donald William
  Loescher, Ann Dull
Salem
  Johnston, Ginny
Short Hills
  McDonnell, Virginia (Bleecker)
Snow Hill
  Fauset, Jessie (Redmon)
Somerville
  Asch, Frank
  Wylie, Elinor Hoyt
Teaneck
  Ezzell, Marilyn
  Martini, Teri
Trenton
  Crane, Barbara J.
  Elgin, Kathleen
  Foley, June
  Huthmacher, J. Joseph
  Novak, Matt
  Samachson, Joseph
  Wood, Nancy
Union City
  Gurko, Miriam (Berwitz)
  Oriolo, Joseph
Ventnor City
  Bourgeois, Florence
Verona
  Leavitt, Jerome E(dward)
Vineland
  Kempton, Jean Welch
  Koering, Ursula
  Lipman, Matthew
Warren County
  Nyce, Helene von Strecker
Weehawken
  Miller, Edna (Anita)
West Hoboken
  Messmer, Otto
West Long Branch
  Primavera, Elise
Westfield
  Addams, Charles (Samuel)
  St. George, Judith
Wildwood Crest
  Brandenberg, Aliki (Liacouras)
Woodbury
  Grammer, June Amos
  Reid, Eugenie Chazal
Woodstown
  Shinn, Everett
Wyckoff
  Alexander, Vincent Arthur

NEW MEXICO
Albuquerque
  Cosner, Shaaron
  Fergusson, Erna
  Mulcahy, Lucille Burnett
Beulah

Barker, S(quire) Omar
Crown Point
  Nailor, Gerald A.
Deming
  Bellville, Cheryl Walsh
  Clark, Van D(eusen)
  Dean, Anabel
Las Vegas
  Clark, Ann Nolan
Melrose
  Hanna, William
Roswell
  Garretson, Victoria Diane
  Hurd, Peter
Zia Pueblo, Bernalillo
  Herrera, Velino

NEW YORK
  Allison, Bob
  Barry, James E.
  Bull, Charles Livingston
  Compere, Janet
  Draper, Nancy
  Gleick, Beth Youman
  Heit, Robert
  Hilles, Helen (Train)
  Hogeboom, Amy
  Jaworski, Irene D.
  Keith, Hal
  Keller, Charles
  Klein, H(erbert) Arthur
  Lilly, Charles
  Marsh, Corinna
  Meyer, Gerard Previn
  Rose, Carl
  Schwalje, Earl G(eorge)
  Silliman, Leland
  Sootin, Harry
  Throckmorton, Peter
  Willis, Robert J.
  Winder, Viola Hitti
  Yerkow, Charles
Addison
  Howard, Robert West
Afton
  Hayes, Carlton J. H.
Akron
  Brady, Esther Wood
Albany
  Bason, Lillian
  Bratton, Helen
  Harte, Francis Bret(t)
  Kennedy, Brendan
  Kennedy, William
  Korty, Carol
  Lathrop, Dorothy P(ulis)
  Maguire, Gregory
  Olcott, Virginia
  Slobodkin, Louis
  Stillman, Myra (Stephens)
Almond
  Fenner, Phyllis Reid
Alplaus
  Epstein, Anne Merrick
Alton
  Baldridge, Cyrus LeRoy
Amityville

  Munson, Gorham (Bert)
Amsterdam
  Girard, Linda Walvoord
Arverne
  May, Robert Lewis
Astoria
  Auerbach, Marjorie (Hoffberg)
  Wormser, Sophie
Auburn
  Meaker, Marijane
  VanDuyn, Janet
Baldwin
  Myrus, Donald (Richard)
Baldwinsville
  Means, Florence Crannell
Batavia
  Gardner, John (Champlin, Jr.)
Bayport, Long Island
  Madison, Arnold
Bayshore
  Lee, Betsy
Binghamton
  Garis, Howard R(oger)
  Peterson, Helen Stone
Bolivar
  Boardman, Fon Wyman, Jr.
Boonville
  Edmonds, Walter D(umaux)
  Schultz, James Willard
Brentwood, Long Island
  MacLeod, Beatrice (Beach)
Brightwaters, Long Island
  Wisner, William L.
Bronx
  Adoff, Arnold
  Alda, Arlene
  Barrett, Ron
  Bortstein, Larry
  Bryan, Ashley F.
  Callahan, Dorothy M(onahan)
  Chwast, Seymour
  Curtis, Richard (Alan)
  Feiffer, Jules
  Fisher, Lois I.
  Frascino, Edward
  Glaser, Dianne Elizabeth
  Kohl, Herbert
  Lager, Marilyn
  Liberty, Gene
  Munowitz, Ken
  Myers, Bernice
  Pincus, Harriet
  Waldman, Bruce
  Waldman, Neil
  Wyler, Rose
Bronxville
  Adams, Barbara Johnston
  Bell, Frederic
  Billings, Henry
  Clemens, Virginia Phelps
  Meade, Ellen (Roddick)
Brooklyn
  Abisch, Roslyn Kroop
  Abrashkin, Raymond
  Allen, Maury
  Appel, Martin E(liot)
  Arenella, Roy

  Baker, Emilie (Addoms) Kip
  Barnett, Moneta
  Barr, George
  Barrett, Judi(th)
  Bartenbach, Jean
  Bechtel, Louise Seaman
  Becker, Joyce
  Beebe, Charles William
  Behrman, Carol (Helen)
  Bennett, Jay
  Berelson, Howard
  Berg, David
  Berger, Melvin H.
  Berger, Phil
  Bethancourt, T(omas) Ernesto
  Blaisdell, Elinore
  Bolognese, Elaine Raphael
    (Chionchio)
  Bossom, Naomi
  Brady, Maxine L.
  Brenner, Barbara (Johnes)
  Broun, Heywood Campbell
  Brown, Elizabeth M(yers)
  Brown, Margaret Wise
  Buck, Margaret Waring
  Calmenson, Stephanie
  Campbell, R(osemae) W(ells)
  Cassedy, Sylvia
  Clark, Frank J(ames)
  Cohen, Miriam
  Cohen, Paul S.
  Conly, Robert Leslie
  Cook, Joseph J(ay)
  Cook, Marion Belden
  Cooney, Barbara
  Crane, Alan (Horton)
  Crichlow, Ernest T.
  Cuffari, Richard
  Dannay, Frederic
  Dareff, Hal
  Davidson, R(aymond)
  Degen, Bruce N.
  Diller, Angela
  Dillon, Leo
  Dilson, Jesse
  Dinnerstein, Harvey
  Disalvo-Ryan, DyAnne
  Drimmer, Frederick
  DuBois, Theodora
    (McCormick)
  Dueland, Joy V(ivian)
  Elbert, Virginia Fowler
  Ellen, Barbara
  Ellentuck, Shan
  Erikson, Mel
  Fadiman, Clifton (Paul)
  Feelings, Thomas
  Felsen, Henry Gregor
  Field, Edward
  Fleischman, Albert Sid(ney)
  Fleisher, Robbin
  Flynn, James Joseph
  Ford, George (Cephas, Jr.)
  Ford, Paul Leicester
  Fox, Lorraine
  Fox, Sonny
  Frazetta, Frank

Frommer, Harvey
Funk, Thompson
Garraty, John A.
Gaul, Albro T.
Gennaro, Joseph F(rancis), Jr.
Gibbs, Alonzo (Lawrence)
Giff, Patricia Reilly
Goode, Diane (Capuozzo)
Gordon, Sol
Greenberg, Joanne (Goldenberg)
Greenleaf, Peter
Griffin, Gillett Good
Grinnell, George Bird
Habberton, John
Hafner, Marylin
Hermes, Patricia
Heuman, William
Hill, Helen M(orey)
Hodges, David
Hopkins, Joseph G(erard) E(dward)
Hults, Dorothy Niebrugge
Ilowite, Sheldon A.
Janeway, Elizabeth (Hall)
Jaquith, Priscilla
Jennings, John Edward, Jr.
Johnson, Margaret S(weet)
Jones, Hettie
Juster, Norton
Kahn, Roger
Kalina, Sigmund
Katz, William Loren
Keats, Ezra Jack
Keller, Mollie
Keyes, Daniel
Kimmel, Eric A.
Klagsbrun, Francine (Lifton)
Klass, Morton
Klass, Sheila Solomon
Klevin, Jill Ross
Knight, Charles Robert
Krantz, Hazel (Newman)
Krasilovsky, Phyllis (Manning)
Krupp, Robin Rector
Kunstler, Morton
Kurland, Gerald
Lasker, Joseph Leon
Leach, Maria
Lee, Robert C.
Leeming, Joseph
Lesser, Rika
Lessin, Andrew
Levine, David
Levinson, Riki (Friedberg)
Liebman, Oscar
Liss, Howard
Low, Elizabeth Hammond
Lupoff, Richard A(llen)
Mack, Stan(ley)
Madison, Steve
Maiorano, Robert
Mammen, Edward William
Marks, Mickey Klar
Marlowe, Stephen
McCann, Gerald
McDermott, Beverly Brodsky
McDonald, Barbara Guthrie
McEntee, Dorothy (Layng)
Meyers, Susan (Thompson)
Miers, Earl Schenck
Moran, Eugene Francis
Morgan, Alfred P(owell)
Morressy, John
Mosesson, Gloria R(ubin)
Munro, Eleanor (C.)
Murray, Judith Michele (Freedman)
Myron, Robert
Nash, Bruce M(itchell)
Nichols, Marie C.
Noonan, Julia
Numeroff, Laura Joffe
Paltrowitz, Donna (Milman)
Paltrowitz, Stuart
Paradis, Adrian Alexis
Paterson, Diane (R. Cole)
Peabody, Josephine Preston
Pepe, Phil(ip)
Pinto, Ralph
Plate, Robert
Pollock, Bruce
Pomerantz, Charlotte
Pough, Frederick Harvey
Powers, Bill
Prelutsky, Jack
Rabinowich, Ellen
Rand, Paul
Randall, Florence Engel
Reigot, Betty Polisar
Ressner, Phil(ip)
Reynolds, Quentin James
Richardson, Frank Howard
Richter, Alice
Roche, P(atricia) K.
Roos, Ann
Rosenblum, Richard
Ruchlis, Hy(man)
Sarnoff, Jane
Scheib, Ida
Schlein, Miriam
Schulman, L(ester) M(artin)
Schuyler, Pamela R(icka)
Schwartz, Alvin
Segal, Joyce
Seiden, Art(hur)
Seigel, Kalman
Sendak, Jack
Sendak, Maurice (Bernard)
Seuling, Barbara
Severn, William Irving
Shanks, Ann Zane (Kushner)
Shapiro, Milton J.
Shebar, Sharon Sigmond
Shecter, Ben
Shulman, Irving
Shuttlesworth, Dorothy (Edwards)
Silman, Roberta (Karpel)
Silverman, Burton Philip
Silverstein, Alvin
Singer, Susan (Mahler)
Slackman, Charles B.
Slote, Alfred
Smith, Betty (Wehner)
Smith, E(dric) Brooks
Smith, Robert Kimmel
Smith, Robert Paul
Smith, Ruth Leslie
Snyder, Carol
Soderlind, Arthur E(dwin)
Sohl, Frederic J(ohn)
Sorrentino, Joseph N.
Sowers, Phyllis (Ayer)
Spelman, Mary
Stamaty, Mark Alan
Stambler, Irwin
Steiner, Stan(ley)
Steptoe, John (Lewis)
Stevens, Kathleen
Strong, Charles Stanley
Taylor, Florence M(arian) Tompkins)
Taylor, Herb(ert Norman, Jr.)
Teague, Donald
Teitelbaum, Michael
Terry, Walter
Tinkelman, Murray
Toto, Joe
Trimble, Joe
Ubell, Earl
VanTuyl, Barbara
Versace, Marie Teresa
Vogel, Ray
Wakin, Edward
Waldeck, Theodore J.
Walsh, William B(ertalan)
Warshofsky, Fred
Watson, Aldren A(uld)
Weldon, Martin
Werstein, Irving
Wiley, Karla H(ummel)
Wiseman, B(ernard)
Wolfe, Rinna (Evelyn)
Wolitzer, Hilma
Wood, James Playsted
Wynne, Annette
Zaidenberg, Arthur
Ziner, Florence Feenie

Brooklyn (Bay Ridge)
Ostman, Lempi

Brooklyn (Brownsville)
Charlip, Remy

Brooklyn (Fort Hamilton)
Benet, Laura

Buffalo
Bate, Norman (Arthur)
Birmingham, Lloyd
Bonnell, Dorothy Haworth
Bourne, Miriam Anne (Young)
Case, Marshal T(aylor)
Coatsworth, Elizabeth (Jane)
Cormack, Maribelle B.
Devlin, Dorothy Wende
Ditzel, Paul C(alvin)
Eckert, Allan W.
Facklam, Margery Metz
Fosdick, Harry Emerson
Guillaume, Jeanette G. (Flierl)
Haley, Neale
Hanser, Richard (Frederick)
Holt, Margaret (Cecile)

Horgan, Paul
Howe, Fanny
Hubbell, Harriet Weed
Hyman, Linda
Kassirer, Norma
Kropp, Paul (Stephan)
Lankes, Julius J.
Levy, Elizabeth
Lewin, Ted
Longsworth, Polly (Ormsby)
Myers, Arthur
Paul, James
Pratt, Fletcher
Scabrini, Janet
Schuyler, Remington
Swados, Harvey
Tabrah, Ruth (Milander)
Unterecker, John
VanWoerkom, Dorothy (O'Brien)
Wagner, Glenn A.
Williams, Jay
Willis, Corinne (Denney)
Woodard, Carol
Yates, Brock W(endel)
Yates, Elizabeth
Zirbes, Laura
Buffalo (near)
Wadowski-Bak, Alice
Candor
Trost, Lucille Wood
Canton
Ducornet, Erica
Remington, Frederic (Sackrider)
Carthage
Carpenter, John
Catskill
Marshall, S(amuel) L(yman) A(twood)
Catskill-on-Hudson
Conkling, Hilda
Champlain
Dudley, Ruth H(ubbell)
Chappaqua
Fribourg, Marjorie G.
Charleston
Laurence, Ester Hauser
Chittenango
Baum, L(yman) Frank
Clayton
Comins, Ethel M(ae)
Clifton Springs
Hawes, Charles Boardman
Clinton
Swift, Hildegarde Hoyt
Cohoes
Lord, Athena V.
Cold Brook
Paull, Grace A(lice)
Cold Spring Harbor
Tunis, Edwin (Burdett)
Conklin
Fletcher, Alan Mark
Cooperstown
Bonner, Mary Graham
Copaigue
Stefanik, Alfred T.
Corning

Lattin, Harriet (Pratt)
Cornwall-on-Hudson
Freeman, Margaret
Corona
Alcorn, John
Cortland
Carmer, Carl (Lamson)
Craigville
Wallace, Dillon
Crenessee Valley
Malkus, Alida (Wright) Sims
Delaware County
Lord, Beman
Delhi
Celestino, Martha Laing
Depew
Clifton, Lucille
Dunkirk
Adams, Samuel Hopkins
Martignoni, Margaret E.
East Aurora
Wyeth, Betsy James
East Meadow
Sachar, Louis
Ellenburg
Goodwin, Harold Leland
Elmira
Adams, Katharine
Cunningham, Dale S(peers)
Riskind, Mary (Julia Longenberger)
Flushing
Barry, Scott
Eisenberg, Lisa
Martin, Lynne
Whitney, Alex(andra)
Flushing, Long Island
Jonas, Ann
Flushing, Queens
Lippman, Peter J.
Forest Hills, Long Island
Brooks, Anita
Fredonia
Webster, Alice (Jean Chandler)
Freedom Plains
Schaeffer, Mead
Garden City
Heilbroner, Joan Knapp
Genesco
Thompson, Blanche Jennings
Geneva
Schnirel, James R(einhold)
Zappler, Lisbeth (Moses)
Glen Cove
Gasperini, Jim
Gemming, Elizabeth
Westerberg, Christine
Glens Falls
Adamson, Wendy Wriston
Knight, David C(arpenter)
Gloversville
Kenyon, Raymond G.
Gowanda
Pliss, Louise
Great Neck, Long Island
Hilder, Rowland
Greenport, Long Island

Flack, Marjorie
Greenwich
Moses, Anna Mary (Robertson)
Hamburg
Young, Lois Horton
Harlem
McCannon, Dindga Fatima
Haverstraw
Meriwether, Louise
Hempstead, Long Island
Berman, Linda
Knight, Hilary
Walker, Charles W.
Henderson
Peck, George Wilbur
Highland Falls
Kripke, Dorothy Karp
Hoosick Falls
Bailey, Carolyn Sherwin
Hornell
Sibley, Don
Hudson
Darling, Mary Kathleen
Tamarin, Alfred
Weisberger, Bernard A(llen)
Huntington
Packard, Edward
Ithaca
Hinton, Charles Louis
Makie, Pam
O'Daniel, Janet
Sargent, Pamela
Troy, Hugh
Jamaica, Long Island
Hamberger, John (F.)
Vecsey, George
Jamestown
Anderson, Bradley Jay
Kunz, Roxane (Brown)
Kingston
Petersham, Maud (Sylvia Fuller)
Lake Placid
Woods, George A(llan)
Lancaster
Carroll, Ruth (Robinson)
Livingston Manor
Woolsey, Janette
Livonia
Crane, Irving (Donald)
Lloyd's Neck
Buba, Joy Flinsch
Lockport
Yates, Raymond F(rancis)
Long Beach
Edwards, Harvey
Long Island
Adler, C(arole) S(chwerdtfeger)
Callan, Jamie
Geer, Charles
Gold, Phyllis
Phelps, Ethel Johnston
Lynbrook, Long Island
Keeshan, Robert J.
Manhasset
Rofes, Eric Edward
Maspeth, Long Island
Honig, Donald

Mayville
  Mark, Pauline (Dahlin)
  McKay, Robert W.
Middle Village, Long Isl.
  Pollack, Merrill S.
  Pollack, Reginald Murray
Middletown
  Bullard, Marion (Rorty)
  Oppenheim, Joanne
Mineola
  Benedict, Stewart H(urd)
  Burstein, John
  Humphrey, Henry (III)
Mineola, Long Island
  Forman, James Douglas
Mohawk Valley
  Howe, Gertrude Herrick
Monroe
  Albrecht, Lillie (Vanderveer)
Monticello
  Schongut, Emanuel
Mount Kisco
  Blumberg, Leda
Mount Vernon
  Apfel, Necia H(alpern)
  Buchwald, Art(hur)
  Douty, Esther M(orris)
  Erhard, Walter
  Frankenberg, Robert (Clinton)
  Heinz, W(ilfred) C(harles)
  Kaplan, Jean Caryl Korn
  Lewis, Thomas P(arker)
  Monroe, Marion
  Pyne, Mable Mandeville
  Roberts, Bruce (Stuart)
  Warner, Lucille Schulberg
  White, E(lwyn) B(rooks)
New Rochelle
  Beatty, Jerome, Jr.
  Branley, Franklyn M(ansfield)
  Chenery, Janet (Dai)
  Lantz, Walter
  MacBride, Roger Lea
  McPhee, Richard Byron
  Rockwell, Thomas
  Sterling, Philip
New South Berlin
  Davis, Clive E(dward)
New York
  Abrams, Joy
  Acheson, Patricia Castles
  Adams, Laurie
  Adamson, George Worsley
  Adelson, Leone
  Adler, David A.
  Adler, Robert Irving
  Agard, Nadema
  Ahern, Margaret McCrohan
  Alderson, Sue Ann
  Allen, Richard J.
  Allen, Stephen Valentine Patrick William
  Alsop, Reese Fell
  Alvarez, Joseph A.
  Amerman, Lockhart
  Ames, Lee J(udah)
  Ancona, George

Anderson, Madelyn Klein
Anderson, Mary (Quirk)
Andriola, Alfred J.
Angell, Judie
Anthony, Edward
Anticaglia, Elizabeth
Appel, Benjamin
Arbeiter, Jean S(onkin)
Archer, Jules
Arkin, Alan (Wolf)
Arkin, David
Arnold, Elliott
Arnosky, Jim
Arnstein, Helen S(olomon)
Asinof, Eliot
Austin, Elizabeth S(chling)
Ayer, Jacqueline (Brandford)
Ayer, Margaret
Aymar, Brandt
Bach, Alice (Hendricks)
Bacon, Margaret Hope
Bader, Barbara (Brenner)
Bailey-Jones, Beryl
Baldwin, James (Arthur)
Ball, Robert
Barbera, Joseph Roland
Bare, Arnold Edwin
Barkley, James Edward
Barnett, Leo
Barnett, Lincoln (Kinnear)
Barr, Donald
Barrer-Russell, Gertrude
Barrett, William E(dmund)
Batterberry, Ariane Ruskin
Beach, Edward L(atimer)
Beagle, Peter S.
Beame, Rona
Becker, May Lamberton
Beckhard, Arthur J.
Beech, Linda
Behr, Joyce
Beiser, Arthur
Beitler, Stanley (Samuel)
Benchley, Peter B(radford)
Bendick, Jeanne
Bendick, Robert L(ouis)
Berger, Terry
Bergere, Thea Lindgren
Berlitz, Charles L. (Frambach)
Bernstein, Joanne E(ckstein)
Bernstein, Theodore M(enline)
Bevans, Michael H.
Billington, Elizabeth T(hain)
Bischoff, Ilse Marthe
Black, Algernon David
Blaine, Marge(ry Kay)
Blauer, Ettagale Laure
Blegvad, Lenore (Hochman)
Bliss, Corinne D(emas)
Bloom, Freddy
Bloom, Lloyd
Bloome, Enid P.
Blos, Joan W(insor)
Blue, Rose
Blumberg, Rhoda
Blumenthal, Shirley
Bock, Harold I.

Boegehold, Betty (Doyle)
Bogen, Constance
Bolognese, Don(ald Alan)
Bolton, Henry Carrington
Bond, Jean Carey
Bonsall, Crosby (Barbara Newell)
Bottner, Barbara
Bouchard, Lois Kalb
Boyton, Neil
Bram, Elizabeth
Brann, Esther
Braun, Kathy
Breetveld, Jim Patrick
Brimberg, Stanlee
Brindze, Ruth
Brooks, Anne (Tedlock)
Brown, Judith Gwyn
Brown, Laurene Krasny
Brown, Robert Fletch
Browne, Richard
Brussel-Smith, Bernard
Bunin, Catherine
Burd, Clara M(iller)
Burlingame, William Roger
Burnett, Constance Buel
Burns, Ray(mond Howard)
Burns, William A(loysius)
Busch, Phyllis S.
Bushmiller, Ernie
Byrne, Donn
Cahn, William
Caines, Jeannette (Franklin)
Carey, Ernestine (Moller) Gilbreth
Carlson, Dale Bick
Carlson, Daniel
Carmichael, Joel
Carryl, Charles E(dward)
Carse, Robert
Carter, Samuel III
Cartwright, Sally
Carty, Leo
Casey, Brigid
Cerf, Bennett (Alfred)
Cerf, Christopher (Bennett)
Chafetz, Henry
Chambers, Bradford
Chambers, John W.
Chan, Plato
Chandler, David Porter
Chaneles, Sol
Chardiet, Bernice (Kroll)
Charmatz, Bill
Charosh, Mannis
Chasins, Abram
Chester, Michael (Arthur)
Childs, John Farnsworth
Christesen, Barbara
Chrystie, Frances Nicholson
Clancy, Joseph P(atrick)
Clark, Mary Higgins
Clement, Charles
Clements, Bruce
Clymer, Eleanor (Lowenton)
Clyne, Patricia Edwards
Cobb, Vicki (Wolf)
Cober, Alan E(dwin)

Coen, Rena Neumann
Cole, Lois Dwight
Cole, Walter
Collier, Christopher
Collier, James Lincoln
Colman, Hila (Crayder)
Conford, Ellen (Schaffer)
Conover, Chris
Conrad, Pam(ela)
Conrad, Sybil
Cooper, Lester (Irving)
Coopersmith, Jerome
Copeland, Paul W(orthington)
Corcos, Lucille
Corwin, Judith Hoffman
Corwin, June Atkin
Cott, Jonathan
Craig, M. Jean
Crane, William D(wight)
Crayder, Dorothy
Craz, Albert G.
Cromie, William J(oseph)
Cruz, Ray(mond)
Cullen, Countee Porter
Curtis, Elizabeth
Curtis, Robert H.
Dana, Barbara
Danska, Herbert
Darling, Lois (MacIntyre)
Dauer, Rosamond
Daugherty, Charles Michael
Davenport, Marcia (Gluck)
Davidson, Jessica
Davidson, Margaret (Compere)
Davis, Daniel S(heldon)
Davis, Lavinia (Riker)
DeCamp, Catherine C(rook)
DeCamp, L(yon) Sprague
DeKay, Ormonde, Jr.
DeLage, Ida
DeLarrea, Victoria
Densen-Gerber, Judianne
DePauw, Linda Grant
Deucher, Sybil
Deutsch, Babette
Devaney, John
Deveaux, Alexis
Devereux, Frederick L(eonard), Jr.
Dewey, Ken(neth Francis)
Di Certo, Joseph John
Diamond, Donna
DiFranco, Anthony (Mario)
Diska, Pat
DiValentin, Maria (Messuri)
Dixon, Peter L.
Dodge, Mary (Elizabeth) Mapes
Donahey, Mary (Augusta) Dickerson
Donna, Natalie
Donovan, Frank (Robert)
Doob, Leonard W(illiam)
Dorman, Michael
Dorson, Richard M(ercer)
Dowling, Victor J.
Dragonwagon, Crescent (Zolotow)

Drescher, Joan E(lizabeth)
Duane-Smyth, Diane (Elizabeth)
Ducas, Dorothy
Dupuy, T(revor) N(evitt)
Earle, Eyvind
Edelson, Edward
Edey, Maitland A(rmstrong)
Egan, E(dward) W(elstead)
Egielski, Richard
Ehrlich, Amy
Einsel, Walter
Eisner, Will(iam Erwin)
Elfman, Blossom
Elisofon, Eliot
Ellison, Virginia Howell
Epstein, Perle S(herry)
Ernst, Kathryn (Fitzgerald)
Ernst, Lyman John
Evanoff, Vlad
Faber, Doris (Greenberg)
Faber, Harold
Faithfull, Gail
Farb, Peter
Fassler, Joan (Grace)
Fast, Howard (Melvin)
Feder, Paula (Kurzband)
Feder, Robert Arthur
Feil, Hila
Feinberg, Barbara Jane
Fenten, Barbara D(oris)
Fenten, D(onald) X.
Fenton, Edward
Ferguson, Walter (W.)
Fetz, Ingrid
Fiammenghi, Gioia
Field, Rachel (Lyman)
Finlayson, Ann
Fisher, Barbara
Fisher, Leonard Everett
Fitzgerald, Edward Earl
Fleischer, Lenore
Flender, Harold
Fletcher, Helen Jill
Flexner, James Thomas
Floethe, Louise Lee
Florian, Douglas
Folsom, Michael (Brewster)
Ford, Lauren
Forrester, Frank H.
Fox, Paula
Frank, Josette
Frankel, Bernice
Frankel, Edward
Freedman, Benedict
Freeman, Eugene
Freeman, Lucy (Greenbaum)
Frimmer, Steven
Frisch, Rose E.
Funke, Lewis
Furchgott, Terry
Gallico, Paul (William)
Gamerman, Martha
Gannett, Ruth Stiles
Gardner, Richard A.
Garret, Maxwell R.
Gates, Frieda
Geisel, Helen

Gelman, Jan
Gelman, Steve
Geringer, Laura
Gerson, Virginia
Gevirtz, Eliezer
Gibbs, Wolcott, Jr.
Gillette, Henry Sampson
Gilman, Phoebe
Girion, Barbara
Givens, Janet E(aton)
Glanckoff, Samuel
Glaser, Milton
Gles, Margaret Breitmaier
Golann, Cecil Paige
Goldberg, Herbert S.
Goldberg, Martha
Goldfrank, Helen Colodny
Goldin, Augusta
Goldsmith, Howard
Goldstein, Philip
Goldston, Robert (Conroy)
Gonzalez, Gloria
Goodman, Deborah Lerme
Goodman, Elaine (Egan)
Goodman, Walter
Goodwin, Harold
Gorelick, Molly C.
Gottlieb, Gerald
Gottlieb, Robin (Grossman)
Gottlieb, William P(aul)
Govan, Christine Noble
Graboff, Abner
Graham, Frank, Jr.
Grand, Samuel
Granda, Julio
Grant, Eva (Cohen)
Gray, Lee Learner
Grayson, Marion (Forbourg)
Green, Jane
Green, Sheila Ellen
Greene, Constance C(larke)
Greene, Laura
Greenfeld, Howard
Greenidge, Edwin
Greenleaf, Barbara Kaye
Greisman, Joan Ruth
Gretz, Susanna
Grey, Jerry
Grifalconi, Ann Weik
Groch, Judith (Goldstein)
Grodin, Adams John
Gropper, William
Gross, Sarah Chokla
Grossman, Nancy (S.)
Grossman, Robert
Gutman, William
Gwynne, Fred(erick Hubbard)
Haas, Irene
Haas, James E(dward)
Habenstreit, Barbara (Zeigler)
Haber, Louis
Hackett, Albert
Hadley, Leila (Burton)
Haines, Charles
Hall, Rosalys Haskell
Halliburton, Warren J.
Halsted, Anna Roosevelt

Hamalian, Leo
Hanlon, Emily
Hann, Jacquie
Hano, Arnold
Hansen, Joyce W.
Hargrove, James
Harlan, Elizabeth
Harnan, Terry
Harris, Jonathan
Harris, Leon A., Jr.
Harris, Sherwood
Hart, Bruce
Hartman, Louis F(rancis)
Hatch, Alden
Hautzig, Deborah
Hawes, Judy
Hawthorne, Hildegarde
Hayes, Sheila
Hayes, Will
Hays, H(offmann) R(eynolds)
Hecht, George J(oseph)
Hefter, Richard
Heilman, Joan Rattner
Helfman, Henry
Heller, Linda
Hellman, Harold
Hest, Amy
Heyman, Ken(neth Louis)
Hirsch, Phil
Hirschfeld, Burt
Hoag, Edwin
Hoagland, Edward
Hobson, Laura Z(ametkin)
Hodgetts, Blake Christopher
Hoff, Syd(ney)
Hoffman, Edwin D.
Hoffman, Phyllis M.
Hogner, Dorothy Childs
Hogrogian, Nonny
Holden, Raymond Peckham
Hollander, John
Hollander, Phyllis
Hollander, Zander
Hollingsworth, Alvin C(arl)
Holman, Felice
Hoopes, Lyn L(ittlefield)
Hopkins, Clark
Hornblow, Arthur (, Jr.)
Hornblow, Leonora (Schinasi)
Houston, Joan
Howes, Barbara
Hubley, Faith (Elliot)
Huff, Vivian
Hume, Ruth (Fox)
Hunt, Joyce
Hunter, Evan
Hurd, Clement
Hurwitz, Johanna
Hurwood, Bernhardt J.
Ingraham, Leonard W(illiam)
Irving, Washington
Isaac, Joanne
Isadora, Rachel
Israel, Elaine
Jacobi, Kathy
Jacobs, Francine
Jewett, Eleanore Myers

Jiler, John
John, Joyce
Johnson, Evelyne
Jordan, June (Meyer)
Kahn, Joan
Kalb, Jonah
Kalmenoff, Matthew
Kalusky, Rebecca
Kamen, Gloria
Kandell, Alice S.
Kane, Robert W(illiam)
Kaplan, Anne Bernays
Karp, Naomi J.
Katz, Herbert (Melvin)
Katz, Jane (Bresler)
Kaufmann, Helen (Loeb)
Kaufmann, John
Kavaler, Lucy
Kaye, Danny
Keller, Holly
Kellin, Sally Moffet
Kelly, George Anthony
Kerner, Ben
Kevles, Bettyann
Keyes, Fenton
Kieran, John (Francis)
Kilian, Crawford
Killilea, Marie (Lyons)
King, Cynthia
Kingsley, Emily Perl
Kipniss, Robert
Kissin, Eva H.
Kjelgaard, James Arthur
Klaperman, Gilbert
Klein, David
Klein, Leonore (Glotzer)
Klein, Norma
Klemin, Diana
Komisar, Lucy
Komroff, Manuel
Konigsburg, E(laine) L(obl)
Korach, Mimi
Koren, Ed(ward)
Kovalski, Maryann
Krementz, Jill
Kroll, Steven
Kubie, Nora (Gottheil) Benjamin
Kugelmass, Joseph Alvin
Kunhardt, Dorothy Meserve
Kunhardt, Philip B(radish), Jr.
Kupferberg, Herbert
Kurland, Michael (Joseph)
Kuskin, Karla (Seidman)
L'Engle, Madeleine
Lader, Lawrence
LaFarge, Oliver (Hazard Perry)
LaFarge, Phyllis
Laiken, Deirdre S(usan)
Laite, Gordon
Lambert, Saul
Landeck, Beatrice
Lane, Carl Daniel
Langner, Nola
Langstaff, John (Meredith)
Lanier, Sterling E.
Lash, Joseph P.
Lasker, David

Lauber, Patricia (Grace)
Lavine, David
Lawson, John (Shults)
Lawson, Robert
Leichman, Seymour
Leisk, David (Johnson)
LeShan, Eda J(oan Grossman)
Levin, Betty (Lowenthal)
Levine, Abby
Levine, Betty K(rasne)
Levine, Edna S(imon)
Levine, I(srael) E.
Levine, Joan Goldman
Levine, Rhoda
Levoy, Myron
Lewis, Joseph Anthony
Lewis, Marjorie
Lewis, Mildred
Lewis, Milton
Lewis, Richard
Lewis, Shari
Lewiton, Mina
Liebers, Arthur
Lifton, Betty Jean (Kirschner)
Liman, Ellen (Fogelson)
Limburg, Peter R(ichard)
Lipkind, William
Lipsyte, Robert (Michael)
Lisker, Sonia O(lson)
Littledale, Freya (Lota Brown)
Livingston, Carole
Lobsenz, Norman M(itchell)
Locker, Thomas
Loeb, Jeffrey
Loeb, Robert H., Jr.
Loewenstein, Bernice
Lonette, Reisie (Dominee)
Louie, Ai-Ling
Low, Alice
Lowenfels, Walter
Lozier, Herbert
Lubell, Winifred (Milius)
Luckhardt, Mildred (Madeleine) Corell
Lukas, J(ay) Anthony
Lustig, Loretta
Maas, Julie
MacClintock, Dorcas
MacDonald, Dwight
Mace, Katherine (Keeler)
MacKaye, Percy (Wallace)
Madian, Jon
Maestro, Betsy (Crippen)
Maestro, Giulio (Marcello)
Mali, Jane Lawrence
Malzberg, Barry (N.)
Mann, Peggy
Mantel, S. G.
Marcus, Rebecca B(rian)
Marr, John S(tuart)
Marran, Ray J.
Marrin, Albert
Marshall, Anthony D(ryden)
Marshall, Garry
Martin, George
Martinez, John
Math, Irwin

Matthew, Eunice S.
Matthews, Herbert L(ionel)
Matthiessen, Peter
Matus, Greta
Mayerson, Charlotte Leon
Mayerson, Evelyn White
Mays, Lewis Victor, Jr.
Mazer, Harry
Mazer, Norma Fox
McCarthy, Agnes
McCord, David (Thompson Watson)
McCue, Lillian Bueno
McCurdy, Michael
McElroy, Clifford D., Jr.
McGovern, Ann
McGrady, Mike
McGuire, Leslie (Sarah)
McIntyre, Kevin
McNulty, Faith
Meadowcroft, Enid (LaMonte)
Melville, Herman
Memling, Carl
Mendoza, George
Menuhin, Yehudi
Metter, Bert(ram Milton)
Meyer, Jerome Sydney
Meyers, Robert W.
Miklowitz, Gloria D(ubov)
Milgrom, Harry
Miller, Frances A.
Miller, Mitchell (Alexander)
Mills, Claudia
Mills, Yaroslava Surmach
Milne, Margarey (Joan Greene)
Mincieli, Rose Laura
Mitchell, Isla
Moche, Dinah (Rachel) L(evine)
Mofsie, Louis B.
Mohn, Peter B(urnet)
Mohr, Nicholasa (Golpe)
Moore, Clement Clarke
Moore, Emily R.
Moore, Lilian (Moore Reavin)
Morris, Richard Brandon
Morse, Dorothy B(ayley)
Moscow, Alvin
Moskof, Martin Stephen
Most, Bernard
Mulford, Philippa Greene
Munves, James (Albert)
Munzer, Martha E(iseman)
Musciano, Walter A.
Nagy, Al
Nathan, Robert (Gruntal)
Naylor, Penelope
Nef, Evelyn Stefansson
Nelson, Esther L.
Nesbitt, Esta
Newman, Gerald
Newman, Robert (Howard)
Nivola, Claire (A.)
Noguere, Suzanne
Nordlicht, Lillian
Nordstrom, Ursula (Litchfield)
Nugent, Frances Roberts

O'Brien, Thomas C(lement)
O'Connor, Jane
O'Neill, Eugene (Gladstone)
O'Neill, Mary L(e Duc)
Oakley, Helen (McKelvey)
Orbach, Ruth Gary
Ozer, Jerome S.
Pack, Robert
Palazzo, Anthony D.
Palmer, Robin
Panetta, George
Pantell, Dora (Fuchs)
Panter, Carol (Yeckes)
Parton, Ethel
Pascal, David
Pascal, Francine
Paul, David (Tyler)
Pearl, Richard M(axwell)
Peet, Creighton B.
Perera, Thomas Biddle
Perkins, Al(bert Rogers)
Perl, Lila
Pfeffer, Susan Beth
Phelan, Terry Wolfe
Platt, Kin
Plimpton, George (Ames)
Plotz, Helen (Ratnoff)
Pohl, Frederik
Polatnick, Florence T.
Porte, Barbara Ann
Potok, Chaim
Prager, Arthur
Preiss, Byron (Cary)
Presberg, Miriam Goldstein
Puner, Helen W(alker)
Purdy, Susan Gold
Raiff, Stan
Rapaport, Stella F(read)
Raskin, Edith Lefkowitz
Raucher, Herman
Ravielli, Anthony
Razzi, James
Reed, Thomas (James)
Reid, Barbara
Reiff, Stephanie Ann
Reiner, William B(uck)
Reinfeld, Fred
Reit, Seymour
Resnick, Seymour
Reyher, Rebecca Hourwich
Reynolds, Pamela
Ricciuti, Edward R(aphael)
Rice, Edward E.
Rice, Eve (Hart)
Richards, Ruth
Richelson, Geraldine
Riesenberg, Felix, Jr.
Rinaldi, Ann
Rinkoff, Barbara (Jean Rich)
Ritter, Lawrence S(tanley)
Rivera, Geraldo
Rivoli, Mario
Robertson, Dorothy Lewis
Robinson, Jerry
Robinson, Nancy K(onheim)
Robinson, Ray(mond Kenneth)
Rockwell, Gail

Rockwell, Norman (Percevel)
Rodgers, Mary
Rodman, Selden
Roos, Stephen (Kelley)
Roosevelt, Anna Eleanor (Roosevelt)
Rosenberg, Ethel (Clifford)
Rosenberg, Jane
Rosenberg, Maxine B(erta)
Rosenberg, Nancy Sherman
Rosenberg, Sharon
Rosenbloom, Joseph
Rosenfeld, Sam
Rosenthal, Harold
Ross, David
Ross, Frank (Xavier), Jr.
Ross, John
Roth, Arthur J(oseph)
Roth, David
Rothberg, Abraham
Rothkopf, Carol Z.
Rothman, Joel
Ruffins, Reynold
Rugoff, Milton
Rukeyser, Muriel
Rutz, Viola Larkin
Ryan, Cheli Duran
Ryan, Elizabeth (Anne)
Sachs, Elizabeth-Ann
Sachs, Judith
Sachs, Marilyn (Stickle)
Sagan, Carl
Sagsoorian, Paul
Samachson, Dorothy (Mirkin)
Sammis, John
Samstag, Nicholas
Sapieyevski, Anne Lindbergh
Saunders, Rubie (Agnes)
Schachtel, Roger (Bernard)
Schechter, Betty (Goodstein)
Scheier, Michael
Schell, Orville H.
Scherman, Katharine
Schick, Alice
Schick, Eleanor (Grossman)
Schiff, Ken(neth Roy)
Schindelman, Joseph
Schmiderer, Dorothy
Schoen, Barbara
Schoenherr, John (Carl)
Schonberg, Harold C(harles)
Schrank, Joseph
Schwartz, Daniel (Bennet)
Schwartz, David M(artin)
Schwartz, Sheila (Ruth)
Schwartz, Stephen (Lawrence)
Scott, Henry Joseph
Scott, Jane (Harrington)
Scott, Lenore (Kurtz)
Seaman, Augusta Huiell
Seeger, Pete(r)
Seidman, Laurence (Ivan)
Seitz, Jacqueline
Seixas, Judith S.
Selsam, Millicent E(llis)
Serwer, Blanche L.
Seton, Anya

Shachtman, Tom
Shapp, Martha (Glauber)
Shaw, Arnold
Shaw, Charles (Green)
Shay, Arthur
Shea, George
Shearer, John
Sheedy, Alexandra (Elizabeth)
Sheldon, Muriel
Sherman, Theresa
Shore, Robert
Siegel, Beatrice
Siegmeister, Elie
Silverberg, Robert
Simon, Henry W(illiam)
Simon, Howard
Simon, Norma (Feldstein)
Simon, Seymour
Singer, David (Lin)
Singer, Julia
Singer, Marilyn
Siroff, Harriet
Sitomer, Mindel
Sive, Helen R.
Slepian, Jan(ice B.)
Sloane, Eric
Slobodkin, Florence (Gersh)
Smith, Linell Nash
Smith, Lucia B.
Snow, Richard F(olger)
Snyder, Gerald S(eymour)
Snyder, Jerome
Sobol, Donald J.
Sobol, Harriet Langsam
Solot, Mary Lynn (Marx)
Sommer, Robert
Sonneborn, Ruth (Cantor) A.
Sorel, Edward
Spache, George Daniel
Spar, Jerome
Spicer, Dorothy (Gladys)
Spiegelman, Judith M.
Spilka, Arnold
Splaver, Sarah
Sprague, Rosemary
Springstubb, Tricia
Stearns, Monroe (Mather)
Steig, William
Steinberg, Fred J.
Sterling, Dorothy
Stern, Madeleine B(ettina)
Stern, Marie Simchow
Stevens, Carla M(cBride)
Stevens, Lucy Beatrice
Stevenson, James
Stiles, Norman B.
Stillerman, Robbie
Stoiko, Michael
Strasser, Todd
Straus, Jacqueline Harris
Supraner, Robyn
Sussman, Irving
Sutton, Jane
Swinburne, Laurence
Taback, Simms

Tafuri, Nancy
Tait, Agnes
Talbot, Toby (Tolpen)
Tallon, Robert
Tannenbaum, Beulah (Goldstein)
Tanner, Louise S(tickney)
Tarshis, Jerome
Tarsky, Sue
Taylor, Carl
Taylor, Sydney (Brenner)
Tee-Van, Helen Damrosch
Teltsch, Kathleen
Thacher, Mary McGrath
Thompson, Julian F(rancis)
Thurman, Judith
Titherington, Jeanne
Titus, Eve
Tobias, Tobi
Tooke, Louise Mathews
Torrey, Marjorie
Treat, Lawrence
Trell, Max
Tremain, Ruthven
Tripp, Paul
Trudeau, G(arretson) B(eekman)
Ullman, James Ramsey
Untermeyer, Louis
Vaeth, J(oseph) Gordon
Valen, Nanine
VanDoren, Margaret
VanGelder, Richard G(eorge)
Vaughan, Harold Cecil
Vautier, Ghislaine
Vogel, John H(ollister), Jr.
Walden, Amelia Elizabeth
Walworth, Nancy Zinsser
Ward, Ralph T.
Warner, Susan Bogert
Warren, Mary Phraner
Watson, Clyde (Dingman)
Wechsler, Herman
Weingartner, Charles
Weiser, Marjorie P(hillis) K(atz)
Weiss, Adelle
Weiss, Ellen
Weiss, Harvey
Weiss, Leatie
Weiss, Nicki
Wells, Rosemary
Wels, Byron G(erald)
Wennerstrom, Genia Katherine
Werner, Herma
Wexler, Jerome (LeRoy)
Wharton, Edith
Whelan, Elizabeth M(urphy)
White, Florence M(eiman)
Widdemer, Mabel Cleland
Wilbur, Richard (Purdy)
Wilcox, R(uth) Turner
Wilkinson, John Burke
Williams, Garth (Montgomery)
Wilson, Dagmar
Wilson, Lionel
Windsor, Patricia
Winnick, Karen B(eth) B(inkoff)
Winston, Clara
Winston, Richard

Winter, Paula (Cecelia)
Wise, William
Wiseman, Ann (Sayre)
Wittels, Harriet Joan
Wohlberg, Meg
Wolf, Bernard
Wolff, Diane
Wolkstein, Diane
Wollheim, Donald A(llen)
Wood, Edgar A(llardyce)
Woods, Geraldine
Woods, Harold
Wormser, Richard Edward
Wortis, Avi
Wright, Anna (Maria Louisa Perrot) Rose
Wulff, Edgun Valdemar
Wyckoff, James (M.)
Yolen, Jane H(yatt)
Young, Miriam
Zalben, Jane Breskin
Zarchy, Harry
Zaslavsky, Claudia
Zeiger, Sophia
Zerman, Melvyn Bernard
Ziegler, Jack (Denmore)
Zim, Herbert S(pencer)
Zindel, Bonnie
Zion, Eugene

New York (Almond)
Fenner, Carol (Elizabeth)
Newburgh
Brick, John
Maxwell, Edith (Smith)
Niagara Falls
Acker, Helen
Cornell, James (Clayton, Jr.)
McKinney, Roland Joseph
Pilarski, Laura
North Tonawanda
Benedict, Lois Trimble
Norwich
Scoville, Samuel, Jr.
Nyack
Comfort, Barbara
Deyrup, Astrith Johnson
Jukes, Mavis
Oceanside
Gardner, Beau
Kaplan, Boche
Ogdensburg
Wende, Philip
Olean
LeBar, Mary E(velyn)
Oneida
Howe, James
Irwin, Wallace (Admah)
Oneonta
Tharp, Louise Hall
Ontario
Clifford, Mary Louise (Beneway)
Orange County
Arthur, Timothy Shay
Ossining
Swanson, Arlene Collyer
Oswego

Duvall, Evelyn Millis
Foster, Genevieve (Stump)
Wheeler, Post
Parish
Tallcott, Emogene
Peekskill
Peterson, Harold L(eslie)
Pekin
Orton, Helen (Fuller)
Pelham
Balducci, Carolyn Feleppa
Penn Yan
Bode, Janet
Jensen, David E(dward)
Piermont-on-Hudson
Peck, Anne Merriman
Pierpont
Bacheller, Irving (Addison)
Port Chester
Abels, Harriette Sheffer
Edwards, Anne
Portchester
Suggs, Robert Carl
Poughkeepsie
Maar, Leonard (F., Jr.)
Queens
Carrick, Carol (Hatfield)
Fitzgerald, F(rancis) A(nthony)
Mayer, Marianna
Otfinoski, Steven
Quogue
Scribner, Charles, Jr.
Randolph
Fosdick, Charles Austin
Rochester
Albion, Lee Smith
Alden, Isabella (Macdonald)
Ames, Gerald
Baker, Mary Elizabeth (Gillette)
Bill, Alfred Hoyt
Bracker, Charles Eugene
Brittain, William
Brown, Marcia (Joan)
D'Amato, Janet (Potter)
Dudley, Martha Ward
Eichner, James A.
Gliewe, Unada (Grace)
Gorsline, Douglas (Warner)
Haviland, Virginia
Jones, Penelope
Katz, Fred(eric Phillip)
Knight, Clayton
Mangione, Jerre
Merrill, Jean (Fairbanks)
Nolan, Paul T(homas)
Pringle, Laurence P.
Pundt, Helen Marie
Reynolds, Marjorie (Harris)
Rico, Don(ato)
Sauer, Julia (Lina)
Simon, Joseph H.
Smiley, Virginia Kester
Tensen, Ruth Marjorie
Weilerstein, Sadie Rose
Wilder, Alec
Wilkin, Eloise (Burns)
Rockville Center

Hooker, Ruth
Rockville Centre
Glovach, Linda
Rome
Brooks, Walter R(ollin)
Mooney, Elizabeth C(omstock)
Moore, Eva
Rowe, Dorothy
Roslyn
Yorinks, Arthur
Roslyn Heights
Curtis, Bruce (Richard)
Roxbury
Burroughs, John
Rushford
Wood, Harrie
Rye
Beers, Dorothy Sands
McLoughlin, John C.
Nash, Frederic Ogden
Sag Harbor, Long Island
Mulvihill, William Patrick
Saranac Lake
Longtemps, Kenneth
Sarasota Springs
Bruchac, Joseph III
Saratoga Springs
Chiefari, Janet D.
Walton, Richard J.
Saugerties
Crump, J(ames) Irving
Schenectady
Ball, John (Dudley), Jr.
Kinzel, Dorothy
Mayer, Ann M(argaret)
Reig, June
Rogers, Grenville Cedric Harry
Westervelt, Virginia (Veeder)
Yepsen, Roger B(ennet) Jr.
Scotia
Ross, Dave
Sherrill
Austin, Mary C(arrington)
Somerville, Long Island
Geary, Clifford N.
Southampton
McDonnell, Christine
Staten Island
Cole, William (Rossa)
Spollen, Christopher
Stair, Gobin (John)
Waugh, Carol-Lynn Rossel
Zindel, Paul
Stillwater
Bunce, William Harvey
Sullivan County
Adler, Ruth
Syosset
Forshay-Lunsford, Cin
Syracuse
Barss, William
Beim, Lorraine Levy
Buckley, Helen E(lizabeth)
Canfield, Jane White
Carle, Eric
Coville, Bruce

Farley, Walter (Lorimer)
Friedman, Frieda
Greene, Wade
Johnson, Charlotte Buel
King, Robin
Morgan, Tom
Paige, Harry W.
Parnall, Peter
Sugarman, Tracy
Wilson, Sarah
Tarrytown Heights
Kent, Rockwell
Ticonderoga
Smith, Anne Warren
Troy
Anderson, David Poole
Barker, Will
Boxer, Devorah
Grohskopf, Bernice (Appelbaum)
Tyll, Al
Tuckahoe
Austin, Oliver L(uther) Jr.
Epple, Anne Orth
Tuxedo Park
Rushmore, Robert (William)
Union Springs
Berger, William Merritt
Doremus, Robert
Utica
Clarke, Clorinda
Hunt, Clara Whitehill
Mandry, Kathy
Sortor, June Elizabeth
Waterport
Nearing, Penny
Wellsville
Hill, Grace Livingston
West Bloomfield
Hall, Anna Gertrude
West Hills, Long Island
Whitman, Walt(er)
West Point
McGee, Dorothy Horton
Westfield
Berry, B(arbara) J.
White Plains
Adler, Larry
Edwards, Linda Strauss
Gannon, Robert (Haines)
Gridley, Marion E(leanor)
Mannetti, Lisa
Payson, Dale
Tether, Cynthia Graham
Webb, Jean Francis (III)
Whitestone
Coffin, Joseph (John)
Woodstock
Holsinger, Jane Lumley
Yonkers
Eagle, Mike
Fink, William B(ertrand)
Heuer, Kenneth John
Morse, Flo
Murray, John
Nevins, Albert J.
Tomes, Margot (Ladd)
Vosburgh, Leonard (W.)

Yorkville
  Soglow, Otto

NORTH CAROLINA
Ahoskie
  Koch, Dorothy (Clarke)
Asheville
  Daugherty, James (Henry)
  Fletcher, Beale
  Weston, Martha
Biltmore
  Brock, Betty (Carter)
Brown Summit
  Sparks, Mary W.
Bunnlevel
  Newton, Suzanne (Latham)
Charlotte
  Bearden, Romare (Howard)
  Byars, Betsy (Cromer)
  Haley, Gail E(inhart)
  Reid, John Calvin
Concord
  Street, Julia Montgomery
Durham
  Brown, Margery (W.)
  Davis, Burke
  Wilkinson, Sylvia (J.)
Eastern Cherokee Reservat
  Tsisghwanai, Traveller Bird
Elizabeth City
  Saunders, Keith
Elkin
  Ainsworth, Catherine Harris
Fayetteville
  James, Harold (Laymont)
  Williams, Edward G.
Gastonia
  McCarter, Neely Dixon
  Ray, Ralph
Greensboro
  Lobsenz, Amelia (Freitag)
  Porter, William Sydney
  Shaw, Richard
Greenville
  Bridgers, Sue Ellen
Hertford
  Hallman, Ruth
High Point
  Hauser, Margaret L(ouise)
Jefferson
  Gillett, Mary (Bledsoe)
Kannapolis
  Gilliam, Stan
Maiden
  Throneburg, James
Middlesex
  Stokes, Olivia Pearl
Nash County
  Powledge, Fred
Newport
  McCain, Murray (David, Jr.)
Parmele
  Greenfield, Eloise (Little)
  Little, Lessie Jones
Raleigh
  Anderson, Helen Jean
  Daniels, Jonathan

  Searcy, Margaret Zehmer
Rich Square
  Burgwyn, Mebane H(oloman)
Rutherfordton
  Shelton, William Roy
Sladesville
  Credle, Ellis
Statesville
  Taylor, Theodore (Langhans)
Stumpy Point
  Wechterr, Nell Wise
Tarboro
  Bunin, Sherry
Wadesboro
  Chandler, Linda S(mith)
Whiteville
  Hooks, William H(arris)
Wilmington
  Broadhead, Helen Cross
  Henderson, Nancy Wallace
  Richardson, Willis
  Worth, Kathryn
Winston-Salem
  Davis, Paxton
  Jacobs, Linda C.

NORTH DAKOTA
Bottineau
  Teal, Val(entine M.)
Carson
  Peterson, Esther (Allen)
Crosby
  Laughlin, Florence (Young)
Devils Lake
  Angell, Madeline
Ellendale
  Oppenheimer, Joan L(etson)
Fargo
  Emery, Anne (Eleanor
    McGuigan)
Grand Forks
  Tweton, D. Jerome
Jamestown
  Cadwallader, Sharon
  Camp, Charles Lewis
Kulm
  Kessel, Joyce Karen
LaMoure
  McQueen, Mildred Hark
Medora
  Denniston, Elinore
New Rockford
  Fanning, Leonard M(ulliken)
Sheldon
  McGrath, Thomas
Straubville
  Montgomery, Rutherford
    (George)
Valley City
  McPherson, James M.
Wales
  Sypher, Lucy Johnston
Williston
  Johnson, Charles R.

OHIO
  Anderson, Ethel Todd

  Bailey, John (Swartwout)
  Comins, Jeremy
  Fuchs, Lucy
  Heavlin, Jay
  Martin, Charles Morris
Ada
  McMillen, Wheeler
Akron
  Auth, William Anthony, Jr.
  Batiuk, Thomas M(artin)
  Kessler, Leonard P.
  Marks, Burton
  Marks, Rita (Weiss)
  Oana, Katherine D.
Alliance
  Turkle, Brinton (Cassady)
Ashtabula Harbor
  McGinnis, Lila S(prague)
Athens
  Bryson, Bernarda
  Katona, Robert
Bascom
  Smith, Nancy Covert
Bellefontaine
  Flora, James (Royer)
Berea
  Root, Shelton L., Jr.
Bowersville
  Peale, Norman Vincent
Bucyrus
  Fuller, Catherine L(euthold)
  Kendall, Carol (Seeger)
Canton
  Chittum, Ida (Hoover)
  Erlanger, Ellen (Louise)
  Tolan, Stephanie S.
Chillicothe
  Bennett, John
  Finley, Martha
  Foster, Laura Louise (James)
  Jacobs, Susan
  Stevenson, Burton E(gbert)
Cincinnati
  Allen, Lee
  Barnett, Naomi
  Beard, Dan(iel Carter)
  Black, Susan Adams
  Brosnan, James Patrick
  Buff, Mary Marsh
  Clifford, M(argaret) C(ort)
  Davidson, Alice Joyce
  Fillmore, Parker H(oysted)
  Hines, Anna G(rossnickle)
  Hoobler, Thomas
  Huffman, Tom
  Jacobs, William Jay
  Jahn, Joseph Michael
  Knoepfle, John
  Kohler, Julilly H(ouse)
  McAllister, Mariana Kennedy
  McFall, Christie
  Mearian, Judy Frank
  Mitchell, Kathy
  Moe, Barbara
  Prieto, Mariana B(eeching)
  Quammen, David
  Ransohoff, Doris

Self, Margaret Cabell
Spielberg, Steven
Stewart, Anna Bird
Washburne, Heluiz Chandler
Wibbelsman, Charles J(oseph)
Cleveland
Abdul, Raoul
Adams, Hazard
Allen, Marie Louise
Bollen, Roger
Brondfield, Jerome
Burton, Katherine (Kurz)
Cable, Mary
Calvert, James
Carrighar, Sally
Carruth, Elia (Kaiser)
Chesnutt, Charles Waddell
Climo, Shirley
Colver, Anne
Cooper, Kay
Corrigan, Helen Adeline
Crofut, William E. III
Dietz, David H(enry)
Falkner, Leonard
Fodor, Ronald V(ictor)
Foster, Elizabeth
Foster, Marian Curtis
Giblin, James Cross
Gilman, Esther
Gould, Marilyn
Hahn, Mona Lynn
Haseley, Dennis
Himler, Ronald (Norbert)
Huntsberry, William E(mery)
Jeschke, Susan
Linderman, Frank B(ird)
Madden, Don
McCaslin, Nellie
Morrow, Elizabeth (Reeve Cutter)
Mosel, Arlene (Tichy)
Moser, Don(ald Bruce)
Norton, Alice Mary
Ogle, Lucille (Edith)
Okimoto, Jean Davies
Pallas, Norvin
Pallister, John C(lare)
Petrovich, Michael B(oro)
Phillips, Elizabeth Louise
Pierce, Ruth (Ireland)
Pollock, Penny
Prescott, Orville
Pucci, Albert John
Pugh, Ellen T(iffany)
Rahn, Joan Elma
Robertson, Don
Rourke, Constance (Mayfield)
Sarasy, Phyllis Powell
Schaefer, Jack (Warner)
Scheele, William Earl
Schraff, Anne E(laine)
Shulman, Alix Kates
Simon, Shirley (Schwartz)
Stadtler, Bea
Stephens, Henrietta Henkle
Stover, Allan C(arl)
Suid, Murray

Swiger, Elinor Porter
Thomas, Art(hur Lawrence)
Waniek, Marilyn (Nelson)
Watson, Emily
Watson, Sara Ruth
Weber, Devora
Weber, William John
Woolsey, Sarah Chauncy
Young, Bernice Elizabeth
Zelazny, Roger (Joseph Christopher)
Cleveland (Lakewood)
Kubinyi, Kalman
Columbus
Allen, Samuel (Washington)
Berliner, Don
Carson, Julia Margaret (Hicks)
Eaton, Jeanette
Epstein, Beryl (M. Williams)
Gregg, Walter H(arold)
Jackson, Jesse
Mayer, Albert Ignatius, Jr.
Melin, Grace Hathaway
Schwartz, Elizabeth Reeder
Serage, Nancy
Stine, Robert Lawrence
Thurber, James (Grover)
Wahl, Jan (Boyer)
Conneaut
Loomis, Robert D.
Cuyahoga Falls
Yamaguchi, Marianne Illenberger
Dayton
Babbitt, Natalie (Moore)
Cappel, Constance
Carter, William E(arl)
Cleven, Kathryn Seward
Dunbar, Paul Laurence
Faulhaber, Martha
Graham, Ada
Guisewite, Cathy
Hazen, Barbara Shook
Holmgren, Virginia C(unningham)
Jacobs, Lou(is), Jr.
Knebel, Fletcher
Margolis, Vivienne
Ostendorf, Arthur Lloyd, Jr.
Webb, Robert N.
Defiance
Knight, Ruth Adams (Yingling)
Delaware
Hoffmann, Margaret Jones
Delphos
Peltier, Leslie C(opus)
East Liberty
Donze, Sara Lee (Hathaway)
East Liverpool
Curry, Jane L(ouise)
Seeger, Ruth Porter (Crawford)
Elyria
Brother Ernest,
Findlay
Crouse, Russell M.
Raymond, John F(rancis)
Fostoria
Markle, Sandra L(ee)
Franklin

Carter, Mary Kennedy
Gallipolis
Adkins, Jan
Jobb, Jamie
Geneva
Barnum, Jay Hyde
Ellis, Edward S(ylvester)
Glendale
Woodward, Landon Cleveland
Greenfield
Hoover, Helen (Drusilla Blackburn)
Greenville
Gould, Jean R(osalind)
Grover Hill
Beckman, Delores
Hamilton
DeLeeuw, Adele (Louise)
DeLeeuw, Cateau (Wilhelmina)
Halter, Jon C(harles)
McCloskey, John Robert
Highland
Moore, David William
Hillsboro
Caniff, Milton (Arthur)
Kenton
Machetanz, Frederick
Kilbourne
Hickman, Janet
Knoxville (near)
Eshmeyer, R(einhart) E(rnst)
Lakewood
Jacob, Helen Pierce
Nathanson, Laura Walther
Sears, Stephen W.
Leipsic
Bowman, James Cloyd
Lima
Jones, Weyman (B.)
Olney, Ross R.
Wissmann, Ruth H(elen Leslie)
Lorain
Moore, Carman Leroy
Morrison, Toni (Chloe Anthony Wofford)
Luray
Catherwood, Mary Hartwell
Mansfield
Angle, Paul M(cClelland)
Klimowicz, Barbara (Tingley)
Marietta
Buell, Ellen Lewis
Havighurst, Marion (Boyd)
Hymes, Lucia M(anley)
Woodburn, John Henry
Martins Ferry
Rankin, Robert H(arry)
Siculan, Daniel
Martinsville
Dwiggins, William Addison
Massillon
Wagoner, David (Russell)
McConnelsville
Crew, Fleming H.
Gall, Alice Crew
Middletown
Crout, George C(lement)

Lucas, Jerry
Montpelier
Bauer, Fred
Morgan County
Christy, Howard Chandler
Mt. Vernon
Taylor, Louise Todd
Newark
Dengler, Sandy
Oberlin
Leighton, Margaret (Carver)
Ottawa
Horwich, Frances R(appaport)
Parkman
Norton, Frank R(owland) B(rowning)
Paulding County
Swayne, Sam(uel F.)
Pemberville
Hiser, Iona Seibert
Piney Fork
Scagnetti, Jack
Port Clinton
Wells, Peter
Portsmouth
Robinson, Barbara (Webb)
Provident
Susac, Andrew
Ravenna
Riddle, Maxwell
Reily
Fichter, George S.
Ross County
Lee, Norma E.
Scio
Logsdon, Lois Irene (Kupfer)
Somerset
Rarick, Carrie
Springfield
Lenski, Lois (Lenore)
Murphy, Barbara Beasley
Olds, Helen Diehl
Plagemann, Bentz
Renick, Marion (Lewis)
Smith, Philip M.
Stark County
Hoover, H(elen) M(ary)
Sylvania
Cosgrove, Margaret (Leota)
Tiffin
Bell, Corydon Whitten
Toledo
Carris, Joan Davenport
Castillo, Edmund Luis
Chapin, Henry
Collier, Ethel
Dank, Gloria Rand
Eager, Edward (McMaken)
Evans, Mari
Fife, Dale (Odile)
Osborne, Leone Neal
Shreve, Susan Richards
Smith, William A(rthur)
Vogt, Marie Bollinger
Whitney, Thomas P(orter)
Union City
Ness, Evaline (Michelow)

Union Furnace
Schell, Mildred
Upper Sandusky
Logsdon, Richard Henry
Urbana
Hull, Jessie Redding
Warren
McKinley, Jennifer Carolyn Robin
Wellston
Moore, John Travers
Westchester
Donahey, William
Wigginsville
Foley, Anna Bernice Williams
Wilmington
McDonald, Gerald D(oan)
Moon, Carl
Woodington
Thomas, Lowell (Jackson)
Wooster
Allmendinger, David F(rederick), Jr.
Schreiber, Ralph W(alter)
Yellow Springs
Hamilton, Virginia (Esther)
Youngstown
Alger, Leclaire (Gowans)
Arora, Shirley Lease
DeWit, Dorothy (May Knowles)
Liston, Robert A.
McGuffey, Alexander Hamilton
Zanesville
Laycock, George (Edwin)

OKLAHOMA
Bartholomew, Barbara (G.)
Flack, Naomi (John White)
Whitebead, Baida
Apache
Houser, Allan C.
Bartlesville
Ernst, Lisa Campbell
Boswell
Kelleam, Joseph E(veridge)
Cleveland
Smith, LeRoi
Colgate
Heck, Bessie Holland
Collinsville
Vogt, Esther Loewen
Cordell
Searight, Mary W(illiams)
Darlington
West, Walter Richard
Douglas
Allen, T(erril) D(iener)
Duncan
Nixon, Hershell Howard
Enid
Wellman, Paul I(selin)
Fort Sill
Osborne, Mary Pope
Starbird, Kaye
Headrick
Stepp, Ann
Henrietta
Matthews, William Henry III

Hooker
Maves, Mary Carolyn
Jet
Benedict, Rex (Arthur)
Lambert
Keith, Harold (Verne)
Lawton
Momaday, N(avarre) Scott
Mangum
Cooper, Lee (Pelham)
Marshall
Johnson, B(urdetta) F(aye)
McAlester
Blair, Mary Robinson
Schone, Virginia
Mountain Park
Kimball, Yeffe
Muskogee
Anderson, LaVere (Francis Shoenfelt)
Norris
Robinson, Millian Oller
Oklahoma City
Brown, Walter R(eed)
Clark, Margaret Goff
Cutchen, Billye Walker
Kennell, Ruth E(pperson)
Morriss, James E(dward)
Springer, Marilyn Harris
Tolles, Martha
Wisler, G(ary) Clifton
Okmulgee
King, Seth S.
Paoli
Laklan, Carli (Laughlin Aiello)
Pawnee
Gould, Chester
Picher
Barton, Harriett
Ponca City
Thomas, Joyce Carol
Scraper
Rawls, Woodrow Wilson
Shawnee
Ashabranner, Brent (Kenneth)
Kelling, Furn L.
Springdale
Wilson, Charles Banks
Tulsa
Dean, Nell Marr
Gardner, Martin
Hammer, Charles
Hinton, S(usan) E(loise)
Hinton, Sam
Keegan, Marcia
Wardville
Stilley, Frank
Weatherford
Whitcomb, Jon

OREGON
Brown, Conrad
Cram, L. D.
Upington, Marion
Arlington
Newell, Edythe W.
Baker

Atwater, Montgomery Meigs
Knight, Damon
Banks
Hunt, Lawrence J.
Bend
Baldwin, Stan(ley C.)
Coquille
Vernon, Elda Louise A(nderson)
Corvallis
Bethers, Ray
Lewis, Claudia (Louise)
MacKinnon Groomer, Vera
Marchette, Katharine E.
Dallas
Lampman, Evelyn (Sibley)
Enterprise
Newberry, Clare Turlay
Eugene
Archer, Marion Fuller
Hayden, Gwendolen Lampshire
Simon, Paul
Garibaldi
Parenteau, Shirley (Laurolyn)
Grants Pass
Sullivan, Mary W(ilson)
Gresham
Wees, Frances Shelley
Klamath Falls
Moeri, Louise (Healy)
McMinnville
Cleary, Beverly (Bunn)
Merrill
Barks, Carl
Mt. Angel
Olson, Helen Kronberg
Myrtle Point
Brown, William Louis
Newburg
Dyer, T(homas) A(llan)
Oakland
Marino, Dorothy Bronson
Ontario
Brady, Irene
Fox, William Wellington
McGinley, Phyllis (Louise)
Oregon City
Markham, Edwin
Portland
Adair, Margaret Weeks
Austin, Margot
Baldwin, Gordon C.
Beatty, John (Louis)
Beatty, Patricia (Robbins)
Burn, Doris
Butler, William
Carr, Mary Jane
Cone, Ferne Geller
Davidson, Judith
Elmer, Irene (Elizabeth)
Goodsell, Jane Neuberger
Haas, Merle S.
Hoyt, Edwin P(almer), Jr.
McDonald, Lucile Saunders
McIntosh, Frank
Nathan, Dorothy (Goldeen)
Nelson, Roy Paul
Price, Harold

Rice, Inez
Stirnweis, Shannon
Taylor, Kenneth N(athaniel)
Wangerin, Walter, Jr.
White, Dori
Wittman, Sally (Anne Christensen)
Reedsport
Stone, D(avid) K(arl)
Salem
McKillip, Patricia A(nne)

PENNSYLVANIA
Andre, Evelyn M(arie)
Bristow, Joan
Culp, Louanna McNary
Gwynne, John Harold
Jaszi, Jean Yourd
Jefferson, Robert Louis
Lewin, Betsy
Steurt, Marjorie Rankin
Wheeling, Lynn
Abington
Ault, Rosalie Sain
Smith, Jacqueline B.
Allentown
Gackenbach, Dick
Gerson, Corinne (Schreiberstein)
Marko, Katherine D(olores)
Schuon, Karl
Weiss, Renee Karol
Williams, Leslie
Altoona
Servello, Joe
Titler, Dale Milton
Ambler
Hook, Frances
Ambridge
Angeles, Peter A.
Ardmore
Porter, Jean Macdonald
Ashland
Jeppson, J(anet) O(pal)
Loeper, John J(oseph)
Avondale
Lewis, Richard William
Bath
Christopher, Matt(hew) F.
Beaver
Linn, Charles F.
Bethelehem
Benet, Stephen Vincent
Pavel, Frances
Bloomsburg
Bakeless, Katherine Little
Baker, Betty (Lou)
Keeler, Ronald F(ranklin)
Boyertown
Schealer, John M(ilton)
Brackenridge
Leister, Mary
Braddock
Miller, Donald G(eorge)
Bradford
Hane, Roger
Newell, Hope (Hockenberry)
Bristol

Anderson, Poul (William)
Brooklyn
Cruickshank, Helen Gere
Bryn Mawr
D'Ignazio, Fred(erick)
Butler
Aaron, Chester
Lyons, Grant
McClung, Robert Marshall
Schneider, Rex
Camp Hill
Ford, Nancy K(effer)
Canonsburg
McVicker, Charles (Taggart)
Carlisle Barracks
Bakeless, John (Edwin)
Chester
Friedman, Ina R(osen)
Friedman, Marvin
Clairton
Berg, Jean Horton
Clearfield County
Yost, Edna
Conneautville (near)
Power, Effie Louise
Connellsville
Pierce, Tamora
Coraopolis
Low, Joseph
Crawford County
Honore, Paul
Darby Township
Covington, John (P.)
Dauphin
Feaser, Daniel David
DuBois
Moore, Margaret R(umberger)
Duquesne
Skurzynski, Gloria (Joan)
Easton
Brennan, Joseph L(omas)
Moore, Ruth (Nulton)
Simonetta, Sam
Welch, Martha McKeen
Erie
Brown, Marc (Tolon)
Cooper, Elizabeth Keyser
Samson, Joan
Spencer, William
Evansville
Rublowsky, John M(artin)
Fishing Creek (Mill Hall)
Marston, Hope Irvin
Ford City
Chandler, Caroline A(ugusta)
Frankford
Kyle, Anne D.
Franklin
Dolson, Hildegarde
Germantown
Alcott, Louisa May
Price, Hattie Longstreet
VanDyke, Henry Jackson, Jr.
Greencastle
Walck, Henry Z(eigler)
Greensboro
Mocniak, George

Grove City
   Dodds, John W(endell)
Harrisburg
   Blust, Earl R.
   Pennington, Lillian Boyer
Hartford
   DeMuth, Flora Nash
Hatfield
   Bock, William Sauts Netamux'we
Haverford
   Bowen, Catherine Drinker
   Kerigan, Florence
   Morley, Christopher (Darlington)
Hollidaysburg
   Sweney, Frederic
Jeanette
   Sussman, Cornelia (Silver)
Jenkintown
   Ewing, Kathryn
   Nonnast, Marie
Jim Thorpe (Mauch Chunk)
   Parke, Margaret Bittner
Johnstown
   Erlich, Lillian (Feldman)
   Meyer, Louis A(lbert)
   Sandak, Cass R(obert)
Kanter
   Berkebile, Fred D(onovan)
Lancaster
   Andrews, F(rank) Emerson
   Brecht, Edith
   Fleur, Anne (Elizabeth)
Lancaster County
   Seyfert, Ella Maie
Lansdale
   Hoban, Russell (Conwell)
   Williams, Edgar
Lansdowne
   Wallace, John A(dam)
Latrobe
   Mays, Lucinda L(a Bella)
   Rogers, Fred (McFeely)
Lehman
   Booth, Ernest Sheldon
Lewistown
   Hopper, Nancy J.
   Meyer, Carolyn (Mae)
Lititz
   Eitzen, Ruth (Carper)
Mauch Chunk
   Frace, Charles
McKeesport
   Clay, Patrice
   Connelly, Marc(us Cook)
   Milton, Joyce
Meadville
   Barnaby, Ralph S(tanton)
   Glick, Virginia Kirkus
Media
   Browin, Frances Williams
   Sechrist, Elizabeth (Hough)
Middletown
   Shirk, Jeannette Campbell
Mildred
   Hood, Robert E(ric)
Millertown
   Anderson, Ruth I(rene)

Millvale
   Osterritter, John F(erdinand)
Morris
   Myers, Caroline Elizabeth (Clark)
Mount Pleasant
   Gantos, John (Bryan), Jr.
Mountainhome
   Rosenburg, John M.
Myerstown
   Mohn, Viola Kohl
   Russell, Helen Ross
New Alexandria
   Turnbull, Agnes Sligh
New Castle
   Rice, Dale R(ichard)
New Hope
   Spencer, Ann
New Kensington
   Berkey, Barry Robert
   Froehlich, Margaret Walden
   Willard, Mildred Wilds
Norristown
   Spinelli, Jerry
Oak Hill
   Parker, Kay Peterson
Oakmont
   Blair, Anne Denton
   McGough, Elizabeth (Hemmes)
Odin
   Sutton, Margaret (Beebe)
Oil City
   Conn, Frances (Goldberg)
   VanderVeer, Judy
Palmerton
   Boyer, Robert E(rnst)
Philadelphia
   Abrahams, Robert D(avid)
   Albert, Marvin H.
   Alexander, Lloyd (Chudley)
   Alexander, Raymond Pace
   Asher, Sandy (Fenichel)
   Atene, Rita Anna
   Auslander, Joseph
   Baldwin, Anne Norris
   Barksdale, Lena
   Barnes, Catherine J.
   Barringer, Daniel Moreau, Jr.
   Barthelme, Donald
   Bates, Barbara S(nedeker)
   Begley, Kathleen A(nne)
   Benasutti, Marion
   Berenstain, Jan(ice Grant)
   Berenstain, Michael
   Berenstain, Stan(ley)
   Bernstein, Ralph
   Borten, Helen Jacobson
   Bova, Ben(jamin William)
   Burchardt, Nellie
   Callahan, Claire Wallis
   Castor, Henry
   Cavallo, Diana
   Cherry, Lynne
   Connor, James
   Cooke, Donald Ewin
   Dank, Milton
   Darley, F(elix) O(ctavius) C(arr)
   Davis, Christopher

   Davis, Richard Harding
   Day, A(rthur) Grove
   DeMartelly, John Stockton
   Denslow, W(illiam) W(allace)
   DiFiori, Lawrence
   Docktor, Irv
   Duncan, Lois S(teinmetz)
   Einsel, Naiad
   Elkins, Dov Peretz
   Elliott, Elizabeth Shippen Green
   Esherick, Joseph
   Evslin, Bernard
   Fairman, Joan A(lexandra)
   Feelings, Muriel (Grey)
   Freed, Alvyn M.
   Freund, Rudolf
   Frost, A(rthur) B(urdett)
   Gladstone, Gary
   Glazer, Tom
   Goll, Reinhold W(eimar)
   Gordon, Cyrus Herzl
   Gorham, Charles Orson
   Gould, Lilian
   Gray, Elizabeth Janet
   Greenberg, Harvey R.
   Gross, Ruth Belov
   Hall, Adele
   Hanff, Helene
   Harmon, Margaret
   Hartman, Gertrude
   Haywood, Carolyn
   Herron, Edward A(lbert)
   Hoban, Lillian
   Hoban, Tana
   Hogan, Bernice Harris
   Hoobler, Dorothy
   Hood, Joseph F.
   Hunt, George Pinney
   Hunt, Morton
   Hunter, Kristin (Elaine Eggleston)
   Hyde, Margaret Oldroyd
   Hyman, Trina Schart
   Iannone, Jeanne (Koppel)
   Johnson, Eric W(arner)
   Jones, Wilfred J.
   Joseph, Joseph M(aron)
   Keane, Bil
   Kelly, Walt(er Crawford)
   Knipe, Alden Arthur
   Knipe, Emilie Benson
   Kohn, Bernice (Herstein)
   Kumin, Maxine (Winokur)
   Landau, Jacob
   Lazarevich, Mila
   Leckie, Robert (Hugh)
   Lee, Mary Price
   Levin, Marcia Obrasky
   Lieb, Frederick George
   Lippincott, Bertram
   Lippincott, Joseph Wharton
   Lippincott, Sarah Lee
   Longstreth, T(homas) Morris
   Masey, Mary Lou(ise Leach)
   Matthias, Catherine
   McCaffery, Janet
   McCoy, J(oseph) J(erome)
   Mead, Margaret

Mellor, William Bancroft
Merriam, Eve
Mezey, Robert
Milhous, Katherine
Miller, Albert G(riffith)
Modell, Frank B.
Moran, Tom
Munce, Ruth (Livingston) Hill
Needleman, Jacob
Neilson, Frances Fullerton (Jones)
Newsome, Arden J(eanne Bokeeno)
Obrant, Susan
Parrish, Frederick Maxfield
Phillips, Mary Geisler
Pinkney, Jerry
Pitz, Henry C(larence)
Poole, Gray (Johnson)
Rachlin, Harvey (Brant)
Ray, Deborah (Kogan)
Repplier, Agnes
Roever, J(oan) M(arilyn)
Roth, Arnold
Scarf, Maggi(e)
Schemm, Mildred Walker
Schwartz, Joel L.
Scott, Ann Herbert
Scott, Elaine
Scott, John
Sheldon, Walt(er J.)
Silverstein, Virginia B(arbara Opshelor)
Smith, Jessie Willcox
Smith, Nora Archibald
Smith, Ralph Lee
Snyderman, Reuven K.
Spanfeller, James J(ohn)
Spinelli, Eileen
Stine, G(eorge) Harry
Stone, A. Harris
Stone, Helen (Virginia)
Strachan, Margaret Pitcairn
Sweeney, James B(artholomew)
Terkel, Susan N(eiburg)
Thompson, Ruth Plumly
Vaughan, Sam(uel) S.
Waber, Bernard
Wagner, Frederick (Reese, Jr.)
Walters, Audrey
Weaver, Jack
Webster, David
Weiss, Malcolm E.
White, William, Jr.
Wiggin, Kate Douglas (Smith)
Wilson, Ruth
Wister, Owen
Woldin, Beth Weiner
Wolters, Richard A.
Worcester, Gurdon Saltonstall
Worth, Valerie
Yap, Weda
Philadelphia (Blockley)
Stockton, Francis Richard
Phoenixville
Jeffers, Harry Paul
Pine Grove
Richter, Conrad (Michael)
Pittsburgh
Anderson, Lucia (Lewis)
Arnold, Caroline
Belden, Wilanne Schneider
Block, Irvin
Borhegyi, Suzanne Catherine Sims de
Breisky, William J(ohn)
Carey, Valerie Scho
Cathon, Laura E(lizabeth)
Cavin, Ruth (Brodie)
Commager, Henry Steele
Crawford, John E(dmund)
Dahlstedt, Marden (Armstrong)
Davis, Lou Ellen
Demas, Vida
Dietz, Lew
Dillard, Annie
Dodson, Susan
Dotts, Maryann J.
Feldman, Anne (Rodgers)
Fiedler, Jean(nette Feldman)
Galinsky, Ellen
Glass, Andrew
Graham-Barber, Lynda
Green, Phyllis
Grimm, William C(arey)
Hall, Natalie Watson
Haney, Lynn
Heide, Florence Parry
Hilton, Suzanne (McLean)
Hine, Al
Hoke, John (Lindsay)
Holding, James (Clark Carlisle, Jr.)
Holl, Adelaide (Hinkle)
Hosford, Dorothy (Grant)
James, Elizabeth
Kessler, Ethel
Levine, Sarah
Manes, Stephen
Marx, Robert F(rank)
McClary, Jane Stevenson
McSwigan, Marie
Meade, Marion
Miller, Madge
Munsch, Robert N.
Oakley, Don(ald G.)
Oakley, Thornton
Ormes, Zelda J.
Pier, Arthur Stanwood
Price, Olive (M.)
Reed, Betty Jane
Ripper, Charles L(ewis)
Schulman, Janet
Shapiro, Irwin
Thompson, Mozelle
Vance, Eleanor Graham
Venable, Alan (Hudson)
Wilson, Ellen (Janet Cameron)
Pittsburgh (near)
Keith, Joseph Joel
Plumville
Murphy, Mabel (Ansley)
Plymouth
Baker, Liva
Pottsdown
Shenton, Edward
Pottsville
Leonard, Constance (Brink)
Lloyd, Norman
Punxytawney
Micale, Albert
Reading
Brancato, Robin F(idler)
Miller, Shane
Nyce, Vera
Walker, Barbara M(uhs)
Ridgway
Craig, Margaret Maze
Kisinger, Grace Gelvin (Maze)
Ridley Park
Murphy, Robert (William)
Rochester
Bentel, Pearl B(ucklen)
Sandy Lake
Thomas, Patricia J(ack)
Sayre
Latham, Donald Crawford
Schuylkill Haven
Singmaster, Elsie
Scranton
Boyce, George A(rthur)
Cross, Wilbur Lucius III
Hallstead, William F(inn) III
Harris, Mark Jonathan
Hoexter, Corinne K.
Hopkins, Lee Bennett
Jenkins, William A(twell)
MacKinstry, Elizabeth
Mikolaycak, Charles
Sewickley
Jorgensen, Mary Venn
Stewart, George Rippey
Sharon
Bethell, Jean (Frankenberry)
Feague, Mildred H.
Shillington
Updike, John (Hoyer)
Shippensburg
Bugbee, Emma
Springfield
Carson, Rachel (Louise)
State College
McDonnell, Lois Eddy
Valens, Evans G., Jr.
Susquehanna
Motz, Lloyd
Swissville
Dazey, Agnes J(ohnston)
Tarentum
Rosenbaum, Eileen
Trymville
Daugherty, Harry R.
Uniontown
Bolton, Carole (Roberts)
Warren
Hazeltine, Alice Isabel
Hoh, Diane
Washington
Carlstrom, Nancy White
Gustkey, Earl
McGuffey, William Holmes

Stevenson, Drew
Wheatley, Arabelle
Wayne
Crawford, Charles P.
Waynesboro
Wallower, Lucille
Weatherly
Bell, Raymond Martin
Wilkes-Barre
Baron, Virginia Olsen
Flory, Jane Trescott
Foster, Elizabeth Vincent
Kelley, Leo P(atrick)
Rifkin, Lillian
Savitt, Sam
Wilkinsburg
Ormondroyd, Edward
Robinson, Maurice R.
Worthington
Graff, S. Stewart
Wyalusing
Stern, Philip Van Doren
York
Klaveness, Jan O'Donnell

PUERTO RICO
Delacre, Lulu
Cidra
Belpre, Pura
San Juan
Alegria, Ricardo E.
Colorado (Capella), Antonio Julio
Santurce
Figueroa, Pablo
Pelaez, Jill

RHODE ISLAND
Central Falls
Belair, Richard L.
East Greenwich
Bailey, Ralph Edgar
Newport
Barry, Robert (Everett)
Pawtucket
Barton, Byron (Theodore Vartanian)
Madison, Winifred
Providence
Barker, Melvern (J.)
Brown, Edna Adelaide
Brown, Lloyd Arnold
Caroselli, Remus F(rancis)
Dahl, Mary B(artlett)
Goldstein, Ernest A.
Green, Norma B(erger)
Grose, Helen Mason
Hale, Linda (Howe)
Hatlo, Jimmy
Joslin, Sesyle
Lane, Carolyn (Blocker)
Lansing, Elisabeth Carleton (Hubbard)
Marsoli, Lisa Ann
Meader, Stephen W(arren)
Sewall, Marcia (Osgood)
Slocum, Rosalie
Wilbur, C. Keith

Warren
Butterworth, Hezekiah
Westerly
Gordon, Bernard Ludwig
Woonsocket
Gelinas, Paul J.

SOUTH CAROLINA
Bang, Betsy (Garrett)
Charleston
Childress, Alice
Halacy, D(aniel) S(tephen, Jr.)
Heyward, Du Bose
Hirschmann, Linda (Ann)
Columbia
Brawley, Benjamin Griffith
Rosen, Winifred
Ehrhardt (near)
St. John, Wylly Folk
Greenville
Burgess, Mary Wyche
Steele, Henry Max(well)
Greenwood
Lloyd, Mary Norris
Hilton Head Island
Patterson, Lillie G.
Kingstree
Waldeck, Jo Besse McElveen
Manning
Parish, Margaret Cecile
Pageland
Barnwell, D. Robinson
Ridge Spring
Bodie, Idella F(allaw)
Spartanburg
Edwards, Sally (Cary)
Summerville
Lee, Manning de V(illeneuve)
Sumter
Edens, Bishop David

SOUTH DAKOTA
Fuller, Alice Cook
VanderBoom, Mae M.
Baltic
Eckblad, Edith Berven
Carthage
Crary, Margaret (Coleman)
Chamberlain
Sweetland, Nancy A(nn Rose)
De Smet
Lane, Rose Wilder
Freeman
Hiebert, Ray Eldon
Waltner, Willard H.
Lead
Gadler, Steve J.
Lennox
Alberts, Frances Jacobs
Manchester
Dunn, Harvey T(homas)
Martin
Deloria, Vine (Victor), Jr.
Mitchell
Feig, Barbara Krane
Parker
Leekley, Thomas B(riggs)

Rosebud
Sneve, Virginia Driving Hawk
Sioux Falls
Croll, Carolyn
Giegling, John A(llan)
Spencer
Wendt, Lloyd
Virgil
Cleaver, Vera (Allen)
Wall (near)
Rounds, Glen (Harold)
Watertown
Fox, Robert J.
Jance, J(udith) A(nn)
Johnson, Spencer
Underhill, Alice Mertie (Waterman)
Yankton
Waltner, Elma

TENNESSEE
Carter, Forrest
Julian, Nancy R.
Kassem, Lou
Bell Buckle
Fults, John Lee
Bolivar
Bishop, Curtis (Kent)
Brownsville
Halliburton, Richard
Camden
Wilford, John Noble, Jr.
Centerville
Foster, F. Blanche
Chattanooga
Chapman, Mary Hamilton Illsley
Huffaker, Sandy
Jones, Betty Millsaps
Moser, Barry
Pahz, James Alon
Steele, Mary Q(uintard Govan)
Stephens, William M(cLain)
Wallace, Beverly Dobrin
Clarksville
McGaw, Jessie Brewer
Seltzer, Richard (Warren, Jr.)
Zach, Cheryl (Byrd)
Del Rio
Justus, May
Franklin
Steele, William O(wen)
Johnson City
Marshall, Sarah Catherine
Jonesboro
Wells, Rhea
Kingsport
Showell, Ellen Harvey
Knoxville
Giovanni, Nikki
Sharpe, Mitchell R(aymond)
Lebanon
Farr, Finis (King)
Garner, Elvira (Carter)
Maryville
Burger, Carl (Victor)
McMinnville
Snow, Dorothea J(ohnston)

Memphis
  Anton, Michael J(ames)
  Fitzhugh, Louise (Perkins)
  Greene, Bette
  Pinkwater, Daniel Manus
  Rockwell, Anne (Foote)
  Sanders, Scott R(ussell)
  Seligman, Dorothy Halle
Morganton
  Beals, Frank Lee
Morrison
  Brown, Buck
Morristown
  Wagner, Jane
Nashville
  Blackburn, John(ny) Brewton
  Burt, Jesse Clifton
  Friedman, Estelle (Ehrenwald)
  Helmer, Jean Cassels
  Jarrell, Randall
  Laughbaum, Steve
  McKissack, Fredrick L(emuel)
  McKissack, Patricia (L'Ann) C(arwell)
Newbern
  Parks, Edd Winfield
Paris
  Davis, Louise Littleton
Rockwood
  Brown, Robert Joseph
Smyrna
  Wood, Linda C(arol)
Summertown
  Sanger, Frances Ella (Fitz)
Tullahoma
  Urmston, Mary

TEXAS
  Catlin, Wynelle
  Haynes, Nelma
  Ray, Ophelia
  Stewart, Arvis L.
  Whitehead, Ruth
  Wilson, Walt(er N.)
Abilene
  Byfield, Barbara Ninde
  Coalson, Glo
  Crane, Roy(ston Campbell)
  Stanley, Diane Z.
Alamo
  Smith, Garry (VanDorn)
Austin
  VanOrden, M(erton) D(ick)
Baytown
  Shefelman, Janice (Jordan)
Blanco
  Alexander, Frances (Laura)
Bonham
  Burroughs, Jean Mitchell
Castroville
  Davis, Mary Octavia
Childress
  Edwards, Margaret (Alexander)
Clarksville
  Egypt, Ophelia Settle
Clifton
  Mauzey, Merritt

Coleman
  Rice, James
  Waltrip, Lela (Kingston)
College Station
  Nelson, Mary Carroll
Corpus Christi
  Cason, Emille Mabel Earp
Dalhart
  Constant, Alberta Wilson
Dallas
  Angrist, Stanley W(olff)
  Cardwell, Paul, Jr.
  Crowley, Arthur M(cBlair)
  Geisert, Arthur (Frederick)
  Gramatky, Hardie
  Hook, Martha
  Johnson, Siddie Joe
  Jones, Mary Alice
  Lange, Suzanne
  Lehr, Delores
  Lunn, Janet
  Robinson, Louie, Jr.
  Smith, Hugh L(etcher)
  Stevens, Janet
  Tinkle, Julien Lon
  Trotter, Grace V(iolet)
Dickinson
  Carona, Philip B(en)
Dublin
  Leslie, Robert Franklin
Dundee
  Capps, Benjamin (Franklin)
El Paso
  Malcolmson, David
  Maynes, J. Oscar, Jr.
  Roddenberry, Eugene Wesley
  Schilling, Betty
Fort Worth
  Barkin, Carol
  Burton, William H(enry)
  Campbell, Camilla
  Newsom, Carol
  Pritchett, Elaine H(illyer)
  Tolliver, Ruby C(hangos)
Fredonia
  Cameron, Edna M.
Frost
  Edmonds, I(vy) G(ordon)
Galveston
  Kempner, Mary Jean
  Wilson, Peggy
Goliad
  Hayes, William D(imitt)
Hamilton
  Baity, Elizabeth Chesley
Hillsboro
  Booher, Dianna Daniels
Houston
  Christian, Mary Blount
  Crump, Fred H., Jr.
  McGraw, Eloise Jarvis
  Richards, John Paul
  Sazer, Nina
  Vlahos, Olivia
  Westheimer, David
Hughes Springs
  Hargis, John Edwin

Indian Creek
  Porter, Katherine Anne
Kerrville
  Burleson, Elizabeth
  Coppock, Charles
Kilgore
  Joyner, Jerry
Laredo
  Luttrell, Ida (Alleene)
Live Oaks County
  Dobie, J(ames) Frank
Longview
  Crawford, Thelmar Wyche
Lubbock
  Halsell, Grace
Marfa
  O'Leary, Frank(lin J.)
Marshall
  Rice, Elizabeth
Mason
  Gipson, Fred(erick Benjamin)
McAllen
  Miner, Jane Claypool
Memphis
  Stanley, George Edward
Midlothian
  Winchester, James H(ugh)
Minden
  Arnold, Oren
Mineral Wells
  Munro, Roxie
Munday
  Cousins, Margaret
Nacogdoches
  Baker, Charlotte
New Boston
  Bruce, Mary
Odessa
  Bromley, Dudley
Orange
  Lowrey, Janette Sebring
  McDonald, Forrest
Pampa
  Oates, Stephen B.
Paris
  Soule, Gardner (Bosworth)
Pasadena
  Hancock, Sibyl
Ranger
  Boyd, Mildred Worthy
Rosenburg
  Waltrip, Rufus (Charles)
San Angelo
  Blanton, Martha Catherine
San Antonio
  Baylor, Byrd
  Boeckman, Charles
  DuBose, LaRocque (Russ)
  Eberle, Irmengarde
  Foster, Brad W.
  Marshall, James (Edward)
  Newcomb, Covelle
  Saunders, Susan
  Shefts, Joelle
San Benito
  Fehrenbach, T(heodore) R(eed, Jr.)

Shepherd
  Turner, Eloise Fain
Stamford
  Means, Elliott
Texarkana
  Chastain, Madye Lee
Timpson
  Mayhar, Ardath
Trent
  Call, Hughie Florence
  Campbell, Wanda Jay
Uvalde
  Dunn, Mary Lois
Venus
  Balch, Glenn
Vernon
  Sebestyen, Ouida (Dockery)
Waco
  Bible, Charles
  Jameson, Malcolm
  Laux, Dorothy
  O'Brien, Esse Forrester
  Rogers, Carol
  Walker, James Brazelton
  Weaver, John L.
Wellington
  Vaughn, Ruth
Weslaco
  Smith, Vesta (Henderson)
Wichita Falls
  Daves, Michael
  Grant, Bruce
  Singer, Jane Sherrod
  Waide, Jan
Willis
  Hall-Quest, Edna Olga
    Wilbourne

UTAH
  Fitzgerald, John D(ennis)
Brigham City
  Chapin, Alene Olsen Dalton
Filmore
  Jameson, Johnette H.
Heber
  Stevenson, Anna (M.)
Kanab
  Parr, Lucy
Logan
  Harmer, Mabel
  Swenson, May
Moab
  Keller, Frances Ruth
Ogden
  Hughes, Dean
Price
  Arrowood, McKendrick Lee
    Clinton
  Luce, Willard (Ray)
Provo
  Jones, Helen Hinckley
  Luce, Celia (Geneva Larsen)
  Sorensen, Virginia (Eggersten)
  Taylor, Barbara J.
Richfield
  Lauritzen, Jonreed
Salt Lake City
  Arnold, Susan (Riser)
  Bird, E(lzy) J(ay)
  Downey, Fairfax D(avis)
  Embry, Margaret (Jacob)
  Hatch, Mary Cottam
  Hill, Donna (Marie)
  Hoopes, Roy
  Metos, Thomas H(arry)
  Pedersen, Elsa (Kienitz)
  Russell, Solveig Paulson
  Sabin, Louis
  Sanberg, Karl C.
  Sheffield, Janet N.
  Stretton, Barbara (Humphrey)
  Wellman, Alice
  Williams, Barbara (Wright)
Scipio
  Selman, LaRue W.
St. George
  Cottam, Clarence

VERMONT
  Coblentz, Catherine Cate
  Peck, Robert Newton, III
  Rowand, Phyllis
Arlington
  Scott, Sally Fisher
Brandon
  Chittenden, Elizabeth F.
Bristol
  Allen, Merritt Parmalee
Burke Hollow
  Smith, Elva S(ophronia)
Burlington
  Betancourt, Jeanne
  Farrar, John C(hipman)
  Hill, Ralph Nading
  Hurd, Thacher
  Newcombe, Jack
  Waugh, Dorothy
Hardwick
  Mitchell, Joyce Slayton
Highgate
  Saxe, John Godfrey
Middlebury
  Fregosi, Claudia (Anne Marie)
Middletown
  Avery, Kay
Newport
  Holbrook, Stewart Hall
Northfield
  Sargent, Robert Edward
Springfield
  Dubanevich, Arlene
  Mathieu, Joseph P.
St. Albans
  Frost, Frances
Walden
  Chickering, Marjorie
Windsor
  Ipcar, Dahlov Zorach

VIRGINIA
  Brooks, Bruce
  Doughtie, Charles
  Phelps, Margaret (Nelson)
Alexandria
  Boatner, Mark Mayo III
Bedford
  Harrison, Deloris
Big Stone Gap
  Cummings, Betty Sue
Black Creek Valley
  Cather, Willa (Sibert)
Boydton
  Turner, Nancy Byrd
Buena Vista
  Jennings, Gary (Gayne)
  Jennings, Michael
Canton
  Woodson, Carter Goodwin
Charlottesville
  Morris, Robert A(da)
Franklin
  Jones, Hortense P.
Greenbackville
  Carter, Katharine J(ones)
Hale's Ford, Franklin Cty
  Washington, Booker T(aliaferro)
Hampton
  Zweifel, Frances
Hopewell
  Rylant, Cynthia
Inman
  Whitehead, Don(ald) F.
Lexington
  Armstrong, William H(oward)
Lynchburg
  Faulkner, Nancy (Anne Irvin)
  Horner, Dave
  Taylor, L(ester) B(arbour), Jr.
Newport News
  Gayle, Addison
  Iverson, Genie
  Rees, Ennis (Samuel, Jr.)
Norfolk
  Buck, Lewis
  Hutchinson, William M.
  Long, Judith Elaine
  Parker, Robert Andrew
  Turlington, Bayly
  Zolotow, Charlotte S(hapiro)
Oakland
  Page, Thomas Nelson
Portsmouth
  Andrews, Virginia Cleo
  Creekmore, Raymond (L.)
Quantico
  McCullough, Frances Monson
Richlands
  Davis, Hubert J(ackson)
Richmond
  Bryan, Joseph (III)
  Chappell, Warren
  Elam, Richard M(ace, Jr.)
  Fox, Mary Virginia
  Hammerman, Gay M(orenus)
  Hill, Robert W(hite)
  Johnson, Maud Battle
  Larsen, Suzanne Kesteloo
  Monsell, Helen (Albee)
  Scheer, George F(abian)
  Scheer, Julian (Weisel)
  Woodson, John Waddie, Jr.

Roanoke
 Evans, Eva Knox
 Roberson, John R(oyster)
 Sargent, Sarah
 Showalter, Jean B(reckinridge)
Rockingham County
 Smith, Susan Mathias
Salem
 Randall, Ruth Painter
Smithfield
 Batten, Mary
Virginia Beach
 Dunrea, Olivier
Warrenton
 Roy, Jessie Hailstalk
White Post
 Chrisman, Arthur Bowie
Whitewood
 White, Ruth C.
Winchester
 Carlson, Natalie Savage
 Larrick, Nancy G(ray)
 Woodrich, Mary Neville

VIRGIN ISLANDS
St. Thomas
 Olugebefola, Ademole

WASHINGTON
Aberdeen
 Daugherty, Richard D(eo)
Bellingham
 Mercer, Jessie
 Robinson, Tom D.
 Werner, Vivian
Bremerton
 Gardner, Richard (M.)
 Hirschi, Ron
Centralia
 Evans, Shirlee
Chehalis
 Laure, Jason
Dayton
 Meier, Minta
Hoquiam
 Morey, Walt(er Nelson)
Medical Lake
 Leyson, Burr Watkins
Mercer Island
 Rand, Ted
Olympia
 Espy, Willard R(ichardson)
 McKenny, Margaret
 Redford, Lora Bryning
Pasco
 Crowell, Pers
 Norling, Ernest Ralph
Pomeroy
 Overholser, Wayne D.
Port Townsend
 McNamee, James
Prosser
 Tompkins, Walker Allison
Seattle
 Antoncich, Betty (Kennedy)
 Arkhurst, Joyce (Cooper)
 Campbell, Hope
 Cleaver, William Joseph
 DeClements, Barthe
 Deyneka, Anita
 Douglas, John Scott
 Engle, Eloise Katherine
 Hodge, P(aul) W(illiam)
 James, Robin (Irene)
 Johnston, Dorothy Grunbock
 Ketcham, Henry King
 Komoda, Beverly
 Matson, Emerson N(els)
 McNamara, Margaret (Craig)
 Orlob, Helen Seaburg
 Pierce, Meredith Ann
 Sherburne, Zoa (Morin)
 Shortall, Leonard W.
 Stapp, Arthur D(onald)
 Suttles, Shirley (Smith)
 Walker, Stephen J.
 Watson, Sally (Lou)
 Wier, Ester (Alberti)
 Wriggins, Salley Hovey
South Bend
 Robinson, Irene Bowen
Spokane
 Battles, Roxy Edith (Baker)
 Blair, Walter
 Brautigan, Richard (Gary)
 Brown, Eleanor Frances
 Cosgrove, Stephen E(dward)
 Cunningham, Julia W(oolfolk)
 Hawkins, Helena Ann Quail
 Hunt, Linda Lawrence
 Jones, Charles M(artin)
 Offord, Lenore (Glen)
 Piowaty, Kim Kennelly
 Scribner, Joanne L.
 Villiard, Paul
Sunnyside, Yakima Valley
 Showers, Paul C.
Tacoma
 Arntson, Herbert E(dward)
 Cone, Molly (Lamken)
 Edwards, Audrey
 Freeman, Lydia
 Handforth, Thomas (Schofield)
 Herbert, Frank (Patrick)
 Larson, Gary
 Vaughan, Marcia
 Wilson, Beth P(ierre)
Walla Walla
 Clark, Patricia (Finrow)
 Lewis, Alice C.
 Whitehouse, Jeanne
Waverly
 Rosenberg, Dorothy
Yakima
 Johnson, Robert E.
 Newton, James R(obert)

WEST VIRGINIA
 Felts, Shirley
 Rush, William Marshall
 Sutton, Felix
Belington
 Latham, Frank B(rown)
Buckhannon
 Latham, Jean Lee
Clarksburg
 Adams, Julia Davis
 Smith, Agnes
Elkins
 Goode, Stephen
Fairmont
 Knowles, John
 Lomask, Milton (Nachman)
 Scherf, Margaret (Louise)
French Creek
 Brooks, Maurice (Graham)
Grafton
 Bee, Clair (Francis)
Grant Town
 Wilson, Tom
Hillsboro
 Buck, Pearl S(ydenstricker)
Hinton
 Gondosch, Linda
Hollidays Cove
 Slate, Joseph (Frank)
Hominy Falls
 Lefler, Irene (Whitney)
Huntington
 Christian, Samuel T(erry)
 Fischbach, Julius
 Partridge, Benjamin W(aring), Jr.
Martinsburg
 Myers, Walter Dean
Moundsville
 Hannum, Sara
Mount Clare
 Musgrave, Florence
Northfork
 Cooney, Nancy Evans
Parkersburg
 Icenhower, Joseph Bryan
 Johnson, Lois S(mith)
 Lichello, Robert
South Charleston
 Brown, Drollene P.

WISCONSIN
 Dresser, Lawrence
 Kennedy, T(eresa) A.
 Walters, Helen B.
Algoma
 Rietveld, Jane Klatt
Almond
 Harshaw, Ruth H(etzel)
Angelica
 Simon, Martin P(aul William)
Appleton
 Hanson, Joan
 Havighurst, Walter (Edwin)
 Milotte, Alfred G(eorge)
 White, David Omar
Beaver Dam
 Ehlert, Lois (Jane)
 Ellis, Mel(vin Richard)
Beloit
 Andrews, Roy Chapman
 Jackson, Jacqueline (Dougan)
 Shafer, Robert E(ugene)
Berlin
 Hancock, Mary A.

Cashton
　King, Frank O.
Clintonville
　Hyde, Wayne F(rederick)
Curtiss
　Trowbridge, Leslie W(alter)
Deer Park
　Seymour, Alta Halverson
Denmark
　Sutton, Eugenia Geneva (Hansen)
East Troy
　Hickok, Lorena A.
Eau Claire
　Regli, Adolph Casper
Edgerton
　North, Sterling
Elkhorn
　Lawson, Marion Tubbs
　Petrie, Catherine
　Roop, Constance Betzer
Elroy
　Sherin, Ray
Fairwater
　Haskell, Helen (Eggleston)
Fond du Lac
　Butler, Beverly (Kathleen)
　Taylor, Paula (Wright)
　Watson, Jane Werner
　Wise, Winifred E.
Grafton
　Joosse, Barbara M(onnot)
Hayward
　McCord, Jean
Janesville
　Briggs, Carole S(uzanne)
　Pond, Alonzo W(illiam)
Kaukauna
　Icks, Robert J.
Kenosha
　Karlin, Eugene
La Crosse
　Larson, William H.
　Robinson, Jean O. (Kroner)
　Toland, John (Willard)
LaCrosse
　Fox, Dorothea M.
Ladysmith
　Young, Rodney Lee Patrick (, Jr.)
Lake Pepin
　Wilder, Laura (Elizabeth) Ingalls
Madison
　Caraway, Caren
　Clish, Lee Marian
　Fargo, Lucile Foster
　Godrog, Judith (Allen)
　Kampen, Owen
　Link, Martin
　Smith, Beatrice S(chillinger)
　Wilber, Donald N(ewton)
Manitowoc
　Brennan, Gale Patrick
Marinette
　Hubley, John
Millville
　Simak, Clifford D(onald)

Milwaukee
　Aiken, Clarissa (Lorenz)
　Artis, Vicki Kimmel
　Aylward, William James
　Balian, Lorna (Kohl)
　Belton, John Raynor
　Bornstein, Ruth
　Carlsen, Ruth C(hristoffer)
　Carpenter, Patricia (Healy Evans)
　Davis, Gibbs
　Davis, Grania
　Fijan, Carol
　Forman, Harrison
　Fox, Charles Philip
　French, Dorothy Kayser
　Friedman, Judi
　Gault, William Campbell
　George, John Lothar
　Greenberg, Polly
　Holberg, Richard A.
　Holberg, Ruth (Langland)
　Houlehen, Robert J.
　House, Charles Albert
　Johnson, Milton
　Kahl, Virginia (Caroline)
　Kennedy, Dorothy M(intzlaff)
　Klug, Ron(ald)
　Kraus, Robert
　Larsen, Rebecca
　Millstead, Thomas Edward
　Nash, Mary (Hughes)
　Polland, Barbara K(ay)
　Raskin, Ellen
　Reiss, John (J.)
　Reitci, Rita Krohne
　Romano, Louis G.
　Schultz, Gwendolyn
　Shane, Harold Gray
　Teague, Robert
　Toschik, Larry
　Weinstock, Herbert
Milwaukee (N. Greenfield)
　Ets, Marie Hall
Mineral Point
　Ludden, Allen (Ellsworth)
Mt Horeb
　Jordan, Hope (Dahle)
Neillsville
　Eunson, Dale
Newton
　Wernecke, Herbert Henry
North Bay
　Erickson, Phoebe
Oconto County
　Parkinson, Ethelyn M(inerva)
Oshkosh
　Malmberg, Carl
　Osborn, Robert Chesley
　Summers, James L(evingston)
Phillips
　Gilge, Jeanette
Pine Creek
　Pellowski, Anne
Portage
　Gale, Zona
Prairie du Chien (near)

　Munroe, Kirk
Racine
　Haas, Dorothy F.
　Henkes, Kevin
　Kanetzke, Howard W(illiam)
　Kherdian, David
　Marcher, Marion Walden
Rhinelander
　Brow, Thea
Rice Lake
　Cameron, Ann
River Falls
　Brier, Howard M(axwell)
Rosendale
　Portteus, Eleanora Marie Manthei
Sauk City
　Derleth, August (William)
Sheboygan
　Hemschemeyer, Judith
　Mueller, Virginia
　Pape, D(onna) L(ugg)
Shorewood
　Sherwan, Earl
Somers
　Landon, Margaret (Dorothea Mortenson)
South Milwaukee
　Roberts, Nancy Correll
Spring Green (near)
　Reely, Mary Katharine
Superior
　Beecroft, John William Richard
　Wheeler, Opal
　Wohlrabe, Raymond A(dolph)
Thorp
　Tolford, Joshua
Watertown
　Sandin, Joan
Waukesha
　Stewig, John Warren
Waupaca County
　Ashmun, Margaret Eliza
Wausau
　Jahsmann, Allan Hart
　Lapp, Eleanor J.
West Salem
　Garland, Hannibal Hamlin
Wiergor Township
　Boyd, Waldo T.
Wilton
　Phillips, Irv(ing W.)

WYOMING
Casper
　Dines, Harry Glen
Cheyenne
　MacLachlan, Patricia
Kemmerer
　Cetin, Frank Stanley
Midwest
　Radlauer, Ruth (Shaw)
Moose
　Burt, Nathaniel
Riverton
　Dobler, Lavinia G.
Torrington

Swayne, Zoa Lourana (Shaw)

AUTHORS BORN OUTSIDE THE UNITED STATES

AFRICA
Luanda, Angola
Dodson, Kenneth M(acKenzie)

ARGENTINA
Norris, Gunilla B(rodde)
Sandstrom, George F.
Buenos Aires
Frasconi, Antonio
Hornos, Axel
Obligado, Lilian (Isabel)
Pendle, Alexy
Stevens, Patricia Bunning

AUSTRALIA
Melbourne
Marks, Geoffrey
Sydney
Buchan, Stuart
Kaula, Edna Mason
Macknight, Ninon
Sydney, New South Wales
Jacobs, Joseph

AUSTRIA
Chernoff, Goldie Taub
Knight, Max
Koffler, Camilla
Marek, George R(ichard)
Roth, Harold
Schachner, Erwin
Zimmer, Dirk
Czernowitz
Jagendorf, Moritz (Adolf)
Graz
Lacher, Gisella Loeffler
Lemberg
Sharp, William
Lwow
Ewen, David
Meran, Tirol
Bemelmans, Ludwig
Olmutz, Moravia
Weiss, Emil
Styria Mountains
Dobias, Frank
Vienna
Apsler, Alfred
Buchwald, Emilie
Butterworth, Emma Macalik
D'Harnoncourt, Rene
Erdoes, Richard
Fleischer, Max
Gregor, Arthur
Gruenberg, Sidonie M(atsner)
Guiterman, Arthur
Matulay, Lazlo
Merkling, Erica
Moskin, Marietta D(unston)
Orgel, Doris (Adelberg)
Pauli, Hertha (Ernestine)
Perl, Susan
Rethi, Lili
Segal, Lore (Groszmann)
Sibal, Joseph
Siebel, Fritz (Frederick)
Siegl, Helen
Singer, Kurt D(eutsch)
Smith, Theresa Kalab
Steiner, Charlotte
Trapp, Maria (Augusta) von
Weidhorn, Manfred
Weihs, Erika
Weil, Lisl
Wiesner, William
Vienna (near)
Dombrowski, Kathe Schonberger von

AUSTRIA-HUNGARY
Buchach
White, Bessie (Feistiner)

BAVARIA
Eggenhofer, Nicholas

BELGIUM
Antwerp
Rose, Anne K.
Schisgall, Oscar
Schneider, Nina (Zimet)
Brussels
Basilevsky, Helen
Schreiber, Georges
Webb, Francoise
Wondelgem
Sarton, Eleanor May

BERMUDA
Paget
Burland, Brian (Berkeley)

BOHEMIA
Ruzicka, Rudolph

BOLIVIA
Chulumani
Sotomayor, Antonio

BRAZIL
Belem
Maynard, Olga
Sao Paulo
Boulet, Susan Seddon

BRITISH WEST INDIES
Trinidad
Dalgliesh, Alice

BULGARIA
Dabcovich, Lydia
Leskovitz
Katchamakoff, Atanas

BURMA
Rangoon
Stevens, William Oliver

BYELORUSSIA
Kolba, Tamara

CANADA
Collins, Ruth Philpott
Jennison, Keith Warren
MacFarlan, Allan A.
Walker, Nedda
Bath, New Brunswick
MacLeod, Charlotte (Matilda Hughes)
Belleville, Ontario
Shannon, Monica
Brampton, Ontario
Price, Norman Mills
Brantford, Ontario
Costain, Thomas B(ertram)
Duncan, Norman
Calgary, Alberta
Cohen, Morton N(orton)
Noble, Iris (Davis)
Dryden, Ontario
Hayes, John F.
Edmonton, Alberta
Darby, Ray(mond) K.
Ilsley, Velma (Elizabeth)
Fassett, Quebec
Keating, Leo Bernard
Granby, Quebec
Cox, Palmer
Halifax, Nova Scotia
Foster, Harold Rudolf
MacDonald, Zillah Katherine
Hamilton, Ontario
Burman, Alice Caddy
Grant, Myrna (Lois)
Highfield, Ontario
Verral, Charles Spain
Kamsack, Saskatchewan
Coerr, Eleanor (Page)
London, Ontario
Smith, Lillian H(elena)
Montreal
Chalmers, Audrey
Nova Scotia
Marshall, James
Stirling, Lilla
Ontario
Laut, Agnes C(hristina)
Wright, Dare
Ottawa, Ontario
James, Harry Clebourne
Vermes, Jean C(ampbell Pattison)
Peterborough, Ontario
Price, Willard (DeMille)

Quebec
　Williamson, Margaret
Quebec City, Quebec
　Kerman, Gertrude Lerner
Quesnel, British Columbia
　Skinner, Constance Lindsay
Rush Lake, Saskatchewan
　Corey, Dorothy
Saskatchewan
　Metcalfe, June M.
Somerset, Nova Scotia
　Robinson, Boardman
St. Catharines, Ontario
　Kovalik, Nada
St. John, New Brunswick
　Boyd, Frank
Stouffville, Ontario
　Mercer, Charles (Edward)
Toronto
　Haycraft, Molly Costain
Toronto, Ontario
　Brasier, Virginia
　Carter, Helene
　Cole, Sheila R(otenberg)
　Crawford, Mel
　Duff, Annis (James)
　Foley, Mary Louise Munro
　Graham, Margaret Bloy
　Houston, James A(rchibald)
　Lazare, Gerald John
　Lonergan, Pauline Joy
　　(MacLean)
　Milne, Lorus J(ohnson)
　Mintz, Lorelie Miller
　Starrett, Charles Vincent
　　Emerson
　Zaid, Barry
Vancouver, B. C.
　Luger, Harriett M(andelay)
Vancouver, B.C.
　Beckett, Sheila
　Scarry, Patricia (Murphy)
Victoria, British Columbia
　Kinney, C. Cle(land)
Waldheim, Saskatchewan
　Baerg, Harry J(ohn)
Winnipeg, Manitoba
　Brand, Oscar
　Cameron, Eleanor Frances
　　(Butler)
　MacAgy, Douglas (Guernsey)
　Molloy, Paul
　Thorne, Diana

CANADA (MANITOBA)
Portage La Prairie
　MacKenzie, Garry

CANADA (SUMMERSIDE)
Prince Edward Island
　Strand, Mark

CHIAPUS
Isthmus of Tehuantepic
　Shields, Karena

CHILE

Santiago
　Fabres, Oscar

CHINA
　Tang, You-Shan
　Turner, Alice K.
Canton
　Chin, Richard (M.)
　Moy, Seong
　Selden, Samuel
Chengtu
　Vander els, Betty
Chinkiang
　Yaukey, Grace S(ydenstricker)
Futsing
　Caldwell, John C(ope)
Hankow
　Carr, Rachel (Elizabeth)
　Fritz, Jean (Guttery)
Kiu-Kiang
　Chiang, Yee
Nanking
　Chu, Daniel
Ningpo
　Harmelink, Barbara (Mary)
Peking
　Liang, Yen
　Lyle, Katie Letcher
　Miller, Grambs
　Moyler, Alan (Frank Powell)
　Namioka, Lensey (Chao)
　Stilwell, Alison
　Stoddard, Edward G.
Shanghai
　Alexander, Anna B(arbara
　　Cooke)
　Lattimore, Eleanor Frances
　Lord, Bette Bao
　Poston, Martha Lee
　Stauffer, Dwight G.
Soochow
　Wallace, Barbara Brooks
Swatow
　Rau, Margaret
Tientsin
　Hersey, John (Richard)
　Sze, Mai-Mai
　Young, Ed
Tsing-Tsiang pu
　Paterson, Katherine (Womeldorf)
Tsintao
　McMullan, James

COSTA RICA
　Crespi, Pachita
　DeOsma, Lupe

CUBA
Camaguey
　Ada, Alma Flor
Preston
　Gessner, Lynne

CZECHOSLOVAKIA
　Shyer, Marlene Fanta
Hlomovec
　Schiller, Andrew
Pisek
　Fuka, Vladimir
Prague
　Lustig, Arnost
　Sis, Peter
　Vojtech, Anna
　Winn, Marie
Prostejov
　Duchacek, Ivo D(uka)
Trnovany or Teplitz-Schoe
　Kohner, Frederick
Vlachovo Brezi
　Matulka, Jan

DENMARK
　Drescher, Henrik
　Helweg, Hans H.
　Kristofferson, Eva M(argaret
　　Stiegelmeyer)
Aarhus
　Hillcourt, William
　Minarik, Else Holmelund
Copenhagen
　Allen, Nina (Stromgren)
　Blegvad, Erik
　Bodecker, N(iels) M(ogens)
　Nielsen, Kay (Rasmus)
　Ohlsson, Ib
Nykobing Falster
　Freuchen, Peter
Odense
　Hofsinde, Robert

EAST GERMANY
　Degens, T.
　Prud'hommeaux, Rene

EGYPT
Alexandria
　Nadler, Robert
Cairo
　Forester, C(ecil) S(cott)

ENGLAND
　Bell, Clare
　Bolton, Ivy May
　Garrigue, Sheila
　Harris, Benjamin
　Klein, Mina C(ooper)
　Marshall, Jim
　Pole, James T.
　Smaridge, Norah (Antoinette)
　Trevor, Elleston
　Wilson, Christopher B.
　Wilson, Erica
Barrow-in-Furness
　MacPherson, Thomas George
Bath
　Quin-Harkin, Janet
Bolton
　Fox, Michael Wilson
Bournemouth
　Kirmse, Marguerite
Burton-on-Trent
　Macaulay, David Alexander

Cheetham Hill, Manchester
  Burnett, Frances (Eliza) Hodgson
Chester
  Best, Oswald Herbert
Church Crookham
  Holme, Bryan
Dorset
  Morgan, Shirley
Dover, Kent
  Oliver, John Edward
Gedney
  Vigna, Judith
Guildford, Surrey
  Wodehouse, P(elham) G(renville)
Harrow
  Smith, Susan Vernon
Heathfield, Sussex
  Simmons, Dawn Langley
Hereford
  Oz, Frank (Richard)
Lancashire
  Hilton, James
Leeds
  Lubell, Cecil
Liverpool
  Briscoe, Jill (Pauline)
London
  Baker, Alan
  Bianco, Margery (Williams)
  Bianco, Pamela
  Birch, Reginald B(athurst)
  Boardman, Gwenn R.
  Bobbe, Dorothie (de Bear)
  Booth, Graham (Charles)
  Bowden, Joan Chase
  Chapman, John Stanton Higham
  Chermayeff, Ivan
  Chittenden, Margaret
  Coggins, Jack Banham
  Collier, Zena
  Coolidge, Olivia E(nsor)
  Daly, Kathleen N(orah)
  Dickens, Monica (Enid)
  Earle, Olive (Lydia)
  Fooner, Michael
  Foote, Timothy (Gilson)
  Frank, Mary
  Garrison, Barbara
  Godwin, Edward Fell
  Godwin, Stephanie Mary (Allfree)
  Hall, Brian P(atrick)
  Hallward, Michael
  Hitchcock, Alfred (Joseph)
  Ish-Kishor, Sulamith
  Kepes, Juliet A(ppleby)
  LeGallienne, Eva
  Leighton, Clare (Veronica Hope)
  Marks, Margaret L.
  Maxwell, Arthur S.
  Nelson, Cholmondeley M.
  Nordhoff, Charles (Bernard)
  Orleans, Ilo
  Peterson, Betty Ferguson
  Price, Christine (Hilda)
  Rocker, Fermin
  Scott, John Anthony
  Thomas, Lowell (Jackson), Jr.
  Vaughan-Jackson, Genevieve
  Watts, Mabel Pizzey
Maidenhead, Berkshire
  Lofting, Hugh
Manchester
  Samuels, Gertrude
Menston, Yorkshire
  Knight, Eric (Mowbray)
New Brighton
  Carey, M(ary) V(irginia)
Newcastle
  Batterberry, Michael (Carver)
Northampton
  Whitehouse, Arthur George
Nottingham
  Chetwin, Grace
  Mason, Edwin A.
Pendleton
  Kramer, Nora
Portsmouth
  Katz, Jacqueline Hunt
Sanderstead, Surrey
  Doss, Helen (Grigsby)
Sheffield
  Herford, Oliver
South Shields, Durham
  Seton, Ernest (Evan) Thompson
Southport, Lancashire
  Newman, Daisy
Surbiton, Surrey
  Unwin, Nora S(picer)
Surrey
  Goble, Paul
Walsall, Staffordshire
  Bromhall, Winifred
Walton-on-Thames, Surrey
  Edwards, Julie (Andrews)
Warwickshire
  Rhodes, Frank H(arold Trevor)
Willesden, Sussex
  Finger, Charles J(oseph)
Woodford, Essex
  Perceval, Don

ESTONIA
  Maas, Selve
  Kay, Mara
  DeVeyrac, Robert
  Marokvia, Mireille (Journet)

FRANCE
Ales
  DeMessieres, Nicole
Brittany
  Bishop, Claire Huchet
Decize
  Billout, Guy Rene
Le Bourget du Lac, Savole
  Bernard, Jacqueline (de Sieyes)
Lodeve, Herault
  Seignobosc, Francoise
Mulhouse
  Brustlein, Daniel
Paris
  Amon, Aline
  Brevannes, Maurice
  Brodin, Pierre Eugene
  Carbonnier, Jeanne
  Carlisle, Olga A(ndreyev)
  Charlot, Jean
  DuChaillu, Paul (Belloni)
  Gerassi, John
  Joseph, Alexander
  Marsh, Reginald
  Martin, Rene
  Nebel, Gustave E.
  Nicolay, Helen
  Olcott, Frances Jenkins
  Perard, Victor Semon
  Simont, Marc
  Surany, Anico
  Zacks, Irene
St. Raphael
  LeTord, Bijou

GERMANY
  Forberg, Beate Gropius
  Karen, Ruth
  Palmer, Ruth Candida
  Switzer, Ellen
  Von Hippel, Ursula
  Wallner, Alexandra
Baden
  Meng, Heinz (Karl)
Berlin
  Barry, Katharina (Maria Watjen)
  Busoni, Rafaello
  George, Renee
  Gidal, Sonia (Epstein)
  Guggenheim, Hans
  Kaufman, Bel
  Kuttner, Paul
  Landshoff, Ursula
  Lasell, Elinor H.
  Levitin, Sonia (Wolff)
  Ley, Willy
  Lowenstein, Dyno
  Lutzker, Edythe
  Max, Peter
  Neier, Aryeh
  Schaller, George B(eals)
  Skorpen, Liesel (Moak)
  VanZwienen, Ilse (Charlotte Koehn)
  Wronker, Lili (Cassel)
Bremen
  Balet, Jan (Bernard)
  Gode von Aesch, Alexander (Gottfried Friedrich)
Breslau
  Stern, Catherine (Brieger)
  Vogel, Ilse-Margret
Cassel
  DeWitt, Cornelius Hugh
Cologne
  Eichenberg, Fritz
Dessau
  Jupo, Frank J.
Dortmund
  Hartley, Ellen (Raphael)
Dresden
  Broekel, Rainer Lothar
  Hahn, Hannelore
  Hamilton, Edith

Plume, Ilse
Dusseldorf
Arndt, Ursula (Martha H.)
Erfurt
Hess, Lilo
Essen
Floethe, Richard
Frankfurt
McFadden, Dorothy Loa (Mausolff)
Sommer, Elyse (Vorchheimer)
Gumbinnen
Olschewski, Alfred (Erich)
Hamburg
Penzler, Otto
Rey, H(ans) A(ugusto)
Rey, Margret (Elizabeth Waldstein)
Winterfeld, Henry
Hannover
Loebl, Suzanne (Bamberger)
Hanover
Stern, Ellen N(orman)
Heide
Dirks, Rudolph
Karlsruhe
Odenwald, Robert P(aul)
Klafeld, Westphalia
Schatzki, Walter
Landau
Nast, Thomas
Leipzig
Bettmann, Otto Ludwig
Bostelmann, Else W. von Roeder
Golbin, Andree
Vass, George
Werth, Kurt
Limbach
Chevalier, Christa
Lunden, Schleswig-Holstein
Koerner, W(illiam) H(enry) D(avid)
Mannheim
Altschuler, Franz
Arno, Enrico
Casewit, Curtis
Haber, Heinz
Memel
Jacobson, Morris K(arl)
Michelstadt, Odenwald
Kredel, Fritz
Minden
Wiese, Kurt
Munich
Berg, Bjorn
D'Aulaire, Edgar Parin
Fischer, Anton Otto
Gidal, Tim N(ahum)
Hoffmann, Hilde
Jauss, Anne Marie
Neumeyer, Peter F(lorian)
Wimmer, Helmut Karl
Zimmermann, Arnold E(rnst Alfred)
Munich, Bavaria
Scharl, Josef
Nordhausen

Mueller, Hans Alexander
Nuremburg
Myller, Rolf
Russ
Jordan, E(mil) L(eopold)
Saarbruecken
Benary-Isbert, Margot
Stuttgart
Kranzler, George G(ershon)
Marokvia, Artur
Thorn, John
Weilheim
Holyer, Erna Maria
Wiesbaden
Brahm, Sumishta
Wirsitz
Braun, Wernher von

GREECE
Gianakoulis, Theodore
Kastoria
Giovanopoulos, Paul (Arthur)

GUATEMALA
Sarg, Tony

GUYANA
Agricola
Carew, Jan (Rynveld)

HOLLAND
Amsterdam
Barnouw, Adriaan Jacob
Koningsberger, Hans
Rotterdam
VanLoon, Hendrik Willem
Winterswijk
Reiss, Johanna de Leeuw

HONG KONG
Cheng, Judith

HUNGARY
Beregszasz
Siegal, Aranka
Budapest
Bakacs, George
Candell, Victor
Cellini, Eva
Cellini, Joseph
Domjan, Joseph
Galdone, Paul
Gergely, Tibor
Holisher, Desider
Horvath, Ferdinand Huszti
Ivan, Gustave
Kalnay, Francis
Karasz, Ilonka
Lengyel, Emil
Rogers, Matilda
Seredy, Kate
Suba, Suzanne
Szasz, Suzanne Shorr
Csabdi
DeMiskey, Julian
Gyor
Kelen, Emery

Kolozsvar
Teleki, Geza
Szeged
Pogany, William Andrew
Toeroekszentmiklos
Petersham, Miska
Turkeve
Finta, Alexander

INDIA
McGavran, Grace Winifred
Bombay
Gobhai, Mehlli
Calcutta
Baynes, Ernest Harold
Georgiou, Constantine
Mukerji, Dhan Gopal

IRAQ
Mosul
Lovejoy, Bahija Fattouhi

IRELAND
Bennett, Richard
Floherty, John Joseph
Lappin, Peter
Ballyroney, County Down
Reid, Thomas Mayne
Belfast
Bunting, Glenn (Davison)
Castletown Berehaven
Sheehan, Ethna
County Down
Dunne, Mary Collins
County Longford
Welsh, Mary Flynn
County Tyrone
Daly, Maureen (McGivern)
Dublin
FitzGerald, Cathleen
Kerr, Jessica (Gordon)
Leamy, Edmund (Stanislaus)
Wibberley, Leonard (Patrick O'Connor)
Longford
Colum, Padraic
Maghera
Bunting, A(nne) E(velyn Bolton)
Mountcharles, Cy. Donegal
MacManus, Seumas

ISRAEL
Schweitzer, Iris
Tel Aviv
Joseph, Joan

ISRAEL (PALESTINE)
Jerusalem
Chaikin, Miriam

ITALY
Augelli, John P(at)
Bufano, Remo
D'Amato, Alex
Alessandria
Roselli, Luciana
Bussolengo

Montresor, Beni
Cadegliano
  Menotti, Gian Carlo
Florence
  Mochi, Ugo (A.)
  Saviozzi, Adriana
Foggia
  Tusiani, Joseph
Genoa
  Dobkin, Alexander
Massarosa, Tuscany
  Angelo, Valenti
Milan
  Gobbato, Imero
Pinerolo
  Roland, Albert
Reggio Calabria
  Negri, Rocco (Antonio)
Rodi
  D'Attilio, Anthony
Rome
  Collins, Michael
  Fava, Rita F.
  Fermi, Laura (Capon)
  Lipinsky de Orlov, Lino
    S(igismondo)
  Marzani, Carl (Aldo)
  Orbaan, Albert F.
  Salvadori, Mario (George)
Roteglia
  Palladini, David (Mario)
Trieste
  DeMejo, Oscar
Turin
  Ranucci, Renato
Venice
  Eiseman, Alberta
Voghera
  Gatti, Attilio

JAPAN
Ashiya
  Wartski, Maureen (Ann Crane)
Echigo
  Sugimoto, Etsu Inagaki
Kagoshima
  Iwamatsu, Jun Atsushi
Kawakeera
  Mizumura, Kazue
Morioka
  Fleming, Elizabeth P.
Osaka
  DeForest, Charlotte B(urgis)
Saijo-Shi, Ehime
  Komoda, Kiyo(aki)
Shizuoka
  Watanabe, Shigeo
Tokyo
  Mitsuhashi, Yoko
Toyko
  Yamaguchi, John Tohr
Yokohama
  Bond, Felicia
  Say, Allen
  Whitney, Phyllis A(yame)

KOREA

Minja, Park
Bookchong
  Park, Thomas Choonbai

LATVIA
  Parker, Fan(ia M. Pockrose)
Riga
  Mango, Karin N.
  Sidjakov, Nicolas
  Stubis, Talivaldis
Riga (near)
  Siegel, William

LEBANON
Beirut
  Rugh, Belle Dorman

LITHUANIA
  Gullahorn, Genevieve
Kovno (Kaunas)
  Shahn, Ben(jamin)

MALAYA
Penang
  Wehen, Joy DeWeese

MEXICO
Chihuahua
  Purdy, Claire Lee
Mazatlan
  Mehdevi, Alexander (Sinclair)
Mexico City
  Covarrubias, Miguel
  Ebel, Alex
Nuevo Laredo
  Hutto, Nelson (Allen)
San Pedro, Coahuila
  Hader, Berta (Hoerner)
Tampico
  Ayres, Patricia Miller

NETHERLANDS
Alkmaar
  Shemin, Margaretha (Hoeneveld)
Amsterdam
  Masselman, George
  Spier, Peter (Edward)
Amsterdam, Holland
  Lionni, Leo(nard)
Arnheim
  Flesch, Yolande (Catarina)
Arnhem, Holland
  DeJong, Dola
Blija, Friesland
  DeJong, David C(ornel)
Herwynen
  VanCoevering, Jan Adrian
Rotterdam
  VanStockum, Hilda (Gerarda)
The Hague
  Barnouw, Victor
  VanderHaas, Henrietta
Wierum
  DeJong, Meindert

NEW ZEALAND
Christchurch, Canterbury

Russell, Franklin (Alexander)

NORWAY
  Thorne-Thomsen, Gudrun
Baerum, Oslo
  Bergaust, Erik
Frederiksvarn
  Boyesen, Hjalmar Hjorth
Kongsberg
  D'Aulaire, Ingri (Maartenson)

PAKISTAN
Karachi
  Skofield, James

PERU
  Friedrich, Priscilla
Arequipa
  Llerena-Aguirre, Carlos Antonio
Huaras
  Montgomery, Elizabeth Rider

PHILIPPINES
  Hereford, Robert A.
Baquiro, Luzon
  White, Robb
Iloilo
  Thomson, Peter
Manila
  Aruego, Jose
  Mehdevi, Anne (Marie) Sinclair
  Stiles, Martha Bennett

POLAND
  Bronowski, Jacob
  Nurnberg, Maxwell
  Sapieha, Christine
  Stasiak, Krystyna
  Weiner, Sandra (Smith)
Biala
  Tworkov, Jack
Bielsko
  Klein, Gerda Weissmann
Krakow
  Laskowski, Jerzy
  Lobel, Anita (Kempler)
Kreschov
  Schneider, Herman
Lodz
  Szyk, Arthur
Lvov
  Ulam, S(tanislaw) M(arcin)
Podhajce
  Suhl, Yuri
Poznaw
  Benda, Wladyslaw Theodore
Pultusk
  Pine, Tillie S(chloss)
Radzymin
  Singer, Isaac (Bashevis)
Rzesna
  Mars, W(itold) T(adeusz, Jr.)
Vilna
  Hautzig, Esther (Rudomin)
  Shub, Elizabeth
Warsaw
  Benet, Sula

Borski, Lucia Merecka
Domanska, Janina
Greenhaus, Thelma Nurenberg
Gurko, Leo
Lorentowicz, Irena
Raynor, Dorka
Rodman, Bella (Kashin)
Shulevitz, Uri
Sokol, William
Szulc, Tad
Wojciechowska, Maia (Teresa Rodman)
Zamosc
Lieblich, Irene

PORTUGESE WEST AFRICA
Kamundongo, Angola
Wellman, Manly Wade

ROMANIA
Speevack, Yetta
Bucharest
Cohn, Angelo
Dorian, Marguerite
VandeBovencamp, Valli
Vasiliu, Mircea
Kishinev
Morton, Miriam (Bidner)
Riedman, Sarah R(egal)
Lassy
Daniel, Anita
Sighet
Wiesel, Elie(zer)
Timisoura
Tichy, William

RUSSIA
Cottler, Joseph
Eisenberg, Azriel
Haney, Erene Cheki
Leokum, Arkady
Norman, Charles
Polushkin, Maria
Posell, Elsa Z(eigerman)
Regehr, Lydia
Richter, Mischa
Sitomer, Harry
Steinberg, Fannie
Varley, Dimitry V.
Astrakhan
Shimin, Symeon
Batoum
Seroff, Victor I(ilyitch)
Bessarabia
Gaer, Joseph
Charkov, Ukraine
Bobritsky, Vladimir
Cheliabinsk, Siberia
Slobodkina, Esphyr
Chernigov
Rudolph, Marguerita
Chernigov, Ukraine
Baker, Rachel (Mininberg)
Kharkov, Ukraine
Artzybasheff, Boris (Miklailovich)
Kiev
Kutcher, Ben

Lissim, Simon
Nazaroff, Alexander I.
Kobiantkari, Georgia
Papashvily, George
Kobrin
Cohen, Jene Barr
Kolinkovich
Simon, Solomon
Komarno, Ukraine
Bloch, Marie Halun
Melitopol, Ukraine
Hyndman, Jane (Lee) Andrews
Minusinsk, Siberia
Kalashnikoff, Nicholas
Mitava
Rojankovsky, Feodor (Stephanovich)
Moscow
Daugherty, Sonia Medwedeff
Solonevich, George
Narevke
Globe, Leah Ain
Nemirov, Ukraine
Falstein, Louis
Nogaisk
Raskin, Joseph
Odessa
Gordon, Dorothy (Lerner)
Pylypcze, Ukraine
Hnizdovsky, Jacques
Rostovna-Donu
Alajalov, Constantin
Shavli
Choron, Jacques
Siberia
Shtainmetz, Leon
Slonim
Becker, Beril
St. Petersburg
Bock, Vera
Gollomb, Joseph
Janson, H(orst) W(oldemar)
Mordinoff, Nicolas
Tulchin
Avinoff, Andrey
Ukraine
Dotzenko, Grisha F.
White, Anne Terry
Vobruisk
Garelick, May

SCOTLAND
MacDonald, James
McNaught, Harry
Aberdeen
Michie, Allan Andrew
Taylor, David
Dumferline
Ross, Alexander
Dunbar
Muir, John
Dunure, Ayrshire
Curry, Peggy Simson
Edinburgh
Sanderson, Ivan T(erence)
Stevenson, Lionel
Todd, Ruthven

Falkirk
Keller, Irene (Barron)
Glasgow
MacInnes, Helen
MacKellar, William
McShean, Gordon
Wilson, Edward A(rthur)
Gorebridge
Anderson, Margaret J(ean)
Kirkcudbright
Sayers, Charles Marshall

SICILY
Taormina
Winwar, Frances

SOUTH AFRICA
Cape Town
Linfield, Esther
Spilhaus, Athelstan
Durban
Langley, Noel
Peitermaritzburg
Paton, Alan (Stewart)
Port Elizabeth
Stein, Mini
Sir Lowry Pass
Marais, Josef

SPAIN
Alhabia, Almeria
Castellon, Federico
Almeria
Gonzalez, Xavier
Castellon
Aragones, Sergio
Reus, Tarragona
Matte, Encarnacion L'Enc
Santander
Quintanilla, Luis

SWEDEN
Leydon, Rita (Floden)
Santesson, Hans Stefan
Gothenburg
Ringi, Kjell Arne Sorensen
Magra
Tenggren, Gustaf (Adolf)
Stockholm
Alcock, Gudrun
Stoede
McHugh, Berit Elisabet

SWITZERLAND
Basel
Holland, Isabelle
Bern (Biel)
Baum, Willi
Geneva
Abernethy, Robert G(ordon)
Bloch, Lucienne
Duvoisin, Roger (Antoine)
Palmer, Heidi
Lachen
Brandenberg, Franz
Lausanne
Delessert, Etienne

Fatio, Louise
Speicher
  Buff, Conrad
Zurich
  Gekiere, Madeleine
  Glenn, Mel

SYRIA
Tripoli
  Hewes, Agnes Danforth

TAIWAN
  Yang, Jay

THAILAND
Bangkok
  Goettel, Elinor
  Laugesen, Mary E(akin)

TRINIDAD
Port-of-Spain
  Cartey, Wilfred George Onslow

TURKEY
Adana
  Terzian, James P.
Istanbul
  Miller, Elizabeth
Mardin
  Emrich, Duncan (Black Macdonald)

UGANDA
Kampala
  Gill, Derek L(ewis) T(heodore)

USSR
  Salzman, Yuri
Bobruisk, Minsk
  Ginsburg, Mirra
Crimea
  Wayne, Kyra Petrovskaya
Kiev
  Gregori, Leon
Petrikow
  Klaperman, Libby Mindlin
Petrovichi
  Asimov, Isaac

VIETNAM
Hue
  Vo-Dinh, Mai

WALES
Cardiff
  Fletcher, Colin
Nelson, Glamorgan
  Zaring, Jane (Thomas)

WALES (SOUTH)
Pembrok,
  Harries, Joan

WEST AFRICA
Cameroon
  Gault, Frank

WEST GERMANY
Bremen
  Wilhelm, Hans
Celle
  Mannheim, Grete (Salomon)

WEST INDIES
Jamaica
  Kirkpatrick, Oliver Austin
  Miller, Don
Kingston, Jamaica
  Chen, Anthony (Young)
Maypen, Jamaica
  Shearer, Ted
Port of Spain, Trinidad
  Cabral, O(lga) M(arie)
Trinidad
  Guy, Rosa (Cuthbert)

WHITE RUSSIA
Starchevicvhi
  Bleeker, Sonia

YUGOSLAVIA
Belgrade
  Kostich, Dragos D.
Zagreb
  Costabel, Eva Deutsch